Tax Planning and Compliance for Tax-Exempt Organizations

WILEY NONPROFIT LAW, FINANCE, AND MANAGEMENT SERIES

The Art of Planned Giving: Understanding Donors and the Culture of Giving by Douglas E. White
Beyond Fund Raising: New Strategies for Nonprofit Investment and Innovation by Kay Grace
Charity, Advocacy, and the Law by Bruce R. Hopkins
The Complete Guide to Fund Raising Management by Stanley Weinstein
The Complete Guide to Nonprofit Management by Smith, Bucklin & Associates
Critical Issues in Fund Raising edited by Dwight Burlingame
Developing Affordable Housing: A Practical Guide for Nonprofit Organizations, Second Edition by Bennett L. Hecht
Financial and Accounting Guide for Not-for-Profit Organizations, Fifth Edition by Malvern J. Gross, Jr., Richard F. Larkin,
　　Roger S. Bruttomesso, John J. McNally, Price Waterhouse LLP
Financial Empowerment: More Money for More Mission by Peter C. Brinckerhoff
Financial Management for Nonprofit Organizations by Jo Ann Hankin, Alan Seidner and John Zietlow
Financial Planning for Nonprofit Organizations by Jody Blazek
The Fund Raiser's Guide to the Internet by Michael Johnston
Fund-Raising: Evaluating and Managing the Fund Development Process by James M. Greenfield
Fund-Raising Fundamentals: A Guide to Annual Giving for Professionals and Volunteers by James M. Greenfield
Fund-Raising Regulation: A State-by-State Handbook of Registration Forms, Requirements, and Procedures by Seth Perlman
　　and Betsy Hills Bush
Grantseeker's Toolkit: A Comprehensive Guide to Finding Funding by Cheryl S. New and James Quick
High Performance Nonprofit Organizations: Managing Upstream for Greater Impact by Christine Letts, Allen Grossman,
　　and William Ryan
Intermediate Sanctions: Curbing Nonprofit Abuse by Bruce R. Hopkins and D. Benson Tesdahl
International Guide to Nonprofit Law by Lester A. Salamon and Stefan Toepler & Associates
The Law of Fund-Raising, Second Edition by Bruce R. Hopkins
The Law of Tax-Exempt Healthcare Organizations by Thomas K. Hyatt and Bruce R. Hopkins
The Law of Tax-Exempt Organizations, Seventh Edition by Bruce R. Hopkins
The Legal Answer Book for Nonprofit Organizations by Bruce R. Hopkins
A Legal Guide to Starting and Managing a Nonprofit Organization, Second Edition by Bruce R. Hopkins
Managing Affordable Housing: A Practical Guide to Creating Stable Communities by Bennett L. Hecht, Local Initiatives
　　Support Corporation, and James Stockard
Managing Upstream: Creating High-Performance Nonprofit Organizations by Christine W. Letts, William P. Ryan, and
　　Allan Grossman
Mission-Based Management: Leading Your Not-for-Profit Into the 21st Century by Peter C. Brinckerhoff
Mission-Based Marketing: How Your Not-for-Profit Can Succeed in a More Competitive World by Peter C. Brinckerhoff
Nonprofit Boards: Roles, Responsibilities, and Performance by Diane J. Duca
Nonprofit Compensation and Benefits Practices by Applied Research and Development Institute International, Inc.
The Nonprofit Counsel by Bruce R. Hopkins
The Nonprofit Guide to the Internet by Robbin Zeff
Nonprofit Investment Policies: A Practical Guide to Creation and Implementation by Robert Fry, Jr.
The Nonprofit Law Dictionary by Bruce R. Hopkins
Nonprofit Compensation, Benefits, and Employment Law by David G. Samuels and Howard Pianko
Nonprofit Litigation: A Practical Guide with Forms and Checklists by Steve Bachmann
The Nonprofit Handbook, Second Edition: Volume I—Management by Tracy Daniel Connors
The Nonprofit Handbook, Second Edition: Volume II—Fund Raising by Jim Greenfield
The Nonprofit Manager's Resource Dictionary by Ronald A. Landskroner
Nonprofit Organizations' Business Forms: Disk Edition by John Wiley & Sons, Inc.
Partnerships and Joint Ventures Involving Tax-Exempt Organizations by Michael I. Sanders
Planned Giving: Management, Marketing, and Law by Ronald R. Jordan and Katelyn L. Quynn
Private Foundations: Tax Law and Compliance by Bruce R. Hopkins and Jody Blazek
Program Related Investments: A Technical Manual for Foundations by Christie I. Baxter
Reengineering Your Nonprofit Organization: A Guide to Strategic Transformation by Alceste T. Pappas
Reinventing the University: Managing and Financing Institutions of Higher Education by Sandra L. Johnson and Sean C.
　　Rush, Coopers & Lybrand, LLP
The Second Legal Answer Book for Nonprofit Organizations by Bruce R. Hopkins
Special Events: Proven Strategies for Nonprofit Fund Raising by Alan Wendroff
Strategic Communications for Nonprofit Organizations: Seven Steps to Creating a Successful Plan by Janel Radtke
Strategic Planning for Nonprofit Organizations: A Practical Guide and Workbook by Michael Allison and Jude Kaye,
　　Support Center for Nonprofit Management
Streetsmart Financial Basics for Nonprofit Managers by Thomas A. McLaughlin
A Streetsmart Guide to Nonprofit Mergers and Networks by Thomas A. McLaughlin
Successful Marketing Strategies for Nonprofit Organizations by Barry J. McLeish
The Tax Law of Charitable Giving by Bruce R. Hopkins
The Tax Law of Colleges and Universities by Bertrand M. Harding
Tax Planning and Compliance for Tax-Exempt Organizations : Forms, Checklists, Procedures, Third Edition by Jody Blazek
The Universal Benefits of Volunteering: A Practical Workbook for Nonprofit Organizations, Volunteers and Corporations by
　　Walter P. Pidgeon, Jr.
The Volunteer Management Handbook by Tracy Daniel Connors

Tax Planning and Compliance for Tax-Exempt Organizations

Forms, Checklists, Procedures
Third Edition

Jody Blazek
BLAZEK & VETTERLING LLP

John Wiley & Sons, Inc.

New York • Chichester • Weinheim • Brisbane • Singapore • Toronto

*This book was made possible through
the loving patience of my husband,
David Crossley,
and wonderful sons,
Austin and Jay Blazek Crossley,
to whom it is dedicated.*

This book is printed on acid-free paper. ∞

Copyright © 1999 by John Wiley & Sons. All rights reserved.

Published simultaneously in Canada.

This publication is designed to provide accurate and authoritative information in regard to the subject matter covered. It is sold with the understanding that the publisher is not engaged in rendering legal, accounting, or other professional services. If legal advice or other expert assistance is required, the services of a competent professional person should be sought.

Library of Congress Cataloging-in-Publication Data:

Blazek, Jody.
    Tax planning and compliance for tax-exempt organizations: forms, checklists, procedures / Jody Blazek.—3rd ed.
      p. cm. — (Wiley nonprofit law, finance, and management series)
    Includes bibliographical references and index.
    ISBN 0-471-29380-6 (cloth: alk. paper)
    1. Nonprofit organizations—Taxation—Law and legislation—United States.   2. Tax exemption—Law and legislation—United States. 3. Tax planning—United States. I. Title. II. Series.
KF6449.B58 1999
343.7305' 266—dc21   98-44950

Printed in the United States of America.

10 9 8 7 6 5 4 3 2

About the Author

Jody Blazek is a partner in Blazek & Vetterling, LLP, a Houston CPA firm focusing on tax and financial planning for exempt organizations and the individuals who create, fund, and work with them. BV serves over 200 nonprofit organizations providing financial reports and tax compliance and planning services.

Jody began her professional career at KPMG, then Peat, Marwick, Mitchell & Co. Her concentration on exempt organizations began in 1969; she was assigned to study the Tax Reform Act that completely revamped the taxation of charities and created private foundations. From 1972 to 1981, she gained nonprofit management experience as treasurer of the Menil Interests where she worked with John and Dominique de Menil to plan the Menil Collection, The Rothko Chapel, and other projects of the Menil Foundation. She reentered public practice in 1981 to found the firm she now serves.

She is the author of three books in the Wiley Nonprofit Series: *Tax Planning and Compliance for Tax-Exempt Organizations, 3rd Edition, Financial Planning for Nonprofit Organizations* (1996), and *Private Foundations: Tax Law and Compliance* (1997) co-authored with Bruce R. Hopkins.

Jody serves on the Tax-Exempt Organizations Committee of the American Institute of Certified Public Accountants, the national editorial board of Tax Analysts' *The Exempt Organization Tax Review,* and the Volunteer Service Committee of the Houston Chapter of Certified Public Accountants. She is a founding director of Texas Accountants and Lawyers for the Arts and a member of the board of the Anchorage Foundations, Houston Artists Fund, and the River Pierce Foundation. She is a frequent speaker at nonprofit symposia, including University of Texas Law School Nonprofit Organizations Institute, Institute for Board Development, and Nonprofit Resource Center's Nonprofit Legal and Accounting Institute, among others.

Blazek received her BBA from University of Texas at Austin in 1964 and attended South Texas School of Law. She and her husband, David Crossley, nurture two sons, Austin and Jay Blazek Crossley.

Preface

Tax-exempt organizations comprised between 10–12% of the gross domestic product of the United States during the past 20 years. Revenues and assets of exempt organizations during that period tripled according to the IRS Statistics of Income Division. Marcus Owens, Director of the IRS Exempt Organization (EO) Division, warns that the sector's size will bring enhanced scrutiny from Congress and many others. This book is designed to aid nonprofit organizations pass any tests that come their way in obtaining and maintaining tax-exempt status.

One of my goals in writing this book is to remind the nonprofit community that tax-exempt organizations are taxpayers. Although privileges are afforded to organizations determined to be exempt under Internal Revenue Code (IRC) §501(c), the code imposes a wide variety of income and excise taxes and penalties for late filings and noncompliance. As with most tax provisions, the rules are often gray and impinge upon the particular facts and circumstances of the particular organization. To compound the wealth of information necessary to comply with the rules, Congress in recent years has passed significant tax legislation pertaining to exempt organizations. This third edition incorporates the new provisions: intermediate sanctions, charitable donation and return disclosures, lobbying expense limitations, and classification of unrelated business income, among others. New Internal Revenue Service (IRS) revenue rulings and procedures and court cases have changed the standards for exempt organization/business joint ventures, low income housing projects, compensation, and royalty income. These issues among scores of other developments since 1992 are incorporated in this edition.

A parallel objective of this book is to aid nonprofit organizations and their advisors in satisfying their public disclosure requirements. If you, your clients, your board, or anybody else is questioning why a nonprofit organization should give top priority to correctly completing Form 990, be aware that the form has entered the electronic age where it is now accessible to all on the World Wide Web. An organization's public reporting responsibilities have a new dimension and deserve careful attention. In March 1997, the IRS contracted with the Urban Institute of Washington, D.C. to receive and place on CD-ROM Forms 990 for the years 1996 through 2001.

In a coordinated effort, Philanthropic Resources, Inc., will be digitizing the information so that it can be sorted and searched. Information from prior 990s of some 40,000 public charities is already in their database and can be found at *http://www.guidestar.org*. A site for the 990s filed by charities that help people with AIDS can be found at *http://www.accountabilityproject.com*. The Multi-State Filer Project site (*http://www.form990.org*) instructs nonprofit groups how to electronically store, receive, and transmit 990 information. Eric Mercer's *http://www.muridae.com/publicaccess.html* offers software that allows organizations to display their forms in accordance with public disclosure requirements.[1] Between 1984 and

---

[1] According to chart listed in "Return of the Future," an article in the December 17, 1998, issue of *The Chronicles of Philanthropy*.

eof

1996, an organization had to allow anyone who knocked on its door a look at its Forms 990 and 1023 or 1024 in its office. Beginning sometime in 1999 (60 days after the effective date of final regulations under §6104(e)) both public charities and private foundations must furnish copies of the three most recent year's returns in return for a modest fee, as described in Chapter 27. Expect Forms 990 and 1023 to ask for email and Web site addresses in the future.

With the IRS hope that new technology will help stretch its declining budget, an EO Home Page entitled "Exempt Organizations" is now accessible by dialing *www.irs.ustreas.gov* and clicking *Tax Information for Business.* The topics on which one may click include Types of Tax-Exempt Organizations (Publication 557), Tax-Exempt Organization Tax Kit (forms), Exempt Organization Search (Publication 78 which incidentally sometimes "fails to load"), FAQs (frequently asked questions), IRS Exempt Organizations Continuing Professional Education Technical Instruction Programs (indexed articles from the very useful CPE Text), Customer Service, and Application Process (instructions for submission of Form 1023 and 1024).

I applaud a parallel IRS project to develop an electronic filing system for 990s. The goal is to eliminate the paperwork altogether and allow the agency to monitor exempts in a statistical and focused fashion. One study reported that only 2% of the requests for copies of Form 990-PF sent to the IRS yielded a correct and full return after the first request.[2] Shockingly, direct requests sent by the researchers to corporate foundations yielded a pathetic 10% full cooperation despite public disclosure rule requirements and penalties for noncompliance, as described in Chapter 27.

This book is organized around five subjects essential to all nonprofits seeking federal recognition and maintenance of tax-exempt status.

Part I: Qualification for Exemption

Starting with Chapter 1, this book describes the characteristics of tax-exempt organizations and distinguishes them from for-profit organizations. Checklists designed to gauge the suitability of a project for tax-exempt status, along with other start-up tax and financial considerations, are provided. The types of organizations that can qualify and the characteristics that determine program qualification are presented. Throughout Part I, I try to explain the rationale underlying the distinctions.

Chapter 2 deserves study by anyone working with an organization seeking to obtain and maintain exemption as a charity under IRC §501(c)(3). The standards for serving a charitable class, for meeting the commensurate test (devoting enough money to charitable programs), for being educational (versus action oriented), and other issues should be carefully studied. An understanding of the vague and sometimes contradictory meaning of these tests is very useful in applying the rules.

Chapters 3–10 provide a framework for determining an organization's qualification for exempt status. Churches, schools, civic associations, social clubs, business leagues, labor unions, and title-holding companies are compared and the

---

[2] O'Connor and Paprocki, *Corporate Grantmaking: Giving to Racial Ethnic Populations—Phase Three.* (Washington, D.C.: National Committee for Responsive Philanthropy, 1997).

particular requirements of each of the major §501(c) exemption sections are fleshed out. Lists of the revenue rulings and procedures that contain the standards and definitions applicable to the many different types of organizations within each category allow one to discern a project's qualification for exemption. Readers may be amazed by the seemingly outdated footnotes from the 1960s and 1970s. Yes, they still serve as the governing guidance. Between 1974 and 1990, over 400 revenue rulings concerning exempt organizations were issued; none were issued between 1991 and 1996. Private letter rulings (PLR's) are often the only source of IRS thinking on an issue. Even though they are not precedential, the reader will find them discussed throughout the text as they often provide a reasonable basis for decision making.

Civic associations, unions, and business leagues must calculate the portion of the organization's dues spent on lobbying activities that became nondeductible to members unless the organization chooses to pay a proxy tax on such expenditures. Making this important choice involves following intricate rules found in Chapter 6. The IRS's battle to tax certain associate members' dues for labor unions is chronicled in Chapter 7. The somewhat different criteria for identifying members of business leagues and the impact on revenues collected for rendering member services is reviewed and updated in Chapter 8.

How a charitable organization can qualify for and maintain status as a public charity is presented in Chapter 11. The impact of the distinctions between public and private tax-exempt organizations is discussed, along with a presentation comparing and contrasting the various types of public charities. You will discover how the IRS distinguishes government grants treated as donations from grants considered as fees for services, when a membership fee is classified, and the kinds of donations not counted as public support. Support organizations and the labyrinth of tests that apply to them are illustrated.

Part II: Private Foundations

Privately funded charities are subject to complex sanctions imposed by Congress in 1969, when it set out to discourage the formation of private foundations and to strictly curtail their activities. Despite the absolute tone of the sanctions, many exceptions apply. The dizzying array of excise taxes, definitions, and applicability can be simplified following the discussion, checklists, and examples in Chapters 12–17. Between 1970 and 1984 and January 1, 1995 through May 31, 1996, only the donor's cost basis for properties donated to a private foundation was deductible. Philanthropists can now regularly plan to create and fund private foundations relying upon a permanent extension of the on-again-off-again rule that permits a contribution deduction for the fair market value of *qualified appreciated stock* donated to a private charity.

Techniques for reducing the excise tax private foundations pay on investment income are presented in Chapter 13. The self-dealing rules outlined in Chapter 14 sound absolutely draconian and essentially say no money can ever be paid to a disqualified person by a private foundation. Through the years, however, the rules have evolved as the IRS has used a very practical approach to permit transactions that benefit the foundation. Exceptions applicable are presented by type of financial transactions: sales or leases of property, loans, compensation, payments on behalf of officers and directors, and nonmonetary payments. A private foundation must make *minimum distributions,* or pay out a percentage of certain assets annually, and Chapter 15 discusses which assets are included in the formula and various methods of valuation. Restraints are placed on business ownership by a private foundation with the prohibition on *excess business holdings.* Chapter 16 presents the permitted holdings and disposition periods for excesses received as gifts, along with a discussion of the types of speculative investments considered to be jeopardizing for a foundation.

Chapter 17 discusses the *taxable expenditure* rules that govern the manner in which a private foundation spends its money. This chapter shows that a foundation's spending parameters are actually very broad if enhanced documentation is maintained. As long as charitable purposes are served, a private charity can conduct a breadth of activity similar to a public charity.

Part III: Recognition of Exempt Status

Chapter 18 provides a blueprint for seeking approval for exempt status from the Internal Revenue Service, including specific suggestions for answering each question on Forms 1023 and 1024. Insights into the rationale behind the information requested by the IRS and the interaction between the questions will enable the preparer to mold the prospective organization into an acceptable form. This chapter walks you through the steps involved in the approval process and provides practical advice on the alternatives available in contesting IRS determinations.

Part IV: Maintaining Exempt Status

According to Marcus Owens, "Absence of documentation is at the heart of just about every inurement and private benefit case that is pending in my division now and is a problem we constantly see with unrelated business income (UBI) cases."[3] This refrain forms the structure of the long-awaited published guidance on incentive compensation paid by hospitals reported in Chapter 4 and regulations on Intermediate Sanctions discussed in Chapter 20. Organizations that conduct activities similar to those performed by commercial companies, such as healthcare providers, consulting or referral services, and research programs, for example, present a challenge for professionals representing them. For such organizations, contemporaneous documentation of the process it uses to determine the tax-exempt purposes served by activities is now crucial.

After securing initial IRS approval, annual compliance measures assure ongoing exemption and can aid in accumulating appropriate *documentation of process.* Chapter 19 contains checklists for use by both public and private charities and for non-(c)(3) organizations. We use these checklists annually to review our clients' local, state, and federal filing matters, evaluate reporting and documentation requirements, and to hopefully uncover any troublesome activity.

To qualify for exemption initially and on an ongoing basis, a tax-exempt organization must operate to benefit its exempt constituency, not its creators, direc-

---

[3] Remarks at a meeting of the American Bar Association Exempt Organization Committee, May 9, 1997.

tors, or other self-interested persons. Chapter 20 defines impermissible private inurement or benefit, discusses the range of its application, and explains how the rules apply to different types of financial transactions. Yes, a salary can be paid to a member of the board of directors if such compensation is reasonable. Factors that determine the reasonableness of salaries, loans, asset sales and purchases, conversion of a for-profit to a nonprofit, joint ventures, and other financial arrangements are discussed. The Intermediate Sanction rules now applicable to public charities and civic associations that pay excess benefits to their insiders are presented.

As a source of funding, many exempt organizations charge for services they render or goods they produce. Most exempt organizations are not necessarily prohibited from conducting such income-producing activity, particularly if the revenue stems from an activity that accomplishes its exempt purposes. When an activity is unrelated to the mission, income tax may be due on the profits. A *commerciality test* is applied to decide when the level of income-producing activity is like a commercial business, indicating the organization's underlying exempt status could be challenged. Chapter 21 describes the unrelated business income tax and its endless exceptions and modifications. The convoluted nature of the relevant code sections and the number of conflicting guidelines behoove organizations and their advisors to continually seek up-to-date information on this subject and to pay attention to potential new legislation on the subject of UBI. The small business lobby continues to make suggestions in this regard—most recently forcing enhanced requirements for travel tours. Exclusive marketing agreements and management service agreements are candidates for new IRS initiatives.

After extensive Congressional hearings during the late 1980s, the Treasury Department recommended against making any changes in these rules because the task force proposals would not "significantly improve tax administration with respect to UBI" nor "command a broad base of support." Meanwhile, a section was added to the Forms 990 on which revenue sources are classified. The codes and columns completed in this part serve a variety of purposes for the IRS. Most potentially important unrelated income is labeled. During 1997, social clubs failing to file Forms 990-T to report their investment income (about 40%) were identified with this part and chosen for examination. The statistics are reported to Congressional committees and other interested parties.

Creation of an affiliated organization of another exemption category, spin-off of an activity into a for-profit subsidiary organization, hiring a manager under a profit-sharing agreement, and forming a joint venture with business organization are astute survival methods an organization might need to take in today's economic climate. These important options are available to exempt organizations seeking enhanced efficiency and economies of scale. Forms 990 now request "Information Regarding Transfers, Transactions, and Relationships with Other Organizations" to enable the IRS to scrutinize such relationships. Chapter 22 addresses the issues involved when a tax-exempt organization has such relationships.

To accomplish their goals, many nonprofit organizations engage in lobbying or otherwise attempt to influence lawmaking. Participation in the election of lawmakers—political intervention—is allowed for certain types of exempt organizations and strictly prohibited for others. The restraints on lobbying and electioneering are discussed in Chapter 23 and must be carefully studied before an organization contemplates such actions. Charitable organizations (other than private foundations) can spend an insubstantial part of their resources on attempts to influence elected officials to change the laws of the land. Permissible amount of such lobbying effort is, however, limited by one of two very different tests. The pros and cons of making the IRC §501(h) election and the fate of an organization whose purposes can only be accomplished through the passage of legislation (cannot qualify for charitable exemption) must be studied.

Beginning in 1988, the IRS conducted an Exempt Organization Charitable Solicitations Compliance Improvement Program that emphasized the fact that the tax deduction for a donation to charity is reduced by the value of any goods and services received by the donor in connection with the gift. First the IRS examined fund-raising programs in which premiums, free admissions, dinners, raffles, and other benefits were used to entice donors. Once the list of such events was compiled from the charity's records, the IRS examined the donors to find out whether the tax deduction was overstated. The results were poor. Congress eventually enacted strict disclosure requirements that cause charities to value and report benefits provided to those who sponsor and support charitable events. The substantiation requirements and suggestions for their implementation can be found in Chapter 24.

Prior to 1988, IRS exempt organization examiners did not review payroll tax matters. When they began to look, the results of their examinations caused concern; they found too many employees classified as independent contractors. Millions of dollars of taxes were assessed when the IRS examined colleges and hospitals during the 1990s. For any size organization, payroll tax and associated employee benefit costs represent a significant cost and thus provide a significant temptation to treat workers as nonemployees. Chapter 25 outlines the issues and reporting requirements on this important issue.

Significant organizational changes, such as a merger or other combination with another nonprofit, bankruptcy, or termination, are not anticipated in the heyday of an organization's formation and plenty and are uncommon for most tax-exempt organizations. Nevertheless, such changes may be necessary—the unthinkable does happen. Chapter 26 reviews the tax consequences and filing requirements during such life changes for an exempt organization and considers the consequences, both on the organization and its contributors, when an EO loses its exempt status.

Part V: Communicating with the IRS

The task of communicating successfully with the IRS once exempt status is granted may be made easier by consulting Chapters 27 and 28. Detailed suggestions for the completion of Forms 990, 990T, 990-PF, and 990EZ are presented. The reason questions are asked and the import of the answers is explained. Where an item of income or expense may be reportable on more than one line, the choice is discussed and compared. Guidance for reporting expenses, with particular emphasis on cost allocations is provided.

It has been my experience that the IRS EO Branch is staffed with folks that mirror those working in the nonprofit community. They view their job as facilitating projects of publicly spirited citizens wishing to benefit society. The EO

PREFACE

Division centralized and began to reorganize well before Congress mandated IRS improvements in 1998. The examination guidelines found in Chapter 28 were graciously updated by the chief of the Houston EO office, Jason Kall. The various reasons why an exempt organization might report back to or might hear from the IRS subsequent to initial qualification for exempt status are outlined and suggestions for achieving a good answer are provided.

I hope readers will find this book useful throughout a tax-exempt organization's life and welcome this opportunity to contribute to our great nonprofit sector.

JODY BLAZEK

Houston, Texas
December 1998

Acknowledgments

The response to the second edition of this book was positive and encouraging; I am grateful for the opportunity to comprehensively update and consider many of the issues in greater depth. In 1969, when KPGM assigned me the task of studying, interpreting, and communicating the new private foundation rules to our Houston clients, I searched for interpretive information and often found it lacking. This book represents a compendium of checklists, client memoranda, and interpretive materials developed over the years to provide guideposts for compliance and tax planning for exempt organizations.

My experience has been enriched by a myriad of wonderful people with ideas for improving the human condition and saving the earth. The wealth of altruism and kindness shared by benefactors and volunteers in the nonprofit community is an inspiration. From the vantage of the funder who wants to create a private foundation, the healer who senses the ability to cure a disease, and the artist who wants to paint a public mural, among many others, I have had the privilege of responding to a mandate to figure out the best financial and tax mode in which to establish an entity that can accomplish those goals. My years as a KPGM tax specialist, under the able tutelage of John Herzfeld and Lloyd Jard, taught me that tax rules are not black and white; answers are complex and often gray. Achieving the best tax answer requires an exacting search, an ability to weigh alternatives, and the willingness to defend your choice.

As treasurer and chief financial officer of the Menil Foundation and the Rothko Chapel—the Houston-based charitable ventures of Dominique and John de Menil—I had a unique hands-on opportunity to manage nonprofit organizations. Returning to public practice in 1982, I continued my commitment to nonprofit organizations and started an accounting firm that focuses on exempt organizations and the people who work with and create them. In the early eighties, a group of professionals started the Texas Accountants and Lawyers for the Arts. Our purpose was to improve the technical expertise and expand the body of law applicable to nonprofit organizations. With this goal in mind, seminars were organized and technical issues were researched and reported. Since that time, the number of trained and willing volunteers has multiplied many times. This book is partly a result of the questions asked during those seminars. It is intended to be a practical guide to establishing and maintaining tax-exempt status for nonprofit organizations.

I also want to acknowledge the people who played an instrumental role in making this book possible. Bruce Hopkins, the series editor, and Jeffrey Brown, publisher at John Wiley & Sons, in 1986, originally found merit in my materials and I thank them for their confidence. Martha Cooley, my editor, pushed me to prepare this third edition and provided endless encouragement and invaluable assistance. Robin Goldstein performed some miracles in overseeing the production. Anne Burnell combed through the maze of checklists, exhibits, and appendixes, and greatly facilitated the process. Thanks to you all.

ACKNOWLEDGMENTS

On a professional level, I am indebted to my colleagues at Blazek & Vetter-ling, particularly my assistant, Gabriele Schweigart, for merging the second edition and supplement texts and freeing my time for writing. My clients and colleagues ask me the questions that provide the fuel for the materials I write and I thank them as well. Lastly, I am forever indebted to my husband and clients for their patience and support while I devoted time to this project.

Contents

CONTENTS

CONTENTS

PART III: IRS RECOGNITION

PART IV: MAINTAINING TAX EXEMPT STATUS

CONTENTS

CONTENTS

PART V: COMMUNICATING WITH THE IRS

Qualifying for Exemption

CHAPTER ONE

Distinguishing Characteristics of Tax-Exempt Organizations

The world of exempt organizations includes a broad range of nonprofit institutions: churches, schools, charities, business leagues, political parties, schools, country clubs, and united giving campaigns all conducting a wide variety of pursuits intended to serve the public good. All exempt organizations (EOs) share the common attribute of being organized for the advancement of a group of persons, rather than particular individuals or businesses. Most exempt organizations are afforded special tax and legal status precisely because of the unselfish motivation behind their formation.

The common thread running through the various types of exempt organizations is the lack of private ownership and profit motive. A broad definition of an exempt organization is a nonprofit entity operated without self-interest to serve a societal or group mission that pays over none of the income or profit to private individuals—its members and governing officials.

Federal and state governments view nonprofits as relieving their burdens by performing certain functions of government. Thus, many nonprofits are exempted from the levies that finance government, including income, sales, and ad valorem and other local property taxes. This special status recognizes the work they perform essentially on behalf of the government. In addition, for charitable nonprofits, labor unions, business leagues, and other types of exempt organizations the tax deductibility of dues and donations paid to them further evidences the government's willingness to forego money in their favor. At the same time, deductibility provides a major fund-raising tool. For complex reasons, some of which are not readily apparent, all nonprofits are not equal for tax deduction purposes, and not all "donations" are deductible, as discussed in Chapter 24.

On the federal level, Internal Revenue Code (IRC) §501 exempts some 30 specific types of nonprofit organizations, plus pension plans (§401), political organizations (§527), homeowner's associations (§528), and qualified state tuition programs (§529) from income tax. Although exempt organizations are often perceived as charitable, many other types of nonprofits are classified as tax-exempt under the federal income tax code. Labor unions, business leagues, community associations, cemeteries, employee benefit societies, social clubs, and many other types of organizations are listed in IRC §501. Exhibit 1-1 contains the Internal Revenue Service (IRS) master chart listing all categories of exempt organizations and illustrates the wide variety.

For purposes of federal tax exemption, each category has its own distinct set of criteria for qualification. Chapters 2 through 10 discuss the requirements for the most common types, compare the categories, explain the attributes that distinguish them from each other, and consider instances in which they overlap. Chapter 11 presents the rather complicated rules governing the preferred type of §501(c)(3) organization—public charities. Those §501(c)(3)s unable to be treated as public because of their narrow funding sources are called private foundations and are subject to special sanctions found in Chapters 12–17. The always-challenging task of applying for recognition of tax-exempt status is considered in Chapter 18. The information submitted must draw a picture of the prospective exempt organization both in words and numbers to enable the IRS to perceive the fashion in which it will serve exempt purposes. Suggestions for answering those questions the import of which is not readily apparent can be found in this important chapter along with filled-in forms. Chapter 19 contains annual tax compliance checklists for both charitable and noncharitable organizations. These lists are designed to be used by nonprofit managers and advisors each year to verify ongoing qualification for exempt status and satisfaction of the various filing requirements. Chapters 20 through 26 cover special issues that face a tax-exempt organization during its life—transactions with insiders, unrelated business income, relationships with other organizations and businesses, lobbying and electioneering, payroll taxes, mergers, and bankruptcy. Lastly, Chapters 27 and 28 focus on a tax-exempt's relationship to the IRS. Suggestions for completing the various Form 990s with line-by-line comments and filled-in forms are provided. Chapter 28 discusses reasons why an organization might need to communicate with the IRS and the alternatives in doing so.

This introductory chapter presents the issues to be considered prior to establishing an exempt organization, along with checklists to serve as a guide. An enlightening and thorough legal treatise on exempt organizations, written by the senior editor of the John Wiley & Sons Nonprofit Law, Finance, and Management Series, is *The Law of Tax-Exempt Organizations* by Bruce R. Hopkins, now in its seventh edition. It is an extremely valuable resource for in-depth historical context and explanation.

Throughout the book, and particularly in the next few chapters, you will note revenue rulings issued mostly in the 1960s and 1970s. These citations still re-

Exhibit 1–1

ORGANIZATION REFERENCE CHART

Section of 1986 Code	Description of organization	General nature of activities	Application Form No.	Annual return required to be filed	Contributions allowable
501(c)(1)	Corporations Organized Under Act of Congress (including Federal Credit Unions)	Instrumentalities of the United States	No Form	None	Yes, if made for exclusively public purposes
501(c)(2)	Title Holding Corporation For Exempt Organization	Holding title to property of an exempt organization	1024	990[1] or 990EZ[8]	No[2]
501(c)(3)	Religious, Educational, Charitable, Scientific, Literary, Testing for Public Safety, to Foster National or International Amateur Sports Competition, or Prevention of Cruelty to Children or Animals Organizations	Activities of nature implied by description of class of organization	1023	990[1] or 990EZ[8], or 990-PF	Yes, generally
501(c)(4)	Civic Leagues, Social Welfare Organizations, and Local Associations of Employees	Promotion of community welfare; charitable, educational or recreational	1024	990[1] or 990EZ[8]	No, generally[2,3]

[1] For exceptions to the filing requirement, see chapter 2 and the Form instructions.

[2] An organization exempt under a Subsection of Code Sec. 501 other than (c)(3) may establish a charitable fund, contributions to which are deductible. Such a fund must itself meet the requirements of section 501(c)(3) and the related notice requirements of section 508(a).

[3] Contributions to volunteer fire companies and similar organizations are deductible, but only if made for exclusively public purposes.

[4] Deductible as a business expense to the extent allowed by Code section 192.

[5] Deductible as a business expense to the extent allowed by Code section 194A.

[6] Application is by letter to the address shown on Form 8718. A copy of the organizing document should be attached and the letter should be signed by an officer.

[7] Contributions to these organizations are deductible only if 90% or more of the organization's members are war veterans.

[8] For limits on the use of Form 990EZ, see chapter 2 and the general instructions for Form 990EZ (or Form 990).

[9] Although the organization files a partnership return, all distributions are deemed dividends. The members are not entitled to "pass-through" treatment of the organization's income or expenses.

Exhibit 1–1 (continued)

Section of 1986 Code	Description of organization	General nature of activities	Application Form No.	Annual return required to be filed	Contributions allowable
501(c)(5)	Labor, Agricultural, and Horticultural Organizations	Educational or instructive, the purpose being to improve conditions of work, and to improve products and efficiency	1024	990[1] or 990EZ[8]	No[2]
501(c)(6)	Business Leagues, Chambers of Commerce, Real Estate Boards, Etc.	Improvement of business conditions of one or more lines of business	1024	990[1] or 990EZ[8]	No[2]
501(c)(7)	Social and Recreation Clubs	Pleasure, recreation, social activities	1024	990[1] or 990EZ[8]	No[2]
501(c)(8)	Fraternal Beneficiary Societies and Associations	Lodge providing for payment of life, sickness, accident, or other benefits to members	1024	990[1] or 990EZ[8]	Yes, if for certain Sec. 501(c)(3) purposes
501(c)(9)	Voluntary Employees' Beneficiary Associations	Providing for payment of life, sickness, accident, or other benefits to members	1024	990[1] or 990EZ[8]	No[2]
501(c)(10)	Domestic Fraternal Societies and Associations	Lodge devoting its net earnings to charitable, fraternal, and other specified purposes. No life, sickness, or accident benefits to members	1024	990[1] or 990EZ[8]	Yes, if for certain Sec. 501(c)(3) purposes
501(c)(11)	Teachers' Retirement Fund Associations	Teachers' association for payment of retirement benefits	No Form[6]	990[1] or 990EZ[8]	No[2]
501(c)(12)	Benevolent Life Insurance Associations, Mutual Ditch or Irrigation Companies, Mutual or Cooperative Telephone Companies, Etc.	Activities of a mutually beneficial nature similar to those implied by the description of class of organization	1024	990[1] or 990EZ[8]	No[2]

Section	Description of Organization	Activities	Application Form No.	Annual Return Required	Contributions Allowable
501(c)(13)	Cemetery Companies	Burials and incidental activities	1024	990[1] or 990EZ[8]	Yes, generally
501(c)(14)	State Chartered Credit Unions, Mutual Reserve Funds	Loans to members	No Form[6]	990[1] or 990EZ[8]	No[2]
501(c)(15)	Mutual Insurance Companies or Associations	Providing insurance to members substantially at cost	1024	990[1] or 990EZ[8]	No[2]
501(c)(16)	Cooperative Organizations to Finance Crop Operations	Financing crop operations in conjunction with activities of a marketing or purchasing association	No Form[6]	990[1] or 990EZ[8]	No[2]
501(c)(17)	Supplemental Unemployment Benefit Trusts	Provides for payment of supplemental unemployment compensation benefits	1024	990[1] or 990EZ[8]	No[2]
501(c)(18)	Employee Funded Pension Trust (created before June 25, 1959)	Payment of benefits under a pension plan funded by employees	No Form[6]	990[1] or 990EZ[8]	No[2]
501(c)(19)	Post or Organization of Past or Present Members of the Armed Forces	Activities implied by nature of organization	1024	990[1] or 990EZ[8]	No, generally[7]
501(c)(21)	Black Lung Benefit Trusts	Funded by coal mine operators to satisfy their liability for disability or death due to black lung diseases	No Form[6]	990-BL	No[4]
501(c)(22)	Withdrawal Liability Payment Fund	To provide funds to meet the liability of employers withdrawing from a multi-employer pension fund	No Form[6]	990 or 990EZ[8]	No[5]
501(c)(23)	Veterans Organization (created before 1880)	To provide insurance and other benefits to veterans	No Form[6]	990 or 990EZ[8]	No, generally[7]
501(c)(25)	Title Holding Corporations or Trusts with Multiple Parents	Holding title and paying over income from property to 35 or fewer parents or beneficiaries	1024	990 or 990EZ	No
501(c)(26)	State-Sponsored Organization Providing Health Coverage for High-Risk Individuals	Provides health care coverage to high-risk individuals	No Form[6]	990[1] or 990EZ[8]	No

Exhibit 1–1 (continued)

Section of 1986 Code	Description of organization	General nature of activities	Application Form No.	Annual return required to be filed	Contributions allowable
501(c)(27)	State-Sponsored Workers' Compensation Reinsurance Organization	Reimburses members for losses under workers' compensation acts	No Form[6]	990[1] or 990EZ[8]	No
501(d)	Religious and Apostolic Associations	Regular business activities. Communal religious community	No Form	1065[9]	No[2]
501(e)	Cooperative Hospital Service Organizations	Performs cooperative services for hospitals	1023	990[1] or 990EZ[8]	Yes
501(f)	Cooperative Service Organizations of Operating Educational Organizations	Performs collective investment services for educational organizations	1023	990[1] or 990EZ[8]	Yes
501(k)	Child Care Organization	Provides care for children	1023	990 or 990EZ[8]	Yes
501(n)	Charitable Risk Pools	Pools certain insurance risks of 501(c)(3) organizations	1023	990[1] or 990EZ[8]	Yes
521(a)	Farmers' Cooperative Associations	Cooperative marketing and purchasing for agricultural producers	1028	990-C	No

[1] For exceptions to the filing requirement, see Chapter 2 and the form instructions.

[2] An organization exempt under a Subsection of Code Sec. 501 other than (c)(3), may establish a charitable fund, contributions to which are deductible. Such a fund must itself meet the requirements of section 501(c)(3) and the related notice requirements of section 508(a).

[3] Contributions to volunteer fire companies and similar organizations are deductible, but only if made for exclusively public purposes.

[4] Deductible as a business expense to the extent allowed by Code section 192.

[5] Deductible as a business expense to the extent allowed by Code section 194A.

[6] Application is by letter to the address shown on Form 8718. A copy of the organizing document should be attached and the letter should be signed by an officer.

[7] Contributions to these organizations are deductible only if 90% or more of the organization's members are war veterans.

[8] For limits on the use of Form 990EZ, see chapter 2 and the general instructions for Form 990EZ (or Form 990).

[9] Although the organization files a partnership return, all distributions are deemed dividends. The members are not entitled to "pass-through" treatment of the organization's income or expenses.

flect the precedential IRS view on the particular issue involved. Their age reflects an IRS policy, started in the late 1970s due to staffing limitations, to issue private letter rulings that eventually lead to almost no published rulings. Instead, throughout the text, in the interest of indicating IRS current opinions on the topics, the private rulings are cited.

1.1   DIFFERENCES BETWEEN EXEMPT AND NONEXEMPT ORGANIZATIONS

An exempt organization (or simply an "exempt") is distinguished from a nonexempt organization by its ownership structure, the motivation or purpose for its operations, its activities, and the sources of revenue with which it finances its operations. Exempts are commonly called nonprofit or not-for-profit organizations under state law, which leads to a certain amount of confusion. The term "nonprofit" is a contradiction in one respect. To grow and be financially successful, an exempt can and often must generate profits. Many pay income tax on unrelated business income they are permitted to conduct to raise a part of their funding. Exempts are fascinating because they are full of such paradoxes and surprises.

Although businesses do not often give away food or house the poor, they do operate schools, hospitals, theaters, galleries, publishing companies, and conduct other activities that are also carried on by exempt organizations. The nature of the activity or business is often the same for both. One goal of this book is to provide the tools for understanding the differences between exempt and nonexempt organizations.

The requirements for nonprofit status vary from state to state, and few generalizations apply. Exempt charitable institutions are called "public benefit" corporations in some states. Business leagues and social clubs are sometimes called "mutual benefit" corporations. Rather than being organized to generate profits for owners or investors, exempt organizations instead generate resources to accomplish the purposes of their broadly based public or membership constituents.

(a)   Choosing a Category

Do not expect the distinctions among the categories to be clear or logical. The group of exempt organizations has expanded considerably since the Tariff Act of 1894 established a single category of exempt organizations, which included charitable, religious, educational, fraternal, and certain building and loan, savings, and insurance organizations. Since then, the number of categories has expanded to include at least 30 distinct types.

As with all federal tax matters, the Internal Revenue Code expresses general concepts subject to endless interpretation. For example, only scholars of legislative history can explain why agricultural organizations and labor unions are coupled together. Why are agricultural groups not considered business leagues? Why are agricultural auxiliaries classified as business leagues? Why was a separate category carved out for real estate title-holding companies with multiple parents, instead of placing them in the original §501(c)(2) for single parent organizations?

The choice of category is driven by a number of different factors that are presented in Chapters 2 through 10 along with cited examples of those that do qualify for exemption compared to those that do not. Often the choice is influenced by the desire to receive tax deductible revenues. To receive a charitable donation, a §501(c)(3) charitable or (c)(19) veterans' group classification is required. However, the freedom to lobby is constrained by the (c)(3) category, so that the §501(c)(4) structure might be chosen instead by a charitable project that can only be accomplished through the passage of legislation as discussed in Chapters 6 and 23.

(b) Businesslike Behavior

Ironically, in order to be financially successful, a nonprofit can operate in a businesslike fashion—efficiently and often profitably. Most of the financial management tools applied by for-profit businesses—strategic planning, investment management, responsive organizational structure, budgeting, and others—are appropriately used by an exempt. A thorough consideration of this subject can be found in my book *Financial Planning for Nonprofit Organizations.*[1]

The distinguishing characteristic of an exempt organization in this regard is the motivation for undertaking an activity that generates revenue. The fact that a nonprofit charges for the services it performs is not determinative. A school, a hospital, or any other type of exempt organization may pay all of its costs with fees paid by students, patients, and others using its facilities and services. Whether a hospital is exempt, for example, depends on whether it was created and operated to provide health care for the purpose of promoting the general public's health (see Chapter 4), not upon a deficiency of patient revenues in comparison to its expenditures.

An exempt organization can generate revenues in excess of its expenses and accumulate a reasonable amount of working capital or fund balances. It can save money to purchase a building, to expand operations, to protect itself with a reserve for lost or reduced funding, to ensure a flow of cash to pay for continuous operations, or for any other valid reason serving its underlying exempt purposes. Many private foundations are endowed with assets that are as much as 20 times their annual expenditures since they are only required to spend 5% of the value of their investment assets each year as explained in Chapter 15. There is no specific tax limitation on the amount of assets other types of exempt organizations can accumulate so long as the amount does not evidence a lack of exempt purpose as discussed in 2§2. Too high a level of assets in relation to expenditures, however, can hamper an organization's fund-raising efforts. Public charities, business leagues, clubs, and other membership organizations that depend upon annual support commonly have modest asset levels. The level of accumulated assets may also be influenced by funders that are sometimes reluctant to make grants to an exempt with significant reserve funds.

An exempt organization can also seek to borrow money from private lenders to finance its activities—to establish a new office or acquire an asset, for example. Basically, an exempt can operate without a profit motive and still produce a profit! It can pay salaries and employee benefits comparable to those of a nonexempt business. So long as the overall compensation is reasonable, as discussed in Chapter 20, an exempt entity can offer incentive compensation to its employees. What it

---

[1] John Wiley & Sons, 1996, 275 pages.

normally cannot do with its net profit is distribute it as a return on capital to the persons who control the organization.

The focus and purpose of an exempt organization's activity are outward, unselfish, and directed at accomplishing a public purpose. One way to think of this characteristic is as a one-way street. Much of the money received by an exempt is one-way money—donations or dues paid out of pure generosity with nothing being received or expected in return. Nonprofits are permitted to operate on a two-way street as it regards selling goods and services that accomplish its exempt purpose. Such revenue activity cannot be conducted strictly with the intention of producing a return on investment. In contrast, privately owned businesses operate totally on a two-way street. Their activity is directed at selling goods and services for the purpose of reaping return for their owners' investment.

On a limited basis, an exempt is allowed to compute directly with nonexempt businesses and operate a business that does not advance exempt purposes. The Internal Revenue Code places such an exempt on the same footing as competing businesses by imposing a regular income tax on profits from such activity. If the unrelated business activity becomes too substantial, the exempt can lose its exemption. Chapter 21 considers the question of when a business activity is unrelated, describes the level of business activity allowed, and presents the myriad of exceptions and modifications that allow much of this type of income to escape taxation.

1.2 NOMENCLATURE

The complexity of this subject is illustrated by the fact that the Internal Revenue Code does not contain the word nonprofit—it refers only to exempt organizations. The term nonprofit, or not-for-profit, describes the type of organization created in most states, and is widely used to identify tax-exempt organizations. The terms are often used interchangeably, as they are in this book.

Another factor coloring the distinctions is the language of the code. Tax rules are gray and not necessarily made clear by IRS rulings and decisions. In many cases, the terms used do not necessarily possess their dictionary definitions. To obtain exempt status, an organization applies for a *determination* by the Exempt Organization branch of the IRS. Form 1023 or 1024 is submitted to allow the IRS to determine whether exempt status is appropriate. If the organization plans certain activities within an initial fiscal year of at least eight months, a *definitive determination* is granted. When the operation is prospective, a five-year *advance ruling* is granted, subject to a subsequent final determination, as discussed in Chapter 18.

An exemption qualified under §501(c)(3) must be organized *exclusively* for exempt purposes within the specific terms described in the code, and must operate *primarily* for such purposes. The primary test is applied by deciding whether *substantially all* of the activity is exempt. "Exclusively" does not mean 100%, and "primarily" can mean a little more than 50%. The *facts and circumstances* are examined in each case to ascertain qualification. The regulations provide a few specific numerical tests, which are indicated in the checklists when applicable. A numerical test is most often applied to gross revenues, but it can also be applied to net profits, direct costs, contributions, and the like. In each case, the IRS examines the exact facts to determine whether exemption is in order.

1.3 OWNERSHIP AND CONTROL

As a general rule, directors or trustees may control and govern an exempt organization but may not beneficially own it. Upon dissolution, a charitable exempt may not return any of its funds to its individual contributors or to controlling parties. Instead, its funds can only be paid to other charitable organizations or beneficiaries. A business league, however, can rebate an accumulated surplus to its members upon dissolution, if the accumulation of such a reserve was not a primary purpose of the league. A mutual insurance company continually reduces premiums by the profits earned on investments.

The code of conduct for directors of exempt organizations is most often found in state law defining fiduciary responsibility and embodies the duties of care, loyalty, and obedience. Those who control an exempt are expected to manage the organization in the best interest of its exempt constituents, i.e., its charitable class or membership, not to benefit themselves or their families. IRC §§501(c)(3) and (4) provide that no profits or assets can inure to the benefit of the exempt's officers and directors, but give very meager guidance regarding officer and director responsibility and constraints. For private foundations, specific rules prohibit self-dealing transactions between the foundation and its governors as explained in Chapter 14. Special limitations concerning private inurement in insider transactions for public charities are outlined in Chapter 20.

A common question concerning exempts is whether paid staff members can serve on the organization's board of directors. Such a dual position creates a conflict of interest. To evidence that the interests of the organization rather than the conflicted person are served, paid directors should not participate in votes approving their compensation or in other financial transactions that affect them. In Texas, a director or trustee may serve in a staff capacity for compensation so long as the pay is reasonable and not in violation of his or her fiduciary responsibility. However, in California, no more than 49% of the board members may be staff members. Funders sometimes impose restraints about this matter. This question should be investigated under the laws of the state in which the exempt conducts its activities.

There is no federal tax rule that prohibits a paid staff member from also serving as a board member. Private foundations can compensate its officials for services they provide subject to penalties for unreasonably high payments as discussed in Chapter 14. Congress in 1996 subjected public charities and civic welfare organizations to similar sanctions called *intermediate sanctions*. Penalties can be imposed upon persons receiving excessive compensation or other benefits from §§501(c)(3) and (4) organizations and those officials approving the transaction are also penalized as discussed in Chapter 20.

1.4 THE ROLE OF THE INTERNAL REVENUE SERVICE

The IRS giveth and taketh away an organization's tax-exempt status. Only §501(c)(3) organizations technically need IRS consent, called a *determination*, of their qualification. A (c)(3) organization is not classified as exempt until it makes its request for such status by filing Form 1023. For all other kinds of exempts, being established and operated according to the characteristics described in the tax code is sufficient. However, most exempts seek IRS determination to secure proof of their status for local authorities, members, and in some cases, the IRS itself, and to insure against penalties and interest due on their income if they do not qualify. Chapter 18 explains the process by which application is made.

To qualify for exemption from inception, a prospective §501(c)(3) organization must file a determination application within 27 months of its creation. Later filing will result in a determination only from the date of filing, unless the IRS grants retroactive relief, which is unlikely. Careful timing in the formative stage is critical.

Annual information returns (Form 990 or 990-PF) are filed by most exempt organizations. Detailed balance sheets, income statements, lists of directors and officers and their compensation, and descriptions of activities must be submitted, along with reports of any changes in the organization's form or purposes. The returns contain descriptions of the organization's exempt activity along with financial information, and are open to public inspection. Chapter 27 contains examples and guidelines for completion of the forms.

A special division of the IRS handles exempt organization matters from four regional offices located in Los Angeles, California (West), Dallas, Texas (Midstates), Brooklyn, New York (Northeast), and Baltimore, Maryland (Southeast), a central office in Cincinnati, Ohio for processing exemption applications, a centralized services center for annual returns located in Ogden Utah, and a national office located in Washington, D.C. This division examines returns of exempts to ascertain that continued tax exemption is allowed and, subject to the statute of limitations, can propose revocation. Due to reduced funding over the past years, this IRS division has reduced its personnel and published guidance issued to construe the rules. Chapter 28 outlines matters that bring an organization into contact with the IRS, such as changes in purpose, public status, and fiscal year and offers suggestions for successful communication with the IRS.

1.5 SUITABILITY AS AN EXEMPT ORGANIZATION

Before embarking on the creation of an exempt organization, some basic questions that may influence the decision to go forward should be addressed. Although certain requirements are applied precisely according to published guidelines, the rules are often ambiguous and subject to varying interpretations. The IRS determination branch is highly skilled and thorough in its evaluation of applications for exemption and its taxpayer assisters are helpful. Nevertheless, the determination process and annual tax compliance responsibilities for exempt organizations are at best very similar to those required of profit-motivated taxpayers. Professional assistance from accountants and lawyers familiar with nonprofit matters should be sought to facilitate the process. If funds are limited, a qualified volunteer can be sought. In many states, pro bono assistance is available through technical support centers staffed by volunteers from CPA, Bar, and other professional associations.

Before a prospective project is formally established, four major questions should be asked to determine whether a proposed organization is suitable for qualification for tax-exempt status and ongoing operation as a nonprofit project.

Question 1   Is a new organization really necessary?   Could the project be carried out under the auspices of an existing organization? Several factors can indicate that a new organization is not necessary. If it is a short-term or one-time project with no prospect for ongoing funding, it probably is not worth the trouble to set up an exempt to handle it. Maybe the project can operate as a branch of an existing exempt organization. If a local branch of an organization holding a group exemption is available through a national organization, starting a new exempt may not be a wise idea. If there would be a costly duplication of administrative effort, or if the cost of obtaining and maintaining independent exemption would be excessive in relation to the total budget, it makes sense to opt for another route.

Question 2   Which category of exemption is appropriate?   If the proposed organization passes the first test, the category of exemption best suited to the goals and purposes of the project must be chosen. Due to the rigidity and limitations of the §501(c)(3) exemption rules, certain activities may only be suitable for other categories of exemption. The (c)(3) rules include a complete prohibition against involvement in political campaigns, and limitations on legislative and grassroots lobbying, as explained in Chapter 23. For such projects, a §501(c)(4) organization may be more suitable for the purposes of the founding group.

As explained in Chapters 6–9, some projects can conceivably qualify for more than one category. There are garden clubs classified as charities under §501(c)(3), civic welfare societies under §501(c)(4), and social clubs under §501(c)(7). An association of business persons, such as the Rotary Club or the Lions Club, most often qualifies as a business league. If the activities of the group involve educational and/or charitable efforts, (c)(3) status, rather than (c)(6) status, might be sought, or two organizations—a (c)(3) and a (c)(6) might be suitable. A breakfast group composed of representatives of many different types of businesses may not qualify under §501(c)(6), but might instead easily qualify under §501(c)(7). The tax deductibility of member dues and taxability of income influences the desired choice of category, as discussed later. The creation of a nonexempt nonprofit can also be considered if profits are expected to be minimal.

Question 3   Do expected revenue sources indicate nonprofit character?   Next, the proposed sources of revenues expected to support the project must be examined. Exempt organizations are traditionally supported by donations, member dues, and fees for performing its exempt functions, such as admission to museum or fees for certification of professional standing. Certain sources of revenue are not suitable for exemption. Among them are sales of goods produced by members and income from services rendered in competition with nonexempt businesses (for example, insurance or legal services). Less than half of the exempt's revenues may come from unrelated businesses, as discussed in Chapter 21. Self-dealing and certain other transactions are prohibited, and certain sources of support could result in the exempt organization being designated a private foundation (see Chapter 11).

Question 4   Are creators motivated by selfish goals?   A tax-exempt organization as a rule must be established to serve persons other than its creators (though creators can participate in its affairs). This question examines the reasons why persons seek to establish the nonprofit. Do the organization's creators desire economic benefits from the formation or ongoing operation of the organization? Will the organization be operated to serve the self-interested purposes of its creators? If so, it is likely the project cannot qualify for tax-exempt status. The one-way street characteristic of nonprofits is crucial to ongoing qualification for tax exemption. If the founders desire incentive compensation based on funds raised, or wish to gain from profits generated, an exempt organization may not be the appropriate form or organization. Reasonable compensation for services actually and genuinely rendered can be paid, as discussed in Chapter 20, but no private benefit to insiders or significant participants can result from the exempt's activities.

For a variety of reasons, it is sometimes desirable to convert a for-profit business into a nonprofit one. In the health and human service field, for example, funding is often available from both for-profit and nonprofit sources. An organization's direction may change or funds may become available only for tax-exempt organizations, such as for health issue research programs. When an exempt is created to take over the assets and operations of a for-profit entity, the buyout terms will be carefully scrutinized. Too high a price, ongoing payments having the appearance of dividends, and assumptions of liability that take the creators off the hook are among the issues faced in this situation, as also discussed in Chapter 20.

When a tax-exempt organization ceases to exist, its assets remaining upon dissolution must essentially be used for the same exempt purposes for which the organization was initially granted tax exemption. Charities exempt under §501(c)(3) can only distribute funds to another (c)(3) organization or in support of a charitable project, and their charters must contain a binding dissolution clause. Its assets must be permanently dedicated to charitable purposes. Again, the one-way street concept exemplifies the character of a tax-exempt organization. The creators must understand and intend from inception that they will gain no personal economic benefit from the organization's operations and benefits. Exhibit 1-2 can be used to review the considerations in forming a new exempt organization.

1.6 START-UP TAX AND FINANCIAL CONSIDERATIONS

A project that meets the criteria in the previous section indicating a new nonprofit organization is suitable under the federal tax rules also has significant financial issues to consider before the nonprofit is formed. One important issue that must be thoroughly considered is organizational structure—whether to form a corporation versus a trust, how the board will be chosen, and what bylaw provisions are suitable, among others. Financial issues should be considered and quantified—projections prepared, feasibility studies conducted, and seed money sources identified. Operational plans should commence—financial management, recordkeeping requirements, staffing, and other issues outlined in Exhibit 1-3.

(a) Preliminary Planning

An important start-up question concerns the type of entity to be created. Founders must decide the type of organization that should be formed—a corporation, trust, or association. Each structure has its benefits and drawbacks, as addressed in Chapter 1§7.

Exhibit 1–2

SUITABILITY FOR TAX-EXEMPT STATUS CHECKLIST

> *A predominance of "yes" answers to the following questions indicate the proposed organization is NOT a suitable candidate for tax-exempt status or that special rules may apply. Chapter sections can be studied for more discussion of each issue.*

1. Is a new organization necessary, or could the project be carried out as a branch of an existing organization?

	Yes	No
■ Life of the project is short.	☐	☐
■ It is a one-time project with no prospect for ongoing funding.	☐	☐
■ Project could operate under auspices of another EO.		
■ Duplication of administrative effort is too costly.	☐	☐
■ Cost of obtaining and maintaining independent exemption is excessive in relation to total budget (Ch. 18).	☐	☐
■ Group exemption is available through a national EO (Ch. 18§2f).	☐	☐

2. Which §501(c) category of exemption is appropriate to the goals and purposes of the project?

	Yes	No
■ The organization participates in efforts to influence elections or otherwise participate in political campaigns (Ch. 23).	☐	☐
■ Purposes of the organization can only be accomplished through legislative and grassroots lobbying activity (Ch. 6 and 23).	☐	☐
■ Activities benefit a group of business persons or a social group? (Ch. 7, 8, and 9).	☐	☐
■ Persons benefitted by the proposed activities represent a limited group rather than a charitable class? (Ch. 2§2a).	☐	☐

3. Are the sources of revenue suitable for an exempt organization?

	Yes	No
■ Organization plans to sell goods produced by members indicating a cooperative (Ch. 2§2e).	☐	☐
■ A significant amount of the revenues will come from services to be rendered in competition with nonexempt businesses, such as legal services or insurance? (Ch. 21§8).	☐	☐
■ Over half of revenues will be from unrelated businesses operated in competition with for-profit companies? (Ch. 21§4(b)).	☐	☐
■ A majority of the funding will come from a particular individual, family, or limited group of people that may require classification as a private foundation (Ch. 11–17).	☐	☐

4. Do the creators desire economic benefits from the operation of the organization?

	Yes	No
■ Transactions with related parties are anticipated (Ch. 20§1).	☐	☐
■ Proposed financial arrangements with creators will pay portion of revenues to insiders as rent, royalty, or interest (Ch. 20§6).	☐	☐
■ Creators wish to be paid incentive compensation based upon funds raised or profitability of the organization (Ch. 2§1(c) and 20§2(c)).	☐	☐

Exhibit 1–2 (*continued*)

	Yes	No
■ Assets will be purchased and/or debts of creators assumed (Ch. 20§6).	☐	☐
■ Project will operate in partnership with for-profit investors (Ch. 22).	☐	☐
■ Services and activities will be available to a limited group of persons or members instead of a public class? (Ch. 2§2(a) and 8§2).	☐	☐
■ Upon dissolution of the organization, assets can be returned to creators and/or major donors (Ch. 2§1b).	☐	☐

Future sources of funds to operate the proposed nonprofit should next be projected in the planning stage for several reasons. First and foremost, creators should evaluate the financial feasibility of their ideas. It is laudable to want to feed the poor in one's county; the question to ask at this stage is can the group forming the program put together enough funds to do so. Second, many categories of exempt organization have special attributes and standards measured by their sources of funding for reasons explained in the chapter pertaining to that particular type of organization. If the exempt organization wishes to be classified as a charity, for example, it is time to see whether the organization will qualify as a public charity or a private foundation. Expected donation levels must be quantified to measure public support, as described in Chapter 11. Social clubs are subject to strict numerical limits on the amount of nonmember revenues they may receive. Business leagues and labor unions, like charities, cannot generate too much unrelated business income. The specific plans for the proposed organization should be tested at this point from a financial standpoint, using the basic rules for qualifying as a tax-exempt organization.

Whether the organization will operate as a membership group must be decided. The term "membership" is often misunderstood and misused. Some organizations use the term "member" to designate contributors who actually have no voting rights. Technically, a membership organization is one whose members elect the persons on the governing board. The democracy afforded by such a form of organization may or may not be desirable. A self-perpetuating board retaining control in the hands of a few persons may be appropriate.

The rules governing the organization's future decision-making procedures are outlined in the bylaws. The answers to the following questions, among many others are found in the bylaws: How will officers be elected? When will meetings be held and who can call them? Who will serve as advisors? Who signs checks? What credentials will be required of board members, and what length of term will they serve? A skilled attorney can be very helpful in designing appropriate bylaws. The IRS and some states are not particularly interested in parliamentary procedures. No sample bylaws are provided in IRS Publication 557, *Tax-Exempt Status for Your Organization*. On the other hand, this guide prescribes very particular provisions that must be contained in an organization's articles of organization for

Exhibit 1–3

BASIC TAX AND FINANCIAL CONSIDERATIONS
IN STARTING A NEW NONPROFIT ORGANIZATION

Organizational Issues:

Suitability for exempt organization status (See Exhibit 1-2.) ☐

Form of organization—corporation, trust, or association (Ch. 1§7) ☐

Organizational Documents:
   Mission statement/purpose clause (Ch. 2§1) ☐
   Membership or not ☐
   Provisions of bylaws ☐
   Board composition and terms for advisors ☐

Choose name and check availability ☐

Federal tax considerations
   Qualification for tax exemptions (Ch. 2–10) ☐
   Amount of business activity planned (Ch. 21) ☐
   Transactions with creators, directors, and officers (Ch. 14 and 20) ☐
   Private vs. public charity (Ch. 11) ☐

Financial Considerations:

Capitalization needs
   Future need for capital and ability to raise funds ☐
   Reliability of funding sources ☐

Financial planning systems
   Long- and short-range financial plans (budgets) ☐
   Maximizing cash flow and investment income ☐
   Billing, collection, and bill-paying policies ☐

Internal control systems ☐

Recordkeeping Systems:
   Primary accounting records (banking records, original invoices,
      and customer/patron/client billings) ☐
   Secondary records (cash, general, payroll, and other ledgers) ☐
   Cash vs. accrual method ☐
   Cost accounting systems ☐
   Fund accounting and donor/member database software ☐

Filing systems
   Paid bills in alphabetical order ☐
   Permanent assets (individual files by objects or type) ☐
   Establish "throwaway" date system ☐
   Exempt activity records (archives) ☐

Exhibit 1–3 (*continued*)

Tax compliance systems (Ch. 19)
 Application for federal identification number and exemption ☐
 Complete federal tax compliance checklist ☐
 State and local registration, permits, and/or taxes ☐

Employees vs. independent contractors (Ch. 25)
 Tax aspects: proper classification, withholding,
  and reporting requirements ☐
 Personnel policies: vacation, sick leave, written contracts,
  and job descriptions ☐
 Fringe benefits ☐
 Travel and expense documentation requirements ☐

exemption to be granted. For groups affiliated with a state or national group, model articles and bylaws may be available. The minimal bylaws typically used in Texas are included in the sample Form 1023 in Chapter 18.

This is a good time to think about what name to bestow on the organization. A name that accurately presents the organization's purpose should be chosen. The words "fund" or "foundation" might not be a suitable name for a nonprofit that intends to do fund raising because the words connote it already has resources. Similarly the word "center" connotes a place where people gather for a variety of reasons, "institute" a place where people meet to talk and study. The name cannot repeat or conflict with names already in use. If there is already a Center for Genetic Research chartered in the state, a newly created Center for Genetic Study may not be permitted. The availability of the chosen name can be investigated through the local and state authorities. In Texas, the office of the secretary of state can be called to check availability and to reserve a name.

(b) Financial Management

In a nutshell, to be successful, a nonprofit organization should be financially managed just like a business. To be financially viable, an exempt organization needs sufficient capitalization similar to a for-profit organization—and it cannot float a stock issue. The reliability of funding sources should be evaluated to ensure sustainable spending levels. Before the final decision to establish a new organization is made, the exempt's future needs for capital and its ability to raise money must be projected.

The initial projections can be a starting point for an ongoing planning process that can improve the financial well being for an exempt organization. Short-range budgets and long-range financial plans should be maintained and continually updated. Operating and capital budgets are recommended. Plans for maximizing yield on cash and other investment assets should be formulated. As much of the exempt organization's money as possible should be kept in interest-bearing accounts, and professional investment managers can be sought once capital reserves exceed immediate needs.

An accounting system and procedure should be established to record, report, and internally control the financial resources in accordance with generally accepted accounting principles. This system should also maximize cash flow by billing customers and collecting from contributors as quickly as possible, while at the same time delaying payment of the organization's own bills for as long as is reasonable. Consult my book, *Financial Planning for Nonprofit Organization* for guidance.

1.7 CHOOSING THE BEST FORM OF ORGANIZATION

The three common structural forms for a nonprofit organization are nonprofit corporation, trust, or unincorporated association. The choice of organizational form is influenced by the laws of the states in which the nonprofit will operate. Certain categories of §501 organizations are limited in their choice of form. A title-holding company, for example, must be a corporation. Some §501 categories of exemption apply to clubs, associations, leagues, and posts, and may have unique organizational structures. An experienced attorney knowledgeable about nonprofit organizations can be extremely valuable in making this choice. If the project needs to seek volunteer, or pro bono assistance due to limited funds, the local bar association and accountants' society may have such a program.

Whichever form of organization is chosen, the federal tax code and regulations often have differing requirements from those of the state in which the nonprofit is established. Particularly for those seeking classification as a §501(c)(3) organization, the standards for federal exemption are very specific and commonly more stringent than those of the state. A charter that allows a nonprofit to conduct those activities permitted under local law may not necessarily qualify for federal exemption. Caution must be used in drafting a charter, as more thoroughly discussed in Chapters 2 and 18.

(a) Corporation

Corporate status is said to be the most flexible form of organization for a nonprofit and is the form of choice in most states. The American Bar Association and the Association of Attorneys General have developed uniform exempt statutes that have been adopted by many states.

Creating a corporation as a separate entity creates a corporate veil that may shield the individuals governing and operating the nonprofit from liabilities incurred by the organization, unless they are negligent or somehow remiss in their duties. Some states have adopted immunity laws augmenting protection against liability for directors and officers of nonprofits. In Texas, the Charitable Immunity and Liability Act of 1987 applies to §501(c)(3) organizations. This statute shields a charity's officers, directors, and volunteers, regardless of the form of organization, thus obviating one of the advantages in establishing a corporation. These rules are different for the particular state(s) in which the nonprofit operates and should be carefully studied. In California, for example, only corporations are provided such immunity.

Though historically many nonprofit organizations had members, an exempt corporation can be formed with or without members. Unless the charter provides otherwise, members are presumed in some states. The primary role of members in this context is to elect the board of directors, who in turn govern the organization. In a privately funded organization, the members may be family representatives whose job is to retain control. The founder of a charity can be named the only member. With most public benefit corporations, members broaden the base of financial support and involve the community in the organization's activities. In such cases, there may be hundreds or thousands of individual contributors who, as a group, control the organization because they elect the directors. Mutual benefit societies, unions, clubs, and the like are usually controlled by their dues-paying members.

The other choice is to allow the board of directors to govern the organization. Closer control can be maintained by a small, self-perpetuating board that chooses its own successors. The charter may also appoint representatives of specified organizations or institutions to occupy board positions. A city arts council board might automatically have a representative of the city museum, the college art department, the symphony orchestra, and an individual artist alongside those directors elected by members. A charity seeking classification as a supporting organization must very carefully design its governing structure to satisfy one of the tests found in IRC §509(a)(3) as discussed in Chapter 11.

Bylaws must be adopted to provide rules of governance, such as the number of directors, duration of their terms, and procedures for removing them. Bylaws typically also address the frequency of meetings, notice procedures, type and duties of officers, delegation of authority to committees, and the extent of member responsibility. The manner in which the bylaws can be amended should also be covered in the bylaws. Indemnity to directors may be provided.

An advantage of the corporate form, as compared to a trust, is that its organizational documents can be amended. Usually, the currently serving board has authority to make changes to both the bylaws and the charter. Though such changes would require approval of both the state and the IRS, they are allowed. For consideration of choices to be made in seeking IRS approval see Chapter 27. A nonprofit corporation's articles can (and normally do) allow its directors and members to mold and change its provisions as the organization evolves throughout its existence.

(b) Trust

The trust form of organization is often chosen for an individually- or family-funded charitable organization. A trust created while one is living is called an inter vivos ("among the living") trust. A trust created by a bequest in the creator(s)' will is called a testamentary trust. A trust is favored by some because unlike a corporation, a trust can be totally inflexible. A trust can be created without provisions allowing for changes in its purpose or trustees. Thus, a donor with specific wishes may prefer this potentially unalterable form for a substantial testamentary bequest. Another advantage of a trust is that some states require no registration.

There is some argument that charitable trusts can violate the rule against perpetuities. To get around this potential obstacle, some trusts contain a provision allowing the trustee(s) to convert the trust into an exempt corporation with identical purposes and organizational restraints if the trust form becomes disadvantageous.

Exhibit 1–4

COMPARISON OF REQUIREMENTS AND TAX ATTRIBUTES
FOR IRC §§501(c)(2), (3), (4), (5), (6), AND (7)

	(c)(2)	(c)(3)	(c)(4)	(c)(5)	(c)(6)	(c)(7)
Exemption application required.	Y	Y	N	N	N	N
Time limit for filing IRS application for exemption (15 months)	N	Y	N	N	N	N
Form 1023 filed.	N	Y	N	N	N	N
Form 1024 filed.	Y	N	Y	Y	Y	Y
REGARDING CHARTER/INSTRUMENT:						
Purpose clause limiting.	Y	Y	N	N	N	N
Dissolution clause required.	N	Y	N	N	N	N
Activity limitations required.	Y	Y	N	N	N	N
REGARDING PAYMENTS TO EO:						
Receive tax deductible contributions.	N	Y	N	N	N	N
Receive tax deductible business dues.	N	N	N/Y	Y/N	Y/N	Y/N
REGARDING REVENUES:						
Annual support test for private foundation class.	N	Y	N	N	N	N
Membership primary income source.	N	N/Y	Y/N	Y	Y	Y
Amount of nonmember income limited.	N	N	N	N	N	Y
REGARDING UBIT:*						
Investment income exempt from UBIT unless investment indebted.	Y	Y	Y	Y	Y	N
Volunteer and donated property exceptions available for UBIT.	Y	Y	Y	Y	Y	Y
Convenience exception.	N	Y	N	N	N	N
Amount of UBI† must be limited.	N	Y	Y	N	N	Y
REGARDING ACTIVITIES:						
Can engage in political campaigns.	N	N	N/Y	Y	Y	Y
Can engage in lobbying.	N	N/Y	Y	Y	Y	Y
Lobbying activity limited.	Y	Y	N	N	N	N
Broad purposes can be pursued.	N	Y	Y	N	N	N
Private inurement/benefit prohibited.	Y	Y	Y	Y	Y	Y
Operations must primarily be exempt.	Y	Y	Y	Y	Y	Y
Can carry out active projects.	N	Y	Y	Y	Y	Y

*Unrelated business income tax.
†Unrelated business income.

Exempt organization immunity statutes do not apply to trusts in some states, and more stringent fiduciary standards are often imposed upon trustees than on corporate directors. As a rule, trustees are more exposed to potential liability for their actions than are corporate directors. The tax rates on unrelated business income of a trust are higher than the rate applied to corporations (see Chapter 27§14).

(c) Unincorporated Association

The unincorporated association form of nonprofit organization is the easiest to establish and correspondingly, to reform. To qualify for exemption, an association must have organizing instruments outlining the same basic information found in a corporate charter or trust instrument. Rules of governance must be provided, and it must have regularly chosen officers. Particularly for §501(c)(3) status, the IRS requires specific provisions in the documents prohibiting certain activities.[2] The constitution or articles of association must be signed by at least two persons.[3] There are few established statutes or guidelines to follow. National, statewide, and nonprofits with branches or chapters can facilitate orderly governance for their subordinates by furnishing a uniform structure document.

An unincorporated group faces substantial pitfalls. The primary concern is lack of protection from legal liability for officers and directors. Banks and creditors may be reluctant to establish business relationships without personal guarantees by the officers or directors.

Once a decision has been made that a tax-exempt entity is suitable and the necessary organizational requirements can be satisfied, the specific category of exemption can be chosen. Exhibit 1-1 lists the more than 30 types of organizations included in the Internal Revenue Code. Chapters 2 through 10 discuss the particulars of the first seven types. Exhibit 1-4 compares the filing requirements and primary characteristics of categories (c)(2) through (c)(7).

[2] Outlined in Chapter 2§1.
[3] Form 1023, Application for Recognition of Exemption, p. 3.

CHAPTER TWO

Qualifying Under IRC §501(c)(3)

2.1 Organizational Test
- (a) Charter, Constitution, or Instrument
- (b) Dissolution Clause
- (c) Inurement Clause
- (d) Purpose Clause
- (e) Political Activities
- (f) Private Foundations

2.2 Operational Test
- (a) Charitable Class
- (b) Amount of Charitable Expenditures
- (c) Income Accumulations
- (d) Commensurate Test
- (e) Business Activity
- (f) Importance of Sources of Support
- (g) Action Organization
- (h) Feeders and the Integral Part Test

Organizations that qualify for exemption under Internal Revenue Code (IRC) §501(c)(3) include "Corporations, and any community chest, fund, or foundation, organized and operated exclusively" for one of eight specific charitable purposes and meet the specific criteria listed below:[1]

- It operates for religious, charitable, scientific, testing for public safety, literary, or educational purposes, or to foster national or international amateur sports competition (but only if no part of its activities involves the provision of athletic facilities or equipment), or for the prevention of cruelty to children or animals;

- No part of its net earnings inures to the benefit of any private shareholder or individual;

- No substantial part of its activities is carrying on propaganda, or otherwise attempting to influence legislation (except as otherwise provided in subsection (h)), and

---

[1] Reg. §1.501(c)(3)-1(a).

- It does not participate in, or intervene in (including the publishing or distributing of statements) any political campaign on behalf of (or in opposition to) any candidate for public office.

IRC §501(c)(3) organizations as a group are commonly referred to as "charitable," partly because they qualify for the charitable deduction income, estate, and gift tax purposes. The title of IRC §170 is "Charitable, etc., Contributions and Gifts." Note, however, that "charitable" is only one of the eight categories listed in §501(c)(3).

Our concept of charity in the United States is very broad, including far more than giving alms to the poor—the traditional European notion. Charity is an evolving concept that has changed over the years to meet societal needs and occasionally to advance public policy thought appropriate by those currently making the laws. Private schools, for example, are allowed exempt status only if they adopt a policy prohibiting discrimination against persons on the basis of their race. The tax laws evidence an intention to encourage private sector initiatives in social programs—health care, education, research, among many other social concerns that typically are governmental responsibilities in the rest of the developed world. Interestingly, the U.S. philanthropic model has been used by Mexico and the former satellites of the Soviet Union as they developed their tax systems during the 1990s.

Chapters 2 through 5 detail the requirements for qualifying under §501(c)(3), along with criteria for the different categories of exemption thereunder. This classification contains both the most numerous categories and the most controversial. Each category is the subject of myriad rulings and case decisions. *The Law of Tax-Exempt Organizations*[2] contains more than 150 pages about charitable organizations and contains a wealth of information beyond the scope of this book.

Although this discussion provides guideposts for determining qualification under §501(c)(3), it offers few hard-and-fast rules because the rules are broad and often vague. By far the largest body of law and written material concerning exempt organizations deals with those classified as charities. The possibilities for qualification are endless, and success lies in a thorough review of the alternatives. In a deceptively simple fashion, there are two tests for qualification for §501(c)(3) status called the organizational and operational tests.

2.1 ORGANIZATIONAL TEST

The organizational test dictates certain rules of governance of a qualifying charitable organization and restricts its purposes and goals primarily to those eight specifically listed in the statute. Language in the governing instrument empowering the organization to conduct activities (except insubstantial ones) beyond the specified purposes are not permitted.[3] The organizational documents of a private foundation must literally, or by operation of state law, prohibit violations of the

---

[2] Bruce R. Hopkins, *The Law of Tax-Exempt Organizations, Seventh Edition* (New York: Wiley, 1998).
[3] Reg. 1.510(c)(3)-1(b).

special sanctions to which it is subject as discussed below in §2.1(f). Assets must be permanently dedicated to §501(c)(3) exempt purposes in the organizational rules pertaining to dissolution, inurement, purpose, and prohibited activities.

(a) Charter, Constitution, or Instrument

To receive IRS approval of exempt status, an organization must be created with properly executed documents filed and approved by appropriate state officials. A formless aggregation of individuals cannot be exempt, nor can a partnership.[4] The IRS determination procedures generally assume two types of organizational documents:

1. Articles of incorporation or association or a trust instrument, and

2. Rules of governance under which the exempt organization is operated, usually bylaws.

Bylaws alone are not an organizing document for a nonprofit corporation, but merely the internal rules and regulations of the organization. For trusts and unincorporated associations, the charter or constitution and bylaws are combined into one document. The form of organization must be a "corporation, community chest, fund, or foundation." Individuals, partnerships, and formless groups of individuals cannot qualify.[5] A model charter exemplifying the provisions that minimally satisfy this test have been developed by the American Bar Association. IRS Publication 557, *Tax-Exempt Status for Your Organization,* also contains samples and should be consulted to ensure that proper provisions are included.

A charter that is defective because it does not contain the four required components cannot be cured by the organization's bylaws. The IRS routinely requires revision of deficient articles prior to issuing a positive determination of (c)(3) exempt status. Although they allow for amendment of deficient charters during the review process, sometimes qualification is issued effective from the date of such an amendment. Where the charter is complete and appropriate, exemption is granted retroactively to the original incorporation date. A defective charter is also not overcome merely because the organization's activities are actually charitable; likewise, an acceptable charter cannot overcome nonexempt activity.[6]

IRS policy is to require the dissolution, inurement, purpose, and political action clauses of a proposed (c)(3) exempt organization to contain the literal term "501(c)(3)." Descriptive language limiting the activity solely to charitable purposes (without specifically mentioning (c)(3)) may be acceptable, but other language may not be, as discussed in §2.1(e). In response to a request that the IRS verify exempt status for a 10-year-old organization, an organization with which the author is familiar was required to reform its charter to meet the specific requirements even though their original charter had been approved by the IRS upon initial determination.

[4] Exempt Organizations Handbook (IRM 7751) §321.1.
[5] IRS Instructions to Form 1023, at page 2; see Chapter 1§7 for consideration of the different forms of organization.
[6] Exempt Organizations Handbook (IRM 7751) §320(2); Rev. Proc. 84-47, 1984-1 C.B. 545.

The Tax Court disagreed with this policy in *Colorado State Chiropractic Society*.[7] A charitable organization, in the court's opinion, need not satisfy the organizational test solely by language in its corporate articles. Other factual evidence in addition to the charter, such as the bylaws, can be considered in determining passage of the test. Nevertheless, in the author's experience, the IRS continues to require the language specifically limit the purposes to charitable ones, and preferably using the term "501(c)(3)."

The IRS does not ordinarily question the validity of the corporate status of an organization that has satisfied the formal requirements for such status under the law governing its creation.[8] However, the minimum requirement for establishing a nonprofit organization in some states, such as Texas, is deficient by federal standards. The range of activities permitted a nonprofit corporation is commonly broader, for example, and a charter granting all powers provided under a state's nonprofit corporation act may not qualify.[9] The charter must be approved or registered with the applicable state agency, usually the secretary of state, before submission to the IRS.

Since many nonprofit organizations have similar names, it is very useful to investigate name availability before the documents are submitted to the state. Unlike a business corporation, a nonprofit may not necessarily be required to use the words "corporation," "company," or "incorporated." A trust instrument need not necessarily be registered with the state in which the nonprofit is established, but must contain the four operating rules specified in the regulations and listed at the beginning of this chapter.

(b) Dissolution Clause

Specific language in the nonprofit's charter must describe the manner in which its assets will be distributed in the event of dissolution. Assets may not be returned to contributors, directors, or any non-501(c)(3) organization or purposes.[10] It is not sufficient to say that the assets will be dedicated to "nonprofit purposes," since nonprofit purposes include activities that are broader than the eight specific (c)(3) purposes. Remaining assets at the time of dissolution must be either expended for (c)(3) purposes or given to another (c)(3) organization. To avoid any questions from the determination group, the IRC section should be specifically mentioned by number.

Some state statutes make these provisions automatic unless otherwise stated in the corporate charter. The IRS has a list identifying states whose dissolution clauses qualify.[11] Even so, specific mention in the charter is advisable to avert IRS challenges to the charter when the application exemption is filed.

(c) Inurement Clause

The inurement clause required in the charter must forbid distribution of any part of the organization's net earnings to its directors, officers, trustees, or to any pri-

---

[7] *Colorado State Chiropractic Society v. Commissioner,* 93 T.C. 39 (1989).
[8] Exempt Organizations Handbook (IRM 7751) §321.2.
[9] Gen. Coun. Memo. 39,633.
[10] Reg. §1.501(c)(3)-1(b)(4); *Church of Nature of Man v. Commissioner,* 49 T.C.M. 1393 (1985).
[11] Rev. Proc. 82-2, 1982-1 C.B. 367.

vate individual.[12] Although IRC §503 now only applies to §501(c)(17) and (18) organizations, it is instructive to study its list of the type of insider transactions that are still essentially prohibited for §501(c)(3) organizations.[13] The five prohibited transactions listed in §503 as causes for revocation of exemption are:

1. Lending any part of its income or corpus, without receipt of adequate security and reasonable rate of interest.

2. Paying any compensation, in excess of a reasonable allowance for salaries or other compensation for personal services actually rendered.

3. Making any part of its services available on a preferential basis.

4. Selling any substantial part of its securities or other property, for less than an adequate consideration in money or money's worth.

5. Engaging in any other transaction that results in a substantial diversion of its income or corpus to the EO's creator, substantial contributors, family members, or controlled corporations of such persons.

In other words, a (c)(3) organization cannot use its assets to benefit its insiders. Chapter 20 defines *insiders* and considers the vague difference between private inurement and private benefit and thoroughly outlines the criteria used to evaluate transactions to identify inurement. Chapter 22 discusses a variety of business transactions and associations between one exempt organization and another and between an exempt organization and private individuals or businesses and presents the standards under which such relationships might be deemed to represent impermissible inurement.

Despite the fact that no evidence was submitted to prove the person(s) forming The Fund for Anonymous Gifts did so to derive financial benefit, the court found its true purpose was to provide investment management services to the donors—or to privately benefit the donors.[14] Donors were explicitly allowed to retain full control over the investment of their assets and also retained a high degree of control over how to choose grantees. The IRS argued that the fund was designed to circumvent the restrictions on private foundations and limitations on charitable deductions and was therefore not organized and operated exclusively for an exempt purpose. To some extent control is similarly retained by donors to community foundations[15] and charitable funds created by investment companies.

(d) Purpose Clause

Organizational documents must limit the purposes of the exempt organization to one or more of the eight specific 501(c)(3) purposes listed below. To qualify under 501(c)(3), an exempt organization must also operate exclusively for one of these purposes. The only permitted purposes are:

---

[12] Reg. §1.501(c)(3)-1(c)(2).

[13] This code section was replaced for private foundation in 1969 by the self-dealing rules discussed in Chapter 14 and for public charities in 1996 by the intermediate sanction rules discussed in Chapter 20§9.

[14] *Fund for Anonymous Gifts v. IRS*, No. 95-1629 (D.D.C. 1997).

[15] See Chapter 11§3(c).

1. Religious

2. Charitable

3. Scientific

4. Testing for public safety

5. Literary

6. Educational

7. Fostering national or international amateur sports competition

8. Preventing cruelty to children or animals

Ideally, the charter will describe one or more of the eight, such as charitable, charitable and scientific, or scientific and educational, along with the qualifier, "as defined in (or within the meaning of) §501(c)(3) of the Internal Revenue Code." Words having similar meaning to those listed above cannot be used unless they are so qualified. The term "eleemosynary" may mean charitable but is not acceptable standing alone. "Civic welfare," although listed as a charitable pursuit in the regulations, also does not, standing alone, qualify under (c)(3)—although such words are suitable under (c)(4). Also, combining permissible with impermissible purposes is not acceptable.[16] The IRS provides the following examples:

ACCEPTABLE: "XYZ Organization is created to receive contributions and pay them over to the organizations which are described in §501(c)(3) and exempt from income taxation under §501(a)."[17] It is also acceptable "to grant scholarships to deserving junior college students residing in Gotham City."[18]

NOT ACCEPTABLE: "MD, Inc. will operate a hospital (with no stipulation that the operation be charitable.)"[19] Nor is it acceptable to state that "ABC will conduct adult education classes," without also stating that the organization is formed for educational or charitable purposes.[20]

In what is called the *Better Business Bureau* test, an organization that has a substantial nonexempt purpose cannot qualify for exemption under (c)(3). Reciting detailed descriptions of the organization's purpose in its charter is not necessarily advisable. Such explanations are more suitable placed in the bylaws or mission statement. An organization's activities tend to evolve over the years and it is best to avoid the need to make formal charter changes that require approval by the state. Bylaws can normally be altered by the organization's governing body. Any changes to the organizational documents must be submitted to the IRS in connection with filing the annual Form 990.[21]

---

[16] Rev. Rul. 69-279, 1969-1 C.B. 152; Rev. Rul 69-253, 1969-1 C.B. 151.
[17] Reg. §1.501(c)(3)-1(b)(1)(ii).
[18] Exempt Organizations Handbook (IRM 7751) §322.2
[19] Id. §322.2.
[20] Reg. §1.501(c)(3)-1(b)(1)(ii). This regulation essentially says that conducting classes is not necessarily educational unless the articles specify that term or the term "charitable."
[21] See Chapter 28 for discussion of circumstances and the methods in which an organization seeks overt IRS approval of such changes.

(e) Political Activities

A charity's organizational documents must absolutely prohibit political campaign involvement with the following language:

> The organization shall not participate in, or intervene in (including the publication or distribution of statements) on behalf of or in opposition to any candidate for public office.[22]

A campaign management school organized to train individuals for professional careers in managing political races, for example, was denied exemption because it was formed to be operated to benefit the Republican party. Most of the school graduates were associated with Republican candidates and committees supporting them. In its application for exemption, the American Campaign Academy revealed that it was an outgrowth of a National Republican Congressional Committee project and that its funding was provided solely by the National Republican Congressional Trust. The academy argued, nevertheless, that it met all the definitions of a school and did not discriminate on the basis of political preference, race, color, or national or ethnic origins in its admission policies. The Tax Court agreed with the IRS that the facts—actual curriculum and admission applications—showed narrow partisan interests. The court found that the size of the class and number of Republican party members did not per se transform the benefitted class into a charitable class.[23]

Nonpartisan voter registration drives do not constitute prohibited political activity if they are truly nonpartisan under the standards outlined in Chapters 17§2 and 23§2. The fact that all candidates in the race are given a platform to discuss universal issues, rather than issues of concern to a particular political party, evidence an educational effort. When the facts indicated that an organization is formed to engage in nonpartisan analysis, study, and research and to conduct educational programs for voters, it may qualify for exemption.[24]

Legislative lobbying must be limited by the following language: "No substantial part of the activities of the organization shall be the carrying on of propaganda, or otherwise attempting to influence legislation."[25] Note the word "substantial." A limited amount of lobbying can be conducted by a charity (except a private foundation). The permissible limits apply to both grassroots and direct lobbying efforts. These limitations are outlined in Chapter 23.

(f) Private Foundations

Enhanced requirements are placed on charities classified as private foundations. A private foundation's charter, or laws of the state in which it operates, must specifically prohibit actions that would cause the imposition of excise taxes. Laws have been passed to automatically incorporate the required language into a private foundation's charter in most states and the IRS has issued a ruling approving

---

[22] Reg. §1.501(c)(3)-1(b)(3)(ii).
[23] *American Campaign Academy v. Commissioner*, 92 T.C. 66 (1989).
[24] Priv. Ltr. Rul. 9117001.
[25] Reg. §1.501(c)(3)-1(d)(1)(ii).

the list.[26] To be cautious, some counselors recommend inclusion of the prohibition against incurring excise taxes for all foundations, but they may not be necessary. A private foundation generally is a nonprofit organization qualifying for tax-exemption that receives its funding from investment income or donations of a limited number of people, usually a family or a particular individual, as more fully explained in Chapter 12.

2.2 OPERATIONAL TEST

To qualify under §501(c)(3), an organization must also meet an operational test. A nonprofit exempt under (c)(3) must operate *exclusively* to accomplish one of the eight purposes listed at §2.1(d) and discussed subsequently in Chapters 3, 4, and 5. The term "exclusively" for this purpose does not mean 100%, so some amount of nonexempt activity is permitted for all (c)(3)s except private foundations. The words used in the statute, "operated exclusively," mean "primarily."[27] To satisfy this test, an organization must operate to accomplish one of the eight named charitable (and public) purposes, rather than a private purpose. A qualifying organization promotes the general welfare of society rather than the private interests of its founders, those who control it (directors, trustees, or key employees), or its supporters (members or major contributors). Evidence for the operational test is found not only in the nature of the nonprofit's activities but also in its sources of financial support, the constituency for whom it operates, and the nature of its expenditures. The presence of a single nonexempt program, if substantial in nature, will destroy the exemption regardless of the number or importance of the truly exempt purposes.[28]

The benefit to an individual participating in an exempt organization's programs is acceptable when the activity itself is considered a charitable pursuit. Examples of such benefits are the advancement a student receives from attending college and the relief from suffering experienced by a sick person. As outlined in Chapters 3, 4, and 5, the standards of permissible individual benefit are different for certain of the eight categories of charitable purpose and the distinctions are sometimes vague. For example, promoting amateur sports competition is listed as a permitted exempt purpose but providing recreational athletic facilities was found not to be an exempt purpose because of the benefit to the individual members of a sports club.[29] A fitness center set up as part of a medical center qualified under the theory that it promoted health, as discussed in Chapter 4§6(f). Visiting a museum or attending a play is recognized as educational (discussed in Chapter 5§1) but attending a semiprofessional baseball game is not.[30] The Greater Kansas City Community Foundation is allowed to operate the Kansas City Royals base-

---

[26] Rev. Rul. 75-38, 1975-1 C.B. 161.

[27] Reg. §1.501(c)(3)-I(d)(1)(ii), as ratified by the Supreme Court in *Better Business Bureau of Washington, D.C. v. United States*, 326 U.S. 279 (1945).

[28] *Better Business Bureau of Washington, D.C. v. U.S.*, 326 U.S. 279, 284 (1945).

[29] *I Media Sports League Inc. v. Commissioner*, 52 T.C.M. 1093 (1986).

[30] *Hutchinson Baseball Enterprises, Inc. v. Commissioner*, 73 T.C. 144 (1979), *aff'd* 696 F.2d 757 (10th Cir. 1982).

ball team for whatever period is necessary to sell the team to a purchaser that would agree to keep the team in Kansas City to relieve the burdens of government, as discussed in Chapter 4§3.

(a) Charitable Class

To be exempt as a charitable organization under (c)(3), an organization must operate to benefit an indefinite class of persons—a charitable class—rather than a particular individual or a limited group of individuals. It may not be "organized or operated for the benefit of private interests such as designated individuals, the creator's family, or shareholders of the organization or persons controlled, directly or indirectly, by such private interests."[31] A trust established to benefit an impoverished retired minister and his wife cannot qualify.[32] Likewise, a fund established to raise money to finance a medical operation, rebuild a house destroyed by fire, or provide food for a particular person does not benefit a charitable class. An organization formed by merchants to relocate homeless persons ("throw the bums out") from a downtown area was found to serve the merchant class and promote their interests, rather than those of the homeless or the citizens.[33] In explaining the meaning of the word *charitable,* the regulations also deem federal, state, and local governments to be a charitable class by stipulating that relieving their burdens is a form of charitable activity qualifying for §501(c)(3) exemption.[34]

A comparatively small group of individuals can be benefited as long as the group is not limited to identifiable individuals. The class need not be indigent, poor, or distressed.[35] A scholarship fund for a college fraternity that provided school tuition for deserving members was ruled to be an exempt foundation.[36] On the other hand, a trust formed to aid destitute or disabled members of a particular college class was deemed to benefit a limited class. The IRS General Counsel stated that the "general law of charity recognizes that a narrowly defined class of beneficiaries will not cause a charitable trust to fail unless the trust's purposes are so personal, private or selfish as to lack the element of public usefulness."[37] Criteria for selection of eligible beneficiaries should be specified and evidence used to choose eligible individuals—case histories, grade reports, financial information, recommendations from specialists, and the like—should be maintained.

The some 9,000 current and former employees, volunteers, and families of a §501(c)(3) health care provider were found to be a sufficiently large enough class

---

[31] Reg. §1.501(c)(3)-1(d)(1)(ii).

[32] *Carrie A. Maxwell Trust, Pasadena Methodist Foundation v. Commissioner,* 2 T.C.M. 905 (1943).

[33] *Westward Ho v. Commissioner,* T.C. Memo. 1992-192.

[34] Reg. 1.501(c)(3)-1)d(2); see Chapter 4§3 for discussion of standards for qualifying as "Lessening the Burdens of Government." See also "How the Concept of Charity Has Evolved," a presentation for the American Bar Association Exempt Organization Committee, reprinted in the *Exempt Organization Tax Review,* March 1997, Volume 16, No. 3, pages 403–412.

[35] *Consumer Credit Counseling Service of Alabama, Inc. v. U.S.,* 78-2 USTC ¶9468 (D.C. 1979), but see *El Paso del Aquila Elderly,* T.C. Memo., 1992.441. Making burial insurance available at cost for the elderly is a charitable activity only if distress is relieved (by allowing indigents to participate) and the community as a whole benefits.

[36] Rev. Rul. 56-403, 1956-2 C.B. 307.

[37] Gen. Coun. Memo. 39876 (July 29, 1992).

of beneficiaries to qualify as a charitable class. Gifts to the assistance fund created by a hospital were deductible as charitable gifts because they were not earmarked for any specific person. The IRS also noted that the contributions were not made with the expectation of individual financial benefit, but instead were voluntary gifts to provide assistance to financially needy persons suffering economic hardship due to accident, loss, or disaster.[38]

A genealogical society tracing the migrations to and within the United States of persons with a common name was found to qualify as a social club, not a charity. Although there was educational merit in the historical information compiled, the private interest of the family group predominated.[39] If membership in the society is open to all and its focus is educational—presenting lectures, sponsoring exhibitions, publishing a geographic area's pioneer history—an organization may be classified as charitable.[40] In contrast, a society limiting its membership to one family and compiling research data for family members individually cannot qualify.[41]

A simple way to prove that an organization operates to benefit a charitable class is for the organization to regrant its moneys only to another §501(c)(3) public charitable organization. Congress imposed such a system on private foundations in 1969 to constrain their grant-making freedom, as described in the expenditure responsibility rules found in Chapter 17. Private foundations can grant moneys to individuals and nonpublic entities for a charitable purpose, but only if they enter into a formal contractual agreement with the grant recipient or obtain IRS approval in advance for individual grant programs. Although there are no such formal rules for public charities, a similar burden to prove that grant funds reach a charitable class exists. The Internal Revenue Service inserts the following language in the determination letters of grant-making public charities:

> This determination is based upon evidence that your funds are dedicated to the purposes listed in section 501(c)(3). To assure your continued exemption, you should maintain records to show that funds are expended only for such purposes. If you distribute funds to other organizations, your records should show whether they are exempt under section 501(c)(3). In cases where the recipient organization is not exempt under section 501(c)(3), there should be evidence that the funds will remain dedicated to the required purposes and that they will be used for those purposes by the recipient.

The National Defense Council, Inc.'s exempt status was revoked because it failed to prove that its individual refugee relief payments were made to members of a charitable class. The IRS agreed to reinstate the exemption only if all payments were made directly to §501(c)(3) organizations, governmental units, or organizations that would otherwise qualify as public charities (presumably foreign relief

---

[38] Priv. Ltr. Rul. 9316051.

[39] *The Callaway Family Association, Inc. v. Commissioner*, 71 T.C. 340 (1978); Rev. Rul. 67-8, 1967-1 C.B. 142.

[40] Rev. Rul 80-301, 1980-2 C.B. 180.

[41] Rev. Rul. 80-302, 1980-2 C.B. 182; see also exemption letter issued to *Legal Assistance for Vietnamese Asylum Seekers*.

groups such as the World Health Organization or the United Nations Relief Agency).[42] Similarly, New Faith, Inc. lost its tax-exempt status for lack of evidence that it served a charitable class.[43] The organization operated canteen-style lunch trucks and argued the food was provided to needy persons on a donation or "love offering basis." The evidence found lacking by the court included:

- There was no record of the number of persons, if any, receiving food items for free or below cost nor the number of customers that were impoverished or needy persons.

- No tally of sales below fair market value was maintained.

- Written statements of the organization did not show that food was offered to anybody free or below cost.

A subset of this issue concerns designated funds. A charity must take responsibility and control the use of its funds—it cannot act as a conduit particularly for funds directed to be paid to particular individual scholarships, medical emergency grants, a foreign organization, religious "deputies," or other grant recipients for which a donor is not entitled to claim a contribution deduction if the payment is made directly to the ultimate recipient.[44] One aspect of the issue is whether the organization accepting the conduit donations can qualify as a public charity or rather as a private foundation. The parallel issue is whether the donations are being paid to individuals.

Serving both charity and an individual is not permitted. A split interest trust that pays a fixed annual percentage of its income to its creator and pays the balance to a named charity is not exempt.[45] Nor is a trust paying a fixed annual sum for perpetual care of the creator's cemetery lot, with the balance paid to charities.[46]

(b) Amount of Charitable Expenditures

IRC §501(c)(3) does not require a specific amount of annual expenditures by a charitable organization. Presumably, it is left to the contributors and supporters of an organization to require that their money be spent for worthy causes and to monitor the manner in which funds are expended. Some states have rules governing spending by nonprofit organizations to monitor particularly the level of administrative and fund-raising costs in relation to program costs. The IRS applies a commensurate test discussed in §2.2(d).

A private foundation, partly because it is not scrutinized by public contributors, is subject to a *minimum distribution* requirement. At least 5% of the average annual value of its investment assets must be expended annually in making

[42] Exemption letter dated Mar. 24, 1993.
[43] *New Faith, Inc. v. Commissioner,* TCM 47,411(M); Dec. 48,572(M) (Tax Court, 1993).
[44] Rev. Rul. 62-113, 1962-2 CB 10 9; *Peace,* 43 TC 1 (1964) (support of specific missionaries), and *Davis,* 495 U.S. 472, 65 AFTR 2d 90-1052. (These citations all involving donations to missionary organizations earmarked for particular individuals.) See also Fund for Anonymous Gifts cited in footnote 14.
[45] Rev. Rul. 69-279, 1969-1 C.B. 152.
[46] Rev. Rul. 69-256, 1969-1 C.B. 151.

grants, conducting programs, or purchasing assets used in charitable activities as explained in Chapter 15.

A subset of this issue is the inurement test discussed in §2.1(c). A nonprofit cannot qualify as a 501(c)(3) organization if more than an insubstantial amount of its expenditures are devoted to activities that do not advance its exempt purposes.[47]

(c) Income Accumulations

There is no prohibition per se against a (c)(3) organization accumulating revenues in excess of its expenditures. Nonetheless, a criterion applied by the IRS to measure whether an organization operates exclusively for charitable purposes is the portion of its revenues actually expended on charitable projects. Where funds are accumulated, the organization has a burden of proving to the IRS and those from whom it is seeking financial support how its charitable purposes are better served by increasing its resources.

This issue arises particularly in connection with publicly funded charities— those organizations that annually raise funds to support their programs through donations or fees charged for services rendered (often both). When fundraising efforts are unusually successful, operations are cost efficient, or for whatever reason an organization generates revenues in excess of expenses, the question arises, will the excess revenues jeopardize exempt status? Can the organization save the income? Must it spend it and if so, how soon? Some profit—excess of revenues over expenditures—can be accumulated so long as the purpose for increasing fund balances is to better advance the charitable interests of the organization over a period of time. Acceptable reasons why funds might be accumulated include:

- To maintain sufficient working capital to ensure ongoing, continuous provision of charitable services. Working capital can be saved to protect against years when income declines due to loss of grants, lower donations, reduced investment income, and other uncontrollable outside forces. The standards concerning for-profit corporation earnings accumulations can be applied—ask how investors would view the accumulated funds. Liquid assets equal to one year's operating budget is thought by some to be a minimally reasonable amount of working capital though in the author's experience, some funding agencies consider such an asset level excessively high.

- To replace obsolete equipment, to acquire a new building, or to establish a new program dedicated to charitable purposes. Saving funds until the organization can self-finance new or improvement projects may be prudent because it allows the organization to avoid indebtedness. In other instances, a sinking fund might be established to ensure the organization can meet its annual obligation to pay off the mortgage on a new building.

---

[47] Reg. §1.501(c)(3)-1(c)(1); see Tech. Adv. Memo. 9711003 where the IRS opined that the amount of money spent was not determinative but rather the scope and extent of charitable activities.

- To establish new programs or expand services for charitable constituents when the funds required exceed current available resources. Savings to self-finance expansion can be accumulated.

A useful context in which to consider this issue are the standards applicable to foundations. A private foundation is only required to distribute 5% of the fair market value of its investment assets each year for charitable purposes.[48] The required charitable expenditure level is determined without regard to the actual annual return on investments; a foundation that is able to earn above 5% on its assets may accumulate the excess income.

(d) Commensurate Test

Another criteria applied by the IRS is the commensurate test. Are the expenditures commensurate in scope to the financial resources of the nonprofit? The theory was first espoused in 1964 in looking at what portion of an organization's assets could be invested in unrelated business activities.[49] In addition to operating exclusively for charitable purposes, a charity's primary purpose must also be charitable. The distinction between the two tests is blurry and no exact mathematical test is provided. It is sufficient to say that both must be satisfied to ensure maintenance of exempt status. Beginning in 1990, revenue agents examined fund-raising organizations with professional fund raisers to see if they receive an excessive portion of the funds they raise for charity. State charitable regulators continue to be concerned and may have specific limitations on such payments.

The commensurate test was used to revoke the exempt status of United Cancer Council, Inc. (UCC), a charity that solicited funds by mail. Out of over $7 million raised during 1986, UCC spent less than $300,000 on patient services and research and paid the balance to its fund-raising counsel, Watson & Hughey.[50] Needless to say, the commensurate test was failed. Bingo operations paying excessive operating costs and salaries, with little or no profits left for charity, also fail the test.[51] In the published determination letter of Temple City High School Bingo, the IRS applied a 15% of gross receipts guideline to evaluate whether a commensurate amount of the receipts actually were paid to the high school the organization was formed to raise funds for.[52]

A nonprofit the sole purpose of which is to raise money for other organizations must devote or pay a sufficient amount of the money it raises to charitable purposes to qualify for exemption under §501(c)(3). Other aspects of its operations and policies may also be indicative of its charitable nature. In a published exemption letter, the Sacramento Charities, Inc., an entity organized to conduct an annual golf tournament, agreed to the following IRS conditions to qualify for exemption.[53]

[48] Discussed in Chapter 15.
[49] Rev. Rul. 64-182, 1964 (Part 1) C.B. 186.
[50] *United Cancer Council, Inc. v. Commissioner,* 109 T.C. 326.
[51] Priv. Ltr. Rul. 9132005. For a good history of the commensurate issue, read Gen. Coun. Memo. 32689 published in 1963, Gen. Coun. Memo. 34682 in 1971, and Gen. Coun. Memo. 38742 in 1982.
[52] IRS Exemption Letter July 6, 1992.
[53] Exemption letter dated June 2, 1993; see also Priv. Ltr. Rul. 9711003.

- All net income was payable to other §501(c)(3)s;

- Recipient organizations were local charities chosen on the basis of their community involvement, use of the funds, and fund-raising ability;

- Grants would not be related to the recipient's volunteer efforts toward the annual event;

- Charitable aspects of the tournament were emphasized in publicity materials about the event;

- Mission statement was printed in the tournament program; and

- New board members who better reflect charitable interests and broadly represent the community would be added to the board.

In meeting the commensurate test, it is the way in which the organization's revenues are expended, rather than their source that is determinative. A nonprofit corporation may be recognized as exempt—the typical private foundation when it receives all of its income from passive investment sources.[54] The IRS says, "It is well established that organizations that do nothing but make contributions to other charitable organizations can qualify for exemption."[55]

(e) Business Activity

The receipt of unrelated business income can jeopardize an organization's exempt status. An organization that conducts a trade or business as a substantial part of its activities can be exempt only if the operation of the business furthers its exempt purpose, i.e., is related. The primary purpose of an organization exempt under (c)(3) must not be to carry on an unrelated trade or business.[56] What is meant by *substantial* is not numerically expressed and is measured by taking all of the facts and circumstances of the organization's operations into account. The size and extent of the trade or business in relation to the organization's exempt activity is determinative. The customary measure of "primaryness" is the portion of the organization's overall budget produced by the business and the time expended by its managers on business versus charitable activities.

It is "likely exempt status of an organization will be revoked where it regularly derives over one-half of its annual revenue from unrelated activities."[57] The regulations, however, provide no specific numerical percentage level. The Second Circuit Court of Appeals thought one-third was excessive.[58] Another court indicated that a safe level of unrelated income would be under 20 to 25% of the organization's overall revenues.[59]

---

[54] Rev. Rul. 64-182, 1964-1 C.B. 186, concerning a nonprofit corporation that owned and maintained for commercial tenants an office building.

[55] Priv. Ltr. Rul. 9417003.

[56] Reg. §1.501(c)(3)-1(e); Rev. Rul. 64-182, 1964 (Part I) C.B. 186.

[57] Gen. Coun. Memo. 39108.

[58] *Orange County Agricultural Society, Inc. v. Commissioner,* 893 F.2d 647 (2d Cir. 1990). *aff'g* 55 T.C.M. 1602 (1988).

[59] *Manning Association v. Commissioner,* 93 T.C.M. 596, 603-604 (1989).

The operation of a trade or business that furthers, or is related to, an organization's exempt purposes is permitted. Proving that a business is related, rather than unrelated, may be necessary for an organization to achieve or maintain exempt status. In evaluating the relatedness of a business enterprise, the purpose toward which the activity is directed, rather than the nature of the activity itself, determines whether the activity serves an exempt purpose.[60] In other words, if a resale shop run with handicapped workers provides a livelihood for workers not otherwise able to support themselves, the fact that the shop is in business competing with commercial resale shops does not prevent relatedness. Consider Goodwill Industries: As a part of a job-training program, handicapped workers repair and refurbish furniture and other items for resale. The primary motivation is to provide training and livelihood for the disadvantaged workers (a charitable purpose), not to operate the stores. An unlimited amount of such related business is permitted.

The profit from business activity that is unrelated to the organization's exempt purpose is subject to income tax. See Chapter 21 for a discussion of permitted amounts of unrelated business activity, methods of calculating the tax, and commerciality test. Spinning excess business activity off into an independent subsidiary corporation saved the exemption application for the Ark Environmental Foundation U.S., Inc. Since a substantial part of its activity was the sale of environmentally friendly products, exempt status was initially denied in the key district. The national office, upon reconsideration, decided that if a truly separate subsidiary was created with a bona fide business purpose, exempt status would be available for the parent.[61]

(f) Importance of Sources of Support

The classic (c)(3) organization receives its financial support from voluntary contributions and from investment income produced from contributions it retains in an endowment or working capital fund. Its charitable nature is evidenced by its ability to attract such donations (one-way street gifts) in support of its activities. The IRS applies support ratio tests in its determinations and examinations. Support coming from a limited group of donors may dictate or result in private foundation status. An absence of or limited amount of donations may imply noncharitable status.

The level of public support normally differs according to the type of organization. For example, a grant-making United Fund would receive the bulk of its revenues from donations; a university would receive a sizable part of its revenues from student tuition (exempt function income). See Chapter 11 for detailed definitions of various categories of public charities and requirements for obtaining public status.

(g) Action Organization

An organization whose purposes can only be accomplished through the passage of legislation—changing local, state, or federal laws—is called an *action organization*

---

[60] *Junaluska Assembly Housing, Inc. v. Commissioner,* 86 T.C.M. 1114, 1121 (1986).
[61] Exemption letter dated May 26, 1993.

and cannot qualify for exemption as a charity under (c)(3).[62] When a substantial part of the organization's activity is attempting to influence legislation by propaganda or otherwise, it is considered an action organization. Attempting to influence legislation means:

- Contacting or urging the public to contact members of a legislative body (the Congress, any state legislature, local council, or similar governing body or the public in a referendum) for the purpose of proposing, supporting, or opposing legislation, or

- Advocating the adoption or rejection of legislation

The test of whether an organization's legislative activity is substantial is applied subjectively with no specific mathematical test. One early case applied a 5% limitation.[63] In another case, the use of a percentage test was rejected and instead the balance of an organization's activities in relation to its objectives and circumstances was considered.[64] Due to the uncertainty, Congress added an elective test containing percentage limitations for measuring permissible lobbying—the expenditure test of IRC §501(h).

Another kind of action organization is one that participates or intervenes, directly or indirectly, in any political campaign on behalf of or in opposition to any candidate for public office. Chapters 6 and 23 discusses these rules in detail, including when to consider the formation of a (c)(4) organization.

(h) Feeders and the Integral Part Test

Each separately organized nonprofit organization must seek to qualify for exemption unless it is included in a group exemption.[65] For legal and/or management reasons, an existing nonprofit may create another organization to conduct high-risk activities, to hold investment assets, or a variety of other reasons. The new nonprofit can qualify for exemption if it performs essential services directly to or for its parent or affiliate or to the class of direct beneficiaries of the exempt activities of its parent.[66] Such an entity is said to be an *integral part* of the parent. Services can be rendered to the natural constituency of its creator, such as the students and faculty of a university or the patients of a hospital. The affiliate can be exempt despite the fact that it makes a profit from its dealings with the parent organization. It cannot, however, be exempt if its activities would produce unrelated income in the hands of the parent.

The relationship between the related organizations is significant. Performing services for a group of similar, but unrelated, organizations is an unrelated activity.[67] The regulations say, "An exempt organization is not related to another

---

[62] Reg. §1.501(c)(3)-1(b)(3).

[63] *Seasongood v. Commissioner*, 227 F.2d 907 (10th Cir. 1955).

[64] *Christian Echoes Ministries v U.S.*, 470 F.2d 849 (10th Cir. 1972), *cert denied*, 414 U.S. 864 (1974).

[65] Discussed in Chapter 18§2(f).

[66] Rev. Rul. 78-41, 1978-1 C.B. 148; *Squire v. Students Book Corp.*, 191 F.2d 1018 (9th Cir. 1951).

[67] Discussed in Chapter 21§8(b).

merely because they both engage in the same type of exempt activities."[68] Being an integral part essentially means to operate as a subsidiary of, although the nature of the control relationship is not stipulated. The word *feeder* is used to describe an organization that provides or conducts an unrelated business (provides its services or sells products to unrelated parties) and pays all of—or *feeds*—its profits to one or more other exempt organizations. Feeder entities are specifically prohibited from exempt status by IRC §502. A separately incorporated nonprofit entity selling pharmaceuticals to a hospital's patients would only qualify for exemption if the nonpatient sales were insubstantial. It would have to prove that its primary purpose was to sell drugs to patients to be classified as an integral part.

[68] Reg. §1.502-1(b).

CHAPTER THREE

Religious Organizations

3.1 Types of Religious Organizations
  (a) Ideology or Dogma Not Essential
  (b) Examples of Qualifying Organizations
  (c) Peripheral Religious Activity
  (d) Secular Groups
  (e) Pseudo-Religious Groups

3.2 Churches
  (a) Special Aspects of a Church
  (b) Definition of Church
  (c) Conventions and Auxiliaries
  (d) IRS Examination Protection

3.3 Religious Orders

3.4 Religious and Apostolic Associations

The first type of (c)(3) organization listed in the statute is *religious*. An organization whose primary purpose is to conduct religious activities qualifies for exemption. However, the regulations do not define religious purposes, presumably to maintain the separation of church and state, and the IRS says that the term cannot be defined precisely.[1]

3.1 TYPES OF RELIGIOUS ORGANIZATIONS

A religious organization is basically one that concerns itself with a person's relationship to divine or superhuman powers, either to worship them through ritual or to study human manifestations of their teachings. The major American religions—Catholic, Baptist, Jewish, and so on—clearly qualify as religious organizations and furthermore as churches. However, there are many nonchurches that qualify for exemption as religious organizations. Churches have a special set of qualifications as discussed in § 3.2.

(a) Ideology or Dogma Not Essential

Religion is not confined to a particular sect or ritual. A court has noted that the symbols of one religion may be anathema to another.[2] Another stated that judgments

[1] Exempt Organizations Handbook (IRM 7751) §344.2.
[2] *Unity School of Christianity*, 4 B.T.A. 61 (1962), *acq.* VI-IC.B. 6 (1927).

about the validity or truth of the organization's beliefs must be avoided by the courts: "It is not the province of government officials or courts to determine religious orthodoxy."[3] Religions that do not believe in a supreme being in the Judeo-Christian sense, such as Taoism, Buddhism, and secular humanism, are eligible for exemption.[4] It is unnecessary to inquire into the nature of the beliefs of an organization. A religion with thousands of adherents based upon supernatural revelations to its founder was found to operate for religious purposes, despite its total control by the founder and lucrative publication sales.[5]

Although a formal written dogma, such as the Christian Bible or the Catholic catechism, may not be necessary, to be classified as religious, an organization must adhere to or promote religious beliefs. The Supreme Court in the *Seeger* case used a two-pronged test to identify a religious belief:

1. The beliefs must be deeply and sincerely held by its members, and

2. Those beliefs must involve a matter of ultimate concern to the person to which all else is subordinate (such as the Catholic notion of God as the supreme being).

A series of questions was asked by one court to evaluate the existence of religion:[6]

- Does the system of beliefs address the meaning of life and death, man's role in the universe, and the proper moral code of right and wrong?

- Is the system of beliefs comprehensive? (More than one single moral teaching is expected.)

- Are there any formal, external, or surface signs that may be analogized to accepted religions (such as services, ceremonial functions, the existence of clergy, structure and organization, efforts at propagation, observation of holidays, and other similar manifestations associated with traditional religions)?

(b) Examples of Qualifying Organizations

Although religious orders and churches unquestionably qualify as religious organizations, a vast array of organizations conducting related activities also qualify under the religious category. To illustrate the concepts, the following list compares qualifying organizations to other organizations with a similar focus that do not qualify for exemption.

- Weekend retreat center, open to individuals of diverse Christian denominations, where organized religious programs are presented and recreational time is limited, can qualify.[7] In contrast, an organization sponsoring

---

[3] *Teterud v. Burns*, 522 F. 2d 357 (8th Cir. 1975).
[4] *U.S. v. Seeger*, 380 U.S. 163 (1965).
[5] *Saint Germain Foundation*, 26 T.C. 648 (1956), *acq.*, 1956-2 C.B. 8.
[6] *Malnak v. Yogi*, 592 F. 2d 197 (3d Cir. 1979).
[7] Rev. Rul. 77-430, 1977-2 C.B. 1914.

religious cruises including extensive social and recreational activities was not permitted exemption.[8] Nor was a retreat center that held unscheduled and nonrequired religious activity available for its visitors, to encourage individual meditation and prayer. (It looked too much like a spa or vacation place).[9]

- Kosher food preparation and inspection of commercial products for compliance with religious belief advances religion and can be exempt.[10] However, a Seventh-Day Adventist Church affiliate was denied exemption for its vegetarian restaurant and food store that provided food stuffs in accordance with church doctrines. Although not so stated, perhaps the fatal flaw was the fact that the stores were open to the general public, evidencing a commercial purpose beyond that of ministering to the spiritual needs of the church members.[11]

- A religious publishing house that disseminates literature to promote its own beliefs can qualify for exemption.[12] Also, publication of a nondenominational newsletter is an exempt activity.[13] If, instead, the publishing house sells a wide variety of religious publications and supplies in a profitable commercial manner, it looks to the IRS and the courts like a business venture and cannot qualify for exemption.[14]

- Communal living groups that practice religious functions also provide food, shelter, and other basic human needs that give individual benefit to the commune members. Newly formed new age communes were found not to qualify as exempt religious organizations in the late 1970s.[15] Later, the IRS recanted its seeming discrimination against alternative religions. When the living quarters and provisions are minimal and "do not exceed those strictly necessary," and few of the members work outside the community, and the group has a religious focus, the IRS may rule favorably.[16] Groups of monks, nuns, and other clerics traditionally have been allowed to qualify as religious organizations, and are often exempt as an integrated auxiliary of a church.[17] Special rules for religious orders and apostolic associations are discussed in §§3.3 and 3.4.

[8] Rev. Rul. 77-366, 1977-2 C.B. 192.
[9] *The Schoger Foundation v. Commissioner,* 76 T.C. 380 (1981).
[10] Rev. Rul. 74-575, 1974-2 C.B. 161.
[11] *Living Faith, Inc. v. Commissioner,* T.C.M. Dec. ¶46,860, 60 T.C.M. 710, 1990-484.
[12] *Presbyterian and Reformed Publishing Co. v. Commissioner,* 743 F. 2d 148 (3rd Cir. 1984); *St. Germain Foundation, supra* note 5; *Unity School of Christianity, supra* note 2; *Pulpit Resource v. Commissioner,* 70 T.C. 594 (1978).
[13] Rev. Rul. 68-306, 1968 1 C.B. 257.
[14] *Scripture Press Foundation v. U.S.,* 285 F. 2d 800 (1961), *cert. den.* 368 U.S. 1985, *Fides Publishers Association v. U.S.,* 263 F. Supp. 924 (1967); *Incorporated Trustees of the Gospel Workers Society v. U.S.,* 520 F. Supp. 924 (D.D.C. 1981).
[15] *Martinsville Ministries, Inc. v. U.S.,* 80-2 USTC ¶9710 (D.C. 1980); *Canada v. Commissioner,* 82 T.C. 973 (1984); *Beth El Ministries, Inc. v. U.S.,* 79-2 USTC ¶9412 (D.C. 1979).
[16] Gen. Coun. Memo. 38827 (1981).
[17] Priv. Ltr. Rul. 7838028-7838036.

(c) Peripheral Religious Activity

Other types of organizations conducting activities associated with religious matters include:

- A religious burial service provided by an exempt organization, the purpose of which was to support and maintain basic tenets and beliefs of a religion regarding burial of its members.[18]

- A coffee house for college students to meet with church leaders, educators, and business leaders for discussion and counseling on religion, current events, social and vocational problems is exempt.[19]

- Radio and television broadcasts of religious materials and worship services is an exempt religious activity, and an organization presenting such broadcasts can qualify even when the station holds a commercial license, as long as the amount of broadcasting devoted to advertisements is insignificant.[20]

(d) Secular Groups

Spirituality, rather than secular or worldly issues, should be the focus of a religious organization. An organization practicing a doctrine of ethical egoism by holding dinner meetings and publishing a newsletter is not religious.[21] A nationwide broadcast ministry that engages in substantial legislative activity is also denied exemption.[22] In the absence of "any solid evidence of a belief in a supreme being, a religious discipline, a ritual, or tenets to guide one's daily existence," the Neo-American Church, whose beliefs focused on psychedelic substances, was denied exemption.[23]

An organization teaching "Gay Imperative" was denied exemption because it was a secular group.[24] The organization was dedicated to "religious explorations and a secular lifestyle for men and women who won't worship a god who oppresses gays." Although the court accepted the sincerity of their belief, it found that the group's beliefs were not religious. The basis of the decision was threefold:

1. Religious beliefs must address fundamental and ultimate questions concerning the human condition—issues of right and wrong, life and death, good and evil. Focusing singularly on sexual preference and lifestyle was found not to be a religious question.

---

[18] Rev. Rul. 79-359, 1979-2 C.B. 226.

[19] Rev. Rul. 68-72, 1968-1 C.B. 250.

[20] Rev. Rul. 68-563, 1968-2 C.B. 212, *amplified by* Rev. Rul. 78-385, 1978-2 C.B. 174, which added the comments about advertisements.

[21] *First Libertarian Church v. Commissioner*, 74 T.C. 396 (1980).

[22] *Christian Echoes National Ministry, Inc. v. U.S.*, 470 F. 2d 849 (10th Cir., 1972), *cert. den.*, 414 U.S. 864 (1972).

[23] *U.S. v. Kuch*, 288 F. Supp. 439, 443-444 (D.C. 1968).

[24] *Church of the Chosen People (North American Panarchate) v. U.S.*, 1982-2 USTC ¶9646 (Minn. 1982).

2. The beliefs must be comprehensive in nature and constitute an entire system of belief, instead of merely an isolated teaching. The court found no outward characteristics analogous to those of other religions. There is no published literature explaining its tradition, no formal written documentation of beliefs, such as the Bible or Koran, nor an oral literature reflecting its beliefs or history.

3. The beliefs must be manifested in external form. This group held no regular ceremonies or services.

(e) Pseudo-Religious Groups

Partly because of the lack of specific definitions, pseudo-religious groups formed to take advantage of favorable tax status afforded to ministers have proliferated over the years. The primary reason such groups are denied exemption is that they provide private benefits to their members, who are often their founders. The classic example is the mail-order, or personal, church. For a few hundred dollars, one buys a church—a charter, ordination papers, or other ministerial credentials—through the mail. In the typical scenario, the buyer takes a "vow of poverty" and gives all of his or her property to the church. Afterwards, the church pays all of the person's living expenses in a purportedly nontaxable manner. It has been easy for the IRS and the courts to find that these organizations serve the private interests of their creators and cannot qualify for exemption.[25]

3.2 CHURCHES

Churches are an important subset of the religious exemption category, but there is no definition of church in the regulations under §501(c)(3). A brief definition of churches is found in the regulations on contributions and unrelated business income: the term "church" includes a religious order or organization if such entity (1) is an integral part of a church, and (2) is engaged in carrying out the functions of a church. What constitutes proper church conduct is to be determined by the tenets and practices of a particular religious body constituting a church. The functions of a church include only two activities according to the regulations:[26]

1. Ministration of sacerdotal functions (communion, marriages, and so on)

2. Conduct of religious worship

[25] *Basic Bible Church v. Commissioner*, 74 T.C. 846 (1980); Rev. Rul. 81-94, 1981-1 C.B. 330; *Church of the Transfiguring Spirit, Inc. v. Commissioner*, 76 T.C. 1 (1981); *Bubbling Well Church of Universal Love, Inc. v. Commissioner*, 74 T.C. 531 (1980); *American Guidance Foundation, Inc. v. U.S.*, 80-1 USTC ¶9452 (D.C. 1980); *Unitary Mission Church of Long Island v. Commissioner*, 74 T.C. 36 (1980); *Tony and Susan Alamo Foundation v. Commissioner*, T.C. Memo 199-155, Dec.48.078.

[26] Reg. §1.170-2 (b) (2) and §1.511-2 (a) (3) (ii).

(a) Special Aspects of a Church

Apparently for reasons of respecting the separation of church and state, churches benefit from several special rules:

- A church and its integrated auxiliaries are automatically exempt from tax and need not seek recognition of exemption.

- No annual filing of Form 990 is required, and a high degree of abuse must be present for the IRS to seek to examine a church.[27]

- Parsonage allowances are exempt from income tax, and ministers have special employment tax rules (see Chapter 25).

- A church qualifies under IRC §170(b)(1)(a)(i) as a public charity without regard to its sources of support.

(b) Definition of Church

The IRS has developed a very specific set of characteristics that a church must possess to gain such favorable tax status. The fourteen attributes are:[28]

1. Distinct legal existence

2. Recognized form of worship and creed

3. Definite and distinct ecclesiastical government

4. Distinct religious history

5. Formal code of doctrine and discipline

6. Membership not associated with any other church or denomination

7. Organization of ordained ministers

8. Ordained ministers selected after completing prescribed courses of study

9. Literature of its own

10. Places of worship

11. Regular congregations

12. Regular religious services

13. Sunday schools for religious instruction for youths

14. Schools for preparation of its ministers

Items 5, 7, 11, 12, and 13 were cited as the most significant attributes in a presentation at an IRS annual training seminar for exempt organization special-

---

[27] IRC §7611.
[28] Exempt Organizations Handbook (IRM 7751) §321.3; Rev. Rul. 59-129, 1959-1 C.B. 58.

ists.[29] "At a minimum, a church includes a body of believers or communicants that assembles regularly in order to worship. Unless the organization is reasonably available to the public in its conduct of worship, its educational instruction, and its promulgation of doctrine, it cannot fulfill this associational role," according to the IRS Exempt Organizations Handbook.

This 14-point test for qualifying as a church was applied by the Eighth Circuit Court of Appeals in 1991.[30] The church in question was founded for the stated purpose of spreading "God's love and hope throughout the world." It conducted bimonthly programs with prayers and gospel music in an amphitheater. It built a small chapel for unsupervised meditational activities and individual prayer, but did not conduct religious services in the chapel. Although the society argued that the test discriminated against new, rural, and poor religious organizations, the court agreed that the IRS's standard for qualification as a church was appropriate. The failure to meet three particular criteria influenced the court:

1. The society did not have a regular congregation and its attendees did not consider it their church.

2. It did not ordain ministers but held services conducted by guest ministers.

3. It did not conduct school for religious instruction of the young.

A television ministry known as the Foundation for Human Understanding had its status as a church challenged by the IRS because about one-half of its budget went to pay for the broadcasts to its 30,000 regular listeners. Its estimated total audience was two million persons. There was no question that television broadcasts alone do not qualify an organization as a church. This entity, however, conducted regular services at two locations for 50 to 350 persons under the guidance of an ordained minister. Religious instruction was provided and it had a "distinct, although short, religious history." Therefore the court felt it possessed most of the criteria to some degree, the critical factors were satisfied, and church classification was permitted.[31]

(c) Conventions and Auxiliaries

Conventions or associations of churches also qualify as churches.[32] Such organizations customarily undertake cooperative activities for churches of the same denomination, and for some groups, such as the United States Catholic Conference, represent a governing body. An interdenominational cooperative association of churches may also qualify as a church, as long as it otherwise qualifies as a religious organization.[33]

---

[29] Exempt Organizations Continuing Education Technical Instruction Program for 1981, Training 3177-20 (1-18), TPDS 87196 at 44.

[30] *Spiritual Outreach Society v. Commissioner,* 91-1 USTC ¶50, 111 (8th Cir. 1991).

[31] *Foundation for Human Understanding v. Commissioner,* 88 T.C. 1341 (1987).

[32] IRC §170 (b) (1) (a) (i).

[33] Rev. Rul. 74-224, 1974-1 C.B. 61.

An integrated auxiliary of a church is afforded the same benefits as a church. Church schools, missionary groups, youth organizations, theological seminaries, and women's and men's fellowship associations are listed in the regulations as examples of qualifying auxiliary organizations. Hospitals, retirement homes, orphanages, and some schools do not perform religious functions and so may not necessarily qualify as auxiliaries. To qualify as an integrated auxiliary of a church before 1995, the organization needed to operate exclusively for religious purposes and be controlled by a church or an association of churches.[34]

The regulations defining a church's integrated auxiliary were revised, effective in December 1995, to encompass a financial support test and eliminate an exclusively religious test.[35] An auxiliary can now be independently controlled as long as it has a legal structure similar to a supporting organization.[36] Note that the definition of a religious order continues to require that the activities be exclusively religious. The amended regulations now provide that the auxiliary cannot finance itself with public donations and charges for services to the general public. Instead, its money must come from church constituents. Specifically an integrated auxiliary of a church is defined as an organization that:

- Is affiliated with a church or a convention or association of churches, and

- Receives its primary financial support (over 50%) from internal church sources rather than public or governmental sources, or is "internally supported."

From an organizational standpoint, an auxiliary is considered affiliated if it:

- Is covered by a group exemption,

- Is operated, supervised, or controlled by or in connection with a church (relationship of a type embodied in 509(a)(3)), or

- One of the following facts and circumstances show that it is so affiliated:

- The organization affirms in its charter, trust instrument, bylaws, articles of association, or other organizing documents that it shares common religious doctrines, principles, disciplines, or practices with the church,

- The organization's name indicates an institutional relationship,

- Reports of financial and general operations are made at least annually to the church,

- The church affirms the organization's affiliation with it, and

- In the event of dissolution, the affiliate's assets are required to be distributed to the church.

The support requirement is written negatively to say that an organization is internally supported unless it both:

---

[34] Reg. §1.6033-2(g) before its revision.
[35] Reg. §1.6033-2(h) essentially codifying Rev. Rul. 86-23, 1986-1 C.B. 564.
[36] Defined in Chapter 11§6.

- Offers admissions, goods, services, or facilities for sale, on other than an incidental basis, to the general public, and

- Normally receives more than 50% of its support from a combination of governmental sources, public solicitation of contributions, and exempt function receipts.

Ministers employed by an integrated auxiliary of a church qualify for special employment tax treatment.[37] For that purpose, the IRS provided a good list of criteria for defining what in 1972 it called an *integral agency*.[38] The following factors given in that ruling can be applied to ascertain when an auxiliary is controlled by the church:

- Whether the religious organization incorporated the institution

- Whether the corporate name of the institution indicates a church relationship

- Whether the religious organization continuously controls, manages, and maintains the institution

- Whether the trustees or directors of the institution are approved by or must be approved by the religious organization or church

- Whether trustees or directors may be removed by the religious organization or church

- Whether annual reports of finances and general operations are required to be made

- Whether the religious organization or church contributes to the support of the institution

- Whether, in the event of dissolution of the institution, its assets would be turned over to the religious organization or church

The ruling provides that the absence of one or more of these characteristics will not necessarily be determinative in a particular case. Church-affiliated organizations that are exclusively engaged in managing funds or maintaining retirement programs can also be treated as an integrated auxiliary of a church.[39]

(d) IRS Examination Protection

The IRS has limited information and power to review the tax-exempt status of a church. As discussed in Chapters 18 and 27, churches are not required to file an application for recognition of exemption on Form 1023, nor annual information return on Form 990. The IRS must be able to prove an extraordinary abuse of the tax law to request to examine the records of a church. A church may only be audited by the IRS if the principal internal revenue officer for the IRS region in which the

---

[37] Discussed in Chapter 25§2.
[38] IRC §3121 (w); Rev. Rul. 72-606, 1972-2 C.B. 78.
[39] Rev. Proc 96-10, 1996-1 C.B. 577.

church is located or the Secretary of the Treasury reasonably believes on the basis of written facts and circumstances that the church is not exempted or may be carrying on an unrelated trade or business.[40]

The Church of Scientology and some of its branches have won significant court battles with the IRS about the application of these rules. The church won a limitation of the IRS's right to request information under the IRC §7611(b)(1)(A) summons provisions when the court found that the records were not necessary, rather than merely relevant, to determining the church's tax liability.[41] In similar battles in Florida and California, the government was more successful.[42] The church in Los Angeles sued the IRS under the Freedom of Information Act for details of a "tax shelter litigation project" designating the church and its parishioners.

After 30 years of battle, the Church of Scientology received favorable IRS determination letters recognizing the tax-exempt status of some 20 of its related organizations in October 1993. A Scientology booklet titled *Information on Taxes and Your Donation* said, "The Internal Revenue Service's action has two consequences of utmost interest to Scientologists. First, this action signifies that the IRS—and the United States Government as well—has formally recognized that the Church operates exclusively for religious purposes and that Scientology, as a bona fide religion, is beneficial to society as a whole. Second, the action means that the donations you make to the church—including donations for auditing and training—qualify as charitable contributions and can be claimed as deductions on your federal and state income tax return!" Payments for training sessions had been considered by the IRS and the Supreme Court[43] to represent nondeductible quid pro quo[44] donations. In a decision surprising to some observers,[45] the IRS Exempt Organization division, as a part of its settlement of Scientology, agreed effective January 1, 1993, to overturn the Supreme Court. The IRS agreed to drop all pending cases involving deductibility of payments to the church and discontinue any audits already under way.

3.3 RELIGIOUS ORDERS

The IRS has a list of criteria for qualifying as a religious order. The following characteristics are considered by the IRS, but only the first factor must necessarily be present.[46]

---

[40] IRC §7611 (a).

[41] *U.S. v. Church of Scientology of Boston, Inc.,* 90-2 USTC ¶50,349 (D.C. Mass). The report was subsequently released based upon a suit brought by tax analysts.

[42] In *U.S. v. Church of Scientology Flag Service Org., Inc.,* 90-1 USTC ¶50,019 (M.D. Fla. Dec. 1989) the church essentially lost when the case was referred to a magistrate to decide which requested items were necessary. Also, in *U.S. v. Church of Scientology Western United States* and *U.S. v. Church of Scientology International, et al.,* CV 90-2690-HLH (Central D. Cal. Feb. 11, 1991) the court ordered the organizations to produce documents that the court found necessary to the IRS determinations.

[43] *Hernandez v. Commissioner,* 109 S. Ct. 2137 (1989).

[44] See Chapter 24 for more information about deductibility of such payments.

[45] "Recap—What We Know About the Scientology Closing Agreement," by Paul Streckfus, 9 *Exempt Organization Tax Review* 247 (Feb. 1994) and "Church of Spiritual Technology's Explanation to the IRS," 8 at p. 983 (Dec. 1993).

[46] Rev. Proc. 91-20, 1991-10 IRB 26.

- The order is an organization otherwise qualifying for exemption under IRC §501(e)(3).[47]

- The order is, directly or indirectly, under the control and supervision of a church or convention or association of churches.

- The members of the order vow to live under set rules of moral and spiritual self-sacrifice of their material well-being and to dedicate themselves to the goals of the organization.

- Members make a long-term commitment, normally more than two years, to the organization after successful completion of the training and probationary period.

- The organization's members ordinarily live together in a community and are held to a significantly stricter level of moral and religious discipline than that required of lay church members.

- Members work or serve full-time on behalf of the religious, educational, or charitable goals of the organization.

- Members regularly participate in public or private prayer, religious study, teaching, care of the aging, missionary work, or church reform or renewal.

Status as a religious order is significant for groups whose members wish to claim exemption from participation in the Social Security system under IRC §1402(c)(4).[48]

3.4 RELIGIOUS AND APOSTOLIC ASSOCIATIONS

Religious and apostolic organizations that cannot qualify for exemption under IRC §501(c)(3) because they engage in business for the common good of their members may instead be classified as exempt from income tax under IRC §501(d). Such organizations are not eligible to receive tax deductible donations,[49] but need not pay income tax on annual profits, if any, that the organization itself generates. The members of such organizations, however, do pay income tax.

The spirit of this exemption is to prevent what Congress perceived in 1936 to be an unfair double tax on both the apostolic organizations and their members.[50] Since the rules of apostolic organizations, such as the House of David and the Shakers, prevent members from being holders of property in an individual capacity, the undistributed profits tax should not be imposed on their corporations. The organization must possess the following attributes:

- A common or community treasury must be maintained. Each member is not required to make a vow of poverty nor contribute private property to the organization.[51] It is the organization's property and earnings that are

---

[47] Meets the organizational and operational tests discussed in Chapter 2.
[48] See Form 4361.
[49] Rev. Rul. 57-574, 1957-2 C.B. 161.
[50] 80 *Congressional Record* 9074 (1936).
[51] *Twin Oaks Community, Inc. v. Commissioner,* 87 T.C. 1233 (1986).

shared, placed in a common fund, and used for the maintenance and support of the members.

- Each member reports as dividends his or her pro rata share of income (distributed or undistributed) from business conducted for the common benefit of the members.[52]

The earnings of such organizations are reported annually on Form 1065, U.S. Partnership Return of Income. Each member is treated as a partner and is taxed on his or her proportionate share of the organization's profits.[53] The income is not subject to self-employment tax.[54] No form is provided for making application for exemption under this section. Instead, a letter describing the attributes of the association that cause it to qualify is submitted to the IRS.[55]

[52] Reg. §1.501(d)-(1)(a).
[53] Reg. §1.6033-1(a)(5); Reg. §1.501(d)(1)(b).
[54] Priv. Ltr. Rul. 7740009.
[55] Rev. Proc. 72-5, 1972-1 C.B. 709.

CHAPTER FOUR

Charitable Organizations

The second type of activity qualified for exemption under Internal Revenue Code (IRC) §501(c)(3) is *charitable*, which is expansively defined "in its generally accepted legal sense," meaning much more than relief of the poor.[1] Charity is an evolving concept, fashioned over the years by societal need and perceived abuses. The definition sometimes also depends upon the policies of the administration currently in the White House: A shelter to house Vietnamese refugees qualified for exemption in 1978; but in 1987, the application for exemption for a similar shelter for Central American refugees was denied because the activity was "against government policy."

Charity connotes broad public benefit that is accomplished either by giving direct financial support to individuals and organizations or by operating projects that benefit the community at large. The courts have reminded the Internal Revenue Service (IRS) that community benefit is not limited to housing the homeless or feeding the poor.[2] The education, culture, and health of the public are also charitable concerns. Although the IRS does not always agree, an organization that charges for its services and excludes those that cannot pay *may* qualify as a charitable one.

---

[1] Reg. §1.501(c)(3)-1(d)(2).
[2] *Consumer Credit Counseling Service of Alabama, Inc. v. U.S.*, 78-2 ¶9660 (D.C. 1978).

Particularly in the health care arena, the requirement that the poor be served to achieve charitable classification has been for years the subject of a seesaw battle that continues. The two most important criteria for achieving and maintaining tax-exempt status are whether a broad enough charitable class benefits and whether the services convey a public benefit rather than an individual or private benefit.[3]

Application of the criteria is exemplified by comparing two entities. A performing arts center supported by the sale of $40–$100 tickets per performance is considered charitable because it advances culture and educates the people in its community. Its public is considered broad enough despite the fact it is essentially unavailable to many people who cannot afford to buy the tickets. A community center located in a subdivision in a poor neighborhood where the residents own their own homes may not be classified as charitable, because it benefits them as individual owners. Such an entity would more likely be considered as a homeowners' association.[4] Under each category outlined in the following sections, the evolving character of charitable class and the consequence of charging for services is discussed in detail.

The regulations contain the following list of charitable purposes:[5]

- Relief for the poor and distress of the underprivileged

- Advancement of religion

- Advancement of education or science

- Erection or maintenance of public buildings, monuments, or works

- Lessening of the burdens of government, and

- Promotion of social welfare by organizations designed to accomplish one of the previously listed purposes, or

- To lessen neighborhood tensions

- To eliminate prejudice and discrimination

- To defend human and civil rights secured by law, or

- To combat community deterioration and juvenile delinquency.

This regulation specifies that "the fact that an organization, in carrying out its primary purpose, advocates social or civic changes or presents opinions on controversial issues with the intention of molding public opinion or creating public sentiment or an acceptance of its views does not preclude such organization from qualifying as long as it is not an *action* organization."[6] It also provides that the receipt of voluntary contributions from the indigent persons whom the organization is operated to benefit will not necessarily prevent the organization from being exempt as charitable. This comment can be interpreted to permit an organization to charge for the services it renders—a policy that many tax-exempt organizations,

[3] Rev. Rul. 75-74, 1975-1 C.B. 152.
[4] IRC §528; see Chapter 6§3.
[5] Reg. §1.501(c)(3)-1(d)(2).
[6] Reg. §1.501(c)(3)-1(c)(3); see Chapter 2§2(g).

including schools, hospitals, health centers, and other service-providing organizations, adopt.

4.1 RELIEF OF THE POOR

Relief of the poor and distressed can include a vast array of programs. Examples of the types of organizations that qualify are those that focus on

- Promotion of rights and welfare for public housing occupants[7]
- Vocational training[8]
- Low-cost housing[9]
- Legal aid[10]
- Transportation for the handicapped and elderly[11]
- Counseling for senior citizens[12]
- Money management advice[13]
- Assistance to widow(er)s and orphans of police officers[14]
- Prisoner rehabilitation[15]
- Disaster relief[16]
- Day care for needy parents[17]
- Marketing of products made by the blind in programs designed to provide employment (including distribution of modest profits to the handicapped individuals)[18]

An organization seeking qualification because it relieves the poor and distressed is not precluded from exemption because it charges a fee for the services it provides to its charitable constituents. When services are provided for a fee, the factor that evidences charitable status is the basis on which the fees are determined. The fee structure must be distinguishable from that used by a commercial

---

[7] Rev. Rul. 75-283, 1975-2 C.B. 201.
[8] Rev. Rul. 73-128, 1973-1 C.B. 222; Priv. Ltr. Rul. 9150052.
[9] Rev. Rul. 70-585, 1970-2 C.B. 115.
[10] Rev. Rul. 78-428, 1978-2 C.B. 177; Rev. Rul. 76-22, 1976-1 C.B. 148.
[11] Rev. Rul. 77-246, 1977-2 C.B. 190.
[12] Rev. Rul. 75-198, 1975-1 C.B. 157.
[13] Rev. Rul. 69-441, 1969-2 C.B. 115.
[14] Rev. Rul. 55-406, 1955-1 C.B. 73.
[15] Rev. Rul. 70-583, 1970-2 C.B. 114; Rev. Rul. 67-150, 1967-1 C.B. 133; Rev. Rul. 76-21, 1976-1 C.B. 147.
[16] Rev. Rul. 69-174, 1969-1 C.B. 149.
[17] Rev. Rul. 70-533, 1970-2 C.B. 112.
[18] *Industrial Aid for the Blind v. Commissioner*, 73 T.C. 96 (1979), *acq.* C.B. 1980-2, 1.

business. Typically a charity would charge on a sliding scale according to the recipients' ability to pay—reduced-price services for groups of persons identified to be poor or economically distressed. In other noncommercial pricing systems, the price would be set to recoup the organization's cost with no profit added on top of cost or the charge might be only that amount not reimbursed by another funding agency.

Without regard to the amount of fees charged, a charitable organization must always benefit a charitable class.[19] To clarify this distinction, consider two projects that the IRS ruled did not qualify as charitable. An employee benefit program for needy retired workers of a particular business[20] was not exempt apparently for the unexpressed reason that the organization relieved the burden in the company. Also, a discount pharmaceutical service for senior citizens[21] could not qualify because it made no provision for free or reduced-price drugs for the poor, and was therefore indistinguishable from a commercial business.

How the IRS views charges for services varies for different types of exemption categories. The pricing method for different types of nonprofit organizations is interesting to ponder because the rules stem from historical custom and public policy, rather than economics. Although many hospitals serve the poor, the tax rules allow nonprofit health care providers to charge full price for services they provide without any requirement under the federal tax rules that price reductions be provided for those unable to pay.[22] A small business incubator providing financial and management consulting services is not treated as tax-exempt if it charges full price to anyone able to pay.[23] Many museums and libraries, on the other hand, are open for modest, if any, charge to all with little if any governmental funding.

4.2 PROMOTION OF SOCIAL WELFARE

Promotion of social welfare is another mission considered legitimate for charitable organizations. One of the vaguest categories, it includes working to:

- Eliminate discrimination and prejudice in the workplace,[24] neighborhoods,[25] housing,[26] and against women[27]

- Defend human and civil rights,[28] including the right to work[29]

---

[19] See Chapter 2§2(a).
[20] Rev. Rul. 56-138, 1956-1 C.B. 202.
[21] *Federation Pharmacy Service, Inc. v. U.S.,* 625 F.2d 804 (8th Cir. 1980), *aff'g* 72 T.C. 687 (1979).
[22] The author would speculate this situation exists partly because of available Medicare and Medicaid funding for the aged and indigent.
[23] Particularly if it lacks focus on a charitable class, such as a minority group or the unemployed; see Chapter 21§8(b).
[24] Rev. Rul. 68-70, 1968-1, C.B. 248; Rev. Rul. 75-285, 1975-2 C.B. 203.
[25] Rev. Rul. 68-655, 1968-2 C.B. 613.
[26] Rev. Rul. 68-438, 1968-2 C.B. 609; Rev. Rul. 67-250, 1967-2 C.B. 182.
[27] Rev. Rul. 72-228, 1972-1 C.B. 148.
[28] Rev. Rul. 73-285, 1973-2 C.B. 174.
[29] *National Right to Work Legal Defense and Education Foundation, Inc. v. U.S.,* 487 F. Supp. 801 (E.D. N.Car. 1979).

- Combat community deterioration,[30] lessen neighborhood tensions, and combat juvenile delinquency[31]

- Improve the economic climate in a depressed area[32]

- Encourage building of low-cost housing[33] and monitor zoning regulations[34]

- Acquire, restore, and maintain historic properties[35]

- Preserve and protect the environment,[36] including instituting litigation as a party plaintiff to enforce environmental protection laws,[37] and conducting legal research to settle international environmental disputes through mediation[38]

- Promote world peace, except through illegal protests[39]

- Maintain and set aside public parks and wildlife areas[40]

Organizations qualifying in this category operate to benefit the community, which may be a town, the state, or the world. Under the social welfare umbrella, legislative initiative is one of the tools used to accomplish the organization's goals. If the social welfare can only be promoted through passage of legislation, the action organization rules may prevent charitable status.[41]

(a) Low-Income Housing

Low-income housing and economic development projects receive significant government funding. As a result, the policies affecting them are subject to change as the persons in charge of their local, state, and federal funding sources change and, correspondingly, the standards for tax-exemption change. Most low-income housing units constructed before 1980 were privately owned. The significant income tax benefits and federal funding available made low-income housing a favored investment, typically in the limited partnership form. As government funding was cut and eliminated during the 1980s and the 1986 Tax Reform Act virtually killed the tax advantages of passive ownership, low-income housing lost its appeal. Renovations and owner attention waned and many such properties were put up for sale or foreclosed. Congress and the Resolution Trust Company responded to the need to protect the tenants by adopting policies encouraging charities to acquire such units.

[30] Rev. Rul. 76-147, 1976-1 C.B. 151.
[31] Rev. Rul. 68-15, 1968-1 C.B. 244.
[32] Rev. Rul. 76-419, 1976-2 C.B. 146; Rev. Rul. 77-111, 1977-1 C.B. 144.
[33] Rev. Rul. 67-138, 1967-1 C.B. 129.
[34] Rev. Rul. 68-15, *supra*, n. 26.
[35] Rev. Rul. 86-49, 1986-1 C.B. 243.
[36] Rev. Rul. 67-292, 1967-2 C.B. 184; Rev. Rul. 76-204, 1976-1 C.B. 152.
[37] Rev. Rul. 80-278, 1980-2 C.B. 175.
[38] Rev. Rul. 80-279, 1980-2 C.B. 176.
[39] Rev. Rul. 75-384, 1975-2 C.B. 204.
[40] Rev. Rul. 70-186, 1970-1 C.B. 128; Rev. Rul. 75-85, 1978-1 C.B. 150.
[41] An action organization may qualify under IRC §501(c)(4); see Chapters 6 and 23§4.

Acquisition and maintenance of low-income housing units has long been considered a charitable activity because it accomplishes several purposes: relieving the suffering of the poor, eliminating discrimination, relieving the burdens of government, combating community deterioration, and promoting social welfare.[42] The IRS adopted a baseline, or minimum level of low-income residents, of 75% in 1993 when factors indicating whether the housing project serves a charitable class were added to the Internal Revenue Manual.[43] The new standards were effective, prospectively enabling existing units to continue to be tax-exempt as operated. The standards were again revised in 1995, and in 1996, the safe harbor proposals were finalized in a new revenue procedure.[44] The preamble to those guidelines says that they are intended to help charities involved in low-income housing and facilitate the exemption application process and would again be applied prospectively. It behooves existing projects to conform, if possible, to the safe harbor rules, particularly when the more lenient facts and circumstances might apply.[45]

- At least 75% of the units are occupied by residents who qualify as low-income individuals.

- Either 20% of the residents renting units must qualify as very low income, or 40% of the units must be occupied by residents whose income does not exceed 120% of the area's very low-income limit.

- Up to 25% of the units may be rented at market rates to persons whose income exceeds the low-income limit.

A project not meeting the safe harbor percentages can still seek to qualify for exemption by demonstrating qualification through facts and circumstances, such as combating community deterioration, lessening the burdens of government, and eliminating discrimination and prejudice. The facts and circumstances that can be considered include:

- A substantially greater percentage of residents than required by the safe harbor with incomes up to 120% of the area's very low-income limit

- Limited degree of deviation from the safe harbor percentages

- Limitation of rents to ensure that they are affordable to low-income and very low-income residents

- Participation in a government housing program designed to provide affordable housing

[42] Rev. Rul. 70-585, 1970-2 C.B. 115.

[43] Notice 93-1, 1993-1 I.R.B. 172, announcing addition of the guidelines in Internal Revenue Manual 7664.34; *see also* Priv. Ltr. Rul. 9311034 for application of the guidelines to a charity formed by a commercial real estate company for the purposes of buying low-income housing from the Resolution Trust Company.

[44] Rev. Proc. 96-32, 1996-20 I.R.B. 1.

[45] IRS Announcement 95-37, 1995-20 I.R.B. 18. See the IRS Exempt Organization 1996 CPE Text, Topic B, *Recent Developments in Housing Regarding Qualification Standards and Partnership Issues* by Lynn Kawecki and Marvin Friendlander.

- Operation through a community-based board of directors, particularly if the selection process demonstrates that community groups have input into the organization's operations

- The provision of additional social services affordable to poor residents

- Relationship with an existing §501(c)(3) organization active in low-income housing for at least five years, if the existing organization demonstrates control

- Acceptance of residents who, when considered individually, have unusual burdens such as extremely high medical costs that cause them to be in a condition similar to persons within the qualifying income limits, in spite of their higher incomes

- Participation in a home ownership program designed to provide home ownership opportunities for families that cannot otherwise afford to purchase safe and decent housing

- Existence of affordability covenants or property restrictions

Financing for low-income housing projects is often provided partly or wholly by commercial investors, either as lenders or owners, so the criterion listed here deserves careful consideration. A California nonprofit corporation established to serve as general partner and essentially lend its tax status to a low-income housing project was deemed to serve the private interests of its investors and did not qualify for exemption.[46] To obtain property tax reductions, local law required that a nonprofit serve as manager of housing projects. Housing Pioneers, Inc.'s only duty was to maintain sufficient records to retain the property exemption; it "served as managing partner in name only." Although it used its modest fee for services to finance job training, counseling, and rent subsidies for the low-income residents, these activities were insufficient to outweigh the significant tax benefits flowing to the individual investors who also controlled its board.[47]

(b) Economic Development

Society's welfare may be promoted by exempt organizations working in concert with for-profit businesses, rather than directly with members of a charitable class. Supporting business programs that provide job training and placement, loans, and other services available in a commercial setting may be treated as a charitable activity. Although the private business owners may stand to gain from the activity, such a program that has significant public benefit may qualify for exemption. Evaluating relative benefits is difficult and the line separating them is often very thin. Again the rules may be influenced by the current opinion of lawmakers in regard to using tax policy to support social programs.

Economic development corporations (EDCs) typify this sort of charity. EDCs relieve poverty, combat community deterioration, lessen neighborhood tension,

---

[46] *Housing Pioneers, Inc. v. Commissioner,* T.C. Memo. 1993-120, *aff'd* (9th Cir. June 20, 1995).
[47] This decision does not mention and can be construed to conflict with the *Plumstead Theatre* decision discussed in Chapter 22§3; see Rev. Rul. 98-15 discussed in §4.6(b).

and strive to reduce the economic effect of prejudice and discrimination against minorities. An EDC qualifying as a charitable organization must be established to benefit disadvantaged members of the public.[48] Examples of programs approved as charitable by the IRS include:

- Making loans and purchasing equity interests in businesses unable to obtain conventional loans because of their location in an economically depressed urban area and/or ownership by members of a minority or other disadvantaged group[49]

- Establishing an industrial park in an economically blighted area to attract tenants willing to give employment and training opportunities to unemployed or underemployed residents in return for favorable lease terms[50]

- Having a small business investment company provide low-cost or long-term loans to businesses not able to obtain funds from conventional commercial sources, with preference given to businesses that provide training and employment opportunities for the unemployed or underemployed residents of economically depressed areas[51]

Conversely, an organization formed to increase business patronage for stores in economically depressed areas was *non*charitable.[52] The balance of private/public interests tilted too far in favor of private. The IRS said the absentee, nonminority owners suffered no distress as a result of their operation in the depressed area, and deemed that the projects' efforts to increase sales served to promote the private business owners who had formed the organization. An economic development subsidiary of an accredited college of engineering and management was instead found to be charitable by the IRS based upon the following three factors distilled from the published rulings:[53]

1. Assistance is provided to help local businesses or to attract new local facilities of established businesses or to attract new local facilities of established outside businesses.

2. The type of assistance provided has noncommercial terms and the potential to revitalize the disadvantaged area.

3. There is a nexus between the business entities assisted and relieving the problems of the disadvantaged area, or between the businesses and a disadvantaged group, like a minority, in the area.

EDCs may qualify as exempt under §501(c)(3), (4), and/or (6), further indicating the complexity of the fine private/public line evidencing charitable status.

[48] Gen. Coun. Memo. 39883 (Oct. 10, 1992); see discussion of charitable class in Chapter 2§2(a).
[49] Rev. Rul. 74-587, 1974-2 C.B. 162.
[50] Rev. Rul. 76-419, 1976-2 C.B. 146.
[51] Rev. Rul. 81-284, 1981-2 C.B. 130.
[52] Rev. Rul. 77-111, 1977-1 C.B. 144.
[53] Priv. Ltr. Rul. 9240001.

(c) Public Interest Law Firms

Organizations performing legal services must successfully answer a series of questions to prove that their law practice serves charitable purposes. One concern is whether their clients qualify as members of a charitable class, such as the poor, persons who are discriminated against, or persons whose freedom is jeopardized. Another concern is how their business policies are distinguishable from those of commercial law firms.

The expectation of a legal fee or award cannot be a motivating factor in selection of cases, and the organization cannot withdraw from a case if the client later becomes unable to pay. Also, charges may not exceed the actual cost of the litigation. In essence, charges based upon the client's ability to pay, rather than the amount of work involved, support designation as an exempt organization. Some portion of the organization's financial support must come from donations of cash and services.

Guidelines providing specific sanctions for public interest law firms (PILFs) were issued in 1992 (effective retroactively to taxable years beginning after December 31, 1987). To be exempt, the organization must possess the following characteristics:

- Litigation must not represent a private interest, but must instead be "said to be in representation of a broad public," such as class actions, suits seeking injunctions against actions harmful to the public, or test cases where the private interest is small.

- Litigants are not represented in actions between private persons when the financial interests at stake would warrant private legal representation, except that the PILF can serve as a friend of the court when an issue in litigation affects or will have an impact on a broad public interest.

- The nonprofit must achieve its objectives through legal and ethical means with no disruption of the judicial system, illegal activity, or violations of applicable canons of ethics.

- Litigated cases are described in detail annually on Form 990, including a rationale for the determination that they would benefit the public generally. Fees sought and recovered in each case must also be reported.

- Organizational authority, including approval of policies, programs, and compensation arrangements, rests with an independent board of trustees or a committee that is not controlled by employees or litigators.

- There must be no arrangement to accept donations from litigants to cover costs.

- The nonprofit may not be operated, through sharing of office space or otherwise, in a manner so as to create identification or confusion with a particular private law firm.

- Fees charged to clients may not exceed the cost of providing the legal services, and, once representation is started, the PILF cannot withdraw because the litigant is unable to pay the contemplated fee.

- Out-of-pocket cost reimbursements may be accepted from clients.

- Total attorney fees, both court-awarded and received from clients, may not exceed 50% of the nonprofit's total costs of performing litigation services, calculated on a five-year rolling average basis. If an exception to this limit "appears warranted," a ruling request may be submitted.

- Attorneys must be paid on a straight salary basis; compensation levels must be reasonable and not established by reference to any fees received in connection with the cases they have handled; and the fees must be paid to the organization, not to the individual attorneys.[54]

4.3 LESSENING THE BURDENS OF GOVERNMENT

Lessening the burdens of government overlaps social welfare and may include providing services usually rendered by a governmental agency, i.e., those facilities and services ordinarily furnished at taxpayer expense. Proving that a nonprofit will lessen the burden of government requires also that there be agreement on what those burdens are and whether it is the responsibility of the government to relieve them, which sometimes becomes a political philosophy question. Particularly when the government is not shouldering its burden, it may be difficult to qualify for this exemption. Some disparate examples of projects qualifying as charitable under this category are:

- Erecting or maintaining public buildings, monuments, or works[55]

- Combating drug traffic[56]

- Extending public transportation to an isolated community[57] or making grants to a city transit authority[58]

- Maintaining a professional standards review committee to oversee Medicare or Medicaid programs[59] or conducting cash/risk management services for public school systems[60]

- Maintaining volunteer fire departments[61] and police performance award programs[62]

- Assisting police and fire departments during disasters[63]

---

[54] Proc. 92-59, 1992-29 I.R.B. 11. For historical background, see Rev. Ruls. 75-47, 75-75, and 75-76, 1975-1 C.B. 152.
[55] Reg. §1.501(c)(3)-1(d)(2).
[56] Rev. Rul. 85-1, 1985-1 C.B. 177.
[57] Rev. Rul. 78-68, 1978-1 C.B. 149.
[58] Rev. Rul. 71-29, 1971-1 C.B. 150.
[59] Rev. Rul. 81-276, 1981-2 C.B. 128.
[60] Priv. Ltr. Rul. 9711002.
[61] Rev. Rul. 74-361, 1974-2 C.B. 159.
[62] Rev. Rul. 74-246, 1974-1 C.B. 130.
[63] Rev. Rul. 71-99, 1971-1 C.B. 151.

To test a proposed organization for qualification under this section, ask whether individual citizens normally provide the services for themselves. In some cities, the municipality provides garbage pickup for individuals, but not for businesses. Thus, an organization picking up commercial organizations' garbage would not lessen governmental burdens. It could, however, possibly qualify under the promotion of health category, if proper disposal of garbage can be shown to promote public health.

Whether or not an organization lessens the burdens of government is a matter of what a government "objectively manifests" its burdens to be. A high degree of cooperation and involvement with the governmental body whose burdens are lessened is required.[64] Public statements of support, direct government funding, joint activities with the supervision by the government, appointment and approval of board members by the government, and local bond initiatives and tax exemptions all manifest the requisite connection. Without either written delegation of such responsibility or enabling legislation providing the framework, tax-exempt status is difficult to obtain. A two-part test is applied:

1. Are the activities the nonprofit engages in ones that a governmental unit considers to be its burden, and does the governmental unit recognize that the nonprofit is acting on its behalf?

2. Does the nonprofit's performance of the activities actually lessen the burden of government?

During the early 1990s, applications for exemption for organizations seeking to relieve the burdens of government could be approved only by the Washington office, not by the key district offices. The strictness with which the IRS determination branch applies this test was illustrated by a prison-related organization that failed to receive tax-exempt status. Although it was created in respect of federal and some state statutes that encourage productivity of prisoners and programs providing for their rehabilitation, the rules specifically prohibit sales to the public in competition with private enterprise—the program that Prison Industries, Inc. planned. Thus, exempt status was denied.[65]

In an interesting situation, the IRS permitted a community foundation (CF) to purchase and operate the Kansas City Royals baseball team and finance it with tax deductible contributions.[66] The CF's ownership of the Royals was found to be a charitable activity because all levels of the Kansas City government considered it their burden to retain the club in their city. Additionally, the private foundation, created under the will of the Royals' now-deceased owner, could claim qualifying distributions and would not be self-dealing, because its grant to the CF was earmarked and restricted to purchase of the Royals. Lastly, the private investment group participating in a small part of the financing was deemed not to reap private inurement from the arrangements.

---

[64] Rev. Rul. 85-2, 1985-1 C.B. 178; Gen. Coun. Memos. 38693 (1981), 38347 and 38348 (1982), 39682 (1987), 39761 (1988), and 39864 (1991).
[65] *Prison Industries, Inc. v. Commissioner,* T.C.M. Dec. 47, 104(M), January 8, 1991.
[66] Priv. Ltr. Ruls. 9530024, 9530025, and 9530026.

The "mere fact that the nonprofit's activities might improve the general economic well-being of the nation or a state or reduce any adverse impact from the failure of government to carry out such activities is not enough" to prove that an organization is relieving the burden of government."[67] The fact that the government is not conducting the program may indicate that it is not the burden of government. Operating a state motor vehicle registration office for the government for a fee is not relieving the burdens of government.[68]

Note that this category applies to organizations operating independently of government, not as a branch, division, or agency of a governmental body. Instrumentalities of states and cities are technically not exempt under §501(c)(3), but rather under a concept of governmental immunity. Interestingly, governmental organizations do qualify to receive charitable contributions.[69]

4.4 ADVANCEMENT OF RELIGION

Advancement of religion is included on the list of charitable purposes in the regulations, but there is no explanatory information. This category might include a religious publishing house or broadcast radio or TV station, a retreat center, a burial group, or other peripheral religious activity outside the realm of sacerdotal functions. These groups are discussed in Chapter 3.

4.5 ADVANCEMENT OF EDUCATION AND SCIENCE

Advancement of education and science reiterates two purposes specifically named in §501(c)(3). Perhaps it was added to clarify that auxiliary activities carried on separately from established educational or scientific institutions are entitled to tax-exemption. Organizations qualifying under this category include those sponsoring:

- Scholarship programs,[70] even for members of a particular fraternity,[71] but not for contestants who had to participate in the Miss America Beauty Pageant to qualify[72]

- Low-interest college loans[73] and student food and housing programs[74]

---

[67] *B.S.W. Group, Inc. v. Commissioner*, 70 T.C. 352, 359 (1978); 838 F.2d 465 (4th Cir. 1988), *aff'g* 88 T.C. 1, 21 (1987).

[68] Tech. Adv. Memo. 9208002. Conceivably such an organization established to promote public safety by removing unsafe cars from the road might qualify.

[69] IRC §170(b)(1)(A)(v); see Chapter 10 for the definition of a governmental unit.

[70] Rev. Rul. 69-257, 1969-1 C.B. 151; Rev. Rul. 66-103, 1866-1 C.B. 134.

[71] Rev. Rul. 56-403, 1956-2 C.B. 307.

[72] *Miss Georgia Scholarship Fund, Inc. v. Commissioner*, 72 T.C. 267 (1979).

[73] Rev. Rul. 63-220, 1963-2 C.B. 208; Rev. Rul. 61-87, 1961-1 C.B. 191.

[74] Rev. Rul. 67-217, 1967-2 C.B. 181.

- Vocational training for unemployed workers,[75] but not operation of a grocery store's training program[76]

- National honor societies[77]

- Foreign exchange programs[78]

- Film series and bookstores[79]

- Maintenance of library collections and bibliographic computer information networks[80]

- Research journals[81] and law reviews[82]

- Medical seminars to provide postgraduate education to physicians[83]

4.6   PROMOTION OF HEALTH

Promotion of health as a charitable pursuit is conspicuously absent from the regulations, which contain no guidance on the requirements to be classified as pursuing this very important charitable purpose. The fact that for-profit and nonprofit health care providers operate side by side in a somewhat indistinguishable fashion complicates this category of exemption. To identify a health care organization that can qualify for exemption under 501(c)(3), it is important to first review the organizational and operational standards outlined in Chapter 2. The qualifying organization must be able to prove it will operate to benefit a charitable class rather than the health care professional that created and operates it. The particular tax rules pertaining to various segments of the health care industry must also be considered.

In 1974, a court had to remind the IRS that promotion of health is a charitable purpose listed under the tax statute and the law of charitable trusts.[84] This broad category encompasses hospitals, clinics, homes for the aged, hospices, medical research organizations, mental health facilities, blood banks, home health agencies, organ donor retrieval centers, health maintenance organizations (HMOs), medical centers, hospital holding companies, and many other entities that perform health care that promotes health.

The criteria for exemption under this category have been developed to distinguish charitable entities from privately owned businesses that provide identical health services. The issues primarily involve private inurement: Who benefits

---

[75] Rev. Rul. 73-128, 1973-1 C.B. 222.
[76] Rev. Rul. 73-129, 1973-1 C.B. 221.
[77] Rev. Rul. 71-97, 1971-1 C.B. 150.
[78] Rev. Rul. 80-286, 1980-2 C.B. 179.
[79] *Squire v. Students Book Corp.,* 191 F.2d 1018 (9th Cir. 1951).
[80] Rev. Rul. 81-29, 1981-1 C.B. 329.
[81] Rev. Rul. 67-4, 1967-1 C.B. 121.
[82] Rev. Rul. 63-235, 1963-2 C.B. 210.
[83] Rev. Rul. 65-298, 1965-2 C.B. 163.
[84] *Eastern Kentucky Welfare Rights Organization v. Simon,* 506 F.2d 1278, 1287 (D.C. Cir. 1974).

from the health care entity's operations, the sick or the private doctors and investors who are in control? The rules are constantly evolving; any organization seeking qualification under this category must carefully study the latest developments and be particularly careful when completing Schedule C of Form 1023 (Appendix 18-1). As the cost of medical care began to accelerate in the 1980s and the number of persons to whom such care was unavailable rose, pressure mounted on Congress to change the rules. Ironically as this edition is prepared in 1998, the health care industry has reformed itself and costs have leveled off. Unfortunately the number of uninsured persons without adequate care has increased and the pressure on nonprofit organizations to meet this societal need remains.

Charity Care. A tax-exempt health care provider must serve its charitable class—the sick—rather than those that manage it. The IRS's initial opinion on this subject was that a charity hospital "must be operated to the extent of its financial ability for those not able to pay for the services rendered and not exclusively for those who are able and expected to pay."[85] In 1969, the IRS eased this policy and recognized that the charitable purpose of promoting health is served even if the cost is borne by patients and insurance companies.[86] Later, the IRS refined its position: "[T]o be exempt a hospital must promote the health of a class of persons broad enough to benefit the community and must be operated to serve a public rather than a private interest."[87] Management style and financial facts that distinguish an exempt hospital from a for-profit one provide the evidence of public purpose. Indicators of a hospital's charitable nature as originally set out by the IRS,[88] and still cited today, are called the community benefit standards and include:

- Control by a community-based board of directors with no financial interest in the hospital

- Open medical staff with privileges available to all qualified physicians

- Emergency room open to all (unless this duplicates services provided by another institution in the area)

- Provision of public health programs and extensive research and medical training

- No unreasonable accumulation of surplus fund

- Limited funds invested in for-profit subsidiaries

- A high level of receivables from uncollected billings

(a) Private Inurement

To achieve and maintain tax exemption, a health care organization cannot allow its earnings or properties to benefit its medical staff or other private individuals.

---

[85] Rev. Rul. 56-185, 1956-1 C.B. 202.
[86] Rev. Rul. 69-545, 1969-2 C.B. 117.
[87] Exempt Organizations Handbook (IRM 7751) §343.5(2); Rev. Rul. 83-157, 1983-2 C.B. 94.
[88] Rev. Rul. 69-545, note 86.

The IRS closely scrutinizes contractual relationships with physicians and, until 1996, maintained a policy that no more than 20% of the board members can be physicians. Under a *Community Board and Conflicts of Interest Policy,*[89] the IRS eased this policy if less than 50% of the board is constituted of physicians and the organization in question has an adequate conflict of interest policy.[90] Other factors that the IRS has said evidence private inurement to physicians include:

- Favorable rental rates and exclusive use of facilities by a limited group of doctors[91]

- Profitable services (e.g., a lab) operated by private owners[92]

- A newly established nonprofit paying a high price to purchase a proprietary hospital[93]

- Excessive compensation to medical staff[94] and joint ventures[95]

After many years of private rulings and guidelines, the IRS issued a formal revenue ruling on incentives that a tax-exempt hospital may offer to recruit private practice physicians to join its staff or work in its medical community.[96] The ruling stipulates that it only applies to hospitals that have the following characteristics:[97]

- The hospital is a §501(c)(3) organization that operates to promote health (its exempt purpose) by the standards for exemption set forth in Rev. Rul. 69-545[98]

- The hospital meets the operational test and engages, to a substantial extent, in activities that further its exempt purposes and are reasonably related to accomplishing that purpose in keeping with the standards described in Rev. Ruls. 80-278 and 80-279[99]

- The physicians do not have a substantial influence over the affairs of the hospitals recruiting them so that they would be treated as disqualified persons under §4958[100] nor do they have any personal or private interest

---

[89] 1997 CPE Text for Exempt Organizations, Chapter C, *Tax-Exempt Health Care Organization Community Board and Conflicts of Interest Policy,* Lawrence M. Brauer and Charles F. Kaiser.
[90] The IRS granted exemption to the C.H. Wilkinson Physician Network, despite the fact that, in compliance with Texas law, all board members were physicians.
[91] *Harding Hospital, Inc. v. U.S.,* 505 F.2d 1068 (6th Cir. 1974); *Sonora Community Hospital v. Commissioner,* 46-T.C. 519 (1966), *aff'd,* 397 F.2d 814 (9th Cir. 1968).
[92] Rev. Rul. 69-383, 1969-2 C.B. 113.
[93] *State v. Wilmar Hospital,* 2 N.W. 2d 564 (Sup. Ct. Minn. 1942).
[94] Rev. Rul. 97-21, 1997-18 IRB 115; see also Chapter 20.
[95] Rev. Rul. 98-15, 1998-12 IRB 6; see also Chapter 22.
[96] Rev. Rul. 97-21 formalizing IRS Announcement 95-25 issued March 15, 1995.
[97] This ruling is cited to evaluate reasonableness of compensation paid to university scientists in the Exempt Organization CPE Text for 1999, Chapter B, *Intellectual Property.*
[98] *Ibid.* note 64.
[99] 1980-2 C.B. 175–176.
[100] See Chapter 20§9.

in the hospital that could result in private inurement. The recruitment package must not be structured as a device to distribute net earnings of the hospital to the physician

- The hospital must not engage in substantial unlawful activities inconsistent with charitable purposes

The ruling states the determination of whether the recruitment incentives cause the organization to violate the operational test is based upon all relevant facts and circumstances and contains five scenarios illustrating their position. The first four provide for acceptable recruitment incentives that do not result in private inurement to the physicians. In Situation 5, the hospital is found to operate for substantial nonexempt purposes and fails to qualify for exemption.

Situation 1.   Hospital A is the only hospital within a 100-mile radius and designated by the U.S. Public Health Service as a Health Professional Shortage Area for primary medical care professionals. The hospital has a demonstrated need for ob/gyns in its service area. The hospital recruits a physician who has recently completed an obstetrics and gynecological residency to establish and maintain a full-time practice in its service area and become a member of its medical staff. A signing bonus is paid, professional liability insurance premium is paid for a limited period of time, below-market office rent for a limited number of years (after which time the rent will be at fair value; again number not given) is provided, the physician's residential mortgage is guaranteed, and start-up financial assistance bearing "reasonable terms" is provided. The written incentive package is negotiated in an arm's length fashion in accordance with guidelines that are adopted, monitored, and reviewed regularly by the hospital's board of directors to ensure its exempt purposes are being served. A committee responsible for medical staff contracts approves the agreement. No benefits other than those stipulated in the agreement are provided.

Situation 2.   Hospital B is located in an economically depressed inner-city area of City W and has conducted a community needs assessment indicating both a shortage of pediatricians in its service area and difficulties Medicaid patients are having obtaining pediatric services. Hospital B recruits a physician to relocate and establish a full-time pediatric practice in its service area, join its medical staff, and treat a reasonable number of Medicaid patients. Again in an arm's length negotiation approved by its board, the physician is offered payment of moving expenses, professional liability "tail" coverage for the former practice, and a guaranteed level of private practice income for a limited number of years. The amount guaranteed falls within the range of compensation paid to physicians in similar positions according to regional or national surveys.

Situation 3.   Hospital C, also located in an economically depressed inner-city area, conducts a community needs assessment and finds indigent patients are having difficulty getting access to care because of a shortage of obstetricians in its area willing to treat Medicaid and charity care patients. A member of its current medical staff is recruited to provide these services in return for payment of professional liability insurance during the year the services are provided. The agreement is written and approved in the same fashion as described in Situation 1. The ruling finds the amount paid to the physician is reasonable and that any private benefit to the physician is outweighed by the public purposes served by the agreement.

Situation 4. Hospital D is located in a medium- to large-size metropolitan area. It maintains a minimum of four diagnostic radiologists to ensure adequate coverage and a high quality of care for its radiology department. When two of its radiologists resign, it recruits a radiologist currently working for another hospital in the city. The hospital agrees in a properly approved and written document to supplement the physician's income to the extent the private practice does not generate a certain level of net income for the first few years.

Situation 5. Hospital F was criminally convicted of knowingly and willfully violating the Medicare and Medicaid antikickback statute in its physician recruitment practices. The activities resulting in the violations were substantial.

The examples in the ruling emphasize the board and duly authorized units operating under the aegis of the board analyzing the institution's ability to accomplish its exempt purpose. With that focus, a board can develop a methodology for meeting its charitable needs and take appropriate steps using reasonable standards for determining fair value and the terms of the arrangements deemed necessary to accomplish the exempt purposes. All exempt organizations, particularly hospitals, are expected to have "contemporaneous documentation of process" to evidence the tax-exempt nature of their financial decisions.[101]

(b) Hospital Joint Ventures

While the national and state legislatures, the administration officials in the White House, and the general populace debated the need to reform health care delivery in the United States, no significant changes in the law were passed, but the health care industry voluntarily reformed itself. Managed care became the normal method for dispensing health care; mergers, consolidations, and buyouts of nonprofit providers with and by for-profit entities frequently occurred. Combinations of health care providers happened at such a pace that the IRS was often unable to keep up. Because of reduced staff levels, the Exempt Organization Group during the mid-1990s could not consider requests for private letter rulings within the time frame projects required. Significant transactions involving nonprofit hospitals that previously would have been undertaken only after approval by the IRS now go without.[102] The significant issue in determining a hospital's qualification as a (c)(3) organization is whether it operates to provide public benefit or yields private inurement to those that manage and operate it.

To finance expansion and improve their health care facilities, tax-exempt hospitals have opportunities to enter into associations with for-profit companies

---

[101] Remarks of Marcus Owens at a meeting of the American Bar Association Exempt Organizations Committee, May 9, 1997.

[102] An article on this complex and ever-changing subject, entitled *Virtual Mergers—Hospital Joint Operating Agreement Affiliations,* in the 1997 CPE Text for Exempt Organizations, provided seven meager pages of guidance.

and investors. When the use and control of hospital assets is altered by entering into a joint venture or partnership, the hospital may maintain its tax-exempt status as long as the venture's activity is primarily charitable and the private interests of the for-profit partners are only incidentally served by the arrangement. Importantly, under concepts of partnership taxation, the activities and income of the venture are treated as those of the partners in the venture. The IRS illustrated venture terms it considers to serve charitable interests as compared to those it deems serve private interests in Rev. Rul. 98-15.

Charitable venture. A (c)(3) hospital, in need of additional funding, forms a limited liability company (LLC) with investors. All of the hospital's assets are contributed to the venture in return for an ownership interest proportional to their value. The LLC board has three representatives of the hospital and two chosen by the investors (hospital controls). Governing documents require that the venture operate to further charitable purposes by promoting health for a broad cross section of its community and can only be amended by the hospital-controlled board. The board must also approve major decisions relating to the venture operations, such as capital and operating budgets, distribution of earnings, selection of key executives, contracts in excess of $x a year, changes in types of services hospital offers, and renewal or termination of management agreements.

Commercial venture. A tax-exempt hospital (the "exempt") in need of capital forms a LLC with a for-profit hospital. Similar to the charitable venture, each venturer receives ownership in proportion to the value of their respective assets contributed. Otherwise the venture agreement evidences to the IRS that ownership of the LLC will not serve the exempt's purposes. The purpose clause of the governing documents does not dedicate the LLC to charitable purposes. The governing body that is empowered to amend the documents and make major decisions consists of three individuals chosen by each venturer (the exempt is not in control). The LLC is to be operated by a management company owned by the for-profit hospital (major decisions delegated to the for-profit). As a part of the agreement, the exempt agrees to approve of two for-profit executives to serve as the LLC's chief executive and financial officers. The IRS found the absence of a binding obligation on the LLC to serve a charitable purpose meant the venture could "deny care to segments of the community, such as indigents."

The first chapter in the 1999 EO CPE Text is entitled "Whole Hospital Joint Ventures" and states the IRS in issuing Rev. Rul. 98-15 "does not seek to curb" all such ventures. When an exempt enters into a venture, the IRS expects charitable purposes supersede profit maximization purposes, that health care services benefit the community as a whole, and that the venture does not result in greater than incidental private benefit to the taxable partner or other private parties. The CPE Text contains a list of 24 questions the exempt organization division used in its examinations of such ventures as part of its 1999 work plan. How ventures that stray from the acceptable venture in the ruling remains to be seen. What if the charter constrains the operations to be charitable but the for-profit partners control, for example? Readers should be alert for new developments as a result of the examinations and the Tax Court litigation of Redlands Surgical Services pending as this edition is prepared.

(c) Physician Clinics

A clinic providing private medical care to individuals is traditionally owned by the doctors, operated for their profit-making purposes, and not qualified for tax exemption even though it operates for the exempt purpose of promoting health. When a clinic has no private ownership, provides a reasonable level of free or reduced charge care to members of a charitable class, and otherwise distinguishes itself as a charitable organization, exemption can be sought under the standards previously listed under *Charity Care.*

Clinics operated in conjunction with charity hospitals and medical schools, so-called "faculty practice plans," have traditionally been granted exemption, but there are few clear precedents in the area. In one case approving exemption for such a clinic, the physicians were staff members of a teaching hospital and full-time medical school faculty members.[103] About 25% of the patients were indigent or students, and medical research was conducted, evidencing a significant element of charitable purpose in addition to the promotion of health.

(d) Integrated Health Care Delivery Systems

Health care organizations often combine all service providers—the doctor's clinic, the hospital, the HMO, the pharmacy, and so on—into a consolidated group, called an integrated health delivery system or IDS. The doctors sell their practices to the IDS, become hospital employees, and provide medical services on behalf of one branch, usually the hospital. For management and legal liability reasons, the respective parts of the IDS may remain separately incorporated and individually maintain tax-exempt status. Such a related group of organizations can function as a unit of separate, but integrated, exempt organizations.[104] The IRS in 1993 had some difficulty originally approving IDSs for charitable status.

A favorable ruling for this type of entity depended upon proof that the private doctors do not get favorable treatment in the deal, or do not reap private inurement. To give an idea of the policies an organization must adopt to prove they benefit the community[105] rather than the individual doctors, the conditions under which one IDS was granted exemption are described here. Facey Medical Foundation, a newly created holding company that planned to control 12 tax-exempt hospitals and also create a taxable subsidiary to purchase a private medical practice, received a favorable determination that it qualified as a §501(c)(3) organization.[106] The nonexempt sub planned to buy a 48-physician practice, along with the tangible

---

[103] *University of Maryland Physicians, P.A. v. Commissioner,* 41 T.C.M. 732 (1981); see also *University of Massachusetts Medical School Group Practice v. Commissioner,* 74 T.C. 1299 (1980).

[104] Discussed in Chapter 2§2(h).

[105] The community benefit standard was originally set out by the IRS in Rev. Rul. 69-545, 1969-2 C.B. 117.

[106] Exemption letter dated March 31, 1993; see also exemption letter of *Friendly Hills Healthcare Network* issued on February 8, 1993. For comparison of the two letters, read special report of Michael W. Peregrine and Bernadette M. Broccolo entitled "New 'IDS' Determination Letter Offers Promise, Sparks Controversy," and also "A Practical Examination of the IRS and OIG Rules for Integrated Delivery Systems" by Gerald R. Peters, 7 *The Exempt Organization Tax Review* 757 (May 1993).

and intangible assets, including trade name, medical service contracts, noncompetition agreements, and patient files. Following IRS policy that the purchase of goodwill is inconsistent with exempt status, there was no compensation for goodwill. Facey leased back the assets and provided management services and nonphysician support for the medical practice. The selling doctors receive a set percentage of Facey's gross income for the first two years only, with their compensation subsequently to be negotiated in arm's-length negotiations. The favorable determination was based upon the following significant factors that apparently proved to the IRS that there was sufficient community benefit[107] rather than private benefit to the doctors whose practices were being purchased:

- The organization's board of directors will be controlled by members of the community, with no more than 20% of the board members being doctors.

- A substantial number of the physicians will give emergency room care without regard to a patient's ability to pay.

- The hospitals will provide at least $400,000 worth, not counting bad debts, of charity care annually.

- Facey will participate in both the Medicare and MediCal Insurance program in a nondiscriminatory manner.

- Significant clinical research and public education programs will be conducted.

- Facey will comply with antikickback provisions of the Social Security Act.[108] Essentially, the buyout and compensation arrangements with physicians cannot induce or reward referrals.

The published determination letters of other integrated delivery systems issued since that time can be studied to further clarify the IRS's thinking on this subject.[109]

A pair of professional service organizations, operated in conjunction with the State University of New York at Buffalo's medical and dental schools to assign residents to local teaching hospitals, was denied tax-exempt status. The court found that the organizations were "appendages rather than integral parts of the educational or hospital organizations they serve" (organizational documents themselves stated the service organizations were ancillary to the primary purpose

---

[107] The community benefit standard was originally set out by the IRS in Rev. Rul. 69-545, 1969-2 C.B. 117.

[108] §1128(b) of the Social Security Act, 42 U.S.C. §1230a-7b(b)(1) and (2), prohibiting payment of fees for referrals of patients eligible for Medicare coverage. A General Counsel Memorandum on this issue was promised by Jim McGovern, Associate Chief Counsel for IRS EP/EO Division, at the winter American Bar Association Exempt Organization Section meeting in February 1993.

[109] Friendly Hills Healthcare Network, Geisinger Health Plan, Presbyterian Multi-Specialty Group Practice Foundation (Philadelphia, PA), St. Luke's Medical Associates, Inc. (Kansas City, MO), and Tobey Medical Associates, Inc. (Wareham, MA).

of the school's graduate medical and dental education). Since they serve the university, as well as the hospitals, they also could not qualify as cooperative hospital service organizations under IRC § 501(e)."[110]

(e) Health Maintenance Organizations

Health maintenance organizations (HMOs) providing prepaid medical care to members can be exempt if a large enough charitable class is benefited and the HMO provides the care itself.[111] HMOs providing commercial-type insurance as a substantial part of their activities are not, however, tax exempt under §501(m), which was enacted as a part of the Tax Reform Act of 1986. Insubstantial insurance activity that does not prevent exemption is subject to unrelated business income tax.

In September 1990, the IRS issued a memo setting forth the criteria it would follow for issuing exemptions to HMOs.[112] The standards were designed to ensure that HMOs operate to benefit the community and were similar to those applied for exemption of hospitals. The criteria are as follows:

- Health care services and facilities are provided.

- Emergency treatment is available without regard to ability to pay and this fact is communicated to the public.

- Membership organizations must make efforts to expand the number of members to spread the cost among more persons, seek individual members, have no age or eligibility barriers, and charge individuals rates similar to those charged groups.

- Nonmembers are served on a fee-for-service basis.

- Medicare, Medicaid, and other publicly assisted patients are accepted, and care is provided at reduced rates for indigents.

- Health education and research programs are provided.

- Health care providers are paid fixed compensation (no incentive pay).

- Operating surpluses are dedicated to improving facilities and health care programs.

- The community is broadly represented on the governing body.

A court agreed with the IRS that an HMO that did not itself provide direct medical services and conducted no programs to satisfy the community benefit standards previously outlined could not qualify as charitable.[113] Although the HMO at issue, Geisinger Health Plan, could conceivably qualify as charitable if it were an integral

[110] *University Medical Resident Services, P.C. v. Commissioner,* T.C. Memo. 1996–251.
[111] *Sound Health Associates V. Commissioner,* 71 T.C. 158, *acq.* 1981-2 C.B.2.
[112] Gen. Coun. Memo. 39828.
[113] *Geisinger Health Plan v. Commissioner,* 985 F.2d 1210 (3d Cir, 1993), *rev'g* 62 T.C.M. 1656 (1991).

part of a parent health care system, its primary activity—the provision of insurancelike contract medical services for private patients—did not qualify for charitable status. Likewise, because its primary focus was serving private patients in addition to those of the hospitals, it could not qualify as an exempt feeder under the integral part test. The decision should be read in detail by any proposed HMO not meeting most of the nine of the IRS criteria previously listed. The Third Circuit revisited the Geisinger Health Plan and again decided that it failed to qualify for exemption.[114] A two-pronged test was applied to determine whether the organization qualified under the integral part test:

- It is not carrying on a trade or business that would be an unrelated trade or business if regularly carried on by the parent.

- The relationship to its parent somehow enhances the subsidiary's own exempt character to the point that, when the boost provided by the parent is added to the contribution made by the subsidiary itself, the subsidiary would be entitled the (c)(3) status.

Nonprofit HMOs exclusively providing services to Medicaid recipients can also qualify for (c)(3) status if the standards described above are satisfied. Such organizations are formed to serve managed care systems established by states following the example of other health care providers.[115]

Look for a new technical advice memorandum the IRS in late December 1998, announced it would be issuing.

(f) Health/Fitness Centers

An increasingly important component of the health care industry is alternative therapies and regimes that prevent illness. Most everyone in America today agrees physical fitness and dietary prudence promotes health. Nonprofit organizations, as well as private industry, address this concern. For both the activity itself is essentially charitable—to promote health. What distinguishes a nonprofit fitness center is the absence of private ownership and operational practices that distinguish it from its commercial counterparts following the standards outlined in Chapter 2.

The provision of a fitness facility to the healthy, however, may not always be considered a charitable activity. A community center that restricts its availability to less than an entire community, for example, cannot be classified as charitable.[116] On the other hand, the operation of a health and fitness center providing access to handicapped persons and offering reduced daily rates for persons of limited financial means serves a health care organization's exempt purposes.[117] As a part of a new medical complex, a sports and physical medicine facility was designed to serve patients referred by the center's hospitals and physicians, as well as the general public.

---

[114] *Geisinger Health Plan v. Commissioner,* 100 T.C. 394 (1993), *aff'd* 30 F.3d 494 (3rd Cir. 1994).
[115] Chapter D of the 1999 EO CPE Text entitled *Exemption of Medicaid HMOs and Medicaid Service Organizations under IRC 501(c)(3)* contains two examples of Medicaid HMOs that do note qualify compared to one that does.
[116] Rev. Rul. 67-325, 1967-2 C.B. 113.
[117] Priv. Ltr. Rul. 8935061.

What primarily distinguishes this center as a charitable facility is its provision of services to patients and employees of the medical center. Its availability to the general public is provided in a noncommercial manner and contributes to the center's exempt purpose of providing health care to the community in which it is located.

A similar conclusion was reached regarding a wellness center created as a joint venture of an acute care hospital, its parent, and an orthopedic hospital. The facilities provide physical rehabilitation services to patients and to the general public. Because the membership fee structure permits access to the general public and the facility serves the creators' exempt health care purposes, the center was considered exempt.[118] An organization sponsoring general fitness programs for youths by operating a track, gymnasium, swimming pool, and courts for racquet ball, handball, and squash, was also found to be accomplishing an exempt purpose.[119] Access to most of its facilities were available upon payment of a nominal annual fee. Its operation of a health club program providing use of a spa, exercise rooms, whirlpool, sauna, and such, was, however, considered an unrelated activity not contributing to its exempt purposes. Club members paid an advance annual fee that was comparable to a commercial health club and sufficiently high to restrict participation in the facility.

(g) Professional Standards Review Organizations

Under Social Security legislation in 1972, Congress authorized the creation of professional standards review organizations (PSROs). PSROs monitor and establish cost and quality controls for hospitals in their area with the intention of reducing overutilization of government-financed health programs. PSRO members must be licensed physicians. The exemption issue is whether the PSRO serves the public or the individual doctor members and the medical profession. A PSRO must possess the following attributes to qualify for exemption as a charity—otherwise, it may qualify as a business league:[120]

- It must operate to ensure quality and care utilization for Medicare and Medicaid patients.

- Membership is open to all physicians without charge.

- The governing body cannot be controlled by or tied to a medical society.

- The PSRO is authorized to act under the federal statutes.

An organization that reviewed the propriety of hospital treatment provided to Medicaid recipients was also found to be exempt because it relieved the burden of government and promoted the health of persons eligible for Medicare and Medicaid.[121]

---

[118] Priv. Ltr. Rul. 9226055.

[119] Rev. Rul. 79-630, 1979-2 C.B. 236; see Priv. Ltr. Rul. 9736047 for IRS rationale for granting exemption to a heart health center operated in conjunction with an acute care hospital; see also Priv. Ltr. Ruls. 9329041, 9226055, and 9110042 which focused on whether fees were set at a level to make the facility available to the general public.

[120] Rev. Rul. 81-276, 1981-2 C.B. 128.

[121] *Professional Standards Review Organization of Queens County, Inc. v. Commissioner*, 74 T.C. 240(1980).

(h) Homes for the Aged

Until 1972, homes for senior citizens were required to provide free or low-cost services.[122] Today, a charitable home may charge full cost for its services so long as it provides for the primary needs of the aging—housing, health care, and financial security. In seeking approval for exemption, a home must furnish detailed information about its proposed or actual operation on Schedule F of Form 1023.[123] The questions address the following specific policies that a home must maintain to qualify as charitable:[124]

- Have a commitment to maintain in the residence any person who becomes unable to pay his or her regular charges, or do all that is possible to make other suitable arrangements for their care

- Provide its services at the lowest feasible cost, taking the facts and circumstances of the home into account (for example, cost of facility or wages in the area)

- Charge fees affordable by a significant segment of the elderly population so as to evidence benefit to the community in which it is located

- Adopt policies to protect itself financially and enable it to meet its obligation not to expel aged residents who become unable to pay

A home may require its applicants to make a deposit upon admission of an amount of assets calculated to secure their care.[125] A home might also permit residents to establish trusts, the income of which is payable to the home during the resident's life. Income from trusts is exempt function income to the home.[126] Charitable status can be allowed for a senior citizen home that allows full-paying elderly to keep their assets, subject to a requirement that such assets could be used, if necessary, to supplement income to meet the monthly charges.[127]

A pharmacy organized to furnish discount drugs to senior citizens was denied exemption because it operated for commercial purposes and had no charitable attributes such as low-cost or free drugs to the indigent.[128]

4.7 COOPERATIVE HOSPITAL SERVICE ORGANIZATIONS

IRC §501(e) provides that a cooperative hospital service organization is a charitable organization. Two or more hospitals, either one of which meets the qualifica-

---

[122] Rev. Rul. 72-124, 1972-1 C.B. 145.
[123] Reproduced in Appendix 18-1.
[124] Rev. Rul. 79-18, 1979-1 C.B. 152.
[125] Priv. Ltr. Rul. 9225041.
[126] Rev. Rul. 81-61, 1981-1 C.B. 355.
[127] Priv. Ltr. Rul. 9307027.
[128] *Federation Pharmacy Service, Inc. v. U.S.*, note 21. Likewise an organization formed to help senior citizens with funeral expenses could not be exempt unless it allowed indigents to participate. *El Paso Del Aquila Elderly,* T.C. Memo, 1992, 441.

tions of IRC §170(b)(1)(A)(iii) or is operated by a governmental unit, may organize and operate under the following rules:

- It must perform, on a centralized basis, the following functions: data processing, purchasing (including insurance), warehousing, billing and collections, food, clinical, industrial engineering, laboratory, printing, communications, record center, and personnel (including selection, testing, training, and education).

- The cooperative cannot accumulate profits, but must distribute all net earnings to its patrons on the basis of services performed for them.

- Any stock issued by the cooperative must be owned by its patrons.

Note that the list does not include laundry—Congress deliberately omitted laundry services. The courts have agreed that only the specified services listed in the code may be performed on a cooperative basis. A group providing laundry service may be treated as a cooperative under IRC §1388.

CHAPTER FIVE

Educational, Scientific, and Literary Purposes and Prevention of Cruelty to Children and Animals

5.1 EDUCATIONAL PURPOSES

Educational purposes include "instruction or training of individuals to improve or develop their capabilities; or instruction of the public on subjects useful to the individual and beneficial to the community."[1] This definition of *educational* encompasses professional or occupational training regarding business capabilities.[2] The regulation gives the following four examples of educational organizations:

[1] Reg. §1.501(c)(3)-1(d)(3).
[2] Subject to standards discussed in §5.1(e).

1. Primary or secondary schools, colleges, or professional or trade schools

2. Public discussion groups, forums, panels, lectures, or similar programs

3. Organizations that present courses of instruction by means of correspondence or through the utilization of television or radio

4. Museums, zoos, planetariums, symphony orchestras, and other similar organizations

In clearing the hurdles to obtain exemption, a potentially tax-exempt nonprofit must first decide whether to claim exemption as a charitable or as an educational organization. A stricter standard, with more fully developed criteria, exists for educational organizations. The Internal Revenue Service (IRS) regulation defining *charitable* organizations says:

> The fact that an organization, in carrying out its primary purpose, advocates social or civic changes or presents opinion on controversial issues with the intention of molding public opinion or creating public sentiment to an acceptance of its views does not preclude such organization from qualifying under IRC §501(c)(3) so long as it is not an "action" organization.[3]

The same regulation in defining *educational* organizations instead says

> An organization may be educational even though it advocates a particular position or viewpoint so long as it presents a sufficiently full and fair exposition of the pertinent facts as to permit an individual or the public to form an independent opinion or conclusion. On the other hand, an organization is not educational if its principal function is the mere presentation of unsupported opinion.[4]

This regulation was held to be unconstitutionally vague in the Big Mama Rag, Inc. case in 1980.[5] The IRS had argued that the newspaper, in celebrating the cause of lesbians, failed to present a "full and fair exposition of the facts" as required by the regulations. The court noted that the regulations do not make clear what groups are advocacy groups that must meet this test, nor do they provide any objective standard for distinguishing facts from opinions.

Without answering the questions posed by the D.C. Circuit, the IRS in November 1986 issued a ruling outlining a methodology test for identifying impermissible advocacy.[6] The presence of any of the following factors indicates that the method used by the organization to advocate its viewpoints or positions is not educational:

- The presentation of viewpoints or positions unsupported by facts is a significant portion of the organization's communications.

[3] Reg. §1.501(c)(3)-1(d)(2); see Chapters 2§2(g) and 23§6.
[4] Reg. §1.501(c)(3)-1(d)(3); discussed in §3.1(j).
[5] *Big Mama Rag, Inc. v. U.S.,* 631 F.2d 1030 (D.C. Cir. 1980), *rev'g* 79-1 USTC 9362 (D.C. 1979).
[6] Rev. Rul. 86-43, 1986-2 C.B. 729.

- The facts that purport to support the viewpoints or positions are distorted.

- The organization's presentations make substantial use of inflammatory and disparaging terms, and express conclusions more on the basis of strong emotional feelings than of objective evaluations.

- The approach used in the organization's presentations is not aimed at developing an understanding on the part of the intended audience or readership because it does not consider their background or training in the subject matter.

The methodology test was designed to "eliminate or minimize the potential for any public official to impose his or her preconceptions or beliefs in determining whether the particular viewpoint or position is educational." It is the method used by the organization to communicate its viewpoint or position to others, not the viewpoint itself, that will be tested. The IRS continues to apply this methodology test that was condoned by the Tax Court in confirming denial of exemption for The Nationalist Movement, a pro-white Mississippi organization advocating social, economic, and political change.[7]

An organization that espouses a particular viewpoint concerning issues that may be the subject of legislation or political debate, such as welfare, abortion, or guns, must first test its methodology for making a sufficient presentation of facts. A parallel, but different, issue is whether its advocacy precludes it from tax-exempt status, as discussed in Chapter 23. Can its purposes only be accomplished through the passage of legislation by persons it hopes to see elected? The House Ethics Committee investigation of Representative Newt Gingrich's work with the Abraham Lincoln Opportunity Foundation and the Progress and Freedom Foundations during 1997 focused on these issues. Were the contents of the foundation programs biased? Were the foundations created to advance the private interests of Gingrich and the Republican Party? The information gathered by the committee was turned over to the IRS for examination.[8]

(a) Schools

Schools, like churches and hospitals, occupy a privileged category of 501(c)(3) organizations that are classified as public charities because of the activity they conduct rather than the sources of their revenue. Consequently the definition of educational organizations that qualify for classification as a school is very specific and embodies what can be thought of as the three "regulars." A school is a formally organized entity that possesses the following attributes:[9]

- Regular faculty of qualified teachers
- Regularly scheduled curriculum

---

[7] *The Nationalist Movement v. Commissioner,* 102 T.C.No. 22 (1994), *aff'd* 37 F3d 216,74 (5th Cir. 1994).

[8] Results are unknown at this time; for discussion of the political intervention prohibitions see Chapters 2§1(e) and 23.

[9] *Id.,* n. 1.

- Regularly enrolled body of students in attendance at the location where the educational activities take place

The following educational organizations have also been ruled to be schools:

- Early childhood education centers[10]

- Boards of education that employ all the teachers in a school system and that supervise all the schools in a district[11]

The presentation of formal instruction must be a primary function of a school. The term includes primary, secondary, preparatory, and high schools, and colleges and universities. Schools publicly supported by federal, state, and local governments qualify for this category by definition, and in some cases also qualify as governmental units.[12] A school possessing this duality might seek recognition of (c)(3) qualification to facilitate fund raising; however, as a (c)(3) the state school could be subject to the intermediate sanctions discussed in Chapter 20§9.

Advisors for a school can test its qualification for this category by studying the IRS examination guidelines for colleges and universities developed for use by its specialists.[13] Factors considered by the IRS in determining that a school can continue to qualify can also be used as a reference for organizations seeking recognition as a school.

What the regulations call "non-educational" activities must be incidental. A recognized university can operate a museum or sponsor concerts and remain a school. A museum's art school, however, does not make the museum a school.[14]

All four elements must be present to achieve recognition as a school: regular faculty, students, curriculum, and facility. A home-tutoring entity providing private tutoring was held not to be an educational organization for this purpose.[15] Likewise, a correspondence school was not approved under this section because it lacked a physical site where classes were conducted.[16]

The word "curriculum" was loosely construed in a ruling that permitted an elementary school to qualify despite the fact that it had no formal course program and espoused an open learning concept.[17] However, leisure learning classes, in the eyes of the IRS, do not present a sufficiently formal course of instruction to qualify as a school. Lectures and short courses on a variety of general subjects not leading to a degree or accreditation do not constitute a curriculum.[18] Also, invited authorities and personalities recognized in the field are not considered to be members of a regular faculty.[19]

---

[10] *Michigan Early Childhood Center, Inc. v. Commissioner,* 37 T.C.M. 808 (1978); *San Francisco Infant School, Inc. v. Commissioner,* 69 T.C. 957 (1978); Rev. Rul. 70-533, 1970-2 C.B. 112.
[11] *Estate of Ethel P. Green v. Commissioner,* 82 T.C. 843 (1984).
[12] Reg. §1.170A-9(b); see discussion in Chapter 10§2.
[13] Exempt Organizations Examination Guidelines Handbook 7(10)69.
[14] Rev. Rul. 76-167, 1976-1 C.B. 329.
[15] Rev. Rul. 76-384, 1976-2 C.B. 57.
[16] Rev. Rul. 75-492, 1975-2 C.B. 80.
[17] Rev. Rul. 72-430, 1972-2 C.B. 105.
[18] Rev. Rul. 62-23, 1962-1 C.B. 200.
[19] Rev. Rul. 78-82, 1978-1 C.B. 70.

The duration of the courses has not been considered a barrier by the IRS. An outdoor survival school whose classes lasted only 26 days, but were conducted with regular teachers, students, and course study, was classified as a school, despite the fact that part of the facilities it used were wide open spaces.[20]

IRC §529, entitled *Qualified State Tuition Programs*, exempts organizations established for prepaid tuition plans and exempts their investment income, except to the extent to which it may be subject to the unrelated business income tax.[21] To qualify, the program must be established or maintained by a state or instrumentality of a state to allow persons to purchase tuition credits and to contribute to an account established to pay the qualified higher education expense of a designated beneficiary. Such expenses include tuition, fees, books, supplies, and equipment required for enrollment or attendance at an eligible education institution.[22]

(b) Race Discrimination

Schools must adopt and practice policies prohibiting racial discrimination. A statement that it has a racially nondiscriminatory policy must be included in its charter, bylaws, or other governing instrument or be effective by resolution of its governing body. The statement of its policy must each year be published in an area newspaper. School brochures, catalogs, and other printed matter used to inform prospective students of the school's programs must state the policy as it relates to admission applications, scholarships, and program participation. Schools must complete a special page of Form 990, Schedule A to inform the IRS that it has met these requirements.[23] Form 5578 is due to be filed by schools that are not required to file Form 990, primarily including church schools that qualify as an integrated auxiliary of a church.[24]

A private school that adopted a nondiscrimination policy in connection with seeking application for recognition of its exemption as an educational organization was denied exemption when the facts revealed that it in fact did discriminate—it failed the good faith test. The Tax Court denied tax exemption for Calhoun Academy because the "clear and convincing evidence" indicated that the school operated in a discriminatory fashion.[25] The school was established concurrently with court-ordered desegregation plans. Although the community in which it was located was 50% black, no black student had ever been admitted. The school argued, unsuccessfully, that none had applied. Although the school had been in existence for 15 years, the nondiscrimination policy was only implemented in connection with the exemption application. The court noted that a school could qualify for tax-exempt status without establishing that it took the specific affirmative acts set forth in the IRS procedures, if in fact it operates in a racially nondiscriminatory manner.

---

[20] Rev. Rul. 73-434, 1973-2 C.B. 71.
[21] Small Business Job Protection Act of 1996, §1806.
[22] See Chapter 10§2 for history of this code section.
[23] Reproduced in Appendix 27-3.
[24] See Chapters 3§2 and 27§1(b); the form is reproduced in Appendix 27-4.
[25] *Calhoun Academy v. Commissioner*, 94 T.C. 17 (1990).

In 1980, a district court issued an injunction presuming any private school formed in Mississippi at the time of court-ordered public school integration was created with a racially discriminatory purpose and could not qualify for tax exemption. A published exemption letter indicates how a Mississippi school that lost its exemption under the injunction can regain exempt status under the following conditions:[26]

- The school adopts a nondiscriminatory admission policy.

- It takes positive steps to recruit black students.

- It provides the IRS, for a period of three years, information concerning the racial composition of its student body, faculty, and students receiving financial aid.[27]

The Bob Jones University Museum was determined to be qualified for exemption despite the fact that it was affiliated with the nontax-exempt Bob Jones University.[28]

The IRS has been accused of discriminating against gay and lesbian groups seeking recognition of exemption. The Lambda Legal Defense and Education Fund representatives wrote to the Commissioner of Internal Revenue, Charles O. Rossotti, to complain about discriminatory treatment by "front-line agents" who initially deal with applications when gay- and lesbian-oriented groups apply for tax-exempt status. Marcus S. Owens, Director of the Exempt Organizations Division, responded by scheduling visits of himself and other IRS officials to field offices to brief agents on the importance of professionalism, impartiality, and fairness in dealing with all organizations.[29]

(c) Day Care Centers

IRC §501(k) states that "providing care of children away from their homes" is an educational, and therefore, exempt purpose if:

- Substantially all of the care (at least 85%) is provided to enable individuals to be gainfully employed (including employees, self-employed, enrolled students or vocational trainees, and individuals who are actively seeking employment).[30]

- The day care is available to the general public. Limitations based upon a geographic or political boundary are permissible. Restricting enrollment to children of employees of a particular employer, however, is not permissible.[31]

---

[26] Exemption letter dated April 7, 1993 to Rebul Academy, Inc., citing *Green v. Connelly*, 330 F. Supp. 1150 (D.D.C. 1971), *aff'd sub nom. Coit v. Green*, 404 U.S. 997 (1971).

[27] These factors are also outlined in Rev. Proc. 75-50, 1975-2 C.B. 587.

[28] See more information in §5.1(g).

[29] Letters reprinted in Vol. 21, No. 3, September 1998 edition of *The Exempt Organization Tax Review*, a publication of Tax Analysts, Arlington, Virginia.

[30] Exempt Organization Handbook (IRM 7751) §345(11)2.

[31] Gen. Coun. Memos. 39613 and 39347.

Whether such an organization created by a consortium of employers could qualify for exemption is an unanswered question in the author's experience.

Providing day care referrals and assistance information to the general public, however, has been treated by the IRS as a service that is ordinarily a commercial activity. Counseling parents and caregivers about day care was found not to be per se an educational or charitable activity. In an entity where 98% of its revenues came from charges for its services, the IRS refused to grant tax-exempt status as an educational institution.[32]

(d) Cooperative Educational Service Organizations

IRC §501(f) was added to the Code to sanction pooled investing by educational institutions. To qualify, the organization must be:

- Organized and operated to hold, commingle, and collectively invest and reinvest in stocks and securities, the moneys contributed by its members and to collect the income therefrom, and pay over the entire amount, less expenses, to the members

- Organized and controlled by its members

- Composed solely of organizations qualifying as schools under IRC §170(b)(1)(A)(ii) or IRC §115(a) (schools operated by an instrumentality of a government—a municipality or state)

(e) Informal Education

Organizations that present instructional materials or training on a less formal basis than a school can qualify as a tax-exempt educational organization if they operate to benefit the general public rather than a particular business. Discussion groups, retreat centers, apprentice training programs, and the many other types of educational programs in the following list are exempt if they can prove they provide the requisite instruction for the benefit of individuals:

- Training programs for bankers,[33] physicians,[34] artists,[35] credit union managers,[36] and dancers[37]

- Travel study tours that provide genuine cultural and educational programs, with no or limited recreational aspects and led by professionals[38]

- Interscholastic high school athletic associations[39] and youth sports organizations[40]

---

[32] Gen. Coun. Memo. 39872, modifying Gen. Coun. Memo. 39622.
[33] Rev. Rul. 68-504, 1968-2 C.B. 211.
[34] Rev. Rul. 65-298, 1965-2 C.B. 163.
[35] Rev. Rul. 67-392, 1967-2 C.B. 191.
[36] Rev. Rul. 74-16, 1974-1 C.B. 126.
[37] Rev. Rul. 65-270, 1965-2 C.B. 160.
[38] Rev. Rul. 70-534, 1970-2 C.B. 113.
[39] Rev. Rul. 55-587, 1955-2 C.B. 261.
[40] Rev. Rul. 80-215, 1980-2 C.B. 174.

- On-the-job training of unemployed and underemployed workers, even if the toys they manufacture are sold[41]

- Trade skill training for American Indians[42]

- Counseling and educational instruction through publications concerning homosexuals[43] and voluntary sterilization methods[44]

- Student and cultural exchange programs[45]

- Studying and publishing reports on Civil War battles[46] or career planning and vocational counseling[47]

- Computer users' groups are not exempt if their membership is limited to persons using a particular type of computer,[48] but they may qualify as business leagues.[49]

An educational organization affiliated with or focused on a particular line of business or product must carefully adhere to the private inurement standards.[50] The list of qualifying organizations found in the regulations defining *educational* does not include instruction and training to improve and develop professional or business skills. Business groups conducting classes and sharing information are eligible for exempt status as educational organizations as long as two significant characteristics are present:

- The organization provides no private benefit to a particular manufacturer, product, software company, accounting firm, or similar private company (certainly should not be controlled, financed, or otherwise too closely connected to a commercial company).

- The group's primary function is education, not selling products or consulting services.

Interesting and unique exemption issues arise when the training and information are transmitted by way of electronic bulletin boards and across the Internet. For what it calls "computer related organizations," the IRS has compiled the historical rulings concerning computer users' groups and updated its guidance on the issue. Advisors to formulators of such groups will want to carefully study this reference prior to seeking recognition of exemption or adopting new programs for existing

[41] Rev. Rul. 73-128, 1973-1 C.B. 222.
[42] Rev. Rul. 77-272, 1977-2 C.B. 191.
[43] Rev. Rul. 78-305, 1978-2 C.B. 172.
[44] Rev. Rul. 74-595, 1974-2 C.B. 164.
[45] Rev. Rul. 80-286, 1980-2 C.B. 179; Rev. Rul. 68-165, 1968-1 C.B. 253.
[46] Rev. Rul. 67-148, 1967-1 C.B. 132.
[47] Rev. Rul. 79-71, 1968-1 C.B. 249.
[48] Rev. Rul. 74-116, 1974-1 C.B. 127.
[49] See Chapter 8.
[50] Discussed in Chapter 2§1(c).

organizations.[51] One can visit the IRS website at *www.irs.ustreas.gov.* at Tax Information for Business for the CPE text and other IRS publications.

(f) Performing Arts

Performing arts organizations presenting music, drama, poetry, film, and dance are classified as cultural, and thus, as educational organizations. Symphony orchestras, theaters, public television and radio, and other performing groups easily gain exempt status if they meet the basic organizational and operational tests. Although most charge admission for performances, such arts organizations are characteristically charitable because they receive a significant portion of their revenues from voluntary contributions. The few rulings on the subject follow:

- Repertory theater established to develop the public's interest in dramatic arts, and a foundation funding local community theaters[52]

- Jazz music appreciation society presenting festivals and concerts[53]

- Weekly workshops, public concerts, and booking agency for young musicians[54]

- Sponsor of annual film festival and symposium promoting unknown independent filmmakers[55]

- Producer of cultural, educational, and public interest films that distributes them through public educational channels[56] or makes equipment available to the public to produce programs[57]

Coproduction of performances or recordings with commercial businesses must be carefully planned by a tax-exempt arts organization. As with all organizations qualifying as under §501(c)(3), a performing arts organization must not operate to yield benefit to private individuals. In forming an association with a commercial entity, the terms must be designed to better promote performing arts with only incidental benefit, if any, to the coproducers. An exempt television production company, for example, was found to be advancing its own exempt purposes in entering into a joint venture to develop children's programming for a commercial network.[58] Permissible joint venture activities are explored in Chapter 22, including the famous Plumstead Theatre case.

---

[51] "Computer Related Organizations," by Cheryl Chasin and Robert Harper, *Exempt Organizations Continuing Professional Educational Technical Instruction Program Textbook,* ch. A (1996).
[52] Rev. Rul. 64-175, 1964-1 (Part 1) C.B. 185; Rev. Rul. 64-174, 1964-1 (Part 1) C.B. 183.
[53] Rev. Rul. 65-271, 1965-2 C.B. 161.
[54] Rev. Rul. 67-392, 1967-2 C.B. 191.
[55] Rev. Rul. 75-471, 1975-2 C.B. 207.
[56] Rev. Rul. 76-4, 1976-1 C.B. 145.
[57] Rev. Rul. 76-443, 1976-2 C.B. 149.
[58] Priv. Ltr. Rul. 9350044.

(g) Museums, Libraries, and Zoos

Organizations that collect and exhibit objects of a literary, artistic, historic, biological, or other educational nature for the general public qualify as exempt educational organizations. Again this type of cultural nonprofit is a prototypical charity because admission charges commonly cover a small portion of a museum's budget with contributions and endowment income providing the lion's share. There are only a few rulings on this type of educational organization but the IRS has ruled that the following activities qualify:

- Acquiring, restoring, preserving, and opening to the public homes, churches, and public buildings having historic significance[59]

- Operating a wild bird and animal sanctuary[60]

- Operating a sports museum[61]

- Operating the library of a bar association[62]

- Organizing an international exposition[63]

- Promoting unknown but promising artists through exhibitions of their work,[64] but cooperative art sales galleries are not exempt[65]

The Bob Jones University's federal tax exemption was revoked in 1983 by the Supreme Court because the university was racially discriminatory.[66] The school art gallery, operated since 1951, was separately incorporated in 1992 to lease the museum facility from the school (at below market price) and operate the facility with the same staff and artwork previously on display, now on loan from the school. The museum was to be open to the public free of charge; approximately 80% of the museum's 20,000 annual visitors had no connection with the school. The museum's major support comes from contributions.[67] The court found the museum qualified for tax exemption and overruled the IRS on all of its following arguments:

- Excessive control: Bob Jones and his son were only two out of five directors, therefore the school did not literally control the museum.

- Payment of rent and salaries: The court stated that an organization is entitled to pay ordinary and necessary operating expenses. The rent was at

---

[59] Rev. Rul. 75-470, 1975-2 C.B. 207.
[60] Rev. Rul. 67-292, 1967-2 C.B. 184.
[61] Rev. Rul. 68-372, 1968-2 C.B. 205.
[62] Rev. Rul. 75-196, 1975-1 C.B. 155.
[63] Rev. Rul. 71-545, 1971-2 C.B. 235.
[64] Rev. Rul. 66-178, 1966-1 C.B. 138.
[65] Rev. Rul. 71-395, 1971-2 C.B. 228.
[66] *Bob Jones University v. United States,* 461 U.S. 574 (1983); nondiscrimination standards discussed in 5§1(b).
[67] *Bob Jones University Museum & Gallery, Inc. v. Commissioner,* T.C.M. 1996-247.

below-market value and, in the court's opinion, did not confer an impermissible private benefit on the school. The employees no longer provided any services to the school, so payment of their salaries by the new museum was also found not to benefit the school.

- Reputation and location: Any enhancement of the school's reputation from the location of the museum was minimal and incidental in the eyes of the court.

(h) Sale of Art Objects

An art gallery that sells the works of art it exhibits must overcome a presumption that it is operating a business, rather than serving a purely educational purpose that would entitle it to exemption. The question is whether taking home the object enhances the customer's educational experience and thereby produces income related to exempt purposes. The answer varies dependent upon whether the object is an original work of craft, an original work of fine art, a reproduction or replica of an object, or a handicraft item. An organization whose unrelated business activity is more than insubstantial (commonly thought to equal about 10–15%) may not qualify for exemption. Chapter 21 has a special section on museums.

(i) Publishing—Print and Electronic

Publishing projects have been a subject of controversy with the IRS. The two issues most debated have been controversial subject matter and commercial activity. It is not sufficient that the subject matter of the published work be religious, cultural, scientific, or educational. An exempt publishing company must also distinguish itself from a commercial one so as to evidence that it is not operating an unrelated business. The factors that identify an educational publication program follow:[68]

- The content of the publication must be educational.

- Preparation of the materials follows methods generally accepted as educational.[69]

- Distribution of the materials is necessary or valuable in achieving the organization's educational and scientific purposes.

- The manner in which the distribution is accomplished is distinguishable from ordinary commercial publishing practices.

Organizations distributing educational materials free[70] or at a nominal price[71] indisputably operate in a noncommercial manner. However, publishing a foreign

[68] Exempt Organizations Handbook (IRM 7751) §345.(10)2; Rev. Rul. 67-4, 1967-1 C.B. 121.
[69] Discussed at the beginning of this chapter.
[70] Rev. Rul. 66-147, 1966-1 C.B. 137.
[71] Rev. Rul. 68-307, 1968-1 C.B. 258.

language magazine on a subscription basis at a price and through channels used by commercial publishers is not an exempt activity.[72] A section on the unrelated business aspects of publishing can be found in Chapter 21.

Electronic publishing is a relatively unexplored area of activity for tax-exempt organizations. In its 1998 training materials, the IRS said, "In the past, Internet Service Providers (ISP) have usually been denied exemption because they are viewed as carrying on a trade or business for profit, or conferring an unmixed private benefit, or both."[73] "Providing communication services of an ordinary commercial nature in a community, even though the undertaking is conducted on a nonprofit basis, is not regarded as conferring a charitable benefit on the community unless the service directly accomplishes one of the established categories of charitable purposes."[74] Both of the IRS training course articles from which the previous quotes are taken should be carefully studied for an ISP seeking tax-exempt status. The articles conclude that exemption may be possible if the ISP is an adjunct or integral part of a university, public school, library system, or a local government. Accountability and control, dependence on government grants rather than user fees, and free use to students, library patrons, and the general public are said to be characteristics that evidence a charitable ISP. Such an ISP might also qualify as relieving the burdens of government.[75] The training manual suggests the IRS technician "peruse to the ISP's home page to evaluate its exempt character as a source of public information and to see if 'placards,' 'banners,' and links to commercial sites constitute advertising that create unrelated business income."[76]

(j) Controversial Materials

As early as 1919, the Bureau of Revenue said an educational organization may include one whose sole purpose is the instruction of the public "but an association formed to disseminate controversial or partisan propaganda is not educational." The American Birth Control League was found not to be educational in 1930. Judge Learned Hand opined a purpose to change the law as an end in itself was not itself exempt regardless of the problem of uncontrolled procreation. He thought "political agitation as such is outside the statute, however innocent the aim."[77]

The more recent "service view is that an organization's mere dissemination of words or a viewpoint to the public does not necessarily benefit the public sufficiently to warrant the organization's tax exemption under 501(c)(3)."[78] The methodology test discussed at the beginning of this chapter applies to determine

---

[72] Rev. Rul. 77-4, 1977-1 C.B. 141.

[73] Fiscal 1999 CPE Text for Exempt Organizations, Chapter C entitled *Internet Service Providers Exemption Issues,* by Donna Moore and Robert Harper.

[74] Fiscal 1997 CPE Test for Exempt Organizations, Chapter A entitled *Computer-Related Organizations,* pages 9–12, by Cheryl Chasin and Robert Harper.

[75] See Chapter 4§3.

[76] See Chapter 21§8(d); Form 1023 now requests the applicant's website address on page 1, see Appendix 18-1.

[77] *Slee v. Commissioner,* 42 F.2d 184 (2d Cir. 1930).

[78] 1997 CPE Text for Exempt Organizations Technical Instruction Program, Chapter H, *Education, Propoganda, and The Methodology Test,* Ward L. Thomas and Robert Fonterose, page 83.

the educational nature of a program. To be educational, information must be useful to the individual and beneficial to the community. The materials presented must contain a sufficiently full and fair exposition of the pertinent facts about a subject, rather than an unsupported opinion.

The Tax Court denied exemption for The Nationalist Movement (TNM), a pro-white Mississippi organization advocating social, economic, and political change in the United States.[79] Denial was based not upon excessive lobbying or political activity, but instead on a finding that the organizational activities were neither educational nor charitable. The court found that the organization did not operate exclusively for an exempt purpose. The opinion quotes extensively from the organization's literature—newsletters, convention programs, and writings of the founder, Richard Barrett. The following quotations are from a fund-raising letter and epitomize the philosophy of the organization. The second quotation, from a TNM newsletter, served, in the court's opinion, to exemplify viewpoints unsupported by facts and therefore not educational.

1. "We'll do for the majority in the 1980s what others did for the minorities in the 1960s. Parading, speaking, rallying, petitioning. Only we won't riot, loot or burn. We'll wave flags, win lawsuits, sing songs, and gain power."

2. "What is Black History anyhow? No such thing. Nary a wheel, building or useful tool ever emanated from non-white Africa. Africanization aims to set up a tyranny of minorities over Americans."

The IRS unsuccessfully argued that the organization served the private interests of Barrett by "supplying a forum to express and promote his personal agenda." The court found that "substantial domination of an organization by its founder does not necessarily disqualify the organization from exemption." The court also noted no evidence that Barrett used the organization to further his political career. TNM argued that it operated social service programs that qualified as charitable (feeding the poor and pursuing public interest litigation). The records about these activities were "inconsistent" in the eyes of the court and did not enable TNM to prove that it operated "exclusively for charitable purposes."

Most importantly, the court found that the messages presented through TNM's radio program and written materials failed the methodology test[80] and were not educational. Because they were TNM's primary activity, the organization did not qualify for exemption. The court also found that the methodology test "is not unconstitutionally vague or overbroad on its face" and reduces the vagueness of the regulation. The criteria "tend toward ensuring that the educational exemption be restricted to material which substantially helps a reader or listener in a learning process." The court essentially condoned the regulation it had earlier found unconstitutional by finding that viewpoints unsupported by facts were not educational. Since a significant portion of the organization's communications

---

[79] *The Nationalist Movement v. Commissioner*, 102 T.C.No. 22 (1994), *aff'd* 37 F.3d 216,74 (5th Cir. 1994).
[80] Rev. Proc. 86-43 discussed at the beginning of this section; see also *National Alliance v. U.S.*, 710 F.2d 868 (D.C. Cir. 1983).

contained such materials, the organization was not educational, even if such presentations were not its principal function.[81]

5.2 LITERARY PURPOSES

In this category, the regulations are silent and contain no definition or criteria for qualification. Since literature is both educational and cultural, a literary organization can be exempt under one or both of those categories. Most often at issue for a literary project is its relationship with those that create the literature. Do the programs advance the private interests of the writers? An organization established to encourage emerging writers by publishing their works in the small press market must prove that it does not primarily benefit the individual writers, but instead promotes literature or culture in a global sense. The IRS customarily requires that the nonprofit own the rights to the intellectual property although it allows writers to be compensated for the value of their work.

Examples of literary pursuits include publishing of literature, including poetry, essays, fiction, nonfiction, and all other forms of written compositions. Other examples include a sponsor of poetry readings, a literary workshop to teach writing skills, a critical journal of reviews, a committee to award a prize for excellence in literature (such as the Pulitzer Prize), and a preservation society for rare books.[82]

5.3 SCIENTIFIC PURPOSES

The IRS admitted in 1966 that the term *scientific* is not one definable with precision.[83] The regulations provide only that *scientific* includes the carrying on of scientific research in the public interest. Further they say, "Research when taken alone is a word with many meanings; it is not synonymous with scientific and the nature of particular research depends upon the purpose which it serves." The determination as to whether research is *scientific* does not depend on whether such research is classified as fundamental, or basic, as contrasted with applied, or practical.[84]

(a) Research in the Public Interest

The apparent ambiguity in the meaning of research is addressed by very exact and specific standards for judging whether scientific research is conducted in the pub-

---

[81] TNM lastly argued unsuccessfully that the test allowed "excessive administrative discretion" and violated its free speech rights under the Constitution. The court pointed out the Supreme Court has found that denial of a tax exemption for engaging in speech consisting of "dangerous ideas" can be a discriminatory limitation of free speech (*Speiser v. Randall*, 357 U.S. 513, 519 (1958)). It chose to follow, however, the Supreme Court's opinion that nondiscriminatory denial of a tax benefit, not aimed at suppressing speech content, does not infringe First Amendment rights (*Cammarano v. U.S.*, 358 U.S. 498, 512-513 (1959)). This case considered the issue of nondeductibility of lobbying expenses.

[82] See the discussion of publishing in Chapters 5§1(i) and 21§14.

[83] Rev. Rul. 66-147, 1966-1 C.B. 137.

[84] Reg. §1.501(c)(3)-1(d)(5).

lic interest qualifying as a tax-exempt activity. To be considered as conducted in the public interest, research—both fundamental and applied—must have the following characteristics:

1. Results of the research, including patents, copyrights, processes, or formulas, must be made available to the public on a nondiscriminatory basis.

2. Research is performed for a federal, state, or local government.

3. Work is directed toward benefiting the public for the following reasons:

   ■ To aid in scientific education of college students;

   ■ To obtain information toward a treatise, thesis, or trade publication, or in any form available to the general public;

   ■ To discover a cure for disease; or

   ■ To aid a community or geographic area in attracting development of new industries.

Scientific research does *not* include activities of a type ordinarily carried on as an incident to commercial or industrial operations, as, for example, the ordinary testing or inspection of materials or products, or the designing or construction of equipment, buildings, and the like.[85]

Retaining ownership or control of more than an insubstantial portion of the patents, copyrights, processes, or formulas resulting from an organization's research and not making them available to the public disqualifies it from exempt status.[86] If granting an exclusive right is the only practical manner in which the patent can be utilized to benefit the public, in the case of research conducted for the government or for the purposes listed under the standards above, the information can be withheld.[87] An exempt organization that performs research only for its non-501(c)(3) creators cannot be classified as a 501(c)(3) organization.[88]

One court has suggested that this regulation can be understood in the context of distinguishing a commercial testing laboratory from a scientific research institute.[89] The definition of scientific research would exclude the repetitive or relatively unsophisticated work done by commercial laboratories to determine whether items tested meet certain specifications, rather than the more sophisticated testing done to validate a scientific hypothesis. Scientific research was said to have three components:

---

[85] Rev. Rul. 65-1, 1965-1 C.B. 226; Rev. Rul. 68-373, 1968-2 C.B. 206.
[86] Rev. Rul. 76-296, 1976-2 C.B. 141 discusses the timing of the release of public information under two different scenarios. Publication as a general rule can be withheld until the patent is issued, but may not be delayed to protect the sponsor's business interests.
[87] Reg. §1.501(c)(3)-1(d)(5)(iv)(b).
[88] Rev. Rul. 69-526, 1969-2 C.B. 115.
[89] *Midwest Research Institute v. U.S.*, 554 F. Supp. 1379 (W.D. Mo. 1983), also discussed in Gen. Coun. Memo. 39883 (October 16, 1992).

1. There must be project supervision and design by professionals.

2. Researchers design the project to solve a problem through a search for demonstrable truth, also called "scientific method." A researcher forms a hypothesis, designs and conducts tests to gather data, and analyzes data for its effect on the verity or falsity of the hypothesis.

3. The research goal must be the discovery of a demonstrable truth. Information on the novelty and importance of the knowledge to be discovered is also important to determine whether a particular activity furthers a scientific purpose.

The IRS has suggested that in differentiating between research and testing, it may be useful to refer to "research and development expenses" qualifying for tax credit under §174.[90] In that situation, all costs are incident to the development of an experimental or pilot model, a product, a formula, an invention, or similar property, and the improvement of already existing property of these categories. The term does not include expenditures such as those for the ordinary testing or inspection of materials for products for quality control purposes or for efficiency surveys, management studies, consumer surveys, advertising, or promotion.

A combined educational and scientific purpose may also qualify an organization for exemption, as the following examples illustrate:

- Surveying scientific and medical literature and abstracting and publishing it free of charge is an exempt activity.[91]

- Developing treatment for human diseases and disseminating the results through physicians' seminars, is also an exempt activity.[92]

- Manufacturing cast reproductions of anthropological specimens for sale to scholars and educational institutions was found to support a charitable research purpose.[93]

- Conducting seed technology research, approving certification of crop seeds within a state, and providing instruction in cooperation with a university are scientific activities, and are therefore exempt.[94]

Design and development of a patentable medical device, under a contract with a medical equipment company, was found not to qualify as scientific research, because the science was incidental to the commercial exploitation aspects of the activity. The organization obligated itself to license any patents for the device exclusively to the company in exchange for a royalty.[95]

---

[90] Gen. Coun. Memo. 39196 (August 31, 1983).
[91] Rev. Rul. 66-147, *supra* n. 73.
[92] Rev. Rul. 65-298, 1965-2 C.B. 163.
[93] Rev. Rul. 70-129, 1970-1 C.B. 128.
[94] *Indiana Crop Improvement Association, Inc. v. Commissioner,* 76 T.C. 394 400 (1981).
[95] T.A.M. 8028004.

(b) Commercialization of Research Results

Scientific research often results in valuable intellectual property capable of producing revenues. Two very different issues are involved when research results are commercially exploited.

1. Does the exploitation indicate that the research is not actually conducted in the public interest and if so, does the scope of the activity evidence a significant nonexempt purpose?

2. Is the revenue subject to the unrelated business income tax?

A research project commissioned by commercial interests can only incidentally benefit its private sponsors. To evaluate this benefit, the proverbial facts and circumstances of a project are examined. Importantly the exploitation activity cannot constitute a substantial nonexempt activity without jeopardy to the organization's tax-exempt status. To reduce this possibility, organizations conducting commercial research can consider creating a separate nonexempt organization to conduct the business.[96]

Private rulings requested by research organizations reflect interesting facts that can be studied to understand the IRS view of exploitation of the results of scientific research. One organization created to educate the public on the need for improvement in the use and design of urban public open spaces and to engage in research and design of open spaces provided a good forum for the IRS to find examples of excessive private interest.[97] Eight specific urban design projects were reviewed and a myriad of citations analyzed. Private interest was found to exist in three projects studying the public's use of private property. Examples included a study of pedestrian flow through a building's government-mandated public spaces and the study of ways to enhance an underutilized plaza. Even though the projects serving private property owners produced some 15% of its revenue and were subject to tax, the organization was found to qualify for exemption.

In another instance, an organization was originally created to conduct basic research in biotechnology to broaden the industrial base and foster job creation through the development of innovations. To become financially independent of state funding, it planned to focus on applied research to produce marketable technology it could commercially license and exploit. Under the plan, its discovery research would be transferred to a university. The ruling also considered the sharing of intellectual property rights. The IRS prefers the nonprofit retain 100% of intellectual property rights using the theory that any allocation of rights to individuals results in private inurement. However, the organization's federal research agreements required it to share royalties from patents with the inventors. One-third of revenues from licensing or other transfer of patents were allocated to the inventor employees. Further consulting fees were shared half-and-half or equally with the employees for services rendered during regular working hours. Individual scientists were allowed to retain all fees for consulting performed on their own time. An additional bonus system rewarded managers and senior scientists.

[96] See discussion in Chapter 22.
[97] Priv. Ltr. Rul. 9414003.

Because the compensation arrangements were a result of arm's-length bargaining and the overall compensation was reasonable, the IRS determined that the royalty, fee-sharing, and bonus system did not result in private inurement. The IRS determined that it could retain its tax-exempt status.[98]

Another organization received approval for a reorganization in which it spun off inventions and products into nonexempt subsidiaries. The plan had several goals: (1) to commercialize technologies developed by the exempt's scientists and engineers, (2) to improve the transfer of technology from the exempt's labs into the public domain, (3) to stimulate economic development, (4) to provide entrepreneurial opportunities for the scientists, and (5) to separate the commercial activities from the basic research function.[99]

Special UBI Exclusions. The unrelated business income tax rules modify, or exclude, income that is essentially derived from research programs conducted in the public interest. Using slightly different language from that found in the 501(c)(3) regulations, the code specifically excludes:[100]

- All income derived from research from the United States, any of its agencies or instrumentalities, or any state or political subdivision thereof;

- In the case of a college, university, or hospital, there shall be excluded all income derived from research performed for any person; and

- In the case of an organization operated primarily for purposes of carrying on fundamental research the results of which are freely available to the general public.

Instead, profits from research carried on for the following purposes would be treated as unrelated income, the receipt of which could jeopardize tax-exempt status.[101]

- Scientific research performed for a private sponsor that is not carried on in the public interest.

- Work for a governmental body or others of a type ordinarily carried on as incident to commercial or industrial operations (such as testing for quality).

Royalty Exclusion. Revenues from research of a type not specifically excluded from the unrelated business income tax may also be modified, or excluded, from

---

[98] Priv. Ltr. Rul. 9316052; see Chapter 20 and the fiscal 1999 CPE Text for Exempt organizations entitled *Intellectual Property*.

[99] See "The Inurement Rule and Ownership of Copyrights," by William T. Hutton and Cynthia R. Rowland, 9 *Exempt Organization Tax Review* 813 (April 1994). The authors propose a revenue procedure containing eight situations exemplifying lack or presence of inurement when an individual retains or receives copyrights for a project financed by an exempt organization.

[100] IRC §§512((b)(7), (8), and (9).

[101] See Chapter 21.

unrelated business income tax if they are paid in the form of royalties and paid in return for licensing intellectual property.[102]

5.4 TESTING FOR PUBLIC SAFETY

The regulations give only one example of an organization qualifying because it tests for public safety. Such an organization tests consumer products, such as electrical products, to determine whether they are safe for use by the general public.[103] Other exempt programs might include testing for structural building strength against violent weather, such as hurricanes and tornadoes, or earthquakes. Testing boat equipment and establishing standards for pleasure craft was also ruled to be an exempt activity.[104]

Similar to the scientific research constraints, testing must be performed to serve a public benefit, rather than the interests of private owners, such as drug manufacturers. This distinction is not always clear. In a published ruling, the IRS found that testing, research, and other work toward developing methods and safety certifications for shipping containers benefited the shipping industry and advanced international commerce and, therefore, was not an exempt organization, despite the fact that the stevedores working with shipping containers constitute a charitable class whose safety is significant and worthy of testing.[105] Similarly, a drug company's testing program prior to approval by the Food and Drug Administration was ruled to serve the manufacturer's private interest.[106] The characteristics of scientific research as contrasted with testing activity is discussed in the foregoing §5.3.

Perhaps because their funds are raised through the provision of services, these testing organizations do not qualify as charitable organizations eligible to receive deductible contributions under IRC §170(c), even though they do qualify as exempt under §501(c)(3). They are excepted from private foundation classification under IRC §509(a)(4) presumably because they are not funded with private donations.

5.5 FOSTERING NATIONAL OR INTERNATIONAL AMATEUR SPORTS COMPETITION (BUT ONLY IF NO PART OF ITS ACTIVITIES INVOLVE THE PROVISION OF ATHLETIC FACILITIES OR EQUIPMENT)

The parenthetical qualification to this exemption category was added in 1976 to prevent athletic or social clubs from qualifying under IRC §501(c)(3), while allowing charitable status to the Olympic and Pan-American Games. In a seemingly redundant provision, Congress in 1982 stipulated in §501(j) that certain qualified organizations are not subject to the restriction in the parentheses. Curiously, the

---

[102] Discussed in Chapter 21 §10(d).
[103] Reg. §1.501(c)(3)-1(d)(4).
[104] Rev. Rul. 65-61, 1965-1 C.B. 234.
[105] Rev. Rul. 78-426, 1978-2 C.B. 175.
[106] Rev. Rul. 68-373, 1968-2 C.B. 206.

definition of those organizations that qualify is identical to the words used in §501(c)(3). The regulations concerning the 1976 changes were withdrawn in 1984.

The only reported case in this area involved the International E22 Class Association.[107] The organization was established to formulate and enforce measurements of a particular type of racing sailboat used in international competition. In addition to setting the standard, the association sold tools to measure compliance during construction of the boats and during races. The IRS argued that such devices were athletic equipment and refused to grant the organization an exemption. The Tax Court disagreed, saying that the measurement tools were not facilities, as clubhouses, swimming pools, and gymnasiums are. Equipment means property used directly in athletic endeavors. The court was not aware of any athletic exercise, game, competition, or other endeavor in which the tools could be used.

Local amateur athletic groups, like the Little Leagues, need not necessarily qualify under this category. Such a group can instead qualify under the charitable category because it prevents juvenile delinquency and advances education.[108] The IRS decided that a national high school athletic association created in 1942 could continue to be classified as a charitable and educational entity rather than be reclassified under 501(j). The organization coordinated the efforts of state high school associations by sponsoring meetings and conferences, setting activity rules, publishing educational materials, and serving as the national governing body.[109] Promoting recreational sports for a limited membership, however, may not be an activity benefiting the requisite charitable class.[110]

5.6 PREVENTION OF CRUELTY TO CHILDREN OR ANIMALS

This is another exemption category without explanation in the IRS regulations. Thankfully, a few published rulings provide guidelines, as the following examples of exempt activities indicate:

- Animal protection accomplished by accreditation of animal care facilities that supply, keep, and care for animals used by medical and scientific researchers[111]

- Preventing birth of unwanted animals by providing low-cost spaying and neutering operations[112]

- Monitoring of hazardous occupations for violations of state laws and unfavorable work conditions, in order to protect child workers[113]

---

[107] *International E22 Class Association v. Commissioner*, 78 T.C. 93 (1982).
[108] Rev. Rul. 80-215, 1980-2 C.B. 174.
[109] Tech. Adv. Memo. 9211004.
[110] See Chapter 2§2.
[111] Rev. Rul. 66-359, 1966-2 C.B. 219.
[112] Rev. Rul. 74-194, 1974-1 C.B. 129.
[113] Rev. Rul. 67-151, 1967-1 C.B. 134.

5.6 PREVENTION OF CRUELTY TO CHILDREN OR ANIMALS

A troublesome case might be the provision of veterinary services to individual pet owners. While it could be argued that such services prevent cruelty, there is an additional burden to prove the public usefulness of the effort. Certain treatments probably deserve and could gain charitable status, such as rabies control, but the absence of individual benefit ultimately has to be proved in order to obtain exemption.

CHAPTER SIX

Civic Leagues and Local Associations of Employees: §501(c)(4)

It is well-established that an organization may be created to carry out its purposes through the development and implementation of programs designed to have an impact on community, state, or national policymaking.[1] Environmental protection, housing, civil rights, aid to the poor, world peace, or other public issues may be involved. The pursuit of such subjects is the focus of both (c)(3) and (c)(4) organizations. The term *social welfare* appears in the regulations defining *charitable* for (c)(3) purposes. This chapter focuses on the factors that distinguish a (c)(3) from a (c)(4) organization and the category of exemption most appropriate for organizations that pursue matters of public policies.

    The regulations for Internal Revenue Code (IRC) §501(c)(4) were adopted in 1959 and cover only half a page. They list two basic types of organization that fall into this category:

---

[1] B. Hopkins, *The Law of Tax-Exempt Organizations, Sixth Ed.* (New York: Wiley, 1992), p. 549.

Type 1. A civic league or organization that is organized for nonprofit purposes and operated exclusively for promotion of social welfare. "To promote social welfare means to promote in some way the common good and general welfare of the people of the community."[2] The concept includes bringing about civic betterment and social improvements. A civic league may focus on environmental protection, civil rights, aid to the poor, world peace, and other issues of public concern. The regulations state that a social welfare organization may qualify for exemption as a charitable organization unless it is an *action organization*.[3]

Since this type of (c)(4) is often created to be active, meaning to change the laws, it cannot qualify under (c)(3). As a (c)(4), however, lobbying can be its primary function, as long as the legislative activity promotes in some way the common good and general welfare of the people of a community. The phrase "exclusively operated for civic welfare" does not prohibit an organization from earning some unrelated business income.

Type 2. A local association of employees whose membership is limited to the employees of a designated person or persons in a particular municipality and whose net earnings are devoted exclusively to charitable educational or recreational purposes.[4]

6.1 COMPARISON OF (c)(3) AND (c)(4) ORGANIZATIONS

The term *social welfare* appears in the regulations defining *charitable* for (c)(3) purposes. Since social welfare can be the focus of both §§501(c)(3) and (c)(4) organizations, it is important to carefully choose which category is most appropriate for any particular organization.

IRC §501(c)(4) organizations have several elements in common with §501(c)(3) groups. They conduct similar social welfare activities—lessening neighborhood tensions, eliminating prejudice and discrimination, defending human and civil rights secured by law, and combating community deterioration and juvenile delinquency. Other parallels include:

- Neither type of organization may be organized or operated for profit.
- Both must benefit the "community," defined as a charitable class (for example, a poor group, a minority group, or the population of an entire city, country, or the world).
- Membership in both types of organizations must be open, and cannot be restricted to a limited or select group of individuals or businesses.
- No private inurement or benefit to a select group of insiders is permitted.

The following four characteristics of a §501(c)(4) organization are very different and serve to distinguish it from a §501(c)(3) organization:

[2] Reg. §1.501(c)(4)-1(a)(1)(2)(i).
[3] Discussed in Chapter 2§2(g).
[4] Reg. §1.501(c)(4)-1(b).

- A §501(c)(4) organization can engage in extensive *action* or lobbying efforts to influence legislation by propaganda and other means.

- A §501(c)(4) organization is not required to have a specific dissolution clause in its charter; its only organizational test is that it not be operated for profit-making purposes.

- Participation in political campaigns cannot be the primary purpose of a §501(c)(4) organization, but there is no absolute prohibition. Participation in political campaigns is not considered to be the promotion of social welfare, and §527 taxes the organization to the extent of its political expenditures.[5]

- Donations to §501(c)(4) organizations are not deductible as charitable gifts under IRC §170.

(a) Choosing to Apply under (c)(4) versus (c)(3)

It is possible for some organizations to qualify for exemption under both §§501(c)(3) and (c)(4), so an important choice must be made when a project promoting the social welfare applies for its exempt status. Those that plan action and expect to engage in extensive lobbying beyond the limits permitted under (c)(3) must seek (c)(4) status. There are very few circumstances when (c)(4) would be chosen in preference to (c)(3), particularly when tax deductible contributions can be sought.

Proper timing is important for an existing (c)(3) organization since conversion is not allowed after an organization loses its exempt status due to excessive lobbying. An existing (c)(3) organization that expects its future lobbying efforts will cause it to lose its charitable status can, however, apply to convert before the excessive activity occurs.

The right choice is critical. A (c)(3) organization that loses its exemption because it engages in excessive lobbying cannot then convert to the (c)(4) class, but instead loses its exempt status and becomes a taxable entity.[6] Intentional avoidance of this rule was anticipated by Congress. A transfer of assets by a (c)(3) to create a separate (c)(4) organization may result in loss of its exempt status. The excessive activity is attributed to a (c)(3) spinning off assets to carry on the lobbying in the following circumstances:[7]

- Over 30% of the net fair market value of the (c)(3)'s (other than a church) assets or 50% of the recipient organization's assets are transferred to a controlled non-(c)(3) entity, which then conducts excessive lobbying.

- The transfer is within two years of the discovery of excessive lobbying.

- Upon transfer or at any time within ten years following such a transfer, the transferee is controlled by the same persons who control the transferor.

---

[5] Rev. Rul. 81-95, 1981-1 C.B. 332; see Chapter 23.
[6] IRC § 504.
[7] Reg. §1.504-2(e) and (f).

> *Control* for this purpose means that the persons in authority can, by using their voting power, require or prevent the transferee's spending of funds.[8]

(b) Affiliated (c)(3) and (c)(4) Organizations

It is common for (c)(4) organizations to operate in affiliation with charitable organizations. Social welfare programs often encompass issues that are both the subject of legislative proposals and also entail research, public education, and other activities that qualify as charitable. When it is anticipated that the advocacy efforts will make charitable status difficult to obtain or maintain, two organizations can be formed from the inception—a (c)(4) to carry out lobbying activities and a (c)(3) for strictly charitable activities.

Affiliated (c)(3) and (c)(4) organizations can operate side by side, can share resources, such as office space, equipment, and personnel, and often have similar names—the Sierra Club and the Sierra Club Legal Defense Fund, for example. The financial affairs of each organization, however, must be kept separate, as discussed in Chapter 22§2. Documentation evidencing the fashion in which common costs are shared must be maintained. Form 990, Schedule A, requires very detailed information be reported about such sharing.[9]

While overlapping board members are permissible, common control can suggest a lack of independence. The safest relationship is for each organization to have independent control. Staff overlap must be carefully documented with time records and evidence of staff activity. Shared facilities, memberships, funding campaigns, publications, and other overt products of activity deserve careful expense allocations based upon time spent, space occupied, or other suitable indicator of respective use.[10]

A grant from the (c)(3) to the (c)(4) can be made if the grant is restricted to charitable purposes, such as research disassociated with particular legislative proposals. If allocated to lobbying, the grant should not be for a sum that would violate the (c)(3)'s limitations. Clearly, the (c)(3) organization should not raise general support funds to be transmitted to the (c)(4), but the reverse would be allowable.

(c) Conversion to (c)(3) Status

Circumstances of an organization qualified under (c)(4) may change. If legislative activity declines or for other reasons such as those outlined in the following, an organization may consider converting its tax-exempt status to (c)(3). To explore the issues involved in such a conversion, consider two examples:

Example 1. Representing the population of a planned community of 100,000 residents qualifies for §501(c)(4) status, not (c)(3), in the opinion of the Tax Court.[11] Columbia Park and Recreation Association (CPRA) was a nonprofit organization formed to build and operate "facilities and services for the common good and so-

---

[8] Reg. §53.4942(a)-3(a)(3).
[9] Reproduced in Appendix 27-3.
[10] Cost accounting concepts and documentation methods are discussed in Chapter 27.
[11] *Columbia Park and Recreation Association, Inc. v. Commissioner,* 88 T.C. 1 (1987).

cial welfare of the people" of Columbia, Maryland; to represent property owners and residents with respect to owner assessment and collection of fees for such services; and to enforce property covenants.

The CPRA built the public utility and transportation systems, parks, pools, neighborhood and community centers, and recreational facilities such as tennis courts, golf courses, a zoo, an ice rink, boat docks, and athletic clubs for the community. CPRA essentially functions like a municipality, but is not a political subdivision of the county in which it is located. CPRA was formed by the private developers of Columbia. Columbia has "villages" that have formed separate civic associations.

For the first 12 years of CPRA's existence, it was classified as a §501(c)(4) organization. To qualify for tax-favored bond financing, CPRA sought reclassification as a §501(c)(3) organization in 1982. The IRS denied the (c)(3) exemption based upon failure of both the operational and organizational test, as follows:

- *Private benefit and control.* Regardless of the size of the group benefited (there was no argument that Columbia resembles a city that would qualify), CRPA is owned and controlled by the homeowners and residents, and serves their private interests. Every property owner possesses an ownership right in CPRA's facilities and services. The facilities open to the public represented less than two percent of the total, and out of 110,000 families, only 190 received reduced fees.

- *Funding source.* Another factor distinguishing CPRA from a §501(c)(3) organization was its source of funds—no voluntary contributions were solicited from the public, and the sole source of financing was property owner fees, which are nondeductible for §170 purposes.

- *No charitable purpose.* The CPRA did not lessen the burdens of government. There was no proof that the State of Maryland or Howard County accepted such responsibilities and based upon documents regarding the public transportation system, Columbia was expected to bear the cost.

- *Dissolution clause.* The CPRA's charter names three possible recipients of its assets upon dissolution: Howard County, an agency or instrumentality of the county, or one of the village associations. The first two qualify as §501(c)(3) recipients, but the last does not because village associations are (c)(4) organizations. Thus, the assets are not dedicated permanently to §501(c)(3) purposes.

Example 2.   A civic welfare organization operated to meet the financial and emotional needs of individuals employed in an industry worldwide was allowed to merge itself into its subsidiary §501(c)(3) organization, since it possessed the requisite charitable characteristics, as follows:[12]

- *Contributions.* More than one third of the organization's support is received from contributions from the general public (i.e., nonindustry members).

[12] Priv. Ltr. Rul. 9019046.

- *Charitable services.* Gerontology, social services (legal and emotional counseling), job placement for the unemployed, and scholarships were considered charitable services.

- *Charitable class.* Because of its size (over 10,000 members), its dedication to members of a particular industry was ruled not to negate its charitable purposes.

In both examples, note that the organizational activities benefit a limited class of individuals. What distinguishes the two is (1) the character of the activities and (2) the sources of support. Relieving suffering in distress situations is generally considered charitable, as is promotion of health and education. Recreation, preservation of property values, and commuting to work are not generally classified as charitable activities. See Chapter 22§2 on relationships between §501(c)(3) and §501(c)(4) organizations.

6.2 QUALIFYING AND NONQUALIFYING CIVIC ORGANIZATIONS

The primary characteristic of a qualifying civic league is that it operates to benefit the members of a community as a whole, be it the world or a small town, as opposed to operating a social club for the benefit, pleasure, or recreation of particular individuals. Social events sponsored by civic leagues are permitted, if they are incidental to the group's primary function.[13] One court stated that "the organization must be a community movement designed to accomplish community ends."[14] Another said, "In short, social welfare is the well-being of persons as a community."[15] The following projects have been determined to be qualifying activities for civic leagues:

- Tenants' legal rights defense groups[16]

- Renewal projects in blighted areas of cities

- Unemployment relief efforts organized to provide loans to purchase and develop land and facilities to create jobs,[17] and a credit counseling service to prevent bankruptcy in the community[18]

- Amateur baseball league[19] and a sports organization promoting the interest of youths by giving them free tickets to sporting events, thereby providing wholesome entertainment for the welfare of the community's youths (might also qualify under (c)(3))[20]

---

[13] Rev. Rul. 74-361, 1974-2 C.B. 159; Rev. Rul. 66-179, 1966-1 C.B. 139.
[14] *Erie Endowment v. U.S.*, 361 F.2d 151 (3rd Cir. 1963).
[15] *Commissioner v. Lake Forest, Inc.*, 305 F.2d 814 (4th Cir. 1962).
[16] Rev. Rul. 80-206, 1980-2 C.B. 185.
[17] Rev. Rul. 64-187, 1964-1 C.B. (Part 1) 354; Rev. Rul. 67-294, 1967-2 C.B. 193.
[18] Rev. Rul. 65-299, 1965-2 C.B. 165.
[19] Rev. Rul. 69-384, 1969-2 C.B. 112.
[20] Rev. Rul. 68-118, 1968-1 C.B. 261.

- Bus line providing transportation from a suburb to major employment centers in a metropolitan area.[21] A bus operation for the convenience of employees of a particular corporation would not qualify.[22]

- Junior chambers of commerce customarily qualify[23]

- Antiabortion league formed to educate the public, promote the rights of the unborn, and lobby for legislation to restrict women's access to abortions[24]

- Society presenting an annual festival to preserve ethnic culture[25]

- Parks or gardens for beautification of a city, including a group formed to maintain the public areas of a particular block[26]

- County recreation facilities

- Garden club to bring civic betterment and social improvement (note a garden club can conceivably qualify under 501(c)(3), (4), (5), or (7))[27]

- Bridge club providing recreational activity for a nominal fee to a community[28]

A civic organization that benefits private individuals or operates for profit cannot qualify as a (c)(4) organization. The following groups have failed to receive exemption:

- Tenants' association for a particular apartment complex, and condominium management[29] or residential real estate management associations (see IRC §528).

- Individual practice association of local doctors benefited the member physicians, not a community.[30]

- Pirate ship replica operation and staging of annual mock invasion and parade was for the benefit of its members.[31]

- An ethnic group, whose members live in an area and receive sickness and death benefits, operates for its members.[32]

[21] Rev. Rul. 78-69, 1978-1 C.B. 156.
[22] Rev. Rul. 55-311, 1955-1 C.B. 72.
[23] Rev. Rul. 65-195, 1965-2 C.B. 164.
[24] Rev. Rul. 76-81, 1976-1 C.B. 156.
[25] Rev. Rul. 68-224, 1968-1 C.B. 222. A kennel club focused on presenting an annual show that draws over 25,000 visitors and is broadcast on television to millions of people was allowed to qualify as a civic association since its social functions were incidental according to Priv. Ltr. Rul. 9805001.
[26] Rev. Rul. 68-14, 1968-1 C.B. 243, *as distinguished by* Rev. Rul. 75-286, 1975-2 C.B. 210.
[27] Rev. Rul. 66-179, 1966-1 C.B. 139; see also IRS Priv. Ltr. Rul. 9805001.
[28] Tech. Adv. Memo. 9220010.
[29] Rev. Rul. 74-17, 1974-1 C.B. 130.
[30] Rev. Rul. 86-98, 1986-2 C.B. 74.
[31] *Ye Krewe of Gasparilla*, 80 T.C. 755, Dec. 40,052.
[32] Rev. Rul. 75-159, 1975-1 C.B. 48.

- Television antenna group organized on a cooperative basis to improve reception for a remote area on a fee basis to members does not qualify,[33] but a group with the same purpose supported by voluntary contributions and available to all that live in the area can qualify.[34]

- An educational camp society formed to provide a rural retreat for a school's faculty and students, does not benefit the community.[35] Also, a vacation home established and controlled by a corporation for its female employees, despite the facts that it was open for public use and the general public used it 20% of the time.[36]

- An antiwar protest group that encourages people to commit illegal acts during demonstrations operates against public policy and is not exempt.[37]

- A lake association formed to provide recreational services to its members as residents of a particular community cannot qualify under (c)(4) but instead is allowed to qualify as a social club under (c)(7).[38]

6.3 NEIGHBORHOOD AND HOMEOWNER ASSOCIATIONS

To qualify under §501(c)(4), an organization must serve a constituency that constitutes a community rather than a limited group of individuals. The homeowner association exemplifies the type of group not qualified for (c)(4) tax-exempt status; but the distinction between those that qualify and those that do not is vague. One IRS definition of *community* says "The term has traditionally been construed as having reference to a geographic unit bearing a reasonably recognizable relationship to an area ordinarily identified as a governmental subdivision or a unit or district thereof."[39] A community is sometimes hard to define and the facts and circumstances of each case are determinative.[40] Taken as a whole, the rulings indicate that to prove that an organization operates for the benefit of the community as opposed to individual residents, the following factors must be present:[41]

- The association does not maintain private residences, either exterior or interior. Such services are evidence that an organization is operated for private benefit.[42]

[33] Rev. Rul. 54-394, 1954-2 C.B. 131.
[34] Rev. Rul. 62-167, 1962-2 C.B. 142.
[35] *The People's Educational Camp Society, Inc. v. Commissioner,* 331 F.2d 923 (2d Cir. 1964), *aff'g* 39 T.C. 756 (1963), *cert. den.,* 379 U.S. 839 (1964).
[36] Rev. Rul. 80-205, 1980-1 C.B. 184, issued by the IRS to say that it will not follow *Eden Hall Farm v. U.S.,* 389 F. Supp. 858 (W.D. Penn. 1975), which held that a farm did qualify because the group of working women it served represented a community.
[37] Rev. Rul. 75-384, 1975-2 C.B. 204.
[38] April 1994 Determination Letter published by IRS National Office EO Technical Division.
[39] Rev. Rul. 74-99, 1974-1 C.B. 131.
[40] Rev. Rul. 80-63, 1980-1 C.B. 116.
[41] Rev. Rul. 67-6, 1967-1 C.B. 135; Rev. Rul. 72-102, 1972-1 C.B. 149, mod. by Rev. Rul. 76-147, 1976-1 C.B. 151.
[42] Rev. Rul. 74-99, *supra n.* 39.

- Common areas, including streets, sidewalks, and parks, are open to the general public for their use and enjoyment without controlled access restricted to members. Subdivisions often form a separate social club to operate a swimming pool or other recreational facility from which they want to exclude the public.

- Association is not limited to a particular commercial development unless it conducts only those activities customarily reserved to a municipality. This question is sometimes difficult, as the *Columbia Park* case discussed previously indicates.[43]

- The organization must not have as its sole purpose providing basic services to residents (such as garbage pickup and security patrol).

- Enforcing covenants for architectural appearance and limitations on commercial or multitenant occupancy with the intention of preserving the community provides a public benefit, despite the fact that it may serve also to maintain property values of the individual owners.[44]

- Revenue for a civic league comes from a variety of usage fees, governmental grants, and voluntary donations, as distinguished from a homeowner association, which normally finances all of its costs from member assessments.

(a) Characteristics of Homeowner Associations

Although it may have some activities that benefit the community, the typical homeowner association will not qualify for §501(c)(4) exemption if its primary focus is to benefit individual owners—the first four items in the previous list. To stop some of the controversy, clarify the rules, and allow tax relief for such associations, Congress in 1976 enacted IRC §528, which provides a special exemption section for homeowner associations. Two types of associations qualify—condominium management associations and residential real estate management associations.[45] The basic requirements for qualifying include:

- An annual election to be so taxed pursuant to the section is made and filed by the due date of the return, including extensions.[46]

- The nonprofit must be organized and operated to acquire, construct, manage, maintain, and care for association property, whether held in common for the owners, held privately by the owners, or held by a governmental unit for use by the owners.[47]

---

[43] *Columbia Park and Recreation Association, Inc. v. Commissioner, supra n. 7.*
[44] Rev. Rul. 72-102, *supra n. 41.*
[45] Reg. §1.528-2.
[46] IRS Instructions to Form 1120-H at 2. This election cannot be revoked retroactively to take advantage of a net operating loss. However, permission was granted by the IRS for revocation when an association had relied on inadequate tax advice provided by a professional tax advisor. Rev. Rul. 83-74, 1983-1 C.B. 112.
[47] Reg. §1.528-3.

- Sixty percent or more of its gross income must be "exempt function income," i.e., membership dues, fees, or assessments from member owners of residential units. A settlement for past underassessments of dues paid by a real estate developer is exempt function income.[48]

- Ninety percent or more of its expenditures in a tax year must be for "exempt function purposes." These purposes include capital expenditures for property improvements or replacement costs, salaries of managers, clerical, maintenance, and security personnel, gardening, paving, street signs, property taxes, repairs to association property, and all other disbursements to acquire, construct, manage, and maintain the property.

- Eighty-five percent or more of the condominium, subdivision, development, or similar area related to the association must be used by individuals as residences. Vacant units are included if they were residences before they became unoccupied.[49]

- No part of its net earnings can inure to the benefit of any private shareholder or individual.

(b) Calculating the Tax

The tax relief is only partial. While all of a qualifying civic league's income is exempt from income tax, a homeowner's association pays tax. It can elect to pay *either* a flat 30% tax on its nonexempt function income (basically, its investment in common area facilities, passive investment income, and any unrelated business income less deductions), *or* the normal corporate tax payable on all of its income. Exempt function revenues are those received from the member property owners as dues or assessments unless such fees or assessments represent payments for services rendered to the members. Taxable revenues[50] for §528 purposes include:

- Interest earned on deposits and investments held in a sinking fund for improvements or repairs, including tax exempt interest

- Member assessments for mortgage principal, interest, and real estate taxes on association property

- Amounts received for work performed on privately owned property

- Assessments for maintenance, trash collection, or snow removal

- Nonmember usage fees, as well as member fees for special services

Deductions from the listed income items include expenses directly connected with producing the nonexempt function income, and there is a $100 exemption. No deduction for net operating loss or dividends received is allowed.

---

[48] Rev. Rul. 88-56 1988-2 C.B. 126.
[49] Reg. §1.528-4.
[50] Reg. §1.528-9.

(c) Annual Election

A homeowner's association has an annual choice of electing to pay as a normal corporation rather than to pay the flat 30% tax on its investment income. For taxable income of up to $50,000 the normal corporate tax rate for 1998 was 15% and 25% for the next $25,000. For an association with modest income taxable, the election to pay the 30% tax may not be suitable. The decision turns on factors that should be quantified in each case to make the correct choice. The tax rate is one factor and is influenced by both the amount of the income and by the kind of income that is taxable. The part of an association's net income that is considered exempt function income is not taxed if the election is made, but it is taxed if the association elects to be taxed as a normal corporation.

A nonelecting homeowners association is subject to a deduction limitation rule,[51] which allows deduction of expenses attributable to owner activities only to the extent of owner income. It is extremely important, therefore, to understand the interplay of the deduction limit in IRC §277 and the flat tax of IRC §528, which contains the exclusions from income. In other words, even though the association's financial statements show no net profit, it may have taxable income.

Once the election is made or not made, the association may seek permission from the IRS to revoke or elect pursuant to the relief provision of IRC §9001. When the wrong decision was made based upon the recommendation of a professional advisor, revocation has been allowed.[52]

Form 1120H filers need not pay quarterly estimated tax. The balance of tax is due by the fifteenth day of the third month following the end of the taxable year. For further details, see IRS Publication 588, *Tax Information for Homeowners Associations*.

6.4 DISCLOSURES OF NONDEDUCTIBILITY

(a) Notice of Noncharity Status

Social welfare organizations and certain other tax-exempt organizations not eligible to receive gifts deductible as charitable contributions must say so on fundraising solicitations.[53] Exempts subject to the disclosure requirement include:

- Organizations not described in §170(c) that are exempt from tax under §501(c) or §501(d) and political organizations defined in §527(e), including political campaign committees and political action committees

- Organizations whose gross annual receipts exceed $100,000 (multiple organizations created to circumvent this limit can be combined by the IRS)

An express statement that payments (whether called dues, gifts, contributions, or something else) are not tax deductible must be printed on written requests for payments and announced in solicitations made by phone, radio, television, and

---

[51] IRC §227.
[52] Priv. Ltr. Rul. 9233025; Rev. Rul. 83-74, 1983-1 C.B. 112.
[53] IRC §6113.

presumably the internet although such a communication device was not anticipated in 1988. Certain types of payment requests are excluded, such as a fee for newsletter ad, registration for an educational conference, premium for insurance program, community association fee for police and fire protection, and other payments for specific services rendered by the nonprofit.

The disclosure must be "conspicuous and easily recognizable." The statement of nondeductibility must be clearly legible in type of the same size as the primary message of the written piece. It cannot be obscured by placement, color, shape, or other means, or buried in some part of the solicitation materials that ordinarily would not be noticed and read by the recipient. The script of telephone, radio, and television (and presumably website) solicitations must contain a statement that the payments are not tax deductible.[54] The penalty for failure to disclose is $1,000 a day up to $10,000 each year.

The IRS imposed the maximum penalty for nondisclosure on a §527 political organization in the first ruling issued on the subject. No notice was included in its telemarketing script. It argued that it had relied upon the "inadequate compliance information supplied to it by its national umbrella organization" so that the penalty should be excused for "reasonable causes." The IRS found that the organization was "not run by inexperienced individuals ignorant of the tax laws, but by experienced, knowledgeable individuals with paid staff having access to information concerning the rules."[55]

(b) Dues Not Deductible as Business Expense

Congress listened to President Bill Clinton's suggestion that almost all lobbying expenses be made nondeductible for income tax purposes. Before 1994, a business expense deduction was not allowed for political campaign activity and grassroots lobbying attempts to influence the public at large, but expenses of direct efforts to influence lawmakers were deductible. IRC §162(e) was revised[56] to add two new types of nondeductible lobbying and political activity—for both for-profit and nonprofit entities—bringing the total to four as follows:

1. Influencing legislation
2. Contacts with certain senior executive branch officials in attempts to influence official actions or positions of such officials
3. Political campaign activities
4. Grassroots lobbying

(c) Definition of Legislation

"Influencing legislation" is defined by §162(e)(4) to mean "any attempt to influence any legislation through communicating (oral or written) with any member or employee of a legislative body or with any government official or employee who

---

[54] IRS Notice 88-120, 1988-2 C.B. 454.
[55] Priv. Ltr. Rul. 9315001.
[56] The Omnibus Budget Reconciliation Act of 1993.

may participate in the formulation of legislation." Influencing legislation is additionally defined by the regulations to include "[a]ll activities, such as research, preparation, planning, and coordination, including deciding whether to make a lobbying communication, engaged in for a purpose of making or supporting a lobbying communication, even if not yet made."[57] Note that no guidance has yet been offered on the definition of "grassroots lobbying" or "communications with executive branch officials." The term *legislation* includes actions with respect to acts, bills, resolutions, or similar items by Congress; any state legislature, local council, or similar governing body; or the public in a referendum, initiative, constitutional amendment, or similar procedure.[58]

Action is limited to the introduction, amendment, enactment, defeat, or repeal of acts, bills, resolutions, or similar items. The IRS has deemed confirmation of a judicial nominee to be "similar to" legislation.[59] Actions of federal or state administrative or special purpose bodies, such as auditing or issuing rulings, are not included.[60] Proposed regulations of the Treasury Department would not be considered legislation nor, apparently, would administrative activities. The legislative provisions contain no exceptions for nonpartisan research and study of issues germane to legislative actions, as found in §4911. Some guidance as to when an issue becomes a legislative proposal is provided in the regulations, as discussed in §6.4(h), under "look-back rule." The congressional conferees did say that any "communication compelled by subpoena, or otherwise compelled by federal or state law, does not constitute an attempt to influence legislation or an official's actions, and therefore is not subject to the general disallowance rules."[61]

Local Councils. A special exception was carved out to permit the deduction of expenses of attempting to influence legislation of "any local council or similar governing body."[62] Any legislative body of a political subdivision of a state, such as a county or city council, comes within the exception for local lobbying.[63] State-level lobbying expenses associated with legislative actions of a state legislature are treated on a par with federal lobbying. Note, however, that communications with state officials are not subject to the disallowance provisions for federal officials.

Communications with Executive Branch. A brand new category of lobbying was created. Expenses paid to make a direct communication with high officials in the executive branch of the federal government in an attempt to influence their official actions are not deductible. The disallowance applies when the communique concerns administrative actions as well as pending or proposed legislation. The covered executive branch officials include:

- The president and the vice president

---

[57] Reg. §1.162-29(b)(1).
[58] Defined by referring to the language of §4911(e)(2) applicable to lobbying by charities.
[59] Gen. Coun. Memo. 39694 (January 22, 1988).
[60] H.R. Rep. 103-213 (Conference Report) at 605, n. 57.
[61] Conf. Rep. at 607.
[62] IRC §162(e)(2).
[63] Conf. Rep. at 605.

- Cabinet members, others having Cabinet-level status, and their immediate deputies

- The two most senior officers of each agency within the Executive Office of the President, such as the National Security Agency

- An employee of the Executive Office of the President

A communication regarding proposed Treasury Department regulations may or may not be a direct communication. Comments about regulations submitted through normal channels to lower-level employees are not generally regarded as a communication with a cabinet member. Direct contact with the Secretary of the Treasury and his or her deputy, however, would be. The cost of research and analysis conducted to gather information intended to be communicated to a covered official is also nondeductible.

A communique addressed to a noncovered official can be treated as a direct communication if the covered official is the intended recipient.[64] The fact that a Cabinet-level official must ultimately approve or sign off on a regulation does not make the lower-level contact a nondeductible activity.[65] It is important to distinguish regulation and procedural communications from those involving legislation. Communication with a member of the executive branch on any level concerning legislation being formulated will be treated as an attempt to influence legislation. Concerning the charitable lobbying rules, the IRS has stated that a treaty required to be submitted by the president to the Senate is considered "legislation" from the moment a U.S. representative begins negotiations with the other country's delegates.[66]

(d) Nondeductible Membership Dues

Dues paid to membership organizations, including a civic league, labor union, or business league, are no longer deductible to the extent the money is spent on nondeductible lobbying.[67] The disallowance applies to dues paid to organizations that spend more than $2,000 annually on "in-house" expenses—what the code calls a de minimis amount.[68] Allocated overhead costs, third-party payments, dues to other organizations, grassroots lobbying, political campaign intervention, and foreign lobbying are not considered in-house expenses. Also, certain organizations whose members ordinarily do not deduct their dues are excluded.

Exempt organizations, other than (c)(3)s, that spend nondeductible monies for lobbying expenses associated with legislative- and executive-branch communications have a choice under the new rules. The first choice Congress gives a lobbying organization is to disclose the nondeductible amount to its members. Under this choice, members are informed of the portion of nondeductible lobbying expenses paid with or allocable to the dues. With the proper notice to members, the

[64] Id.
[65] Conf. Rep. at 607.
[66] Reg. §56.4911-2(d)(1)(i).
[67] IRC §162(e)(4)(B), as amended by the Revenue Reconciliation Act of 1993.
[68] IRC §162(2)(5)(B).

organization can essentially pass through its nondeductible lobbying. Choice 2 allows the organization to choose instead to pay unrelated business income tax, called a *proxy tax*.

Documents seeking payment of dues from members must contain notice of an estimated amount of the nondeductible portion of dues or pay the proxy tax on its lobbying expenditures.[69] Form 990 has been revised to allow the organization to report the total amount of dues received that are allocable to lobbying.[70] The calculation of member dues payments allocable to nondeductible lobbying is made on a first-in, first-out basis so that disallowed expenses are assumed to be paid out of member dues rather than other funds or revenues of the organization. If member dues total less than the amount of nondeductible lobbying in any one year, the excess expense is carried over to the succeeding year. Obviously Congress expected that some creative exempts might use savings or other resources every other year or so to reduce the bad member relations that might result from nondeductibility of dues.

(e) Proxy Tax

The league or union that fails to notify its members of the nondeductible amount or chooses not to notify can itself pay a proxy tax. The tax is payable at the highest corporate tax rate, currently 35%.[71] The choice can be made (or imposed because of a mistake) annually. The tax is due on the portion of member dues allocable to expenditures for nondeductible lobbying activities, but cannot exceed the amount of dues received during a year.[72]

(f) Excepted Organizations

Organizations that establish to the satisfaction of the secretary that substantially all of the dues or other similar amounts paid by persons to such organization are not deductible without regard to §162(e) are excluded from this disclosure and disallowance provisions. The IRS explains the application of this exception by category of organization.[73]

Automatically Excluded. The IRC §6033(e)(3) does not apply to organizations recognized by the IRS as exempt from taxation under §501(a) other than those exempt under §501(c)(4), (5), or (6).

- *(c)(4) Organizations:* Those (c)(4) organizations are excluded if either:
  - The largest amount of annual dues (or similar amounts) paid by any member is $50 indexed, for 1999 the amount is $77 or less and not more than 10% of the total amount of annual dues or similar amounts come from members paying more than $75 annually (originally $50), *or*

---

[69] IRC §6033(e)(1)(A)(ii).
[70] Reproduced in Appendix 27-2, page 4.
[71] IRC §6033(e)(1)(A).
[72] Conf. Rep. at 608.
[73] Rev. Proc. 95-35, 1995-32 I.R.B. 1; updated by Rev. Proc. 98-19, 1998-7 IRB 30.

- More than 90% of all annual dues are received from organizations described in §501(c)(3), state or local governments, or entities whose income is exempt under §115.

- *(c)(5) Organizations:* Same rule as (c)(4)s.

- *(c)(6) Organizations:* Excluded only if more than 90% of all annual dues are received from organizations described in §501(c)(3), state or local governments, or entities whose income is exempt under §115.

Excluded by Nondeductibility.   An exempt organization that cannot satisfy the automatic exclusions may still be excluded if it:

- Maintains records establishing that 90% or more of the annual dues (or similar amounts) paid to it are not deductible without regard to §162(e), and

- Notifies the IRS that it is excluded by §6033(e)(3) when it files its annual Form 990.

The procedure defines the significant terms of §6033(e)(3) as follows:

- *Annual dues* are the amount an organization requires a person, family, or entity to pay to be recognized by the organization as a member for an annual period.

- *Similar amounts* include, but are not limited to, voluntary payments made by persons, families, or entities; assessments made by the organization to cover basic operating costs; and special assessments imposed by the organization to conduct lobbying activities.

- *Member* is used in its broadest sense and is not limited to persons with voting rights in the organization.

The definition of *annual dues* is straightforward and clear. However, the meanings of *similar amounts* and *member* are extremely vague and broad. Assume that a group of individuals creates an organization to lobby the state legislature for more school funding. A self-perpetuating board creates a nonmembership not-for-profit corporation and seeks (c)(4) status. Using a direct mail campaign, the organization seeks support from citizens statewide. There is no mention of membership or dues nor assessment. But it is receiving voluntary payments that, under a strict reading of the IRS definition, could be construed as *similar amounts.* To be prudent, such a group should notify supporters of the nondeductibility of their payments.

The vague definition of the term *member* for this purpose is quite contrary to the definition suggested by the IRS in trying to tax associate member dues of labor unions and business leagues.[74] For that purpose, the IRS says a member is a person who has a formal relationship with specific rights and obligations in relation to the organization.

---

[74] Discussed in Chapter 8§6.

(g) Cost of Lobbying

To tally up its lobbying costs, an organization includes:

- Third-party costs, or amounts spent specifically on lobbying—daily fees paid to professional lobbyists, expenses of travel to Washington, or cost of an opinion poll
- An allocable portion of the organization's overall operating expenses
- Expenses of preparing, planning, or coordinating lobbying activities
- Research and monitoring costs which, upon "looking back," are shown to lead up to lobbying.

The preamble to the regulations says that costs properly allocable to lobbying activities are to be calculated using any reasonable method consistently applied.[75] The method must, however, follow specific rules for the exclusion or inclusion of labor. The labor hours (and presumably the cost of the labor, dependent upon the method used) of persons spending less than 5% of their time on lobbying may be ignored as de minimis, unless the time is spent in direct contact lobbying.

Two distinct categories of cost are allocable: labor costs and general and administrative (G&A) costs. G&A is said to include depreciation, rent, utilities, insurance, maintenance costs, security costs, and other administrative department costs (for example, payroll, personnel, and accounting). The regulations suggest, but do not limit the organization to, use of one of the three following allocation methods:

Type 1—Ratio Method. A percentage of the organization's overall operating costs, not including third-party lobbying expense, is allocated to lobbying. The ratio compares the total number of hours the organization's personnel spend directly engaged in lobbying to the total number of hours personnel work. Any reasonable method may be used to determine labor hours. The opening explanation suggests, as examples of records to be maintained, daily time reports or daily logs. Absent exact records, it may be assumed that full-time personnel spend 1,800 hours a year on the "taxpayer's trade or business." Support personnel labor— "persons engaged in secretarial, maintenance, and similar activities"—may be excluded from both the numerator and denominator of the ratio calculation.

$$\frac{\text{Lobbying labor hours} \times \text{Total cost of operation}}{\text{Total labor hours}}$$

Type 2—Gross-Up Method. Under this method, the total lobbying cost is:

$$\text{Third-party costs} + (\text{basic labor costs} \times 175\%).$$

"Basic labor costs" means salary or other payment for services plus payroll taxes. Pension, profit-sharing, employee benefits, and supplemental unemployment

[75] Reg. §1.162-28, effective July 21, 1995.

benefit plan costs, as well as other similar costs, are not included. The lobbying activities of many nonprofits are conducted by volunteers. This method cannot be used by organizations that do not incur reasonable labor costs for persons engaged in lobbying—by volunteers.[76]

Type 3—§263A Cost System.   The cost system provided for manufacturing businesses can be used. Lobbying activity is treated as a service department or function to which costs are allocated, using a step methodology. The regulations contain a detailed example that can be studied to consider the viability of this choice. Under normal tax accounting ruling, the choice of method is binding and only altered with IRS permission.[77]

(h) Look-Back Rule

Internal Revenue Code §162(e)(5)(c) broadens the definition of what constitutes monies spent to influence legislation to include "any amount paid or incurred for research, or preparation, planning, or coordination of any such activity." Merely monitoring legislative activity is not an attempt to influence it but an organization must look back and reclassify monitoring expenses as nondeductible[78]

> in cases where a taxpayer (including a tax-exempt organization) monitors legislation and subsequently attempts to influence the formulation or enactment of the same (or similar) legislation, the costs of the monitoring activities generally will be treated as incurred 'in connection with' nondeductible lobbying activity

Likewise, if the organization conducts research and prepares presentations, meetings, and communications with underlings of a covered executive branch official "with a view toward directly communicating with the top official," all of the costs are nondeductible.[79]

The regulations recognize that an organization might be involved in matters of legislative import for multiple reasons and suggest that all of the facts and circumstances surrounding an activity be considered to identify the "purpose of an expenditure." The organization may treat an activity partially as related to a legislative initiative and partially for a nonlobbying purpose. The IRS suggests that the following facts would determine the purpose of engaging in an activity:[80]

- Whether the activity and the lobbying communication are proximate in time

- Whether the activity and the lobbying communication relate to similar subject matter

- Whether the activity is performed at the request of, under the direction of, or on behalf of a person making the lobbying communication

[76] Reg. §1.162-28(b)(2).
[77] Discussed in Chapter 28§2.
[78] Conf. Rep. at 606.
[79] Id. at 607.
[80] Reg. §1.162-29(c).

- Whether the results of the activity are also used for a nonlobbying purpose
- Whether, at the time the taxpayer engages in the activity, there is specific legislation to which the activity is related.

The final regulations helpfully list the activities that will be treated as having no purpose to influence legislation:

- Determining the existence or procedural status of specific legislation, or the time, place, and subject of any hearing to be held by a legislative body with respect to specific legislation
- Preparing routine, brief summaries of the provisions of specific legislation
- Performing an activity to comply with any law, such as satisfying state or federal securities law filings
- Reading any publications available to the general public or viewing or listening to other mass-media communications
- Merely attending a widely attended speech

Six detailed examples in the regulations can be studied by an organization wishing to distinguish between activities that have lobbying import and those that have no purpose to influence legislation.

CHAPTER SEVEN

Labor, Agricultural, and Horticultural Organizations: §501(c)(5)

Internal Revenue Code (IRC) §501(c)(5) encompasses three specific kinds of organizations: labor unions, agricultural groups, and horticultural groups. An organization qualifying under this section may have no net earnings inuring to the benefit of any member. These worker-oriented groups may only serve the three purposes provided in regulations that have not been revised since 1958:

1. Betterment of conditions of those engaged in such pursuit.

2. Improvement of the grade of their products.

3. Development of a high degree of efficiency in their respective occupations.[1]

7.1 LABOR UNIONS

The Internal Revenue Service (IRS) defines a labor organization as an "association of workers who have combined to protect or promote the interests of the members by bargaining collectively with their employers to secure better working conditions, wages, and similar benefits." The term includes labor unions, councils, and

---

[1] Reg. §1.501(c)(5)-1(a)(2).

committees.[2] However, it is not mandatory that the membership be exclusively employees though the character of revenue received from nonmembers might be treated differently as is discussed in §7.1(e). The purpose for which the nonprofit is formed determines exempt status.

(a) Organizational Structure and Documents

The Internal Revenue Code and Regulations impose no requirements regarding organizational structure. Form 1024,[3] however, makes a very clear requirement: "If the organization does not have an organizing instrument, it will not qualify for exempt status. The bylaws of an organization alone are not an organizing instrument. They are merely the internal rules and regulations of the organization." IRS Publication 557, *Tax Exempt Status for your Organization,* makes the following suggestion to enable a proposed union to achieve recognition of its exempt status:

> To show that your organization has the purpose of a labor organization, you should include in the articles of organization or accompanying statement (submitted with your exemption application) information establishing that the organization is organized to carry out the betterment of the conditions of workers, the improvement of the grade of their products, and the development of a higher degree of efficiency in their respective occupations.

(b) Scope of Activities

Promoting and protecting the interests of workers can be accomplished in a variety of ways. Labor unions whose activities are limited to representing employee members are automatically granted exemption. Some peripheral activities have been allowed to qualify under the labor organization classification. Examples of permissible activities include:

- Improvement of professional abilities of members through seminars, courses, and participation in conventions; securing better salaries and working conditions for workers through collective bargaining and processing grievance procedures[4]

- Worker dispatch systems to provide equitable allocation of available work and to adjudicate and settle grievances[5]

- Provision of strike benefits[6] and mutual death, sickness, accident, and similar benefits for union members only (from member-contributed funds),[7] but not accounting and tax services[8]

---

[2] Exempt Organizations Handbook (IRM 7751) §521.
[3] Reproduced in Appendix 18-2.
[4] Rev. Rul. 76-31, 1976-1 C.B. 157.
[5] Rev. Rul. 75-473, 1975-2 C.B. 213.
[6] Rev. Rul. 67-7, 1967-1 C.B. 137.
[7] Rev. Rul. 62-17, 1962-1 C.B. 87.
[8] Rev. Rul. 62-191, 1962-2 C.B. 146.

- Apprenticeship committees with union and employer representatives to establish standards of employment and qualification in skilled crafts, and to arbitrate in apprentice-employer disputes[9]

- A nurses' association established to bargain collectively with health institutions[10]

- Seminars and training programs, newspapers,[11] conventions, and legal defense and litigation activities[12] by individual unions or associations of labor organizations and unions

- Labor "temples" or centers containing offices, meeting and recreation halls, and a barbershop, and otherwise providing a home to 162 unions, and which are owned by the unions[13]

(c) Non-(c)(5) Activities

Activities outside the historical role of unions may not be conducted as a primary purpose of a (c)(5) organization. Whether the union itself, a directly affiliated organization, or a totally separate group undertakes the activity can be determinative. The IRS has generally allowed unions to have concerns other than wages, working hours, and working conditions, but only when they are mutually beneficial to union members. Among the activities that have resulted in denial of union status are:

- Savings plans for individual members established under a collective bargaining agreement to collect money and disburse them annually to members, and unrelated to strikes or wage levels[14]

- Businesses formed to provide employment for members.[15] The fact that the profits from such a business go to a union does not help.

- An association formed to collect and pay over federal and state employment taxes on behalf of a group of manufacturers[16]

- An organization formed by individuals (not by a union) to pay weekly income to workers in the event of a strike called by the members' union, but not to represent the workers in employment matters, does not qualify.[17] But a labor union's provision of financial assistance to its members during a strike is an exempt activity.[18]

[9] Rev. Rul. 59-6, 1959-1 C.B. 121.
[10] Rev. Rul. 77-154, 1977-1 C.B. 148.
[11] Rev. Rul. 68-534, 1968-2 C.B. 217.
[12] Rev. Rul. 74-596, 1974-2 C.B. 167; Rev. Rul. 75-288, 1975-2 C.B. 212.
[13] *Portland Co-operative Labor Temple Ass'n v. Commissioner*, 39 B.T.A. 450(1939), *acq.* 1939-1 C.B. 29.
[14] Rev. Rul. 77-46, 1977-1 C.B. 147.
[15] Rev. Rul. 69-386, 1969-2 C.B. 123.
[16] Rev. Rul. 66-354, 1966-2 C.B. 207.
[17] Rev. Rul. 76-420, 1976-2 C.B. 153.
[18] Rev. Rul. 67-7, *supra. n.* 5.

- Unions of individual business owners[19]

A labor organization that primarily conducts exempt functions may also have a limited amount of unrelated business activity without necessarily losing its exempt status as discussed in Chapter 21.

(d) Political Activities

Political action is permissible for a (c)(6) organization on a limited basis.[20] Lobbying and other attempts to influence legislation relating to labor union concerns can be a major activity of a union. Whether lobbying could be the primary activity (representing more than half the annual expenditures) is questionable.

Campaigning on behalf of candidates for public office is not specifically prohibited, as it is for organizations exempt under §501(c)(3).[21] However, campaigning cannot be a primary purpose. Funds expended in efforts to influence elections, to the extent of the organization's investment income, are taxable under IRC §527. A segregated fund could be created to clearly delineate the activity and its income from the union's other sources of funds.

(e) Membership

Membership in a labor organization traditionally includes employees, employers, and others whose participation in the union is to advance a focused field of work—the auto workers, pipefitters, or teachers, for example. To qualify for tax exemption, a union must be an association of workers formed to seek better working conditions, wages, and similar benefits.[22] When the union has membership classes for persons not directly involved in its type of work, two related but different questions arise. The first issue is qualification for tax exemption—the union must show it operates to benefit workers. A nurses' association[23] and a plumbers' group[24] composed mostly of employees were allowed to qualify even though a limited number of their members were independent contractors working in the field. If, instead, most of the members are independent contractors, exemption must be sought under IRC §501(c)(6) as a business league.[25]

A union with associate membership classes also faces a question of character for the revenues paid by its members. The IRS once insisted that membership denotes a formal relationship in which a person, whether specifically described as a member or not, has specific rights and obligations. Dues revenues paid by nonvoting associate members represented unrelated business income in the IRS's eyes. Unions and the IRS fought about this question for some years, as described below for historical context.

---

[19] Rev. Rul. 78-288, 1978-2 C.B. 179.
[20] Exempt Organizations Handbook (IRM 7751) §544.
[21] *Marker v. Schultz*, 485 F.2d 1003 (D.C. Cir. 1973).
[22] See footnote 2.
[23] Rev. Rul. 77-154, *supra, n.* 10.
[24] Rev. Rul. 74-167, 1974-1 C.B. 134.
[25] Rev. Rul. 78-288, *supra,* n. 19.

To clarify the issue, the IRS issued formal guidance in 1995.[26] A primary purpose test was provided which asks, "Is the associate member category created and used to further the organization's exempt purposes or simply to produce unrelated income?" Further in applying this principle "the Service looks to the purposes and activities of the organization rather than of its members." The IRS noted in the guidance that (c)(5) organizations often receive dues payments not only from members who are accorded full privileges in voting but also from associate members who are given less than full, or no, voting privileges. The IRS said it would not treat associate member dues as unrelated business income unless the facts indicate the membership category was created to produce unrelated income. Membership categories for students studying in the field and retired persons should not be questionable in this regard, nor should layers of membership according to years of service or amount of compensation. Note Congress chose not to give unions the special exception discussed in §7.2(c) that was given to agricultural groups. Labor unions must be alert to documenting the purpose of creating various membership classes.

Two cases involving insurance plans administered by the Office of Personnel Management through the Federal Employee Health Benefits Act (FEHBA) provide some insight into this issue. The first case involved the American Postal Workers Union (APWU).[27] The IRS took the position that a portion of the associate (nonpostal worker) member dues was attributable to the group health insurance plan and thereby produced unrelated business income, essentially saying that associate member concerns were unrelated to the basic purpose of serving postal worker members. Thus, the IRS assessed unrelated business income tax on the profits from the associate member group insurance.

After reviewing the charter and bylaws of the union, the district court found that the APWU was organized to serve not only postal workers but any classified federal employee, and was not limited to those employed by the U.S. Postal Service. This broad scope of coverage for all federal employees is permissible under the §501(c)(5) regulations pertaining to labor unions, which state, "a labor union is a voluntary association of workers that is organized to pursue common economic and social interests." Any union is free to define its constituents. Furthermore, the court found that there were "no requirements in the Internal Revenue Code that a union member receive any particular quantum of benefit in order to be considered a bona fide member." Likewise, the court found that the IRS's position that members had to have the right to vote was wholly without authority.

The court decided that the APWU's sponsorship of a group insurance plan served an exempt purpose as a mutual benefit organization. The court also found that the insurance program was not undertaken to make a profit, and that "providing economic benefits to members in return for dues is not a trade or business," citing the 1921 Congressional Record.

The appeals court, however, disagreed and found that the provision of insurance to nonpostal workers was not related to the union's stated focus on the interests of postal employees. The judge admitted that the case was difficult because

---

[26] Rev. Proc. 95-21, 1995-15 IRB 1.
[27] *American Postal Workers Union, AFL-CIO v. U.S.*, 925 F.2d 480 (D.C. Cir. 1991), *rev'g* 90-1 USTC ¶50,013 (D.C. 1989).

nothing in the regulations or any other authoritative source defined the exempt purposes of a labor union. However, based upon a review of the organization's constitution, the court found that privileges of membership were granted only to active members, and that provision of insurance benefits to nonmembers could not be substantially related to the union's exempt purpose. The court was also swayed by the substantial profit generated by nonmember fees.

In a somewhat similar case, the Court of Claims decided that the National Association of Postal Supervisors (NAPS) was taxable on its health insurance activity, because this was an unrelated trade or business operated to produce a profit and was in competition with taxable insurance providers.[28] The NAPS case facts were distinguishable from APWU in one important respect: The NAPS court decided that the associate members were not members. The nonpostal employee members were called "limited members." Their dues were calculated to produce a profit, they did not participate in other union programs, and their memberships were dropped if they failed to continue coverage in the health plan. Although it was not stated, perhaps the deciding factor in the NAPS case was the fact that within five years of starting the insurance program, the limited benefit members made up 71% of the total members in the plan. Thus, the facts supported the IRS's position that the insurance program's purpose was primarily to produce profit, not to serve members. Yet another postal union was made to pay tax on its insurance program because the court found "providing insurance to persons who are not members in any other sense" cannot be substantially related to the union's exempt purpose.[29]

7.2 AGRICULTURAL GROUPS

Agricultural associations are subject to the same basic requirements and constraints outlined previously for labor groups. Again, the code, regulations, and IRS Handbook are silent about the form of organization. In practice and for purposes of filing Form 1024, organizational documents must be adopted to establish governance rules and prohibit private inurement. The purpose must reflect that the organization is devoted to techniques of production, betterment of conditions to those engaged in agriculture or horticulture, development of efficiency, or improvement of the grade of products.

(a) Types of Crops

The IRS Exempt Organizations Handbook separately defines agriculture on the land and the sea because, until 1976, aquaculture was excluded. The handbook first defines "agriculture" to include "the art and science of cultivating the ground, especially in fields or large quantities, including the preparation of the soil, planting of seeds, raising and harvesting of crops, and rearing, feeding, and management of livestock, that is tillage, husbandry, and farming."[30]

---

[28] *National Association of Postal Supervisors v. U.S.,* 90-2 USTC ¶50,445 (Ct.Cl. 1990).
[29] *National League of Postmasters v. Commissioner,* T.C. Memo 1995-205.
[30] Exempt Organizations Handbook (IRM 7751) §531.

Next, it explains that IRC §501(g), added in 1976, includes the "harvesting of aquatic resources" and says that Congress now intends agriculture to include fishing and related pursuits such as the taking of lobsters and shrimp. Both freshwater and saltwater occupations are to qualify, along with the cultivation of underwater vegetation, such as edible sea plants. Finally, the handbook says that agriculture includes the "cultivation of any edible organism." In addition to cattle, crops, and fish, fur-bearing animals and their pelts[31] have also been ruled to be agricultural products. An association formed to guard the purity of the Welsh pony breed also qualified.[32] Agricultural products and pursuits do not include the following:

- Mineral resources, such as limestone. (But what about minerals used in vitamin supplements for human consumption?)

- Dogs not used as farm animals.[33]

- Horse racing, despite the fact that the horses are raised on a farm (unless the racing is a part of an agricultural fair and stock show).[34]

(b) Qualifying Activities

A broad range of activities associated with and supportive of agriculture may qualify under this category. The organization itself need not be directly involved in cultivation. Examples of agricultural groups which the IRS views as exempt include:

- State and county farm bureaus[35]

- Promoters of artificial insemination of cattle[36]

- A group to study aquatic harvesting of seaweed or organic gardening

- A crop seed certification, seed technology research group[37]

- A rodeo sponsor[38]

- An association of farm women[39]

- A producers' association formed to negotiate crop prices (but not to market the crops as a sales agent)[40]

---

[31] Rev. Rul. 56-245, 1956-1 C.B. 204.
[32] Rev. Rul. 55-230, 1955-1 C.B. 71.
[33] Rev. Rul. 73-520, 1973-2 C.B. 180.
[34] *Forest City Livestock and Fair Co. v. Commissioner,* B.T.A. Memo, 32, 215 (1932).
[35] Exempt Organizations Handbook (IRM 7751) §532.1(1)(a).
[36] *East Tennessee Artificial Breeders Ass'n v. U.S.* 63-2 USTC ¶9748 (E.D. Tenn 1963).
[37] *Indiana Crop Investment Association, Inc. v. Commissioner* 76 T.C. 394 (1981).
[38] *Campbell v. Big Spring Cowboy Reunion,* 54-1 USTC ¶9232 (5th Cir. 1954).
[39] Rev. Rul. 74-118, 1974-1 C.B. 134.
[40] Rev. Rul. 76-399, 1976-2 C.B. 147.

(c) Services to Members

Providing a direct business service for the economic benefit of members cannot be the primary purpose of an agricultural group. The rules generally place more constraints on agricultural groups than on unions. Activities which the IRS has deemed to convey such benefits, rather than advancing the "betterment of conditions of those engaged in agriculture," and which are therefore not appropriate activities for an exempt agricultural association, include:

- Management, grazing, and sale of members' cattle[41]

- A housing and labor pool for transient workers[42]

- Cooperative marketing of products (as opposed to monitoring or controlling pricing)[43]

- Leasing a facility to weigh, sort, grade, and ship livestock[44]

- A butter and cheese manufacturers institute (because butter is an agricultural by-product—milk is the agricultural product).[45]

- Provision of welfare aid and financial assistance to members[46]

To better illustrate the distinction between service to members and advancement of the industry, compare a producers' group formed to process production data for its members' use in improving their herds' milk production[47] with a nationwide organization that gathers milk production statistics for the U.S. Department of Agriculture.[48] The former group was not granted exemption because it relieved the individual farmers of work they would have had to perform themselves, and did not necessarily improve the conditions of the milk industry.

Agricultural or horticultural organizations gained a special exception from allocation of portions of their members' dues as unrelated business income.[49] The IRS has been aggressive and successful in treating the associate member dues collected by unions from nonunion members as unrelated business income as described in §7.1(e). Effective retroactively for taxable years beginning after December 31, 1986, agricultural groups were afforded special protection from such a position for required annual member dues of up to $100 (indexed annually, for 1999, $110). IRC §512(d) reads:

> If an agricultural or horticultural organization described in section 501(c)(5) requires annual dues to be paid in order to be a member of such organization, and the amount of such required annual dues does

---

[41] Rev. Rul. 74-195, 1974-1 C.B. 135.
[42] Rev. Rul. 72-391, 1972-2 C.B. 249.
[43] Rev. Rul. 66-105, 1966-1 C.B. 145.
[44] Rev. Rul. 77-153, 1977-1 C.B. 147.
[45] Rev. Rul. 67-252, 1967-2 C.B. 195.
[46] Rev. Rul. 67-251, 1967-2 C.B. 196.
[47] Rev. Rul. 70-372, 1970-2 C.B. 118.
[48] Rev. Rul. 74-518, 1974-2 C.B. 166.
[49] Small Business Job Protection Act of 1996, §1115, adding new IRC §512(d).

not exceed $100 (indexed), in no event shall any portion of such dues be treated as derived by such organization from an unrelated trade or business by reason of any benefits or privileges to which members of such organization are entitled.

7.3 HORTICULTURAL GROUPS

According to the IRS, horticulture is the cultivation of a garden or orchard, and the science or art of growing fruits, vegetables, and flowers or ornamental plants. Under the IRS guidelines, horticulture is a division of agriculture and is subject to the same rules. No specific guidance or rules are provided exclusively for horticulture. To ponder the interesting dilemma presented by a group of rose growers—conceivably eligible to qualify under both (c)(5) and (c)(6)—refer to Chapter 8§9. A garden club might qualify under (c)(3), (c)(4), or (c)(7) depending on the focus of its activities.

7.4 DISCLOSURES OF NONDEDUCTIBILITY

Certain labor, agricultural, and horticultural organizations must make two different types of disclosures to their members in connection with soliciting payments as follows:

1. *Nondeductibility as charitable contribution.* A nonprofit organization exempt under (c)(5) that has gross revenue of $100,000 must print an express statement that payments to it, whether called dues, gifts, contributions, or something else, are not deductible as charitable contributions.

2. *Nondeductible dues attributable to lobbying.* Members must be informed of that portion of their annual dues that are to be expended on lobbying and therefore are not tax deductible at all.

Failure to make the required disclosures are subject to penalties. These rules are discussed in detail in Chapter 6§4. The lobbying expense disclosure may not apply to many labor unions. An organization that is able to show that 90% or more of its members do not benefit from the deduction of their dues, because of the 2% threshold for employee business expenses, is excluded from the rules.

CHAPTER EIGHT

Business Leagues: §501(c)(6)

Internal Revenue Code (IRC) §501(c)(6) provides exemption for business and professional associations not organized for profit and no part of the earnings of which inure to the benefit of private individuals or shareholders, and specifically names

- Business leagues
- Chambers of commerce
- Real estate boards
- Boards of trade
- Professional football leagues

8.1 BASIC CHARACTERISTICS

To qualify under §501(c)(6), a business league must have the following attributes:[1]

- It is an association of persons having some common business interest.

[1] Reg. 1.501(c)(6)-1.

- Its organizational purpose is to promote such common interest and to improve conditions of one or more "lines of business."

- It does not engage in a regular business of a kind ordinarily carried on for profit.

- It does not perform services for individuals or organizations as a primary activity.

- It is not organized for profit, and no private inurement accrues to individuals.

8.2 MEANING OF "COMMON BUSINESS INTEREST"

To qualify as a business league, the members of the association must have a "common business interest." This essentially means that they form the league to advance a mutual goal of improving an industry or profession, not their individual interests. Their purpose in joining together is to improve the overall economic condition of their field. Each member of the league typically conducts a profitable business operation in competition with the other members, some of whom can be involved in a variety of functions operating in the profession or line of business. Examples include:

- *Physicians, Lawyers, and Accountants.* Professional groups such as the American Medical Association, the American Bar Association, and the American Society of Certified Public Accountants are classic examples of groups formed to advance a particular profession. The activities of such organizations unquestionably advance the interests of the members as a profession. Programs considered to advance the profession include (1) establishing standards that control and monitor admission into the profession, (2) conducting educational programs to maintain the technical performance of the members and to advance the body of knowledge about the field, and (3) sponsoring numerous other programs designed to promote the reputation and quality of work performed by the members.

- *Business Leagues.* Business leagues may also conduct educational and charitable activities, such as presenting public lectures, conducting research, maintaining libraries, and disseminating useful information.[2] An association conducting professional certification programs protects and benefits the general public, as well as the particular profession and its members, and arguably could qualify as both a 501(c)(3) and 501(c)(6) organization. However, the Internal Revenue Service (IRS) says certification programs are "directed in whole or in part to the support and promotion of the economic interests" of the members, not the public, and therefore could not qualify the organization for (c)(3) status.[3] See §8.11 for discussion concerning formation of a separate charitable organization.

[2] Rev. Rul. 71-504, 1971-2 C.B. 231, 232.
[3] Gen. Coun. Memo. 39721.

- *American Automobile Association.* The AAA illustrated a lack of common business interest when it failed both IRS and judicial scrutiny in its attempt to be classified as a business league. The interest of its members was found not to be common since it is open to individual motorists for their personal needs without regard to their trade or business association.[4]

- *Women's Leagues.* An organization formed to promote the acceptance and advancement of women in business and professions can qualify due to the shared business interest of its members.[5]

- *Dogs and Horses.* The American Kennel Club lost its fight to qualify as a business league because its member clubs were held to have a common sporting rather than a business interest.[6] On the other hand, the Jockey Club's members, breeders and owners of thoroughbred horses, were considered to have "some common business interest."[7]

- *Investors and Stock Exchanges.* The IRS regulations specifically state that an association engaged in furnishing information to prospective investors to enable them to make sound investments is not serving a common business interest, nor does a stock or commodity exchange.[8]

- *Future Business Interests.* A group of students pursuing a single profession formed a qualifying business league even though they were not yet engaged in the profession. The organization promoted their common business purpose as future members of the profession.[9]

- *Professional Sports Leagues.* The regulations refer specifically to football leagues and fail to mention baseball, basketball, hockey, or other types of sports. In explaining its view of this omission, the IRS says, "Since other professional sports leagues are indistinguishable in any meaningful way from football leagues, we think it is fair to conclude that by formally blessing the exemption it knew football leagues had historically enjoyed, Congress implicitly recognized a unique historical category of exemption under section 501(c)(6). The specific enumeration of football leagues can be viewed as merely exemplary of the category thus recognized. . . . accordingly it is appropriate to continue the Service's 50-year practice of ruling [all] professional sports leagues exempt."[10] The service emphasized that its extension of the statutory language to other professional sports leagues had no implication for extending exemption under section 501(c)(6) to other organizations that were not professional sports leagues.

---

[4] *American Automobile Association,* 19 T.C. 1146 (1953).

[5] Rev. Rul. 76-401, 1976-2 C.B. 175.

[6] *American Kennel Club v. Hoey,* 148 F.2d 290 (2d Cir. 1945); see Priv. Ltr. Rul. 9805001 for a Kennel club qualifying as a (c)(4)

[7] *The Jockey Club v. United States,* 137 F.Supp. 419 (Ct.Cl. 1956), *cert. denied,* 352 U.S. 834 (1957).

[8] Reg. §1.501(c)(6)-1.

[9] Rev. Rul. 77-112, 1977-1 CB 149.

[10] Gen. Coun. Memo. 38179.

8.3 LINE OF BUSINESS

Understanding what constitutes a "line of business" is the key to identifying groups that qualify as business leagues because they share a common business interest. A "line of business" is a trade or occupation, entry into which is not restricted by a patent, trademark, or similar device that would allow private parties to restrict the right to engage in the business.[11]

The term *business* is construed broadly to include almost any enterprise or activity conducted for remuneration. The term encompasses professions as well as mercantile and trading businesses.[12] To qualify, a league's line of business must be broad; it must encompass the common business interest of an entire industry or one of its components, or an industry within a particular geographic area.

(a) User Groups

The computer industry provides good examples both of organizations deemed to serve a common business interest and nonexempt private groups. In 1974, the IRS decided that an organization qualified as a business league because it was formed to stimulate the development of a free exchange of information about computer systems and programming. The membership was diverse, including businesses that owned, rented, or leased computers of a variety of manufacturers. It sponsored semiannual conferences, open to the public, to discuss technical and operational issues. Conversely, organizations formed for the same purposes by users of particular manufacturers' computers are denied business league status.[13] The user groups are deemed to promote the particular computer vendors, rather than to benefit the entire industry or all components of an industry within an area. The Guide International Corporation, limiting in membership to IBM mainframe computer users, was denied exemption because it benefited IBM, a large but nonetheless particular segment of the computer business, not the computer business in general.

Unlike Prime and Guide, the Corporation for Open Systems International found another way to achieve exempt status for its newly created Open Systems Research and Educational Corporation.[14] The entity was organized to conduct and disseminate the results of its research. It sought and achieved recognition as a charitable (c)(3) organization, not a business league. The Form 1023 stated that its research would benefit the general public and "the users of products or services of more than one industry or segment of an industry." The application was initially denied exemption, presumably because the IRS thought there would be excessive private benefit from the research to the computer manufacturer. Upon appeal, the IRS National Office approved charitable status for the following reasons:

---

[11] IRS Exempt Organizations Handbook (IRM 7751) §652(1).

[12] Rev. Rul. 70-641, 1970-2 CB 119.

[13] Rev. Rul. 83-164, 1983-2 CB 95; *National Prime Users Group Inc. v. United States*, 667 F.Supp. 250 (D.Md. 1987); *Guide International Corporation v. United States*, 90-1 USTC 50,304 (N.D. Ill. 1990).

[14] Determination letter released by the IRS National Office's Exempt Organizations Technical Division.

- The proposed entity would follow the IRS guidelines for research organizations.[15]

- Results of its work would be made available to the public through the Internet and printed documents.

- Any research performed for Open Systems would be intended to benefit all users of computers, software, and/or telecommunications products or services, and only incidentally to provide benefit to Open Systems.

(b) Dealer Associations

Associations of dealers and manufacturers of particular brands have been determined not to qualify for exemption as business leagues, because they failed to represent a "line of business."

An association of Midas Muffler dealers formed to represent the dealers in negotiations with the manufacturer failed to convince the Supreme Court that it constituted a "line of business." It was deemed unfair to allow exemption to a group, the purpose of which is to compete with another group within an industry.[16] Earlier the Pepsi-Cola Bottlers' Association was allowed an exemption, a decision which the IRS promptly announced that it would not follow.[17]

An association of licensed dealers of a patented product (held by the association) was deemed to be engaged in furthering the business interest of its member-dealers and not benefiting competing manufacturers of products of the same type covered by the patent.[18]

A shopping center merchants' association promotes too narrow an interest when its sole activity is to place advertisements to attract customers to the center and its membership is restricted to merchants in the one-owner shopping center.[19] If, instead, membership is open to all merchants within the neighborhood and if the association is not concerned with landlord–tenant matters relating to the shopping center, exemption is allowed.[20]

Dealers selling a particular type of car do not promote the automobile industry.[21] Franchisees of a particular chain, such as McDonald's restaurants, would similarly be precluded from forming an exempt group, but a league of franchise holders open to all types of merchants or food establishments would qualify.

(c) Hobby or Recreational Groups

Hobby groups do not qualify as business leagues because a hobby is not a business.[22] To be characterized as a business, the activity must be entered into with the

---

[15] See Chapter 5§3.
[16] *Pepsi-Cola Bottlers' Association v. United States*, 369 F.2d 250 (7th Cir. 1966). The IRS announced its disagreement with this case in Rev. Rul. 68-182, 1968-1 CB 263.
[17] *National Muffler Dealers Association v. United States*, 440 U.S. 472, 477-479 (1979).
[18] Rev. Rul. 58-294, 1958-1 CB 244.
[19] Rev. Rul. 73-411, 1973-2 CB 180.
[20] Rev. Rul. 78-225, 1978-1 C.B. 159.
[21] Rev. Rul. 67-77, 1967-1 CB 138.
[22] Rev. Rul. 66-179, 1966-1 CB 139.

intention of producing a profit. For income tax purposes, an activity is presumed to be a hobby if it loses money for more than two years in a five year period.[23]

Gardeners, pet owners, card players, and collectors of antiques, baseball cards, fine art, and so on, form groups for purposes somewhat similar to those of typical business leagues. However, unless the members are pursuing their hobby interests for personal profit, and therefore for individual business purposes, exemption is not available for the group under §501(c)(6). Such a group may, however, qualify in other categories of exemption, such as social club, civic welfare organization, or (rarely) charitable, depending upon its purposes.

8.4 RENDERING SERVICES FOR MEMBERS

A qualifying business league must devote its efforts primarily to promoting the industry. A §501(c)(6) association may not, as a significant activity, engage in a regular business of a kind ordinarily carried on for profit.[24] Services rendered for members aimed at improving the industry or maintaining its standards are treated as related, or nonbusiness activity, and the rendering of such services will not jeopardize the exemption. Services benefiting the individual members, however, produce unrelated business income (UBI). Examples of the types of services that have been held to be "related" or to serve the industry as a whole, rather than the individual members, follow.

(a) Services Benefiting the Industry

- Industrywide advertising to encourage use of products[25]

- Testing for quality control[26]

- Examination and certification of professionals, peer review, and ethics audits[27]

- Mediation service to settle disputes within the industry[28]

- Research and publication of technical information,[29] but only if the information is available to the industry as a whole, rather than being available only to paying members[30]

- Referral services available to the general public, if there is evidence of benefit to the public rather than to individual service providers[31]

[23] IRC §183.
[24] *Supra*, n. 1.
[25] *Washington State Apples, Inc. v. Commissioner,* 46 B.T.A. 64 (1942).
[26] Rev. Rul. 81-127, 1981-1 C.B. 357; Rev. Rul. 70-187 1970-1 C.B. 131.
[27] Rev. Rul. 73-567, 1973-2 C.B. 178; Rev. Rul. 74-553, 1974-2 C.B. 168.
[28] *American Fisherman's Tuna Boat Association v. Rogan,* 51 F.Supp. 933 (S.D. Cal. 1943).
[29] Rev. Rul. 70-187, 1970-1 C.B. 131.
[30] Rev. Rul. 69-106, 1969-1 C.B. 153 and *Glass Container Industry Research Corp.,* 70-1 USTC ¶9214.
[31] Rev. Rul. 80-287, 1980-2 C.B. 185. Also see *Kentucky Bar Foundation, Inc. v. Commissioner,* 49 T.C. 921, 930 (1982).

- A bid registry established and operated to encourage fair bidding practices with the industry[32]

- Insurance associations that serve their industry without charge and essentially do not sell insurance. See §8.4(b) for discussion of nonqualifying insurance groups.

- Lobbying groups presenting information, trade statistics, and group opinions to government agencies and bureaus[33]

(b) Disqualifying Services to Individual Members

Services giving benefit to the members as individuals rather than to the industry as a whole may disqualify a business league as an exempt league, if such services constitute a substantial and major activity of the organization. Individual benefit services are taxed as unrelated business income.[34]

The distinction is often vague, but several factors evidence the difference. Of primary importance is the manner in which persons are charged for receiving the services, and whether the services are available to the general public. When the services are rendered in return for a specific charge or the services are only available to members, individual benefit is generally found. Activities for which individual members are not expected to pay are evidence of intangible industrywide benefit. Making services available to all also reflects cooperative effort. By contrast, when members buy and the association sells services for member convenience or cost savings, individual benefit results. Examples of services that have been considered as providing individual benefit follow:

- Publication of catalogs containing advertisements for products manufactured by members[35] or a tourism promotion yearbook made up of advertisements from the association's members.[36] Compare these to ads promoting the entire industry.

- Group insurance plans provided for members[37]

- Real estate multiple listing services[38]

- Employment placement services[39]

- Credit rating or information services[40]

---

[32] Rev. Rul. 66-223, 1966-2 C.B. 224.
[33] Rev. Rul. 61-177, 1961-2 C.B. 117.
[34] See Chapter 21§8(b).
[35] Rev. Rul. 56-84, 1956-1 C.B. 201.
[36] Rev. Rul. 65-14, 1965-1 C.B. 236.
[37] *Oklahoma Cattlemen's Association v. U.S.*, 310 F.Supp. 320 (W.D. Okla. 1969); Rev. Rul. 70-95, 1970-1 C.B. 137; Rev. Rul. 67-176, 1967-1 C.B. 140.
[38] Rev. Rul. 59-234, 1959-2 C.B. 149 and *Evanston-North Shore Board of Realtors*, 63-2 USTC ¶9604, 320 F.2d 375 (Ct. Cl. 1963), *cert. denied*, 376 US 931 (1964).
[39] Rev. Rul. 61-170, 1961-2 C.B. 112.
[40] Rev. Rul. 68-265, 1968-1 C.B. 265 and Rev. Rul. 70-591, 1970-2 C.B. 118 and *Oklahoma City Retailers Ass'n*, 64-1 USTC ¶9467, 331 F.2d 328 (10th Cir. 1964).

- Collective bargaining agreement records

- A luncheon or social meeting hall for members without a program for professional improvement did not qualify;[41] contrast this with a luncheon group devoted to discussion, review, and consideration of problems in a particular industry directed to the improvement of business conditions, which can qualify.[42]

- Trade shows organized primarily to allow members to sell merchandise individually, rather than to educate the audience, do not constitute qualifying business league activity.[43] Shows organized instead to attract persons to an industry by educating the public represent exempt activity.[44] See Chapter 21§9(c) for a discussion of §513(d)(3) "Qualified Convention and Trade Show Activities," which provides the parameters for shows that are excluded from the unrelated business income tax.

- Sale of standardized forms for use by the profession and the public is a debatable type of service. The IRS thinks such activity is an unrelated trade or business.[45] The courts, however, felt that the San Antonio Bar Association improved relations between the bar, bench, and the public with its forms. Similarly, the Texas Apartment Association's lease forms and landlord manuals prevented controversy and maintained fairness in the industry.[46] In a private ruling, the IRS said a national association operated a "commercial" trade or business selling its standard forms partly because more than half of the forms were sold to the general public.[47]

- Insurance company associations present a gray area. When the association provides its services or information to insurance companies without charge and is not selling the insurance itself, the requisite industry benefit is present. An association created to carry out state-mandated rules concerning uninsured parties[48] and an association of casualty companies settling claims against insolvent companies[49] were ruled exempt. In both cases, all companies within a state were required to be members and the expenses of the association were paid from member dues. On the other hand, an association of insurance companies that maintained a data bank and exchange for confidential life insurance underwriting information, made available for a fee to its members (who wrote 98% of the legal reserve life insurance in force in the United States), was determined to serve

[41] *The Engineers Club of San Francisco v. United States*, 609 F.Supp. 519 (N.D. Cal. 1985).
[42] Rev. Rul. 67-295, 1967-2 C.B. 197.
[43] Rev. Rul. 58-224, 1958-1 C.B. 242; *Men's and Boys' Apparel Club of Florida*, 64-2 USTC ¶9840; *Indiana Hardware Ass'n, Inc.*, 66-2 USTC ¶9691, 366 F.2d 998 (Ct.Cla. 1966).
[44] *American Woodworking Machinery and Equipment Show, Inc.*, 66-1 USTC ¶9219, 249 F.Supp. 393 (D.C. N.C. 1966).
[45] Rev. Rul. 78-51, 1978-1 C.B. 165.
[46] *San Antonio Bar Association v. United States*, 80-2 U.S.T.C. ¶9594 (W.D. Texas 1980); *Texas Apartment Association v. United States*, 869 F.2d 884 (5th Cir. 1989).
[47] Priv. Ltr. Rul. 9527001.
[48] Rev. Rul. 76-410, 1976-2 C.B. 155.
[49] Rev. Rul. 73-452, 1973-2 C.B. 183.

the individual interests of the members and not to qualify for exemption.[50] Likewise, an association furnishing medical malpractice insurance to health care providers was not exempt.[51] A thorough reading of the rulings and cases is warranted prior to forming such an association.[52]

The details of a pair of cases and a private ruling on this subject help to identify the types of facts and circumstances applied to determine the character of a program as accomplishing an exempt function. The American Academy of Family Physicians' information clearing house for physician placement fostered the "appropriate distribution of physicians to provide health care for the nation." The court found that this stated objective advanced the organization's exempt purposes so that the fees charged to access the information were related income.

In a second issue, the Eighth Circuit Court of Appeals affirmed a Missouri federal district court's opinion that payments to the business league by an insurance company did not stem from profit-motivated business activity, but instead represented passive interest income not taxable as unrelated business income. Member insurance services were handled by an independent company that was required by the association to maintain reserves to pay claims and pay a fixed percentage of the reserves annually to the league without regard to the profitability of the insurance program. The court noted that the association's involvement did not possess the general characteristics of a trade or business—it furnished a list of its members, allowed the use of its name, and monitored the insurance products to assure that the needs of its members were met. The league did not underwrite or administer the policies or have any other activities the court could equate to operating a business.[53]

Another physician recruitment program, called Medical Opportunities in Michigan, was found not to jeopardize the tax-exempt status of the Michigan Health Council, a §501(c)(3) organization.[54] The program was established to bring physicians, physician assistants, nurse practitioners, nurse midwives, and certified registered nurse anesthetists to the underserved and growing communities in Michigan. A priority-neutral computerized database of available positions, with no advertisements or logos of health care entities, was made available free of charge to prospective medical workers. The facts indicated about 72% of Michigan's counties had primary care physician shortages and that 62% of the physicians trained in Michigan left the state to begin their medical practices. These facts, plus a finding that the registry was "clearly distinguishable from commercial placement services," allowed the IRS to find that the database promoted health and consequently served a charitable purpose. The IRS also found that no private benefit existed, because there was a broad cross section of potential subscribers and most of the job postings were for nonprofit hospitals, clinics, and community health centers.

---

[50] *MIB, Inc.,* 84-1 USTC ¶9476, 734 F.2d 71 (1st. Cir. 1984).

[51] Rev. Rul. 81-175, 1981-1 C.B. 337, distinguishing Rev. Rul. 71-155, 1971-1 C.B. 152.

[52] *North Carolina Association of Insurance Agents, Inc.* 84-2 USTC ¶9668, 739 F.2d 949 (4th. Cir. 1984); Priv. Ltr. Rul. 8841003, June 24, 1988.

[53] *American Academy of Family Physicians v. U.S.,* No. 95-2791 WM (8th Cir. 1996), *aff'g* 95-1 U.S.T.C. ¶ 50,240 (W.D. Mo. 1995).

[54] Priv. Ltr. Rul. 9617040.

The IRS noted that the Tax Court had found organizations that further exempt purposes through sponsoring legal or medical referral services do not confer private benefits so long as the service was open to a broad representation of professionals and no select group of professionals was the primary beneficiaries of the service.[55]

(c) Avoiding the Exploitation Rule

A business league that partly finances its activities by earning unrelated business income faces limitations on deductions that can offset such income. In calculating the tax on unrelated business income, the "exploitation rule" disallows the deduction of expenses attributable to the league's member or exempt function activities.[56] Losses incurred in membership activities cannot be deducted against business income. Despite the economic fact that the league has a loss overall, it may have to pay tax as more fully described in Chapter 27§14(d).

To avoid this situation, one might think that the league should abandon its exempt status and file as a normal corporation showing no profit, but IRC §277 is designed to prevent this tactic. Membership expenses are only deductible to the extent of membership income, and cannot be deducted against business income for a nonexempt taxpayer.

8.5   SOURCES OF REVENUE

The portion of total support received from members is a factor in determining qualification. The IRS expects "meaningful membership support," although the code and regulations contain no specific numerical support requirement. Revenue received in rendering services to individuals that do not benefit the industry as a whole cannot provide a major portion of the league's budget. As is true for other categories of exempt organizations, there is no prohibition against a league earning such income as long as the amounts are insubstantial, but there is no exact numerical test. When a league's income from providing such services is excessive, its exempt status is jeopardized and the income is taxable. A safe rule of thumb is more than 50% of the league's support should come from member dues and exempt function charges. Decisions that illustrate the IRS's view on revenue sources follow:

- City contract revenue received by a tourism promotion organization was deemed to be related income and therefore member income. The ruling noted a high degree of member involvement, and opined that the organization should not lose its exemption "merely because a significant portion of its income was derived from other than traditional member sources."[57]

- "Incidental" television advertising activity and provision of laboratories for testing quality control on a fee basis was not enough to cause revocation of a league's exemption.[58]

[55] *Kentucky Bar Foundation v. Commissioner,* 78 T.C. 921 (Tax Ct. 1982); *Fraternal Medical Specialist Services, Inc. v. Commissioner,* T.C. Memo. 1984-644.
[56] Reg. §1.512(a)-1(d)(1).
[57] Priv. Ltr. Rul. 9032005.
[58] *American Plywood Ass'n,* 67-2 USTC ¶9568, 267 F.Supp. 830 (1967).

8.6 MEMBERSHIP CATEGORIES

An exempt business league may have different classes of members, as long as the purpose is to advance the interests of the profession and all members share the same common business interest. Junior, senior, retired, associate, student, supporters and other types of categories are common, in recognition of age, stature, or active versus peripheral involvement in the business. Varying levels of dues can also be charged to different types of members, presumably based upon their ability to pay or their involvement in league activities. Those members required to have continuing education might pay more than inactive or student members who are not required to participate in classes, for example. Member dues and assessments are deductible as business expenses for members who are actively engaged in a trade or business, except for the amount of the dues allocable to political activity or grassroots lobbying.[59]

The charging of substantially greater dues to associate members has been said to evidence private inurement benefiting the active members, although higher associate dues were permissible when the revenues benefited the entire industry by allowing more extensive programs.[60] Dues paid by associate or other subclass members who joined to market their products or obtain association benefits, such as group insurance, may be taxable as unrelated business income.[61] In one instance, industry suppliers could promote their products in the association publications and obtain the mailing list by becoming associate (nonvoting) members. Since the motivation of association members was to sell products to members rather than to advance the industry, their dues represented taxable advertising revenue.[62]

The IRS before 1997 asserted membership assumes some right to participate in the organization's direction as well as an obligation to help support the organization through regular financial contributions. "Most importantly, members have voting rights and have a voice in the administration and direction of the organization." Labor unions and the IRS battled about the character of associate members for some years as described in Chapter 7§1(c). The IRS eventually eased its stance and issued formal guidance on the character of member dues, originally only for labor unions[63] and later extended to (c)(6) organizations.[64] The procedure sets forth a primary purpose test. The test asks, "Was the associate member category created and used to further the organization's exempt purposes or simply to produce unrelated income?" Where members serve only to buy unrelated goods and services (insurance or advertising, for example), their dues will be treated as unrelated income. The procedure gives no specific criteria for applying the test except to say the IRS will look to the purposes and activities of the organization rather than its members. In a private letter ruling issued after the procedure, the IRS was asked to consider the status of "allied members" of a professional association. Al-

---

[59] See §8.12.
[60] Priv. Ltr. Rul. 9128002, August 17, 1990.
[61] See Chapter 7§1(e).
[62] Priv. Ltr. Rul. 9345004; this position also espoused in Priv Ltr. Rul. 8834006.
[63] Rev. Proc. 95-21, 1995-15 IRB 1.
[64] Rev. Proc. 97-12, 1997-4 IRB 1.

though their rights were not as extensive as those accorded regular members, the associates could vote and serve as officers at a chapter level and their dues were similar to those of regular members. The IRS thought therefore that the dichotomy between regular and allied members did not evidence an organization purpose to generate unrelated income.[65]

Tax-exempt organizations may also be members of a qualifying league, despite the fact that the regulations define a business league as an association of persons. A labor union and a business league have been permitted to form a qualifying league.[66]

8.7   MEMBER INUREMENT

The league may not allow its assets to inure to the benefit of individual members or otherwise operate primarily to benefit its members. The league may not, as its primary activity, provide direct services of benefit to individual members, but it can provide a whole host of services designed to benefit their common interests. The IRS Exempt Organization Handbook[67] and the courts have provided some additional guidance as to when inurement results, as follows:

- A charter provision that permits distributions of remaining assets to members upon dissolution of the league will not in and of itself preclude exemption.[68] However, regular distributions of income or accumulated surplus would constitute inurement.[69]

- A league cannot be organized as a stockholding company with members holding the shares.[70]

- Newsletters and member "informational materials" do not provide impermissible benefit.

- Preferential pricing for members results in private inurement *unless* it is shown that the league supports the activity from member dues and the pricing reflects that revenue.[71]

- Refunds of dues paid proportionately to all classes of members is permitted.[72]

- A partial rebate of trade show advance deposits to exhibitors is permitted if all participants receive a share.[73] Rebates paid to members only out of income-producing activity represents inurement.[74]

---

[65] Tech. Adv. Memo. 9742001.

[66] Rev. Rul. 70-31, 1970-1 C.B. 130. See also Rev. Rul. 82-138, 1982-2 C.B. 106.

[67] Exempt Organizations Handbook §640.

[68] *Crooks v. Kansas City Hay Dealers Association*, 37 F.2d 83 (1929).

[69] Exempt Organizations Handbook §630.

[70] *Northwest Jobbers Credit Bureau v. Commissioner*, 37 F.2d 880 (1930) Ct. D. 206, C.B. IX-2, 228.

[71] Exempt Organizations Annual Technical Review Institutes for 1979, page 354.

[72] Rev. Rul. 81-60, 1981-1 C.B. 335.

[73] Rev. Rul. 77-206, 1977-1 C.B. 149.

[74] *Michigan Mobile Home and Recreational Vehicle Institute v. Commissioner*, 66 T.C. 770 (1976).

- Financial aid and welfare services provided to members represents benefit to the individual members, in the eyes of the IRS.[75]

- Payment of malpractice defense costs and paying judgments rendered in such suits creates individual inurement.[76]

- Payment of excessive compensation or purchase price for property or services to a member, particularly to persons controlling the league, results in inurement of earnings. See Chapter 20 for standards applied to measure reasonable values.

8.8   CHAMBERS OF COMMERCE AND BOARDS OF TRADE

A chamber of commerce or board of trade is distinguishable from a business league because it serves the general economic welfare of a community. Membership is typically open to all lines of business within a geographic area. Its activities must be directed at the promotion of the area's business and usually include the promotion of tourism, publishing directories of resources available in the area, developing programs to promote the business climate, conducting studies, and similar projects. The following activities have been ruled to be suitable for a chamber of commerce:

- Development of an industrial park to attract new businesses to an area, including the offering of below-cost rents and other subsidies.[77]

- Encouraging national organizations to hold their conventions in a city.[78]

- A "neighborhood community association" whose membership is open to all and whose purpose is to improve the business conditions of a neighborhood, as opposed to a particular subdivision or shopping area, can qualify.[79]

8.9   COMPARISON TO §501(c)(5)

The basic difference between §501(c)(5) and §501(c)(6) is sometimes gray, due both to industry type and to congressional logic. While (c)(5) is narrow and applies only to agricultural groups and labor unions, (c)(6) is broad and includes almost any business enterprise or activity.[80]

To contrast the two categories of §501(c) classification, consider a rose growers' association. Except for the roses, such an association would qualify as a business league under §501(c)(6). Nevertheless, the organization will be classified

---

[75] Rev. Rul. 67-251, 1967-2 C.B. 196.
[76] *National Chiropractor Association v. Birmingham,* 96 F.Supp. 824 (D.C. Iowa 1951).
[77] Rev. Rul. 70-81, 1970-1 C.B. 131; Rev. Rul. 81-138, 1981-1 C.B. 358.
[78] Rev. Rul. 76-207, 1976-1 C.B. 1578.
[79] Rev. Rul. 78-225, 1978-1 C.B. 159.
[80] Rev. Rul. 70-641, 1970-2 C.B. 119.

under §501(c)(5) as horticultural if its members are all directly involved in the cultivation of roses with the purpose of bettering the conditions of persons growing roses, improving the grade of roses, and developing growing systems. However, if group membership includes nongrowers such as shippers, pesticide suppliers, and florists, it will not qualify under §501(c)(5) and will instead have to meet the tests for §501(c)(6).

In many ways, the two categories are identical. For both, unrelated business income is taxed and must not be a substantial revenue source or activity. For both categories, economic benefits and services cannot generally be rendered to individual members. However, labor unions can provide mutually funded benefits for life, health, and accident insurance.

Neither political activity nor lobbying is prohibited under either §501(c)(5) or §501(c)(6). Advocacy of legislation beneficial to the common business interest can conceivably be the group's primary purpose, if the activity is undertaken to improve working conditions, production, or efficiencies.[81] Whether an activity is "primary" is generally measured by dollars expended on that function in relation to the league's total budget. For both, the portion of member dues spent on lobbying efforts is nondeductible and specific disclosures must be made to members.[82]

8.10   RECOGNITION OF EXEMPT STATUS

(a) Federal Recognition

Form 1024 is filed to achieve recognition of exemption. Statutorily, a league essentially qualifies if it meets the §501(c)(6) definitions and need not seek IRS approval to qualify. As a practical matter, however, the IRS requires filing of Form 1024 to avoid subjecting the league's income to tax. Suggestions for completion of Form 1024 can be found in Chapter 18. The information return, Form 990 or 990EZ, that is filed annually to report activity and allow the IRS to review continued qualification is illustrated in Chapter 27.

The non-(c)(3) categories of tax-exempt organizations are not subject to a specific organizational requirement, as discussed in Chapter 7§1(a) concerning labor unions. The instructions to Form 1024, however, say that exemption will not be approved unless organizing documents are attached. They go on to say that bylaws are internal rules and are not, by themselves, organizational documents.

(b) State Exemptions

A business league may be qualified for state and local tax exemptions. In Texas, for example, an automatic exemption from the corporate franchise tax is granted for organizations furnishing their IRS determination letter evidencing their qualification as a §501(c)(6) organization. The sales tax exemption is only granted to "a chamber of commerce or a convention and tourist promotional agency representing a Texas city or county," and then only if the entity is not organized for profit and no part of its earnings inure to a private shareholder or other individual. Most

---

[81] Rev. Rul. 61-177, 1961-2 C.B. 117.
[82] See §8.12.

Texas business leagues are subject to the sales tax on items they buy, lease, or consume. The rules of the particular state(s) in which a league operates must be investigated.

8.11   FORMATION OF A RELATED CHARITABLE ORGANIZATION

Business, trade, and professional associations described in §501(c)(6) can create a separate organization to pursue their educational, cultural, scientific, or other charitable interests. The motivation is usually financial—to form an entity able to seek funding from those who desire a charitable deduction for their support or those (such as another foundation) whose grants can only be paid for charitable purposes. Say for example, an association wishes to create a library of educational materials. Rather than increasing overall dues, members capable of paying more can be asked to voluntarily contribute to the library. Gifts to the league itself for its use in establishing the library would not be deductible as contributions (could be a business expense), but a gift to the league's separate charity for the purpose of maintaining a library would be so long as it is open to the general public.[83] Grants from foundations, corporations, and testamentary bequests from members can also be sought. See discussion of sponsorships in Chapter 21§8(e) for circumstances under which such payments may be treated as advertising taxable as unrelated business income to the league.

A charitable organization established by a business league must meet the standards for qualification as a §501(c)(3) organization that require it to operate exclusively to benefit the general public, rather than to benefit the league and its members. In the IRS view, "the foundation cannot serve to improve the reputation and business interest of the association's members and the profession of which they form a part. For this reason, an organization that administers a national certification exam, presents seminars, and seeks to serve the public interest by maintaining high standards in the accounting profession cannot qualify as an educational organization.[84] A foundation can present educational programs, such as classes leading to certification in a particular line of business or continuing education. A foundation should not be responsible for certification, enforcement of a code of ethics for those that are certified, or other activities germane to an association of persons having a common business interest (definition of (c)(6) organization).[85] The foundation can conduct research on subjects pertaining to the business of the association members, but the results of the research must be available to the general public and conducted under the standards for charitable research organizations.[86] An engineering society conducting research that is made available to universities on a cost basis was allowed to convert to a (c)(3) because it did not police its profession or undertake a public relations program (so that it did not qualify as a business league).[87] The foundation can make scholarship grants to persons

---

[83] Rev. Rul. 58-293, 1958-1 C.B. 146 and Rev. Rul. 66-79, 1966-1 C.B. 48.
[84] Gen. Coun. Memo. 39721.
[85] A professional (standards) review organization created to oversee medicare treatment is afforded (c)(3) status as discussed in Chapter 4§6.
[86] Discussed in Chapter 5§3.
[87] Rev. Rul. 71-506, 1971-2 C.B. 233.

aspiring to enter the business, but should not sponsor an essay contest designed to increase public interest in its members and the line of business they represent.[88]

A business league and the foundation it creates can share common or overlapping board members or trustees; the league can, and for management reasons often does, absolutely control its affiliated foundation. Facilities, personnel, and other costs can be shared. When such a sharing arrangement exists, documentation must be maintained to evidence that the foundation's funds are not used for association purposes.[89] Furnishing of administrative services to the foundation for free is a charitable activity on the league's part that should not jeopardize its (c)(6) status if it is inconsequential to the league's overall operations.[90]

A controlled charitable subsidiary of a business league (or a (c)(4) or (c)(5) organization) may qualify as a public charity for one of three reasons. If its annual support is received from a broad range of contributors it may qualify under 509(a)(1). If its primary source of support comes from sales of educational programs and materials, it may qualify under 509(a)(2). Lastly it may be entirely funded and controlled by its affiliated (c)(6) organization and eligible under 509(a)(3). The charity's charter and organizational rules must be carefully drawn to meet the specific requirements for the last category, referred to as a supporting organization.[91] The third type may be desirable for a foundation that is receiving funding from a variety of sources because it avoids the need to maintain detailed public support information to prove that the affiliate is not a private foundation.

Rather than forming a new, separate charitable organization, it is conceivable that an organization classified as a (c)(6) might be able to requalify itself as a (c)(3) if its resources are devoted primarily to educational activities. The determinative factors are whether the organization promotes and protects the profession or business of its members and/or engages in extensive legislative activity.[92] Sponsoring semiannual law institutes, moot court proceedings, and providing legal assistance to indigents were agreed to be charitable and educational activities for a city bar association. Establishing minimum fee schedules, enforcing standards of conduct, and studying ways to make the practice of law more profitable instead promote the common business purpose of the bar's members. Thus, a bar association conducting both educational and professional standard-type activities was not allowed to be reclassified as a (c)(3).[93]

8.12 DISCLOSURES FOR LOBBYING AND NONDEDUCTIBILITY

Certain business leagues must disclose the fact that gifts to the association are not deductible as charitable contributions, and also must inform their members of the

---

[88] Gen. Coun. Memo. 37579.

[89] See Chapter 27§3.

[90] Tech. Adv. Memo. 8418003.

[91] Chapter 11 presents the various categories of public charities in detail.

[92] Rev. Rul. 71-504, 1971-2 C.B. 231, in which a medical society sought unsuccessfully to be reclassified from (c)(6) to (c)(3).

[93] Rev. Rul. 71-505, 1971-2. C.B. 232; see also Rev. Rul. 73-567, 1973-2 C.B. 178 (medical board to certify specialists), Rev. Rul. 74-553, 1974-2 C.B. 168, Rev. Rul. 80-287, 1980-2 C.B. 185, and Gen. Coun. Memos. 35861 and 37853.

portion of dues attributable, if any, to lobbying activity and therefore not deductible. See Chapter 6§4 for details of the rules.

The Revenue Act of 1993 repealed §162(e) and added direct lobbying expense to the list of nondeductibles. Leagues who currently finance such lobbying with member dues payments may have to reallocate their resources. Chapter 6§4 describes the limitation on deductibility of dues attributable to an organization's lobbying activity. The rules may not apply to some leagues. An association that is able to show that 90% or more of its members do not benefit from the deduction of their dues, because of the 2% threshold for employee business expenses, is excluded from the rules.

Amounts expended in connection with political campaigns are also not deductible and federal election laws generally prevent a business league from itself expending funds for electioneering. The association that wants to afford its members the opportunity to influence elections must, therefore, create a separate fund generally known as a political action committee (PAC). See Chapter 23 for definitions and limitations on activities of PACs and tax imposed on political expenditures if paid with organizational funds.

CHAPTER NINE

Social Clubs: §501(c)(7)

Social clubs are defined in Internal Revenue Code (IRC) §501(c)(7) as "clubs organized for pleasure, recreation, and other nonprofitable purposes, substantially all of the activity of which are for such purposes and no part of the net earnings of which inures to the benefit of any private shareholder." The tax exemption is based on the logic of allowing individuals to pool their funds for recreational purposes, and is fundamentally very different from other types of exemptions. A club is not exempt because it provides public benefit, but rather because it serves to benefit private individuals. It is designed to allow individuals to join together on a mutual basis for personal reasons without tax consequences.[1] The types of organizations that typically qualify as social clubs include

- Country clubs
- Amateur hunting, fishing, tennis, swimming, and other sport clubs

---

[1] Exempt Organizations Handbook (IRM 7751) §710.

- Variety clubs

- Local women's and men's clubs

- Hobby clubs

- College sororities and fraternities operating chapter houses for students

The most significant tax attributes of a social club are that:

- Members are bound together with a common social goal.

- No part of the club's assets inure to the benefit of any private shareholder.

- Primary source of support is membership fees, dues, and assessments.[2]

- The club has specific criteria or standards for membership.

- Passive income from dividends, interest, and other investments is taxed.

- Limited revenues come from nonmembers and other business activities, subject to specific numerical tests.

9.1 ORGANIZATIONAL REQUIREMENTS

(a) Purpose Clause and Activities

The charter and bylaws of a social club should provide that the club is organized for pleasure, recreation, or other nonprofitable purposes and that the club does not provide for discrimination on the basis of race, color, or religion.[3] A club operating under a defective charter will qualify for exemption from the date it commenced operation if it has not conducted any of the proscribed activities permitted by the charter.[4] If impermissible activities have been conducted, exemption is only allowed beginning with the year of the revision.

Substantially all of the club's activities must be in pursuit of its recreational and social purposes. The charter should not expressly authorize the club to conduct activities beyond this (c)(7) scope, except that there can be provision for charitable, educational, and other (c)(3) purposes. A charitable deduction can offset the club's unrelated business income.[5]

The activities of a social club must encourage and permit members to join together, that is, the opportunity for social mingling and fellowship on a mutual basis must be present in club functions. Commingling by members must play a material part in the life of the organization.[6] Lack of personal contact may be an indication that the basic purpose of the organization is only to provide personal goods and services in a manner similar to commercial counterparts.[7]

---

[2] See numerical tests applied to measure qualification in §9.4.
[3] Reg. §1.501(c)(7).
[4] Exempt Organizations Handbook (IRM 7751) §722(4).
[5] Discussed in §9.5(g)
[6] Rev. Rul. 58-589, 1958-2 C.B. 266.
[7] Rev. Rul. 69-635, 1969-2 C.B. 126 concerning a nonprofit automobile club.

(b) Examples of Qualifying and Nonqualifying Clubs

A wide variety of groups of persons with common interests have formed qualifying social clubs.

- A pet club,[8] a dog club,[9] bowling tournament club,[10] a family historical society,[11] a garden club,[12] and a mineralogical and lapidary club[13] have been ruled to be exempt social clubs.

- Owning a building and operating the social facilities in it for a tax-exempt lodge,[14] for a fraternity chapter house,[15] and for a veterans organization[16] also is considered to be qualifying activity for a social club. However, an organization whose primary activity was leasing building lots to members with peripheral recreational activity is not exempt.[17] The organization must itself be social or recreational in nature. If social activity predominates, rental activities restricted to members will usually be compatible with exemption as a social club. A fraternity can rent rooms to its members for their private use, for example.[18]

- Gambling, even though illegal under local law, was ruled to be a permissible social club focus when it was conducted only for members and their guests.[19] Similarly, a Calcutta wagering pool conducted by a club in connection with its annual golf tournament was deemed exempt.[20]

Two different flying clubs illustrate the rule. A hobby flying group that held informal meetings for members and owned an airplane that the members maintained, repaired, and flew together in small groups, qualified as a social club.[21] In contrast, a group that only provided "economical" facilities for members' plane storage, but held no meetings or other commingling activity for them, did not qualify as a social group.[22] Lack of a physical facility for regular gatherings implies lack of social purpose.

Examples of nonqualifying groups include the following:

---

[8] Rev. Rul. 73-520, 1973-2 C.B. 180.
[9] Rev. Rul. 71-421, 1971-2, C.B. 229; Rev. Rul. 73-520, 1973-2 C.B. 180.
[10] Rev. Rul. 74-148, 1974-1 C.B. 138.
[11] Rev. Rul. 67-8, 1967-1 C.B. 142.
[12] Rev. Rul. 66-179, 1966-1 C.B. 139.
[13] Rev. Rul. 67-139, 1967-1 C.B. 129.
[14] Rev. Rul. 56-305, 1956-2 C.B. 307.
[15] Rev. Rul. 64-118, 1964-1 (Part I) C.B. 182.
[16] Rev. Rul. 66-150, 1966-1 C.B. 147.
[17] Rev. Rul. 68-168, 1968-1 C.B. 269.
[18] Exempt Organizations Handbook (IRM 7751) §742.
[19] Rev. Rul. 69-68, 1969-1 C.B. 153.
[20] Rev. Rul. 74-425, 1974-2 C.B. 373.
[21] Rev. Rul. 74-30, 1974-1 C.B. 137.
[22] Rev. Rul. 70-32, 1970-1 C.B. 140.

- A breakfast club established to assist its members working in business through study and discussion of problems at weekly meetings is not classified as a social club, but may qualify as a business league.[23]

- A television antenna service group formed to share the costs, but with no member mingling activities, is not a social group.[24]

- A community association operating a swimming pool that serves a social function for residents cannot qualify if it also maintains the streets, collects the trash, and pays the police and fire departments.[25] Separating the functions could result in a (c)(7) pool facility and a (c)(4) community service provider.

- A club with mixed purposes—both a social club and provider of benevolent life insurance to members—cannot qualify (although two independent organizations separately conducting such activities can independently qualify).[26]

- An automobile club providing lower cost services to its members, but no social activities in which its members mingle cannot qualify.[27]

- A club owning a multistory urban building in which it conducted a number of "nontraditional business activities" is not a qualifying club in the Internal Revenue Service's (IRS) eyes. Operation of a parking garage, gas station, barber shop, flower shop, and liquor store, despite the fact that they were open only to members and their guests, does not serve a social purpose, but instead is the rendering of commercial services. Long-term rental of at least 10% of the rooms for members' principal residences is also a nonexempt activity.[28]

- Sale of take-out food for members' consumption off club premises is not a social function[29] or a veteran's group operation of bar with gambling, golf course, swimming pool, and restaurant all open to the public.[30]

- A Florida club sold a portion of its property to participate in a land price boom and distributed the proceeds to the members. The sale was found to be a "violent departure" from the club's normal behavior and not merely incidental to the regular functions of the club. Because financial gain was the aim, the club's exemption was revoked.[31]

---

[23] Rev. Rul. 69-527, 1969-2 C.B. 125.

[24] Rev. Rul. 83-170, 1983-2 C.B. 97; G.C.M. 39063.

[25] Rev. Rul. 75-494, 1975-2 C.B. 214.

[26] *Allgemeiner Arbeit Verein v. Commissioner,* 24 T.C. 371 (1955), *aff'd,* 237 F.2d 604 (1956) 3rd Cir.; Rev. Rul. 63-190, 1963-2 C.B. 212.

[27] *Keystone Auto Club v. Commissioner,* 181 F.2d 420 (3rd Cir. 1950), *aff'g* 12 T.C. 1038 (1949); Rev. Rul. 69-635, 1969-2 C.B. 126.

[28] Gen. Coun. Memo. 39115 (January 12, 1984).

[29] Tech. Adv. Memo. 9212002.

[30] Priv. Ltr. Rul. 9815061.

[31] *Juniper Hunting Club v. Commissioner,* 28 B.T.A. 525 (1933). The 35/15 test would now be applied to measure continued qualification for exemption as discussed in §9.4.

9.2   MEMBER INUREMENT PROHIBITED

The charter or organizational document establishing the club should provide that no private benefit can inure to any individual member of the club.[32] Chapter 20 defines and explores inurement concepts in depth. Under two different circumstances, the governing rules can provide distributions to members that do not result in private benefit to the individual members:

- Upon dissolution or termination of the club, payment of liquidation distributions to club members is acceptable.[33]

- Upon an individual member's withdrawal from the club, the member's shares can be redeemed at their book value. A payment equal to the member's proportionate share of the underlying value of the club's assets is permitted.

Essentially, members can be reimbursed their original membership cost, plus their share of increases in the value of club property and accumulated surpluses.[34] Dissolution payments can differ by membership category if they parallel and are attributable to differing levels of initiation fees or type of members. Lower dues rates for a voting class of membership at the expense of higher-paying nonvoting members is viewed as providing inurement to the voting members.[35] Such a dues structure may reflect inurement, as does the lowering or reduction of member charges or dues with profits earned from nonmember activities. When there is some other reason for the difference, such as enhanced privileges, benefits may not inure.[36]

(a)   Inurement from Nonmember Revenues

Reductions in member dues, facilities fees, and enhancement of club facilities, when financed by nonmember revenues, constitute member inurement.[37] Distribution of proceeds from sale of club land or property to members may be viewed as providing impermissible private inurement, if the sale is profit motivated. When club land is sold to take advantage of a land price boom with the profits distributed to the members, private benefit is found and the club's exemption revoked.[38] If, however, the club property is taken by a condemnation proceeding[39] or is sold by a club because of encroaching urbanization and trespasses,[40] distribution of the proceeds to the members (with or without dissolution) has not been deemed to produce unallowed benefit.

[32] *West Side Tennis Club v. Commissioner,* 111 F.2d 6 (2nd Circ. 1940).
[33] Rev. Rul. 58-501, 1958-2 C.B. 262.
[34] Rev. Rul. 68-639, 1968-2 C.B. 220.
[35] Rev. Rul. 70-48, 1970-1 C.B. 133.
[36] *Pittsburgh Press Club v. U.S.,* 536 F.2d 572 (3rd Cir. 1976).
[37] Rev. Rul. 58-589, 1958-2 C.B. 266.
[38] *Juniper Hunting Club v. Commissioner,* 28 B.T.A. 525 (1933).
[39] Rev. Rul. 65-64, 1965-1 C.B. 241.
[40] Rev. Rul. 58-501, 1958-2 C.B. 262.

(b) Direct Inurement to Members

Direct services rendered to members beyond the social purposes of the club may result in inurement. Examples of services that have been found to provide direct inurement, rather than to serve the social purposes of the club, include:

- Sale of packaged liquor to members for off-premises consumption[41]
- Sickness and death benefit payments to members[42]
- Leasing building lots to members on a long term basis[43]

9.3 MEMBERSHIP REQUIREMENTS

(a) Discrimination

Racial and religious discrimination by social clubs is strictly prohibited.[44] The charter, bylaws, or other governing instrument or written policy statement may contain no provision providing for discrimination against any person based upon race, color, or religion. Note that the code does not contain the word "sex." A written policy against discrimination is not absolutely necessary as long as the club obeys the spirit of the prohibition. It is actual discrimination that will cause revocation of exemption. Two specific types of religious organizations are permitted to discriminate based upon religion, and are relieved from this sweeping requirement:

- A fraternal beneficiary society, order, or association limiting its members to a particular religious group.
- A club which in good faith limits it membership to the members of a particular religion in order to further the teachings or principles of that religion, and not to exclude individuals of a particular race or color.[45]

IRS policy does not to permit exemption for religious groups falling outside those specified above, and not for ethnic groups.[46]

Sexual discrimination is not prohibited by the tax code so that exemption is permitted for clubs that discriminate in favor of a particular sex. Such clubs may be challenged under the broader civil rights legislation. Princeton's last two "male only" social clubs were ordered to admit women by the Supreme Court of New Jersey in July 1990. However, the Massachusetts Commission Against Discrimination refused in March 1990 to require the Harvard Fly Club to admit women.

---

[41] Rev. Rul. 68-535, 1968-2 C.B. 219.
[42] Rev. Rul. 63-190, *supra,* n. 26.
[43] Rev. Rul. 68-168, 1968-1 C.B. 269.
[44] IRC §501(i), added to the Code in 1976.
[45] IRC §501(i)(1) and (2).
[46] Priv. Ltr. Rul. 8317004.

(b) Classes of Membership

The shared interest of social club members is evidenced by the limitations and prerequisites of its membership structure.[47] Membership requirements cannot be broad or vague, but should serve to limit membership to a clearly defined constituency. Different classes of members, however, are permitted. Membership distinctions based on amount of dues paid, age, residency, and facilities used do not, in and of themselves, indicate lack of social purpose. Different voting rights and different dissolution rights for different classes of membership are also permissible. A health club with 25 active members and 25,000 nonvoting associate members, however, "clearly was not of an exempt character."[48] For geographically broad-based social clubs, mingling of members within each local chapter will suffice to meet IRS requirements.[49]

(c) Company Memberships

A social club must be a nonprofit membership organization of individuals. If corporate memberships are offered, individual representatives of the corporation must be subject to approval by the membership committee and must be granted the same privileges as other individual members.[50] The company can pay the bill as long as the charges are for member use.[51] If, instead, the club allows member corporations to designate their representatives, the club cannot qualify for exemption.[52]

(d) Subterfuge Clubs

Clubs actually doing business with the public under the guise of a social club cannot qualify for exemption. Clubs created to "circumvent liquor laws, zoning ordinances, or laws enforcing civil rights" are among those considered as subterfuges by the IRS. The following factors evidence nonqualifying clubs:[53]

- The membership requirements are broad or vaguely stated.
- Initiation charges or dues are so low that one-time transient use of the facilities by the general public is encouraged.
- Management conducts vigorous public solicitations to expand club membership.
- The club is closely associated with a for-profit hotel, restaurant, or health facility that also provides the management, the food services, and so on.

---

[47] *Arner v. Rogan*, 40-2 USTC ¶9567 (D.C. 1940).
[48] Rev. Rul. 58-588, 1958-2 C.B. 265.
[49] Rev. Rul. 67-248, 1967-2 C.B. 204.
[50] Rev. Rul. 74-168, 1974-1 C.B. 139.
[51] Rev. Rul. 71-17, 1971-1 C.B. 683.
[52] Rev. Rul. 74-489, 1974-2 C.B. 169.
[53] Exempt Organizations Handbook (IRM 7751) §727.

9.4 REVENUE TESTS

IRC §501(c)(7) was revised in 1976 to require that "substantially all" of a social club's activities involve the pleasure, recreation, and other nonprofit purposes of its members. Congress expressed an intention that no more than 35% of a qualifying social club's gross revenues come from investment and nonmember income, with nonmember income equaling no more than 15% of its gross revenue.[54] This gross receipts test is referred to as the *35/15 test* and establishes a specific numerical test that is used to measure a club's ongoing qualification for exemption under §501(c)(7). Prior to 1976, clubs had to operate "exclusively" for nonprofit purposes, and the regulations[55] provided that a club that engaged in business activity was not exempt, but no precise numerical test existed. Note that this regulation, originally proposed in 1956 and adopted in 1958, has not been revised since.

(a) 35/15 Test

The revenue test is two-pronged. First, an overall test requires that nonmember receipts, including investment income, cannot equal more than 35% of the club's "traditional, normal and usual activity." Extraordinary and nonrecurring income, such as gain on the clubhouse sale or member initiation and capital assessment fees, are excluded from the denominator and numerator for this test. Irregularly held events (but not annual events) are not counted. The revenues from a golf tournament held every twenty years were not counted in the test, although it was subject to the tax on unrelated business income.[56] Capital gains from investment activity and unrelated business income (including that set aside for charity) are also included in gross receipts.[57] The second prong of the test regards nonmember revenue only. The IRS provides the following guidelines for measuring nonmember usage and revenue:[58]

- Gross receipts from the general public (nonmember) facility and service charges may not exceed 15% of total receipts.

- The revenue generated from guest charges can be attributed to members if the guests are bonafide and the member pays for the guest charges.

- Reciprocal membership arrangements do not turn a visitor into a member of a visited club.[59]

For auditing purposes, the IRS guidelines say groups of eight or fewer persons that include one member are counted as a member receipt. For larger parties, guests may be treated as members if 75% or more of the particular group using

---

[54] P.L. 94-568, 94th Cong. 2d Sess. (1976).
[55] Reg. §1.501(c)(7)-1(b).
[56] Priv. Ltr. Rul. 7838018.
[57] Senate Report 94-1318, 2nd Session, 1976-2 C.B. 597, 599.
[58] Rev. Proc. 71-17, 1971-1 C.B. 683.
[59] Gen. Coun. Memo. 39343; Rev. Proc. 71-17.

club facilities are members of that group. Typical business luncheon clubs hosting the Rotary Club, tax study forums, and similar groups have a hard time meeting this test.

(b) Failing the Test

Failure of the 35/15 test in one year does not necessarily cause immediate revocation of exemption. The facts and circumstances of each case can be considered individually when the club makes its case for continued exemption. The IRS is more likely to be sympathetic if an organization fails the test because of an unusual or occasional special event, as opposed to receiving regular, perhaps daily, funds from nonmembers.[60] If the club experiences a one-year failure out of a number of years—as opposed to small and recurring annual failures—continued qualification is more likely. The purpose for which facilities are made available to nonmembers will also be considered.

Accounting records are essential to document nonmember use and proper categories of gross receipts. The IRS procedures[61] contain detailed criteria which clubs serving nonmembers must study carefully to distinguish between member and nonmember income. The total income of a club failing to keep the required details may become subject to the unrelated business income tax. The type of records a club should maintain regularly include:

- Date and description of club usage
- Number in each party, indicating members and nonmembers
- Total charges attributable to members and nonmembers
- Charges paid by nonmembers (based upon signed statements regarding reimbursements, including those of employers).

9.5   UNRELATED BUSINESS INCOME TAX

Social clubs are significantly different from other tax-exempt entities in one important respect: the definition of their revenues that are subject to the unrelated business income (UBI) tax. IRC §512(a)(3)(A) provides a special definition for social clubs, as well as voluntary employee benefit associations (VEBAs), group legal services plans, and supplemental unemployment funds. Taxable income for such groups is defined expansively to include all gross income other than exempt function income. Many of the exceptions and modifications that exclude investment and passive income from tax for other types of tax-exempt organizations, including the corporate dividend deduction, are not available to shelter a club's unrelated income.[62]

Exempt function income of a social club is "gross income from dues, fees, charges, or similar amounts paid by members of the organization as consideration

---

[60] Exempt Organizations Handbook (IRM 7751) §733(1).
[61] Rev. Proc. 71-17, *supra,* n. 51.
[62] See Chapter 21 for discussion of these rules.

for providing such members or their dependents or guest goods, facilities, or services constituting the basis for exemption." All other social club income is subject to regular income tax, including nonmember revenues, special events, open golf tournaments, royalties, rents, dividends, interest, and other unrelated business income. Losses attributable to nonmember club usage are not necessarily deductible against other types of taxable income.

In view of the limited tax exemption permitted to social clubs, such groups have to carefully consider the advisability of seeking or maintaining tax-exempt status. Due to the interaction of the limitation on the deduction of nonmember losses and the taxability of investment income, some groups might incur a higher tax bill as an exempt entity. A previously taxable social club must carefully project the potential tax savings, if any, from conversion to exempt status. To compound the problem, appreciation inherent in a club's assets may be reportable upon the conversion as taxable gain pursuant to regulations under §337(d).[63]

(a) Rationale for Different UBI Treatment

In extending the unrelated business income tax to social clubs in 1969, Congress reiterated its intention to allow individuals to join together to provide recreational or social facilities or other benefits on a mutual basis without tax consequences. However, it made clear that tax exemption is proper applied only to sources of income generated from membership activity. When the club receives income from sources outside the membership, such as interest income on its savings or charges to outsiders for use of its facilities, it is taxed. Exempting such income from tax would allow club members to use tax-free dollars to pay for recreational and pleasure pursuits.

(b) Limitations on Deductions

As a general rule, unrelated business taxable income means the gross income derived by any organization from any unrelated trade or business regularly carried on by it, less the deductions allowed by this chapter (of the Internal Revenue Code) that are directly connected with the carrying on of such business.[64] Concepts used to identify a direct connection of an expense to a particular type of revenue are fairly vague and sometimes difficult to apply.[65] Calculating permissible expense deductions is difficult where exempt functions are carried on in connection with nonexempt activities. For social clubs, this problem is particularly an issue for member and nonmember services.

(c) Nonmember Losses

Unless club facilities and services are made available to nonmembers with the intention of producing a profit—as opposed to simply recouping costs—losses from serving nonmembers are not deductible against club income subject to the unre-

---

[63] See discussion in Chapter 21§10(e).
[64] IRC §512(a)(1).
[65] See Chapter 27§14(d).

lated business income tax. During the 1980s, the IRS and social clubs fought in the courts about offsetting losses from nonmember activities against investment income. The battle was fought on two different fronts: (1) how to calculate the loss, that is, what portion of the club's fixed, or indirect, expenses are deductible, and (2) the deductibility of the loss itself. Permissible deductions are those expenses that are directly connected with the production of gross income otherwise allowed by the code, that is, ordinary and necessary business expenses allowed to for-profit businesses under §162. Beginning in 1981, the IRS took the position that a profit motive must be present for the income-producing activity for associated expenses to qualify as allowable trade or business expenses so that activities without profit motive could not be aggregated with those with profit motive.[66]

In a 1985 memorandum decision, the Tax Court adopted a narrower position in deciding that expenses attributable to nonmember activity were not "connected with the production of" income at all. In 1986, the Second Circuit Court of Appeals overruled the decision and held that all ordinary and necessary expenses of producing nonmember income, including investment income, were deductions only so long as they were incurred for the purpose of producing a profit.[67] North Ridge Country Club[68] lost its battle on this front in 1989 after the Cleveland Athletic Club[69] convinced the Sixth Circuit to allow such losses. In June 1990 the Supreme Court unanimously decided that the Portland Golf Club's nonmember activity losses were not deductible against investment income, because the activity was neither profitable nor profit motivated. To calculate the loss for both purposes, direct and indirect costs had to be taken into account.[70] The Supreme Court agreed with the IRS's long-standing position that fixed and indirect expenses, which the club incurs whether or not it serves nonmembers, are not deductible to the extent they exceed nonmember income. Essentially, a social club cannot deduct an allocable portion of its basic member fixed expenses against its investment income, unless the nonmember activity is profit motivated. The Court looked to the hobby loss standards of IRC §183 to test the profit motivation, particularly because the Portland Gold Club incurred losses in every year from 1975 through 1984.

(d) Direct and Indirect Costs

The issue of deductible expenses is even more complicated, because two types of expenses are involved in calculating the profit or loss from any activity of the club:

1. *Fixed or indirect expenses,* such as club facility costs, insurance, mortgage interest, depreciation, utilities, managers, and other overhead, which the club incurs to serve its basic membership and sustains whether or not nonmembers are served ("but for expenses")

---

[66] Rev. Rul. 81-69, 1981-1 C.B. 351.

[67] *The Brook, Inc. v. Commissioner,* 86-2 U.S.T.C. §9646 (2nd Cir. 1989), *rev'g* 50 T.C.M. 959, 51 TCM 133 (1985).

[68] *North Ridge Country Club v. Commissioner,* 89-1 U.S.T.C. §9363 (9th Cir. 1989), *rev'g* 89 T.C. 563 (1987).

[69] *Cleveland Athletic Club, Inc. v. U.S.,* 86-1 U.S.T.C. §9116 (6th Cir. 1986).

[70] *Portland Golf Club v. Commissioner,* 90-1 U.S.T.C. §50,332 (110 S. Ct. 2780, 1990).

2. *Variable or direct expenses,* such as food, waiters, golf caddies, and other expenses incurred in direct relationship to number of persons served, including members and nonmembers

The confusion starts from the fact that terms normally used in cost accounting texts—fixed and variable, direct and indirect—are absent from the code. The regulations only add a stipulation that the expenses must have a proximate and primary relationship to the income and provide for allocation of expenses attributable to both related and unrelated income.

(e) How to Measure Profit Motive

A secondary, but important, aspect of the *Portland Golf Club* case was an argument about how to measure profit motive. Are both direct and indirect costs taken into account? Or is the fact that the nonmember direct income covers nonmember direct expenses (without any reduction for allocable indirect expense) sufficient evidence of profit motive? The Portland Golf Club argued that since its nonmember income exceeded its nonmember direct expenses, it had a profit motive. The Court disagreed, and unless Congress acts to change the tax laws, profit motive for this purpose is calculated by deducting both direct and indirect costs associated with nonmember income.

Another issue to consider is whether one cost allocation method can be used to measure profit motive while another method is used to calculate taxable income. This issue was not settled in Portland Golf Club, although most justices thought that only one method can be used for both purposes. The question then becomes which method to use. Any method reasonably calculated to arrive at a fair allocation, and consistently applied, can be used. The regulations under IRC §512 provide that allocations must be made on a reasonable basis. The two basic methods used in the social club field are:

1. *Gross-to-gross method.* Actual gross revenues from members and nonmembers are used to allocate the costs.

2. *Actual use method.* Square footage occupied and hours of actual use are tabulated to calculate fixed cost allocations. Here, the numerator of the equation is important. In a case involving a football stadium, the IRS and taxpayers have argued whether the proper divisor is the total number of hours in the year or the total number of hours the stadium was used. See Chapter 27§14 for further discussion of cost allocations.

(f) Aggregating Nonmember Activities

The last issue is whether all nonmember activities can be aggregated to evaluate profit motive and allocable costs. The Tax Court sided with the Atlanta Athletic Club to allow aggregation. Losses from nonmember food and beverage sales and facility fees (e.g., golf greens, tennis, pool) were deductible against profits from two professional golf tournaments. The club argued that there was a common business purpose for promoting its nonmember undertakings, but the IRS said that each activity had to be considered separately, and any profitable activities taxed. The club's victory was only partial. The overall loss from nonmember activity was not deductible against other investment income because the court found the requisite profit motive lacking, following the Portland rationale.[71]

(g) Charitable Set-Asides

A special provision contained in IRC §512(a)(3)(B)(i) excludes income otherwise taxable as unrelated business income from tax to the extent the funds are set aside for charitable purposes. Essentially an unlimited charitable deduction is allowed to a social club for income paid directly for charitable purposes described in IRC §170(c) and for funds accumulated or earmarked for such purposes in the future. This deduction is claimed in a specially designed portion of Form 990-T.[72]

Setting aside means something more than simply showing that a club expended a portion of its overall funds annually on charitable projects. Specific board action or stated policy, isolation or designation of the funds, or other overt actions are necessary to prove that funds are earmarked or set aside exclusively for (c)(3) purposes. In the case of a cooking club, the club's records did not show or prove that investment income, rather than subscriptions and membership fees, had been used to pay to publish an educational magazine.[73] Lacking proof that some other funds rather than investment income had paid, no set-aside deduction was permitted. Similarly a court ruled that the Phi Delta Theta fraternity magazine was not educational, but rather served the recreational purposes of the members. Endowment income used to support the publication did not qualify for the charitable set-aside donation.[74]

(h) Sales of Real Estate

A gain from sale of real estate used in regular club activity to perform its exempt function may also be classed as unrelated business income to the extent that the proceeds are *not* reinvested one year before or three years after the date of its sale.[75] The phrase "used in regular club activities" does not necessarily include property contiguous to the club held for possible future expansion or simply to protect the club from the suburbs.[76] Only that property in actual, direct, continuous, and regular use for social and recreational purposes qualifies. For example, a steep buffer tract heavily wooded with thick undergrowth, was found not to be used directly in exempt functions. Even though it served to isolate the club from the surrounding developed area and roads, its physical condition indicated that it was not devoted to exempt activity. Proceeds from granting a permanent easement for passage and

---

[71] *Atlanta Athletic Club v. Commissioner,* T.C. Memo. 1991-83 (1991).
[72] Schedule G is reproduced in Appendix 27-7.
[73] *Confrerie de la Chaine des Rotisseurs v. Commissioner,* T.C. Memo. 1993-637.
[74] *Phi Delta Theta Fraternity v. Commissioner,* 887 F.2d 1302 (6th Cir. 1989), *aff'g* 90 T.C.B. 1033 (1988).
[75] IRC §512(a)(3)(D).
[76] *Cleveland Athletic Club v. Commissioner,* T.C. Memo. 1991-83 (1991); *Framingham Country Club v. U.S.,* 659 F. Supp. 650 (D. Mass. 1987).

use of the buffer produced taxable gain.[77] But where the proceeds of sale of a scenic easement to view the club's golf course were reinvested in improving the course, the proceeds were not taxable.[78]

Because social clubs, particularly country clubs, often own highly appreciated real estate, the reinvestment rule requires particular attention. A sale of such property can have two negative consequences: (1) a significant tax liability if the proceeds are not used to purchase other property to be used by the club and (2) loss of exempt status due to failure of the 35/15 test[79] when the sale of the property is treated as nonmember revenue. The cutting of timber from a wildlife preserve necessary to maintain its usefulness was not, in the IRS's opinion, a business activity because the club's exempt purposes were furthered. Nonetheless, the sale generated unrelated business income because the activity was not a direct exempt function.[80] Additional developments concerning the treatment of gains on sales of club real estate as taxable unrelated business income are presented in Chapter 21§8(g).

(i) IRS Compliance Program

When the IRS applied its Exempt Organization Returns and Inventory Classification System (EORICS) to social clubs in September 1996 it found over 1400 social clubs with investment income reflected on their Form 990 that had not filed Form 990-T. Though they did not collect significant revenues, the IRS conducted audits of some 500 social clubs. They announced a program of public education for clubs. The IRS handbook applicable to social clubs was updated[81] and a new publication 3079, *Gaming Publication for Tax-Exempt Organizations* was issued.

9.6 FILING AND DISCLOSURE REQUIREMENTS

Social clubs file Form 1024[82] for recognition of tax exemption under IRC §501(c)(7) and file Form 990 or 990EZ annually to report financial activity to the IRS. Form 990T is filed to report income subject to UBI tax.[83] A nonexempt membership club (or one whose exemption has been revoked) files Form 1120 as a regular corporation. A taxable club is subject to the special limitations of IRC §277. Essentially expenses attributable to membership activities are only allowed as a deduction to the extent of membership income.

Tax-exempt social clubs must disclose the fact that payments to the organization are not deductible as charitable contributions. The nondeductibility disclosure must be printed on all invoices issued to members in soliciting dues and other payments as described in detail in Chapter 6§4.

---

[77] Tech. Adv. Memo. 9225001.
[78] Priv. Ltr. Rul. 9824045.
[79] Described in §9.4.
[80] Gen. Coun. Memo. 39688 (December 18, 1987).
[81] Chapter 38 of IRM 7.8.2, Exempt Organizations Technical Guidelines Handbook.
[82] Explained and illustrated in Chapter 18.
[83] Reproduced in Appendix 27-7 and discussed in Chapter 27§14.

Social club dues are generally not deductible as a business expense. Effective January 1, 1994, the code disallows a deduction for amounts paid or incurred for membership in any club organized for business, pleasure, recreation, or other social purpose.[84] The limitation applies to clubs the principal purpose of which is to conduct entertainment activities for its members or their guests or to provide access to entertainment facilities. Examples given are country clubs, golf and athletic clubs, airline clubs, hotel clubs, and clubs operated to provide meals under circumstances generally considered to be conducive to business discussion. Dues paid to professional, civic, or public service organizations, such as the Rotary or Lions Club, are deductible if paid for business reasons and the principal purpose of the group is not to conduct entertainment activities.[85] Before 1994, dues or fees paid to social clubs were deductible when it could be shown business discussions occurred.

[84] §274(a)(3).
[85] Reg. §1.274-2(a)(iii).

CHAPTER TEN

Instrumentalities of Government and Title-Holding Corporations

10.1 §501(c)(1) INSTRUMENTALITIES OF THE UNITED STATES

The Internal Revenue Code (IRC) §501(c)(1) exempts "instrumentalities" of the United States organized specifically under an act of Congress. Among these instrumentalities are the following:

- Federal Deposit Insurance Corporation (FDIC)

- Federal Home Loan Banks

- Federal Land Banks

- Federal Intermediate Credit Banks

- Federal National Mortgage Association (FNMA)

- Federal Reserve Bank

- Federal Crop Insurance Corporation

- United States Housing Authority

- Pennsylvania Avenue Development Corporation

- Federal Credit Unions

- Pension Benefit Guaranty Corporation

These creations of Congress are considered exempt because they are wholly owned by the United States government. They are not required to file annual information returns nor to apply for exemption from income tax.

10.2   GOVERNMENTAL UNITS

States, their municipalities, and other divisions thereof, interestingly, are not exempted by any part of §501(c) though they by definition could qualify under IRC §501(c)(3) because they relieve the burdens of government.[1] Although a governmental unit is separately organized, it is not entitled to exemption because of its sovereign powers to tax and to exercise eminent domain and police powers.[2] IRC §170(b)(1)(A)(v) provides for a charitable contribution deduction for a *governmental unit* defined as:

> A State, a possession of the United States, or any political subdivision of any of the foregoing, or the United States or the District of Columbia, but only if the contribution or gift is made for exclusively public purposes.

The regulations under IRC §170 do not define what is meant by a *political subdivision*. One must look to the rules of IRC §103, Interest on State and Local Bonds, to find out what the term denotes:

> Any division of any State or local governmental unit which is a municipal corporation or which has been delegated the right to exercise part of the sovereign power of the unit. As thus defined, a political subdivision of any State or local governmental unit may or may not include special assessment districts so created, such as road, water, sewer, . . . and similar districts.

The term most simply means a jurisdictional or geographical component of a state, such as a county and city. A 1944 court complicated the meaning by saying it must be broad and comprehensive and denotes any division of the state made by the proper authorities thereof, acting within their constitutional powers, for the purpose of carrying out a portion of these functions of the state that by long usage and the inherent necessities of government have always been regarded as public.[3]

To clarify their federal filing requirements, the IRS in 1995 added two more classes of organizations to the IRC §6033 list of those not required to file Form 990—governmental units and affiliates of governmental units. An organization is treated as a governmental unit for this purpose if:[4]

- It is a state or local governmental unit as defined in Reg. §1.103-1(b);

[1] See discussion in Chapter 4§3.
[2] Rev. Rul. 60-384, 1960-2 C.B. 172; see also the IRS 1996 Exempt Organizations CPE Text, Chapter F. *State Institutions -Instrumentalities,* by Joseph O'Malley, Elizabeth Mayer, and Marvin Friedlander.
[3] *Commissioner v. Estate of Alexander J. Shamburg,* 3 T.C. 131, *aff'd,* 144 F.2d 998 (2d Cir.), *cert. denied,* 323 U.S. 792 (1944).
[4] Rev. Proc. 95-48, 1995-47 I.R.B. 13.

- It is entitled to receive deductible charitable contributions as an organization described in IRC §170(c)(1) of the Code; or

- It is an Indian tribal government, or a political subdivision thereof, under IRC §§7701(a)(40) and 7871.

An organization is treated as an affiliate of a governmental unit if it meets one of two sets of criteria as follows:

1. It has a ruling or determination from the IRS that:

    - Its income, derived from activities constituting the basis for its exemption under IRC §501(c), is excluded from gross income under IRC §115.

    - It is entitled to receive deductible charitable contributions under IRC §170(c)(1) on the basis that contributions to it are "for the use of" governmental units.

    - It is a wholly owned instrumentality of a state or a political subdivision thereof, for employment tax purposes.

2. It does not have an IRS determination, but:

    - It is either "operated, supervised, or controlled by" governmental units, or by organizations that are affiliates of governmental units, or the members of the organization's governing body are elected by the public at large, pursuant to local statute or ordinance;

    - It possesses two or more of the affiliation factors in the following list; or

    - Its filing of Form 990 is not otherwise necessary to the efficient administration of internal revenue laws.

Affiliation factors that are considered for this purpose include:

- The organization was created by one or more governmental units or a government affiliate, or by public officials acting in their official capacity.

- The organization's support is received principally from taxes, tolls, fines, government appropriations, or fees collected pursuant to statutory authority. Amounts received as government grants or other contract payments are not qualifying support for this purpose.

- The organization is financially accountable to one or more government units or affiliates thereof.

- One or more governmental units or affiliates exercises control over, or oversees, some or all of the organization's expenditures.

- Upon dissolution, its assets will be distributed to one or more governmental units or affiliate thereof.

Before issuance of the 1995 procedure, the definition of a governmental unit was found in IRS rulings issued in the 1970s. These rulings required that organizations qualified as governmental units have three important powers—to tax, to enforce laws, and to exercise eminent domain—a requirement is not contained in the procedure outlined above. Examples of entities qualifying as governmental units in rulings compared to those that do not follow:

- A rapid transit authority created by a state legislative act was empowered to issue bonds, exercise police powers, set rates, enforce its rules with a security force, and realize indirect benefit from taxes imposed and eminent domain exercised by participating local governmental bodies. The authority had sufficient sovereign powers of the state to constitute a governmental unit.[5]

- A community development authority similarly created under state laws to collect service and user fees for the construction, operation, and maintenance of community facilities was not classed as a governmental unit. It lacked the power to tax, power of eminent domain, and control over zoning, policy, and fire protection.[6]

- A state university without the three powers may not qualify as a political subdivision.[7]

- An unincorporated intergovernmental cooperative organization established by an act of the Texas legislature on behalf of a consortium of eleven Texas public school districts was found to be a private foundation, not a governmental unit, for two reasons:[8]

  1. Its source of support was a particular private foundation that granted it the money to undertake its curriculum research and development.

  2. It was not a governmental unit. Although the cooperative arguably was an instrumentality of the state because it had the required sovereign powers of eminent domain, it did not have the power to assess and collect taxes nor did it have police powers. The fact that it was an integral part of a group of governmental units—the public schools by which it was established—did not make it a governmental unit.

The Michigan Education Trust fought an interesting battle to qualify for tax exemption. It was created as a state agency to collect and receive advanced state college tuition, its board members were appointed by the governor, and its investments were managed by employees of the state treasury. Its assets, however, were not available to state creditors and were returnable to the "investors" upon dissolution. The IRS and a district court agreed that the trust was neither an instrumentality of the state nor a governmental unit and instead benefited the individual students who were to earn tax-free interest on their college savings. The Sixth Circuit Court disagreed and found the trust to be an integral part, or political subdivision, of the State of Michigan.[9]

[5] Rev. Rul. 73-563, 1973-2 C.B. 24.
[6] Rev. Rul. 77-164, 1977-1 C.B. 20.
[7] Rev. Rul. 77-165, 1977-1 C.B. 21.
[8] *Texas Learning Technology Group v. Commissioner,* 96 T.C. 28 (April 30, 1991).
[9] *Michigan v. United States,* 40 F.3d 817 (6th Cir. 1994), *rev'g* 92-2 USTC ¶50,424 (W.D. Mich. 1992); Priv. Ltr. Rul. 8825027.

Congress responded to the pressure about the Michigan decision and the 11 other states that, by July 1996, had tuition prepayment plans in place (Alabama, Alaska, Florida, Kentucky, Louisiana, Massachusetts, Michigan, Ohio, Pennsylvania, Texas, and Wyoming) by creating a new category of exempt organization. IRC §529, entitled *Qualified State Tuition Programs,* exempts such plans and their investment income, except to the extent to which they may be subject to the unrelated business income tax.[10] A *qualified program* is defined as one established or maintained by a state or instrumentality of a state under which a person may purchase tuition credits or may contribute to an account established to pay the qualified higher education expense of a designated beneficiary. Such expenses include tuition, fees, books, supplies, and equipment required for enrollment or attendance at an eligible education institution.

10.3 §501(c)(2) TITLE-HOLDING CORPORATIONS

According to IRC §501(c)(2), "Corporations organized for the exclusive purpose of holding title to property, collecting income therefrom, and turning over the entire amount thereof, less expenses, to an organization that itself is exempt" under IRC §501 are title-holding companies (THCs). After some years of confusion and hesitation, IRC §501(c)(25) was added in 1986 to permit THCs with multiple parents.

Essentially, a title-holding corporation is a passive entity whose tax exemption stems from its subservient relationship to another exempt organization. The full range of §501 organizations discussed in this part and pension plans are permissible beneficiaries. If the organization on whose behalf the property is held loses its tax exemption, the THC also does.[11] A THC is traditionally formed to shelter the property transferred to it and assets it purchases from exposure to liability for claims asserted against its creator(s) although the reverse can occur if the property has inherent risk. A separate property-owning arm may also be created for administrative or management reasons, or to permit joint ownership under §501(c)(25).

(a) Organizational and Operational Requirements

As its names implies, a qualifying IRC §501(c)(2) title-holding corporation cannot be a trust, joint venture, or other unincorporated form of organization. It must be a corporation or an association classified as a corporation.[12] The *exclusive purpose* clause of the statute is strictly applied. The THC's purpose is reflected by its charter, its activities, and the facts and circumstances under which it was created. All of these factors are taken into account by the IRS in evaluating evidence that a THC's purposes are strictly limited to those provided in the statute. A THC will not be granted exemption if it engages in any business other than that of holding title to property and collecting income therefrom.[13] The income can be generated

[10] Small Business Job Protection Act of 1996, §1806.
[11] Rev. Rul. 68-371, 1968-2 C.B. 204.
[12] IRC §7701(a)(3).
[13] Reg. §1501(c)(2)-1; Senate Report No. 2375, 81st Congress, 2d Session (1950), 1950-2 C.B. 483, 504.

by normal investment sources such as interest income on bonds held or rental income to commercial tenants.[14] A charter containing language that empowers the organization to engage in broader activities is not acceptable.[15] When the charter language contains the appropriate constraints but the organization's proposed or actual activity goes beyond the limits, exemption may be denied. The (c)(25) THC must also comply with the specific requirements regarding beneficiary organizations and activities.

Connection to Beneficiary Organization.   The amount of control and the relationship that must exist between the title-holding corporation and the exempt organization it benefits are not specified in the statute or in the regulation (which is only two paragraphs long). However, the IRS *Exempt Organizations Handbook* provides some guidelines.

A parent–subsidiary relationship is the most common form for a THC. As a rule, the THC must be controlled by and be responsive to the exempt organization for which it holds property, despite the lack of specific requirements in the statute or regulations. In the IRS's view, the elements of control necessary include owning the voting stock of the THC, possessing the power to select nominees to hold the voting stock, or having the ability to appoint the directors.[16] A group of philanthropists was not allowed to establish a THC that would have essentially circumvented the private foundation rules.

A single controlling beneficiary organization is ostensibly required for §501(c)(2) entities. The long-standing policy of the IRS was to consider multiple parents as evidence of asset pooling, not mere holding of title.[17] However, for some years the IRS debated the possibility that "conceivably a title-holding company might hold title for more than one kind of exempt."[18] Fortunately, in 1986 Congress created §501(c)25, allowing pooled ownership in real estate by a group of tax-exempt organizations.

The method of a title-holding company's formation may be influenced by state or local rules. In one example, a title-holding company was approved despite its being controlled by a broad individual base of members (a college fraternity), when the stock conferred no rights to dividends or distributions to members. All of the income from the property was payable to the §501(c)(7) organization.[19] A THC controlled by and created to benefit a private foundation is subject to the additional constraints explained in Chapters 12 through 17.

Restrictions on Activity.   The operating powers of a THC must be limited to those required to hold title to, conserve, keep up the property, and remit income to the beneficiary organization. The property held by a (c)(2) THC can include real and personal property, investments, and exempt function assets.[20] A (c)(25) THC,

---

[14] Rev. Ruls. 69-381, 1969-2 C.B. 113 and 81-108, 1981-1 C.B. 327.
[15] Rev. Rul. 58-455, 1958-2 C.B. 261.
[16] Rev. Rul. 71-544, 1971-2 C.B. 227.
[17] Gen. Coun. Memo. 39341 and 37551.
[18] IRS Exempt Organizations Handbook (IRM 7751) §281.
[19] Rev. Rul. 68-222, 1968-1 C.B. 243.
[20] Rev. Rul. 76-335, 1976-2 C.B. 141.

however, can only hold real estate. Traditionally, the title-holding corporation holds assets that need protection from exposure to operational liability, but can also hold property that would expose the benefited organization to unacceptable risks. There is no express reason why operational or exempt function assets, real or personal, cannot be kept in a (c)(2) holding company. Actively operating exempt functions by the THC within the facility, however, is not permissible because it goes beyond "title-holding." A subsidiary of a veterans organization that held title to a building *and* operated the social facilities located in the building was not permitted THC status.[21]

An activity that generates unrelated business income (UBI) is generally not appropriate to be carried on by a THC, although certain types of UBI associated with real estate operations can be earned. Such income includes debt-financed income under IRC §514, net profits-based rental transactions, personal property rentals (alongside real property), and investment income earned by a title-holding entity taxed because it benefits a social club or voluntary employee benefits association (VEBA).[22]

Effective January 1, 1994, a (c)(2) or (c)(25) title-holding company is permitted to receive up to 10% of its gross income as unrelated income so long as the income is incidentally derived from ownership of real estate, such as parking lot fees. Such income is still subject to the unrelated business income tax, but will not cause the title-holding company to lose its exemption.

Passive investments suitable as (c)(2) THC holdings include stocks and bonds, rental real estate, and oil and gas royalties or production payments. Equipment related alongside real estate is also acceptable, and is common among universities and hospitals. Operating a merchandise store, managing a hotel, providing investment management services,[23] holding a working interest in an oil well, and other active business pursuits are not permitted.[24] When business activity is anticipated, the property should instead be spun off or transferred to a taxable "feeder" subsidiary.[25]

For UBI purposes, IRC §511(c) provides that the THC is to be treated as being organized for the same purposes for which its parent is organized, if it meets two requirements:

1. It turns over all of the net income to the parent; and

2. It files a consolidated return with the parent.

(b) Turning Over the Income

Accumulation of surplus income by a title-holding corporation generally is contrary to the statutory theme of *turning over the income*. As a rule, all net income must be paid over to the beneficiary organization. Deductions for depreciation[26]

---

[21] Rev. Rul. 66-150, 1966-1 C.B. 147.
[22] Reg. 1.501(c)(2)-1(a); see Chapter 21 for a more detailed definition of UBI.
[23] Rev. Rul. 69-528, 1969-2 C.B. 127.
[24] Rev. Rul. 66-295, 1966-2 C.B. 207.
[25] As defined in IRC §502.
[26] Rev. Rul. 66-102, 1966-1 C.B. 133.

and reserves or sinking funds to make current or future mortgage payments[27] are allowed to be withheld from income required to be turned over. A reasonable provision for maintenance or restoration of the property can also be deducted from distributable income. Rents can also be used to repay an interest-free construction loan through an organization also controlled by the THC's parent.[28] Regarding the timing for distribution of funds, there is no specific requirement, but a delay with no justification, as evidenced by a substantial surplus, might be expected to bring IRS scrutiny.

Payment to the beneficiary is customarily made in the form of cash dividends, or grants in the case of a nonstock corporation. When the THC owns the building occupied by the parent and no rent is paid, there may be no income generated and available to be paid. In such cases, the rent-free use of the building fulfills the statutory scheme.

(c) Why Form a Title-Holding Corporation?

A number of factors must be considered before deciding to form a title-holding corporation. Among the advantages of a THC are the opportunity it provides to shelter some assets from operating fund liabilities and the possibility of increasing the beneficiary organization's borrowing power. Setting up a THC can also facilitate separate management and administration of a corporation's physical plant. A THC might also be created to serve as a nonmember form of property ownership for a member-controlled organization.

There is, of course, a down side to the formation of a title-holding corporation. First, it increases paperwork burdens: Form 1024 must be filed to seek IRS recognition of its exemption and a separate Form 990 must be filed annually if gross receipts normally exceed $25,000. Some relief of the compliance burden may be gained by filing a consolidated tax return, which is permitted by IRC §1504(e).

On the other hand, there are situations in which the formation of a THC is ill-advised. The tax exemption of the THC is dependent upon the continued qualification of its beneficiary. If the parent company loses its exemption, the THC automatically loses its §501(c)(2) status.[29] Also, the THC cannot be used as a fundraising vehicle, because donations to a THC generally do not qualify as charitable contributions under IRC §170. In a private ruling, the IRS has held that gifts to the parent but dedicated expressly to a charitable project conducted by a THC were deductible.[30]

10.4 §501(c)(25) TITLE-HOLDING CORPORATIONS

An IRC §501(c)(25) title-holding corporation serves a very narrow but significant purpose: to facilitate pooled purchasing and holding of real estate by a group of nonprofit organizations. It can hold no other type of asset and is only available to

---

[27] Rev. Rul. 77-429, 1977-2 C.B. 189.
[28] Priv. Ltr. Rul. 9213027.
[29] Rev. Rul. 68-371, 1968-2 C.B. 204.
[30] Priv. Ltr. Rul. 8705041.

four specified types of tax-exempt organizations. Multiple unrelated exempt organizations may form a THC so long as it possesses the following characteristics:

- It must be a corporation or a trust;
- It must have no more than 35 shareholders or beneficiaries;
- It must have only one class of stock or beneficial interest;
- It must be organized for the exclusive purposes of acquiring real property, holding title to and collecting the income from such property, and remitting the income (net of expenses) to one or more qualifying shareholders or beneficiaries; and
- Its shareholders must be one of the following types of organizations:
  - §501(c)(3) organization,
  - §401(a) qualified employee plan,
  - §414(d) government plan, or
  - Federal, state, or local government agency or instrumentality.

Since this type of exempt organization was created in 1986, the IRS has issued two notices providing detailed guidance for their establishment, which must be carefully studied by anyone contemplating the creation of a (c)(25) THC. The expanded criteria for qualification as fleshed out by the IRS include:[31]

- The articles of incorporation, bylaws, or trust document must contain language that clearly demonstrates that the entity satisfies the five statutory requirements previously listed.
- Removal of the investment advisor must be permitted by a majority vote of the beneficial owners.
- Termination of a beneficiary's interest must be allowed in one of only two ways: (1) By selling or exchanging its stock or interest to another qualifying (c)(25) organization (provided that the total number of shareholders remains below 35), or (2) Upon 90 days notice, by having its shares or beneficial interest redeemed.

---

[31] IRS Notice 87-18, 1987-1 C.B. 455; IRS Notice 88-121, 1988-2 C.B. 457. There are no regulations nor published or private rulings on this code section as this chapter is being updated in 1998.

CHAPTER ELEVEN

Public Charities

The significance of "public charity" status for organizations tax exempt under Internal Revenue Code (IRC) §501(c)(3) is multifaceted, and is of utmost importance to both private and public exempt organizations. Knowing the meaning of the four parts of IRC §509 is the key to understanding public charities. *All* §501(c)(3) organizations, other than those listed in §509(a)(1), (2), (3), and (4) are private foundations, and are subject to the operational constraints outlined in Chapters 12 through 17. The specific requirements of each of the §509 categories are described below. Briefly, the four categories of public charities are:

- §509(a)(1)—Organizations engaging in inherently public activity and those supported by the general public

- §509(a)(2)—Organizations supported by charges for services

- §509(a)(3)—Supporting organizations

- §509(a)(4)—Organizations that test for public safety

11.1 DISTINCTIONS BETWEEN PUBLIC AND PRIVATE CHARITIES

Private foundations must comply with a variety of special rules and sanctions, so it is useful, when possible, to obtain and maintain public status. The important attributes of private foundations (PFs), compared to public charities (in parentheses) include:

- The deduction for contributions by individuals to PFs is limited to 30% of the donor's adjusted gross income (AGI) for cash gifts, and 20% for appreciated property gifts.[1] (Up to 50% of a donor's AGI can be deducted for cash gifts to public charity, and 30% for gifts of appreciated property.) To illustrate, assume that a generous taxpayer with an income of $1 million wants to annually give $500,000 in cash for charitable pursuits. Only $300,000 of the annual gift would be deductible if it is given to a private foundation. The full $500,000 is deductible if it is given to a public charity.

- Appreciated property (other than corporate stock for which a quotation is readily available on an established securities market) is not fully deductible when given to a PF—only the basis of real estate, closely held company stock, or other types of property is deductible.[2] (A full fair market value (FMV) deduction is potentially available for a gift of such property to a public charity.)

- An excise tax of two percent must be paid on a PF's investment income.[3] (There is no tax on investment income for a public charity.)

- A PF cannot buy or sell property, nor enter into most self-dealing transactions with its directors, officers, contributors, or their family members, under any circumstances.[4] (Public charities can have business dealings with their insiders, within limits.)[5]

- Annual returns must be filed by all PFs regardless of support levels and value of assets. (No return is required for certain public organizations, and an EZ form is available for many others.)[6]

[1] IRC §170(b)(1)(B).
[2] IRC §170(e)(1)(B) and (e)(5); unless the property is redistributed; see Chapter 15§4(a).
[3] Outlined in Chapter 13.
[4] Discussed in Chapter 14.
[5] Discussed in Chapter 20.
[6] See Chapter 27.

- Fund raising between PFs is constrained by expenditure responsibility requirements that prohibit one private foundation from giving to another without contractual agreements and follow-up procedures.[7] (No such policing of grant paid is required for public charities.)

- Absolutely no lobbying activity by PFs is permitted.[8] (Limited amount of lobbying permitted for public charities under two different systems for measuring permissible amount.)[9] Absolutely no *political* activity is permitted either for public or private charities.

- A PF's annual spending for grants to other organizations and charitable projects must meet a "minimum distribution" requirement.[10] (A public charity has no specific spending requirement.)[11]

- Holding more than 20% of a business enterprise, including shares owned by board members and contributors, is prohibited for PFs as are jeopardizing investments.[12] (No such limits are placed on public charities.)

- The full FMV of appreciated property, such as land, art works, or a partnership interest, is not deductible when the property is donated to a private, nonoperating, foundation. Stocks for which market quotations are readily available are deductible.[13] (A full deduction is potentially available for most types of property donated to a public charity and private operating foundation.)

- A PF cannot buy or sell property, nor enter into self-dealing transactions with its directors, officers, contributors, or their family members, under most circumstances. (Public charities can have business dealings with their insiders, within limits, subject to reasonableness standards. If excessive salaries or purchase price is paid to an insider, intermediate standards may be imposed.)[14] Exhibit 11-1 summarizes these differences.

11.2 "INHERENTLY PUBLIC ACTIVITY" AND BROAD PUBLIC SUPPORT: §509(a)(1)

A wide variety of organizations qualify as public charities under IRC §509(a)(1). The (a)(1) category includes all those organizations tax-exempt under IRC §501(c)(3) that are described in IRC §170(b)(1)(A)(i)–(vi), which lists organizations

---

[7] See Chapter 17.

[8] See Chapter 17.

[9] See Chapter 23.

[10] Described in Chapter 15§3.

[11] Except for the commensurate test discussed in Chapter 2.

[12] Discussed in Chapter 16.

[13] IRC §170(e)(5)(D); this on-again-off-again provision was made permanent by the Omnibus Consolidated and Emergency Supplemental. See Chapter 15§5 for more details.

[14] See Chapter 20 concerning private inurement standards applicable to both private foundations and public charities. See Chapter 20§9 for discussion of intermediate sanctions applicable to public charities, and Chapter 14 for discussion of self-dealing rules applicable to private foundations.

Exhibit 11–1

DIFFERENCES BETWEEN PUBLIC AND PRIVATE CHARITABLE ORGANIZATIONS

	Charitable Deduction	Excise Tax	Activities	Minimum Distribution Requirements	Annual Filings
Private Foundations	■ limited to 30% of AGI* for cash and qualified appreciated stock gifts; other property is limited to 20% and basis	■ 2% of investment income ■ 5–15% of amount of disqualified transactions	■ grants to other organizations ■ limits on grants to other PFs ■ self-initiated projects ■ no lobbying	■ 5% of fair market value of investment assets	■ all must file Form 990-PF ■ newspaper notice
Private Operating Foundations	■ limited to 30% for appreciated property, 50% for cash	■ same as for PFs	■ carries out self-initiated projects	■ $3\frac{1}{3}$% fair market value investment assets	■ same as for private
Public Charities	■ same as for private operating foundation	■ no tax on income (except UBI) ■ excise tax on excess lobbying and intermediate sanctions	■ can lobby ■ grant-making or carry out own projects	■ none, unless excess accumulation of surplus	■ file if gross revenue over $25,000. Form 990 or 990EZ.

* Adjusted gross income.

eligible to receive deductible charitable contributions. The definition is complicated and rather unwieldy because it includes six distinct types of exempt entities. Because of the code's design, the categories are labeled with numerical letters.

The first five categories include those organizations that perform what the Internal Revenue Service (IRS) calls "inherently public activity."[15] The first three achieve public status because of the nature of their activities without regard to sources of funds with which they pay their bills—even if they are privately supported. The fourth and fifth are closely connected with governmental support and activities. Last but certainly not least, because it includes a wide variety of charities, the sixth category includes those organizations balancing their budgets with donations from a sizable group of supporters, such as the United Way or American Red Cross. They must meet a mathematically measured contribution base formula and can be referred to as *donative public charities*. A consideration of the rules that pertain to both donative public charities and service provider entities is important to understanding public charities. A comparison of the differences between the categories can be found in §11.5.

(a) Churches

The first category includes a "church, convention, or association of churches." Churches are narrowly defined and not all religious organizations are regarded as churches. Chapter 3 is devoted to these distinctions. Perhaps due to the need to separate church and state, neither the Internal Revenue Code nor the IRS regulations define a church.[16]

(b) Schools

Although the title does not say "school," the second category basically includes formal schools. A school is an "educational organization that normally maintains a regular faculty, has a regular curriculum, and normally has a regularly enrolled body of pupils or students in attendance at the place where its educational activities are regularly carried on." The IRS very strictly scrutinizes what are referred to as the four regulars in granting classification as a school. Note that the world of educational organizations for purposes of IRC §501(c)(3) is much broader.[17]

(c) Hospitals and Medical Research Organizations

This class of public charity includes hospitals, the principal purpose or function of which is providing medical or hospital care, medical education, or medical research. An organization directly engaged in continuous, active medical research in conjunction with a hospital may also qualify if, during the year in which the contribution is made, the funds are committed to be spent within five years.

---

[15] 1992 Exempt Organizations Continuing Professional Education Technical Instruction Program, p. 216.
[16] Discussed in Chapter 3§2.
[17] Discussed in Chapter 5§1.

Medical care includes the treatment of any physical or mental disability or condition, on an inpatient or outpatient basis. A rehabilitation institution, outpatient clinic, or community mental health or drug treatment center may qualify. Convalescent homes, homes for children or the aged, handicapped vocational training centers, and medical schools are not considered to be hospitals.[18] An animal clinic was also found not to be a hospital.[19] The issues involved in qualifying for exemption as a hospital are evolving, and close attention must be paid to the latest information. These issues are discussed in Chapter 4§6.

Medical research is the conduct of investigations, experiments, and studies to discover, develop, or verify knowledge relating to the causes, diagnosis, treatment, prevention, or control of physical or mental diseases and impairments of man. "Appropriate equipment and qualified personnel necessary to carry out its principal function must be regularly used." The disciplines spanning the biological, social, and behavioral sciences, such as chemistry, psychiatry, biomedical engineering, virology, immunology, biophysics, and associated medical fields must be studied.[20] Such organizations must conduct research directly. Granting funds to other organizations, while possible, may not be a primary purpose.[21] The rules governing a research organization's expenditure of funds and its endowment levels are complicated, and the regulations must be studied to understand this type of public organization. A participant in a joint venture is considered to conduct the activity of the venture. Tax-exempt participants in a whole hospital joint venture remain providers of hospital care for purposes of qualification as a public charity under IRC §170(b)(1)(A)(iii).[22]

(d) College and University Support Organizations

An entity operating to receive, hold, invest, and administer property and to make expenditures to or for the benefit of a college or university qualifying under 170(b)(1)(A)(ii) are public charities. Such entities must normally receive a substantial part of their support from governmental grants and contributions from the general public, rather than exempt function revenue.

(e) Governmental Units

The United States, District of Columbia, states, possessions of the United States, and their political subdivisions are classified as governmental units. They are listed as qualifying as a public charity although they are not actually tax-exempt under IRC §501(c)(3). In essence they are public charities because they are responsive to all citizens. IRC §170(c)(1) permits a charitable contribution deduction for gifts to governmental units. The regulations contain no additional definition or explanation of the meaning of this term, but IRS rulings and procedures and the courts have provided some guidance, as presented in Chapter 10§2.

[18] Reg. §1.170A-9(c)(1).
[19] Rev. Rul. 74-572, 1974-2 C.B. 82.
[20] Reg. §1.170A-9(c)(2)(iii).
[21] Reg. §1.170A-9(c)(2)(v)(c); see also Chapter 5§3.
[22] 1999 IRS Exempt Organizations CPE Text, Chapter A, *Whole Hospital Joint Ventures,* by Mary Jo Salins, Judy Kindell, and Marvin Friedlander, page 15; see Chapter 22.

(f) Publicly Supported Organizations

Public charities in this category are those organizations that normally receive at least 33⅓% of their annual support in the form of donations from members of the general public (not including fees and charges for performing exempt functions).[23] "Normally" is based on an aggregation of the four years preceding the year in question and the succeeding year: for 1999 and 2000, the revenue for 1995 through 1998 is used.[24] A five-year period is applied during an organization's initial advanced ruling period. The calculation is illustrated in Exhibit 11-2, the IRS training form provided to its specialists. It mirrors the page in Schedule A of Form 990[25] that is used to test an organization's ongoing qualification under this public support test. Before 1996, the Schedule A version did not include lines 13 and 14 that reflect the percentage of public support. To arrive at includable donations for this type of public charity, a number of factors must be considered.

Support. The 33⅓% support formula for donative public charities does not include revenues the organization receives from performing its exempt activities— student tuition or patient fees, for example—as does the formula for service providers.[26] Donations of services for which a contribution deduction is not allowed[27] are also excluded. Donations from other donative public charities and governmental entities are fully included in the numerator and denominator for this test but other type of donations are partly or fully excluded as next explained. An organization that is primarily dependent upon exempt function revenues may qualify as a donative public charity[28] but only if it receives more than an insignificant amount of donations from governmental units and the general public.

Two Percent Gifts. There is a 2% ceiling for donations included as public support. Contributions from each donor, whether an individual, corporation, trust, private foundation, or other type of entity (after combining related parties) during each four-year period are only counted up to 2% of the charity's total support. For example, say an organization receives total support during the four-year test period of $1 million. In such a case, contributions from each donor of up to $20,000 could be counted as public donations. If one person gave $20,000 each year for a total of $80,000 for four years, only $20,000 is counted. The $1 million organization must receive at least $333,333 in public donations of $20,000 or less from each donor to satisfy the one-third support test. It could receive $666,666 from one source and $10,000 from 33 sources or $20,000 from 17 sources, for example.

> A public donation = Up to and no more than 2% of total support
> $20,000 = 2% of $1 million.

---

[23] Reg. §1.170A-9(e)(2).
[24] Reg. §1.170A-9(e)(4).
[25] Illustrated in Appendix 27-3.
[26] Reg. §1.170A-9(e)(7).
[27] IRC §170(e).
[28] Reg. §1.170A-9(e)(7)(ii).

Exhibit 11–2

INTERNAL REVENUE SERVICE TRAINING FORM

4. Making the Calculation

   a. A Support Test Worksheet for IRC 509(a)(1)/170(b)(1)(A)(vi) Organizations

Preceding Years	(a) 1st	(b) 2nd	(c) 3rd	(d) 4th	(e) Total
1 Gifts, grants and contributions received (Do not include unusual grants)					
2 Membership fees received					
3 Gross income from interest, dividends, amounts received from payments on securities loans (IRC 512(a)(55)), rents, royalties and unrelated business taxable income (less IRC 511 taxes) from business acquired by the organization after June 30, 1975					
4 Net income from unrelated business activities not included in line 3					
5 Tax revenues levied for the organization's benefit and either paid to it or expended on its behalf					
6 The value of services of facilities furnished by a governmental unit without charge. Do not include the value of services or facilities generally furnished to the public without charge.					
7 Other income. Do not include gain (or loss) from sale of capital assets					
8 Total of lines 1 through 7					

9 Enter 2% of line 8(e) . . . . _____

10 Add lines 1(e), 2(e), 5(e), and 6 (e) . . . . _____

11 Less: Contributions of individual donors in excess of 2% of aggregate total support (line 9) . . . . _____

12 Total public support (numerator) . . . . _____

13 Aggregate total support from line 8(e) (denominator) . . . . _____

14 Public support percentage (line 12 divided by line 13) . . . . _____

       If line 14 is 33$\frac{1}{3}$% or more, the organization qualifies under IRC 509(a)(1)/170(b)(1)(A)(vi). If line 14 is less than 33$\frac{1}{3}$%, consider the facts and circumstances 10% test.

1992 Exempt Organizations Continuing Professional Education Technical Instruction Program, p. 223.

Public Charity Grants. Voluntary grants and donations received by a donative public charity from other charities listed in 170(b)(1)(A) and from governmental units, including foreign governments,[29] are not subject to the 2% limit and instead are fully counted as donations from the general public,[30] unless the gift was passed through as a donor-designated grant over which donor has control.[31] A grant from a service providing entity[32] and a grant from a supporting organization is subject to the 2% inclusion limitation.[33]

(g) Facts and Circumstances Test

When the percentage of an organization's public donations fall below the precise $33\frac{1}{3}\%$ test, it may be able to sustain public charity status by applying the *facts and circumstances test.* The history of the organization's fund-raising efforts and other factors are considered as an alternative method to the strict mathematical formula for qualifying for public support under (a)(1). This test is not available for charities qualifying as public under §509(a)(2). An organization can seek to apply this test to prove it qualifies for public status by submitting the information in the following lists when originally filing Form 1023. The applicant should spare no details to prove it meets the test. Brochures, board lists, program descriptions, and fund solicitations can be furnished. In that instance, the IRS will scrutinize the facts and issue its approval or disapproval. When an organization needs to apply the test later in its life because its support has fallen below the $33\frac{1}{3}\%$ level, it has two choices. The information can be submitted as an attachment to Schedule A of its annual Form 990. The problem with this choice is that the IRS does not customarily respond to such a filing. Though prior IRS approval is not required, an organization might choose to seek approval by submitting the information to the Cincinnati office responsible for determinations.[34]

For the facts and circumstances test to apply, the following series of factors must be evidenced.[35] The first two factors in the following list must be present and a sufficient number of the other favorable factors must indicate the organization is responsive to public interests. In the author's experience, control of the board by major contributors or their family members is a fatal flaw. The factors that are considered are fully explained in the regulations that should be carefully studied in preparation of information evidencing satisfaction of the test.

1. Public support must be at least 10% of the total support, and the higher the better.

2. The organization must have an active "continuous and bona fide" fund-raising program designed to attract new and additional public and governmental support. Consideration will be given to the fact that, in its

---

[29] Rev. Rul. 75-435, 1975-2 C.B. 215.
[30] Reg. §1.170A-9(e)(6)(i).
[31] As discussed in §11.3(c).
[32] Reg. §1.170A-9(e)(6)(i) and (v).
[33] Priv. Ltr. Rul. 9203040.
[34] See Chapter 28§2.
[35] Reg. §1.170A-9(e)(3).

early years of existence, it limits the scope of its solicitations to those persons deemed most likely to provide seed money in an amount sufficient to enable it to commence its charitable activities and to expand its solicitation program.

3. The composition of the board is representative of broad public interests (rather than those of major contributors).

4. Some support comes from governmental and other sources representative of the general public (rather than a few major contributors).

5. Facilities and programs are made available to the general public, such as a museum or symphony society.

6. Programs appeal to a broadly based public (and in fact the public participates).

7. The fact that an organization is an educational or research institution that regularly publishes scholarly studies that are widely used by colleges and universities and the general public.

8. The participation in, or sponsorship of, the programs of the organization by members of the public having special knowledge or expertise, public officials, or civic or community leaders.

9. For a membership organization, the solicitations for dues-paying members is designed to enroll a substantial number of persons in the community or area and the dues amount makes members available to a broad cross section of the interested public.

(h) Unusual Grants

When inclusion of a substantial donation(s) causes an organization to fail the $33\frac{1}{3}\%$ public support test, public charity status may still be sustained by excluding such gift(s). A qualifying *unusual grant* can be excluded from gross revenue in calculating total support for both (a)(1) and (a)(2) purposes. A grant is unusual if it is an unexpected and substantial gift attracted by the public nature of the organization *and* received from a disinterested party. A number of factors are taken into account, no single factor is determinative, and not all factors need be present. The eight positive factors are shown in the following list, along with their opposites in parentheses:[36]

1. The contribution is received from a party with no connection to the organization. (The gift is received from a person who is a substantial contributor, board member, manager, or related to one.)

2. The gift is in the form of cash, marketable securities, or property that furthers the organization's exempt purposes. (The property is illiquid, difficult to dispose of, and not pertinent to the organization's activities—useless, in other words.) A gift of a painting to a museum, or a gift of

---

[36] Regs. §1.170A-9(e)(6)(ii) and §1.509(a)-3(c)(4).

wetlands to a nature preservation society would be useful and appropriate property.[37]

3. No material restrictions are placed on the gift. (Strings are attached.)

4. The organization attracts a significant amount of support to pay its operating expenses on a regular basis, and the gift adds to an endowment or pays for capital items. (The gift pays for operating expenses for several years and is not added to an endowment.)

5. The gift is a bequest. (The gift is an inter vivos transfer.)

6. An active fund-raising program exists and attracts significant public support. (Fund solicitation programs are unsuccessful.)

7. A representative and broadly based governing body controls the organization. (Related parties control the organization.)

8. Prior to the receipt of the unusual grant, the organization qualified as publicly supported. (The unusual grant exclusion was relied upon in the past to satisfy the test.)

If the grant is payable over a period of years, it can be excluded each year, but any income earned on the sums would be included.[38] The IRS has provided a set of "safe harbor" reliance factors to identify unusual grants. If the first four factors just listed are present, unusual grant status can automatically be claimed and relied upon. As to item 4, the terms of the grant cannot provide for more than one year's operating expense.[39]

11.3 COMMUNITY FOUNDATIONS

More than $16 billion in charitable assets are held in the United States by public charities called *community foundations or trusts* (CFs). The first such organization was created in 1914 in Cleveland, Ohio—The Cleveland Foundation. Now there are about five hundred. The primary purpose of a CF is to raise funds and maintain endowments to support projects benefiting a particular local community or area. A prototype CF is controlled by a governing body representing the city or area it serves and receives a broad base of support from many sources so that it meets the mechanical $33\frac{1}{3}\%$ support test or the facts and circumstances test.[40] Typical CFs solicit and receive lifetime and testamentary gifts. They may collect donations in the form of modest gifts from individuals and businesses and major donors. Some affluent philanthropists want to avoid the administrative costs and labyrinth of rules applicable in creating and operating one's own independent private foundation. They instead choose to establish a fund within a community

---

[37] See Rev. Rul. 76-440, 1976-2 C.B. 58 concerning gift of large tract to be used in perpetuity to preserve the natural resources of a town.
[38] Reg. §1.170A-9(e)(6)(ii)(c).
[39] Rev. Proc. 81-7, 1981-1 C.B. 621.
[40] Explained in §11.2(g).

foundation. Such donors often wish to maintain some control over their funds and to designate and restrict the manner in which funds are expended. As CFs have evolved through the years, two very different organizational structures are used:

- Sole or single nonprofit corporation or trust

- Composite organization of otherwise taxable trusts, corporations; or unincorporated restricted funds that are treated as a single entity for exemption purposes. New York Community Trust, for example, has a number of different banks acting as its trustees, each holding one or more of its trusts and funds. The IRS says CFs "are akin to holding companies."[41]

The regulations governing CFs create the legal fiction of a single entity and were designed to limit donor control. When more stringent rules were imposed on privately funded charities in 1969, some existing private foundations were collapsed into community foundations. CFs also became an attractive vehicle for new entities seeking to avoid the PF rules. Two different regulations refer to such conversions and affect the establishment of a new community foundation.[42]

Interestingly the §507 regulation governing CFs refer to *community trusts* and without mention of a corporation. The IRS has addressed qualification of a CF in a combined corporate/trust form.[43] In its training literature, the IRS says "many CFs combine both forms of organization," but it also admits the issue is unsettled.[44] The IRS fought recognition of one corporate CF, the National Foundation, in 1987 because it felt donors had too much control over their funds.[45] Donors were allowed to recommend charitable projects subject to National's acceptance. The standard agreement forms, though, provided that once the donor committed the funds, National fully controlled them and was free to use or not use them as the donor suggested. The IRS argued that National was merely a conduit and provided evidence that National ordinarily honored requests for redistribution of funds without exercising independent judgment about needs most deserving of support. The court disagreed and approved National's recognition as a charitable and "unitary" organization without mention of the regulation. The Fund for Anonymous Givers lost a similar challenge because it not only gave donors discretion over grants but also control over investment of assets they contributed.[46] Although the IRS has recognized their exempt status, funds created by financial institutions, such as the Fidelity Gift Fund, have been carefully scrutinized. Fidelity has imposed an annual distribution requirement on its accounts equivalent to the 5% minimum distribution.

---

[41] 1993 (for FY 1994) *Exempt Organizations Continuing Professional Education Technical Instruction Program Textbook*, Topic K, at 136.

[42] Regs. §§1.170A-9(e)(10)-(14) and 1.507-2(a)(8)(iii).

[43] G.C.M. 37818 (Jan. 11, 1979); G.C.M. 38812 (Aug. 21, 1981).

[44] *CPE Textbook, supra* n.41, at 135.

[45] *National Foundation, Inc. v. U.S.*, 13 Cl. Ct. 486 (1987); also see G.C.M. 39748, released in 1988 and withdrawn in 1992.

[46] *The Fund for Anonymous Gifts v. IRS*, 79 AFTR 2d ¶97874.

Fundamentally, the IRS will apply two tests to determine if a new CF can qualify for tax-exempt status:

1. Single entity test
2. Component part test

(a) Single Entity Test

All of the legally separate entities operating under the aegis of a particular community foundation that meet the criteria outlined here are treated as part of a single entity, rather than as separate funds. The individual funds associated with a CF—whether trusts, not-for-profit corporations, unincorporated associations, or combination thereof—are not treated as separate legal entities for tax purposes. Essentially, they are considered as part of a consolidated group and do not separately apply for recognition or exemption.[47]

- *Name.* The organization must be commonly known as a community trust, fund, foundation, or other similar name conveying the concept of a capital or endowment fund to support charitable activities in the community or area it serves.

- *Common Instrument.* All funds of the organization must be subject to a common governing instrument or a master trust or agency agreement, which may be embodied in a single or several documents containing common language. Making the component fund subject to the CF's governing instrument in the transfer documents is acceptable.

- *Common Governing Body.* A single or common governing body or distribution committee must control all components. Any restricted funds dedicated to a particular purpose or organization must be monitored by the governing body.

- *Power to Modify or Remove.* The CF's governing body must have the power—in the governing instrument, instrument of transfer, bylaws, or other controlling documents—to modify any restriction or condition on the distribution of funds if such restriction or condition becomes, in effect, unnecessary, incapable of fulfillment, or inconsistent with the charitable needs of the community or area served.

- *Exercise of Powers.* There must be a written resolution to replace any participating trustee, custodian, or agent for breach of fiduciary duty under state law, including failure to produce a reasonable return on assets.

- *Common Reports.* The periodic financial reports must be presented in a consolidated manner treating all funds as CF funds.

The variety of funds cited by the IRS as acceptable examples of component funds that can be offered or maintained within a CF include:[48]

---

[47] Reg. §1.170A-9(e)(11)(i) for purposes of §§170, 501, 507, 508, 509, and chapter 42.
[48] *CPE Textbook, supra* n.41, at 139.

- *Unrestricted Funds.* The CF has unfettered use of these funds—both income and principal. No restrictions or conditions on the management or distribution of the monies exist. The CF, not the donor, identifies community needs and distributes funds according to those needs.

- *Memorial Funds.* Funds named after particular persons, family, private foundation, or historic event or catastrophe.

- *Field of Interest Funds.* These funds are dedicated to a particular area of charitable need or concern—the arts, the poor, the homeless, higher education, religion, and so on. The types of interests for which funds are made available may be broad or narrow and can be designated or requested by the donors. The manner in which the interest is pursued, however, is up to the CF itself (whether to directly conduct a program or regrant the funds to another organization serving the interest).

- *Advised Funds.* The donor is given the right to make nonbinding suggestions as to the specific organization or projects to receive funding. The CF retains final authority to determine use of its income. See further discussion later in this section regarding limitations on donor designations.

- *Designated Funds.* The donor may specify the particular charitable purpose or organization to be supported with his or her funds.

- *Agency Endowments.* A designated fund supporting a particular local charity is established within the CF. The charity solicits donations made payable into the fund for its benefit. Such an agency arrangement may be advantageous to the local from an investment management standpoint.

- *Pooled Income Funds.* The income is paid to the donors during their lives and upon the donors' death the principal and income is distributed to the CF.

(b) Component Part Test

Each qualifying component must be created by a gift, bequest, legacy, device, or other transfer to a community trust treated as a single entity and the gifts may not be directly subjected by the transferor to any material restriction or condition within the meaning of the §507 regulations. A donor may not encumber a fund with a restriction that prevents the CF from "freely and effectively employing the transferred assets, or the income derived therefrom, in furtherance of its exempt purposes."[49] Essentially, the regulations are intended to prevent the creation of miniprivate foundations under an umbrella CF. The following donor-imposed restrictions are not considered material and are therefore allowed:

- *Name.* The fund may take the name of a private foundation, the fund's creator, or the creator's family.

- *Purpose.* The donor may designate that the income and principal be used for specified charitable purposes or one or more §509(a)(1), (2), or (3) organization. The CF's governing body must be given the power to stop dis-

---

[49] Reg. §1.507-2(a)(8).

tributions and recover any funds that were not used for the CF's exempt purposes.

- *Administration.* A separate or identifiable fund may be required by the donor. Distribution of some or all of the principal can be delayed in time.

- *Required Retention of Gift.* A donor may require the CF to keep the property if, because of the property's peculiar features, its retention is important to accomplishing the exempt purposes of the community, such as a historic property or wildlife preserve.

(c) Donor Designations Versus Donor Directions

Donors may designate the purposes for which their funds are to be expended before or at the time the gift is made—not later. Reservation of the right to choose grantees or programs (donor direction) is not permitted once the fund is established. Recognizing that moral suasion can be imposed by philanthropists even without written direction, the regulations provide a list of factors that indicate donors have not reserved a right to designate:[50]

- CF investigates the donor's advice and its investigation shows that the advice is consistent with specific charitable needs most deserving of support in the community.

- CF has published guidelines listing the specific charitable needs of the community and the donor's advice is consistent with those guidelines.

- CF has begun an educational program advising donors and other persons of its guidelines that list the specific charitable needs most deserving of support. These needs must be consistent with its charitable purposes.

- CF disburses other funds to the same or similar organizations or charitable needs as those recommended by the donor. Other funds are from sources other than, and in excess of, those distributed from the donor's fund.

- CF's solicitation for funds specifically states that it will not be bound by any advice the donor offers.

Impermissible donor *retention* of control is evidenced, according to the regulations, by the presence of two or more of the following factors:[51]

- The only criterion considered by the CF in making a distribution of income or principal from the donor's fund is the donor's advice.

- Solicitations of funds by the CF state or imply that the donor's advice will be followed. Also considered is a pattern of conduct by the CF that creates an expectation that the donor's advice will be followed.

---

[50] Reg. §1.507-2(a)(8)(iv)(A)(2); see also 1997 IRS CPE Text, Chapter 1.
[51] Reg. §1.507-2(a)(8)(iv)(A)(3).

- Donor's advice is limited to distributions of amounts from his or her fund and the CF has not (1) done an independent investigation to evaluate whether the donor's advice is consistent with the charitable needs most deserving of support in the community, or (2) established guidelines that list the specific charitable needs of the community.

- CF solicits advice regarding distributions from the donor's fund only from the donor and no procedure is provided for considering advice from others.

- CF follows the advice of all donors concerning their funds substantially all the time.

(d) Public Support Test

A community foundation must each year on Form 990 complete financial information to calculate its percentage of public support. Part IV of Schedule A[52] contains a separate box to identify an organization as a "community trust." The regulations specifically say a CF must meet the 33⅓% public support test or, if not, the facts and circumstances test.[53]

11.4 SERVICE-PROVIDING ORGANIZATIONS: §509(a)(2)

Like those organizations said to conduct "inherently public" activities—churches, schools, and hospitals—the second major category of public charity includes entities that also provide services to the public—museums, libraries, low-income housing projects, and the like. Unlike churches, schools, and hospitals that qualify without regard to their sources of support, (a)(2) service providers must meet public support tests. Also unlike donative public charities that disregard fee for service revenue in calculating public support, service providers count exempt function revenues and donations and grants as support as shown in Exhibit 11-3. Thus, this category usually includes organizations receiving a major portion of their support from fees and charges for activity participation, such as day care centers, animal shelters, theaters, and educational publishers. A two-part support test must be met to qualify under this category:

1. Investment income cannot exceed ⅓ of the total support. (Total support basically means the organization's gross revenue except for capital gains.)

2. More than ⅓ of the total support must be received from exempt function sources (called "gross receipts") made up of a combination of the following:

   - Gifts, grants, contributions, and membership dues received from non-disqualified persons. Unusual grants[54] can be excluded.

---

[52] Reproduced in Appendix 27-3.
[53] Reg. §1.170A-10.
[54] Explained in §11.2(h).

Exhibit 11–3

INTERNAL REVENUE SERVICE TRAINING FORM

E. A Support Test Worksheet for IRC 509(a)(2) Organizations

Preceding Years	(a) 1st	(b) 2nd	(c) 3rd	(d) 4th	(e) Total
1 Gifts, grants and contributions received (Do not include unusual grants)					
2 Membership fees received					
3 Gross receipts from admissions, merchandise sold or services performed or furnishing of facilities in any activity that is not a business unrelated to the organization's charitable, etc., purposes					
4 Gross income from interest, dividends, amounts received from payment on securities loans (IRC 512(a)(5)), rents, royalties, and unrelated business taxable income (less IRC 511 taxes) from businesses acquired by the organization after June 30, 1975					
5 Net income from unrelated business activities not included in line 4					
6 Tax revenues levied for the organization's benefit and either paid to it or expended on its behalf					
7 The value of services or facilities furnished by a governmental unit without charge. Do not include the value of services or facilities generally furnished to the public without charge					
8 Other income. Do not include gain (or loss) from sale of capital assets					
9 Total of lines 1 through 8					
10 Enter 1% of line 9					

11 Add lines 1(e), 2(e), 3(e), 6(e) and 7(e) . . . . _____

12 Deduct: Income from disqualified persons . . . . _____
   Exempt function income exceeding $5,000/1% limit . . . . . . _____

13 Line 11 less line 12 = public support (numerator) . . . . _____

14 Total support from line 9(e) (denominator) . . . . _____

15 Public support percentage (line 13 divided by line 14) . . . . _____

> If line 15 is 33⅓% or more, the public support test is met. Go on to gross investment test. If line 15 is less than 33⅓%, the organization will not qualify under IRC 509(a)(2).

16 Investment income from line 4(e) . . . .

17 Unrelated business income on line 5(e) less tax paid on that income . . . . .

18 Total of lines 16 and 17 (numerator) . . . .

19 Total support from line 9(e) (denominator) . . . .

20 Gross investment percentage (line 18 divided by line 19) . . . .

> If line 20 is less than 33⅓%, the gross investment test is met. If line 20 is 33⅓% or more, the organization will not qualify under IRC 509(a)(2).

1992 Exempt Organizations Continuing Professional Education Technical Instruction Program, p. 231.

- Admissions to exempt function facilities or performances, such as theater or ballet performance tickets, museum or historic site admission fees, movie or video tickets, seminar or lecture fees, and athletic event charges.

- Fees for performance of services, such as school tuition, day care fees, hospital room and laboratory charges, psychiatric counseling, testing, scientific laboratory fees, library fines, animal neutering charges, athletic facility fees, and so on.

- Merchandise sales of goods related to the organization's activities, including books and educational literature, pharmaceuticals and medical devices, handicrafts, reproductions and copies of original works of art, by-products of a blood bank, and goods produced by handicapped workers.

- Exempt function revenues received from one source are not counted if they exceed $5,000 or 1% of the organization's support for the year, whichever is higher.

A qualifying service provider cannot receive more than $\frac{1}{3}$ of its revenue from investment income. Dividends, interest, payments with respect to security loans, rents, royalties, and net unrelated business income (less the unrelated business income tax (UBIT)) are treated as investment income for this purpose.[55] Program-related investments, such as low-income housing loans, do not produce investment income but rather exempt function gross receipts.[56]

11.5 DIFFERENCE BETWEEN §509(a)(1) AND §509(a)(2)

Some organizations, including most churches, schools, and hospitals, can qualify for public status under both §509(a)(1) and (a)(2). In such cases, the (a)(1) class will be assigned by the IRS to identify the organization's category of public status. For purposes of annual reporting, unrelated business, limits on deductions for donors, and most other tax purposes, the two categories are virtually the same, with one important exception. To receive a terminating distribution from a private foundation upon its dissolution, the charity must be an (a)(1) organization.[57]

(a) Definition of Support

The items of gross income included in the requisite "support" are different for each category, and do not equal total revenue under either class. "Support" forms the basis of public status for both categories, and the calculations are made on a four-year moving average basis using the cash method of accounting.[58] Those Form 990 filers reporting income and expense on an accrual basis for financial purposes are also directed to follow that method for most other tax purposes. Ac-

---

[55] IRC §509(e).
[56] Reg. §1.509(a)-3(m). For discussion of program-related investments, see Chapter 16§2(d).
[57] IRC §507(b)(1)(A). Also see Chapter 12§4 regarding termination of private foundations.
[58] Gen. Coun. Memo. 39109 and Reg. §1.509(a)-3(k).

cordingly, an organization computing its qualification as a public charity based upon its sources of revenue must essentially keep detailed revenue records on both a cash and accrual method as discussed in Chapter 27 § 12(c).

For (a)(1) purposes, certain revenues are not counted as support and are not included in the numerator or the denominator.[59]

- Exempt function revenue, or that amount earned through charges for the exercise or performance of exempt activities, such as admission tickets, patient fees, and such

- Capital gains or losses

- Unusual grants

- Donations of in-kind services and facilities (do count facility and service donations from governmental units)

For (a)(2) purposes, total revenue less capital gains or losses, unusual grants, and in-kind service and facility donations equals total support.

(b) Major Gifts

Contributions received are counted as public support differently for each category. For planning purposes, these rules are extremely important to consider. Under the (a)(1) category, a particular giver's donations are counted only up to an amount equal to 2% of the total "support" for the four-year period, as discussed under Chapter 11§2(f). Gifts from §170(b)(1)(A)(vi) public charities and governmental entities are not subject to this 2% floor; grants from those classified as public under §170(b)(1)(A)(i)–(v) are counted only up to 2%.

For (a)(2) purposes, all gifts, grants, and contributions are counted as public support, except those received from disqualified persons.[60] Such a person may be a substantial contributor, or one who gives over $5,000 if such amount is more than 2% of the organization's aggregate contributions for its life, or a relative of such a person.[61] For (a)(2) purposes, gifts from these insiders are not counted at all. Subject to the 2% ceiling, their gifts are counted for (a)(1) purposes. Grants from other public charities classified under 509(a)(1) are fully counted. Although they are excluded from the definition of substantial contributors under IRC §507, another 509(a)(2), a 509(a)(3), or other category of 501(c) organization is treated as disqualified persons and their grants subject to limitations on their inclusion in public support for this purpose.

(c) Types of Support

Not all revenue is counted as support. The basic definition of "support" for both excludes capital gains from the sale or exchange of capital assets. Some types of gross revenue are counted differently under differing circumstances.

---

[59] Reg. §1.170A-9(e)(7).
[60] "Disqualified persons" are defined in IRC §4946 and discussed in Chapter 12.
[61] See Chapter 12§2 for definitions of these terms.

Membership fees for both classes may represent donations or charges for services rendered. In some cases a combined gift and payment for services may be present. The facts in each circumstance must be examined to properly classify the revenue. A membership fee is a donation if it is paid by a person to support the goals and interests they have in common with the organization rather than to purchase admission, merchandise, services, or the use of facilities. The regulations say that when services are provided to members as a part of overall activity, the payment may still be classed as member dues[62] (donations) rather than exempt function receipts. Under the enhanced scrutiny of the IRS's Special Emphasis Program[63] on deductibility of charitable gifts, some organizations realized that their members are not necessarily making contributions. Particularly for (a)(1) purposes, this distinction is very important, because exempt function fees are not included in the public support calculations. See Chapter 24§4(b) for classification of member benefits.

Grants for services to be rendered for the granting organization, such as a state government's funding for home health care, are treated under both categories as exempt function income, not donations or grants.[64] A grant is normally made to encourage the grantee organization to carry on certain programs or activities in furtherance of its own exempt purposes; no economic or physical benefit accrues to the grant-maker.[65] "Gross receipts," however, result whenever the recipient organization performs a service or provides a facility or product to serve the needs of the government agency.

Under both categories, this distinction is important to determine amounts qualifying as contributions. For (a)(2) status, the distinction has yet another dimension. Only the first $5,000 of fees for such services received from a particular person or organization is includable in public support.[66] Moneys received from a third party payor, such as Medicare or Medicaid patient receipts[67] or blood bank charges collected by a hospital as agent for a blood bank,[68] are considered as gross receipts from the individual patients.

Pass-through grants received from another public charity are totally counted toward public support unless the gift represents an indirect grant expressly or implicitly earmarked by a donor to be paid to a subgrantee organization. In that case, the donor is the individual.[69] *Donor-designated* grants therefore require careful scrutiny. The basic question is whether the intermediary organization received the gift as an agent or whether it can freely choose to regrant the funds. Donations received by donor-advised funds and community foundations qualify as public

---

[62] Reg. §509(a)-3(h).

[63] See Chapter 24.

[64] Rev. Rul. 83-153, 1983-2 C.B. 48 provides similar treatment for state agency payments to a youth care facility.

[65] Reg. §1.509(a)-3(g).

[66] IRC §509(a)(2)28(ii).

[67] Rev. Rul. 83-153, 1938-2 C.B. 48 says that these payments are gross receipts from an exempt function, not a government grant, because individuals choose their own health care providers.

[68] Rev. Rul. 75-387, 1975-2 C.B. 216.

[69] Reg. §1.509(a)-3(j).

support to the initial recipient organization (and again to the ultimate recipient) if the fund retains ultimate authority to approve the regrants.[70]

In-kind gifts are counted differently for each category. For (a)(1) purposes, the regulation specifically says support does not include "contributions of services for which a deduction is not allowable."[71] For (a)(2) purposes, the regulation says support includes the fair market or rental value of gifts, grants, or contributions of property or use of such property on the date of the gift.[72] Under (a)(1), the regulations and the IRS instructions to Form 990 are silent about gifts of property that are deductible. It is not stated whether the full fair market value of property the deductibility of which is limited to the donor's tax basis, such as a gift of clothing to the charity resale shop, is counted at full value or at basis. For accounting purposes, the organization would count such gifts at their full value.

Supporting organization grants and split-interest trust gifts to an (a)(1) public charity are subject to the 2% limit. For (a)(2) entities such gifts retain their character as investment income for purposes of limiting the amount of investment income it is allowed to receive.[73]

(d) Change of Public Charity Category

Sometimes the sources of a public charity's support change, causing it to fail to qualify under one category or another. When the change indicated is reclassification from (a)(1) to (a)(2) or vice versa, the factors discussed in Chapter 28§2 can be considered. Simply reporting the financial information on Schedule A is sufficient to allow an organization to continue its public status; the issue is whether to seek overt IRS approval and a new determination letter.

(e) Loss of Public Status

A more serious situation arises when the changes in support cause the organization to lose its public charity status. Importantly the loss of status is not immediate; if the financial tally submitted with the organization's 1999 return reflects support for the years 1995–1998 was less than the requisite one-third, public status continues through the year 2000. If a material change in the organization's sources of support occurs that is not caused by an unusual grant, a five-year testing period may apply.[74] Special rules also apply for new organizations.[75] Until a change of status is announced in the Internal Revenue Bulletin, contributors are entitled to rely upon the latest IRS letter. A donor who is responsible for or otherwise aware of the changes is not entitled to such reliance.[76] This issue is particularly troublesome for private foundations as discussed in Chapter 17§4(a).

---

[70] Gen. Coun. Memo. 39748 was issued in 1988 to clarify this subject, and was later withdrawn with Gen. Coun. Memo. 39875.
[71] Reg. §1.170A-9(e)(7)(b).
[72] Reg. §1.509(a)-3(f)(3).
[73] Reg. §1.509(a)-5(a)(1); Priv. Ltr. Rul. 9203040.
[74] Reg. §§1.170A-9(e)(4) and 1.509(a)-3(c)(1)(ii).
[75] Reg. §§1.170A-9(e)(5) and 1.509(a)-3(c)(1)(iv).
[76] Reg. §§1.170A-9(e)(5)(iii) and 1.509(a)-3(c)(1)(iii).

11.6 SUPPORTING ORGANIZATIONS: §509(a)(3)

The third category of organizations that escape the stringent requirements placed upon private foundations is a *supporting organization* (SO). If such organizations are sufficiently responsive to and controlled or supervised by or in connection with one or more public charities, they are classified as public charities themselves, even if they are privately funded.

Basically, supporting organizations dedicate all of their assets to one or more public charities that need not necessarily control them (except an SO cannot be controlled by disqualified persons). Beneficiary organization(s) must be specified, but can be changed under certain conditions. This flexibility makes SOs popular with benefactors who want neither to create a private foundation nor to make an outright gift to an established charity. The rules are not entirely logical and the regulations are quite detailed and extensive. The questions that must be answered on Form 1023, Schedule D[77] for organizations seeking this classification are also instructive. An SO must meet three unique organizational and operational tests as follows:

1. It must be organized, and at all times thereafter, operated exclusively for the benefit of, to perform the functions of, or to carry out the purposes of one or more specified public charities (purpose);

2. It must be operated, supervised, or controlled by or in connection with one or more public charities (*organizational test*); and

3. It cannot be controlled, directly or indirectly, by one or more disqualified persons.[78]

The IRS chart in Exhibit 11-4 provides an excellent overview of the complex tests that have to be satisfied for an organization to gain the SO classification.[79] One of three very different types of relationship must exist between the supporting organization and the organization(s) it supports as described in the following paragraphs:

(a) Purpose Clause

A supporting organization must be organized, and at all times thereafter be operated exclusively:

- For the benefit of,

- To perform the functions of, or

- To carry out the purposes of one or more specified IRC §509(a)(1) or (2) organizations, a "public charity."[80]

---

[77] Reproduced in Appendix 18-1.
[78] IRC §509(a)(3)(A).
[79] 1992 Exempt Organizations Continuing Professional Education Technical Instruction Program, page 233.
[80] IRC §509(a)(3)(A).

Exhibit 11–4

BASIC STEPS IN MAKING AN IRC §509(a)(3) DETERMINATION

Of the tests set forth in the statute, the relationship test of IRC §509(a)(3)(B) is the most important. Therefore, whether there is a proper relationship between the organizations should be determined first. The order to proceed in making a determination under IRC §509(a)(e) is as follows:

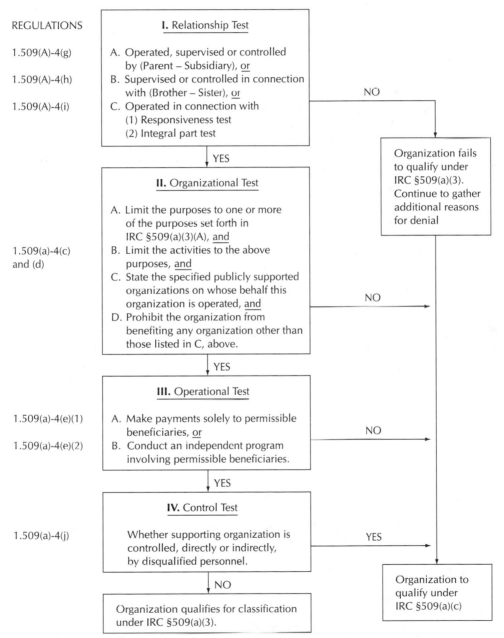

REGULATIONS

I. Relationship Test

1.509(A)-4(g)   A. Operated, supervised or controlled by (Parent – Subsidiary), or
1.509(A)-4(h)   B. Supervised or controlled in connection with (Brother – Sister), or
1.509(A)-4(i)   C. Operated in connection with
                         (1) Responsiveness test
                         (2) Integral part test

NO

Organization fails to qualify under IRC §509(a)(3). Continue to gather additional reasons for denial

YES

II. Organizational Test

A. Limit the purposes to one or more of the purposes set forth in IRC §509(a)(3)(A), and
1.509(a)-4(c) and (d)   B. Limit the activities to the above purposes, and
C. State the specified publicly supported organizations on whose behalf this organization is operated, and
D. Prohibit the organization from benefiting any organization other than those listed in C, above.

NO

YES

III. Operational Test

1.509(a)-4(e)(1)   A. Make payments solely to permissible beneficiaries, or
1.509(a)-4(e)(2)   B. Conduct an independent program involving permissible beneficiaries.

NO

YES

IV. Control Test

1.509(a)-4(j)   Whether supporting organization is controlled, directly or indirectly, by disqualified personnel.

YES

NO

Organization qualifies for classification under IRC §509(a)(3).

Organization to qualify under IRC §509(a)(c)

Source: Chart prepared by Jeanne S. Gessay, Chief of Exempt Organization Rulings Branch II, IRS National Office, Washington, DC.

The articles of organization must limit the purposes to those previously listed, in addition to the regular constraints on operations imposed upon 501(c)(3) organizations.[81] The categories of purpose—whether charitable, religious, or educational—may be very broad. Classic examples of suitable SO purposes would be to raise money for the publicly supported hospitals in an urban medical center, to fund the medical library of the center, or to build and maintain a chapel for the center.

(b) Specified Public Charities

Supporting organizations most commonly operate to benefit one or more specified public charities as literally required by the code and regulations. Nonetheless a complex labyrinth of terms allows nondesignation to occur. When the Type A relationship exists ("operated, supervised or controlled by"), a class of organizations dedicated to a specific purpose can be named.[82] A class of beneficiary organizations, such as "Catholic churches in Milwaukee" or "institutions of higher learning in California" may be named (rather than naming individual churches or schools) if the public charities are in control. The SO's charter can have the following latitude:[83]

- It may permit the substitution of public charities;

- It may permit new or additional beneficiaries of the same class; and

- It may permit the SO to vary the amount of support among different public organizations within the class.

Slightly different rules exist for Type B, or entities "operated in connection with." First and foremost, specific beneficiaries must be named in the charter. However, the articles may permit certain changes.[84] Particularly when one of the benefited organizations loses its tax exemption, fails, or abandons operations, substitution is permitted. However, it is not permissible to retain the right to change when the supported organization becomes "unnecessary, undesirable, impractical, impossible, or no longer adapted to the needs of the public."[85]

(c) Operational Control

The supporting organization must have one of three special types of relationship described below with its supported public charity(ies).[86] Simply turning over all of the SO's income to a specifically named charity in accordance with the SO's articles of incorporation is not sufficient. An entity may not meet this operational

---

[81] Reg. §1.509(a)-4(c)(1); see discussion in Chapter 2.
[82] Reg. §1.509(a)-4(d).
[83] Reg. §1.509(a)-4(d)(3).
[84] Reg. §1.509(a)-4(d)(4).
[85] *William F., Mable E., and Margaret K. Quarrie Charitable Fund v. Commissioner*, 70 T.C. 182, 187 (1978), *aff'd*, 603 F. 2d 1274 (7th Cir. 1979).
[86] IRC §509(a)(3)(A), (B), and (C).

test even though it satisfies the §501(c)(3) operational tests. The three types of relationships are as follows:[87]

- *Type A: Operated, Supervised, or Controlled By.* An SO is operated, supervised, or controlled by its beneficiary organization(s) when it essentially functions in a parent–subsidiary relationship. A substantial degree of direction is exercised by the parent over programs, policies, and activities. The SO, or subsidiary, is accountable and responsible to the parent, or supported organization. This type is found when a majority of the controlling officials of the SO are appointed by the supportees, although any one of a group of beneficiaries need not control if all are represented.

- *Type B: Supervised or Controlled in Connection With.* This type of relationship exists when the same persons control both the supporting and the supported organization, or in other words, there is common control or supervision.

- *Type C: Operated in Connection With.* This type of SO is the most independent of its supportee(s), as it may have a totally independent board with specific named beneficiary organization(s). Because of its relative freedom, it must meet two additional tests to qualify: the responsiveness and the integral part tests.

Responsiveness. To meet the responsiveness test, the supported organization must have a significant voice in the SO's governance.[88] This voice is gained when one or more officers or directors of the SO are appointed or elected by the supported organization's board or officers. In the case of a charitable trust, responsiveness is present when the supportee is named, and the named supportee has the power to enforce the trust and to compel an accounting under state law.

Integral Part. The integral part test essentially determines whether the supportee is dependent upon the SO for the type of support it provides.[89] The SO must maintain a significant involvement in and devote its assets to the supportee's activities. The SO can conduct active programs; it might provide and maintain facilities or equipment; it might conduct a function or activity that the supportee itself would normally carry out; and it can simply grant its income to the supportee (if the attentiveness test is satisfied).[90] The SO might also conduct fund-raising programs and unrelated businesses (on a limited scale) to raise funds in support of its publicly supported organization.

The amount of an SO's income that must be expended to meet the integral part test is, as a general rule, substantially all of its annual income. Income for this purpose is defined by reference to the private operating foundation rules[91] and includes short-term, but not long-term, capital gains.[92] Some 85% of annual

---

[87] Reg. §1.509(a)-4(f).
[88] Reg. §1.509(a)-4(i)(2).
[89] Reg. §1.509(a)-4(i)(3).
[90] Reg. §1.509(a)-4(e)(2).
[91] IRC §4942(f)(1).
[92] Priv. Ltr. Ruls. 9714006 and 9730002 based upon the definition as interpreted by Rev. Rul. 76-208, 1976-1 C.B. 161.

income is the substantial amount the IRS wants to see distributed each year.[93] All of the income need not be paid over in the year in which it is earned, but can be accumulated if a good reason can be shown.[94]

Attentiveness. A subset of the income test portion of the integral part test is called "attentiveness" and says the SO's support must be sufficient in amount to assure that the supported organization will be attentive to its operations.[95] The regulations suggest that the test is passed when it can be shown that the funds are needed to avoid an interruption of the supported organization's particular functions or activities. Attentiveness manifested by required reporting, investment oversight, or scope of accomplishments is taken into consideration. The IRS has privately ruled that merely granting the supportee organization's annual income to the supported organization is insufficient to constitute "performs(ing) the functions of, or carrying out the purposes of" test.[96] A trust that paid all of its income to a city to maintain a science center named after its creator was found to fail the first part of the Integral Part test. To compare a good example of suitable attentiveness, see Cockerline Memorial Fund[97] and compare Roe Foundation Charitable Trust as an entity that failed to meet the "in connection with" relationship test.[98]

The IRS 1997 Exempt Organizations CPE Text contains a chapter entitled *Public Charity Status on the Razor's Edge* that reviews the fine distinctions made in evaluating satisfaction of these tests.

(d) Control by Disqualified Persons

An SO cannot be controlled by disqualified persons other than its own managers or the public charities that it benefits.[99] Indirect control is also not allowed; a funder's employees, for example, cannot substitute for the funder. An organization will be considered controlled by disqualified persons if, by aggregating their votes or positions of authority in the organization, they can require the organization to perform any act that significantly affects its operations. Lack of control is evidenced when the disqualified persons have under 50% of the voting power or lack the right to veto actions of the board.

(e) Conversion to Private Foundation

If the circumstances of the benefited organization or the funders change, it is possible for an SO to cease to operate solely to benefit the current public charity(ies), and convert itself into a private foundation (or a public charity if requisite support is received). Two important questions arise in such a conversion:

---

[93] Rev. Rul. 76-208, 1976-1 C.B. 161.
[94] Gen. Coun. Memo 36523.
[95] Reg. §1.509(a)-4(i)(3)(iii)(d).
[96] Priv. Ltr. Rul. 9730002.
[97] *Cockerline Memorial Fund v. Commissioner*, 86 T.C. 53 (1986).
[98] *Roe Foundation Charitable Trust v. Commissioner*, T.C.M. 1989-566 (1989).
[99] IRC §509(a)(3)(C); Reg. §1.509(a)-4(j).

1. The supported organization should agree to ceasing to be supported. As a practical matter, since it normally controls the SO, this factor is almost always present. There may be a price for agreement. In one situation, a retiring public charity supportee was given about half of the foundation's assets upon the SO's conversion.[100]

2. The conversion must not be part of a plan arranged when the SO was created, to enable the creators or donors to circumvent some tax limitation or private foundation sanction.

A supporting organization is often formed when the property to be given is closely held corporate stock. A private foundation cannot hold more than 2% of the shares of a company owned more than 20% by the PF and the persons who control or created it, and such "excess business holdings" must be sold by the PF within five years of their receipt. Thus, in the case of conversion of an eight-year-old SO to a private foundation in the same year that its stock holdings were purchased in a public offering, it might well be asked if such a conversion was originally intended. Without question, a conversion within a few years of original creation would be suspect, when the SO's public status afforded the donors a contribution carryover or higher percentage limitation on deductions than that allowed to a private foundation.

(f) Noncharitable Beneficiaries

Business leagues, chambers of commerce, civic leagues, social welfare organizations, labor unions, and agricultural and horticulture organizations normally are publicly supported under the IRC §509(a)(2) support tests. For that reason, they may also be a beneficiary organization of an SO. Since the SO qualifies for receipt of deductible contributions, an SO formed with such a beneficiary must, of course, meet the organizational and operational tests of §501(c)(3).[101] In other words, an organization performing the charitable or other IRC §170(c)(2) purpose activities for an IRC §501(c)(4),(5), or (6) organization *and* meeting the IRC §509(a)(3)(B) control tests may qualify as a supporting organization.

11.7 TESTING FOR PUBLIC SAFETY: §509(a)(4)

An organization that is organized and operated exclusively for testing for public safety is also treated as a public charity. This category is of limited use, however, because IRC §170 does not provide for deductibility of donations to such organizations. Thus, organizations seeking this status must also satisfy the requirements for a research organization in order to qualify to receive donations.[102]

---

[100] Priv. Ltr. Rul. 9052055.
[101] See Chapter 2.
[102] See Chapter 5.

PART TWO

Private Foundations

CHAPTER TWELVE

Private Foundations— General Concepts

Private foundations were segregated by Congress in 1969 from public charities—those organizations that traditionally receive their contributions from a wide range of supporters—rather than from particular individuals. In the exempt organization community and throughout this book, private foundations are sometimes referred to as PFs. The persons who create, contribute to, and manage PFs are "disqualified persons" and are sometimes referred to as DPs.

12.1 WHY PRIVATE FOUNDATIONS ARE SPECIAL

Private foundations are viable and valuable types of nonprofit organizations, despite the fact that the special rules applicable to them warrant six chapters in this book.[1] A PF is often the best tool to accomplish an individual's philanthropic goals. Unfortunately, some professional advisors discourage the formation of PFs because of the sanctions outlined in Exhibit 12-1. Granted, the rules are a bit more

---

[1] For an expanded consideration of this subject, see B. Hopkins and J. Blazek, *Private Foundations: Tax Law and Compliance* (New York: Wiley, 1997).

Exhibit 12–1

PRIVATE FOUNDATION EXCISE TAXES

Sanction	Tax Imposed On		Initial Tax		Additional Tax	
	Private Foundation	Managers	1st Tier Rate	Amount Imposed	2nd Tier Rate	Assessed
Section 4940 Investment Income Tax	X		2%	of investment income imposed annually when Form 990-PF filed	N/A	not applicable
	X		1%	tax reduced by one percent for PFs increasing grants annually	N/A	not applicable
Section 4941 Self-Dealing		on self-dealer X	5%	of "amount involved" for each year transaction outstanding	200%	if self-dealing not "corrected"
		on manager X	2½%	of "amount involved" for each year transaction outstanding; participating managers jointly and severally liable; can agree to allocate among themselves; maximum for managers $10,000	50%	if manager refuses to agree to part or all of correction. Maximum additional tax $10,000
Section 4942 Underdistribution	X		15%	of "undistributed income" for each year undistributed	100%	for each year income remains undistributed

Section		Initial Tax		Additional Tax	
Section 4943 Excess Business Holdings	X	5%	on fair market value of excess holdings each year	200%	of excess holdings at end of "taxable period"
Section 4944 Jeopardizing Investments	X	5%	on amount so invested for each year of "taxable period"	25%	of amount not removed from jeopardy
	X	5%	on amount so invested for each year of investment; participating managers jointly and severally liable for maximum tax of $5,000 per investment	5%	of amount on managers who refused to agree to part or all of removal from jeopardy; maximum for management $10,000
Section 4945 Taxable Expenditures	X	10%	of each taxable expenditure	100%	of uncorrected expenditure at end of "taxable period"
	X	2½%	of each taxable expenditure for any manager who knew of and agreed to the expenditure; maximum for all managers $5,000	50%	of expenditure manager who refuses to correct all or part of taxable amount; maximum amount $10,000

complicated than those for publicly supported charities, but they can be mastered and become easy once their logic is understood. All organizations qualifying for exemption under 501(c)(3)—private and public—are technically subject to a requirement that they not provide private benefits to those that create and manage them.[2] For years, some suggested that all charities should be subject to rules similar to those applicable to private charities. For reasons more thoroughly described in Chapter 20, Congress in 1996 added penalties, called intermediate sanctions, for public charities that pay excess benefits to certain individuals.

Private foundations are a perfect vehicle for funders who do not want a public board. A charitable trust or corporation whose sole trustee/director is also the creator can qualify for exemption. Commonly, the donor and his or her children comprise the board of a private foundation. Although financial transactions with the creators, and certain other activities, are strictly constrained by the PF rules, nothing prevents absolute control of the organization by founders and their families.

Funders who wish to be flexible in their grant-making programs may prefer a privately controlled foundation for a similar reason. A modest grant payout requirement, annually equal to 5% of the PF's investment assets,[3] must be maintained. The private operating foundation[4] is a perfect example of this latitude. The funder can establish a PF, hire a staff, and work to further his or her own charitable purposes, as long as genuine public interest programs are undertaken and the rules are followed.

Another positive attribute is the fact that family members or other disqualified persons[5] can be compensated for work they perform in serving on the organization's board. Disqualified persons can also be paid salaries for services genuinely rendered in a staff capacity. Those who learn the rules and plan well to adhere to them need not allow sanctions to discourage creation of a private foundation.

Finally, a private foundation can serve as a perfect income and estate tax planning tool for taxpayers with charitable interests. The classic example is a philanthropist who is ready to realize a large capital gain on the sale of corporate stock. A PF can be created in the year of sale, preferably gifting the shares to the foundation thereby avoiding tax on the gain. As much as 30% of the philanthropist's income can be given to an operating foundation (up to 20% to a normal PF) to substantially reduce his or her income tax burden.[6] The best part is that the money given to create the foundation need not be given away immediately. The foundation must essentially spend only a minimum of 5% of the value of the capital gift for its charitable purposes.

Philanthropists who make charitable bequests under their wills can create private foundations to begin to receive a portion of the bequests as donations while they are still living, and thereby obtain a double deduction. Current gifts to the PF are deductible and increase the estate by reducing income tax. The property gifted to the PF and the undistributed income accumulating in the PF are not sub-

[2] Discussed in Chapters 2§2 and 20.
[3] Described in Chapter 15.
[4] Discussed in Chapter 15§5.
[5] Defined in §12.2(c).
[6] IRC §170(e)(5) was extended permanently by the Taxpayer Relief Act of 1998.

ject to estate tax. The foundation can also serve as the beneficiary of a charitable remainder trust created during one's lifetime. Such plans usually result in more after-tax money for the charity and for other beneficiaries. There are many possibilities for the charitably minded taxpayer though a detailed discussion of the giving rules is beyond the scope of this book.

12.2 SPECIAL RULES PERTAINING TO PRIVATE FOUNDATIONS

(a) What is a Private Foundation?

Private foundations are defined negatively by what they are not. Any domestic or foreign charity qualifying for exemption under IRC §501(c)(3) is presumed to be a private foundation *unless* it is a church, school, hospital or affiliated medical research organization, donative or service providing charity, supporting organization, or an entity that tests for public safety.[7]

Those charities not able to qualify as public are those most often supported by a particular individual, family group, corporation, or endowment that do not restrict their activities to supporting activities. They accomplish their charitable purposes by making grants to public organizations of the types listed in the previous paragraph and, less frequently, by spending money directly for charitable projects. It is interesting to note, however, that the first four categories of public organizations listed are public, even if they are privately supported, because of the nature of their activities.

Throughout this part of the book, note the importance of public charities to PFs, both as the usual recipients of their annual gift-giving bounty and as potential recipients of "terminating distributions." Exhibit 11-1 charts some of the distinctions between public and private charitable organizations, and may make it easier to recall the differences. IRS Publication 578, *Tax Information for Private Foundations and Foundation Managers,* can still be used as a guide, if it's available. Last updated in 1989, the IRS has begun again to distribute it; but one may not find it on their website.

The burden of proving non-PF status rests with each exempt organization. A charitable exempt organization cannot qualify as a 501(c)(3) entity and is presumed to be a private foundation until proper notice is filed with the IRS on Form 1023.[8] If the exempt organization fails to file its notice for determination on time, it is treated as a taxable entity until the date of filing. The IRS does not count support received during the delinquency period in determining qualification as a public charity, and only an advance ruling can be obtained.

Unless state law effectively does so automatically, the charter or instrument creating a PF must contain language that prohibits violation of the private foundation sanctions. Every state except Arizona and New Mexico has passed such a statute.[9] Without proper organizational restraints, the PF cannot be exempt, nor is it eligible to receive charitable contributions.

---

[7] IRC §509(a); see Chapter 11 for a thorough explanation of each category of public charity.
[8] IRC §508(b); the determination process is discussed in Chapter 18.
[9] Rev. Rul. 75-38, 1975-1 C.B. 161.

If circumstances change or if its creators, for whatever reason, wish it, a PF can terminate its status. For example, its public support might have increased to the point that it can qualify as a public charity. It can also distribute all of its assets to a public charity, or to another private foundation, and go out of business. It can split itself into two or more parts. Voluntary and involuntary termination of PF status are discussed in §12.4.

(b) Special Sanctions

When Congress segregated privately funded charities and gave them special status, it was in an antifoundation mood resulting in the following sections being added to the Internal Revenue Code. These sections have operational constraints to govern the conduct of private foundations and impose excise taxes for failures to adhere to the rules. The first section is actually imposed on all private foundations—an annual tax of 2% of the foundation's investment income.[10] This tax is calculated annually on the foundation's Form 990-PF.[11]

- IRC §4940 Excise Tax Based on Investment Income

- IRC §4941 Taxes on Self-Dealing

- IRC §4942 Taxes on Failure to Distribute Income

- IRC §4943 Taxes on Excess Business Holdings

- IRC §4944 Taxes on Investments Which Jeopardize Charitable Purpose

- IRC §4945 Taxes on Taxable Expenditures

- IRC §4946 Definitions and Special Rules

- IRC §4947 Application of Taxes to Certain Nonexempt Trusts

- IRC §4948 Foreign Private Foundations

Appendix 12-1 contains capsule definitions of these provisions to use as a reference guide. Sanctions for failure to comply with PF rules of §§4941 through 4945 potentially include a tax (called the Chapter 42 tax) on both the PF and its disqualified persons, loss of exemption, and repayment of all tax benefits accrued during the life of the PF. Exhibit 12-1 tabulates the tax rates and the entity(ies)—sometimes several—subject to the tax. The standards for imposing the penalties on taxable events are somewhat different for each section, as described in Chapters 14–17. Form 4720, Return of Certain Excise Taxes on Charities and Other Persons under Chapters 41 and 42 of the IRC,[12] is filed to report the incidents and calculate any taxes due. Under abatement provisions explained in Chapter 16§2(c), certain of the taxes imposed upon a foundation and its managers can be abated if the vio-

---

[10] Discussion of this tax and ways to reduce it follow in Chapter 13.
[11] See Chapter 27§13 for suggestions about the unique issues faced in completing this form.
[12] Reproduced in Appendix 27-6.

lation was due to reasonable cause, rather than for willful and intentional reasons,[13] and if the violation is corrected. Self-dealing penalties cannot be abated.

(c) Definitions of Special Terms

The special sanctions applicable to private foundations contain unique and specific definitions of those persons whose actions are curtailed and of those that will be held responsible when violations of the rules occur.

Disqualified Persons. To determine who is in control of a private foundation and thereby subject to restraints against self-dealing and other sanctions, persons and entities in certain relationships to a foundation are treated as disqualified persons (DPs).[14] Individuals, corporations, trusts, partnerships, estates, and other foundations can be DPs. The list of DPs encompasses substantial contributors to the foundation, foundation managers, entities that own more than 20% of a "substantially contributing" business, family members, and corporations, trusts, or estates that are more than 35% owned by disqualified persons.

Substantial Contributors. Using the cumulative total of all contributions and bequests received during the PF's existence, a substantial contributor (SC) is one who has given more than $5,000 or two percent of the total aggregate contributions the organization has ever received, whichever is greater. A creator of a trust is also a substantial contributor, regardless of support level.

    With one exception, once one becomes an SC, one remains an SC, regardless of changing PF support levels or death. The exception is this: If, for ten years, an SC has made no contribution to the PF, is not a manager, and his, her, or its aggregate contributions are insignificant, that person ceases to be treated as an SC.[15]

    One becomes a substantial contributor the moment after the transaction in which he or she (or it) makes the substantial gift, as a result of the transaction.[16] Thus, self-dealing does not occur with respect to the transaction in which one becomes an SC. A testamentary bequest causes the testator to become an SC, so her or his children and ancestors become disqualified persons upon the testator's death.

Foundation Managers. A private foundation's officers, directors, and trustees, and individuals having similar powers or responsibilities, are its managers.[17] If an employee has actual or effective responsibility or authority for the foundation's action or failure to act, he or she is a manager. A person is considered to be an officer if he or she is specifically so designated under the certificate of incorporation, bylaws, or other constitutive documents of the PF, or if he or she regularly exercises general authority to make administrative or policy decisions on behalf of the PF. Advisers, engaged as independent contractors with no direct legal authority,

---

[13] IRC §§4961, 4962, and 4963.
[14] IRC §4946(a).
[15] IRC §507(d)(2)(c). Note: A disqualified person for reasons of being a manager or stockholder ceases to be a DP the day that status changes. See Priv. Ltr. Rul. 9210029 for example of use of this rule to avoid self dealing.
[16] Reg. §1.507-6(b).
[17] IRC §4946(b); Reg. §53.4946-1(f).

are not managers. However, employees of a bank that serves as a PF trust officer—although employees of the bank, not the PF—are treated as PF managers for accounts over which "they are free, on a day-to-day basis, to administer the trust and distribute the funds according to their best judgment.[18]

20%+ Owners.   An owner of more than 20% of a substantially contributing business is a DP. Ownership is measured differently for different businesses.[19]

- For a corporation, it means ownership of over 20% of the "combined voting power."

- For a partnership, it means ownership of an interest of 20% or more of net profits.

- For an unincorporated business, the distributive share of profits determines ownership. If there is no fixed agreement, the portion of the entity's assets receivable upon dissolution determines.

- For a trust, ownership is actuarially calculated.

Family Members.   A family member of any person listed above—a disqualified person, a substantial contributor, a foundation manager, or a 20% + business owner—is also considered as a disqualified person. The term "family member" includes:[20]

- Spouse

- Ancestors

- Children, grandchildren, and great-grandchildren

- Spouses of children, grandchildren, and great-grandchildren

- Legally adopted children

Not defined as family members for this purpose are siblings, cousins, aunts, uncles, nieces, nephews, and any more distant relatives.

35%+ Business.   A corporation of which more than 35% of the total combined voting power is owned by one or more disqualified persons is disqualified itself, as is a partnership of which more than 35% of the profit interest is owned by a DP. If a disqualified person owns more than 35% of the beneficial interest of a trust or estate, then the trust or estate is also considered a DP.[21]

Other Disqualified Persons.   For two limited purposes, other private foundations and government officials are treated as disqualified persons.

[18] Rev. Rul. 74-287, 1974-1 C.B. 327.
[19] Reg. §53.4946-1(a)(3).
[20] IRC §4946(d).
[21] IRC §4946(a)(1)(E), (F), and (G).

Related Private Foundations. For the sole purpose of calculating excess business holdings,[22] another private foundation that is effectively controlled, either directly or indirectly, by the PF in question is treated as a DP. The related PF's stock ownership is therefore attributed to the other PF. A PF that, for its entire existence, has received at least 85% of contributions from the same persons contributing to another PF is also related for this purpose.[23]

Government Officials. For self-dealing purposes only, a government official is a DP with whom financial transactions are generally prohibited. A person who, at the time of the act of self-dealing, holds one of the following offices is a governmental official:[24]

1. An elective public office in the executive or legislative branch of the government of the United States

2. An office in the executive or judicial branch of the United States government that is appointed by the president

3. A position in the executive, legislative, or judicial branch of the government of the United States which is listed in schedule C of rule VI of the Civil Service Rules, or the compensation for which is equal to or greater than the lowest rate of compensation prescribed for GS-16 of the General Schedule under IRC §5332 of Title 5 of the United States Code

4. A position under the House of Representatives or the Senate of the United States held by an individual receiving gross compensation at an annual rate of $15,000 or more

5. An elective or appointive public office in the executive, legislative, or judicial branch of the government of a state, possession of the United States, or political subdivision or other area of any of the foregoing, or of the District of Columbia, held by an individual receiving gross compensation at an annual rate of $20,000 or more

6. A position as personal or executive assistant or secretary to any of the foregoing

12.3 APPLICATION OF TAXES TO CERTAIN NONEXEMPT TRUSTS

Trusts and estates are permitted an unlimited charitable deduction against their otherwise taxable income for donations made pursuant to their governing instrument.[25] Though a nontax-exempt trust cannot qualify as recipient of an income tax deductible charitable contribution, it can escape income tax itself by paying out all of its income to 501(c)(3) organizations. To prevent the creation of trusts for the purpose of avoiding the PF rules, a wholly charitable trust is treated as a private foundation despite the fact that it does not have formal recognition as an exempt charitable organization.[26] To be so classified, "all of the unexpired interests of the trust"

[22] Discussed in Chapter 16.
[23] Reg. §4946-1(b).
[24] IRC §4946(a)(c); Reg. §53.4946-1(g).
[25] IRC §642.
[26] IRC §4947(a)(1); Reg. §53.4947-1(b).

must be devoted to charitable purposes[27] and income, estate, or gift tax deductions must have been allowed for gifts made to the trust. The tax on investment income and all the other PF sanctions are imposed on a wholly charitable trust; Form 990PF is filed annually and possibly Form 990-T if the trust has unrelated business income.

Split-interest trusts, or those holding property devoted to both charitable and noncharitable beneficiaries, are subject to some of the PF rules.[28] For example, such a trust might have a remainder interest payable to a named charity with the current income payable to the creator's son. Such a trust cannot formally seek tax-exempt status because of its unexpired noncharitable interests, but a deduction is allowable for the value of the charitable interests placed in them. The sanctions against self-dealing (Chapter 14) and excess business holdings and jeopardizing investments (Chapter 16) apply to such trusts as if they were private foundations. Form 1041, accompanied by 1041-A, and Form 5227 are filed annually for charitable remainder and lead trusts and pooled income funds.

12.4 TERMINATION OF PRIVATE FOUNDATION STATUS

A private foundation may wish to voluntarily terminate its existence for a number of reasons, or the IRS may cause it to be involuntarily terminated for reasons of repeated violations of the PF sanctions. In either case, the PF must carefully follow the rules for ceasing to exist, as the termination tax can be very costly.

(a) Involuntary Termination

The ultimate penalty for failure to play by the excise tax rules Congress designed to curtail PF operations is involuntary termination, also called the *third tier tax*. When a PF has willfully repeated flagrant act(s) or failure(s) to act giving rise to the imposition of the sanctions set out in IRC §§4941 through 4945, the IRS will notify the PF that it is liable for a termination tax.[29] The termination tax equals the lower of the aggregate tax benefit resulting from §501(c)(3) status or the PF's net assets.

Aggregate Tax Benefit. The sum of the tax benefits resulting from the PF's exempt charitable status is potentially due to be paid—all of the income, estate, and gift taxes saved by the PF's contributors. The amount equals the total tax that would have been payable if deductions for all contributions made after February 28, 1913 had been disallowed.

Repeated Acts. At least two acts or failures to act, which are voluntary, conscious, and intentional, must be committed.[30] The offense must appear to a reasonable person to be a gross violation of the sanctions, and the managers must have "known" that they were violating the rules. The "knowing" rules are discussed in Chapter 16§2(c).

---

[27] According to IRC §170(c)(2)(B); Reg. §53.4947-1(b)(2)(i).
[28] IRC §4947(a)(2).
[29] IRC §507(a).
[30] Reg. §1.507-1(c)(1).

Foreign Private Foundations.   The termination tax does not apply to termination of a foreign private foundation that has received substantially all of its support, other than gross investment income, from sources outside the United States.[31]

(b) Voluntary Termination

When the directors or trustees decide for whatever reason that they cannot continue to operate a private foundation, they can avoid the termination tax in several ways. All of the foundation's assets can be given away to a public charity. The foundation can convert itself into a public charity by virtue of activities it will begin to conduct—operate as a church, school or hospital—or by seeking public funding that will equal at least one-third of its annual revenues. Or a private foundation can—only after notifying the IRS of its intent and receiving approval for abatement of the termination tax—contribute its assets to another private foundation.[32]

(c) Transfer of Assets to a Public Charity

A PF that wishes to cease to exist, or terminate, can transfer or donate all of its assets to one or more public charities qualified under IRC §509(a)(1). The terminating PF must not have had any flagrant or willful acts or failure to act giving rise to the penalty taxes.

Qualifying Recipients.   The recipient organization must have been in existence for at least 60 continuous months.[33] Only churches, schools, hospitals, and donative public charities qualify as recipients.[34] Organizations classified as public under IRC §509(a)(2) and §509(a)(3)—organizations supported primarily by their exempt function revenues (symphony societies, theaters, and scientific research organizations for examples) do not qualify.[35]

Filing Requirements.   Advance notice to or approval by the IRS prior to termination in this fashion is not necessary. Some states require notice of intent to dissolve a nonprofit corporation or trust. Complete details should be included in Form 990-PF for the year of the termination, as described in Chapter 27.[36] Proof of public status must be maintained in the files of the terminating PF.

Restrictions and Conditions.   "All right, title, and interest in and to all of the net assets" must be transferred. No material restrictions or conditions can be imposed preventing free and effective use of the assets by the public charity. The following questions are used to find restrictions:[37]

---

[31] IRC §4948.
[32] IRC §507(g).
[33] IRC §507(b)(1)(A); Reg. §1.507-2(a)(2).
[34] Described in Chapter 11§2.
[35] Reg. §1.507-2(1)(3).
[36] Reg. §1.507-2(a)(6); IRC 6043(b).
[37] Reg. §1.507(a)(8).

- Does the public charity become owner in fee of the transferred assets?

- Are the assets used by the public charity for its exempt purposes? Are the assets subject to liabilities, leases, or other obligations limiting their usefulness?

- Does the public charity's governing body have ultimate authority and control over the assets?

- Is the public charity operated separately and independently of the PF?

- Were members of the public charity board chosen by the PF?

It is permissible for the public charity to name a fund to hold the assets after the terminating PF or its founders. The charitable purpose for which the transferred funds are to be used can be designated. Finally, the transferor can require that the property be retained and not sold when it is important to the charitable purpose, such as a nature preserve or historic property, but not simply as an endowment to produce income.

(d) Conversion of a Private Foundation to a Public Charity

A private foundation can change its method of operation or sources of support and become a public charity.[38] Basically, the PF adopts plans to qualify under IRC §509(a)(1), (2), or (3) and submits an application for approval to the Cincinnati district office. All of the information outlined in the regulations[39] must be submitted. Beware, as timing here is very important—the termination notice must be filed in advance of the year in which it is effective.

60-Month Termination. This type of conversion is called a 60-month termination because the requirements are to be met throughout and by the end of the continuous period of 60 months. The foundation does not have to qualify as publicly supported at the beginning of the termination period. The statute of limitations is extended during the 60 months to impose excise taxes for any year in which the reformed PF fails to qualify as publicly supported. Actually, the converted PF could revert from public back to PF status if its plans fail in the sixth, sixteenth (or whatever) year beyond sixty months. Form 990-PF is filed during the 60-month period. Subject to an extension of time for its assessment, the excise tax is not paid as long as public status is achieved.

Why Convert? A variety of circumstances could arise to make conversion to a public charity desirable. For example, because of a delay in start-up of operations and attendant fund-raising programs, an organization classified as public during its advance ruling period might mathematically fail to receive over one-third of its support from the general public. The current year support levels might qualify it as public, but the cumulative totals for the first five years do not. Thus it becomes classified as a private foundation during its advance ruling period. In a timely

---

[38] IRC §507(b)(1)(B).
[39] Reg. §1.507-2(b) and (d).

fashion, this organization might be able to continue its public status by adopting a 60-month termination. The possibility of using the facts and circumstances test or unusual grant rules to retain public status should also be explored as explained in Chapter 11§4.

Another example would be a privately endowed operating foundation, say a museum, that plans to undertake a major public campaign to expand its operations. It is privately funded in the early years, but converts as soon as possible to public status. Sometimes a private foundation ceases grant making and converts its operations to a type that qualifies for public status, such as a hospital or school.

(e) Transfer Assets to Another PF

A PF desiring to terminate can also transfer all or part of its assets to one or more existing or newly created PFs.[40] This transfer is simple because the old foundation is deemed not to terminate. Assets transferred to the recipient PF carry transferee liability and retain characteristics possessed by the transferring PF. Any previously undistributed income, for example, must be distributed by the recipient PF; likewise, prior excess distributions can be carried over. The transferring PF must exercise expenditure responsibility over the transferred assets unless it distributes all of its assets. Most significantly, the recipient bears any burden for a termination tax, in the unlikely event that one is assessed.

IRS Private Letter Rulings 9033054 and 9033044 make it clear that the division of all assets of one PF to two other PFs, to enable the trustees to pursue their divergent charitable interests, does not terminate the transferor's PF status or result in §507(c) termination tax. The IRS's conclusion was based on two facts: The transferor had not given notice of intent to terminate, and there was no evidence that the original PF had violated any of the PF sanctions so as to cause the IRS to terminate it involuntarily.

The treatment of the old and new organizations in a private foundation split-up was further clarified in a 1991 ruling.[41] According to the IRS, neither the old nor the newly created organization are treated as newly created (a seemingly impossible situation). The attributes of the old organization are attributed proportionately to each of the "new-old" PFs.

The tax attributes that carry over to a successor private foundation include excess qualifying distributions pursuant to IRC §4942.[42] The amount of the carryover attributable to one of several distributees is calculated in proportion to the value of assets each receives from the terminating foundation.[43] The private letter rulings issued by the IRS offer many examples of split-ups that have been blessed by the IRS as follows:

- A merger of two private operating foundations to manage a recreational complex; a merger of two PFs into one.[44]

[40] IRC §507(a)(2); Reg. §1.507-3(c)(1); see also the IRS Private Foundation Handbook Chapter 17.5, as revised.
[41] Priv. Ltr. Rul. 9121036; also see Priv. Ltr. Rul. 9814047 and 9805020.
[42] Discussed in Chapter 15.
[43] Priv. Ltr. Rul. 9342057.
[44] Priv. Ltr. Ruls. 9052025, 9814047, and 9805020.

- Three new organizations—one public organization to receive half of the assets and two private foundations each to receive one-fourth of the assets—formed from one private foundation.[45]

- A private foundation's legal structure converted to a nonprofit corporation from its original form as a charitable trust.[46]

- One private foundation split into three.[47]

- A combination of three commonly controlled foundations into one,[48] or two into one.[49]

The transferor PF, in a case of transfer of less than all of its assets, is expected to exercise expenditure responsibility[50] as it regards grants paid to the successor organization.[51]

(f) Conversion to a Taxable Entity

Listed first in the statute, but the least likely choice for termination, is a voluntary termination by conversion to a taxable entity.[52] PF can notify the IRS of its intent to terminate and request abatement (very unlikely) or pay tax, which, of course, it will probably have to pay at a confiscating level.

In most cases, the assets remain dedicated to charitable purposes under charter provisions or a trust instrument, and thereby, under state law. Once notice is given, the PF is treated as a newly created organization. If, for some unlikely reason, it wanted to resecure tax-exempt status, it would have to refile Form 1023 to be recognized as exempt.[53]

---

[45] Priv. Ltr. Ruls. 9101020, 9751044, and 9814040.
[46] Priv. Ltr. Rul. 9103035.
[47] Priv. Ltr. Ruls. 9204016 and 9750009.
[48] Priv. Ltr. Ruls. 9132052.
[49] Priv. Ltr. Ruls. 9115057, 9751044, and 9814046.
[50] See Chapter 17.
[51] Reg. §1.507-3(a)(7).
[52] IRC §507(a)(1).
[53] Reg. §1.507-1(b)(3).

Brief Description of Tax Sanctions Applicable to Private Foundations

A private foundation is given special treatment by the federal income tax code because it is funded by a single donor (or a particular family or small number of persons). The U.S. Congress, in 1969, added provisions to the tax code to prevent the operation of a private foundation for the benefit of its creators and insiders. The rules, in a negative fashion, call those that fund and control the foundation *disqualified persons*. The disqualified persons and the foundation can be subject to excise tax rules if the rules contained in Chapter 42 of the Internal Revenue Code are violated. The rules are sometimes identified by the code section numbers, §4940 to §4946. This memo briefly described those code sections and is not intended to fully inform one about the rules, but only to provide enough information to enable one to know when to ask a question.

EXCISE TAX ON INVESTMENT INCOME—§4940 TAX

A private foundation must annually pay an excise tax on the income earned on its investments, including dividends, interest, royalties, rents, and capital gains from properties producing such income. The tax rate is 2%, but can be reduced to 1% in a year in which the foundation's percentage of charitable giving in relation to its total assets increases. Essentially, some say the foundation can choose to give away half of the tax to grantees rather than to the government.

To illustrate, if a foundation receives a net investment income of $100,000, for example, the foundation would owe a tax of $2,000 (2% of the income). This excise tax is paid with tax deposit vouchers at a federal bank throughout the year on a quarterly basis following the similar system for paying the estimated income tax.

See Chapter 13 for tax planning and reporting issues. This tax is calculated on the Form 990-PF all private foundations are required to file annually. See Chapter 27.

SELF DEALING—§4941

In 1969 Congress felt private foundations were being used as extra pocketbooks for funds not necessarily available to a foundation's related parties from other sources and set out to completely eliminate self-interested financial activity between a privately funded charity and its insiders. A foundation is constrained from having financial transactions with persons that create, control, and fund it as a general rule. The prohibition applies even if the foundation benefits from the transactions. As an absurd example, a foundation cannot buy for $1 an asset owned by a funder that is worth $1 million.

As with many tax rules, some exceptions may apply. Though the following list of specific transactions that constitute prohibited self-dealing forbids the use of property, the PF's creator can provide rent-free office space. Similarly, although payment of compensation is literally prohibited, director's fees and salaries can be paid so long as the amount is reasonable for the services rendered. If a prohibited self-dealing transaction occurs, the money must be returned and the insider is subject to a 5% excise tax. Directors or trustees who approved the transaction may also be penalized. The following specific transactions between the foundation and its disqualified persons are identified as self-dealing and forbidden by the code, although exceptions apply as discussed in Chapter 14:

- Sale, exchange, or leasing, of property between a PF and a DP.

- Lending of money or other extension of credit between PF and DP.

- Furnishing of goods, services, or facilities by PF to DP and vice versa.

- Payment of compensation/reimbursement of expenses by PF to the DP.

- Transfer to, or use by, or for benefit of, a DP of any income or assets belonging to the PF.

- Agreement by the PF to pay a government official.

MINIMUM DISTRIBUTION REQUIREMENT—§4942

The foundation must annually spend a minimum amount for grants and other charitable disbursements. The required amount of the charitable payments, called *qualifying distributions,* is 5% of the average fair market value of the PF's investment assets for the preceding year. A PF in its first year of existence has no distribution requirement. Assume for simplicity, a foundation's investments have an average value of $1 million during year 1. Its mandatory distribution amount for year 2 is $50,000 payable before the end of year 2. In each succeeding year of its existence, the foundation must continue to distribute the mandatory amount based upon the prior year's average asset value. If charitable disbursements in a year exceed the required amount, the excess can be carried over five years to offset the mandatory amount in succeeding years. See Chapter 15.

EXCESS BUSINESS HOLDINGS—§4943

A private foundation, when its ownership in an active business corporation or partnership is combined with the holdings of its disqualified persons, cannot own more than 20% of the total shares of that enterprise, unless the PF itself owns not more than 2%. A foundation cannot operate its own business, or be what is called a *proprietor* of a business. If a foundation receives a donation of property that creates an excess business holding, the PF is allowed five years in which to dispose of the excessive amount. See Chapter 16.

JEOPARDIZING INVESTMENT—§4944

A private foundation's directors and trustees must exercise prudence and good business judgment in investing the foundation's assets. They are penalized if they invest any amount in a manner that jeopardizes the PF's ability to carry out its tax-exempt purposes. This rule parallels state laws under which the managers of a PF have a fiduciary responsibility to safeguard its assets on behalf of its charitable constituents. The long- and short-term financial needs of the PF can be taken into account in evaluating the inherent risk of an investment in accord with the Institutional Investor Act adopted by many states. The *Prudent Investor Rules* outlined by the American Bar Association in its *Restatement of the Law Trust Series* contain guidance on this subject. See Chapter 16.

TAXABLE EXPENDITURES—§4945

Lastly a foundation must devote its income and principal exclusively to the charitable purposes for which it was created and maintain records that prove its disbursements accomplish a charitable purpose. Payments made for noncharitable purposes and those without suitable documentation are called *taxable expenditures* and are subject to a 10% excise tax. Most PFs make grants to support the activities of churches, schools, hospitals, museums, and other publicly supported tax-exempt organizations and can rely upon the recipient's IRS status as proof of the charitable nature of the grant made. The suggested Grants Checklist, Grant Agreement, and Grant Payment Transmittal found in Chapter 17 can be used as a guide in gathering the appropriate documentation for such grants. It is very important the foundation ascertain—*before* it pays a grant—the public charity status of proposed grant recipients.

Although special documentation is required, one private foundation's support of another private foundation and individual scholarship and research grants can also serve its charitable purposes. A foundation that makes individual scholarship grants must seek advanced IRS approval for its program as evidenced by a written plan designed to ensure such grants are awarded on an objective and nondiscriminatory basis that allows no benefit to the foundation's insiders. One foundation granting funds to another must enter into a contract with the other foundation, called an expenditure responsibility agreement, and make special reports to the IRS, also discussed in Chapter 17.

ADMINISTRATIVE ISSUES

Grant Documentation.   A foundation should maintain a permanent file for each of its grant recipients. At minimum, a grant application should be required for each potential grantee and a Grants Checklist should be completed prior to the issuance of any grant payment. Due to the specific rules governing their charitable expenditures and the paperwork involved in the grant-making process, a private foundation must carefully describe its charitable mission and the specific types of programs it supports. Even if the foundation's charter contains a broad charitable purpose, its grant decision makers may find it useful to narrow the categories of programs it supports. Some foundations develop written grant criteria to inform interested persons of the purposes for which the foundation will grant funds. It is very important that the information entered in Part XV of Form 990-PF be accurate because it is published nationwide in printed and electronic directories for grant seekers.

Many foundations ask if they are required to keep the paperwork regarding grants that are not awarded. For federal tax purposes there is no requirement, but some foundations find it useful to keep such requests for a few years (in alphabetical order) for reference in the event the organization reapplies or someone inquires about the grant deliberation process.

Donation Acknowledgments.   Just like all other charitable organizations, a private foundation must provide the type of receipt shown in Exhibit 24-1 to its contributors to acknowledge their donation and reveal whether any goods or services of value were provided in connection with the donation(s). Note the furnishing of goods or services might constitute prohibited self-dealing, as discussed in Chapter 14.

Tax Compliance. Although private foundations are exempt organizations under IRC §501(c)(3), they are taxpayers in other respects. Persons engaged to serve the foundation may be employees from whom the foundation must withhold deposit, and report employment taxes as discussed in Chapter 25. Real and personal property held for investment may be subject to state and local property taxes. Certain types of business income may be taxed as unrelated income as explained in Chapter 21. A foundation selling books, reproductions, or other items may be required to collect local sales tax. The annual tax filing requirements outlined in Exhibit 27-8 should be studied.

CHAPTER THIRTEEN

Excise Tax Based on Investment Income: IRC §4940

To pay the cost of "extensive and vigorous" enforcement of sanctions imposed upon privately funded charities, Congress in 1969 adopted a tax on private foundation investment income. Congress felt that foundations should continue to be exempt from income tax, so the tax was enacted as an excise tax rather than the normal income tax imposed by Internal Revenue Code (IRC) §1.

The private foundation excise tax on investment income was described by the Congress as a "charge or audit fee" and was initially set at 4% of the foundation's investment income. When the tax being collected was revealed to actually be much more than the cost of examining foundations, the tax was cut to 2% in 1978.

In 1984 the tax was reduced again, but only for foundations that essentially pay out part of the tax in the form of charitable grants and projects as described fully in §13.4(b). If the foundation sustains its historical percentage of giving in relation to the current value of its investment assets, it can divert the 1% tax to grantees and need not pay it to the government—it only pays a 1% tax.[1]

[1] IRC §4940(e).

To discourage foundations from purposefully losing exempt status to avoid this excise tax, IRC §4940(b) provides that a taxable foundation must still pay the 2% excise tax *plus* the unrelated business income tax, unless the ordinary income tax on its overall income is higher.

During 1997, the IRS examined a sampling of "smaller" private foundations (PF) with under $1 million in assets. According to Marcus Owens, Director of the IRS Exempt Organizations Division, the most common problem with the exams dealt with the calculation of the 4940 tax.[2] Look for Owens' promised increased guidance on the IRS home page and improved instructions to Form 990-PF, but fewer exams.

13.1 FORMULA FOR TAXABLE INCOME

The excise tax is imposed on the foundation's *net investment income* for each taxable year, which equals:

Gross Investment Income	+	Net Capital Gain	−	Allowable Deductions	=	Net Investment Income

(a) Gross Investment Income

Only five specifically named types of income are included *in gross investment income* for a private foundation: interest, dividends, rents, payments with respect to securities loans,[3] and royalties from all sources. Any such income subject to the unrelated business income tax (UBIT) of IRC §511 is not taxed twice and, therefore, is excluded from the excise tax.[4] The income and associated deductions are reportable using the method of accounting, either cash or accrual, normally used by the foundation for financial reporting purposes, with certain exceptions discussed below.[5] Income of the specifically named five types listed that is produced by both investment and exempt function assets is taxed.[6]

(b) Interest

Interest income is taxed if it is earned on the following types of obligations and investments:

- Bank savings or money market accounts, certificates of deposit, commercial paper, and other temporary cash investment accounts

[2] Remarks to the Exempt Organizations Committee of the Washington D.C. Bar Association on September 25, 1997.
[3] As defined in IRC §512(a)(5).
[4] IRC §4940(c)(2) and Reg. §53.4940-1(d).
[5] Reg. §53.4940-1(c); Rev. Rul. 80-18, 1980-1 C.B. 103.
[6] Reg. §53.4940-1(d)(1).

- Commercial paper, U.S. Treasury bills, notes, bonds and other interest-bearing government obligations, and corporate bonds

- Interest on student loans receivable,[7] on mortgage loans to purchasers in low income housing projects, and loans to minority business owners as a program-related investment

- Payments on collateral security loans

- Municipal bond interest paid by state and local government is excluded and is not taxed and any expenses allocable to the nontaxable interest are not allowable as deductions. Municipal interest is included in "adjusted net income" for a private operating foundation.

- Series E bond interest, not previously reported by a decedent or by the estate, is taxed to the foundation.[8]

Distributions attributable to interest income earned by an estate do not retain their character as interest but instead are treated as contributions to the foundation. Proceeds of a qualified employee plan, except for interest accrued after the date the gift is effective, are not among the specified types of income. Plan proceeds are deferrred compensation and do not constitute investment income and are not taxable under IRC §4940.[9] Look for promised IRS guidance on this matter.

(c) Dividends

Dividends that are taxable include the following:

- Dividends paid on all types of securities, whether listed and marketable or privately held and unmarketable

- Mutual fund dividends (capital gain portion is also taxed, but as a capital gain)

- For-profit subsidiary dividends

- Corporate liquidating distributions classified as dividends under IRC §302(b)(1), but not including payments on complete redemption of shares that are classified as capital gains.[10]

The redemption of stock from a private foundation to the extent necessary to avoid the excess business holdings tax is a sale or exchange not equivalent to a

---

[7] Reg. §53.4940-1(d)(1).

[8] Rev. Rul. 80-118, 1980-1 C.B. 254; retirement plan proceeds payable to a foundation were deemed to be income in respect of a decedent in Priv. Ltr. Rul. 9818009. Watch for a subsequent ruling in which it is expected the IRS will address the issue of taxability for excise tax purposes.

[9] Fiscal 1999 CPE Text for Exempt Organizations, Chapter P, p. 316 and Priv. Ltr. Rul. 9341008; though in Priv. Ltr. Rul. 9818009 concerning a Keogh plan the IRS took a contrary view, the training text clarifies that matter.

[10] Priv. Ltr. Ruls. 8512090, 8326125, 8043112, and 8001046.

dividend, and the proceeds are not taxed as investment income.[11] Similarly a conversion of the foundation's shares in a tax-free reorganization is not considered as taxable investment income.[12]

(d) Rentals

Amounts paid in return for the use of real or personal property, commonly called rent, are taxable—whether the purpose for renting the property is an investment purpose or is related to the foundation's exempt activities.[13] Rental income that is earned on property that is debt financed is taxed as unrelated income, and therefore excluded from the investment income excise tax.[14]

(e) Royalties

Payments received in return for assignments of mineral interests owned by the foundation, including overriding royalties, are taxed. Only cost, not percentage, depletion is permitted as an offseting deduction. Royalty payments received in return for use of a foundation's intangible property, such as the foundation's name or a publication containing a literary work commissioned by the foundation, are also taxable. Income from a working interest in a mineral property is excluded. Instead it is UBI (and the property may be an excess business holding).

(f) Estate or Trust Distributions

Payments to the foundation from an estate or trust do not generally "retain their character in the hands" of the foundation. In other words, such payments do not pass through to the foundation as taxable income.[15] Part of the reason for this rule lies in the fact that the wholly charitable trust pays its own 2% investment income tax, and its distributions are not taxed again to the foundation upon their receipt. Income earned during administration of an estate that is set aside, or earmarked for payment to a foundation is deductible as a charitable contribution. Such income is therefore not taxable to either the estate or the foundation (unless administration is unreasonably continued).[16]

Payments from a split-interest trust created after May 26, 1969 do pass through to the foundation as taxable income if they are attributable to trust income from interest, dividends, or the other specific types of taxable investment income. However, capital gains distributed from a split-interest trust are treated as donations and do not retain their character as capital gains.[17]

---

[11] Rev. Rul. 75-336, 1975-2 C.B. 110.
[12] Priv. Ltr. Rul. 7847049.
[13] Instructions to Form 990-PF, Part I, column (b), at p. 6.
[14] IRC §514(a)(1) and 4940(1)(2).
[15] Reg. §53.4940-1(d)(2).
[16] Priv. Ltr. Rul. 8909066.
[17] IRC §§642(c) and 663(a)(2).; Reg. §53.4940-1(f) and Priv. Ltr. Rul. 9724005.

13.2 CAPITAL GAINS

Net short- and long-term capital gains from the sale of property used for the production of the specific types of income subject to the investment income tax—interest, dividends, royalties, rents, and security loan payments—are also taxed.[18] Mutual fund capital gain dividends, both short- and long-term, are classified as investment income.[19] Gains or losses from sales of assets used directly by the foundation in conducting its exempt activities are not taxed, including program-related investments.[20] The investment-use portion of a dually used property is taxed. The gain from property used in an unrelated trade or business is not taxed if it is subject to the normal income tax.

Capital losses only offset capital gains including capital gain dividends. Losses may not offset other investment income and a net capital loss for a year cannot be used to offset gains in a succeeding or preceding year.[21] Year-end tax planning to avoid a net capital loss for the year is very important to a foundation with security investments.

(a) Basis

The tax basis for calculating gain or loss is equal to the amount paid by the PF for the assets it purchases or constructs, less any allowable depreciation or depletion. Assets acquired by gift, however, retain the donor's, or a so-called carryover, basis.[22] Under accounting principles, a foundation records donated property at its value on the date the property is given. For tax purposes, however, it may not step-up the tax basis to such value. Essentially, the PF pays the tax unpaid by the donor (even when the alternative minimum tax applies). A foundation holding low basis securities may be able to reduce this tax burden if it can dispose of the shares in a year (other than its first year) in which its tax rate is reduced to 1%, as illustrated in §13.4(b).

The basis of inherited property is equal to its Form 706 (estate tax return) value, which is ordinarily its value on the date of the decedent's death. For property held by a foundation on December 31, 1969—the date when the tax became effective—special rules apply. The tax basis for any property held on that date is equal to its December 31, 1969, valuation, unless a loss is realized on the sale using such a value.[23] The IRS *Private Foundation Handbook* contains 25 pages of stock quotations from that date for reference.[24] Property held in a trust or in an estate created before 1969 may also use the 1969 basis.[25]

---

[18] IRC §4940(c)(4)(A).
[19] Rev. Rul. 73-320, 1973-2 C.B. 385.
[20] Priv. Ltr. Rul. 9320054.
[21] IRC §4940(c)(4)(A).
[22] Reg. §53.4940-1(f)(2) refers to IRC §1015.
[23] IRC §4940(c)(4)(B); Rev. Rul. 74-403, 1974-2 C.B. 381.
[24] IR Manual 7752, Exhibit (12)00-1.
[25] Rev. Rul. 76-424, 1976-2 C.B. 367. See also Priv. Ltr. Ruls. 8539001 and 8150002 regarding property distributed after a life tenant's death.

(b) Questionable Types of Gain

Gain from sale of property capable of producing the specific types of income (interest, dividends, rents, security loans, and royalties) are taxed even if the property is disposed of immediately after the foundation receives it. Since the statute applies to "property used for the production" of the specified income, clever foundations in the early days were hopeful they could escape the tax on low-basis property gifts by selling them as soon as the property was given.[26] The foundations argued that they never held the property to produce the specified types of income, so the tax should not apply. Effective December 31, 1972, a sentence was added to the regulations to provide that the tax applies even if the property is immediately disposed of upon its receipt, if "the property was of a type which generally produces interest, dividends, rents, royalties or capital gain through appreciation (for example rental real estate, stocks, bonds, mineral interests, mortgages, and securities).[27] The courts agreed with the IRS.[28]

A case involving a sale of timberland further clarified the application of the tax to such properties. Even though it was conceivable that the real estate in question could have been used to produce rental income, it was not. Instead, it was "economically prudent and reasonable" for the Zemurray Foundation to grow and cut the timber. Since the foundation did not use the land to produce a type of income specified in the statute, gain on its sale was not subject to the tax. The court held that only property that "can be reasonably expected to generate one or more of the five types of income" is subject to the tax.[29] Other assets that fall into this nontaxable category include collectibles such as art works, gold, antiques, cattle, and undeveloped raw land. Non-dividend-paying common stock is, for example, a type of property *capable* of producing dividends and the appreciation is, therefore, subject to the tax.

(c) Nontaxed Gains

Certain capital gains are not taxed:

- Gain from sale of exempt function assets, including program-related investments. Such property producing "incidental" income is fully excluded from the tax. Property used both for exempt and income-producing purposes, such as an office building partly used for administrative offices and partly rented to paying tenants, however, will produce *pro rata* nontaxable and taxable gain or loss.[30]

---

[26] Rev. Rul. 74-404, 1974-2 C.B. 382.

[27] Reg. §53.4940-1(f)(1).

[28] *Ruth E. and Ralph Friedman Foundation, Inc. v. Commissioner,* 71 T.C. 40 (1978); *Greenacre Foundation v. U.S.,* 762 F.2d 965 (Fed. Cir. 1985, aff'g 84-2 U.S.T.C. ¶9789 (Ct. Cl. 1984): and *Balso Foundation v. U.S.,* 573 F. Supp. 191 (D. Conn. 1983).

[29] *Zemurray Foundation v. U.S.,* 84-1 U.S.T.C. ¶9246 (E.D. La. 1983), *aff'd* 755 F.2d 404 (5th Cir. 1985).

[30] Reg. §53.4940-1(f)(1); Priv. Ltr. Rul. 8425114.

- Distribution of property for charitable purposes is not considered a sale or other disposition for purposes of this tax. Thus, the gain inherent in appreciated property distributed as a grant to another charity is not taxed.[31]

- Gain from disposition of "excess business holdings" held on December 31, 1969 (or received as a bequest under a trust irrevocable on May 26, 1969), and sold to or redeemed by a disqualified person to reduce the holdings[32]

- Gain realized in a merger or corporate reorganization ruled to be tax free under IRC §368 or other section of IRC Subchapter C[33]

- Appreciation on warrants or options to purchase securities[34]

- Capital gains distributed by a split-interest trust[35]

13.3 DEDUCTIONS FROM GROSS INVESTMENT INCOME

Gross investment income can be reduced by "all the ordinary and necessary expenses paid or incurred for the production or collection of property held for the production of gross investment income or for the management, conservation, or maintenance of property held for the production of such income." A private foundation's operating expenses include compensation of officers, other salaries and wages of employees, outside professional fees, office rent, interest, rents and taxes on property used in the foundation's operations and other administrative expenses[36] Expenses must be paid or accrued and have a connection or nexus to taxable income. A termination fee paid by a foundation upon receipt of the remainder interest in a trust was, accordingly, not deductible (value of the property received is also not taxable).[37] Interest expense paid on debt attributable to bonds to be used for construction of an exempt facility was deductible only to the extent of income from temporary investment of the bond proceeds.[38]

Where a private foundation's officers or employees engage in activities on behalf of the foundation for both investment purposes and for exempt purposes, their compensation and salaries must be allocated. No particular expense allocation method is prescribed, so that the foundation can use any reasonable method that is used consistently from year to year. For personnel costs, the preferred allocation method is for the employees involved to maintain actual records of their time devoted to investment and exempt activities. The concepts and rules applicable to

---

[31] Reg. §53.4940-1(f)(1); see discussion in §13.4(c).

[32] Reg. §53.4940-1(d)(3); Priv. Ltr. Rul. 8214023.

[33] Priv. Ltr. Ruls. 8906013 and 8730061.

[34] Priv. Ltr. Ruls. 8852001, 8846005, 8752033, and 8650049.

[35] See §13.1.(f).

[36] IRC §4940(c)(3); Reg. §53.4940-1(e)(1)(i).

[37] *Lettie Pate Whitehead Foundation, Inc. v. U.S.*, 606 F.2d 523 (5th Cir. 1979) *aff'g* 77-1 U.S.T.C. ¶9157 (N.D. Ga. 1977).

[38] *Indiana University Retirement Community, Inc. v. Commissioner*, 92 T.C. 891 (1989).

deductible expenses for unrelated business income tax purposes can be used as a guideline.[39] Documentation should be maintained to evidence the manner in which the allocations are made.

(a) Deductions Allowed

The following deductions are permitted:

- Depreciation on property the income of which is taxed using a straight line method, but no accelerated system is allowed.[40] The basis for calculating depreciation for purchased or constructed assets is equal to their cost. Donated property retains the donor's, or a carryover, basis. The normal income tax rules are used to measure basis.[41] Special rules apply to assets held by a foundation before 1969 when it began to claim depreciation for the first time in 1970.

- Cost, but not percentage, depletion on mineral interests.[42]

- Investment management and counseling fees, except for that portion attributable to tax-exempt interest.

- Legal and accounting fees allocable to investment income activity. A private foundation can ask its advisors to render billings specifically identifying such an allocation based upon time actually spent.[43]

- Taxes, insurance, maintenance, and other direct and specifically identifiable costs paid for property producing rental income, and an allocable part of such costs for administrative offices. Space rental would be similarly deductible to the extent the space is occupied by persons responsible for managing the properties that produce income subject to the excise tax.

- A proportionate part of operating expenses, including officer and staff salaries and associated costs, office and clerical costs, professional fees, and bank trustee fees.

- An allocable portion of expenses paid or incurred incident to a charitable program that produces investment income is deductible to the extent of the income earned.[44]

- Bond premium amortization deductible under IRC §171.[45]

(b) Deductions Not Allowed

No deduction is permitted for costs associated with a foundation's grant making and other charitable or exempt function projects. When a project or asset produces

[39] See Chapter 27§14.
[40] IRC §4940(c)(3)(B)(i).
[41] IRC §1015.
[42] IRC §4940(c)(3)(B)(ii).
[43] Rev. Rul. 75-410, 1975-2 C.B. 446.
[44] Reg. §53.4940-1(e)(2)(iv) and Priv. Ltr. Rul. 8047007.
[45] Rev. Rul. 76-248, 1976-1 C.B. 353.

or is operated to produce some income, the deductions for the activity are allocated between the exempt and investment uses.[46] With such joint purpose activities, the primary motivation for undertaking the project (investment or gratuitous) must be determined. When the expenses are incurred in connection with an exempt function project, allocable expenses are deductible only to the extent of the gross investment income from the project.[47] An investment project conceivably could result in a deductible loss. The typical historic restoration project is not expected to produce net income. Since admission charges for visiting such buildings are normally incidental to the overall cost of the project, it would be hard to prove that the building loss is deductible against other investment income. The following items are examples of nondeductible expenses for investment income purposes:

- Charitable distributions and administrative expenses associated with grant-making program costs are not deductible.[48] Similarly, expenses of programs directly conducted by the foundation are not deductible.

- Purchase of exempt function assets, depreciation of their cost, and cost of their maintenance, repair or conservation are not deductible.[49]

- Capital losses in excess of capital gains are not deductible, nor is a carryover permitted to the succeeding year.[50] This is a potentially costly rule to a foundation that does not properly time its asset dispositions.

- Operating losses incurred in a preceding year do not carry forward from year to year.[51]

- The allocable portion of expenses of exempt function income-producing property or activity in excess of the income produced therefrom and reportable as investment income.[52]

- Expenses allocable to taxable unrelated business income. (The income is also not includable.)[53]

- Interest paid on borrowing to acquire exempt function assets is not deductible. For example, interest paid on a bond issue floated to finance building a retirement community is not paid on behalf of an investment.[54] If the building is rental property, however, the interest and other property maintenance and operational expenses should be deductible[55] but subject to possible limits on loss deductions.

---

[46] Reg. §53.4940-1(e)(1)(ii).

[47] *Supra*, n. 43.

[48] *Julia R. and Estelle L. Foundation, Inc.*, 79-1 U.S.T.C. ¶9363 (2d Cir., 1979), *aff'g* 70 T.C. 1, Dec. 35,086; no charitable deduction similar to IRC §170 or §642(c) is permitted.

[49] *Historic House Museum Corp.*, 70 T.C. 12, Dec. 35,087.

[50] Reg. §53.4940-1(f)(3).

[51] Reg. §53.4940-1(e)(1)(iii).

[52] *Supra*, n. 31.

[53] Reg. §53.4940-1(e)(1)(i).

[54] Priv. Ltr. Rul. 8802008; Rev. Rul. 74-579, 1974-2 C.B. 383.

[55] *Indiana University Retirement Community, Inc.*, 92 T.C. 891, Dec. 45, 674 (Acq.).

- Interest paid to borrow funds that a foundation relends to another charitable organization (presumably low or interest-free) has been ruled not deductible. Such interest expense is deductible only to the extent of any interest income collected from the relending or temporary income earned on the funds.[56]

- A trust termination fee paid by the sole beneficiary private foundation was not paid for the production of income, nor were the unused deductions from the final trust return (customarily deductible to a noncharitable beneficiary under §642(h)(2)) deductible to the PF.[57]

- The special corporation deductions including the dividends received deduction are not allowed.[58]

13.4 TAX PLANNING IDEAS

This section explores the interaction of the §4940 excise tax on investment income, the §4942 minimum distribution requirements, and the §170 deduction for appreciated property donations. As the excise tax rate on foundation investment income has fallen over the past 30 years, the PF excise tax has become an accepted cost of retaining private control over donated funds. Perhaps because of the tax rate, very little is written on the subject. Its modest annual amount may be less than the cost of engaging advisers to perform year-end tax planning. Given the right circumstances, substantial savings can result from taking advantage of two relatively simple tax planning methods systematically over a period of years. Say for example, a foundation with net investment income of $500,000 pays an annual excise tax of $10,000. Although this tax is modest in some eyes, most foundations could reduce and partly avoid the tax using the techniques described in the following sections.

(a) Distributing, Rather Than Selling, Property

For several very different—but interacting—reasons, a foundation might sell assets that result in recognized capital gains subject to tax. The typical foundation invests its assets for *total return*.[59] Under this investment philosophy, more than 50% of the average security portfolio is invested in common stocks. The aim is a combined income from current dividends, interest, and capital appreciation. It is expected that capital gains will be regularly earned as portfolio holdings are sold in response to market changes. When the desired result—capital gain—occurs, tax is due.

The dividends and interest, sometimes referred to as the *current return*, from a total return security portfolio often equal less than the foundation's 5% payout requirement.[60] A foundation with such a portfolio essentially distributes its capital

---

[56] Rev. Rul. 74-579, 1974-2 C.B. 383.
[57] *L. P. Whitehead Foundation, Inc. v. U.S.,* 79-2 U.S.T.C. ¶9706 (5th Cir. 1979).
[58] IRC §4940(c)(3) and Reg. §53.4940-1(e)(1)(iii).
[59] *Foundation Management Report* (7th ed., Council on Foundations, 1993).
[60] See Chapter 15§3.

gains to meet the requirement. Thus, tax occurs for the second reason: securities are sold to raise the cash to make qualifying distributions. Herein also lies one possibility for tax savings. *If the securities (or other property), rather than cash from their sale, are distributed to grantees, the capital gain earned on the property is not taxed. Such a distribution is not treated as a sale or other distribution for excise tax purposes.*[61]

For example, suppose that one-half, or $500,000, of a PF's $1 million of income is capital gains on highly appreciated securities. Assume also that the PF plans to make grants of $100,000 each to five charitable grantees. As much as $10,000 in tax is saved if the grants are paid with the securities themselves ($500,000 × 2% tax). The higher the untaxed gain in a PF's portfolio, the greater the possibility for savings. The tax basis for calculating the gain for donated securities is equal to the donor's basis, meaning that many PFs have a good chance to realize the savings. Readily marketable securities are most suitable for delivery to grantees, because of the ease with which they can be converted to cash. However, any investment property producing dividends, interest, rents, or royalties is subject to this special tax exception; such property might include a bond or a rental building.

Implementing the savings requires some advance planning and cooperative grantees. Grants are normally pledged and paid in round numbers ($5,000 or $50,000). Securities do not normally sell for round numbers, and the price changes constantly. The grantee rather than the granting PF will have to pay the sales commission. The PF may want to gross up the number of shares to be delivered to ensure that the grantee receives the intended funding. The potential savings can be compared to the costs before such noncash grants are made. The size of the grant and the likelihood that the grantee will retain the securities in its own portfolio can enhance the attractiveness of this medium for grant funding.

Consider an example. A foundation is funded with zero-basis shares donated by a now publicly traded company's founding family. The PF keeps a supply of stock certificates in a variety of share numbers. When a grant is due to be paid, one or more certificates for the number of shares approximating the amount pledged are delivered to the grantee. If the shares are selling for $60 and a $100,000 grant is due, approximately 1,670 shares would be delivered (the few extra shares cover the commission). The full fair market value of the shares on the delivery date is treated as a qualifying distribution. Thus, the difference between the value and the foundation's basis ($100,000 of capital gain in this example) is not taxed, saving the PF $2,000.

(b) Qualification for 1% Tax Rate

A foundation's excise tax rate on investment income is reduced to 1% for each year, not including its first year, during which the foundation's qualifying distributions equal a hypothetical distribution amount plus 1% of net investment income.[62] The average of the foundation's annual *qualifying distributions* as a portion

---

[61] Reg. §53.4940-1(f)(1). The regulations specifically say, "For purposes of this paragraph, a distribution of property for purposes described in section 170(c)(1) or (2)(B) which is a qualifying distribution under section 4942 shall not be treated as a sale or other disposition of property."
[62] IRC §4940(e).

of its average investment assets each year is calculated. For example, a foundation has $1 million of assets and makes grants of around $60,000 each year. Its distribution payout ratio is 6% of its assets. Taking into account the payout percentage for the five-year period preceding the current year, an average payout ratio is determined. If the current year's distributions equal the average plus 1% of the current year investment income, only a 1% excise tax is due. See the sample completed Form 990-PF in Appendix 27-5 for an illustration of the calculation.

Some say that a PF can essentially choose to distribute 1% of its investment income to charitable recipients rather than the U.S. Treasury. The qualifying formula, as illustrated here, basically calculates an historic minimum distribution ratio by applying the past five-year average percentage of distributions to the current endowment value and adding half of the normal tax. If the foundation makes distributions equal to and $1 more than its past percentage (times the current fair market value), it can qualify for a reduced tax of 1% rather than 2%. The calculation briefly compares:

Average monthly FMV × 5-year average payout: ($2,000,000 × 5%)	$100,000
+1% of PF's net investment income	1,000
Baseline to compare to current distributions	$101,000
Qualifying distributions for the year	$102,000

Because the qualifying distributions made by this hypothetical foundation during a year equal or exceed the $101,000, the PF's tax rate is 1% rather than 2%. Essentially a PF may be able to pay half of the tax to grantees. Note, though, that the calculation is based on the average monthly value of the foundation's investment assets, including the last day of its year; hence planning for the savings is not easy. Since this tax reduction opportunity came into effect in 1985, foundations that realize the reduction often do so by accident rather than by specific planning. Unless the value of the PF's assets fluctuates widely, it is possible to deliberately time grant payments to reduce the tax to 1% in alternate years. For a foundation paying $20,000 to $30,000 in tax, a $10,000 biannual savings may be worth the trouble. To illustrate, Exhibit 13-1 contains a six-year projection for XYZ Foundation, which potentially redirects $48,000 in tax.

(c) Redistributing Donated Property

A donation to a nonoperating private foundation is not necessarily fully deductible, under a number of §170 constraints. The fair market value of noncash gifts, other than readily marketable securities to nonoperating private foundations is not fully deductible. For a donor to receive a deduction for full fair market value (FMV) of long-term capital gain property, the foundation essentially must give away the full value of the gift, or the gift itself, within 2½ months after the end of its year in which the donation was received.[63] A noncash donation retained by the

---

[63] IRC §170(b)(1)(E)(ii).

Exhibit 13-1

XYZ FOUNDATION—1995

	Qualifying Distribution	FMV Inv. Assets	Distribution Ratio
1994	1,000,000	20,000,000	5.00%
1993	950,000	19,000,000	5.00%
1992	1,100,000	22,000,000	5.00%
1991	1,000,000	20,000,000	5.00%
1990	900,000	18,000,000	5.00%
A. Average—five years			5.00%
B. Average FMV Assets		1995	21,000,000
Factor A × B			1,050,000
Add 1% taxable income			20,000
Base line for qualification			1,070,000
1995 DISTRIBUTIONS (Qualifies for 1% tax rate)			$1,300,000

XYZ FOUNDATION—1996

	Qualifying Distribution	FMV Inv. Assets	Distribution Ratio
1995	1,280,000	21,000,000	6.09%
1994	1,000,000	20,000,000	5.00%
1993	950,000	19,000,000	5.00%
1992	1,100,000	22,000,000	5.00%
1991	1,000,000	20,000,000	5.00%
A. Average—five years			5.21%
B. Average FMV Assets		1996	22,000,000
Factor A × B			1,146,200
Add 1% taxable income			20,000
Base line for qualification			1,166,200
1996 DISTRIBUTIONS (Does not qualify for 1% tax rate)			$1,000,000

XYZ FOUNDATION—1997

	Qualifying Distribution	FMV Inv. Assets	Distribution Ratio
1996	1,000,000	22,000,000	4.55%
1995	1,290,000	21,000,000	6.09%
1994	1,000,000	20,000,000	5.00%
1993	950,000	19,000,000	5.00%
1992	1,100,000	22,000,000	5.00%
A. Average—five years			5.13%
B. Average FMV Assets		1997	23,000,000
Factor A × B			1,180,000
Add 1% taxable income			30,000
Base line for qualification			1,210,000
1997 DISTRIBUTIONS (Qualifies for 1% tax rate)			$1,200,000

Exhibit 13-1 (*continued*)

XYZ FOUNDATION—1998

	Qualifying Distribution	FMV Inv. Assets	Distribution Ratio
1997	1,270,000	23,000,000	5.52%
1996	1,000,000	22,000,000	4.55%
1995	1,280,000	21,000,000	6.09%
1994	1,000,000	20,000,000	5.00%
1993	950,000	19,000,000	5.00%
A. Average—five years			5.23%
B. Average FMV Assets		1998	$23,500,000
Factor A × B			1,229,000
Add 1% taxable income			30,000
Base line for qualification			1,259,000
1998 DISTRIBUTIONS (Does not qualify for 1% tax rate)			$900,000

XYZ FOUNDATION—1999

	Qualifying Distribution	FMV Inv. Assets	Distribution Ratio
1998	900,000	23,500,000	3.83%
1997	1,270,000	23,000,000	5.52%
1996	1,000,000	22,000,000	4.55%
1995	1,280,000	21,000,000	6.09%
1994	1,000,000	20,000,000	5.00%
A. Average—five years			5.00%
B. Average FMV Assets		1999	22,000,000
Factor A × B			1,100,000
Add 1% taxable income			20,000
Base line for qualification			1,130,000
1999 DISTRIBUTIONS (Qualifies for 1% tax rate)			$1,250,000

XYZ FOUNDATION—2000

	Qualifying Distribution	FMV Inv. Assets	Distribution Ratio
1999	1,220,000	22,000,000	5.55%
1998	900,000	23,500,000	3.83%
1997	1,270,000	23,000,000	5.52%
1996	1,000,000	22,000,000	4.55%
1995	1,280,000	21,000,000	6.09%
A. Average—five years			5.10%
B. Average FMV Assets		2000	22,000,000
Factor A × B			1,122,000
Add 1% taxable income			30,000
Base line for qualification			1,152,000
2000 DISTRIBUTIONS (Does not qualify for 1% tax rate)			$900,000

foundation and essentially added to its endowment is limited in its deductibility to the donor's tax basis for calculating gain or loss for federal income tax purposes.[64]

During the years 1984 to 1994, and again after July 1, 1996 (the rule is now permanent),[65] the redistribution issue does not apply to gifts of certain securities. A special exception for marketable securities applies to encourage inter vivos gifts that would build endowments for private foundations. A full fair market value deduction is permitted for the donation of *qualified appreciated stock* or shares of a corporation for which "market quotations are readily available on an established securities market."[66]

For gifts of property other than securities, foundations must make distributions equal to the FMV of the appreciated property to afford their donors an income tax deduction for the full value of the property. Such a foundation must choose whether to redistribute the property itself or cash. Choosing redistribution of the property rather than sell it or other property may present an opportunity for the foundation to avoid paying the excise tax on the capital gain.

For the redistribution "not [to] be treated as a sale or other distribution of property" so as to qualify the gain for exclusion from excise tax, the foundation must grant property in a manner that is considered a *qualifying distribution* under §4942(g). The grant must be made for purposes described in §170(c)(1) or (b)(2) and must basically be made payable to an unrelated and uncontrolled public charity.[67] Additionally, the gift must be treated as a distribution out of corpus.[68] The fact that the distribution is charged to corpus (to meet the §170 requirement), rather than applied as a current distribution, should not cause the redistribution to fail as a *qualifying distribution*. Thus, a literal reading of the two applicable tax code sections and referenced regulation seems to allow the gain inherent in the redistributed property to be excluded from the excise tax.

13.5 FOREIGN FOUNDATIONS

As a general rule, foreign private foundations are taxed at a rate of 4% on their U.S. source (IRC §861) investment income calculated under the IRC §4940(c)(2) rules discussed previously.[69] Tax treaties with some foreign countries, including Canada, provide an exemption from the tax.[70]

A foreign organization may be eligible to be classified as a public charity under IRC 509§(a)(1), (2), or (3). If it operates a school, church, hospital, or receives sufficient revenues from public sources to satisfy the more than $33\frac{1}{3}\%$ support test, it is a public charity by definition, as discussed in Chapter 11. Such an organization would, therefore, not be subject to this tax. When such an organization

---

[64] IRC §170(e)(1)(A)(ii).
[65] Full deductibility without redistribution temporarily restored by the Small Business Job Protection Act of 1996, §1206.
[66] IRC §170(e)(5).
[67] IRC §170(e)(5); §4942(g).
[68] IRC §170(e)(5); §4942(g).
[69] IRC §4948(a).
[70] Rev. Rul. 74-183, 1974-1 C.B. 328.

might seek recognition of its exempt status to be readily eligible for grants from private foundations is discussed in Chapter 17§4(c).

13.6   TIMELY PAYMENT OF EXCISE TAX

The balance of any excise tax shown due on Form 990-PF is payable by the return due date, or 4½ months after the year-end (May 15 for a calendar year PF). Any unpaid tax is subject to an underpayment penalty of ½ of 1% per month unless an extension of time to pay has been allowed.[71] Interest at the current prevailing rate is also charged.[72] Additionally, a penalty may be imposed if the foundation fails to pay adequate estimated tax as discussed in the following paragraph.

Effective for the 1987 tax year, the excise tax is payable in advance under the corporate estimated tax system when a foundation's tax liability is $500 or more. The tax for each year is estimated or projected, and paid quarterly on or before the fifteenth day of the fifth, sixth, ninth, and twelfth months of the tax year.[73] Form 990-W is used to calculate the quarterly liability. The foundation's unrelated business income tax liability must similarly be prepaid. As in the corporate system, most foundations can make "safe" payments based upon the immediately preceding tax year. As long as 100% of the prior tax year's liability is paid quarterly, or 90% of the tax actually due for the year is paid, no penalty is imposed on any balance of tax due at year end. Form 2220 is attached to Form 990-PF to calculate any penalty.

Large foundations whose annual income was $1 million or more in any one of its three preceding years can base only the first quarterly payment on the prior year tax.[74] For the second, third, and fourth installment, the tax must be projected based upon actual income and deductions earned through the end of the month before the payment is due. At the other end of the scale, a foundation whose tax is $500 or less is excused from paying the excise tax in advance.

Any excise tax due must be deposited with an authorized federal depository bank using preprinted depository receipts (Form 8109) or through electronic transfer if the tax exceeds $50,000. The forms are customarily sent to a new foundation when it is issued an employer identification number.

13.7   EXEMPT OPERATING FOUNDATIONS

No excise tax is due from a special category of private foundation known as an exempt operating foundation, created in 1984 by Congress.[75] This rule is intended to eliminate tax liability for endowed museums and libraries. To be exempt, the foundation must have the following characteristics:

[71] IRC §6651.
[72] IRC §6621.
[73] IRC §6655.
[74] Since Form 990PF is not due until the fifteenth day of the fifth month following the close of the foundation's fiscal year, this exception is convenient.
[75] IRC §4940(d), added by H. Rep. No. 98-861, 98th Cong. 2d Sess. 1084 (1984).

- It qualifies as a private operating foundation.[76]

- It has been publicly supported for at least 10 years.[77]

- At least 75% its board members cannot be disqualified persons[78] and numbers must be broadly representative of the general public.

- No officer can be a disqualified person at any time during the taxable year.

[76] See Chapter 15§5.
[77] See Chapter 11§2.
[78] Defined in Chapter 12§4.

CHAPTER FOURTEEN

Self-Dealing: IRC §4941

Despite the general prohibition against inurement of a charity's assets to the benefit of its insiders,[1] Congress in 1969 found certain loans and stock bailouts between privately funded organizations and their creator's families troubling. Former Internal Revenue Code (IRC) §503 (now repealed) permitted such transactions as long as a reasonable rate of interest was charged and the fair market value (FMV) was paid. Nevertheless, Congress felt that private foundations were being used as extra pocketbooks for funds not necessarily available from other sources. This chapter describes the labyrinth tax code section designed to prevent most

---

[1] See Chapters 2§1(d) and 20.

financial transactions between foundations and the persons who create, fund, and manage them. In 1996, Congress imposed similar sanctions on excessive compensation or other benefits paid by public charities.[2]

14.1 DEFINITION OF SELF-DEALING

As a basic concept, all direct and indirect financial transactions are prohibited between a private foundation (PF) and its disqualified persons (DPs)—those persons who control, manage, and fund the foundation. There are exceptions, but most of the rules are draconian. It is immaterial whether the transaction results in a benefit or a detriment to the foundation.[3] Even if only $1 is paid by the PF for a director's $1,000,000 building, such a bargain sale is absolutely prohibited, regardless of the financial benefit to the charity. Such a sale can occur between the PF and a person who at the time of the sale is not a disqualified person, even though the transaction causes the person to become a substantial contributor and consequently a DP. Also drawn into the web are "indirect acts," those between the DPs and organizations controlled by the PF, or vice versa. This chapter addresses the complex subject of self-dealing from several different perspectives by presenting:

- The six absolute rules as found in the Internal Revenue Code
- Exceptions found both in the statute and in the regulations
- Examples of acceptable and unacceptable self-dealing transactions
- Suggestions for documenting associations that could conceivably produce self-dealing
- Procedures and rules to follow if self-dealing occurs

(a) Statutory Language

Six specific acts of prohibited self-dealing between a private foundation and a disqualified person are listed in the statute.[4] The specified transactions cannot occur directly between the PF and its insiders, nor indirectly through an entity controlled by such DPs or by the PF. These transactions are:

1. Sale, exchange, or leasing of property
2. Lending of money or other extension of credit
3. Furnishing of goods, services, or facilities
4. Payment of compensation (or payment or reimbursement of expenses)
5. Transfer to, or use by or for the benefit of, a DP of any income or assets of the PF
6. Agreement to pay a government official

[2] See Chapter 11.
[3] Reg. §53.4941(d)-1(a).
[4] IRC §4941(d)(1).

(b) Statutory Exceptions

What the statute calls "Special Rules" provide both clarification and certain exceptions, remove some of the absoluteness of the "six sins," and bring some reasonableness to the rules. The basic concept underlying these exceptions is to permit certain transactions that actually provide benefit to the PF without producing economic benefit to any DPs. The following transactions are permitted.[5]

- Transfer of indebted real or personal property is considered a sale to the PF, if the foundation assumes a mortgage or similar debt, or if it takes the property subject to a debt placed on the property by the DP within a 10-year period ending on the date of gift.

- A DP can make a loan that is without interest or other charge to the PF if the funds are used exclusively for 501(c)(3), or charitable, purposes.

- Offering a no-rent lease or furnishing free use of a DP's goods, services, or facilities to the PF is permissible, as long as they are used exclusively for exempt purposes.

- Furnishing a DP with exempt-function goods, facilities, or services that the private foundation regularly provides to the general public is not self-dealing, if conditions and charges for the transaction are the same as for the public.

- Reasonable compensation, payment of expenses, and reimbursement of expenses for a DP can be paid by the PF to a DP, if the amounts are reasonable and necessary to carry out the PF's exempt purposes. The definition of reasonable compensation relied upon by the Internal Revenue Service (IRS) national office is "such amount as would be ordinarily paid for like services by like enterprises under like circumstances."[6]

- Proceeds of a corporate liquidation, merger, redemption, recapitalization, or other corporate adjustment, organization, or reorganization, can be received by a PF if "all securities of the same class as that held by the PF are subject to the same terms and such terms provide for receipt by the PF of no less than FMV."

- Certain scholarship, travel, and pension payments to elected or appointed federal and state government officials are not considered self-dealing, as discussed in §14.6.

- Leasing by a DP to a PF of space in a building with other unrelated tenants is acceptable if:

---

[5] IRC §4941(d)(2).

[6] Reg. §1.165-7(b)(3): Tech. Adv. Memo. 9008001. A December 11, 1997 article in *The Chronicle of Philanthropy* reported that the median salary of a foundation chief executive officer was $84,000—with a regional median of $108,000 in the Northeast and $72,500 in the Midwest. The same article reported the names of 37 PF chief executives whose annual compensation exceeds $200,000. The National Center for Nonprofit Boards in September, 1997, reported the majority of charity CEOs make less than $75,000 annually.

- The lease was binding on October 9, 1969, or pursuant to renewals of such lease.

- Execution of the lease was not a prohibited transaction under former IRC §503, now repealed.

- The lease terms and its renewals reflect an arm's-length transaction.

(c) Exceptions Provided in Regulations

Additional exceptions to the (at first glance) absolute rules are found in the regulations, which provide that the following types of "indirect" transactions also do not constitute self-dealing:[7]

- Certain business transactions between an organization controlled by the PF and its DPs. Control, for purposes of these exceptions, means that the PF or its managers, acting in their capacity as such, can cause the transaction to take place.

- A grant to an uncontrolled intermediary organization that plans to use the funds to make payments to governmental officials is not self-dealing, as long as the intermediary is in fact in control of the selection process and makes its decision independently.

- Transactions during administration of an estate or revocable trust in which the PF has an interest or expectancy, if the specific requirements are satisfied.[8]

- Transactions totaling up to $5,000 a year and arising in the "normal course" of a retail business are permitted between a DP and a controlled business, as long as the prices are the same as for other customers.

- Stocks owned on May 26, 1969, and required to be distributed to avoid the IRC §4943 tax on excess business holdings can be sold, exchanged, or otherwise disposed of to a DP.[9]

14.2 SALE, EXCHANGE, OR LEASE OF PROPERTY

Sales and exchanges of property between a PF and its DPs are absolutely prohibited by rules that are strictly applied by comparison to those applicable to compensation for services. Even the "sale of incidental supplies" is self-dealing.[10] A PF's purchase of a mortgage held by its bank trustee (a DP) was found to be self-dealing, even when the rate or interest was much more favorable than would otherwise have been available to the foundation. The self-dealing occurred because the bank was selling its own property, not simply handling the purchase of an in-

---

[7] Reg. §53.4941(d)-1(b).
[8] See §14.9.
[9] Reg. §53.4941(d)-4(b)(1); Rev. Rul. 75-25, 1975-1 C.B. 359.
[10] Reg. §53.4941(d)-2(a).

vestment instrument issued by an independent source.[11] The sale to an unrelated party of an option to buy shares in a corporation that is a disqualified person is not self-dealing, even though the exercise of the option by the PF would be.[12]

(a) Transactions through Agents

A sale handled by an outside agent will not necessarily circumvent the rules, but can be attributed to the foundation. In a case involving an art object consigned to a commercial art auction house, the purchase of the object by a DP constituted self-dealing.[13] However, even though the same banking institution served as trustee for both parties, a sale to a PF by a testamentary trust (which is not a DP of the purchasing PF) was not considered as self-dealing.[14] A sale to the bank itself by either party would be self-dealing, because the bank is a DP of both parties—neither is to the other. The leasing of property to a DP by a management company resulted in self-dealing when the PF controlled the manager's actions through a retained veto power.[15]

(b) Exchanges

A transfer of shares of stock in payment of an interest-free loan is "tantamount to a sale or exchange."[16] Similarly, a transfer of real estate equal to the amount of the DP's loan (in an effort to correct self-dealing) was ruled to be a second act of self-dealing.[17] However, a transfer of real estate in satisfaction of a pledge to pay cash or readily marketable securities was held not to be a "sale or exchange" because the pledge was not legally enforceable and because a pledge is not considered a debt.[18] No self-dealing resulted in such a transfer because it is essentially a gift.[19]

An exchange of a PF's securities in a reorganization or merger of a corporation that is a DP is not necessarily an act of self-dealing. When all of the securities of the same class as those held by the foundation (prior to the transaction) are subject to the same, or uniform, terms and the foundation receives the full FMV for its securities, no self-dealing occurs.[20]

The partition of property a foundation holds as a tenant-in-common with a disqualified person did not produce reportable gain or constitute self-dealing for a foundation.[21] Without saying so directly, the IRS deems a partition not a prohibited sale or exchange. The foundation had received the undivided interest in the unproductive property as a gift from the DP. Local law prohibited a nonprofit corporation

---

[11] Rev. Rul. 77-259, 1977-2 C.B. 387.
[12] Priv. Ltr. Rul. 8502040.
[13] Rev. Rul. 76-18, 1976-1 C.B. 355.
[14] Rev. Rul. 78-77, 1978-1 C.B. 378.
[15] Priv. Ltr. Rul. 9047001.
[16] Rev. Rul. 77-379, 1977-2 C.B. 387.
[17] Rev. Rul. 81-40, 1981-1 C.B. 508.
[18] See §14.5(e).
[19] Priv. Ltr. Rul. 8723001.
[20] Reg. §53.4941(d)-3(d)(1).
[21] Priv. Ltr. Rul. 8136085; also see Priv. Ltr. Ruls. 8141074, 8038049, and 8327051.

from holding unproductive property and the PF wanted to make the property marketable by creating a divided interest.

(c) Use of Property

Property can be provided to a private foundation for rent-free use, but the foundation cannot permit a DP to use its property unless there is some exempt purpose. No rent can be charged, neither by the PF nor by the DP, for use of property. Permissible payments include those for janitorial services, utilities, and other maintenance costs, as long as payments are not made directly or indirectly to the DP.[22] There are circumstances in which property can be used.

Assume that a private foundation borrows an art object from its creator at no cost to display in its museum. The PF pays the maintenance and insurance to independent parties. The IRS has ruled that this "use of property" is not self-dealing, and has provided some interesting facts. First, the PF is allowed to pay the DP's costs of owning the art object, which, in these days of high auction prices, represents a substantial benefit. It is important to note that the PF did not reimburse the DP; it paid the costs directly to unrelated parties. The reason for permitting this arrangement is that the public benefits: Art that would not otherwise be available can now be seen. However, placement of PF art in the DP's private home, away from public view, is clearly not allowed.[23] Displaying art on the DP's property that is open to the public has been permitted, but only because the PF's collection was displayed throughout the city, primarily on public lands, as a part of a comprehensive Outdoor Museum program.[24]

Furnishing living quarters in a historic district to a substantial contributor (who worked 25 to 35 hours a week overseeing the complex and managing the foundation's financial affairs) was also found not to be self-dealing, as long as the fair value of the space is treated as compensation,[25] and as long as the total compensation is reasonable.[26]

A PF's rental of a charter aircraft from a charter aircraft company that is itself a disqualified person, is an act of self-dealing.[27] Donating use of the plane to the PF, however, would be allowed. If the charter company officials travel on bona fide foundation business, the foundation could directly pay for their direct out-of-pocket expenses, such as fuel or hanger rental in the city visited, as long as the goods and services were purchased from an independent party.[28]

---

[22] Reg. §53.4941(d)-2(b)(2).

[23] Rev. Rul. 74-600, 1974-2 C.B. 385.

[24] Tech. Adv. Memo. 9221002. But see Priv. Ltr. Rul. 8824001 for the opposite result when, due to the fact that the sculptures were placed on the DP's private residential grounds not physically open to the public but only available for viewing from the street, self-dealing occurred. See also Priv. Ltr. Rul. 9119009 in which the "unavoidable driving of the antique automobiles by a foundation's creator from time to time on behalf of the foundation to maintain and show them" did not result in self-dealing.

[25] Regardless of whether it is actually taxable under IRC §119.

[26] Priv. Ltr. Rul. 8948034; also see Priv. Ltr. Rul. 9327082 concerning housing on a ranch.

[27] Rev. Rul. 73-363, 1973-2 C.B. 383.

[28] §14.7 explores permissible sharing of spaces, people, and expenses and provides samples of required documentation.

(d) Co-owned Property

Mere co-ownership of a property by a foundation and its disqualified person(s) does not result in self-dealing.[29] Therefore, a PF can receive and hold a gift or bequest of an undivided interest in property from its DPs. The catch is that only the PF can "use the property," because the statute specifically prohibits the use of any income or assets of the PF by the DP.[30] A transitional exception to the rule provided by Congress applies only to property jointly owned before October 9, 1969.

Essentially the PF may hold and use co-owned property; the DP co-owner can hold but cannot use or otherwise reap any benefit from the property. A number of private rulings have illustrated why limited-use or shared ownership can still be of some advantage to the DPs retaining an interest. In one case, a decedent and his spouse owned an extensive art collection that they planned to bequeath to a museum they were creating. Upon the husband's death, the PF museum and the spouse became joint tenants holding an undivided interest in each object in the art collection. The IRS would not permit the spouse to display a small portion of the co-owned objects in her home and strictly applied the statute to prohibit her use of the art in any way.[31] On a positive note, the museum was permitted to pay the insurance on all of the art works, similar to the rules discussed previously.[32]

A gift of an undivided interest in property the donor planned to subsequently sell was sanctioned.[33] The donor relinquished all rights to use the improved real estate and retained only the right to inspect the property. Expenses were to be shared proportionately between the donor and the PF. Upon subsequent sale of co-owned property, the proceeds were divided proportionately. No self-dealing resulted from the gift, from holding the property jointly, or from the sale. The restrictions on use have also been found to include the making of improvements to the property.[34]

An alternative to holding property as co-owners—becoming partners—has been sanctioned by the IRS.[35] A limited partnership interest given to a charitable remainder trust treated as a private foundation was distinguished from the "jointly owned property" contemplated by the regulations because "the holding and use of separate interests in a limited partnership is not the use of jointly owned property." Instead of donating an undivided interest in a shopping center, the donors contributed the property and became general partners in a limited partnership. Formation of a partnership between a private foundation and its three benefactor §4947(a)(2) split-interest charitable lead trusts did not result in self-dealing.[36] Caution must be used in planning such arrangements to ensure that the terms of partnership agreement permit each partner to have exclusive control, *or use*, of their respective interests, and create no common or shared interests.

---

[29] Priv. Ltr. Rul. 7751033.
[30] IRC §4941(d)(1)(E).
[31] Priv. Ltr. Rul. 8842045.
[32] See §14.2(c).
[33] Priv. Ltr. Rul. 7751033.
[34] Priv. Ltr. Rul. 8038049.
[35] Priv. Ltr. Ruls. 9114025 and 7810038.
[36] Priv. Ltr. Rul. 9015070.

14.3 LOANS

The lending of money or extension of credit is a self-dealing act. Even if a circuitous route is followed, with the foundation not being the first lender, indebtedness payable to or from the foundation is prohibited. If a PF sells property in return for a mortgage to a third party who later resells the property to a DP in relation to the PF, self-dealing occurs with the second sale.[37] A loan without interest from a DP to a PF is permitted[38] if the proceeds of the loan are used exclusively in carrying out the foundation's exempt activities. Repayment of such a loan with property other than cash is an act of self-dealing.[39]

A gift of a whole life insurance policy subject to a cash surrender loan is also an act of self-dealing, unless the loan was placed on the policy more than ten years before the gift. Even though the insurer does not demand repayment of the loan and failure to repay simply reduces the death benefits, the loan is valid indebtedness that causes self-dealing.[40] The date on which the loan is made, not when the loan or line of credit was approved, is the date from which the 10-year exception is measured. It is normally the date a lien is actually placed on the property for purposes of the exception.[41]

A gift of stock in a rental property holding company that was indebted to the substantial contributor was ruled not to result in self-dealing. The loan was made for business reasons prior to the transfer of the shares.[42] A future obligation to pay expenses to maintain gifted property is not indebtedness for this purpose. Similarly a loan by the PF to an individual before he or she becomes a disqualified person is not self-dealing even though the transaction causes the person to become a DP.[43] However, the loan cannot remain outstanding beyond the first day of the year in which the loan is made; an act of self-dealing occurs in each year in which there is an uncorrected extension of credit.[44]

14.4 COMPENSATION

An extremely important and frequently used exception to the self-dealing sanctions is the provision allowing payment of compensation for personal services provided by PF insiders. Though the code literally says payment of compensation is self-dealing, exceptions permit such payments. A foundation can pay reasonable (i.e., not excessive) salaries and fees and reimburse expenses incurred in serving a foundation. The services rendered must be "personal" and be rendered by

---

[37] Reg. §53.4941(d)-2(c)(1).
[38] Reg. §53.4941(d)-2(c)(2).
[39] Rev. Rul. 77-379, 1977-2 C.B. 387.
[40] Rev. Rul. 80-132, 1980-1 C.B. 255.
[41] Rev. Rul. 78-395, 1978-2 C.B. 270.
[42] Priv. Ltr. Rul. 8409039.
[43] Reg. §53.4941(d)-1(a).
[44] See §14.3 and Priv. Ltr. Ruls. 9343033, 9417018, and 9530032 concerning a loan to a newly hired PF executive director to purchase a home. Initially the transaction was sanctioned on the rationale that the loan was part of compensation; the IRS later reconsidered and ultimately revoked the ruling.

an individual, a partnership, or other form of service provider.[45] It is very important to note that excessive compensation results not only in self-dealing but also a taxable expenditure.[46]

It is sometimes difficult to decide what constitutes permitted personal services. The regulations only name the services of a broker acting as agent for the foundation, legal services, investment counseling, and commercial banking services as examples. By contrast, payments under a contract to manufacture microscopes is deemed not to constitute a permissible payment for personal services.[47] Presumably, the personal services are rendered for the company making the scopes and not for the PF purchasing the finished product. Why the rental of a safety deposit box and maintenance of a checking account are treated as personal services under the regulation could be debated. What about remodeling a building or painting the office? Is the result different if the PF pays the workers directly rather than through a separate company? The Tax Court agreed with the IRS, in a case involving property management, that this exception is limited to payments that are "essentially professional and managerial in nature."[48]

(a) Definition of Reasonable

The factors for evaluating whether private inurement has occurred can be applied to determine whether PF compensation is reasonable.[49] The IRC §162 regulations are prescribed as the standard to follow in this regard.[50] To prove that compensation is reasonable, a foundation must show that the pay is equal to "such amount as would ordinarily be paid for like services by like enterprises under like circumstances." Annual compensation 75% higher than the average for a private foundation of comparable size listed in the *Council on Foundations' 1986 Foundation Management Report,* which also represented 35% of the foundation's grant expense, for example, was found to be excessive and an act of self-dealing.[51]

All payments to or made on behalf of a disqualified person are tallied up to determine total compensation—salaries, bonuses, fringe benefits (medical and life insurance, nonaccountable auto allowance, and child care, for example), qualified and nonqualified deferred compensation, retirement plan contributions, contractor fees, and the like. In a schedule where officers, directors, trustees, and key employees must be individually listed, the instructions to Form 990-PF direct the foundation to report "all forms of cash and noncash compensation received by each person whether paid currently or deferred.[52]

---

[45] Reg. §53.4941(d)-3(c)(1).

[46] Defined in Chapter 17.

[47] Reg. §53.4941(d)-3(c)(2), example (4).

[48] *Madden, Jr. v. Commissioner,* T.C. Memo. 1997-395(1997); see also Priv. Ltr. Rul. 8732064 in which the IRS sanctioned payments to conduct a six-week scientific research project with a monthly retainer for chemical advisory services; Priv. Ltr. Rul. 8351111 concerning architectural services; and 1995 IRS Exempt Organizations CPE Text, Topic O, pages 247, 269–274 that discusses personal services.

[49] See Chapter 20.

[50] Reg. §1.162-7.

[51] Priv. Ltr. Rul. 9008001.

[52] Part VIII of Form 990-PF, reproduced in Chapter 27, Appendix 27-5.

Foundation payment of board member's and manager's expenses of attending board meetings and otherwise participating in conduct of foundation activities are not considered compensation. Property and services that qualify as de minimus working condition fringe benefits—whether provided to compensated or noncompensated persons—are also not counted in determining total compensation.[53] That portion of the foundation's liability insurance premiums attributable to the Chapter 42 taxes is, however, treated as compensation paid to the directors, officers, and managers though it is considered a nontaxable fringe benefit.[54] Expenses paid on behalf of or reimbursed to disqualified persons should be carefully documented to evidence their connection to the accomplishment of the foundation's exempt purposes.

(b) Commissions

Compensation based on a percentage of sales of a foundation's property or the value of the property managed is permitted. The terms for payment of commissions should be based on a customary scale prevailing in the normal marketplace for sale of the property (i.e., the amount was reasonable). Commissions paid to a DP/art dealer, for example, were found not to be self-dealing when sold by the same dealer who had represented the artist while living. Funds were to be used to fund the foundation's programs. The IRS set out "comparability factors" the foundation should use to determine whether commissions were reasonable, including[55]

- Commissions charged by nondisqualified persons for selling the (same) artist's work

- Commissions paid by the artist during his or her lifetime to persons who are now disqualified persons and to others

- Commissions that agents charge to sell art of the same school as the artist

- Commissions that are received by agents who sell art generally from the foundation's geographic area

Brokerage commissions and investment management fees can similarly be paid to an investment manager that is a related party as long as the amount is customary and normal for the industry. Total compensation that included the normal transactions fees plus 50% of the account's annual equity value increases in excess of 15%, was deemed reasonable because it was consistent with practices in the industry.[56]

(c) Advances

Advances that are "reasonable in relation to the duties and expense requirements of a foundation manager" are permitted.[57] Cash advances should not ordinarily exceed $500 (a 1970 amount often too low by current standards) according to the

---

[53] Reg. §53.4941(d)-2(f)(8).
[54] Discussed below in §14.5(a).
[55] Priv. Ltr. Rul. 9011050.
[56] Priv. Ltr. Rul. 9237035.
[57] Reg. §53.4941(d)-3(c)(1).

regulations. If the advance is to cover anticipated out-of-pocket current expenses for a reasonable period (such as a month), self-dealing will not occur:

- When the PF makes an advance,

- When the PF replenishes the funds upon receipt of supporting vouchers from the manager, or

- When the PF temporarily adds to the advance to cover extraordinary expenses anticipated to be incurred in fulfillment of a special assignment, such as long distance travel.

(d) Bank Fees

Banks and trust companies often serve as foundation trustees, and in this role often face self-dealing possibilities. Certain functions that the bank performs for all of its customers can be performed for a foundation. Taking into account a fair interest rate for the use of the funds by the bank, reasonable compensation can be paid. The "general banking services" permitted are:[58]

- Checking accounts, as long as the bank does not charge interest on any overdrafts. Payment of overdraft charges not exceeding the bank's cost of processing the overdraft have been ruled to be acceptable.[59]

- Savings accounts, as long as the foundation may withdraw its funds on no more than 30 days' notice without subjecting itself to a loss of interest on its money for the time during which the money was on deposit

- Safekeeping activities

Transactions outside the scope of these three relationships may be troublesome. When a PF left funds earning no interest in a DP's bank, self-dealing was found.[60] The bank's purchase of securities owned by independent parties for a PF's account is not self-dealing, but purchase of the bank's own mortgage loans would be.[61] The purchase of certificates of deposit by a PF is unacceptable if the certificates provide for a reduced rate of interest if they are not held to the full maturity date.[62] Purchase of a foreign currency with which the foundation purchased foreign securities (unrelated to the bank) was found not to result in self-dealing.[63]

14.5 TRANSACTIONS THAT BENEFIT DISQUALIFIED PERSONS

The use of a foundation's income or assets by or for the benefit of a disqualified person generally constitutes self-dealing.[64] Self-dealing can occur even if money is

[58] Reg. §53.4941(d)-2(c)(4).
[59] Rev. Rul. 73-546, 1973-2 C.B. 384.
[60] Rev. Rul. 73-595, 1973-2 C.B. 384.
[61] Rev. Rul. 77-259, 1977-2 C.B. 387.
[62] Rev. Rul. 77-288, 1977-2 C.B. 388.
[63] Priv. Ltr. Rul. 9616040.
[64] IRC §4941(d)(1)(E).

not transferred directly to or from the foundation and its insiders. A foundation may not pay an insider's obligations but it can allow him or her to receive recognition for foundation programs. This somewhat vague standard—no use of assets or income—is exemplified in the following situations:

- The purchase or sale of securities by the foundation for the purpose of manipulating the price of the stock or other securities to the advantage of a disqualified person.[65]

- Foundation investment assets taken into account to satisfy a disqualified person's security investment margin requirement is an act of self-dealing.[66]

- Guarantee of a disqualified person's loan by a foundation is considered self-dealing as is indemnification of the lender.[67]

- A student loan guarantee program funded by a foundation through a public charity resulted in self-dealing when a DP's children received loans.[68]

(a) Indemnification of Disqualified Persons

An act of self-dealing does not occur, as a general rule, when a foundation indemnifies its managers with respect to civil[69] judicial or administrative proceedings involving the private foundation sanctions and state laws relating to mismanagement of funds of charitable organization. Liability insurance to reimburse the foundation for costs associated with indemnifying its DPs also does not result in self-dealing.[70] The indemnification can extend to all expenses including attorneys fees, judgments, and settlements (other than taxes, penalties, or expenses of correction of Chapter 42 violations) if the following conditions exist:[71]

- Such expenses are reasonably incurred by the manager in connection with the proceedings.

- The manager is successful in the defense, or the proceedings are terminated by settlement and the manager has not acted willfully and without reasonable cause with respect to the act or failure to act which led to liability for tax under IRC Chapter 42.

Insurance premiums must be allocated between that amount attributable to Chapter 42 taxes and other matters. The portion allocable to Chapter 42 taxes must be included in the manager's compensation for purposes of determining its reasonableness.[72] After some years of confusion, the fringe benefit regulations now make

[65] Reg. §53.4941(d)-2(f)(1).
[66] Tech. Adv. Memo. 9627001.
[67] Reg. §53.4941(d)-2(f)(1).
[68] Rev. Rul. 77-331, 1977-2 C.B. 388.
[69] Priv. Ltr. Rul. 8202082.
[70] Rev. Rul. 82-223, 1982-2 C.B. 301.
[71] Reg. §53.4941(d)-2(f) as amended; see B. Hopkins and J. Blazek, *Private Foundations: Tax Law and Compliance* (New York: Wiley, 1997), Chapter 5§6, for a history of these rules.
[72] Reg. §53.4941(d)-2(f)(4); see §14.4(a).

it clear that such premiums can be classified as nontaxable fringe benefits to the foundation managers—both those that are salaried and those that serve as volunteers.[73]

A PF's payment of legal defense fees awarded by a court on behalf of a director, who brought suit against the other directors to require them to carry on the foundation's charitable program, was held not to constitute an act of self-dealing.[74]

(b) Excise Taxes

A foundation cannot pay the excise taxes imposed upon disqualified persons for their participation in a violation of any of the private foundation sanctions. The payment is considered a transfer of PF property for the benefit of the DP, and is therefore self-dealing.[75]

(c) Memberships and Galas

Payment of church membership dues for a foundation donor was found to be self-dealing because the membership provided a direct economic benefit to the individual.[76] It is common for grant recipient organizations to identify contributors as members eligible for special privileges. When the foundation makes such a gift, the individual trustees or other foundation representatives are customarily provided such member benefits. The question in such a situation is whether the individual can accept such benefits as a representative of the PF. It is also important to ascertain whether the PF is satisfying a personal obligation of the DP to support the grantee. Some foundations disclaim membership perks or have their managers pay for their own individual memberships to avoid any question in this regard.

A similar problem arises in connection with fund-raising event benefits. Self-dealing was found when a foundation shared the cost of purchasing benefit tickets with a disqualified person. The foundation paid the donation portion of the ticket; the DP paid that part of the ticket price allocable to the FMV of the dinner and entertainment.[77] To be able to attend the benefit, the individual would have been required to pay full price for the ticket. The IRS found the DP reaped benefit when the foundation paid an expense he would otherwise have been expected or required to pay. Thus, the partial purchase of the ticket by the PF constituted direct economic benefit to the DPs, and resulted in self-dealing. Some foundations argue that it is appropriate for their DPs to attend fund-raising events as representatives of the foundation, and that private benefit does not result. In an earlier ruling, the IRS agreed the cost of benefit tickets used by foundation officers were "reasonable administrative expenses." Tickets given to a disqualified person not serving as an officer was deemed to result in self-dealing and a taxable expenditure.[78]

---

[73] Reg. 1.132-5(r), effective on December 30, 1992.
[74] Rev. Rul. 73-613, 1973-2 C.B. 385.
[75] *Id.*
[76] Rev. Rul. 77-160, 1970-1 C.B. 351.
[77] Priv. Ltr. Rul. 9021066.
[78] Priv. Ltr. Rul. 8449008.

(d) Charitable Pledges

If a foundation satisfies a charitable pledge made by one of its disqualified persons and thereby relieves the DP of an obligation, self-dealing may occur.[79] Payment of church membership dues for a DP was found to be self-dealing when the membership provided a personal benefit to the individual.[80] A foundation created by a group of corporations committed an act of self-dealing when it paid pledges entered into by and legally binding on the corporations before the PF was established.[81] However, pledges obligating a DP to make a gift to the PF itself may not create self-dealing. The regulations say:

> The making of a promise, pledge or similar arrangement to a PF by a DP, whether evidenced by an oral or written agreement, a promissory note, or other instrument of indebtedness, to the extent motivated by charitable intent and unsupported by consideration, is not an extension of credit before the date of maturity.[82]

Modification of a DP's charitable pledge to a foundation prior to its maturity is acceptable. The IRS looked at the case of a PF that operated both with current contributions from its substantial contributor and with loans made by a bank against pledges made periodically by the DP. When the DP reduced his current promised payments before their maturity, but pledged a larger amount later, self-dealing was held not to occur.[83]

A foundation created and funded by a corporation was allowed to match the contributing corporation's employees' gifts to various charities.[84] Similarly, a grant by the corporate foundation to a museum that would be open to the public primarily to display articles manufactured by the corporation was found not to be an act of self-dealing.[85]

Return of a conditional gift by the PF to a contributor who stipulated that it be returned if his donation were disallowed was found not to be self-dealing.[86]

(e) Name Recognition

What the regulations call "incidental or tenuous benefit" can be bestowed upon a disqualified person without adverse consequence.[87] Any public recognition or prestige that a person may receive, arising from the charitable activities of a PF to which that person is a substantial contributor, does not, in itself, result in self-dealing.[88]

A PF grant to a public charity made on the condition that the charity change its name to that of the PF's substantial contributor (and that it not change it again

---

[79] Reg. §53.4941(d)-2(f)(1) and Rev. Rul. 77-160, 1977-1 C.B. 351.
[80] Rev. Rul. 77-160, 1970-1 C.B. 351.
[81] Priv. Ltr. Rul. 8128072.
[82] Reg. §53.4941(d)-3(c).
[83] Tech. Adv. Memo. 8723001.
[84] Priv. Ltr. Rul. 8130172.
[85] Priv. Ltr. Rul. 8719041.
[86] *G. M. Underwood, Jr. v. U.S.,* 78-2 USTC ¶9831 (N.D. Tex. 1978).
[87] Reg. §53.4941(d)-2(f)(2).
[88] Rev. Rul. 77-331, 1977-2 C.B. 388.

for 100 years) did not result in self-dealing.[89] Grants by a PF to charity, private or public, with interlocking board members are permitted.[90] The fact that the board members are recognized for causing the grants to be awarded does not amount to self-dealing.

The name recognition Corporation Y receives (through promotions planned by the Corporate Foundation X it funds) was found to be tenuous and incidental and therefore not to result in self-dealing. The foundation intended to celebrate its anniversary by conducting a publicity campaign discussing and reviewing its support of American education through grants for enhanced teaching and learning and the management of schools, colleges, and universities. The publicity was intended to stimulate the general public to support education and also to make Y's shareholders more aware of its public service so as to be supportive of future gifts to the foundation.[91]

The goodwill generated by a company foundation scholarship program is also treated as incidental. As long as the program meets the "objective and nondiscriminatory" requirements,[92] the awarding of grants to children of the corporation's employees is not self-dealing. Similarly, the fact that a corporation plans to recruit and hire graduates of a university engineering program results only in an incidental benefit. The company's foundation can fund the program without self-dealing unless the corporation is given preferential treatment in access to the graduates.[93]

It is important to again note excessive compensation may not only result in self-dealing but also a taxable expenditure.[94]

14.6 PAYMENTS TO GOVERNMENT OFFICIALS

The basic statutory provision absolutely prohibits payments to government officials, but there are a number of exceptions. Self-dealing results if a private foundation enters into an agreement to make payments of money or other property to a government official[95] *other than* an agreement to employ the person, unless the official's government service is terminating within 90 days of the date of the offer.[96] Certain de minimus payments to government officials are permitted, as follows:[97]

- A prize or award that is not includable in gross income under IRC §74(b), if the government official receiving the prize is selected from the general public. (The prize must be paid over to a charitable institution.)

[89] Rev. Rul. 73-407, 1973-2 C.B. 383.
[90] Rev. Rul. 80-310, 1980-2 C.B. 319; Rev. Rul. 82-136, 1982-2 C.B. 300, clarifying Rev. Rul. 75-42, 1975-1 C.B. 359.
[91] Priv. Ltr. Rul. 9615046.
[92] See Chapter 17§3(c).
[93] Rev. Rul. 80-310, 1982-2 C.B. 319.
[94] See Chapter 17.
[95] Defined in Chapter 12.
[96] IRC §4941(d)(1)(F).
[97] IRC §4941(d)(2)((G); Reg. 53.4941(d)-3(e).

- A scholarship or fellowship grant that is excludable from gross income under IRC §117(a) and that is to be utilized for study at an IRC §151(e)(4) educational institution (but only for tuition, fees, and books)

- Certain types of pension plans and annuity payments

- Contributions, gifts, services, or facilities provided to or made available to a government official totaling no more than $25 in any one year

- Government employee training program payments

- Reimbursement of the actual cost of travel within the United States for attendance at a charitable function, not to exceed 125% of the prevailing per diem rate

14.7 SHARING SPACE, PEOPLE, AND EXPENSES

As a practical matter, many private foundations are operated alongside their creators—corporations, family groups, and individuals. At least until the foundation achieves a certain volume of assets with consequential grant activity (and maybe thereafter), rental of a separate office and engagement of staff is beyond the PF's reasonable economic capability, particularly when such expenditures take funds away from grant-making activity.

(a) Can the Foundation Pay for Its Share?

When can a foundation pay for its portion of the expenses in such a sharing situation? The tax code specifically prohibits the "furnishing of goods, services or facilities" between (to or from) a PF and a DP. The types of property intended to be covered by this rule include office space, automobiles, auditoriums, secretarial help, meals, libraries, publications, laboratories, and parking lots.[98]

When Congress imposed these strict rules in 1969, it provided a transitional period until 1980, during which existing and contractual sharing arrangements could be phased out.[99] As time passed and the costs of the absolute rule became unreasonable in certain circumstances, the IRS in private letter rulings relaxed what looked like an impenetrable barrier to any arrangements in which a PF and DPs share space, people, or other expenses. Three very important factors have been present in the private rulings issued by the IRS:

- The foundation pays its share of cost directly to an independent vendor.

- Time and other suitable usage records are maintained to measure and evidence the portion of the shared costs attributable to the foundation.

- Space and personnel are used by the foundation in conducting its charitable programs.

[98] Reg. §53.4941(d)-2(d)(1).
[99] Reg. §53.4941(d)-4(d).

Office Space.   A number of foundations sought and received approval for shared expenses. One foundation was permitted to rent contiguous space with a common reception area, but with separate offices, from its disqualified persons. Separate leases were entered into and the DPs received no benefit in the form of reduced rent because of the PF's rental in the related space.[100] Another PF was allowed to purchase its part of a duplicating machine and hired a shared employee with its creators. Time records were kept to determine each entity's share of the cost of the machine and the allocable time of the employee. Because "nothing was paid directly or indirectly to the DP" and there was "independent use" by the PF that was measurable and specifically paid for to outside parties, no self-dealing resulted from what certainly appears to have been a "sharing arrangement," supposedly phased out and consequentially prohibited by the code.[101]

Different and safer terminology was used to secure IRS approval for payment to the DPs' family management corporation for rendering accounting, tax, and asset management services.[102] The corporation operated on a cost-recovery basis to serve the business needs of "family assets held in trusts, foundations, and partnerships." While the arrangement was essentially a sharing one, the IRS ruled that payment of a fee based on costs was reasonable compensation for services rendered and not an act of self-dealing.[103] Similarly, the IRS has permitted payments directly to a partnership in which one of the PF's directors was a partner, for shared accounting services. The payment was not excessive and "services were reasonable and necessary for the foundation's exempt purposes."[104]

Group Insurance.   Employee insurance policies present similar situations. Corporate and other conglomerate groups funding private foundations have been allowed to include their private foundation employees in a common health insurance policy. The foundation pays directly for the premiums allocable to its employees, or reimburses the company. Direct payment is strongly preferred, but if it is impracticable, reimbursement has been allowed. The rationale for reimbursements is found in the *Special Rules* that permit lending of money to a foundation if no interest is charged and the money is used for exempt purposes.[105] Exhibit 14-1 suggests an expenditure documentation agreement suitable to document a sharing arrangement between a foundation and its donors and managers.

(b) Public Facilities

A private foundation that operates a museum, maintains a wildlife preserve, publishes essays, or conducts other programs for which it charges is faced with a decree that it must not furnish goods, services, or facilities to its DPs. Taken literally, the rule prevents DPs from visiting the sites or purchasing the journal. A PF's furnishing of goods, services, or facilities normally open to the general public to a DP,

---

[100] Priv. Ltr. Rul. 8331082.
[101] Tech. Adv. Memo. 7734022; see also Priv. Ltr. Ruls. 8824010, 9226067, 9307026, and 9312022.
[102] Priv. Ltr. Rul. 9019064.
[103] Due to the §4941(d)(2)(E) exception.
[104] Priv. Ltr. Rul. 8235092.
[105] IRC §4941(d)(2)(B).

Exhibit 14–1

EXPENDITURE DOCUMENTATION POLICY

Sample Foundation

Introduction

As a private foundation (PF), Sample Foundation (Sample) is responsible for proving that all of its expenditures are made for charitable purposes, and that it makes no expenditures on behalf of nor has any financial transactions with its "disqualified persons" (DPs), meaning major contributors and managers. Sample will establish its headquarters and laboratory in the office building owned by its president and contributor, XYZ, who is a DP in relation to Sample. Therefore, Sample wishes to adopt procedures to adhere to the self-dealing provisions of the tax code that prohibit the following:

- Sale, exchange, or lease of property between the PF and DP, except at no charge

- Lending of money or extension of credit between PF and DP

- Furnishing of goods, services, or facilities between a PF and DP, unless the DP furnishes them to the PF without charge

- Payment of compensation or reimbursement of expenses from the PF to the DP, unless such payments are reasonable and necessary to carrying out the exempt purposes of the PF.

Policy

To ensure adherence to these requirements, Sample adopts the following rules:

Office Space. Sample is entering into a lease agreement with XYZ stipulating that the space is furnished to Sample at no charge. Maintenance, repair, and utilities attributable to the space occupied by Sample will be paid by Sample directly. For example, the space leased to Sample represents _____% of the total square footage of the building. Therefore, _____% of the utility bill will be paid by Sample. Any expenses not directly attributable to Sample space will be paid by XYZ.

Personnel. Sample will hire a project manager, and possibly other personnel, to work exclusively on foundation projects. Because Sample is small and is just getting started, it does not need a full-time secretary or accountant. It will enter into a separate agreement to hire XYZ receptionist and business manager whom it is expected will devote approximately half of their time to Sample's business. Therefore, half of their salaries, employee benefits, and taxes will be paid by Sample. Each person will maintain a record of his or her actual time and the ratio will be evaluated periodically.

Office Furnishings and Equipment. XYZ owns a telephone system, copy machine, computers, and other equipment that Sample is allowed to use rent-free. To the extent that Sample incurs direct costs in connection with such equipment, it will pay the bills directly. For example, long distance phone

Exhibit 14–1 (*continued*)

> calls, photocopy paper, and other expendable supplies directly related to foundation activities will be paid by Sample.
>
> *Automobile.* XYZ is furnishing Sample with a vehicle for its use in connection with foundation projects. Sample will pay the expenses attributable to its actual use of the vehicle. A mileage log will be maintained to evidence the usage.
>
> *Asset Purchases and Sales and Debt Payments.* Sample hereby adopts a policy that it will not engage in any financial transactions with XYZ or with any other DP that would cause it to "self-deal" as defined in §4941.

however, comes within another of the useful exceptions to the general rules. Such activity is not self-dealing *if* :[106]

- The property involved is "functionally related to the exercise or performance by the PF of its charitable, educational, or other purpose or function forming the basis for its exemption";

- The number of persons (other than the DPs) who use the facility is substantial enough to indicate that the general public is genuinely the primary user; and

- The terms for DP usage are not more favorable than the terms under which the general public acquires or uses the property.

A PF's library meeting room used regularly by the community at large for exempt function-related affairs can be used by a government official who is also a disqualified person.[107] Similarly, the use of a public thoroughfare situated on the foundation's property was permitted for access to the headquarters and manufacturing plant of its corporate disqualified person.[108] The road apparently provided access to both the PF's museum and to the company facility, and the company paid for the road's upkeep. An allocation of cost was not mentioned but could be permitted as discussed in §14.7(a).

14.8 INDIRECT DEALS

Transactions between a disqualified person and an organization controlled by a foundation may be classified as an indirect act of self-dealing as to the foundation itself, even though the funds never touch the PF. Say, for example, a private foundation owns a 70% interest in a real estate rental partnership and two of the PF's directors own a construction company. The partnership, because it is controlled by

---

[106] Reg. §53.4941(d)-3(b).
[107] Rev. Rul. 76-10, 1976-1 C.B. 355.
[108] Rev. Rul. 76-459, 1976-2 C.B. 369.

the PF, cannot hire the construction company owned by its DPs to repair its apartment buildings. An indirect transaction is defined by describing circumstances in which a business transaction will not be considered as self-dealing. The regulations provide that indirect self-dealing does not occur in the following situations:[109]

- Transactions in place prior to the creation of the control relationship that caused the self-dealing are allowed.

- Transactions at least as favorable to the controlled organization (CO) as an arm's length transaction with an unrelated party would have been allowed, but only if (1) the CO could have engaged in the transaction with someone other than the DP only at a severe economic hardship to the CO, or (2) because of the unique nature of the product or services provided by the CO, the DP could not have engaged in the transaction with anyone else.

- De minimus transactions with a CO engaged in a retail business with the general public, such as office supplies, are not indirect self-dealing if the transactions' total amount in one year does not exceed $5,000.[110]

The first self-dealing case to be decided involved an impermissible transfer of indebted property from a corporation owned by a trustee to a foundation's wholly owned subsidiary.[111] Another foundation was found guilty of indirect self-dealing when space in a building it owned was leased to a company controlled by one of its DPs. The entire building was subleased to an independent management company which, in turn, subleased the spaces, so that the foundation was not a party to the building subleases. The master lease granted the PF, as landlord, the power of approval over the form and content of any long-term leases entered into by the management company. Thus, the PF essentially controlled the management company and, for self-dealing purposes, became a party to the lease with the DP.[112] Special rules also apply to transactions between a foundation's intermediary grantee organization and a government official.[113]

14.9 PROPERTY HELD BY FIDUCIARIES

A trustee or estate executor may find that property bequeathed to a foundation, such as an undivided interest in property, is not suitable to be held by the foundation. At times, the best solution to the situation is a self-dealing transaction, either direct or indirect. Because the property has not yet become the property of the foundation, a fair degree of leeway is allowed to the estate or revocable trust officials in allocating or

---

[109] Reg. §53.4941(d)-1(b)(1).
[110] Reg. §53.4941(d)-1(b)(6).
[111] *Adams v. Commissioner,* 70 T.C. 373 (1978), *aff'd* (unpublished) 2d Cir. 1982 and 70 T.C. 446 (1978).
[112] Priv. Ltr. Rul. 9047001; see also Priv. Ltr. Rul. 9325061 in which provision of "commercial services" by businesses owned by DPs to limited partnerships and corporations holding real estate for the PF and the DPs was deemed indirect self-dealing.
[113] Reg. §53.4941(d)-1(b)(2).

selling assets among beneficiaries. Transactions during administration regarding the foundation's interest or expectancy in property (whether or not encumbered) held by the estate (regardless of when title vests in the PF on the date of death under local law) are not self-dealing, if all five of the following conditions are met:[114]

1. The executor, administrator, or trustee has authority to either sell the property or reallocate it to another beneficiary, or is required to sell the property by the terms of the trust or will;

2. A probate court having jurisdiction over the estate approves the transaction. It is unclear whether this approval must be granted specifically for the transaction, or whether the court's acceptance of the final estate accounting and its release of the parties is sufficient;

3. The transaction occurs before the estate or trust is terminated;

4. The estate or trust receives FMV for the PF's portion of the property; and[115]

5. The PF receives an interest at least as liquid as the one given up for an exempt function asset, or receives an amount of money equal to that required under an option binding upon the estate.

The purchase of stock by a disqualified person (that otherwise would have been transferred to a foundation) for less than its FMV constituted self-dealing.[116] The division of properties owned by an artist's estate in order to fund a statutory one-third life estate in favor of his wife did not result in self-dealing, despite the exchanges of property inherent in the settlement. The agreement satisfied the five regulation requirements. A substitution of art they preferred for objects specifically bequeathed to the artist's daughters, however, would result in self-dealing. An exchange of specific property, rather than a partitioning or dividing of property essentially owned by the estate, would occur and §4941(d)(1)(A) would apply despite the fact that the PF's art collection purportedly would be enhanced by the trade.[117]

Where the foundation is bequeathed the residuary of an estate, a provision that estate taxes are to be paid from the portion given to the PF was ruled not to result in self-dealing. The IRS ruled that the taxes were being paid from property not owned by the PF because it only had a vested interest in the estate after the payment of taxes.[118] Payments out of an estate's residuary funds made pursuant to the

---

[114] Reg. §53.4941(d)-1(b)(3).

[115] See also *Rockefeller v. U.S.*, 572 F. Supp. 9 (E.D. Ark. 1982), *aff'd*, 718 F.2d 290 (8th Cir. 1983), *cert. den.*, 466 U.S. 962 (1984), in which it was found that the full FMV was not paid for the estate's shares and, consequently, indirect self-dealing occurred. See also Priv. Ltr. Rul 9210040.

[116] *Rockefeller v. U.S.*, 572 F. Supp. 9 (D.C. Ark. 1982), *aff'd* 718 F.2d 290 (8th Cir. 1983), *cert. den.*; see also *Reis Estate v. Commissioner*, 87 T.C. 1016 (1986) involving sales of Mark Rothko's art work by his executor/dealer and the foundation created under his will.

[117] Priv. Ltr. Rul. 9252042.

[118] Priv. Ltr. Rul. 9307025; in Priv. Ltr. Rul. 9308045 the IRS approved the receipt and operation (as a functionally related business) of a business corporation formed to perpetuate its creator's name and musical compositions.

settlement of a will contest have been ruled not to be an act of self-dealing. The decedent had left his residuary estate entirely to a foundation. The will left nothing to the son except an option to purchase certain assets from the residuary estate. After controversy surrounding the purchase, a settlement was entered into giving the son part of the shares and placing part of the shares in a 20-year unitrust for the son's benefit with remainder to the foundation. Because the regulation requirements previously discussed were met, the IRS ruled that no self-dealing had occurred.[119] The IRS has also approved transactions with a living trust[120] and with a QTIP trust.[121]

14.10 ISSUES ONCE SELF-DEALING OCCURS

Once it has been determined that self-dealing has occurred, the self-dealing must be corrected and an excise tax return must be filed on Form 4720. The steps involved in repairing the damage include "undoing" the deal, assigning an "amount" attributable to the self-dealing, deciding who has to pay an excise tax, and advancing any reasonable cause to reduce or avoid the tax. Unlike other foundation penalties imposed by IRC §§4942–4945, the initial excise tax imposed upon self-dealing transactions cannot be abated.

(a) Undoing the Transaction

To undo self-dealing, the deal must be corrected and rescinded (i.e., the property returned) if possible. The financial position of the private foundation after the correction must be no worse than it would have been if the original transaction had not occurred. Specific rules govern sales by or to the PF, uses of property and compensation deals and are outlined very specifically in the regulations.[122]

Sales by the Foundation.   The sale must first be rescinded. If the purchaser still holds the property, the foundation must take back the property. Next the foundation is to repay the purchaser the sales price or the current FMV of the property at the time of the correction, whichever is less. Any income earned by the DP buyer from the property in excess of the PF's earnings on the money (from investment of the sales proceeds) during the self-dealing period should be restored to the foundation, essentially reducing the repayment of the purchase price by the foundation. If the property has been resold, the foundation is to receive the greater of the original proceeds that it received or what the DP received upon the resale.

Sales to the Foundation.   Again, rescission of the sale is required. Fair market value and resale considerations similar to those previously mentioned are taken into account, to ensure that the foundation is restored to the financial position it

---

[119] Priv. Ltr. Rul. 8929087. See also Priv. Ltr. Ruls. 8707065 and 8527091, which reach a similar result.
[120] Priv. Ltr. Rul. 9814050.
[121] Priv. Ltr. Rul. 9752071.
[122] Reg. §53.4941(e)-1(c).

would have been in had it not purchased the property. For example, say a PF sold 100 shares of stock to a DP for $4000 in 1998, at a time when the FMV was $3,500. The DP sells the shares in 1999 for $6,000 although the shares had been quoted at $6,700 at one point during the year. The PF must be paid $6,700 to cure the transaction. The first-tier tax will be charged based on the $5,000. If the self-dealing is not corrected and the second-tier tax applies, the tax is calculated based on $6,700. Care must be exercised if property other than cash is used to correct a transaction to avoid yet another act of self-dealing.[123]

Uses of Property by a DP.   The use must be stopped. If the rent paid exceeded the FMV, an imputed rent factor based on fair market differentials, if any, must be repaid to the foundation. Different corrections are specified in the regulations, depending on whether the PF or the DP rented the property.

Uses of Property by the PF.   Again, the lease must be terminated and the FMV differential repaid.

Unreasonable Compensation.   When excessive or unreasonable salaries have been paid to a DP, the excess must be repaid to the foundation. However, termination of the employment or independent contractor arrangement is not required.

(b) Amount Involved

The penalties for entering into a self-dealing transaction are based on the *amount involved,* which is defined as follows:

> The greater of the amount of money and the fair market value of the other property given or the amount of money and the fair market value of the other property received.[124]

Thus where a PF leases office space from a DP for $30,000, but the FMV of the space is $25,000, the amount is $30,000. If a PF loans a DP money at a below-market interest rate, the amount equals the principal of the loan plus the interest that would have been charged at the prevailing market rate at the time the loan is made.[125] The highest fair market value during the correction period is the amount involved in second- and third-tier taxes discussed in the following paragraphs.

Compensation.   In the case of compensation paid for personal services to persons other than government officials, the amount is the portion of the total compensation in excess of the amount that would have been reasonable.

Stock Redemptions and Other Permitted Dealings.   Sometimes a transaction that is permitted by the statutory exceptions[126] goes amiss, and a tax is imposed.

---

[123] Rev. Rul. 81-40, 1981-1 C.B. 508, 509.
[124] Reg. §53.4941(e)(2) and §53.4941(e)-1(b)(2).
[125] Reg. §53.4941(e)-1(b)(4).
[126] Listed in §14.1(b).

This occurs particularly often under exceptions 6 and 8, in which the value is determinative. In such cases, the "amount involved" is only the amount by which the redemption price is deficient (i.e., the amount by which the property was undervalued) or the taxable self-dealing. Two conditions must be present to show that the parties made a good faith effort to determine the FMV (so that only the excess is taxed):

1. The appraiser who arrived at the value must be competent to make the valuation, must not be a DP, and must not be in a position, whether by stock ownership or otherwise, to derive an economic benefit from the value utilized; and

2. The method utilized in making the valuation must be a generally accepted method for valuing comparable property, stock, or securities for purposes of arm's length business transactions in which valuation is a significant factor.

For example, say a corporation that is a DP as to a PF redeems the PF's stock for $200,000. Assume that the correct valuation is later determined to be $250,000. Self-dealing has occurred in the amount of $50,000.

To calculate the *first-tier* tax initially imposed on a sale, exchange, or lease of property, the amount involved is determined as of the date on which the self-dealing occurred. If the self-dealing goes uncorrected and the additional or *second-tier* tax is calculated, the valuation is equal to the highest value during the period of time the self-dealing continued uncorrected. For a complicated saga of one foundation's attempts to cure a self-dealing transaction, see the Dupont case.[127]

(c) Who Pays What Tax?

The penalty tax is imposed on the individual(s) or corporate self-dealer(s) participating in the prohibited transaction, but not on the PF itself. The self-dealer pays an initial tax of 5% of the amount involved in each year in the taxable period even if he or she was unaware that a rule was being violated. A $2\frac{1}{2}$% tax is also imposed on any persons (including the self-dealer) who approved the transaction if the following conditions exist:[128]

- An initial tax is imposed on the self-dealer;

- The foundation manager knows that the act is an act of self-dealing; and

- The manager's participation is willful and not due to reasonable cause.

A foundation manager is expected to be aware of the PF sanctions and to remain sufficiently informed of the PF's affairs to prevent any violations of the sanctions.[129] The term *participation* not only includes affirmative actions of a manager, it also includes silence or inaction on the part of a manager where he is under a

---

[127] *Dupont v. Commissioner,* 74 T.C. 498 (1980).

[128] IRC §4941(a)(2); Reg. §53.4941(a)-1(b).

[129] Reg. §53.4941(a)-1(b)(3); see also Chapter 16§2(c).

duty to speak or act; voting against the deal excuses the tax. A person is considered to have participated *knowingly* only if:

- He has actual knowledge of sufficient facts so that, based solely upon such facts, such transaction would be an act of self-dealing;

- He is aware that such an act under these circumstances may violate the provisions of federal tax law governing self-dealing; and

- He negligently fails to make reasonable attempts to ascertain whether the transaction is an act of self-dealing, or he is in fact aware that it is such an act.

The managers are jointly and severally liable for the tax imposed upon them, up to a maximum of $10,000.[130] The tax is not imposed on a PF manager if a full disclosure of the facts was made to counsel, a *reasoned legal opinion* was issued, and the manager relied upon that opinion in deciding that no sanctions were violated.[131] The terms applied to determine if a manager knew are defined further in Chapter 16.2(c).

The *taxable period* begins with the date on which the transaction occurred and ends on the earliest of the date of mailing of the notice of deficiency with respect to the initial tax, the date on which the initial tax is assessed, or the date on which correction of the transaction is completed.[132] The second-tier (but not the first) tax may be abated if the act was due to reasonable causes and not to willful neglect, and if it is corrected.[133]

An additional tax of 200% of the amount involved is imposed on the self-dealer if the correction is not made. A foundation manager who refuses to agree to the correction faces a penalty of 50% of the amount involved.[134] A *third tier* tax—the IRC §507 termination tax—can be charged if the transactions are never cured.[135] A foundation that conducts repeated and willful violations of the PF sanctions is liable to be terminated, with all tax benefits it and its contributors have ever received being repaid to the government—very likely, all of the assets held in the PF. Exhibit 12-1 lists all of the rates of tax and the parties upon whom the tax is imposed.

[130] IRC §4941(c).
[131] Reg. §53.4941(a)-1(b)(6).
[132] IRC §4941(e)(1).
[133] IRC §4962.
[134] IRC §4941(b).
[135] See Chapter 12.

CHAPTER FIFTEEN

Minimum Distribution Requirements: IRC §4942

Before 1970, all Internal Revenue Code (IRC) §501(c)(3) exempt organizations were subject to a vague and unenforceable prohibition against accumulating income unreasonably. Assets could be invested in a no- or low-income producing manner, with very little money being given to charity. A family could take tax deductions, in some years offsetting as much as 90% of its income, for placing shares of the family business in a foundation. The company could pay out no dividends to the shareholders and instead pay whatever money as salaries the family needed to live on. The only persons benefiting from such arrangements were the family members, not the intended beneficiaries of charitable organizations.

To stem such abuses, Congress enacted IRC §4942, which requires private foundations (PFs) to satisfy a strict numerical test for making annual expenditures for charitable projects and grants. A PF must annually make "qualifying distributions," or charitable grants or project expenditures, equal to its prior year's minimum investment return (MIR). The MIR is approximately 5% of the value of the PF's investment assets.

Before 1982, PFs were required to distribute the higher of MIR or actual net investment income. When interest rates were close to 20%, the actual income was often a much higher amount. Foundation representatives convinced Congress that they needed to reserve some of their income against future inflation.

15.1 ASSETS USED TO CALCULATE MINIMUM INVESTMENT RETURN

Stated most simply, a private foundation annually is required to spend or pay out for charitable and administrative purposes at least 5% of the average fair market value (FMV) of its investment assets for the preceding year, less the amount of any debt incurred to acquire the property and a $1\frac{1}{2}\%$ provision for cash reserves.

$$(\text{PF Investment Assets} - \text{Debt} - \text{Cash Reserves}) \times 5\% = \text{MIR}$$

The 5% distribution rate is reduced for a foundation with a short taxable year.[1] The percentage for a short year is calculated by multiplying the number of days in the year by 5% and dividing the result by 365. Say, for example, a foundation is created on September 1 and chooses a calendar year end. Its MIR for the first short year is calculated as follows:

$$\frac{\textit{Days in short year} - 122 \textit{ days} \times 5\% = 1.67\%}{\text{Days in year} - 365 \text{ days}}$$

Successful calculation of MIR depends upon distinguishing investment assets from exempt function assets. This concept of exempt function versus investment is an important key to understanding MIR. If the foundation holds an asset as an investment, 5% of its value is payable annually for charitable purposes, even if it is not producing any current income. This scheme is very different from the rules for calculating the excise tax on investment income under which income from certain types of assets is excluded from tax.[2]

(a) What Are Investment Assets?

The statute applies the percentage to the aggregate FMV of all assets other than those that are used (or held for use) directly in carrying out the foundation's ex-

---

[1] Reg. §53.4942(a)-2(c)(5)(iii).
[2] See Chapter 13.

empt purposes, over (i.e., less) the acquisition indebtedness with respect to such assets and a cash reserve of $1\frac{1}{2}$% of investment assets.[3] The typical PF investment portfolio of stocks, bonds, certificates of deposit, and rental properties usually forms the basis for calculating the distributable amount. Funds of all sorts—current, deferred grants, capital, endowment, and similar types of reserves—are all includable in the formula. If a property is used for both investment and program purposes, its value is allocated.[4] Business properties, such as cattle and other fixtures of a working ranch donated to a foundation, are included, as would be an interest in a partnership.

(b) Future Interests or Expectancies

Certain assets provide beneficial support to the PF in an indirect fashion. Assets over which the PF has no control and in which it essentially holds no present interest are not included in the MIR formula. These assets most often are not actually in the possession or under the control of the PF, nor are they customarily included in the financial records or statements of the foundation. These include:[5]

- Charitable remainders and other future interests in property created by someone other than the PF itself, until the intervening interests expire or are otherwise set apart for the PF. If the foundation is able to take possession of the property at its will or to acquire it readily upon giving notice, the property is included. The rules of constructive receipt for determining when a cash basis taxpayer receives an item of income are relevant.

- Present interests in a trust, usually called a *charitable lead trust*. However, income from any such trusts created after May 26, 1969, is includable in the adjusted net income and can affect a private operating foundation.[6]

- Pledges of money or other property to the PF, whether or not the pledges are legally enforceable.

- Property bequeathed to the PF is excluded while it is held by the decedent's estate. If and when the IRS treats the estate as terminated because the period of administration is prolonged,[7] the assets are treated as PF assets from the time of such Internal Revenue Service (IRS) determination.

- Options to sell property that are not readily marketable and are without an ascertainable value. Listed options to buy or sell common stocks that are traded on a security exchange are includable as investment assets.

(c) Exempt Function Assets

Income need not be imputed to property held by and actually used by the foundation in conducting its charitable programs. Such assets are called *exempt function*

---

[3] IRC §4941(f)(1)(A); Reg. §53.4942(a)-2(c)(1).
[4] See §15.1(d) for discussion of dual-use property.
[5] Reg. §53.4942(a)-2(c)(2).
[6] *The Ann Jackson Family Foundation v. Commissioner,* 97 TC 4, No. 35.
[7] See Reg. §1.1641(b)-3 for circumstances under which administration of an estate is considered to be unreasonably prolonged.

assets, and are not usually held for the production of income (although they do in some cases), but instead are "used (or held for use) directly in carrying out the foundation's exempt purpose." To be excluded, such assets must actually be in use; cash earmarked for purchase of art work, for example, is not an exempt function asset. The most common type of assets excluded from the MIR formula follow.[8]

Administrative offices, furnishings, equipment, and supplies used by employees and consultants in working on the foundation's charitable projects are not counted. However, the same property, if used by persons who manage the investment properties or endowments, is treated as investment property.

Buildings, equipment, and facilities used directly in projects are clearly not counted as investment property. Examples include:

- Historic buildings, libraries, and the furnishings in such buildings

- Collections of objects on educational display, such as works of art or scientific specimens, including art works loaned to other organizations[9]

- Research facilities and laboratories, including a limited access island held vacant to preserve its natural ecosystem, history, and archaeology[10]

- Print shops and educational classrooms

- Property used for a nominal or reduced rent by another charity. No figures are furnished in the regulations. The asset test for private operating foundations, however, defines a rental property leased to carry out an exempt purpose. The property is considered to be exempt property if the rent is less than the amount that would be required to be charged in order to recover the cost of property purchase and maintenance.[11]

Reasonable cash balances are considered to be necessary to carry out exempt functions. One and one-half percent of the included investment assets is presumed to be a reasonable cash balance, even if a smaller cash balance is actually maintained.[12] If the foundation's programs require a higher amount to cover expenses and disbursements, the PF can apply to the IRS to permit a higher amount.[13]

Future Use Property. An asset acquired for use in the future may be treated as exempt function property where the foundation has definite plans to commence such use within a reasonable period of time (usually one year) as discussed in §15.1(e). Funds designated for a set-aside project are treated as investment assets.

Program-related investments and functionally related businesses[14] are not considered as investment assets. Examples include a low-rent indigent housing facility and student loans receivable. Stock of a restaurant and hotel complex operated by

---

[8] Reg. §53.4942(a)-2(c)(3)(ii).
[9] Rev. Rul. 74-498, 1974-2 C.B. 387.
[10] Rev. Rul. 75-207, 1975-1 C.B. 361.
[11] Reg. §53.4942(b)-2(a)(2).
[12] Rev. Rul. 75-392, 1975-2 C.B. 447.
[13] Reg. §53.4942(a)-2(c)(3)(iv).
[14] See Chapter 16§2(b).

a separate taxable corporation within a historic village and an educational journal for which advertising is sold are given as examples in the regulations.[15] Such properties are not included in investment assets because they are related businesses.[16]

(d) Dual-Use Property

In many cases, a PF owns and uses property for managing or conducting both its investments and its charitable projects. In such situations, an allocation between these two uses must be made. For assets used 95% or more for one purpose, the remaining 5% is ignored. An office building housing the foundation would be allocated based on the functions performed by the persons occupying the spaces. Consider the following example:

Investment department	1,125 square feet	25%
Program offices	3,375 square feet	75%
	4,500	100%

In such a case, 25% of the building's value would be treated as an investment asset. In a very large foundation, the formula may be more complicated. A third category, administration, may need to be included in the formula when the staff is sophisticated and separate personnel, accounting, and central supply departments serve the investment and program groups. For property that is partly used by the foundation and partly rented to others, the IRS has ruled that an allocation based on the fair rental value of the respective spaces, rather than the square feet, is appropriate.[17]

(e) Assets Held for Future Use

Sometimes it takes a number of years to piece together a project using hard assets like land, buildings, and equipment. When a PF has future plans for use of property and "establishes to the satisfaction of the Commissioner" (i.e., obtains IRS approval) that its immediate use of the property is impractical, an asset held for future use is excluded. Definite plans must exist to commence use within a reasonable period of time, and all of the facts and circumstances must prove the intention to devote the property to such use. The concepts are similar to set-asides.[18] Property acquired to be devoted to exempt purposes may be treated as exempt function property from the time it is acquired, even if it is temporarily rented.

Acquisition of future use property is also treated as a qualifying distribution. The rental status must be for a reasonable and limited period of time and only

---

[15] Reg. §53.4942(a)-2(c)(3)(iii).
[16] IRC §512; see Chapter 21.
[17] Rev. Rul. 82-137, 1982-2 C.B. 303.
[18] Reg. §53.4942(a)-2(c)(3)(i). See §15.4(c).

while the property is being made ready for its intended use, such as during re-modeling or acquisition of adjacent pieces of property. IRS approval is not necessary if the property conversion takes only one year. However, if the property is rented for more than a year, it is treated as investment property during the second year and thereafter until it is devoted to exempt purposes. This change is also reflected for qualifying distribution purposes. Property reclassified as investment property would be treated as a negative distribution.[19]

15.2   MEASURING FAIR MARKET VALUE

The minimum investment return is based on a percentage, now 5%, of the average FMV of the includable investment assets. Different methods, revaluation times, and frequencies are provided for various types of investment assets that a private foundation might need to value.

(a) Valuation Methods

Any "commonly acceptable method of valuation" may be used, as long as it is reasonable and consistently used. Valuations made in accordance with the methods prescribed for estate tax valuation are acceptable.[20] Presumably, the rules governing valuation of charitable gifts would also be acceptable.[21] The opinion of an independent appraiser is only required for real estate. For all other assets, the PF itself can establish a consistent method for making a good faith determination of the value of most of its assets. Mistakes in valuation, if unintentional, can be corrected.[22]

(b) Date of Valuation

Different valuation dates are prescribed for different kinds of assets:

Asset Valuation Dates

Cash	Monthly
Marketable securities	Monthly
Real estate	Every five years
All other assets	Annually

Cash is valued on a monthly basis by averaging the amount of cash on hand on the first and last day of each month. Assets valued annually can be valued on any date, as long as approximately the same date is used each year.[23] Likewise, real es-

[19] See §15.3.
[20] Reg. §53.4942(a)-2(c)(4)(i)(*b*) and (iv)(*c*) refers to IRC §2031 regulations.
[21] Described in IRS Publication 561.
[22] See §15.6(c).
[23] Reg. §53.4942(a)-2(c)(4)(vi).

tate valuation should be done on approximately the same date every fifth year. No precise date is prescribed for valuation of property newly acquired by a foundation. The price actually paid for property of a sort valued annually should serve as its value for the year of purchase absent abnormal acquisition circumstances. Property received by the foundation as a gift should be valued within a reasonable time of its receipt of the property. The value used by the donor for income and gift tax purposes can be used if the foundation obtains appropriate evidence of the value.

The average value of an asset held by the foundation for part of a year is calculated by using the number of days in the year that the asset was held as the numerator, and 365 is the denominator. The includable value is thereby reduced to equate to the partial year holding period. For example, for a $100,000 piece of real estate acquired on July 1, the includable amount would be

Asset Held for Partial Year

$$\$100,000 \times 182/365 = \$50,000$$

(c) Readily Marketable Securities

Securities for which a market quotation is readily available must be valued monthly, using any reasonable and consistent method.[24] Securities include (but are not limited to) common and preferred stocks, bonds, and mutual fund shares.[25] The monthly security valuation method applies to:

- Stocks listed on the New York Stock Exchange, the American Stock Exchange, or any city or regional exchange in which quotations appear on a daily basis, including foreign securities listed on a recognized foreign national or regional exchange

- Stocks regularly traded in a national or regional over-the-counter market, for which published quotations are available

- Locally traded stocks for which quotations can readily be obtained from established brokerage firms.

The *quotation system* can be one of a variety of methods, again as long as a consistent pattern is followed. The following examples are given in the regulations.[26]

- The classic method averages the high and low quoted price on a particular day each month, which could be the first, fifth, last, or any other day.

- A formula averaging the first, middle, and last day closing prices for each month.

---

[24] Reg. §53.4942(a)-2(c)(4)(i)(*a*).
[25] Reg. §53.4942(a)-2(c)(4)(v).
[26] Reg. §53.4942(a)-2(c)(4)(e).

- The average of the bid and asked price for over-the-counter stocks or funds on a consistent day, using the nearest day if no quote was available on the regular day.

Portfolio reports generated by a computer pricing system and prepared monthly for securities held in trust by a bank or in an account of a financial institution may be acceptable. The bank's or investment advisor's system must be accepted as a valid method for valuing securities for federal estate tax purposes. The foundation has a responsibility to inquire of the bank as to its method of valuation, and to obtain evidence that its system is approved. Banks commonly have certification from bank examiners, and investment advisory firms have their license renewals from the Securities and Exchange Commission. In the author's experience, the IRS has not required proof that the bank's system has specific IRS approval, even though the regulations require it.

Blockage discounts of up to 10% are permitted to reduce the valuation of marketable securities when a foundation can "show that the quoted market prices do not reflect FMV"[27] for one or more of the following reasons:

- The block of securities is so large in relation to the volume of actual sales on the existing market that it could not be liquidated in a reasonable time without depressing the market.

- Sales of the securities are few or sporadic in nature, and the shares are in a closely held corporation.

- The sale of the securities would result in a forced or distress sale because the securities cannot be offered to the public without first being registered with the Securities and Exchange Commission.

Essentially, a foundation is permitted to use the price at which the securities could be sold by an underwriter outside the normal market. The discount is limited to 10% for unrestricted listed securities, and is unlimited otherwise.[28] Where the foundation's shares represent a controlling interest, the price at which shares of others are sold is not necessarily an accurate value of the shares.[29]

(d) Cash and Other Assets

Cold hard dollars are valued by taking the average of the cash on hand at the beginning and end of each month. Thus, a foundation cannot easily manipulate its cash balance. An imputed amount of cash, $1\frac{1}{2}\%$ of all investment assets, is excluded in calculating the MIR.

Common Trust Funds. Foundation funds invested in a common trust fund[30] can use the fund's valuation reports. Fund participants typically receive periodic val-

---

[27] Reg. §53.4942(a)-2(c)(4)(i)(*c*).
[28] IRC §4942(e)(2).
[29] Reg. §53.4942(a)-2(c)(4)(I)(c)(3); for more discussion see Chapter 6§3(c) of B. Hopkins and J. Blazek, *Private Foundations: Tax Law and Compliance*. (New York: Wiley, 1997).
[30] Defined in IRC §584.

uations of their interests from the fund manager throughout the year, and can calculate the average of these valuation reports. If the fund issues valuations quarterly, the simple average of the four reported valuations is an acceptable measure of the fund's value for this purpose.

Real Estate. A certified, independent appraisal made in writing by a qualified person who is not a disqualified person with respect to, or an employee of, the foundation is required to be made every five years for investment real estate held by a foundation.[31] An appraisal is considered *certified* only if it includes a statement that, in the opinion of the appraiser, the values placed on the land appraised were determined in accordance with valuation principles regularly employed in making appraisals of such property using all reasonable valuation methods. Due to the significant cost that can be entailed in such appraisals, gifts of modest parcels of real estate to a PF (or sale soon after a gift) should be avoided.

More frequent valuations can be made when circumstances dictate, as for example when real estate has declined substantially in value (starts a new five-year period). The IRS will not disturb a valuation properly made during the five year period even when the valuation has increased materially.[32]

Other Types of Assets. *Mineral interest* valuations are based on reserve studies conducted by independent petroleum evaluation engineers. These studies are customarily updated every five years, like real estate, although there is no mention of oil properties in the IRS literature on the subject.

A *closely held business* can be valued on any day of the year (but consistently from year to year). Estate tax valuation methods apply.

Valuations of *computers, office equipment, and other tangible assets used in managing the investment activity* can be obtained from the local newspaper's classified advertisements for used equipment, or by obtaining a quotation from a used office furniture dealer.

The value of a *whole life insurance policy* is its cash surrender value.

Notes and accounts receivable are included at their net realizable value or their face value discounted for any uncollectable portion.

Collectibles such as gold, paintings, and gems are valued under estate tax valuation rules.

15.3 DISTRIBUTABLE AMOUNT

To arrive at what the Internal Revenue Code calls the distributable amount (DA), or the amount required to be paid out annually, the PF follows this formula:

$$A + B - C = \text{Distributable Amount}$$

---

[31] Reg. §53.4942(a)-2(c)(4)(iv)(*b*).
[32] *Id.*

A = Minimum investment return (5% of value of investment assets)[33] plus

B = Any amounts previously included as qualifying distributions, but now not qualifying, such as:

- Grants, student loans, and program-related investments repaid or returned to the foundation for any reason.[34]

- An asset that ceases to be an exempt function asset, whose purchase or conversion was previously included as a qualifying distribution. The sale proceeds or FMV at the time of conversion of the asset is the amount added back.

- Unused set-aside funds that are no longer earmarked for a charitable project or which are ineligible because of excessive time lapse.

C = Less the excise tax on investment income and unrelated business income tax imposed for the year.

The distributable amount must be paid out before the end of the next succeeding year. For example, a foundation must, before September 30, 1999, distribute the amount calculated and shown on its September 30, 1998 year-end return. This one-year time lag essentially gives a new foundation two years in which to establish its grants systems and to earn the income needed to be distributed by the end of its second year. Additionally the MIR percentage for a short year is prorated according to the number of months in the year, and assets held less than a year are similarly prorated.[35]

The distributable amount is calculated each year on Form 990-PF. A summary schedule entitled "Undistributed Income" is also completed to compare the qualifying distributions (discussed next) to the required amount. Though a foundation is penalized if it underdistributes, a five-year carryover is allowed for excess distributions.[36] A foundation that changes its fiscal year ending (which it incidentally can do automatically by filing Form 990-PF within 4½ months of the end of the short year) must pay out the distributable amount by the end of the short period.

Controversial Addition. In spite of the fact that IRC §4942(d) literally does not, Part XI of Form 990PF, the instructions to the form, and the regulations[37] require that income paid or payable by certain trusts be added to the distributable amount of all foundations. Since 1982, this addition has only been applicable to private operating foundations[38] in calculating their *adjusted gross income*.[39] Prior to 1982, all

---

[33] See §15.1.

[34] See IRC §4945 for grant agreements and expenditure responsibility grants.

[35] Reg. §53.4942(a)-2(c)(4)(vii) and (5) (iii); see §§15.1 and 15.2(b).

[36] See §15.6 for discussion of satisfying the distribution test.

[37] Reg. §53.4942(a)-2(b)(2); IRS Publication 578, *Tax Information for Private Foundations and Foundation Managers* (last revised in January 1989), also contains this requirement.

[38] Discussed in §15.5.

[39] Defined by IRC §4942(f) to include the guaranteed annuity amount paid or payable to a foundation by a split-interest trust attributable to amounts placed in trust after May 26, 1969.

foundations were required to distribute either their adjusted gross income, including such trust distributions, or the hypothetical minimum investment return, whichever was higher. To preserve the principal value of their assets, foundations convinced Congress to lower the annual distribution requirement solely to the minimum investment return adjusted as shown previously for the excise tax and recoveries of amounts previously claimed as qualifying distributions. Nonetheless the IRS form continues to prompt addition of distributions, actually paid or payable, from split-interest trusts.

The Ann Jackson Family Foundation challenged the IRS and convinced the Tax Court that the regulation was an "unwarranted extension of the statutory provision."[40] Interestingly enough, another section of the regulations pertaining to distribution requirements provides that the corpus of a split-interest trust is not counted as an investment asset for purposes of calculating the foundation's minimum investment return.[41] Thus a foundation that is a beneficiary of a split-interest trust faces a dilemma in view of this controversy.

15.4 QUALIFYING DISTRIBUTIONS

An excise tax is due when a foundation has undistributed income for the year defined as the distributable amount less *qualifying* distributions.[42] Not all contributions or disbursements qualify or count when a foundation tallies up its expenses to see if it meets the minimum distribution requirements. There are two sets of tests to meet: Of primary importance is that the expenditure must be in pursuit of a charitable purpose.[43] Second, distributions are only counted on a cash basis of accounting—the foundation must actually let go of its cash or other property. Pledging to pay in the future or earmarking funds for a restricted purpose does not constitute a distribution. Grants paid with borrowed funds are treated as a distribution when the grant is paid, not when the loan is made or repaid.[44]

The rules are designed to ensure that the distributable amount is used to serve broad charitable purposes each year. Various types of qualifying distributions are described below and in summary are defined by the tax code to include:[45]

- Any amount, including reasonable and necessary administrative expenses, paid to accomplish one or more tax-exempt purposes,

- Any amount paid to acquire an asset used or held for use directly in carrying out tax-exempt purpose(s); and

- Qualified set-asides and program-related investments.

---

[40] *Ann Jackson Family Foundation v. Commissioner*, 97 T.C. No. 35 (1991), *aff'd*, 94-1 U.S.T.C. 50068 (9th Cir. 1994).
[41] Reg. §53.4942(a)-2(b)(2)(iii).
[42] Illustrated in §15.6.
[43] As defined in IRC §170(c)(1) or (c)(2)(B).
[44] Reg. §53.4942(a)-3(a)(4). Interest on such debt is not itself counted as a qualifying distribution, nor as a reduction of investment income for excise tax purposes.
[45] IRC §4942(g)(1).

(a) Direct Grants

Charitable grants paid directly to publicly supported charitable organizations,[46] for general support or for a wide range of specific charitable purposes, comprise by far the bulk of qualifying distributions made by private foundations. A grant can also be paid to an instrumentality of a national, state, or local government. Grants to accomplish a charitable purpose to any type of exempt or nonexempt organization anywhere throughout the world can qualify, if the proper procedures are followed.[47] Although a foundation is not prevented from making such grants, payments to two particular types of organization do not qualify to offset the distributable amount:

1. A grant to another private foundation does not count unless the receiving PF redistributes the funds or is an unrelated private operating foundation.

2. A controlled organization, either private or public, again does not count, unless the funds are properly redistributed.

The recipient organization (or donee, in the language of the regulations) is controlled by the PF or by one or more of its disqualified persons if any of such persons can, by aggregating their votes or positions of authority, require the recipient organization to make an expenditure, or prevent it from making an expenditure, regardless of the method by which control is exercised or exercisable.[48] Control for this purpose is determined on an organizational level. It is acceptable for the foundation to designate which of the grantee's programs it chooses to support, but not to direct the fashion in which a program is operated. The creation of a separate fund or special budgetary controls can be required, but there must be no material restriction on how the recipient uses the funds to accomplish its own exempt purposes.[49] Funds cannot be earmarked for lobbying, a specific individual grant, or any other expenditures that the PF itself would not be permitted to make.

Redistribution by the controlled organization or unrelated foundation is accomplished where not later than the close of the first taxable year after the donee organization's taxable year in which such contribution is received, such donee organization makes a distribution equal to the full amount of such contribution. Additionally, the donee may not count the distribution toward satisfying its own requirement, but instead must treat its regranting of the money as a payment out of corpus. The donor foundation must obtain proof that the redistribution was accomplished in the form of a donee statement containing specific information described in the regulations.[50]

---

[46] See Chapter 11.
[47] See Chapter 17 for a discussion of grant-making requirements and particularly Chapter 17§5 for discussion of educational grants to social fraternities and Chapter 17§4 for grants to foreign organizations.
[48] Reg. §53.4942(a)-3(a)(3).
[49] Reg. §53.4942(a)-3(a)(3) refers back to §1.507-2(a)(8) to define materials restriction.
[50] Reg. §53.4942(a)-3(c).

Conduit foundation. The income tax deduction for gifts of appreciated property (other than cash and marketable securities) is limited to the donor's tax basis *unless* the PF redistributes the property or other assets of equal value. To qualify the gift for full FMV deduction, the PF must become what is called a "conduit foundation" for the year. It must redistribute 100% of all donations received by the 15th day of the third month of the following year *and* the redistribution cannot be counted as a qualifying distribution.[51]

In-kind gifts not paid in cash, such as rent-free use of space, are not counted.[52] To avoid this result, a foundation could grant funds with which the grantee could pay the rent. Except any excise, and possibly an unrelated business income, tax[53] that might be due on profits from the rental activity, this alternative might yield a better result.

Pledges to make a gift in the future, likewise, do not qualify as an actual distribution. The word *paid* means that a distribution is counted in the year in which cash or property is actually paid out, not the year in which a donation is approved or promised.[54] Thus, a foundation that pledged a gift to a public charity to help build a museum could not count the gift until the funds were actually paid. Holding the funds to earn interest for the three-year period before construction began so that the PF could earn interest precludes treating the funds as distributed.[55] Certain *set-asides* can be counted as discussed in § 15.4(c).

Noncash Grants. A qualifying grant can be paid in either cash or property. The FMV of the property is counted as a distribution and importantly, the unrealized gain inherent in the property is not taxed. This significant tax advantage makes it important for a foundation to consider distributing appreciated property to a grantee, rather than selling the property to be able to give it cash.[56] The value of distributed property must be reduced by any amount previously treated as a qualifying distribution. For example, when a building purchased by the foundation for use in its own exempt activities was subsequently donated to another charity, only the current FMV in excess of its cost in the property was counted.[57]

(b) Direct Charitable Expenditures

Amounts paid to accomplish a charitable purpose, including a portion of the foundation's reasonable and necessary administrative expense, are eligible to be treated as a qualifying distribution. The following are examples of the types of nongrant expenditures that qualify as qualifying distributions.

---

[51] For a more thorough discussion, see B. Hopkins and J. Blazek, *Private Foundations: Tax Law and Compliance* (New York: Wiley, 1997), Chapter 3§2.

[52] Priv. Ltr. Rul. 8719004.

[53] See Chapter 13§1(d).

[54] Priv. Ltr. Rul. 8839003; see also Priv. Ltr. Rul. 8750006 concerning the proper reporting for deferred grant awards.

[55] Rev. Rul. 79-319, 1979-2 C.B. 388; but see Rev. Rul. 77-7, 1977-1 C.B. 354.

[56] See this and other tax planning ideas in Chapter 13§4.

[57] Rev. Rul. 79-375, 1979-2 C.B. 389.

Exempt function assets[58] purchased used or held for use in conducting a foundation's programs, rather than as investment assets, are treated as charitable disbursements. The full purchase price of the asset is counted even if part or all of the purchase price is borrowed. Depreciation does *not* count.[59]

Conversion of an asset previously held for investment purposes to use as an exempt function asset is counted. For example, a building rented to commercial tenants might be converted to rent-free use by a public charity. The distribution amount is equal to the FMV on the date of conversion. The date on which the foundation approves the plan for conversion, rather than the date the conversion is completed, is the effective date of change.[60]

Administrative expenses expended by the foundation in conducting its exempt activities, rather than managing its investments, are includable as qualifying distributions. The design of Form 990-PF prompts a foundation to allocate its expenditures between those associated with its investments and charitable programs.[61] Expenses directly attributable to grant-making activity might include program officer salaries and associated costs, computerized grant tracking systems, and grantee technical assistance. Organizational administrative costs not solely related to grants, including personnel costs, professional advisors, facilities, and other expenses must be allocated on some reasonable basis. Legal fees paid in a suit involving an exempt charitable trust seeking to clarify its beneficiaries were treated as a qualifying distribution, for example.[62]

For years beginning after 1984 and before 1991, a limitation was placed on the amount of administrative expense added to qualifying distributions. During that time, no more than 0.65% of a foundation's net investment assets over a three-year period could be claimed.

Self-sponsored charitable program expenses paid directly (of a sort a private operating foundation must incur) by the traditional private foundation also count. Examples are numerous, including operating a museum or library, running a summer camp for children, conducting research and publishing books, and preserving historic houses. Charitable projects can be carried out in any location. There is no constraint against a private foundation conducting activities outside the United States.

Individual grants count as qualifying distributions if they are paid under a program meeting the nondiscrimination requirements.[63] Academic grants are considered to be fully counted when the recipients can expend a portion of the funds granted on child care, as long as such spending enables the grantees to continue research and are not made in accordance with individuals' personal or family needs.[64]

---

[58] Defined in §15§1(c).

[59] Rev. Rul. 74-560, 1974-2 C.B. 389; also see Priv. Ltr. Rul. in which the cost of a feasibility study for development of a museum was deemed a qualifying distribution rather than acquisition of an exempt function asset.

[60] Rev. Rul. 78-102, 1978-1 C.B. 379.

[61] See Part I of the filled-in form in Chapter 27.

[62] Rev. Rul. 75-495, 1975-2 C.B. 449.

[63] See Chapter 17§5.

[64] Priv. Ltr. Rul. 9116032.

Program-related investments that satisfy the jeopardizing investment and taxable expenditure rules,[65] including interest-free or low-interest loans to other exempt organizations or individuals, also are counted as qualifying distributions.

(c) Set-Asides

Money set aside or saved for specific future charitable projects rather than being paid out currently, can be considered to be qualifying distributions in the year saved.[66] Such funds are treated as a foundation liability and charged against corpus, rather than being counted again, when they are actually paid out in a subsequent year.[67] The amount set aside need not be increased by income earned on the funds, but the income and set-aside funds are treated as investment assets for mandatory payout purposes. There are two very different types of set-asides. For the first type, the foundation must have plans to use the money within 60 months after its set-aside for a specific project and meet a *suitability* test. Prior IRS approval is required before reserved funds can be claimed as a qualifying distribution for this type.[68] In a second type, a newly created organization must simply satisfy a mathematical test.

Type 1—The Suitability Test. To qualify for this type of set-aside, the foundation must convince the IRS that a project is worthy and that it can be better accomplished with several years of income (but not more than five, initially) which it plans to save rather than pay out. Approval must be sought before the end of the year of set-aside. To be approved, the project should include "situations where relatively long-term grants or expenditures must be made to assure the continuity of particular charitable projects or program-related investments, or where grants are made as part of a matching grant program."[69] This type of program would include, for example:

- A plan to erect a museum building to house the foundation's art collection, even though the exact location and architectural plans have not been finalized

- A plan to purchase an art collection offered for sale as a unit at a price in excess of one year's income[70]

---

[65] See Chapters 16 and 17.

[66] IRC §4942(g)(2); Reg. §53.4942(a)-3(b).

[67] Rev. Rul. 78-148, 1978-1C.B. 380.

[68] To obtain approval, a PF must write to the IRS National Office in Washington and submit detailed information as outlined in IRS Publication 578, *Tax Information for Private Foundations and Foundation Managers*.

[69] Rev. Rul. 77-7, 1977-1 C.B. 540.

[70] In Priv. Ltr. Rul. 9302015, because the date of availability and the cost of artworks are unpredictable and the cost could be prepaid, the IRS agreed that additional set-aside periods would best accomplish the museum's goals as long as the museum funds pledged were actually expended on artworks; see also Priv. Ltr. Rul. 9409025.

- A plan to fund a specific research program of such magnitude as to require an accumulation of funds before beginning the research, even though not all of the details of the program have been finalized[71]

However, setting aside all three years of the pledged amount of fixed-sum research grants and renewable scholarships did not qualify.[72]

The set-aside period can be extended by the IRS where good cause can be shown.[73] An extension was granted, for example, because a local building moratorium caused a delay in acquiring the necessary property.[74] A foundation that initially applied the cash distribution test was allowed to continue set-asides for its self-help construction program for the poor.[75]

Type 2—The Cash Distribution Test. For a new foundation that plans a specific project that can be better accomplished by accumulating funds, reduced distributions may be permitted without prior IRS approval.[76] Essentially such a foundation's distributable amount is reduced during its first four years following the year it was established in what is called a *start-up period minimum amount* as follows:

- First Year: 20% of the normal distributable amount paid out in qualifying distributions

- Second Year: 40% of the normal distributable amount paid out in qualifying distributions

- Third Year: 60% of the normal distributable amount paid out in qualifying distributions

- Fourth Year: 80% of the normal distributable amount paid out in qualifying distributions

- Fifth Year: Normal distributable amount paid out in qualifying distributions

Distributions in excess of the minimum amounts can also be carried forward to offset future distributable amounts. Details of how a foundation plans to meet these requirements must be attached to the Form 990-PF. The rules are very specific, so it is important to study the regulations and instructions to Form 990-PF in detail before claiming such a set-aside.[77]

---

[71] Reg. §53.4942(a)-3(b)(2); see also Priv. Ltr. Rul. 9619070 in which due to excessive rainfall, a foundation was unable to complete its planned wildlife habitat restoration project.

[72] Rev. Rul. 75-511, 1975-2 C.B. 450; see also Priv. Ltr. Rul. 9616041 in which a foundation was permitted to set aside funds while it sought approval to expand geographic area in which it was permitted to make scholarship grants.

[73] Reg. §53.4942(a)-3(b)(1).

[74] Priv. Ltr. Rul. 7821141.

[75] Priv. Ltr. Rul. 9305018.

[76] IRC §4942(g)(2)(A) added to the code in 1976; Reg. §53.4942(a)-3(b)(4)(I).

[77] Reg. §53.4942(a)-3(b)(3) and (4). See Priv. Ltr. Rul. 9301022 in which a foundation that failed to claim the Type 2 set-aside on its original return was allowed to elect to treat the amounts as a qualifying distribution on amended returns.

15.5 PRIVATE OPERATING FOUNDATIONS

Internal Revenue Code §4942(j)(3) creates a special type of foundation that is essentially a cross between a private foundation and a public organization. A private operating foundation (POF) is a charity that does its own thing, or, in the language of the statute, "actively conducts activities constituting the purpose or function for which it is organized and operated." In other words, a POF makes qualifying distributions by sponsoring and managing its own charitable projects rather than merely making grants to other organizations.[78] One type of operating foundation is an endowed institution operating a museum, library, or other charitable pursuit not included in the list of organizations that qualify as public charities without regard to their sources of support.[79] Many POFs are privately funded entities started by a person of means who has strong ideas about charitable objectives he or she wants to accomplish through self-initiated projects.

A POF must meet two annual distribution requirements: one based on its income levels and another on its assets or sources of its revenues. Most importantly for its funders, donations to a private operating foundation are afforded the higher deductibility limits allowed for gifts to public charities.[80]

(a) Active Charitable Programs

The most significant attribute of a POF is sometimes the most difficult quality to possess. To qualify as a POF, the foundation must focus—it must be *significantly involved* in its own projects in a continuing and sustainable fashion. To be involved might mean the foundation purchases goods and services to operate a museum, to conduct scientific research, to develop low-income housing, or to conduct some other charitable program. A POF maintains a staff of researchers, teachers, curators, or other program specialists. Its staff can be partly or wholly made up of volunteers and can include its funders or trustees, if their work involvement is genuine.

The typical operating foundation acquires and maintains program assets used in its programs—buildings, art works, research facilities, and the like. A POF might buy, restore, and rent historic houses to preserve them. It would engage realtors, architects, contractors, and other specialists needed to acquire and fix up the property. It would pay utility, maintenance, and insurance costs, engage property managers, and pay administrative expenses necessary to operate the properties. Optimally, a POF is identified in the public eye with and by its projects. The regulations provide the following examples.[81]

Ghetto Improvement Project. An organization is created to improve conditions in an urban ghetto. Ten percent of its income is spent to conduct surveys of the

---

[78] Reg. §53.4942(b)-1(b).

[79] Churches, schools, hospitals, and certain medical research organizations as described in Chapter 11.

[80] For a more thorough presentation on private operating foundations, see B. Hopkins and J. Blazek, *Private Foundations: Tax Law and Compliance* (New York: Wiley, 1997), Chapter 3.

[81] Reg. §53.4942(b)-1(d).

ghetto's problems. The remaining 90% is used to make grants to other nonprofit organizations doing work in the ghetto. Since only 10% of its funds is directly expended, it cannot qualify as a POF. If, instead, it spent all of the money directly to analyze the results, develop recommendations, publish the conclusions of its studies, and hire community advisors to assist business developers and other organizations working in the area, it might qualify.

Teacher Training Program.   An entity is formed to train teachers for institutions of higher education. Fellowships are awarded to students for graduate study leading toward advanced degrees in college teaching. Pamphlets encouraging prospective college teachers and describing the POF's activity are widely circulated. Seminars attended by fellowship recipients, POF staff, and consultants and other interested parties are held each summer, and papers from the conference are published. Despite the fact that a majority of the organization's money is spent for fellowship payments, the program is comprehensive and suitable to qualify as an active project.

Medical Research Organization (MRO).   An MRO is created to study heart disease. Physicians and scientists apply to conduct research at the MRO's center. Its professional staff evaluates the projects, reviews progress reports, supervises the projects, and publishes the resulting findings.

Historical Reference Library.   A library organization is established to hold and care for manuscripts and reference material relating to the history of the region in which it is located. Additionally, it makes a limited number of annual grants to enable postdoctoral scholars and doctoral candidates to use its library. Sometimes, but not always, the POF can obtain the rights to publish the scholar's work.

Set-asides of funds for a specific future project are permitted for POFs. The requirements discussed in §15.4(c) must be met for the amounts set aside to be counted as qualifying distributions.

(b) Grants to Other Organizations

While one or more other charitable organizations may be involved in some manner, an operating foundation must expend a prescribed amount of its funds directly. The regulations provide that:

> Qualifying distributions are not made by a foundation directly for the active conduct unless such distributions are used by the foundation itself, rather than by or through one or more grantee organizations.[82]

A grant to another organization is presumed to be indirect conduct of exempt activity, even if the activity of the grantee organization helps the POF accomplish its goals. However, in one instance a grant to another organization was found to qualify as direct involvement on a charitable trust's part. The trust granted all of its income to a conduit organization that had been established for liability reasons

---

[82] Reg. §53.4942(b)-1(b).

to serve in a fiduciary capacity on behalf of the trust. Although the corporation actually operated the cultural center, its activities were attributed to the POF.[83]

It is important to note that a POF is not prohibited from making grants to other organizations; such grants simply do not count toward satisfying the POF's distribution requirements. So long as the POF distributes the requisite annual amount for its active programs, it may in addition make grants to other organizations. A special limitation applies if the operating foundation's minimum investment return is less than its adjusted net income. If its active project distributions are less than adjusted gross income, more than 85% of the total qualifying distributions must be active.[84] The point is that as long as the POF meets the income and asset tests, it may spend additional amounts on any form of charitable activity it chooses.

(c) Individual Grant Programs

Payments to individuals under a scholarship program, a student loan fund, a minority business enterprise capital support project, or similar charitable effort can qualify as appropriate activity for a POF.[85] The facts and circumstances surrounding the project must indicate that the POF is *significantly involved*. Merely selecting, screening, and investigating applicants for grant or scholarships is insufficient. When the recipients perform their work or studies alone, such as in pursuit of a doctoral degree or exclusively under the direction of some other organization, the individual grants are not considered to be direct qualifying payments. The administrative costs of such screening and investigation, as opposed to the individual grants themselves, may be treated as direct activity disbursements.

Significant involvement of the POF and its staff exists when the individual grants are part of a comprehensive program. The regulations say the test is qualitative, rather than quantitative, and give two examples of such programs. In one, the POF's purpose is to relieve poverty and human distress, and its exempt activities are designed to ameliorate conditions among the poor, particularly during national disasters. The POF provides food and clothing to such indigents, without the assistance of an intervening organization or agency, under the direction of the POF's salaried or voluntary staff of administrators, researchers, or other personnel who supervise and direct the activity.

In the second example, a POF develops a specialized skill or expertise in scientific or medical research, social work, education, or the social sciences. A salaried staff of administrators, researchers, and other personnel supervise and conduct the work in its particular area of interest. As a part of the program, the POF awards grants, scholarships, or other payments to individuals to encourage independent study and scientific research projects and to otherwise further their involvement in the POF's field of interest. The POF sponsors seminars, conducts classes, and provides direction and supervision for the grant recipients. Based on

---

[83] Rev. Rul. 78-315, 1978-2 C.B. 271; see also Priv. Ltr. Rul. 9203004.
[84] Reg. §53.4942(b)-1(a)(1)(i).
[85] Reg. §53.4942(b)-(1)(b)(2).

these facts, the individual grants are treated as active and thus qualify under the POF distribution test.[86]

(d) Tests to Qualify as a Private Operating Foundation

To qualify as a private operating foundation, the private foundation must meet two tests:

1. The income test[87]

2. The asset, endowment, or support test[88]

Income Test. Under this test, the POF must expend substantially all (85%) of the lesser of its adjusted net income or its minimum investment[89] on its actively conducted projects.

Asset Test. To meet this test, at least 65% of the FMV of the POF's assets must be devoted to the active conduct of its charitable activities, a functionally related business, or stock of a controlled corporation substantially all of the assets of which are so devoted. The concepts of exempt function and dual-use assets used in calculating the MIR are followed to identify assets qualifying for this test.[90] An asset that is not capable of being valued, such as a botanical garden, can be included at its historical cost.[91]

Endowment Test. For this test, the POF's annual distributions must equal at least two-thirds of its minimum investment return ($3\frac{1}{3}\%$ of investment assets). This test is designed to prevent a private foundation from seeking POF status to take advantage of the income test that requires distribution of income or MIR, which is lower. Assuming a PF holds marketable securities that pay no dividends, the income test, taken alone, would require no current charitable spending. A POF with a portfolio of low current yield securities would have to distribute part of its principal or contributions received to meet this test.[92]

Support Test. Under this test, the POF's support (meaning donations and not including investment income) must be received from the general public and from five or more noncontrolled §501(c)(3) organizations, with none giving more than 25% of the POF's support. An organization wishing to meet this test must carefully study the regulations.[93]

---

[86] See also *The Elizabeth D. Leckie Scholarship Fund v. Commissioner,* 87 T.C. 250919860.
[87] Reg. §53.4942(b)-1(a)(1).
[88] Reg. §53.4942(b)-2.
[89] MIR is the same as for standard private foundations as discussed in §15.1.
[90] See §15.1(c). One distinction is made in the regulations that, in a possibly confusing fashion, say amounts receivable under a charitable loan program (students, disabled persons, or the like) are treated as investment assets for this purpose.
[91] Reg. §53.4942(b)-2(a)(4).
[92] Reg. §53.4942(b)-2(b)(1).
[93] Reg. §53.4942(b)-2(c).

(e) Adjusted Net Income

Before 1982, all private foundations were required to distribute their adjusted net income or their MIR, whichever was higher. For traditional foundations effective for years beginning in 1982, only MIR need be paid out, and adjusted net income is not relevant. Private operating foundations, however, distribute their MIR or the adjusted net income, whichever is *lower.* Adjusted gross income is calculated using the following formula:[94]

$$A - B - C - D = \text{Adjusted Net Income}$$

A = Gross income of all types for the year (not limited to income subject to the investment income tax)

B = Long term capital gains

C = Contributions received

D = Ordinary and necessary expenses paid or incurred for the production or collection of gross income or for the management, conservation, or maintenance of property held for the production of such income[95]

Over the years, a few rulings have been published to clarify the amounts includable in adjusted net income. A brief summary follows:

- Bond premium amortization is permitted, following the rules of IRC §171.[96]

- Annuity, IRA, and other employee benefit plan payments are includable to the extent that the amount exceeds the value of the right to receive the payment on the decedent's date of death.[97]

- Capital gain dividends paid or credited for reinvestment by a mutual fund are *not* included, because they are considered as long term by IRC §852(b)(3)(B).[98]

(f) Compliance Period

The income test and the asset, endowment, or support tests are applied each year for a four-year period that includes the current and past three years. The POF has a choice of two methods to calculate its compliance with the tests but it must use the same method for both tests:

1. All four years can be aggregated, that is, the distributions for four years are added together. The POF must use only one of the asset, endowment, or support tests for all four years.

---

[94] Reg. §53.4942(a)-2(d)(1); IRS Form 990-PF Instructions, p. 8.
[95] Reg. §53.4942(a)-2(d)(4); also see Chapter 13§3.
[96] Rev. Rul. 76-248, 1976-1 C.B. 353.
[97] Rev. Rul. 75-442, 1975-2 C.B. 448.
[98] Rev. Rul. 73-320, 1973-2 C.B. 385.

2. For three of the four years, the POF meets the income test and any one of the asset, endowment, or support tests.

If the POF fails to qualify for a particular year, it is treated as an ordinary private foundation for that year. It can return to POF classification as soon as it again qualifies under both the income test and the assets, endowment, or support test. There is no requirement that a POF applying method 2 make up the deficient year.[99]

New organizations generally must meet the test in their first year. If application for exemption is made prior to the completion of the proposed POF's first fiscal year, the IRS will accept the organization's assertion, based on a good faith determination, that it plans to qualify.[100] Form 1023 and its instructions contain a workpaper for submitting the appropriate information.[101] Failure in the first year can be remedied if the POF does in fact qualify in its second, third, and fourth years.

An IRS advance ruling is not technically required for a PF to convert to operation as a POF. The foundation is qualified if it meets the tests by changing its method of operation or mix of assets. However, most trustees seek the comfort of an IRS determination to sanction the conversion. The question arises because the transition takes four years and the one-year time lag for making charitable distributions is lost. For a converting traditional foundation, distributions are accelerated with the payment of both the prior year distributable amount and active program distributions before year-end.

(g) Advantages of Private Operating Foundations

Private operating foundations have several special advantages.

- *Contribution deduction limits are preferential.* The percentage limits for charitable deductions are higher for POFs than for private foundations. They are the same as the deductions permitted for public charities. A full 50% of an individual's income can be sheltered by contributions to a POF, but only 30% of one's income can be deducted for gifts to a normal PF. The full FMV of real estate, art works, and other appreciated property is deductible for donations to a POF. Subject to an on-again off-again rule, only marketable securities donated to a traditional foundation are fully deductible.[102]

- *Distributable amount may be lower.* The minimum distribution requirement for a POF may be lower than for normal private foundations. In some cases, given a sufficient return on investment, a POF can better build an endowment over the years. It must only distribute its actual net income when it is lower than MIR and only need to pay out two-thirds of its MIR.

The primary *disadvantage* is that the one-year delay afforded to PFs to meet the minimum distribution requirement is lost. The POF must distribute either its adjusted net income for the year in question or its MIR.

[99] Priv. Ltr. Rul. 9509042.
[100] Reg. §53.4942(b)-3.
[101] See Appendix 18-1 for an example.
[102] IRC §170(e)(5).

15.6 EXCISE TAX FOR FAILURE TO DISTRIBUTE

Each year a normal private foundation is required to make qualifying distributions equal to its distributable amount (DA) for the prior year reduced by any carryovers of prior year excess distributions. A private foundation that fails to pay out this amount and has *undistributed income,* must make up the deficiency and a penalty tax may apply. A private operating foundation is not subject to this tax but instead to losing its operating status as discussed previously. Failure to correct a deficiency and repeated deficiencies can result in loss of exemption. Undistributed income equals:

> Current year DA[103]
> less
> Qualifying Distributions[104] that are not
> applied either to offset prior deficits or to corpus.

An initial tax of 15% is imposed for each year that the deficit goes uncorrected.[105] The underdistribution must be corrected by making grants that are *qualifying distributions.*

(a) Timing of Distributions

To identify a deficiency of distributions and to correct the condition, one must understand how payments are applied. A foundation's charitable expenditures that are considered qualifying distributions are totaled for each year in which they are paid, but they are not necessarily applied in that year. The terminology can be confusing here because the current year DA is based on the prior year's minimum investment return.[106] Nevertheless, qualifying distributions are applied as follows:[107]

- First, to make up any prior year's deficiency of DA (for a year in which the PF has undistributed income subject to the excise tax)

- Next, the remaining qualifying distributions are applied to the current year's DA (essentially, the prior year's adjusted MIR)

- Finally, any remaining distributions are taken out of corpus.[108] Remember, the redistribution of a grant received by one PF from another PF must be charged against corpus and cannot reduce the donee PF's own DA. See § 15.4(a). Also, a gift from a contributor who wishes to receive a higher percentage contribution deduction limitation must be paid from corpus.[109]

---

[103] Defined in §15.3.
[104] Defined in §15.4.
[105] IRC §4942(a)(1).
[106] Defined in §15.3.
[107] IRC §4942(h).
[108] Reg. §53.4942(a)-3(d).
[109] IRC §170(b)(1)(E).

Distributions in excess of the DA applied to corpus are carried forward for five years and can offset the future DA as shown in Exhibit 15-1. The IRS Chief Counsel has issued a memorandum entitled "Adjustments of Excess Distribution Carryovers from Closed Years," taking the position that adjustments to years closed by the statute of limitations is permissible.[110] The memorandum recognizes the fact that in any one year, a nonoperating PF has excessive or deficient distributions and, therefore, a carryover of excess distributions is an accumulation of all post-1969 years. It is an unusual foundation that pays out the exact minimum distribution amount.

A single error in calculating the amount required to be distributed or qualifying distributions in any one year causes all years to be wrong. Thus, the IRS takes the position, as yet unchallenged in court, that the years from 1970 forward are open years for this purpose.[111] The excesses (designated as out of corpus) are applied over a five-year period in the order in which they occur so that (in the exhibit) by 1999, no 1996 excess remains because it offset the 1995 and 1998 deficits. The 1999 excess of $20 can be carried to 2004.

(b) Calculating the Tax

A foundation that fails to make the required charitable expenditures in a timely manner is subject to an excise tax of 15% on the undistributed amount. The tax is charged for each year or partial year that the deficiency remains uncorrected. Essentially, the tax calculation starts on the first late day and continues until a notice

Exhibit 15–1

DISTRIBUTION APPLICATION AND CARRYOVERS

Corpus	1995	1996	1997	1998	1999	2000	Carryovers
Qualifying Distributions	0	250	70	40	160	100	
Distributable Amount	100	100	100	100	100	100	
Net Distributions	−100	150	−30	−60	60	0	
Application of annual amounts:							
Apply '96 to '95	+100	−100					+50 '96 yr end
Apply '96 to '97		−30	+30				+20 '96 yr end
Apply '96 to '98		−20		+20			0
Apply '99 to '98				+60	−60		+20 '99 yr end
Balance	0	0	0	0	+20	0	
Balance	0	0	0	0	20	0	

[110] IRS Gen. Coun. Memo. 39808.
[111] Priv. Ltr. Rul. 9116032.

of the deficiency is issued by the IRS (but in whole year increments). This taxable period also closes on the date of voluntary payment of the tax.[112] Note there is no tax on the foundation managers.

Assume that a calendar year PF fails to distribute $50,000 of its 1997 DA by December 31, 1998. If the amount is distributed within the first year after the deadline (by December 31, 1999), a 15% tax is due. If the correction takes two years, or is not fixed until the second year after it was due (on or before January 1, 2000), another 15% is due, or a total of 30%. The additional 15% would be due even if the payment is made on January 2, 2000.

An additional 100% tax is triggered if the PF fails to make up the deficient distributions within 90 days of receiving IRS notification of the problem. *The allowable correction period* is 90 days after the date of mailing of the deficiency notice.[113] The notice date is critical to calculating the tax. If the deficiency is self-admitted on the face of Form 990-PF, Part XIII or XIV, an accompanying Form 4720 is due to be filed to calculate the tax due. If the deficiency is not self-admitted, the IRS computers should recognize the problem and generate a notice within a few months beyond the return filing date.

In the more common situation, the underdistribution is found by the IRS upon examination, and the notice is mailed when the examination is completed. The PF has 90 days from the date of the notice to correct the problem by making grants. If it does not, the 100% additional penalty tax is imposed.

(c) Abatement of Penalty

Valuation Mistakes.   When a PF fails to make the required annual charitable distributions due solely to an incorrect valuation of assets, the statutory sanction may be excused. In the interest of being fair, the underdistribution can essentially be corrected if four conditions for abatement listed in the code are satisfied:[114]

1. The failure to value the assets properly was not willful and was due to reasonable cause.

2. The deficiency is distributed as a qualifying distribution by the PF within 90 days after receipt of the IRS notice of deficiency.

3. The PF notifies the IRS of the mistake by submitting information on its Form 990-PF and recalculating its qualifying distributions.

4. The extra distribution made to correct the deficiency is treated as being distributed in the deficiency year.

To prove that the undervaluation was *not willful* and was *due to reasonable cause*, the PF must show that it made all reasonable efforts in good faith to value the assets correctly.[115] A system regularly maintained for collecting the information, such as saving month-end copy of stock quotes, evidences good faith. Reliance on

[112] Reg. §53.4942(a)-1(c)(1)(ii).
[113] IRC §4942(j)(2).
[114] IRC §4942(a)(2).
[115] Reg. §53.4942(a)-1(b)(2).

an invalid appraisal received from an unrelated, but accredited, appraiser, based upon fully disclosed information pertaining to the property to be valued, should be considered as reasonable.

Underdistribution Mistakes. The IRS has discretion to abate the first-tier, or 15%, penalty. §4962 gives the IRS discretion to abate the penalty if a private foundation violates a sanction imposed by IRC §§4942, 4943, 4944, or 4945 (note absence of §4941). A private foundation that fails to meet the minimum distribution requirement may be excused from penalty in certain cases. The second-tier taxes may also be abated under IRC §4961. The exception applies if:

- The taxable event was due to reasonable cause and not to willful neglect.

- The event was corrected within the correction period for such event.

The standards for evaluating reasonable cause are discussed in chapter 16§2(c). A foundation seeks abatement of the penalty by filing Form 4720 along with an explanation of the reasons why the penalty should be forgiven. In the author's experience, the IRS has been fair in permitting abatement where reasonable cause can be shown. See Appendix 27-6 for a filled-in Form 4720.

The second-tier taxes may also be abated under circumstances described in IRC §4961.

CHAPTER SIXTEEN

Excess Business Holdings and Jeopardizing Investments: IRC §§4943 and 4944

16.1 EXCESS BUSINESS HOLDINGS

A private foundation's level of ownership in an operating business, other than one conducted as a charitable activity, is limited by Internal Revenue Code (IRC) §4943, entitled "Excess Business Holdings." A foundation is entitled to receive a gift that causes it to have impermissible ownership in a business but cannot retain it. Specific time periods are prescribed for disposition of such holdings received by a foundation through donation or inheritance. The basic rule is that the combined ownership of the private foundation (PF) and those that fund and manage it (its insiders that are formally referred to as disqualified persons) in a business enterprise of any legal form—a corporation, partnership, joint venture, or other unincorporated company—must not exceed 20%. If it can be proved the foundation and its insiders lack control of the business, the allowable percentage rises to 35%. A foundation may own up to 2% of a business (other than a solely owned proprietorship) without regard to the ownership of its insiders.

(a) Definition of Business Enterprise

The tax code only provides a negative definition of a *business enterprise* by saying what is not.[1] The two enterprises it says can be owned without limitation include a functionally related business and a business 95% of whose income is from passive sources. The regulations define *business enterprise* broadly as follows:

> A business enterprise includes the active conduct of a trade or business, including any activity which is regularly carried on for the production of income from the sale of goods or the performance of services and which constitutes an unrelated trade or business under IRC §513.[2]

The ownership limits apply regardless of whether the business produces a profit. A bond or other form of indebtedness is treated as a business holding if it is essentially a disguised equity holding. A leasehold interest in real estate, the rent from which is based, in whole or part, on profits, is customarily not considered to be a business interest, unless the leasehold constitutes an interest in the lessor's business.[3]

Functionally Related Business. A business conducted to accomplish program-related purposes is not treated as a business enterprise.[4] Such businesses include those that are excused from the unrelated business income tax as being basically not businesslike, and include:[5]

- A business the conduct of which is substantially related (aside from the mere provision of funds for the exempt purpose) to the exercise or performance by the private foundation of its charitable, educational, or other purpose or function constituting the basis for its exemption. A music publishing company concentrating on classical or serious music was considered related to the purposes of a PF promoting music education and the choice of music as a career[6]

- A business in which substantially all of the work is performed for the foundation without compensation

- A business carried on by the foundation primarily for the convenience of its members, students, patients, officers, visitors, or employees, such as a cafeteria operated by a hospital or museum

- A business that consists of selling merchandise, substantially all of which has been received by the foundation as gifts or contributions

- An activity carried on within a larger combination of similar activities related to the exempt purposes of the foundation

[1] IRC §4943(d)(3).
[2] Reg. §53.4943-10(a).
[3] Reg. §53.4943-10(a)(2).
[4] IRS Publication 578, *Tax Information for Private Foundations and Foundation Managers*, Chapter X, p. 32.
[5] Defined by reference to Reg. §53.4942-2(c)(3)(iii) regarding businesses that are not unrelated pursuant to IRC §513(a)(1), (2), and (3).
[6] Priv. Ltr. Rul. 8927031.

Passive Holding Company.   A company that obtains at least 95% of its gross income from the passive sources listed in IRC §512(b)(1), (2), (3), and (5) is not considered a business. The word "passive" was provided in this Code section in 1969, well before the Tax Reform Act of 1986 gave it another dimension. For purposes of excess holdings, passive income is classified as investment income, and includes the following.[7]

- Dividends, interest, and annuities

- Royalties, including overriding royalties, whether measured by production or by gross or taxable income from the property. Working interests in mineral properties are active businesses[8]

- Rental income from real property and from personal property leased alongside real property, if the rent is incidental (less than 50% of the total rent)

- Gains or losses from sales, exchanges, or other dispositions of property other than stock in trade held for regular sale to customers

- Income from the sale of goods if the seller does not manufacture, produce, physically receive or deliver, negotiate sales of, or keep inventories in the goods

Income classified as passive for this purpose does not lose its character merely because the property is indebted so as to make the foundation's income from the holding subject to the unrelated business income tax.[9]

(b) Corporate Holdings

Permitted holdings of business enterprises by a private foundation vary according to the form of ownership, type of entity, and other variables. A foundation may hold 20% of the voting stock of an incorporated business enterprise, reduced by the percentage of voting stock owned by all disqualified persons (DPs).[10] In other words, the foundation and its contributors and managers and their families cannot generally together control more than 20% of a corporation.

Nonvoting Stock.   If all of the insiders together own no more than 20% of the corporation's voting stock, the foundation can own any amount of nonvoting stock.[11] Stock carrying contingent voting rights is treated as nonvoting until the event triggering the right to vote occurs. An example is preferred stock that can be voted only if dividends are not paid; such shares are considered nonvoting until the voting power is exercisable. This exception only applies to an incorporated entity, not to a partnership or other form.[12] Entering into a binding agreement (scripted on

---

[7] Reg. §53.4943-10(c)(2).
[8] Priv. Ltr. Rul. 8407095.
[9] Reg. §53.4943-10(c)(2).
[10] IRC §4943(c)(2); Reg. §53.4943-3(b)(1).
[11] IRC §4943(c)(2).
[12] Reg. §53.4943-3(c)(4)(i).

the shares and transferable to any purchaser of the shares) not to vote the PF's stock does not reduce excess business holdings.[13]

Thirty-five Percent. Up to 35% ownership in a corporate business can be held aggregately by the foundation and its insiders, when the foundation establishes to the satisfaction of the Internal Revenue Service (IRS) that the enterprise is controlled by a *third person* (unrelated parties). Control for this purpose means possession, directly or indirectly, of the power to direct or cause the direction of the management and policies of the enterprise, whether through ownership of voting stock, the use of voting trusts, contractual arrangements, or otherwise. It is the reality of control that is decisive, not its form or the means by which it is exercisable.[14] The IRS has required actual proof of outside party control.[15]

Two Percent. The PF can own up to 2% of voting stock and up to 2% in value of all outstanding shares of all classes of stock, called a de minimus amount, regardless of the insider's holdings.[16] Any commonly controlled PF's holdings are combined with the PF's for this purpose.

(c) Partnerships, Trusts, and Proprietorships

The permitted holdings in partnerships and other forms of ownership are determined using the same concepts as those applicable to corporations—using different terms to identify the ownership. For a general or limited partnership or a joint venture, the terms *profit interest* and *capital interest* are substituted for *voting stock* and *nonvoting stock*.[17] The interest of the foundation and its insiders in a partnership is determined using the distributive share concepts of IRC §704(b). Absent a formal partnership agreement, the foundation's ownership is measured by the portion of assets that the foundation is entitled to receive upon withdrawal or dissolution, whichever is greater.

A private foundation's interest in a partnership makes it an owner of a proportionate part of the properties owned by the partnership for purposes of measuring excess business holdings. The 20/35% limitations apply as if the foundation owned the property directly. Therefore, a foundation owning 45% of a partnership is deemed to own 45% of properties owned by the partnership. Say, for example, the partnership owned 50% of the outstanding shares of a corporation. The PF is considered to own 45% of 50%, or 22.5% of such corporation. Unless the foundation can prove the corporation is controlled by third parties, as discussed previously, excess business holdings are present and the partnership's share of the corporation must be reduced. If instead the foundation holds a limited partnership interest, 35% may be permitted.[18] A right on the part of the limited partner PF to veto the general partner's actions may constitute sufficient control to cause the lower 20% limit to apply.[19]

---

[13] Priv. Ltr. Ruls. 9325046 and 9124061.
[14] Reg. §53.4943-3(b)(3).
[15] Rev. Rul. 81-811, 1981-1 C.B. 509.
[16] IRC §4943(c)(2)(C); Reg. §53.4943-3(b)(4).
[17] IRC §4943(c)(3); Reg. §53.4943-3(c)(2).
[18] Reg. §53.4943-3(b)(3)(ii).
[19] Priv. Ltr. Rul. 9250039.

For trusts, the term *beneficial interest* is used to measure ownership, and the permitted holdings are limited to 20%.

A foundation may not hold an interest in a proprietorship.[20] An interest in a proprietorship given or bequeathed to a foundation (but not purchased) must be disposed of within five years. An interest of less than 100% of a proprietorship is treated as an interest in a partnership.

(d) Constructive Ownership

The stock or other interest owned, directly or indirectly, by or for a corporation, partnership, estate, or trust is considered as being owned proportionately by or for its shareholders, partners, or beneficiaries.[21] Corporations engaged in active business are exempt from this attribution rule.[22] Stock held in a split-interest trust for which the foundation has only an income interest or is a remainder beneficiary is not considered constructively owned by the foundation unless the foundation can exercise primary investment discretion with respect to such interest.[23]

Powers of Appointment. Any interest in a business enterprise over which the foundation or a disqualified person has a power of appointment exercisable in favor of the PF or the DP is also treated as owned by the PF or person holding the power of appointment.

Material Restrictions. If the PF disposes of any interest in a business with the retention of any material restrictions or conditions that prevent free use of or prevent disposition of the transferred shares, then the PF is treated as owning the interest until the restrictions or conditions are eliminated.[24]

(e) Disposition Periods

Five-Year Period. A private foundation is given five years to dispose of excess business holdings acquired by gift or bequest. During the disposition period, the foundation is not treated as owning the shares. The statute says:

> If there is a change in the holdings in a business enterprise (other than by purchase by the private foundation or by a disqualified person) which causes the PF to have excess holdings, the interest of the PF shall be treated as held by a disqualified person during the five-year period beginning on the date of such change in holdings.[25]

For shares received under a will or from a trust, the five-year period begins at the time of actual distribution from the fiduciary.[26] If the foundation already holds

---

[20] IRC §4943(c)(3)(B); Reg. §53.4943-3(c)(3).
[21] Reg. §53.4943-8.
[22] Reg. §53.4943-8(c).
[23] IRC §4943(d)(1); Reg. §53.4943-8(b)(2).
[24] Reg. §53.4943-2(a)(1)(iv).
[25] IRC 4943(c)(5).
[26] Reg. §53.4943-6(b)(1).

excess shares of the business at the time it is given additional shares, special rules apply.[27]

Extension of Time.   A foundation that is attempting to sell its excess business holdings within the permissible time period (ending on or after November 1, 1983) but is unable to do so can request an additional five-year extension of the time. To obtain permission, the foundation must demonstrate that:[28]

- The gift is an unusually large gift or bequest of diverse business holdings or holdings with complex corporate structures;

- It has made diligent efforts to dispose of the holdings within the initial five-year period;

- Disposition of the holdings was not possible during the first five years because of the size and complexity or diversity of the holdings, except at a price substantially below fair market value (FMV). Congressional hearing testimony considered 5% below FMV to be substantial; and

- Before the close of the first five years, the foundation submits a disposition plan to the IRS and seeks approval of its state attorney general (or similar responsible authority).

Private letter rulings show a favorable pattern of granting extensions for PFs that have "made diligent effort" to dispose of their excess holdings.[29] A plan developed by an independent financial consultant to assist the foundation to sell its holdings, in conjunction with the substantial contributor's family members who also owned the same holdings, was approved by the IRS.[30]

Ninety-Day Period.   When a purchase by a DP creates excess business holdings, the PF has 90 days from the date it knows, or has reason to know, of the event which caused it to have such excess holdings.[31] The excise tax is not applied if the holdings are properly reduced within the 90-day period. The period can be extended to include any period during which a foundation is prevented by federal or state securities law from disposing of the excess holdings.

No Period.   An interest purchased by the PF itself that causes the combined ownership to exceed the limits must be disposed immediately, and the foundation is subject to tax. If the foundation had no knowledge, nor any reason to know, that its holdings had become excessive, the 90-day period is applied and the tax is excused.

---

[27] Reg. §53.4943-6(a)(i)(iii).
[28] IRC §4943(c)(7).
[29] Priv. Ltr. Rul. 8514098, 8508114, 8737085, and 9029067. In the 1990 ruling, the IRS found that the PF had not been diligent and denied an extension.
[30] Priv. Ltr. Rul. 9115061.
[31] Reg. §53.4943-2(a)(1)(ii).

Twenty, Fifteen, and Ten Years. Interests held on May 26, 1969 (when these rules were added to the code) were called *present interests.* Any excess ownership held at that time was disposable over 10, 15, or 20 years, depending on the amount of combined ownership. An interest received from a trust irrevocable on May 26, 1969, or from a will in effect and never revised since that date, is still subject to these longer time periods.[32] The selling off of excess business holdings by many PFs during the 1970s and 1980s was a major undertaking. The regulations contain 30 pages of instructions, exceptions, downward ratchet rules, and complicated procedures that must be carefully studied by any PF under such disposition period.

(f) Business Readjustments

Any increases in a foundation's holdings due to a *readjustment* are treated as if they were not acquired by purchase. This means that the PF either has 90 days or 5 years to dispose of them, as a general rule.[33] A readjustment may be a merger or consolidation, a recapitalization, an acquisition of stock or assets, a transfer of assets, a change in identity, form or place of organization, a redemption, or a liquidating distribution.[34] If the readjustment results in the PF owning a larger percentage than owned prior to the change, a taxable event may occur, and the rules need to be carefully studied.

(g) Tax on Excess Holdings

If the excess holdings are not disposed of within the time periods previously described, an initial tax is due. The tax is imposed only on the private foundation and is equal to 5% of the highest value of the excessive amount of the shares during each year. The tax is payable for each tax year during what is called the *taxable period.* Form 4720 is filed to calculate and report the tax due.[35] The valuation is determined under the estate tax rules.[36]

Taxable Period. The taxable period begins with the first day that excess business holdings exist, and ends on the earlier of the following dates:

- The date on which the IRS mails a deficiency notice under §6212,

- The date on which the excess is eliminated, or

- The date on which the tax is assessed. If the deficiency is self-admitted by voluntarily filing Form 4720, the period ends when the return is filed. Excess holdings found by the IRS upon examination results in the IRS issuing the assessment.

---

[32] IRC §4943(c)(4); Reg. §53.4943-4 and 5.
[33] Reg. §53.4943-6(d).
[34] Reg. §53.4943-7(d)(1).
[35] The form is reproduced in Appendix 27-6.
[36] IRC §4943(a); Reg. §53.4943-2(a).

Additional Tax.   If excess holdings exist at the end of the taxable period, an additional 200% tax is imposed on the value of the excess still held.[37] In an egregious case, a third-tier, or termination tax can be assessed.[38]

Tax Abatement.   The IRC §4962 tax abatement rules discussed in Chapter 16§2(c) may also apply, if the excess holdings were due to reasonable cause and not to willful neglect. The excess holding condition must be corrected by disposing of the excess before the penalty can be abated.

16.2   JEOPARDIZING INVESTMENTS

The managers of a private foundation have a fiduciary responsibility under most state laws to safeguard the assets on behalf of the foundation's charitable constituency. In a similar spirit, the tax code says that a private foundation should not:

> invest any amount in such a manner as to jeopardize the carrying out of any of its exempt purposes.[39]

To deter a foundation from making investments that might imperil its assets, an excise tax is imposed on the foundation itself and on any of its managers that approve of the making of a jeopardizing investment. Managers are expected to use a high degree of fiduciary responsibility in investing foundation funds. The purpose is to shield private foundation assets from risk, so as to maximize both capital and income available for charity.

Investments made to advance a charitable purpose, such as student loans or low-income housing, are classified as program-related investments and not subject to the same standards of risk/reward applicable to normal investments. The following investments are not considered to be jeopardizing:

- Program-related investments the primary purpose of which is to accomplish one or more charitable purposes rather than to produce income[40]

- Property received as gifts or by gratuitous transfers are not jeopardizing, unless the foundation F pays some consideration in connection with the gift, such as a bargain sale[41]

- Stock received in a corporate reorganization within the meaning of IRC §368 is not jeopardizing

(a) Identifying Jeopardy

A manager fails to exercise the appropriate level of responsibility if he or she fails to exercise:

[37] IRC §4943(b); Reg. §53.4943-2.
[38] See Chapter 12§4.
[39] IRC §4944(a)(1).
[40] Discussed in §16.2(d).
[41] Reg. §53.4944-1(a)(2)(ii).

> [o]rdinary business care and prudence, under the facts and circumstances prevailing at the time the investment is made, in providing for the long- and short-term needs of the foundation to carry out its exempt purposes.[42]

The existence of jeopardy is made on an investment-by-investment basis, in each case taking into account the foundation's portfolio as a whole. The identification of jeopardy is based on facts available to the foundation managers at the time the investment is made, not subsequently on the basis of hindsight. Once it is ascertained that an investment is prudent and not jeopardizing, the investment, according to the regulations, can never be considered to be a jeopardizing one, even though the foundation ultimately loses money. A change in the form or terms of an investment is considered to be a new investment as of the date of the change, and a new determination is to be made at that time.[43]

Certain types of investments are said by the regulations to possess a higher degree of risk and must be closely scrutinized. After conceding that no category of investment will be treated as per se jeopardizing, the following types are listed as investments requiring close scrutiny:

- Trading in securities purchased on margin
- Trading in commodity futures
- Working interests in oil and gas
- Puts, calls, and straddles
- Purchases of warrants
- Selling short

In April 30, 1998, the IRS expanded the list of investments that require close scrutiny to include what it calls recent investment strategies (that by reference are not necessarily prohibited) to include:[44]

- Investment in junk bonds
- Risk arbitrage
- Hedge funds
- Derivatives
- Distress real estate
- International equities in third world countries

The IRS expansion of the list reflects the reality of financial markets in the 1990s, which were not anticipated when the regulations were written in 1970. The

---

[42] Reg. §53.4944-1(a)(2).
[43] Reg. §53.4944-1(a)(2).
[44] Internal Revenue Manual 7.8.3, *Private Foundation Handbook*, Chapter 16.

American Law Institute (ALI) revised its *Restatement of the Law, Trusts: Prudent Investor Rule,* a compendium of the basic rules governing the investment of trust assets in 1992.[45] The ALI guide reflects modern investment concepts and practices apparently now recognized by the IRS. The prudent investor rule acknowledges that return on investment is related to risk, that risk includes the risk of deterioration of real return owing to inflation, and that the risk/return relationship must be taken into account in managing trust assets. Based on this rule, maintaining all of a foundation's assets in certificates of deposit or other fixed money obligations—a policy thought by many to be secure—could theoretically be treated as a jeopardizing situation.[46]

There is precious little guidance on the subject from a tax code standpoint. The regulations, unchanged since issuance in 1972, contain three examples that describe three stocks and contrast factors that indicate jeopardy with those that do not:

- Corporation X has been in business a considerable time, its record of earnings is good, and there is no reason to anticipate a diminution of its earnings. (Not jeopardizing).

- Corporation Y has a promising product, has had earnings in some years and substantial losses in others, has never paid a dividend, and is widely reported in investment advisory services as seriously undercapitalized. (Is jeopardizing unless Y's shares are purchased in a new offering of an amount intended to satisfy Y's capital needs.)

- Corporation Z has been in business a short period of time and manufactures a product that is new, is not sold by others, and must compete with a well-established alternative product that services the same purpose. (Is jeopardizing unless the management has a demonstrated capacity for getting new businesses started successfully and Z has received substantial orders for its new products.)

Another example finds E Foundation's purchase of unimproved real estate not to be jeopardizing where E was following the advice of a professional manager. E sought recommendations on how best to diversify its investments to provide for its long-term financial needs and protect against inflation. E's short-term financial needs could be satisfied with its other assets.

The only published ruling on jeopardizing investments concerns a whole life insurance policy. A PF received a gift of an indebted policy covering an insured with a 10-year life expectancy. Based on the scheduled death benefit, the PF could expect to pay more in premiums and loan interest than it would receive. Each payment on the policy was found to be a jeopardizing investment.[47] In the only court case, placement of the entire foundation corpus in a Bahamian bank without in-

---

[45] American Law Institute Publishers, St. Paul, Minnesota.

[46] See Chapter 5, Asset Management, in J. Blazek, *Financial Planning for Nonprofit Organizations* (New York: Wiley, 1996) for more information and Chapter 8§2, Prudent Investments, in J. Blazek and B. Hopkins, *Private Foundations: Tax Law and Compliance* (New York: Wiley, 1997).

[47] Rev. Rul. 80-133, 1980-1 C.B. 258.

quiring as to the integrity of the bank was found to be jeopardizing since the bank at the time had actually lost its license to do business.[48]

In private rulings, the IRS has approved investments of the type that it says require close scrutiny. In one ruling, gold stocks purchased as a hedge against inflation were not jeopardizing despite a net loss of $7,000 on a $14,500 investment. The PF bought the shares over three years, made money on one block, and lost on two others. The ruling noted that the PF had realized $31,000 in gains and $23,000 in dividends during the same period on its whole portfolio. Importantly, the portfolio performance as a whole was found to enable the PF to carry out its purposes.[49]

A "managed commodity trading program" was found to give diversity to a PF's marketable security portfolio and not to be a jeopardizing investment. Since commodity futures have little or no correlation to the stock market, the added diversity may provide less risk for the PF's overall investment. The foundation invested 10% of its portfolio.[50]

Distressed real estate, a U.S. hedge fund, commodities, oil and gas funds, and limited partnerships were also deemed not to be jeopardizing investments by the IRS. Based on advice that its stock and bond portfolio be diversified, a foundation asked if it could increase its investment in those "nontraditional investments" by a "certain percentage."[51] The foundation also was advised that it could invest about 10% of its portfolio in a market-neutral fund. Though no ruling has discussed the subject, selling covered options against stocks in an investment portfolio is considered under the prudent investor rules to enhance yield without risk.

(b) Program-Related Investments

A program-related investment is not subject to the same standards of risk/reward applicable to normal investments because it serves a charitable, rather than an income-producing, purpose. Program-motivated investments are not treated as jeopardizing investments even if they bear no interest or dividend and possess a high degree of risk of loss. They are best described by the criteria used in the code and regulations to define them:[52]

- The primary purpose of the investment is to accomplish an exempt charitable purpose;

- No significant purpose of the investment is the production of income or the appreciation of property; and

- No purpose of the investment may be the furthering of substantial legislative or political activities.

Such investments "would not have been made" but for the relationship between the investment and the accomplishment of the foundation's exempt purposes. In evalu-

---

[48] *Thorne v. Commissioner,* 99 T.C. 67(1992).
[49] Priv. Ltr. Rul. 8718006.
[50] Priv. Ltr. Rul. 9237035.
[51] Priv. Ltr. Rul. 9451067.
[52] IRC §4944(c); Reg. §53.4944-3(a)(1).

ating the foundation's motivation, it is "relevant whether investors solely engaged in investment for profit would be likely to make the investment on the same terms as the foundation." The following regulation examples illustrate the concept:[53]

- A small business enterprise, X, is located in a deteriorated urban area and is owned by members of an economically disadvantaged minority group. Conventional sources of funds are unwilling or unable to provide funds to the enterprise. A PF makes a below-market interest rate loan to encourage economic development.

- The PF described above allows an extension of X's loan in order to permit X to achieve greater financial stability before it is required to repay the loan. Since the change is not motivated by attempts to enhance yield, but by an effort to encourage success of an exempt project, the altered loan is also considered to be program related.

- Assume instead that a commercial bank will loan X money if it increases the amount of its equity capital. PF's purchase of X's common stock, to accomplish the same purposes as the loan described in 1 and 2, is a program-related investment.

- Assume instead that substantial citizens own X, but continued operation of X is important for the economic well-being of the low-income persons in the area. To save X, PF loans X money at below-market rates to pay for specific projects benefiting the community. The loan is program related.

- The PF wants to encourage the building of a plant to provide jobs in a low-income neighborhood. The PF loans the building funds at below-market rates to SS, a successful commercial company that is unwilling to build the plant without such inducement. Again, the loan is program related.

- A PF loans X, a socially and economically disadvantaged individual, funds to attend college interest-free.

- A loan program established to make low-interest rate loans to blind persons unable to obtain funds through commercial sources constitutes a program-related investment.[54]

- Land purchased for land conservation, wildlife preservation, and the protection of open and scenic spaces is program related.[55]

A change in the terms of a program-related investment will not create jeopardy if the change continues to advance the exempt purposes for which the investment was originally made and is not made to produce income or appreciation.[56] A

---

[53] Reg. §53.4944-1(b).
[54] Rev. Rul. 78-90, 1978-1 C.B. 380.
[55] Priv. Ltr. Rul. 8832074; see also Priv. Ltr. Rul. 9109068 in which a tract of undeveloped land located along a city harbor was found a program-related investment because it was part of a plan to encourage civic beautification.
[56] Reg. §53.4944-3(a)(3).

program-related investment is treated as a qualifying distribution by the foundation at the time the investment is made.[57] Very importantly, such an investment must be monitored and reported to the IRS throughout its life under the expenditure responsibility rules.[58]

(c) Penalty Taxes

An initial tax of 5% on the amount invested for each year in the taxable period is imposed on both the private foundation and certain of its managers for any investment that jeopardizes carrying out the private foundation's charitable purposes. The taxable period begins on the date the amount is so invested and ends on the earliest of the following:[59]

- Date of mailing of a notice of deficiency with respect to the tax;

- Date on which the tax is assessed; or

- Date on which the amount so invested is removed from jeopardy.

An investment is removed from jeopardy when it is sold or otherwise disposed of and the proceeds are not reinvested in a jeopardizing fashion. Correction may be difficult or impossible if the asset is not marketable. Evidence that the foundation is making every effort to maximize available funds from the investment may help to avoid the additional tax.

Foundation managers who participate in making a decision to purchase an investment knowing that it is a jeopardizing one are taxed unless their participation is not willful and is due to reasonable cause. A manager is treated as *knowing* only if three factors are present:[60]

1. She or he has actual knowledge of sufficient facts so that, based solely on such facts, such investment would be a jeopardizing one;

2. She or he is aware that such an investment under such circumstances may violate IRC §4944; and

3. She or he negligently fails to make reasonable attempts to ascertain whether the investment is a jeopardizing investment, or she or he is in fact aware that it is such an investment.

Knowledge.   Knowing does not mean having reason to know an investment was jeopardizing. The question is whether the manager actually did know. The actual facts and circumstances are examined to find out why the manager did not know. To be excused, the manager has to be essentially ignorant of the facts that indicate a bad deal. Assume that a foundation's board has ten members, with a three-member finance committee. The written investment policy of the foundation provides

---

[57] See Chapter 15§4(b).
[58] See Chapter 17§5.
[59] IRC §4944(e).
[60] Reg. §53.4944-1(b)(2).

that the board approves investment actions proposed by the finance committee, based on the advice of independent counselors. Nonfinance committee board members should not be expected to be aware of details discussed in finance committee meetings.

Willfulness. A manager's participation must be willful to subject him or her to tax. Voluntary, conscious, and intentional ignorance of the facts pointing to jeopardy is willful participation (reports of pending difficulties withheld by others).

Reasonableness. The manager must have a good reason for not knowing. To show reasonable cause for not knowing, the manager must prove that good business judgment was exercised with ordinary business care and prudence.

Participation. Any manifestation of approval of the investment in question is considered to be participation in the decision to make the investment. Clearly, a vote as a board member to approve a purchase is participation. Board members who do not attend meetings but sanction investment decisions may be derelict in their fiduciary responsibility, but their inability to participate in the decision and resulting lack of knowledge may shield them from the tax. If they receive a board information packet revealing the questionable investment, they have knowledge, but the tax only applies if they participate in the approval.

Advice of Counsel. A manager who relies on outside advisors will not be treated as *knowingly* and *willfully* participating in a jeopardizing investment, and may be excused from the tax. The factual situation must be fully disclosed to the outside advisor. The fact that a manager failed to seek advice is one of the factors pointing to willful participation.[61] The types of reliance permitted may be different for different types of investments:

- For *program-related investments,* a manager may rely on a reasoned written legal opinion that a particular investment would not jeopardize the carrying out of any of the foundation's exempt purposes. The opinion must state that, as a matter of law, the investment is a program-related one not classified as a jeopardizing investment under the Internal Revenue Code.

- For *financial investments* from which the PF derives its operating income, it is appropriate to rely on qualified investment counselors. Again, all facts must be disclosed to the advisor. Advisors must render advice "in a manner consistent with generally accepted practices" of persons in their business. The written advice must recommend investments that provide for the foundation's long- and short-term financial needs.

Managers found to be guilty are jointly and severally liable for the tax.[62] On a positive note, the maximum tax in the case of the first-tier tax for managers (5% rate) is $5,000 and for the second-tier (25% rate), the maximum is $10,000 for all.

---

[61] Reg. §53.4944-1(b)(2)(v).
[62] IRC §4944(d).

Additional Tax.   If the jeopardy is not removed within the *taxable period*, the foundation must pay an additional 25% tax. Managers that refuse to agree to part or all of the removal of the investment from jeopardy must pay an additional tax of 5%.

Abatement.   IRC §§4942, 4943, 4944, and 4945 contain no exception, or excuse, for imposition of the penalty on the private foundation itself for failure to comply with the specific provisions of these code sections. The regulations under these sections do contain relief for those foundation managers who do not condone, or participate in the decision to conduct, a prohibited action. Until 1984, the penalties were strictly applied. Congress in 1984 added IRC §§4961, 4962, and 4963 to permit abatement of the penalties imposed on both the foundation and its managers if it is established to the satisfaction of the Secretary (by the IRS under responsibility delegated by the Treasury Department) that:

- The taxable event was due to reasonable cause not to willful neglect, and

- The event was corrected within the correction period for such event.

To allow abatement, it is the actions of the responsible foundation officials that must be considered. Although IRC §4962 is entitled "Definitions," neither it nor the regulations define the terms "reasonable cause" or "willful neglect." There have been no court decisions concerning abatement of these penalties and the author could find no private rulings construing their meaning for this purpose. In a ruling concerning a taxable expenditure penalty for failure to seek advance approval of a scholarship plan there was no mention of abatement.[63] The Congressional committee reports says, "A violation which was due to ignorance of the law is not to qualify for such abatement."[64]

The regulations pertaining to the penalties imposed upon self-dealers, upon managers approving of self dealing, jeopardizing investments, and taxable expenditures, however, do contain definitions that hopefully can be applied to justify abatement of the penalties. The definition of reasonable cause and willful neglect are the same as those listed above. The PF officials must show they used good business judgment exercised with ordinary business care and prudence. They must show they made a good faith effort to follow the rules by seeking the advice of qualified professionals. All of the facts and circumstances of the foundation's activities must be fully disclosed to such advisors.

For the foundation's penalty to be abated, its managers must also prove the failure was due to reasonable causes and not to willful neglect. These terms are not defined in the code or regulations under §4962 or 4963. No clarifying rulings have been issued to date nor is the term defined for this purpose in the IRS CPE Texts.[65] A bankruptcy judge found a trustee had not demonstrated conscious, intentional, or reckless indifference in failing to file a return or obtain an extension so that reasonable cause for abating penalties existed.[66]

[63] Priv. Ltr. Rul. 9825004.
[64] P. L. 98-369, Deficit Reduction Act of 1984.
[65] The *IRS Exempt Organizations Continuing Education Technical Training Program* for 1985 at page 16 mentions the then new abatement provision but contains no definitions.
[66] *U.S. Bankruptcy Court of Central District of California re Molnick's Inc.*, 95-1 USTC¶ 95751.

Under the general rules pertaining to tax penalties in Reg. §6664-4(b), the determination of whether a taxpayer's actions were due to reasonable cause in good faith is made on a case-by-case basis. According to this regulation, "Generally, the most important factor is the extent of the taxpayer's effort to access the taxpayer's proper tax liability. Circumstances that may indicate reasonable cause and good faith include an honest misunderstanding of fact or law that is reasonable in light of all of the facts and circumstances, including the experience, knowledge, and education of the taxpayer." These regulations say that reliance upon the advice of a professional tax advisor does not necessarily demonstrate reasonable cause and good faith. However, such reliance constitutes reasonable cause and good faith if, under all the circumstances, such reliance was reasonable and the taxpayer acted in good faith. Reliance on the opinion or advice of a professional is considered reasonable cause if:

1. The taxpayer did not know, or should not have known, that the advisor lacked knowledge in the relevant aspects of federal tax law.

2. The advice was based upon all pertinent facts and circumstances of the transaction(s) and the tax law as it relates the matter involved, including the taxpayer's purpose for entering into the transaction and for structuring a transaction in a particular manner.

3. The advice is based upon reasonable factual or legal assumptions and does not unreasonably rely on the representations, statements, findings, or agreements of the taxpayer or any other person.

The second-tier taxes may also be abated under circumstances described in IRC §4961.

(d) Double Jeopardy

The private foundation excise taxes are not applied exclusively. As a result, an investment can conceivably cause three taxes to occur simultaneously.[67] If the foundation buys a disqualified person's 40% share of an insolvent computer software development company the following occurs: (1) self-dealing[68] (because the purchase takes place between the PF and a DP), (2) excess business holdings (because the combined ownership exceeds 20%), and (3) a jeopardizing investment (assuming the foundation is not focused on scientific or scholarly development of software and the company is not a functionally related business). The unrelated business income tax might also apply to the income from such a business investment.

---

[67] Reg. §53.4944-1(a)(2)(iv).
[68] See Chapter 14§2.

CHAPTER SEVENTEEN

Taxable Expenditures: IRC §4945

In response to abuses uncovered by the Filer Commission and reported to the Congress,[1] a sanction was added to the Internal Revenue Code (IRC) to limit the manner in which a private foundation (PF) can spend its money to accomplish its exempt purpose. Whereas other types of exempt organizations can engage in some amount of nonexempt activity without losing their exempt status, private foundations have no such leeway and are subject to a tax on any violations.

A private foundation (a "foundation") must first meet the organizational and operational tests of IRC §501(c)(3)[2] that require it operate *exclusively*—meaning its major focus, but not necessarily 100 percent—for charitable purposes. IRC

---

[1] Summarized in Rep. Wright Patman's reports to the House Select Committee on Small Business during 1963–1968 entitled *Tax Exempt Foundations and Charitable Trusts: Their Impact on Our Economy.*
[2] Described in Chapter 2.

§4945, however, adds the absolute. Thus a foundation operates under a higher standard within the constraints outlined in this chapter—it can conduct absolutely no nonexempt activity such as lobbying. Potential foundation creators and managers need not be discouraged by this fact, however. The rules are actually broader than many realize. Once the rules are understood and procedures are in place to review compliance, a PF has a fairly high degree of latitude in developing its grant and program activity. Efforts directed at improving matters of broad social and economic impact, such as health care or the environment, have needlessly been foregone by some foundations. Educational and scientific efforts involving such subjects are not necessarily legislative efforts, even if the problems are of a type that government would be ultimately expected to deal with.[3]

Essentially, IRC §4945 prohibits transactions called *taxable expenditures*. The private foundation and its disqualified persons (DPs) will incur an excise tax, and possibly lose its tax-exempt status, if any amounts are paid or incurred for the following purposes:[4]

- To carry on propaganda or otherwise attempt to influence legislation

- To influence the outcome of any specific election, or to carry on any voter registration drive, except efforts involving at least five states

- As a grant to an individual for travel, study, or other similar purpose, except according to a preapproved plan

- As a grant to an organization unless

  - It is a publicly supported §501(c)(3) organization as defined in IRC §509(a)(1), (2), or (3);

  - It is an exempt operating foundation,[5] a special type of PF controlled by a public board[6]; or

  - The PF making the grant exercises expenditure responsibility.

- For any purpose not specified in IRC §170(c)(2)(B), that is, religious, charitable, scientific, literary, educational, to foster national or international amateur sports competition, or to prevent cruelty to children or animals

17.1 LOBBYING

A private foundation is strictly prohibited from carrying out propaganda or otherwise attempting to influence legislation—defined to *include any attempt to influence any legislation* through:

- An attempt to affect the opinion of the general public or any segment thereof (called *grassroots lobbying*); or

[3] Reg. §53.4945-2(d)(4).
[4] IRC §4945(d).
[5] IRC §4940(d)(2).
[6] See Chapter 13§7.

- An attempt to influence legislation through communication with any member or employee of a legislative body, or with any other government official or employee who may participate in the formulation of the legislation (except technical advice or assistance provided to a governmental body or to a committee or other subdivision thereof in response to a written request by such body or subdivision, as the case may be), other than through making available the results of nonpartisan analysis, study, or research.[7]

The definition of lobbying for PF purposes is cross-referenced to the regulations applicable to those public charities that elect to lobby.[8] While there was some uncertainty before these regulations were finalized, PFs can participate in educational activity involving public issues that may eventually be the subject of legislation.[9]

(a) Germane Lobbying

A foundation can spend its money to make an appearance before, or communicate to, any legislative body with respect to a possible decision of such body that might affect the existence of the PF, its powers and duties, its tax-exempt status, or the deduction of contributions to it.

The existence of the organization is not affected, in the IRS's view, by a possible loss of economic support.[10] Lobbying in favor of an appropriations bill funding a program under which the PF has received support in the past is not self-defense. Similarly, a PF that provides care for the elderly is lobbying when its executive director appears before the state legislature to favor or oppose a bill authorizing the state to provide nursing care for the aged. Likewise, a PF receiving governmental grants to support its research programs is lobbying when it testifies about the advisability of continuing the program (unless it was asked to testify). It is the economic condition and the resulting scope of the PF's operation, not its underlying existence, that is at issue in these examples. On the other hand, an effort to influence a state's reformation of its charitable corporation statutes to include provisions not now present in a PF's charter would be self-defense and therefore permissible legislative activity.

(b) Broad Social, Economic, and Similar Problems

Sponsoring discussions or conferences, conducting research, and publishing educational materials about matters of broad social and economic subjects, such as human rights or war and peace, are appropriate and permissible activities for a private foundation. Such topics are often the subject matter of legislation, involve public controversy, and raise the possibility of the foundation being treated as conducting prohibited legislative activity. However, a foundation can sponsor

---

[7] IRC §4945(e).
[8] Reg. §53.4945-2(a)(1).
[9] See Chapter 23 for definition of lobbying.
[10] Reg. §53.4945-2(d)(3)(ii), Examples 3 & 4.

such discussions examining such issues when three specific factors are *not* present. The PF's written communications, either directly with members of the general public or with the legislators themselves, may not:

- Mention or refer in any way to specific legislation;

- Take a position on any legislation; or

- Recommend that the reader take any steps to contact legislators, employees of legislators, or government officials or employees involved in legislation, or contain a so-called *call to action*.[11]

(c) Nonpartisan Analysis, Study, or Research

A private foundation can conduct an independent and objective exposition or study of particular subject matters, and can make the information or results of its work available to the general public and to governmental bodies, officials, or employees. When a communiqué distributing the results presents a particular viewpoint or position—for example, that oil tankers should have double hulls to lessen the possibility of oil spills—the materials must be educational in content. Mere opinion, unsupported by pertinent facts enabling individuals to form their own opinions, is not nonpartisan. The regulations contain twelve examples that can be studied for more examples.[12]

A broadcast or publication series must meet the same standards as printed matter. One of the presentations can contain biased information if another part of the series (broadcast within six months of the initial viewing) contains contrary information or the other side of the argument. If the PF selects the time for presentation of information to coincide with a specific legislative proposal, the expenses of preparing and distributing that part of the study may be treated as lobbying and result in a taxable expenditure.[13]

(d) Grants to Public Charities That Lobby

As a general rule, a PF can make a grant to a public charity that conducts legislative lobbying, regardless of whether the grant recipient has made the §501(h) election, but the foundation's money cannot be earmarked for lobbying. There must be no agreement, oral or written, that the granting PF can direct the manner in which the funds are expended.[14] Also, the PF's grant cannot be more than the amount needed to fund the recipient organization's budget for nonlobbying projects. If, after a grant satisfying these rules is paid, the grant recipient loses its exempt status due to excessive lobbying, the money paid is not a taxable expenditure only if:

- The grant was not earmarked for lobbying,

---

[11] *Supra,* note 3.
[12] Reg. §53.4945-2(d)(1)(vii); also see Chapter 5§1 for definition of educational.
[13] Reg. §53.4945-2(d)(1)(ii).
[14] Reg. §53.4945-2(a)(5) and (6).

- The recipient had a valid determination of its public status,

- Notice of the revocation was not published when the grant was made, and

- The PF does not control the public charity.[15]

(e) Summary of Permissible Activity

To summarize this important constraint, a private foundation and its managers can participate in efforts that involve matters of public policy. Such activities do not constitute legislative intervention in the following situations:

- Self-defense (or *germane*) lobbying

- Technical assistance or expert testimony given upon request

- Grants (not earmarked for lobbying) to public charities that lobby

- Nonpartisan analysis, study, or research

- Programs involving topics that are the subject of legislation

- Direct communication with government officials, including legislators, and also with the general public, without reference to and not in support of specific legislation

- Efforts to influence regulations or other administrative rules clarifying and interpreting existing laws

- Lobbying efforts of managers acting on their own behalf

17.2   VOTER REGISTRATION DRIVES

All charitable §501(c)(3) organizations, including foundations, are prohibited from participating or intervening in elections of public officials with the intent to influence the outcome. Certain educational efforts in connection with the electoral process may, however, be permitted. What a foundation is specifically forbidden to do *is [t]o attempt to influence the outcome of any specific public election, or to carry on, directly or indirectly, any voter registration drive.*[16] In the South during the early 1960s, certain foundations financed voter drives aimed specifically at registering blacks to vote, in connection with the foundations' effort to eliminate discrimination. Partly as a result, very specific rules govern a PF's participation in such efforts. A foundation is permitted to make a grant to another organization, including another PF, that itself conducts a voter registration drive if the recipient organization meets the following requirements:

- The organization is a charitable one exempt under IRC §501(c)(3);

---

[15] Reg. §53.4945-2(a)(7).
[16] IRC §4945(d)(2).

- Activities of the organization are nonpartisan, are not confined to one specific election period, and are carried on in five or more states;

- At least 85 percent of the organization's income is spent directly on the active conduct of its charitable purposes;

- At least 85 percent of its support (other than gross investment income as defined in IRC §509(e)) comes from other tax-exempts, the general public, and governmental units, and not more than 25 percent comes from a single organization; and

- Contributions for voter registration drives cannot be earmarked for particular states or political subdivisions.[17]

17.3   GRANTS TO INDIVIDUALS

A private foundation may make grants to individuals for travel, study, or other similar purposes, but only may do so under the terms of a written plan that has been preapproved by the Internal Revenue Service.[18] A taxable expenditure results if such individual grants are not paid pursuant to an approved plan. Individual grants also cannot be earmarked to be used for political, legislative, or other noncharitable activities.[19] Travel, study, or similar purpose grants must also be one of the following:

- A grant constituting a scholarship or fellowship grant that would be subject to the provision of IRC §117(a) as it was in effect prior to the Tax Reform Act of 1986 to be used at an educational institution described in IRC §170(b)(1)(A)(ii).

- A prize or award[20] paid to a recipient selected from the general public.

- A grant to achieve a specific objective, produce a report or other similar product, or improve or enhance a literary, artistic, musical, scientific, teaching, or other similar capacity, skill or talent of the grantee[21]

(a) Meaning of "Travel, Study or Other Purposes"

Only grants paid to individuals for the three purposes specified above are subject to the prior plan approval rules. The concepts are well illustrated in three scenarios.[22] In the first, the grant is not subject to IRS approval but in the second and third, approval is required.

Scenario 1.   A PF organized to promote the art of journalism makes awards to persons whose work represent the best example of investigative reporting on mat-

---

[17] Reg. §53.4945-3(b)(1).
[18] Reg. §53.4945-4(a)(5).
[19] IRC §4945(d)(3).
[20] Defined under IRC §74(b).
[21] IRC §4945(g).
[22] Rev. Rul. 77-380, 1977-2 C.B. 419.

ters concerning the government. Potential recipients are nominated; they do not apply for the award (thus, the IRC §74 exclusion may apply). The awards are granted in recognition of past achievement and are not intended to finance any specific activities of the recipients nor to impose any conditions on the manner in which the award is expended by the recipient. Therefore, since the payments are not to finance study, travel, or a similar purpose, the awards project was not subject to prior approval.

Scenario 2.   Assume instead that the annual award recipients are required to take a three-month summer tour to study government at educational institutions. These awards are subject to prior approval because the payment is required to be used for study and travel.

Scenario 3.   The facts are the same as in Scenario 1, except that the award must be used to pursue study at an educational institution and qualifies as a scholarship under IRC §117(a). Again, prior approval is required. A similar conclusion was reached in a ruling concerning grants to science fair winners that required them to use the prizes for their education. The program was a scholarship plan requiring approval.[23]

Other Purposes.   The meaning of grants for *other similar purposes* is elusive. The regulations say that student loans and program-related investments constitute such grants.[24] If the payment is given with the expectation or requirement that the recipient perform specific activities not directly of benefit to the foundation, a grant occurs. Research grants, and payments to allow recipients to compose music or to choreograph a ballet, are all examples of awards for *similar purposes* when the recipient must perform to earn the award. Grants and interest-free loans made to persons that incur extraordinary medical expenses, funeral or burial costs, or suffer financial hardship due to medical emergencies, natural disasters, or violent crimes are not grants for *other purposes*. Such grants are awards to relieve suffering, not to finance study, travel, or similar purpose. Therefore, a corporate foundation that established a hardship grant and loan program was not technically required to obtain advance approval for its program to avoid the payments being classified as taxable expenditures.[25]

No Strings Attached.   Grants given with no strings attached are not subject to the preapproval rules. A payment to an indigent individual for the purchase of food or clothing is not subject to these rules.[26] Awards paid to winners of a craft school competition on an unconditional and unrestricted basis were also deemed not to be grants for this purpose.[27] Grants in recognition of literary achievement not given to finance future activity; not imposing any future condition on the recipient; not paid for travel, study, or other purpose were ruled not to be grants.[28]

[23] Rev. Rul. 76-461, 1976-2 C.B. 371.
[24] Reg. §53.4945-4(a)(2).
[25] Priv. Ltr. Rul. 9314058.
[26] Reg. §53.4945-4(a)(3)(i).
[27] Rev. Rul. 76-460, 1976-2 C.B. 371.
[28] Rev. Rul. 75-393, 1975-2 C.B. 451 and Priv. Ltr. Rul. 9151040.

(b) Compensatory Payments

Payments for personal services, such as salaries, consultant fees, and reimbursement of travel and other expenses incurred on behalf of the foundation, for work performed in working on the foundation's own project(s), are not grants requiring a preapproved plan. A foundation can freely hire persons to assist it in planning, evaluating, and developing projects and program activity by consulting, advising, and participating in conferences organized by the foundation.[29] Persons hired to develop model curricula and educational materials, for example, are not grant recipients.[30]

In 1986, Congress gutted the tax-free treatment of scholarships, fellowships, and prizes. As a result, all payments other than those paid for tuition, books, and fees, are taxable to grant recipients. Certain scholarships and, particularly, teaching fellowships are taxable for another reason—the fact that the recipient is expected to render services in return for receiving the grant. Where there is a quid pro quo, or exchange of services for pay, the grant is made primarily for the benefit of the granting foundation, and the approval rules do not apply. Scholarships paid by one foundation formed to aid worthy college students planning to teach in state public schools were found to have strings attached. As a condition of the grant, recipients had to indicate they were willing to teach for two years in state public schools after receiving their degrees. Even though the obligation carried no financial guarantee and was only a moral obligation of the student, the IRS found that such scholarships were not described in IRC §177(a) and, therefore, that prior approval was not required.[31]

Since 1986, the traditional award systems have lost their appeal since part of the grant payments are taxable to the recipients. Rather than fund research under a grant program, a foundation can avoid the approval process by establishing internal research projects. Nonperformance, nonstudy grants in recognition of achievement grants also do not require preapproval. Such awards, however, should still be made on a nondiscriminatory basis to ensure they are awarded to members of a charitable class.

(c) Selection Process

Once a foundation chooses to make grants subject to the approval process, it must adopt a suitable plan. The primary criterion for approval of a plan for making individual grants is that the grants must be awarded on an "objective and nondiscriminatory basis." The plan must contain the following provisions:[32]

- An "objective and nondiscriminatory" method of choice, consistent with the PF's exempt status and the purpose of the grant, is used.

- The group from which grantees are selected is sufficiently broad so as to constitute a charitable class.[33] The size of the group may be small if the purpose of the grant so warrants, such as research fellows in a specialized field.

---

[29] Reg. §53.4945-4(a)(2).
[30] Rev. Rul. 74-125, 1974-1 C.B. 327.
[31] Rev. Rul. 77-44, 1977-1, C.B. 118.
[32] IRC §4945(g); Reg. §53.4945-4(b) and (c).
[33] Defined in Chapter 2§2(a).

- Criteria used in selecting the recipients include academic performance, recommendations from instructors, financial need, and/or motivation and personal character.

- Selection committee members are not in a position to derive a private benefit, directly or indirectly, if one person or another is chosen.

- Grants are awarded for study at an academic institution, or as fellowships, prizes or awards for study or research involving a literary, artistic, musical, scientific, or teaching purpose.

- Procedures to obtain reports are provided for scholarships, fellowships, and research or study grants.

Class of Potential Grantees. The second item in the list above requires the group from which the grantees are chosen to be sufficiently broad. A group including all students in a city or all valedictorians in a state clearly qualifies. The regulations sanction a plan to grant 20 annual scholarships to members of a certain ethnic minority living within a state.[34] However, a group of girls and boys with at least one-quarter Finnish blood living in two particular towns was found to be a discriminatory group and not sufficiently broad.[35] Likewise, a plan that gave priority to family members and relatives of the trust's creator, if their qualifications were substantially the same as an unrelated party, was found to be discriminatory.[36]

Scholarships and Fellowships. A report of the grantee's courses taken and grades earned in each academic period must be collected at least once annually and verified by the educational institution. For grantees whose work does not involve classes but only the preparation of research papers or projects, such as a doctoral thesis, the foundation should receive an annual report approved by the faculty members supervising the grantee or other school official. Upon completion of a grantee's study, a final report must also be obtained.

Research or Study Grants. At least annually, a report of progress and use of funds is due. A final report describing the grantee's accomplishments and funds expended with respect to the grant must also be made.

Investigation of Diversions. Procedures must be established to investigate when no reports are filed, or when reports indicate that funds are being diverted. The PF will not be treated as making a taxable expenditure if the recipient has not previously misused funds and if the PF takes the following steps during its investigation:

- During the investigation, the PF must withhold additional payments until it receives the grantee's assurances that future diversions will not occur, and must require the grantee to take extraordinary precautions to prevent future diversions from occurring.

- The PF must take reasonable steps to recover the funds.

[34] Reg. §53.4945-4(b)(5), Example 2.
[35] Priv. Ltr. Rul. 7851096.
[36] Rev. Rul. 85-175, 1985-2 C.B. 276.

- If a grantee was reprieved after an initial investigation and the PF reinstituted the grant only to have the funds diverted for a second time, a taxable expenditure will not occur if the same steps are repeated and the diverted funds are recovered.[37]

Record Keeping. A foundation making individual grants must maintain and keep available for IRS examination documentation that the recipients are chosen in a nondiscriminatory manner and that proper follow-up is accomplished. The following records must be kept:

- Information used to evaluate the qualification of potential grantees;

- Reports of any grantee/director relationships;

- Specification of amount and purpose of each grant; and

- Grade reports or other progress reports approved by a faculty member must be received annually.

(d) Company Scholarship Plans

The regulations and countless rulings have approved scholarship plans established by a company's foundation for children of the company's employees.[38] The issue with such plans is whether they discriminate in favor of the corporate executives or shareholders and thus represent a means of paying additional compensation. Specific guidelines exist and should be carefully studied prior to application for approval of such a plan.[39] Similar rules apply to a company foundation's educational loan program.[40] The primary criteria are:

1. The scholarship plan must not be used by the employer, the PF, or the organizer thereof, to recruit employees or to induce continued employment;

2. The selection committee must be wholly made up of totally independent persons, not including former employees, preferably including persons knowledgeable about education;

3. Identifiable minimum requirements for grant eligibility must be established and eligibility should not depend on employment-related performance, although up to three years of service for the parent can be required;

4. Selection criteria must be based on substantial objective standards such as prior academic performance, tests, recommendations, financial need, and personal interviews;

---

[37] Reg. §53.4945-4(c)(5)(ii).
[38] Reg. §53.4945-4(b)(5), example 1; Priv. Ltr. Rul. 9115061.
[39] Rev. Rul. 76-47, 1976-2 C.B. 670, clarified by Rev. Proc. 81-65, 1981-2 C.B. 690, and amplified by Rev. Proc. 77-32, 1977-2 C.B. 541; see also Rev. Proc. 85-51, 1985-2 C.B. 717.
[40] Rev. Proc. 80-39, 1980-2 C.B. 772.

5. A grant may not be terminated because the recipient or parent terminates employment;

6. The courses of study for which grants are available must not be limited to those of particular benefit to the employer;

7. The terms of the grant and course of study must allow recipients to obtain an education in their individual capacities solely for their personal benefit and must not include any commitments, understandings, or obligations of future employment; and

8. No more than 10% of the eligible persons and no more than 25 percent of the eligible persons who submitted applications and were considered by the selection committee, can be awarded grants. A fraction of one-half greater can be rounded up to determine plan qualification in calculating the allowable percentage of children of employees permitted to receive scholarships.[41]

Due to the self-dealing rules, no grants can be paid to children of disqualified persons. The plan must avoid a disproportionate amount of grants to executives' children. Application for approval is the same as for other scholarship plans, although satisfaction of the eight tests just listed must be outlined.

(e) Seeking Approval

Application for approval of a scholarship plan is a ruling request and is submitted to the IRS Service Center in Cincinnati, Ohio.[42] The approval process is intended to review the foundation's standards, procedures, and follow-up designed to meet the code's requirements for the PF's individual grant programs.[43] The PF submits its proposed procedures for awarding grants (Exhibit 17-1), including the methods of meeting the selection process requirements. Written approval is not sent by the IRS to successful applicants; instead, silence signifies approval. If within 45 days after submission of the plan, no notification is received that the procedures are unacceptable, the PF can consider the plan approved.

The user fee for making application for approval of an individual grant program in 1998 was $2,100 ($600 for organizations with annual gross receipts less than $150,000).[44] In the author's experience during 1998, this fee was not required. Newly created foundations can seek approval for their plans in connection with filing Form 1023 and need not make a separate application.[45]

(f) Individual Grant Intermediaries

A foundation wishing to avoid the administrative burden and cost of applying for approval and disbursing scholarships directly can instead fund a grant program

[41] Rev. Proc. 94-78, 1994-52 I.R.B. 38.
[42] The procedures for issuing rulings for exempt organizations are updated by the IRS in a revenue procedure issued each spring. The ruling effective as of publication date was Rev. Proc. 99-4, 1999-1 IRB 115.
[43] Reg. §53.4945-4(d)(1).
[44] Rev. Proc. 93-23, 1993-1 C.B. 538.
[45] See Schedule H in Appendix 18-1.

Exhibit 17–1

SAMPLE REQUEST FOR IRS APPROVAL OF INDIVIDUAL GRANT PROGRAM

Internal Revenue Service, District Director
IRS Center
P.O. Box 192
Covington, KY 41012-0192

> RE: Sample Foundation
> ID #70-0000000
> Approval of Scholarship Plan

Dear IRS Representative,

From 1950 to 19XX, the Sample Foundation operated a medical research facility and was classified as a public charity pursuant to Internal Revenue Code (IRC) §509(a)(1). During that time a scholarship fund was established in the memory of Dr. XYZ, one of the founders of Sample. For the past 20 years, scholarship grants have been paid annually. As of MMM, 19XX, Sample discontinued the research facility and was reclassified as a private foundation. Your approval for the scholarship program is hereby sought.

The XYZ Scholarship will further Sample's educational purposes by enabling deserving men and women to complete a medical-related education in the graduate schools of their choice, so that they will be able to serve honorably and effectively in their chosen medical field. The scholarship will be a "grant" within the meaning of IRC §4945(d)(3) and will satisfy the requirements of IRC §4945(g) in all respects.

The grant will be awarded on an objective and nondiscriminatory basis. The grant will be excluded from gross income under IRC §117(a), to the extent that it is used for tuition, books, and equipment required for educational courses. The purpose of the grant is to promote medical-related education for graduate degree candidates, and the recipient of the grant will be selected from the population of graduate school medical students.

As provided by IRS Publication 578, Chapter VI, and the regulations, the grant-making procedures will be as follows:

- *Grantee class.* Any graduate college student seeking a degree in medical-related education may be considered for the scholarship.
- *Selection criteria.* The selection criteria for the scholarship will include, but not be limited to, the student's demonstrated academic ability and desire, character, good citizenship, and economic necessity. A recipient cannot be related to a member of the committee or to any "disqualified persons" in relation to Sample.
- *Selection committee.* The selection committee shall be composed of members of the board of directors of Sample. Members of the selection committee will not be in a position to receive private benefit, directly or indirectly, if certain potential grantees are selected over others.
- *Progress reports.* The scholarships will be about $5,000 per semester and can be renewed annually for a maximum of three years, provided that the student is not on academic or disciplinary probation and is making satisfactory progress toward completion of a medical-related degree. A student need not have an "A" average, but should be of a caliber to indicate an abil-

Exhibit 17–1 (*continued*)

ity to profit from and be intellectually equal to work on a graduate level. Progress reports will be obtained and verified with the educational institution each semester. Upon completion of the grantee's study, a final report will be collected from the grantee.

- *Report follow-up.* If no report is filed by the student, or if reports indicate that the funds are not being used in furtherance of the scholarship purpose, a member of the board of directors will investigate the grant. While conducting this investigation, Sample will withhold further payments from the grantee and will take reasonable steps to recover grant funds until it has determined that the funds are being used for their intended exempt purpose.
- *Record keeping.* The foundation will retain all records submitted by the grantees and their educational institutions. Sample will obtain and maintain in its file evidence that no recipient is related to the foundation or to any members of the selection committee.

Sample trusts that the above criteria and purpose for its educational scholarship satisfy the requirements of IRC §4945 and respectfully requests approval for its grant procedures. Under penalties of perjury, I declare that I have examined this request, including accompanying documents, and to the best of my knowledge and belief, the facts presented in support of the request are true, correct, and complete.

Date

Sample Officer

at an independent public charity. The foundation may be involved in the process. As long as the foundation has no control over the choice of recipients, it is not considered to have made the grants directly to the individuals.[46] There must be no agreement, oral or written, that the PF can dictate the selection of particular individuals. No earmarking is permitted, only suggestions.

The parameters of the grant, such as the study discipline—medicine or law, for example—or qualifications, such as grades or civic achievement, can be stipulated by the foundation; though the class of grantees should be relatively broad. A grant to fund scholarships for children of employees may be considered grants by the company foundation itself, not by the college administering the plan.[47] Actually suggesting the individual grantee is permitted, as long as there is an objective manifestation of the public charity's control over the selection process. Maintaining the right to veto a potential recipient is de facto control.[48] Likewise, a research grant disbursed by a college was found to be a direct grant when the funding was contingent on supervision by the professor designated by the PF with reserved rights to patents, inventions, and publications arising from the research, and the

[46] Reg. §53.4945-4(a)(4).
[47] Rev. Rul. 81-217, 1981-2 C.B. 217.
[48] Priv. Ltr. Rul. 8542004.

PF retained authority to approve the professor's project and any of his scientific work.[49] The regulations contain useful examples for further study.[50]

17.4 GRANTS TO PUBLIC CHARITIES

Most private foundations make grants to public charities, or those grant recipients specifically excluded from the taxable expenditure list in IRC §4945(d)(4)(A). This is true partly because so much charitable work is performed by those organizations and private foundations have traditionally used their endowments to fund such institutions. A private foundation can make a grant to a public charity without exercising expenditure responsibility.[51]

A foundation is, however, permitted to make a grant to any type of entity, exempt or nonexempt, if it properly documents its purposes in making the grant and ensures the transaction with *expenditure responsibility* agreements. The purpose of these rules is to see that PF funds are used to benefit the public, not the private interests of their creators. Grants to public charities are preferred by most PFs because they require less documentation and public charities serve a broad constituency that monitors their responsiveness to public needs and use of their funds for charitable purposes.

Definition of Public Charity. Such charities qualify first as exempt organizations under IRC §501(c)(3)[52] and are further classified as public by IRC §509(a)(1), (2), and (3).[53] The definition is a bit convoluted because the bulk of organizations so qualifying are those defined in IRC §170(b)(1)(A). The list includes churches, schools, hospitals, medical research organizations, branches of the government, states, cities and municipalities, and organizations receiving their support from the general public, such as a United Way agency, a community foundation, or the American Red Cross. Exempt operating foundations are treated as public for this purpose.[54] A grant to an instrumentality of a foreign government is also considered to be a grant to a public charity, as long as it is made for charitable purposes,[55] likewise, an instrumentality of a U.S. political subdivision is treated as a public charity.[56]

Proof of Public Status. A grant-making private foundation must establish a system for documenting the tax character of its grant recipients. The checklist in Exhibit 17-2 can be used to document the foundation's verification of each grantee tax status. Additionally this checklist asks that the charitable nature of the grant be well documented with a grant request or other information. It also documents the

[49] Rev. Rul. 73-564, 1973-2 C.B. 28.
[50] Reg. §53.4945-4(a)(4)(iv).
[51] Discussed next in §17.5.
[52] See Chapter 2.
[53] See Chapter 11.
[54] IRC §4940(d)(2).
[55] Reg. §53.4945-5(a)(4).
[56] Rev. Rul. 81-125, 1981-1 C.B. 515.

Exhibit 17–2

PRIVATE FOUNDATION GRANT APPROVAL CHECKLIST

The following documentation should be obtained by a private foundation before it issues a check for a grant.

1. Obtain the grant proposal indicating the exempt purpose of the grant. If the PF is unilaterally giving a grant to an established charity for an exempt project, a transmittal letter stating that it is for general support will suffice. A grant agreement and completion of this checklist is recommended.

2. Read the proposal to ensure that the grant will not be expended for:

   - A political campaign or influencing voters.

   - Influencing legislation at the national, state, or local level.

   - Individual grants (unless the recipient's choice is totally under the control of the recipient organization).

   - A grant to another private foundation, unless there is an expenditure responsibility contract.

   - A commercial venture (except for related projects and unless there is an expenditure responsibility agreement).

3. Obtain a determination letter stating that the recipient is exempt under IRC §501(c)(3) and is publicly supported under IRC §509(a)(1), (2), or (3), or that it is an exempt operating foundation.

4. Verify the recipient's public status either in the printed IRS Publication 78, *Cumulative List of Organizations Described in IRC §170* or on *www.irs.ustreas.gov* and check additions and deletions announced in the *Internal Revenue Bulletin* since its latest update.

5. Ascertain the possibility that this grant will cause the recipient to lose public status (see Rev. Proc. 89-23 and Chapter 17§4(a)).

6. Request a grant agreement from the recipient if there is any question about its status or the exempt nature of its project. See Exhibit 17-3 or 17-4.

---

grant will not be used for a prohibited purpose. The checklist should become a part of the foundation's permanent file for each grant paid. The effort to document tax status begins for most foundations when they request that a copy of the IRS determination letter accompany grant requests. Based on the name registered with the IRS as shown on that letter, the foundation next verifies that the organization is still listed in Publication 78, the IRS master list of qualifying 501(c)(3)s. The public or private classification of each entity is noted in Publication 78. The foundation must also decide if it can rely on the published information as discussed in the next section.

Exhibits 17-3 and 17-4 can also be used to ask that the grantee overtly verify its public status and agree to use the moneys only for the charitable purposes for which they were granted.

(a) The Reliance Problem

A private foundation can rely on its grantee organization's proof—the IRS determination letter stating that it is a public charity—until a notice of its revocation is published in the weekly *Internal Revenue Bulletin* or is otherwise made public.[57] A prudent PF obtains copies of this list. The IRS also updates its Publication 78 three times a year to provide a master list of charitable organizations, along with their public or private status.[58] The list is also available on the internet at *www.irs .ustreas.gov* after a click on *Tax Information for Business.*

Exhibit 17–3

GRANT AGREEMENT

This letter requests tax status information before a grant is paid.

Grantee Organization
Address

Dear Grant Recipient:
As a private foundation, Sample Foundation must ascertain that your organization is exempt from income tax under Internal Revenue Code §501(c)(3) and is classified as a publicly supported organization under IRC §509(a)(1), (2), or (3).

According to the information that was furnished to us with the proposal, your organization is so qualified. Please inform us only if there has been a change in your tax status since then.

In addition, we must be assured that our grant will be expended for an educational, scientific, literary, or other charitable purpose. We ask that you use our funds exclusively to carry out the project described in the application. Also, we ask you not to use any of our funds to influence legislation, to influence the outcome of any election, or to carry on any voter registration drive.

Finally, we ask that any funds not expended for the purposes for which the grant is being made be returned to us.

Please signify your agreement with these conditions by returning a signed copy of this letter to us. Thank you.

_____
For Sample Foundation

Acknowledged by: _____

Date:_____

---

[57] Reg. §§1.170A-9(e)(4)(v)(b) and 1.509(a)-3(c)(1)(iii)(a).
[58] The printed version of Publication 78 can be ordered from the IRS Reading Room, 1111 Constitution Avenue, Washington, D.C.

Exhibit 17–4

GRANT PAYMENT TRANSMITTAL

This letter conveys the grant payment check for repeating grant recipients.

Grant Recipient
Address

Dear Grant Recipient:
We are happy to enclose our check for $_____ in payment of a grant for [name] project as described in your request dated [date].

As a private foundation, we must document that our grant is expended for a charitable or educational purpose. We must ask that you use our funds exclusively to carry out the project described in our request. You must not use any of our funds to influence legislation, to influence the outcome of any election, or to carry on any voter registration drive.

We must have proof that your organization continues to be exempt under Internal Revenue Code §501(c)(3) and is still classified as a publicly supported organization pursuant to IRC §509(a)(1), (2), or (3). Kindly send us a copy of your most recent Internal Revenue Service tax determination letter, your financial statements, Form 990, and any annual report for the year in which our grant funds are expended.

Finally, we must ask that any funds not expended for the purposes for which the grant is being made be returned to us. Please indicate your agreement with these conditions by returning a signed copy of this letter.

Thank you.

_____
For Sample Foundation

Acknowledged by: _____

Date:_____

If the grantee organization is not controlled by the foundation, that is, the PF cannot cause it to act or prevent its acts, the PF need not investigate the effect of its grant on the recipient.[59] When the foundation has a relationship with the grantee organization, and certainly if the PF controls it, the foundation also has a responsibility to determine whether its grant will cause the recipient organization to lose its public status. This situation is referred to as "tipping." When a public entity undergoes a "substantial and material change," the PF has three choices if it chooses to make a grant:

1. The PF can satisfy itself that it was not responsible for the change by reviewing financial information from the grantee's officers. The grantor is not responsible if its gift in a year is less than 25% of the recipient's total gifts for the immediately preceding four years.

[59] Rev. Proc. 89-23, 1989-1 C.B. 844.

2. The PF can ascertain that the grant is an unusual one that will not cause the grantee to lose public status.

3. The PF can exercise expenditure responsibility.[60]

(b) Controlled Grantees

Public charities are free to make grants to individuals, to support a newly created but yet-unrecognized organization, to finance lobbying efforts, and to conduct a host of other projects that might not be permissible for a PF. Accordingly, there is a temptation for a PF to funnel or pass money through a public charity for such a project that the PF itself cannot undertake or for which it does not wish to exercise expenditure responsibility. An earmarked grant to a public charity to do something the PF itself is not permitted to do can result in a taxable expenditure.

A foundation grant to an intermediary organization—also called a fiscal agent—may be treated as a grant by the PF to the ultimate grantee if the foundation has control over the regrant.[61] The rules are similar to the rules applicable to designating scholarship recipients discussed in §17.3(f). A *look-through rule* applies when the PF earmarks its grant in an oral or written manner. If the regrant is to another public charity, there is no problem (unless the grant is earmarked for lobbying or for a particular individual). If the regrant is to be made to another PF or for some other purpose described in IRC §4945, a taxable expenditure may occur. When a foundation grants funds to an organization or fiscal agent in this fashion, the grant should be carefully documented.[62]

(c) Foreign Organizations

A foreign government and any agency or instrumentality thereof is treated as a public organization for this purpose. Certain international organizations also qualify as public charities, such as the World Health Organization, the United Nations, the International Bank for Reconstruction and Development, the International Monetary Fund, and others designated by the president.[63]

A foreign charitable organization that does not have an IRS determination letter, but that is equivalent to and would in fact qualify as a public charity if it sought approval, may also be treated as a public entity. The PF is allowed to make a good faith determination of the foreign organization's status. An affidavit from the foreign entity or an opinion of counsel should be obtained, and sufficient facts concerning the operations and support of the grantee should be revealed in a manner that would allow the IRS to determine whether the organization would qualify as a public charity.[64]

---

[60] Priv. Ltr. Rul. 8542004; Rev. Proc. 81-6, 1981-1 C.B. 620.

[61] Reg. §53.4945-5(a)(5).

[62] See Gregory L. Colvin, *Fiscal Sponsorships: 6 Ways to Do It Right* (San Francisco: San Francisco Study Center, 1993).

[63] Reg. §53.4945-5(a)(4)(iii). The international organizations are designated by executive order under 22 U.S.C. §288.

[64] Reg. §53.4945-5(a)(5); see Rev. Proc. 92-94, 1992-46 I.R.B. 34 for contents of a "currently qualified" affadavit from the grantee.

The equivalency method of proving public status does not necessarily apply to a foreign organization with over 15 percent of its gross income from U.S. sources. Such a foreign organization might instead directly apply for recognition of its exempt status. IRC §4948(b) denies the application of section 508 (notice of exemption) for a foreign organization that receives substantially all of its support (other than gross investment income) from sources outside the United States. The definition for the term *substantial* used for purposes of defining a private operating foundation is 85 percent.[65] The volunteer exception for excluding income from an unrelated business is commonly applied using an 85 percent test.[66] Thus it would seem a foreign public charity with more than 15 percent to 20 percent of its support (other than investment income) from United States sources is able to give 508 notice by filing for recognition of its qualification for tax-exempt status under 501(c)(3).

Such an organization thereby avoids the 4 percent tax on its U.S.-based investment income under §4948 and the corresponding withholding required by IRC §1443(b). It also has proof of public charity equivalency for purposes of seeking grants from U.S.-based private foundations. Very importantly, however, achieving recognition as a §501(c)(3) tax-exempt organization does not make a foreign organization qualify under §170 for charitable donations. What it does is qualify them for exemption from U.S. tax on investment income and to seek grants without the need to exercise expenditure responsibility. The author finds little guidance on this subject and would welcome feedback.

Documentation. Seeking the appropriate information from a foreign organization is often troublesome due to language, currency, and legal differences. Because of these difficulties, PFs sometimes find it more comfortable to treat such foreign grants as expenditure responsibility grants to avoid unexpected results. The paperwork may be simpler and the possibility for a taxable expenditure is less.[67]

Charitable Deduction Connection. Among the reasons why a private foundation would involve itself in foreign projects is the IRC §170 rule that disallows income deductions for gifts to foreign charities. When the U.S. charity's board (private or public) has control and discretion as to the use of the funds raised, the fact that the funds are contributed to the PF specifically for projects outside the United States does not render contributions nondeductible.

A PF's gifts to a pair of organizations established to build a basketball stadium in the foreign country and to sponsor and operate the games in the foreign country were allowed by the IRS and by reference qualification for exempt status sanctioned. Interestingly, only one organization was designed to qualify for U.S. charitable deductions. Organization 1 raised funds to regrant to Organization 2 and to build and own the stadium in which Organization 2 would operate. The ruling continues the tax policy regarding charity, which recognizes the exempt nature of the activity, regardless of its location.[68]

---

[65] Reg. §53.4942(b)-1(c).
[66] See Chapter 21§9(a).
[67] Priv. Ltr. Ruls. 8030104 and 8515070 indicate the extent to which some PFs go in ensuring that their grants to foreign organizations meet the expenditure responsibility test.
[68] Priv. Ltr. Rul. 9129040.

The tax treaty between Mexico and the United States, adopted in 1994, establishes a protocol under which Mexican charitable organizations can be recognized as public charities for private foundation purposes. The treaty also provides for an income tax deduction against a U.S. resident's Mexican-source income reportable in the United States and vice versa. Private foundations that are interested in supporting charitable activities in Mexico and other foreign countries should be alert for similar provisions in income tax treaties impacting the status of such organizations.[69]

17.5 EXPENDITURE RESPONSIBILITY GRANTS

To ensure accountability for grants and program-related investments by private foundations, record-keeping requirements are more stringent when a grant is made to:

- Another private foundation or a private operating foundation;

- An organization exempt under a §501(c) category other than (3); or

- A nonexempt business for a direct charitable program or a program-related investment.[70]

Grants to such organizations are *not* prohibited—a foundation is not the "insurer of the activities of grantee."[71] The PF can make the grant "as long as it exerts all reasonable efforts and establishes adequate procedures" to

- See that the grant is spent solely for the purpose for which it is made; and

- Obtain required reports with respect to the expenditures and submit information on Form 990-PF.

Unique grant recipients. As one example of the latitude available, a PF may make a grant to a social club if the grant is suitably dedicated for charitable purposes. A PF made a grant to a social fraternity's §501(c)(2) title-holding organization to build a study room in the chapter house. The facility was to contain exclusively educational equipment and furniture, along with computers linked to the university's mainframe. The university sanctioned the grant by certifying in writing that the room benefits the school by supplementing its resources, alleviating overcrowding in its library and study areas, and providing additional computer terminals. The fraternity agreed to return any grant funds not used for construction of the study space. There was no time period stipulated for this guarantee, but the foundation required that it be able to inspect the room annually.[72]

[69] Milton Cerny outlined the rules pertaining to nonprofit organizations in the February 1995 issue of *The Exempt Organizations Tax Review,* in an article entitled "The Americas: An Expanding Nonprofit Sector."
[70] Reg. §53.4945-6(c).
[71] Reg. §53.4945-5(b)(1).
[72] Priv. Ltr. Ruls. 9050030, 9219033, and 9306034.

Another example was an "urban enterprise association" established to operate a recycling facility to provide jobs for a city's unemployed.[73] The PF's grant, in addition to commercial loans, provided start-up funds for the project. The project's purpose was to train workers and find them permanent employment. A public charity partner planned to turn the facility into a viable self-sustaining business (presumably related), the net income of which would go to the public charity. Note that the regulations permit such a grant to be made to a nonexempt business as long as the charitable purposes of the activity are clearly evident.

To exercise expenditure responsibility, a foundation must take very specific steps. All seven of the following steps and those in Exhibit 17-5 must be followed:

1. Conduct a *pregrant inquiry* of the sort outlined in Exhibit 17-6.

2. Establish proper terms for the grant or program-related investment.

3. Enter into a written agreement requiring the terms to be followed and establishing a reporting system for the grantee.

4. Follow up by receiving and reviewing grantee reports.

5. Investigate any diversions of funds.

6. Annually disclose proper information on Form 990-PF evidencing compliance with the steps.

7. Keep documentation of these steps for IRS inspection.

(a) Pregrant Inquiry

The first step in exercising expenditure responsibility is to investigate the grantee organization and its proposed project. A pregrant inquiry is a limited investigation directed at obtaining enough information to "give a reasonable man assurance that the grantee will use the grant for the proper purposes."[74] The inquiry should concern itself with matters such as:

- The identity, prior history, and experience (if any) of the grantee organization and its managers. Is the other organization capable of accomplishing the grant purposes?

- Information about the management, activities, and practices of the grantee organization, obtained either through the PF's prior experience and association with the grantee or from other readily available sources.

The scope of the inquiry is expected to be tailored to the particular grantee's situation, the period over which the grant is to be paid, the nature of the project, and the PF's prior experience with the grantee. The regulation examples present the following profiles of successful inquiries:[75]

---

[73] Priv. Ltr. Rul. 9310044.
[74] Reg. §53.4945-5(b)(2).
[75] Reg. §53.4945-5(b)(2)(ii).

Exhibit 17–5

EXPENDITURE RESPONSIBILITY CONTROL CHECKLIST

Sample Organization

This questionnaire is used to document the seven steps required for expenditure responsibility grants.

Do Not Proceed to Next Step Until Each Step Is Completed!

	Date	Initial
Step 1. Pregrant inquiry completed.	_____	_____
Step 2. Expenditure responsibility contract signed.	_____	_____
Step 3. Grant timetable prepared.	_____	_____
Step 4. Form 990-PF attachment prepared (Reg. §53.4945-5(d)).	_____	_____
Step 5. Delinquent reports or diversions investigated.	_____	_____
Step 6. Withhold payments.	_____	_____
Step 7. Documents segregated in a manner to assure that they are saved for four years.	_____	_____

Approved by: _____

- A PF is considering a grant to a newly created drug rehabilitation center located in a neighborhood clinic and classified as a §501(c)(4) organization because it is an "action" organization. One of its directors, they are informed, is an ex-convict. The PF determines that he is fully rehabilitated and that the board as a whole is well qualified to conduct the program, since they are members of the community and more likely to be trusted by drug offenders.

- A grant recipient provides medical research fellowships. It has conducted the program for years and receives a large number of other PF grants. Another PF that supports this recipient informs the PF that it is satisfied that its grants have been used for the purposes for which they were made.

If the grantee has received prior expenditure responsibility grants from the PF and has satisfied all of the reporting requirements, a pregrant inquiry is not necessary. Likewise, for a grant to a split-interest trust that is required by its instrument to make payments to a specified public charity, a less extensive inquiry would be necessary.[76] Exhibit 17-5 can be used to monitor the information gathered and form the basis for the grant decision as a result of the pregrant inquiry.

[76] Id.

Exhibit 17–6

PREGRANT INQUIRY

Sample Foundation

Name of Proposed Grantee:_____

Tax status?   501(c)(3)_____   501(c)(4)_____   Other _____
               509(a)(1)_____   509(a)(2)_____   509(a)(3)_____

Copy of IRS documentation letter obtained:	☐ Yes	☐ No
Publication 78 verification made:	☐ Yes	☐ No
Written request with full details received:	☐ Yes	☐ Get one
Complete financial information submitted:	☐ Yes	☐ No
Form 990:	☐ Yes	☐ Get one
Financial statements:	☐ Yes	☐ Get

Contacts: Name   Date of meeting/call

                _____   _____

                _____   _____

                _____   _____

References: _____   _____

                _____   _____

                Year   Purpose

Prior grants: _____   _____

                _____   _____

Reports on time: Yes_____ No_____ If not, why_____

Reasons grantee
is qualified:_____

_____

Is project achievable? _____

_____

Supplemental information (not required, but helpful):

Organizational history	Publications/reports of projects
List of board members	Projects of grantee
Letters of reference	Annual report
Organization budgets	Needs analysis

(b) Grant Terms

An officer, director, or trustee of the grant recipient must sign a written commitment (See Exhibits 17-7 and 17-8) that, in addition to stating the charitable purposes to be accomplished, obligates the grantee to do the following:

- Repay any portion of the amount granted that is not used for the purposes of the grant;

- Submit full and complete annual reports on the manner in which the funds are spent and the progress made in accomplishing the purposes of the grant;

- Maintain records of the receipts and expenditures, and make its records available to the grantor at reasonable times; and

- Not use any of the funds for electioneering, lobbying, or other purposes that result in taxable expenditures according to IRC §4945(d).[77]

When making a grant to an organization that is not a §501(c)(3), the private foundation must require the grantee to establish, and maintain as long as grant funds remain, a separate fund dedicated to the charitable purposes for which the grant is made.

Program-Related Investments. In addition to the previously listed information required, the recipient of program-related investment funds must also agree to:

- Repay the funds not invested in accordance with the agreement, but only to the extent permitted by applicable law concerning distributions to holders of equity interests;

- Submit financial reports of a type ordinarily required by commercial investors under similar circumstances, and a statement that it has complied with the terms of the investment; and

- Maintain books and records of a type normally required by commercial investors.[78]

Foreign Grants. An agreement with a foreign entity should phrase the restrictions in appropriate terms under foreign law or custom. While not specifically required, an affidavit or opinion of counsel stating that the agreement is valid under the foreign laws is "sufficient."[79] Translation of the agreement into applicable languages may be appropriate.

(c) Grantee Reports

Each year, details must be provided for each grant upon which "any amount or any report is outstanding at any time during the taxable year." The grantor PF

---

[77] Reg. §53.4945-5(b)(3)(i), (ii), (iii), and (iv).
[78] Reg. §53.4945-5(b)(4).
[79] Reg. §53.4945-5(b)(5).

Exhibit 17–7

EXPENDITURE RESPONSIBILITY AGREEMENT

(Version 1)

Name of Grantee Organization
Address

Dear _____,

_____ (Name of Grantor) is pleased to inform you that its board of directors has approved a grant of $_____ to the _____ (Name of Grantee) pursuant to the grant application dated _____.

Since your organization and ours are private foundations, we must again enter into an expenditure responsibility agreement.

Use of Funds

Our grant must be expended for charitable, scientific, literary, or educational purposes as defined under Internal Revenue Code §501(c)(3), and more specifically for _____ (Description of purpose of grant, title if any) or general support of the grantee. ANY FUNDS NOT SO EXPENDED MUST BE RETURNED TO _____ (Grantor). Funds may not be used to influence legislation or the outcome of any election, to carry on a voter registration drive, or to make grants to individuals for travel or study.

Annual Report

_____ (Grantee) will provide a narrative and financial report to us by _____ (Date). The narrative portion should include a copy of publications, catalogs, and other materials describing the accomplishments of the program or project. The financial report must be attested to by an outside accountant and must contain details of expenditures, such as salaries, travel, supplies, and the like.

Although grant funds need not be physically separated, reports of receipts and expenditures under the grant, as well as copies of the report furnished to us, should be kept available for our inspection until _____(four years from grant).

Payment Terms

Payments under the grant will be made on the following dates, after receipt of a signed copy of this agreement:

_____   _____

_____   _____
(Date)   (Amount)

Exhibit 17–7 (*continued*)

Sign and Return

If this agreement meets with your approval, kindly sign it and return one copy to us. On behalf of _____ (Grantor), I extend every good wish for the success of this endeavor.

Acknowledged by:

_____   _____
For Sample Foundation   For Grantee Organization

_____   _____
Date   Date

---

must receive a report on the use of the grant funds reflecting the nature of the expenditures—salaries, travel, supplies, and so on. For a general support grant, an annual financial report or Form 990-PF (or 990) may be sufficient. In addition to financial information, the report should state the grantee is in compliance with the terms of the grant and describe the progress made by the grantee toward achieving the purposes for which the grant was made. The reports are to be made at the end of the grantee's fiscal year for each year the grant is outstanding, and should be received within a reasonable time after the close of the year. For multiyear grants, a final report summarizing all expenditures, should be submitted.[80]

Endowment Grants.   A grant of endowment funds or funds for the purchase of capital equipment or other capital purposes must be monitored for the year of the grant and for the two following years. The use of the principal and income (if any) from the grant funds is to be reported.[81] Such grants are outstanding for 990-PF purposes for three years. If it is reasonably apparent before the end of the second succeeding year that the funds have been used for the purpose granted, the reports can be suspended.

Program-Related Investments.   A grantee report must be received for each year during which the investment is in existence. The Charles Stewart Mott Foundation found out the hard way that program-related investments must be reported for the life of the loan or as long as the investment is held (in its case, 12 years).[82] Mott had relied upon the three-year endowment reporting requirement.

[80] Reg. §53.4945-5(c)(1); examples of grantee reports can be found in Chapter 9 of B. Hopkins and J. Blazek, *Private Foundations: Tax Law & Compliance* (New York: Wiley, 1997).
[81] Reg. §53.4945-5(c)(2).
[82] *Charles Stewart Mott Foundation v. U.S.,* 91-2 USTC ¶50,340 (6th Cir. 1991).

Exhibit 17–8

EXPENDITURE RESPONSIBILITY AGREEMENT

(Version 2)

Grantee:_____

Amount of Grant   Grant Payment Dates

_____   _____   _____

_____   _____   _____

_____   _____   _____

_____   _____   _____

Total Grant Awarded $_____

Grant Term in Years:_____

Purpose of Grant: _____

_____

_____

_____

_____

and as further described in your grant request dated _____.

Terms of Grant:
A. Funds granted will be expended only for the purposes for which the grant is being made. You will notify us if there are any changes in your plans. ANY FUNDS NOT SO USED MUST BE RETURNED TO SAMPLE FOUNDATION.

B. A financial report attested to by an independent accountant must be furnished annually by _____(date), along with a narrative report of accomplishments and any reports, publications, or other materials prepared in connection with the project.

C. Financial records pertaining to the grant such as receipts and other documentation evidencing the nature of the disbursements in connection with the grant will be maintained for at least four years and be open to our inspection at any time during that period.

Exhibit 17–8 (*continued*)

D. None of our funds may be used to:

- Carry on propaganda, or otherwise attempt to influence legislation (IRC §4945(d)(2))

- Influence the outcome of any specific public election, or carry on, directly or indirectly, any voter registration drive (as defined in IRC §4945(d)(3))

- Make an individual grant or regrant funds to another organization unless the requirements of IRC §4945 are met; or

- Advance any purpose other than one specified in IRC §170(c)(2)(B)

E. If Sample Foundation becomes aware that the funds are not being used for the purposes described above, we reserve the right to be reimbursed for the amounts so diverted, and will withhold any future grant payments.

Acknowledged by:

_____

For Sample Foundation

_____

For Grantee Organization

_____

Date

_____

Date

Private Foundation Successor Organizations.   A private foundation that distributes part of its assets to another private foundation in a termination distribution,[83] has a duty to exercise expenditures responsibility indefinitely until all of its assets are distributed.[84]

Grantee Accounting Records.   The recipient grantee need not maintain separate bank accounts or books for the grant unless the PF requires it. However, records of the manner in which the funds are expended must be maintained for at least four years after completion of the use of the funds. The grantor PF is entitled to rely on information submitted by its grantees.

(d) Reporting to the IRS

Each year, a foundation must provide information about each "outstanding" expenditure responsibility grant as an attachment to Form 990-PF. No special form is provided. An example of the report required to be attached to Form 990-PF can be found in Appendix 27-5. The regulations specify the following data be submitted:

[83] Discussed in Chapter 12.
[84] Reg. §§53.4945-5(b)(7) and 1.507-3(a)(7) and (8).

- Name and address of grantee

- Date and amount of the grant

- Purpose of the grant

- Amounts expended by grantee based upon the most recent report

- Whether (to the knowledge of the grantor) the grantee has diverted any portion of the funds, or income therefrom in the case of an endowment, from the intended purpose

- Dates of any reports received from the grantee

- Dates and results of any verification of grantee reports undertaken because the PF doubted their accuracy or reliability.[85]

The IRS has strictly enforced the expenditure responsibility reporting requirement. Before 1984, reporting the information on an amended return did not correct the taxable expenditure.[86] Stiff penalties were upheld against a group of three commonly controlled organizations in *Hans S. Mannheimer Charitable Trust*.[87] Their Form 990-PF contained no report. The foundation argued unsuccessfully that all of its internal documents, meeting transcriptions, and actual observations of the activities amounted to the exercise of expenditure responsibility. Despite the facts and the foundation's argument that its failure to report was due to an oversight, the penalty assessment was upheld. Effective beginning in 1984, the mistake can be corrected.[88]

(e) Grant Diversions

Rules similar to those governing scholarship fund diversions apply to grant fund diversions. The grant is not considered to be a taxable expenditure even though the grantor PF finds that any or all of the funds were used for improper purposes if the grantor PF:

- Takes all reasonable and appropriate steps either to get the funds back or to cause the grantee to use other funds to satisfy the grant terms; and

- Withholds, as soon as it discovers the problem, any further payments to the grantee until it receives the grantee's assurance that future diversions will not occur, and requires the grantee to take extraordinary precautions to prevent future diversion from occurring.[89]

If a grantee fails to make reports, a taxable expenditure will result unless the PF

---

[85] Reg. §53.4945-5(d)(2).
[86] Rev. Rul. 77-213, 1977-1 C.B. 357.
[87] *Hans S. Mannheimer Charitable Trust v. Commissioner,* 93 T.C. 5 (1989).
[88] See §17.7.
[89] Reg. §53.4945-5(e)(1)(iii).

- Originally made the grant following the appropriate procedures[90]

- Complied with all reporting requirements

- Makes a reasonable effort to obtain the required report; and

- Withholds any future payments on the specific grant and on any other grants to the same grantee[91]

17.6 NONCHARITABLE EXPENDITURES

The term *taxable expenditure* includes any amount paid or incurred for a noncharitable purpose.[92] The IRS has provided a list of expenditures that will not be classified as noncharitable, even though they are neither grants nor project expenditures. The list includes

- Payments to acquire investments entered into for the purpose of obtaining income or funds to be used in furtherance of charitable pursuits

- Payment of taxes

- Expenses deductible against unrelated business income

- Payments constituting a qualifying distribution under IRC §4942 or a deduction against investment income under IRC §4940

- Reasonable expenses to evaluate, acquire, notify, and dispose of a program-related investment

- Business expenses by the recipient of a program-related investment[93]

- Return of contingent contributions[94]

Conversely, the following expenses are taxable expenditures:

- Unreasonable administrative costs, including consulting fees

- Payment of unreasonable compensation[95]

- Payment of legal costs and settlement amounts to defend officers and directors in an unsuccessful state mismanagement action[96]

- Payments to a cemetery company eligible to receive charitable contributions under IRC §170(c)(5)[97] (because they are not technically a public charity under IRC §509(a)(1)).

[90] Listed at the beginning of §17.5.
[91] Reg. §53.4945-5(e)(2).
[92] IRC §4945(d)(5).
[93] Reg. §53.4945-6(b).
[94] *Underwood v. U.S.*, 461 F. Supp. 1382 (N.D. Tex. 1978).
[95] *Kermit Fisher Foundation v. Commissioner*, T.C. Memo 1990-300.
[96] Rev. Rul. 82-223, 1982-2 C.B. 301.
[97] Rev. Rul. 80-97, 1980-1 C.B. 257.

17.7 EXCISE TAXES PAYABLE

A tax of 10 percent of the amount of any taxable expenditure is imposed on the private foundation making the expenditure. A 2½ percent tax is payable by any foundation manager who willfully agreed to the expenditure knowing that it was such an expenditure, up to a maximum of $5,000. These taxes may possibly be abated as discussed at the end of this section.

To be subject to the tax, the manager must intentionally agree to the expenditure knowing that it is taxable. *Knowing* does not necessarily mean having reason to know. Such manager must have agreed to make the expenditure willfully and without reasonable causes, such as reliance on the written advice of outside or inside counsel. Only those managers in a position to decide what expenditures are paid and approve such disbursements are subject to the tax.[98]

If the taxable expenditure is not corrected before the date of mailing a notice of deficiency or the date on which the initial tax is assessed, known as the taxable period, an additional tax of 100 percent of the expenditure is imposed on the foundation.[99] The knowing managers are jointly and severally liable for an additional tax of 50 percent, up to a maximum of $10,000.

Correcting the taxable expenditure is accomplished when the PF takes whatever corrective steps the IRS recommends, including the following:[100]

- Requiring that any unpaid funds due the grantee be withheld

- Requiring that no further grants be made to the grantee

- Requiring additional, possibly quarterly, reports to be made

- Improving methods of exercising expenditure responsibility

- Improving methods of selecting recipients of individual grants

If the taxable expenditure was caused by inadequate reporting by grantees, receipt of the appropriate reports is a correction. For failure to obtain advance approval for a scholarship or fellowship grant program, obtaining such advance approval for grant-making procedures is a correction.

The IRS has the discretionary authority to abate the first and second tier tax where the PF establishes that the violation was due to reasonable cause, not due to willful neglect, and a timely correction is made. See Exhibit 17-9 for a sample Letter to the IRS. Form 4720 is filed to inform the IRS that a potential taxable expenditure occurred but the foundation took steps to make the required corrections. See Appendix 27-6 for a sample Form 4720. The rules for excusing the foundation and its managers and the possible abatement of the tax are the same as those outlined in Chapter 16§2(c).

---

[98] Reg. §53.4945-6(b); see Chapter 16§2(c) for further discussion of these terms.
[99] IRC §4945(i)(2).
[100] Reg. §53.4945-1(d).

Exhibit 17–9

SAMPLE ATTACHMENT TO FORM 4720

SAMPLE FOUNDATION   #44-4444444
ATTACHMENT TO FORM 4720
for Fiscal Year Ending June 30, 1997

STATEMENT regarding CORRECTION OF TAXABLE EXPENDITURE

In submitting its Form 990-PF for the fiscal year ending June 30, 1998, the SAMPLE FOUNDATION (Sample) inadvertently failed to submit information regarding an expenditure responsibility grant. This failure is corrected in this return by making a complete report of the seven required items properly included as an attachment to Part VII-B, Statement Regarding Activities for which Form 4720 may be Required, of this year's Form 990-PF.

Sample, during its fiscal year ending June 30, 1996, made an endowment grant to ABC FOUNDATION (ABC), a private foundation. The required expenditure responsibility agreement was executed in a timely fashion and the grant information reported in Sample's 1995 Form 990-PF. Additionally ABC reported that the endowment and its income were dedicated to charitable purposes as its agreement with Sample required. Sample duly submitted the seven points of information on its 1995 Form 990-PF for the fiscal year ending June 30, 1996. ABC further made a second year's report for the 1997 fiscal year in its 1996 return.

A taxable expenditure occurred, however, when Sample failed to include a statement of the required information on its 1997 Form 990-PF. Sample had made expenditure responsibility grants in past years, but had not previously made an endowment grant that required multiple year reporting. Sample's controller who prepared the return failed to include the report because he was following the pattern established for non-endowment grants. Sample's grant department had engaged outside counselors to prepare the agreement regarding the grant. They were advised Sample needed to receive and submit to the IRS two years of monitoring reports and also to report the grant in the year in which it was made. The controller was not furnished a copy of the counselors' letter describing this requirement.

Pursuant to Internal Revenue Code §4962, Sample respectfully requests that the first tier §4945 penalty for failure to report, or initial tax of $15,000, be abated because the failure was due to reasonable causes and without willful neglect. The mistake was discovered by Sample's executive director when she was reviewing the 1997 Form 990-PF prior to submitting it to me for signature. The inclusion of the proper report in this 1997 return effectively corrects the failure to report. Therefore, Sample submits it is entitled to an abatement of the tax because it meets the requirements of §4962 and the instructions to Form 4720.

I swear that this information is true and correct and that the foundation's failure to make the third year's report of ABC's endowment grant was inadvertent, accidental, and without intention or knowledge on my part or on the part of any of Sample's other officers.

J. B. Sample, President

PART THREE

IRS Recognition

Chapter Eighteen
Obtaining Recognition of Exempt Status

CHAPTER EIGHTEEN

Obtaining Recognition of Exempt Status

Internal Revenue Service (IRS) approval, called recognition, of an organization's exempt status is secured by submitting Form 1023 or 1024. The desired result is a determination letter describing the category of exemption granted (shown in Exhibit 18–4).

Effective October 1, 1997, all applications for recognition of tax-exempt status and letters regarding changes in the activities or organizational documents of an exempt organization are to be sent to the centralized processing office in Cincinnati, Ohio.[1] All applications are now submitted to the IRS Center, P.O. Box 192, Covington, KY 41012-0192. Do not be confused by this address, which is located across the river from the Cincinnati Key District Office.

The IRS has designated four commercial delivery services—FedEx, United Parcel, DHL Worldwide Express, and Airborne Express—as carriers (as of October 1998) whose dated receipts will be recognized as valid for timely filing purposes.[2] The surface address for such deliveries is Internal Revenue Service, 201 West Rivercenter Blvd., Attn: Extracting, Stop 312, Covington, KY 41011. The Cincinnati office now has a toll free number (877) 829-5500. The choices for assistance are:

1. To inquire about the tax-exempt status of an organization.

2. To check on the status of Form 1023 already submitted.

3. To seek assistance with completion of Form 1023.

4. To inquire about an advanced ruling for forms and publications.

Applications are first procedurally and technically screened and added to the master tracking system in Ohio. During 1997–98 (and "until the new center is fully staffed"), applications requiring "further development" were worked on by specialists in the former key district offices.

Completing these forms is actually a healthy exercise for a new organization's creators. All aspects of the organization's structure, purposes, finances, and relationships are explored in the process of answering the questions. Proposed activities and grant programs are to be described, along with information about where the money will come from and how much will be spent. Fund-raising plans are to be fleshed out and solicitation letters submitted. Gathering the necessary information provides a good opportunity for strategic planning for the proposed organization and allows the organizers to focus on realizable goals and discard any ill-conceived or potentially nonexempt projects.

The terms used to define organizations qualifying for exemption connote different meanings to different people. What is religious to one may be sacrilegious to another. The Key District Office specialist responsible for approving or denying an application construes the meaning of a proposed organization's exempt purpose within the context of his or her understanding of the rules. The girth of chapters 2 through 10 indicates the vagaries of the rules and different standards applicable to each type of exempt activity. Although the IRS specialists are knowledgeable and cooperative, they may not perceive a proposed organization in the same light as its creators. Therefore applications must be prepared with care after reviewing the criteria for qualifying as compared to nonqualifying organizations found in Chapter 2–10.

Before plunging into the time-consuming process of preparing and submitting the application (the IRS estimates it takes 68 hours and 13 minutes at a mini-

[1] IRS Announcement 97-89, 1997-36 I.R.B.1.
[2] IRS Notice 97-26, 1997-26, IRB 6.

mum), the following questions, distilled from Exhibits 1–2 and 1–3, should be evaluated.

- Is there a need to create a new organization, rather than carry out the project through an existing organization?

- What is the best form of organization: nonprofit corporation, trust, or unincorporated association?[3]

- Which category of exemption is appropriate to the goals and purposes of the organization: Internal Revenue Code (IRC) §501(c)(3) or §§501(c)(4)-(27)?

- Can the organizational and operational tests be met?[4]

- Might a profit-making organization be preferable? Are the creators or managers willing to forego potential profits? Will business activity be substantial?[5] Are prospects for raising venture capital better than for getting grants?

- Should more than one exempt organization (EO) be created in view of differing purposes or funding sources? A supporting organization?[6] A lobbying branch qualified under IRC §501(c)(4)?[7] A for-profit subsidiary?[8]

- Is a broadly based governing board appropriate? Should the organization be controlled by its membership?

One should also evaluate whether any of the following advantages will be useful to the proposed organization.

- Exemption from federal income tax, except on unrelated business income. Exemption from other taxes, such as the federal unemployment tax and state and local taxes.

- Eligibility to receive tax deductible charitable contributions for income, estate, and gift tax purposes.

- Qualification for grant funding from foundations and government entities.

- Potential for other benefits, such as tax-deferred gifts and postal rate privileges.

18.1   FORM 1023: EXEMPTION UNDER IRC §501(C)(3)

This chapter contains strategies for obtaining IRS recognition of exempt status. It will take you step by step through Form 1023, Application for Recognition of

---

[3] See Chapter 1.
[4] See Chapter 2.
[5] See Chapter 21.
[6] See Chapter 11.
[7] See Chapter 6.
[8] See Chapter 22.

Exemption Under Section 501(c)(3) of the Internal Revenue Code.[9] It discusses the statutory requirements for exemption and explains how to complete the form, including important deadlines and group exemptions. Strategies for solving problems, such as denial of the application or late filing, are presented. A copy of favorable determination letters issued by the IRS are available for 30 days after their issuance in its Washington Freedom of Information Reading Room.[10] Organizations approved for qualification under IRC §501(c)(3) are listed in IRS Publication 78 available in printed copy or on the Internet.[11]

(a) Statutory Requirements for Exemption

In order to qualify for exemption under IRC §501(c)(3), an organization must be a corporation, community chest, fund, or foundation, organized and operated exclusively for one of the following eight very specific purposes:

1. Religious

2. Charitable

3. Scientific

4. Testing for public safety

5. Literary

6. Educational

7. To foster national or international amateur sports competition (but only if no part of its activities involve the provision of athletic facilities or equipment)

8. For the prevention of cruelty to children or animals

Furthermore, the organization's documents must require that:

- No part of its net earnings shall inure to the benefit of any private shareholder or individual;

- No substantial part of its activities shall be the carrying on of propaganda, or otherwise attempting to influence legislation (except as otherwise provided in IRC §501(c)(h)); and

- The organization shall not participate in or intervene in (including publishing or distributing statements) any political campaign on behalf of (or in opposition to) any candidate for public office.

One or more of the eight specified purposes must be named in the organization's organizing documents. An entity established "to promote community bene-

---

[9] Appendix 18–1 has a filled-in example.
[10] IRS Notice 92-28, 1992-25 I.R.B. 5.
[11] *www.irs.ustreas.gov.*, Tax Information for Business.

fits" and "to develop the art of dance" would not qualify, unless its charter also stated that such activities were to be conducted for exclusively educational or charitable purposes. The standards discussed in Chapter 2 concerning the organizational and operation tests should be reviewed in connection with preparing Form 1023. IRS Publication 557, *Tax-Exempt Status for Your Organization,* contains sample documents and provides a comprehensive resource for issues the IRS deems important in this regard. Chapters 3, 4, and 5 should be consulted regarding the characteristics and special rules applicable to each category of qualifying 501(c)(3) organization.

(b) Proper Timing

No Charitable Status until Filing.   Even though a newly formed organization meets all of the qualifications to be exempt under (c)(3), it is not treated as a tax-exempt organization until it properly notifies the IRS of its qualification by filing Form 1023.[12] An exempt organization is also presumed to be a private foundation unless its properly completed Form 1023 furnishes information proving its public status. Organizations that qualify under other subsections of §501(c) are exempt without filing such notice, although they usually file Form 1024 to obtain proof of exemption.[13]

Due Date.   According to the statute and the general instructions to Form 1023, an application for recognition of exemption is due to be filed 15 months after the end of the month the organization is *formed.*[14] Since 1992, an automatic 12-month extension is available simply by checking a box on Form 1023 and filing within 27 months of the organization's formation.[15] *A reasonable action and good faith standard* applies to allow the extension but no information is submitted with the form. When the 27 months have passed, the deadline can again be extended automatically and without submission of excuses for the delay if the filing is made before the organization is contacted by the IRS and the interests of the government are not prejudiced by the extension. While it seems too good to be true, voluntary filing within any period of time before the IRS discovers the failure is presumed to evidence good faith.[16]

If the IRS discovers that the application is late,[17] all is still not lost. An extension can still be obtained by submitting "reasons specific to your particular organization and situation." The Form 1023 instructions suggest the following information be provided to show good cause for granting an extension:

- Whether the organization consulted an attorney or accountant knowledgeable in tax matters or communicated with a responsible IRS employee

[12] IRC §508(d)(3)(B).
[13] Discussed in §18.3.
[14] Form 1023, General Instructions, pg. 1; Rev. Proc. 90-27, 1990-1 C.B. 514.
[15] Rev. Proc. 92-85, I.R.B. 1992-42 (Oct. 1, 1992), superseding Rev. Proc. 79-63 and 80-31.
[16] See IRS Publication 557, *Tax-Exempt Status for Your Organization.*
[17] Because, for example, Forms 1099 are filed to report interest income paid to a nonprofit that files no Form 1120 or 990. Filing Form SS-4 to obtain an identification number for a new nonprofit organization does not register a requirement to file Form 990 or 1120 in the IRS systems. Federal income tax filing requirements are based instead on the receipt of income.

(before or after the organization was created) to ascertain the organization's federal filing requirements and, if so, the names and occupation or titles of the persons contacted, the approximate dates, and the substance of the information obtained

- How and when the organization learned about the 15-month deadline for filing Form 1023

- Whether any significant intervening circumstances beyond the organization's control prevented it from submitting the application timely or within a reasonable time after it learned of the requirement to file the application within the 15-month period

- Any other information that you believe may establish good cause for not filing timely or may otherwise justify granting the relief sought.

Effective Date of Exemption. A nonprofit's tax-exempt status is effective retroactively to its *date of organization* if the application is timely filed and accepted by the IRS. Applications not treated as timely filed are effective only from the date of filing. A late-filing organization can request tax-exempt status as a (c)(4) organization for the period between formation and the effective (c)(3) exemption date; otherwise income taxes may be due on income received prior to the effective date of exemption.

To prove timely filing, it is preferable that the application be sent by certified mail, return receipt requested. The postmark stamped on the envelope transmitting the application determines the date of filing. Absent such a postmark, the date the application is stamped as received by the IRS is the receipt date.[18] If the application is simply dropped into a post box and is subsequently lost, the EO has no way to prove that it was sent. The designated commercial delivery services—Federal Express, United Parcel, DHL Worldwide Express, and Airborne Express—(as of October, 1998) date stamps are recognized as valid for timely filing purposes.[19]

Date Organization Formed. Timely filing is measured from the date the organization is *formed,* or the date it becomes a legal entity.[20] For a corporation, this would be the date that the articles of incorporation are approved by the appropriate state official. For unincorporated organizations, it is the date the constitution or articles of association are adopted. The date of formation is the date on which the organization comes into existence under applicable state law.

Incomplete Applications. The regulations take a surprisingly lenient position regarding incomplete applications.

The failure to supply, within the required time, all of the information required to complete the form, is not alone sufficient to deny exemp-

---

[18] Rev. Rul. 77-114, 1977-1 C.B. 153.
[19] IRS Notice 97-26, 1997-26, IRB 6.
[20] Form 1023, Instructions to Part I, Line 5; Rev. Proc. 90-27, 1990-1 C.B. 514.

tion from the date of organization to the date such complete information is submitted by the organization. If the organization supplies the necessary additional information at the request of the Commissioner within the additional time period allowed by him (her), the original notice will be considered timely.[21]

The instructions to Form 1023 provide that an incomplete application may be returned for resubmission with the missing information and attachments. "This will delay the processing of the application and may delay the effective date of your organization's exempt status." In practice, the IRS often requests information needed to complete the application. What constitutes a complete return is described in the procedures for filing a declaratory judgment to appeal an adverse determination. A "substantially complete" application contains the following elements:[22]

- Signature of an authorized individual.

- Employer identification number or Form SS-4.

- Information regarding previously filed federal income tax and exempt organization information returns.

- Statement of receipts and expenditures and balance sheet for the current and three preceding years (or all years of existence if less than four). A two-year proposed budget is submitted for new organizations.

- Statement of proposed activities and description of anticipated receipts and contemplated expenditures.

- Conformed copy of organizing documents with evidence they were approved by state authorities if applicable.

- Copy of bylaws.

- Correct user fee.

(c) Expeditious Handling

It normally takes from 90 to 120 days after filing a complete and unquestioned application to receive a determination letter. The timing depends upon the IRS's workload, which is usually heavier in the fall at year-end tax planning time, when many organizations are formed to receive deductible gifts from substantial contributors. Absent approval for special handling, submission of a complete and clearly prepared application can save considerable time in obtaining approval. Paying the filing fee with a cashier's check or money order eliminates the wait for the check to clear.

When approval is needed as soon as possible, a speedy determination or expeditious handling can be requested. Such a request may be granted when the EO

[21] Reg. §1.508-1(a)(2)(ii).
[22] Rev. Proc 90-27, 1990-1, I.R.B. 514.

can prove that it will lose a significant grant or source of funding without a determination of its exempt status. A good candidate for expeditious handling would be a newly created organization with an offer for a major grant from a private foundation that wishes to satisfy its minimum distribution requirements before the determination can reasonably be expected, but which will not make the grant without an IRS determination. The specific steps to take in requesting expeditious handling include the following:

- A cover letter requesting special handling and describing the reason why speed is necessary. Good reasons include the emergency nature of the project, such as disaster relief, or the possibility that a grant will not be received if approval is delayed.

- Independent documentation of reasons, such as a letter from a prospective funder denying funds if there is a delay.

(d) National Office

Applications that present questions not specifically answered by stature, regulation, IRS ruling, or court decision—at the discretion of the district director—may be forwarded to Washington, D.C., for determination by the national office.[23] From time to time, the exempt organizations branch reserves issues about which there is controversy or rules that are in transition. In past years, the IRS has withheld rulings regarding hospital reorganizations, relieving the burdens of government, sheltering Central American refugees, and issuers of tax-exempt bonds, among other issues.

For the period February 1993 to July 1994, for example, applications for exemption for organizations that plan to issue tax-exempt bond financing were evaluated with a "risk assessment worksheet." Applications were scored from answers to 25 questions designed to measure whether the bond proceeds will be used for the private benefit of the organization's insiders. If the score was too high, the determination had to be made in the National Office. An acceptable score left the application in the Key District Office, subject to another set of inquiries. A "yes" answer to a question caused the application to be sent to the National Office. Specialists have now been trained to handle these applications. Guidelines that EO specialists follow can be found in the Internal Revenue Manuals.

An organization that believes its case involves an issue on which there is no precedent or nonuniformity between the districts can ask the key district to obtain technical advice from the IRS National Office.

(e) Organizations That Need Not File

Three types of organizations are excused from filing Form 1023 to achieve tax-exempt status because they are automatically treated as tax-exempt.[24] Despite

---

[23] Rev. Proc. 98-4, 1998-1 IRB 113, also see Chapter 28§2 for consideration of seeking a national office ruling.
[24] IRC §508(c)(3).

their exception from the requirement, some such organizations find it desirable to file nonetheless, for a number of reasons. They may need written IRS approval of their exempt status to evidence eligibility to receive tax deductible donations. Exempt status in some states is dependent upon federal approval. Nonprofit mailing privileges and other benefits of EOs are most readily obtained by organizations that can furnish a federal IRS determination letter.

Churches.   The first type of nonprofit organization excused from seeking recognition of its exempt status is churches, including local affiliates and integrated auxiliaries,[25] and conventions or associations of churches. Even though filing is not required, IRS determination may be desirable to remove uncertainty in the case of an unrecognized sect or a branch of a church established outside the United States. The IRS has developed a 14-point definition of a church contained in Schedule A of Form 1023.[26] Churches are generally granted favorable status; for example, they need not file annual Form 990 and may receive more liberal local tax exemptions. Employment tax reporting rules for ministers are also favorable.[27]

Modest Organizations.   The second type of organization that does not need to file is one whose gross revenue is normally under $5,000 and which is not a private foundation. The term "normally" means that the organization received $7,500 or less in gross receipts in its first taxable year, $12,000 or less during its first two tax years combined, and $15,000 or less total gross receipts for its first three tax years combined. If an organization has gross receipts in excess of the minimal amounts above during any year after its formation, it must file Form 1023 within 90 days after the close of that year.[28]

Subordinate Nonprofits.   The third type of organization that need not file Form 1023 is the subordinate organization covered by a group exemption, for which the parent annually submits the required information.

(f) Group Exemptions

To reduce overall compliance efforts, the parent organization of an affiliated group of organizations centralized under its common supervision or control can obtain a *group exemption letter* recognizing tax-exempt status for itself and members of its group.[29] A central organization may be a subordinate itself, such as a state organization that has subordinate units and is itself affiliated with a national organization. Subordinate chapters, posts, or local units of a central organization, such as the Girl Scouts of America or the National Parent-Teacher Association, need not separately seek recognition by filing separate applications if they are covered by the group letter. All of the subordinate organizations in the group must qualify for the same category of exemption (for example, §501(c)(3) for an educational group),

---

[25] Defined in Chapter 3§2(c).

[26] Reproduced in Appendix 18–1 and discussed in Chapter 3§2(b).

[27] Discussed in Chapter 25§2.

[28] Reg. §1.508-1(a)(3)(ii).

[29] Rev. Proc. 80-27, 1980-1 C.B. 677.

although the parent can have a different category from its subordinates. The group may not include private foundations or foreign organizations.

Information Submitted. The parent organization files Form 1023 to obtain recognition of its own exemption. Then, it separately applies by letter to the IRS Key District for approval of its group.[30] A letter requesting recognition of the parent's group is submitted, along with a $500 filing fee. The letter must contain the following information:

- A letter signed by a principal officer of the central organization verifying the existence of the relationship with its subordinates including a list of names, addresses, federal employer identification numbers (each subordinate must have a separate number), description of purpose, proposed activities, and financial projections. Any subordinate that already has a separate determination should be identified.

- Sample copy of the uniform governing instruments to be adopted by subordinates, which reflect general supervision and control of affiliate organizations by the parent.

- Affirmative statement that all subordinates have given written authorization to be included in the group exemption and recognized that they are under the control of the central EO.

- Statement that all subordinates qualify for exemption under the same paragraph of IRC §501(c) (though not necessarily the same paragraph under which the central organization is exempt).

- Statement that every organization in the group agrees to have the same accounting fiscal year.

For a (c)(3) group, two additional issues must be addressed. First, the effective date of organization of all entities must be furnished to ascertain timely filing. If a member of the group has been in existence longer than 27 months (and was not excused from seeking recognition), the group exemption may only be issued from the date of filing. Also, public charity status must be indicated, since no private foundations can be included with public charities.

New Group Members. Subordinates created after issuance of the IRS group determination letter report only to the central organization for recognition of exemption, not to the IRS. The new group member executes organizing documents and requests inclusion in the group. To qualify as tax-exempt under 501 (c)(3) from the date of its formation, the subordinate should seek inclusion before the end of the 15th month of its formation.[31]

Update of Affiliate Information. Annually, at least 90 days before the end of the accounting period, the central organization must submit information to update

---

[30] IRS Publication 557, *Tax-Exempt Status for Your Organization* (Rev. May, 1997), pg. 4.
[31] As discussed in §18.1(c), this time period is automatically extended to 27 months.

the master list of its subordinates with the Internal Revenue Service Center in Ogden, Utah. Three separate lists must be submitted to report the following information:

1. Subordinates that have changed their names or addresses during the year.

2. Subordinates no longer to be included in the group exemption letter because they have ceased to exist, disaffiliated, or withdrawn their authorization to the central organization.

3. Subordinates to be added to the group exemption letter because they are newly organized or affiliated or they have newly authorized the central organization to include them.

Each list must show the name, mailing address (including postal ZIP codes), actual address if different, and employer identification number of the affected subordinates. An annotated directory of subordinates will not be accepted for this purpose. If there were none of the above changes, the central organization must submit a statement to that effect.

Form 990.   The parent organization must file its own Form 990.[32] Affiliated organizations may file a separate return for themselves or be included in a group return. A group Form 990 is filed by the parent by combining the financial information for two or more (or all) of its subordinates. A subordinate must in writing declare, under penalty of perjury, that it authorizes its inclusion in a group return and that the information it submits for inclusion is true and complete. A list of the names, addresses, and identification numbers of included subordinates is attached to the group return.

Withdrawal from Group.   For a variety of reasons, a subordinate organization covered by a group exemption may wish to withdraw from the group and operate independently. To secure its ongoing and uninterrupted tax-exempt status, the withdrawing subordinate must seek its own recognition of exemption in the time frame provided for a new organization.[33]

(g) Form 8718: User Fee

A user, or filing fee, is due to be paid and attached to Form 8718, User Fee for Exempt Organization Determination Letter Request, and must accompany Forms 1023 and 1024.[34] The IRS will not process the application until the fee is paid and will send the application back if it is omitted. Submission of a cashier's check payable to the IRS, rather than a bank check requiring clearing, may speed the process. The fees are subject to update at the beginning of each year. The charges effective January 1, 1999,[35] are as follows:

---

[32] See Chapter 27 for suggestions for filing Form 990.
[33] Gen. Coun. Memo. 39833, released December 10, 1990.
[34] Reproduced in Appendix 18–3.
[35] Rev. Proc. 99-1 C.B. 1998-1 I.R.B. 229, updated annually.

Organizations with gross receipts averaging not more than $10,000 annually	$150
Gross annual receipts exceed $10,000	$500
Group exemption	$500
Final letter of termination of private foundation	$200

18.2 SUGGESTIONS FOR COMPLETING FORM 1023

A fill-in Form 1023 for a fictitious entity—the Campaign to Clean Up America—is included as Appendix 18–1 and can be used as a guide for completing a Form 1023. A depth of information is needed to evidence an organization's qualification for exemption; the application should paint a picture of the new organization as it will operate with both words and numbers. This section contains suggestions for completing each part of Form 1023; the reader may find it helpful to have a blank copy of Form 1023 to follow along with the text and to use the preparation checklist in Exhibit 18–1 before completing Form 1023.

Note in the upper left-hand corner of Appendix 18–1 that the reproduced Form 1023 was revised in September 1998. The IRS periodically issues a new version and preparers should use the latest version.

(a) Part I: Identification of Applicant

Line 1, Full name of organization. The name "exactly" as it appears on the organizational documents must be entered here. The determination will be issued in that name. If, for some reason, the organization plans to conduct its activities in some other name, the new name should be shown in parentheses. If the organization intends to abandon the name on its organizing documents, registering a formal change of name with state authorities prior to application might be preferable. This may save time explaining to donors why the determination letter has a different name. The form now asks for the EO's website address.

Line 2, Employer identification number. For all federal tax filing purposes, starting with Form 1023, an EO must secure and use a federal employer identification number (EIN). Form SS-4 is used to request the number. The IRS Center, not the determination office, assigns EINs, and no special category or type of identifying number is issued to tax-exempt organizations. Although the Form SS-4 may accompany Form 1023 if a number has not yet been obtained, it may slow the process. It is preferable to obtain the number separately. The application can be submitted by phone or facsimile by following the instructions to the form that can be obtained on the Internet.

Line 3, Person to contact. The name and telephone number of the person (or persons) to contact during business hours for additional information is requested. The instructions to the form suggest choosing a person familiar with the EO's activities, preferably an officer, director, or authorized representative. A good choice is someone qualified to answer any IRS telephone inquiry and to prepare written

Exhibit 18–1

PREPARATION CHECKLIST FOR FORM 1023

APPLICATION FOR RECOGNITION OF EXEMPTION
AS A § 501(C)(3) ORGANIZATION

A. *SUITABILITY (Chapter 1§5)*

☐ 1. Has the suitability checklist been completed indicating that establishment of a tax-exempt organization is desirable? _____

☐ 2. Verify (c)(3) is the appropriate category of exemption (Exhibit 1–2). If not, complete Form 1024. _____

B. *PROCEDURAL MATTERS (Chapter 18)*

☐ 1. Read the six pages of Form 1023 instructions prior to completing the form to get a sense of why the IRS asks certain questions. Note some items require detailed attachments; others do not. The objective is to paint a picture of the organization with words and numbers that prove it will be organized and operated exclusively for charitable purposes and therefore qualified as a § 501(c)(3) organization. _____

☐ 2. Verify place of filing, signatures, conforming attachments, and other specific instructions as set out by IRS. This checklist is designed for use alongside the instructions and does not repeat items clearly explained by the IRS. _____

C. *USER FEE*

☐ 1. Attach Form 8718, User Fee for Exempt Organization Determination Letter Request (current version) along with appropriate amount of the filing fee. _____

☐ 2. Forms submitted without payment will be returned. _____

☐ 3. Attach a cashier's check to avoid delay in processing. The applications are held until a check attached in payment clears. _____

D. *DUE DATE (Chapter 18§2)*

☐ 1. What date was the organization formed—date of incorporation, execution of trust instrument or articles of association—(Chapter 18§2(d))? _____

☐ 2. What is the due date of the application (15 months from D1 date)? _____

☐ 3. If not late, but a completed application cannot be prepared timely, should a request to extend the due date be filed? _____

☐ 4. If late, can the organization qualify for automatic 12-month extension (Chapter 18§2(e))? _____

Exhibit 18–1 (*continued*)

☐ 5. If late, is a prospective exemption effective on the filing date acceptable? Would the organization qualify as a (c)(4) organization prior to the filing date? _____

☐ 6. Consider request for expeditious handling if new organization's funding is awaiting IRS determination (Chapter 18§2(g)). _____

E. *FORM OF ORGANIZATION (Chapter 1§7)*

☐ 1. Do the creators wish to permanently stipulate organizational and operational policies and purposes so that an irrevocable trust is preferable? _____

☐ 2. Should a more informal and flexible unincorporated association be formed? _____

☐ 3. Should the most commonly adopted form, a nonprofit or not-for-profit corporation, be established? _____

☐ 4. How will the organization be controlled? By a board of directors only, or by its members who elect the board? _____

    a. If by members, how will they be chosen? Should members be permanent and named in the articles, should they be appointed by some other entity or official, or should the class of members essentially represent supporters paying annual dues or making contributions? _____

    b. Is a self-perpetuating board of directors desired and, if so, how will the directors be chosen? _____

    c. Should the board include representatives of institutions, such as the head of the local United Way, school superintendent, or chair of the arts council? _____

    d. If a private foundation, is it desirable to name only family members to control the PF, or should outsiders be included? _____

☐ 5. Do the organizing documents (separately adopted bylaws for a corporation) reflect policies and procedures for governing the organization? _____

    a. How will persons in control be chosen? How they can resign, be removed, or be replaced? _____

    b. Stipulate time for regular meetings at least annually. _____

    c. Provide rules for giving notice or calling meetings. _____

    d. Designate officers and their responsibilities. _____

    e. Make provisions for opening bank accounts, signing checks, entering into contracts, accepting gifts, maintaining books

Exhibit 18–1 (*continued*)

and records, indemnifying officers and directors, and handling other procedural matters. _____

    f.   Choose a fiscal year (see Chapter 18§3(a)). _____

    g.   Stipulate manner in which document can be amended, if at all. _____

F. *ORGANIZATIONAL TEST (Chapter 2§1)*

☐ 1. Do the organizing documents meet the organizational test? _____

    a.   *Purpose clause:* The organization is exclusively formed to accomplish one or more of the eight specified 501(c)(3) purposes—charitable, religious, educational, scientific, testing for public safety, literary, fostering national or international amateur sports competition, or preventing cruelty to children or animals? _____

    b.   *Use of assets:* The assets are permanently dedicated and substantially all of the funds must be spent for (c)(3) purposes. _____

    c.   *Dissolution clause:* If the organization dissolves or otherwise ceases to operate, its assets must be paid over to another (c)(3) organization. _____

    d.   *Electioneering:* The organization is prohibited from participating or intervening in any political campaign on behalf of any candidate for public office (Chapter 23). _____

    e.   *Lobbying activity:* No substantial part of the activities of the organization will be directed to conducting propaganda or otherwise attempting to influence legislation (Chapter 23). _____

    f.   *Private inurement:* No part of the net earnings of the organization, except for payment of reasonable compensation for services rendered, can be devoted to the personal or private interest of the directors, officers, or other individuals. No payments will be made to individuals upon dissolution (Chapter 20). _____

☐ 2. Does state law permit actions not suitable for a (c)(3) organization? If so, should the organizing documents specifically restrain or prohibit it from such acts? _____

☐ 3. Are shares authorized? If so, will they be held only by other (c)(3) organizations? _____

☐ 4. If a private foundation is being created, should the documents specifically prohibit actions that would cause the imposition of sanctions under §§4941–4945? (Chapters 13–17). _____

Exhibit 18–1 (*continued*)

G. CHARITABLE ACTIVITIES (Chapters 2–5)

☐ 1. Do the anticipated activities accomplish the (c)(3) purposes described in the organizing documents? _____

☐ 2. Flesh out the organization by describing the nature or scope of the activity it will conduct during the first few years to prove that the organization will: _____

    a. Serve a sufficiently large number of persons from the general public to constitute a charitable class (Chapter 2§2(a))? _____

    b. Spend an amount of money for charitable purposes that is commensurate with financial resources (Chapter 2§2(d))? _____

    c. If the projections indicate there will be surpluses or accumulations of income, are the reserves reasonable and necessary for prudent fiscal management? _____

    d. Arrangements to use property of or hire members of the board and officers and their relatives evidence no favoritism or excessive amounts (Chapter 20)? _____

    e. Financial arrangements with unrelated constituents or employees, such as artists, doctors, or research fellows, do not provide excessive amounts (Chapter 20§4–5)? _____

☐ 3. Review qualifications for particular type of charitable activity. _____

    ■ **Churches** complete Schedule A to prove they can meet the 14-point test (Chapter 3§2). _____

    ■ **Schools** complete Schedule B to show the IRS (1) they will operate a school as defined by the tax regulations and (2) the planned admission, student aid, faculty, or student privilege policies will not racially discriminate in any way (Chapter 5§1). _____

    ■ **Hospitals and medical research organizations** complete Schedule C to prove they operate to benefit the public rather than the medical staff (Chapter 4§6). _____

    ■ **Supporting organizations** complete Schedule D to describe their relationship with the organization(s) they support (Chapter 11§5). _____

    ■ **Private operating foundations** complete Schedule E to mathematically prove they will meet the income distribution and exempt asset tests (Chapter 15§5). _____

    ■ **Old folks and handicapped persons' homes** complete Schedule F to prove they will operate on a charitable basis (Chapter 4§6(d)). _____

Exhibit 18–1 (*continued*)

- **Day care centers** show they meet the very specific requirements for charitable status and complete Schedule G (Chapter 5§1(c)). _____

- **Scholarship and student aid providers** complete Schedule H (Chapters 2§2(a) and 17§3). _____

- **A for-profit organization** converting to nonprofit completes Schedule I (Chapter 20§8). _____

- **Low-income housing providers** meet the requirements outlined in the Internal Revenue Manual 7664.34 (Chapter 4§2(a)). _____

- Organizations claiming they **relieve the burdens of government** must prove there is a governmental body that wants to delegate its burdens and possibly pass scrutiny from the IRS National Office (Chapter 4§3). _____

- **Relief of the poor** efforts must establish guidelines by which they identify persons who are poor and eligible members of their charitable class (Chapter 4§1). _____

- **Publishing projects** must distinguish themselves from commercial publishers (Chapters 5§1(i) and 21§20). _____

- **Religious orders** may not qualify for exemption under (c)(3) because they conduct business activity for the common good of their members and may instead qualify under § 501(d). Do not file Form 1023 (Chapter 3). _____

- Service-rendering organizations must advance their own exempt purposes in **performing services for other exempts** and meet the Rev. Rul. 70-535 requirements (Chapter 21§8(a)). _____

- Activist organizations planning to attempt to **influence legislation** must prove they are not an "action" organization (Chapter 2§2(g)), limit amounts spent on lobbying efforts, and decide whether to elect to lobby. To elect, Form 5768 is separately filed with IRS Center (Chapter 23). _____

H.   SOURCES OF REVENUE (Chapters 21 and 24)

☐ 1. Will all of the organization's funds come from voluntary contributions or grants from other (c)(3)s, with no return benefits or services provided by the organization? If so, go to I. _____

☐ 2. If services will be rendered for exempt constituents—patients, students, or attendees of cultural events, for example—consider the following; _____

    a. Will the charges be reasonable? _____

Exhibit 18–1 (*continued*)

b. Will any of the services be provided for free or on a sliding fee scale? _____

c. Is the pricing established to produce a profit? To break even? At a loss to be covered by contributions? _____

d. Are the services of convenience to those participating in the organization's activities—a student dormitory, museum coffee shop, or hospital pharmacy? _____

☐ 3. If the organization plans to sell goods, consider the following: _____

a. Are the goods by-products of an exempt function activity—blood platelets or handicrafts produced by students? _____

b. Do the objects sold educate or assist in some way the participants in the organization's exempt activities, such as student books, art reproductions, Bibles, or baseball uniforms? _____

c. Is the sales activity run in a businesslike fashion that competes with for-profit businesses selling the same goods (Chapter 21§9)? _____

■ Are the goods donated? _____

■ Is the shop run by volunteers? _____

■ Does the sale or auction only occur once a year or quarterly? _____

☐ 4. If membership dues are to be solicited, what benefits will be provided to members? _____

a. Do membership requirements limit admission to a select group? _____

b. Do the terms reflect a social tone? _____

c. Do they evidence discrimination? _____

☐ 5. Does the organization plan to accumulate funds either as an endowment or as working capital? _____

a. Will the funds be maintained to produce income following the prudent investor rules? _____

b. Will the investments produce "passive income," i.e., dividends, interest, rents, royalties, and capital gains, or will unrelated business income be earned (Chapter 21§10)? _____

c. Are joint ventures with business enterprises and/or related parties proposed? If so, is information furnished to prove the project serves the new exempt's charitable purposes, not the private interests of others (Chapters 20§8 and 22§3)? _____

Exhibit 18–1 (*continued*)

I. PROJECTED EXPENDITURES (Chapter 20)

☐ 1. Do the proposed budgets or actual expenditures reflect expenditure of funds to advance the exempt purposes described in G above? _____

☐ 2. Do the proposed salary and fee levels for personal services appear too high (Chapter 20§2 and 20§10)? _____

　　 a. Are details of proposed compensation furnished, giving position or job description and compensation? Attach any contracts. _____

　　 b. For services competitively priced, such as investment advisors or building managers, explain how the fee was determined. _____

　　 c. For major expenditures, such as research services or building construction, explain how contractors were chosen. Were bids solicited? _____

　　 d. If the parties engaged are unrelated, say so. If related, explain why no conflict of interest exists (meaning no private inurement will occur). _____

　　 e. If director's fees are proposed, how often will the directors meet? Describe their responsibilities. _____

J. PUBLIC CHARITY VERSUS PRIVATE FOUNDATION STATUS (Chapters 11 and 12)

☐ 1. Consider the differences between public and private charitable organizations outlined on Exhibit 11–1. _____

☐ 2. Will the new organization qualify as public because of the activities it will conduct—a church, school, hospital, or medical research organization—without regard to its sources of support? _____

☐ 3. Can the organization qualify for a definitive ruling because it has completed an eight-month tax year? _____

☐ 4. Should the organization seek an advanced ruling because the initial public support indicates a private foundation? _____

responses to questions—ideally an accountant or attorney experienced in exempt organization matters that is engaged to prepare the form.

　　If representatives are used, Form 2848, Power of Attorney and Declaration of Representative, or Form 8821, Tax Information Authorization, must be completed and attached to the application, and the representative's name(s) are entered on Line 3.

Line 4, Accounting year. The choice of fiscal year is influenced by several factors, including the type of ruling being sought. A definitive ruling "cannot be issued before the close of an organization's first fiscal year having at least eight months."[36] In many cases, an advance ruling is sought, so any fiscal year can be chosen to accommodate this requirement.

Another factor in choosing the fiscal year is the organization's programming period. Schools and performing arts organizations normally operate on a September 1 to August 31 or August 1 to July 31 year, for example. Exempt organizations funded by federal government grants often find it convenient to match the federal year that ends September 30 or August 31. A summer or fall fiscal year end is sometimes chosen to accommodate accountants' workload.

Be sure that the fiscal year shown on the application agrees with the organization's bylaws and Form SS-4. If an incorrect fiscal year was indicated on a separately filed Form SS-4, or if for any other reason the organization needs to change its fiscal year, see Chapter 28§2.

Line 5, Date incorporated or formed. See previous discussion in §18.1(b).

Line 6, Activity code. The correct choice of activity code is very important and sometimes difficult. The wrong choice can lead to enhanced or misleading scrutiny from the determination specialist. The list printed on the back of Form 1023 includes all types of exempt organizations and is identical to the Form 1024 list. Sprinkled among some 300 possibilities are many non-(c)(3) activities. For example, "Advocacy, attempts to influence public opinion" is included in a list of more than 30 social issues such as gun control, birth control methods, and ecology. An exempt organization that chooses any of these codes will be required to prove that it is not an action organization.[37] Many codes fall into more than one exemption category. For example, a nurses' register might be a (3) or (6); a community center or a voter education project might be classed as a (c)(3) or (4); a horticulture society might fall into (c)(3), (4), (5), (6), or (7). The codes are to be entered in order of their significance to the organization's overall activities. Only one or two codes may be appropriate.

Line 7, Miscellaneous categories. In addition to (c)(3)s, the following organizations also file Form 1023:

- IRC §501(e), cooperative hospital service organization (see Chapter 4§7)

- IRC §501(f), cooperative educational service organization (see Chapter 5§1(d))

- IRC §501(k), organization providing child care (see Chapter 5§1(c))

Line 8, Other applications. The IRS wants to know if the applicant has previously applied for recognition of exemption, and if so, under what category. As discussed in Chapter 6§1, a (c)(3) that loses its status because of excess lobbying cannot later qualify as a (c)(4). Conversely, the IRS wants to be alerted up front if a (c)(4) or any other type of EO is applying to convert to a (c)(3).

---

[36] Form 1033, Instructions to Part III, Line 10 at page 6. See 18§5 regarding definitive and advance rulings.

[37] Discussed in Chapter 2§2(g).

Line 9, Form 990 required. This question allows the IRS to record the type of return to expect to be filed annually in the future by the applicant. Most applicants should check the "yes" block. The instructions direct a private foundation applicant to answer "N/A." A church and its integrated auxiliaries are not required to file 990s and consequently answer "no."

Line 10, Prior returns. To enable the IRS to verify compliance with annual filing requirements, the applicant is asked whether any prior returns have been filed—either an income tax return or an exempt organization information return. An EO in existence for more than one year may be responsible to file a return. An exempt organization more than one year old that was not required to file because it had less than $25,000 of gross receipts should say so.

Line 11, Organizational documents. Conformed copies of the documents legally establishing the organization are attached as follows:

- Articles of incorporation (including amendments and restatements) signed by the directors and "approved (certified, in most states) and dated by the Secretary of State or other appropriate state official," along with the adopted bylaws; or

- Constitution or articles of association, including evidence that the organization was formed by two or more persons; or

- Trust instrument.

The document copies must be "conformed," or ones that agree with the original and all amendments to them. A sworn statement (not necessarily notarized) signed by an officer or director, that reads: "I swear that the attached copies of the charter and bylaws (and amendments, if any) are true and correct copies of the originally executed documents," is sufficient.

These documents are used by the IRS to conclude that the organization meets the organizational test. Faulty limitations on activities and/or dissolution clauses will cause the IRS to return the application and deny exemption until the faults are cured. If the organization is relying on state law to impose dissolution or other provisions, the statute should be cited and summarized.[38] Review Chapter 2§1 for more details on this extremely important subject.

(b) Part II: Activities and Operational Information

This part fleshes out the candidate for exemption and paints a picture of the proposed organization. The IRS wants to know where the money to operate the organization will come from, the manner in which it will be obtained, how it will be spent, who will decide, who gets to participate or receive benefits, why the organization was created, whether it evolved from a previous life, whether it will benefit a limited group of people (particularly those who control it), and other information to determine that it will qualify as a charitable organization.

Successful preparation of Form 1023 involves weighing the material facts that should be submitted against their potential for generating controversy with

---

[38] Form 1033, Instructions to Part I, line 10, at pg. 3.

the IRS. While the facts must be accurate, there is room for judgment in the presentation of a potentially nonexempt activity. If there is a reasonable chance that a potentially unrelated activity might be approved and the EO is prepared to agree not to undertake the activity if it is not acceptable, inclusion is warranted.

Another important aspect to consider is that the organization will be somewhat constrained to operate in the manner presented in Form 1023. The organizers must look to the future and the possibilities must be surveyed before the application is submitted. Any future "substantial change" in operations may necessitate resubmission or communication with the IRS.[39] Finally, the application will be viewed by many persons in the future for a number of reasons. The organization's managers should periodically review the original Form 1023 to ensure everyone understands why the IRS considers the organization to be exempt, and to see if there has been a "material change" in its operations. The application must also be available for inspection by anyone who asks to see it or to buy a copy of it.[40]

Line 1, Narrative description of activities. The essence of the applicant's charitable nature is reflected in the description of proposed activities. The space allotted may suffice in some cases (and the IRS is suggesting by the limited amount of space that the description should be concise). However, a complete picture of the organization must be painted. Spare no words, but choose them carefully.

Information submitted in the narrative description must be coordinated with answers to other questions as well. If a website address is provided, the information contained therein should be reviewed with a view to qualification for tax-exempt status. If, for example, the description states that monetary assistance will be provided to needy families, the IRS technician may want to know how the recipients will be chosen, and will look to line 11(b) for a description of the criteria.

As another example, assume that the description states that the organization is established for literary purposes and that it plans to encourage emerging writers. The IRS will want to know how those writers will be chosen, how their works will be published, and who will own the copyright to the works. In this situation, the answers for both lines 11(a) and (b) are relevant as well as the projected financial information in Part IV. Most importantly, the answers must indicate to the IRS how the activity furthers the exempt interests of the general public while, as a by-product of accomplishing its purpose, it also may provide some benefits to individual writers. Retention of copyright by private individuals is thought by the IRS in most cases to provide private inurement. Payment of royalties to the writers in amounts intended not to exceed reasonable compensation may be acceptable but must be carefully explained.

The proposed activities to be carried out in accomplishing the exempt purposes must be described with a view to the particular standards for exemption pertaining to organizations conducting such activities. Chapters 2, 3, 4, or 5 should be studied to review the specific rules applicable to the organization. The standards, criteria, procedures, or other means adopted or planned for choosing participants and recipients of the organization's programs must be explained in sufficient detail to indicate the activity will benefit a charitable class. For example, a low-income housing project is subject to specific rules outlined in Chapter 4 and a

---

[39] Discussed in Chapter 28.
[40] IRC §6104(e) discussed in Chapter 27§2.

research organization to those found in Chapter 5. Special schedules are attached for churches, schools, and others as described in the suggestions for Part III and shown in Form 1023 in Appendix 18–1.

A mere restatement of the organization's exempt purposes, with a declaration that proposed activities will further such purposes, is *not* sufficient. The author prefers to answer Line 1 in outline form, highlighting categories of activities as shown in Exhibit 18–2.

Line 2, Sources of financial support. The EO's anticipated revenue sources should be summarized briefly according to the categories on the statement of revenue and expense in Part IV. The proportions should agree with the financial information presented in the proposed budgets or actual financial results. This line alerts the technician to private foundation status and to possible unrelated business income issues. The form asks that sources be listed in order of size. It is useful to indicate size with percentages similar to these:

Individual membership dues	30%
Government grants	20
Private foundation grants	20
Contributions from disqualified persons	15
Exempt function revenues	10
Investment income	5
	100%

Line 3, Fund-raising program. A thorough description of both actual and planned fund-raising activities is crucial to a complete application for most EOs other than private foundations. A private foundation (PF) might simply say it plans no public fund-raising activities. For others, the instructions define solicitations for contributions, functionally related activities, and unrelated business activities as fund-raising activities that must be explained. Significant issues can be raised by the answers to this question including:

- Possible private inurement to fund-raisers through payments of unreasonable salaries or fees based upon a high percentage of the contributions collected. If professionals are to be hired, it is very important to fully disclose the terms and their relationship, if any, to the EO. If there is no plan to compensate the fund-raisers, it's advisable to say so.

- Businesslike taint of purported exempt revenues, such as research fees, advertising, sales of books or other publications, premiums from group insurance, or income from a restaurant may be questioned. IRS specialists are also alert to other unrelated business activity disguised as a donation program—for example, premiums with a cost in excess of $7.20 offered in return for contributions.[41]

[41] Unrelated business income tax issues are discussed in Chapter 21.

Exhibit 18–2

SAMPLE NARRATIVE DESCRIPTION OF ACTIVITIES

XYZ was organized and will operate exclusively for charitable and educational purposes. XYZ is a newly formed organization located in an area of the city with a high degree of poverty. XYZ's primary purpose is to lessen the suffering of the poor (*or* XYZ is an outgrowth of a citizens committee formed by the STU Community Center informally assisting underprivileged members of the area). XYZ will conduct the following activities in space donated rent-free by the STU Community Center.

Educational Programs. XYZ will hold weekly public forums. Representatives of local, county, state, and national government agencies that provide assistance for the poor will be invited to speak to members of the community about services and financial assistance available to them. XYZ will publicize the forums by circulating fliers throughout the community. XYZ will hold tutorial classes for children after school to assist them in succeeding in their schoolwork and to keep them from dropping out of school. (Activity will comprise about 65% of our time.)

Nutritional Counseling. XYZ will seek a volunteer nurse to conduct a class at STU Community Center to teach nutrition. Health education of children and pregnant women will be emphasized, as well as substance abuse information. (Time: 10%)

Credit and Debt Counseling. XYZ plans to establish a group of business volunteers to counsel and assist community members in debt. Free income tax assistance will be offered during tax time. XYZ will contact the Better Business Bureau and other agencies offering help to the poor in gathering information to structure the program. (Time: 15%)

Grocery Cooperative. XYZ will provide management assistance for members of the community to operate a food cooperative previously sponsored by the STU Community Center. The cooperative will be run with volunteers and will enable the poor to purchase vegetables, grains, and high-protein foods to provide better nutrition for their families. The nutritional courses will be coordinated with foods purchased. (Time: 10%)

Future Programs. Although no definite plans are being made at this time because of funding constraints, funding for drug and job counseling programs will be sought. The state agencies providing such funding require that the organization be in existence for over two years before applying for funds.

- The proper distinctions between deductible and nondeductible portions of benefit dinners, auctions, and other events might be scrutinized.[42]

- Satisfaction of the "commensurate test" is evaluated here. This test measures the net profit produced by fund-raising programs. If promoter fees and other expenses are excessive, the organization itself may be deemed to operate to benefit the fund-raisers rather than the required charitable constituency.[43]

It is possible (but not necessarily desirable) to state that the fund-raising program has not yet been developed. If the projected sources of support consist primarily of grants from other exempt organizations, a lack of plans will probably not pose problems. If fund-raising events and exempt function revenues are to be the primary sources of support, the IRS expects detailed information. At a minimum, the organizers should submit mock-ups of letters requesting contributions for attachment.

The answers given for types of assets and charges for services to be rendered on lines 8 and 11 of Part II may signal the need to submit income-producing information. Conversely, answers about the fund-raising program should be reflected in those questions and also in the financial data of Part IV.

Line 4, Governing body. The questions about board membership enable the IRS to determine whether unreasonable salaries will be paid, whether the board includes political officials or disqualified persons, and what types of financial transactions are planned with insiders. To qualify for tax-exemption as a (c)(3), the nonprofit must not use its assets or income for the private benefit of its governing officials.

Line 4a, Names and addresses. Fill in the names, addresses, and titles of officers, directors, trustees, or other governing officials. Although it is no longer requested, their expertise and occupations can be submitted. A factor useful in proving the "public" nature of a project might be the presence of a broadly based board of independent experts. Take, for example, an organization that is being formed to support the work of a particular scientist. The occupations and expertise of outside directors might improve its chances for approval. Advisory board members who have no voting authority are not commonly included, nor are their names requested. If their stature adds to the organization's credibility and shows responsiveness to the public, such information could be voluntarily submitted.

Line 4b, Compensation. A key question in evaluating an exempt organization's qualification for charitable status is the possibility of "inurement of earning" to members of the board by virtue of payment of unreasonable compensation to them. While there is no prohibition against such payments, they will be scrutinized. A private foundation proposing to pay compensation to its directors should carefully review the self-dealing rules and consider submission of information evidencing the amounts will be reasonable.[44] Other (c)(3)s compensating the persons who govern them should review the intermediate sanction rules for similar reasons.[45]

---

[42] See Chapter 24.
[43] See Chapters 2§2 and 20.
[44] See Chapter 14.
[45] See Chapter 20§9.

Total annual compensation is to be reported, including salary, bonus, and other forms of payment to the individual for services while employed by the organization. Though the instructions do not direct that pension or other fringe benefits be included, for most purposes they are treated as part of one's compensation.

Line 4c, Public officials. Persons who serve on the governing body by reason of being public officials or being appointed by public officials are to be named here and their method of selection described. If the answer is "yes," the proposed (c)(3) organization must be mindful of the prohibition against intervening in or otherwise attempting to influence the election of such persons. The self-dealing sanctions specifically govern a private foundation's relationship to officials.[46]

A "yes" answer might be positive proof that the organization will be responsive to public scrutiny, particularly when the officials are designated by position and will rotate as their terms expire. For example, a drug prevention program might benefit from participation by the director of the local health department. On the other hand, a voter education project might not be allowed to have representatives of a particular political party as members.

Line 4d, Disqualified persons. For purposes of constraining their financial relationship with the organization, the Internal Revenue Code identifies certain insiders as disqualified persons (DPs). DPs can serve as members of the board, can be paid reasonable compensation for services they actually render, and stand in relationship to the organization just as any other person. They are simply "red flagged" for scrutiny. For purposes of this question, disqualified persons are defined to include

- Substantial contributors (generally over $5,000)

- Creators of trusts regardless of contribution level

- Foundation managers

- A member of the family of those listed above

- Controlled corporations, partnerships, trusts, or estates (over 35%)

- Another exempt organization controlled by the EO itself or by the same persons.

This question asks the preparer to explain if any members of governing body are disqualified persons. Typically, their names and the relationship are reported, although there is no specific instruction as to additional information to include. This question formerly asked if assets would be assigned. Now it is mostly answered "no" because Form 1023 is typically filed before the organization has any financial activity that would cause a person to become disqualified. Although it is not now required, anticipated donations by major contributors can be explained here, particularly if they involve the answers to other questions.

Line 5, Control of/by another organization. The first of this two-part question simply asks if the applicant controls or is controlled by any other organization and the instructions ask for no additional information. Control for this purpose is based upon a 50% overlap of persons governing the organizations. The second

---

[46] See Chapter 14§6.

part asks if the organization is an outgrowth of or specially related to another organization.

Control is not necessarily a negative factor; the issue is whether the charitable interests will be respected and advanced by the association. When the answer is "yes," the prudent applicant should explain the manner in which control is effected, whether with bylaw provisions, appointment of directors by the other organization, contractual terms, or otherwise. The following situations warrant answers to this question:

- Creation and control of a charitable EO by an EO of a different exemption category, such as a business or civic league or a social club (also requires information on Line 6).

- Facilities and other costs shared with a substantial contributor or the business creating the organization.

- The exempt organization is a successor to a nonexempt entity. The issue is whether the predecessor reaps any gain from the takeover. As with the problems anticipated in line 4d, if liabilities are being assumed, there must be no indication that the new charity is ending up in a positive financial position. Schedule I, Successors to "For Profit" Institutions, must be completed in such situations and can be referred to in answer to this question.

- A new supporting organization reveals its relationship with its supported organization by referring to the answers on Schedule D.

Line 6, Transactions with non-(c)(3)s. The details of any transactions anticipated to occur between the applicant and a non-(c)(3) nonprofit organization(s) must be revealed and will be carefully scrutinized. This question is asked again each year on Form 990, and seeks to ensure that the charitable (c)(3) is not operated to benefit a (c)(4) or other non-(c)(3) nonprofit organization.

Line 7, Accountability to another organization. If the exempt organization is financially accountable to another organization, the terms, written agreements, reporting forms, or other requirements should be described here. Sometimes the question is whether to report potential requirements. For example, assume a newly created organization hopes to become a United Way agency or to receive substantial governmental funding. It could include a statement of the possibility and the fact that extensive annual reporting will be required if it is successful. If available, grant-reporting forms might be attached.

A §509(a)(3) supporting organization should carefully describe any formal system it has developed for reporting to its supported organization and refer to the answers it provides in Schedule D.

Line 8, Exempt function assets. This question adds facts to complete the picture of the exempt organization in a physical sense. No information concerning investment assets or endowments is requested (as was the case in the 1986 and prior versions of the form). Examples of possible answers include:

- XYZ will operate from a rent-free building for use by other charities. Administrative assets, including computers, photocopiers, and office equipment, will be purchased. As funds become available, it is hoped that a vehicle for transporting neighborhood children, display cases for the food cooperative, and desks, speaker systems, and other assets to enhance the educational classes and other uses of the building will be obtained.

- ABC is a grant-making private foundation that will obtain administrative assets, such as computers, telephone systems, file cabinets, and other office equipment and furniture.

- DEF will operate a hospital. As reflected on the attached capital budget projections, a building will be constructed and furnished with equipment necessary to operate the hospital, its laboratories, cafeteria, and other patient care facilities.

Line 9, Tax-exempt bond financing. An organization answering this question "yes" must follow IRS procedures.

Line 10a, Facilities manager. With this question, the IRS is looking for the possibility of private inurement that might result through such an agreement. If either question is answered "yes," Chapter 20 must be carefully studied. The types of questions the IRS specialists asks him or herself in evaluating any contracts include the following:

- Do management arrangements in any way take unfair advantage of the charity?

- Is the fee reasonable for services to be rendered?

- How does it compare to prevailing rates charged other businesses? To the EO's overall budget?

- Is the fee related to performance, for example, a percentage of profits or other arrangement reflecting a business transaction?

- Are contracts entered into with related parties?

Except for a private foundation, there is no prohibition against a board member managing an exempt organization's property or engaging in other business transactions with the organization, but such a transaction will be carefully scrutinized to verify the fairness.

Line 10b, Leases. The applicant must attach a copy of any leases it is a party to, along with an explanation of the relationship between the organization and the lessor, if any. Arrangements for office space and equipment rentals are the most common examples. An arm's length agreement with an unrelated party needs no explanation beyond the lease itself. For a related party lease, evidence that the terms of the lease are fair must be submitted, along with other information described in Chapter 20.

Line 11, Membership organizations. For governance purposes, a nonprofit organization is a membership organization if it has members granted voting control pursuant to its governing documents. Some EOs designate financial supporters as members without delegating any control to them. For purposes of this question, a membership organization exists if three factors are present:

- Members share the common goal for which the organization was created;

- Members actively participate in achieving the organization's purposes; and

- Members pay dues.

The membership questions seek to determine whether the organization's membership aspect allows members to receive private benefit of a sort that would prevent exemption. When members are contributors and receive no monetary benefits, there is no problem. Among membership requirements that suggest nonexempt characteristics are a high membership fee with only members eligible to participate in exempt activities. Membership open only to a narrow group, such as those living in a particular subdivision or on a specific street, would also be troublesome. An art appreciation society whose membership is limited to persons who own works of a particular living artist might not qualify as benefiting a charitable class.[47]

Line 11a, Membership requirements and dues. A description of membership requirements and a schedule of membership dues (established with private inurement and charitable class standards in mind) must be attached.

Line 11b, Efforts to attract members. The present and proposed efforts to attract members are to be described and membership solicitation brochures or flyers are to be attached. This information must be coordinated with the responses to Questions 3 and 12 of this part and the financial information in Part IV. If the organization's services and benefits are offered exclusively to members, exemption may not be allowed. Membership discounts or reduced prices are acceptable so long as nonmembers have access to the activities. In such situations, estimates of those that will participate might be useful to reflect the organization's public nature. For example, a research organization may limit use of its laboratories to members but have a policy of publishing results and conducting seminars.

Line 11c, Benefits to members. This question is a two-edged sword. Of most concern is the issue of whether the organization operates to benefit only its members rather than a charitable class of individuals. Second, certain membership benefits are treated as consideration provided by the exempt organization. The value of such benefits must be disclosed to members and may reduce the contribution portion of members' dues. Proposed fund-raising materials will be scrutinized by the IRS specialist for adherence to the disclosure rules discussed in Chapter 24. The unrelated business aspects of members' transactions will also be evaluated.

Line 12a, Charges for exempt services/products. If the exempt organization plans to charge for services it renders or products it sells, the method of determining the charges must be described. Services do not have to be provided for free to be charitable but the concepts of private inurement and charitable class must be kept in mind in setting such policies. There is no prohibition against some amount of built-in profit, as the prices of private college tuition and hospital stays exemplify. This information, however, allows the IRS specialist to evaluate the possibility of unrelated business activity, particularly for services that are customarily provided by for-profit businesses, such as credit counseling or job placement.[48] Some possible answers follow:

---

[47] Defined in Chapter 2§2(a).
[48] See Chapter 21.

- Classes, workshops, and educational materials will be priced according to their direct cost; overhead expenses will be covered by donations.

- Charges for hospital services will be determined in accordance with the guidelines for Medicare/Medicaid reimbursements and the currently prevailing rate for comparable services in the community. Charges will be waived for persons who prove that they are unable to pay.

- Donated clothing will be resold in a volunteer-run shop at prices similar to those of other nonprofit and for-profit resale shops in the city.

- Charges for legal services will be determined on a sliding scale according to the client's family income level. See attached client engagement letter and fee arrangement for details.

Line 12b, Limitation on service recipients. How the charitable class of beneficiaries is selected, if there is a limitation, is to be explained here. Restrictions can cause denial of exemption. For example, schools must adopt a nondiscrimination policy and comply with requirements outlined in the Schedule B attachment for schools. A hospital might be denied exemption unless its provides free care to indigents or can otherwise prove its charitable nature.[49] An artists' cooperative that exhibited only work of its members has been found to serve its members, not the general public, and was therefore not exempt, despite the educational nature of the art.[50]

Line 13, Lobbying. A private foundation must answer this question "no." For other (c)(3)s, a "yes" answer is OK. Public charities may spend a limited amount on attempts to influence legislation by contacting members of a legislative body directly or by advocating to the general public adoption or rejection of legislation. Permissible lobbying is measured, however, by two very different tests—*expenditure* and *no substantial part*—and the choice for an exempt organization that plans to lobby should be made on the application. Issues to consider in making the decision are outlined in Chapter 23.

An organization electing to use the expenditure test to measure permissible lobbying attaches Form 5768, Election/Revocation of Election by an Eligible Section 501(c)(3) Organization to Make Expenditures to Influence Legislation.[51] The form actually has no mathematical information. The financial projections submitted with the application should quantify expected lobbying expenditures; such amounts should be within the allowable percentage limitations.

Although the form does not request it, a non-electing organization should attach details of its planned lobbying efforts, including:

- Dollar amount to be expended annually and calculation of percentage of total budget

- Amount of time to be expended by organization representatives (both paid and unpaid) on behalf of the EO, in connection with lobbying efforts

[49] Discussed in Chapter 4§6.
[50] Rev. Rul. 71-395, 1971-2 C.B. 228.
[51] Reproduced in Appendix 23-1.

- Description of issues involved and method proposed for carrying out lobbying activities

- Any written materials published or disseminated to the public or to government officials

Line 14, Political campaigns. The answer to this question must be "no!" To receive a determination that it qualifies as a (c)(3) organization, the applicant cannot intervene in any way in an election campaign, and its organizational documents must prohibit such involvement.

(c) Part III: Technical Requirements

Line 1–6, Timely filing. It is highly desirable that Line 1 be answered "yes" and the remaining lines 2–6 not be relevant. If the application is being filed more than fifteen months beyond the end of the month when the organization was established, refer to the Proper Timing discussion in §18.1(b) to complete this page.

If §501(c)(3) status is not available because the application is late, question 6 provides the opportunity to be classified as a (c)(4) organization for the period between organization and filing. Although the contribution deduction is lost for any gifts the organization has received before the filing date, at least none of the income will be taxable. Consult Chapter 6 for discussion of the similarities between (c)(3)s and (c)(4)s that indicate why this temporary classification is possible.

Line 7, Private foundation status. The new organization must state whether it is a private foundation.

Line 8, Private operating foundations. A private foundation planning to conduct self-initiated projects may qualify as an operating foundation.[52] If so, Schedule E is also to be completed.

Line 9, Public charity classification. One of ten blanks must be checked by organizations claiming to qualify for public charity status. Organizations qualify as public for one of three reasons. Types (a), (b), (c), (d), and (f) are public by virtue of the activities they conduct. They may claim a definitive ruling from their inception, as long as they can satisfy the requirements for those classifications. Types (e) and (g) operate to benefit another type of public entity. Types (h) and (i) may qualify based upon their revenue sources.

- (a) Churches complete Schedule A and must meet a strict fourteen-point test.[53]

- (b) Schools must complete Schedule B.[54]

- (c) Hospitals and medical research groups are subject to evolving rules and must complete Schedule C.[55]

- (d) Governmental units must meet special standards.[56]

---

[52] For qualifications see Chapter 15§5.
[53] Outlined in Chapter 3§2.
[54] See Chapter 5§1(b).
[55] See Chapter 4§6.
[56] See Chapter 10§2.

- (e) Supporting organizations check this blank and complete Schedule D.[57]

- (f) Entities testing for public safety.[58]

- (g) A supporting organization benefiting a college or university that is a governmental unit.

- (h) Publicly supported organizations qualifying because their support comes from a broad segment of the public (also known as §509(a)(1) organizations) must meet the mechanical tests illustrated in Exhibit 11–2 and proceed to line 10.

- (i) Service-providing organizations must satisfy the tests shown in Exhibit 11–3 and also proceed to line 10.

- (j) Entities that are not sure which category they qualify under check this blank to request the IRS decide. The disadvantage of this choice is the extra time needed to allow the IRS to request information.

Line 10, Definitive ruling. As the name connotes, a definitive ruling is essentially a "permanent ruling" of public status, effective until the organization's sources of support cause it to fail the public support tests mathematically. Ongoing qualification is based on a calculation made annually when Form 990, Schedule A is filed. The IRS has found that it can make up its mind about the public status of most organizations that have been in existence for a taxable year of at least eight months. A definitive ruling need not be chosen if, during the first year of activity, sufficient public support has not been received. Such an organization can request an advance ruling to avoid private foundation classification.

A newly created organization with limited operational history receives an advance ruling that it will be treated as a publicly supported organization, subject to a redetermination at the end of five years. At the end of the advance ruling period, the organization must furnish a detailed report of its sources of support during the past five years to allow the IRS to make a final determination of public charity status.

An organization receiving an advance ruling must agree to extend the statute of limitations during the five years. Form 872-C, Consent Fixing Period of Limitation Upon Assessment of Tax under IRC §4940 of the Internal Revenue Code, must be signed and filed (in duplicate) to evidence agreement to pay the private foundation excise tax on investment income earned during the advance ruling period if public status is not achieved.

A report of support sources is to be filed five years later, within 90 days after the period ends. Failure to file can result in reclassification as a private foundation. Placing a tickler on a reliable person's or firm's calendar is very important. Donors may rely upon the public status determination until the IRS publishes a notice of revocation, unless the donors are in a position to cause or be aware of the organization's failure to qualify. The significance of definitive versus advance rulings is discussed in §18.5.

---

[57] See Chapter 11§6.
[58] See Chapter 11§7.

Line 11, Unusual grants. To calculate an organization's qualification as a publicly supported organization under type (h) or (i), unusual grants can be omitted. These are significant grants from unrelated parties having the characteristics described in Chapter 11§2(h).

Line 12, Under two percent donors. See Chapter 11§2(f) to understand the information requested on this line. The calculation would be based on financial information submitted in Part IV.

Line 13, $5,000 fees. See Chapter 11§4 before answering this part.

Line 14, Carefully check the blanks on this line, because each "yes" check requires an attached schedule.

(d) Part IV: Financial Data

Section A of Part IV.   *A Statement of Revenue and Expenses* is required for all organizations, both newly formed ones presenting projected or proposed financial data and those having actual financial history. If the information is prepared on a method of accounting other than cash, an explanation is to be attached. Although the instructions to this part do not request details for many of the revenue and expense categories, the author's experience indicates furnishing details avoids requests for them. Keep in mind the successful application paints a picture of the organization in the reviewer's mind. Detailed pricing schedules, circulation and attendance numbers, donations by types of payors (individuals, businesses, governmental grants, private foundations), personnel listings with salary for each position and a brief job description, and contracts proposed for fund-raisers or architects are examples of the kind of details that the IRS routinely requests if they are not furnished. Particularly as it regards compensation for personal services, the more information the better.

Financial information for the current year must end within 60 days of the application date. An organization that has been in existence less than one year should include financial statements to date, plus projected budgets for the next two years. The IRS may request information for up to four years. Depending on the organization's chosen fiscal year, an organization filing on November 1 might include four sets of numbers. For example, an EO chartered on January 1 and choosing a fiscal year ending in June submits the following period of information:

- Column (a) A six month statement as of June 30—the first tax year.

- Column (b) Two month statement for July and August.

- Column (c) Ten month projection ending June 30 of the second year (or for full year).

- Column (d) An additional year's projection.

The arrangement of the lines for reporting the financial information is different from Forms 990 and 990-PF, but the contents are basically the same. Suggestions for choosing the lines on which to input financial information and details to supply follow.[59]

---

[59] Chapter 27 can also be consulted if there is any question about choice of lines.

Line 1, Gifts, grants and contributions received. Income reported on Part I, line 1 of Forms 990, 990-PF, and 990EZ are submitted on this line. No detailed listing of contributors is requested. Unusual grants are reported separately on line 12. For organizations seeking a definitive ruling of their public status based on their sources of support, sufficient details of contributor revenue should be submitted in Part III, lines 13 and 14 to allow the IRS to calculate its qualification. Voluntary submission of expected donors might be advisable for an organization that expects to receive extensive fee for service revenues. The receipt of donative support evidences a charitable project.

Line 2, Membership fees. Amounts paid by members to support the organization are reported on this line. Charges for member services (such as admissions, merchandise, or use of facilities) are included on line 4 or 9, not here. Line 3 of Forms 990 and 990EZ contains the same revenue. The issues discussed under Part II, line 11 and 12 should be revisited for organizations with membership revenue.

Line 3, Gross investment income. Dividends, interest, payments on security loans, rents, and royalties are the common forms of investment income. Interest received for program-related investments, such as student loans, are reported on line 8. This amount equals that reported on lines 4–7 on Form 990, lines 3–5 on Form 990-PF, and line 4 of Form 990EZ.

Line 4, Unrelated business net income. Income from unrelated businesses that are regularly carried on in a businesslike manner and reportable on Form 990-T are included on line 4. If such income is excepted from taxability because it is operated by volunteers, for member convenience, or some other exception, it is not included here but instead on line 8.[60] There is no comparable reporting on Forms 990.

Line 5, Beneficial tax levies. Amounts collected by local tax authorities from the general public and either paid to or spent on behalf of the organization are to be reported here. Schools and human service organizations receive this type of revenue, which is commonly reportable on line 1 of Forms 990 unless the amounts are paid in return for services the organization renders.

Line 6, Governmental unit "in kind" donations. Facilities and services donated to the organization from a governmental unit are reported on this line. Other donations of services and use of facilities are not reported in the financial data.

Line 7, Other income. In the author's experience, an amount is seldom reported on this line. If any amount is reported, it should be described in an attachment.

Line 9, Exempt function income. This line asks for gross receipts (meaning without reduction for related costs) paid to the organization by participants in charitable, educational, or other exempt activities. Student tuition, hospital charges, publication sales, and laboratory fees are good examples. Unlike on Forms 990, nontaxable unrelated business income is also included here. Fund-raising events and projects, raffles, bingo, thrift shop, and other revenue-producing activities are to be recorded here, except for the donation portion that is put on line 1. Although an explanation is not required, the application is more understandable if the details of this revenue are submitted and coordinated with the answer to Part II, line 11a. For example, the description for exempt function might say:

---

[60] See Chapter 21.

Tuition charges from students	$100,000
Sale of textbooks	8,000
Student activity fees	10,000
Laboratory usage fees	5,000
	$123,000

Line 11, Capital gains or losses. Property held by an organization as investment and property used in performing exempt functions constitutes its capital assets. A description of each asset sold, the name of the person to whom it was sold, and the amount received is to be reported in detail for capital transactions. For security sales through a brokerage company, the name of the purchaser is not required. Sales of objects held for resale in both an exempt function and fund-raising context are reported on line 9.

Line 14, Fund-raising expenses. The IRS's concern for this subject is shown by its appearance as the first expense item. Full disclosure of the engagement of a professional including the contract, if there is one, must be disclosed. The IRS will ask what the relationship, if any, of the fund-raiser is to the organization. However, neither Form 990EZ nor 990-PF reflect this amount as a single item. On Form 990, page 1, the direct costs associated with fund-raising events and inventory sales are deducted against the gross revenue to arrive at total revenue on page 1; other fund-raising expenses are displayed in a separate column on page 2. The instructions to this line suggest that "total expenses incurred in soliciting contributions, gifts, grants, etc." be included and logically, cost of goods sold should be included. Such expense could also be reported on line 22.

Line 15, Grants paid. A schedule is to be attached, showing the name of each recipient, a brief description of the purposes or conditions of payment, and the amount paid. If the organization is new and has made no actual payments, the total amount projected to be paid with a reference back to Part II, line 1 (where the grant program is described) may be suitable. If scholarship grants are planned, this information should be coordinated with Schedule H. Similar information is submitted on Forms 990.

Line 16, Disbursements for members. A schedule should be submitted showing the name of each recipient, a brief description of the purposes or conditions of payment, and the amount paid. This category of expense is potentially a red flag area as discussed under Part II, lines 11 and 12. Member benefits that serve a charitable purpose, such as an educational newsletter, go on line 22.

Line 17, Officer, director, and trustee compensation. This line calls for the name of each officer, his or her office or position, the average amount of time devoted to the organization per week or month, and the amount of annual compensation. This information should agree with Part II, line 4b. Not for this purpose, but for Forms 990, fringe benefit and expense account information is to be furnished. The question the IRS is asking on this line is whether the compensation is so excessive as to result in private inurement.

Line 18, Employee salaries. All other compensation paid to persons treated as employees for whom income tax is withheld is to be reported on this line. Consultants, accountants, lawyers, and other independent contractors are reported on line 22, except for fund-raisers reported on line 14. Again, private benefit could be an issue. It is advisable to include a detailed listing of positions with a brief job description and compensation to be paid.

Line 19, Interest expense. Total interest expense, except that reported as occupancy expense because it is paid on a mortgage on the building used by the organization, is reported here. It is unusual for a new organization to have such expense, except for equipment purchases. If interest is paid on a loan from a disqualified person, the organization should explain how the loan serves its exempt purposes. Details of loans are also furnished as an attachment to the balance sheet.

Line 20, Occupancy. The total cost of the physical space occupied by the organization for offices and exempt function activities is to be presented, including rent, mortgage interest, taxes, utilities, maintenance, and other costs of the facilities.

Line 21, Depreciation and depletion. Fixed assets that the organization plans to acquire are not deducted in full. Instead this part reflects depreciation and depletion calculated by the organization for accounting purposes. For a private foundation, this expense may not be shown on page 1 of Form 990-PF because assets purchased for exempt purposes are treated totally as a charitable disbursement in the year acquired. No detail is requested here, but instead should be provided as an attachment to line 8 of the balance sheet.

Line 22, Other. All other "significant" expenses not listed on some other line are to be reported. The instructions suggest that a single total may be reported if the amount is not substantial. In the interest of avoiding questions that may delay the application process, detail is recommended unless the amount is under five percent of the total and is truly miscellaneous. Use page 2 of Form II, Statement of Functional Expenses on Form 990[61] as a guide to the suitable types of expense categories.

Line 24, Excess of revenue over expenses. This excess is not totaled in column (e) because the amounts may include projections as well as actual results. When actual financial results are reported in columns (a)–(d), this bottom line 24 should tie to line 17 of Part IV Section B, or the total fund balance on the balance sheet for the current tax year.

Section B of Part IV. *A Balance Sheet* as of the end of the current tax year is requested. In the example at the beginning of this section, September 30 would be its date. The information is to be presented according to the generally accepted accounting principles used by the organization for maintaining its books and records, although the categories may be different than those reflected on the organization's independent auditor's report. It may also be useful to note that the balance sheet does not segregate assets of an unrelated business activity and instead combines them with investment assets as is customary for financial reporting purposes. A new organization that has not yet begun operation may simply say it has no assets.

Line 1, Cash. All cash assets, including checking, petty cash, savings, money market, and certificates of deposits and U.S. Treasury obligations due in less than one year are included on this line.

Line 2, Accounts receivable. Amounts due to be paid to the organization that arose from the sale of goods or performance of services (related and unrelated) are presented here. For example, a university might report tuition receivable,

---

[61] Shown in Appendix 27–1.

amounts due on a grant paid on a reimbursement basis, accounts receivable for its literary press, football season ticket holder balances, and insurance reimbursements due to the health center. Charitable gifts receivable under a pledge system would be reported on line 10.

Line 3, Inventories. Materials, supplies, and goods purchased or manufactured by the organization and held to be sold or used in some future period are considered inventory. The university's bookstore, science lab, football team, fundraising department, and property management office might all have inventory. Although items that produce both related and unrelated income are reported here, the proceeds of selling them is reportable either on line 4 or 9 of the Statement of Revenue and Expense.

Line 4, 5, and 7, Investments. Organizations owning bonds, notes receivable, stocks, buildings, land, mineral interests, or any other investment assets report them on these lines. Details are requested and in the case of stocks, both the book and fair market value must be reported. The instructions ask for specifics and should be consulted.

Line 6, Loans. Rather innocently, the instructions ask for details about each loan—the borrower's name, purpose of the loan, repayment terms, interest rate, and the original amount of the loan. It does not ask if the lender is a related party; a fact that would be indicated by the director list in Part II, line 4. Related party loans may evidence private inurement and deserve special consideration.

Line 8, Buildings and equipment. Real and tangible personal property not held for investment, but used instead for exempt purposes, is reported here. A detailed list of the assets should be attached, along with the depreciation information to coordinate with line 21 of the Expense Statement.

Line 9, Land. Land held for exempt purposes, not for investment, is presented here. Land purchased for exempt use in the future is included if it is not income producing; otherwise, it would be shown as an investment.

Line 12, Accounts payable. Amounts due to be paid to suppliers and others, such as salaries, accrued payroll taxes, and interest accrued on notes payable are reported here.

Line 13, Grants payable. Commitments for grants and contributions to other organizations and individuals due to be paid in the future and booked under the organization's method of accounting (accrual) are reportable as due to be paid.

Line 14, Mortgages and notes payable. Details including the lender, terms for repayment and interest, purpose of the loan, and the original amount, are called for. This line should be coordinated with line 19 on the Expense Statement and possibly line 8 of Part II.

Line 17, Fund balance or net assets. All of the organization's assets are reported in total on the balance sheet. If the organization uses fund accounting, all funds are combined. Likewise, all cash accounts are reported on line 1 and are not segregated by fund.

(e) Schedules for Certain Organizations

The following types of organizations must answer specific questions to enable IRS specialists to satisfy themselves that the organization can qualify for such a category of (c)(3) exemption.

Schedule A: Churches. To preserve the separation of church and state, churches are granted automatic exemption and actually need not file Form 1023. For groups not formed as a part of the established Judeo-Christian religions, proving that they are a church often requires such filing. This schedule's 19 questions are designed to ascertain whether the church meets the IRS's 14-part test.[62] The questions probe for genuine sacerdotal character and private benefit to the church's creators.

Schedule B: Schools, Colleges, and Universities. The special nondiscriminatory requirements for schools are covered in the ten questions asked on this schedule.

Schedule C: Hospitals and Medical Research Organizations. The rules governing the charitable status of hospitals began to evolve in the late 1980s and are still in a state of flux. The evolving rules are presented in Chapter 4§6. The concerns, as evidenced by the questions, are twofold: provision of health services to the nonpaying public, and private inurement to the physicians. Private benefit in the form of low rents, excessive salaries, or royalties from research patents paid to doctors can prevent exemption, as can profit motive evidenced by lack of indigent care, academic connections, or public interest research.

Schedule D: IRC §509(a)(3) Supporting Organizations. This part seeks information to prove that the requisite control and relationship exist between the newly created organization and the public charity it is organized to support (PSO). The rules for qualification as a supporting organization are complex and the distinctions sometimes unclear, as indicated by the Code designations, which allow three types:[63]

- An EO operated, supervised, or controlled by the PSO;

- An EO supervised or controlled in connection with the PSO; or

- An EO operated in connection with the PSO.

While Form 1023 seeks information to prove the connection, it does not explain why the questions are asked.

Schedule E: Private Operating Foundation. A private operating foundation (POF) is a private foundation (PF) that dedicates its assets and its income to self-initiated projects. The typical PF only makes grants to other organizations. A POF may make direct grants, but only in addition to spending the minimally required amounts on its own activities. A POF endowed with $1 million must spend $33,333 annually on projects it institutes and conducts directly with its own staff and facilities.

Schedule E may be difficult to complete without an understanding of certain terms peculiar to PFs. Study Chapter 15§5 before attempting to calculate the answers. Very generally, a POF must first meet an income test requiring that it spend a minimal amount annually, three and one-third percent of its investment assets, on its direct charitable activities. Secondly, the POF must meet either the asset, endowment, or support test. In brief:

---

[62] Discussed in Chapter 3§2.
[63] Discussed in Chapter 11§6.

- *Asset test:* More than 65% are exempt function assets.

- *Endowment test:* More than $3\frac{1}{3}$ of the average value of investment assets is spent on direct charitable projects.

- *Support test:* More than 25% of support comes from the general public or from five or more other exempts.

Schedule F: Homes for the Aged or Handicapped. This schedule is largely self-explanatory.[64]

Schedule G: Child Care Organizations. Day care centers must generally answer questions 1, 4, and 5 "yes," as explained in Chapter 5§1(c). If the exempt organization concurrently operates a school, it must also complete Schedule B.

Schedule H: Organizations Providing Scholarship Benefits, Student Aid, Etc., to Individuals. Private foundations must obtain advance IRS approval of their scholarships plans.[65] The purpose is to establish that individual grants will be made in an objective and nondiscriminatory manner. The form is designed to ensure that no favoritism is given to certain individuals, particularly not to family members of founders, directors, trustees, or other interested parties. In addition, plans may not discriminate according to race or creed. This schedule is used by new private foundations to seek approval. Although public charities are not required to receive advance permission, they may not make grants that convey private benefit.

Schedule I: Successors to "For Profit" Institutions. A nonprofit organization created to receive the assets and operations of a for-profit entity has the burden of proving that the transfer creates no unacceptable benefits to the for-profit owners. Private benefit may be indicated by the terms of the deal, the price being paid for the predecessor's assets, liabilities being assumed, excessive rental for privately owned facilities or equipment, and other benefits to insiders or controlling individuals. This schedule fishes for such factors.[66]

18.3 FORM 1024: EXEMPTIONS OTHER THAN IRC §501(c)(3)

Form 1024 is filed to seek application for recognition of exemption for organizations exempt under IRC §501 (other than (c)(3)) and IRC §120). The instructions to the form and Part I are almost identical for both applications. The introductory discussion and suggestions in §18.2 regarding Part I should be referred to as an aid in preparation of Form 1024. Due to ongoing IRS reorganizations, instructions for the most recent version of the form should be read to see that applications are still filed in the Cincinnati, Ohio IRS District Office. The current user fees should also be verified.

In Part II, questions 1–5, also explained in §18.2 are basically the same as in Form 1023 except that question 3 is omitted. Again, the reader should obtain a

[64] See Chapter 4§6(d).
[65] IRC §4945(g).
[66] Discussed in Chapter 20§6.

blank copy of the form to read along with this section. The completed Form 1024 of a mock organization, the Disposable Bottle Action Committee, is provided as Appendix 18–2.

(a) Special Aspects of Form 1024

In Part II, beginning with Question 6, there is a perceptible change in tone from Form 1023. The questions begin to probe for information regarding member benefits. Schedules A–M continue to solicit information necessary for qualification for the different types of exempt organizations. The reasons why these questions are asked, and the rules that have been developed by the IRS and the courts in granting exempt status to some of these entities, are discussed in Chapters 6–9. The distinctive issue for a non (c)(3) organization is whether its revenue sources indicate whether it serves its members as its primary function, rather than nonmembers. The reader can also study the parts of IRS Publication 557, *Tax-Exempt Status for your Organization,* applicable to the particular type of exempt organization for which the application is being prepared.

 With Form 1024, it is again important to paint a complete picture of the organization and its proposed activities. Membership solicitation materials, brochures, and newsletters are requested as evidence of how the organization presents itself to the public. Such materials should be prepared with a view toward depicting the proposed organization comprehensively and accurately. The financial data is to be presented in a similar manner to that required for Form 1023. Consult §18.2(d) for suggestions on completion of this part.

(b) Timing

Exempt status for organizations filing Form 1024 does *not* depend on when the form is filed. The critical need for (c)(3) organizations to file Form 1023 in a timely manner, explained in §18.1, is absent here, because qualification is based on meeting the definitions in the tax code, regulations, and applicable rulings and court cases. If an exempt organization meets the requirements for any category, exempt status is automatically granted with no action on the organization's part. There is no deadline for filing Form 1024.

(c) Evidence of Exemption

As a practical matter, even though exemption for non-(c)(3)s is automatic without action on the organization's part, many choose to request a determination letter from the IRS to remove any uncertainty. Particularly when an organization plans to enter into unrelated business activity or projects that might be questioned by the IRS, it is prudent to settle the questions early in the life of the organization. Also, filing Form 990 triggers a request for an exemption application.

 Some states also rely on the federal determination letter to grant exemption for income, franchise, sales, or other tax purposes. Having the federal letter also makes U.S. Postal Service nonprofit bulk mailing permits easier to obtain.

18.4   GETTING A POSITIVE IRS DETERMINATION

Once Form 1023 or 1024 is completed with adequate information to allow the IRS to evaluate qualification, the next requirement is patience. It normally requires 80 to 120 days to receive a determination letter. If the examining specialist questions any of the facts or circumstances or denies the organization's eligibility for exemption, some methods of responding are more effective than others.

(a) Application Processing System

An IRS notice of receipt, Form 5548 (Exhibit 18–3), may be expected to arrive a month to six weeks from the date of original filing. A case number and contact person are assigned, and an estimated time the case will take to process is provided in the notice of receipt. Subsequent inquiries about the application should be referenced with the case number. Failure to receive such notice means that something is amiss and the Cincinnati District Office should be contacted particularly if timely filing might be an issue. The toll-free telephone at time of writing was (877) 829-5500. At this point, the case has not been assigned to a particular technical specialist.

(b) Best Case Scenario

In the best case scenario, a determination letter (Exhibit 18–4) is received within the processing time. This letter may be the single most important piece of paper an exempt organization possesses. It is often the document furnished to state and local authorities to obtain their recognition of tax exemption. Without it, contributions for (c)(3)s from some sources such as private foundations, are difficult if not impossible. Obtaining a replacement copy can be a time-consuming process.

(c) When Questions Are Asked

IRS exempt organization specialists often seek additional information through standard letter 1312 (Exhibit 18–5). Nonsubstantive amendments are often made during this time and do not alter the effective date of the application in most cases.[67] For example, the agent might recommend one of the following tactics:

- Amend the charter's dissolution or purpose clause to specifically name IRC §501(c)(3) in order to restrict distributions and activities to (c)(3) purposes. In some states, the standard nonprofit charter acceptable to the state does not contain this restriction distinction, which is necessary to meet the federal requirements. Review Chapter 2§1 concerning charter requirements for (c)(3)s and Chapters 6 through 9 for other types of exempt organizations.

- Change the public status category from §509(a)(2) to §509(a)(1), or vice versa. The IRS policy is to grant §509(a)(1) status in all cases when the organization qualifies for both types of public status. See Chapter 11 for the details of these categories.

[67] Rev. Proc. 90-27, 1990-1 C.B. 514; IRS Pub. 557 (revised May 1997) page 4.

Exhibit 18–3

IRS LETTER FORM 5548: NOTICE OF RECEIPT

Internal Revenue Service   Department of the Treasury
District Director   Southeast Region
Internal Revenue Service Center   F - 5548' 'ALS
P.O. Box 2508   **Refer Reply To:**
Cincinnati OH 45201   1733131004 :JT/67

Date: March 4, 1997

Campaign to Clean Up America
1111 Any Street
Hometown, TX 77777

Re:

        Document Locator Number: 11111- 111- 11111- 1
              User Fee Paid: $ 465

ACKNOWLEDGEMENT OF YOUR REQUEST

We have received your application for recognition of exemption from Federal income tax and have assigned it document locator number 11111 -111 -11111 -1. You should refer to that number in any communication with us concerning your application.

We will review your application and send a reply as soon as possible. However, we must process applications in the order that we receive them.

You may normally expect to hear from us within (120 days). If you do not hear from us within that period and choose to write again, please include a copy of this letter with your correspondence. Also, please provide a telephone number and the most convenient time to call if we need to contact you. If you wish, you may call E. Wolf between the hours of 7:00 a.m. and 3:30 p.m. Eastern Standard Time at (513) 684-3957 for assistance.

Thank you for your cooperation.

Form 5548 EOP ALS

Exhibit 18–4

IRS LETTER FORM 1045: DETERMINATION LETTER

INTERNAL REVENUE SERVICE   DEPARTMENT OF THE TREASURY
DISTRICT DIRECTOR
P. O. BOX 2508
CINCINNATI, OH 45201

Employer Identification Number:
Date: APR 13 1998   44-4444444

DLN:

Campaign to Clean Up America   17053357081007
1111 Any Street   Contact Person:
Hometown, TX 77777   D. A. DOWNING
      Contact Telephone Number:
      (513) 241-5199
      Accounting Period Ending:
      December 31
      Foundation Status
      Classification:
      509(a)(1)
      Advance Ruling Period Begins:
      December 15, 1997
      Advance Ruling Period Ends:
      December 31, 2001
      Addendum Applies:
      No

Dear Applicant:

Based on information you supplied, and assuming your operations will be as stated in your application for recognition of exemption, we have determined you are exempt from federal income tax under section 501(a) of the Internal Revenue Code as an organization described in section 501(c)(3).

Accordingly, during an advance ruling period you will be treated as a publicly supported organization, and not as a private foundation. This advance ruling period begins and ends on the dates shown above.

Within 90 days after the end of your advance ruling period, you must send us the information needed to determine whether you have met the requirements of the applicable support test during the advance ruling period. If you establish that you have been a publicly supported organization, we will classify you as a section 509(a)(1) or 509(a)(2) organization as long as you continue to meet the requirements of the applicable support test. If you do not meet the public support requirements during the advance ruling period, we will

---

Exhibit 18–4 (*continued*)

classify you as a private foundation for future periods. Also, if we classify you as a private foundation, we will treat you as a private foundation from your beginning date for purposes of section 507(d) and 4940.

Grantors and contributors may rely on our determination that you are not a private foundation until 90 days after the end of your advance ruling period. If you send us the required information within the 90 days, grantors and contributors may continue to rely on the advance determination until we make a final determination of your foundation status.

If we publish a notice in the Internal Revenue Bulletin stating that we will no longer treat you as a publicly supported organization, grantors and contributors may not rely on this determination after the date we publish the notice. In addition, if you lose your status as a publicly supported organization, and a grantor or contributor was responsible for, or was aware of, the act or failure to act, that resulted in your loss of such status, that person may not rely on this determination from the date of the act or failure to act. Also, if a grantor or contributor learned that we had given notice that you would be removed from classification as a publicly supported organization, then that person may not rely on this determination as of the date he or she acquired such knowledge.

If you change your sources of support, your purposes, character, or method of operation, please let us know so we can consider the effect of the change on your exempt status and foundation status. If you amend your organizational document or bylaws, please send us a copy of the amended document or bylaws. Also, let us know all changes in your name or address.

As of January 1, 1984, you are liable for social security taxes under the Federal Insurance Contributions Act on amounts of $100 or more you pay to each of your employees during a calendar year. You are not liable for the tax imposed under the Federal Unemployment Tax Act (FUTA).

Organizations that are not private foundations are not subject to the private foundation excise taxes under Chapter 42 of the Internal Revenue Code. However, you are not automatically exempt from other federal excise taxes. If you have any questions about excise, employment, or other federal taxes, please let us know.

Donors may deduct contributions to you as provided in section 170 of the Internal Revenue Code. Bequests, legacies,

Exhibit 18–4 (*continued*)

devises, transfers, or gifts to you or for your use are deductible for Federal estate and gift tax purposes if they meet the applicable provisions of sections 2055, 2106, and 2522 of the Code.

Donors may deduct contributions to you only to the extent that their contributions are gifts, with no consideration received. Ticket purchases and similar payments in conjunction with fundraising events may not necessarily qualify as deductible contributions, depending on the circumstances. Revenue Ruling 67-246, published in Cumulative Bulletin 1967-2, on page 104, gives guidelines regarding when taxpayers may deduct payments for admission to, or other participation in, fundraising activities for charity.

You are not required to file Form 990, Return of Organization Exempt From Income Tax, if your gross receipts each year are normally $25,000 or less. If you receive a Form 990 package in the mail, simply attach the label provided, check the box in the heading to indicate that your annual gross receipts are normally $25,000 or less, and sign the return.

If a return is required, it must be filed by the 15th day of the fifth month after the end of your annual accounting period. A penalty of $20 a day is charged when a return is filed late, unless there is reasonable cause for the delay. However, the maximum penalty charged cannot exceed $10,000 or 5 percent of your gross receipts for the year, whichever is less. For organizations with gross receipts exceeding $1,000,000 in any year, the penalty is $100 per day per return, unless there is reasonable cause for the delay. The maximum penalty for an organization with gross receipts exceeding $1,000,000 shall not exceed $50,000. This penalty may also be charged if a return is not complete. So, please be sure your return is complete before you file it.

You are not required to file federal income tax returns unless you are subject to the tax on unrelated business income under section 511 of the Code. If you are subject to this tax, you must file an income tax return on Form 990-T, Exempt Organization Business Income Tax Return. In this letter we are not determining whether any of your present or proposed activities are unrelated trade or business as defined in section 513 of the Code.

You are required to make your annual return available for public inspection for three years after the return is due. You are also required to make available a copy of your exemption application, any supporting documents, and this

Exhibit 18–4 (*continued*)

exemption letter. Failure to make these documents available for public inspection may subject you to a penalty of $20 per day for each day there is a failure to comply (up to a maximum of $10,000 in the case of an annual return).

You need an employer identification number even if you have no employees. If an employer identification number was not entered on your application, we will assign a number to you and advise you of it. Please use that number on all returns you file and in all correspondence with the Internal Revenue Service.

Revenue Ruling 77-208, published in Cumulative Bulletin 1977-1, on page 153, states that if an organization does not apply within 15 months of its formation, we will not consider financial information for the period prior to the application date in determining an organization's private foundation status. Accordingly, your advance ruling covers the period beginning and ending on the advance ruling period dates shown in the heading of this letter. Contributions by donors would be deductible beginning December 15, 1997.

You have agreed on your application for exemption under section 501(c)(3) of the Code that your exemption is effective December 15, 1997, the date your completed application was filed.

This determination is based on evidence that your funds are dedicated to the purposes listed in section 501(c)(3) of the Code. To assure your continued exemption, you should keep records to show that funds are spent only for those purposes. If you distribute funds to other organizations, your records should show whether they are exempt under section 501(c)(3). In cases where the recipient organization is not exempt under section 501(c)(3), you must have evidence that the funds will remain dedicated to the required purposes and that the recipient will use the funds for those purposes.

If you distribute funds to individuals, you should keep case histories showing the recipients' names, addresses, purposes of awards, manner of selection, and relationship (if any) to members, officers, trustees or donors of funds to you, so that you can substantiate upon request by the Internal Revenue Service any and all distributions you made to individuals. (Revenue Ruling 56-304, C.B. 1956-2, page 306.)

If we said in the heading of this letter that an addendum applies, the addendum enclosed is an integral part of this letter.

Exhibit 18–4 (*continued*)

Because this letter could help us resolve any questions about your exempt status and foundation status, you should keep it in your permanent records.

We have sent a copy of this letter to your representative as indicated in your power of attorney.

If you have any questions, please contact the person whose name and telephone number are shown in the heading of this letter.

Sincerely yours,

District Director

Enclosure(s):
Form 872-C

Exhibit 18–5

IRS LETTER FORM 1312: REQUEST FOR INFORMATION

DISTRICT DIRECTOR
P.O. BOX 2508
CINCINNATI, OH 45201

Date: June 10, 1998

Campaign to Clean Up America
1111 Any Street
Hometown, TX 77777

Please reply to:
  INTERNAL REVENUE SERVICE
  ROOM 105-EO 7202
  20719 WATERTOWN ROAD
  WAUKESHA, WI 53186
Employer Identification
Number:
  44-4444444
Contact Person:
  JULIA WIECZOREK
Contact Telephone Number:
  (414) 798-8320
Response Due Date:
  July 03, 1998

Dear Applicant:

Before we can recognize your organization as being exempt from Federal income tax, we must have enough information to show that you have met all legal requirements. You did not include the information needed to make that determination on your Form 1023, Application for Recognition of Exemption Under Section 501(c)(3) of the Internal Revenue Code.

We will be glad to consider your application when you submit the items listed on the attached sheet by the Response Due Date shown above. An extension of time to submit the requested information may be granted for good cause. If you need an extension, you must request it before the response due date.

If we do not hear from you within that time, we will assume you do not want us to consider the matter further and will close your case. In accordance with Code section 6104(c), we will notify the appropriate state officials that we are unable to recognize you as an organization described in Code section 501(c)(3). Your user fee payment will be forfeited after 90 days and another fee will be required if you wish to re-apply at a later date.

In addition, if you do not provide the requested information in a timely manner, we will consider that you have not taken all reasonable steps to secure the determination you requested. Under Code section 7428(b)(2), this may be considered as failure to exhaust administrative remedies available to you within the Service and you may lose your rights to a declaratory judgement under Code Section 7428.

Exhibit 18–5 (*continued*)

If you have any questions, please contact the person whose name and telephone number are shown in the heading of this letter.

Thank you for your cooperation.

Sincerely yours,
Julia Wieczorek
Exempt Organizations
Specialist
Letter 1312 (DC/PL)

The copy of your Articles of Amendment submitted with your application does not bear evidence that the document was filed and approved by the Secretary of State. Please send us a copy which shows the "FILED" stamp of the Secretary of State and the date of filing.

Please submit copies of any grant applications and indicate their status.

Please provide a proposed budget for 1998 and 1999.

Please submit a breakdown and explanation of the following amounts shown on Page 8 of the application for 1996 and 1997:

-line 14: Development & Outreach

One of the documents submitted with your application is a resolution to create an objective commission to recommend revision of the U.S. environmental laws. Will your organization promote this resolution or similar resolutions in the future?

How will your organization account for any direct lobbying or grassroots expenditures? For your convenience I am enclosing Publication 557 which has additional information on lobbying expenditures.

Please send correspondence to the address shown below:

INTERNAL REVENUE SERVICE
ROOM 105-EO 7202
20719 WATERTOWN ROAD
WAUKESHA, WI 53186

Letter 1312 (DC/PL)

- Reclassify sources of support to reflect the deductibility of fund-raising revenues. See Chapter 24.

- Change level of lobbying activity planned and propose classification as a (c)(4) rather than a (c)(3) organization. See Chapter 23.

(d) Eligibility for Exemption Questioned

What if the IRS questions the application? It is extremely important to request the "basis in law" for suggestions made by the EO specialists. It is useful to realize the published revenue rulings issued in the 1960s and 1970s and still **precedential** in making IRS determinations are sometimes not relevant to a contemporary situation. A specialist's personal bias and experiences may also play a part in their opinions. For example, if it is suggested the organization should have independent outsiders (not staff) on the board, ask for a citation to IRS procedures or policy. Question why an artists' press must satisfy the requirements found in a revenue ruling pertaining to a spiritual publishing company? Why does a discussion group have to meet the qualifications for a school? Why cannot the organization question the policy of the president sending troops to fight in a foreign land?

Consider seeking the assistance of a knowledgeable professional if the exempt organization is unwilling to make a change or is skeptical about the need for the change. If funds are not available to hire a professional, a volunteer may be found through a public service agency. While most IRS EO specialists are well trained, helpful, and cooperative, the organization seeking exemption must remember that the rules are broad and vague. The specialists apply published revenue rulings to judge the newly established organization, even though it is unique and distinguishable. In these cases, the organization may find knowledgeable advisers particularly useful.

If the examiner suggests a negative answer, submit a brief indicating the reasons and citing authority for the position that the organization should be exempt. Before an adverse determination is issued, the case will be reviewed. The brief can make it easier for the specialist's superior to overturn the recommendation for denial.

The policies followed by the examiners are contained in IRS Manual 7751: *Exempt Organizations Handbook,* Manual 7752: *Private Foundations Handbook,* and the annual *Exempt Organizations Continuing Professional Educational Technical Instruction Program.*

Occasionally, the Key District specialist is unable to consider an application and will refer it to the national office for determination. Such a referral is made automatically for any type of organization whose exempt status is pending in litigation or is under consideration within the IRS. In the past, hospital reorganizations, publications with advertising, mail-order churches, and other controversial exemptions have been sent to Washington.

(e) Disputed Cases

When the IRS specialist cannot make a favorable determination, there are a number of steps an organization can take. The choice of alternatives is guided primarily by the strength of the case. If the organization clearly qualifies for exemption, but the facts and circumstances are apparently being misunderstood by the examining agent, an appeal may be indicated.

Appeal. Allow the examiner to issue an adverse report denying exemption and follow the appeal procedure. A protest of the determination may be filed within 30 days from the date of the adverse letter. Request a conference in the Appeals Office. See IRS Publication 557, page 3, for more information, and seek competent counsel. Proper appeal procedures must be followed to be able later, if desired, to file an appeal in court.

Amend. If the reasons for denial are curable and negotiations remain amicable, the organization can request (or the IRS may offer) the opportunity to amend the application, altering planned projects or fund-raising activities to eliminate the ones not considered appropriate for a tax-exempt organization. Usually, the EO examiner gives the organization 60 to 90 days to reform itself and essentially resubmit the application. When the organization has already commenced operations and the changes are substantive, the exemption may be granted only prospectively, from the effective date of the changes in operations.

Withdraw. An application can be withdrawn at any time before issuance or denial of a determination letter. The effects of withdrawing an application are outlined by the IRS under three different scenarios. As a rule, the withdrawal cancels previous notice, the time period prior to withdrawal is lost, and a resubmitted application is treated as a new filing, so that exemption will be effective prospectively from the date of resubmission.[68] The IRS considered the following possibilities:

- *Scenario 1.* Form 1023 seeking §501(c)(3) status is filed 10 months after the organization is created, but is withdrawn. Two years later it is re-organized, the application is resubmitted, asserting that the organization had operated as exempt from "day one" and, therefore, that exemption should be allowed from the original date of filing.

- *Scenario 2.* Same facts as Scenario 1, except upon withdrawal, the organization requests classification as a §501(c)(4) from date of formation through date of resubmission.

- *Scenario 3.* A subordinate member of a group exemption withdraws from the group and, within fifteen months of withdrawal, submits an independent application.

In the first scenario, under the old rules, exemption was effective only from the date of resubmission. Due to the automatic extension policy,[69] a resubmission within 27 months of the organization's creation can be granted retroactively. The second example now applies for organizations resubmitting 27 months beyond date of organization. In the third scenario, exemption is effective from the original inclusion in a group continuing on with new timely filing when such notice was required.

Withdrawal may be appropriate when an organization has failed to file income tax or other returns that were required of it as a nonexempt organization.

---

[68] Rev. Rul. 90-100, 1990-2 C.B. 156.
[69] Discussed in §18.1(b).

Upon withdrawal, it has not been customary for notification to be made to the Internal Revenue Service Center. Upon denial, however, the center is notified. Procedurally, it is desirable to voluntarily file delinquent returns and to request relief from any penalties for failure to file, rather than being notified of the need to file.

A principal officer or representative with a power of attorney must make a written withdrawal request. No information submitted to the IRS will be returned but it can be used by the IRS in any subsequent examination of the organization's returns or requests.

(f) Declaratory Judgment

When all administrative remedies have been exhausted in negotiating a positive determination of exempt status and the IRS persists in denying exemption, a declaratory judgment may be requested with the assistance of a qualified attorney. See IRS Publication 556 for appeals to the courts. It is important to remember that the correct steps must be taken first, and court is the last resort.

18.5 ADVANCE VERSUS DEFINITIVE RULINGS

In response to a Form 1023 or 1024 application, the IRS determines whether the organizational and operational plans of organization entitle it to be classified as an exempt organization. For Form 1023 filers, a determination is also made as to whether the exempt organization is a public charity or a private foundation. Public status is based either on the organization's sources of support and revenue, or its activities. Churches, schools, hospitals, and certain types of charities listed in Part III, line 9 of Form 1023 qualify as public due to their activities without regard to their support sources. For public status due to sources of support, either a definitive or an advance determination is made by the IRS.

(a) Definitive Ruling

A definitive, or final, determination as to public status for a charitable organization listed in §§170(b)(1)(A)(i)-(v) and 509(a)(3)—a church, school, hospital, governmental unit, or supporting organization—can be made before the organization has any financial activity based on the nature of its activity. Those organizations classified as public charities for reasons of their sources of support can only be issued a final determination after they have completed a tax year of at least eight months.[70] The choice of fiscal year is therefore important for an organization seeking advance determination based on sources of support. For example, an entity incorporated in June that adopts a year ending December 31 cannot seek a definitive ruling if it files before its next succeeding year-end. It would have to choose a year ending between December and April to receive a definitive ruling. Such an organization can subsequently change its tax year if necessary, according to the rules set out in Chapter 28.

Second, the organization's sources of support and revenue and activities must be clearly and unquestionably suitable for public status. If the ratios are too

---

[70] Instruction to Form 1023, Part III, line 10, at pg. 6.

close or if fund-raising plans are insufficient, the IRS may prefer to make the tentative, or advance, ruling. A final determination is only effective so long as the organization's sources of support continue to provide it with the requisite 1/3 ratio. A continuing four-year moving average of support is calculated annually throughout the organization's life when it files Form 990. There is essentially a two-year time lag between the year the ratio is deficient and the year the organization becomes classified as a private charity. As more thoroughly explained in Chapter 11§§2 and 4, public support status for the current year is based on the next preceding year's ratio. Except for a contributor or grantor that has reason to know their support will cause loss of public status, donors are entitled to rely upon the IRS determination of public charity status until notice of the change is published in the *Internal Revenue Bulletin*.

(b) Advance Ruling

An advance determination is a final determination as to operations and structure, but is tentative as to public versus private foundation status. An advance ruling is effective for the exempt organization's first five tax years.[71] For all purposes, the exempt organization is considered a public charity during the advance period. Contributors who were not in a position to know that the exempt organization would not qualify for public status are entitled to calculate their income tax deductions based on public status.[72] Eligibility for advance determination is indicated by two very different factors.

1. First tax year is less than eight months.

2. Contributions and activities during start-up phase.

The information furnished to the IRS for the newly created organization must indicate that the organization can reasonably be expected to meet the public support tests. The "pertinent facts and circumstances taken into account by the IRS" include:

- *Composition of governing body.* Is the board made up of persons representing a broad segment of the community in which the charity is organized? Does it include persons having specialized knowledge relevant to the organization's activities? Is the entity a membership organization anticipating a broad base of individual members? A small board made up of major donors indicates private status.

- *Initial funding.* Will the organization's initial funding come from a few contributors or from many? Are the anticipated projects the type that will attract a broad base of support, or are they attractive only to a few contributors? Initial funding from only a few contributors must be offset with anticipated public appeal.

---

[71] Reg. §1.509(a)-3(d). The regulation provides for a two year advance period because it was adopted prior to passage of the Deficit Reduction Act of 1984, by which Congress extended the period to five years.
[72] Reg. §1.509(a)(3)(e)(2).

- *Fund-raising plans.* Are concrete solicitation programs implemented or anticipated to reach a broad group of contributors? Are there firm funding commitments from or working relationships established with civic, religious, charitable, or similar community groups?

- *Government or public grants.* Will part of the revenue be received from governmental agencies or public charities in support of its community services, such as slum clearance and employment opportunity programs?

- *Membership dues.* Will the organization enroll a substantial number of persons in a community, area, profession, or field of special interest as contributing members?

- *Exempt function revenues.* Does the organization plan to conduct exempt activities for which it will charge, such as theater performances, job counseling, or educational classes?[73]

(c) Reporting Back to the IRS

It is important to emphasize the temporary nature of an advance determination, because failure to report at the end of the advance period results in reclassification as a private foundation. An EO holding an advance recognition as a public charity must report back to the district director's office in charge of determinations at the end of its first five years of operation. Under current rules, the EO is to report within 90 days of an advance determination's ending date. Since this step is critical to ongoing public status, this filing deadline should be verified and noted on a responsible person's calendar.

Adequate revenue information must be submitted to show whether it has gained the requisite base of public support to receive a final determination of its non-PF status. If the amounts of contributions or exempt function revenues are sufficient, the IRS issues a definitive or permanent ruling. Chapter 11 describes the various types of revenues qualifying as public support in detail.

In a 1990 report entitled "Tax Administration: IRS Can Improve Its Process of Recognizing Tax-Exempt Organizations," the General Accounting Office (GAO) suggested that the IRS expand its advance ruling follow-ups to include consideration of activities.[74] The GAO report criticizes the IRS for making no effort to look at the manner in which the charities use their support, and recommends that the advance ruling process be expanded to include a review of activities. The GAO observed that "the expenditures data as well as revenue data could provide IRS insight into whether the organization is fulfilling its exempt purpose and whether there are other potential issues, such as private inurement or unreported unrelated business income." To date this recommendation has not been followed.

(d) Failure to Meet Support Tests

If the exempt organization fails to meet the public support tests and is reclassified as a private foundation after its advance period, it must pay the excise tax on in-

---

[73] Reg. §1.509(a)-3(d)(3).
[74] GAO/GGD-90-55 (1990).

vestment income, plus interest, for income earned during the advance ruling period. Even if the organization receives sufficient public support, failure to report back to the Key District can cause the organization to be reclassified as a private foundation unless relief is allowed for reasonable causes. In such a circumstance, the public entity would have to apply to terminate its private foundation status, according to the procedures discussed in Chapter 12§4.

18.6 RELIANCE ON DETERMINATION LETTER

After a positive determination letter is issued, the exempt organization can rely on the IRS's approval of its exempt status as long as there are no substantial changes in its purposes, operations, or character. Absent such changes, the IRS can only revoke exemption due to changes in the law or other good causes, and usually can do so only prospectively. Thus, it is very important that Form 1023 accurately portray the proposed operations. Now that the filing deadline is essentially 27 months from the date an exempt organization is established, it may sometimes be useful to delay filing until adequate plans are developed to file an accurate application—if collection of revenues from donors can await the delay.

Contributors, however, cannot necessarily rely upon the IRS's original determination of overall exempt status and qualification for public charity status dated sometime in the past. A critical question for givers and grant makers to publicly supported §501(c)(3)s, particularly private foundations, is whether an organization's status is the same as originally stated in its determination letter. Has a publicly supported organization become a private foundation?

(a) Checking Current Status

Current status must be checked in two different IRS publications. The first place to check on the status of a (c)(3) organization is the IRS master list of exempt organizations, Publication 78, *Cumulative List of Organizations Described in IRC §170(c) of the Internal Revenue Code of 1986.* This publication lists all organizations currently qualifying under IRC §501(c)(3) and indicates their public or private status. The list is issued annually with semiannual updates and includes organizations qualifying according to the IRS master file. The list is also available on the IRS website at *www.irs.ustreas.gov.*

The second place to check is the *Internal Revenue Bulletin.* Revocation of exemption and removal from the list is reported to the general public in this weekly bulletin in a deletions list. Until the IRS communicates a deletion, contributors are entitled to rely upon Publication 78 unless the contributor was responsible for or aware of the organization's loss of such status.[75] When the IRS failed to publish notice in the Bulletin when it revoked a school's exemption, the Tax Court ruled that mere omission of the school's name from Publication 78 was sufficient notice.[76]

It is important to remember that the reliance cushion is different for insiders or donors who are in a position to be aware of organizational changes. For them,

---

[75] Rev. Proc. 82-39, 1982-17 I.R.B. 18; Reg. §1.170A-9(e)(5).
[76] *Estate of Sally H. Clopton,* 93 T.C. 25 (1989).

the change in status is effective retroactively to the time the change occurred. A private foundation making a grant to another organization whose revocation has not been announced can rely upon the determination letter, unless the public charity is controlled by the PF.[77]

(b) Names Missing from Publication 78

Absence from the list does not necessarily mean that the entity has lost its exempt status. The IRS in the past automatically excluded organizations that have not filed annual Form 990s (for two years). This policy omits a significant group of charities, including churches and their affiliates, state colleges and universities, and those not technically required to file Form 990 because their annual gross revenue is under $25,000. The United States Catholic Conference and some state universities, among others, have specifically sought group exemptions, despite the fact that filing is not required, to ensure their inclusion in Publication 78.

Individuals and organizations must complete a thorough investigation of a proposed grant recipient's tax status and cannot rely totally upon inclusion in or exclusion from Publication 78. The IRS has reinforced its policy that omission from Publication 78 is sufficient notice of loss of exemption. The omission of nonfilers may continue as well as other errors of omission or name changes, leaving the burden to prove exempt status on each individual organization.[78]

(c) Contact the IRS

A call to the IRS EP/EO Group in Cincinnati Ohio at (877) 829-5500 (toll free) or (513) 241-5199 may yield an answer. This number reaches a customer service representative who has the ability to look up an organization on the master list. Knowing the federal identification number of the organizations makes the process easy. Name searches do not always yield the right answer due to the alphabetizing method or some change in the name since recognition.

An organization that has lost its determination letter or has one evidencing an expired advance ruling period can also call to request verification of its continued exempt status. See Chapter 28 for more information regarding communication with the IRS, when to report back to the IRS, and the consequences to donors and tax filing status of an organization that loses its exemption.

18.7 STATE TAX EXEMPTIONS

Many states allow exemption from some or all of their income, franchise, licensing fees, property, sales, or other taxes to religious, charitable, and educational organizations and other §501(c) organizations. The process for obtaining such exemptions varies with each state and locality. Each new exempt organization should obtain current information and forms directly from the appropriate state or local authorities.

---

[77] Rev. Proc. 89-23, 1989-1 C.B. 844.
[78] Gen. Coun. Memo. 39809.

By way of example, in Texas the state filing schedule starts when a nonprofit charter is filed with the Secretary of State. There is no filing or registration for trusts or unincorporated associations. A status report is next filed with the Comptroller of Public Accounts, indicating which category of federal exemption is being sought. No formal application process is required for exemption. State exemption is automatically granted when the exempt organization furnishes a copy of its federal exemption to the comptroller's office. The organization may furnish a copy of its completed Form 1023 and a letter requesting state exemption, if it desires state recognition prior to receiving the federal approval. Sample letters to and from the comptroller are shown in Exhibits 18–6 and 18–7.

The effective date of Texas sales and franchise tax exemption is the date of qualification for §501(c) exemption. If the federal exemption process is delayed one year, a franchise tax may be due to be filed. That tax is refundable once the exemption is approved.

Two significant cases have considered eligibility for exemption from local sales taxes. The Supreme Court decided in *Jimmy Swaggart Ministries v. Board of Equalization of California*[79] that a sales tax could be imposed upon the sale of religious articles if it is equally imposed on other nonprofit organizations. The arguments focused primarily upon the First Amendment protection of the free exercise of religion.

In *Texas Monthly, Inc. v. Bullock,* the Supreme Court held that state sales tax exemption for religious publications violates the establishment clause of the First Amendment when religious organizations are the only beneficiaries of the exemption.

Local property tax exemptions may also be available. Some (but not all) §501(c)(3) organizations qualify under the Texas Property Tax Code for exemption, for example. YWCAs and YMCAs have faced challenges to their local property tax exemptions in California and in Oregon, with conflicting results. The primary issue has been the level of free services furnished to the needy. In Utah, a hospital system conglomerate's local property tax exemption was revoked. Tax authorities in Pennsylvania tried to revoke property tax exemptions for private colleges.

Charitable solicitation registration is required in certain municipalities and states, as discussed in Chapter 24.

---

[79] January 17, 1990.

Exhibit 18–6

SAMPLE LETTER TO THE COMPTROLLER

July 21, 1998

Ms. Judy Evanicky
Comptroller of Public Accounts
Exempt Organizations Section
State of Texas
Austin, Texas 78774

      Re: Campaign to Clean Up America
              44-4444444
              Classification: 501(c)(3)

Dear Ms. Evanicky:

On behalf of our client, we are writing to inform you that the Campaign to Clean Up America is organized and operated for charitable purposes and has received a determination of exemption from federal income tax as an organization defined under Internal Revenue Code 501(c)(3) as of April 13, 1998. A copy of the Internal Revenue Service determination letter is enclosed for your reference.

We respectfully request that you issue the Campaign to Clean Up America an exemption from the Texas sales, excise, and use tax pursuant to Section 151.310 of the Texas Tax Code and also that you recognize the organization as exempt from franchise tax pursuant to Section 171.063 of the Texas Tax Code.

Thank you for your consideration. If we can furnish any additional information, please call on us.

Sincerely,

Gabriele Schweigart

Enclosure

cc:

Exhibit 18–7

SAMPLE LETTER FROM THE COMPTROLLER

COMPTROLLER OF PUBLIC ACCOUNTS
STATE OF TEXAS
AUSTIN, TEXAS 78774-0100

August 4, 1998

Gabriele Schweigart
Blazek & Vetterling, LLP
3101 Richmond, Ste. 220
Houston, TX 77098-3013

Dear Ms. Schweigart:

I am pleased to report that Campaign to Clean Up America, Taxpayer No. 1- 11111- 111 -1, qualifies for exemption from the franchise tax as a 501(c)(3) organization effective March 5, 1998. Since the account is in the process of being updated, you should disregard any franchise tax notices for periods covered by the exemption. In the event we have reason to believe the organization no longer qualifies for exemption, we will notify the registered agent that the exempt status is under review.

This corporation also qualifies for exemption from the state and local sales taxes effective March 5, 1998, as a 501(c)(3) organization. It may now issue an exemption certificate instead of paying the sales tax on taxable items if they relate to the purpose of the exempt organization and are not used for the personal benefit of a private stockholder or individual. The certificate does not require a number to be valid and may be reproduced in any quantity.

If the organization makes any sales of taxable items or services, please contact our Tax Assistance Section at 1-800-252-5555 to determine if a sales tax permit is needed. The regular number is 512/463-4600.

If the organization changes its name, registered agent or registered office address, it is required to notify the Secretary of State.

If you have any questions, please call me toll free at 1-800-531-5441, extension 3-4726. My direct number is 512/463-4726.

Sincerely,
Judy Evanicky
Exempt Organizations Section

SM/74

Appendix 18–1

FORM 1023

Form **1023** (Rev. September 1998) Department of the Treasury Internal Revenue Service	**Application for Recognition of Exemption Under Section 501(c)(3) of the Internal Revenue Code**	OMB NO. 1545-0056 If exempt status is approved, this application will be open for public inspection.

Read the instructions for each Part carefully.
A User Fee must be attached to this application.
If the required information and appropriate documents are not submitted along with Form 8718 (with payment of the
appropriate user fee), the application may be returned to you.
Complete the Procedural Checklist on page 8 of the Instructions.

Part I   Identification of Applicant

1a Full name of organization (as shown in organizing document) **Active Projects Fund**		**2** Employer identification number (EIN) (If none, see page 3 of the instructions) **33-3333333**
1b c/o Name (if applicable)		**3** Name and telephone number of person to be contacted if additional information is needed
1c Address (number and street) **1111 Any Street**	Room/Suite	**A. Good Accountant (444)222-3333**
1d City, town, or post office, state, and ZIP + 4. If you have a foreign address, see Specific Instructions for Part I, page 3. **Hometown, Texas 77777-7777**		**4** Month the annual accounting period ends **June**
		5 Date incorporated or formed **01-29-99**

1e Web site address
www.betternpos.org

6   Check here if applying under section:
501(e) [ ]   501(f) [ ]   501(k) [ ]   501(n) [ ]

7 Did the organization previously apply for recognition of exemption under this Code section or under any
other section of the Code? . . . . Yes [ ]   No [X]
If "Yes," attach an explanation.

8 Is the organization required to file Form 990 (or Form 990-EZ)? . . . . [ ] N/A   Yes [X]   No [ ]
If "No," attach an explanation (see instructions).

9 Has the organization filed Federal income tax returns or exempt organization information returns? . . . . Yes [ ]   No [X]
If "Yes," state the form numbers, years filed, and Internal Revenue office where filed.

10 Check the box for the type of organization. ATTACH A CONFORMED COPY OF THE CORRESPONDING ORGANIZING
DOCUMENTS TO THE APPLICATION BEFORE MAILING. (See Specific Instructions, Part I, Line 10, on page 3.) Get
Pub. 557, Tax-Exempt Status for Your Organization, for examples of organizational documents.)

a [X] Corporation -   Attach a copy of the Articles of Incorporation, (including amendments and restatements) showing
approval by the appropriate state official; also include a copy of the bylaws.

b [ ] Trust -   Attach a copy of the Trust Indenture or Agreement, including all appropriate signatures and dates.

c [ ] Association -   Attach a copy of the Articles of Association, Constitution, or other creating document, with a declaration
(see instructions) or other evidence the organization was formed by adoption of the document by more
than one person; also include a copy of the bylaws.

If the organization is a corporation or an unincorporated association that has not yet adopted bylaws, check here . . . . [ ]

I declare under the penalties of perjury that I am authorized to sign this application on behalf of the above organization and that I have examined this application, including the
accompanying schedules and attachments, and to the best of my knowledge it is true, correct, and complete.

**Please
Sign
Here**   _John J. Emminenta CPA_   Secretary/Treasurer   2/1/xx
            (Signature)   (Title or authority of signer)   (Date)

For Paperwork Reduction Act Notice, see page 7 of the instructions.   (HTA)

Appendix 18–1

FORM 1023 *(continued)*

Form 1023 (Rev. 9-98)	Active Projects Fund	33-3333333	Page 2

Part II   Activities and Operational Information

1   Provide a detailed narrative description of all the activities of the organization - past, present, and planned. DO NOT MERELY REFER TO OR REPEAT THE LANGUAGE IN THE ORGANIZATIONAL DOCUMENT. List each activity separately in the order of importance based on the relative time and other resources devoted to the activity Indicate the percentage of time for each activity. Each description should include, as a minimum, the following: (a) a detailed description of the activity including its purpose and how each activity furthers your exempt purpose; (b) when the activity was or will be initiated; and (c) where and by whom the activity will be conducted.

Active Projects Fund was created and will operate exclusively for charitable and educational purposes as defined in IRC 501(c)(3). Specifically Active Projects Fund is dedicated to improving the quality of management and operation of nonprofit organizations. Active Projects Fund will accomplish its purpose by conducting seminars, providing technical assistance, and writing and disseminating educational materials.

Seminars: APF will hire an executive director with significant experience in nonprofit management. He or she will develop courses on financial and management issues such as personnel policies, budgeting, fund-raising, office efficiency, computer use, and other issues relevant to the management of a nonprofit organization. APF will seek to identify qualified professionals in the community who will be willing to volunteer their time as teachers. APF also expects to hire teachers with special expertise.

Technical Assistance: APF plans to encourage effective management by facilitating solutions to problems nonprofits face. APF will develop, and keep open regularly, a library of technical books, publications, and computer programs on nonprofits. APF will seek to foster exchanges of information and encourage networking. For example, roundtable-type meetings will be held, possibly groups with similar concerns will be formed. APF will develop a database of problems faced and solutions found as a reference tool. APF also expects to develop, as a resource tool, lists of companies, professionals, and other information useful to its exempt constituents.

Publications: APF plans to publish a newsletter that contains technical articles on topics of interest to nonprofits. The newsletter will also serve to announce seminars, roundtable meetings, library news, and other information. The publication will be distributed free and will contain no advertising. APF will seek legal, accounting, and other professionals to donate articles and information. The newsletter will also be used to announce educational seminars and courses to be presented; it has not yet been written.

2   What are or will be the organization's sources of financial support? List in order of size.

Donations from substantial contributors	85%
Seminar fees and publication sales	15%

3   Describe the organization's fundraising program, both actual and planned, and explain to what extent it has been put into effect. Include details of fundraising activities such as selective mailings, formation of fundraising committees, use of volunteers or professional fundraisers, etc. Attach representative copies of solicitations for financial support.

Active Projects Fund does not plan to conduct fundraising to seek public donations. APF does plan to make modest charges for seminars and publications as explained in Question 12.

Appendix 18–1

FORM 1023 (continued)

Form 1023 (Rev. 9-98)	Active Projects Fund	33-3333333	Page 3

Part II Activities and Operational Information (Continued)

4 Give the following information about the organization's governing body:

a Names, addresses, and titles of officers, directors, trustees, etc.	b Annual Compensation
Jane D. Environmentalist , President	None
John J. Environmentalist, Secretary/Treasurer	None
John J. Environmentalist, Jr. Vice-President	None
Address for all: **1111 Any Street** **Hometown TX 77777-7777**	

c Do any of the above persons serve as members of the governing body by reason of being public officials or being appointed by public officials? . . . . Yes [ ] No [X]
If "Yes," name those persons and explain the basis of their selection or appointment.

d Are any members of the organization's governing body "disqualified persons" with respect to the organization (other than by reason of being a member of the governing body) or do any of the members have either a business or family relationship with "disqualified persons"? (See Specific Instructions, Part II, Line 4d, on page 3.)   Yes [X]   No [ ]
If "Yes," explain.

Jane D. and John J. Environmentalist will be substantial contributors.

5 Does the organization control or is it controlled by any other organization? . . . . Yes [ ] No [X]
Is the organization the outgrowth of (or successor to) another organization, or does it have a special relationship with another organization by reason of interlocking directorates or other factors? . . . . Yes [ ] No [X]
If either of these questions is answered "Yes," explain.

The creators of Active Projects Fund were also the creators and substantial contributors of Environmentalist Fun an affiliated and commonly controlled private foundation. The two foundations function separately.

6 Does or will the organization directly or indirectly engage in any of the following transactions with any political organization or other exempt organization (other than 501(c)(3) organization): (a) grants; (b) purchases or sales of assets; (c) rental of facilities or equipment; (d) loans or loan guarantees; (e) reimbursement arrangements; (f) performance of services, membership, or fundraising solicitations; or (g) sharing of facilities, equipment, mailing lists or other assets, or paid employees? . . . . Yes [ ] No [X]
If "Yes," explain fully and identify the other organizations involved.

7 Is the organization financially accountable to any other organization? . . . . Yes [ ] No [X]
If "Yes," explain and identify the other organization. Include details concerning accountability or attach copies of reports if any have been submitted.

Appendix 18–1

FORM 1023 (*continued*)

| Form 1023 (Rev. 9-98) | Active Projects Fund | 33-3333333 | Page 4 |

Part II   Activities and Operational Information (Continued)

8   What assets does the organization have that are used in the performance of its exempt function? (Do not include property producing investment income.) If any assets are not fully operational, explain their status, what additional steps remain to be completed, and when such final steps will be taken. If "None," indicate "N/A."

Active Projects Fund will obtain computers and office furnishings needed to conduct its program.

9   Will the organization be the beneficiary of tax-exempt bond financing within the next 2 years? . . . . Yes ☐   No ☒

10a Will any of the organization's facilities or operations be managed by another organization or individual under a contractual agreement? . . . . Yes ☐   No ☒

b   Is the organization a party to any leases? . . . . Yes ☐   No ☒

If either of these questions is answered "Yes," attach a copy of the contracts and explain the relationship between the applicant and the other parties.

No lease has been signed to date.
Active Projects Fund expects to lease, from an unrelated party at market price, enough space with offices and meeting rooms, one of which must serve up to 100 persons at a time.

11 Is the organization a membership organization? . . . . Yes ☐   No ☒

If "Yes," complete the following:

a   Describe the organization's membership requirements, and attach a schedule of membership fees and dues.

b   Describe the organization's present and proposed efforts to attract members and attach a copy of any descriptive literature or promotional material used for this purpose.

c   What benefits do (or will) the members receive in exchange for their payment of dues?

12a If the organization provides benefits, services, or products, are the recipients required, or will they be required, to pay for them? . . . . ☐ N/A   Yes ☒   No ☐

If "Yes," explain how the charges are determined, and attach a copy of the current fee schedule.

Active Projects Fund will charge a modest amount, $10-25, dependent upon time and instructors, for its educational seminars. The library and newsletter will be made available free of charge.

b   Does or will the organization limit its benefits, services, or products to specific individuals or classes of individuals? . . . . ☐ N/A   Yes ☐   No ☒

If "Yes," explain how the recipients or beneficiaries are or will be selected.

Active Projects Fund's offices, library, and newsletters will be available free of charge to employees, volunteers, board members, and others interested in its program.

13 Does or will the organization attempt to influence legislation? . . . . Yes ☐   No ☒

If "Yes," explain. Also, give an estimate of the percentage of the organization's time and funds that it devotes or plans to devote to this activity.

14 Does or will the organization intervene in any way in political campaigns, including the publication or distribution of statements? . . . . Yes ☐   No ☒

If "Yes," explain fully.

Appendix 18–1

FORM 1023 (*continued*)

Form 1023 (Rev. 9-98)	Active Projects Fund	33-3333333	Page 5

Part III   Technical Requirements

1   Are you filing Form 1023 within 15 months from the end of the month in which your organization
was created or formed? . . . .   Yes [X]   No [ ]
If you answer "Yes," do not answer questions on lines 2 through 7.

2   If one of the exceptions to the 15-month filing requirement shown below applies, check the appropriate box and proceed to
question 7.
Exceptions - You are not required to file an exemption application within 15 months if the organization:

  [ ]   **a**   Is a church, interchurch organization of local units of a church, a convention or association of churches, or an
integrated auxiliary of a church. See Specific Instructions, Line 2a, on page 4;

  [ ]   **b**   Is not a private foundation and normally has gross receipts of not more than $5,000 in each tax year; or

  [ ]   **c**   Is a subordinate organization covered by a group exemption letter, but only if the parent or supervisory organization
timely submitted a notice covering the subordinate.

3   If the organization does not meet any of the exceptions on line 2 above, are you filing Form 1023 within
27 months from the end of the month in which the organization was created or formed? . . . . . .   Yes [ ]   No [ ]

  If "Yes," your organization qualifies under Regulation section 301.9100-2, for an automatic 12-month
extension of the 15-month filing requirement. Do not answer questions 4 through 6.

  If "No," answer question 4.

4   If you answer "No" to question 3, does the organization wish to request an extension of time to apply
under the "reasonable action and good faith" and the "no prejudice to the interest of the government"
requirements of Regulations section 301.9100-3? . . . .   Yes [ ]   No [ ]

  If "Yes," give the reasons for not filing this application within the 27-month period described in question 3.
See Specific Instructions, Part III, Line 4, before completing this item. Do not answer questions 5 and 6.

  If "No," answer questions 5 and 6.

5   If you answer "No" to question 4, your organization's qualification as a section 501(c)(3) organization
can be recognized only from the date this application is filed with your key District Director. Therefore,
do you want us to consider the application as a request for recognition of exemption as a section
501(c)(3) organization from the date the application is received and not retroactively to the date the
organization was created or formed? . . . .   Yes [ ]   No [ ]

6   If you answer "Yes" to the question on line 5 above and wish to request recognition of section 501(c)(4) status for
the period beginning with the date the organization was formed and ending with the date the Form 1023
application was received (the effective date of the organization's section 501(c)(3) status)   [ ] , check here
and attach a completed page 1 of Form 1024 to this application.

Appendix 18–1

FORM 1023 (*continued*)

Form 1023 (Rev. 9-98)	Active Projects Fund	33-3333333	Page 6

Part III Technical Requirements (Continued)

7 Is the organization a private foundation?
- [X] Yes (Answer question 8.)
- [ ] No   (Answer question 9 and proceed as instructed.)

8 If you answer "Yes" to the question on line 7, does the organization claim to be a private operating foundation?
- [X] Yes (Complete Schedule E)
- [ ] No

After answering question 8 on this line, go to line 14 on page 7.

9 If you answer "No" to the question on line 8, indicate the public charity classification the organization is requesting by checking the box below that most appropriately applies:

THE ORGANIZATION IS NOT A PRIVATE FOUNDATION BECAUSE IT QUALIFIES:

a	[ ]	As a church or a convention or association of churches (CHURCHES MUST COMPLETE SCHEDULE A.)	Sections 509(a)(1) and 170(b)(1)(A)(i)
b	[ ]	As a school (MUST COMPLETE SCHEDULE B.)	Sections 509(a)(1) and 170(b)(1)(A)(ii)
c	[ ]	As a hospital or a cooperative hospital service organization, or a medical research organization operated in conjunction with a hospital (These organizations, except for hospital service organizations, MUST COMPLETE SCHEDULE C.)	Sections 509(a)(1) and 170(b)(1)(A)(iii)
d	[ ]	As a governmental unit described in section 170(c)(1).	Sections 509(a)(1) and 170(b)(1)(A)(v)
e	[ ]	As being operated solely for the benefit of, or in connection with, one or more of the organizations described in a through d, g, h, or i (MUST COMPLETE SCHEDULE D.)	Section 509(a)(3)
f	[ ]	As being organized and operated exclusively for testing for public safety.	Section 509(a)(4)
g	[ ]	As being operated for the benefit of a college or university that is owned or operated by a governmental unit.	Section 509(a)(1) and 170(b)(1)(A)(iv)
h	[ ]	As receiving a substantial part of its support in the form of contributions from publicly supported organizations, from a governmental unit, or from the general public.	Sections 509(a)(1) and 170(b)(1)(A)(vi)
i	[ ]	As normally receiving not more than one-third of its support from gross investment income and more than one-third of its support from contributions, membership fees, and gross receipts from activities related to its exempt functions (subject to certain exceptions).	Section 509(a)(2)
j	[ ]	The organization is a publicly supported organization but is not sure whether it meets the public support test of block h or block i. The organization would like the IRS to decide the proper classification.	Sections 509(a)(1) and 170(b)(1)(A)(vi) or Section 509(a)(2)

If you checked one of the boxes a through f in question 9, go to question 14.
If you checked box g in question 9, go to questions 11 and 12.
If you checked box h, i, or j, in question 9, go to question 10.

FORM 1023 (*continued*)

Form 1023 (Rev. 9-98)	Active Projects Fund	33-3333333	Page 7

Part III   Technical Requirements   (Continued)

10 If you checked box h, i, or j on line 9, has the organization completed a tax year of at least 8 months?

☐ Yes - Indicate whether you are requesting:

☐ A definitive ruling (Answer questions on lines 11 through 14.)

☐ An advance ruling (Answer questions on lines 11 and 14 and attach two Forms 872-C completed and signed.)

☐ No - You must request an advance ruling by completing and signing two Forms 872-C and attaching them to the application.

11 If the organization received any unusual grants during any of the tax years shown in Part IV-A, attach a list for each year showing the name of the contributor; the date and the amount of the grant; and a brief description of the nature of the grant.

12 If you are requesting a definitive ruling under section 170(b)(1)(A)(iv) or (vi), check here ☐ and:

a Enter 2% of line 8, col. (e), total, of Part IV-A   **n/a**

b Attach a list showing the name and amount contributed by each person (other than a governmental unit or "publicly supported" organization) whose total gifts, grants, contributions, etc., were more than the amount entered on line 12a.

13 If you are requesting a definitive ruling under section 509(a)(2), check here ☐ and:

a For each of the years included on lines 1, 2, and 9 of Part IV-A, attach a list showing the name of and amount received from each "disqualified person." (For a definition of "disqualified person," see Specific Instructions, Part II, Line 4d, on pg 3.)

b For each of the years included on line 9 of Part IV-A, attach a list showing the name of and amount received from each payer (other than a "disqualified person") whose payments to the organization were more than $5,000. For this purpose, "payer" includes, but is not limited to, any organization described in sections 170(b)(1)(A)(i) through (vi) and any governmental agency or bureau.

14 Indicate if your organization is one of the following. If so, complete the required schedule. (Submit only those schedules that apply to your organization. Do not submit blank schedules.)

	Yes	No	If "Yes," complete Schedule:
Is the organization a church?		X	A
Is the organization, or any part of it, a school?		X	B
Is the organization, or any part of it, a hospital or medical research organization?		X	C
Is the organization a section 509(a)(3) supporting organization?		X	D
Is the organization a private operating foundation?	X		E
Is the organization, or any part of it, a home for the aged or handicapped?		X	F
Is the organization, or any part of it, a child care organization?		X	G
Does the organization provide or administer any scholarship benefits, student aid, etc.?		X	H
Has the organization taken over, or will it take over, the facilities of a "for profit" institution?		X	I

Appendix 18–1

FORM 1023 (*continued*)

Form 1023 (Rev. 9-98) Active Projects Fund 33-3333333 Page 8

Part IV Financial Data

Complete the financial statements for the current year and for each of the 3 years immediately before it. If in existence less than 4 years, complete the statements for each year in existence. If in existence less than 1 year, also provide proposed budgets for the 2 years following the current year.

A. Statement of Revenue and Expenses

Revenue	Current tax year	3 prior tax years or proposed budget for 2 years			(e) TOTAL
	(a) From to	(b) 1999-2000	(c) 2000-2001	(d) 19	
1 Gifts, grants, and contributions received (not including unusual grants)		300,000	300,000		600,000
2 Membership fees received					0
3 Gross investment income (see instructions)	new	3,000	6,000		9,000
4 Net income from organization's unrelated business activities not included on line 3	organization				0
5 Tax revenues levied for and either paid to or spent on behalf of the organization					0
6 Value of services or facilities furnished by a governmental unit to the organization without charge (not including the value of services or facilities generally furnished the public without charge) . . .		See attachment to this part for details of projection.			0
7 Other income (not including gain or loss from sale of capital assets) (attach schedule)					0
8 Total (add lines 1 through 7)	0	303,000	306,000	0	609,000
9 Gross receipts from admissions, sales of merchandise or services, or furnishing of facilities in any activity that is not an unrelated business within the meaning of section 513. Include related cost of sales on line 22.		30,000	50,000		80,000
10 Total (add lines 8 and 9	0	333,000	356,000	0	689,000
11 Gain or loss from sale of capital assets (att. sch.)					0
12 Unusual grants					0
13 Total revenue (add lines 10 through 12)	0	333,000	356,000	0	689,000
Expenses					
14 Fundraising expenses . . .					
15 Contributions, gifts, grants, and similar amounts paid (attach schedule)					
16 Disbursements to or for benefit of members (attach schedule)					
17 Compensation of officers, directors, and trustees (attach schedule)					
18 Other salaries and wages		150,000	166,000		
19 Interest					
20 Occupancy (rent, utilities, etc.) . . .		36,000	37,000		
21 Depreciation and depletion		5,000	5,000		
22 Other (attach sch.)		90,000	78,000		
23 Total expenses (add lines 14 through 22)	0	281,000	286,000	0	
24 Excess of revenue over expenses (line 13 minus line 23)	0	52,000	70,000	0	

Appendix 18–1

FORM 1023 (*continued*)

Form 1023 (Rev. 9-98)	Active Projects Fund	33-3333333	Page 9

Part IV   Financial Data   (Continued)

B. Balance Sheet (at the end of the period shown)		Current tax year
		NEW ORGANIZATION

Assets

1	Cash	1	NO ASSETS
2	Accounts receivable, net	2	
3	Inventories	3	
4	Bonds and notes receivable (attach schedule)	4	
5	Corporate stocks (attach schedule)	5	
6	Mortgage loans (attach schedule)	6	
7	Other investments (attach schedule)	7	
8	Depreciable and depletable assets (attach schedule)	8	
9	Land	9	
10	Other assets (attach schedule)	10	
11	Total assets (add lines 1 through 10)	11	0

Liabilities

12	Accounts payable	12	
13	Contributions, gifts, grants, etc., payable	13	
14	Mortgages and notes payable (attach schedule)	14	
15	Other liabilities (attach schedule)	15	
16	Total liabilities (add lines 12 through 15)	16	0

Fund Balances or Net Assets

17	Total fund balances or net assets	17	
18	Total liabilities and fund balances or net assets (add line 16 and line 17)	18	0

If there has been any substantial change in any aspect of the organization's financial activities since the end of the period shown above, check the box and attach a detailed explanation . . . . ☐

Appendix 18–1

FORM 1023 (*continued*)

| Form 1023 (Rev. 9-98) | Active Projects Fund | 33-3333333 | Page 21 |

Schedule E. Private Operating Foundation

Income Test	Amounts projected		Most recent tax year
1a Adjusted net income, as defined in Regulations section 53.4942(a)-2(d)		**1a**	3,000
b Minimum investment return, as defined in Regulations section 53.4942(a)-2(c)		**1b**	7,500
2 Qualifying distributions:			
a Amounts (including administrative expenses) paid directly for the active conduct of the activities for which organized and operated under section 501(c)(3) (attach schedule)		**2a**	276,000
b Amounts paid to acquire assets to be used (or held for use) directly in carrying out purposes described in section 170(c)(1) or 170(c)(2)(B) (attach schedule)		**2b**	25,000
c Amounts set aside for specific projects that are for purposes described in section 170(c)(1) or 170(c)(2)(B) (attach schedule)		**2c**	
d Total qualifying distributions (add lines 2a, b, and c)		**2d**	301,000
3 Percentages:			
a Percentage of qualifying distributions to adjusted net income (divide line 2d by line 1a)		**3a**	10033.33%
b Percentage of qualifying distributions to minimum investment return (divide line 2d by line 1b) . . . . (Percentage must be at least 85% for 3a or 3b)		**3b**	4013.33%
Assets Test			
4 Value of organization's assets used in activities that directly carry out the exempt purposes. Do not include assets held merely for investment or production of income (attach schedule)		**4**	N/A
5 Value of any stock of a corporation that is controlled by applicant organization and carries out its exempt purposes (attach statement describing corporation)		**5**	
6 Value of all qualifying assets (add lines 4 and 5)		**6**	
7 Value of applicant organization's total assets		**7**	
8 Percentage of qualifying assets to total assets (divide line 6 by line 7 - percentage must exceed 65%)		**8**	0.00%
Endowment Test			
9 Value of assets not used (or held for use) directly in carrying out exempt purposes:			
a Monthly average of investment securities at fair market value		**9a**	0
b Monthly average of cash balances		**9b**	150,000
c Fair market value of all other investment property (attach schedule)		**9c**	
d Total (add lines 9a, b, and c)		**9d**	150,000
10 Acquisition indebtedness related to line 9 items (attach schedule)		**10**	
11 Balance (subtract line 10 from line 9d)		**11**	150,000
12 Multiply line 11 by 3 1/3% (2/3 of the percentage for the minimum investment return computation under section 4942(e)). Line 2d above must equal or exceed the result of this computation		**12**	5,000
Support Test			
13 Applicant organization's support as defined in section 509(d)		**13**	N/A
14 Gross investment income as defined in section 509(e)		**14**	
15 Support for purposes of section 4942(j)(3)(B)(iii) (subtract line 14 from line 13)		**15**	
16 Support received from the general public, five or more exempt organizations, or a combination of these sources (attach schedule)		**16**	
17 For persons (other than exempt organizations) contributing more than 1% of line 15, enter the total amounts that are more than 1% of line 15		**17**	
18 Subtract line 17 from line 16		**18**	0
19 Percentage of total support (divide line 18 by line 15 - must be at least 85%)		**19**	0.00%
20 Does line 16 include support from an exempt organization that is more than 25% of the amount of line 15? . . . . Yes ☐			No ☐
21 Newly created organizations with less than 1 year's experience: Attach a statement explaining how the organization is planning to satisfy the requirements of section 4942(j)(3) for the income test and one of the supplemental tests during its first year's operation. Include a description of plans and arrangements, press clippings, public announcements, solicitations for funds, etc.			**See attachment**
22 Does the amount entered on line 2a include any grants that the applicant organization made? . . . . . Yes ☐ If "Yes," attach a statement explaining how those grants satisfy the criteria for "significant involvement" grants described in section 53.4942(b)-1(b)(2) of the regulations.			No ☒

For more information, see back of Schedule E.

FORM 1023 (*continued*)

Form **2848** (Rev. December 1995) Department of the Treasury Internal Revenue Service	**Power of Attorney and Declaration of Representative** For Paperwork Reduction and Privacy Act Notice, see the instructions.	OMB No. 1545-0150 For IRS Use Only Received by: Name _____ Telephone _____ Function _____ Date

Part I   Power of Attorney   (Please type or print.)

1   Taxpayer Information (Taxpayer(s) must sign and date this form on page 2, line 9.)

Taxpayer name(s) and address Active Projects Fund 1111 Any Street Hometown TX 77777-7777	Social security number(s) _____	Employer identification number 33-3333333
	Daytime telephone number (444) 423-2222	Plan number (if applicable)

hereby appoint(s) the following representative(s) as attorney(s)-in-fact:

2   Representative(s) (Representative(s) must sign and date this form on page 2, Part II.)

Name and address
    A Good Accountant
    1011 Main Street
    Hometown TX 77777-7777
	CAF No. 2200-22222R
	Telephone No. (444) 222-3333
	Fax No. (444) 222-3444
	Check if new: Address [ ] Telephone No. [ ]

Name and address	CAF No. Telephone No. Fax No. Check if new: Address [ ] Telephone No. [ ]
Name and address	CAF No. Telephone No. Fax No. Check if new: Address [ ] Telephone No. [ ]

to represent the taxpayer(s) before the Internal Revenue Service for the following tax matters:

3   Tax Matters

Type of Tax (Income, Employment, Excise, etc.)	Tax Form Number (1040, 941, 720, etc.)	Year(s) or Period(s)
Exemption Recognition	1023	
Income & Excise Tax	990-PF	1999-2001

4 Specific Use Not Recorded on Centralized Authorization File (CAF). - If the power of attorney is for a specific use not recorded on CAF, check this box. (See Line 4 - Specific Uses Not Recorded on CAF on page 3.) . . . . [   ]

5 Acts Authorized. - The representatives are authorized to receive and inspect confidential tax information and to perform any and all acts that I (we) can perform with respect to the tax matters described in line 3, for example, the authority to sign any agreements, consents, or other documents. The authority does not include the power to receive refund checks (see line 6 below) or the power to sign certain returns (see Line 5 - Acts Authorized on page 4).
List any specific additions or deletions to the acts otherwise authorized in this power of attorney:

....

Note: In general, an unenrolled preparer of tax returns cannot sign any document for a taxpayer. See Revenue Procedure 81-38, printed as Pub. 470, for more information.
Note: The tax matters partner/person of a partnership or S corporation is not permitted to authorize representatives to perform certain acts. See the instructions for more information.

6 Receipt of Refund Checks. - If you want to authorize a representative named in line 2 to receive, BUT NOT TO ENDORSE OR CASH, refund checks, initial here _____ and list the name of that representative below.

Name of representative to receive refund check(s)

(HTA)   Form 2848 (Rev. 12-95)

Appendix 18–1

FORM 1023 (*continued*)

Form 2848 (Rev. 12-95)	Active Projects Fund	33-3333333	Page 2

7 Notices and Communications. - Original notices and other written communications will be sent to you and a copy to the first representative listed in line 2 unless you check one or more of the boxes below.

a If you want the first representative listed on line 2 to receive the original, and yourself a copy, of such notices or communications, check this box . . . . ☐

b If you also want the second representative listed to receive a copy of such notices and communications, check this box . . . . ☐

c If you do not want any notices or communications sent to your representative, check this box . . . . ☐

8 Retention/Revocation of Prior Power(s) of Attorney. - The filing of this power of attorney automatically revokes all earlier power(s) of attorney on file with the Internal Revenue Service for the same tax matters and years or periods covered by this document. If you do not want to revoke a prior power of attorney, check here . . . . ☐
YOU MUST ATTACH A COPY OF ANY POWER OF ATTORNEY YOU WANT TO REMAIN IN EFFECT.

9 Signature of Taxpayer(s). - If a tax matter concerns a joint return, both husband and wife must sign if joint representation is requested, otherwise, see the instructions. If signed by a corporate officer, partner, guardian, tax matters partner/person, executor, receiver, administrator, or trustee on behalf of the taxpayer, I certify that I have the authority to execute this form on behalf of the taxpayer.
IF NOT SIGNED AND DATED, THIS POWER OF ATTORNEY WILL BE RETURNED.

Signature	Date	Title (if applicable)
John J. Environmentalist	1/31/xx	Secretary/Treasurer
John J. Environmentalist — Print Name		
Signature	Date	Title (if applicable)
Print Name		

Part II Declaration of Representative

Under penalties of perjury, I declare that:
* I am not currently under suspension or disbarment from practice before the Internal Revenue Service;
* I am aware of regulations contained in Treasury Department Circular No. 230 (31 CFR, Part 10), as amended, concerning the practice of attorneys, certified public accountants, enrolled agents, enrolled actuaries, and others;
* I am authorized to represent the taxpayer(s) identified in Part I for the tax matter(s) specified there; and
* I am one of the following:

    a Attorney - a member in good standing of the bar of the highest court of the jurisdiction shown below.
    b Certified Public Accountant - duly qualified to practice as a certified public accountant in the jurisdiction shown below.
    c Enrolled Agent - enrolled as an agent under the requirements of Treasury Department Circular No. 230.
    d Officer - a bona fide officer of the taxpayer organization.
    e Full-Time Employee - a full-time employee of the taxpayer.
    f Family Member - a member of the taxpayer's immediate family (i.e., spouse, parent, child, brother, or sister).
    g Enrolled Actuary - enrolled as an actuary by the Joint Board for the Enrollment of Actuaries under 29 U.S.C. 1242 (the authority to practice before the Service is limited by section 10.3(d)(1) of Treasury Department Circular No. 230).
    h Unenrolled Return Preparer - an unenrolled return preparer under section 10.7(a)(7) of Treasury Department Circular No. 230.

IF THIS DECLARATION OF REPRESENTATIVE IS NOT SIGNED AND DATED, THE POWER OF ATTORNEY WILL BE RETURNED.

Designation - Insert above letter (a-h)	Jurisdiction (state) or Enrollment Card No.	Signature	Date
B	Texas	*a good accountant*	1/31/xx

Appendix 18–1

FORM 1023 (*continued*)

Form **8718**	**User Fee for Exempt Organization Determination Letter Request**	**For IRS Use Only**
(Rev. January 1998) Department of the Treasury Internal Revenue Service	Attach this form to determination letter application. (Form 8718 is NOT a determination letter application.)	Control number _____ Amount paid _____ User fee screener

1 Name of organization **Active Projects Fund**	2 Employer Identification Number 33-3333333

Caution: Do not attach Form 8718 to an application for a pension plan determination letter. Use Form 8717 instead.

3 Type of request   **Fee**

a ☐ Initial request for a determination letter for:

      * An exempt organization that has had annual gross receipts averaging not more than $10,000 during the preceding 4 years, or

      * A new organization that anticipates gross receipts averaging not more than $10,000 during its first 4 years.   **$150**

      Note: If you checked box 3a, you must complete the Certification below.

Certification

I certify that the annual gross receipts of ....

                                           name of organization

have averaged (or are expected to average) not more than $10,000 during the preceding 4 (or the first 4) years of operation.

Signature   Title

b ☒ Initial request for a determination letter for:

      * An exempt organization that has had annual gross receipts averaging more than $10,000 during the preceding 4 years, or

      * A new organization that anticipates gross receipts averaging more than $10,000 during its first 4 years . . .   **$500**

c ☐ Group exemption letters **$500**

Attach
Check
or
Money
Order
Here

(HTA)   Form 8718 (Rev. 1-98)

Appendix 18–1

FORM 1023 *(continued)*

ACTIVE PROJECTS FUND   **EIN # 77-7777777**

Attachment to Form 1023 – Part I , Question 11

I swear that the attached copies of the nonprofit Articles of Incorporation and Bylaws are true and correct copies of the originals.

Author's Note: The model nonprofit charter and bylaws for Active Projects Fund were provided by the Texas Lawyers and Accountants for the Art.

John J. Environmentalist, Secretary/Treasurer   Date

FORM 1023 (*continued*)

The State of Texas

SECRETARY OF STATE

CERTIFICATE OF INCORPORATION
OF

ACTIVE PROJECTS FUND
33-3333333

The undersigned, as Secretary of State of Texas, hereby certifies that the attached Articles of Incorporation for the above named corporation have been received in this office and are found to conform to law.

ACCORDINGLY, the undersigned, as Secretary of State, and by virtue of the authority vested in the Secretary by law, hereby issues this Certificate of Incorporation.

Issuance of this Certificate of Incorporation does not authorize the use of a corporate name in this state in violation of the rights of another under the federal Trademark Act of 1946, the Texas trademark law, the Assumed Business or Professional Name Act, or the common law.

> Dated: January 31, 1999
> Effective: January 31, 1999

_____
Secretary of State   RR

Attachment 1

Appendix 18–1

FORM 1023 (*continued*)

ARTICLES OF INCORPORATION
of
ACTIVE PROJECTS FUND
(A Non-Profit Corporation)

I, the undersigned natural person of the age of eighteen (18) years or more, acting as incorporator of a corporation under the Texas Non-Profit Corporation Act, do hereby adopt the following Articles of Incorporation for such Corporation:

ARTICLE ONE
Name

The name of the Corporation is **Active Projects Fund**.

ARTICLE TWO
Nonprofit Corporation

The Corporation is a nonprofit corporation.

ARTICLE THREE
Duration

The period of the Corporation's duration is perpetual.

ARTICLE FOUR
Purposes

Section 4.01. The Corporation is organized exclusively for charitable and educational purposes as defined in Section 501(c)(3) of the Internal Revenue Code.

Section 4.02. Notwithstanding any other provision of these Articles of Incorporation:

a. No part of the net earnings of the Corporation shall inure to the benefit of any director of the Corporation, officer of the Corporation, or any private individual (except that reasonable compensation may be paid for services rendered to or for the Corporation affecting one or more of its purposes); and no director, officer or any private individual shall be entitled to share in the distribution of any of the corporate assets on dissolution of the Corporation. No substantial part of the activities of the Corporation shall be the carrying on of propaganda, or otherwise attempting to influence legislation, and the Corporation shall not participate in, or intervene in (including the publication or distribution of statements) any political campaign on behalf of any candidate for public office.

b. The corporation shall not conduct or carry on any activities not permitted to be conducted or carried on by an organization exempt from taxation under Section 501(c)(3) of the Internal Revenue Code and its Regulations as they now exist or as they may hereafter be amended, or by an organization, contributions to which are deductible under 170(c)(2) of the Internal Revenue Code and Regulations as they now exist or as they may hereafter be amended.

Appendix 18–1

FORM 1023 (*continued*)

c. Upon dissolution of the Corporation or the winding up of its affairs, the assets of the Corporation shall be distributed exclusively to charitable organizations which would then qualify under the provisions of Section 501(c)(3) of the Internal Revenue Code and its Regulations as they now exist or as they may be hereafter amended.

d. The Corporation is organized pursuant to the Texas Nonprofit Corporation Act and does not contemplate pecuniary gain or profit and is organized for nonprofit purposes which are consistent with the provisions of Section 501(c)(3) of the Internal Revenue Code and its Regulations as they now exist or as they may be hereafter amended.

ARTICLE FIVE
Membership

The Corporation shall have no voting members

ARTICLE SIX
Initial Registration Office and Agent

The street address of the initial registered office of the Corporation is 1111 Any Street, Hometown, Texas 77777, and the name of the initial registered agent at such address is Jane D. Environmentalist.

ARTICLE SEVEN
Directors

The number of Directors constituting the initial Board of Directors of the Corporation is three (3), and the names and addresses of those people who are to serve as the initial Directors are:

Name	Address
Jane D. Environmentalist	1111 Any Street Hometown, Texas 77777
John J. Environmentalist	1111 Any Street Hometown, Texas 77777
John J. Environmentalist, Jr.	1111 Any Street Hometown, Texas 77777

ARTICLE EIGHT
Indemnification of Directors and Officers

Each Director and each officer or former Director or officer may be indemnified and may be advanced reasonable expenses by the Corporation against liabilities imposed upon him or her and expenses reasonably incurred by him or her in connection with any claim against him or her, or any action, suit or proceeding to which he or she may be a party by reason of his or being, or having been, such Director or officer and against such sum as independent counsel selected by the Directors shall deem reasonable payment made in settlement

Appendix 18–1

FORM 1023 (*continued*)

of any such claim, action, suit or proceeding primarily with the view of avoiding expenses of litigation; provided, however, that no Director or officer shall be indemnified (a) with respect to matters as to which he or she shall be adjudged in such action, suit or proceeding to be liable for negligence or misconduct in performance or duty, (b) with respect to any matters which shall be settled by the payment of sums which independent counsel selected by the Directors shall not deem reasonable payment made primarily with a view to avoiding expense of litigation, or (c) with respect to matters for which such indemnification would be against public policy. Such rights of indemnification shall be in addition to any other rights to which Directors or officers may be entitled under any bylaw, agreement, corporate resolution, vote of Directors or otherwise. The Corporation shall have the power to purchase and maintain at its cost and expense insurance on behalf of such persons to the fullest extent permitted by this Article and applicable state law.

ARTICLE NINE
Limitation On Scope Of Liability

No director shall be liable to the Corporation for monetary damages for an act or omission in the Director's capacity as a Director of the Corporation, except and only for the following:

a.   A breach of the Director's duty of loyalty to the Corporation;

b.   An act or omission not in good faith by the Director or an act or omission that involves the intentional misconduct or knowing violation of the law by the Director;

c.   A transaction from which the Director gained any improper benefit whether or not such benefit resulted from an action taken within the scope of the Director's office; or

d.   An act or omission by the Directors for which liability is expressly provided for by statute.

ARTICLE TEN
Informal Action by Directors

Any action required by law to be taken at a meeting of Directors, or any action which may be taken at a meeting of Directors, may be taken without a meeting if a consent in writing setting forth the action so taken shall be signed by a sufficient number of Directors as would be necessary to take that action at a meeting at which all of the Directors were present and voted. All consents signed in this manner must be delivered to the Secretary or other officer having custody of the minute book within sixty (60) days after the date of the earliest dated consent delivered to the Corporation in this manner. A facsimile transmission or other similar transmission shall be regarded as signed by the Director for purposes of this Article.

ARTICLE ELEVEN
Incorporator

The name and address of the incorporator is:

Name	Address
Jane D. Environmentalist	1111 Any Street Hometown, Texas 77777

IN WITNESS WHEREOF, I have hereunto set my hand, this 25th day of January, 1999.

Jane D. Environmentalist

Appendix 18–1

FORM 1023 (*continued*)

BYLAWS

OF

ACTIVE PROJECTS FUND

a Texas Non-Profit Corporation
* * * * * * * * * * * * * * *

ARTICLE ONE - OFFICES

Section 1.01. Principal Office. The principal office of the Corporation in the State of Texas shall be located in the City of Hometown, County of Lone Star. The Corporation may have such other offices, either within or without the State of Texas, as the Board of Directors may determine or as the affairs of the Corporation may require from time to time.

Section 1.02. Registered Office and Registered Agent. The Corporation shall have and continuously maintain in the State of Texas a registered office, and a registered agent whose office is identical with such registered office may be, but need not be, identical with the principal office of the Corporation in the State of Texas, and the address of the registered office may be changed from time to time by the Board of Directors.

ARTICLE TWO - PURPOSES

Section 2.01. Organizational Purposes. The Corporation is organized exclusively for charitable, literary and educational purposes including fostering and nurturing active projects. The corporation is established as a permanent organization in Texas seeking to enrich the local community through activities promoting active projects. The Corporation may engage in any activities which further its purposes.

No part of the net earnings of the Corporation shall inure to the benefit of any Director of the Corporation, officer of the Corporation, or any private individual (except that reasonable compensation may be paid for services rendered to or for the Corporation affecting one or more of its purposes), and no Director or officer of the Corporation, or any private individual shall be entitled to share in the distribution of any of the corporate assets on dissolution of the Corporation. No substantial part of the activities of the Corporation shall be the carrying on of propaganda, or otherwise attempting to influence legislation, and the Corporation shall not participate in, or intervene in (including the publication or distribution of statements) any political campaigning on behalf of any candidate for public office.

Notwithstanding any other provision of these Bylaws, the Corporation shall not conduct or carry on any activities not permitted to be conducted or carried on by an organization exempt from taxation under Section 501(c)(3) of the Internal Revenue Code and its Regulations as they now exist or as they may hereafter be amended, or by an organization, contributions to which are deductible under Section 170(c)(2) of the Internal Revenue Code and Regulations, as they now exist or as they

FORM 1023 (*continued*)

may hereafter be amended.

Upon dissolution of the Corporation or the winding up of its affairs, the assets of the Corporation shall be distributed exclusively to charitable organizations which would then qualify under the provisions of Section 501(c)(3) of the Internal Revenue Code and its Regulations as they now exist or as they may hereafter be amended.

ARTICLE THREE - MEMBERS

Section 3.01. The corporation shall have no voting members.

ARTICLE FOUR - BOARD OF DIRECTORS

Section 4.01. General Powers. The affairs of the Corporation shall be managed by its Board of Directors. Directors need not be residents of Texas.

Section 4.02. Number, Tenure and Qualifications. The number of Directors shall be not less than three (3) nor more than fifteen (15).. The initial Directors shall serve terms of one, two and three years, as provided by the Board. Afterwards, each director shall serve for one (1) year, thereby providing for staggered terms. The initial terms of additional Directors shall be fixed to ensure than a disproportionate number of Directors (more than one-half) will not be up for election in any given year.

Section 4.03. Regular Meetings. The Board of Directors shall provide for by resolution the time and place, either within or without the State of Texas, for the holding of the regular annual meeting(s) of the Board, and may provide by resolution the time and place for the holding of additional regular meetings of the Board, without other notice than such resolution. However, there shall never be less than one annual meeting of the Board of Directors.

Section 4.04. Annual Meetings. Beginning in 1999, an annual meeting of the Board of Directors shall be held at the date, time and place determined by the Board of Directors.

Section 4.05. Special Meetings. Special meetings of the Board of Directors may be called by or at the request of the President, or any two Directors. The person or persons authorized to call special meetings of the Board may fix any place, either within or without the State of Texas, as the place for holding any special meetings of the Board called by them.

Section 4.06. Meetings Utilizing Electronic Media. Members of the Board of Directors or members of any committee designated by the Board of Directors may participate in and hold a meeting of that Board or committee, respectively, by means of conference telephone or similar communication equipment, provided that all persons participating in such a meeting shall constitute presence in person at such meeting, except where a person participates in the meeting for the express purpose of objecting to the transaction of any business on the ground that the meeting is not lawfully created.

FORM 1023 (*continued*)

Section 4.07.   Notice. Notice of any special meeting of the Board of Directors shall be given at least three (3) business days previously thereto by oral or written notice delivered personally or sent by mail, telegram, facsimile or messenger to each Director at his or her address as shown by the records of the Corporation. If mailed, such notice shall be deemed to be delivered when deposited in the United States mail so addressed with postage thereon prepaid. If notice be given by telegram, such notice shall be deemed to be delivered when the telegram is delivered to the telegram company. Any Director may waive notice of any meeting. The attendance of a Director at any meeting shall constitute a waiver or notice of such meeting, except when a Director attends a meeting for the express purpose of objecting to the transaction of any business because the meeting is not lawfully called or convened. Neither the business to be transacted at, nor the purpose of, any regular or special meeting of the Board need be specified in the notice or waiver of notice of such meeting, unless specifically required by law or by these Bylaws.

Section 4.08.   Quorum. A majority of the Board of Directors, but never less than three (3), shall constitute a quorum for the transaction of business at any meeting of the Board; but if less than a quorum of the Directors is present at said meeting, a majority of the Directors present may adjourn the meeting from time to time without further notice.

Section 4.09.   Manner of Acting. The act of a majority of the Directors present at a meeting at which a quorum is present shall be the act of the Board of Directors, unless the act of a greater number is required by law or by these Bylaws.

Section 4.10.   Vacancies.   Any vacancy occurring in the Board of Directors, and any directorship to be filled by reason of an increase in the number of Directors, shall be filled by the Board of Directors. A Director elected to fill a vacancy shall be elected for the unexpired term of his or her predecessor in office. However, vacancies need not be filled unless such a vacancy would result in fewer than three directors remaining on the board.

Section 4.11.   Compensation. Directors as such shall not receive any stated salaries for their services, but by resolution of the Board of Directors a fixed sum and expenses of attendance, if any, may be allowed for attendance at each regular or special meeting of the Board; but nothing herein contained shall be construed to preclude any Director from serving the Corporation in any other capacity and receiving compensation therefor.

Section 4.12.   Informal Action by Directors. Any action required by law to be taken at a meeting of Directors, or any action which may be taken at a meeting of Directors, may be taken without a meeting if a consent in writing setting forth the action so taken shall be signed by a sufficient number of Directors as would be necessary to take that action at a meeting at which all the Directors were present and voted. Each such written consent shall be delivered, by hand or certified or registered mail, return receipt requested, to the Secretary or other officer or agent of the Corporation having custody of the Corporation's minute book. A written consent signed by less than all of the Directors is not effective to take the action that is the subject of the consent unless, within sixty (60) days after the date of the earliest dated consent delivered to the Corporation in the manner required by this Article, a consent or consents signed by the required number of Directors is delivered to the Corporation as provided in this Article. For purposes of this Article, a telegram, telex,

FORM 1023 (*continued*)

cablegram, or similar transmission by a Director or a photographic, photostatic, facsimile or similar reproduction of a writing signed by a Director shall be regarded as signed by the Director.

Section 4.13. Resignation. Any Director may resign by giving written notice to the President. The resignation shall be effective at the next called meeting of the Board of Directors, of which meeting the resigning Director shall receive notice.

Section 4.14. Removal. Any Director may be removed with or without cause by a two-thirds majority of the remaining Directors.

Section 4.15. Indemnification. The Corporation may indemnify and advance reasonable expenses to directors, officers, employees and agents of the Corporation to the fullest extent required or permitted by Article 2.22A of the Texas Non-Profit Corporation Act, subject to the restrictions, if any, contained in the Corporation's Articles of Incorporation. The Corporation shall have the power to purchase and maintain at its cost and expense insurance on behalf of such persons to the fullest extent permitted by Article 2.22A of the Texas Non-Profit Corporation Act.

ARTICLE FIVE - OFFICERS

Section 5.01. Officers. The officers of the Corporation shall be a President, one or more Vice Presidents (the number thereof to be determined by the Board of Directors), a Secretary, a Treasurer, and such other officers as may be elected in accordance with the provisions of this Article. The Board of Directors may elect or appoint such other officers, including one or more Assistant Secretaries and one or more Assistant Treasurers, as it shall deem desirable, such officers to have the authority and perform the duties prescribed, from time to time, by the Board of Directors. Any two or more offices may be held by the same person, except the offices of President and Secretary.

Section 5.02. Election and Term of Office. The officers of the Corporation shall be elected by the Board of Directors at the annual meeting of the Board of Directors. If the election of officers shall not be held at such meeting, such election shall be held as soon thereafter as conveniently may be. New offices may be created and filled at any meeting of the Board of Directors. Each officer shall hold office until his or her successor shall have been duly elected and shall have qualified.

Section 5.03. Removal. Any officer elected or appointed by the Board of Directors may be removed with or without cause by a two-thirds majority vote of the Board of Directors, but such removal shall be without prejudice to the contract rights, if any, of the officer so removed.

Section 5.04. Vacancies. A vacancy in any office because of death, resignation, disqualification, or otherwise, may be filled by the Board of Directors for the unexpired portion of the term.

Section 5.05. President. The President shall be the principal executive officer of the Corporation and shall, in general, supervise and control all of the business and affairs of the Corporation. He or she shall preside at all meetings of the Board of Directors. The President may sign, with the Secretary or any other proper officer of the Corporation authorized by the Board of

FORM 1023 (*continued*)

Directors, any deeds, mortgages, bonds, contracts, or other instruments which the Board of Directors has authorized to be executed, except in cases where the signing and execution thereof shall be expressly delegated by the Board of Directors or by these Bylaws or by statute to some other officer or agent of the Corporation; and in general he or she shall perform all duties as may be prescribed by the Board of Directors from time to time, including participating in various committee meetings as a member or chairperson thereof. He or she shall also be responsible for informing the Board of Directors of possible programs, meetings, and functions of the corporation.

Section 5.06. <u>Vice President</u>. In the absence of the President or in the event of his or her inability or refusal to act, the Vice President (or in the event there be more than one Vice President, the Vice Presidents in order of their election) shall perform the duties of the President, and when so acting shall have all the powers of and be subject to all the restrictions upon the President. Any Vice President shall perform such other duties as from time to time may be assigned to him or her by the President or Board of Directors.

Section 5.07. <u>Treasurer</u>. If required by the Board of Directors, the Treasurer shall give a bond for the faithful discharge of his or her duties in such sum and with such surety or sureties as the Board of Directors shall determine. He or she shall have charge and custody of and be responsible for all funds and securities of the Corporation; receive and give receipts for moneys due and payable to the Corporation from any source whatsoever, and deposit all such moneys in the name of the Corporation in such banks, trust companies, or other depositories as shall be selected in accordance with the provisions of these Bylaws; he or she shall keep proper books of account and other books showing at all times the amount of funds and other property belonging to the Corporation, all of which books shall be open at all times to the inspection of the Board of Directors; he or she shall also submit a report of the accounts and financial condition of the Corporation at each annual meeting of the Board of Directors; and in general perform all the duties incident to the office of Treasurer and such other duties as from time to time may be assigned to him or her by the President or by the Board of Directors.

Section 5.08. <u>Secretary</u>. The Secretary shall keep the minutes of the meetings of the Board of Directors in one or more books provided for that purpose; give all notices in accordance with the provisions of these Bylaws or as required by law; be custodian of the corporate records and of the seal of the Corporation, and affix the seal of the Corporation to all documents, the execution of which on behalf of the Corporation under its seal is duly authorized in accordance with the provisions of these Bylaws; and, in general, perform all duties incident to the office of Secretary and such other duties as from time to time may be assigned to him or her by the President or Board of Directors. The Board of Directors and Officers shall give bonds of the faithful discharge of their duties in such sums and with such sureties as the Board of Directors shall determine. The Assistant Treasurer and Assistant Secretaries, in general, shall perform such duties as shall be assigned to them by the Treasurer or the Secretary or by the President or the Board of Directors.

ARTICLE SIX - <u>COMMITTEES</u>

Section 6.01. <u>Appointment</u>. The Board of Directors shall appoint members of committees

FORM 1023 (*continued*)

established by the Board of Directors. The Board of Directors shall appoint the chairperson of each committee. These committees shall perform such functions and make such reports as the President or Board of Directors shall determine. Both Directors and members of the Advisory Board may serve on all committees except the Executive Committee.

Section 6.02. Committees of Directors. The Board of Directors, by resolution adopted by a majority of the Directors in office, may designate and appoint one or more committees, each of which shall consist of two or more persons, a majority of who are Directors, which committees, to the extent provided in said resolution shall have and exercise the authority in the management of the Corporation of the Board of Directors. However, no such committee shall have the authority of the Board of Directors in reference to amending, altering, or repealing the Bylaws; electing, appointing, or removing any member of any such committee or any Director or officer of the Corporation; amending the Articles of Incorporation; adopting a plan of merger or adopting a plan of consolidation with another Corporation; authorizing the sale, lease, exchange, or mortgage of all or substantially all of the property and assets of the Corporation; authorizing the voluntary dissolution of the Corporation or revoking proceedings therefor; adopting a plan for the distribution of the assets of the Corporation; or amending, altering, or repealing any resolution of the Board of Directors which by its terms provides that it shall not be amended, altered or repealed by such committee. The designation and appointment of any such committee and the delegation thereof of authority shall not operate to relieve the Board of Directors, or any individual Director, of any responsibility imposed on it or him or her by law.

Section 6.03. Executive Committee. The Board of Directors may from among its members appoint an Executive Committee consisting of the officers and any additional members as deemed necessary by the Board to serve at the pleasure of the Board. The President, unless absent or otherwise unable to do so, shall preside as Chairperson of the Executive Committee. The Committee shall meet at the call of the President or the Board of Directors, or any two (2) members of the Committee, and shall have and may exercise when the Board of Directors is not in session the power to perform all duties, of every kind and character, not required by law or the charter of the Corporation to be performed solely by the Board of Directors. The Executive Committee shall have authority to make rules for the holding and conduct of its meetings, keep records thereof and regularly report its actions to the Board. A majority but never less than three of the members of the Committee in office shall be sufficient to constitute a quorum at any meeting of the Committee, and all action taken at such a meeting shall be by a majority of those present all acts performed by the Executive Committee in the exercise of its aforesaid authority shall be deemed to be, and may be certified as, acts performed under authority of the Board of Directors. Vacancies in the Executive committee shall be filled by appointment by the Board of Directors. All actions of the Executive Committee shall be recorded in writing in a minute book kept for that purpose and a report of all action shall be made to the Board of Directors at its next meeting. The minutes of the Board of Directors shall reflect that such a report was made along with any action taken by the Board of Directors with respect thereto.

Section 6.04. Nominating Committee. The President shall, with thirty (30) days advance notice to the Board of Directors, appoint the members of the Nominating Committee created by the Board of Directors. The members shall be members of the Board of Directors and Advisory Board

FORM 1023 (*continued*)

appointed to nominate candidates for officers and directors. Additional nominations may be made by Directors at the annual meeting.

Section 6.05. Advisory Committee. The Board of Directors may appoint an Advisory Committee at such times as it deems necessary. The function and purpose of the Advisory Committee shall be to advise the Board of Directors on matters relating to the purpose of the organization and to suggest projects which the Corporation may undertake.

Section 6.06. Other Committees. Other committees not having and exercising the authority of the Board of Directors in the management of the Corporation may be designated by a resolution adopted by a majority of the Directors present at a meeting at which a quorum is present. Except as otherwise provided in such resolution, the President of the Corporation shall appoint the members of each such committee. Any member thereof may be removed by the person or persons authorized to appoint such member whenever in their judgment the best interests of the Corporation shall be served by such removal. Members of such committee or committees may, but need not be, Directors.

Section 6.07. Term of Office. Each member of a committee shall continue as such until the next annual meeting of the members of the Board of Directors and until his or her successor is appointed, unless the committee shall be sooner terminated, or unless such member be removed from such committee, or unless such member shall cease to qualify as a member thereof.

Section 6.08. Chairperson. One member of each committee shall be appointed chairperson by the person or persons authorized to appoint the members thereof.

Section 6.09. Vacancies. Vacancies in the membership of any committee may be filled by appointments made in the same manner as provided in the case of the original appointments.

Section 6.10. Quorum. Unless otherwise provided in the resolution of the Board of Directors designating a committee, a majority of the whole committee shall constitute a quorum and the act of a majority of the members present at a meeting at which a quorum is present shall be the act of the committee.

Section 6.11. Rules. Each committee may adopt rules for its government not inconsistent with these Bylaws or with rules adopted by the Board of Directors.

Section 6.12. Committee Dissolution. The Board of Directors may, in its sole discretion, dissolve any committee with or without cause. Except for the Executive Committee, such dissolution shall require approval by a majority of the quorum. The Executive Committee shall only be dissolved by approval of two-thirds or more of all members of the Board of Directors.

ARTICLE SEVEN - CONTRACTS, CHECKS, DEPOSITS, AND GIFTS

Section 7.01. Contracts. The Board of Directors may authorize any officer or officers, agent or agents of the Corporation, in addition to the officers so authorized by these Bylaws, to enter into

Appendix 18–1

FORM 1023 (*continued*)

any contract or execute and deliver any instrument in the name of and on behalf of the Corporation. Such authority may be general or confined to specific instances.

Section 7.02. <u>Checks and Drafts, Etc</u>. All checks, drafts, or orders for the payment of money, notes, or other evidence of indebtedness issued in the name of the Corporation shall be signed by such officer or officers, agent or agents of the Corporation and in such manner as shall from time to time be determined by resolution of the Board of Directors. In the absence of such determination by the Board of Directors, such instruments shall be signed by the Treasurer or an Assistant Treasurer and countersigned by the President or a Vice President of the Corporation.

Section 7.03. <u>Deposits</u>. All funds of the Corporation shall be deposited from time to time to the credit of the Corporation in such banks, trust companies, or other depositories as the Board of Directors may select.

Section 7.04. <u>Gifts</u>. The Board of Directors may accept on behalf of the Corporation any contribution, gift, bequest, or devise for the general purposes or for any special purpose of the Corporation.

ARTICLE EIGHT - <u>BOOKS AND RECORDS</u>

Section 8.01. <u>Books and Records</u>. The Corporation shall keep correct and complete books and records of account of the activities and transactions of the Corporation including, a minute book which shall contain a copy of the Corporation's application for tax-exempt status (IRS Form 1023), copies of the organization's IRS information and/or tax returns (For example, Form 990 and all schedules thereto), and a copy of the Articles of Incorporation, By-Laws, and Amendments. The Corporation shall also keep minutes of the proceedings of its Board of Directors and any committees having the authority of the Board of Directors. All books and records of the Corporation may be inspected by any Director or his or her agent or attorney for any proper purpose at any reasonable time. Representatives of the Internal Revenue Service may inspect these books and records as necessary to meet the requirements relating to federal tax form 990. All financial records of the Corporation shall be available to the public for inspection and copying to the fullest extent required by law.

ARTICLE NINE - <u>FISCAL YEAR</u>

Section 9.01. <u>Fiscal Year</u>. The fiscal year of the Corporation shall be as determined by the Board of Directors.

ARTICLE TEN - <u>SEAL</u>

Section 10.01. <u>Seal</u>. The Board of Directors may authorize a corporate seal.

FORM 1023 (*continued*)

ARTICLE ELEVEN - <u>WAIVER OF NOTICE</u>

Section 11.01. <u>Waiver of Notice</u>. Whenever any notice is required to be given under the provisions of the Texas Non-Profit Corporation Act or under the provisions of the Articles of Incorporation or the Bylaws of the Corporation, a waiver thereof in writing signed by the person or persons entitled to such notice, whether before or after the time therein, shall be deemed equivalent to the giving of such notice.

ARTICLE TWELVE - <u>AMENDMENTS TO BYLAWS</u>

Section 12.01. <u>Amendments to Bylaws</u>. These Bylaws may be altered, amended, or repealed and new Bylaws may be adopted by a majority of the Directors present at any regular meeting or at any special meeting, if at least one day's written notice is given of an intention to alter, amend, or repeal these Bylaws or to adopt new Bylaws at such meeting.

ARTICLE THIRTEEN - <u>AMENDMENTS TO ARTICLES</u>

Section 13.01. <u>Amendments to Articles</u>. The Articles of Incorporation of the Corporation may, to the extent allowed by law, be altered, amended, or restated and new Articles of Incorporation may be adopted by a two-thirds majority of the Directors present at the regular meeting or at any special meeting, if at least one day's written notice is given of an intention to alter, amend, or restate the Articles of Incorporation or to adopt new Articles of Incorporation at such meeting.

CERTIFICATE

I HEREBY CERTIFY that the foregoing is a true, complete and correct copy of the Bylaws of **Active Projects Fund**, a Texas non-profit corporation, in effect on the date hereof.

IN WITNESS WHEREOF, I hereunto set my hand and affix the seal of the Corporation, this 25th day of January, 1999.

_____
Signature

Appendix 18–1

FORM 1023 *(continued)*

ACTIVE PROJECTS FUND   **EIN #: 33-3333333**
Attachment to Form 1023

Part IV - Financial data

Revenue, Line 1 - Contributions

Jane D. & John J. Environmentalist plan to donate about 1,000 shares of Clean Air
Industries annually, or some $300,000, to the Fund. The shares are listed on the
NYSE and will be sold upon receipt to support the Fund's programs.

Expenses, line 18 - Other salaries & wages

	1999-2000	*2000-2001*
Executive Director (full time)	$75,000	$80,000
Administrator (full time)	30,000	32,000
Librarian/publicist (part time)	14,000	16,000
Assistants (2 part time)	15,000	20,000
	134,000	148,000
Fringe benefits and payroll tax	16,000	18,000
Total other salaries	$150,000	$166,000

Expenses, Line 21 - Depreciation

Active Projects Fund plans to spend up to $ 25,000 buying computers,
office furnishings, tables and chairs, projectors, and similar equipment.
The depreciation will be calculated on a five year straight-line basis.

Expenses, Line 22 - Other Expense

Library books and publications	$20,000	$10,000
Computer programs for demonstration purposes	20,000	10,000
Printing & design of:		
Seminar materials	10,000	15,000
Monthly newsletter	10,000	12,000
Mailing newsletter	12,000	14,000
Seminar refreshments	5,000	6,000
Legal fees	4,000	1,000
Accounting fees	2,000	2,000
Office supplies & expenses	5,000	6,000
Insurance	2,000	2,000
Total other expenses	$90,000	$78,000

Appendix 18–1

FORM 1023 *(continued)*

ACTIVE PROJECTS FUND   EIN #: 33-3333333
Attachment to Form 1023

SCHEDULE E: PRIVATE OPERATING FOUNDATIONS

Active Projects Fund projects the following information
that indicate it will meet the Income and Endowment Tests
and be eligible for classification as an operating foundation.

Income Test

		1999-2000	2000-2001
Line 1a	Adjusted net income	3,000	5,000
Line 1b	Minimum investment return	7,500	8,000
Line 2a	Qualifying distributions	276,000	281,000
Line 2b	Acquisition of exempt function assets	25,000	0
Line 2d	Total qualifying distributions	301,000	281,000
Line 3a	Percentage of qualifying distributions to ANI	> 100%	>100%
Line 3b	Percentage of qualifying distribution to MDR	> 100%	>100%

Endowment Test

Line 9	Value of assets not used directly in exempt activities.		
Line 9a	Projected monthly average of investment securities	0	0
Line 9b	Projected average of cash balances	150,000	160,000
Line 9c	Projected value of other investment property	0	0
Line 9d	Total	150,000	160,000
Line 10	Acquisition indebtedness	0	0
Line 11	Balance	150,000	160,000
Line 12	Multiple line 11 by 3-1/3%	$4,995	$5,328

Note line 2d exceeds the amount on line 12.

Active Projects Fund has made a good faith determination that it will satisfy the
income test and the endowment test set forth above for its first taxable year and
and the years thereafter based upon projections of income and expenditures and
the opinion of our counsel. See Part II, Question 1 for description of the planned
activities. We have made no public announcements or had press coverage to date.

Appendix 18–1

FORM 1023 (*continued*)

Schedule A. Churches (Continued)

10 Does the organization have a school for the religious instruction of the
young? . . . . Yes ☐   No ☐

11 Were the current deacons, minister, and/or pastor formally ordained after a prescribed
course of study? . . . . Yes ☐   No ☐

12 Describe the organization's religious hierarchy or ecclesiastical government.

**NOTE: Applicants choose and attach the schedule indicated
by answer in Part III, Question 14**

13 Does the organization have an established place of worship? . . . . Yes ☐   No ☐

If "Yes," provide the name and address of the owner or lessor of the property and the
address and a description of the facility.

If the organization has no regular place of worship, state where the services are held and how the
site is selected.

14 Does (or will) the organization license or otherwise ordain ministers (or their equivalent)
or issue church charters? . . . . Yes ☐   No ☐

If "Yes," describe in detail the requirements and qualifications needed to be so
licensed, ordained, or chartered.

15 Did the organization pay a fee for a church charter? . . . . Yes ☐   No ☐

If "Yes," state the name and address of the organization to which the fee was paid,
attach a copy of the charter, and describe the circumstances surrounding the chartering.

16 Show how many hours a week your minister/pastor and officers each devote to church work and the
amount of compensation paid to each of them. If the minister or pastor is otherwise employed, indicate
by whom employed, the nature of the employment, and the hours devoted to that employment.

Appendix 18–1

FORM 1023 (*continued*)

Form 1023 (Rev. 9-98)   Page 13

Schedule A. Churches (Continued)

17 Will any funds or property of the organization be used by any officer, director, employee, minister, or pastor for his or her personal needs or convenience? . . . . Yes ☐   No ☐

If "Yes," describe the nature and circumstances of such use.

18 List any officers, directors, or trustees related by blood or marriage.

19 Give the name of anyone who has assigned income to the organization or made substantial contributions of money or other property. Specify the amounts involved.

Instructions

Although a church, its integrated auxiliaries, or a convention or association of churches is not required to file Form 1023 to be exempt from Federal income tax or to receive tax-deductible contributions, such an organization may find it advantageous to obtain recognition of exemption. In this event, you should submit information showing that your organization is a church, synagogue, association or convention of churches, religious order or religious organization that is an integral part of a church, and that it is carrying out the functions of a church.

In determining whether an admittedly religious organization is also a church, the IRS does not accept any and every assertion that such an organization is a church. Because beliefs and practices vary so widely, there is no single definition of the word "church" for tax purposes. The IRS considers the facts and circumstances of each organization applying for church status.

The IRS maintains two basic guidelines in determining that an organization meets the religious purposes test:

1. That the particular religious beliefs of the organization are truly and sincerely held, and

2. That the practices and rituals associated with the organization's religious beliefs or creed are not illegal or contrary to clearly defined public policy.

In order for the IRS to properly evaluate your organization's activities and religious purposes, it is important that all questions in Schedule A be answered accurately.

The information submitted with Schedule A will be a determining factor in granting the "church" status requested by your organization. In completing the schedule, consider the following points:

1. The organization's activities in furtherance of its beliefs must be exclusively religious, and

2. An organization will not qualify for exemption if it has a substantial nonexempt purpose of serving the private interests of its founder or the founder's family.

NOTE THERE IS NO PAGE 14 or 26

Appendix 18–1

FORM 1023 (*continued*)

Schedule B. Schools, Colleges, and Universities

1 Does, or will, the organization normally have: (a) a regularly scheduled curriculum, (b) a regular faculty of qualified teachers, (c) a regularly enrolled student body, and (d) facilities where its educational activities are regularly carried on? . . . . Yes ☐   No ☐
   If "No," do not complete the rest of Schedule B.

2 Is the organization an instrumentality of a state or political subdivision of a state? . . . . Yes ☐   No ☐
   If "Yes," document this in Part II and do not complete items 3 through 10 of this Schedule B.
   (See instructions on the back of Schedule B.)

3 Does or will the organization (or any department or division within it) discriminate in any way on the basis of race with respect to:

   a Admissions? . . . . Yes ☐   No ☐

   b Use of facilities or exercise of student privileges? . . . . Yes ☐   No ☐

   c Faculty or administrative staff? . . . . Yes ☐   No ☐

   d Scholarship or loan programs? . . . . Yes ☐   No ☐
     If "Yes" for any of the above, explain.

4 Does the organization include a statement in its charter, bylaws, or other governing instrument, or in a resolution of its governing body, that it has a racially nondiscriminatory policy as to students? . . . . Yes ☐   No ☐

   Attach whatever corporate resolutions or other official statements the organization has made on this subject.

5a Has the organization made its racially nondiscriminatory policies known in a manner that brings the policies to the attention of all segments of the general community that it serves? . . . . Yes ☐   No ☐

   If "Yes," describe how these policies have been publicized and how often relevant notices or announcements have been made. If no newspaper or broadcast media notices have been used, explain.

   b If applicable, attach clippings of any relevant newspaper notices or advertising, or copies of tapes or scripts used for media broadcasts. Also attach copies of brochures and catalogues dealing with student admissions, programs, and scholarships, as well as representative copies of all written advertising used as a means of informing prospective students of the organization's programs.

6 Attach a numerical schedule showing the racial composition, as of the current academic year, and projected to the extent feasible for the next academic year, of: (a) the student body, and (b) the faculty and administrative staff.

7 Attach a list showing the amount of any scholarship and loan funds awarded to students enrolled and the racial composition of the students who have received the awards.

8a Attach a list of the organization's incorporators, founders, board members, and donors of land or buildings, whether individuals or organizations.

   b State whether any of the organizations listed in 8a have as an objective the maintenance of segregated public or private school education, and, if so, whether any of the individuals listed in 8a are officers or active members of such organizations.

9a Indicate the public school district and county in which the organization is located.

   b Was the organization formed or substantially expanded at the time of public school desegregation in the above district or county? . . . . Yes ☐   No ☐

10 Has the organization ever been determined by a state or Federal administrative agency or judicial body to be racially discriminatory? . . . . Yes ☐   No ☐

   If "Yes," attach a detailed explanation identifying the parties to the suit, the forum in which the case was heard, the cause of action, the holding in the case, and the citations (if any) for the case. Also describe in detail what changes in the organization's operation, if any, have occurred since then.

For more information, see back of Schedule B.

Appendix 18–1

FORM 1023 (*continued*)

Instructions

A "school" is an organization that has the primary function of presenting formal instruction, normally maintains a regular faculty and curriculum, normally has a regularly enrolled student body, and has a place where its educational activities are carried on.

The term generally corresponds to the definition of an "educational organization" in section 170(b)(1)(A)(ii). Thus, the term includes primary, secondary, preparatory and high schools, and colleges and universities. The term does not include organizations engaged in both educational and noneducational activities unless the latter are merely incidental to the educational activities. A school for handicapped children is included within the term, but an organization merely providing handicapped children with custodial care is not.

For purposes of Schedule B, "Sunday schools" that are conducted by a church are not included in the term "schools," but separately organized schools (such as parochial schools, universities, and similar institutions) are included in the term.

A private school that otherwise meets the requirements of section 501(c)(3) as an educational institution will not qualify for exemption under section 501(a) unless it has a racially nondiscriminatory policy as to students.

This policy means that the school admits students of any race to all the rights, privileges, programs, and activities generally accorded or made available to students at that school and that the school does not discriminate on the basis of race in the administration of its educational policies, admissions policies, scholarship and loan programs, and athletic or other school-administered programs.

The IRS considers discrimination on the basis of race to include discrimination on the basis of color and national or ethnic origin. A policy of a school that favors racial minority groups in admissions, facilities, programs, and financial assistance will not constitute discrimination on the basis of race when the purpose and effect is to promote the establishment and maintenance of that school's racially nondiscriminatory policy as to students.

See Rev. Proc. 75-50, 1975-2 C.B. 587, for guidelines and recordkeeping requirements for determining whether private schools that are applying for recognition of exemption have racially nondiscriminatory policies as to students.

Line 2

An instrumentality of a state or political subdivision of a state may qualify under section 501(c)(3) if it is organized as a separate entity from the governmental unit that created it and if it otherwise meets the organizational and operational tests of section 501(c)(3). (See Rev. Rul. 60-384, 1960-2 C.B. 172.) Any such organization that is a school is not a private school and, therefore, is not subject to the provisions of Rev. Proc. 75-50.

Schools that incorrectly answer "Yes" to line 2 will be contacted to furnish the information called for by lines 3 through 10 in order to establish that they meet the requirements for exemption. To prevent delay in the processing of your application, be sure to answer line 2 correctly and complete lines 3 through 10, if applicable.

Appendix 18–1

FORM 1023 (*continued*)

Schedule C. Hospitals and Medical Research Organizations

☐ Check here if claiming to be a hospital; complete the questions in Section I of this schedule; and write "N/A" in Section II.

☐ Check here if claiming to be a medical research organization operated in conjunction with a hospital; complete the questions in Section II of this schedule; and write "N/A" in Section I.

Section I   Hospitals

1a How many doctors are on the hospital's courtesy staff? . . . .

  b Are all the doctors in the community eligible for staff privileges? . . . . Yes ☐   No ☐
If "No," give the reasons why and explain how the courtesy staff is selected.

2a Does the hospital maintain a full-time emergency room? . . . . Yes ☐   No ☐
  b What is the hospital's policy on administering emergency services to persons without apparent means to pay?

  c Does the hospital have any arrangements with police, fire, and voluntary ambulance services for the delivery or admission of emergency cases? . . . . Yes ☐   No ☐
Explain.

3a Does or will the hospital require a deposit from persons covered by Medicare or Medicaid in its admission practices? . . . . Yes ☐   No ☐
If "Yes," explain.

  b Does the same deposit requirement, if any, apply to all other patients? . . . . Yes ☐   No ☐
If "No," explain.

4 Does or will the hospital provide for a portion of its services and facilities to be used for charity patients? . . . . Yes ☐   No ☐
Explain the policy regarding charity cases. Include data on the hospital's past experience in admitting charity patients and arrangements it may have with municipal or government agencies for absorbing the cost of such care.

5 Does or will the hospital carry on a formal program of medical training and research? . . . . Yes ☐   No ☐
If "Yes," describe.

6 Does the hospital provide office space to physicians carrying on a medical practice? . . . . Yes ☐   No ☐
If "Yes," attach a list setting forth the name of each physician, the amount of space provided, the annual rent, the expiration date of the current lease and whether the terms of the lease represent fair market value.

Section II   Medical Research Organizations

1 Name the hospitals with which the organization has a relationship and describe the relationship.

2 Attach a schedule describing the organization's present and proposed (indicate which) medical research activities; show the nature of the activities, and the amount of money that has been or will be spent in carrying them out. (Making grants to other organizations is not direct conduct of medical research.)

3 Attach a statement of assets showing their fair market value and the portion of the assets directly devoted to medical research.

For more information, see back of Schedule C.

FORM 1023 (*continued*)

Additional Information

Hospitals

To be entitled to status as a "hospital," an organization must have, as its principal purpose or function, the providing of medical or hospital care or medical education or research. "Medical care" includes the treatment of any physical or mental disability or condition, the cost of which may be taken as a deduction under section 213, whether the treatment is performed on an inpatient or outpatient basis. Thus, a rehabilitation institution, outpatient clinic, or community mental health or drug treatment center may be a hospital if its principal function is providing the above-described services.

On the other hand, a convalescent home or a home for children or the aged is not a hospital. Similarly, an institution whose principal purpose or function is to train handicapped individuals to pursue some vocation is not a hospital. Moreover, a medical education or medical research institution is not a hospital, unless it is also actively engaged in providing medical or hospital care to patients on its premises or in its facilities on an inpatient or outpatient basis.

Cooperative Hospital Service Organizations

Cooperative hospital service organizations (section 501(e)) should not complete Schedule C.

Medical Research Organizations

To qualify as a medical research organization, the principal function of the organization must be the direct, continuous, and active conduct of medical research in conjunction with a hospital that is described in section 501(c)(3), a Federal hospital, or an instrumentality of a governmental unit referred to in section 170(c)(1).

For purposes of section 170(b)(1)(A)(iii) only, the organization must be set up to use the funds it receives in the active conduct of medical research by January 1 of the fifth calendar year after receipt. The arrangement it has with donors to assure use of the funds within the 5-year period must be legally enforceable.

As used here, "medical research" means investigations, experiments, and studies to discover, develop, or verify knowledge relating to the causes, diagnosis, treatment, prevention, or control of human physical or mental diseases and impairments.

For further information, see Regulations section 1.170A-9(c)(2).

Appendix 18–1

FORM 1023 (*continued*)

Schedule D. Section 509(a)(3) Supporting Organizations

1a Organizations supported by the applicant organization: Name and address of supported organization	**b** Has the supported organization received a ruling or determination letter that it is not a private foundation by reason of section 509(a)(1) or (2)?	
....	☐ Yes	☐ No
....	☐ Yes	☐ No
....	☐ Yes	☐ No
....	☐ Yes	☐ No
....	☐ Yes	☐ No

c If "No" for any of the organizations listed in 1a, explain.

2 Does the supported organization have tax-exempt status under section 501(c)(4), 501(c)(5), or 501(c)(6)? . . . . Yes ☐   No ☐
If "Yes," attach: (a) a copy of its ruling or determination letter, and (b) an analysis of its revenue for the current year and the preceding 3 years. (Provide the financial data using the formats in Part IV-A (lines 1-13) and Part III (lines 12, 13, and 14).)

3 Does your organization's governing document indicate that the majority of its governing board is elected or appointed by the supported organizations? . . . . Yes ☐   No ☐
If "Yes," skip to line 9.
If "No," you must answer the questions on lines 4 through 9.

4 Does your organization's governing document indicate the common supervision or control that it and the supported organizations share? . . . . Yes ☐   No ☐
If "Yes," give the article and paragraph numbers. If "No," explain.

5 To what extent do the supported organizations have a significant voice in your organization's investment policies, in the making and timing of grants, and in otherwise directing the use of your organization's income or assets?

6 Does the mentioning of the supported organizations in your organization's governing instrument make it a trust that the supported organizations can enforce under state law and compel to make an accounting? . . . . Yes ☐   No ☐
If "Yes," explain.

7a What percentage of your organization's income does it pay to each supported organization?

b What is the total annual income of each supported organization?

c How much does your organization contribute annually to each supported organization?

For more information, see back of Schedule D.

FORM 1023 (*continued*)

Schedule D. Section 509(a)(3) Supporting Organizations (Continued)

8 To what extent does your organization conduct activities that would otherwise be carried on by the supported organizations? Explain why these activities would otherwise be carried on by the supported organizations.

9 Is the applicant organization controlled directly or indirectly by one or more "disqualified persons" (other than one who is a disqualified person solely because he or she is a manager) or by an organization that is not described in section 509(a)(1) or (2)? . . . . Yes ☐   No ☐
If "Yes," explain.

Instructions

For an explanation of the types of organizations defined in section 509(a)(3) as being excluded from the definition of a private foundation, see Publication 557, Chapter 3.

Line 1
List each organization that is supported by your organization and indicate in item 1b if the supported organization has received a letter recognizing exempt status as a section 501(c)(3) public charity as defined in section 509(a)(1) or 509(a)(2). If you answer "No" in 1b to any of the listed organizations, please explain in 1c.

Line 3
Your organization's governing document may be articles of incorporation, articles of association, constitution, trust indenture, or trust agreement.

Line 9
For a definition of a "disqualified person," see Specific Instructions, Part II, Line 4d, on page 3 of the application's instructions.

Appendix 18–1

FORM 1023 (*continued*)

Instructions

If the organization claims to be an operating foundation described in section 4942(j)(3) and-

   a. Bases its claim to private operating foundation status on normal and regular operations over a period of years; or

   b. Is newly created, set up as a private operating foundation, and has at least 1 year's experience;

provide the information under the income test and under one of the three supplemental tests (assets, endowment, or support). If the organization does not have at least 1 year's experience, provide the information called for on line 21. If the organization's private operating foundation status depends on its normal and regular operations as described in a above, attach a schedule similar to Schedule E showing the data in tabular form for the 3 years preceding the most recent tax year. (See Regulations section 53.4942(b)-1 for additional information before completing the "Income Test" section of this schedule.) Organizations claiming section 4942(j)(5) status must satisfy the income test and the endowment test.

A "private operating foundation" described in section 4942(j)(3) is a private foundation that spends substantially all of the smaller of its adjusted net income (as defined below) or its minimum investment return directly for the active conduct of the activities constituting the purpose or function for which it is organized and operated. The foundation must satisfy the income test under section 4942(j)(3)(A), as modified by Regulations section 53.4942(b)-1, and one of the following three supplemental tests: (1) the assets test under section 4942(j)(3)(B)(i); (2) the endowment test under section 4942(j)(3)(B)(ii); or (3) the support test under section 4942(j)(3)(B)(iii).

Certain long-term care facilities described in section 4942(j)(5) are treated as private operating foundations for purposes of section 4942 only.

"Adjusted net income" is the excess of gross income determined with the income modifications described below for the tax year over the sum of deductions determined with the deduction modifications described below. Items of gross income from any unrelated trade or business and the deductions directly connected with the unrelated trade or business are taken into account in computing the organization's adjusted net income.

Income Modifications

The following are income modifications (adjustments to gross income):

   1. Section 103 (relating to interest on certain governmental obligations) does not apply. Thus, interest that otherwise would have been excluded should be included in gross income.

   2. Except as provided in 3 below, capital gains and losses are taken into account only to the extent of the net short-term gain. Long-term gains and losses are disregarded.

   3. The gross amount received from the sale or disposition of certain property should be included in gross income to the extent that the acquisition of the property constituted a qualifying distribution under section 4942(g)(1)(B).

   4. Repayments of prior qualifying distributions (as defined in section 4942(g)(1)(A)) constitute items of gross income.

   5. Any amount set aside under section 4942(g)(2) that is "not necessary for the purposes for which it was set aside" constitutes an item of gross income.

Deduction Modifications

The following are deduction modifications (adjustments to deductions):

   1. Expenses for the general operation of the organization according to its charitable purposes (as contrasted with expenses for the production or collection of income and management, conservation, or maintenance of income-producing property) should not be taken as deductions. If only a portion of the property is used for production of income subject to section 4942 and the remainder is used for general charitable purposes, the expenses connected with that property should be divided according to those purposes. Only expenses related to the income-producing portion should be taken as a deduction.

   2. Charitable contributions, deductible under section 170 or 642(c), should not be taken into account as deductions for adjusted net income.

   3. The net operating loss deduction prescribed under section 172 should not be taken into account as a deduction for adjusted net income.

   4. The special deductions for corporations (such as the dividends-received deduction) allowed under sections 241 through 249 should not be taken into account as deductions for adjusted net income.

   5. Depreciation and depletion should be determined in the same manner as under section 4940(c)(3)(B).

Section 265 (relating to the expenses and interest connected with tax-exempt income) should not be taken into account.

You may find it easier to figure adjusted net income by completing column (c), Part 1, Form 990-PF, according to the instructions for that form.

An organization that has been held to be a private operating foundation will continue to be such an organization only if it meets the income test and either the assets, endowment, or support test in later years. See Regulations section 53.4942(b) for additional information. No additional request for ruling will be necessary or appropriate for an organization to maintain its status as a private operating foundation. However, data related to the above tests must be submitted with the organization's annual information return, Form 990-PF.

Appendix 18–1

FORM 1023 (*continued*)

Schedule F. Homes for the Aged or Handicapped

1   What are the requirements for admission to residency? Explain fully and attach promotional literature and application forms.

2   Does or will the home charge an entrance or founder's fee? . . . . Yes ☐   No ☐
    If "Yes," explain and specify the amount charged.

3   What periodic fees or maintenance charges are or will be required of its residents?

4a What established policy does the home have concerning residents who become unable to pay their regular charges?

b   What arrangements does the home have or will it make with local and Federal welfare units, sponsoring organizations, or
    others to absorb all or part of the cost of maintaining those residents?

5   What arrangements does or will the home have to provide for the health needs of its residents?

6   In what way are the home's residential facilities designed to meet some combination of the physical, emotional, recreational,
    social, religious, and similar needs of the aged or handicapped?

7   Provide a description of the home's facilities and specify both the residential capacity of the home and the current number
    of residents.

8   Attach a sample copy of the contract or agreement the organization makes with or requires of its residents.
    For more information, see back of Schedule F.

Appendix 18–1

FORM 1023 (*continued*)

Instructions

Line 1

Provide the criteria for admission to the home and submit brochures, pamphlets, or other printed material used to inform the public about the home's admissions policy.

Line 2

Indicate whether the fee charged is an entrance fee or a monthly charge, etc. Also, if the fee is an entrance fee, is it payable in a lump sum or on an installment basis?

Line 4

Indicate the organization's policy regarding residents who are unable to pay. Also, indicate whether the organization is subsidized for all or part of the cost of maintaining those residents who are unable to pay.

Line 5

Indicate whether the organization provides health care to the residents, either directly or indirectly, through some continuing arrangement with other organizations, facilities, or health personnel. If no health care is provided, indicate "N/A."

Appendix 18–1

FORM 1023 (*continued*)

Form 1023 (Rev. 9-98)   Page 25

Schedule G. Child Care Organizations

1   Is the organization's primary activity the providing of care for children away from their homes?
    homes? . . . . Yes ☐   No ☐

2   How many children is the organization authorized to care for by the state (or local governmental unit), and what was the average attendance during the past 6 months, or the number of months the organization has been in existence if less than 6 months?

3   How many children are currently cared for by the organization?

4   Is substantially all (at least 85%) of the care provided for the purpose of enabling parents to be gainfully employed or to seek employment? . . . . Yes ☐   No ☐

5   Are the services provided available to the general public? . . . . Yes ☐   No ☐
    If "No," explain.

6   Indicate the category, or categories, of parents whose children are eligible for the child care services (check as many as apply):

    ☐ low-income parents

    ☐ any working parents (or parents looking for work)

    ☐ anyone with the ability to pay

    ☐ other (explain)

Instructions

Line 5
If your organization's services are not available to the general public, indicate the particular group or groups that may utilize the services.

REMINDER - If this organization claims to operate a school, then it must also fill out Schedule B.

Appendix 18–1

FORM 1023 (*continued*)

Schedule H. Organizations Providing Scholarship Benefits, Student Aid, Etc., to Individuals

1a Describe the nature and the amount of the scholarship benefit, student aid, etc., including the terms and conditions governing its use, whether a gift or a loan, and how the availability of the scholarship is publicized. If the organization has established or will establish several categories of scholarship benefits, identify each kind of benefit and explain how the organization determines the recipients for each category. Attach a sample copy of any application the organization requires individuals to complete to be considered for scholarship grants, loans, or similar benefits. (Private foundations that make grants for travel, study, or other similar purposes are required to obtain advance approval of scholarship procedures. See Regulations sections 53.4945-4(c)and (d).)

b If you want this application considered as a request for approval of grant procedures in the event we determine that the organization is a private foundation, check here . . . . ☐

c If you checked the box in 1b above, check the boxes for which you wish the organization to be considered.

☐ 4945(g)(1)   ☐ 4945(g)(2)   ☐ 4945(g)(3)

2 What limitations or restrictions are there on the class of individuals who are eligible recipients? Specifically explain whether there are, or will be, any restrictions or limitations in the selection procedures based upon race or the employment status of the prospective recipient or any relative of the prospective recipient. Also indicate the approximate number of eligible individuals.

3 Indicate the number of grants the organization anticipates making annually . . . .

4 If the organization bases its selections in any way on the employment status of the applicant or any relative of the applicant, indicate whether there is or has been any direct or indirect relationship between the members of the selection committee and the employer. Also indicate whether relatives of the members of the selection committee are possible recipients or have been recipients.

5 Describe any procedures the organization has for supervising grants (such as obtaining reports or transcripts) that it awards, and any procedures it has for taking action if the terms of the grant are violated.

For more information, see back of Schedule H.

FORM 1023 (*continued*)

Additional Information

Private foundations that make grants to individuals for travel, study, or other similar purposes are required to obtain advance approval of their grant procedures from the IRS. Such grants that are awarded under selection procedures that have not been approved by the IRS are subject to a 10% excise tax under section 4945. (See Regulations sections 53.4945-4(c) and (d).)

If you are requesting advance approval of the organization's grant procedures, the following sections apply to line 1c:

4945(g)(1) -   The grant constitutes a scholarship or fellowship grant that meets the provisions of section 117(a) prior to its amendment by the Tax Reform Act of 1986 and is to be used for study at an educational organization (school) described in section 170(b)(1)(A)(ii).

4945(g)(2) -   The grant constitutes a prize or award that is subject to the provisions of section 74(b), if the recipient of such a prize or award is selected from the general public.

4945(g)(3) -   The purpose of the grant is to achieve a specific objective, produce a report or other similar product, or improve or enhance a literary, artistic, musical, scientific, teaching, or other similar capacity, skill, or talent of the grantee.

Appendix 18–1

FORM 1023 (*continued*)

Schedule I. Successors to "For Profit" Institutions

1 What was the name of the predecessor organization and the nature of its activities?

2 Who were the owners or principle stockholders of the predecessor organization? (If more space is needed, attach schedule.)

Name and address	Share or interest

3 Describe the business or family relationship between the owners or principal stockholders and principal employees of the predecessor organization and the officers, directors, and principal employees of the applicant organization.

4a Attach a copy of the agreement of sale or other contract that sets forth the terms and conditions of sale of the predecessor organization or of its assets to the applicant organization.
  b Attach an appraisal by an independent qualified expert showing the fair market value at the time of sale of the facilities or property interest sold.

5 Has any property or equipment formerly used by the predecessor organization been rented to the applicant organization or will any such property be rented? . . . . Yes ☐   No ☐
    If "Yes," explain and attach copies of all leases and contracts.

6 Is the organization leasing or will it lease or otherwise make available any space or equipment to the owners, principal stockholders, or principal employees of the predecessor organization? . . . . Yes ☐   No ☐
    If "Yes," explain and attach a list of these tenants and a copy of the lease for each such tenant.

7 Were any new operating policies initiated as a result of the transfer of assets from a profit-making organization to a nonprofit organization? . . . . Yes ☐   No ☐
    If "Yes," explain.

Additional Information

A "for profit" institution for purposes of Schedule I includes any organization in which a person may have a proprietary or partnership interest, hold corporate stock, or otherwise exercise an ownership interest. The institution need not have operated for the purpose of making a profit.

Appendix 18–2

FORM 1024

Form **1024** (Rev. September 1998) Department of the Treasury Internal Revenue Service	**Application for Recognition of Exemption Under Section 501(a)**	OMB No. 1545-0057 If exempt status is approved, this application will be open for public inspection.

Read the instructions for each Part carefully.
A User Fee must be attached to this application.
If the required information and appropriate documents are not submitted along with Form 8718 (with payment of the appropriate user fee), the application may be returned to the organization.
Complete the Procedural Checklist on page 6 of the Instructions.

Part I.   Identification of Applicant   (Must be completed by all applicants; also complete appropriate schedule.) Submit only the schedule that applies to your organization. Do not submit blank schedules.

Check the appropriate box below to indicate the section under which the organization is applying:

- a ☐ Section 501(c)(2) - Title holding corporations (Schedule A, page 7)
- b ☒ Section 501(c)(4) - Civic leagues, social welfare organizations (including certain war veterans' organizations), or local associations of employees (Schedule B, page 8)
- c ☐ Section 501(c)(5) - Labor, agricultural, or horticultural organizations (Schedule C, page 9)
- d ☐ Section 501(c)(6) - Business leagues, chambers of commerce, etc. (Schedule C, page 9)
- e ☐ Section 501(c)(7) - Social clubs (Schedule D, page 11)
- f ☐ Section 501(c)(8) - Fraternal beneficiary societies, etc., providing life, sick, accident, or other benefits to members (Sch. E, p. 13)
- g ☐ Section 501(c)(9) - Voluntary employees' beneficiary associations (Parts I through IV and Schedule F, page 14)
- h ☐ Section 501(c)(10) - Domestic fraternal societies, orders, etc., not providing life, sick, accident, or other benefits (Sch. E, p. 13)
- i ☐ Section 501(c)(12) - Benevolent life insurance associations, mutual ditch or irrigation companies, mutual or cooperative telephone companies, or like organizations (Schedule G, page 15)
- j ☐ Section 501(c)(13) - Cemeteries, crematoria, and like corporations (Schedule H, page 16)
- k ☐ Section 501(c)(15) - Mutual insurance companies or associations, other than life or marine (Schedule I, page 17)
- l ☐ Section 501(c)(17) - Trusts providing for the payment of supplemental unemployment compensation benefits (Sch. J, p. 18)
- m ☐ Section 501(c)(19) - A post, organization, auxiliary unit, etc., of past or present members of the Armed Forces of the United States (Schedule K, page 19)
- n ☐ Section 501(c)(25) - Title holding corporations or trusts (Schedule A, page 7)

1a Full name of organization (as shown in organizing document) **Disposable Bottle Action Committee**	**2** Employer identification number (EIN) (If none, see Specific Instructions on page 2) 42-2222222
1b c/o Name (if applicable)	**3** Name and telephone number of person to be contacted if additional information is needed
1c Address (number and street) Room/Suite **1111 Any Street**	
1d City, town or post office, state, and ZIP + 4 If you have a foreign address, see Specific Instructions for Part I, page 2. **Hometown TX 77777-7777**	**A. Good Accountant** **(444) 222-3333**

1e Web site address **www.savebottles.org**	**4** Month the annual accounting period ends **June**	**5** Date incorporated or formed **1-1-xx**

6 Did the organization previously apply for recognition of exemption under this Code section or under any other section of the Code? If "Yes," attach an explanation.   Yes ☐   No ☒

7 Has the organization filed Federal income tax returns or exempt organization information returns?
If "Yes," state the form numbers, years filed, and Internal Revenue office where filed.   Yes ☐   No ☒

8 Check the box for the type of organization. ATTACH A CONFORMED COPY OF THE CORRESPONDING ORGANIZING DOCUMENTS TO THE APPLICATION BEFORE MAILING.

- a ☒ Corporation - Attach a copy of the Articles of Incorporation (including amendments and restatements) showing approval by the appropriate state official; also attach a copy of the bylaws.
- b ☐ Trust - Attach a copy of the Trust Indenture or Agreement, including all appropriate signatures and dates.
- c ☐ Association - Attach a copy of the Articles of Association, Constitution, or other creating document, with a declaration (see instructions) or other evidence that the organization was formed by adoption of the document by more than one person. Also include a copy of the bylaws.

If this is a corporation or an unincorporated association that has not yet adopted bylaws, check here . . . . ☐

I declare under the penalties of perjury that I am authorized to sign this application on behalf of the above organization, and that I have examined this application, including the accompanying schedules and attachments, and to the best of my knowledge it is true, correct, and complete.

Please Sign Here   _Cary G. Generous_   (Signature)   **Director**   (Title or authority of signer)   _2/1/xx_ (Date)

For Paperwork Reduction Act Notice, see page 5 of the instructions.   (HTA)

Appendix 18–2

FORM 1024 (*continued*)

Form 1024 (Rev. 9-98)	Disposable Bottle Action Committee	42-2222222	Page 2

Part II. Activities and Operational Information   (Must be completed by all applicants)

1   Provide a detailed narrative description of all the activities of the organization - past, present, and planned. Do not merely refer to or repeat the language in the organizational document. List each activity separately in the order of importance based on the relative time and other resources devoted to the activity. Each description should include, as a minimum, the following: (a) a detailed description of the activity including its purpose and how each activity furthers your exempt purpose; (b) when the activity was or will be initiated; and (c) where and by whom the activity will be conducted.

       See attachment for this part

2   List the organization's present and future sources of financial support, beginning with the largest source first.

Membership dues	**75%**
Exempt function sales	**25%**

Appendix 18–2

FORM 1024 (*continued*)

Form 1024 (Rev. 9-98)	Disposable Bottle Action Committee	42-2222222	Page 3

Part II. Activities and Operational Information (continued)

3 Give the following information about the organization's governing body:

a Names, addresses, and titles of officers, directors, trustees, etc.	**b** Annual compensation
Gary G. Generous President 222 Fifth Street, Hometown, Texas 77777	None
Samantha Zealot Vice President 404 University Dr., Austin, Texas 78777	None
Linda Lockard Secretary/Treasurer 982 Pine Valley, Dallas, Texas 75555	None
Jane D. Environmentalist Director 333 First Street, Hometown, Texas 77777	None

4 If the organization is the outgrowth or continuation of any form of predecessor, state the name of each predecessor, the period during which it was in existence, and the reasons for its termination. Submit copies of all papers by which any transfer of assets was effected.

Not Applicable

5 If the applicant organization is now, or plans to be, connected in any way with any other organization, describe the other organization and explain the relationship (e.g., financial support on a continuing basis; shared facilities or employees; same officers, directors, or trustees).

Disposable Bottle Action Committee (DBAC) is being formed by individuals who also serve as directors of a private foundation, Environmentalist Fund, and a publicly supported EO, Campaign to Clean Up America. There will be no financial relationship between the organizations and the individuals will not control DBAC.

6 If the organization has capital stock issued and outstanding, state: (1) class or classes of the stock; (2) number and par value of the shares; (3) consideration for which they were issued; and (4) if any dividends have been paid or whether your organization's creating instrument authorizes dividend payments on any class of capital stock.

Not Applicable

7 State the qualifications necessary for membership in the organization; the classes of membership (with the number of members in each class); and the voting rights and privileges received. If any group or class of persons is required to join, describe the requirement and explain the relationship between those members and members who join voluntarily. Submit copies of any membership solicitation material. Attach sample copies of all types of membership certificates issued.

Membership is open to all persons who can pay the basic dues of $10.

8 Explain how your organization's assets will be distributed on dissolution.

Assets would be distributed to Campaign to Clean Up America, a publicly supported 501(c)(3) organization.

Appendix 18–2

FORM 1024 *(continued)*

Form 1024 (Rev. 9-88)   Disposable Bottle Action Committee   42-2222222   Page 4

Part II. Activities and Operational Information (continued)

9   Has the organization made or does it plan to make any distribution of its property or surplus funds
to shareholders or members? . . . .   Yes ☐   No ☒
If "Yes," state the full details, including: (1) amounts or value; (2) source of funds or
property distributed or to be distributed; and (3) basis of, and authority for, distribution or
planned distribution.

10   Does, or will, any part of your organization's receipts represent payments for services performed or
to be performed? . . . .   Yes ☐   No ☒
If "Yes," state in detail the amount received and the character of the services performed or
to be performed.

11   Has the organization made, or does it plan to make, any payments to members or shareholders for
services performed or to be performed? . . . .   Yes ☐   No ☒
If "Yes," state in detail the amount paid, the character of the services, and to whom the
payments have been, or will be, made.

12   Does the organization have any arrangement to provide insurance for members, their dependents,
or others (including provisions for the payment of sick or death benefits, pensions or annuities)? . . . . . .   Yes ☐   No ☒
If "Yes," describe and explain the arrangement's eligibility rules and attach a sample copy of
each plan document and each type of policy issued.

13   Is the organization under the supervisory jurisdiction of any public regulatory body, such as a social
welfare agency, etc.? . . . .   Yes ☐   No ☒
If "Yes," submit copies of all administrative opinions or court decisions regarding this supervision,
as well as copies of applications or requests for the opinions or decisions.

14   Does the organization now lease or does it plan to lease any property? . . . .   Yes ☒   No ☐
If "Yes," explain in detail. Include the amount of rent, a description of the property, and any
relationship between the applicant organization and the other party. Also, attach a copy of
any rental or lease agreement. (If the organization is a party, as a lessor, to multiple leases
of rental real property under similar lease agreements, please attach a single,
representative copy of the leases.)
     DBAC will lease one room on a month to month projected cost basis of $200 per month.
     The building is owned by an unrelated party.

15   Has the organization spent or does it plan to spend any money attempting to influence the selection,
nomination, election, or appointment of any person to any Federal, state, or local public office or to
an office in a political organization? . . . .   Yes ☐   No ☒
If "Yes," explain in detail and list the amounts spent or to be spent in each case.

16   Does the organization publish pamphlets, brochures, newsletters, journals, or similar printed
material? . . . .   Yes ☐   No ☒
If "Yes," attach a recent copy of each.

Appendix 18–2

FORM 1024 (*continued*)

Form 1024 (Rev. 9-98)   Disposable Bottle Action Committee   42-2222222   Page 5

Part III. Financial Data   (Must be completed by all applicants)

Complete the financial statements for the current year and for each of the 3 years immediately before it. If in existence less than 4 years, complete the statements for each year in existence. If in existence less than 1 year, also provide proposed budgets for the 2 years following the current year.

A. Statement of Revenue and Expenses

Revenue	(a) Current Tax Year	3 Prior Tax Years or Proposed Budget for Next 2 Years			(e) Total
	From / To	(b) 19	(c) 19	(d) 19	
1 Gross dues and assessments of members	No financial activity to date.				
2 Gross contributions, gifts, etc.					
3 Gross amounts derived from activities related to the organization's exempt purpose (Include related cost of sales on line 9.)	See projections attached				
4 Gross amounts from unrelated business activities (attach sch.) . . .					
5 Gain from sale of assets, excluding inventory items (attach sch.)					
6 Investment income (see inst.)					
7 Other revenue (attach schedule) . .					
8 Total revenue (add lines 1 through 7)					
Expenses					
9 Expenses attributable to activities related to the organization's exempt purposes					
10 Expenses attributable to unrelated business activities					
11 Contributions, gifts, grants, and similar amounts paid (attach sch.) . . .					
12 Disbursements to or for the benefit of members (attach schedule) . . .					
13 Compensation of officers, directors, and trustees (attach schedule) . . .					
14 Other salaries and wages					
15 Interest					
16 Occupancy					
17 Depreciation and depletion					
18 Other expenses (attach sch.)					
19 Total expenses (add lines 9 - 18) . . .					
20 Excess of revenue over expenses (line 8 minus line 19)					

B. Balance Sheet (at the end of the period shown)

Assets		as of	Current Tax Year New Organization No assets
1 Cash		1	
2 Accounts receivable, net		2	
3 Inventories		3	
4 Bonds and notes receivable (attach schedule)		4	
5 Corporate stocks (attach schedule)		5	
6 Mortgage loans (attach schedule)		6	
7 Other investments (attach schedule)		7	
8 Depreciable and depletable assets (attach schedule)		8	
9 Land		9	
10 Other assets (attach schedule)		10	
11 Total assets		11	
Liabilities			
12 Accounts payable		12	
13 Contributions, gifts, grants, etc., payable		13	
14 Mortgages and notes payable (attach schedule)		14	
15 Other liabilities (attach schedule)		15	
16 Total liabilities		16	
Fund Balances or Net Assets			
17 Total fund balances or net assets		17	
18 Total liabilities and fund balances or net assets (add line 16 and line 17)		18	

If there has been any substantial change in any aspect of the organization's financial activities since the end of the period shown above, check the box and attach a detailed explanation . . . . ☐

Appendix 18–2

FORM 1024 (*continued*)

Form 1024 (Rev. 9-98)	Disposable Bottle Action Committee	42-2222222	Page 8

Schedule B   **Organizations Described in Section 501(c)(4) (Civic leagues, social welfare organizations (including posts, councils, etc., of veterans' organizations not qualifying or applying for exemption under section 501(c)(19)) or local associations of employees.)**

1   Has the Internal Revenue Service previously issued a ruling or determination letter recognizing the applicant organization (or any predecessor organization listed in question 4, Part II of the application) to be exempt under section 501(c)(3) and later revoked that recognition of exemption on the basis that the applicant organization (or its predecessor) was carrying on propaganda or otherwise attempting to influence legislation or on the basis that it engaged in political activity?   Yes ☐   No ☒

If "Yes," indicate the earliest tax year for which recognition of exemption under section 501(c)(3) was revoked and the IRS district office that issued the revocation.

2   Does the organization perform or plan to perform (for members, shareholders, or others) services, such as maintaining the common areas of a condominium; buying food or other items on a cooperative basis; or providing recreational facilities or transportation services, job placement, or other similar undertakings? . . . .   Yes ☐   No ☒

If "Yes," explain the activities in detail, including income realized and expenses incurred. Also, explain in detail the nature of the benefits to the general public from these activities. (If the answer to this question is explained in Part II of the application (pages 2, 3, and 4), enter the page and item number here.)

3   If the organization is claiming exemption as a homeowners' association, is access to any property or facilities it owns or maintains restricted in any way? . . . .   N/A   Yes ☐   No ☐

If "Yes," explain.

     Not Applicable

4   If the organization is claiming exemption as a local association of employees, state the name and address of each employer whose employees are eligible for membership in the association. If employees of more than one plant or office of the same employer are eligible for membership, give the address of each plant or office.

     Not Applicable

Appendix 18–2

FORM 1024 (*continued*)

Disposable Bottle Action Committee

Attachments to Form 1024

Author's notes: This model application does not include a charter, bylaws, or Forms 8718 or 2848. See Appendix 18-1, the model 1023, for examples.

Form 1024, pages 1 through 5 are completed by all applicants. Pages 6 through 19 contain questions germane to particular categories of 501(c) exemption. An applicant chooses and completes the appropriate page for their proposed category. All pages are included in this appendix for illustration purposes.

Reader will note Disposable Bottle Action Campaign completes page 8.

Appendix 18–2

FORM 1024 (*continued*)

Disposable Bottle Action Committee   EIN #: 42-2222222
Attachment to Form 1024 - Part II, question 1

Description of Proposed Activities

Disposable Bottle Action Committee (DBAC) was formed to initiate a nationwide campaign to propose and pass legislation to eliminate disposable containers and reward recycling efforts. By reducing trash, encouraging the conservation of resources, and curtailing pollutants to our land, water, and air, DBAC's goal is to advance the community welfare.

LEGISLATION -- DBAC plans to be an action organization, whose purposes are accomplished through passage of legislation. Model legislation will be drafted (based upon the California and Washington state models) for passage of a comprehensive waste management law based upon eventual elimination of disposable containers and other toxic wastes. Committees will be formed in as many states as possible to conduct petition campaigns to lobby congress people to support the legislation.

RESEARCH -- The Ecology Department of Michigan State University and Northwestern University were contacted and have agreed to cosponsor a year long research project to evaluate the economic and ecological consequences of disposable containers. While DBAC will not contribute financially to the efforts, the results of the studies will be available for use in the legislative efforts. It is hoped that the University of California at Berkley or a similar West Coast institution will be convinced to study the consequences of their existing beverage container laws.

FUND RAISING and PUBLIC EDUCATION -- Committees will be formed in key states to raise funds to finance the campaign and to raise public consciousness about the issue of wastes and the need for reducing garbage through recycling and elimination of disposable containers. Funds will be raised through voluntary donations, memberships, and sale of bumper stickers, buttons, and other campaign materials.

Attachment to Part II, Question 1

Appendix 18–2

FORM 1024 (*continued*)

Disposable Bottle Action Committee
Attachment to Form 1024

EIN #: 42-2222222

Proposed Budgets - Part III

	20XX	20XX
REVENUES:		
Membership dues	$ 25,000	$ 50,000
Exempt function sales:		
Bumper stickers	5,000	10,000
Posters	2,000	5,000
Buttons	2,000	5,000
Model legislation	2,000	5,000
Total	36,000	75,000
EXPENSES:		
Campaign coordinator*	$ 10,000	$30,000
Telephone/web site	5,000	12,000
Mailing	5,000	12,000
Printing	5,000	12,000
Cost of stickers, posters, buttons	2,000	6,000
Occupancy**	2,000	3,000
	29,000	75,000
Working capital reserve	7,000	0
Total	$ 36,000	$ 75,000

*The Campaign coordinator is an independent contractor who serves as consultant to nonprofit organizations conducting lobbying campaigns. Compensation is based upon actual time expended at the rate of $20 per hour plus reimbursement of direct out-of-pocket expenses. DBAC will be operated primarily by volunteers.

**DBAC will sublease one room in an office building owned by an unrelated party. The rent is expected to be about $200 per month with a month-to-month lease.

Attachment to Part III

Appendix 18–2

FORM 1024 (*continued*)

Part IV. Notice Requirements (Sections 501(c)(9) and 501(c)(17) Organizations Only)

1 Section 501(c)(9) and 501(c)(17) organizations:

Are you filing Form 1024 within 15 months from the end of the month in which the organization was created or formed as required by section 505(c)? . . . .   Yes ☐   No ☐

If "Yes," skip the rest of this Part.

If "No," answer question 2.

2 If you answer "No" to question 1, are you filing Form 1024 within 27 months from the end of the month in which the organization was created or formed? . . . .   Yes ☐   No ☐

If "Yes," your organization qualifies under Regulation section 301.9100-2 for an automatic 12-month extension of the 15-month filing requirement. Do not answer questions 3 and 4.

If "No," answer question 3.

3 If you answer "No" to question 2, does the organization wish to request an extension of time to apply under the "reasonable action and good faith" and the "no prejudice to the interest of the government" requirements of Regulations section 301.9100-3? . . . .   Yes ☐   No ☐

If "Yes," give the reasons for not filing this application within the 27-month period described in question 2. See Specific Instructions, Part IV, Line 3, page 4, before completing this item. Do not answer question 4.

If "No," answer question 4.

Note: Applicants choose and attach the schedule on page 6-19 applicable to the category under which exemption is sought.

4 If you answer "No" to question 3, your organization's qualification as a section 501(c)(9) or 501(c)(17) organization can be recognized only from the date this application is filed. Therefore, does the organization want us to consider its application as a request for recognition of exemption as a section 501(c)(9) or 501(c)(17) organization from the date the application is received and not retroactively to the date the organization was created or formed? . . . .   Yes ☐   No ☐

FORM 1024 (*continued*)

Schedule A   **Organizations described in section 501(c)(2) or 501(c)(25)**   **(Title holding corporations or trusts)**

1   State the complete name, address, and employer identification number of each organization for which title to property is held and the number and type of the applicant organization's stock held by each organization.

2   If the annual excess of revenue over expenses has not been or will be not be turned over to the organization for which title to property is held, state the purpose for which the excess is or will be retained by the title holding organization.

3   In the case of a corporation described in section 501(c)(2), state the purpose of the organization for which title to property is held (as shown in its governing instrument) and the Code sections under which it is classified as exempt from tax. If the organization has received a determination or ruling letter recognizing it as exempt from taxation, please attach a copy of the letter.

4   In the case of a corporation or trust described in section 501(c)(25), state the basis whereby each shareholder is described in section 501(c)(25)(C). For each organization described that has received a determination or ruling letter recognizing that organization as exempt from taxation, please attach a copy of the letter.

5   With respect to the activities of the organization.

    a   Is any rent received attributable to personal property leased with real property? . . . .   Yes ☐   No ☐
       If "Yes," what percentage of the total rent, as reported on the financial statements in Part III, is attributable to personal property?

    b   Will the organization receive income which is incidentally derived from the holding of real property, such as income from operation of a parking lot or from vending machine? . . . .   Yes ☐   No ☐
       If "Yes," what percentage of the organization's gross income, as reported on the financial statements in Part III, is incidentally derived from the holding of real property?

    c   Will the organization receive income other than rent from real property or personal property leased with real property or income which is incidentally derived from the holding of real property? . . . .   Yes ☐   No ☐
       If "Yes," describe the source of the income.

Instructions

Line 1.- Provide the requested information on each organization for which the applicant organization holds title to property. Also indicate the number and types of shares of the applicant organization's stock that are held by each.

Line 2.- For purposes of this question, "excess of revenue over expenses" is all of the organization's income for a particular tax year less operating expenses.

Line 3.- Give the exempt purpose of each organization that is the basis for its exempt status and the Internal Revenue Code section that describes the organization (as shown in its IRS determination letter).

Line 4.- Indicate if the shareholder is one of the following:

1. A qualified pension, profit-sharing, or stock bonus plan that meets the requirements of the Code;
2. A government plan;
3. An organization described in section 501(c)(3); or
4. An organization described in section 501(c)(25).

Appendix 18–2

FORM 1024 (*continued*)

Form 1024 (Rev. 9-98)   Page 9

Schedule C	Organizations described in section 501(c)(5) (Labor, agricultural, including fishermen's organizations, or horticultural organizations) or section 501(c)(6) (business leagues, chambers of commerce, etc.)

1 Describe any services the organization performs for members or others. (If the description of the services is contained in Part II of the application, enter the page and item number here.)

2 Fishermen's organizations only. - What kinds of aquatic resources (not including mineral) are cultivated or harvested by those eligible for membership in the organization?

3 Labor organizations only. - Is the organization organized under the terms of a collective bargaining agreement? . . . .   Yes ☐   No ☐

If "Yes," attach a copy of the latest agreement.

Appendix 18–2

FORM 1024 (*continued*)

Form 1024 (Rev. 9-98)   Page 11

Schedule D   **Organizations described in section 501(c)(7) (Social clubs)**

1 Has the organization entered or does it plan to enter into any contract or agreement for the management or operation of its property and/or activities, such as restaurants, pro shops, lodges, etc.? . . .   Yes ☐   No ☐

If "Yes," attach a copy of the contract or agreement. If one has not yet been drawn up, please explain the organization's plans.

2 Does the organization seek or plan to seek public patronage of its facilities or activities by advertisement or otherwise? . . . .   Yes ☐   No ☐

If "Yes," attach sample copies of the advertisements or other requests.
If the organization plans to seek public patronage, please explain the plans.

3a Are nonmembers, other than guests of members, permitted or will they be permitted to use the club facilities or participate in or attend any functions or activities conducted by the organization? . . . . . .   Yes ☐   No ☐

If "Yes," describe the functions or activities in which there has been or will be nonmember participation or admittance. (Submit a copy of the house rules, if any.)

b State the amount of nonmember income included in Part III of the application, lines 3 and 4, column (a) . . . .   . _____

c Enter the percent of gross receipts from nonmembers for the use of club facilities . . . . _____

d Enter the percent of gross receipts received from investment income and nonmember use of the club's facilities . . . . _____

4a Does the organization's charter, bylaws, other governing instrument, or any written policy statement of the organization contain any provision that provides for discrimination against any person on the basis of race, color, or religion? . . . .   Yes ☐   No ☐

b If "Yes," state whether or not its provision will be kept.

c If the organization has such a provision that will be repealed, deleted, or otherwise stricken from its requirements, state when this will be done . . . . _____

d If the organization formerly had such a requirement and it no longer applies, give the date it ceased to apply . . . . _____

e If the organization restricts its membership to members of a particular religion, check here and attach the explanation specified in the instructions . . . . ☐

See reverse side for instructions

Appendix 18–2

FORM 1024 (*continued*)

Instructions

Line 1.- Answer "Yes," if any of the organization's property or activities will be managed by another organization or company.

Line 3b, c, and d.- Enter the figures for the current year. On an attached schedule, furnish the same information for each of the prior tax years for which you completed Part III of the application.

Line 4e.- If the organization restricts its membership to members of a particular religion, the organization must be:

    1. An auxiliary of a fraternal beneficiary society that:

    a. Is described in section 501(c)(8) and exempt from tax under section 501(a), and

    b. Limits its membership to members of a particular religion; or

    2. A club that, in good faith, limits its membership to the members of a particular religion in order to further the teachings or principles of that religion and not to exclude individuals of a particular race or color.

If you checked 4e, your explanation must show how the organization meets one of these two requirements.

Appendix 18–2

FORM 1024 (*continued*)

Form 1024 (Rev. 9-98)   Page 13

Schedule E — **Organizations described in section 501(c)(8) or 501(c)(10) (Fraternal societies, orders, or associations)**

1 Is the organization a college fraternity or sorority, or chapter of a college fraternity or sorority? . . . . . .   Yes ☐   No ☐
If "Yes," read the instructions for Line 1, below, before completing this schedule.

2 Does or will your organization operate under the lodge system? . . . .   Yes ☐   No ☐
If "No," does or will it operate for the exclusive benefit of the members of an organization operating
under the lodge system? . . . .   Yes ☐   No ☐

3 Is the organization a subordinate or local lodge, etc.? . . . .   Yes ☐   No ☐
If "Yes," attach a certificate signed by the secretary of the parent organization, under the
seal of the organization, certifying that the subordinate lodge is a duly constituted body
operating under the jurisdiction of the parent body.

4 Is the organization a parent or grand lodge? . . . .   Yes ☐   No ☐
If "Yes," attach a schedule for each subordinate lodge in active operation showing: (a) its name
and address; (b) the number of members in it; and (c) how often it holds periodic meetings.

Instructions

Line 1.-   To the extent that they qualify for exemption from Federal income tax, college fraternities and sororities generally qualify as organizations described in section 501(c)(7). Therefore, if the organization is a college fraternity or sorority, refer to the discussion of section 501(c)(7) organizations in Pub. 557. If section 501(c)(7) appears to apply to your organization, complete Schedule D instead of this schedule.

Line 2.-   Operating under the lodge system means carrying on activities under a form of organization that is composed of local branches, chartered by a parent organization, largely self-governing, and called lodges, chapters, or the like.

Appendix 18–2

FORM 1024 (*continued*)

Schedule F   **Organizations described in section 501(c)(9)**   **(Voluntary employees' beneficiary associations)**

1   Describe the benefits available to members. Include copies of any plan documents that describe such benefits and the terms and conditions of eligibility for each benefit.

2   Are any employees or classes of employees entitled to benefits to which other employees or classes of employees are not entitled? . . . .   Yes ☐   No ☐

     If "Yes," explain.

3   Give the following information for each plan as of the last day of the most recent plan year and enter that date here. If there is more than one plan, attach a separate schedule . . . . ▸ _____

                                                                             (mo.) (day) (yr.)

     a Total number of persons covered by the plan who are highly compensated individuals (See instructions.) . . . . ▸ _____
     b Number of other employees covered by the plan . . . . ▸ _____
     c Number of employees not covered by the plan . . . . ▸ _____
     d Total number employed * . . . . ▸ _____

       * Should equal the total of a, b, and c - if not, explain any difference. Describe the eligibility requirements that prevent those employees not covered by the plan from participating.

4   State the number of persons, if any, other than employees and their dependents (e.g., the proprietor of a business whose employees are members of the association) who are entitled to receive benefits . . . . ▸ _____

Instructions

Line 3a.- A "highly compensated individual" is one who:

   (a) Owned 5% or more of the employer at any time during the current year or the preceding year.

   (b) Received more than $80,000 (adjusted for inflation) in compensation from the employer for the preceding year, and

   (c) Was among the top 20% of employees by compensation for the preceding year. However, the employer can choose not to have (c) apply.

Appendix 18–2

FORM 1024 (*continued*)

Schedule G	Organizations described in section 501(c)(12) (Benevolent life insurance associations, mutual ditch or irrigation companies, mutual or cooperative telephone companies, or like organizations)

1 Attach a schedule in columnar form for each tax year for which the organization is claiming exempt status. On each schedule:

a Show the total gross income received from members or shareholders.

b List, by source, the total amounts of gross income received from other sources.

---

2 If the organization is claiming exemption as a local benevolent insurance association, state:

a The counties from which members are accepted or will be accepted.

b Whether stipulated premiums are or will be charged in advance, or whether losses are or will be paid solely through assessments.

---

3 If the organization is claiming exemption as a "like organization," explain how it is similar to a mutual ditch or irrigation company, or a mutual or cooperative telephone company.

---

4 Are the rights and interests of members in the organization's annual savings determined in proportion to their business with it? . . . .   Yes ☐   No ☐

If "Yes," does the organization keep the records necessary to determine at any time each member's rights and interests in such savings, including assets acquired with the savings? . . . .   Yes ☐   No ☐

---

5 If the organization is a mutual or cooperative telephone company and has contracts with other systems for long-distance telephone services, attach copies of the contracts.

Instructions

Mutual or cooperative electric or telephone companies should show income received from qualified pole rentals separately. Mutual or cooperative telephone companies should also show separately the gross amount of income received from nonmember telephone companies for performing services that involve their members and the gross amount of income received from the sale of display advertising in a directory furnished to their members.

Do not net amounts due or paid to other sources, against amounts due or received from those sources.

Appendix 18–2

FORM 1024 (*continued*)

Form 1024 (Rev. 9-98)

Schedule H	Organizations described in section 501(c)(13) (Cemeteries, crematoria, and like corporations)

1 Attach the following documents:

a Complete copy of sales contracts or other documents, including any "debt" certificates, involved in acquiring cemetery or crematorium property.

b Complete copy of any contract your organization has that designates an agent to sell its cemetery lots.

c A copy of the appraisal (obtained from a disinterested and qualified party) of the cemetery property as of the date acquired.

2 Does your organization have, or does it plan to have, a perpetual care fund? . . . .   Yes ☐   No ☐
If "Yes," attach a copy of the fund agreement and explain the nature of the fund (cash, securities, unsold land, etc.)

3 If your organization is claiming exemption as a perpetual care fund for an organization described in section 501(c)(13), has the cemetery organization, for which funds are held, established exemption under that section? . . . .   Yes ☐   No ☐
If "No," explain.

Appendix 18–2

FORM 1024 (*continued*)

Schedule I	Organizations described in section 501(c)(15) (Small insurance companies or associations)

1   Is the organization a member of a controlled group of corporations as defined in section
    831(b)(2)(B)(ii)? (Disregard section 1563(b)(2)(B) in determining whether the organization
    is a member of a controlled group.) . . . .   Yes ☐   No ☐

If "Yes," include on lines 2 through 5 the total amount received by the organization and all other members
of the controlled group.

If "No," include on lines 2 through 5 only the amounts that relate to the applicant organization.

	(a) Current Year	3 Prior Tax Years		
	From To	(b) 19	(c) 19	(d) 19
2 Direct written premiums				
3 Reinsurance assumed				
4 Reinsurance ceded				
5 Net written premiums ((line 2 plus line 3) minus line 4)	0	0	0	0

6   If you entered an amount on line 3 or line 4, attach a copy of the
    reinsurance agreements the organization has entered into.

Instructions

Line 1.-   Answer "Yes," if the organization would be considered a member of a controlled group of corporations if it were not exempt from tax under section 501(a). In applying section 1563(a), use a "more than 50%" stock ownership test to determine whether the applicant or any other corporation is a member of a controlled group.

Line 2.-   In addition to other direct written premiums, include on line 2 the full amount of any prepaid or advance premium in the year the prepayment is received. For example, if a $5,000 premium for a 3-year policy was received in the current year, include the full $5,000 amount in the Current Year column.

FORM 1024 (*continued*)

Form 1024 (Rev. 9-98)   Page 18

| Schedule J | Organizations described in section 501(c)(17) (Trusts providing for the payment of supplemental unemployment compensation benefits) |

1 If benefits are provided for individual proprietors, partners, or self-employed persons under the plan, explain in detail.

2 If the plan provides other benefits in addition to the supplemental unemployment compensation benefits, explain in detail and state whether the other benefits are subordinate to the unemployment benefits.

3 Give the following information as of the last day of the most recent plan year and enter that date here . . . . . ․ _____
a Total number of employees covered by the plan who are shareholders, officers, self-employed persons, or highly compensated (See Schedule F instructions for line 3a on page 14.) . . . . ․ _____
b Number of other employees covered by the plan . . . . ․ _____
c Number of employees not covered by the plan . . . . ․ _____
d Total number employed * . . . . ․ _____
  * Should equal the total of a, b, and c - if not, explain the difference. Describe the eligibility requirements that prevent those employees not covered by the plan from participating.

4 At any time after December 31, 1959, did any of the following persons engage in any of the transactions listed below with the trust: the creator of the trust or a contributor to the trust; a brother or sister (whole or half blood), a spouse, an ancestor, or a lineal descendant of such a creator or contributor; or a corporation controlled directly or indirectly by such a creator or contributor?

Note: If you know that the organization will be, or is considering being, a party to any of the transactions (or activities) listed below, check the "Planned" box. Give a detailed explanation of any "Yes" or "Planned" answer in the space below.

a Borrow any part of the trust's income or corpus? . . . .   Yes☐   No☐   Planned☐
b Receive any compensation for personal services? . . . .   Yes☐   No☐   Planned☐
c Obtain any part of the trust's services? . . . .   Yes☐   No☐   Planned☐
d Purchase any securities or other properties from the trust? . . . .   Yes☐   No☐   Planned☐
e Sell any securities or other property to the trust? . . . .   Yes☐   No☐   Planned☐
 f Receive any of the trust's income or corpus in any other transaction? . . .   Yes☐   No☐   Planned☐

5 Attach a copy of the Supplemental Unemployment Benefit Plan and related agreements.

Appendix 18–2

FORM 1024 (*continued*)

Form 1024 (Rev. 9-98)   Page 19

| Schedule K | Organizations described in section 501(c)(19) - A post or organization of past or present members of the Armed Forces of the United States, auxiliary units or societies for such a post or organization, and trusts or foundations formed for the benefit of such posts or organizations. |

1 To be completed by a post or organization of past or present members of the Armed Forces of the United States.

  a Total membership of the post or organization . . . .

  b Number of members who are present or former members of the U. S. Armed Forces . . . .

  c Number of members who are cadets (include students in college or university ROTC programs or at armed services academies only), or spouses, widows, or widowers of cadets or past or present members of the U. S. Armed Forces . . . .

  d Does the organization have a membership category other than the ones set out above? . . . .   Yes ☐   No ☐

     If "Yes," please explain in full. Enter number of members in this category . . . . _____

  e If you wish to apply for a determination that contributions to your organization are deductible by donors, enter the number of members from line 1b who are war veterans, as defined below . . . . _____

     A war veteran is a person who served in the Armed Forces of the United States during the following periods of war: April 21, 1898, through July 4, 1902; April 6, 1917, through November 11, 1918; December 7, 1941, through December 31, 1946; June 27, 1950, through January 31, 1955; and August 5, 1964, through May 7, 1975.

2 To be completed by an auxiliary unit or society of a post or organization of past or present members of the Armed Forces of the United States.

  a Is the organization affiliated with and organized according to the bylaws and regulations formulated by such an exempt post or organization? . . . .   Yes ☐   No ☐
     If "Yes," submit a copy of such bylaws or regulations.

  b How many members does your organization have? . . . .

  c How many are themselves past or present members of the Armed Forces of the United States, or are their spouses, or persons related to them within two degrees of blood relationship? (Grandparents, brothers, sisters, and grandchildren are the most distant relationships allowable.) . . . .

  d Are all of the members themselves members of a post or organization, past or present members of the Armed Forces of the United States, spouses of members of such a post or organization, or related to members of such a post or organization within two degrees of blood relationship? . . . .   Yes ☐   No ☐

3 To be completed by a trust or foundation organized for the benefit of an exempt post or organization of past or present members of the Armed Forces of the United States.

  a Will the corpus or income be used solely for the funding of such an exempt organization (including necessary related expenses)? . . . .   Yes ☐   No ☐
     If "No," please explain.

  b If the trust or foundation is formed for charitable purposes, does the organizational document contain a proper dissolution provision as described in section 1.501(c)(3)-1(b)(4) of the Income Tax Regulations? . . . . .   Yes ☐   No ☐

PART FOUR

Maintaining Tax Exempt Status

CHAPTER NINETEEN

Maintaining Exempt Status

Once an organization's tax-exempt status is recognized by the Internal Revenue Service (IRS), applicable states, and other authorities, the task is to maintain such status. This chapter contains checklists that outline compliance requirements and areas of primary concern. The checklists are designed to remind an exempt organization that it is a taxpayer and to allow its managers and professionals who assist exempt organizations of areas of concern deserving annual review. The objective is to ensure an organization's ongoing qualification for exemption.

The sheer number of items on the lists is evidence of the complexity and scope of issues involved in maintaining exempt status. As you first read the opening checklist, do not expect to understand all the terms if you are not a nonprofit organization specialist. Many of the issues are considered in depth in other chapters, and they will hopefully become clear as the materials are studied.

The Annual Tax Compliance Checklist for 501(c)(3)s (Exhibit 19–1) can be used yearly to test compliance with a variety of requirements, including the organizational test, the operational test, identification of unrelated business income, payroll tax compliance, public support tests, private foundation sanctions, filing requirements, excise and estimated tax requirements, property contributions, fund-raising event disclosures, public inspection requirements, and group exemption filing requirements.

The Annual Tax Compliance Checklist for Exempt Organizations other than 501(c)(3)s (Exhibit 19–2) asks similar questions. It is completed for exempt organizations qualifying in categories 501(c)(2), (4), (5), (6), (7), and so on.

The Short Form Exempt Organization Annual Tax Compliance Checklist (Exhibit 19–3) provides an abbreviated checklist for use with all types of organizations.

The sections referred to after the questions are sections of this book where more complete explanations can be found.

Exhibit 19–1

ANNUAL TAX COMPLIANCE CHECKLIST FOR §501(C)(3) ORGANIZATIONS

Organization_____

Prepared by_____Reviewed by_____Date_____

ORGANIZATIONAL ISSUES

Federal tax exemption

New organization: Has Form 1023 been filed within 15 (or 27) months after organizational date? [§18.1]   _____

Young organization (1–5 yrs): If advanced ruling received, has IRS report been filed 90 days of ending date? [§18.5]   _____

All organizations: Review Form 1023, IRS correspondence, and determination letter for exempt purposes originally represented to IRS to verify category of exemption. See if current activities in keeping with original purposes.   _____

State and local taxes

Must the organization file any state returns?   _____

Obtain a copy of state tax exemption(s) letter or prepare application for exemption(s). [§18.7]   _____

Does the organization use the proper form for exemptions it is entitled to claim?   _____

Must the EO collect sales tax on goods or services sold? Are timely returns filed? Is tax deposited on time?   _____

Does the organization pay real or personal property tax?   _____

Would use of property qualify it for exemption?   _____

For property classed as exempt, is it devoted to exempt use or has it been converted to commercial use?   _____

Charter and bylaws

Were there any changes to the charter or bylaws this year?   _____

If so, obtain copy for attachment to Form 990.   _____

Were there any substantial changes in structure or purpose that require reporting to the IRS?   _____

Change reported on Form 990? [§27.10]   _____

New 1023 required? [Exhibit 28–2]   _____

Review the minutes of directors' meetings. Do they reflect the purpose of the EO's activities?   _____

Exhibit 19–1 (*continued*)

OPERATIONAL ISSUES

Private Inurement or Benefit

Does the EO provide benefits to persons that control, manage, or fund it? [§20.1] _____

Have excess benefits been paid to disqualified persons [§20.9]? _____

Is compensation paid to officers, directors, and others or price paid for goods or services reasonable? [§20.2] _____

Are loans made to officers or directors? [§20.5] _____

Does the organization benefit a charitable class or a limited number of persons? [§2.2(a)] _____

Does the organization sell services or goods produced by its staff or members? [§2.2(e)] _____

Exempt Activities

Do activities further the purposes for which the organization was determined to be exempt (as described in Form 1023 or subsequently reported to IRS)? _____

Are files maintained to document or provide an archive of the nature of activities? For example: copy of exhibition invitations, class schedules, grants paid? _____

Does the EO have a record retention policy? _____

Does the organization lobby? If so, should the §501(h) election be made by filing Form 5768? [§23.4(b)] _____

If lobbying is conducted, does EO meet the limitations? [§23.5] _____

Has the organization participated in any political campaigns? Review newsletters for mention of candidates/issues. [§23.1] _____

Does EO have unrelated business income (UBI)? [§21.5] If so, complete Form 990-T [Appendix 27–7] and UBI checklist. _____

Does the EO make payments for personal services? If so, complete *Employee vs. Ind. Contractor Status* [Exhibit 25–1]. _____

Does the EO have a policy for distinguishing between employees and contractors? [§25-1] Are Forms W-9 on file? _____

Does EO comply with federal and state payroll withholding and reporting requirements? [Exhibit 25–3] _____

Are payroll taxes deposited in a timely fashion? _____

Must Forms 5500 be filed for employee benefit plans? _____

Has the IRS ever examined the organization? Review reports for compliance with any changes. [§28.3] _____

Exhibit 19–1 (*continued*)

Complete the "publicly supported" or "private foundation" checklist. [§11-1]   _____

For hospitals, review IRS Audit Guidelines.   _____

For college or university, review IRS Audit Guidelines.   _____

Filing Requirements

FORM 990EZ: (c)(3)s with gross receipts <$100,000 and assets <$250,000, includes Schedule A. [Appendix 27–1]   _____

FORM 990: (c)(3)s with gross receipts >$100,000 or assets >$250,000 file long form plus Schedule A. [Appendix 27–2]   _____

FORM 990-PF: Private foundations and PFs converting to public file regardless of support levels. [Appendix 27–5]   _____

If the EO is exempt from filing, consider filing. [§27.1] Keeps address current for IRS announcements, maintains Pub. 78 listing, and statutory time starts.   _____

Was an extension of time requested? [Form 2758]   _____

If the return is being filed late, has penalty abatement been requested? [§27.1]   _____

Does the EO need to change its fiscal year or its accounting method for tax purposes? With proper planning, can the change be made automatically? [§28.2]   _____

Property Contributions

Has the organization received gifts of property (other than listed securities) for which Form 8283 is required?   _____

Must sales of $5,000+ donated property made within two years from date of gift be reported on Form 8282?   _____

Validity of Financial Information

Has a compilation, review, or audit checklist been completed to ensure proper financial reporting and adherence to accounting principles?   _____

Should an amended return be filed to reflect restatement of prior year(s)? [§28.2]   _____

UNRELATED BUSINESS INCOME

Does the EO sell goods or services in an activity that does not relate to or further its exempt purposes? [§21.8]   _____

Does the "related business" have a commercial taint? If so, complete Commerciality Test in Exhibit 21–1.   _____

Exhibit 19–1 (*continued*)

Is the business activity substantial (as measured by gross revenue or staff time devoted to it) in relation to the organization's exempt activity? [§21.3] _____

Does the organization do any of the following?

- Sell advertisements in its publications? [§21.8(d) and Exhibit 21–4 for calculation of taxable portion]. _____

- Accept corporate sponsorships? [§21.8(e)] _____

- Rent personal or real property? [§21.8(a)] _____

- Earn any income from indebted property, margin accounts, or loans? [§21.12] _____

- Sell its mailing list? [21.9(h)] _____

- Operate a bookstore, restaurant, or parking lot for member convenience? If so, are any sales made to unrelated parties causing the fragmentation rule to apply? [§21.4(c)] _____

- Furnish or sell services? [§21.8(b)] _____

- Carry out any of the above activities through a separate, but controlled, business corporation or partnership? [§22.4] _____

Do any exceptions or modifications apply?

- The activity is not regularly carried on. [§21.6] _____

- Substantially all (85 percent) work in carrying out the trade or business is performed by volunteers. [§21.9(a)] _____

- The facility is operated for the convenience of persons participating in the organization's activities. [§21.9(c)] _____

- Items sold are either donated, educational, or directly related to the exempt function. [§21.9(b)] _____

- Items are "low-cost" premiums sold for significantly more than their value. [§21.9(g)] _____

- The income is of a passive nature (e.g., dividends, interest, rents, or royalties). [§21.10] _____

Is the rental property indebted? [§21.12] _____

Filing Issues

Do accounting records reflect allocation for expenses? _____

- Time records for staff. [§27.14] _____

- Square footage of spaces used. _____

- Allocation of membership dues to publications. _____

Exhibit 19–1 (*continued*)

Was Form 990-T filed in prior years? _____

Is IRS alerted 990-T is required because Form 990, page 6, Part VII, column B contains a number? [§27.11] _____

Does the gross income exceed $1,000? If loss realized, 990-T required and useful to establish net operating loss carryover or carryback and start statute of limitation time period. _____

Should estimated tax payments be made? Are federal tax deposit coupons (Form 8109) available? _____

If 990-T is required, complete *Checklist for Preparation of Form 990-T.* [Exhibit 27–4] _____

PUBLICLY SUPPORTED ORGANIZATIONS

Can the EO meet its public support tests under §509(a)(1) or §509(a)(2)? Note Schedule A now reveals passage of test. _____

Does EO maintain cash basis records of support? [§27.12(c)] _____

If the organization claims to be a supporting organization, can satisfaction of the "responsiveness" or "control and supervision" tests be documented? [§11.6] _____

Are deadlines for filing a report scheduled before the 60-month termination date? [§18.5] _____

Is fund-raising conducted in a state that requires reports? Does a state charitable solicitation act apply? _____

Do fund-raising solicitations reflect fair market value (FMV) of benefits offered to donors in return for gifts? For +$75 payments, is disclosure of deductible portion complete? [§24.2] _____

Is the method for calculation for FMV of benefits provided to donors reasonable and documented? [§24.3] _____

Has EO furnished copies of Forms 990 and 1023 to members of public requesting to see them? [§27.2] _____

Does the EO have excess lobbying expense [§23.5], political expenditures [§23.2(d)], or intermediate sanctions [§20.9] subject to excise tax? Form 4720 filed? [Appendix 27–6] _____

Reconsider the need to elect Section 501(h) for lobbying activities, in view of Section 4912. [§23.4(b)] _____

Are expense allocations and shared expenses with related 501(c)(4), (c)(5), or (c)(6)s documented? [§22.4] _____

Exhibit 19–1 (*continued*)

PRIVATE FOUNDATION TAX CHECKLIST

§4940—Excise Tax on Income

Does the PF have any nontaxable investment income? [§13.1 and §13.2] _____

Does the PF have records to support expense allocation among investment, administrative, and exempt activities? _____

Is the allocation consistent with prior years? [§13.3] _____

Is the tax basis of assets (donee's basis for gifts received) maintained separately from the book basis? [§13.2(a)] _____

Should estate income distributions be delayed? [§13.1(f)] _____

Does the PF have substantially appreciated property it could distribute to grantees (rather than cash) to reduce excise tax on capital gain from sale of the property? [§13.4] _____

Should the PF make extra qualifying distributions to reduce its excise tax to 1 percent? [§13.4(b)] _____

Are quarterly payments of tax due for 990-T or 990-PF? [§27.13(F)] _____

Must large corporation method for estimating be used? _____

Are federal tax deposit coupons (Form 8109) available? _____

§4941—Self-Dealing

Did the PF pay money to disqualified persons? If, so: Was the payment for reasonable compensation? [§14.4] _____

Did the PF reimburse exempt function expenses? [§14.7] _____

Was interest-free loan being repaid? [§14.3] _____

Did the <$5,000 transaction occur during "normal course" of retail business? [§14.2(c)] _____

Were benefit tickets accepted for grant? [§14.5(c)] _____

Does the PF pay for memberships? [§14.5(c)] _____

Does the PF indirectly do business with a DP? [§14.8] _____

For bequeathed property, should distributions from estate be delayed until property sold or divided? [§14.9] _____

§4943: Calculate percentage of stock holdings to identify excess business holdings. [§16.1] _____

§4944: Review PF's investment portfolio to evaluate presence of jeopardizing investments. [§16.2] _____

Exhibit 19–1 (*continued*)

§4942: Minimum Distribution Requirement

Evaluate calculation of minimum investment return: [§§15.1 and 15.2]

- Is method of valuation consistently applied? _____

- Are appraisals of nonreadily marketable assets updated? _____

- Are exempt function assets excluded? _____

- Can > $1^{1}/_{2}$% cash reserves be justified? _____

Compete Part XII and XIII to determine whether minimum distribution requirement are satisfied? [§15.3 and 15.6] _____

Determine if adjustments to qualifying distributions are needed for the following? [§15.4] _____

- Sale of exempt assets previously classified as distribution? _____

- Amounts not redistributed in a timely manner by another private foundation or controlled organization? _____

- Set-asides not used for an approved purpose? _____

§4945 Taxable Expenditures

Did the PF spend money for any of the following?

- Political campaign? [§17.1] _____

- Lobbying or a grant to finance lobbying? [§17.1] _____

- Unapproved individual grant? [§17.3] _____

- Grant to another PF or non-(c)(3) entity? [§17.5] _____

- If so, attach expenditure responsibility reports. [§17.5(d)] _____

Verify questions in Part VII *Statement Regarding Activities* on Form 990-PF [Appendix 27–5] are answered correct. *No* is not the right answer to all questions. [§27.13(g)] _____

Should the foundation consider conversion to a public charity? [§12.4] Or to a private operating foundation? [§15.5] _____

Violations of §4941/4945 Sanctions

Is Form 4720 required? [Appendix 27–6] _____

Can penalty be abated for reasonable cause under §4962? [§16.2(c)] _____

Has violation been corrected? [§14.10, §15.6, §16.1(a), §16.2(c), §17.7] _____

Exhibit 19–2

ANNUAL TAX COMPLIANCE CHECKLIST FOR NON 501(C)(3)s

Organization:_____

Completed by_____Reviewed by:_____Date_____

ORGANIZATIONAL ISSUES

Federal Tax Exemption

New organization: Has Form 1024 been filed? If not, consider need for proof that proposed operation qualifies for exemption and proper listing for IRS filing status? [§18.3]   _____

All organizations: Review Form 1024, IRS correspondence, determination letter for exempt purposes originally represented to IRS to verify category of exemption. Are activities in keeping with expressed purposes.   _____

State and Local Taxes

Does EO have any state or local filing requirements?   _____

Is the EO entitled to any state tax exemptions?   _____

Obtain a copy of any state tax exemption(s) certificates or prepare application for exemption(s). [§18.7]   _____

Does the organization use the proper form to claim exemptions it is entitled to?   _____

Must the EO collect sales tax on goods or services sold? Are timely returns filed? Is tax deposited on time?   _____

Does the organization pay real or personal property tax?   _____

Would use of property qualify it for exemption?   _____

For property classed as exempt, is it devoted to exempt use or has it been converted to commercial use?   _____

Charter and Bylaws

Were there any changes to the charter or bylaws this year?   _____

If so, obtain copy for attachment to Form 990.   _____

Were there any substantial changes in structure or purpose that require reporting to the IRS?   _____

> Change reported on Form 990? [§27.10]
> New 1024 required? [Exhibit 28–2]

Review the minutes of director's meetings. Do they reflect the mission-related purpose of the organization's activities?   _____

Exhibit 19–2 (*continued*)

OPERATIONAL ISSUES

Private Inurement or Benefit

Does the EO provide benefits to persons that control, manage, or fund it? [§20.1]   _____

Have excess benefits been paid to a disqualified person by a (c)(4) organization? [§20.9]   _____

Is the compensation paid to directors, officers, and others reasonable? [§20.2]   _____

Are loans made to officers or directors? [§20.5]   _____

Does the organization benefit an identifiable class of exempt constituents? [Chapters 6–10]   _____

Does the organization sell services or goods produced by its staff or members? [§8.4 and §21.8]   _____

Validity of Financial Information

Has a compilation, review, or audit checklist been completed to insure proper financial reporting and adherence to accounting principles?   _____

Exempt Activities

Do activities further the purposes for which EO was determined to be exempt (as described in Form 1024 or subsequently reported to IRS)?   _____

Are files maintained to document or provide an archive of the nature of activities? For example: copy of program notices, peer review boards, member services, etc?   _____

Does the EO lobby? If so, is it germane to purposes? [§23.6]   _____

Has the organization participated in any political campaigns? Does campaigning further the exempt purpose? [§23.1]   _____

Should Form 1120POL be filed? [§23.3]   _____

Are expense allocations and expenses shared with related 501(c)(3), (4), (5), or (6)s accurately calculated?   _____

If a social club, can it meet the gross revenue tests? [§9.4]   _____

Does EO have unrelated business income? [§21.5] If so, complete Form 990-T [Appendix 27–7] and UBI checklist.   _____

Does the EO make payments for personal services? If so, complete Employee vs. Ind. Contractor Status. [Exhibit 25–1].   _____

Does the EO have a policy for distinguishing between employees and contractors? [§25.1] Are Forms W-9 obtained for all contractors?   _____

Exhibit 19–2 (*continued*)

Does EO comply with federal and state payroll withholding and reporting requirements? [Exhibit 25–3] _____

Are Forms 5500 due to be filed for employee benefit plans? _____

Are payroll taxes deposited in a timely fashion? _____

Has the IRS ever examined the organization? Review reports for compliance with any changes. [§28.3] _____

Should an amended return be filed to reflect restatement of prior year(s)? [§28.2(d)] _____

Filing Requirements

FORM 990EZ: EOs with gross receipts <$100,000 and assets <$250,000 [Appendix 27–1] _____

FORM 990: EOs with gross receipts >$100,000 or assets >$250,000 file long form [Appendix 27–2] _____

If the EO is exempt from filing, consider filing. [§27.1(c)] Address is kept current and statutory time starts. [§27.1(f)] _____

Is the EO a chapter or affiliate of a central organization holding a group exemption? If so, [§18.1(f)]

- Must the chapter file its own 990? _____
- Will the central EO file a group 990? _____
- Have changes in address been reported to central? _____

Was an extension of time requested? [Form 2758] _____

If the return is being filed late, has penalty abatement been requested? [§27.2] _____

Does the EO need to change its fiscal year or its accounting method for tax purposes? [§28.2] _____

Notice of Nondeductibility

Fund-raising solicitations must "conspicuously" say payments do not qualify for charitable deduction. [§6.4(a)] _____

For (c)(4),(5), and (6) organizations that lobby, has the portion of member dues attributable to lobbying been calculated? If so, have members been informed of nondeductible amount? [§6.4(b)] _____

Has the EO chosen to pay proxy tax for lobbying expenses? If so, has Form 990-T been paid? [§6.4(e)] _____

Do accounting records identify lobbying expense? [§6.4(g)] _____

Public Inspection Requirements

Has the EO furnished copies of Forms 990 and 1024 to persons asking to inspect them? [§27.2] _____

Exhibit 19–3

ANNUAL TAX COMPLIANCE FOR TAX-EXEMPT ORGANIZATIONS
SHORT FORM

Name of Organization_____Prepared by_____

ORGANIZATIONAL TEST

Have all exemptions been applied for in a timely manner? [Ch. 18]   _____

Federal final determination received? [Ch.18§5]   _____

State franchise, income, sales, property tax, or other exemptions in place? [Ch. 18§7]   _____

Were there changes in charter, bylaws, or purposes?   _____

OPERATIONAL TEST

Were there transactions with board members, officers, or other insiders? If so did private inurement occur? [Chs. 20 and 22]   _____

Are activities in furtherance of exempt purposes? [Chs. 3–10]   _____

Do new activities need to be reported to IRS? [Ch. 2§2]   _____

Are files maintained to document nature of activities?   _____

If EO lobbies, should Form 5768 be filed? [Ch. 23]   _____

Any political activity? [Ch. 23]   _____

Is there excessive unrelated business income? [Ch. 21]   _____

Is payroll tax withholding required? [Ch. 25]   _____

Are exempt disbursements sufficient for commensurate test? [Ch. 2§2(d)]   _____

Are fund balances excessive? [Ch. 2§2(c)]   _____

FILING REQUIREMENTS

Is Form 990 required? If so, can and should EZ be filed? [Ch. 27]   _____

Is Form 990-T required? (Complete UBI checklist.) [Chs. 21 and 27]   _____

Are payroll and information returns filed? (Complete checklist.) [Exhibit 25–3]   _____

Should extension of time to file be requested?   _____

Has change of accounting method occurred? [Ch. 28]   _____

Should tax filing year be changed? [Ch. 28]   _____

Is Form 4720 required for excise taxes? [Appendix 27–6]   _____

Is Form 8283 or 8282 due for property gifts received?   _____

Exhibit 19–3 (*continued*)

Do fund solicitations reveal fair market value or nondeductibility of
benefits to donors? [Ch. 24]   _____

For non-(c)(3) is nondeductibility conspicuously disclosed or dues
attributable to lobbying? [Ch. 6]   _____

Are Forms 990 and 1023 made available for public inspection? [Ch. 27]   _____

If EO is part of a group, should group exemption be obtained? [Ch. 18]   _____

Has there been an IRS examination? Changes to consider? [Ch. 28]   _____

Is there a signed engagement letter in the file?   _____

If EO is a PF, complete private foundation checklist.   _____

If EO is a (c)(7), complete social club revenue tests.   _____

CHAPTER TWENTY

Private Inurement and Intermediate Sanctions

Organizations exempt under most categories of Internal Revenue Code (IRC) §501 must meet two separate tests in order to retain exemption. The first test, called the organizational test, ensures that no one owns an exempt organization. No dividends are paid; shareholders exist only in certain membership organizations; and the circumstances under which funds can be returned to the members in the business league, social club, or other category are very limited. When recognizing an organization's exempt status, the Internal Revenue Service (IRS) applies this test to review the charter, bylaws, and other organizational documents.

The second test, though, is an ongoing one. Exempt organizations of all categories must continually operate "exclusively" for their particular exempt purposes, whether charitable, agricultural, or advancement of a line of business. An exempt organization (EO) must not devote itself to benefiting private individuals. To describe the requirements of tax-exempt status, IRC §501 uses the word "inures" to limit the activities of §501(c)(3), (4), (6), (7), (9), (10), (13), and (19) organizations. These subsections all require that, "no part of the net earnings inure to the benefit of any private shareholder or individual."

The last of the six definitions of "inure" found in *Webster's Deluxe Unabridged Dictionary,* second edition, is the one applied for federal tax exemption purposes: "to serve to the use or benefit of, as a gift of land inures to the heirs of a grantee or it inures to their benefit." The IRS 1981 Continuing Professional Education manual for EO agents[1] comments that inurement is "likely to arise where the organization transfers financial resources to an individual solely by virtue of the individual's relationship with the organization, and without regard to accomplishing exempt purpose, or more plainly stated, a private person cannot pocket the organization's funds." Whether private benefit is incidental to overall public benefit or interest turns on the nature and quantum of the activity under consideration and the manner by which the public benefit is derived. The 1983 manual asserts that "the forms which inurement can take are limited only by the imagination of the insiders involved."[2]

Private inurement potentially occurs whenever a person receives funds or property from an exempt organization in return for which he or she gives insufficient consideration—in other words, pays less for something than it is worth or gives less than he or she receives. An organization that devotes too much of its funds to providing private inurement does not qualify for exemption.

To eliminate the possibility of private inurement in a privately funded charity, Congress in 1969 introduced the concept of self-dealing.[3] As a rule, all financial transactions with insiders are absolutely prohibited for private foundations (PFs). The fact that the transaction actually benefits the PF (a bargain sale, for example) does not lift the ban. Neither will the facts that the transaction is at arm's length and for fair market value rescue the transaction from self-dealing sanctions (as these facts would for a public charity). A few limited exceptions, involving compensation for personal services, expense reimbursements, no-interest loans, and no-rent leases, are pointed out in the following sections.[4]

To provide a tool to punish a public charity or civic league that paid excessive amounts to its insiders, Congress in 1996 added intermediate sanctions to the tax code as discussed in §20.9. Until that time, the only penalty the IRS could impose on such an organization was revocation of their exempt status. Thus, as the word intermediate implies, sanctions that stop short of revocation can now be imposed when inurement occurs. This new regime for scrutiny of insider transactions does not replace the inurement standards discussed in this chapter but can be thought of as a new construct within which to evaluate the presence of inurement.

20.1 DEFINING INUREMENT

To ensure that it operates to benefit its exempt constituents, an exempt organization must monitor its financial relations with "private shareholders or individuals," a very broad group. The regulations narrow the group somewhat by saying

---

[1] Exempt Organizations Continuing Professional Education Technical Instruction Program for 1981, p. 92; Gen. Coun. Memo. 38459.
[2] Exempt Organizations Continuing Professional Education Technical Instruction Program for 1983, p. 50.
[3] Defined in IRC §4941.
[4] See Chapter 14 for more details.

that it "refers to persons having a personal and private interest in the activities of the organization."[5] While this language does not specifically say so, the "interest" commonly stems from control.

(a) Persons Involved

Expressed most simply, the rule is usually (but not always) applied to insiders, including:

- Someone with the ability to decide (e.g., vote) to authorize payments (e.g., a member of the board, trustee, executive committee member, or officer)
- A member of the family of such a person
- A substantial contributor able to influence the EO
- A business controlled or owned by one of the above types of insider

The intermediate sanction rules are imposed on insiders called *disqualified persons,* defined as those in a position to exercise substantial influence over the affairs of the organization.[6] Private foundation insiders are also called disqualified persons.[7]

Persons not on the above insider list—outsiders—can also receive unacceptable advantage or gain. Persons having a relationship that might produce some private benefit equivalent to inurement include employees, consultants, and exempt function beneficiaries (those persons who participate in the organization's activities and are the intended recipients of its services). The IRS and the courts have not limited their finding of private benefit to members of the board or other persons in direct authority, but instead find the following relationships can embody compensation arrangements that jeopardize exempt status:

- Doctors and the hospitals that need to attract their services[8]
- Ministers whose churches pay them lavishly[9]
- Fund-raising consultants who receive a large percentage of funds raised[10]

(b) Identifying Inurement

For most exempt organizations financial transactions involving insiders are not specifically prohibited, but instead are constrained and subject to scrutiny. In each case, the same criteria are applied to evaluate the presence of disqualifying inurement to insiders and their family members. The IRS agents are instructed to examine contracts for supplies and services, loan and lease agreements, and compensation contracts, and to be alert "to the appearance of insiders' names in a context

---

[5] Reg. §1.501(a)(1)-1(c).
[6] See §20.9 for detailed definition for that purpose.
[7] See Chapter 12§2(c).
[8] Gen. Coun. Memo. 39862.
[9] *Founding Church of Scientology v. U.S.,* 412 F.2d 1197 (Ct.Cl. 1969).
[10] *United Cancer Council, Inc. v. Commissioner,* 109 T.C. 326.

indicating that the individuals are not acting as representatives of the exempt organization."[11] The answer will be based on the facts of each case. The burden of proof is on the exempt organization.

- *Reasonableness*. Is the amount paid reasonable?

- *Documentation*. Is the transaction properly documented?

- *Independent approval*. Is the transaction sanctioned by disinterested persons or by an independent appraiser?

- *State law*. Does the deal violate fiduciary responsibility law or state fund solicitation regulations?

Transactions between related for-profit businesses are subject to reallocation among the parties if the IRS finds they were not conducted at arm's length. The rules to test for fair pricing in intellectual property transactions use twelve factors.[12] These income tax rules on reallocations can be instructive in evaluating possible inurement between an exempt organization and its related parties.

1. Prevailing rates in the same industry or for similar property

2. Offers of competing transferors or bids of competing transferees

3. Terms of the transfer, including limitations on the geographic area covered and the exclusive or nonexclusive character of any rights granted

4. The uniqueness of the property and the period for which it is likely to remain unique

5. The degree and duration of protection afforded to the property under the laws of the relevant countries

6. Value of services rendered by the transferor to the transferee in connection with the transfer

7. Prospective profits to be realized or costs to be saved by the transferee through its use or subsequent transfer of the property

8. Capital investment and start-up expenses required of the transferee

9. Availability of substitutes for the property transferred

10. Arm's-length rates and prices paid by unrelated parties when the property is resold or sublicensed to such parties

11. Cost incurred by the transferor in developing the property

12. Any other fact or circumstance which unrelated parties would have been likely to consider in determining the amount of an arm's-length consideration for the property.

---

[11] Exempt Organizations Examination Guidelines (IRM 7(10-69)), §153.
[12] Reg. §1.482-2(d)(2)(iii).

(c) Meaning of Net Earnings

For inurement or private benefit to result, the organization's net earnings must be paid in an impermissible fashion to one or more individuals. The meaning of *net earnings* is *not* the customary accounting definition—gross revenues less associated expenses.[13] Instead, the term is very broadly construed to mean all assets an exempt organization holds as permanent capital, restricted funds, current or accumulated surpluses, or net profits. An exempt organization is treated as having earned each penny it has accumulated. A prohibited distribution of net earnings or profits is not limited to an arrangement based on some sharing agreement, incentive, or ownership. It can take many forms, including but not limited to those discussed in the following sections of this chapter.

20.2 SALARIES AND OTHER COMPENSATION

Reasonable compensation for personal services rendered can be paid to insiders in the form of salaries, directors' fees, or other payment. The IRS position on compensation is expressed in its training literature.

> The National Office has found that benefit to an exempt organization's employees, so long as it constitutes no more than reasonable compensation for services rendered, is not necessarily incompatible or inconsistent with the accomplishment of the exempt purpose of the employer. Exempt organizations can establish and operate incentive plans that devote a portion of receipts to reasonable compensation of productive employees so long as the benefits derived from the plans generally accrue not only to the employees but also to the charitable employers through, for instance, increased productivity and cost stability, thus aiding rather than detracting from the accomplishment of exempt purpose.[14]

The exempt organization must be able to substantiate that the payments are not excessive for the work performed, because the payment of excessive compensation clearly will jeopardize exempt status.[15] When compensation is found to be unreasonably high, the recipient may be treated as having received an excess benefit that must be returned. Not only must be the excess be repaid, penalties may be imposed upon both the recipient and those approving of the payments.[16]

An evaluation of the reasonableness of compensation should also include an analysis of the need for the position. Consideration of the exempt purposes served by the job performed within the context of the organization's programs is expected by the IRS. The board must analyze the needs of an institution and come up with a "methodology for meeting a need and then take appropriate steps using reasonable standards for fair market value and reasonable standards for terms

---

[13] Exempt Organizations Annual Technical Review Institutes for 1983, p. 41.

[14] *Ibid.* p. 46, n.2.

[15] *Birmingham Business College, Inc. v. Commissioner,* 276 F.2d 476 (5th Cir. 1960).

[16] See §20.9 and Chapter 14§4.

and conditions of arrangements."[17] The types of questions asked to measure the reasonableness of compensation, the answers to which must be maintained, include:

- Is the amount of any payment for personal services excessive or unreasonable?[18]

- Are the payments ordinary and necessary to carry out the exempt purposes of the EO? (Apply the same tests used under IRC §162 to judge the reasonableness of business deductions.)[19]

- What are the individual's responsibilities and duties? Is there a written job description, a contract for services, or personnel procedures?

- Is the person qualified for the job through experience, education, or other special expertise?[20] How much time is devoted to the job?

- To evaluate compensation accurately, count not only salary but all benefits,[21] including:

  - Salary or fees (current and deferred)

  - Fringe benefits

  - Contribution to pension or profit-sharing plans

  - Housing or automobile allowances

  - Directors' and officers' liability insurance

  - Expense reimbursements

  - Clubs, resort meetings, or other lavish items

  - Compensation to family members

- Does the method of calculation imply inurement? Paying a percentage of profits from operations or fund-raising efforts may suggest inurement. The IRS has not always won this one, particularly when the overall pay is reasonable.[22]

- Are adequate accounting records, such as time sheets or diaries, maintained to document the actual time expended on the job?

- How does the individual's salary compare to those of other staff members and to the total organization budget?

---

[17] Remarks of Marcus S. Owens, Director of the IRS Exempt Organization Division, in describing the need for "contemporaneous documentation of process," in discussing the physician recruitment ruling (Rev. Rul. 97-25, discussed in Chapter 4§6) before the American Bar Association Exempt Organization Committee members on May 9, 1997.

[18] *The Labrenz Foundation, Inc. v. Commissioner,* 33 T.C.M. 1374 (1974).

[19] *Enterprise Railway Equipment Company v. U.S.,* 161 F. Supp. 590 (Ct.Cl. 1958).

[20] *B.H.W. Anesthesia Foundation, Inc. v. Commissioner,* 72 T.C. 681 (1979).

[21] *John Marshall Law School vs. U.S.,* 81-2 T.C. 9514 (Ct.Cl. 1981); Rev. Rul. 73-126, 1973-1 C.B. 220.

[22] *World Family Corporation v. Commissioner,* 81 T.C. 958 (1983); see §20.2(c).

- How does the compensation structure compare to those of similar exempt organizations or commercial businesses of similar size?[23] Compare the exempt organization to commercial businesses of similar size, if possible. There is no ruling that says that nonprofit employees or consultants cannot be paid salaries commensurate with businesses', nor that they need to donate their services.

(a) Finding Salary Statistics

Comparative information is critical to evaluating the reasonableness of a salary. The most appropriate comparison is made to similar exempt organizations in the same field of endeavor (for example, health care, academia, music, or college administration). Surveys of compensation in the EO's area of interest can be obtained, and should be retained for IRS scrutiny.

A personnel consulting and executive search firm can be engaged to recommend appropriate levels of compensation for the organization. Such independently commissioned surveys satisfy the rebuttable presumption of reasonableness that is required to avoid intermediate sanctions, as discussed in §20.9.

Another way to obtain compensation information is to look at Forms 990 for relevant organizations. The forms must be made available upon request at the organization's office and may be available on the Internet. Any amounts paid to officers and directors for compensation, employee benefit plans, and expense accounts are to be reported, along with their titles and average amounts of time devoted to the position each week. For charitable organizations only, Form 990, Schedule A also reports the same information for the top five employees (other than key employees) receiving over $50,000 a year. Additionally, the top five independent professional contractors paid over $50,000 during the year are listed by name and amount.

The Council on Foundations publishes a biennial *Foundation Management Report* which contains private foundation compensation levels by size of foundation, position, and area of the country. The Society for Nonprofit Organizations annually publishes *Compensation for Nonprofit Organizations,* a comprehensive survey of salaries and benefits by size of organization, by focus or purpose of the entity (health, education, day care, and so on), and by positions (executive director, controller, clerical assistant, program manager, and so on). In Houston, Texas, the Management Assistance Program of the United Way of the Texas Gulf Coast compiles a similar annual survey of area compensation.

(b) Avoiding Conflict of Interest

When compensation is paid to directors, officers, or other controlling members of an organization, additional proof of the reasonableness of compensation is required. It is critical that local conflict of interest statutes be observed to prove that the payments do not violate fiduciary responsibility concepts. Persons who have significant control over an organization are treated as an insider for this purpose.[24]

---

[23] Reg. §1.162-7(b)(3).
[24] *United Cancer Council, Inc. v. Commissioner,* 109 T.C. 326.

Most organizations should adopt conflict of interest policies to evidence its good faith in securing independent and impartial approval for compensation payments. Such policies should require, at a minimum, that interested parties abstain from approving their own compensation and that there are enough noncompensated members of the board to achieve independent or disinterested approval for the compensation.[25] A compensation committee comprised of knowledgeable persons should gather data and make recommendations.

(c) Incentive Compensation

Compensation that is measured by the results of activities—net profits, number of patients served, funds raised, and so on—are subject to enhanced scrutiny. The intermediate sanctions rules have a special section on "transactions in which the amount of economic benefit is determined in whole or in part by the revenues of one or more activities of an organization."[26] One court has said that "there is nothing insidious or evil about a commission-based compensation system," and decided that procuring contributions with a six percent commission was reasonable, despite the absence of a ceiling on the total commission that could be paid.[27]

In evaluating a "fixed percentage of income" formula, the IRS dissected one hospital's policies and intentions in evaluating a radiologist hired to run the radiology department. His compensation was a fixed percentage of the department's gross revenues less bad debts. The IRS found this incentive compensation method to be acceptable because the physician had no control over compensation decisions, either managerial or governance position. He was simply an employee. It also noted that the negotiations over compensation were conducted at arm's length.[28] According to the IRS training literature, the following factors are used to find reasonableness in incentive compensation. Not all factors need be present:[29]

- The contingent payments serve a real and discernible business purpose of the organization itself, not the financial need of the employee. The risk of paying the higher salary due to higher revenues is self-insured by its tie to revenue or profit level.

- Compensation amount is not dependent upon curtailing expenses or skimping on services, but instead is based upon accomplishment of exempt purposes, such as serving more patients, writing more books, or increasing test scores. A plan to pay a percentage of revenues exceeding the budgeted amount has even been sanctioned.[30]

- Actual operating results show that prices for services are comparable to those at similar organizations, and are not manipulated to increase the compensation.

[25] The rebuttable presumption rules used to evaluate application of the intermediate sanctions should be followed in this regard; see §20.9.
[26] See §20.9.
[27] *National Foundation, Inc. v. U.S.*, 87-2 USTC ¶9602 (Ct.Cl. 1987).
[28] Rev. Rul. 69-383, 1969-2 C.B. 113.
[29] Exempt Organization Annual Technical Review Institutes for 1983, p. 45.
[30] Gen. Coun. Memo. 39674. Also see Gen. Coun. Memos. 32453, 36918, 39498, and 39670.

- There is a ceiling or maximum amount of compensation, so as to avoid "the possibility of windfall benefit to the employee/professional based upon factors bearing no direct relationship to the level of services provided."[31]

In the health care context, the IRS in 1997 updated its guidance regarding incentive compensation package used to recruit physicians.[32]

Stock options or employee stock purchase plans are commonly available for employees of for-profit corporations. A nonprofit corporation may wish to offer shares of its for-profit subsidiary to key employees of the subsidiary as incentive compensation. Encouragement of personnel by issuing a minority interest was found acceptable for an exempt organization.[33] The president of a newly created for-profit subsidiary received 4% of the shares as a part of his compensation. The plan was found to be consistent with the charity's purpose of providing the employee an incentive to maximize commercial exploitation of the charity's technology transferred to the subsidiary. The value of the shares would be counted in evaluating the presence of inurement due to unreasonable compensation. To document the amount of compensation at the time of issuance, a comprehensive and preferably independent opinion as to the value of the shares should be obtained.

20.3 HOUSING AND MEALS

An exempt organization may have a good reason to provide housing or meals, or allowances for these purposes, to its officers, directors, or employees. Using the four basic criteria outlined in §20.1(b), amounts actually incurred for meals and other travel expenses incurred on exempt organization business can be paid. Questions to ask to ensure that the four criteria are met include the following:

- Is the insider a staff member whose presence is required on the premises of the EO at all hours (a school or home for orphans, for example)?

- Does the housing allowance or provision qualify for IRC §119 income exclusion from insider income because it is furnished for the convenience of the employing EO?

- Is the location of the project remote or temporary? Is the research conducted on an island or in a city away from the EO's and the employee's permanent residence?

- Is the housing lavish or unreasonably expensive?[34]

- Are board meetings held in resort locations?

Documentation is essential to prove both the amount and nature of each expense, as well as its connection to organization affairs. A diary should be kept of meetings, persons entertained, and the project to which discussions relate.

[31] *People of God Community v. Commissioner,* 75 T.C. 127, 132 (1980).
[32] Rev. Rul. 97-25; see Chapter 4§6.
[33] Priv. Ltr. Rul. 9311032.
[34] *John Marshall Law School,* n. 21.

Due to the self-dealing rules, scrutiny can be expected, but a private foundation can reimburse its disqualified persons for "reasonable expenses" incurred in conducting the foundation's affairs as discussed in Chapter 14§4. Daily expenses in excess of the federal per diem reimbursement rate would require explanation.

20.4 PURCHASE, LEASE, OR SALE OF PROPERTY OR SERVICES

An exempt organization can buy, lease, or sell property to or from an insider in certain circumstances. The appropriateness of any such transaction depends partly on whether the property is devoted to exempt functions, such as administrative offices, or to production of income, that is, an investment. The standards for reasonable compensation discussed previously may also be applicable to sales of property. The intermediate sanctions apply to property transactions.[35] When a property transaction takes place between an insider and an exempt organization, the following tests must be satisfied:

- Is no more than the current fair market value (FMV) being paid for the property or services which the organization is buying? At least full FMV must be paid for the property being sold or purchased.[36]

  - Is there a readily established market price for the property being purchased or leased?[37]

  - If not, was an appraisal or other independent evidence of its value obtained? Does the appraisal consider a number of different valuation factors, such as income forecast, resale value of underlying property, goodwill, and comparative prices?

  - Was the organization established to promote the insider's business, as was found in cases involving a travel agent,[38] a musical instructor,[39] a doctor who established a hospital,[40] or a minister?[41]

- Are the terms for payment of the purchase price favorable?

  - Is the rate of interest on a mortgage equal to or less than prevailing rates for similar commercial mortgages (if the EO is buying), or more than these rates (if the insider is buying)?

  - If the property is encumbered, can the income generated by the property carry the note and provide a reasonable return? Or does the amount of the debt exceed the value of the property purchased or given?[42]

---

[35] See §20.9.

[36] *Anclote Psychiatric Center, Inc. v. Commissioner,* T.C. Memo. July 1998.

[37] Priv. Ltr. Rul. 8234084 and 9130002.

[38] *International Postgraduate Medical Foundation v. Commissioner,* 56 T.C.M. 1140 (1989).

[39] *Horace Heidt Foundation v. U.S.,* 170 F. Supp. 634 (Ct.Cl. 1959).

[40] *Kenner v. Commissioner,* 33 T.C.M. 1239 (1974).

[41] *Church by Mail, Inc. v. Commissioner,* 48 T.C.M. 471 (1984).

[42] Rev. Rul. 76-441, 1967-2 C.B. 147.

- Does the purchase, lease, or sale make economic sense?

  - Is the proportion of organization capital devoted to the purchase reasonable in relation to the capital needed to carry out exempt purposes?

  - Will the income yield a rate of return commensurate with the organization's overall financial needs?

  - Does the amount of cash paid down deprive the organization of needed working capital?

  - Is the arrangement beneficial for the organization? The rates or rents should be favorable.[43]

- Does the purchase or sale serve an exempt function?

Although a PF is absolutely prohibited from buying, selling, or leasing anything to or from its disqualified persons for any price—even one dollar—a rent-free lease to the PF is allowed if it serves the organization's objectives. A PF can pay its proportion of occupancy costs, but "sharing arrangements" can present problems.[44]

20.5 LOANS AND GUARANTEES

An exempt organization should think very carefully before lending money to or borrowing from an insider. One court has commented that the very fact that an exempt organization was a source of credit for an insider represented inurement.[45] Loans are subject to the same criteria as leases and sales of property, and many of the same questions apply. Additionally, one should ask:

- Is the EO serving exempt purposes by making the loan?[46]

- Are the rates and terms favorable to the EO?[47]

- Is there substantial market risk inherent in the loan?

- Is there adequate security for the loan?

- Is it a good investment? Is the rate of return good?[48]

- Does a low- or no-interest loan to an employee or director serve a permissible compensatory purpose?

A private foundation is prohibited from borrowing money from or lending money to a disqualified person. A gift of indebted property to a PF is prohibited unless the

---

[43] *Texas Trade School v. Commissioner,* 30 T.C. 642 (1958), *aff'd,* 272 F.2d 168 (5th Cir. 1959); *Founding Church of Scientology, supra,* n. 9.
[44] See Chapter 14§7.
[45] *Lowry Hospital Association v. Commissioner,* 66 T.C. 850 (1976).
[46] *Best Lock Corp. v. Commissioner,* 31 T.C. 1217 (1959).
[47] *Hancock Academy of Savannah, Inc. v. Commissioner,* 69 T.C. 488 (1977).
[48] *Donald G. and Lillian S. Griswold,* 39 T.C. 620 (1962), *acq.,* 1965-1 C.B. 4.

debt was placed on the property 10 years before the gift.[49] Essentially the PF's taking over responsibility for the debt is treated as compensation or a loan to the donor.

20.6 FOR-PROFIT TO NONPROFIT AND VICE VERSA

Contributing a business to a nonprofit organization with purely gratuitous motivation does not necessarily result in private inurement or benefit to the donor, but such transactions are closely scrutinized. If such a transfer occurs for tax avoidance purposes, as when the donor retains the right to occupy the property and essentially continues to operate the business for his or her own purposes, the level of private interest prevents tax-exempt status for the new nonprofit organization.[50]

When the conversion is basically a sale to the exempt organization, the purchase must be examined for unreasonable price or terms favorable to the seller.[51] In a sale of a proprietary school to a newly created educational organization, the consideration paid for goodwill was found to be excessive.[52] Payments for intangible earning capacity are not, however, prohibited per se. When an exempt organization intends to operate a facility and will clearly benefit from the goodwill that has been established, the intangible assets will contribute to the new organization's exempt functions and can be paid for. The IRS has ruled that the "capitalization of excess earnings" formula is an acceptable manner by which to value such an intangible asset.[53]

The health care industry during the 1990s provided countless examples of the purchase of a nonprofit provider by a for-profit company and vice versa. Whether private inurement occurs is a significant question in such situations to be judged by standards developed by the IRS particularly for the industry.[54] For an excellent discussion of the other circumstances in which a for-profit might convert itself to a nonprofit, and the tax consequences to shareholders, refer to the transcript of the May 1995 meeting of the American Bar Association Exempt Organization Committee.[55]

The transfer of substantially all of the assets of a taxable corporation to a tax-exempt organization is essentially treated as a taxable sale of the transferred assets at their fair market value under the so-called *General Utilities Doctrine*.[56] Thus the conversion of a taxable entity to a tax-exempt one is treated as a transaction in which gain may be recognized.

Converting a Nonexempt Nonprofit into an Exempt Nonprofit.   For a variety of reasons, an entity organized as a nonprofit may not seek approval for tax-exempt status or may lose its exempt status. Converting such a nonprofit into a tax-

---

[49] IRC §4941 (d)(2)(A).

[50] Rev. Rul. 69-266, 1969-1 C.B. 151.

[51] Under standards discussed in §20.4.

[52] *Hancock Academy of Savannah, Inc., supra* n. 47.

[53] Rev. Rul. 68-609, 1968-2 C.B. 227.

[54] Discussed in Chapter 4§6.

[55] May 19, 1995 meeting in Washington, D.C., Panel I, entitled "Conversions To and From Exempt Status," presented by Doug Mancino, LaVerne Woods, and Lauren McNulty and reprinted in *The Exempt Organization Tax Review,* vol. 12, no. 1, July 1995.

[56] Reg. §337(d)-4.

exempt entity may require a number of steps. The charter or other organizing documents might have to be revised to include constraints required for the particular category of exemption.[57] If the nonexempt entity has relationships with persons who control it, such entanglements may have to be undone. The second issue is whether the future operations would qualify under the desired category of exemption. Third, the proposed exempt would have to prove that no private inurement resulted from the conversion. If, for example, the entity has incurred debt, the assets should be sufficient to retire the debt. In particular, debt owed to persons controlling the organization would be questioned as to its reasonableness, rate of interest, and why it exists. The IRS might require that the debt be retired prior to the conversion. Other business relationships, such as space rental and management service contracts, are also scrutinized.[58]

20.7 SERVICES RENDERED FOR INDIVIDUALS

When does the rendering of services to members or insiders result in private benefit and evidence that the organization does not operate to benefit the public? When is service revenue classified as unrelated business income, as discussed in Chapter 21? As a general proposition, these questions are of most concern to §501(c)(3) organizations, but all exempt organizations must serve some exempt constituency—be it the poor, the pipefitters, or the social set—in a group sense, not on an individual level. For (c)(3) organizations, the basic question is whether the charitable class is sufficiently broad that the individuals are served as a means of achieving the public purpose. The distinction is best made through examples, although the logic is not necessarily clear (See also chapter 2§2(a)).

(a) Services Providing Public Benefit

Certain types of services provide public benefit even though they are furnished to individuals, because they serve a societal purpose that is considered as charitable. Examples include:

- Medical services, including hospitals and health maintenance organizations
- Schools, both private and public
- Cultural providers, such as art galleries and all types of performing arts
- Grants of money, food, housing, or other services to poor people or students

(b) When Private Benefit is Found

Some services produce more than incidental private benefit to individual recipients, and therefore cause the activity to be considered nonexempt. Examples of such services include:

[57] For §501(c)(3)s, see Chapter 2§1; for (c)(4) through (c)(7) organizations, see Chapters 6–9.
[58] Discussed in §20.2 through §20.4.

- A bus service for private school students[59]

- Cooperative art gallery management[60]

- Preferential housing to employees of one of the exempt organization's directors[61]

- A genealogical society for a particular common name[62]

- Financial planning for charitable giving[63]

- Management consulting for small businesses[64]

- Real estate multiple listing services[65]

(c) Membership Perks

Member benefit is an especially confusing aspect of this issue. In the §501(c)(3) and (c)(4) context, a membership composed of contributors can be given preferential treatment in certain circumstances. For example, reduced or free admission, discounts in bookstores, attendance at conferences or receptions, and other benefits directly connected with the exempt organization's mission are permitted when their value is small in relation to the charges, as discussed in Chapter 24. However, services construed to benefit individuals on a personal level unrelated to the exempt activities, such as group insurance plans, are troublesome.

Because (c)(5), (c)(6), and (c)(7) organizations are formed to benefit members, they have wider latitude in providing services. Nevertheless, services still must be directed toward the particular objectives of the exempt organization.

Labor unions provide a wide range of work-related services, including day care, job training, and placement services germane to their members' gainful employment. A union might incur nonexempt function income and potential unrelated business income tax from its sale of housing, food, or medical products. The IRS *Exempt Organizations Handbook* instructs the specialist to refer any inurement questions concerning a labor union to the national office, due to the lack of published precedents.

Business leagues run afoul of the inurement test more often than unions, and a clearer distinction is possible. Such a league must carry out programs that benefit an industry or locality, and while incidental individual benefit can result, the overriding purpose must be to serve the industry. For example, the American Institute of Certified Public Accountants can perform peer reviews and administer qualifying tests that maintain the standards of its profession, but running an executive search department to secure job placement for individual members would be an unrelated business. Many examples of individual benefits can be found in Revenue Rulings, such as:

---

[59] Rev. Rul. 69-175, 1969-1 C.B. 149.
[60] Rev. Rul. 71-395, 1971-2 C.B. 228.
[61] Rev. Rul. 72-147, 1972-1 C.B. 147.
[62] *The Callaway Family Association, Inc. v. Commissioner*, 71 T.C. 340 (1978).
[63] *Christian Stewardship Assistance, Inc. v. Commissioner*, 70 T.C. 1037 (1978).
[64] *B.S.W. Group, Inc. v. Commissioner*, 70 T.C. 352 (1978).
[65] Rev. Rul. 59-234, 1959-2 C.B. 149.

- Group purchases of supplies or inventory[66]

- A trading stamp program[67]

- Research made available only to members, not to the industry as a whole[68]

20.8   JOINT VENTURES

Private inurement occurs when an exempt organization's assets are placed at unreasonable risk of loss in comparison to the assets of private investors joining it in a venture. Of equal importance is whether the exempt organization receives a share of ownership equivalent to the non-EO investors. As usual, there is also the burden of proving that the transaction serves the exempt purposes of the EO.

The IRS has repeatedly refused to allow §501(c)(3) organizations to be general partners in any venture, in order to prevent them from "taking on an obligation to further the private financial interests of their other partners." Only when the venture is buying exempt function property (not investment property), such as a school building or opera production, has the IRS allowed an exempt organization to be a general partner. The Plumstead Theatre Society[69] won a decision that yielded the following characteristics of a limited investor venture:

- The venture served an exempt purpose: to produce a play;

- The amount invested by and provided for return to the limited partners was reasonable;

- The transaction was at arm's length;

- Plumstead was not obligated to return the invested capital;

- Investors had no control over Plumstead's operations; and

- Investors were not officers or directors of Plumstead.

The medical community has been fraught with controversy about private inurement. There have been hundreds of private letter rulings seeking approval of hospital reorganizations involving sales of nonprofit hospitals, purchases of medical practices, for-profit subsidiaries, and other rearrangements of health care entities. The standards for joint ventures are outlined in Chapter 22 and the particular rules applicable to hospitals can be found in Chapter 4§6. Private foundations are not only prohibited from entering into joint ownership with their disqualified persons, but also face the possibility that a joint venture could be classified as a jeopardizing investment or an excess business holding.[70]

---

[66] Rev. Rul. 66-338, 1966-2 C.B. 226.
[67] Rev. Rul. 65-244, 1965-2 C.B. 167.
[68] Rev. Rul. 60-106, 1969-1 C.B. 153.
[69] *Plumstead Theatre Society, Inc. v. Commissioner*, 74 T.C. 1324 (1980).
[70] See Chapter 16.

20.9 INTERMEDIATE SANCTIONS

To better enforce the existing rule that no private individual unfairly reap benefit from a §501(c)(3) or (4), the Taxpayer Bill of Rights 2 added penalties called *intermediate sanctions*.[71] Unlike the sanctions on self-dealing by private foundations,[72] the only recourse available to the IRS before IRC §4958 to punish a public charity paying excessive salaries to its key employees was to revoke its exemption. IRC §501(c)(3) organizations, and as a part of this legislation (c)(4)s, must operate exclusively to benefit the exempt class they are formed to serve—the poor, culture seekers, or the sick, for example. An organization that pays excessive salaries (as a relatively minor part of its expenditures) often also serves its charitable constituents and is thereby entitled to retain exempt status. Despite the private inurement, it operates substantially and devotes most of its assets to the charitable purposes.[73] IRC §4958 serves to complement, not to alter, the requirements for tax-exempt status under 501(c)(3). Both revocation and tax can be invoked in a circumstance that the level of excess benefits reflects a question of whether the organization as a whole functions as a charity (footnote 15 in legislative history).

Exemption revocation was considered an ineffective sanction because it deprived the public of needed services and did not recover the excessive benefits paid. IRC §4958 requires that the excessive compensation or benefits be repaid and imposes a 25% initial, or first-tier, penalty tax (the intermediate sanction) on the *disqualified person* who receives *excess benefits* from a §501(c)(3) (other than a private foundation) or (4) organization in a transaction that occurred on or after September 14, 1995.[74]

The *managers* who participated in the excess benefit transaction, knowing that it was such a transaction, unless such participation was not willful and was due to reasonable cause, are liable for a tax equal to 10% of the excess benefit, subject to a maximum of $10,000. If more than one person is subject to the tax, they are jointly and severally liable for the tax. A manager that receives excessive benefits may be liable for both taxes plus return of excess benefits.

A *manager* is any officer, director, or trustee of an organization and those individuals that have and actually exercise power and responsibility similar to those of officers, directors, or trustees. Independent contractors, acting in a capacity as attorneys, accountants, and investment managers and advisors, are not officers.[75] Any person who has authority merely to recommend particular administrative or policy decisions, but not to implement them without approval of a superior, is not an officer. A person serving on a committee of the governing body of the organization that invokes the rebuttable presumption of reasonableness based on the committee's actions, is treated as a manager for purposes of the 10% tax regardless of whether they are an officer, director, or trustee.

---

[71] H.R. 2337, §§1311–1314. 104th Cong., 2d Sess. (1996).

[72] See Chapter 14.

[73] The organizational and operational requirements for qualification as a tax-exempt organization are discussed in Chapter 2. These tests require that substantially all, but not 100%, of the organization's efforts be charitable.

[74] Prop. Reg. §53.4958-1(c).

[75] Prop. Reg. §53.4958-1(d).

A manager *participates knowing* if he or she had reason to know that an excess benefit transaction would result from payments being authorized under standards outlined in Chapter 14§10(c). A manager is excused from the penalty if he or she, after full disclosure of the facts, relies upon the advice of outside or in-house counsel expressed in a reasoned written legal opinion that the transaction is not an excess benefit transaction.

If the excess is not corrected (repaid to the organization), an additional second-tier tax of 200% can be assessed against disqualified person(s) (not the managers). Note that *no* tax is imposed on the organization. These rules are in transition as this edition is being prepared and are complicated. The Wiley Nonprofit Series has a book dedicated exclusively to the subject.[76]

The definition of those treated as **disqualified persons** is far broader than the definition of the same terms under the private foundation rules (contrary to what some expected before the proposed regulations were issued). The proposed regulations define the term generally to mean a "person in a position to exercise substantial influence over the affairs of the organization, whether they are an exempt organization manager, officer, director, or trustee."[77] Those persons with and without substantial influence over the organization are listed in the proposed regulations as follows:

Group A. A person is a disqualified person with respect to a transaction if the person is a member of the family of the person with substantial influence. Members of the family and related businesses are defined for this purpose as the following "statutory categories of disqualified persons":

- Family members[78] (spouses, ancestors, children, grandchildren, great-grandchildren, and siblings and their spouses).

- A 35% controlled entity meaning corporations in which disqualified persons own more than 35% of the combined voting power and partnerships, trusts, and estates in which disqualified persons own more than 35% of the profits or beneficial interest.

Group B. Certain persons are disqualified persons by virtue of the fact that they have powers or responsibilities of the sort included in the following list:

- Persons serving on the governing body who are entitled to vote (evidence that one did not participate in a decision may be important);

- Presidents, chief executive officers, or chief operating officers;

- Treasurers and chief financial officers; and

- Persons with material financial interest in a provider-sponsored organization.

---

[76] Bruce R. Hopkins and D. Benson Tesdahl, *Intermediate Sanctions: Curbing Nonprofit Abuse* (New York: Wiley, 1997).

[77] IRC §4958(f)(1); Prop. Reg. §53.4958-3.

[78] Determined by reference to IRC §4946(d) except for the inclusion of whole and half-blood siblings.

Group C. Persons deemed not to have substantial influence include:

- Another organization tax exempt under (c)(3) (proposed regulations conspicuously omitted (c)(4)).

- Persons receiving economic benefits in an amount less than that used to define highly compensated employees for pension plan purposes[79] who are not substantial contributors.

Group D. Persons not listed in Group A or B may still be treated as a disqualified person based upon the facts and circumstances of his or her relationship to the organization.[80] The following facts tend to indicate a person has substantial influence.

- The person founded the organization;

- The person is a substantial contributor;

- The person's compensation is based on revenues derived from activities of the organization that he or she controls;

- The person has authority to control or determine a significant portion of the organization's capital expenditures, operating budget, or compensation for employees (such as a school headmaster);

- The person has managerial authority or serves as a key advisor to a person with managerial authority; or

- The person owns controlling interest in a corporation, partnership, or trust that is a disqualified person.

Group E. Facts tending to indicate a person does not have control over an organization include the following:

- The person has taken a bona fide vow of poverty as an employee or agent of a religious organization.

- The person is an independent contractor, such as an attorney, accountant, or investment manager, unless such person stands to economically benefit with respect to transactions.[81]

An **excess benefit transaction** is one in which the economic benefit the insider receives, directly or indirectly, exceeds the value of the consideration (worked performed or price paid) he or she gives back to the organization, also

---

[79] Pursuant to IRC §414(q)(1)(B)(i) or $80,000; some suggest IRS Notice 95-55, 1995-2 C.B. 336 may apply to tie this number to COLAs.

[80] Prop. Reg. §53.4958-3(e).

[81] The proposed regulations by example say this condition exists if the advisor's firm has a policy prohibiting economic benefit aside from fees received for professional services rendered. Prop. Reg. §53.4958-4, Example 9.

called a non-fair market value transaction.[82] The excess benefit is the difference between the FMV, or *reasonable* amount, and the higher amount actually paid. The following types of payments are disregarded for this purpose:

- Reasonable expenses for members of the governing body to attend meetings, not including luxury or spousal travel;
- Economic benefit received solely as a member, or volunteer to, an organization of a sort provided to the public in exchange for membership fee of $75 or less per year; and
- Benefits received as a member of a charitable class the organization intends to benefit, such as admission to a park or educational information.

Excess benefit transactions cause the sanctions to be imposed unless reasonableness is evidenced by certain *rebuttal presumptions*.[83] The three specific types of excess benefit transactions include:

- A non-FMV transaction occurs between the insider and the exempt organization;
- Unreasonable compensation (including expense allowances and deferred benefits) is paid by the exempt organization to an insider; or
- A *revenue-sharing arrangement* based on the organization's income violates the private inurement standards.

Excess benefit transactions can be direct or indirect.[84] A payment of the type listed previously made by an exempt organization's controlled subsidiary to a person that is an insider of the organization is subject to the sanction.

A **rebuttable presumption** of reasonableness exists if a compensation arrangement or property transaction is approved by a board of directors or trustees (or committee) that

- Is composed entirely of independent individuals unrelated to and not subject to control by the disqualified person involved (no conflict of interest occurs);
- The amount paid is based upon *appropriate data* as to comparability of value; and
- Adequate documentation of data forming the basis for the approval is accumulated and maintained by parties authorizing the transaction.

The rebuttable presumption does not apply to payments to disqualified persons that are not reported by the organization and the individual as compensation. Contemporaneous documentation of process is extremely important for an organization to maintain in this regard according to Marcus Owens, Chief of the Exempt

---

[82] Prop. Reg. §53.4958-4.
[83] Prop. Reg. §53.4958-6.
[84] IRC §4958(b)(1)(A).

Organizations Division of the IRS. Not only must the procedures for arriving at the amount of all payments be documented, the organization and the recipient must treat them as compensation. Except for nontaxable fringe benefits and expense reimbursements, payments must be treated as compensation on Forms W-2, 1099, 990, the recipient's 1040, and other relevant tax returns. The fact that payments are unreported evidences an intention to make excess benefits even if the unreported payments, when combined with reported amounts, result in reasonable compensation.[85]

In determining when an excess benefit transaction has occurred, one must consider whether the total of all types of compensation paid to an individual is unreasonable. The IRS has developed extensive rules pertaining to definition of and reporting of wages, fringe benefits, fees to independent contractors, and other forms of compensation, or economic benefits, paid by an exempt organization to persons that perform services for it. Form 990, Part V, entitled List of Officers, Directors, and Trustees, requires the names and addresses, position and time devoted, compensation, employee benefit and deferred compensation plan contributions, and expense account and other allowances paid to each individual officer, director, trustee, or key employee.[86] For the rebuttable presumption to apply, it is important that all forms of compensation—taxable and nontaxable—be reported on Form 990. Premiums for liability insurance coverage for penalties imposed by these rules must be treated as compensation, albeit a nontaxable fringe benefit, to avoid classification as excess benefits themselves.[87]

Compensation is **reasonable** if it is in an amount that would ordinarily be paid for like services by like enterprises under like circumstances. Relevant information sufficient to prove reasonable should be gathered and maintained by persons for measuring reasonableness—independent compensation surveys, price paid for similar services available in the area, actual written offers from similar institutions competing for the person's services, and in the case of property, independent appraisals. For an organization with annual gross receipts of less than $1 million, data on compensation paid by five comparable organizations in the same or similar communities or of similar services is considered appropriate data. Total compensation of no more than $80,000 is presumed to be reasonable according to the proposed regulations.

The conditions existing at the time of the contract or other arrangement for engagement of services is the preferred time to measure reasonableness. If that is not possible, all of the facts and circumstances of the transaction are considered, up to and including the date of the payment. The fact that a court, state, local legislative body, or agency has approved of the compensation is not determinative of reasonableness. Reasonableness is reevaluated when the terms are modified or the contract extended.

In a **revenue-sharing** transaction the compensation is determined in whole or in part by the revenues from one or more of the organization's activities. Excess benefits in such transactions are to be determined by the facts and circumstances

---

[85] Instructions to 1997 Form 990, Part P, appearing on page 9.

[86] See appendix to Chapter 27 and discussion of this part in §27.9.

[87] Prop. Reg. §53.4958-4(a)(4); the same rule applies to private foundations as discussed in Chapter 14§4(a).

of each situation. The proposed regulations give three examples that should be carefully studied by those considering incentive compensation. A revenue-sharing arrangement can yield excess benefit, without regard to whether the total compensation is reasonable, when it permits a disqualified person to receive additional compensation without providing proportional benefits that contribute to the organization's accomplishment of its mission.[88]

The penalty is not imposed if the reasonableness is evidenced by the **rebuttal presumptions.** Any reimbursement of the penalty tax to the disqualified person by an organization is to be treated as yet another excess benefit transaction subject to tax unless

- The reimbursement is treated as additional compensation during the year it is paid, and

- The total compensation paid, including the reimbursement, is reasonable.

For transactions entered into between September 14, 1995, and December 31, 1996, the parties were entitled to rely upon the rebuttable presumption if, within 90 days of the payment of the excess benefits, the basic requirements for presumption are documented. After January 1, 1997, the requirements must be met before the payment is made.

Appropriate data to be used to evaluate the reasonableness of compensation paid include levels paid by similarly situated organizations, both taxable and tax-exempt, for functionally comparable positions. The location of the organization may be considered, including the availability of similar specialties in the geographic area. Salary levels reflected in independent compensation surveys by nationally recognized firms and actual written offers made to the person by similar institutions competing for his or her services are also appropriate data.

Correction of the transaction occurs when the person repays the excess benefits or otherwise financially restores the organization, or places it in a financial position not worse than it would have been in if the insider transaction had adhered to highest fiduciary standards. If the excessive payments are being made pursuant to a contract, the contract need not be terminated but the terms must be modified to reasonable amounts. Unless the excess is corrected, a second-tier tax of 200% is imposed on the insider (but not the managers approving the transaction). Correction must be made by the earlier of the date of a deficiency notice with respect to the first-tier tax, or the date on which the second-tier tax is assessed.

Paying the §4958 Excise Tax. The person(s) subject to the excise tax must file Form 4720[89] to report the transaction and calculate the tax due. Form 990 of the organization must disclose any excise tax imposed during the year by answering a four-part question regarding the sanctions for excess benefits, lobbying, or political expenditures.[90] Transactions under contracts binding before September 14,

---

[88] Prop. Reg. §53.4958-5; these rules are only to be applied when the regulations are finalized.

[89] Illustrated in Appendix 27–6.

[90] IRC §6033(b); for 1997, question 89 requests this information on page 4 of Form 990 illustrated in Appendix 27–2.

1995, and still in effect and not materially modified, are not covered. The amount of tax imposed and the amount of reimbursement of tax paid to disqualified persons is also reported on Form 990.

The tax imposed on a disqualified person by the intermediate sanction rules can be abated if the overpayment(s) were not due to willful disregard for the law and the excessive amounts are repaid. The standards of IRC §4961 and 1962 are made applicable by the regulations in allowing abatement.[91] Losing exempt status to avoid the tax is not effective because the rules are made applicable to any organization that was exempt from tax at any time during the five-year period ending on the date of the excess benefit transaction.[92]

The excess benefits tax does not apply to a foreign organization that receives substantially all of its support from sources outside the United States.

Readers should be careful to consult the final regulations for changes in this section. The American Institute of Certified Public Accountants, American Bar Association, and many others suggested substantial changes to the proposed regulations.[93] A hearing was scheduled for March 16–17 in Washington with video conferencing for a Los Angeles location. Since the burden of this sanction falls on the person receiving the excess benefit, it is extremely important for the organization's management to pay attention to new developments.

[91] Prop. Reg. §53.4958-1(c)(iv); see Chapter 15.6(c).
[92] Prop. Reg. §53.4958-2.
[93] Letters were reproduced in the *Exempt Organizations Tax Review* in December 1998 and January 1999.

CHAPTER TWENTY-ONE

Unrelated Business Income

Exempt organizations receive two types of income: earned and unearned. Unearned income—income for which the organization gives nothing in return—comes from grants, membership fees, and donations. One can think of it as *one-way street* money. The motivation for giving the money is gratuitous and/or of a nonprofit character with no expectation of gain on the part of the giver; there is donative intent.

In contrast, an organization furnishes services and goods or invests its capital in return for earned income: an opera is seen, classes are attended, hospital care is provided, or credit counseling is given, for example. The purchasers of the goods and services do intend to receive something in return; they expect the street to be *two-way*. An investment company holding the organization's money expects to have to pay reasonable return for using the funds. In these examples, the organization receives earned income. The important issue this chapter considers is when earned income becomes unrelated business income (UBI) subject to income tax.

The tax on unrelated business income applies to all organizations exempt from tax under §501(c) other than corporations created by an act of Congress and also to the following:

- Tax-exempt employee trusts described in IRC §401
- Individual retirement accounts
- State and municipal colleges and universities
- Qualified state tuition programs described in IRC §529
- Education individual retirement accounts described in IRC §530

The rules that govern when earned income becomes unrelated business income are complex. The concepts of UBI are vague and contain many exceptions that have been carved out by special interest groups. The House of Representatives Subcommittee on Oversight held hearings and drafted revisions over a four-year period during 1987 to 1990. Though proposals to limits deductions and tax a variety of items were not passed, two very important changes resulted from the studies. The Internal Revenue Service (IRS) was directed to expand the Form 990 to report details of revenue sources that now reveals when an organization should file Form 990-T.[1] For-profit subsidiary payments in the form of rent, interest, royalties, or other expense deductible to the subsidiary is taxed to the tax-exempt parent when ownership is 50% or more as explained later.

Tax planning of the sort practiced by a good businessperson is in order for organizations receiving UBI. The best method for reducing unrelated business income tax (UBIT) is to keep good records. The accounting system must support the desired allocation of deductions for personnel and facilities with time records, expense usage reports, auto logs, documentation reports, and so on.[2] Minutes of meetings of the board of directors or trustees should reflect discussion of relatedness of any project claimed to accomplish an exempt purpose, if it appears that the activity is unrelated. For example, contracts and other documents concerning activities that the or-

[1] See Part VII of Form 990 reproduced in Appendix 27–2.
[2] Discussed in Chapter 27§14.

ganization wants to prove are related to its exempt purposes should contain appropriate language to reflect the project's exempt purposes. An organization's original purposes can be expanded and redefined to broaden the scope of activities or to justify the proposed activity as related. Such altered or expanded purpose can be reported to the IRS to justify the relatedness of a new activity. If loss of exemption[3] is a strong possibility because of the extent and amount of unrelated business activity planned, a separate for-profit organization[4] can be formed to shield the organization from a possible loss of exemption due to excessive business activity.

Sometimes an exempt organization has facilities that are dually used for exempt and unrelated purposes. If dual-use facilities are partly debt-financed and partly paid for, an organization could purposefully buy the nontaxable exempt function property with debt and buy the unrelated part of the facility with cash available. Or, separate notes could be executed, with the taxable and unrelated property's debt being paid off first.[5]

21.1   IRS SCRUTINY OF UNRELATED BUSINESS INCOME

Beginning in 1989 with the addition of Part VII to Form 990 and Part XVI-A to Form 990-PF, the IRS has a tool with which it can scrutinize the UBI issue. Until this Analysis of Revenue-Producing Activities was added to the forms, UBI was not identified in any special way on Form 990. The UBI was simply included with related income of the same character. The Congressional representatives and the IRS agreed that there was insufficient information to propose changes to the existing UBI rules. Parts VII and XVI-A separate income into three categories:

1. Unrelated income (identified with a business code from Form 990-T that describes its nature)

2. Unrelated income identified by the specific Internal Revenue Code section by which the income is excluded from UBI

3. Related or exempt function income, along with a description of the relationship of the income-producing activity to the accomplishment of exempt purposes

The IRS's first scrutiny of the new information found a 50–60% compliance rate with UBIT requirements. It found a large portion of social clubs were failing to file Form 990-T when it took a look in 1997 and 1998.

21.2   HISTORY OF THE UNRELATED BUSINESS INCOME TAX

Before 1950, a tax-exempt organization could conduct any income-producing activity and, in fact, many operated businesses and paid no income tax on the profits. Under a destination of income test, the income earned from a business was tax free

---

[3] Discussed in §21.3.
[4] Discussed in Chapter 22§4.
[5] See §21.12.

so long as it was expended for exempt activities. In view of its extensive operations, the IRS tried in the late 1940s to tax New York University Law School's profits from its highly successful spaghetti factory.[6] The court decided no tax could be imposed under the then-existing tax code since the profits were used to operate the school.

In response to pressure from businesses, Congress established the unrelated business income tax in 1951 with the intention of eliminating the unfair competition charitable businesses represented, but it did not prohibit its receipt. The Congressional committee thought that the:

> Tax free status of exemption section 501 organizations enables them to use their profits tax free to expand operations, while their competitors can expand only with profits remaining after taxes. The problem . . . is primarily that of unfair competition.[7]

A key question in identifying UBI is, therefore, whether the activity that produces earned income competes with commercial businesses and whether the method of operation is distinguishable from that of a for-profit entity. Another question is, "Does the income producing activity accomplish the organization's exempt purpose?" These questions are sometimes difficult to answer. The distinctions between for-profits and nonprofits has narrowed over the years as organizations search for creative ways to pay for program services. Consider what the difference between a museum bookstore and a commercial one is, other than the absence of private ownership. Privately owned for-profit theaters operate alongside non-profit ones. Magazines owned by nonprofits, such as *National Geographic* and *Harper's,* contain advertising and appear indistinguishable from *Traveler* or *Life Magazine*. The health care profession is also full of indistinguishable examples.

21.3 CONSEQUENCES OF RECEIVING UBI

There are potentially several unpleasant consequences of earning unrelated income.

- *Payment of unrelated income tax.* Unrelated net income may be taxed at corporate or trust rates with estimated tax payments required. Social clubs, homeowner associations, and political organizations also pay the UBI tax on certain passive investment income in addition to the unrelated business income.

- *Exempt status revocation.* The organization's tax-exempt status could be revoked if the unrelated business activity becomes its primary activity, in which case all income is taxed.

- *Excess business holdings.* A private foundation may not operate a business and is limited in the ownership percentage it can hold in a separate business entity.[8]

[6] *C. F. Mueller Co. v. Commissioner,* 190 F.2d 120 (3rd Cir. 1951).
[7] House of Representatives No. 2319, 81st Cong., 2nd Sess. (1950) at 36–37.
[8] See Chapter 16 for rules defining impermissible excess business holdings for private foundations.

- Internal Revenue Code §501 requires a nonprofit organization to be both organized and operated exclusively for an exempt purpose, although *exclusively* does not mean 100%.[9]

In evaluating the amount of unrelated business activity that is permissible, not only the amount of gross revenue but other factors may be taken into consideration. Nonrevenue aspects of the activity, such as staff time devoted or value of donated services, are factors that might be determinative. The basic issue is whether the operation of the business subsumes, or is inconsistent with, the organization's exempt activities.

A complex of nonexempt activity caused the IRS to revoke the exemption of the Orange County Agricultural Society.[10] Its UBI averaged between 29 to 34% of its gross revenue. Private inurement was also found because the society was doing business with its board of directors. In another context, the IRS privately ruled a 50-50 ratio of related to unrelated income was permitted for a day-care center raising funds from travel tours.[11] An organization with unrelated income in excess of 15–20% of its gross revenue must be prepared to defend its exempt status by showing it focuses on its mission purposes rather than on its business activities. An organization can run a business as a substantial part of its activities, but not as its primary purpose.[12]

21.4   DEFINITION OF TRADE OR BUSINESS

To have unrelated business income, the nonprofit must first be found to be engaging in a trade or business. *Trade or business* is defined very broadly to include any activity carried on for the production of income from the sale of goods or performance of services.[13] The tax court, though, said a trade or business is conducted with "continuity and regularity" and in a "competitive manner similar to commercial businesses.[14] This is an area where the tax rules are very gray. The word "income" does not mean receipts or revenue and also does not necessarily mean net income. IRC §513(c) says: "Where an activity carried on for profit constitutes an unrelated trade or business, no part of such trade or business shall be excluded from such classification merely because it does not result in profit."

The regulations couch the definition in the context of unfair competition with commercial businesses, saying that "when an activity does not possess the characteristics of a trade or business within the meaning of Section 162," the UBIT will not apply. However, these regulations were written before the IRC §513(c) profit motive language was added to the code. They are the subject of continuing arguments between taxpayers and the IRS, and the confusion has produced two tests: profit motive and commerciality.

[9] See Chapter 2.
[10] *Orange County Agricultural Society Inc. v. Commissioner,* 90.1 USTC ¶50.076 (2d Cir. 1990), *aff'g* 55 T.C.M. 1602 (1988).
[11] Priv. Ltr. Rul. 9521004.
[12] Reg. §1.501(c)(3)-1(e)(1).
[13] Reg. §1.513-1(b).
[14] *National Water Well Association, Inc. v. Commissioner,* 92 T.C. 75 (1985).

(a) Profit Motive Test

Under the profit motive test, an activity conducted simply to produce some revenue but without an expectation of producing a profit (similar to the hobby loss rules) is not a business.[15] This test is applied by the IRS in situations when a nonprofit has more than one unrelated business. Losses from the unprofitable activity or hobby cannot necessarily be offset against profits from other businesses. Likewise, the excess expenses (losses) generated in fundamentally exempt activity, such as an educational publication undertaken without the intention of making a profit, cannot be deducted against the profits from a profit-motivated project. Social clubs have battled with the IRS about this issue.[16]

(b) Commerciality Test

The commerciality test looks to the type of operation: If the activity is carried on in a manner similar to a commercial business, it constitutes a trade or business. This test poses serious problems for the unsuspecting because there are no statutory or regulatory parameters to follow. A broad range of UBI cases where the scope of sales or service activity was beyond that normally found in the exempt setting have been decided by examining the commercial taint of the activity.[17] Exhibit 21–1 highlights situations that may jeopardize an organization's exempt status.

(c) Fragmentation Rule

Further evidence of the overreaching scope of the term *trade or business* is found in the fragmentation rule.[18] This rule carves out an activity carried on alongside an exempt one and proves that unrelated business does not lose its identity and taxability when it is earned in a related setting. Take, for example, a museum shop. The shop itself is clearly a trade or business, often established with a profit motive and operated in a commercial manner. Items sold in such shops, however, often include both educational items, such as books and reproductions of art works, and souvenirs. The fragmentation rule requires that all items sold be analyzed to identify the educational, or related, items the profit from which is not taxable and the unrelated souvenir items that do produce taxable income. The standards applied to identify museum objects as related or unrelated are well documented in IRS rulings.[19]

---

[15] *West Virginia State Medical Association*, 89-2 U.S.T.C. §9491 (4th Cir. 1989); 91 T.C. 651 (1988), *Commissioner v. Groetzinger*, 480 U.S. 23 (1987).

[16] Discussed in Chapter 9§5.

[17] *Better Business Bureau v. U.S.*, 326 US. 279, 283 (1945); *United States National Water Well Association, Inc. v. Commissioner*, 92 T.C. 7 (1989); *Scripture Press Foundation v. U.S.*, 285 F.2d 800 (Ct.Cl. 1961); *Greater United Navajo Development Enterprises, Inc. v. Commissioner*, 74 T.C. 69 (1980); also see Priv. Ltr. Rul. 9636001 for Christian school's textbook publishing department earning UBI because it was indistinguishable from commercial publishing company.

[18] IRC §513(c).

[19] See §21.13.

Exhibit 21–1

COMMERCIALITY TEST CHECKLIST

"YES" answers to these questions are warnings signs that signal the EO's exposure to a challenge that the organization operates in a commercial manner and may not be exempt.

☐ COMPETITIVENESS: Does the exempt organization's activity compete with for-profit businesses conducting the same activity? Is there a counterpart for the activity in the business sector, particularly a "small" business?

☐ PERSONNEL MOTIVATION: Do managers receive generous compensation? Is the activity run by well-paid staff members?

☐ SELLING TECHNIQUES: Are advertising and promotional materials utilized? Are retailing methods, such as mail order catalog or display systems, similar to for-profit enterprise used?

☐ PRICING: Is the highest price the market will bear charged for goods and services? There are no scaled or reduced rates available for members of a charitable class.

☐ CUSTOMER PROFILE: Are the organization's services and goods for sale to anyone? Are they available to the general public on a regular basis, rather than only for persons participating in the organization's other exempt activities?

☐ ORGANIZATION'S FOCUS—GOOD WORKS RATIO: Does the organization conduct significant other charitable program activity? Is the income-producing activity its primary focus rather than exempt ones?

☐ CHARACTER OF ORGANIZATION'S SUPPORT: Does very little or none of the organization's support come from voluntary contributions and grants or other unearned sources?

21.5   WHAT IS UNRELATED BUSINESS INCOME?

Unrelated business income is defined as the gross income derived from any *unrelated trade or business regularly carried on,* less the *deductions connected* with the carrying on of such trade or business, computed with *modifications and exceptions.*[20] The italicized terms are key to identifying UBI. Exhibit 21–2 shows them graphically. All four prongs of the circle surrounding the circle must be considered to determine what earned income is to be classified as UBI.

---

[20] IRC §512(a)(1).

Exhibit 21–2

COMPONENTS OF UNRELATED BUSINESS INCOME

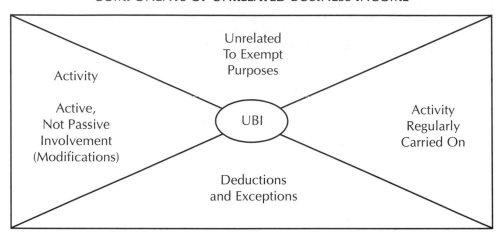

21.6 "REGULARLY CARRIED ON"

A trade or business regularly carried on is considered to compete unfairly with commercial business and is fair game for classification as a taxable business. In determining whether an activity is regularly carried on, the IRS looks at the frequency and continuity of an activity when examined by comparison to commercial enterprises. The normal time span of comparable commercial activities can also be determinative.[21] Exhibit 21–3 compares regular and irregular activities.

(a) Meaning of Irregular

Intermittent activities may be deemed *regularly carried on* or commercial unless they are discontinuous or periodic. For example, the revenue from a weekly dance is more likely to be taxed than the profits from an annual fund-raising event. By the same token, ads sold for a monthly newsletter would be classed as commercial; program ads sold for an annual ball might not. Where the planning and sales effort of a special event or athletic tournament is conducted over a long span of time, the IRS may argue that the activity itself becomes regularly carried on despite the fact that the event occurs infrequently.[22] Events held once a year have been the subject of much argument as to their regularity. Congress specifically mentioned *income derived from annual athletic exhibition* in stating that the UBI applies only to business regularly carried on.[23] When the IRS proposed taxing broadcast rights, it argued that preparatory time, not the actual playing time, determines regularity. If an event or program takes the entire year to produce, the span

---

[21] Reg. §1.513-1(c).
[22] See the NCAA advertising sales discussion following under Agency Theory and §21.8(h).
[23] S. Rep. 91-552, 91st Cong., 1st Sess. (1969).

Exhibit 21–3

DETERMINING REGULAR ACTIVITY	
Irregular	Regular
Sandwich stand at annual county fair.	Cafe open daily.
Annual golf tournament.	Racetrack operated during racing "season."
Nine-day antique show.	Antique store.
Gala Ball held annually.	Monthly dance.
Program ads for annual fund-raising event.	Advertisements in quarterly magazine.

of time spent negotiating contracts and otherwise working on the event is considered. Examples of the arguments follow:

- Time spent by volunteers in soliciting advertisements or sponsorships were to be considered in evaluating the time span of the activity.[24]

- An eight-month concert season program was ruled to be comparable to commercial entertainment operations and thereby regularly carried on.[25]

- The National College Athletic Association (NCAA) convinced the court that an independent company's year-round effort to sell ads for the Final Four championship basketball tournament program was not attributable to the NCAA. The three-week duration of the tournament made it irregular and the program income excludible from UBIT even though the activity was an unrelated business.[26]

- Year-round sales effort for ads in a labor organization's yearbook, in IRS eyes, meant the activity is regularly carried on. The facts indicated that the yearbook had relevance to the members throughout the year and "the vast majority of advertisements carry a definitely commercial message."[27]

- One private ruling, however, said it would be difficult to conclude that an annual ball, which occurs only once each year, is regularly carried on.[28]

- Biannual publication of a business league's directory was also ruled to be a regular activity; the every-other-year publication cycle was regular or normal in commercial settings. The IRS opined that "continuity" did not

[24] Rev. Rul. 75-201, 1975-1 C.B. 164.
[25] Rev. Rul. 75-200, 1975-1 C.B. 163. See also *Suffolk County Patrolmen's Benevolent Association, Inc. v. Commissioner*, 77 T.C. 1314 (1981), *acq.* 1984-1 C.B. 2. The fact that the solicitors spent 16 weeks organizing the event makes the activity regular in the IRS's eyes.
[26] *National College Athletic Association v. Commissioner*, 914 F.2d 1417 (10th Cir. 1990). The IRS strongly disagrees with this opinion; see Priv. Ltr. Ruls. 9044071 and 9721001.
[27] Priv. Ltr. Rul. 9304001.
[28] Priv. Ltr. Rul. 9417003.

necessarily mean "continuously," but rather having a connection with similar activities in the past that will be carried forward into the future.[29]

(b) Seasonal Activity

Activities conducted during a period traditionally identified as seasonal, such as Christmas, if conducted during the season, will be considered regular and the income will not qualify to be excluded from UBIT. Christmas card sales during October or November, or Independence Day balloons sold in June/July, would be regular sales activity.

21.7 "SUBSTANTIALLY RELATED"

An activity is substantially related only when it has a causal relationship to the achievement of the organization's exempt purpose[30] (that is, the purpose for which the organization was granted exemption based upon its Form 1023 or 1024 and subsequent Form 990 filings). This requirement necessitates an examination of the relationship between the business activities (producing and distributing goods or performing services) that generate the particular income in question and the accomplishment of the organization's exempt purposes.[31]

> Any business the conduct of which is not substantially related (aside from need to make money) to the performance of an organization's charitable, educational, or other purposes or function constituting the basis of its exemption is defined as unrelated.[32]

The size and extent of the activity itself and its contribution to exempt purposes are determinative. The nexus (association, connection, or linkage) between the activity and accomplishment of exempt purposes is examined to find relatedness. The best way to illustrate the concept is with examples.

(a) Examples of Related Activity

Related income-producing activities include:

- Admission tickets for performances or lectures

- Student or member tuition or class fees

- Symphony society sale of symphonic musical recordings

- Products made by handicapped workers or trainees[33]

- Hospital room, drug, and other patient charges

[29] Priv. Ltr. Rul. 9302035.
[30] IRC §513(a).
[31] Reg. §1.513-1(d).
[32] Reg. §1.513-1(a).
[33] Rev. Rul. 73-128, 1973-1, C.B. 222; Priv. Ltr. Rul. 9152039.

- Agriculture college sale of produce or student work

- Sale of educational materials (see §21.13 for museum issues)

- College golf course usage by students and faculty[34]

- Secretarial and telephone answering service training program for indigent and homeless[35]

- Operation of diagnostic health devices, such as CAT scans or magnetic imaging machines by a hospital or health care organization[36]

- Sale of online bibliographic data from EO's central databases[37]

- "Public entertainment activities," or agricultural and educational fair or exposition (Section 21.9(d))

- "Qualified conventions and trade shows" (§21.9(e))

- Producing tapes of endangered ethnic music[38]

- Birthing center operated as a part of a church in respect of its religious tenets and belief that birth is a sacred and spiritual event[39]

(b) School Athletic and Entertainment Events

College-sponsored events have traditionally been thought to foster school spirit and advance the educational purposes of the schools. Revenues produced through sales of admission tickets, event programs, refreshments, and similar items have not normally been treated as UBI. Legislative history underlying the UBI provisions states "athletic activities of schools are substantially related to their educational functions. For example, a university would not be taxable on income derived from a basketball tournament sponsored by it, even where the teams were composed of students from other schools."[40]

Payments for radio and television broadcast rights, however, have been controversial. In 1977, the IRS advised Texas Christian University, Southern Methodist University, University of Southern California, and the Cotton Bowl Athletic Association that revenue derived by the universities from the telecasting and radio broadcasting of athletic events constituted unrelated trade or business income. In 1978, the IRS reversed its position after a challenge by the Cotton Bowl and National College Athletic Association.[41] In 1979, the IRS further expanded its position regarding such events and provided a good outline of the issues:[42]

---

[34] Usage by spouses, alumni, and donors was not considered as related in Priv. Ltr. Rul. 9645004.

[35] Priv. Ltr. Rul. 9009038.

[36] Tech. Adv. Memo. 8932004.

[37] Priv. Ltr. Rul. 9017028.

[38] Priv. Ltr. Rul. 9210026.

[39] Priv. Ltr. Rul. 925037, citing Rev. Ruls. 80-114, 79-359, and 71-580.

[40] S. Rep. 2375 and H. Rep. 2319, 81st Cong., 2d Sess. 109 (1950).

[41] Priv. Ltr. Rul. 7851004.

[42] Priv. Ltr. Rul. 7930043.

- Sales of broadcast rights were regularly carried on and the activity looked at as a profit-motivated trade or business activity, with extensive time expended training the teams and preparing for the game.

- The events were regularly carried on (systematic and consistent, not discontinuous or periodic).

- Games, however, were related to the Cotton Bowl's exempt purpose. Income from sale of the game broadcast was a by-product because it was presented in its original state and provided a simultaneous extension of the exempt-function game to the general public.

A long series of IRS proclamations on the subject were issued in following years concerning the sale of broadcast rights by colleges, all of which ruled that such sales produced related income.[43] In 1981, the IRS applied the commerciality test[44] to find the promotion of rock concerts in a "multipurpose college auditorium" a taxable unrelated activity. The college's goal to maximize revenue to the exclusion of other considerations indicated the facility was not operated as an educational program. The nature of the entertainment and the audience were not the criteria used to judge the activity's relatedness; instead, the detrimental fact was the college's selection of events based upon their profitability. The facts outlined in the ruling evidencing the businesslike manner of conduct were as follows:[45]

- During the school year, 45 ticket events were held, 44% of which were rock concerts.

- Contemporary professional entertainers comprised 40% of the concert season.

- The facility was managed by a director with more than 30 years' experience in promoting commercial events.

- The school's fine arts department had no involvement in the selection of events to be held at the center and normally did not participate.

- Twenty-six percent of the tickets were sold to nonstudents.

- Tickets were sold through a commercial ticket service.

- Ticket prices for students were not discounted.

- Concerts were generally indistinguishable by price or type of performance from similar events provided by commercial impresarios.

- Compensation to the performers was negotiated and generally the same as compensation paid by for-profit centers.

---

[43] Priv. Ltr. Ruls. 7851005, 7930043, 7948113; Rev. Ruls. 80-295 and 80-296; and Priv. Ltr. Rul. 8643091. See §21.8(e) for special consideration of corporate sponsorship of such events.
[44] See §21.4(b).
[45] Priv. Ltr. Rul. 9147008.

Spouses and children of students, spouses and dependents of a university's employees, university alumni, members of President's Club (big donors and guests) were deemed to be unrelated users of a university's golf course. The IRS ruled that only use by full- and part-time students and employees was substantially related and that there was no causal relationship between the university's educational purposes and use of its golf course by any other persons.[46]

21.8 UNRELATED ACTIVITIES

The types of income that can potentially be treated as unrelated income are numerous, as the following controversial types of income illustrate. The examples do not always follow a logical pattern because courts and the IRS do not always agree, and the IRS has not always been consistent in its rulings. Further rules applicable to one type of income are not necessarily applied to another type.

(a) Rentals

Rentals of equipment and other personal property (such as computers or telephone systems) to others are specifically listed in IRC §512(b)(3) for inclusion in UBI. Such rental presumably is undertaken only to collect revenue to cover costs, with no direct connection to the organization's own exempt purposes; it *exploits* the exempt holding of the property. However, the following situations should be noted:

- Renting to (or sharing with) another nonprofit (or, conceivably, an individual or a for-profit business) is related if the rental expressly serves the landlord's exempt purposes, such as a museum's rental of art works—that would otherwise be kept in its storage—to other institutions to ensure maximum public viewing of the work or relieve storage needs.

- Mailing list rentals produce UBI according to the IRS, except for narrow exceptions allowed to §501(c)(3) organizations for exchanges of lists with other (c)(3)s.[47] A growing number of organizations have successfully claimed that list rentals are excludible royalty income as discussed in §21.10(d).

- Real estate rentals are also excluded from UBI under the passive exceptions, but only if the property is unencumbered as discussed in §21.12 regarding debt-financed property.[48]

Whether rental charges are at, below, or above cost can be determinative in evaluating relatedness. A full fair market value rental arrangement does not evidence exempt purposes (although the taint can be overcome by other reasons for the rental, such as dissemination of specialized educational information).

[46] Priv. Ltr. Rul. 9645004.
[47] IRC §513(h).
[48] IRC §512(b)(3).

(b) Services

Services Provided to Another Nonprofit. Rendering services (such as billing, technical assistance, administrative support) to other nonprofits does not serve the exempt purposes of the service provider and is unrelated, according to the IRS. The fact that sharing creates efficiencies that allow all the nonprofits involved to save money does not necessarily sway the IRS. Only where the services themselves represent substantive programs better accomplished by selling the services to other organizations is the revenue considered related.

- The Tax Court sanctioned the sharing of computer database technology for a group of libraries based upon the concept that if an activity was a necessary component part of the operation of one library, it served an exempt purpose to provide the service to other exempt organizations.[49]

- Training courses furnished by a university to a business was sanctioned.[50]

- An HMO service provider created to provide management consulting to other exempt HMOs was not itself exempt.[51] Similarly the exempt status of an organization providing management and administrative services to rural hospitals was revoked despite the fact that it had been a tax-exempt organization since 1956.[52]

Cooperative Efforts. Where an organization is created to serve a consortium of organizations with a common building or pooled investment funds, the IRS has generally allowed its exemption when the new organization itself is partly supported by independent donations. When services are program related, the cooperative performance of charitable or educational functions has generally been acceptable to the IRS.[53]

- Certain cooperative service organizations have been specifically exempted by Congress. IRC §501(e) grants exempt status to cooperative hospital organizations formed to provide on a group basis specified services including data processing, purchasing (including the purchase of insurance on a group basis), warehousing, billing and collection, food, clinical, industrial engineering, laboratory, printing, communications, record center, and personnel (including selection, testing, training, and education of personnel services). Note that laundry is not on the list.

- Cooperative services organizations established to "hold, commingle, and collectively invest" stocks and securities of educational institutions are also provided a special exempt category under IRC §501(f).

[49] *Council for Bibliographic & Information Technology,* T.C.M. 1992-364 (Tax Ct. 1992). See also Tech. Adv. Memo. 9032005 in which a §501(c)(6) tourist and convention bureau provided related services to businesses planning conventions but received taxable commissions from hotel referrals.
[50] Priv. Ltr. Rul. 9137002.
[51] Priv. Ltr. Rul. 9232003.
[52] Priv. Ltr. Rul. 9822004.
[53] See Priv. Ltr. Rul. 9237034.

- IRC §513(e) allows a special exclusion from UBI for the income earned by a hospital providing the types of services listed in IRC §501(e) to another hospital that has facilities to serve fewer than 100 patients, provided the price for such services is rendered at cost plus a "reasonable amount of return on the capital goods used" in providing the service.

Member Services.   Services furnished to members must also accomplish an exempt purpose to be treated as related. Services provided by churches, schools, hospitals, and most other charitable organizations are ordinarily treated as related. Classification of member services by business leagues, labor unions, and other non-(c)(3) organizations is not always clear. The question is whether the service yields private inurement to the individual member or to the profession as a whole and therefore the general public. Excessive unrelated member services can imperil an association's exempt status. Chapters 7 and 8 have extensive consideration of this issue.

(c) Licensing Use of the Organization's Name

Licensing the use of an organization's name normally is accomplished by a contract permitting use of the organization's intangible property—its name—with the compensation constituting royalty income that is excluded from UBI.[54] However, such arrangements may constitute commercial exploitation of an exempt asset in arrangements that usually require the nonprofit to furnish its mailing lists, endorse products, distribute materials on behalf of the list renter, and perform other services associated with use of its intangible property.[55] Since 1981, the IRS has been trying to tax organizations on the sale of their names in connection with insurance programs, affinity sales, and other commercial marketing schemes.[56]

To add flavor to the problem, in April 1990, the IRS reversed its position that a *royalty arrangement* licensing an organization's name, logo, and mailing list to an insurance agent (to promote life insurance to its membership) did not produce UBI for the exempt organization.[57] Because of the extensive involvement (active, not passive) of the exempt organization in servicing the membership lists, the narrow exemption of mailing lists,[58] and the agency theory discussed in §21.8(h), the IRS ruled that the supposed royalty arrangement produced UBI. The American Bar Association lost a similar battle in 1986, although its case was made more complicated by an arrangement whereby its members made substantial donations of the program profits.[59]

Affinity card revenues are UBI, as far as the IRS is concerned, that do not qualify for the royalty exception. When first ruling on affinity cards, the IRS allowed royalty exclusion for a fraternal order's card income.[60] By 1988, it had reversed this

---

[54] Under modifications discussed in §21.10(d).

[55] In Priv. Ltr. Rul. 9705001 a business league earned royalty income from licensing its name without its mailing list or other services.

[56] Rev. Rul. 81-178, 1981-2 C.B. 135.

[57] Priv. Ltr. Rul. 9029047.

[58] See §21.9(h).

[59] United States v. American Bar Endowment, 477 U.S. 105 (1986).

[60] Priv. Ltr. Rul. 8747066.

position.[61] While use of the organization's name and logo alone can produce royalty income, the credit card arrangements often depend on an accompanying sale of the organization's mailing list and, in some cases, endorsements and promotion by the organization in its publications and member/donor correspondence. The IRS therefore again applies an agency-type theory to deem that the nonprofit itself, rather than the intermediary organization, performed valuable services that produced unrelated income. Some organizations try to avoid this problem by bifurcating the royalty and mailing list aspects of the contract. The IRS position is to see them as one transaction, in reality, one contract, and apply UBIT.[62]

(d) Advertising

Sale of advertising in an otherwise exempt publication is almost always considered unrelated business income by the IRS. The basic theory is that the advertisements promote the interests of the individual advertiser and cannot therefore be related to the charitable purposes of the organization. The following examples are indicative of IRS thinking:

- The American College of Physicians was unsuccessful in arguing that the drug company ads in its health journal published for physicians educated the doctors. The college said the ads provided the reader with a comprehensive and systematic presentation of goods and services needed in the profession and informed physicians about new drug discoveries, but the court disagreed.[63]

- A college newspaper training program for journalism students enrolled in an advertising course produced related income.[64]

- Institutional or sponsor ads produce UBI if they are presented in a commercial fashion with a business logo, product description, or other sales information. Only when sponsors are listed without typical advertising copy can the money given for the listing be considered a donation. Different sizes for different amounts of money may not cause the ad to be classified as commercial.[65]

- Advertising revenues received by a police troopers' labor union from sale of business listings and ads in its annual publication were found to be unrelated business income.[66] The firm hired to sell the ads and produce the

---

[61] Priv. Ltr. Rul. 8823109.

[62] See additional discussion at §21.10(d).

[63] *American College of Physicians v. U. S.*, 457 U.S. 836 (1986); ads complementing the text concerning developments in manufacturing technology were held to similarly produce unrelated income in Priv. Ltr. Rul. 9724006.

[64] Reg. §1.513-1(d)(4)(iv), Example 5.

[65] *Fraternal Order of Police, Illinois State Troopers Lodge No. 41 v. Commissioner*, 833 F.2d 717 (7th Cir. 1987), *aff'g* 87 T.C. 747 (1986); Priv. Ltr. Rul. 8640007.

[66] *State Police Ass'n of Massachusetts v. Commissioner*, T.C.M. 1996-407 (Sept. 1996), *cert. denied*, 123 F.3d 1 (1st Cir. 1997).

Constabulary was acting on the union's behalf and under its control in an agency relationship[67] similar to that found in the NCAA case.

- Despite classification of ad revenues as UBI, the formula for calculating the taxable UBI sometimes yields surprising results that permit some ad sale programs to escape tax. This exploitation formula is discussed in Chapter 27§14.

(e) Sponsorships

Corporate sponsorships of a wide variety of events—golf tournaments, fun runs, football bowl games, public television, art exhibitions, and so on—are a favorite form of corporate support for exempt organizations. The appeal of wide public exposure for sponsoring worthy causes and cultural programs has gained extensive popularity. The *Wall Street Journal* ran a series of articles during 1991 discussing the extent of such support and reasons why it made good business sense.

The Cotton Bowl Association's payments from Mobil Oil Company were, in 1991 after a lengthy controversy, treated as UBI.[68] The IRS found substantial benefit in the form of advertising was given to Mobil. After an outcry from the exempt community, and in the face of proposed legislation to exempt such payment, the IRS issued proposed regulations concerning the character of sponsorship payments in 1993.[69] The proposals were said to reflect an IRS policy decision not to be responsible for hampering an exempt organization's need to raise private support. The regulation intended to distinguish between commercial advertising and benevolent payments.

In 1997, the 1993 proposed regulations were codified to delineate between those sponsorship payments that constitute a donation from those that represent payment for an advertisement taxable as UBI. The new tax code provision reduced the uncertainty of reliance upon a proposed regulation, but significantly narrowed the definition of an acceptable acknowledgment. The code says the term *unrelated trade or business* does not include the activity of soliciting and receiving qualified sponsorship payments and defines that term as follows:[70]

> The term *qualified sponsorship payment* means any payment made by any person engaged in a trade or business with respect to which there is no arrangement or expectation that such person will receive any substantial return benefit other than the use or acknowledgement of the name or logo (or product lines) or such person's trade or business in connection with the activities of the organization that receives such payment. Such a use or acknowledgement does not include advertising such person's products or services (including messages containing qualitative or comparative language, price information, or other indications of savings or value, an endorsement, or an inducement to purchase, sell, or use such products or services).

[67] Discussed in §21.8(h).
[68] Priv. Ltr. Rul. 9147007.
[69] Prop. Reg. §1.513-4, entitled *Certain Sponsorship Not Unrelated Trade or Business.*
[70] IRC §513(i)(2)(A) added by the Taxpayer Relief Act of 1997.

Note the code only specifically allows the use or acknowledgement of the sponsor's name and logo. Anyone watching public TV or radio sees and hears not only the sponsor's name and logo, but their address, phone number, and often extensive "value-neutral descriptions" of their business as permitted under the proposed regulations. A typical sponsor announcement says "Black, Brown & White is a 90-year old plaintiff's law firm with offices around the world serving a broad base of international business clients." The proposed regulations broaden the definition and allow listing addresses and product descriptions in addition to the name and logo.

Unfortunately neither the new code nor the committee reports explain the meaning of *substantial return benefit*. The House Committee Report stipulates services, benefits, facilities or other privileges provided to a sponsor in connection with an event have no bearing on the determination of whether the payment is a qualified sponsorship payment. The report essentially says the substantial rules apply to evaluate the value of privileges as a separate transaction. In other words, if a $50,000 sponsor is provided $1,000 worth of football tickets by a university, the donation is $49,000. See Priv. Ltr. Rul. 9805001 for examples of privileges not required to be valued.

Two types of sponsorship payments are subject to the unrelated business income tax rules:

- A contingent payment, or any payment that is "contingent upon the level of attendance at one or more events, broadcast ratings, or other factors indicating the degree of public exposure to one or more events."

- Periodical and trade show payments that "entitle the payor to the use or acknowledgement of the name or logo (or product line) of the payor's trade or business in regularly scheduled and printed materials published by or on behalf of the payee organization that is not related to and primarily distributed in connection with a specific event conducted by the payee organization . . . or any payment made in connection with any qualified convention or trade show activity."

The House Committee Report says a payment based on a contingency that the event actually take place does not create unrelated income. The report also permits, similar to the proposed regulations, the display, sale, and free distribution of the sponsor's products at a sponsored event. Again the code contains important new language the meaning of which is uncertain until guidance is issued.

The proposed regulations delineate sponsorship revenue as either an advertisement that is selling or promoting a product or an acknowledgment to express thanks to a supporter. Specifically with respect to sponsorship of the activities of an exempt organization, the regulation says:

[a]dvertising means any message or other programming material which is broadcast or otherwise transmitted, published, displayed or distributed in exchange for any remuneration, and which promotes or markets any company, services, facility or product. Advertising includes any activity that promotes or markets any company, services, facility or product. Advertising does not include an acknowledgment.

Acknowledgments are mere recognition of sponsorship payments. Acknowledgments may include the following, provided that the effect is identification of the sponsor rather than promotion of the sponsor's products, services or facilities; sponsor logos and slogans that do not contain comparative or qualitative descriptions of the sponsor's products, services, facilities or company; sponsor locations and telephone numbers; value-neutral descriptions, including displays or visual depictions of a sponsor's product line or services; and sponsor brand or trade names and product or service listings. Logos or slogans that are an established part of a sponsor's identity are not considered to contain comparative or qualitative descriptions.

Messages or other programming material that include the following constitute advertising: qualitative or comparative language; price information or other indications of savings or value associated with a product or service; a call to action; an endorsement; or an inducement to buy, sell, rent or lease the sponsor's product or service. Distribution of a sponsor's product by the sponsor or the exempt organization to the general public at the sponsored event, whether for free or for remuneration, is not considered an inducement to buy, sell, rent or lease the sponsor's product or service for purposes of this regulation. If any activities, messages or programming material constitute advertising with respect to a sponsorship payment, then all related activities, messages or programming material that might otherwise be acknowledgments are considered advertising.

The proposals were much more lenient than expected by the exempt community and are very helpful in providing specific guidelines. Happily for many organizations, making facilities, services, or other privileges available to sponsors—front row seats, dinner with the golf pro, or a reception with major donors—is permitted and "does not affect the determination of whether a sponsorship payment is advertising income." It is promotion of the sponsor's product by reflecting prices, comparisons, and other praises of the sort found in commercial advertisements that will cause the transaction to result in UBI.

The proposals contain eight examples that can be studied for additional guidance for organizations anticipating solicitation of sponsorships. Very importantly, the examples indicate that sponsorship payments in excess of the fair market value of the "advertising" can be excluded from UBI when the excess can be clearly demonstrated. Also significantly, amounts treated as advertising are still eligible to be excluded under other UBI rules, such as for ads sold by volunteers or an activity irregularly carried on.

The proposals add expense allocation examples for calculating the tax on such revenues. The first example allocates expenses of a college bowl game among the related and unrelated revenues from the game when the sponsorship is treated as an acknowledgment rather than advertising. The bowl game example is expanded by adding unrelated leasing of the college's stadium during the year.[71]

---

[71] Id., Example 3.

Allocation formulas for photographic museum advertising revenue for promoting a sponsor's photographic products are also given.[72]

(f) Insurance

Group insurance programs have been a subject of active litigation among trade unions, business leagues, and the IRS, with the IRS prevailing in classifying revenues produced in an internally managed insurance program for members as UBI.[73] Instead of conducting the insurance program directly, creative nonprofits have instead licensed their membership lists to insurance providers in return for what they hope will be nontaxable royalty income. Similar to the factors considered in affinity card rulings and other mailing list licensing cases, the issue is to what extent the organization renders personal services in connection with the arrangement. It is also important to note in this context that organizations that provide commercial-type insurance cannot qualify for tax-exempt status under 501(m).

The criteria used to evaluate group insurance programs were outlined in a private ruling requested by a business league serving the public health community.[74] The facts leading the IRS to conclude that valuable services were provided, causing the payments to be classified as taxable UBI rather than royalties excluded by §512(b)(2), were as follows:

- The insurance company acted as the league's agent in choosing suitable policies for its members, marketing the program to members, and performing administrative services such as creation of presentation brochures, seeking enrollments, and handling the premium collections.

- The league agreed to endorse the program and allow the insurance agent to use its logo, name, and membership list to promote the program to its members.

- The league retained the right to approve the form and content of mailings to its members, endorse the plan, and advise its members of its availability, and include plan information in new member packets.

- The league's involvement was direct and extensive and represented the rendering of valuable personal services, so that the so-called licensing payments did not qualify as royalty income.

Careful structuring of the contractual arrangements for such plans can allow the revenues to be bifurcated resulting in some unrelated taxable income and some nontaxable royalty. Such an agreement would separate the requirements and compensation regarding services to be rendered. Terms for payments due for use of the organization's name can be clearly identified as royalty payments made strictly for use of intangible property, without regard to the service requirements.

---

[72] Id., Example 4.
[73] *Louisiana Credit Union League v. United States*, 693 F.2d 525 (5th Cir. 1982); *Texas Farm Bureau v. United States*, 93-1 U.S.T.C. ¶ 50, 257 (C.D. Tex. 1993), *rev'd*, 95-1 U.S.T.C. ¶ 50,297 (5th Cir. June 1, 1995).
[74] Priv. Ltr. Rul. 9316045.

At best, two separate agreements could be reached to prove that the obligation to pay royalties is dissociated from services required to be performed.

(g) Real Estate

Real estate development projects can be characterized as related (low-income or elderly housing), as a trade or business (subdivision, debt-financed rental, hotel), as an investment (unindebted rental), or sometimes as a combination of all three. Any nonprofit anticipating such a program should study Private Letter Ruling 8950072, in which the IRS outlines the UBI consequences of four different methods of developing an unindebted piece of raw land owned by an exempt organization. Leasing or selling raw land unquestionably produced no UBI because of the passive income modifications. Completion of the preliminary development work of obtaining permits and approval prior to the property's sale did not convert the sale into a business transaction. But total development of the property prior to the sale converts the property into a business asset and produces UBI.

Development of an apartment building and parking garage as a part of an urban renewal effort is a related business for an organization whose purpose is to combat community deterioration. The organization operated to assist the city by encouraging revitalization of its downtown area. While the activity would result in UBI if conducted for investment, in this case the activity served the organization's exempt purposes.[75]

A Catholic religious order received IRS sanction for a UBI exclusion of gain earned in a one-time liquidation of vacant land that had been used as part of its exempt facility. The order proposed to convert the land into 75+ residential lots. The order obtained the permits, subdivided the land, and made the minimum physical improvements necessary to sell the lots, but an independent broker was to market and sell the lots. As explained in §21.10(b), the issue was whether the order was selling property "held for sale to customers in the ordinary course of a trade or business." The fact that the order took the steps necessary to prepare the land for sale and maintained control over the development process did not constitute active business activity.[76]

(h) Agency Theory

An agency theory may be applied to look through certain arrangements. To avoid UBI classification for potentially unrelated activities previously listed, an organization might engage an independent party to conduct the activity in return for a royalty or a rental payment. Inherently passive activities for which compensation is paid in the form of rent or royalty are not subject to UBIT, even if the activity is deemed unrelated. The question is, however, whether the IRS can look through the transactions and attribute the activity of the independent party back to the organization, as it did in the following example.

The National Collegiate Athletic Association (NCAA) hired an unrelated commercial publishing company to produce its tournament programs. NCAA

---

[75] Priv. Ltr. Rul. 9208033; see also Priv. Ltr. Ruls. 9337027, 9616039, and 9619069.
[76] Priv. Ltr. Rul. 9337027.

gave the publisher a free hand in soliciting the advertisements, designing the copy, and distributing the programs, in return for a percentage of the advertising and direct sales revenues. Because it had little or no involvement in the activity, the NCAA treated the income as a passive and irregularly carried on activity not subject to the unrelated business income tax. There was no argument that selling the program itself produces related income; nor was there any question that the advertising income is unrelated. The tournament lasts only three weeks.

The issue considered by the Tax Court[77] was whether the NCAA had sufficiently disengaged itself under the contract. Did it sell the right to use its name or did it engage in the ad activity itself? The Tax Court adopted an agency theory and held that because the publisher acted as the NCAA's agent, the activity was totally attributable to the NCAA. The Tenth Circuit Court agreed with the Tax Court but reversed the decision (because the activity was irregularly carried on and not in competition with business); the agency theory was not disputed. The IRS disagrees with the appellate decision regarding irregularity.[78]

Another athletic tournament-sponsoring organization also failed the agency test. The independently hired promoter's efforts during a 15-month ad campaign were attributed to the organization.[79] The agency theory was escaped, however, by an organization that turned over the publication of its monthly journal to a commercial company, retaining one-third of the net revenues from subscriptions and reprints. All advertising income, two-thirds of the circulation revenues, and all the risk of publication expenses were borne by the company. The IRS decided, under the circumstances, that the company was acting on its own behalf, not as agent for the charity. No advertising revenue was allocated to the charity.[80]

Earnings of an ostensibly independent for-profit subsidiary may also be allocated back to the nonprofit parent using the agency theory. The subsidiary's business is treated as separate only if it is managed at arm's length without the parent taking part in daily operations. The factors necessary to prove that the subsidiary's operation is separate are discussed in detail in Chapter 22§4.

21.9 THE EXCEPTIONS

Despite their literal inclusion in the "unrelated" prong of the UBI rules, certain types of revenue-raising activities are not subject to UBIT, presumably because they are not businesslike and do not compete with commercial businesses.[81] Charitable §501(c)(3) organizations qualify for all of the following exceptions. Certain exceptions do not apply to non-501(c)(3) organizations, as noted under the particular exception.

---

[77] *National Collegiate Athletic Association v. Commissioner,* 90-2 U.S.T.C. §50513 (10th Cir. 1990), *rev'g* 92 T.C. No. 27 (1989). See also Priv. Ltr. Rul. 9137002 and 9211004.

[78] Priv. Ltr. Rul. 9306030; see also Priv. Ltr. Ruls. 9721001 and 9712001.

[79] Tech. Adv. Memo. 8932004; Priv. Ltr. Rul. 9150047.

[80] Tech. Adv. Memo. 9023003; similar result in Priv. Ltr. Rul. 9137002 and 7926003; contrary result in Priv. Ltr. Ruls. 9309002 and 9306030.

[81] IRC §513(a).

(a) Volunteers

Any business in which substantially all the work is performed without compensation is excluded from UBI. *Substantially* for this purpose means at least 80 to 85% of the total work performed, measured normally by the total hours worked. A paid manager or executive, administrative personnel, and all sorts of support staff can operate the business if most of the work is performed by volunteers. This rule is the reason the countless boxes of candy, coupon books, and other items sold by school children to raise funds for parent-teacher organizations do not result in unrelated business income to the school or PTA.[82]

In most cases the number of hours worked, rather than relative value of the work, is used to measure the percent test. This means that the value of volunteer time need not necessarily be quantified for comparison to monetary compensation paid. In the case of a group of volunteer singing doctors, the value of the doctors' time was considered. Because the doctors were the stars of the records producing the income, their time was counted by the court at a premium, which offset administrative personnel whose time was compensated modestly.[83] Having 77% of its labor donated by volunteers, however, was not enough to allow a bingo operation to avail itself of this exception. The 23% compensated workforce ratio was substantial enough to cause an Elks Lodge to pay tax on its bingo profits.[84]

Expense reimbursements, in-kind benefits, and prizes are treated as compensation if they are compensatory in nature. Particularly when the expenses enable the volunteers to work longer hours and serve the convenience of the organization, the payments need not be counted in measuring this exception. However, solicitors for a religious organization that traveled in vans and lived a "very Spartan life" were not unpaid volunteers, as the organization had claimed, because their livelihood was provided by the organization.[85] Similarly when food, lodging, and other living expenses were furnished to sustain members of a religious group, the members working for the group's businesses were not treated as volunteers.[86]

The court in the Shiloh case found it to be a communal organization that provided for its members' needs. The fact that Shiloh's doctrine expressed a belief that "God commanded them to work," and that members were required, not only to display a willingness to work, but to in fact work convinced the court that the workers were not volunteers. It was also noted that Shiloh's support came primarily from payments for services its work teams performed for a variety of service-oriented businesses.

The result for members of a religious order was different.[87] Under a *but-for* test it was decided that food, shelter, clothing, and medical care received by brothers in a religious order were paid without regard to whether they worked. The members of the order were under a vow of poverty and were provided necessities

---

[82] Priv. Ltr. Rul. 9704012.

[83] *Greene County Medical Society Foundation v. U.S.*, 345 F. Supp. 900 (W.D. Mo. 1972).

[84] *Waco Lodge No. 166, Benevolent & Protective Order of Elks v. Commissioner*, T.C. Memo 1981-546, *aff'd per curiam*, 696 F.2d 372 (5th Cir. 1983).

[85] Priv. Ltr. Rul. 9652004.

[86] *Shiloh Youth Revival Centers v. Commissioner*, 88 T.C. 579 (1987).

[87] *St. Joseph Farms of Indiana Brothers of the Congregation of Holy Cross, Southwest Province, Inc. v. Commissioner*, 85 T.C. 9 (July, 1, 1985).

by the order without regard to their particular assignment. The court deemed the benefits provided were not compensatory. There was not a connection between the services and benefits because it was not the case that "but for rendering of services, the payments would not have been made." It was also noted that only 14 out of St. Joseph's 167 members worked on the farm and that the court had no doubt that, if the farm ceased to operate, the farm-working brothers would continue to receive their livelihood. The farm revenue was therefore excluded from UBI.

(b) Donated Goods

The selling of merchandise, substantially all of which is received by the organization as gifts or contributions, is not treated as a taxable activity. Thrift and resale shops selling donated goods are afforded a special exception from UBI for donated goods they sell. A shop selling goods on consignment as well as donated goods must distinguish between the two types of goods. Under the fragmentation rules,[88] the consigned goods sales would be separated, or fragmented, from the donated goods and any net profit from those sales included in UBI. Note consignment sales by volunteer-run resale shops would be excluded under the volunteer exception.

(c) Convenience

For §501(c)(3) organizations only, a cafeteria, bookstore, residence, or similar facility used in the organization's programs and operated for the convenience of patients, visitors, employees, or students is specifically excepted from UBI.[89] Recovery of patients is hastened when family and friends visit or stay with them in the hospital, and the cafeteria facilitates the visits. Museum visitors can spend more time viewing art if they can stop to rest their feet and have a cup of coffee.

When the cafe, shop, dorm, or parking lot is also open to the general public, the revenue produced by public use is unrelated income. It is thought by some that the whole facility becomes subject to UBIT if the facility's entrance is on a public street. At best, the income from a facility used by both qualified visitors and the disinterested public off the street is fragmented. The taxable and nontaxable revenues are identified and tabulated and the net taxable portion is calculated under the dual use rules discussed in Chapter 27§14.

Parking lots for the exclusive use of participants in an exempt organization's activities can also be excluded from UBI under the convenience exception. A lot open to both visitors and nonvisitors is fragmented into its visitor convenience and nonvisitor parts. If the lot is operated by an independent party under a lease arrangement in which the exempt organization performs no services, the nonvisitor revenue can be classified as rental income excludable from UBI by the passive income modifications. If the organization itself operates the lot, the revenue from general public usage is a trade or business.[90]

The *IRS Examination Guidelines for Colleges and Universities*[91] contains useful criteria for applying the convenience exception for UBI purposes. Most importantly, the

---

[88] Discussed in §21.4(c).
[89] IRC §513(a)(2).
[90] Gen. Coun. Memo. 39825.
[91] Final version contained in IRS Announcement 94-112.

IRS admits that the facts and circumstances of each situation are determinative. The items sold to students, officers, and employees in the school book stores are essentially individually judged. First, the relatedness of an item is evaluated. Books and materials required and recommended for classes, supplies such as notebooks, pencils, and computers (one a year), and athletic gear necessary to participate in physical education programs are listed as items that advance the educational institution's exempt purposes. Materials that "further the intellectual life of the campus community," such as books, tapes, records, and compact discs, are also deemed related.

Items considered as unrelated to academic pursuits are those that might be merely conveniences to the students. The unstated presumption is that students or staff can spend more time studying (they need not travel to the mall) if they have toiletries, novelty items bearing the institution's insignia, candy, cigarettes, magazines, greeting cards, film, cameras, and small appliances easily available to them. Sales to alumni, parents, and other outsiders are unrelated and not excludable under the convenience exception.

(d) Bingo Games

Bingo games not conducted in violation of any state or local law are excluded from UBI. IRC §513(f) defines bingo as any game of bingo of a type in which usually (1) wagers are placed, (2) winners are determined, and (3) distribution of prizes or other property is made, in the presence of all persons placing wagers in such game. The regulations expand the definition as follows:

> A bingo game is a game of chance played with cards that are generally printed with five rows of five squares each. Participants place markers over randomly called numbers on the cards in an attempt to form a pre-selected pattern such as a horizontal, vertical, or diagonal line, or all four corners. The first participant to form the pre-selected pattern wins the game. Any other game of chance including but not limited to, keno, dice, cards, and lotteries, is not bingo (and will create UBI).[92]

Pull-tabs and other forms of instant bingo are not bingo in the IRS's opinion, and produce UBI despite the fact that such variations of the bingo game are so classified by the state bingo authority. During 1990, the IRS aggressively examined nonprofits in the Southwest District and assessed tax on any bingo variations not strictly meeting the code and regulation definitions.[93] Publication 3079, entitled "Gaming Publication for Tax-Exempt Organizations," was issued in April, 1998 to explain these rules comprehensively.

(e) Entertainment, Conventions, and Trade Shows

Public entertainment is defined as that traditionally conducted at fairs or expositions promoting agricultural and educational purposes (including but not limited

---

[92] Reg. §1.513-5.

[93] *Julius M. Isreal Lodge of B'nai B'rith No.2113 v. Commissioner,* 78AFTR 2d ¶96-5482 (5th Cir.), *aff'g.* TCM 1995-439; see also *Women of the Motion Picture Industry, et.al. v. Commissioner,* T.C. Memo. 1997-518.

to animals or products and equipment) and does not produce UBI for §501(c)(3), (4), or (5) organizations. Internal Revenue Code §513(d)(2) requires that the event be held in conjunction with an international, national, state, regional, or local fair, or be in accordance with provisions of state law that permit such a fair.

A *convention or trade show* is intended to attract persons in an industry generally (without regard to membership in the sponsoring organization), as well as members of the public, to the show for the purpose of displaying industry products, or stimulating interest in and demand for industry products or services, or educating persons engaged in the industry in the development of new products and services or new rules and regulations affecting the industry. A "qualified" show is one conducted by §501(c)(3), (4), (5), or (6) organizations in conjunction with an international, national, state, regional, or local convention, annual meeting, or show. Exhibitors are permitted to sell products or services and the organization can charge for the display space.

Priv. Ltr. Rul. 9835001 should be studied by groups owning exhibition facilities. The IRS found a tax-exempt agricultural fair organization received both taxable and nontaxable rental income from leasing its facilities during its offseason ($10\frac{1}{2}$ months of year). Free admission for its shareholders (essentially members) was found not to result in private inurement because such admissions only constituted 3% of the tickets given away.

(f) Indian Tribes

Income earned by a federally recognized Indian tribe from the conduct of an unincorporated business or a corporation incorporated under the Indian Reorganization Act of 1934 (IRA) is not subject to federal income tax.[94] A corporation formed instead under the laws of the state in which the tribe is located, however, would be subject to tax even though it is owned and controlled by an Indian tribe or members of a tribe. The basis of this distinction lies in the definition of an Indian tribe. Section 1 of the Internal Revenue Code subjects individuals, trusts, and estates to tax; Section 11 taxes corporations. A tribe is not such a taxable entity; a separately incorporated business would be.[95]

In 1981 the IRS ruled that a properly established Indian tribal corporation (under the IRA) had the same tax status as an Indian tribe as it regarded activities carried on within the boundaries of the reservation.[96] This restriction to on-reservation activity was reconsidered and removed in the 1994 ruling. The ruling says that because an Indian tribe is not a taxable entity, any income earned by it—on or off the reservation—is not taxable. The ruling states that it applies only to federal income taxes. It does not affect the application of other federal taxes, such as employment and excise taxes (including excise taxes on wagering), to Indian tribes or tribal corporations. A draft of an IRS "Guide to Indian Taxation Issues" was reviewed with tribal representatives on March 3, 1994, but not formally issued. The IRS issued temporary (and has yet to finalize) procedural and adminis-

---

[94] Rev. Rul. 94-16, 1994-1 C.B. 19.
[95] Rev. Rul. 67-284, 1967-2 C.B. 55, 58.
[96] Rev. Rul. 81-295, 1981-2 C.B. 15, relying on *Mescalcro Apache Tribe v. Jones*, 411 U.S. 145,157 (1973).

trative tax regulations under the Indian Tribal Governmental Tax Status Act of 1982 that can be studied in this regard. Regulation §305.7701-1 defines an Indian tribal government and Reg. §305.7871-1 considers Indian tribal governments treated as States for certain purposes.

(g) Low-Cost Articles

For §501(c)(3) and veterans groups, gift premiums distributed with no obligation to purchase in connection with the solicitations of contributions are not treated as a sale of the gift premium. The gift must be part of a fund-raising campaign and must cost (not fair market value) the organization no more than $7.20 (during 1999; indexed annually for inflation). The recipient of the premium must not request or consent to receive the premium. Literature requesting a donation must accompany the premium along with a statement that the recipient may keep the low-cost article regardless of whether a charitable donation is made. If the donation is less than $36 (during 1999; indexed annually), the fair market value of the premium reduces the deductible portion of the donor's gift.[97]

A program for distribution of low-cost articles cannot qualify for this exception if it presents unfair competition to nonexempt businesses and is conducted like a commercial enterprise.[98] A religious group's "donation solicitations" in return for caps, T-shirts, and similar items at public sporting and entertainment events was found to be conducted in a profit-seeking fashion in competition with for-profit vendors.[99] For this reason as well as its failure to prove it distributed the items with no obligation to purchase, the revenues were treated as unrelated business income.

(h) Mailing Lists

Again for the organizations eligible to receive charitable donations under §170—primarily §501(c)(3) and veteran organizations—a business involving the exchange or renting of mailing lists between such organizations only is excluded from UBI classification. This special treatment was added by Congress in 1986 based upon IRS recommendation.[100] Sale or exchange of mailing lists by such organizations to others and sales by all other types of §501(c) organizations ostensibly by omission create UBI. Courts have found, much to the consternation of the IRS, that §513(h) does not overrule the passive royalty income exception that modifies revenues from licensing of mailing lists for all types of tax-exempt organizations.[101]

A program allowing credit card holders to direct the bank's affinity card program to pay rebates to named charities is a charitable giving program. When the cardholder voluntarily designated a specific charity, the bank was acting as an

---

[97] Rev. Proc. 90-12 (Feb. 1990), supplemented by Rev. Proc. 92-58, 1992-2 IRB 10; and updated annually for COLA, latest revision 98-61, 1998-52 IRB 1. See Chapter 24§3 for more information about the de minimus rules.

[98] *Hope School v. Commissioner,* 612 F. 2d 298 (CA-7, 1980).

[99] Priv. Ltr. Rul. 9652004.

[100] IRC §513(h).

[101] See §21.10(d).

agent so that its transfer of the funds to the charity on behalf of the cardholder qualified as a charitable contribution.[102] The furnishing of the charity's mailing list to the card company did not constitute rental of the list because the revenue stemmed from cardholders' voluntary action.

21.10 INCOME MODIFICATIONS

For §501(c) organizations other than social clubs, voluntary employee benefit associations, supplemental unemployment plans, and veterans groups, specified types of investment income are modified, or excluded, from UBI unless the underlying property is subject to debt. IRC §512(b) excludes "all dividends, interest, royalties, rents, payments with respect to security loans, and annuities, and all deductions connected with such income." Passive income of a sort not specifically listed is not necessarily modified or excluded from UBI.

(a) Dividends and Interest

Dividends and interest paid on amounts invested in savings accounts, certificates of deposit, money market accounts, bonds, loans, preferred or common stocks, and payments in respect to security loans and annuities, net of any allocable deductions are excluded from UBI.

In 1978, the general exclusion of interest and dividends was expanded to include the words "payments in respect of security loans." For some time there was uncertainty regarding techniques such as "strips," interest rate swaps, and currency hedges. It is now recognized that such investments are *ordinary and routine* and income earned from such transactions in security portfolios is considered as investment income for §512 purposes.[103]

When securities producing dividends and interest are acquired with indebtedness, the income is swept back into UBI by IRC §514. An organization must be careful to use new money to acquire each element of investment in its portfolio. A pension fund owning five-year certificates of deposit (CDs) in 1979 (after interest rates had risen over 5 points) realized UBI when it purchased new CDs using its old CDs as collateral. Although the fund escaped an early withdrawal penalty and received a higher rate of interest, the new CD was a debt-financed asset purchase. Thus, the fund's original CD produced "modified" or nontaxable income, and the new higher-rate CD acquired with the loan proceeds was held to be taxable as unrelated debt-financed income.[104] The CD switch, incidentally, was not a permissible "payment in respect of a security loan." Such a loan allows a broker to use an organization's securities in return for a fee, not as a loan against which the securities are used as collateral.

The Omnibus Budget Reduction Act of 1993 amended §512 to provide that gain and loss received from unexercised options on investment assets such as se-

---

[102] Priv. Ltr. Rul. 9623035.
[103] Prop. Reg. §§1.509(a)-3, 1.512(b)-1 and 53.4940-1.
[104] *Kern County Electrical Pension Fund v. Commissioner,* 96 T.C. No. 41 (June 20, 1991).

curities and real estate, as well as loan commitment fee forfeitures, are excluded from the UBI.

(b) Capital Gains

Gains from sale, exchange, or other disposition of property is classified as UBI dependent upon the character of the property sold. Generally the normal income tax rules of IRC §§1221 and 1231 for identifying capital, versus ordinary income, property apply to identify property covered by this exception. Sales of stock in trade or other inventory-type property, or of property held for sale to customers in the ordinary course of trade or business, produce UBI.

Options/Shorts. Gains on lapse or termination of covered and uncovered options, if written as a part of investment activity, are not taxable.[105] Short-term capital gain from a short sale of publicly traded stock through a broker was ruled not to create UBI. Although a short sale technically creates an obligation for the purchaser to pay for any loss that may occur on covering the short position, this possible loss is not treated as acquisition indebtedness.[106]

Timber. Timber standing on real estate owned by the exempt organization can be treated as a capital asset if the organization retains an economic interest in the timber.[107] The somewhat complicated rules must be studied for organizations owning such property to ensure proper tax treatment. Percentage depletion may apply, and specific rules for allocating the cost basis of the underlying property between the real estate and the timber are provided.[108]

Social Club Issues. A gain from the sale of real estate used by a social club in regular club activities (its exempt function) is not classed as UBI to the extent the proceeds are reinvested one year before or three years after the date of the sale.[109] Because social clubs often own valuable and desirable real estate, particularly country clubs and old-line city clubs, this exception can be valuable. When the property is considered as nonexempt function, the club must treat the revenue as nonmember revenue and also face the possibility of failing a so-called 35/15 test necessary to maintain ongoing exemption.

---

[105] IRC §512(b)(5).
[106] Rev. Rul. 95-8, 1995-14 I.R.B. 1; see §21.12.
[107] IRC §613(b).
[108] Reg. §1.613-2; Priv. Ltr. Rul. 9252028 discusses a private foundation's sale of timber and concludes that the timber sale produces capital gain income not subject to the UBIT and further that the arrangement did not represent a "business enterprise" subject to the excess business holdings rules. See Chapter 16§1. See also Priv. Ltr. Rul. 9608002, in which a fishing club's sale of timber was classified as the sale of exempt function property not taxable, except for failure on the club's part to reinvest the sales proceeds in another exempt activity within the four-year period.
[109] IRC §512(a)(3)(D). Priv. Ltr. Rul. 9307004 says it is insufficient that the club bought the land with the intention of using it for club activities. Actual use is required.

Harvesting pine timber to preserve the usefulness of a club's property as a wildlife habitat was found to further advance the club's exempt purposes. The club, created in 1870, owned a five-square-mile fish and game preserve and historic clubhouse building adjacent to public land areas maintained in a natural state. The club, beginning in 1983, engaged professional foresters to plan timber harvesting to improve the habitat for wild game and to control gypsy moths. Sale of the timber pursuant to the plans did not create unrelated business income.[110]

A Florida club sold a portion of its property to participate in a land price boom and distributed the proceeds to the members. The court said the sale was a "violent departure" from the club's normal behavior and not merely incidental to the regular functions of the club. Because financial gain was the aim, the court revoked the club's exemption.[111]

Property contiguous to a club and held for possible future expansion, or simply protecting the club from the suburbs, is not exempt function property. Only property in actual, direct, continuous, and regular use for social and recreational purposes qualifies. Accordingly, a golf club was taxed on gain from selling off road frontage. The land was originally acquired with the expectation that it would be used for club facilities, but in actuality was not.[112]

Use of vacant land containing no physical improvements but was used for jogging, picnics, kite-flying contests, and other outdoor activities was found to constitute direct use by club members. The court said, "It is certainly conceivable that joggers derive as much pleasure and recreation from that pastime as golfers do from their rounds on the links."[113] A "buffer tract," containing a steep incline and heavily wooded with thick undergrowth, however, was found not to be used directly in exempt functions. Even though it isolated the club from the surrounding developed area and roads, its physical condition indicated it was not devoted to exempt activity. Proceeds from granting a permanent easement for passage and use produced UBI.[114]

(c) Rentals

Rental income is considered a passive type of investment income that is not modified (excluded) from UBI, except:

- Personal property rentals are taxable unless they are rented incidentally (not more than 10% of rent) with real property.

- A fluctuating rental agreement that calculates the rent based on net profits from the property is unrelated income; rent based on gross revenue is not UBI.

---

[110] Priv. Ltr. Rul. 9535051.

[111] *Juniper Hunting Club v. Commissioner*, 28 B.T.A. 525 (1933).

[112] *Framingham Country Club v. United States*, 659 F. Supp. 650 (D.C. Mass. 1987); IRS Priv. Ltr. Rul. 9307003.

[113] *Atlanta Athletic Club v. Commissioner*, 93-1 U.S.T.C. ¶ 50,051 (10th Cir.), *rev'g* T.C.M. 1991-83, 61 T.C.M. 2011, Dec. 47,195(M).

[114] Tech. Adv. Memo. 9225001. See also Priv. Ltr. Rul. 9630001, in which adjacent land was also found not to qualify as exempt function property.

When substantial services are rendered, such as the rental of a theater complete with staff or rental of a hotel room complete with room service, the rental is not considered passive.[115]

Sharecrop arrangements for farm land owned by an organization may or may not be treated as excludable from UBI under the rent exception. The method for calculating the rent and risk borne by the organization is determinative. The issue is whether the exempt is a joint venturer participating in the farming operations. The following factors were considered in two court cases on the subject.[116]

- Organization is not involved in the day-to-day operation of the farm; it simply provides the land and buildings.

- Organization bears no risk of loss from accidents.

- Organization is not required to contribute to any losses from the operation, but only pays an agreed portion of the operating expenses (in one case 50%).

- The rent is equal to a fixed percentage of the gross sale of the crop or a fixed amount, not a percentage of net profits.[117]

Parking lot rental presents a similar situation. Rental of the bare real estate to another party that operates the lot (where the organization has no relationship or responsibility whatsoever to the parkers) clearly produces passive rental income.[118] If the exempt provides some services to the operator, UBI taint may occur. The regulations speak of "services rendered . . . primarily for the convenience and other than those usually or customarily rendered in connection with the rental of rooms or other space for occupancy only." Providing maid service, but not trash hauling, in renting a room is the example provided.[119] Operation of a parking lot for the benefit of employees and persons participating in an exempt organization's functions, rather than disinterested persons, should be a related activity.[120] A parking rate structure "not consistent with commercially operated for-profit facilities in the same metropolitan area" was found to reflect an organization's desire to provide a necessary service to the public.

Substantial services were provided to corporate and business patrons who rented an educational organization's facilities for receptions in the evenings. The services provided included maintenance and security personnel and liquor service (because the organization held the license). The IRS was not convinced that the

---

[115] While agreeing there was some educational benefit from the site, a museum renting its exhibition halls for private receptions provided substantial services to its tenants that caused the usage fees to be unrelated income in Priv. Ltr. Rul. 9702003.

[116] *Trust U/W Emily Oblinger v. Commissioner,* 100 T.C. No. 9 (Feb. 23, 1993); *Harlan E. Moore Charitable Trust v. U.S.,* 812 F. Supp. 130 (C.D. Ill. 1993) *aff'd,* 93-2 USTC ¶ 50,601 (7th Cir.). Similarly see *Independent Order of Odd Fellows v. U.S.,* No. 4-90-CV-60552 (S.D. Iowa 1993); and *White's Iowa Manual Labor Institute v. Commissioner,* T.C. Memo. 1993-364.

[117] IRC §512(b)(3)(A)(ii).

[118] Priv. Ltr. Rul. 9301024.

[119] Reg. §1.512(b)-1(c)(5).

[120] Priv. Ltr. Rul. 9401031; also see the convenience exception discussed supra in §21.9(c).

rentals served an exempt purpose in finding the programs were primarily social or business-oriented and included such items as cocktails, dinner-dances, awards presentations, and holiday celebrations. While there was some educational benefit to the attendees of viewing exhibits, they were ancillary to the events' principal purpose.[121] The IRS noted the holding would be different if request was for the organization to create an educational event in its space, with the food and services provided only incidentally.

(d) Royalties

The fact that the term *royalties* is not defined under the code or regulations pertaining to unrelated income has caused significant controversy. The IRS and the courts have very different notions about the application of this exception. The IRS insists a royalty must be received in an activity that is passive to qualify. Most courts have said instead that a royalty paid for the use of intangible property rights is excluded from UBI. The battle has focused on licensing of mailing lists, EO logos, and associated issuance of affinity cards.

The regulations provide that royalties, whether measured by production or by the gross or taxable income from the property, are modified, or excluded from UBI.[122] Income from an oil and gas working interest for which the organization is responsible for its share of development costs is not modified or excluded from UBI.[123]

Initially the IRS insisted that none of the revenue paid in return for licensing the use of an organization's mailing list is treated as a royalty payment.[124] While agreeing that mailing lists are intangible property, the IRS argued the activity exploiting the lists was conducted like an active business. The Tax Court in 1993, however, ruled that it could find no evidence that Congress intended to limit the royalty exception to passively held or investment properties.[125]

The Ninth Circuit Court of Appeals partially agreed with the Tax Court.[126] As to list rentals, the club engaged list managers that marketed the lists and per-

---

[121] Priv. Ltr. Rul. 9702003.

[122] IRC §512(b)(2).

[123] Reg. §1.512(b)-1(b).

[124] Gen. Coun. Memo. 39827; Priv. Ltr. Rul. 9029047.

[125] *Sierra Club, Inc. v. Commissioner*, TCM 47751(M) Dec. 49025 (M) (1993).

In 1994, the Tax Court (*Sierra Club, Inc. v. Commissioner*, 103 T.C. No. 17) again ruled in favor of the Sierra Club. The sole issue in question was whether the club was in the business of selling financial services that could produce unrelated business income. The court found no intention on the part of the club to form a joint venture to share in a "mutual proprietary interest in net profits," nor did it bear any risk or loss or expense. The fact that the club was required to solicit members and keep records of their names and addresses did not, in the court's eyes, indicate that the club had control over the financial institution's actions for such actions to be imputed to the club. The Tax Court decision in this case, referred to as *Sierra II; also see Alumni Ass'n of Univ. of Or. Inc. v. Commissioner*, T.C. Memo 1996-63; *Oregon State Univ. Alumni Ass'n Inc. v. Commissioner*, T.C. Memo 1996-34.

[126] *Sierra Club v. Commissioner*, 96-2 U.S.T.C. ¶ 503r6 (9th Cir. 1996). Another pair of cases are also on appeal to the 9th Circuit, *Alumni Ass'n of Univ. of Oregon v. Commissioner*, T.C. Memo 1996-63 and *Oregon State University Alumni Ass'n Inc. v. Commissioner*, T.C. Memo 1996-34. The IRS decided not to appeal another defeat in the *Mississippi State Alumni v. Commissioner* (T.C. Memo. 1997-37) case.

formed all of the necessary services. The club simply provided the lists and retained the right to review rental requests and approve contents. It found the licensing did not unfairly compete with businesses and that the agreement did not create an agency transaction.[127] When Sierra licensed its lists to a bank for an affinity card program, however, it agreed to promote the program. The case was remanded to the Tax Court to reexamine "extras" the Sierra Club was required to provide in satisfying provisions of its contract with the bank. The question was whether the club receives compensation for services. The IRS may resume its contest of these court decisions; watch for new developments.

To ensure revenues from licensing its mailing list be treated as nontaxable royalty income, an organization must avoid performing the type of services rendered by the Disabled American Veterans (DAV) in regard to its lists. The DAV lost its battle to escape tax deficiencies of over $4 million based on $279 million of revenue.[128] There was no argument that DAV managed the activity in a businesslike manner. Several persons worked full-time to keep the list current (not a volunteer operation), DAV placed conditions on the name usage, required advance approval of the client copy, and had a complicated rate structure that it widely circulated on rate cards. It belonged to the Direct Mail Marketing Association, a trade association composed of organizations using direct mail in their operations.

This issue is of particular interest in the scientific and medical fields, where considerable sums are earned from royalties paid for the use of patented devices and methods. Perhaps because the licensing of intellectual property rights for patents involves complex legal issues and potential for liability, the agreements are very carefully structured. There is usually no question that the EO assigns all responsibility for services performed in developing the patent to the license. Thus the revenue received by the EO is unquestionably passive and eligible to be modified, or excluded from UBI.[129]

What appears from the facts to be the Interscholastic League also failed in its effort to turn advertising revenues into royalties. Under licensing agreements with sporting goods manufacturers and insurance providers, the league was required to perform services and provide free advertising for the commercial concerns.[130] To confuse this issue, IRC §513(h)(1)(B) excludes revenues attributable to the exchange of lists between entities eligible to receive charitable contributions.[131]

(e) Subsidiary Payments

Payments of interest, rents, royalties, or annuities excluded under the general rules are includable in UBI if paid by either a controlled taxable subsidiary or a controlled tax-exempt subsidiary. On August 5, 1997, the percentage of ownership

---

[127] See §21.8(h).
[128] *Disabled American Veterans v. Commissioner, rev'g* 91-2 U.S.T.C. §50.336 (6th Cir. 1991), 94 T.C. 60 (1990).
[129] See the fiscal 1999 CPE Text for Exempt Organizations, Chapter B, entitled *Intellectual Property* by Roderick Darling and Marvin Friedlander,
[130] Tech. Adv. Memo. 9211004.
[131] Discussed in §21.9(h).

constituting control for this purpose was reduced from 80% to 50%.[132] Specifically the code now defines control as follows:

- In the case of a corporation, ownership (by vote or value) of more than 50% of the stock in such corporation

- In the case of a partnership, ownership of more than 50% of the profits, interests, or capital interests of the partnership

- In any other case, ownership of more than 50% of the beneficial interests in the entity

The inclusion portion of amounts received is essentially that amount of the payment that would have been taxable to the controlled organization as UBI had it not paid the interest, rent, or royalty that could be claimed as a deductible expense. For a nonexempt controlled entity, the taxable amount is equal to that portion of such entity's taxable income that would have been UBIT had it been a tax-exempt entity.

There is no specific at this time regarding the meaning of beneficial interests in a nonprofit entity. Under regulations issued before the 1997 amendment to this section, control of a nonstock organization resulted from interlocking directors. If at least 80% (now read as 50) of the directors of one organization are representatives of the second organization or have the right to appoint or control the board of the second, control exists.

The attribution rules of IRC §318 apply for purposes of determining constructive ownership of stock in a corporation. Similar principles shall apply for purposes of determining ownership of interests in any other entity. Before mid-1997, amounts paid by a second-tier subsidiary were nontaxable and not subject to inclusion because this section at that time contained no attribution or indirect ownership requirement that would treat the parent as controlling its subsidiary's subsidiary.[133] Although not a tax issue for the tax-exempt organization itself, a financial issue that arises for an exempt organization owning a subsidiary is the so-called General Utilities doctrine. The transfer of substantially all of the assets of a taxable corporation to a tax-exempt organization (commonly as its parent) is essentially treated as a taxable sale of the transferred assets at their fair market value.[134] The conversion of a taxable entity to a tax-exempt one is similarly treated as a transaction in which gain must be recognized. A transfer of assets the exempt will use to conduct an unrelated business are not taxed at the time of transfer (because they will be taxed when eventually sold).

(f) Research

Research income is not taxable if the research is performed for the United States, its agencies, or a state or political subdivision thereof by any exempt organization.[135] In addition:

---

[132] IRC §512(b)(13) as amended by Taxpayer Relief Act of 1997.
[133] Priv. Ltr. Rul. 9338003.
[134] Reg. §1.337(d)-4; the February issue of *Exempt Organizations Tax Review*, p. 259.
[135] IRC §512(b)(7).

- A college, university, or hospital can exclude all research income from private or governmental contractors.[136]

- An exempt organization performing fundamental research, the results of which are freely available to the general public, can also exclude all research income.[137]

See Chapter 5§3 and 5§4 for discussion of the distinction between scientific research that is treated as related income and testing that is considered a commercial and unrelated enterprise.

(g) Partnerships and S Corporations

A tax-exempt organization's share of income from a partnership, regardless of whether distributed or paid to the organization, flows through to the nonprofit partner and retains its character as rent, interest, business, or other type of income.[138] If the partnership conducts a trade or business that is unrelated to the organization's exempt purpose, the organization's share of the business income, less associated deductions, must be reported as unrelated business taxable income. The exceptions and modifications[139] pertaining to passive income apply to exclude the organization's share of interest or other passive income distributed by the partnership. This rules applies to organizations that are general and limited partners.[140]

Until January 1, 1994, distributions from publicly traded partnerships were fully taxable to the tax-exempt partner, including retirement plans. Since 1994, the partnership's income is fragmented to allow each type of income to flow through to the tax-exempt partner according to the general rule outlined above. Thus, partnership income or loss retains its character as either taxable business income or passive investment income in the hands of the tax-exempt partner.[141] A publicly traded partnership is one for which interests in it are traded on an established securities market or are readily tradable on a secondary market.[142]

Organizations exempt under §501(c)(3) and 401(a) are eligible, effective for tax years beginning after December 31, 1997, to become shareholders of an S corporation.[143] New IRC §512(e), however, says that stock in an S corporation represents an interest in an unrelated trade or business. Accordingly, the code now also provides the following:

> All items of income, loss, or deduction taken into account under IRC §1366(a), and any gain or loss on disposition of the stock in the S corporation, shall be taken into account in computing the unrelated business taxable income of such organizations.

---

[136] IRC §512(b)(8).

[137] IRC §512(b)(9).

[138] IRC §513(c)(1).

[139] Discussed in §21.9 and §21.10.

[140] *Service Bolt Nut Co. Profit Sharing Trust v. Commissioner*, 724 F.2d 519 (6th Cir. 1983), *aff'g* 78 T.C. 812 (1982).

[141] IRC §513(c)(2), revised effective January 1, 1994.

[142] IRC §469(k)(2).

[143] The Small Business Job Protection Act of 1996, §1316.

Unlike a partnership, all of the income distributed to an exempt organization by an S corporation flows through to it as unrelated business income, including passive income otherwise modified from tax.[144] Gain or loss on the sale of S corporate shares is also treated as UBI. Thus where possible, an exempt organization's investment in an entity that will produce a significant amount of passive income should preferably be held in partnership form.

21.11 CALCULATING AND MINIMIZING TAXABLE INCOME

When an otherwise tax-exempt organization has taxable UBI, the tax is calculated under the normal income tax rules. Gross UBI, minus allowable deductions and exemptions, is subject to tax. As long as the percentage of an organization's UBI is modest in relation to its overall revenues,[145] the only problem UBIT presents is the reduction in profit because of the income tax paid. Maximizing deductions to calculate the income is important. The income tax sections of the Internal Revenue Code of 1986 govern and the same concepts apply, including:

- *Form 990-T.* The UBIT is calculated on Form 990-T. Chapter 27§14 has a filled-in form and detailed suggestions for its completion.

- *Tax rates.* The income tax is calculated using the normal tables for all taxpayers, that is, §1(e) for trusts and §11 for corporations. For controlled groups of exempt organizations (also including 80% owned for-profit subsidiaries), the corporate tax bracket must be calculated on a consolidated basis under the rules of §1561. The tax liability is payable in advance during the year, as the income is earned, similar to for-profit businesses and individuals.

- *Alternative minimum tax.* Accelerated depreciation, percentage depletion, and other similar tax benefits may be subject to the alternative minimum tax, just as with for-profit taxpayers with certain levels of income.

- *Ordinary and necessary criteria.* Deductions claimed against the unrelated income must be "ordinary and necessary" to conducting the activity and must meet the other standards of §162 for business deductions. Ordinary means common and accepted for the type of business operated; necessary means helpful and appropriate, not indispensable. The activity for which the expenditure is incurred must also be operated with profit motive.[146] No portion of the organization's basic operating expense theoretically is deductible against UBI because of the exploitation rule. However, when there is an ongoing plan to produce UBI and such revenue is part of the justification affording a particular exempt activity, allocation of overhead is permitted, although it is challenging, as discussed in Chapter 27§14.

- *Profit motive.* To be deductible, an expenditure must also be paid for the production of income, or in a business operated for the purpose of making a profit. IRC §183 specifically prohibits the deduction *of hobby losses*, or

---

[144] IRC §512(e).
[145] See §21.3.
[146] Reg. §1.512(a)-1(a).

those activities losing money for more than two years out of every five. The IRS will challenge the deduction for UBI purposes of any expenditure not paid for the purposes of producing the profit.[147]

- *Depreciation.* Equipment, buildings, vehicles, furniture, and other properties that have a useful life to the business are deductible, theoretically over their life. As a simple example, one-third of the total cost of a computer that is expected to be obsolete in three years would be deductible during each year the computer is used in the business. Unfortunately, Congress uses these calculation rates and methods as political and economic tools, and the code prescribes rates and methods that are not so simple. IRC §§167, 168, and 179 apply and must be studied to properly calculate allowable deductions for depreciation.

- *Inventory.* If the nonprofit keeps an inventory of items for sale, such as books, drugs, or merchandise of any sort, it must use the inventory method to deduct the cost of such goods. The concept is one of matching the cost of the item sold with its sales proceeds. If the exempt organization buys ten widgets for sale and, as of the end of a year, only five have been sold, the cost of the five is deductible and the remaining five are capitalized as an asset to be deducted when those widgets are sold. Again, the system is far more complicated than this simple example, and an accountant should be consulted to ensure use of proper reporting and tabulation methods. IRC §§263A and 471–474 also apply.

- *Capital and nondeductibles.* A host of nondeductible items contained in IRC §§261–280H might apply to disallow deductions, either by total disallowance or required capitalization of permanent assets. Again, all the rules applicable to for-profit businesses apply, such as the luxury automobile limits, travel and entertainment substantiation requirements, and the 50% disallowance for meals.

- *Dividend deduction.* The dividends received deduction provided by IRC §§243–245 for taxable nonexempt corporations is not allowed. As a general rule, a corporation is allowed to exclude 70% of the dividends it receives on its investments; exempt organizations are not. This rule only presents a problem for dividends received from investments that are debt financed. Most dividends received by exempts are excluded from the UBI under the modifications previously discussed.

Net Operating Losses.   A loss realized in operating an unrelated business in one year may be carried back for 2 years and forward for 20 years, for offset against another year's operating income. Gains and losses for different types of UBI earned within any single exempt organization are netted against profits from the various business activities of the organization, including acquisition of indebted investment property. Tax years in which no UBI activity is realized are counted in calculating the number of years for permissible carryovers. Conversely, net operating losses are not reduced by related income.

[147] *Iowa State University of Science and Technology v. U. S.,* 500 F.2d 508 (Ct. Cl. 1974); *Commissioner v. Groetzinger,* 480 U.S. 23 (1987); Reg. §1.513-1(4)(d)(iii).

Exploitation and Fragmentation.   When unrelated business income is generated in a fundamentally exempt activity, such as a museum gift shop or hospital pharmacy, the revenues and expenses are fragmented into the respective related and unrelated parts.[148] Such revenues are said to exploit the exempt function—the expense deductions are limited and a loss from the exploited activity is limited.[149] A social club, for example, cannot offset losses on serving nonmembers against income from its investments, according to the Supreme Court, which sided with the IRS.[150] There were conflicting decisions among the U.S. Circuit Courts of Appeal for several years, and clubs claiming such losses had to file amended returns to report tax resulting from the loss disallowance.

In Rev. Rul. 74-399, a museum restaurant was found to be a related activity because it attracted persons to the museum, allowed more time for viewing of exhibitions, and was conducive to efficient museum operative for the staff. Another museum that allows restaurant customers to eat without paying admission to visit the museum was deemed an unrelated facility. Compounding the problem was the fact that the restaurant was promoted with advertisements in a local monthly magazine and the yellow pages that mentioned the free admission.[151]

It is extremely important for an exempt organization to file Form 990-T despite the fact that it incurs a loss. Reporting the loss allows for carryback or carryover of the loss to offset past or future income. An election is available to carry losses forward and forgo any carryback in situations where the organization has not previously earned UBI.

$1,000 Exemption.   An exemption of $1,000 is allowed.

21.12   DEBT-FINANCED INCOME

The modifications exempting passive investment income, such as dividends and interest, from the UBIT do not apply to the extent that the investment is made with borrowed funds. Debt-financed property is defined as including property held for the production of income that was acquired or improved with borrowed funds and has a balance of acquisition indebtedness attributable to it during the year.[152] The classic examples are a margin account held against the exempt organization's endowment funds or a mortgage financing the purchase of a rental building.

(a) Properties Subject to Debt-Financed Rules

Real or other tangible or intangible property used 85% or more of the time, when it is actually devoted to such purpose and used directly in the organization's ex-

---

[148] See §21.4(f) and §21.13(a).
[149] For discussion see Chapter 27.14(d).
[150] *Portland Golf Club v. Commissioner,* 90-1 U.S.T.C. §50,332; *Iowa State University of Science and Technology v. United States,* 500 F.2d (Ct.Cl. 1974); *Groetzinger, supra* n.6. 110 S.Ct. 2780 (1990).
[151] Tech. Adv. Memo. 9720002.
[152] IRC §514.

empt or related activities, is exempt from these rules.[153] Assume a university borrows money and builds an office tower for its projected staff needs over a 20-year period. If less than 85% of the building is used by its staff and a net profit is earned, the nonuniversity-use portion of the building income is taxable as UBI.

Income included in UBI for some other reason, such as hotel room rentals or a 100% owned subsidiary's royalties, is specifically excluded by the code and is not counted twice because the property is debt financed.[154] Conversely, an indebted property used in an unrelated activity that is excluded from UBI because it is managed by volunteers, is for the convenience of members, or is a facility for sale of donated goods, is not treated as unrelated debt-financed property.[155] Property used in unrelated activities of an exempt organization, the income of which is excepted from UBI because it is run by volunteers for the convenience of members, or sale of donated goods, can be indebted and still not be subject to this classification. Research property producing income otherwise excluded from the UBIT is not subject to the acquisition indebtedness taint. *Future-use land* (not including buildings) acquired and held for use by an exempt organization within 10 years (churches get 15 years) from the date it is acquired, and located in the *neighborhood* in which the organization carries out a project, is exempt from this provision. This exception applies until the plans are abandoned; after five years, the organization's plans for use must be "reasonably certain."[156]

Tax status of the tenant or user is not necessarily determinative. Rental of an indebted medical office building used by staff physicians was found to be related to a hospital's purposes.[157] Although their restoration served a charitable purpose, the rental of restored historic properties to private tenants was deemed not to serve an exempt purpose where the properties were not open to the public.[158] Regulations suggest that all facts and circumstances of property usage will be considered.

Federal funding provided or insured by the Federal Housing Administration, if used to finance purchase, construction, or rehabilitation of residential property for low-income persons, is excluded.

Charitable gift annuities issued as the sole consideration in exchange for property worth more than 90% of value of the annuity is not considered acquisition indebtedness. The annuity must be payable over the life (not for a minimum or maximum number of payments) of one or two persons alive at the time. The annuity must not be measured by the property's (or any other property's) income.

Although investment of a pension fund is admittedly inherent in its exempt purposes, debt-financed investments made by such a fund (or most other exempt organizations) are not inherent in a fund's purposes.[159] The Southwest Texas Electric Cooperative's purchase of Treasury Notes with Rural Electrification Administration (REA) loan proceeds represented a debt-financed investment. The loan

---

[153] Reg. §1.514(b)-1.

[154] Reg. §1.514(b)-1(b)(2)(ii).

[155] IRC §514(b)(1)(B) & (C).

[156] IRC §514(b)(3)(A)–(E).

[157] Reg. §1.514(b)-1(c)(1); Rev. Rul. 69-464, 1969-2 C.B. 132; Tech. Adv. Memo. 8906003.

[158] Rev. Rul. 77-47, 1977-1 C.B. 156; Tech. Adv. Memo. 9017003.

[159] §514(c)(4); *Elliot Knitwear Profit Sharing Plan v. Commissioner,* 71 T.C. 765 (1979), *aff'd* 614 F.2d 347 (3d Cir. 1980).

proceeds were required to be used to pay construction costs. The cooperative's cash flow, however, allowed it to pay part of the construction costs with operating funds. To take advantage of a more than 4% spread in the REA loan and prevailing Treasury Note rates, the cooperative deliberately "drew down" on the REA loan. The Tax Court agreed with the IRS that the interest income was taxable debt-financed income.[160]

Indebted property producing no recurrent annual income, but held to produce appreciation in underlying value, or capital gain, is subject to this rule.[161] A look-back rule prevents deliberate payoff prior to sale to avoid the tax. The portion of the taxable gain is calculated using the highest amount of indebtedness during the 12 months preceding the sale as the numerator.[162]

Schools and their supporting organizations, certain pension trusts, and 501(c)(25) title holding companies may have a special exception for indebted real property. If the property is purchased in a partnership with for-profit investors, profit- and loss-sharing ratios must have substantial economic effect and not violate the disproportionate allocation rules.[163]

(b) Acquisition Indebtedness

Acquisition indebtedness is the unpaid amount of any debt incurred to purchase or improve property or any debt "reasonably foreseen" at the time of acquisition that would not have been incurred otherwise.[164] Securities purchased on margin are debt financed; payments for loan of securities already owned are not. The formula for calculation of income subject to tax is:

$$\frac{\text{income from property} \times \text{average acquisition indebtedness}}{\text{average adjusted basis}}$$

The average acquisition indebtedness equals the arithmetic average of each month or partial month of the tax year. The average adjusted basis is similarly calculated using the straight-line method of depreciation.

The proportion-of-use test is applied to identify property used for exempt and nonexempt purposes and can be based on a comparison of the number of days used for exempt purposes with the total time the property is used, or on the basis of square footage used for each, or on relative costs.[165]

Debt placed on property by a donor will be attributed to the organization when the organization agrees to pay all or part of the debt or makes any payments on the equity.[166] Property that is encumbered and subject to existing debt at the

---

[160] *Southwest Texas Electric Cooperative, Inc. v. Commissioner,* 68 T.C.M. Dec. 50,008(M), T.C. Memo. 1994-363.

[161] Reg. §1.514(b)-1(a).

[162] Reg. §1.514(a)-1(a)(1)(v).

[163] IRC §§ 168(h)(6), 514(c)(9), and 704(b)(2); Reg. §1.514(c)-2.

[164] IRC §514(c).

[165] Reg. §1.514(b)-1(b)(ii), §1.512(b)-1(b)(iii) Example 2; Priv. Ltr. Ruls. 8030105 and 8145087.

[166] Reg. §1.514(c)-1(b).

time it is received by bequest or devise is not treated as acquisition indebted-property for 10 years from its acquisition, if there is no assumption or payment on the debt by the organization. Gifted property subject to debt is similarly excluded, if the donor placed the mortgage on the property over 5 years prior to gift and had owned the property over 5 years, unless there is an assumption or payment on the mortgage by the organization. A life estate does not constitute a debt. When some other individual or organization is entitled to income from the property for life or another period of time, a remainder interest in the property is not considered to be indebted.[167]

(c) Calculation of Taxable Portion

Only that portion of the net income of debt-financed property attributable to the debt is classified as UBI.[168] Each property subject to debt is calculated separately, with the resulting income or loss netted to arrive at the portion includable in UBI. Expenses directly connected with the property are deducted from gross revenues in the same proportion. The capital gain or loss formula is different in one respect: the highest amount of indebtedness during the year preceding sales is used as the numerator. The formula can be better understood by studying Schedule E of Form 990-T illustrated in Appendix 27–7.

21.13 MUSEUMS

Museum gift shop sales and related income-producing activities are governed by the fragmentation[169] and exploitation[170] rules. Since 1973, when it published a ruling concerning greeting cards,[171] the IRS has agreed that items printed with reproductions of images in a museum's collection are educational and related to the exempt purposes so that their sale does not produce UBI. The ruling expressed two different reasons: (1) The cards stimulated and enhanced public awareness, interest in, and appreciation of art; and (2) a self-advertising theory stating that a "broader segment of the public may be encouraged to visit the museum itself to share in its educational functions and programs as a result of seeing the cards."

A second 1973 ruling[172] (still cited today) explored the fragmentation rule and expanded its application to trinkets and actual copies of objects and distinguished items. The IRS felt that educational benefit could be gained from utilitarian items with souvenir value. Since that time, it has been clearly established that a museum shop often contains both related and unrelated items, and the museum must keep exacting records to identify the two.

---

[167] Reg. §1.514(b)-1(c)(3).
[168] IRC §514(a)(1).
[169] Discussed in §21.4(c).
[170] Discussed in Chapter 27§14.
[171] Rev. Rul. 73-104, 1973-1 C.B. 263.
[172] Rev. Rul. 73-105, 1973-1 C.B. 265.

(a) Identifying Related and Unrelated Objects

After the IRS and museums argued for 10 years about the relatedness of a wide variety of objects sold, four exhaustive private rulings were issued in 1983 and are still followed.[173] The primary concern for a museum is to identify the *relatedness* of each object sold in its shops, and to segregate any unrelated sales. The connection between the item sold and achievement of the museum's exempt purpose is evidenced by the facts and circumstances of each object and the policy of the curatorial department in identifying, labeling, and categorizing objects on public view.

The rulings direct the *facts and circumstances* of each object is examined to prove that the objects being sold have educational value and list the following factors to consider in designating an item:

- Interpretive material describing artistic, cultural, or historical relationship to the museum's collection or exhibits

- Nature, scope, and motivation for the sale activity

- Are sales solely for production of income or are they an activity to enhance visitor awareness of art?

- Curatorial supervision in choosing related items

- Reproductions of objects in the particular museum or in other collections, including prints, slides, posters, postcards and greeting cards, are generally exempt.

- Adaptations, including imprinted utilitarian objects such as dishes, ashtrays, and clothing, must be accompanied by interpretive materials and must depict objects or identify an exhibition. Objects printed with logos were deemed unrelated, although in practice, the IRS has been lenient.

- Souvenirs and convenience items are generally unrelated unless imprinted with reproductions or promoting a particular event or exhibition. Souvenirs promoting the town in which the museum is located are not considered related to the museum's purposes.

- Toys and other teaching items for children are deemed inherently educational and therefore related.

(b) Original Works of Art

Original works of art created by living artists and sold by museums are considered unrelated by the IRS. They think it is inconsistent with the purpose of exhibiting art for public benefit to deprive the public the opportunity of viewing the art by selling it to an individual. This policy can apply as well to deceased artists.

---

[173] Priv. Ltr. Ruls. 8303013, 8326003, 8236008, and 8328009; See also Tech. Adv. Memo 9550003, in which the IRS reviewed its rulings and provided an extensive listing of eight categories of items that it considered related to a "living museum's" and six groups of unrelated objects. Importantly, the IRS found off-site sales activity is not, solely for that reason, treated as an unrelated activity, if the museum can show that such sales enhance a broader public appreciation of the art works and encourages visits to the museum facilities.

- A cooperative art gallery established to encourage individual emerging artists was not allowed to qualify as an exempt organization because, in the IRS's opinion, the interests of the general public were not served by promoting the careers of individual artists. The art sales served no exempt purpose and constituted UBI. Because the organization was supported entirely by UBI from the sales of art of the artists, it was not exempt.[174]

- A community art center located in an isolated area with no commercial galleries obtained exemption, and the Tax Court decided that its sales of original art were related to exempt purposes. The decision was based on the fact that no other cultural center existed in the county, the art sales were not the center's sole source of support, and a complex of other educational activities were conducted.[175]

- An unrelated gallery managed by volunteers and/or selling donated works of art produces unrelated income, but the income is not taxable because of exceptions. Exempt status depends on whether the gallery is a substantial part of the organization's activities. See §21.3 for consequences of receiving such income.

21.14 TRAVEL TOURS

Museums and other types of exempt organizations sponsor study tours as promotional, educational, and fund-raising tools. The issue is whether such tours advance the exempt purposes of the exempt organization other than its need for funds. Such tours are commonly professionally organized in a fashion similar to those of travel agents and commercial tour guides. To be related to an exempt function, a tour must be educational rather than recreational. The IRS says the crux of the matter is the intent of the tour-sponsoring organization. One must evaluate the difference between "serendipitous acquisition of knowledge" and a deliberate intent to educate.[176] Regulations were proposed in April, 1998, to "augment guidance on travel tours."[177]

To scrutinize the bona fide educational methodology of the tour, the professional status of leaders and the educational content of the program is considered. Advance preparation, such as reading lists, evidence relatedness. The actual amount of time spent in formal classes and visits to historic sites, mandatory participation for lectures, preparation of reports, and opportunity for university credit are other attributes evidencing the educational nature of a tour.[178] Conversely, a large amount of recreational time allowed to participants, the resort-taint of the places the tour visits, and holiday scheduling suggest predominantly personal pleasure purposes and cause the tour to not qualify as educational.[179] The regulations contain four examples that should be carefully studied by organizations conducting such tours.

---

[174] Priv. Ltr. Rul. 8032028.

[175] *Goldsboro Art League, Inc. v. Commissioner*, 75 T.C. 337 (1980).

[176] Remarks of Marc Owens, Director of IRS Exempt Organization Division, Non-Profits in Travel Conference, on March 9, 1995.

[177] Prop. Reg. §1.513-7.

[178] Rev. Rul. 70-534, 1970-2 C.B. 113.

[179] Rev. Rul. 77-366, 1977-2 C.B. 192.

The proposed regulations suggest documentation of a trip's relatedness start during its planning stage. The EO's records should indicate how and for what reason the destination(s) is chosen, how guides are chosen, and other information evidencing the educational raison d'être of the trip. Proving the educational nature of a tour may be more difficult for an organization whose sole purpose is conducting tours. An organization that uses professional travel companies to arrange tours also has a burden of proving it was not established to benefit the private operators.

Not only the profit from the tour itself, but the *additional donation* requested as an organizational gift from all participants in a travel tour program, may be classed as unrelated income if the tour is not considered as educational.[180]

21.15 PUBLISHING

Exempt organization publications present two very different exposures to trouble: the unrelated income tax and potential revocation of exemption. As discussed previously, the most universal problem is that publication advertising sales create UBI in most cases. A less common, but more dangerous, situation occurs when the underlying exemption is challenged because the publication itself is a business.

(a) Advertising

Revenue received from the sale of advertising in an otherwise exempt publication is considered business income by the IRS, and is taxed unless

- The publication schedule or ad sale activity is irregularly carried on.
- The advertising is sold by volunteers.
- The advertising activity is related to one of the organization's underlying exempt purposes, such as ads sold by college students or trainees.
- The ads do not contain commercial material, appear essentially as a listing without significant distinction among those listed, and represent acknowledgment of contributors or sponsors.

The IRS has continually taken the position that advertising sold using the exempt organization's name is unrelated activity, despite creative contracts attributing the activity to an independent commercial firm.[181]

(b) Readership versus Ad Lineage Costs

Even if ad revenue is classified as UBI, the tax consequence is limited by the portion of the readership and editorial costs allowed as deductions against the ad revenue. The important question is what portion of the expense of producing and distributing the publication can be allocated against the revenue.[182] It is helpful first to study Exhibit 21–4, Calculation of Taxable Portion of Advertising Revenue, a

---

[180] Tech. Adv. Mem. 9027003.
[181] Rev. Rul. 73-424, 1973-2 C.B. 190; IRS Tech. Adv. Memo. 9222001; also see §§21.8(d) and 21.8(h).
[182] Reg. §1.512(a)-1(f)(6); Rev. Rul. 81-1-1, 1981-1 C.B. 352.

Exhibit 21–4

CALCULATING THE TAXABLE PORTION OF ADVERTISING REVENUE

BASIC FORMULA: $\mathbf{A - B - (C - D)} =$ Taxable Income

A = **Gross sales of advertising.**

B = **Direct costs of advertising:**

Occupancy, supplies, and other administrative expenses	$	_____
Commissions or salary costs for ad salespersons		_____
Clerical or management salary cost directly allocable		_____
Artwork, photography, color separations, etc.		_____
Portion of printing, typesetting, mailing, and other direct publication costs allocable in the ratio of total lineage in the publication to ad lineage		
Total direct cost of ads	$	_____

C = **Readership costs:**

Occupancy, supplies, and other administrative expense	$	_____
Editors, writers, and salary for editorial content		_____
Travel, photos, other direct editorial expenses		_____
Portion of printing, typesetting, mailing, and other direct publication costs allocable in ratio of total lineage in publication to editorial lineage (in general, all direct publication costs not allocable to advertising lineage)		_____
Total readership costs	$	_____

D = **Readership (or circulation) revenues:**

If publication sold to all for a fixed price, then readership revenue equals total subscription sales. $ _____

or

If 20% of total circulation is from paid nonmember subscriptions, then price charged to nonmembers times number of issues circulated to members plus nonmember revenue equals readership revenues.   _____

or

If members receiving publication pay a higher membership fee, readership revenue equals excess dues times number of members receiving publication, plus nonmember revenue.   _____

or

If more than 80% of issues distributed to members free, readership revenue is the membership receipts times the ratio of publication costs over the total exempt activities cost including the publication costs.   _____

worksheet reflecting the order in which readership and editorial costs versus advertising costs are allocated.

The formula prorates deductions in arriving at taxable advertising income. Publication costs are first divided into two categories: direct advertising and readership. Because readership costs are exempt function costs, under the *exploitation rule*[183] they theoretically should not be deductible at all against the UBI income. In a limited exception, the regulations allow readership costs, if any, in excess of readership income to be deducted against advertising income. In other words, advertising revenues can be offset with a readership loss. Arriving at a readership loss, however, means the publication's underlying production costs must be more than its revenues.

(c) Circulation Income

Circulation income is income attributable to the production, distribution, or circulation of a periodical (other than advertising revenue), including sale of reprints and back issues.[184] When members receive an organization's publication as a part of their basic membership fee, a portion of the member dues is allocated to circulation income. Other types of member income, such as educational program fees or convention registration, are not allocated.[185] When the publication is given free to members but is sold to nonmembers, a portion of the members' dues is allocated to readership revenue. The IRS formula requires allocation of a hypothetical portion of the dues, as described in the calculation.

- Free copies given to nonmembers are subject to controversy with IRS (check for new decisions).

- If the organization has more than one publication, the IRS and the courts disagree on the denominator of the fraction for calculation of allocable exempt function costs.[186]

(d) Commercial Publication Programs

A publication program can be considered a commercial venture, despite its educational content. Distinguishing characteristics, according to the IRS, are found by examining the organization's management decisions.

Characteristics deemed commercial by the IRS include:

- *Presence of substantial profits.* Accumulation of profits over a number of years evidences a commercial purpose. The mere presence of profits, by itself, will not bar exemption,[187] but other factors will be considered. For

---

[183] Discussed in Chapter 27§14.
[184] Reg. §1.512(a)-(f)(3)(iii).
[185] Tech. Adv. Memo. 9204007; also see Tech. Adv. Memo. 9734002.
[186] *North Carolina Citizens for Business and Industry v. U.S.,* 89-2 U.S.T.C. §9507 (Cl.Ct. 1989).
[187] *Scripture Press Foundation v. U. S.,* 285 F.2d 800 (Ct.Cl. 1961), *cert. denied,* 368 U.S. 985 (1982).

what purpose are profits being accumulated? Do the reserves represent a savings account for future expansion plans?

- *Pricing methods.* The method of pricing books or magazines sold yields significant evidence of commercial taint. Pricing at or below an amount calculated to cover costs shows nonprofit motive. Pricing below comparable commercial publications is not required, but certainly can evidence an intention to encourage readership and to educate, rather than to produce a profit.

- *Other factors.* Other factors can show commerciality:

  - Aggressive commercial practices resembling those undertaken by commercial publishers.[188]

  - Substantial salaries or royalties paid to individuals.

  - Distribution by commercial licensers.

- *Nonprofit publications.* By contrast, nonprofit and noncommercial publications:[189]

  - Rely on volunteers and/or modest wages.

  - Sell some unprofitable books and magazines.

  - Prepare and choose materials according to educational methods, not commercial appeal.

  - Donate parts of press runs to other exempt organizations or members.

  - Balance deficit budgets with contributions.

A Christian school publishing program, for example, was treated as an unrelated activity despite the educational nature of the books it sold.[190] Although the program had significant commercial attributes—more than 1,200 titles produced on presses that ran 16 hours a day and sold throughout the world—the IRS said two particular characteristics caused it to consider the activity as unrelated:

1. The methods used in selling the textbooks are indistinguishable from ordinary commercial sales practices.

2. Fifty percent of the schools' highly compensated employees were sales representatives.

The IRS provided some useful criteria for deciding what constitutes a *periodical* in a 1994 private ruling.[191] The definition is important because that portion of membership dues allocated to published periodicals is treated as taxable unrelated income. An educational organization devoted to the study of reproduction

---

[188] *American Institute for Economic Research v. U. S.,* 302 F.2d 934 (Ct. Cl. 1962).
[189] *Presbyterian and Reformed Publishing Co. v. Commissioner,* 70 T.C. 1070, 1087, 1083 (1982).
[190] Priv. Ltr. Rul. 9636001.
[191] Priv. Ltr. Rul. 9402005.

distributed a variety of publications, some of which were deemed periodicals and others of which were not. A quarterly newsletter and annual meeting programs distributed to members were periodicals for the following reasons:

- Each was published at regular recurring intervals.

- The right to receive the publication was associated with membership or similar status in the organization for which dues, fees, or other charges were received (even though nonmembers may also).

- Each contained editorial materials related to the accomplishment of the organization's exempt purposes; in this case, publicizing scientific developments in the field, technical articles, and reports of annual meeting.

- The newsletter was part of an ongoing series, with each issue indicating its relation to prior or future issues; it contained a regular feature column, president's message, and reports of organizational meetings and activities.

- With respect to the advertising portion of the publications, the purpose was the production of income, each issue of a periodical indicated a relation with prior or subsequent issues.

Relationships with Other Organizations and Businesses

22.1 ORGANIZATIONAL SPIN-OFFS

Sometimes an exempt organization, its board, or its staff wish to undertake an activity not appropriate for the organization itself, but suitable for another form of organization. There are two classic types of spin-offs: One is a title-holding company[1] formed to hold assets for the benefit of the organization. The other is an Internal Revenue Code (IRC) §501(c)(4) organization formed by a §501(c)(3) charity to conduct lobbying activities that would be unallowable for the reasons outlined in Chapter 23.

A new and separate exempt organization might be formed to conduct a program that exposes the organization's assets to unacceptable risk of financial loss.

---

[1] Discussed in Chapter 10.

The motivation is similar to the reasons for forming a title-holding company, except that a title-holding company cannot actively operate programs or projects.

A new organization might also be formed because it can qualify for funding not available to the existing organization. A common example of this type of spin-off is an auxiliary formed to allow the individuals involved in fund-raising to control the funds that they raise while not controlling the underlying organization. The creation of a charity to benefit a business league or labor union can attract deductible gifts that are not available to the benefited organization itself.

The new organization must, of course, meet the requirements for the category of exemption under which it is formed. The application for recognition of exemption must describe in detail the relationship and the reasons why the new organization is being created. While interlocking directorates are not prohibited in either situation, prudence usually dictates that a separate, noncontrolling board be established for the new organization. Criteria for attributing activities back to the creating organization have been developed by the Internal Revenue Service (IRS) to evaluate for-profit subsidiaries.

As a practical matter, the existing organization's assets are not usually transferred as might be implied by the term "spin-off," except in the formation of a title-holding company or supporting organization. In fact, to retain the distinct tax exemption and legal identity, separate and distinguishable operations are imperative. Nevertheless, the two organizations often operate side by side and share employees and facilities. Record keeping may need to be expanded to ensure documentation of the new entity's separate existence.[2]

22.2 CREATION OF (C)(3) BY (C)(4), (5), OR (6)

Business leagues, labor unions, civic clubs, and other noncharitable exempt organizations are typically organized and operated to further the interests of their members. Conversely, a (c)(3), often called a charitable organization, is created to raise funds in support of programs benefiting the general public.[3] The possible motivations for non-(c)(3)s to establish a (c)(3) are many. Often, such organizations already conduct charitable programs and wish to raise grant funds from non-members to support them. A (c)(3) organization might also be created as a vehicle to honor respected members upon their deaths or as the recipient of split-interest trust or life insurance gifts during members' lives. A charitable wing might be created to enhance the public image of the profession through the sponsorship of scholarships and educational programs.

(a) Form of Relationship

The relationship between the two organizations can take many forms. Typically the board members overlap. While it is acceptable for both boards to be identical, they may be totally separate. If public status as a supporting organization is de-

---

[2] See §22.4(c).

[3] Standards for exemption described in Chapter 2; additional considerations for a business league forming a (c)(3) are discussed in Chapter 8§11.

sired, the link must be evident and the purposes and organizational documents must meet the specific requirements found in Chapter 11§6.

(b) Category of Public Charity

Public charity status is an important question in structuring this type of relationship. Though affiliated charities formed by business leagues and other non(c)(3)s are often called foundations, such charities can normally qualify as a public charity rather than as private foundations. The appropriate type of public charity is dictated both by the anticipated sources of funding for the foundation and by scope of its activities. If the majority of the support will be received from the related organization or a small group of members, formation of a supporting organization under IRC §509(a)(3) is clearly indicated. If donations are expected from a wide segment of the membership and general public, the new organization can also qualify for public status under IRC §509(a)(1) or (2). When the proposed organization can qualify as publicly supported under more than one category of IRC §509, a choice must be made. The §509(a)(1) and (2) categories allow the new organization to operate and be controlled more independently than it could as a supporting organization under §509(a)(3). The fact that no public support test calculations are required makes the §509(a)(3) category more desirable. The difference between §509(a)(1) and (a)(2) is primarily mathematical and depends on the sources of revenue.[4]

(c) Donation Collection System

A subset of the public support question arises when the professional society, civic league, or union solicits donations as a part of its annual dues collection process. Typically, the donations to the separate charitable foundation are optional for society members. The notice may suggest an amount or allow members to add whatever amount they choose. The society collects the donations and periodically pays them over to the charity. A question may arise as to who is making the gift—the individual member or the society. Particularly for optional gifts, there is evidence of donative intention on the member's part, rather than the society's. Such donations should be segregated and recorded on the society's books as a liability being held by the society as agent for the foundation.

(d) Grants to and from the (c)(3)

The (c)(3) organization raises the funds to carry out educational, scientific, or other charitable activities on behalf of or in concert with the organization that creates it. The interesting question is whether the (c)(3) must disburse the funds itself and directly undertake charitable projects, or whether it can grant funds to the (c)(4), (5), or (6) to enable it to undertake the activities. Both scenarios are permissible. If the funds are paid over to the parent non(c)(3) organization, the grant should be restricted under a written agreement specifying the qualifying charitable purposes for which the moneys can be spent and, if possible, annual reports should be made back to the funding charity.

---

[4] Chapter 11 explains the intricacies of public status.

Often the society furnishes the charity with office space, personnel, and other necessary operating overhead items. Reimbursement of expenses incurred by either organization is permissible under standards discussed in §22.4(c) for a for-profit subsidiary. However, the charity has the burden of proving that the expenditures do not benefit the society and its members. When it is financially possible, payment of the expenses by the society without reimbursement eliminates questions of this sort.

In one situation, the IRS decided that a related foundation of a business or professional association (§501(c)(6)) was not truly engaged in appropriate tax-exempt activities because it operated primarily for the benefit of the association. The foundation's only activity was to provide a no-rent lease to the related membership association. The IRS concluded that leasing is not usually an inherently charitable activity, and that the charity in this case was only operated to further the interest of the parent organization and therefore did not qualify for exemption.[5] Loaning the foundation's non-(c)(3) parent money to conduct lobbying (or any other noncharitable purpose) is unacceptable.[6]

Respecting the separateness of the (c)(3) is appropriate. The projects it sponsors should be discrete and identifiable as its own though they may often focus on issues of concern to their affiliate business league or union. When the (c)(3) was created by a (c)(4) that conducts extensive lobbying, it is particularly important that adequate records be maintained to evidence allocation of moneys.[7]

22.3 ALLIANCES WITH INVESTORS

In the face of declining governmental support for housing and education during the 1970s, exempt organizations began to turn to the private sector for capital funding for buildings and equipment. In the medical field, the cost of new medical technology and the establishment of health care conglomerates compounded capital needs. Accelerated depreciation rates encouraged such arrangements until 1984[8] and again in 1986, with the advent of longer depreciable lives and the passive loss limitations. Despite the reduced tax benefits, joint ventures with private individuals and businesses still proliferate, both to raise capital and to gain their participation and expertise.

(a) Exempt Organization as General Partner

Originally, the IRS ruled that an exempt organization was completely prohibited from serving as a general partner with private limited partners. Since the general partner has an obligation to maximize profits for the benefit of the limited partners, the IRS took the position that the general partner role violates the basic private inurement standards and automatically causes loss of exempt status. Their

---

[5] Priv. Ltr. Rul. 9017003.
[6] Priv. Ltr. Rul. 9812001.
[7] See Chapter 6 for further discussion about companion (c)(3) and (c)(4) organizations.
[8] IRC §168(j)(9), the so-called tax-exempt entity leasing rules lengthened depreciable lives for certain properties.

words were "the arrangement is inherently incompatible with being operated exclusively for charitable purposes."[9]

By 1980, the IRS relaxed its prohibition and agreed that an exempt organization could serve as a general partner if (but only if) the venture is one that serves its charitable purposes. Each case is to be carefully scrutinized and the facts and circumstances considered in detail to evaluate the purposes served by the venture. First and foremost, the underlying exempt purposes of the EO are considered. Building ventures have been condoned when they attract and keep qualified physicians to a charity hospital.[10] Acquisition of new equipment necessary to serve the community with home health care, made possible with investor funds, has also been condoned.[11]

Not only must exempt purposes be primarily served, but the exempt organization must not bear unreasonable risk to its financial condition. Insulating the exempt partner's assets from venture liabilities is equally important. Among the facts that provide such insulation are:

- Contractual limitation of liability[12]

- Right of first refusal or option to purchase on dissolution or sale granted to the EO[13]

- Limitation or ceiling on returns to limited partners[14]

- Presence of other general partners or managers with responsibility to serve the limited partners[15]

- Organizational control exercised by the exempt partner and attention paid to the charitable mission carried on by the partnership[16]

- Methods for calculating profit sharing, asset purchases, and cost reimbursements designed to protect the EO's interests

The first factor is of primary concern in protecting the exempt organization's assets. The organizational test for continued charitable exemption requires that the assets be dedicated to charitable purposes and that earnings be similarly used. Consequently, liabilities associated with any joint venture must be identifiable and limited, and must not pose a threat to the organization's underlying assets. Such protection can be achieved with insurance coverage, with indemnity agreements specifying the extent of exposure, or by the nature of the activities. For example, a student dormitory building project has less inherent risk than a nuclear

---

[9] Gen. Coun. Memo. 36293 (May 30, 1975).

[10] Priv. Ltr. Rul. 8940039.

[11] Priv. Ltr. Rul. 8943063.

[12] Gen. Coun. Memo. 39546 (August 27, 1986).

[13] Priv. Ltr. Rul. 8344099.

[14] Priv. Ltr. Ruls. 8940039, 8417054, and 8344099; *Plumstead Theatre Society, Inc. v. Commissioner,* 675 F.2d 244 (9th Cir. 1982), *aff'g* 74 T.C. 1324 (1980).

[15] Gen. Coun. Memo. 39005 (June 29, 1983).

[16] Priv. Ltr. Ruls. 9122061, 9122062, 2122070, 9021050; also see Chapter 4§2(b) regarding a low-income housing project, Housing Pioneers, Inc., failure to qualify for exemption.

fission research laboratory, and may provide lower exposure to an exempt general partner.

The second and third factors ensure that the limited partners do not reap unreasonable compensation or gain at the expense of the EO. Conversely, the exempt organization taking the risk of serving as general partner should be appropriately rewarded with the greater share of the return. Another method of protecting the EO's interest is to allow the charity to repurchase the venture asset or to specifically limit the profits. Suitable terms under which a laboratory venture operated can be found in G.C.M. 37852. The discussion regarding management contracts and compensation levels has more examples of fair compensation.[17]

The fourth factor mitigates the fiduciary responsibility problem. An important IRS objection to exempt general partners is the conflict between their responsibilities to create gain for the limited partners and to serve their exempt constituents. In some cases, the exempt organization requires a dual general partner to actually manage the venture to suitably limit its role.

The last two factors were used by the IRS in approving the reorganization of a resonance imaging center established by an exempt hospital group's for-profit corporate subsidiary, partly with its own funds and partly with funds furnished by limited partner physicians. All financial arrangements between the parties were at fair market value, and profits and losses were to be allocated in relation to the investments made and risks assumed. Mutually binding termination and buy-out agreements were in place to protect the charitable interests from undue risk of loss.

Two new forms of organization, limited liability companies (LLC) and limited liability partnerships (LLP), add another dimension to this issue. Such entities are to be judged by the same criteria used to judge partnership arrangements.[18]

(b) Joint Ventures

In 1983, Medicare changed its cost-based reimbursement system for inpatient hospital services to fixed, per case, prospective payments. Cost recoupment became dependent on the number of patients served and hospitals began to adopt policies to enhance patient population. Consequently, the emphasis shifted to admissions and physician referrals. To give tangible encouragement to the doctors, hospitals designed incentive profit sharing arrangements based on patient revenue. As long as the total compensation to the doctor is reasonable, incentive compensation is not necessarily prohibited.

One version of such plans attracted IRS attention—joint ventures to operate certain departments were set up between the hospitals and physicians. The exempt hospital and the doctors both invested funds. The transferability of the doctor partners was restricted. (In one case, there was a mandatory repurchase agreement.) Basically, the patients would still be served in the same manner, and the hospitals retained the equipment, overhead, and so on. The significant factor was that the net revenue stream (discounted to present value) from the department was sold to the venture up front, sometimes with and sometimes without investment by the doctors.

---

[17] See Chapter 22.5.
[18] Comments of Jay Rotz, IRS National Exempt Organization Office, about Priv. Ltr. Rul. 9517029, May 19, 1995, ABA meeting of the Exempt Organization Section.

The IRS initially approved such ventures.[19] In December 1991,[20] it reversed its position in a memorandum that reviewed three net revenue stream ventures and found that the exempt status of the hospital ventures should be revoked. The revenue sharing plans represent two problems—excessive compensation and per se inurement—resulting from assignment of the hospital's assets to individuals who essentially control it and, at the very least, prohibited private benefit. The IRS found very little community or public benefit resulting from the doctor ventures; no new resources, treatment modalities, enhanced patient care, or cost savings results.[21] A permissible joint venture of a for-profit hospital and an exempt supporting organization of another (c)(3) was formed to operate an acute care facility. The following tests were applied to find that the proposed venture would not jeopardize the exempt partner's status:[22]

Relatedness criterion requires that the activity of the partnership or the exempt's participation in the venture further its exempt purposes. In this ruling, the IRS agreed that patients would benefit from the more medically sophisticated programs—state-of the-art systems and services not otherwise available in their region. Lives would be saved for the exempt partner's patients now able to use the trauma center.

Financial benefit criterion was used to measure whether the venture terms adequately protected the exempt organization's financial interest. The agreement required equal sharing of capital contributions, profit and losses, distributions, and assumption of liabilities and use of fair market value to determine amounts. The assets of the exempt and its affiliates were not placed at risk to benefit the for-profit partner. The transactions were to take place at fair market value.

Conflict of interest criterion evaluates whether the venture terms allowed the exempt to operate in furtherance of its organizational objectives. Management of the partnership was by consensus, with each partner placing three members on the controlling board. The exempt had the right to negotiate directly with managed care providers and the for-profit partner had no control over the exempt.

Hospitals participating in similar joint ventures were given the opportunity to undo the relationships without losing exempt status. Such entities were given until September 1, 1992 to enter into closing agreements with the IRS.[23] The factors just enumerated were incorporated into the IRS hospital audit guide.[24]

(c) Fast Forward to 1998

Between 1992 and 1997, the health care industry evolved so fast that the many alliances were formed between tax-exempt and for-profit health care providers without prior IRS approval. Although private rulings were issued on what by then were called *joint operating agreements*, no precedential guidance was issued. A

---

[19] Priv. Ltr. Rul. 8820093; revocation discussed in Priv. Ltr. Ruls. 9231047 and 8942099.
[20] Gen. Coun. Memo. 39862.
[21] October 1992 remarks of T.V. Sullivan of the National Health Lawyers Association Conference in Washington, D.C.
[22] Gen. Coun. Memo. 39862.
[23] Announcement 92-70, 1992-19 IRB.
[24] *Exempt Organizations Examination Guidelines Handbook,* ¶ 333 (IRM 7(10)69-38).

book entitled *The Law of Tax-Exempt Healthcare Organizations* was added to the Wiley Nonprofit Series to focus specifically on this important topic.[25] Finally in 1997, the IRS published Rev. Rul. 97-21 concerning incentive compensation paid to recruit physicians.[26] In March, 1998, Rev. Rul. 98-15 was issued to provide guidance on joint ventures between exempt organizations and for-profit entities.[27] The ruling compares and contrasts two scenarios—one acceptable, the other causing loss of exempt status. The question remains the same. Does the venture provide private inurement to the for-profit investors?

This new published ruling contained two significant factors not outlined in the criterion outlined previously. In the acceptable scenario, the exempt organization controlled the LLC. The organization appointed three of the directors; the for-profit appointed two. The nonexempt venturer had 50-50 control. The documents in the acceptable venture explicitly placed a duty on the governing board to operate the hospital in a manner that furthered a charitable purpose. Documents of the venture failing to qualify as tax-exempt placed no such constraint upon the operation nor in management contracts it entered into with other for-profits. Proposed operating agreements should be tested by this ruling for facts that are similar. Additionally the three criterion outlined in the preceding section can still be applied to evaluate the presence of inurement. The rulings are further discussed in Chapter 4§6.

(d) Trouble-Free Relationships

A joint venture with another exempt organization of the same §501 category, to own and operate exempt function assets or to sponsor a charitable program, poses no threat to either organization's status. A trouble-free example might have three museums buying a Georgia O'Keefe painting, each receiving an undivided one-third interest. The costs are shared equally and each museum exhibits the work one-third of each year. This joint ownership is established to reduce the funds expended by each museum and to enable them to reduce their storage requirements, and thus serves an exempt purpose.

What if the venture borrows money from a private individual to buy the painting? Assume that the loan is to be paid back over a four-year period, as fundraising permits. Interest on the debt is paid at the prevailing prime rate. If the loan is unpaid at the end of four years, the painting can be foreclosed by the lender in return for any principal payments made against the loan, adjusted for any increase in value as determined by an independent outside appraiser. Since (1) purchasing and exhibiting art work advances the educational purposes of the museums, (2) their underlying endowments are not used to purchase the painting (i.e., limited liability), and (3) the museums reap any increase in the value of the art work, this venture involving a private investor should not pose a threat to their exempt status.

Another arrangement is possible when an exempt organization needs to expand. Assume that it needs to acquire a building to provide additional space.

[25] By Thomas K. Hyatt and Bruce R. Hopkins (New York: Wiley, 1994).
[26] 1997-18 I.R.B. 1; see Chapter 4§6.
[27] 1998-12 I.R.B. 6, facts outlined in Chapter 4§6(b).

After meetings with major donors, it is clear that funds cannot be raised entirely through donations. Some of the donors, however, offer to build the facility and lease it back to the organization. If the building serves exempt purposes and the four factors discussed above are present, a tenant–landlord relationship is permissible.[28]

(e) Unrelated Business Income Aspect

Formation of a partnership does not shelter an exempt organization from classification of an activity as an unrelated business. The activity of the partnership is considered those of its partners. The income earned by a partnership (SubS or similar venture) passes directly through to the partners, retaining its same character. The partnership itself pays no tax but submits Form 1065 reporting each partner's distributive share of profits or losses. The exempt organization partner then reports its share of profits or losses directly on its own Form 990 or 990-T and pays an applicable tax directly.

One must also determine whether the business activities of the partnership (or of a corporate subsidiary) will be attributed to the exempt organization, and, if so, will the exempt status of the organization be jeopardized because of the activity? The primary purpose of the exempt organization cannot be to participate in the venture. The IRS applied a "more than incidental" test in a private ruling. When no more than 15% of its computerized database users would be nonexempt users, an organization qualified for exemption.[29]

22.4   CREATION OF A FOR-PROFIT CORPORATE SUBSIDIARY

A customary motivation for forming a corporation instead of a partnership is to segregate the tax aspects of unrelated business activities and to avoid the liability problems inherent in the partnership form of organization. Typically, the subsidiary is formed to conduct a business: to commercially develop patents resulting from research, to operate a restaurant and ski lodge on investment property being held for future expansion, or to establish a computer facility open to the public. When such a corporation is formed without outside investors, the more flexible profit/loss sharing ratios available to a partnership are not needed.

(a) Maintaining Separate Corporate Identity

Attribution of the subsidiary's activities back to its exempt parent defeats the purpose for its formation. Thus, it is important to structure the subsidiary to ensure its separate corporate identity. If the exempt organization owns less than 100% of the stock (for unrelated business income purposes, under 50% is desirable[30]), the outside owners provide the separateness. When the exempt organization owns all of the stock, proof of independence includes a separate board of directors and officers

---

[28] The private inurement rules discussed in Chapter 20 should be reviewed in connection with such a relationship.
[29] Priv. Ltr. Rul. 8636079; also see Chapter 21.
[30] See Chapter 21§10(e).

and independent management of daily affairs.[31] Actual evidence of separate operation should be maintained, such as board meetings, operating budgets, and financial reports. The fact that the parent corporation retains control over significant corporate actions, such as dissolution, does not constitute interference with the subsidiary's day-to-day affairs.[32]

The makeup of the board of directors can be evidence of the subsidiary's independent operation. While there is technically no requirement for it, independent and nonemployee members of the board are noted as a positive factor. A hotel-operating corporation established by a historic village foundation was ruled to be autonomous and "operated at arms' length" partly because of the outsiders sitting on the board of directors.[33] A for-profit subsidiary in a hospital conglomerate group was also found to be valid because of its independent board.[34]

The subsidiary must be established for a valid business purpose to avoid its being considered merely a guise to allow the exempt organization to conduct excess business or other impermissible activity. The subsidiary should not be merely an arm, agency, or integral part of the parent.[35] The creation of a subsidiary by a business league to "isolate into one single taxable entity" all of its unrelated activities was condoned.[36]

The facts and circumstances may be important to prove the separateness of an exempt organization and its subsidiary when customers are referred by the nonprofit to the for-profit. Exempt organizations involved in such relationships will be well served by studying the complex and extensive rules found in IRC §482, Allocation of Income and Deductions among Taxpayers. The IRS is empowered by the section to "distribute, apportion, or allocate gross income, deductions, credits, or allowances between or among" two or more organizations owned or controlled directly or indirectly by the same interests. The regulations contain 12 different factors that may indicate a basis for reallocations.[37]

(b) Subsidiary Pays Its Own Income Tax

As a separate taxpayer, the subsidiary files its own Form 1120 and pays its own income tax. Dividends are therefore paid to the exempt parent with after-tax profits. To avoid circumvention of this rule, payments to a controlled parent (owning 50% or more or the stock) in the form of rent, interest, or royalty are taxed to the parent.[38] In other words, tax on unrelated business income cannot be escaped by paying it back to an exempt parent as a deductible expense. Additionally transfer of assets upon sale or liquidation from the taxable subsidiary to the exempt parent may be taxable.[39]

---

[31] Gen. Coun. Memo. 39326 and 39598.
[32] Priv. Ltr. Rul. 8909029.
[33] Priv. Ltr. Rul. 8952076.
[34] Priv. Ltr. Rul. 9046045.
[35] Gen. Coun. Memo. 33912.
[36] Priv. Ltr. Rul. 9119060; see also Priv. Ltr. Rul. 9305026.
[37] Outlined in Chapter 20§1(b).
[38] IRC §512(b)(13); discussed in Chapter 21§10(e).
[39] Reg. 1.337(d); see Chapter 21§10(e).

(c) Sharing Facilities and/or Employees

Combining exempt organizations of more than one category of §501(c), private foundations, and/or nonexempt organizations into sharing arrangements for office space, employees, group insurance, project management, or a variety of other operating necessities may be permissible. There is no absolute prohibition as long as the following conditions are met:

- The activity (rental of office space, hiring of employees, etc.) serves an exempt purpose of the organization.

- The organization reaps cost savings by combining with others in securing the shared items or services.

- Documentation is maintained to evidence each organization's allocable portion of each expenditure. This may be done through:

  - Time sheets

  - Space utilization

  - Asset cost (e.g., "We buy the copier, you buy the phones.")

  - Automobile and travel logs

- The arrangement does not allow unfair advantage to any of the parties, unless such advantage inures to the 501(c)(3)s involved.

- No exempt organization assumes any risk of loss on behalf of the other organization(s).

- For private foundations, the organization pays its share directly to the outside vendors.[40]

The first condition above is of primary importance in evaluating a sharing relationship between an EO and either another EO or a nonexempt organization. The primary motivation for the expenditure of the organization's funds must always be to serve its own exempt purposes, not those of another. The proof is often easy, however. Space in which to operate the exempt organization is necessary. Why not accept the use of space in a major contributor's building? Significant equipment not owned by the organization may be made available at little or no cost; a lease and/or a deposit may not be required. Often the rent is under market value because it is space not otherwise rentable at the time, although payment of full fair market value is not prohibited.

Another common arrangement is the sharing of employees. If a new charity needs a part-time secretary, it may engage the available time of an associated organization's employee. As long as the compensation paid to such workers is fairly allocated among the organizations for whom each person performs services, there again is no reason why staff cannot be shared.[41] Evidence of the time actually devoted to each organization must be maintained as a basis for allocating salary and associated costs.

[40] See Chapter 14 for rules on self-dealing.
[41] Priv. Ltr. Rul. 8944017.

Combining related organization employees into one group for health insurance has been specifically sanctioned by the IRS.[42] In a hospital conglomerate group, the (c)(3) charitable hospital, its (c)(3) supporting, its fund-raising arm, and two for-profit subsidiaries (a health equipment rental company and an administrative services provider) combined their employees into a self-funded, self-insured major medical plan. The inclusion of the subsidiary employees increased the number of plan participants and resulted in decreased cost of insurance, spreading the risk of loss over more participants. The per-participant cost for all entities was the same. The IRS found that providing employee benefits was consistent with the hospital's exempt purposes. It also noted that the insurance trust was separate from all of the organizations. Presumably this fact was important because the 501(c)(3)s were not assuming any unforeseen risks on behalf of the for-profits.

(d) Individual or Outside Shareholders

For a variety of reasons, an exempt organization's for-profit subsidiary may issue or sell shares to others. An employee stock option plan may be desirable to offer incentive compensation to employees.[43] Investment capital may be raised by selling shares, or the corporation may be formed as a joint venture with others. Such relationships serve the economic or business purposes of the subsidiary; the question is whether the exempt purposes of the nonprofit shareholder are served by it. Selling shares to investors and issuing incentive shares to employees serves the purposes of the exempt as long as the shares are sold and issued at their fair market value.[44] The presence of outside ownership may be useful to prove that the subsidiary has separate corporate identity. The IRS astutely pointed out that this issue should be judged in view of the reasonableness of the executive compensation and whether the prices being paid for the shares are at fair market value.[45]

22.5 ACTIVE BUSINESS RELATIONSHIPS

Partly due to limited access to investment capital and limited ability to compete for qualified permanent personnel, an exempt organization may wish to engage an outside professional, either an individual or a company, to manage a project, facility, or other activity. The issues involved in consideration of such a relationship with a for-profit company are similar to the partnership/subsidiary issues.

(a) Criteria for Approval

The exempt organization must satisfy itself that two important criteria exist before entering into such a relationship. The issues of primary concern are:

1. Are exempt purposes served by the relationship? Can the EO more effectively promote its mission by engaging the commercial manager to set up and administer the new facility?

[42] Priv. Ltr. Rul. 9025089. Priv. Ltr. Rul. 9242039 reaches the same result.
[43] Discussed in Chapter 20§2(c).
[44] Priv. Ltr. Rul. 9242038.
[45] Priv. Ltr. Rul. 9530009.

2. Is the compensation reasonable? Are terms equal to similar commercial arrangements? Is there other evidence of private inurement in the relationship?

Proof that exempt purposes are served could include a broad range of factors. The ability to secure, on a part time basis, the medical staff, development personnel, and insurance claims staff necessary to operate a proposed health care facility, at an estimated cost savings equal to one-half of the organization's reserves, and allowing the facility to obtain licensing and begin serving the public six months earlier than otherwise, are good examples of factors indicating that an arrangement serves the organization's underlying exempt purpose. In the case of a blood bank's joint venture with a commercial laboratory for a plasma fractionation facility, costs were reduced, plasma was more effectively furnished, and thereby the project served the exempt organization's goals.[46]

Particularly if the manager is supervised by representatives of the EO, assuring adherence to the EO's standard of care for charitable constituents, there is no constraint against an EO operating efficiently and with a high level of expertise and professionalism. A university that lacked the skills to operate a first-rate university press and wanted to avoid the financial risks inherent in publishing purely academic works served its purposes in engaging a commercial publisher. It retained 5% of the gross revenues and proprietary rights in the publications.[47] A charitable health care provider can contract with a for-profit medical group to provide its needed radiology services.[48] A day care center can hire a for-profit center operator.[49]

An educational TV production company was permitted to undertake a project to be financed partly with funding from a commercial network.[50] It was noted that the amount was comparable to the typical investment in a commercial animated series on the network's part. In return, the network received exclusive broadcast rights for one year, renewal rights for four years, a percentage of the revenues from home video sales, if any, and programming control for purposes of meeting standards and practices required by the broadcasting industry.

The purchase and resale of a beachfront golf course to private developers, subject to a conservation easement, was found to serve the objectives of an organization focused on preserving the environment. The easement retention ensured protection of the natural habitat for fish and wildlife. Benefits to the developers were incidental to the mission-oriented goal accomplished.[51]

(b) Factors to Evaluate Reasonableness

A number of factors can indicate reasonableness of the compensation of a commercial vendor. An excessive amount, however, cannot be paid to secure such services. To test for reasonableness, another series of questions can be asked:

[46] Priv. Ltr. Rul. 7921018.
[47] Priv. Ltr. Rul. 9036025.
[48] Priv. Ltr. Rul. 9215046.
[49] Priv. Ltr. Rul. 9208028.
[50] Priv. Ltr. Rul. 9350044; see also Rev. Rul. 76-443, 1976-2 C.B. 149.
[51] Priv. Ltr. Rul. 9407005.

- Are the outside managers or professionals totally independent of the organization? Is the compensation being negotiated at arm's length? Are there interlocking directorates or family relationships? In other words, does the exempt organization retain ultimate authority over the activities being managed?[52]

- Are the terms equivalent to (or more favorable than) similar commercial arrangements? Is the price equal to the fair market value? Were competitive bids or comparable price studies obtained? Were CPAs, economists, appraisers, or others capable of determining the value engaged?

- Does the relationship prevent earnings from accruing to the benefit of the private individuals, or does it provide economic gain to the manager(s) at the expense of the exempt organization's charitable public interests?

- How is the compensation calculated: a fixed fee, percentage of gross or net income, or some other basis?

- Does the contract provide for sufficient funds to the exempt organization to compensate for its allocation of resources, the capital it is investing, and the risks it assumes?

- Is the contract period too long or too short?

- Are services rendered for constituents unable to pay? Will the credit policies of the manager recognize the organization's charitable nature and lack of profit motive in conducting the operation?

(c) Net Profit Agreements

A long-standing IRS policy frowns upon net profit agreements. On one hand, maximizing profits assures efficiency and may provide the funds for the exempt organization as well as for the manager, which is usually a desirable result. The quality of services rendered to the exempt constituency, however, must not be compromised by the manager's desire to produce profits. The IRS allows net profits-interest contracts if they contained a ceiling, cap, or maximum amount that the for-profit company or individual is to receive. The cap prevents windfall benefit to the managers.[53]

In any arrangement, it is advisable to require by contract that the compensation terms be alterable, if necessary, to retain tax-exempt status, along with self-serving language that the relationship must be conducted in a fashion that serves the exempt constituents of the engaging organization. Regarding pricing, the IRS has required that charitable services must be provided at the least feasible cost.[54] Again, the contract must require the manager to operate the project in a fashion that serves the organizational objectives.[55]

---

[52] *Broadway Theatre League of Lynchburg, Virginia, Inc. v. U.S.*, 293 F.Supp. 346 (W.D.Va. 1968) and *est of Hawaii v. Commissioner*, 71 T.C. 1067(1979), *aff'd* 647 f.2d 170 (9th Cir. 1981 unpublished).

[53] Gen. Coun. Memo. 38905.

[54] Rev. Rul. 75-198, 1975-1 C.B. 157.

[55] See §22.3 for additional consideration of this subject.

CHAPTER TWENTY-THREE

Electioneering and Lobbying

One possible detriment to achieving 501(c) exempt status is a limitation on an organization's participation in political campaigns and the legislative processes of governments. The amount and extent of the political and legislative activity allowed for any particular type of exempt organization is limited by both the Internal Revenue Code (IRC) of 1986 and the Federal Election Campaign Act (FECA). For organizations exempt under 501(c)(3), there is an absolute prohibition against participation in a political campaign on behalf of a candidate for public office and IRC §4955 places a penalty tax upon a (c)(3) organization and its managers who approved of any prohibited political activities. Private foundations are, in addition, strictly prohibited from conducting either legislative or campaign activity and penalties for such actions are imposed.[1] A (c)(3) organization that loses its exempt

---

[1] IRC §4945 discussed in Chapter 17.

status due to excessive electioneering or lobbying activities cannot thereafter qualify to obtain exemption as a (c)(4) organization.[2]

The regulations pertaining to many types of nonprofits exempt under IRC §501, including charities, civic associations, social clubs, cemetery companies, fraternal societies, and others, specifically require that the organization devote itself exclusively to achieving its defined purpose. "Exclusively" used for this purpose does not mean 100%. Whether political campaign and legislative activities further the exempt purpose of an organization is a question based upon its particular facts and circumstances.

23.1 ELECTION CAMPAIGN INVOLVEMENT

To understand the morass of rules and regulations that pertain to public policy activities, it is important to distinguish politically oriented activity that constitutes electioneering from attempts to influence the legislature, or lobbying activity. *Electioneering* involves intervention in the electoral process—the election or appointment of someone to public office. *Lobbying,* or *legislative,* activity involves attempts to influence those persons once they have been elected or appointed. Both types of activities are commonly referred to as political activity. The specific definition of political campaign activity found in the regulations says that an organization has political activity if it:

> participates or intervenes, directly or indirectly, in any political campaign on behalf of or in opposition to any candidate for public office. The term *candidate* for public office means an individual who offers himself, or is proposed by others, as a contestant for an elective public office, whether such office be national, state, or local.[3]

Efforts to create a new party or to stop a candidate's nomination certainly are treated as influencing the choice of candidates for public office, as well might be an effort to impeach someone in office. Those officials who occupy *public office* must be identified. Public office includes any position that is filled by a vote of the people at the federal, state, or local level. It must also be determined whether an appointment is in fact an election under the applicable local election laws. The answers vary from state to state. Not only is the person nominated by a political party a candidate, but also someone being drafted to run for office.

Organizations have unexpectedly lost exempt status for involvement in school board, water commission, and other local campaigns. The IRS found an organization lost its exempt status due to involvement in political party precinct elections.[4] An analysis of relevant local election laws indicated to the IRS that the precinct committee position possessed the characteristics of public office. The organization's counsel had advised it that the positions were administrative, not political. In another important distinction, appointed members of the federal judicial

---

[2] IRC §504.
[3] Reg. §1.501(c)(3)-1(c)(3)(iii).
[4] Gen. Coun. Memo. 39811.

system are not considered to be elected public officials. Attempts to influence the U.S. Senate confirmation of a nominee to the Supreme Court does not constitute intervention in a political campaign, but instead constitutes influencing or attempting to influence legislation.[5] The absolute ban against participation by (c)(3) organizations in political campaigns has given way to refinements and distinctions among actual campaign intervention, voter education, and other political activities as noted in the following discussion.

The absolute ban on spending money for political purposes by a charitable organization exempt under IRC §501(c)(3) is contained in both the organizational and operational tests for qualification.[6] Most other nonprofit organizations exempt from income tax are not similarly constrained from participating in political campaigns. All Form 990-filing exempt organizations are asked to submit the amount of their "political expenditures, direct or indirect." If any amount is reported, they are further directed to file Form 1120-POL. A(c)(3) organization answering this question with an amount is also penalized.[7] The 990 instructions define a *political expenditure* as one intended to influence the selection, nomination, election, or appointment of anyone to a federal, state, or local public office, or office in a political organization, or the election of presidential or vice presidential electors. The IRS notes it does not matter whether the attempt succeeds. An expenditure for this purpose includes a payment, distribution, loan, advance, deposit, gift of money, or anything of value. It also includes contract, promise, or agreement to make an expenditure, whether or not legally enforceable.

The Fund for the Study of Economic Growth and Tax Reform was formed to fund a project with the same name that became known as the Kemp Commission. It was established by then Senate Majority Leader Bob Dole and House Speaker Newt Gingrich who appointed its all Republican membership. Its purpose was to study ideas for tax reform and create economic opportunity through tax reduction. Though it conducted no overt lobbying, its creators and members were widely quoted making statements such as, "Tax reform is, of course, political (partisan)." The court found it to be an action organization that conferred substantial private benefit to the Republican party and did not qualify for tax exemption under 501(c)(3).[8]

The amount of permitted campaign involvement for each category of exempt organization is different. The basic guidelines are as follows:

- 501(c)(3): An organization qualified as charitable is absolutely prohibited from participation or intervention in a political election campaign.[9]

- 501(c)(4): A civic welfare organization must be "exclusively" devoted to social welfare (not, oddly enough, a 100% test), and the regulations simply

---

[5] The IRS announced that confirmation lobbying may be treated as a political expenditure for purposes of the IRC §527 tax unless the effort is handled in a segregated fund. IRS Announcement 88-114, 1988-37IRB 26.

[6] See Chapter 2.

[7] IRC §4955 discussed in §23.2(d).

[8] *Fund for Economic Growth and Tax Reform v. Commissioner*, 81 AFTR 2d¶98,472 (D.C. Dist.Ct.1998).

[9] Reg. §1.501(c)(3)-1(b)(3) and (c)(3)(iii); Exempt Organizations Handbook (IRM 7751) §370.

state that political activity does not promote social welfare. There is not a complete ban. The IRS has ruled that supporting candidates cannot be a primary purpose of a civic organization, but can be a secondary one.[10]

- 501(c)(5): A labor organization will not "be disqualified merely because it engages in some political activity."[11] Traditionally unions have been significantly involved in political elections.

- 501(c)(6): A business league's permissible political activity is not mentioned in the code, regulations, or handbook. Rulings indicate that, like (c)(5)s, business leagues may have political involvement as long as they devote their primary attention and resources to their exempt purposes.[12]

When political involvement is permitted, the percentage of the annual budget expended on the campaign may be quantified to prove that the activity is not a substantial one. Any amount of money in excess of $100 spent on political activity is taxed under IRC 527(f) with the filing of Form 1120-POL.[13] Federal election laws also make it unlawful for a corporation to make a contribution or expenditure in a federal election. To avoid both tax on an organizational level and controversy regarding the extent of political activity, a 501(c)(4), (5), or (6) or other exempt (but not a (c)(3)) can create a separate political action committee (PAC). Exhibit 23–1 illustrates these important rules.

The *Exempt Organizations Continuing Professional Education Technical Instruction Program for 1985* comments that it is possible for a relationship to exist between a (c)(3) organization and a political organization, as long as the political one is not established by, administered by, solicited for, or funded by the charitable organization. The article further states that a political organization could rent space from the charity at its fair market value or purchase its materials, but notes that this could produce unrelated business income (if the property is indebted).

23.2 VOTER EDUCATION VERSUS CANDIDATE PROMOTION

In addition to direct political campaign involvement, activities focused on public policy issues, such as who should be allowed to emit chemicals suspected of depleting the ozone layer, and the public policy makers who get to decide the issues, may also be classified as prohibited political activity.

Endorsements of political candidates or other electioneering statements by an organization's officers and directors in their individual capacities should not be attributed to the nonprofit organization itself. However, such endorsements will be imputed to the organization and can endanger exempt status of a (c)(3) organization, if the organization directly or indirectly authorized or ratified their actions.[14]

---

[10] Rev. Rul. 81-95, 1981-1 C.B. 332.
[11] Exempt Organizations Handbook (IRM 7751) §544.
[12] Rev. Rul. 61-177, 1961-2 C.B. 117.
[13] See §23.3 for definitions, tax rates, and other guidance regarding paying this tax.
[14] Gen. Coun. Memo. 33912.

Exhibit 23–1

PERMISSIBLE PAC INVOLVEMENT			
	(c)(3)	(c)(4)	(c)(5) or (6)
Establish the PAC	No*	Yes	Yes
Pay administrative costs	No**	Yes	Yes
Control PAC's board	No*	Yes	Yes
Allow PAC to solicit funds from exempt's members	No**	Yes	Yes
Use exempt's name (ABC Charity's PAC)	No***	Yes	Yes
Use exempt's mailing list	If PAC pays	Yes	Yes

*PAC cannot be created by the (c)(3) itself. Individual board or staff members can establish the PAC if they act in their individual capacities. The PAC essentially must be a "non-connected committee" in relation to the (c)(3).

**Election laws, which are generally more lenient than the tax rules, permit a charitable organization to create a PAC, pay for the PAC's overhead and administration, and raise funds from the exempt organization's constituents.

***Use of name implies support or endorsement of the campaign and also represents a donation of the (c)(3)'s intangible asset—its goodwill. State and federal laws conversely require the PAC name to include the name of its corporate, union, or other organizational sponsor.

Voter registration drives do not constitute intervention in a political campaign when conducted in a nonpartisan manner.[15] Drives that are targeted at members of a particular party, or that are in support of or against named candidates, are likely to be classified as political activity.[16] Partisan language on materials handed out to potential voter registrants that implies endorsement of a political persuasion can cause the campaign to be classified as political activity. Private foundations may finance multistate voter registration drives under very specific rules.[17]

(a) Voter Education

The IRS retroactively revoked an ostensible educational organization's exemption due to a variety of political activity. It found the following language to be incriminating:

> Conservatives in the U.S. Senate and House of Representatives are giving us economic prosperity, reducing government intervention and instilling pride in America and our way of life. All of this will be lost if

---

[15] *1992 Exempt Organizations Continuing Professional Education Technical Instruction Program*, Chapter N. Election Year Issues, page 427; standards applied by the Federal Election Commission can be applied to determine nonpartisanship.
[16] *American Campaign Academy v. Commissioner*, 92 T.C. 1053 (1989).
[17] See Chapter 17§2.

Conservatives like you and me do not head off the huge voter registration drive by the liberals.

The ruling contains a broad analysis of voter education and campaign workshops, and is mandatory reading for any organization participating in similar activities.[18] If an organization publishes materials that discuss and, particularly, criticize governmental policies and officials, it important that the information be nonpartisan. The following questions should be asked in evaluating whether the analysis constitutes participation in a campaign:

- Can the discussions be tied to a candidate running for election?
- Are the voting records of government officials reported, compared, or criticized?
- Is there an attempt to affect voter acceptance or rejection of a candidate?
- Are materials distributed only to the membership or to the public?
- Do the evaluations relate directly to the organization's exempt purpose?
- Are the reports based on scientific studies or research?
- Do the comments include "full and fair exposition" of all facts about the issue, or will they be construed as biased opinion?

The following criteria are used to judge whether publication of Congressional representatives' voting records on selected issues constitutes political action:[19]

- Voting records of all incumbents are presented.
- Candidates for re-election are not identified.
- No comment is made on any individual's qualification for public office.
- No candidate is endorsed or rejected.
- No comparison of the candidates is made.
- A statement is included pointing out the inherent limitations of judging a candidate on the basis of selected votes, and stating the need to consider such unrecorded matters as performance on subcommittees and constituent service.
- The organization does not distribute the report widely, but distributes it only to members.
- Publication is not targeted toward particular areas in which elections are occurring, nor timed to concur with elections.

During the 1996 election season, the IRS reiterated the standards used to judge permissible a particular voter education project.[20] Charity M sponsored candidate fo-

---

[18] Priv. Ltr. Rul. 9117001.
[19] Rev. Rul. 80-282, 1980-2 C.B. 154, amplifying Rev. Rul. 78-248, 1978-1 C.B. 154; Gen. Coun. Memo. 38444.
[20] Priv. Ltr. Rul. 9635003 in reliance on Rev. Rul. 86-95, 1986-2 C.B. 73.

rums and issued candidate evaluations. A scientifically selected group of voters chosen to reflect the demographics of the state evaluated the candidates, picked those eligible to debate, and issued their personal opinions on the candidates. The ruling outlined the following factors to consider whether the method used to choose candidates invited to debate was aimed at voter education or at influencing the campaign:

- Whether inviting all legally qualified candidates is impractical

- Whether the organization adopted reasonable, objective criteria for determining which candidates to invite

- Whether criteria were applied consistently and to all candidates

- Whether all candidates are treated fairly and impartially without promoting or advancing a particular candidate over another

Charity M's limiting the candidate forums to less than all the legally qualified candidates was found not to be campaign intervention. The holding of press conferences and publication of the opinions of its voter groups, however, was considered impermissible and, therefore, subject to the penalty tax. The content of a "CC" (presumably Christian Coalition) organization's fund-raising letters were deemed to violate the prohibition against political intervention and result in taxable expenditures under §4955. The letters encouraged readers to imagine certain political candidates as defeated and also saying "together we can change the shape of American politics."[21]

(b) Examples of Permissible Political Education

The IRS has issued the following guidance regarding campaign involvement that is considered educational:

- Public television and radio stations can provide air time to political candidates as long as it does so equally to candidates.[22] The Federal Communications Commission also has procedures for neutral debates or forums that allow candidates to explain their views to the public.

- Publishing a newsletter containing voting records and grading the votes according to the organization's ideals, without any expression of endorsement for or opposition to the candidates themselves, is educational. The newsletter's circulation must be directed at constituents and must not be aimed at affecting an election.[23]

- Disseminating information concerning campaign practices, furnishing teaching aids to political science and civic teachers, and publicizing proposed codes of fair campaign practices without soliciting the signing or endorsement of the code by candidates, are all qualified political education.[24]

---

[21] Priv. Ltr. Rul. 9609007.
[22] Rev. Rul. 74-574, 1974-2 C.B. 160.
[23] Gen. Coun. Memo. 38444.
[24] Rev. Rul. 76-456, 1976-2 C.B. 151.

- As a part of a political science program, a university can require students to participate in political campaigns for candidates of their choice.[25]

- A student newspaper's coverage of political campaigns and student editorial opinions about such elections are not considered to be university political activity.[26]

- An exempt organization established for the purpose of collecting and collating campaign speeches, interviews, and other materials of a candidate for a historically important elective office for donation to a university or public library, was engaged in permissible political education.[27]

The IRS took a surprisingly lenient position regarding peace promotions run during the 1984 Presidential campaign.[28] Advertisements urged the reader to "Think about it when you vote this November," and to "Choose leaders who will lead us away from a nuclear nightmare, not into one." The IRS "reluctantly concluded that the organization probably did not intervene in the campaign," apparently because the ads did not overtly support a candidate (even though everyone knew that the peace candidate was Democratic nominee Walter Mondale).

(c) Impermissible Political Activity

The IRS found political activity that constituted impermissible electioneering for a (c)(3) organization in the following examples:

- Attempting to improve a public school system by campaigning on behalf of candidates for election to the school board is political campaign activity.[29]

- A bar association that published a rating system for elective judicial candidates was also deemed to be intervening in a political campaign.[30]

- Assisting a governor-elect was held to be involvement in a political campaign. The organization interviewed and screened applicants for appointive offices and prepared the legislative message to reflect a party's platform and budget.[31]

A school to train political campaign workers was found to operate for partisan purposes because all of its graduates were affiliated with the Republican party and therefore operated for substantial nonexempt (political) purpose.[32]

---

[25] Rev. Rul. 72-512, 1972-2 C.B. 246.
[26] Rev. Rul. 72-513, 1972-2 C.B. 246.
[27] Rev. Rul. 79-321, 1970-1 C.B. 129.
[28] Tech. Adv. Memo. 8936002.
[29] Rev. Rul. 67-71, 1967-1 C.B. 125.
[30] *The Bar Association of the City of New York v. Commissioner,* 88-2 USTC ¶9535 (2nd Cir. 1988), *rev'g* 89 T.C. 599, 609-610 (1987).
[31] Rev. Rul. 74-117, 1974-1 C.B. 128.
[32] *American Campaign Academy vs. U.S.,* 92 T.C. 1053 (1989).

(d) Penalty Tax on (c)(3) Political Expenditures

Until 1987, the only tool the IRS had to punish a (c)(3) organization for participation in an election campaign was revocation of its exempt status. While making it clear such activity continued to be absolutely prohibited, Congress believed a penalty was a suitable sanction for minor violations of the rule prohibiting political involvement. The primary targets were ostensibly *educational* organizations established to promote the campaign of particular candidates and/or controlled by candidates. To avoid loss of its exempt status, the organization is expected to correct a political expenditure by recovering the money to the extent possible and adopting safeguards to prevent future political expenditures.[33] If the violation is due to reasonable cause and not to willful neglect, the tax may be abated.[34]

A *first-tier* excise tax of at least 10% (up to 100%) is imposed on political campaign expenditures of a (c)(3) organization, in addition to a $2\frac{1}{2}$ percent tax on the *manager(s)* involved in the activity.[35] Managers subject to the tax are those officers, directors, trustees, or other individuals with authority or responsibility to make the expenditure in question.[36] The initial tax is not imposed if the organization and its managers can prove that the political expenditure was not willful and flagrant, that the funds have been recovered, and that the organization has established safeguards to prevent future political expenditures.[37] The tax is reported on Form 4720 (Appendix 27–6). Managers who, after full disclosure of relevant facts, relied upon the advice of counsel in approving the activity, are not ordinarily considered as willfully approving of the expenditure.[38]

The §4955 regulations and accompanying §§6852 and 7409 emphasize the continued and concurrent application of the absolute prohibition against a §501(c)(3) organization's participation in an election campaign. Political expenditures subject to the tax are defined by reference to activity that causes a (c)(3) organization to be classified as an *action organization* due to campaign intervention.[39]

Any expenditures by a *candidate-controlled* organization are treated as political expenses. Such an exempt organization is one both formed *primarily* to and is availed of (operated) primarily to promote a candidate or prospective candidate.[40] An organization is effectively controlled when a candidate or prospective candidate has a continuing, substantial involvement in the organization's day-to-day operations. Mere affiliation with the candidate or acquaintance of the candidate with the organization's directors and officers is not sufficient. Conducting research, study, or other educational activities regarding issues of concern to the candidate likewise do not make the organization candidate controlled. The fact that the research is made available only to the candidate, however, indicates that the purpose of the organization is to promote that person, as will payment of his

---

[33] H.Rep. No. 100-391, 100th Cong., 1st Sess. 1623-1627 (1987).
[34] IRC §§4961-4963.
[35] IRC §4955(a)(1).
[36] IRC §4955(f)(2); Reg. §53.4955-1(b)(2).
[37] Reg. §53.4955-1(b)(2).
[38] Reg. §53.4955-1(b)(7).
[39] Reg. §53.4955-1(c)(1) cross references to Reg. §1.501(c)(3)-1(c)(3)(iii).
[40] IRC §4955(d)(2).

or her traveling expenses.[41] The code specifically lists expenses paid for travel, speeches, polling, surveys, advertising, and similar expenses of a person in office or running for office as examples of such political expenditures.[42]

23.3 TAX ON POLITICAL EXPENDITURES

Until 1968, the tax status of political organizations and political expenditures was uncertain, except for the absolute prohibition against participation by a charitable (c)(3) organization. In that year, the IRS announced that the investment income of a political organization was to be taxed by filing a fiduciary income tax return on Form 1041. Political contributions received would continue to be untaxed as gifts, but would not be deductible for the giver.

Effective in 1975, IRC §527 entitled *Political Organizations* took its place among the code sections governing nonprofit organizations; Form 1120-POL was introduced for reporting the taxable income. Essentially any investment income of an organization that spends money for political (called exempt function) purposes is taxed. A political organization with no more than $100 of investment income need not file. The tax applies to nonprofits devoted solely to political activity and to §501(c) exempt organizations that expend their own funds for political purposes. The definitions and constraints are found both in IRC §527 and in the Federal Election Campaign Act.

(a) What is a Political Organization?

The Internal Revenue Code defines a political organization as:[43]

> A party, committee, association, fund, or other organization (whether or not incorporated) organized and operated primarily for the purpose of directly or indirectly accepting contributions or making expenditures, or both, for an exempt function.

The exempt function for a PAC is:

> The function of influencing or attempting to influence the selection, nomination, election, or appointment of any individual to any federal, state, or local public office or office in a political organization, or the election of presidential or vice-presidential electors, whether or not such individual or electors are selected, nominated, or appointed.

A qualifying campaign group can function in favor of or in opposition to candidate(s).

---

[41] After the House Ethics committee hearings on Newt Gingrich, his organization was examined by the IRS and found to be educational.
[42] IRC §4955(d); Reg. §53.4955-1(c)(2)(ii).
[43] IRC §527(e)(2).

A public office for this purpose is:

> based upon the facts and circumstances based upon the principles consistent with the private foundation rules, which essentially mean the candidate must seek to become a government official.[44]

Elected federal executive or legislative officials, appointed federal executive or judicial officers, elected or appointed officials in any branch of the government in any state that receive pay in excess of $20,000, and certain other government workers are listed in the regulations. The distinction between a public office holder and a public employee is based on whether the individual's activities include performing independent policy-making functions.[45]

A political organization's exempt activities focus on what the regulations refer to as the "selection process." Any amounts spent to advance an individual's campaign for public office or to defeat another, including unannounced candidates, is treated as exempt function. The following examples of qualifying expenditures are provided in the regulations.[46]

- Prospective candidate's expenses to travel throughout a state to rally support for intended race

- Voice and speech lessons taken to improve the candidate's skills

- An officeholder and candidate for reelection's purchase of tickets to attend a testimonial dinner

- Between-election activities to train staff members, draft party rules, implement party reform proposals, and sponsor a party convention

- Conducting seminars and conferences intended to influence persons who attend to support individuals to public office whose political philosophy is in harmony with the organization

- Payment of debts and other expenses, such as reasonable cash awards to campaign workers,[47] incurred after the conclusion of a candidate's campaign

The IRS has also explained exempt function expenditures to include the cost of conducting public opinion polls and voter canvasses,[48] election night parties,[49] direct mail campaigns,[50] and grassroots lobbying focusing on opinions of candidates on selected issues targeted in a geographic area and timed to coincide with an election.[51]

---

[44] Reg. §1.527-2(d).
[45] Reg. §53.4946-1(g).
[46] Reg. §1.527-2(c).
[47] Rev. Rul. 87-119, 1987-2 CB 151.
[48] Rev. Rul. 79-13, 1979-1 CB 208.
[49] Rev. Rul. 87-119, 1987-2 CB 151.
[50] Rev. Rul. 79-13, 1979-1 CB 208.
[51] Priv. Ltr. Rul. 9724005.

A political organization need not engage exclusively in activities that are exempt functions although campaign-related activities should be primary. The distinction between exempt and nonexempt expenses is important because any funds spent for nonexempt functions lose their tax-free status. Exempt function expenses include anything that supports candidates seeking election.[52] The activities need not focus on any one particular candidate or race, though they must involve the selection process.[53] Examples of expenses treated as nonexempt function (because they do not involve choosing a candidate) include:[54]

- Nonpartisan educational workshops
- An incumbent's office expenses
- Nonpartisan voter registration or get-out-the-vote efforts
- Committee to support an initiative or referendum measure

Permissible expenditures by political campaign committees may include certain lobbying efforts although such expenses may be treated as nonexempt function expenses. In a situation where a candidate was named and pictured on the flyer of a statewide referendum on fiscal responsibility, the expense was an exempt function because the candidate was identified as the leader of the effort. Even though the candidate had not yet filed to run for governor, the ruling found that the piece was packaged to identify him as a potential candidate for governor, and was therefore an exempt function expense for the campaign committee.[55]

A political organization must be organized for the primary purpose of carrying on the exempt function of influencing the selection, nomination, or election of public office holders. Formal articles of incorporation, association, or trust are acceptable, but are not required. "Consideration is given to statements of the members as to how they intend to operate the political organization primarily to carry on one or more exempt functions."[56] An officeholder's newsletter fund is taxed as a political organization, but funds cannot be expended for campaign, personal, or any other purposes. Special distinctions, affecting tax rates and permissible activities, apply to segregated funds and to the principal campaign committee of any office seeker. The regulations and legislative history should be studied for those types of organizations.

(b) Taxable Income

Both a §501(c) exempt organization and a political organization that spends any amount directly for a political expenditure as defined by IRC §527 is taxed on such

---

[52] *1992 Exempt Organizations Continuing Professional Education Technical Instruction Program*, Chapter N. Election Year Issues, page 448.
[53] Rev. Ruls. 79-12 and 79-13, 1979-1 C.B. 208.
[54] Reg. §1.527-2(a)(3).
[55] Priv. Ltr. Rul. 913008; see also Priv. Ltr. Ruls. 9516006, 9409003, and 9320002 and *Exempt Organizations Continuing Professional Education Technical Instruction Program Textbook* 1995 (for Fiscal Year 1996) Topic O, "Election Year Issues."
[56] Reg. §1.527-2(a)(2).

expenditure or its net investment income (interest, dividends, rents, royalties, and capital gains), whichever is lower. A grant from one exempt organization to another exempt organization to be used specifically for political purposes will also be taxed to the granting exempt organization. Both organizations exempt under 501(c) that make political expenditures and political organizations file Form 1120-POL where a tax is essentially imposed on investment income. The highest corporate income tax rate applies as a rule.[57] A designated *principal campaign committee* of a congressional candidate is taxed at the appropriate corporate rate for its level of income.[58]

Taxable income is taxed at the highest corporate tax rate (currently 35 percent) and is defined to include:[59]

- Gross income for the year (not including exempt function)

- Less deductions directly connected to production of such income, excluding exempt function expenses, but including an allocable part of dual-use facilities or personnel

- Less a modification (reduction) of $100 (except for newsletter funds).

No net operating loss or dividend received deductions are allowed.[60] Only those exempt function revenues expended for exempt functions are excluded from taxable income. Exempt function revenues for this purpose consist solely of:

- Contributions of money or other property;

- Membership dues or assessments; and

- Proceeds of fund-raising or entertainment events, including sales of political campaign materials not sold in a commercial manner.[61]

A transfer of political contributions or dues collected by an organization to a segregated fund is not treated as a political expenditure.[62] The interest an organization earns by temporarily keeping PAC funds in a general interest-bearing checking account was found to provide administrative efficiency and did not constitute prohibited investment of the funds by the organization.[63] For ease of collection, a professional association and a labor union issued billings for normal dues and PAC contributions together to its membership. Moneys were collected continually throughout the year. For the organizations' convenience, PAC funds were periodically transferred (in one case twice a month and in the other once a month) to the PAC. The "negligible" amount of interest that was earned by the exempt organization on funds it temporarily held was not taxed.

---

[57] IRC §527(b)(1).
[58] IRC §527(h).
[59] IRC §527(c)(1).
[60] IRC §527(c)(2), Reg. §1.527-4.
[61] Reg. §1.527-3(a).
[62] Reg. §1.527-6(e)(3).
[63] Priv. Ltr. Ruls. 9105001 and 9105002.

(c) Segregated Funds (Political Action Committees)

A segregated fund, usually called a political action committee (PAC), can be created by a §501(c) exempt organization, or by any individual, that plans to engage in political activity and wishes to ensure proper identification of the funds subject to tax.[64] A segregated fund is treated as a political organization for tax purposes. Thus, when funds are collected from the members or employees of the exempt organization and are paid directly into the segregated fund, the conduit exempt organization is able to prove that it has not made a political expenditure on its own behalf.

An exempt organization's indirect expenses, such as its accounting department, attributable to the creation of and management of a PAC are not necessarily treated as political expenditures. The regulations direct that they are exempt function expense "to the extent provided" in a reserved, or unissued section. Thus while mentioning the issue, the regulations provide no guidance. The legislative history indicates Congress intended indirect expense not be allowed as deductions against taxable investment income.[65] A prudent organization can ask its PAC to reimburse its expense of soliciting and paying over the funds to avoid this issue.[66]

The Federal Election Campaign Act specifically permits labor unions and business leagues to spend money for internal communications involving support of particular candidates with members and their families, but not with the general public. They are also permitted to establish, administer, and solicit contributions for PACs.

23.4 LOBBYING ACTIVITY OF §501(c)(3) ORGANIZATIONS

Carrying on propaganda or otherwise attempting to influence legislation, commonly referred to as lobbying activity, cannot be a substantial part of the activities of a §501(c)(3) organization. A (c)(3) organization must devote itself *exclusively* to one or more charitable objectives and primarily conduct activities that advance its mission.[67] Organizations that conduct excessive lobbying and those whose purposes can only be accomplished through the passage of legislation are considered *action organizations* that cannot qualify for (c)(3) exempt status.[68]

All exempt organizations, except private foundations and title-holding companies, can engage in lobbying or attempts to influence legislation. The extent of the allowed involvement differs for each category. For (c)(3) exempt organizations, different rules apply for organizations falling in each of three categories:

- Exempt organizations that elect under §501(h) to measure their permissible lobbying activity using the expenditure test.

---

[64] Reg. §1.527-2(b)(1).

[65] S. Rep. No. 93-1374, 93d Cong., 2d Sess. 29 (1974).

[66] For a more thorough discussion of political organizations, see the 23-page article entitled "Political Organizations," by Milton Cerney and Frances R. Hill, published in *The Exempt Organization Tax Review,* vol. 13, no. 4, April 1996.

[67] Reg. §1.501(c)(3)-1(c)(3).

[68] See Chapter 2 § 2(g).

- Nonelecting organizations measuring permissible lobbying under the ill-defined substantial part test.

- Private foundations that can conduct absolutely no lobbying.[69]

The definitions and numerical tests applied to measure the permissible amount of lobbying under the first two tests listed are very different. Only a §501(c)(3) organization electing to calculate its permissible lobbying expenditures under §501(h) can apply those rules. A business league, civic welfare organization, or labor union that discloses the nondeductible portion of dues attributable to lobbying expenditures to its members[70] may spend an unlimited amount of expenditures on lobbying that accomplish its exempt purposes.[71]

In addition to the tax rules, the Lobbying Disclosure Act of 1995 requires, effective beginning in 1996, certain exempt organizations to register to conduct lobbying activities and subsequently to file semiannual reports.[72] Organizations subject to this registration requirement are those that:

- Employ a lobbyist, or one who makes at least two lobbying contacts in a six-month period and devotes at least 20% of his or her time to lobbying, and

- Incur, or expect to incur, lobbying expenditures of $20,000 or more in a six-month period

The fashion in which the tax-exempt organization defines *lobbying* for this purpose is determined by the federal tax rule the organization applies. A §501(c)(3) organization that elects to calculate its permissible lobbying expenditures under §501(h) can apply those rules; a nonelecting charity must follow rather unique standards. A business league, civic welfare organization, or labor union that discloses the nondeductible portion of dues attributable to lobbying expenditures to its members as described in Chapter 6 may apply the federal tax rules for lobbying disclosure purposes. The IRS 1996 training manual contains a 107-page chapter, entitled "Lobbying Issues," that is a must-read for any tax-exempt organization planning to conduct any more than an inconsequential amount of lobbying activity.[73]

(a) Rules for Nonelecting Exempt Organizations

A charitable organization exempt under 501(c)(3) choosing not to make a §501(h) election to govern its lobbying activity is subject to the basic exemption criteria requiring that *no substantial part* of its activities consist of attempting to influence legislation by propaganda or otherwise. The definitions and other rules applied by organizations making an election to report lobbying activity under §501(h) cannot be used to identify and define lobbying for those organizations that do not

---

[69] See Chapter 17.
[70] See Chapter 6§4.
[71] The IRS *Continuing Professional Education, Exempt Organization Technical Instruction Program for FY 1997* entitled "Lobbying Issues."
[72] Form LD-2 due in February and August.
[73] *Exempt Organizations Continuing Professional Education (CPE) Program. Technical Instruction Program for FY 1997*, Topic P.

elect. A portion of an organization's operating expenses is allocable to the lobbying activity, making a detailed allocation of organizational costs necessary absent the election. Nonelecting exempt organizations should carefully study the IRS recommendations for making such allocations to calculate costs associated with lobbying activity.[74] In several instances the IRS suggests such an organization be guided by provisions governing those organizations that elect §501(h). A (c)(3) with substantial legislative activity is an *action organization* and does not qualify for exemption.[75] A (c)(3) organization is regarded as attempting to influence legislation if it:

- Contacts or urges the public to contact members of a legislative body for the purpose of proposing, supporting, or opposing legislation; or

- Advocates the adoption or rejection of particular legislation[76]

Legislation is defined generally for (c)(3) purposes to include "actions by the Congress, by any State legislature, by any local council or similar governing body, or by the public in a referendum, initiative, constitutional amendment, or similar procedure."[77] Administrative bodies are not considered as governing for this purpose.[78] After the Senate hearings on Robert Bork's nomination to the Supreme Court, the IRS issued notice that the U.S. Senate's action of advising and consenting to a judicial appointment *is legislative activity*.[79]

In interpreting the congressional mandate to limit exempt organization lobbying, the IRS has adopted the following clarifying rules:

- The desirability of the legislation (such as protecting the environment, animals, or children, or other issues unquestionably serving the public good) does not influence an activities classification as lobbying.[80] Legislation can include zoning matters if the decisions are under the jurisdiction of a local council or legislative representatives.[81] [Actions by executive, judicial, or administrative bodies are specifically not legislative matters under §4911].[82] Legislation includes proposals for making laws in other countries.[83] Acts undertaken by the organization itself, not by its members or constituents as individuals, are constrained.[84]

---

[74] Rev. Ruls. 78-111, 78-112, 78-113, and 78-114, 1978-1 C.B. 41, 42, 43, and 44 (the so-called Halloween rulings).

[75] See Chapter 2§2(g).

[76] Reg. §1.501(c)(3)-1(b)(3).

[77] Reg. §1.501(c)(3)-1(b)(3)(i); note this definition is the same as contained in Reg. §56.4911-(2)(d)(1)(I) applicable to charities electing §501(h).

[78] IRS *Exempt Organization Technical Instruction Program for FY 1997,* Topic P "Lobbying Issues," page 271.

[79] IRS Notice 88-76. 1988-2 C.B. 392.

[80] Rev. Rul. 67-293, 1967-2 C.B. 185.

[81] Rev. Rul. 67-6, 1967-1 C.B. 135 regarding a historical restoration association.

[82] Reg. §56.4911-2(d)(4).

[83] Rev. Rul. 73-440, 1973-2 C.B. 177.

[84] Rev. Rul. 72-513, 1972-2 C.B. 246; Gen. Coun. Memos. 34631 (Oct. 4, 1971) and 39414 (Feb. 29, 1984).

Supporting activities of an educational nature—study, research, preparation of papers—that concern subjects of legislation may be considered as lobbying expenditures.[85] The time spent discussing public issues, formulating and agreeing upon positions, and studying them preparatory to adopting a position must be taken into account as legislative activity. Information gathered prior to the moment the exempt organization makes a legislative appeal can be associated with the later act of lobbying.[86] Nonpartisan analysis, study, or research of matters pertaining to legislation will not constitute attempts to influence legislation if it does not advocate the adoption or rejection of the legislation.[87] Since nonpartisan analysis is oriented to issues, a fair exposition of both sides of the issue is expected to be presented.[88] It is these vague standards that the 501(h) election seeks to replace as explained in the following section.

There is no precise mathematical test for the *substantial part* test. One court opined that using "a percentage test to determine whether activities were substantial obscures the complexity of balancing the organization's activities in relation to its objectives and circumstances."[89] Nevertheless a common measure of substantial is the actual dollars expended by the organization on lobbying efforts. No specific limit is provided, and as little as 5% of an organization's budget has been questioned.[90] Moreover, the efforts of volunteers, the amount of research and discussion to formulate a position on a legislative matter, the continuous rather than intermittent attention to the matters, and the whole context in which the activity is conducted may also be considered.[91] In a more precise fashion, only actual dollars spent by the organization are considered for an exempt organization electing to use the expenditure test.

For business expense deduction purposes, goodwill advertising or institutional pieces intended to bring the organization's name before the general public by presenting views on economic, financial, social, or other subjects of a general nature is not lobbying if the material does not directly or indirectly propose, support, or oppose legislation.[92] When the information published has some connection to pending legislation, potentially limited grassroots lobbying may be found.[93]

(b) The §501(h) Election

Congress has enacted specific numerical parameters and definitions within which (c)(3)s can conduct lobbying efforts when the organization makes an election provided in IRC §501(h). The tax-exempt status of an electing organization can

---

[85] *League of Women Voters v. U.S.* 180 F. Supp. 379(Ct.Cl. 1960), *cert. denied*, 364 U.S. 882 (1960).

[86] *Kuper v. Commissioner,* 332 F.2d 562(3d Cir. 1964), *cert. denied*, 379 U.S. 920(1964).

[87] *Hasall v. U.S.,* 500 F.2d 1133, 1144 (Ct.Cl. 1974, *cert. denied,* 419 U.S. 1107 (1975); also see Rev. Ruls. 64-195, 1964-2 C.B. 138 and 70-79, 1970-1 C.B. 127.

[88] The IRS applies a *methodology* standard to determine when information is educational as discussed in Chapter 5.

[89] *Christian Echoes National Ministry, Inc. v. U.S.,* 470 F.2d 849 (10th Cir. 1972), *cert. den.,* 414 U.S. 864 (1973).

[90] *Seasongood v. Commissioner,* 227 F.2d 907, 912 (6th Cir. 1955).

[91] *League of Women Voters v. U.S., supra* note 84. Gen. Coun. Memo. 36148 (Jan. 28, 1975).

[92] Reg. §1.162-29(a)(2).

[93] See §23.5(b).

only be revoked if the exempt organization normally has expenditures to carry on propaganda, or otherwise attempt to influence legislation, that exceed prescribed limits. It is important to emphasize that these rules apply *only* to charities electing their application. The regulations under IRC §501(h) and the parallel penalty provision, IRC §4911, total 57 pages, and were proposed and reproposed three times over a four-year period before the final version became effective on August 31, 1990. The rules are surprisingly lenient for public charities. Churches and their integrated auxiliaries, private foundations, supporting organizations of business leagues, unions, and civic associations, and private foundations are not permitted to make the election.[94]

The regulations interact with a number of other provisions: Regulations under IRC §501 (conversion of (c)(3) to a (c)(4)); §501(h); §504 (revocation of exempt status due to excessive lobbying); §4911 (excise tax on excessive lobbying); §4945 (nonpartisan analysis by private foundations); §170, §2055, and §2522 (limitations on charitable donations); and §162(e) (nondeductible dues due to lobbying by business and civic leagues and unions). The following material only skims the surface. A comprehensive treatment of the subject can be found in *Charity, Advocacy, and the Law*,[95] a good reference book for any organization conducting more than an insignificant amount of lobbying.

(c) Definition of Lobbying

Lobbying is defined in IRC §4911 as

- Any attempt to influence any legislation through an attempt to affect the opinions of the general public or any segments thereof, or

- Any attempt to influence any legislation through communication with any member or employee of a legislative body, or with any government official or employee who may participate in the formulation of specific legislation.

The IRS Handbook, however, cautions that lobbying is not limited to these definitions. The regulations contain eight pages of examples on direct and grassroots lobbying alone that should be studied. The facts and circumstances of each communication is to be examined.

(d) What Is Legislation?

Legislation is defined to include "action with respect to acts, bills, resolutions, or similar items by the Congress, any state legislature, any local council, or similar governing body, or by the public in a referendum, initiative, constitutional amendment, or similar item."[96] Legislative bodies do not include executive, judicial, or administrative bodies such as school boards, housing authorities, sewer and water districts, and zoning board, whether they are appointive or elective.

[94] IRC §501(h)(5).
[95] Bruce Hopkins (New York: John Wiley, 1992).
[96] IRC §4911(2); Reg. §56.4911-2(d); essentially same language applied to nonelecting charities.

Specific legislation, as the name implies, includes both legislation that has already been introduced in a legislative body and a specific legislative proposal that the organization either supports or opposes. A referendum or ballot initiative becomes specific legislation when the petition seeking signatures is first circulated among voters.[97] Before a bill is actually formulated, debate about a subject that may become the subject of legislation is not lobbying.

A *similar item*, according to examples in the regulations, includes confirmation of a cabinet level appointee and a Supreme Court nominee.[98] A proposed treaty subject to Senate approval is a legislative matter from the time when treaty negotiations start.[99] Referenda and ballot initiatives are legislative actions in which the members of the general public constitute the legislature, so an attempt to influence a referendum vote is direct lobbying.[100]

(e) What Lobbying Is Not

IRC §4911(d) excludes the following activities from the meaning of the term *influencing legislation:*

- Dissemination of the results of nonpartisan analysis, study, or research

- Provision of technical advice or assistance in response to a written request by a governmental body

- Appearances before, or communications to, any legislative body with respect to a possible decision by that body that might affect the existence of the organization, its powers and duties, its tax-exempt status, or the deduction of contributions to it (self-defense)

- Communications between the organization and its bona fide members with respect to legislation or proposed legislation of direct interest to them, unless the communications directly encourage the members to influence legislation or urge members to contact nonmembers to influence legislation

- Routine communications with government officials or employees, including the executive branch and agencies.[101]

Nonpartisan Analysis.   An independent and objective exposition on a particular subject that advocates a viewpoint on legislation is not considered lobbying if it qualifies as nonpartisan analysis, study, or research.[102] Sufficiently fair and full exposition of the pertinent facts on the subject, not merely unsupported opinion, must be communicated to the general public to enable the public to form an

---

[97] Reg. §56.4911-2(d)(1)(ii).
[98] Reg. §56.4911-2(b)(4)(ii)(B), Example (6).
[99] Reg. §56.4911-2(d)(1)(i).
[100] Reg. §56.4911-2(b)(1)(iii); see also Gregory L. Colvin and Lowell Finley, *Seize the Initiative,* Alliance for Justice, Washington, D.C., 1996.
[101] Reg. §56.4911-2(c).
[102] Reg. §56.4911-2(c)(1).

independent opinion or conclusion. Preparing a paper on a state issue and sending the study to members of state legislature when there is no legislation pending is not legislative lobbying.[103]

The information can be communicated in any form, whether visual or auditory: radio, television, public forums, magazines, publications, or newspapers. No direct encouragement to "take action" may be contained in the materials. If the research material is subsequently used for lobbying purposes, the expenses of preparing the research paid within six months of such use is reclassified as a lobbying expense.[104] The regulations contain eleven pages of examples.

Grassroots Lobbying. Contacting the general public (instead of the legislators themselves) is classified as grassroots lobbying.[105] More restrictive limitations apply to this indirect lobbying method, so the distinction between *direct* and *grassroots* is important. Grassroots expenditures cannot comprise more than 25% of an electing organization's overall lobbying expenditures. The portion of a member's dues attributable to grassroots (and direct) lobbying is not deductible under IRC §162.

This issue has been the focal point of much controversy between the IRS and the exempt community. The regulations somewhat narrowly define grassroots lobbying to include only communications that contain all of the following three elements:

1. It refers to *specific legislation* (including legislation that has already been introduced in a legislative body and specific legislative proposals that the exempt organization either supports or proposes);

2. It reflects a view on such legislation; and

3. It encourages the recipient of the communication to take action with respect to the legislation.[106]

Mass media communication may be classified as lobbying even if it does not meet the three-part definition. When a press release or advertisement sponsored by the exempt organization and taking a position on legislation is published within two weeks before the vote is scheduled, such a publication is considered grassroots lobbying if it either refers to the highly publicized legislation or encourages the public to lobby about the legislation.

A requisite characteristic of a lobbying communication is that it directly urges the public to take action. *Taking action* is urged directly if any one of the first three elements below is present. The fourth attribute, taken alone, does not constitute a call to action.[107]

1. The communication states that the recipient should contact legislators, their employees, or other governmental representatives who may participate in the formulation of the legislation.

---

[103] Reg. §56.4911-2(b)(4) Example (3).
[104] Reg. §56.4911-2(c)(v).
[105] IRC §4911(c)(3); Reg. §56.4911.2(b)(2).
[106] Reg. §56.4911-2(b)(2)(ii).
[107] Reg. §56.4911-2(b)(2)(iii).

2. The address, telephone number, or similar information facilitating contact is furnished on the notice, letter, or other form of communication.

3. A petition, tear-off postcard, or the like is provided for the recipient to communicate views to the appropriate governmental party.

4. One or more legislators who will vote on the legislation is specifically identified as opposing it or undecided, is the recipient's representative, or is a member of the committee considering the legislation.

Attempts to influence highly publicized legislation, such as paid advertisements placed in mass media (television, radio, billboards, and general circulation newspapers and magazines) that do not contain one of the take action elements may still be grassroots lobbying if

- The advertisement is placed within two weeks prior to a vote by a legislative body or a committee (but not a subcommittee).

- The advertisement offers a view on the general subject of the legislation, and either refers to the legislation or encourages the public to communicate with legislators on the general subject of the legislation.[108]

The presumption that an advertisement fits these conditions can be rebutted if the organization can show that

- It regularly publishes such communications without regard to the timing of legislation, or

- The timing of the particular advertisement is unrelated to the legislative action. In other words, if the organization can prove that it placed the advertisement without any knowledge that the vote would occur within two weeks, it may escape its classification as grassroots lobbying.

Member communications are governed by additional standards. The member rules were substantially altered each time the proposed regulations were issued (in 1980, 1986, and again in 1988), becoming more lenient with each new version. Under the following specific conditions, information sent to members is *not* treated as lobbying:

- The communication is directed only at members;

- The communication refers to and reflects a view on specific legislation that is of direct interest to the organization and its members;

- Members are not encouraged to engage in direct lobbying; and

- Grassroots lobbying is not encouraged.

Direct lobbying occurs when the third requirement is failed; grassroots lobbying occurs when the fourth one is failed. A *member* is one who pays dues or makes a

---

[108] Reg. §56.4911-2(b)(5)(ii).

contribution of more than a nominal amount, makes a contribution of more than a nominal amount of time, or is one of a limited number of "life or honorary" members. Prospective members are not considered members. A member of one of an affiliated group of organizations is treated as a member of each of the exempt organizations in the group.[109]

23.5 PERMISSIBLE AMOUNTS OF LOBBYING

Nonelecting 501(c)(3)s must prove that their lobbying activities do not represent a substantial part of their activities. The portion is measured largely, though not entirely, by expenditures. Not only is the cost of time expended by paid staff, but also the value of volunteer board members and others can be considered. For example, an organization that uses its prestige to influence legislation, achieving a high degree of success with a minimal expenditure of money, could be found to conduct excessive lobbying. Regarding the amount of actual expenditures, 5–10% of an organization's overall budget is generally considered a permissible expenditure level.[110] IRC §4912 places an excise tax on nonelecting 501(c)(3)s and their managers when excessive lobbying causes the exempt organization to lose its exemption. When lobbying activities are insignificant and an exempt organization wishes to avoid the increased record keeping and scrutiny presumed to be caused by a §501(h) election, this *nonelective method* may be preferable.

(a) Making the Election

A (c)(3) organization that elects to monitor its lobbying expenditures under IRC §501(h) buys a safe harbor and removes the discretionary factors used in the substantial part test. Under this election, the exempt organization agrees to a mathematical limit based upon a percentage of its exempt purpose expenditures (EPE) to prove that legislative efforts are not substantial. Unless lobbying expenditures exceed 150% of the prescribed amounts over a four-year period, exempt status remains intact.[111]

Form 5768 is filed to make the election.[112] It can be filed with Form 1023 or with an annual Form 990. The election is effective until it is revoked and can be voluntarily revoked at any time, effective for the next tax year. A new election is effective for the following year after at least one intervening nonelection year. For example if a revocation is in effect for 1998, an exempt organization can elect for 1999 anytime between January 1, 1998 and December 31, 1999. Private foundations, churches, and supporting organizations cannot make the election.

(b) Mechanical Test

Overall lobbying expenditures, including direct and grassroots efforts combined, cannot exceed the sum of:[113]

---

[109] Reg. §56.4911-5(f).
[110] Discussed in §23.4(a).
[111] IRC §501(h)(2)(B).
[112] Reproduced in Appendix 23-1.
[113] IRC 501(h); Reg. §1.501(h)-3(e).

- 20% of the first $500,000 of the exempt organization's exempt purpose expenditures (EPE), plus

- 15% of the next $500,000 of EPE, plus

- 10% of the next $500,000 of EPE, plus

- 5% of the rest up to a maximum total lobbying allowance of $1 million for any one organization

Grassroots lobbying expenditures (contacting the general public rather than contacting legislators directly) cannot exceed 25% of the total lobbing limits above.

Exempt purpose expenditures[114] include:

- Amounts paid to accomplish one or more charitable purposes, including grants paid for charitable projects, program expenses, employee compensation (including deferred), and administrative and general expenses, and depreciation on assets used for exempt purposes;

- Lobbying expenditures, including grants to a noncharity earmarked for lobbying;

- Amounts paid for nonpartisan analysis, study, or research, and for examination of broad social, economic, and similar problems; and

- Expenses for responding to requests for technical advice, self-defense efforts, and member nonlobbying communications.

Exempt purpose expenditures do not include expenses incurred for the production of income, including managing an endowment or other investments and an unrelated business activity. Expenses incurred by a separate fundraising unit are also excluded.

Affiliated organizations are consolidated for application of the lobbying tests, to prevent the creation of new entities to avoid the spending limits. An exempt organization that is bound under its governing instrument by the decisions of another exempt organization regarding legislative issues is affiliated. Interlocking directorates also create affiliation.[115]

Accounting for lobbying involves identifying expenditures directly connected with specific legislation, as opposed to matters that are subjects of legislation. It is critical to isolate costs of associated research on issues and review of pending legislation until the exempt organization decides to support or oppose the legislation.

Mixed-purpose expenditures involving both direct and grassroots lobbying activities are presumed to be grassroots, except to the extent that the organization can demonstrate a reasonable allocation between the two types of lobbying.[116] Likewise, the expense of publications or communications sent to members or to the public must be allocated among the various elements of lobbying, fund-raising,

---

[114] Reg. §56.4911-4.
[115] Reg. §56.4911-7; see Priv. Ltr. Rul. 9236028.
[116] Reg. §56.4911-3(a)(2).

and education. The portion of telephone, fax, computer, staff, and other costs attributable to lobbying efforts must be documented with time sheets and usage records.

(c) Penalty Tax and Revocation

A 25% tax is imposed under IRC §4911(a)(1) on excess lobbying expenses of public charities electing to limit their lobbying expenses by IRC §501(h). The taxable excess is the higher excessive overall lobbying expenditures (including grassroots) or excessive grassroots lobbying expenses. If an organization's lobbying expenses normally rise above 150% of the permissible amounts, exempt status is denied.[117] The calculation year and the three preceding years are combined to arrive at the normal amount. A newly electing organization's status will not be revoked until the end of the base period.

(d) Pros and Cons of Election

Although the elective lobbying provisions were expected to eliminate confusion about the consequences of lobbying, the three sets of regulations proposed over the years contain radically different interpretations of the terms. Although there are those who propose the rules should be unified and those who propose that all (c)(3) organizations elect 501(h),[118] uncertainty exists. Due partly to the confusion, very few organizations have made the election. Accordingly, there is meager guidance on the subject and the pros and cons must be carefully considered. Among the advantages of electing are these facts:

Advantages of Electing. The advantages of making the election under IRC §501(h) include the following:

- Volunteers' time and influence are not counted; only actual expenditures count.

- The revocation of exemption calculation is based on a four-year average, not on an ongoing annual test.

- Mathematical limits are specific.

- The degree of certainty provided by specific tests applied to electing organizations is preferable to the subjective and untested standards for nonelecting ones. IRC §501(h) allows examining agents to use the definitive rules only for electing organizations, not for nonelecting ones.

- Some practitioners expect the IRS to scrutinize nonelecting organizations.

---

[117] IRC §501(h); Reg. §1.501(h)-3.
[118] Independent Sector, in August 1998, announced a campaign entitled *Charity Lobbying in the Public Interest*. IS says "Charity Lobbying: It's the Right Thing to Do" in informing charitable organizations of the limits within which lobbying efforts can be undertaken.

- The membership communications exclusion does not classify as lobbying the "objective reporting on the contents and status of legislation" to members.

- Record-keeping requirements may be less because volunteer time need not be recorded.

Advantages of Not Electing. The advantages of not making the election under IRC §501(h) include the following:

- Grassroots lobbying limit is not separately limited to a percentage of lobbying expenditures.

- Record-keeping requirements may be less if the organization need not distinguish between direct lobbying and grassroots efforts. However, the information furnished on Form 990 may need to be more detailed.

- Drawing attention to the organization by making the election is thought by some to possibly trigger an IRS audit. The IRS disavows this view and the author is unaware of such a case.

- Directors and officers can be personally liable for penalties for excess lobbying.

- Affiliated organization's lobbying activities must be consolidated or combined to measure limitations under the election, but are otherwise measured on a per entity basis.

- The maximum amount of expenditures for an electing organization is $1 million. For an exempt organization with a $50,000,000 annual budget, for example, the maximum of $1 million equals 2% of the budget, a de minimus amount in relation to the 5–10% considered permissible by some for a nonelecting exempt organization.

- It may be preferable to avoid the uncertainty caused by the multiple proposed regulations and the controversy surrounding the allocation of indirect expenses.

23.6 LOBBYING LIMITS FOR 501(c)(4), (5), (6), AND OTHER EXEMPT ORGANIZATIONS

There is no specific numerical lobbying limit for exempt organizations other than those recognized as tax-exempt under §501(c)(3). The facts of each case will determine whether the league is focused on accomplishing its *primary* exempt purpose when lobbying or political activities are carried on alongside more traditional activities. In some situations, an EO's purposes can be accomplished only through the passage of legislation. For example, a 1961 ruling allowed a business league to spend all of its money on lobbying as long as the legislation was germane to its specific exempt purpose.[119] Member dues deductions are limited under IRC §162.

[119] Rev. Rul. 61-177, 1961-2 C.B. 117.

To the extent that dues finance political campaigning, grassroots lobbying, or direct lobbying, they are not deductible. If an association spends a substantial portion of its funds for lobbying, the dues deduction is allowed only for that portion that can be clearly identified as attributable to exempt activities.[120]

Lobbying activities are also restricted by the U.S. Postal Service, which denies second and third class mailing permits to nonprofits whose primary purpose is lobbying. Registration of lobbying activities is also required in many states and by federal election laws.

23.7 ADVOCACY AND NONPARTISAN ANALYSIS

Many nonprofit groups are focused on issues with political overtones that are the subject of legislation and positions taken by seekers of public offices. An organization whose mission can only be accomplished by the passage of legislation is treated as an *action organization* not qualified for exemption under §501(c)(3). Since part of the rationale for granting tax exemption is that nonprofits relieve the burdens of government by performing socially useful activities, opinions change over the years regarding the types of actions that exempt organizations can properly take. Stopping commercial development in the national forests may or may not be a concern of a particular administration in the White House and may or may not be accomplished only by the passage of legislation. A nationwide boycott campaign against Exxon in response to its oil spill may or may not primarily serve to preserve the environment. A U.S. District Court allowed the exempt status of the Infant Formula Action Coalition, whose only activity is relieving starving children by boycotting Nestlé, a company that manufactures baby formula for sale in underdeveloped countries.[121]

IRS policies may change according to the current political climate. The following subjects may present problems with the determination and field representatives of the IRS:

- *Issues of race*—segregation, immigration

- *Issues of sex*—sexual preference, discrimination

- *Issues of faith*—abortion, sun worship

- *Economic issues*—tax protesters, communists/capitalists

- *Survival issues*—pollution, nuclear power, no-smoking

- *Human rights issues*—legal representation, refugee centers, freedom of speech, right to life

- *Foreign policy issues*—weapons treaties, apartheid, war or peace

Pursuing one of the above subjects with activities that encourage the passage of legislation can jeopardize exempt status. The regulations describe three different possibilities for classification as an *action organization*:[122]

---

[120] Reg. §1.162-20(c)(2)(i); See Chapter 6§4.
[121] *Infant Formula Action Coalition v. U.S.* (D.D.C. No. 79-0129).
[122] Reg. §1.501(c)(3)-1(c)(3).

1. A (c)(3) that has substantial lobbying;

2. A (c)(3) that participates or intervenes in political campaigns; or

3. A (c)(3) whose primary objectives (as distinguished from its incidental or secondary objectives) may be attained only by legislation or a defeat of proposed legislation, and that advocates or campaigns for such objective (as distinguished from engaging in nonpartisan analysis, study, or research and making the results available to the general public).

The most troublesome provision is the third action category. An exempt organization involved in controversial subjects must be able to pass the following hurdles:

- Prove that its purposes can be accomplished through means other than legislation, such as court intervention to enforce existing laws, publication of educational materials, or direct provision of services not being provided by the government.

- Show that its activity is not illegal or is protected by the rights of free speech and association. Demonstrations, boycotts, strikes, and picketing raise red flags with the IRS.

- Conduct its politically tainted activity, if possible, within a larger complex of traditionally exempt activities.

- Meet the *educational* test for information published in its newsletters, publications, or research reports on topics or issues that are potentially the subject of legislation. "Disparaging terms, insinuations, innuendoes, and suggested implications drawn from incomplete facts" are not educational.[123]

---

[123] Rev. Rul. 68-263, 1968-1 C.B. 256; see discussion of IRS methodology test for defining educational efforts in Chapter 5§1.

Appendix 23–1

FORM 5768

Form **5768** (Rev. December 1996) Department of the Treasury Internal Revenue Service	**Election/Revocation of Election by an Eligible Section 501(c)(3) Organization To Make Expenditures To Influence Legislation** (Under Section 501(h) of the Interest Revenue Code)	For IRS Use Only
Name of organization		Employer identification number
Number and street (or P. O. box no., if mail is not delivered to street address)		Room/suite
City, town or post office, state and ZIP code		

1 Election - As an eligible organization, we hereby elect to have the provisions of section 501(h) of the Code, relating to expenditures to influence legislation, apply to our tax year ending .... and all subsequent tax years until revoked.

(Month, day, and year)

Note: This election must be signed and postmarked within the first taxable year to which it applies.

2 Revocation - As an eligible organization, we hereby revoke our election to have the provisions of section 501(h) of the Code, relating to expenditures to influence legislation, apply to our tax year ending ....

(Month, day, and year)

Note: This revocation must be signed and postmarked before the first day of the tax year to which it applies.

Under penalties of perjury, I declare that I am authorized to make this (check applicable box) ☐ election ☐ revocation on behalf of the above named organization.

_____   _____   _____
(Signature of officer or trustee)   (Type or print name and title)   (Date)

(HTA)   Form 5768 (Rev. 12-96)

CHAPTER TWENTY-FOUR

Deductibility and Disclosures

Tax-exempt organizations must be mindful of the income tax consequence of payments received from their supporters for a couple of reasons. First, an organization can enhance its development activity by seeking payments that are fully deductible either as a contribution or a business expense. Second, organizations are required to disclose the tax character of payments solicited from their supporters. Penalties are imposed on organizations that fail to provide proper tax information. This chapter briefly outlines standards for tax deductibility and thoroughly describes the different types of disclosure rules applicable to §501(c)(3) organizations. Special disclosure rules applicable to social welfare organizations, business leagues, and labor unions are discussed in Chapters 6, 7, and 8.

24.1 OVERVIEW OF DEDUCTIBILITY

Tax-exempt organizations in all categories are eligible to receive payments that are potentially deductible for income tax purposes either as a business expense or as a contribution. A payment's character is determined by the motivation for making the payment, but deductibility may also depend upon the recipient organization's category of exempt status. One pays dues to a (c)(6) business league to maintain and improve one's professional standing thereby making the payment a deductible expense directly related to one's business. One pays dues to the (c)(4) civic association to better one's neighborhood. If such dues are paid for business reasons, they are deductible as a business expense; if paid for personal reasons, the dues are not deductible. As discussed in Chapter 6, certain civic associations qualify as (c)(3) charitable organizations thereby making payments to them deductible as a contribution.

Tax-exempt organizations in only one category, 501(c)(3), are eligible to receive payments that qualify for a contribution deduction for income tax purposes. Interestingly enough, IRC §170 that allows such deductions does not specifically mention 501(c)(3). Instead it describes eligible recipient organizations by using the same words found in 501(c)(3).[1] The tax code defines the term *charitable contribution* by saying it means a contribution or gift to or for the use of

(1) A State, a possession of the United States, or any political subdivision of any of the foregoing, or the United States or the District of Columbia, but only if the contribution or gift is made for exclusively public purposes.

(2) A corporation, trust, or community chest, fund, or foundation

(a) created or organized in the United States or in any possession thereof, or under the laws of the United States, any State, the District of Columbia, or any possession of the United States,

(b) organized and operated exclusively for religious, charitable, scientific, literary, or to foster national or international amateur sports competition (but only if no part of its activities involve the provision of athletic facilities or equipment), or for preventing cruelty to children or animals,

(c) no part of the net earnings of which inures to the benefit or any private shareholder or individual, and

(d) which is not disqualified for tax exemption under section 501(c)(3) by reason of attempting to influence legislation, and which does not participate in, or intervene any political campaign on behalf of (or in opposition to) any candidate for public office.

Another interesting connection between §§170 and 501 lies in the fact that the definition of organizations qualifying as public charities under §509(a)(1) is not found in that section but instead is contained in §170(b) and its associated regulations.[2]

(a) Contribution Defined

In a deceptively simple fashion §170(c) states that an income tax deduction is allowed for "a contribution or gift to or for the use of qualified charitable organizations."[3] Neither the code nor the regulations define the word "contribution." The commonly used definition of a contribution is "a voluntary transfer without consideration." In other words, only a gift for which nothing is received in return is

---

[1] With the exception of organizations that test for public safety reasons. See Chapter 2.
[2] See Chapter 11.
[3] IRC §170(c).

fully deductible. The intention to give with no expectation of financial benefit must be present for a donation to occur.[4] In the Supreme Court's words, "the gift must proceed from detached and disinterested generosity."[5]

When a donor receives services, goods, or other property of value, a rebuttable presumption arises that there is no gift.[6] Therefore, all the moneys paid for attendance at dinners, balls, theatrical performances, and other fund-raising events are presumed to be payments for value received and not deductible. To overcome the presumption, the donor must prove that the fair market value (FMV) of the benefits, entertainment, or other items furnished is less than the amount paid. Since 1994, charitable organizations have been required to provide valuation information as more fully described in §24.2.

The requirement that the payment to a charity be disclosed for deductibility has caused many charities to re-examine donor-designated payments. Amounts paid directly to an individual are, of course, not deductible. What about amounts paid to support a particular program conducted by an individual? The Tax Court found that the naming of two missionaries, unrelated to a decedent, as the beneficiaries of a charitable trust did not defeat the charitable nature of the bequest.[7] The judge thought that the church had sufficient control and enforceable rights over the bequest to ensure that the funds would be used for charitable purposes as required by the statute. Following this logic, a scholarship fund donation accompanied by a suggestion that tuition be awarded to a particular person could conceivably be deductible, although the IRS disagrees.[8]

The IRS also says if a person related to the donor is involved with the recipient organization, specifically in one case a theological seminarian, there is no gift.[9] Such a gift is not made "to" a charity if the charity merely acts as a conduit to a particular person. The test of deductibility is whether the organization has full control of the donated funds, and discretion as to their use, so as to ensure that they will be used to carry out its functions and purposes. The parents who directed that their gift be used to pay their son's tuition argued unsuccessfully that although they designated the use of their gift, they had no right to demand such use. Organizations that currently conduct designated gift programs face the problem of whether they sufficiently control the funds so as to remove any benefit to the donor. Likewise, a church school that allows church members to enroll children for a tuition less than that of nonmembers may need to value the member discount.

(b) Limitations on Deductions

The allowable tax deduction for a gift to a qualifying charitable organization depends on a number of different factors. Limitations that influence the deductible amount include the following:

---

[4] *U.S. v. American Bar Endowment,* 477 U.S. 105, 116–117 (1986).
[5] *Duberstein v. Commissioner,* 363 S. Ct. 278 (1960); *William S. Allen v. U.S.,* 541 F.2d 786 (9th Cir. 1976); Rev. Rul. 86-63, 1986-1 C.B. 88; Rev. Rul. 76-232, 1976-2 C.B. 62.
[6] Rev. Rul. 67-246, 1967-2 C.B. 104, 105.
[7] *Estate of Hubert,* T.C. Memo. 1993-482.
[8] Rev. Rul. 83-104, 1983-2 C.B. 46.
[9] Tech. Adv. Memo. 9405003.

- Varying percentages of the donor's income
- Type of property donated
- Classification of the recipient organization as a public or private charity
- Character of the property given as a capital versus an ordinary income property
- Type of transfer—whether the gift is made outright or in trust and whether the donation is of a taxpayer's entire interest or a partial interest.

The following percentage limitations apply:[10]

- An individual may annually deduct up to 50% of his or her adjusted gross income for gifts of cash and ordinary income property to public charities and operating foundations.
- Up to 30% of an individual's income may be offset by donations of long-term capital gain property to public charities and operating foundations and for gifts of cash to a private foundation.
- Gifts to a private foundation of property other than cash, as a rule, are deductible only up to the taxpayer's cost basis. An on-again-off-again rule, now made permanent, allows a full-value deduction for gifts of certain appreciated securities limited to 20% of an individual's income.
- Corporate donations are deductible up to 10% of the company's pretax income.
- No percentage limitation applies for gift and estate tax charitable deduction purposes.[11]

Carryover.   If the total donations made in any one year exceed the foregoing limits, the excessive amount can be carried over and claimed for up to five subsequent years, again subject each year to the applicable percentage limitations.[12]

Fair Market Value.   The deduction amount for a gift of property other than cash is normally the fair market value (FMV) of the property. According to the IRS, the FMV is the price that property would sell for in the open market. It is the price at which the property would change hands between a willing buyer and a willing seller, neither being under any compulsion to buy or sell and both having reasonable knowledge of relevant facts. If the contribution is made in property of a type which the taxpayer sells in the course of his business, the FMV of the contributed property is the price that the taxpayer would have received if he had sold it in the usual market in which he customarily sells, at the time and place of the contribution and, in the case of a contribution of goods in quantity, in the quantity contributed.[13]

[10] IRC §170(b).
[11] IRC §§2055 and 2522.
[12] IRC §170(d).
[13] Reg. §1.170A-1(c) (2).

The "usual market place" standard means that used clothing must be valued at the price for which it can be sold in a resale shop considering its age, condition, style, and usefulness. In making and supporting the valuation of donated property the IRS recommends that all of the following factors affect value and are relevant:[14]

- The cost or selling price of the item
- Sales of comparable properties[15]
- Replacement cost
- Opinions of experts

Property that is sold in an active market for which information is routinely published, like shares of common stock and used automobiles, are relatively easy to value for donation purposes. Closely held company shares, office buildings, fine art, and similar unique properties have no readily established market value. Consequently, in addition to consideration of the foregoing four factors, IRS procedures require a qualified appraisal be obtained for all donations of property other than money and publicly traded securities where the value of the property is more than $5,000.

Additionally, for such donations, Form 8283 must be acknowledged by both the recipient organization and the independent appraiser and attached to the donor's tax return. To provide the IRS with clues about valuations that should be questioned, a charity that sells property reported on Form 8283 within two years of its receipt must itself file Form 8282 to report to the IRS the price at which the property was sold.

The value of property subject to restrictions on its use or subsequent disposition must reflect the decrease in value attributable to such restriction.

Capital Gain Property.   Except for capital gain property, the contribution deduction is limited to the taxpayer's cost for the property donated. The rule says that for deduction purposes the value of the property must be reduced by the amount of gain that would not have been long-term capital gain had the property been sold by the donor.[16] The definition of capital gain property is property eligible for special tax rates applicable to long-term capital gains tax because of its holding period and investment nature.[17] Goods normally sold in a business activity, such as inventory, are considered ordinary income property not capital in nature. Inventory items used solely for the care of the ill, the needy, or infants and scientific property used for research are subject to a partial limitation.[18] Nicely enough, the untaxed gain inherent in donated property is not taxed.

---

[14] IRS Publication 561 entitled *Determining the Value of Donated Property.*
[15] See Rev. Rul. 80-69, 1980-1 C.B. 55 in which the IRS indicates arm's length sales of similar property are the most probative evidence of fair value.
[16] IRC §170(e).
[17] IRC §§1(h) and 1223; holding period after July 28, 1997 must be at least 18 months. Gains on certain business property may also be considered capital gain property under IRC §1231.
[18] IRC §170(e)(3) & (4).

A donation of personal services is also limited by this rule. One has no tax basis inherent in one's own time. Theoretically, to claim a deduction for volunteer services rendered, one would have to first report the value of the services as income to achieve some tax basis. The charitable donation is reported on the individual income tax form as an itemized deduction and is potentially limited in deductibility even if the service provider recognizes income. Therefore no deductions are available for the value of time contributed to a charitable organization though unreimbursed expenses paid incident to rendering the services are deductible.[19] For Form 990 purposes, donated services are also not reported even where they are valued and shown as contributions for financial reporting purposes.

Tangible Personal Property.   The deduction for gifts of tangible personal property, such as clothing, art, or other collectibles, may be limited unless the charity actually keeps and uses the property. This limitation applies when the use by the donee is unrelated to its charitable purposes constituting the basis for its exemption, or in the case of a governmental unit, its function.[20] When applicable, this rule limits the deduction to the donor's tax basis, ordinarily what was originally paid for the property.

The deduction for property donated to charitable auctions and to resale shops is therefore limited to the taxpayer's basis in the property or the value, whichever is lower. The donor is responsible for valuing such property, but the helpful charity assists the donor in valuing such donations for two reasons. The price for which the charity ultimately resells the goods can be treated as determinative of value. Purchasers at charity auctions traditionally pay more than FMV as a way to make a donation to the charity. Providing a list of auction item values gives the purchaser documentation necessary to calculate the donation amount.

Special Private Foundation Limitations.   When Congress created private foundations in 1969, the rule-makers were intent upon not only enhancing regulation of them,[21] but also upon discouraging their formation. Thus as a general rule property donated to a private foundation is limited in its deductibility to the amount of the donor's tax basis.[22] Further, the percentage of income limits are lower for gifts to a private foundation. A private operating foundation that conducts its own active programs is not subject to these restrictive limitations.

Qualified Appreciated Stock.   From 1984 through 1994 and after July, 1996 (now permanently extended), Congress lifted the deduction reduction to basis limitation for gifts of certain marketable securities to private foundations. The full fair market value of qualified appreciated stocks is allowable as a deduction. To qualify the stock has to possess the following characteristics:[23]

- Market quotations are readily available on an established securities market on the date of contribution,

[19] Reg. §1.170A-1(g).
[20] IRC §170(e)(1)(B)(i).
[21] See Chapters 12–17.
[22] IRC §170(e)(1)(B)(ii).
[23] IRC §170(e)(5).

- Stock is capital gain property,

- The foundation's sale of the stock cannot be limited by securities laws as to the volume or other insider trading rules, and

- The value of the stock contributed, when added to any prior gifts by the donor and his or her family members, cannot exceed 10% of the value of all of the outstanding stock of the corporation.

(c) Planned Gifts

Planned gifts are those donations that occur over a period of time either with the creation of a trust during one's life or as a bequest effective upon death. A classic planned gift separates the property into its income and principal attributes in what is referred to as a "split interest trust." Such a gift is a perfect marriage of a donor's desire to support charity, to avoid the income tax, and to keep some of the benefits. The underlying property is often a low-yield significantly appreciated stock.

Charitable Remainder Trust. As its name implies, a charitable remainder trust is created to pay income to the donor or other person(s) for a period of time after which time the rest or remainder is payable to one or more named charities.[24] The written agreements creating such trusts must provide for specified income distributions at least annually. Such a trust that distributes a percentage of its assets is referred to as a "charitable remainder unitrust," or a CRUT. A "charitable remainder annuity trust," or CRAT, instead annually pays out a fixed sum of money. A CRUT or CRAT can last for a term of up to 20 years or for the income beneficiary's life.

  The deduction allowed for creation of a qualifying trust is essentially the FMV of the properties placed in trust less a calculated value of the retained income interest. The IRS provides tables of life expectancy and prevailing interest rates for this purpose. The tables calculate the present value of the life interest based upon the assumed rate of income to be paid annually and the life expectancy of the person(s) possessing the retained income interest. Both public and private charities can be named as the charitable beneficiary.

Charitable Lead Trust. A charitable lead trust reverses the pattern of a remainder trust by paying a defined percentage of its principal for a defined period of time to charity(s). At the end of the trust's life, or lead period, the property is returned to the donor or other designated beneficiary. The lead trust must be either a qualifying annuity or unitrust. The advantage of this type of planned gift is an immediate tax deduction for the donor equal to the present value of the charity income stream. Unlike the remainder trust, however, the donor is treated as a "grantor" of the trust and must annually report the trust income.[25]

Pooled Income Fund or Charitable Annuity. Two other forms of planned gifts popular with public charities encompass a gift of property directly to the charity

---

[24] IRC §664.
[25] IRC §671 treats the donor as owner of the trust property because of the retained reversionary interest in the principal.

rather than a separate trust. Similar to a CRUT or CRAT, the charity promises to pay income to the donor for some period of time. Essentially such trusts have the same elements as a charitable remainder trust, but are established and managed by the public charity itself.[26]

(d) Business "Donations"

Classifying a corporate, or other type of business, payment as a contribution may not be advantageous, for a number of reasons. The corporate contribution deduction is limited to 10% of a company's taxable profit for the year (before the deduction).[27] A contribution disallowed by the percentage limitations of §170 is not otherwise deductible.[28] Correspondingly, no §162 business expense deduction is allowable if any part of a payment qualifies as a charitable gift under §170.[29] As a practical matter, it is contrary to basic corporate responsibility to private shareholders to make a contribution without some kind of economic motivation. Advertising and promotional expenses have no similar limitation. From a corporation's standpoint, a contribution in many situations is not preferable. A transfer of property to a charitable organization that "bears a direct relationship to the taxpayer's business and is made with a reasonable expectation of financial return commensurate with the amount of transfer" may be deductible as an "ordinary and necessary business expense rather than as a charitable contribution." The following decisions give a flavor to the issue.

- A corporation agreeing to pay a certain amount to a named charity in return for each unit of a particular product it sold (for which a label was returned) incurred a business expense for its payments to the named charity, in an early cause-related marketing case.[30]

- A sewing machine manufacturer was not allowed to claim charitable deductions for discounts given to school districts. Its expectation that the students using the machines would become future customers indicated an anticipated financial return for the discounts.[31]

- Payments made by a newspaper publisher to fund a first-grade reading program in the local school, however, was not a deductible business expense, but instead a charitable contribution. There was no direct relationship between the program and the publishing business, nor a reasonable expectation of commensurate financial return.[32]

The IRS has announced that "whether or not an activity constitutes advertising or acknowledgment for the recipient charity's purposes does not determine whether

[26] IRC §531(c)(5)(A).
[27] §170(b)(2).
[28] Reg. §1.170A-(c)(5).
[29] Reg. §1.162-15.
[30] Rev. Rul. 63-73, 1963-1 C.B. 35.
[31] *Singer Co. v. Commissioner,* 71-2 U.S.T.C. ¶ 9685 (Ct. Claims 1971).
[32] Priv. Ltr. Rul. 8145020.

a sponsor may deduct its payment under §162 or §170."[33] See Chapter 21§8(e) for the corollary rules on corporate sponsorships for unrelated business income tax purposes. Those interested in further exploring the motivations behind corporate giving—social responsibility versus profit maximization—and how the reasons interact with the tax law, should consult the June 1995 issue of *The Exempt Organization Tax Review.*[34]

24.2 THE SUBSTANTIATION AND QUID PRO QUO RULES

Contributors often receive benefits in return for support of their favorite charitable organization: dinner, entertainment, prizes, and a wide variety of premiums are provided to donors to entice their support. Often those valuable items are provided to donors at no cost to the charity because businesses and patrons donate the items of benefit offered to the attendees. In such case, the proceeds of fund-raising events and memberships add directly to an organization's coffers and it seems logical to treat all of a donor's payment as a charitable donation. The trouble with this premise is it belies the basic concept of a charitable donation—a payment made with the intention of making a gift.[35] When one pays the going price for a nice dinner dance with friends, a contrarian might say the minimum price charged for admission to an event establishes its FMV, resulting in no charitable gift being made. It is also reasonable to propose that the social nature of fund-raising events implies lack of donative intent. Partly due to this imprecision, until 1988, a charity was neither expected nor required to assign value to such benefits, or to inform the givers that the ticket price is not fully deductible. "Deductible to the extent allowed by law" was a common refrain.

(a) History of Disclosure Rules

In the late 1980s, the House Budget Committee decided that "charities fail to make sufficient disclosures in soliciting gifts to allow donors to calculate the nondeductible portion of donations." Legislation was passed that made it mandatory for non-501(c)(3) organizations to prominently print on all fund-raising materials that payments were not deductible.[36] The IRS was directed to measure tax revenues lost due to overstated donations to 501(c)(3) organizations and to investigate any abuses found. In response the IRS initiated a special emphasis program entitled Exempt Organization Charitable Solicitations Compliance Improvement Study. It mailed Publication 1381 to the more than 500,000 tax-exempt organizations eligible to receive deductible contributions, sent IRS representatives around the county to give public education talks on the subject, and examined major charities to test compliance.

---

[33] IRS Notice of Proposed Rulemaking, January 19, 1993, concerning corporate sponsorships.

[34] Article entitled "The Paradox of Corporate Giving: Tax Expenditures, The Nature of the Corporation, and the Social Construction of Charity," by Nancy J. Knauer of Temple University School of Law.

[35] See §24.1(a).

[36] IRC §6116 applicable to now-501(c)(3) organizations with gross receipts of over $100,000.

Based on the relatively poor results of the study, Congress ended the deductibility dilemma in 1993 by adding §170(f)(8) and §6115 to the income tax code to require that charities provide information to donors revealing the value of benefits provided. The Senate said, "Taxpayers may not simply rely on a canceled check as substantiation." The Revenue Reconciliation Bill of 1993, passed by the Congress as part of the Omnibus Budget Reconciliation Bill imposed a substantiation rule on persons claiming charitable donations and disclosure rules on the charities themselves effective for gifts after 1993, as follows:

- A written receipt from the donee organization is required for taxpayers claiming a charitable gift of $250 or more. Congress said this burden is on the giver, but it also falls on the organization that must produce the receipt. See Exhibit 24–1.

- A donee organization furnishing economic benefit in the form of goods or services in return for donations in excess of $75 must provide a written statement revealing the deductible portion of donor payments. See Exhibit 24–1.

(b) Substantiation Rules

No charitable deduction is allowed for a gift of $250 or more unless the taxpayer obtains a contemporaneous written acknowledgment from the donee organization with sufficient information to evidence the amount of the deductible contribution.[37] Separate payments are not aggregated; only a single payment of $250 or more requires substantiation. For example, a monthly contribution of $200 resulting in a total of $2,400 for the year is not subject to receipting. The acknowledgment must be written and contain the following information:

- Amount of cash the taxpayer paid and a description (but not necessarily the value) of any property other than cash the taxpayer transferred to the donee organization,

- A statement of whether the donee organization provided any goods or services in consideration, in whole or in part, for any of the cash or other property transferred to the donee organization, and

- If the donee organization provides any intangible religious benefits, a statement to that effect.

Timing. A "contemporaneous acknowledgment" is one obtained on or before the earlier of (1) the actual filing date the taxpayer's original return for the year in which the contribution was made, or (2) the due date (including extensions) for filing the taxpayer's original return for that year. In other words, a donor may not file a return claiming a contribution deduction for a charitable payment of $250 or more without a proper receipt in hand.

---

[37] Reg. §1.170A-13(f).

Exhibit 24–1

SAMPLE DONOR DISCLOSURE RECEIPTS

Failure to disclose the value of benefits provided is subject to a $10 penalty for each donor for each event. The language can vary but three very specific items of information must be provided to satisfy the IRS:

1. Donor name with amount and date of cash paid
2. Description of other property given (without a valuation)
3. Statement of whether or not benefits were provided, and if so, a good faith estimate of the value.

NO BENEFITS PROVIDED—CHARITABLE GIFT OF $250 OR MORE

Donor Name

Thank you for your contribution of _____ in cash and property _____ (description) on _____ (date). Your gift will be devoted to our organizational objectives and we will not provide benefits or services required to be valued in consideration for this gift.

Organization Name

BENEFITS PROVIDED—PAYMENT OF $75.01 OR MORE

Donor Name

Thank you for your contribution of _____ in cash and property _____ (description) on _____ (date). We estimate the fair market value of the benefits we provided to you in consideration for this gift was $_____ per person. We are a §501(c)(3) organization and you may claim a donation deduction for the difference between the cash and property given to the organization and the value of the benefits you received.

Organization Name

INTANGIBLE RELIGIOUS BENEFITS—GIFT OF $250+

Donor Name

Thank you for your contribution of $_____ in cash and _____ (description of property donated) on _____ (date). The church furnishes intangible religious benefits that need not be valued for tax purposes. You may claim the full value of your gift as a donation.

Name of Religious Organization

CHARITABLE BENEFITS—TICKET PRICE $75.01 OR MORE

Donor Name

Thank you for your purchase of benefit tickets for $_____ in cash on _____ (date). We estimate the fair market value of the meal and entertainment furnished in connection with the event was $_____ per person (ticket). We are a §501(c)(3) organization and therefore you may claim a donation deduction for the difference between the cash you paid and the value of the benefits, or $ _____.

Organization Name

Exhibit 24–1 *(continued)*

AUCTION PURCHASE RECEIPT
Purchaser's Name
Thank you for your purchase of auction item #_____ (description) for
$_____ in cash on _____ (date). We estimate the fair market value of this item
is $_____. We are a §501(c)(3) organization and therefore you may claim
a donation deduction for the difference between the cash you paid less the
value of the item, or $_____.

Organization Name

In Consideration Of.   Benefits are treated as being "in consideration of" the donation where there is a connection between the transactions. The charity is
deemed to have provided goods and services in consideration of a donation IF at
the time the taxpayer makes the payment, he or she expects to receive the benefits
in exchange for the payment. It is a matter of the donor's intention. Goods received in a year other than the year of payment are included if the donor had an
expectation of their receipt. An unannounced or irregularly scheduled recognition
dinner held to honor supporters would not be a quid pro quo benefit but a routine
and anticipated dinner could be connected to annual giving.

Good Faith Estimate.   The donor is entitled to rely upon the charity's estimation
of the value of benefits provided unless she has some reason to know the value is
incorrect.[38]

Disregarded Benefits.   Due to the difficulty of valuing certain donor privileges,
the IRS, in August 1995, significantly eased the disclosure requirements by extending the "token item" rules to apply to certain benefits. Benefits can be disregarded if they fall into one of two categories:[39]

1. Goods and services that have insubstantial value, referred to as the token
   items. As discussed in §24.3(a), coffee mugs, posters, calendars or similar
   premiums that cost the organization a modest amount ($7.20 for 1999 and
   annually adjusted), furnished to donors of $36 (adjusted annually) or
   more, do not reduce the deductible contribution.

2. Annual membership rights and privileges offered to members in exchange for a payment of $75 or less per year that consist of:

   - Any rights and privileges that the member can exercise frequently
     (and not limited as to use) during the membership period, including
     but not limited to free or discounted admission or parking, preferred
     access to goods or services, and discounts on purchases of goods or
     services.

---

[38] Benefit valuation issues are discussed in §24.3 and illustrated in Exhibit 24–3.
[39] Reg. §1.170-13(f)(8); Rev. Proc. 98-61, 1998-52 IRB 1.

- Admission to events during the membership period that are open only to members for which the charity reasonably estimates that cost per person is below the prevailing low-cost article amount (determined at the time the membership package is first offered for the year). A reception with light refreshments prior to an opera performance would, for example, be considered of "insubstantial value" if the event costs the organization $7.20 (figure adjusted annually) or less per person.

Members paying amounts above $75 are entitled to disregard (not reduce their contribution) the value of those privileges included in a basic membership priced at $75 or less. The meaning of "frequently exercised" is defined only by example of what is not. Free tickets to all of a theater group's eight summer performances are not disregarded because of the limited (and specific) number of performances. Benefits provided to the member's employees can also be disregarded under this rule without regard to the number of employees who actually use the benefits.

The contemporaneous receipt need not mention the fact that rights and privileges can be disregarded. The receipt can say "no goods or services were provided."[40] Goods and services provided to the employees or partners of the donor can be disregarded if they are the same token benefits offered to all other individual members.

Payroll Deductions.   Contributions paid through a payroll withholding system need not be acknowledged by the donee organization directly to the donor. The substantiation rules apply when $250 or more is withheld for a particular paycheck, not the cumulative amount of the annual deductions. Taxpayers can substantiate a $250+ payroll deduction with a combination of two documents:

- A pay stub, Form W-2, or other document furnished by the taxpayer's employer that evidences the amount withheld from the taxpayer's wages for purposes of payment to a donee organization, and

- A pledge card or other document prepared by the donee organization that includes a statement that the organization does not provide goods or services in whole or partial consideration for any contributions made by payroll deduction.

During united giving campaigns, donors may designate specific amounts to be redistributed by the collecting charity to named charities. For disclosure purposes, the fund-raising and distributing charity is treated as the donee.

Volunteer out-of-pocket expenses are also subject to contemporaneous written receipt rules. Volunteers must themselves keep adequate substantiation (meaning airline tickets, meal chits, and other §274 expense-account-type receipts) plus obtain a disclosure statement containing:

- Description of services provided by the taxpayer,
- Statement that benefits were or were not received and

---

[40] Reg. §1.170A-13(f)(8), Example 2.

- Quid pro quo benefit description plus valuation, if applicable.

Gifts to charitable remainder and lead trusts, but not pooled income fund gifts, are exempted from the $250+ substantiation requirement. The IRS reasoned that the donee of such transfers is often unknown and subject to change. Partnerships and S corporations need not obtain separate substantiation receipts for each partner reporting a contribution deduction passed through to them. The partnership or S corporation is considered as the donor required to obtain a $250+ receipt.

Rights to Buy College Athletic Tickets.   When an amount paid to an institution of higher education entitles the donor to purchase tickets for seating at an athletic event in an athletic stadium of the college or university, 20% of the amount paid is considered as the value of the right to buy tickets.[41]

Tax-Exempt Grantors.   A tax-exempt organization wishing to claim a contribution deduction for unrelated business income tax purposes (see §27.14) must obtain a disclosure receipt for any grants it wishes to claim as a charitable gift for that purpose.

Information Returns.   Instead of furnishing an acknowledgment for each individual $250+ contribution, §170(f)(8)(D) provides an alternative. "If the donee organization files a return, on such form and in accordance with such regulations as the Secretary may prescribe, which includes the information described in §170(f)(8)(B)," individual receipts are not required. Such a form has not been issued as of December 4, 1998.

Whether the charity produces individual substantial receipts or files an information return, the disclosure rules require a communique with donors. As a practical matter, most charities already send a thank-you to donors using computer systems that efficiently generate such mailings. For them, this requirement does not impose a difficult burden. The Conference Committee Managers Report said the acknowledgments need not take any particular form—a postcard, letter, or computer-generated form is acceptable. Sample receipts are shown in Exhibit 24–1.

The IRS publication explaining these provisions is Publication 1771, *Charitable Contributions—Substantiation and Disclosure Requirements.*

(c) Quid Pro Quo Disclosure Rules

When an organization described in §170(c)(2), (3), (4), or (5) receives a quid pro quo contribution in excess of $75, the organization shall, in connection with the solicitation or receipt of the contribution, provide a written statement that:[42]

- Informs the donor that the amount of the contribution that is deductible for federal income tax purposes is limited to the excess of the amount of

---

[41] IRC §170(I); Reg. §1.170A-13(f)(14).
[42] IRC §6115(a).

any money and the value of any property other than money contributed by the donor over the value of goods or services furnished in return, and

■ Provides a good faith estimate of the value of such goods or services.

A quid pro quo contribution is defined by §6115(b) as "a payment made partly as a contribution and partly in consideration for goods or services provided to the payor by the donee organization." The fact that the goods or services were donated to the organization at no cost does not make a quid pro quo payment fully deductible. Neither does the fact that the money will be use exclusively for the organization's exempt purposes.[43] A pure exchange transaction, such as a museum gift shop or church book store sale, has no donative element so that no disclosures are required.

Intangible Religious Benefits.   Payments to religious organizations in return for "intangible religious benefit that generally is not sold in a commercial transaction outside the donative context" are not required to be valued. The regulations provide no guidance on the definition of *intangible religious benefit*. As discussed in Chapter 3§1, our tax policy does not define religion so as to foster the separation of church and state. The results are not necessarily logical or fair. Fees paid for the many weddings and funerals performed outside churches are not deductible. Where it is customary for the church secretary to suggest a $300 "donation" be paid to the minister performing such services in the church, one wonders why payment is not treated as a quid pro quo?

Voluntary Disclosures.   The value of ALL benefits provided in connection with an ostensibly charitable payment must be subtracted from the amount paid to the charity, *regardless of whether the charity is required to disclose such amount to the donor.* Although the charitable disclosure rule requires the value of goods and services be provided where the solicitation is for a gift of more than $75, the helpful charity might choose to value all benefits not excluded by the de minimis rules explained in §24.3(a). The following illustrates the fact that the $50 contributor also needs to receive valuation information to correctly claim the charitable deduction portion of his or her gift.

Charitable event ticket sells for	$50	$100
Fair market value of event is	−40	−40
Amount of donation	$10	$60

Timing.   The disclosure is to be made in "connection with the solicitation or receipt of the donation." The Ways and Means Committee report says it intends for the disclosure to be made in a manner reasonably likely to come to the attention of the donor. "For example, a disclosure of the required information in small print set forth within a larger document might not meet the requirement." Timing of the disclosure can be troublesome. Mostly charities have chosen to disclose an estimated

---

[43] Rev. Rul. 67-246, 1967-2 C.B. 104.

value on the invitation printed well in advance of the actual event. What should a prudent organization do if they find the valuation was mistaken? Do they send a follow-up receipt once the more accurate valuation is available? If possible, at least the required follow-up $250 plus substantiation acknowledgments would reflect the subsequently corrected value.

The charity has issues to consider in deciding where to print the disclosure information. Without question, it is preferable to print the benefit valuation disclosure on the event invitation, not on the RSVP card that is returned (and consequently not available later to the donor). If the value of the benefit is printed on the return card sent back with the donor's check, the charity can expect unnecessary calls at tax filing time from donors who did not keep a copy of the valuation information.

Note that the code seems to give a choice: Information can be furnished at the time the gift is requested or when payment is received. As a practical matter, the charity may not be able to assign an accurate valuation for an event when invitations are mailed. The de minimus rules discussed later do require a statement on the solicitation, and it is unfortunate that Congress provided a choice. The $250+ gift acknowledgment clearly will be provided after the gift is received, perhaps only once a year listing all such gifts by a particular giver.

Donative Intent. The connection between a benefit conferred by a charity and the actual donation is sometimes vague. What if one purchases tickets but does not use them? How does a charity determine when a payment is made in "consideration for" a benefit that was not necessarily expected or bargained for? What if the charity invites potential donors to be guests at a dinner reception worth $50 a person? If no consideration is paid specifically for the dinner, the question is whether the value of the "free" dinner reduces an attendee's subsequent payment. Does the result change if the charity regularly holds such dinners? Does it matter whether a donation is made at the dinner or within a short time after the dinner?

Auctions. Purchases in a charity auction are not quid pro quo transactions, but the purchase can be a partial donation. A bidder who pays more than the FMV for an item for sale in a charitable auction is entitled to treat the amount paid in excess of the value as a charitable gift. A catalog, label, or other evidence of the value of the items should be available and the helpful charity will also print the estimated value on the purchase receipt. Though the charity is not technically required to place a value on the donated items in acknowledging the gift to auction donors, it must do so if it wishes to provide documentation for the purchasers. When the donation portion exceeds $250, an acknowledgment should be provided as discussed previously.

Raffles. A purchase of a raffle ticket is without donative intention and consequently the price paid is not deductible as a charitable gift. The prize value is reportable as taxable income by the winner and the charity sponsoring the raffle has reporting and tax withholding requirements outlined in Exhibit 24–2 and Chapter 25§3(f).

§6714(a) Imposition of Penalty. If an organization fails to meet the disclosure requirements or discloses incomplete or inaccurate information with respect to a

Exhibit 24–2

TAX REPORTING/WITHHOLDING FOR RAFFLES AND DRAWINGS

Prizes awarded as a part of a charitable fund-raising activity may be subject to tax reporting on Form 1099 or W-2G. The fair value of a raffle prize is reported on Form W-2G. A prize received in a drawing for which no separate ticket was purchased to be eligible (door prize-type) is reported on Form 1099 Miscellaneous. Also tax withholding may be required. Imagine how happy the charity will be to take $930 out of its coffers to pay the tax due on a $3000 (donated) cruise!

PRIZE IS $600 OR MORE

- Step 1: Form W-9 requesting the winner's taxpayer federal identification number should be completed and signed by the winner before prize is awarded.
- Step 2: Form W-2G or 1099 Misc. is filed by the charity. If the winner fails or refuses to give their ID number, the charity is required to pay 31 percent of the prize to the IRS as backup withholding. In other words, tax due is payable by the charity if it fails to get the number.

PRIZE OF MORE THAN $5000

- Step 1: Form W-9 requesting the winner's taxpayer ID number must be completed and signed. For a *cash prize,* 28 percent of the net prize must be subtracted or withheld from the prize. For a *noncash prize* (such as a car or a trip), the winner should pay the charity 28 percent of the net prize before the prize is awarded. The net prize is equal to the value of the prize less the wager paid (essentially equal to the amount on which the winner must pay tax). If the winner refuses to furnish ID number the withholding rate is 31 percent
- Step 2: Form W-2G or 1099 Misc. is filed by the charity and furnished to winner by January 31 of the following year.

---

quid pro quo contribution, a $10 penalty for each contribution in respect of which the organization fails to make the required disclosure is due. Form 990 asks "Did the organization comply with the disclosure requirements relating to quid pro quo contributions?" When the answer to this question is "No," the total penalty with respect to a particular fund-raising event or mailing can be up to $5000.

§6714(b) Reasonable Cause Exception. No penalty shall be imposed under this section with respect to any failure if it is shown that such failure is due to reasonable cause. Although an organization relied upon compliance information furnished as "industry standard" by a national organization, it could not escape the penalty. Neither would the IRS relent because the solicitations were made by volunteers.[44]

[44] Priv. Ltr. Rul. 9315001.

24.3 VALUING DONOR BENEFITS

The value of a benefit provided to a donor is the fair market value (FMV), or the amount "a willing buyer will pay a willing seller for the same item, object or service purchased individually in the normal marketplace in which the item is sold."[45] This general rule is hard to follow for many charitable events have no commercial counterpart. The value of a gala is not necessarily equal to the organization's cost, particularly when the items are donated or purchased below market prices. The prescribed method for valuing the use of a museum room for a private reception is the price for hotel space of comparable size. The value of the art collection need not be taken into account.[46] Celebrity presence at an event can similarly be ignored and items of modest value provided in connection with a donation can also be disregarded. Exhibit 24–3 is a list of typical benefits and suggestions for valuing gifts.

Exhibit 24–3

SUGGESTED GUIDELINES FOR VALUING GIFTS

BENEFIT	VALUE ASSIGNED
Objects or services sold normally in stores and by service providers.	Price at which goods or services normally sell.
Discounts on purchases.	Amount of discount given.
Benefit dinner dance in the nonprofit's facility.	Cost of event, including donated goods and services.
Benefit golf tournament.	Normal cost of playing golf on course.
Chance to play with pro.	Price of the chance.
Raffle or door prize ticket.	Price paid for ticket.
Participation in educational tour.	Price of similar commercial tour.
Attendance at performance or movie or admission to facility.	Normal ticket or admission price.
Posters, buttons, bumper stickers, books, and publications.	Comparable market price unless de minimus rules apply.
Goods or services purchased at charitable auction.	Normal selling price in commercial setting.
Name printed in program or on a building.	None.

[45] Reg. §1.170A-1(c)28(2).
[46] Reg. §1.6115-1(a)(3) Example 1.

Who Values.   The burden of proving value of donor benefits has now shifted to charities providing benefits.[47] A charity's good faith estimate of the value of benefits provided can be relied upon by a donor, unless the taxpayer knows, or has reason to know, that the estimate is erroneous. Thus, the charity has a burden to obtain sufficient information to make an accurate valuation, although any reasonable methodology can be used. The factors used should be documented and preferably include independent opinions. While the cost of rendering a service or providing a benefit to members and/or attendees it not the prescribed measure of the value, the cost is often instructive in making a valuation when there is no commercial counterpart. Merchants who donate goods and services inherent in benefits can, for example, be asked to furnish an invoice reflecting the normal cost of the items they contribute. Commercial price lists of similar items can be sought.

Other Valuation Issues.   Where the market value of an event is determined in reference to the cost of the event, there is often a question of which denominator to use. Does one count the number of tickets sold, the number that actually attend, or the number one prepared to serve? The good faith standard expects the charity to arrive at a fair value taking all relevant information into account under the circumstances to value the direct benefit provided.

The organization's administrative staff, facility, and fund-raising costs are not counted as part of the cost of benefits provided for this purpose, for Form 990 reporting purposes, or for financial reporting purposes. Similarly, the nonprofit using actual cost to value entertainment or favors provided for disclosure purposes (due to lack of a comparable commercial event) should exclude overhead costs.

Fortunately, intangible recognition, such as having one's name placed on a building or donor listing, is as a general rule considered to be of incidental or tenuous benefit, and does not reduce the value of the gift.[48]

Failure to use the tickets or privileges does not entitle the purchaser to a deduction, but written refusal of the ticket or privilege from the outset enables the donor to evidence a gift. Returning tickets received can also convert such transactions into a pure gift.[49]

(a) The de Minimus Rule

Premiums or benefits of insubstantial value given in connection with a qualified fund-raising campaign are de minimus and can be ignored.[50] In response to charities' complaints that the valuation process was too difficult and subjective, benefits can be disregarded and do not reduce the donation in the following circumstances:

---

[47] This rule is sometimes confused with the fact that the donor, rather than the charity, is responsible for valuing items of property contributed to a charity.

[48] Reg. §53.4941 (d)-2(f)28(2); Rev. Rul. 66-358, 1966-2 C.B. 216; Rev. Rul. 73-407, 1973-2 C.B. 383.

[49] Rev. Rul. 65-432, 1968-2 C.B. 104.

[50] Rev. Proc. 90-12, IRS News Release IRB 90-20, February 1990; updated by Rev. Proc. 92-58, 1992-2, IRB 10 and Rev. Proc. 97-57, 1997-52 IRB 20.

- The fair market value of all benefits received for the payment is not more than 2% of the payment, or $71, whichever is less (e.g., a benefit worth up to $72 can be given to a $3,660 contributor).

- The donation is $36[51] or more (during 1998 and adjusted annually) and the benefits received are token items (bookmarks, calendars, key chains, mugs, posters, tee shirts, etc.) bearing the organization's name or logo, with a cost (as opposed to FMV) of no more than $7.20 (during 1999 and adjusted annually). All benefits received during a year are aggregated to calculate the total amount furnished. For example, the combined cost of a $4 mug and a $4 tee shirt exceed the de minimus amount, and thus reduce the donation by the entire $8.

Organizations following this procedure are instructed to include this statement in their fund-raising literature:

> Under IRS guidelines, the estimated value of [benefits received] is not substantial; therefore the full amount of your payment is a deductible contribution.

De minimus benefits provided to the employees of a donor or to partners of a partnership may be disregarded.

Qualified Campaign.   A qualified fund-raising campaign has three elements:

1. It is designed to raise tax deductible donations.

2. The charity uses reasonable methods to value benefits offered in return for donations.

3. Solicitations state how much of the donation is deductible and how much is not. (This statement may be written on tickets, or receipts, broadcast, telephoned, or made in person.)

Commercial Quality Publications.   Publications, such as newsletters or program guides, are assigned value if they are commercial quality publications (CQPs). A CQP is one (1) the primary purpose of which is not to inform members about the organization's activities, (2) is available to the general public, (3) contains paid advertising, and (4) contains articles written for compensation.

(b) Benefits That Need Not Be Valued

It is sometimes difficult to tell whether a donor is receiving something of value treated as a quid pro quo, or if the charity is simply fulfilling its exempt functions by furnishing services. Furnishing educational benefits to donors in the form of newsletters, lectures, or training, is normally considered an exempt function. Civil Air Patrol squadron dues entitling members to be trained for rescue missions and to purchase items at a military exchange were deemed to be deductible, because

---

[51] This amount was originally set at $25 and the permissible cost started at $5; see note 39.

the specific benefits were merely incidental to the charitable purposes of the patrol and to the public services rendered by the members.[52] The rights to attend an annual meeting, vote for officers, attend semiannual social functions, and conduct an annual rummage sale did not make a convalescent home member's dues nondeductible.[53]

Intangible Religious Benefits. Goods and services that consist solely of intangible religious benefits are not valued and do not reduce one's donation to a religious organization. Such benefits are those provided by an exclusively religious organization for religious purposes and generally not sold in a commercial transaction outside the donative context.[54] Pew rents, payments for performing weddings, funerals, and other religious services by churches are, for example, classed as charitable donations.[55] The Supreme Court, in 1989, found "auditing fees" of the Church of Scientology to be valuable personal services in upholding IRS disallowance of their deduction as charitable donations.[56] Later the IRS reversed its position, issued a favorable determination letter for the church, and deemed such payments deductible effective January 1, 1993.

Member Privileges. Until 1995, member dues were deemed to represent a pure charitable donation only if members are given no "commensurate rights and privileges" other than the personal satisfaction of being of service to others and furthering the charitable cause in which the members share a common interest.[57] Due to the difficulty of valuing such privileges, the substantiation rules allow certain member privileges to be disregarded under specific conditions.[58]

24.4 UNRELATED BUSINESS INCOME ASPECTS OF FUND-RAISING

Many fund-raising events look like business activities, are conducted in competition with businesses that sell the same goods and services, and are potentially subject to tax as unrelated business income (UBI). Event profits are, however, not often taxable as UBI because exclusions apply. The typical fund-raising event is organized and operated by volunteers,[59] is irregularly carried on,[60] involves the sale of donated merchandise,[61] and/or may be related to the entity's exempt purposes. Special standards apply to determine when a corporate sponsorship can be classified as taxable advertising revenue rather than a donation.[62]

---

[52] *Miller v. Commissioner,* 34 T.C.M. 1207 (1975).
[53] Rev. Rul. 55-70, 1955-1 C.B. 506.
[54] IRC §170(f)(8)(B)(iii).
[55] Rev. Rul. 70-47, 1970-1 C.B. 49.
[56] *Hernandez v. Commissioner,* 109 S.Ct. 2137 (1989).
[57] Rev. Rul. 68-432, 1968-2 C.B. 104 and Rev. Rul. 55-70, 1955-1 C.B. 506.
[58] See §24.2(b).
[59] IRC §513(a)(1).
[60] IRC §512(a)(1).
[61] IRC §513(a)(3).
[62] See Chapter 21§8(e).

The IRS has targeted for examination the types of fund-raisers usually claimed to be excluded from UBI classification because of their relatedness to the organization's exempt purposes, such as travel tours and athletic facilities. For a travel tour to be classified as related to an organization's exempt purposes, the tour must include a fairly high level of educational content and professional direction. The IRS found a typical travel tour program was unrelated, so that all of the proceeds, including the donation element, were subject to the UBI tax.[63] Management of athletic events and rental of school athletic facilities to outsiders is considered business income to a school.

Bingo games are given a special exclusion from UBI if the operation of bingo by the organization does not violate state law.[64] It is extremely important to note that other games of chance (such as raffles, lotteries, and casino parties) do not qualify for this exclusion meaning the profits are potentially taxable unless the volunteer or irregular exclusions apply. The tax code specifically defines bingo to include only those games in which (1) wagers are placed, (2) winners are determined, and (3) prizes or other property are distributed, in the presence of all persons placing wagers in such game. The regulations delineate this definition to include games of chance played with cards that are generally printed with five rows of five squares each, during which participants place markers over randomly called numbers on the cards in an attempt to form a preselected pattern such as a horizontal, vertical, or diagonal line, or all four corners.[65]

The winnings in a game of chance must be reported as taxable income to the winner. The type of reporting, either a Form 1099 or W-2, depends upon the amount of the prize. As outlined in Exhibit 24–2, tax withholding is also required in certain cases.

24.5 STATE AND LOCAL REGULATIONS

Proper disclosures are also of concern on a local level. In all but eight states charitable solicitation statutes require registration by professional fund-raisers and certain organizations. Many cities also have standards and registration requirements for solicitors. The focus of such registration requirements is on truth in the solicitation materials and private benefit to professional fund-raisers. Fund-raising literature that does not reflect the actual amount of money devoted to charitable purposes constitutes a deceptive trade practice under the common law. It is the opinion of the Charitable Trust Section of the Texas Attorney General's office that charities have a fiduciary responsibility to maximize funds available for programs.

The Better Business Bureau, the National Charities Information Bureau, among others, monitor the levels of fund-raising costs. They publish public information reporting cost percentage ratios and other information intended to inform donors about the use of their donations. For a comprehensive view of these rules see *The Law of Fund-Raising*.[66]

[63] Tech. Ad. Memo. 9029001.
[64] IRC §513(f).
[65] Reg. §1.513-5(d).
[66] Bruce Hopkins (New York: John Wiley 1993) supplemented annually.

CHAPTER TWENTY-FIVE

Employment Taxes

Employment taxes and associated payroll costs, such as workers' compensation and health insurance, equal between 10 to 25% of an exempt organization's payroll. These taxes represent a substantial expense to most organizations and there is sometimes a temptation to classify a worker as an independent contractor, in order to avoid such costs. Until 1973, exempt organizations (EOs) were exempt from Social Security taxes, and their employees were only eligible to be covered if the organization elected to participate in the system. Until 1989, Internal Revenue Service (IRS) exempt organization examiners had no authority to look at employment taxes. For these reasons, many EOs ignored the complexities of employment taxes, until the IRS announced its intention to emphasize employment tax issues. This posture was costly to many colleges and universities that were assessed payroll tax liabilities in the millions for part-time student workers after mid-1990 IRS audits.

Since 1978, the IRS's hands have been tied by a congressionally mandated safe harbor that prevents IRS reclassification of workers for an entity that uses some reasonable basis for its policy and files information returns reporting compensation to nonemployees. An organization is presumed to be correct if it relies on IRS precedent, long-standing industry practice, or a prior IRS audit. Generally, exempt organizations have operated under this safe harbor. However, the General Accounting Office and the Treasury Department actively look for ways to enhance collections of income taxes from independent contractors, so new legislation and IRS pronouncements can be expected.

The character of payments made by exempt organizations to individuals—whether employees or independent contractors—is basically governed by the same rules as those applied to nonexempt businesses. There are a few exceptions, but the rules for payroll tax deposits, annual reporting, fringe benefits, and taxability of pensions paid to retirees are mostly the same. If there is any doubt about the importance of employment tax issues to an exempt organization, proof can be found in the 1996–97 tax law changes. Several provisions enacted at that time impact EO employers.

- *Employer-Provided Educational Assistance.* IRC §127(d) retroactively extended the tax-free treatment of nongraduate level educational assistance for up to $5,250 per individual.[1]

- *Medical Research Institution Employee Housing.* IRC §119(d)(4)(A) was added to the code to exempt subsidized housing for employees of certain medical research institutions that are classified as §170(b)(1)(a)(iii) organizations.[2] This exemption previously applied only to schools.

- *Long-Term Care Insurance.* Benefits paid under a qualified long-term care contract are treated like payments from an accident and insurance plan and excluded from income as amounts received for personal injuries and sickness,[3] with a cap of $175 per day. Payments for such plans, effective in 1997, are deductible as medical expenses.[4]

- *Health Insurance Portability.* Group health plans, including health maintenance organizations (HMOs) covering two or more persons must contain provisions intended to enhance continued coverage for employees who change jobs and those with preexisting conditions.[5] Governmental, accident, dental or vision, Medicare supplement, disability income, liability, and certain other insurance plans are not covered.

25.1 DISTINCTIONS BETWEEN EMPLOYEES AND INDEPENDENT CONTRACTORS

Whether a worker is an employee or an independent contractor is a factual question based on common law, which often requires a detailed analysis. The case law

---

[1] Small Business Job Protection Act §1202.
[2] Small Business Job Protection Act §1123.
[3] IRC §§106(c), 125(f), 807(d)(3)(A)(iii), and 4980B(g)(2); Health Insurance Portability and Accountability Act §321.
[4] IRC §§162(1) and 213(d)(1)(C); Health Insurance Portability and Accountability Act §401.
[5] IRC §§9801-9806 and 4980B(f).

and rulings provide some guidance, and the IRS has developed a 20-factor test.[6] The IRS Form SS-8, Determination of Employee Work Status for Purposes of Federal Employment Taxes and Income Tax Withholding, that reflects the 20 factors is shown as Appendix 25–1. The criteria developed by the courts and the IRS are briefly capsulated in Exhibit 25–1, Employee Versus Independent Contractor Status.

(a) Employees

Employees are typically subject to tighter employer controls than independent contractors are: hours of work are regular and specified; the place of work is the employer's; compensation is regular and continuing; and tools, training, and work supplies are normally furnished by the employer, among other benefits and advantages. Employees are given paid vacations and accrue pension and sick pay benefits, and are generally thought to have a more secure position than independent contractors.

The term *contract worker* is often misleading. Typically, workers hired on a part-time or temporary basis are given this title, and are often not treated as employees, partly because they are not given certain advantages of employees. Nonetheless, the fact that a worker is not hired for a permanent position does *not* determine his or her status as an employee, and most such workers are employees subject to withholding.

(b) Independent Contractors

As the title implies, independent contractors work when they please, use their own tools, have independent professional standing, and bear a risk of loss if the job is not completed satisfactorily or within the prescribed time. Outside accountants, computer consultants, fund-raising advisors, and consulting psychologists are examples of independent workers.[7] No vacation or sick pay is provided, no taxes are withheld, pension eligibility is not furnished, and the engagement is for a limited time period for a specific task.

Form SS-8 (reproduced in Appendix 25–1) should be completed to evidence the status of each worker treated as a contractor. This form can be used to show that the organization made a good faith effort to determine a worker's proper classification. The form's length and the variety of criteria developed by the IRS indicate the subjective nature of the distinction and the difficulty that may occur in identifying the proper category for a worker.

The terms of engagement should validate a worker's status as an independent contractor. At the minimum, three important documents evidence the arrangement and prove that the person is not an employee:

1. A contract or other type of engagement letter with the contractor (see Exhibit 25–2) describing the respective responsibilities and terms of the contract, including three important elements:

---

[6] Reg. §31.3401(c)-1(a) and (d); Rev. Rul. 87-41, 1987 1 C.B. 296.
[7] See Priv. Ltr. Rul. 9231011 regarding a part-time grant proposal writer and Priv. Ltr. Rul. 9227025 about a food bank manager—both deemed employees.

Exhibit 25–1

EMPLOYEES VS. INDEPENDENT CONTRACTOR CHECKLIST

Revenue Ruling 87-41 lists the primary characteristics distinguishing employees from independent contractors. These characteristics are listed on this checklist. Whichever blank best describes the predominant characteristic of a worker or position is to be checked. There is no specific mathematical test, although more than one-half of the checkmarks on either line is a strong indication. The facts and circumstances of each payee-payor relationship should be analyzed. Classifying a worker as an employee is seldom challenged; finding justification for treating one as independent is more troublesome. The most common reason for making the distinction is to identify persons—the employees—who are subject to federal income tax withholding and unemployment taxes. Independent contractors are abbreviated as "ICs"

Instruction and Training

☐ Employees are required to comply with instructions as to when, where, and how work is performed, and their training is provided either by formal program or work supervision.

☐ ICs are free to perform work according to their own professional standards, use their own methods, and receive no training from purchasers of their services.

Payment Terms

☐ Employees are paid by the hour, week, or month on a regular, indefinite, and continuous basis. Employees' business expenses are paid. Fringe benefits are usually provided.

☐ ICs are often paid by the engagement with a fee calculated without regard to time spent. ICs are not paid for excess time to perform the task nor given paid vacation or sick leave. ICs pay their own expenses.

Engagement Terms

☐ Employer has the right to discharge an employee; control is exercised with threat of dismissal. Employees have the right to quit without incurring liability.

☐ ICs complete the agreed task without regard to the time it takes and may suffer damages if work is not performed as contracted.

Relation to Entity

☐ Employees' services are an integral part of the ongoing success and continuation of the organization. Services are rendered personally by employees, who work only for, have loyalty to, and do not compete with the employer. Employees are bonded and provided workers compensation.

☐ ICs consult on a per job, limited term, or special project basis. ICs can hire and pay assistants to perform the work. ICs' services are available to the others on a regular basis. Some ICs work under a company name.

Exhibit 25–1 *(continued)*

Work Place and Hours

☐ Employees work on business premises or are physically directed and supervised by employer. Hours of work are established by employer.

☐ ICs often work at their own places of business, and usually set their own time for performing work.

Investment

☐ Employees are dependent upon employer for tools and facilities, and usually make no investment in the job. Employees bear no risk of loss for financial costs of employer.

☐ ICs buy their own tools, hire workers, pay licensing fees, and are responsible for costs of engagement. ICs bear financial risk of losing money.

- The engaging company does not essentially control the work product of the independent contractor;

- The contractor's engagement can be terminated if the work is not performed to specifications and all obligations are met; and

- The contractor has the right to hire and fire assistants.

2. A signed Form W-9 is obtained to show that the contractor claims exemption from withholding and that the organization is not responsible for backup withholding. This step also obtains the federal identification number for purposes of preparing Form 1099.

3. An invoice or periodic billing statement evidences the independence of the contractor. The billing should appear professional and support the organization's position that the worker is independent.

(c) Employee Benefits

Payments made on behalf of employees for fringe benefits, expense reimbursements, and deferred compensation are, as a general rule, not taxed to employees. The rules governing the taxability of such payments are the same as for employees working for nonexempt entities. For example, an exempt organization employee's car allowance is reportable on Form W-2 unless the employee submits an accounting for the mileage.

    An exempt organization can adopt a cafeteria plan to provide day care, tuition, and other benefits.[8] Health insurance and medical reimbursement plans can be established for employees.[9] Most types of qualified pension plans, including defined benefit, defined contribution, thrift, 401(k) plan, and simplified employee

---

[8] IRC §125.
[9] IRC §106.

Exhibit 25–2

SAMPLE CONTRACTOR ENGAGEMENT LETTER

> *This letter is intended to serve only to provide suggestions. Qualified legal assistance may be required.*

In consideration of payment by _____ [name of customer]

Fixed fee or
Hourly rate $_____ per hour times _____ hours = _____

Reimbursable expenses:

_____   _____
_____   _____
_____   _____

Invoices for services will be issued monthly, along with receipts and other documentation for reimbursable expenses listed above. For consideration, we (I) agree to perform the following services:

_____
_____
_____
_____
_____

We (I) agree to perform the specified services in good order in a timely fashion. We (I) are independent contractors, not an employee or agent of _____, and are responsible for all federal and state payroll taxes and insurance in connection with this engagement. This agreement may be terminated by either party at any time after payment for any unpaid charges for services rendered up to termination. In acknowledgment of our understandings, we have both signed below.

By: _____ Date: _____   By: _____ Date: _____

Name of Contractor _____ Name of Organization _____

plans (SEP) can be provided for exempt organization employees. A 403(b) plan can be adopted by a (c)(3) organization. Special limitations are placed on deferred compensation arrangements.[10] A thorough discussion of pension benefits is beyond the scope of this book.

(d) Volunteer Fringe Benefits

An exempt organization may pay certain expenses on behalf of its volunteers, and may reimburse its volunteers for expenses they incur on behalf of the organization

_____
[10] IRC §457.

in conducting its projects. After some years of question, the regulations provide that an exempt organization volunteer who performs services (including services as a director) for an organization or for a federal, state, or local governmental unit, is deemed to have a profit motive for purposes of IRC §162.[11] This means that such expenses, up to the value of services rendered, are not taxable to the individual volunteer and are not reportable by the organization as compensation. Of particular importance to some exempt organizations, this rule applies to officer and director liability insurance and indemnification. Premiums previously had to be reported as compensation to the officers, directors, and volunteers.

(c) Fellowships, Scholarships, and Awards

Although it seems incongruous with the motivation for making grants to individuals, certain individual grants must be reported to the IRS on Form 1099 or Form W-2, and taxes must be withheld as the following discussion outlines.

Tuition and Fees. A scholarship grant is fragmented into two parts. The portion awarded for payment of tuition and related expenses required for enrollment in an educational institution (such as books, fees, supplies, and equipment) is not taxable to the recipient, nor is it reportable to the IRS by the organization. Such payments are called "qualified scholarship" payments and are specifically excluded from gross income of a person who is a candidate for a degree.[12]

IRC 6050S requires reporting of tuition payments by schools. The information reporting requirements were designed to aid parents in calculating their HOPE Scholarship credit under IRC §25A. IRS Notice 97-73 sets out reporting requirements applicable for calendar year 1998. At the time this book was completed, it was not known ultimately whether parent's taxpayer identification number would be required. The notice excused schools from reporting grants and scholarships paid directly to their students and not processed by the school.

Room and Board. Payments for room, board, travel, and any other expenses are includible in income after the 1986 Tax Reform Act. For some reason, however, such taxable payments are not reportable to the IRS as income unless they represent compensation.[13] The 1998 instructions to Form 1099 clearly state, "DO NOT use this form to report scholarship or fellowship grants." They go on to say, "Other taxable scholarship or fellowship payments are not required to be reported by you to the IRS on any form."[14]

Teaching Fellows and Other Student Workers. For income tax purposes, scholarships or fellowships paid on the condition that recipients teach, perform research, or provide other services for the institution granting the scholarship do produce taxable income.[15] Such income is considered to be wages reportable on Form W-2

---

[11] Reg. §1.132-5.
[12] IRC §117.
[13] Prop. Reg. 6041-3(q).
[14] IRS Notice 87-31, 1987-1 C.B. 475.
[15] IRC §117(c).

even though students are eligible to claim an exemption from income tax withholding.[16]

Social Security taxes may or may not need to be withheld, matched, and paid for amounts paid to students for work performed for colleges they attend. Students receiving payments from a state or federal agency that does not participate in the Social Security system are not subject to FICA. IRC §3121(b)(10) provides what is referred to as a *Student FICA exception,* which exempts payments for employment services to a student who is enrolled and regularly attends classes at a school, college or university (whether or not tax-exempt), or an affiliated organization of such an institution. The regulations somewhat vaguely say a student performing services incident to and for the purpose of pursuing a course of study at a school, college, or university qualifies. After significant controversies during examinations of colleges and universities, the IRS issued Rev. Proc. 98-16 to establish specific standards.[17] The ruling contains a series of questions designed to provide answers to schools employing students eligible for exclusion from the FICA tax.

To qualify for the exemption, the student must be a part-time undergraduate or professional student as those terms are defined by the Department of Education. Services of career employees, postdoctoral students and fellows, and medical residents and interns do not qualify. The definitions contained in the procedure should be carefully studied by any institution exempting students from FICA withholding. The IRS previously had taken the position that a student had to take 12 credits of courses and work less than 20 hours a week to be qualified for the exemption.

Awards.   Prizes or awards paid to recognize someone's accomplishment are taxable to the recipient and reported on Form 1099-MISC. Only if the money is paid by the recipient to a charitable organization does the award escape taxation.[18] See discussion in §25.3(f) regarding raffles and gaming awards.

Foreign Grant Recipients.   For foreign grantees, the portion of a scholarship grant paid for study, training, or research in the United States (not including tuition and fees) is also taxable. As a general rule, income tax must be withheld at the rate of 14% on the taxable portion.[19] Treaties may exempt certain of these payments. After a number of years of controversy, the withholding requirements for foreign grant recipients are determined by the *situs* or residence of the person or organization making the payment, in addition to the residence of the recipient.[20] In two circumstances, fellowship or scholarship payments are not subject to withholding:

1. The payor is a U.S.-based citizen, domestic partnership, or corporation, a state, or a federal agency, and payment is made to a non-U.S. person for study pursued outside the United States.

---

[16] Prop. Reg. 1.117-6(d)(4); it is presumed a student's earnings will not exceed the minimum standard deduction.
[17] Rev. Proc. 98-16, 1998-5 IRB.
[18] IRC §74.
[19] IRC §1441(b)(1).
[20] Reg. §1.863-1(d), effective August 25, 1995.

2. The payment is made for study within the United States by a foreign government, international organization, or person other than a U.S. citizen.

The regulations specifically say that this rule does not apply to salary or other compensation for services, but does apply to prizes and awards for artistic, scientific, or charitable achievements. Reporting requirements are outlined in §25.3(d).

25.2 MINISTERS

Duly ordained ministers of a church hold a special place in employment tax procedures. The clergy of some sects take vows of poverty and, as a matter of religious conscience, take no compensation for their work. The procedures for reporting compensation of ministers has evolved with respect for the need to maintain separation of church and state. The result is a set of confusing rules.

(a) Who Is a Minister?

The term *minister* is defined in the Internal Revenue Code and Regulations by a job description. Services provided by a minister in the exercise of his (her) ministries include:[21]

- Ministration of sacerdotal functions (marriage, baptism, funerals, and similar services)

- Conduct of religious worship

- Conduct, control, and maintenance of religious organizations, including religious board, societies, and other integral agencies of such organizations (such as schools)

- Performance of teaching and administrative duties at theological seminaries

A minister need not be ordained, but may also be commissioned, licensed, appointed, or otherwise authorized by a religious organization. The important criterion is that the minister must perform religious duties within the scope and practices of a religious denomination.[22] Interestingly these standards use the term *religious organization*, not *church*, although the criteria for defining organizations performing the foregoing functions apply to churches and their integrated auxiliaries for exempt-status purposes as outlined in Chapter 3§2.

In a 1992 private ruling, the IRS considered whether a particular sect's "commissioned ministers" qualified for the housing allowance exclusion discussed in §25.2(b). The sect ordained ministers who officiated in public administration of the sacraments and led public worship. The commissioned ministers "in some circumstances lead the liturgy in prayer, read the scriptures or perform a baptism but more often served as deacon or director of Christian education." The IRS found

[21] Reg. §1.1402(c)-5(b)(2).
[22] Rev. Rul. 78-301, 1978-2 C.B. 103.

that the commissioned ministers performed full-time ministerial duties. The qualifying functions included classroom teaching; evangelizing; counseling individuals; leading Bible study groups, devotion, worship studies for youth, and a congregation's music ministry; giving the children's service at Sunday worship service; addressing the congregation in worship services; coordinating lay church workers; administering or guiding the congregation's youth ministry events; participating in ministries to those with special needs; and caring spiritually for the sick, the imprisoned, and their families.[23]

Qualifying ministers also include a probationary member of the United Methodist Church,[24] cantors of the Jewish faith,[25] and retired ministers.[26]

Not qualifying as ministers are chaplains not employed by a religious organization or its integral auxiliary. *Ministers* do not include chaplains employed to teach at a university,[27] employed at a human service organization[28] or the Veterans Administration,[29] or chaplains in the Armed Services (chaplains are commissioned officers).[30]

(b) How Ministers Are Special

Ministers are exempt from income tax and Social Security tax withholding[31] and a portion of the compensation for services they perform as a minister may not be subject to income and the self-employment tax in situations listed below. However, if the minister is subject to one or both of these taxes, the compensation is considered to be attributable to the carrying on of a trade or business,[32] which permits the deduction of ordinary and necessary expenses in arriving at taxable income for both income (as an itemized deduction for employees) and self-employment purposes.[33]

Income Tax.   Any amounts paid as compensation to a minister for services are subject to income tax, just as for other individual taxpayers. Offerings and fees received for marriages, baptisms, funerals, and the like are taxable income.[34] Ministers are classified as employees or independent contractors by applying the standards listed in §25.1. If the minister is classified as an employee, the income tax liability is paid either through the estimated tax system or through voluntary income tax withholding. An employed minister receives Form W-2, in most cases re-

---

[23] Priv. Ltr. Rul. 9221025.

[24] *Wingo v. Commissioner,* 89 T.C. 922 (1989).

[25] Rev. Rul. 78-301, 1978-2 C.B. 103; *D. Silverman,* 73-2 USTC ¶9546 (8th Cir. 1973), *aff'g* 57 T.C. 727 (Dec. 31,290).

[26] Rev. Rul. 63-156, 1963-2 C.B. 79.

[27] *L. D. Boyer,* 69 T.C. 521 (Dec. 34,900).

[28] Rev. Rul. 68-68, 1968-1 C.B. 51.

[29] Rev. Rul. 72-462, 1972-2 C.B. 76.

[30] Reg. §1.107-1(a).

[31] Reg. 31.3401(a)(9)-1; IRS Publication 15-A Supplement to Circular E, *Employer's Tax Guide,* For 1998, p. 77.

[32] IRC §1402(c)(2)(D).

[33] Rev. Rul. 80-110, IRB 1980-16, 10.

[34] Reg. §1.162-2(a)(1) and IRS Publication 525, *Taxable and Nontaxable Income.*

flecting only the gross wage amount. If the minister is not an employee, the tax is paid individually through the estimated income tax system, and the church reports the compensation on Form 1099.

Self-Employment Tax. A minister's earnings are excepted from "employment" for the purpose of imposing the Social Security tax.[35] A minister is instead subject to the self-employment tax, unless he or she is one of the following persons:[36]

- Members of a religious order whose members have taken vows of poverty.[37]

- Duly ordained ministers who have not taken a vow of poverty but who make an individual election out of the Social Security system on Form 4361. A statement must be signed indicating that the minister is opposed by conscience or religious principle to the acceptance of any public insurance and is so informing his or her church.

- Clergy members of a church or church-controlled organization that makes the election for its employees to be exempt from Social Security coverage pursuant to IRC §3121(w). This exemption only applies to remuneration of less than $100 per year and generally applies to "vow of poverty" situations.

In a test case, the Tax Court found that a Methodist minister was an employee and not self-employed for purposes of claiming business expense deductions on Schedule C. The expenses were deductible as miscellaneous itemized deductions subject to the 2%-of-adjusted-gross-income floor.[38] The court found a long list of reasons why he was not an independent businessman. He was required to be amenable to the church in the performance of numerous required duties, to provide explanations of his sermons to church officials, could not unilaterally discontinue services or refuse an appointment, was bound by mandatory retirement rules, and was subject to supervision. In addition, he was not required to invest in church facilities, was not in a position to increase his profits as a minister, and received benefits (including a pension, vacation, paternity leave, disability pay, and a guaranteed salary) when not assigned to a church.

Housing Allowances. Amounts designated by a church as housing allowance for its ministers are not taxable for income tax purposes,[39] but are subject to self-employment tax. The allowance must be designated in advance of its payment or

---

[35] IRC §3121(b)(8)(A) for purposes of the Federal Insurance Contributions Act; see IRS Publication 15-A, *Employer's Supplemental Tax Guide.*

[36] IRS Publication 517, *Social Security and Other Information for Members of the Clergy and Religious Workers.*

[37] IRC §1402(c); see also Chapter 3§3.

[38] *Weber v. Commissioner,* 103 T.C. No. 19 (Aug. 25, 1994); *aff'd,* 95-2 USTC ¶ 50,409 (4th Cir. 1995); for cases involving Assembly of God ministers see *Alford vs. U.S.,* Civil No. 94-1074 (D.C. W. Arkansas, 1996) and *Richard G. and Anne C. Greene v. Commissioner,* T.C. Memo. 1996-531.

[39] IRC §107; IRS Publication 525, page 10.

provision, as evidenced by an employment contract, church budget, deacons' resolution, or similar official action. The minister must actually expend the amount provided. Any allowance not used or used for nonresidential purposes is taxed.[40] The taxable amount is equal to the fair rental value of housing (including utilities and other costs). A parsonage may be furnished rent-free, or allowances may be paid to cover the parsonage utilities and other maintenance, or to cover rents, or to cover the minister's costs of individually owning and maintaining a house.

(c) Conscientious Objectors

As noted previously, a minister may make an individual election not to participate in the Social Security system by filing Form 4361, Application for Exemption from Self-Employment Tax for Use by Ministers, Members of Religious Orders and Christian Science Practitioners. A minister, however, is subject to income tax on compensation paid for services he or she renders that is not otherwise excluded as a fringe benefit. Some religious organizations, peace groups, and other exempt organizations employ persons who protest payments of federal income taxes for spiritual reasons. These conscientious objectors have traditionally objected to money allocated to armaments that bring harm to human beings caused by war or to government-supported abortions. How should an organization respond if it is asked not to levy taxes against such an employee? What is the responsibility of the organization to the IRS? The answer is that the IRS basically holds the exempt organization responsible, but may use some leniency.

The Quakers produced answers to some of these questions when they faced a federal district court in December 1990. The judges decided that the collection of taxes applied to all citizens equally, and did not specifically regulate religious practice or beliefs. The church was therefore required to withhold the full amount of taxes from its regular employees' wages. Out of deference to the church's exercise of religious freedom, however, the court imposed no penalties for failure to withhold the taxes in question.[41]

25.3 REPORTING REQUIREMENTS

Whether paid to employees, individual contractors, or individual grant recipients, almost all payments made by exempt organizations to individuals or unincorporated entities are reportable to the IRS. The annual W-2 Form is filed for employees. The Form 1099 Miscellaneous (also called an information return) is filed for most other payments to independent contractors and other nonemployees. Exhibit 25–3 is used to facilitate annual compliance review.

(a) Penalties

The penalty for failure to file an information return is up to $50 per return. However, if the IRS determines that a contractor should have been classified as an employee,

---

[40] Reg. §1.107-1(c).
[41] *U.S. v. Philadelphia Yearly Meeting, Religious Society of Friends*, No. 88-6386 (E.D. Pa), Dec., 19901.

Exhibit 25–3

EMPLOYER TAX REQUIREMENTS CHECKLIST

Nonprofit organization employers are subject to the same rules that govern for-profit employers, including rules administered by the Department of Labor, workers compensation statutes, the Employee Retirement Insurance Security Act (ERISA) rules, and federal and state employment taxes. Since the costs of employee benefits range from 10 to 30 percent of direct payroll costs, these matters deserve close attention. Severe penalties in the Internal Revenue Code are imposed on failure to pay over employment taxes.

1. Does the organization have a policy for distinguishing between employees and independent contractors? ☐

   - Verify satisfaction of at least four factors in Exhibit 25–1, Employee vs. Independent Contractor Checklist. ☐
   - Review questions on Form SS-8, Information for Use in Determining whether a Worker Is an Employee for Federal Employment Taxes and Income Tax Withholding. ☐
   - Does the organization have a contract and a signed Form W-9 (Appendix 25–2) for independent contractors? (See Exhibit 25–1.) ☐
   - Have Social Security numbers been secured?
   - Are invoices obtained from independent contractors to prove their professionalism? ☐

2. Are meals, cars, tuition, or housing allowances furnished to employees? Determine whether they are reportable compensation and whether withholding is required. ☐

3. Does the pension plan adhere to ERISA rules? ☐

4. Is Form 5500, 5500C, or 5500R required for employee plan? ☐

5. Are the terms of any qualified or nonqualified deferred compensation plan being adhered to? ☐

6. Do Consolidated Omnibus Budget Reconciliation Act (COBRA) rules entitle former employees to continued medical benefit coverage? ☐

7. Is workers compensation coverage required? ☐

8. Verify adherence to federal withholding requirements. Study IRS Circular E, *Employer's Tax Guide,* and Publication 15-A for filing requirements and an excellent chart on wages subject to or exempt from taxes. The types of employment taxes are:

   - Income tax withholding. Most wages are subject to this tax, but certain ministers, members of religious orders, student workers, and fellowship or grant recipients are exempt. ☐
   - Social Security tax. Review Circular E chart; wages over $100 are taxable. ☐

Exhibit 25–3 *(continued)*

- Federal unemployment tax. §501(c)(3) organizations are exempt from this tax. Several types of compensation subject to income tax are also exempt. See Circular E. ☐

9. Verify timely filing of the following IRS reports: ☐

- Form 940, federal unemployment tax report (due January 31) (Form 940 is not filed by §501(c)(3) organizations.) ☐
- Form 941, employer's quarterly federal tax return (due January 31, April 30, July 31, and October 31) ☐
- W-2 Forms for all employees (due January 31) ☐
- W-3 Form to IRS with copies of W-2s (due February 28) ☐
- W-4 placed in each employee's file ☐
- Form 1099-MISC for all independent contractors ☐
- Form W-2G Prizes and Awards ☐
- Form W-2P Statement for Recipients of Pensions ☐

10. Verify timely deposit of federal employment taxes. ☐

- Taxes deposited by fifteenth of next month following wage payment. ☐
- Tax deposited biweekly for employers whose tax for prior year exceeded $50,000. ☐
- Tax deposited electronically. ☐

11. Is the exempt organization subject to unemployment taxes? ☐

- On the federal level, only 501(c)(3)s are exempt.
- On the state level, obtain instructions from the employment commission of the state where the worker is employed. The rules differ by state. ☐
- Many states exempt 501(c)(3) EOs with fewer than four employees. ☐
- A *reimbursing* or self-insured employer status may be available. ☐

12. Are state employment (workforce) commission requirements satisfied? ☐

- Are quarterly returns filed and tax paid on time? ☐
- New organizations must first obtain an account number by filing a status report. ☐

13. Verify timely payment of federal unemployment tax liability (if applicable). ☐

- Under $100 per year: pay or deposit when filing Form 940 (January 31) ☐
- Over $100 for quarter: by 30th of next month ☐
- Over $100 per year but under $100 per quarter: by 30th of month after the quarter (or combination of quarters) in which liability exceeds $100 ☐

the exempt organization will be billed for all employment taxes that would have been payable if the worker had been classified as an employee, plus interest and penalties. Before 1997, responsible parties, starting with the board members, were assessed a penalty up to 100% of this amount for failure to withhold the taxes. Congress followed the lead of the many states that encourage board service by allowing a degree of immunity from penalties for volunteers serving on nonprofit organization boards. The IRC §6672 contains an important exception from the penalties for failure to collect and pay employment taxes for an unpaid, volunteer member of a board or a trustee or director of a tax-exempt organization that possesses the following characteristics:[42]

- Is serving solely in an honorary capacity;

- Does not participate in the day-to-day or financial operations of the organization; and

- Does not have actual knowledge of the failure on which such penalty is imposed.

(b) Tax Withholding Requirements

An exempt organization is subject to the income and Social Security tax withholding system for most of its employees.[43] An individual paid less than $100 is not subject to Social Security tax withholding, but is subject to income tax withholding. Special rules apply to ministers and foreigners, as discussed previously and in the special circumstances discussed below.

(c) Unemployment Tax

Only charitable organizations classified as exempt under IRC §501(c)(3) are exempt from the federal unemployment tax; all other exempt organizations are subject to such tax. Exemptions may be available in some states. For example, in Texas the following exemptions apply:

- Charities with fewer than four employees are not subject to the tax.

- A charity may elect to be a *reimbursing employer* by agreeing to directly pay any benefits that may come due as employee claims are made.

(d) Backup Withholding

The backup withholding system allows the U.S. Treasury to collect funds up front from independent contractors who potentially will not pay their taxes. Form W-9, Request for Taxpayer Identification Number and Certification (Appendix 25–2) is furnished by organizations to payment recipients. This is the same form used by banks and stockbrokers to ask individuals to verify their federal identification numbers and to claim exemption from backup withholding.

[42] Taxpayer Bill of Rights §904.
[43] IRS Circular E, *Employer's Tax Guide*.

Unless the organization receives a signed W-9 reflecting a Social Security number from nonemployees receiving payments for services and from individuals receiving taxable grant or fellowship payments, income tax must be withheld from the payments. Absent completion of Form W-9 or when there is some reason to believe that the Social Security number furnished is incorrect, a flat 31% of the amounts paid must be withheld and remitted. The system is designed to cause the organization to collect the tax if the individual is unable or unlikely to do so.

Nonresident Aliens. Reporting and withholding requirements for nonresident aliens depends on the alien's visa status, the existence of a treaty between the alien's home country and the United States, and the character of the payments the alien receives. The IRS has created a Foreign Payments Division to coordinate enforcement issues related to this complicated subject. After some years of confusion and controversy, the IRS wrote regulations governing these withholding requirements under IRC §1441.[44] An organization making such payments may have to file a number of special forms designed particularly for aliens, as follows:

- *Form 1001.* Form furnished by student to the institution to claim exemption from withholding on the taxable portion of any grants or awards that are excluded under treaty provisions with the student's country.

- *Form 1040NREZ.* Individual income tax return specially designed for use by nonresident alien students and professors.

- *Form 1042-S.* Report for each nonresident alien student of the amount of his or her scholarship that is nontaxable (award that is equal to or less than the tuition and fees the alien would be required to pay), the taxable portion (award amounts in excess of fees and tuition and not excluded under a treaty), and the amount of the tax that was withheld (14%) on the taxable portion.

- *Form 8233.* Form completed by institution to report to the IRS treaty-based exemptions for payments for teaching and research services rendered by nonresident aliens. This exemption is not effective until 10 days after filing the form.

(e) Payroll Depository Requirements

Nonprofits with tight cash flows are sometimes tempted to pay the employees the net amount of salary (less taxes) and use the tax money to pay the rent or some other pressing expense. However, the amounts withheld from an employee's salary are held in trust on behalf of the employee, so the money does not belong to the organization. The penalties for failure to pay over such taxes are steep. Taxes withheld are due to be deposited in as few as three days from the date wages are paid. Following is a brief list of late deposit penalties and the corresponding percentage assessed to the organization as a penalty.[45]

---

[44] Reg. §1.1441-4.
[45] IRS Publication 15, *Employer's Tax Guide,* for 1998, p. 20; Reg. §31.6302-1(c)(1).

1 to 5 days late	2%
6 to 15 days late	5%
16 or more days late (also applies to amounts paid to the IRS within 10 days of IRS notice date)	10%
Deposits made at an unauthorized financial institution, paid directly to IRS, or paid with return	10%
Amounts subject to Electronic Federal Tax Payment System (EFTPS) but not paid with EFTPS	10%
Amounts still unpaid more than 10 days after first IRS notice or demand for immediate payment, whichever is earlier.	15%

The deposit schedule for a calendar year is determined from the total taxes reported on Forms 941 in a four-quarter lookback period, which begins on July 1st and ends on June 30th. There are only two depository time periods, as follows:

- *Monthly.* Employers with modest payrolls ($50,000 or less of taxes for the lookback period) are to deposit their tax liability, including both the employee withholding and the matched FICA, by the fifteenth day following month end.

- *Semi-weekly.* Employers whose tax liability exceeds $50,000 a year ($4,166.67 per month) must deposit within three banking days of the date the tax is withheld. If an employer's total deposits were more than $50,000 in 1996, they must make electronic deposits for ALL depository tax liabilities that occur after 1997 using the Electronic Federal Tax Deposit System (EFTPS)

$100,000 Next-Day Deposit Rule.   An employer with a daily tax liability of $100,000 or more must deposit the tax by the next banking day.

No Deposit.   An employer with less than a $500 tax liability during the quarter (line 13 of Form 941) may make a payment with Form 941 instead of depositing it.

(f) Withholding for Bingo, Raffles, and Other Contests

Income taxes are imposed on gambling winnings, including prizes of all sorts won in a raffle, sweepstakes, lottery, or other contest. The rules for exempt organizations are the same as those for nonexempts.[46] A serious trap for the unsuspecting exempt is the 31% withholding requirement placed on an organization (exempt or nonexempt) awarding any prize with a value in excess of $5000 (in 1998).[47] Form W-2G is due to be filed reporting the winnings. See Exhibit 24–2 for a checklist on this subject.

[46] IRC §3402.
[47] Package 1099, *Instructions to Filers of Forms 1099, 1098, 5498, and W-2G;* see Publication 15-A, *Employer's Supplemental Tax Guide,* for special rules applicable to "Distribution of Indian Gaming Profits to Tribal Members."

Cash Prizes.   In the case of a cash prize, the organization must withhold the tax liability from the prize and make a net payment. For example, $200 would be withheld from a $1000 prize, resulting in a cash payment of $800. If the organization pays the winner the full $1000 without withholding the $200 tax, the organization must pay the tax (and hope to be reimbursed). Unless the cash is collected from the winner, the reported prize is increased by the imputed compensation resulting from the organization's payment of the winner's tax liability. The amount is calculated under an algebraic formula found in the regulations.[48]

Noncash Prizes.   Cars, trips, paintings, and other tangible merchandise won as prizes are also taxed, and income tax must be withheld if their value exceeds $5000. The value is equal to the amount a willing buyer would pay a willing seller in the normal marketplace in which such goods are sold. A car donated to a charity auction by a car dealer is not valued at the dealer's cost, but at the price at which the dealer normally sells the car.

   Before releasing a prize having a value that exceeds $5000, the charity should require the winner to pay the tax. Twenty-eight percent of the prize's value should be collected by the awarding organization. The organization is obligated to pay taxes, as described previously under Cash Prizes, regardless of whether the prize winner furnishes the cash.

Tuition and Other Bonuses.   Free admission, tuition, or other valuable services must also be valued with income taxes paid, as described previously. A private school conducting a raffle to award a year of free tuition to a parent is faced with a choice of diluting the gift by requiring the parent to pay the tax, or increasing its fundraising budget by the amount of tax it must pay on behalf of the winner.

[48] Reg. §31.3402(q)-1(d).

Appendix 25–1

FORM SS-8

Form **SS-8** (Rev. June 1997) Department of the Treasury Internal Revenue Service	**Determination of Employee Work Status for Purposes of Federal Employment Taxes and Income Tax Withholding**	OMB No. 1545-0004

Name of firm (or person) for whom the worker performed services	Name of worker	
Address of firm (include street address, apt. or suite no., city, state, and ZIP code)	Address of worker (include street address, apt. or suite no., city, state, and ZIP code)	
Trade name	Telephone no. (include area code)	Worker's social security number
Telephone number (include area code)	Firm's employer identification number	

Check type of firm for which the work relationship is in question:

☐ Individual   ☐ Partnership   ☐ Corporation   ☐ Other (specify) ....

Important Information Needed to Process Your Request

This form is being completed by: ☐ Firm   ☐ Worker

If this form is being completed by the worker, the IRS MUST have your permission to disclose your name to the firm.

Do you object to disclosing your name and the information on this form to the firm? . . . .   ☐ Yes   ☐ No

If you answer "Yes," the IRS cannot act on your request. Do not complete the rest of this form unless the IRS asks for it.

Under section 6110 of the Internal Revenue Code, the information on this form and related file documents will be open to the public if any ruling or determination is made. However, names, addresses, and taxpayer identification numbers must be removed before the information is made public.

Is there any other information you want removed? . . . .   ☐ Yes   ☐ No

If you check "Yes," we cannot process your request unless you submit a copy of this form and copies of all supporting documents showing, in brackets, the information you want removed. Attach a separate statement showing which specific exemption of section 6110(c) applies to each bracketed part.

(HTA)   Form SS-8 (Rev. 6-97)

FORM SS-8 (*continued*)

Form SS-8 (Rev. 6-97)   Page 2

This form is designed to cover many work activities, so some of the questions may not apply to you. You must answer ALL items or mark them "Unknown" or "Does not apply." If you need more space, attach another sheet.

Total number of workers in this class. (Attach names and addresses. If more than 10 workers, list only 10.) _____

This information is about services performed by the worker from _____ to _____
(month, day, year)   (month, day, year)

Is the worker still performing services for the firm? . . . . [ ] Yes   [ ] No

If "No," what was the date of termination? _____
(month, day, year)

1a Describe the firm's business
  b Describe the work done by the worker ....

2a If the work is done under a written agreement between the firm and the worker, attach a copy.
  b If the agreement is not in writing, describe the terms and conditions of the work arrangement ....

  c If the actual working arrangement differs in any way from the agreement, explain the differences and why they occur ....

3a Is the worker given training by the firm? . . . . [ ] Yes   [ ] No
  If "Yes": What kind? ....
  How often? ....
  b Is the worker given instructions in the way the work is to be done (exclusive of actual training in 3a)?   [ ] Yes   [ ] No
  If "Yes," give specific examples ....
  c Attach samples of any written instructions or procedures.
  d Does the firm have the right to change the methods used by the worker or direct that person
  on how to do the work? . . . . [ ] Yes   [ ] No
  Explain your answer ....

  e Does the operation of the firm's business require that the worker be supervised or controlled in
  the performance of the service? . . . . [ ] Yes   [ ] No
  Explain your answer ....

4a The firm engages the worker:
  [ ] To perform and complete a particular job only
  [ ] To work at a job for an indefinite period of time
  [ ] Other (explain) ....
  b Is the worker required to follow a routine or a schedule established by the firm? . . . . [ ] Yes   [ ] No
  If "Yes," what is the routine or schedule? ....

  c Does the worker report to the firm or its representative? . . . . [ ] Yes   [ ] No
  If "Yes," how often? ....
  For what purpose? ....
  In what manner (in person, in writing, by telephone, etc.)? ....
  Attach copies of any report forms used in reporting to the firm.
  d Does the worker furnish a time record to the firm? . . . . [ ] Yes   [ ] No
  If "Yes," attach copies of time records.
5a State the kind and value of tools, equipment, supplies, and materials furnished by:
  The firm ....

  The worker ....

  b What expenses are incurred by the worker in the performance of services for the firm? ....

  c Does the firm reimburse the worker for any expenses? . . . . [ ] Yes   [ ] No
  If "Yes," specify the reimbursed expenses ....

Appendix 25–1

FORM SS-8 (*continued*)

Form SS-8 (Rev. 6-97)   Page 3

6a Will the worker perform the services personally? . . . . ☐Yes ☐No

b Does the worker have helpers? . . . . ☐Yes ☐No
If "Yes," who hires the helpers? ☐Firm ☐Worker
If the helpers are hired by the worker, is the firm's approval necessary? . . . . ☐Yes ☐No
Who pays the helpers? ☐Firm ☐Worker
If the worker pays the helpers, does the firm repay the worker? . . . . ☐Yes ☐No
Are social security and Medicare taxes and Federal income tax withheld from the helpers' pay? . . . . ☐Yes ☐No
If "Yes," who reports and pays these taxes? ☐Firm ☐Worker
Who reports the helpers' earnings to the Internal Revenue Service? ☐Firm ☐Worker
What services do the helpers perform?

7 At what location are the services performed? ☐Firm's ☐Worker's ☐Other (specify)
8a Type of pay worker receives:
☐Salary ☐Commission ☐Hourly wage ☐Piecework ☐Lump sum ☐Other (specify)
b Does the firm guarantee a minimum amount of pay to the worker? . . . . ☐Yes ☐No
c Does the firm allow the worker a drawing account or advances against pay? . . . . ☐Yes ☐No
If "Yes," is the worker paid such advances on a regular basis? . . . . ☐Yes ☐No
d How does the worker repay such advances?
9a Is the worker eligible for a pension, bonus, paid vacations, sick pay, etc.? . . . . ☐Yes ☐No
If "Yes," specify
b Does the firm carry worker's compensation insurance on the worker? . . . . ☐Yes ☐No
c Does the firm withhold social security and Medicare taxes from amounts paid the worker? . . . . . ☐Yes ☐No
d Does the firm withhold Federal income taxes from amounts paid the worker? . . . . ☐Yes ☐No
e How does the firm report the worker's earnings to the Internal Revenue Service?
☐Form W-2 ☐Form 1099-MISC ☐Does not report ☐Other (specify)
Attach a copy.
f Does the firm bond the worker? . . . . ☐Yes ☐No
10a Approximately how many hours a day does the worker perform services for the firm?
b Does the firm set hours of work for the worker? . . . . ☐Yes ☐No
If "Yes," what are the worker's set hours?
c Does the worker perform similar services for others? . . . . ☐Yes ☐No ☐Unknown
If "Yes," are these services performed on a daily basis for other firms? . . . . . . ☐Yes ☐No ☐Unknown
Percentage of time spent in performing these services for:
This firm   Other firms   ☐Unknown
Does the firm have priority on the worker's time? . . . . ☐Yes ☐No
If "No," explain
d Is the worker prohibited from competing with the firm either while performing services or
during any later period? . . . . ☐Yes ☐No
11a Can the firm discharge the worker at any time without incurring a liability? . . . . ☐Yes ☐No
If "No," explain
b Can the worker terminate the services at any time without incurring a liability? . . . . ☐Yes ☐No
If "No," explain
12a Does the worker perform services for the firm under:
☐The firm's business name ☐The worker's own business name ☐Other (specify)
b Does the worker advertise or maintain a business listing in the telephone
directory, a trade journal, etc.? . . . . ☐Yes ☐No ☐Unknown
If "Yes," specify
c Does the worker represent himself or herself to the public as being in business to
perform the same or similar services? . . . . ☐Yes ☐No ☐Unknown
If "Yes," how?
d Does the worker have his or her own shop or office? . . . . ☐Yes ☐No ☐Unknown
If "Yes," where?
e Does the firm represent the worker as an employee of the firm to its customers? . . . . ☐Yes ☐No
If "No," how is the worker represented?
f How did the firm learn of the worker's services?
13 Is a license necessary for the work? . . . . ☐Yes ☐No ☐Unknown
If "Yes," what kind of license is required?
Who issues the license?
Who pays the license fee?

FORM SS-8 (*continued*)

Form SS-8 (Rev. 6-97)   Page 4

14 Does the worker have a financial investment in a business related to the services
performed? . . . . □ Yes   □ No   □ Unknown
If "Yes," specify and give amount of the investment ....

15 Can the worker incur a loss in the performance of the service for the firm? . . . . □ Yes   □ No
If "Yes," how? ....

16a Has any other government agency ruled on the status of the firm's workers? . . . . □ Yes   □ No
If "Yes," attach a copy of the ruling.

b Is the same issue being considered by any IRS office in connection with the audit of
the worker's tax return or the firm's tax return, or has it been considered recently? . . . . . . □ Yes   □ No
If "Yes," for which year(s)?

17 Does the worker assemble or process a product at home or away from the firm's place of business? . . . . □ Yes   □ No

If "Yes," who furnishes materials or goods used by the worker?   □ Firm   □ Worker   □ Other

Is the worker furnished a pattern or given instructions to follow in making the product? . . . . □ Yes   □ No

Is the worker required to return the finished product to the firm or to someone designated by the firm? . . . . □ Yes   □ No

18 Attach a detailed explanation of any other reason why you believe the worker is an employee or an independent contractor.

Answer items 19a through o only if the worker is a salesperson or provides a service directly to customers.

19a Are leads to prospective customers furnished by the firm? . . . . □ Yes   □ No   □ Does not apply

b Is the worker required to pursue or report on leads? . . . . □ Yes   □ No   □ Does not apply

c Is the worker required to adhere to prices, terms, and conditions of sale established by the firm? . . . . □ Yes   □ No

d Are orders submitted to and subject to approval by the firm? . . . . □ Yes   □ No

e Is the worker expected to attend sales meetings? . . . . □ Yes   □ No

If "Yes," is the worker subject to any kind of penalty for failing to attend? . . . . □ Yes   □ No

f Does the firm assign a specific territory to the worker? . . . . □ Yes   □ No

g Whom does the customer pay?   □ Firm   □ Worker
If worker, does the worker remit the total amount to the firm? . . . . □ Yes   □ No

h Does the worker sell a consumer product in a home or establishment other than a permanent
retail establishment? . . . . □ Yes   □ No

i List the products and/or services distributed by the worker, such as meat, vegetables, fruit, bakery products, beverages
(other than milk), or laundry or dry cleaning services. If more than one type of product and/or service is distributed, specify
the principal one ....

j Did the firm or another person assign the route or territory and a list of customers to the worker? . . . . □ Yes   □ No
If "Yes," enter the name and job title of the person who made the assignment ....

k Did the worker pay the firm or person for the privilege of serving customers on the route or in the territory? . . . . □ Yes   □ No
If "Yes," how much did the worker pay (not including any amount paid for a truck or racks, etc.)? $ ....
What factors were considered in determining the value of the route or territory? ....

l How are new customers obtained by the worker? Explain fully, showing whether the new customers called the firm for service,
were solicited by the worker, or both ....

m Does the worker sell life insurance? . . . . □ Yes   □ No
If "Yes," Is the selling of life insurance or annuity contracts for the firm the worker's entire
business activity? . . . . □ Yes   □ No
If "No," list the other business activities and the amount of time spent on them ....

n Does the worker sell other types of insurance for the firm? . . . . □ Yes   □ No
If "Yes," state the percentage of the worker's total working time spent in selling other types of insurance ....
At the time the contract was entered into between the firm and the worker, was it their intention that the worker sell
life insurance for the firm: □ on a full-time basis   □ on a part-time basis
State the manner in which the intention was expressed ....

o Is the worker a traveling or city salesperson? . . . . □ Yes   □ No
If "Yes," from whom does the worker principally solicit orders for the firm? ....
If the worker solicits orders from wholesalers, retailers, contractors, or operators of hotels, restaurants, or other similar
establishments, specify the percentage of the worker's time spent in the solicitation ....
Is the merchandise purchased by the customers for resale or for use in their business operations? If used by the customers
in their business operations, describe the merchandise and state whether it is equipment installed on their premises or a
consumable supply.

Under penalties of perjury, I declare that I have examined this request, including accompanying documents, and to the best of my knowledge
and belief, the facts presented are true, correct, and complete.

Signature   Title   Date

If the firm is completing this form, an officer or member of the firm must sign it. If the worker is completing this form, the worker must sign it.
If the worker wants a written determination about services performed for two or more firms, a separate form must be completed and signed
for each firm. Additional copies of this form may be obtained by calling 1-800-TAX-FORM (1-800-829-3676).

Appendix 25–2

FORM W-9

Form **W-9** (Rev. December 1996) Department of the Treasury Internal Revenue Service	**Request for Taxpayer** **Identification Number and Certification**	Give form to the requester. Do NOT send to the IRS.

Name (if a joint account or you changed your name, see Specific Instructions on page 2.))

Business name, if different from above (See Specific Instructions on page 2.)

Check box: ☐ Individual/Sole proprietor ☐ Corporation ☐ Partnership ☐ Other ....

Address (number, street, and apt. or suite no.)	Requester's name and address (optional)
City, state, and ZIP code	

Part I   Taxpayer Identification Number (TIN)

Enter your TIN in the appropriate box. For individuals, this is your social security number (SSN). For sole proprietors, see the instructions on page 2. For other entities, it is your employer identification number (EIN). If you do not have a number, see How To Get a TIN on page 2.

Note: If the account is in more than one name, see the chart on page 2 for guidelines on whose number to enter.

Social security no.

OR

Employer ID no.

List account number(s) here (optional)

Part II   For Payees Exempt From Backup Withholding
(See Part II instructions on page 2)

Part III   Certification

Under penalties of perjury, I certify that:

1. The number shown on this form is my correct taxpayer identification number (or I am waiting for a number to be issued to me), and

2. I am not subject to backup withholding because: (a) I am exempt from backup withholding, or (b) I have not been notified by the Internal Revenue Service that I am subject to backup withholding as a result of a failure to report all interest or dividends, or (c) the IRS has notified me that I am no longer subject to backup withholding.

Certification Instructions. - You must cross out item 2 above if you have been notified by the IRS that you are currently subject to backup withholding because of underreporting interest or dividends on your tax return. For real estate transactions, item 2 does not apply. For mortgage interest paid, the acquisition or abandonment of secured property, cancellation of debt, contributions to an individual retirement arrangement (IRA), and generally payments other than interest and dividends, you are not required to sign the Certification, but you must provide your correct TIN. (See the instructions on page 2.)

Sign Here	Signature	Date

Form W-9 (Rev. 12-96)

Mergers, Bankruptcies, and Terminations

26.1 MERGERS AND OTHER COMBINATIONS

Strategic alliances, collaborations, networks, duplication of effort, modernization of facilities and methods, constituency changes, human disagreements, and countless other factors might indicate the need for a nonprofit organization to combine with another organization. Achieving economies of scale in the operations, eliminating duplicated services, integrating service delivery, acquiring needed skills and assets, and strengthening administrative capability are just a few of the reasons why one or more organizations might combine themselves through a merger or other type of organizational combination. In some instances, forming a partnership, engaging a professional management company, or entering into a relationship with a for-profit or nonprofit organization can accomplish the needed improvement without a change in the structure of the organization itself. The tax issues to consider in such a situation are discussed in Chapter 22.

Once it is decided that an alliance or some other form of cooperating operation is not suitable, a formal combination with another organization may in some circumstances be appropriate. The terms used to describe such transactions are those normally applicable to businesses—merger or acquisition. This section briefly addresses the tax issues involved when such combinations occur for tax-exempt organizations. The wide range of management and operational issues involved in alliances, mergers, and other combinations are beyond the scope of this book, but good resources are available.[1] The state and local laws regarding mergers must also be considered with local advisors familiar with the rules.

First and foremost, any merger or combination must be entered into cognizant of the fact that a tax-exempt organization of any category is essentially required to devote its assets—both during its life and upon its demise—primarily to the purposes for which it is exempt. As discussed in Chapters 2 through 10, particular standards of formation apply to those organizations qualifying as charitable and other categories. A charitable organization's charter, for example, must specifically require that its assets only be distributed upon dissolution for charitable purposes. Applicable fiduciary responsibilities and responsiveness to members and past supporters must be considered in combinations of all types of tax-exempt organizations. The bottom line in any merger is an obligation that the assets of a nonprofit ideally be distributed to an organization whose purposes will accomplish the goals for which moneys were accumulated by the organization going out of existence. From a federal tax standpoint, in a formal merger, one organization survives. In its simplest form, all of the assets of one organization are assigned, or transferred, to another.

What have been referred to as *virtual mergers* for hospitals are actually joint operating agreements, not a true merger.[2]

For the purposes of this discussion, it is presumed in a merger there will be one surviving organization. All of the parties to the merger presumably have recognition of tax-exempt status and normally are exempt under the same subsection of 501(c)—(c)(3), (c)(4), or (c)(6)s for example. The assets of a (c)(3) should not, as a general rule, be distributed to an organization that is qualified for tax exemption under some other category. On the other hand, a business league might for some good reason contribute its assets to a labor union of persons working in the same profession.

(a) Tax Attributes

Concepts normally applicable to for-profit business combinations can be referred to in evaluating tax attributes that are assigned or attributed to the successor organization in a merger.[3] Conceptually, all of the tax attributes of the entity transferring its property carry over to the recipient organization.[4]

Carryover Basis. A merger is classically a nontaxable transaction, meaning no gain or loss is recognized upon the transfer of assets from one organization to another. This discussion assumes the organizations participating in the merger are themselves tax-exempt and therefore excused from tax on the transaction.[5] Any

---

[1] The reader can consult Thomas McLaughlin, *Nonprofit Mergers and Alliances. A Strategic Planning Guide* (New York: John Wiley, 1998) and Alceste T. Pappas, *Reengineering Your Nonprofit Organization: A Guide to Strategic Transformation* (New York: John Wiley, 1995) for those issues.

[2] Defined in 1997 CPE Text for Exempt Organizations, Chapter J., *Virtual Mergers, Hospital Joint Operating Agreement Affiliations,* Roderick Darling and Marvin Friendlander.

[3] IRC §351.

[4] IRC §381.

[5] See Chapter 21§10(e) regarding distributions from a for-profit subsidiary of a tax-exempt organization.

unrealized gain inherent in the assets is allowed to go untaxed (even if an entity is taxable) because the tax basis of the assets of the transferee is carried over to the surviving organization. Particularly when unrelated business or private foundation assets are involved, this rule serves to permit the transfer. The tax impact comes when the recipient party to the merger disposes of the asset. The asset-holding period of the entity ceasing to exist also carries over. Depreciation for assets transferred, for example, will continue to be calculated in the same manner as before the transfer.

Other Tax Attributes.   Activities classified as an unrelated business to the expiring entity will very likely be considered as such for the recipient organization. Net operating loss, foreign tax, and contribution deduction carryovers and accumulated corporate earnings (ACE) accounts attributable to the unrelated business will carry over to the surviving entity.[6]

Public Charity Status.   The ongoing public status of the surviving organization will depend partly upon the category of Internal Revenue Code (IRC) §509 under which the surviving organization operates. A church, school, hospital, medical research organization, or college support organization that continues to conduct such activities (after it receives assets of another organization) can continue to so qualify.[7] Although the author could find no ruling or procedures addressing the question, it seems logical that the combined, or surviving, organization might be required to calculate its public support test on a combined basis. Conceivably the past revenues of the transferring organization would be added to those of the recipient (surviving) organization to determine qualification as a public charity. The unusual grant rules and facts and circumstances test can be availed of, if necessary, to achieve public status.[8]

(b) Seeking IRS Approval

The Internal Revenue Service (IRS) does not require advanced approval for a distribution in termination of all of the assets of any form of 501(c) organization. The Forms 990, 990-EZ, and 990-PF annually ask whether there have been any changes in the organization's operations, purposes, or governing documents. As explained in §26.3, a complete termination of a tax-exempt organization is essentially accomplished under state law. Full information, including documents approved by appropriate state authorities, must be attached to the final Form 990 filed by the terminating organization. Similar documents are attached to the recipient, or surviving, organization. Private foundations have additional issues that are outlined in Chapter 12§4.

Advance approval for a merger or other transactions involving transfers of significant assets is not required, but may be desirable. In a complicated situation, particularly where there is some question as to the ongoing qualification of the survivor, an IRS ruling prior to completion of the merger might be requested

---

[6] See Chapters 21 and 27§14.
[7] Standards for qualification are outlined in Chapters 3, 4, 5, and 11.
[8] Discussed in Chapter 11§2.

under procedures discussed in Chapter 28.2(a). If prior approval is not requested, another choice is available. The documents, along with full information, can be furnished to the Ohio Service Center (assigned with responsibility for making determinations of tax-exempt status) with a letter request that they decide whether the completed transaction has any impact upon the survivor's qualification. Last, the parties to the transaction can simply furnish full details with the Forms 990 filed for the year of the merger in response to Question 76, and possibly 77 in Part VI. The latter choice has, in the past, brought no overt response from the IRS. The choice of method of informing the IRS depends on a desire for overt approval as discussed in Chapter 28§2.

(c) Other Types of Transformations

A nonprofit organization might also transform itself by splitting up into two or more parts. Sometimes the activities of the organization are of a sort that exposes the organization to liability for claims of damages. In such situations, a title-holding company or a supporting organization might be created by transferring the organization's investment assets and permanent operating assets, such as buildings, into a separate nonprofit corporation. Such a holding company can qualify for independent tax-exemption if it is dedicated to holding the assets and paying over the income generated therefrom to its parent organization.[9] A new Form 1023 or 1024 is filed for the holding company.[10]

In a similar fashion, one organization might split itself into several parts for one of the reasons suggested at the opening of this chapter. Separate, independent organizations might be formed to conduct certain programs and hold certain assets. Again a new Form 1023 or 1024 is required for any newly created trust or corporation receiving a distribution of assets, and the multitude of rules and procedures outlined in Chapters 2–11 must be taken into consideration in determining its proper tax status. Another possibility is for a local organization to reorganize itself to become part of a group exemption.[11] This might be accomplished either with a spin-off of a particular activity or transformation of the entire organization. Private foundations have requested a slew of private rulings for split-ups as discussed in Chapter 12§4.

26.2 BANKRUPTCY

Despite the best intentions and dreams of their creators and managers, exempt organizations on occasion expend funds in excess of their resources. Some organizations are fortunate enough to have philanthropists or other supporters who are willing and able to cover operating deficits they might incur. Sometimes, however, an exempt organization may become insolvent to the point that it must declare bankruptcy. In such cases, the interests of the (normally) for-profit creditors and

---

[9] See Chapter 10.

[10] Rules and procedures for seeking recognition for exemption with Form 1023 or 1024 are discussed in Chapter 18.

[11] See Chapter 18§1(f).

the nonprofit constituents of the organization can be in conflict, and a number of issues must be considered.

A consideration of the federal Bankruptcy Code is also beyond the scope of this book, and any organization facing insolvency and considering bankruptcy should seek an attorney knowledgeable about the field. In most respects, the Bankruptcy Code provides the same rules for nonprofit and for-profit organizations. The intention of the rules is to protect the insolvent organization, to prevent any particular creditor from taking unfair advantage, and to allow an orderly allocation among creditors of the proceeds of the asset liquidation.[12]

The Bankruptcy Code is divided into chapters, with bankruptcy cases referred to by the numbers of the chapters they are brought under. A Chapter 7 bankruptcy allows the organization, under the supervision of a court-appointed trustee, to sell off its assets, allocate the proceeds of such sales among its creditors, dissolve its legal existence, and cease to operate. The other common type of bankruptcy, Chapter 11, allows the organization to reorganize and remain in existence after providing for a payment plan for its indebtedness.

Bankruptcy may be voluntary or involuntary. A voluntary bankruptcy is filed by an insolvent organization to seek the protection from unfriendly creditors. In contrast, an involuntary bankruptcy is filed by a group of three or more creditors. However, only a "moneyed, business, or commercial operation" qualifies for an involuntary bankruptcy, a significant matter on which the Bankruptcy Code provides different treatment for nonprofit corporations. "Moneyed" organizations are profit-motivated ones operated to create income for their shareholders or members. Most tax-exempt organizations would not continue to qualify for exemption if they could meet such a definition. Thus, it is generally the case that an organization qualified for tax exemption under one of the subsections of IRC §501(c) cannot be placed in involuntary bankruptcy. However, failure to qualify for the exception from involuntary bankruptcy can cause the organization to lose its tax-exempt status, because it would show that the assets are not dedicated to exempt purposes.

(a) How Tax Status Is Affected by a Bankruptcy

All categories of IRC §501 organizations—(c)(1-27) plus §501(d), (e), and (f)—must be organized and operated for their specifically defined category as discussed in Chapters 2–10. Charities, social welfare organizations, business leagues, social clubs, and all other types of exempt organizations must permanently dedicate their assets under organizational documents to their specified purposes, and must then, in fact, operate for such purposes throughout the life of the organization to maintain tax-exempt status.

An insolvent exempt organization considering bankruptcy may face a challenge that it did not operate for exempt purposes. Any revocation of exemption would be based on the facts and circumstances of the case. There is no rule that automatically revokes exempt status upon the declaration of bankruptcy, and there are no revenue rulings or other statements of IRS policy on the subject. The questions

---

[12] U.S.C. §303.

that must be asked in reviewing a particular situation (all versions of the same theme) would include:

- Were the activities in which the debt was incurred exempt activities?

- Why was adequate revenue not provided to pay for the exempt activities? Were revenues diverted to some other nonexempt purposes? Are there unrecorded liabilities attributable to restricted donors whose funds were diverted to other purposes?

- If the debts were incurred in connection with an unrelated business activity, did that business subsume the exempt activities and therefore evidence lack of substantial exempt purposes?

- Were exempt assets diverted to some nonexempt project violating the requirement that assets be dedicated to exempt purposes? Were jeopardizing investments purchased? Particularly for a private foundation, this could provide the additional complication of excise taxes.[13]

- How can assets be allocated to creditors when the organization's charter requires that assets be dedicated permanently to exempt purposes?

- Were members of the governing body of trustees or directors in any way fiscally irresponsible in allowing the deficits to occur? Should any of the deficiencies be paid by such directors to preserve the organizational assets for the exempt constituents?

(b) Revocation of Exempt Status

The Bankruptcy Code automatic stay against collection, assessment, or recovery of a claim against the bankrupt organization does not prevent the IRS from revoking exempt status. In abusive situations, that is, when the debts were incurred in providing benefits to insiders rather than in serving the exempt public or membership, an attempt to revoke should be expected. Such a challenge would be bolstered when there are no assets left upon dissolution for distribution for exempt purposes, as is required by any exempt organization's charter.

The revocation has been ruled to be a preliminary step or prerequisite to the collection of tax and not restrained by the filing of bankruptcy.[14] The anti-injunction provision of IRC §7421 prohibits the bankruptcy trustee or others from interfering in the revocation of exempt status when the IRS deems it appropriate. Whether the IRS can be successful in collecting any taxes assessed is another question to be answered by a bankruptcy specialist.

When exempt status is revoked, tax issues including forgiveness of indebtedness, deductions for bad debts, and recapture of tax attributes, among other issues, must be carefully considered. Even if the exempt status is not revoked, such issues would be of consequence in calculating any tax liability for unrelated business income.

---

[13] See Chapter 16.
[14] *Bob Jones University v. Simon*, 416 U.S. 725 (1974); *Heritage Village Church and Missionary Fellowship, Inc.*, 851 F.2d 104 (4th Cir., 1988).

(c) Filing Requirements

After the exempt organization voluntarily files bankruptcy, a new organization does not come into being. Under IRC §1399, the existing entity continues and normal filing requirements continue. As a matter of tax policy, the exempt status of the organization is allowed to remain intact unless factors evident in the bankruptcy indicate that the exempt status of the organization should be revoked, as discussed previously.

The gross annual revenues of the bankrupt organization govern its annual federal filing requirements.[15] As the bankruptcy proceeds, returns are to be filed as usual except in the year of liquidation, dissolution, termination, or substantial contraction. An entity with more than $25,000 but less than $100,000 of gross receipts files Form 990-EZ, and one with more than $100,000 files Form 990. In the contracting or final year, a lower threshold of $5000 of gross receipts sets the limit for required reporting. In other words, the Form 990 must be filed in almost all cases.

Prior to the actual year of dissolution or termination, the filing requirements for other purposes—annual information, payroll, and all other types of federal returns—remain the same during the period of bankruptcy. Even though the organization ceases normal operations and receives no contributions, gross revenue for filing purposes includes proceeds from the sale of its assets. The parties responsible for filing information returns are either the board of directors and the organization's ongoing managers or the bankruptcy trustee appointed to replace the directors or organizational trustees.

Information revealing the bankrupt status should be attached to Form 990 in response to the question "Has the organization engaged in any activities not previously reported to the IRS?" At a minimum, the documents filed with the bankruptcy trustee and a synopsis of the expected outcome should be attached to the return. An explanation of the cause of the bankruptcy and its effects on ongoing operations (under Chapter 11) or on its orderly dissolution (under Chapter 7) should also be attached to the return. It is very important at this point to indicate that the exempt purposes of the organization are not compromised by the bankruptcy, and that the exempt status should not be revoked or jeopardized as a consequence (when it is possible to so argue).

Section 6043 of the IRC contains specific requirements for information to be reported in the year of dissolution of an exempt organization, which apply to organizations dissolving due to bankruptcy. Although the answer is full of innuendo from the question of jeopardy to exempt status, this section specifically requires that the following information be reported in Form 990 for the distribution year:

- Names and addresses of persons receiving the terminating distributions
- Kinds of assets distributed
- Fact that the assets are distributed and dates of distribution
- Each asset's fair market value

[15] See Chapter 27.

When the asset distribution and settlement with creditors takes place over a series of reporting years, the regulations should be carefully considered for determining when a "substantial contraction" occurs, to allow properly timed reporting.

Related Organization.   What if one member of an affiliated group of exempt organizations becomes insolvent and is considering declaring bankruptcy? Particularly in a statewide or nationwide group whose reputation might be damaged by the bad credit rating of a related entity, questions in addition to those listed previously under §26.2(a) should be asked. Will the parent or other affiliates be held responsible in any way for the bankrupt affiliate's debts? Must the group intervene to provide services to ensure the exempt purposes of the group are served? Should the crippled affiliate be given financial assistance? The systems for monitoring, assisting, and controlling related organizations should be reviewed and revised to avoid reoccurrence.

26.3   TERMINATIONS

An organization exempt under IRC §501(a) may cease to operate and dispose of its assets for a number of different reasons (some discussed previously) and in a variety of ways. Most tax-exempt organizations, including private foundations, are free to terminate their existence so long as they do so in a fashion that serves their tax-exempt purposes. There is no procedure under the tax law that requires an organization seek the permission of the IRS to terminate. A private foundation (PF) that has committed repeated and flagrant violations of the special PF sanctions discussed in Chapters 14 through 17 may be involuntarily terminated by the IRS.[16]

Termination of an exempt organization is mainly a matter of local law that should occur with the assistance of a qualified attorney. Those exempt organizations formed as corporations should seek permission to terminate from the appropriate state officials. Exempt organizations formed as trusts may be able to simply follow the provisions set out in their trust instrument. The IRS instructions to Forms 990 ask if there has been a termination or contraction presuming that the reporting organization has followed the suitable procedures on a state or local level.

However it is accomplished, an exempt organization must report its liquidation, dissolution, termination, or substantial contraction to the IRS when it files Form 990 or Form 990-PF.[17] A blank on the front page is provided to be marked "final." The instructions to the forms request a statement be attached to explain what took place. The following specific information is to be attached to the return:

- Statement reporting assets distributed and the date
- Certified copy of any resolution or plan of liquidation or termination with all amendments or supplements not already filed

[16] See Chapter 12§4.
[17] IRC §6043(b).

- Schedule listing the names and addresses of all organizations and persons receiving assets distributed in liquidation or termination, the kind of assets distributed to each, and the asset fair market value.[18]

(a) No Special Filings Required

Certain types of organizations do not have to provide reports of their dissolution, liquidation, termination, or contraction as follows:

- Any organization not required to file Form 990, including all churches, including their integrated auxiliaries, or conventions or associations of churches and an organization, not a private foundation, normally receiving not more than $5,000 a year of gross receipts[19]

- A private foundation terminating its status by converting to a public charity[20]

- Subordinate member covered by a group exemption where the central organization files Form 990 for the group

- Instrumentality of the United States created by an Act of Congress and their title-holding companies

- Certain pension plans and credit unions

(b) Substantial Contraction

A partial liquidation or other major disposition of assets must also be reported on Form 990 or Form 990-PF. The instructions stipulate that such a disposition occurs in two situations:

- At least 25% of the fair market value of the organization's net assets at the beginning of the year are given to another organization.

- Current year grants, when added to related dispositions begun in an earlier year or years, equal at least 25% of the net assets the organization had when the distribution series began.

---

[18] See Chapter 27§10 comments for line 79 in Part VI of Form 990 and line 5 of Part VII-A for 990-PF.

[19] Reg. §1.6043-3(b).

[20] Such a foundation would have first sought approval for its conversion under rules discussed in Chapter 12§4.

PART FIVE

Communicating with the IRS

Chapter Twenty-Seven
Successful Preparation of Forms 990, 990EZ, 990-T, and 990-PF

Chapter Twenty-Eight
Communicating with the Internal Revenue Service

CHAPTER TWENTY-SEVEN

Successful Preparation of Forms 990, 990EZ, 990-T, and 990-PF

The various Forms 990 are designed to accomplish two purposes. First, the basic financial information—the revenues, expenses, assets, and liabilities—are classified into meaningful categories to allow the Internal Revenue Service (IRS), funders, states, and persons who ask to inspect the returns to statistically evaluate the scope and type of an exempt organization's activity. Second, the questions fish for failures to comply with the federal and to some extent, state, requirements for maintenance of tax exempt status, such as those shown below (Form 990 can be found in Appendix 27–2 and Form 990-PF in Appendix 27–5):

- Do the organization's activities focus on an exempt purpose as reflected in Part III of Form 990 and Parts IX-A, IX-B, and XV of Form 990-PF? (See Chapters 3–10)

- Do the fund-raising costs reported in column (d) of Part II, Form 990, equal too high a percentage of the total expenses indicating the EO fails the commensurate test? (See Chapter 2§2(d))

- Does column (d) of Part VII of Form 990 and Part XVI-A of Form 990-PF show a high percentage of unrelated business revenues in relation to the total revenues indicating the EO is devoted to business rather than exempt purposes? (See Chapter 21§3 and 21§4(b))

- Does the EO operate to benefit private individuals as payments in Part II, lines 24–30 of Form 990 and lines 13–16 of Form 990-PF reflect? (See Chapters 14 and 20)

- Has the EO spent too much (PF can spend none) money on lobbying efforts reported on Schedule A, Part VI-A or B? (See Chapters 17 and 23§5)

- Do the EO's sources of support shown on Schedule A (Appendix 27–3) Part IV indicate it receives 33⅓% of its support from the public so it continues to be classified as a public charity? (See Chapter 11)

Accurate and complete preparation of the forms should be given top priority. The forms have entered the electronic age when they eventually will be accessible to one and all on the Internet. An organization's public reporting responsibilities have entered another dimension and deserve careful attention. In March 1997, the IRS contracted with the Urban Institute of Washington, D.C., to receive and place Forms 990 for the years 1996 through 2001 on CD-ROM, and they hope Forms 990s will be available on the Internet. In a coordinated effort, Philanthropic Resources, Inc., began in 1998 to digitize the information so that it can be sorted and searched. Information from prior 990s of some 40,000 public charities already in their database can be found at *http:/www.guidestar.org*. The IRS is also studying an electronic filing system of 990s to eliminate the paperwork altogether and allow them to more effectively monitor exempts in a statistical and focused fashion. One study reported that only 2% of the requests for copies of Form 990-PF sent to the IRS yielded a correct and full return after the first request.[1] Shockingly, requests sent by the researchers directly to corporate foundations yielded a pathetic 10% full cooperation despite public disclosure rules requiring they do so and imposing penalties for failure to as described in §27.2 and 27§13(s).

Forms 990 are essentially public information. Yet another reason for an organization to pay careful attention to completion of the Forms 990 is the requirement that copies of the three most recent year's returns must be given upon request to those that pay a modest fee. Between 1984 and 1997, an organization had to allow anyone who knocked on its door a look at its Forms 990, 1023, and 1024 in its office. Beginning sometime in 1999 (60 days after the effective date of final regulations under §6104(e)), a copy of the forms must be furnished for a fee as discussed in §27.2(a). Forms 990 are also used for a wide variety of state and local purposes. In many states, an exempt organization can satisfy its annual filing requirement by furnishing a copy of Form 990 to the appropriate state authority. Many grant-making foundations request a copy of Form 990 in addition to or in lieu of audited financial statements, to verify an organization's fiscal activity. The open records standards applicable in many states also require all financial reports and records be open to the public.

27.1 FILING FORMS 990

Beginning in January 1997, the annual Forms 990 are submitted to a processing center devoted exclusively to exempt return filings. The IRS centralized the filing of Forms 990, 990EZ, 990-PF, 990-T, 1041-A, 4720, 5227, 5578, and 5768 in the

---

[1] O'Connor and Paprocki, *Corporate Grantmaking; Giving to Racial Ethic Populations—Phase Three* (Washington, D.C.: National Committee for Responsive Philanthropy, 1997).

Ogden, Utah Service Center. The centralization is expected to improve the speed and accuracy of return processing through a consolidation of expertise on exempt organization matters. In a similar fashion, the filing of Forms 1023 and 1024, applications for determination of exempt status, is being consolidated in the Cincinnati, Ohio Key District Office.[2]

The forms have evolved over the years through cooperative efforts between the IRS, nonprofit organizations, the American Institute of Certified Public Accountants (AICPA), the American Business Association (ABA), and state officials. Page 6, added by Congressional mandate reveals the related and unrelated nature of an organization's revenues.[3] Part IV-A and B was added in response to Financial Accounting Standards Board pronouncements in 1995. While no major changes are expected in the near future, readers should always consult the current supplement to this book for revised versions.

(a) Who is Required to File What

The numerous categories of organizations exempt from income tax are reflected in the different types of returns to be filed. Not all organizations are required to file annual reports with the Internal Revenue Service. Churches and their affiliated organizations, in a manner similar to the Form 1023 rules, do not file Forms 990, except for 990-T. Modest-sized organizations may also be excused from filing. The different types of exempt organization annual reports and their basic requirements are as follows:

- *No Form Filed.* Organizations with gross annual receipts "normally" under $25,000, churches and certain of their affiliates, and other types of organizations listed below need not file. (But see why to file at §27.1(c).)

- *Form 990-EZ.* All exempt organizations, except for private foundations, whose gross annual receipts equal between $25,000 and $100,000 and whose total assets are less than $250,000 file Form 990EZ. (There was talk of raising these levels in 1998—check the supplement.) (See Appendix 27–1.)

- *Form 990.* All exempt organizations, except private foundations, whose gross annual receipts are more than $100,000 or that have assets of more than $250,000 must file Form 990. (See Appendix 27–2.) §501(c)(3) organizations that are public charities also file Schedule A. (See Appendix 27–3.)

- *Form 990-PF.* All private foundations (PFs) file Form 990-PF annually, regardless of gross annual receipts (even if the PF has no gross receipts). (See Appendix 27–5.)

- *Form 990-T.* Any organization exempt under IRC §501(a), including churches, and IRC §401 pension plans (including individual retirement accounts) with $1000 or more gross income from an unrelated trade or business must file Form 990-T. (See Appendix 27–7.)

---

[2] Chapter 18 thoroughly outlines the determination process.
[3] Explained in §27.11.

- *Form 990-BL.* Black lung trusts (IRC §501(c)(21)) file an annual Information and Initial Excise Tax Return for Black Lung Benefit Trusts and Certain Related Persons.

- *Form 4720.* Form 4720 is filed to report excise taxes and to claim abatement of such taxes imposed on §501(c)(3) charities and their insiders. (See Appendix 27–6 and Chapters 14–17 regarding private foundations and Chapters 20 and 23 for public charities.)

- *Form 5500.* One of several Forms 5500 may be due to be filed annually by pension, profit-sharing, and stock bonus plans. Form 5500EZ is filed for one-participant pension benefit plans and 5500 C/R is filed for organizations with fewer than 100 participants in their employee plans, among others.

(b) Federal Filing Not Required

The list of organizations not required to file is reproduced each year in the instructions to Form 990. The most recent version should be consulted if there is any question about filing requirements. The instructions for 1998 list the following organizations as being excused from filing:

- Churches and their affiliates including an interchurch organization of local units of a church, a convention or association of churches, an integrated auxiliary of a church (such as a men's or women's society, religious school, mission society, or youth group) or an internally supported, church-controlled organization; See Chapter 3§2 for a discussion of the criteria applied to define organizations qualifying as churches and their affiliates.

- Schools below college level affiliated with a church or operated by a religious order.

- Mission societies sponsored by or affiliated with one or more churches or church denominations, if more than half of the society's activities are conducted in or directed at persons in foreign countries.

- Exclusively religious activities of any religious order.

- State institutions whose income is excluded from gross income under IRC §115.

- IRC §501(c)(1) organizations that are instrumentalities of the United States and organized under an act of Congress.[4]

- Governmental units and their affiliates who have been granted exemption under 501(a).[5] (See Chapter 10.)

- Religious and apostolic organizations described in 501(d) that file Form 1065.

[4] IRC §6033(a)(2) and (3).
[5] Defined in Rev. Proc. 95-48, 1995-47 I.R.B. 13.

(c) Why File Even If Not Required To

Annual filings of Form 990EZ are advisable for organizations whose annual gross receipts hover around the $25,000 mark to ensure that the organization remains on the IRS mailing list to receive the forms for annual filing and other announcements issued by the IRS every year or so. Form 990EZ can be filed with the simple notation, "gross receipts under $25,000," without completing any other information. Prudence also dictates that any organization seeking donations should ensure that its name is listed in IRS *Publication 78*, the master list of qualifying charitable organizations. Omission from the list may cause two problems: disallowance of charitable contribution deduction to donors and unwillingness of private foundations or other donors to grant funds to the organization.

The extended 27-month deadline for submitting applications for recognition of exemption[6] creates a possible dual filing dilemma. An exempt organization should file Forms 990 for the first fiscal year closing even if it has not yet filed Form 1023 or 1024 for recognition of its exempt status. When the new nonprofit organization files an application for a federal identification number, it is considered a taxpaying entity due to file income tax returns. Until exempt status is entered into the master data bank, the IRS expects the yet-to-be-determined exempt status organization to file Form 1120 or 1041. When tax is due, this is an unwelcome burden, even if the tax is ultimately recovered on an amended return. If income tax returns are filed, gross income received in the form of voluntary donations should be treated as nontaxable income because such donations are gifts.[7]

Whether to submit a protective filing for an expectant exempt organization that is not required to file Form 990 can also be a tough call. Say the new organization is technically not required to file a 990 because its gross revenue in the first year or two is less than $25,000 or it is a church or church affiliate. The issue is whether voluntary filing of a protective 990 to start the statute of limitations colors the IRS consideration of its exemption and whether this remote possibility outweighs the value of protection from tax assessments and reduction of penalties. The submission of financial information on a 1023 has been found not to constitute the filing of a return,[8] so penalties for late filing may not be excusable. An added dimension faces a new organization that may possibly be denied exempt status. Filing of Form 990 by a not-yet-recognized organization, in the good faith belief that it qualifies as an exempt organization, starts the period of limitations for collection of income tax.[9] The time required to appeal an adverse determination can be years, so filing 990s may furnish valuable protection from tax assessments for an organization ultimately found not to be exempt. Such a filing may also provide a "reasonable cause" excuse to reduce or eliminate penalties for failure to file Forms 1120 or 1041 and pay the tax due.

The statute of limitations for assessment of the unrelated business income tax (UBIT) on Form 990-T starts to run when the 990 contains sufficient facts

---

[6] Discussed in Chapter 18§2.

[7] IRC §102.

[8] *Colombo Club, Inc.*, 71-2 USTC ¶ 9674, 447 F.2d 1406 (9th Cir. 1971).

[9] Rev. Rul. 60-144, 1960-1 C.B. 636.

(shown in Part VII) from which the UBIT can be determined.[10] Say, for example, an exempt organization lists an amount for affinity card revenues on its 990, Part VII, Column D. The number is reported on line 103, labeled as royalty income, and identified in Column C with the exclusion code 15 for "royalty income excluded by §512(b)(2)." Assume that, after years of fighting in court, the IRS eventually prevails in treating part or all of the royalty payment as unrelated income.[11] The ruling says tax could only be collected for three years prior to the decision. Note that substantial underpayment penalties might be assessed for the open years.[12]

The same treatment as a taxable entity can occur on a state level.[13] In Texas, for example, new nonprofit corporations must either furnish evidence of the federal exemption or seek exemption within approximately 15 months of their creation or pay franchise tax. Otherwise, the charter is revoked. If the IRS grants recognition retroactive to the date of incorporation, the state tax paid may be refunded.

(d) Filing Deadline

The due date for Forms 990 gives tax practitioners and exempt organizations a reprieve. Forms 990 are due to be filed within $4\frac{1}{2}$ months after the end of the organization's fiscal year, rather than the $2\frac{1}{2}$ allowed for Form 1120 (for-profit corporations) and the $3\frac{1}{2}$ months for Form 1041 (trusts). An extension of time can be requested if the organization has not completed its year end accounting soon enough to timely file. For Forms 990-T and 990-PF, the filing extension does *not* extend the time to pay the tax.

The penalty for late filing is $20 a day (up from $10) for organizations with gross receipts under $1 million a year, not to exceed the greater of $10,000 or 5% of the annual gross receipts for the year of late filing.[14] The penalty can also be imposed if the form is filed incompletely. The penalty for a large organization (>$1 million of annual gross receipts) is $100 a day up to a maximum penalty of $50,000.

(e) Group Returns and Annual Affidavit

The parent organization in "general supervision or control" of a group of subsidiary exempt organizations covered by a group exemption letter may assume the burden of filing a consolidated Form 990 for its subordinate organizations.[15] The parent files its own separate 990. The parent and the subordinate member organizations of the group must file separate 990-Ts. To file a group Form 990, there must be two or more consenting local organizations with the following attributes:

- Affiliated with the central organization at the time its annual accounting period ends,
- Subject to the central organization's general supervision or control,

---

[10] Rev. Rul. 69-247, 1969-1 C.B. 303, modifying Rev. Rul. 62-10, 1962-1 C.B. 305 and reflecting the Tax Court decision in *California Thoroughbred Breeders Ass'n*, 47 T.C. 335, Dec. 28,225 (acq).
[11] See Chapter 21§20(d).
[12] IRC §6662.
[13] See Chapter 18§7.
[14] IRC §6652(c)(1)(A) as amended by the Taxpayer Bill of Rights 2, §1314.
[15] For rules pertaining to inclusion in a group exemption see Chapter 18§1(f).

- Exempt from tax under a group exemption letter that is still in effect, and

- Have the same accounting period as the central organization.

When the parent, or controlling member, of the group takes responsibility for filing a consolidated Form 990, each affiliate member covered by the group exemption must annually give written authority for its inclusion in the group return. A declaration, made under penalty of perjury, that the financial information to be combined into the group Form 990 is true and complete is included. A schedule showing the name, address, and employer identification number of included local organizations is attached to the group return. An affiliate choosing not to be included in the group return files its own separate return and checks Block H(c) on page 1 of Form 990. Each year, 90 days before the end of the fiscal year, the parent organization separately reports a current list of subsidiary organizations to the Ogden, Utah, Service Center.[16]

27.2 PUBLIC INSPECTION OF FORMS 990 AND 1023

Effective within 60 days of the date the Treasury Department issues regulations on the subject, an actual copy of Forms 990, 990-PF, or 990EZ for the three most recent years and Form 1023 must be given by tax-exempt organizations to those requesting one.[17] Readers should verify the following information gleaned from the proposed regulations. The regulations had to be revised to reflect elimination for IRC §6104(d) applicable to private foundations by the Omnibus Consolidated and Emergency Supplemental Appropriations Act signed on October 21, 1998. If the request is made in person at the organization's office, the copy must be provided immediately. In response to a written request, the copy must be mailed within 30 days. Between 1987 and 1997, the returns had to be made available for inspection in the organization's offices. The proposed regulations provided the following rules:

- An organization may charge $1.00 for the first page and $0.15 for each subsequent page.

- Payments must be accepted in cash, money orders, personal checks, or credit cards.

- Written requests can be transmitted by mail, electronic mail, facsimile, or private delivery service, or in person and must contain the address to which the copies can be mailed.

- Alternative methods an organization can use to make the forms are widely available through electronic media instead of furnishing copies.

If the organization that charges a fee for copying receives a request containing no payment, it must, within 7 days of receipt of the request, notify the requester of its

---

[16] Rev. Proc. 96-40, 1996-32 I.R.B. 8.
[17] Taxpayer Bill of Rights 2, §1313, amending IRC §6104(e).

prepayment policy and the amount due. If the copy charge exceeds $20 and pre-payment is not required, the organization must obtain the requester's consent to the charge. An organization can satisfy its public inspection requirement by mak-ing its returns available on the Internet either through its own site or a database of other exempt organizations on another site. The Forms 1023, 1024, and 990s will be considered widely available only if they are posted in the same format used by the IRS to post forms and publications on the IRS web site. The site must contain instructions to enable the user to download and print the forms without charge. Watch for update; these requirements were challenged at a public hearing con-cerning the proposed regulations.

If the organization is the subject of a harassment campaign, the proposed regulations contain procedures for applying to the key district office for relief. As an example, the regulation indicates that the receipt of 200 requests following a national news report about the organization is not considered harassment. Receipt of 100 requests from known supporters of another organization opposed to the policies and positions the organization advocates are said to be disruptive to the organization's operations and to thereby constitute harassment.

The disclosure provisions of IRC §6652 impose a penalty of $10 per day for failure to provide a copy. A fine of $5,000 can be imposed for willful failure to dis-close (up from $1,000).[18] An organization having more than one administrative of-fice must have a copy available at each office where three or more full-time em-ployees work. Service-providing facilities are not counted for this purpose if management functions are not performed there. A branch organization that does not file its own Form 990 because it is included in a group return must make the group return available. A request to see a copy of the return can also be sent to the District Director of the Internal Revenue Service in the area in which the organiza-tion is located, or to the National Office of the IRS. Form 4506-A can also be used to request a copy of any return, and a photocopying fee will be imposed.

The penalty for refusing to furnish Form 990 is payable by the responsible person at a rate of $10 per day for each day of failure up to a maximum of $5,000. For withholding Form 1023, another $10 per day is charged and there is no maxi-mum penalty. If the refusal is a willful act, an additional $1,000 can be assessed.[19]

(a) Disclosures Not Required

The names and addresses of the organization's contributors are not subject to pub-lic inspection and can be omitted from the copy made available to the public. All other parts of the form, including officer compensation and Schedule A, must be disclosed. Forms 990-T and 1120-POL are considered nonpublic returns and need not be made available.

(b) Private Foundations

Prior to 1999, the annual return of a private foundation, Form 990-PF, were made available under a system dating from 1969 that differed from the other Form 990

---

[18] Taxpayer Bill of Rights 2, §1313, amending IRC §6685.
[19] IRC §6685.

rules in several respects. The foundation managers made the form open for inspection by any citizen at the principal office during regular business hours, on request made within 180 days after the date of publication of notice of its availability.[20] A notice of availability was placed in a newspaper and contained information outlined in §27.13(s).

27.3   ACCOUNTING ISSUES

Good accounting is the key to successful preparation of federal information returns for nonprofit organizations.[21] The trick is to allocate and attribute revenues and expenses to the proper lines and columns on Forms 990. Particularly for organizations paying tax on unrelated business income,[22] proper identification of allocable expenses is the goal.

Documentation and cost accounting records must be developed to capture revenues and costs in categories and to report them by function, including joint cost allocations. When expenses are attributable to more than one function, organizations must develop techniques that will provide verifiable bases upon which expenses may be related to program or supporting service functions. The functional classification of expenses permits the organization to tell the reader of the financial statements not only the nature of its expenses, but also the purpose for which they were made. At a minimum, all exempt organizations need to maintain the following:

- A staff salary allocation system is essential for recording the time employees spend on tasks each day. The possibilities are endless. Each staff member could maintain an individual computer database or fill out a time sheet. The reports should be completed often enough to ensure accuracy, preferably weekly. In some cases, as when personnel perform repetitive tasks, preparing one week's report for each month or one month each year might be sufficient. Percentages of time spent on various functions can then be tabulated and used for accounting allocations.

- Office/program space utilization charts to assign occupancy costs can be prepared. All physical building space rented or owned must be allocated according to its usage. Floor plans must be tabulated to arrive at square footage of the space allocable to each activity center. In some cases, the allocation is made by using staff/time ratios. For dual-use space, records must reflect the number of hours or days space is used for each purpose.

- Direct program or activity costs should be captured whenever possible. The advantages include reduction of unrelated business income, proof of qualifying distributions for a private foundation, and insurance against

---

[20] IRC §6104(d).

[21] Chapter 6 of the author's book, *Financial Planning for Nonprofit Organizations* (New York: Wiley, 1996) contains a concise outline of basic accounting principles that apply to nonprofits.

[22] See §27.14.

an IRS challenge for low program expenditures. A minimal amount of additional time should be required by administrative staff to accumulate costs by programs. A departmental accounting system is imperative. Some long-distance telephone companies will assist in developing a coding system that quantifies the phone charges by department. As another example, the organization can establish separate accounts with vendors for different departments.

- Joint projects allocations must be made on a reasonable and fair basis recognizing the cause and effect relationship between the cost incurred and where it is allocated. Four possible methods of allocating include: activity-based allocations (identifying departmental costs); equal sharing of costs (e.g., if three projects, divide by three); cost allocated relative to stand-alone cost (e.g., what it would cost if that department had to hire and buy independently); and cost allocated in proportion to cost savings.[23]

- Supporting, administrative, or other management costs should be allocated to departments to which the work is directly related. The organization's size and the scope of administrative staff involvement in actual programs determine the feasibility of such cost attributions. Staff salaries are most often allocable. Say, for example, the executive director is also the editor of the organization's journal. If a record of time spent is maintained, his or her salary and associated costs could be attributed partly to the publication. When allocating expenses to unrelated business income, an *exploitation* of exempt functions rule may apply to limit such an allocation as discussed in §27.14(d).

- A computer-based fund accounting system is preferable, in which department codes are automatically recorded as moneys are expended. The cost of the software is easily recouped in staff time saved, improved planning, and possibly tax savings due to a reduction in income and excise taxes.

(a) Tax Accounting Methods

Plainly and simply, the instructions for Forms 990 say that an organization should generally use the same accounting method on the return to figure revenue and expenses as it regularly uses to keep its books and records.[24] The method must, however, clearly reflect income. If the organization is required to use the accrual method for state reporting purposes, it may also do so for 990 purposes. The cash method of accounting must be used by public charities for purposes of calculating public support percentages under §170(b)(1)(A)(vi) and §509(a)(2) on Schedule A.[25] Private foundations must also tally the §4942 minimum distribution requirements on a cash basis.[26]

---

[23] Dennis P. Tishlian, "Reasonable Joint Cost Allocations in Nonprofits," *Journal of Accountancy,* November 1992, page 66.
[24] In accordance with IRC §446(a).
[25] Discussed in §27.12(c).
[26] Discussed in §27.13(k).

Once an organization adopts either the cash or accrual method for 990 reporting, it must file Form 3115 to change the method under procedures outlined in Chapter 28. An organization that changes its method of reporting contributions and grants to comply with the Financial Accounting Standards Board (FASB) standards, however, is not required to file Form 3115.[27] The prior year effect of such a change is reported on line 20 of Part I of Form 990 and Part III of Form 990-PF, rather than on the beginning balance sheet.

(b) Professional Accounting Standards

The Financial Accounting Standards Board approved three Statements of Financial Accounting Standards (SFAS)—Nos. 116, 117, and 124—that significantly changed the generally accepted methods of accounting applicable to not-for-profit organizations in 1995. The recommended changes were required to be made for all organizations reporting their financial conditions in accordance with generally accepted accounting principles (GAAP) for years beginning after December 15, 1995. A new edition of the AICPA *Audit and Accounting Guide for Not-For-Profit Organizations* was released as of June 1, 1998 to combine guidance previously issued separately for voluntary health and welfare organizations, colleges and universities, and other types of nonprofit organizations.

During 1996 and 1997, a large number of exempt organizations adopted the new standards and made significant changes in their financial reporting systems. The IRS blessedly allowed such organizations to change their tax reporting methods without permission and continues to allow adoption of SFAS No. 116 without permission.[28] Going forward, such changes may need to be made by an organization that has, in its initial years or for whatever reason, not followed GAAP and chooses to begin to do so. Customarily this situation arises when the organization engages a CPA to issue audited reports of its financial condition. A brief introduction to the accounting concepts follows.

Statement of Financial Accounting Standards (SFAS) No. 116, Accounting for Contributions Received and Contributions Made, affects the manner in which contributions are to be reported on GAAP financial statements. This SFAS defines a contribution as "an unconditional transfer of cash or other assets to an entity or a settlement or cancellation of its liabilities in a voluntary nonreciprocal transfer by another entity acting other than as an owner." FASB further provides that the following inflows of assets are not included in the definition of contributions:

- Transfers that are exchange transactions, in which both parties receive goods or services of commensurate value

- Transfers in which the organization is acting as an agent, trustee, or intermediary for the donor (that is, the organization has little or no discretion concerning the use of the assets transferred)

- Tax exemptions, tax incentives, and tax abatements

---

[27] IRS Notice 96-30, I.R.B. 1996-20, issued April 30, 1996.
[28] Id.

Contributions received in the form of *charitable pledges* are included in revenue when the pledge is unconditionally made or promised, rather than when paid in cash or other assets. A condition is a future and uncertain event. Thus, a pledge to match funding from others is conditional and not reported until the matching gifts have been received. For the value of a pledge to be reported, there must be "sufficient evidence in the form of verifiable documentation that a promise was made and received." Restricted and unrestricted gifts of all kinds and in whatever form—cash, securities, other property, or in-kind—are subject to reporting as current revenue under this rule. Factors indicating a bookable pledge are compared in the following list to (those indicating the gift is conditional and therefore not recordable):

- Written evidence exists (no written promise made).

- Documents contain language such as "promise," "agree," "will," or "binding" (no "hope," "intend," "may," or "expect").

- Pledge payments are scheduled for specific dates in the future (no specific payment dates indicated in documents).

- Donor's economic position indicates ability to pay pledged amount (collectibility of pledge is questionable).

- Donor has history of timely payment of pledged amounts (donor has no history).

- Donee has taken specific steps—signed contract to build the new building or sought matching pledges—in reliance on pledge (no action taken or obligation entered into as result of pledge).

- Pledge was made in response to solicitation of formal pledges (promise is unsolicited or funding request sought no pledge).

- Public recognition or announcement of pledge made (no announcement).

Pledges of donations to be received beyond the current year are *discounted* by applying an appropriate rate of interest (return the organization is currently earning on its investments or cash reserves). The increase (called *accretion*) in the value of the pledge each year is reported as a donation in that year. An allowance for uncollectable pledges must be provided to cover the inevitable uncollectable pledge (and reflected as a reduction of the revenue, not as an expense).

Contributed services provided by volunteers are recognized as income for financial purposes (but not for tax purposes) if one of two conditions exists when the services are received:

- The services create or enhance nonfinancial assets (volunteers construct a building or set for a theater performance), or

- Services are of a type that requires specialized skills, are provided by individuals possessing those skills, *and* would typically have to be purchased if not provided by donations. SFAS No. 116 lists by example professions, such as doctors, lawyers, teachers, and carpenters.

Donated facilities produce recognizable income equal to the fair rental value of the facilities but not more than the organization would otherwise pay for its needed facilities. The present value of a binding multiyear lease are reported as income in the year the agreement is arranged. Again note that the value of such a donation is not reported as tax revenue. *In-kind donations* of land, building, equipment, supplies, and other tangible property are recorded for both financial and tax reporting purposes. A *testamentary bequest* is recorded as income when the amount of the bequest can be accurately determined. A specific bequest of a sum certain amount or particular property is recorded when there is no uncertainty about its being subject to death taxes or other obligations of the decedent. The discounted present value of the organization's share of assets in a *split-interest agreement* is reported as a gift of current income in the year its ownership is made certain under the *intention-to-give* concepts defining unconditional gifts.

Increases or decreases in an organization's investment in an *affiliated entity* are reported on line 7 or 11 as other investment income, or possibly as other revenue, depending on the reason why the organization is holding the property. Note that, for tax purposes, affiliated but legally independent exempt organizations must each file their own Forms 990, except for members of an affiliated association holding a group exemption. *Contributions or grants paid out* by the organization are recognized as an expense in the year the promise to pay is made, regardless of whether the cash or other asset is actually disbursed. Matching, conditional, or otherwise contingent promises to pay are booked at the time the uncertainty is removed because the condition is met.

SFAS No. 117, Financial Statements for Not-For-Profit Organizations, redesigned financial statement presentation and made obsolete the different systems previously prescribed for hospitals, colleges, health and welfare, and all other not-for-profit organizations. Donations received are identified as subject to one of three types of restrictions:

- Permanently restricted, such as moneys to be used to pay scholarships only, an endowment fund from which only the dividends and interest may be used, and long-lived assets, such as buildings or collections.

- Temporarily restricted funds given to accomplish a particular program service or to buy certain assets over a period of time.

- Unrestricted net assets will identify all other resources of the not-for-profit organization freely available for use in accomplishing the organization's purposes and subject only to the control of the organization's board or officers.

A *statement of activity* for all organizational funds and programs replaces the statement of financial position and results of operations, also called statement of revenues and expenses. "To help donors, creditors, and others assess an organization's service efforts," the statement of activity reports expenses functionally. In other words, the total cost of major program services is reported along with separate amounts for supporting services (management, fund-raising, and membership development expenses). Additionally, health and welfare organizations report total expenses in their natural categories—personnel, occupancy, interest, grants to others, and so on. For hospitals and all other nonprofits, this report is encouraged but not required. *Current earnings* on all funds, including those permanently restricted, are to be reported on the statement of activity. Revenues subject to restrictions, such as capital gains on endowment funds, are separately identified but still reported as current earnings.

SFAS No. 124, Accounting for Certain Investments Held by Not-for-Profit Organizations, addresses the way in which nonprofit organizations account for equity securities, the value of which is readily determinable, and investments in debt securities. Investments in land, a partnership, a subsidiary corporation, or other investments are not addressed in this SFAS. Marketable equity and debt securities are reported at their fair market value. Such investments are initially reported at their acquisition cost (including brokerage and other transaction fees) if purchased and at fair value if they are received as donations or through an agency transaction. Changes in fair value of such investments are reflected in the statement of activity (income statement) as unrealized gain or loss and increase or decrease unrestricted net assets unless their use is temporarily or permanently restricted by donors to a specified purpose or future period. Such unrealized gains and losses are not recognized for tax purposes, but instead are reflected in Part I, line 20 (990), or Part III, line 3 or 5 (990-PF) as an item reconciling book to tax income. Consequently, the tax gain or loss reported upon sale or other disposition of such investments is different from that reflected for financial purposes. Similarly, the FASB permits investment revenues to be reported net of related expenses, such as custodial fees and investment advisory fees; such expenses are reported in Part II of Form 990.

27.4 FORM 990EZ, THE SHORT FORM

An abbreviated version of Form 990, condensed from six to two pages, can be filed by exempt organizations whose gross receipts are normally more than $25,000 but less than $100,000. Although no filing is required if receipts are under $25,000, the author strongly suggests filing anyway for reasons outlined in §27.1(c). To file Form 990EZ, the EO's total assets shown on line 25, column B for the current year must be under $250,000 and it may not be a private foundation. (PFs file Form 990-PF even if they have no revenue.) Organizations qualified for exemption under IRC §501(c)(3) must also file Schedule A.

The filing requirement is not based solely on the current year's gross revenue but on the amount the organization "normally" receives. Normally receiving under $25,000 of gross receipts occurs in the following circumstances and relieves the organization from filing Form 990EZ:

- *New organization.* An organization up to one year old that receives, or has donors pledging to give, $37,500 or less during its first year;

- *One- to three-year-old organization.* Between one and three years of age, an organization may average $30,000 or less in gross receipts during its first two years and not have to file; and

- *Three- or more-year-old organizations.* All other organizations that receive an average of $25,000 or less in the immediately preceding three tax years, including the year for which the return would be filed, are excused from filing.

Form 990EZ was designed by the IRS to simplify reporting requirements for modest organizations and to reduce their auditing burden. Essentially, Form 990EZ is a condensed version of the six-page Form 990. The information reported is basically the same, but it is combined and abbreviated. Fortunately, the most difficult and dangerous part of the 990—Part VII, *Analysis of Income-Producing Activities* (which pinpoints unrelated business income)—is absent.

The suggestions for completing Form 990 can be used to complete Form 990EZ. To assist the reader, a blank copy of 990EZ referenced to the appropriate book sections that contain instructions for the parallel parts of Form 990 can be found in Appendix 27–1.

27.5 FORM 990, PART I, INCOME AND EXPENSE

The IRS instructions for the various Forms 990 total more than 80 pages and are quite good. They should be read alongside this chapter, which does not repeat the IRS directions, but elaborates on them. Appendix 27–2 is a sample Form 990, filled out for a fictitious organization—Campaign to Clean up America. Note in the example that all nonapplicable questions are answered with "N/A." It is also useful to enter "none" in the blank for any part's total where no amounts are entered. It is especially important to answer the questions on board and staff compensation. The following §27.5 through §27.11 offer practical guidance for completing Form 990, which is divided into parts.

Although the title of Part I is similar to that found in the accountants' financial statement (possibly "Statement of Activity"), its arrangement, and in some cases the amounts, are very different. Also, the tremendous difference in the operations and purposes of different types of exempt organizations adds complexity to completing the form. A few concepts must be defined at the outset.

Contributions are called support on line 1 of this part. *Support* means gratuitous transfer and is essentially a type of revenue received only by an exempt organization. Support represents money given to the exempt organization for which the donor receives nothing in return.[29] Payments for which the payer expects something specific in return are not support. A labor union or a business league reports its member dues on line 3 instead of reporting them as support on line 1. An IRC §501(c)(3) organization reports its member dues payments either on line 1 or line 3, depending upon the value (if any) assigned to the member privileges and benefits. The old refrain used by charities for many years, "deductible to the extent allowed by law," is no longer acceptable. Chapter 24 discusses this issue in detail and provides guidance for valuing such benefits.

Sales of tangible or intangible objects are particularly troublesome because they can be reported on line 2, 8, 9, or 10. Hospitals and colleges using special accounting procedures are allowed to report in accordance with their prescribed categories.

---

[29] For definition for tax purposes see Chapter 24§1 and in accounting terms, see §27.3.

Unrelated business income (UBI) is reported alongside related income without specific identification. Some speculate that lines 10 and 11 are troublesome because they are often the appropriate slot for UBI, although the instructions anticipate that both exempt function and unrelated sales will be included on line 10. It is noteworthy that the statute of limitations for assessment of UBIT runs in three years if sufficient information is submitted with Form 990 to allow the IRS to review the status of each category of revenue, even if Form 990-T is not filed.[30]

The primary goal in classifying an exempt organization's revenues depends upon the exemption category. For a charitable exempt organization, donations that enable it to satisfy the public support tests may be of utmost importance. A labor union is more concerned about distinguishing between member payments that are taxable UBI and those that are dues. All income, including UBI, is reported on page 1. This section discusses types of income that often cause classification questions.

(a) Definition of Gross Receipts

Filing requirements are based on gross receipts as reflected in Part I. An organization's gross receipts include all cash receipts during a year, not including amounts received as an agent for another organization (the recipient organization has no right to keep them but only to serve as custodian), borrowing, interfund transfers, and expense reimbursements. To determine the annual federal filing requirement for Forms 990, gross receipts are calculated from the front page of the form itself. For Form 990, the following lines are added:

- Line 1: Contributions, gifts, and grants
- Line 2: Program service revenue
- Line 3: Membership dues and assessments
- Line 4: Interest on savings and investments
- Line 5: Dividends and interest from securities
- Line 6a: Gross rent
- Line 7: Other investment income
- Line 8a: Gross amount from sale of assets other than inventory
- Line 9a: Gross revenue from special fund-raising events and activities
- Line 10a: Gross sales less returns and allowances
- Line 11: Other revenue

The total can be checked by adding back all the costs deducted on page one on lines 6b, 8b, 9b, and 10b to the total revenue on line 12. Form 990EZ filers can follow the same pattern using the different designations on fewer lines, adding all gross income before the expense deductions.

[30] See discussion in §27.1(c).

(b) Line 1: Contributions, Gifts, Grants, and Other Similar Amounts Received

Most often it is IRC §501(c)(3) and §501(c)(4) organizations that receive voluntary contributions and grants reportable on line 1. Reporting of contributions to be received in the future that are treated as current year revenue under SFAS No. 116 can be reported by an accrual basis exempt organization.[31]

Individual contributions. Volunteer payments motivated by the desire to help finance the exempt organization's exempt activities, or "one-way street receipts," are reported here. Moneys reported on this line include those paid with the intention of making a gift with no expectation of return or consideration other than intangible recognition, such as inclusion of a name on a sponsor list or on a church pew. For a §501(c)(3) organization, amounts that qualify for the IRC §170 charitable deduction appear on this line. Amounts given in return for privileges or goods (see Chapter 24) and investment returns are reported on the other lines.

Corporate donation. Grants from corporations or other businesses are reported as direct public support. Although it seems logical to call it an indirect gift, money raised by a business in a cause-related marketing campaign is reported here. The IRS instructions call such fund-raising *commercial co-ventures*. Typically, a business uses the charity's name in a sales promotion and promises to contribute a stated dollar amount for each item sold or for the occurrence of some action on the public's part. Business sponsorships treated as acknowledgments[32] are reported here; those treated as advertising are reported on Line 11.

Grants from other organizations. Grants received from other charitable organizations for support in operating the organization's programs, building its facilities, conducting its research, and the like are reported on line 1a, along with individual and corporate donations. Restricted grants to be used for a specific purpose, such as acquisition of a work of art to be owned and held by the grantee, are reported on this line. Grants to perform services of benefit to the grantor are reported instead on line 2, as explained below.

Indirect public support. Line 1b includes amounts received through solicitation campaigns of federated fund-raising agencies, such as the United Way or community trust. Support received from a parent or subordinate organization or other group that raises funds on behalf of the organization is also to be reported here, as is money transferred to the charitable arm of a professional society whose members voluntarily add designated donations to their dues payments.

Noncash donations. Gifts of marketable securities, real estate, and other noncash property such as food, clothing, or medical supplies are included on line 1a at their fair market value on the date of gift.[33] For such gifts exceeding $500, the donor must attach Form 8283 to his or her individual return to claim a deduction. When a charity acknowledges a gift of property valued at $5000 or more on Form 8283 and sells the property within 2 years from the date of the gift, Form 8282 must be filed to report the sale. Property distributed for exempt purposes is not so reported.

In-kind contributions. Donations of time, services, or the use of property are *not* reported as support on page 1 or in Schedule A (though gifts of tangible goods

---

[31] See discussion in §27.3.
[32] See Chapter 21§8(e).
[33] The estate tax rules at Reg. §20.2031 prescribe valuation methods.

that are sometimes described as in-kind are). They are not reported even if the services are recorded for financial reporting purposes in accordance with generally accepted accounting principles (GAAP). If they are so recorded, they can be reported for 990-T purposes as discussed in §27.14(f).

Contributor names. A schedule of contributors who gave the organization money or other property worth $5,000 or more during the year is to be attached, except for 509(a)(1) charities that list donors giving $5,000 or 2% of line 1d whichever is higher. Addresses, the date received, and a description of the property must be reported (not open to public inspection). The name of an employer withholding gifts from paychecks that are turned over to the charity, is to be reported, but the individual employee names are not.

Special fund-raising events. Such events produce both contributions and exchange revenues. The donation portion of a payment received in connection with a fund-raiser, as described in §27.5(j), is reported on line 1. Essentially, the total payment less the value of dinner, merchandise, or other benefits provided is reported as a contribution. When the benefits are treated as de minimus,[34] the entire payment is reported on line 1.

Government grants reportable on line 1c are those awards that represent support for the recipient organization to carry on programs or activities that further its organizational objectives.[35] Such grants are said to give a direct benefit primarily to the general public rather than an economic or physical benefit to the payor of the grant. Instead, some grants are payments in exchange for services, and thus are not contributions. When a sale of goods, performance of service, or admission to or use of a facility must be delivered or provided specifically to the grantor, program service revenue reported on line 2 is received; such revenue is referred to under GAAP as exchange transactions.[36] As an example, Medicare funds which a health care provider collects for treatment of patients is reported on line 2. The terms of the grant agreement indicating gross receipts from a service contract, as contrasted to (those terms identifying a contribution), might include the following:

- Specific delivery of services is required within specific time frame (time for performance at discretion of grantee).

- Penalties beyond the amount of the grant can be imposed for failure to perform (only penalty is return of grant for not conducting specific program or other restriction).

- Goods or services furnished or delivered only to grantor (program recipients other than grantor).

Membership dues may represent a charitable donation or fee for services depending on "commensurate rights and privileges" provided to members. A pure donation exists when the benefit is only the personal satisfaction of being of serv-

---

[34] Under Rev. Proc. 90-12 discussed in Chapter 24§3.
[35] Regs. §1.170A-9(e)(8) and §1.509(a)-3(g). Note the definitions are somewhat different under these regulations so that an EO should study the one pertaining to its category of public charity.
[36] See §27.3(b).

ice to others and furthering the charitable cause in which the members have a common interest. Otherwise, an *exchange transaction* occurs and service revenue is realized. Due to the difficulty of valuing certain member privileges, the IRS in August 1995, significantly eased the disclosure requirements by extending the token item de minimus rules to apply to member benefits. Benefits provided to members can be *disregarded* if they are given as a part of a basic annual membership of $75 or less. The IRS reasoned that it was "often difficult to value membership benefits, especially rights or privileges that are not limited as to use, such as free or discounted admission or parking, and gift shop discounts" and decided to allow "limited relief."[37]

Pass-through grants are not recognized as revenue to the organization acting as an agent for another organization. Such grants must be distinguished from indirect public support, or contributions received from a fund-raising agency, such as a united giving campaign, or an affiliated or supporting organization. Pass-through contributions are those that are not the property of the reporting organization, but instead represent a liability to the ultimate donee. Because of the public disclosure requirements (and in some cases, public support test calculations), this distinction has far-reaching impact.

(c) Line 2: Program Service Revenue

Revenues produced from exempt function services rendered, such as student tuition, testing fees, golf course green fees, trade show admission, ticket sales for cultural events, interest on student or credit union loans, low-cost housing rent, or convention registrations are reported on line 2. Fees for services generated in an exempt activity but taxed as unrelated business income are included, such as advertising revenues in an exempt publication. See the instructions in §27.11 for Part VII where this type of income is detailed.

Grants that represent payments for services rendered on behalf of the donor are reported here, for example, a grant received by a scientific laboratory testing for automobile emissions for a state government. Sales of inventory, such as books, posters, reproductions, or other items sold in a bookstore, crafts produced by the handicapped, or tennis balls sold in the country club shop, even though they are related to exempt function activities, are not reported here, but on line 10 instead. Hospitals and colleges whose accounting systems do not allow them to readily extract the cost of goods sold attributable solely to inventory are permitted to report inventory sales on line 2.[38] Line 2 revenues are counted as public support for those (c)(3) organizations qualifying as public charities under §509(a)(2) but not under §509(a)(1).

(d) Line 3: Membership Dues and Assessments

For all exempt organizations with members, the first question in deciding where to report dues is: What do members receive in return for their dues payments? The value attributable to services received by members is reported as membership

---

[37] Reg. §1.170-13(f)(8); see Chapter 24 for details of disclosure rules for contributions.
[38] See more discussion of the character of revenues in Chapter 11§5.

dues and assessments. For most exempt organizations, the total amount of member dues used as general support by the organization is reported on line 3. Separate charges for specific activities, such as an educational seminar conducted by a business league, are reported on line 2.

For a charitable exempt organization, the excess amount of dues over fair market value of benefits and privileges required to be valued is separately reported as a donation on line 1, as explained above. If the rights and privileges of membership are incidental to making the organization function, and if the benefit of membership is the personal satisfaction of being of service to others and furthering the exempt purposes, the membership is a gift.[39] One example of the distinction between dues and donations is that Civil Air Patrol (CAP) members make contributions when their dues entitle them to receive training to perform services for the CAP for the benefit of the public, not for the member.[40] The IRS has ruled that an educational newsletter is incidental to the exempt purposes and is thus not an individual benefit unless it is a "commercial quality" publication.[41] Particularly for 509(a)(1) organizations this distinction is important for Schedule A purposes because membership dues treated as exempt function revenue are not counted as public support.

(e) Line 4: Interest on Savings and Temporary Cash Investments

This line is mostly self-explanatory. Interest earned on a program-related investment, however, goes on line 2 instead. Whether an employee loan is program-related is unclear. Money market interest also presents a question. Clearly, the interest on a bank money market checking or savings account is to be reported on line 4, but the brokerage firm cash fund is reportable as a dividend on line 5.

Interest on a privately placed loan to an individual or a corporation, not representing a security interest (meaning it is not regulated by state or federal securities law), is reported on line 11. If the loan is an investment, the interest is reported on line 7. Interest on a note receivable from the sale of an exempt function asset is also reported as other income on line 11. A labor union loaning funds to a faltering company to protect the jobs of its worker members would report the interest on line 2.

(f) Line 5: Dividends and Interest from Securities

Income payment from investments in stocks, bonds, and security loans are reported on line 5. Mutual fund shares capital gain dividends, however, are reportable on line 8. Dividends from a subsidiary operated as a program-related investment would be reported on line 2; dividends from a for-profit subsidiary would be reported here.

(g) Line 6: Gross Rents

Rents from investment real or personal property are reported on line 6. Rents produced through exempt programs, such as low-income housing, are included on

---

[39] Reg. §1.509(a)-3(h).
[40] *Miller v. Commissioner*, 34 T.C.M. 1207 (1975).
[41] Rev. Proc. 90-12, 1990-1, C.B. 471. See Chapter 24§3(c) for definition of the terms.

line 2. Rental of office space to other unaffiliated exempt organizations are usually reportable as rents on this line. Such rents are only reported on line 2 as exempt function income if the rental rate is well below the fair rental value of the property, and if the rental itself serves the lessor exempt organization's mission.

Expenses directly connected with the rental income are deducted on line 6b, but need not be itemized. Maintenance, interest on mortgages, depreciation, and other direct costs are placed here and are not included on page 2.

(h) Line 7: Other Investment Income

Income produced by Investments—other on line 56 of the balance sheet is reported on line 7. Mineral royalties are a good example. Such income is expected to be explained and the information can be tied to the balance sheet, where an explanation is also requested. The instructions specifically provide that the unrealized gains or losses on investments carried at market value are to be reported, not on this line, but on line 20 as an "other change in fund balance."

(i) Line 8: Capital Gains and Losses

Gains or losses from sales of all types of capital assets (not inventory), including those held for investment, those held for exempt purposes, and those that produce UBI, are reported on line 8. A detailed schedule similar to that included in a normal income tax return is prepared—date acquired and sold, gross sales price and selling expenses, cost basis, and any depreciation. Multiple sales of publicly traded securities can be aggregated and reported as one number. Capital gains distributed from partnerships, trusts, and S corporations are reported here. Unrealized gains reported for financial statement purposes should be reported on line 20.

(j) Line 9: Fund-Raising Events

Amounts paid as admission to events is fragmented on this line. That amount equal to the value of the goods or services provided in connection with payments for tickets or admission are reported, but the excessive payment over the value of services or goods received are reported as donations on line 1 and noted in parentheses on line 9a. Proceeds of an auction, car wash, cookie sales, dinners, and other events would be included here. When the value of goods and services provided in connection with fund-raising efforts—a T-shirt, coffee cup, or poster, for example—are of limited monetary worth, the item or benefit is treated as having no value, or to be de minimus. The total payment made to the organization is then treated as a gift and reported on line 1. No amount is reported on line 9. Also, the expenses associated with purchase of the de minimus items are reported on page 2 as fund-raising expense, not on line 9.

Fund-raising campaign gifts for which donors receive nothing in return for their gifts are totally reported on line 1. The instructions direct §501(c)(3) organizations to keep both their solicitations and the receipts they furnish to participants in events, as well as proof of the method used to determine the noncontribution portion of the proceeds. Services or goods received are to be valued at their fair market value, which is often difficult to determine. The cost of the event is not necessarily determinative. These issues are discussed in Chapter 24§2.

A detailed description of the three largest events sponsored during the year must be furnished; the instructions for this line can be studied for more guidance. The direct costs benefits provided during the event are deducted on line 9b to arrive at the net income. The allocable portion of administrative or fund-raising departments is not reported on this line but on the applicable line of Part II.

(k) Line 10: Gross Sales Minus Returns and Allowances

Sales of inventory property made or purchased for resale, but not sales of capital assets, are reported here. An educational center's books, a retirement home's or a hospital's pharmaceuticals, a thrift shop's used clothing, or other objects purchased for resale constitute inventory items. Prior to 1994, hospitals and colleges could report sales of inventory on line 3, but are now instructed to report them on line 10. Cost of goods sold include direct and indirect labor, materials and supplies consumed, freight, and a portion of overhead expenses. A detailed schedule is requested. Marketing and distribution expenses are reported in Part II.

(l) Line 11: Other Revenues

Interest earned on loans not made as investments, such as an employee advance or officer loan, are cited by the IRS instructions as reportable on this line. Royalties paid for use of the exempt organization's name are also reported here. The author prefers not to use this line.

(m) Lines 13–15: Expense Totals

Organizations that are IRC §501(c)(3) and (4) and IRC §4947(a)(1) charitable trusts must complete these lines. All other Form 990 filers are not required to complete these lines because they do not complete columns b-d on Part II. Totals from Part II on page 2, when expenses are divided into functional categories, are reported here. The organization should note that the ratio between these lines is an evaluation tool used by some readers. For example, assume:

Line 13 Program services	$600,000	67%
Line 14 Management and general	$200,000	22%
Line 15 Fund-raising	$100,000	11%
Line 17 Total expenses	$900,000	100%

Some advisors in the nonprofit community have opinions about the proper level of program spending as compared to general and administrative and fund-raising expenses. The Better Business Bureau thinks that program services equaling at least 80% of the total expense is preferred. Spending 67% as shown above may be questionable in their view.

(n) Line 16: Affiliate Payments

Required payments, such as dues, to a national, state, or other closely related organization under a predetermined formula for sharing support or dues are deducted here. The IRS instructions to the form comprise half a page and provide clear guidance for this line.

(o) Lines 18–21: Fund Balances

The information reported for Form 990 purposes is reconciled to the financial records on these lines. The balance sheet in Part IV is reported according to the organization's financial statements. Differences in reporting treatment might stem from a change in accounting method or from an adjustment of a prior year's mistake in reporting. The exempt organization must decide if a change is significant enough to require amendment of the previously filed Form 990. If not, the difference would be reported on line 20. The IRS may question such a correction if it reflects an overall accounting method change for which permission was not secured in advance, and if the amount is material. Particularly if the change affects UBIT, an amended return may be proper.[42] Another common difference that occurs here is the changes in unrealized gain or loss reported for financial statement purposes not includable on lines 1–11.

27.6 PART II, STATEMENT OF FUNCTIONAL EXPENSES

In this part, all 990 filers report operating expenses in Column A by object classification, such as salaries, occupancy, and so on. The total organizational expenses are reported, including those paid to produce UBI. While it might seem wrong to include UBI expenses with related expenses of program services rendered, the form's design requires it and associated income is reported in Part I. Deductible UBI expenses may appear on any line (but not in Column D). For example, grants reported on line 22 may qualify as a charitable deduction in calculating the UBI tax; §27.14(d) discusses UBI deductions and defines direct and indirect costs—an accounting concept that applies in preparing this part.

The challenge in this part for (c)(3) organizations is dividing the expenses into functional categories of program service, management and general, and fund-raising. The columnar totals allow the IRS and others to evaluate the proportion of costs devoted to exempt activities—optimally, a high proportion. Conversely, fund-raising costs should be low; some states limit them to 20% to 25% of total expenses. The administrative expense level depends on the nature of the organization. Completing columns B, C, and D to break down an organization's total expenses according to its departments for program services, management and general expenses, and fund-raising is optional for:

- Voluntary employee benefits associations and other exempt organizations substituting Department of Labor forms.

- All exempt organizations except §501(c)(3) and §501(c)(4) organizations.

- Organizations whose receipts are normally under $25,000 annually.

---

[42] See discussion in Chapter 28.

Program services are those activities performed to accomplish the purposes for which the organization is exempt (its *exempt function*). Direct expenses specifically incurred in association with a project are included, along with an allocable part of indirect costs, such as salaries of employees directly involved in the project, occupancy cost for space utilized, and the cost of printing the reports. Colleges and hospitals whose internal accounting systems allocate indirect costs into cost centers have options for reporting such costs, and should read the instructions carefully.

Management and general expenses include overhead and administration—those expenses that are not allocable to programs or fund-raising. The executive director or controller and her or his staff and expenses, personnel and accounting departments, auditors, and lawyers are reported in column C. The cost of organizational meetings, such as the annual membership meeting, monthly board, staff, and committee meetings, and other meetings unrelated to a specific program or fund-raising are reported in column C. The investment or cash management function, budgeting, personnel, and staff cafeteria operations typify the costs reported here. Organizational and officer and director liability coverage is a management expense.

Fund-raising includes expenses incurred in soliciting donations, memberships, and grants voluntarily given to the exempt organization, including:

- Annual giving campaign costs of printing, publicity, mailing, staffing, and the like

- Professional fees to plan and execute the campaign or to draw documents for planned giving

- Development or grant-writing department

- Costs of collecting fund campaign pledges

- Portion of event costs not reported on line 8b

- Advertisements soliciting support

Fund-raising expenses do *not* include:

- Unrelated business expenses (these go in column B or C, or possibly only on page 1 if directly related to revenue).

- Fund-raising event, rental, or inventory direct expenses deducted directly from the gross receipts on page 1 (lines 6b, 8b, 9b, or 10b).

- Costs associated with collecting exempt income, such as student tuition or seminar registration fees. Report these in column B.

(a) Line 22: Grants and Allocations

Grants to other exempt organizations and to individuals are reported on line 22. Grants accrued under GAAP but not paid should be listed separately. Attach details summarizing the following information:

- Recipient's name and address and amount given

- Group grants by class or type of grant, such as scholarships, educational research, or building construction

- Relationship, if any, between the grantor and its directors or trustees and an individual grantee. (This information allows the IRS to identify private inurement, discussed in Chapter 20.)

Voluntary payments to affiliated organizations are reported on this line, rather than on line 16. Scholarship, fellowship, and research grants to individuals are reported on line 22, even though it is surprising, given the title of line 23. Only the grant award amounts are reported. The cost of administering the grant program, such as selection of recipients and monitoring compliance, is included on lines 25 through 43. If the grant is made in property rather than cash, more details are required. A description of the property, its book value, how the fair market value was determined, and the date of the gift are to be listed. Any difference between the value and book value of the property granted is reported on line 20 in Part I.

(b) Line 23: Specific Assistance to Individuals

Medical care, food, clothing, or cash to indigents or other members of a charitable class are reported on line 23, with a summary by type of assistance attached. The individual names are not reported. A (c)(3) organization must be alert to defining its charitable class and avoiding challenges, as outlined in Chapter 2§2(a). A grant to a homeless shelter for its operating expenses is reported on line 22, as is payment to the shelter to provide room and board for individuals.

(c) Line 24: Benefits Paid to or for Members

Payment of member benefits is usually antithetical to the purposes of an IRC §501(c)(3) organization, which, as a rule, would avoid such payment. Consult Chapters 7 and 8 for the problems involved with member benefits.

Labor unions, fraternal benefit societies, voluntary employee beneficiary associations, unemployment benefit trusts, and other nonprofit associations are formed to benefit their members in a nonprofit mode, and set aside moneys for such payments as a part of their underlying exempt function. A schedule reflecting the amount and type of benefits paid for sickness, death, unemployment, and the like should be attached and the total reported on line 23. Such payments and the insurance premiums associated with such protection paid on behalf of employees are reported on lines 27 and 28.

(d) Line 25: Compensation of Officers, Directors, etc.

Total officer compensation reported on this line should be coordinated with amounts reported in columns C, D, and E of Part V. Salaries, fees, commissions, and other types of compensation, including pension plan contributions, deferred compensation accruals (even if unfunded), health insurance, and other employee benefits (taxable and nontaxable) are included as further described in the suggestions for Part V. Amounts earned by directors in their capacity as directors and/or as staff or management are reported. The compensation of an officer treated as an independent contractor is also reported on this line. Accurate reporting of these amounts can be critical to satisfy the rebuttable presumption of reasonableness in an Intermediate Sanction dispute.[43]

The total gross wages or fees reported as paid to an individual should also be corroborated with Forms 941, W-2, and 1099 separately filed with the IRS to report the individual compensation and tax withholding. The IRS emphasized this subject during large case examinations in 1992–1997. Chapter 25 can be studied for details of those reporting rules and discussion of taxable compensation for various types of payments made to individuals.

(e) Lines 26, 27, 28, and 29: Salaries, Wages, Pension Contributions, Employee Benefits, and Payroll Taxes

Total payments to all salaried individuals, other than officers reported on line 25, are reported on line 26. Again, other reporting requirements are signaled to the IRS by the numbers on these lines. In addition to payroll taxes mentioned above, state and federal (not for (c)(3)s) unemployment taxes may be due, and Form 5500 may be due for pension plans.

(f) Lines 30, 31, and 32: Professional Fund-Raising, Accounting, and Legal Fees

These lines report compensation paid to independent advisors for fund-raising, accounting, auditing, financial consulting, and legal services. Note that the combination of lines 25–32 represents the direct amounts paid by the organization to individuals for services rendered. If this total number is high in relation to the overall expenses of the organization shown on line 44, an alarm may be sounded in someone's mind—the IRS, the inspecting member of the general public (see §27.2), a news reporter, or potential contributor. The IRS will ask the questions raised in Chapter 20 concerning private inurement.

Some states require charitable registration, and amounts reported on line 32 may signal the need for additional compliance. Consult another book in the Wiley Nonprofit Series, *The Law of Fund-Raising* by Bruce R. Hopkins, for a useful guide to such requirements.

(g) Lines 33–43: Supplies, Telephone, Postage, Occupancy, etc.

These lines are largely explained by their titles though some comments are in order:

Travel. An organization reporting travel should use a system of documentation designed to prove the travel's exempt purpose. Expense vouchers reflecting the nature of the expenditures and indicating any personal elements are appropriate. Staff members using an organization's vehicles must maintain a log of their mileage to prove what use is devoted to organization affairs, as well as any personal use. The personal portion, if any, is part of compensation and reportable on

---

[43] See Chapter 20§9.

line 25, 26, or 28 (and for W-2 purposes). Vehicle expense is reported as a part of travel or shipping.

Interest. Amounts paid for interest on rental property are not reported here but on line 6b of Part I, and, for property occupied by the organization for its own operations, on line 36. Otherwise, interest expense is reported on line 41. The total interest reported on the three lines mentioned should be coordinated with the answer to indebtedness in Part IV, Balance Sheets.

Depreciation. A detailed schedule of depreciation showing how depreciation is computed is attached and should include the current expense, reserves, asset costs, additions and deletions, and possibly date acquired as an attachment for line 42. It is useful to prepare one schedule that reflects depreciation included on line 6b, line 42, and details requested as an attachment for the Balance Sheet of Part IV at lines 55 and 57. If the organization applies MACRS to compute depreciation, Form 4562 is attached.

Joint costs. An organization that has costs associated with a combined educational campaign and fund-raising solicitation included in program costs is asked to explain how it allocates costs. To allocate costs that are of benefit to more than one function of the organization's operations, the IRS suggests, "Use an appropriate basis for each kind of cost." Some expenses, such as salaries, are allocated based on time expended. Occupancy can be based on space assigned or people using it (and may be partly based on their time allocation). The accounting profession provides some guidance for allocating materials that serve both an educational and informational purpose.[44]

27.7   PART III, STATEMENT OF PROGRAM SERVICE ACCOMPLISHMENTS

Due to the fact that a copy of Form 990 must be furnished to anybody who is willing to pay for it[45] and returns are entering the electronic age,[46] the prudent organization carefully prepares this part. It can be considered an opportunity to "toot the organization's horn" and to convince funders to support the organization. At least it should tell the story the organization wants conveyed in electronic media.

Part III asks that the filing organization describe its primary exempt purpose in about five to eight words (depends upon type size) and asks that the organization explain its mission achievements in a "clear and concise manner." To explain the exempt organization's accomplishments, its four major programs are described along with numerical data concerning how many members are served, classes taught, meals served, patients healed, sites restored, books published, products certified, or similar data evidencing benefit to the organization's exempt

---

[44] American Institute of Certified Public Accountants, Statement of Position 98-2, *Accounting for Costs of Activities of Not-for-Profit Organizations and State and Local Governmental Entities That Include Fund-Raising,* issued in March, 1998, as a part of the AICPA Audit and Accounting Guide.
[45] See §27§2.
[46] Discussed at the beginning of this chapter.

constituents. IRS instructions suggests the organization "discuss achievements that are not measurable."

A private elementary school with 400 students can easily answer this question. A 400-bed hospital would report the number of patients served and quantify the amount of charity care, if any. Reasonable estimates can be furnished if the exact number of recipients is not known. If numerical results are not pertinent or available, the project objectives for the return period and the long-range plans can be described. An exempt organization conducting research on heart disease and testing a controlled group of 100 women over a five-year period would say so. Similarly, an organization commissioning a study of an area's history would say it expects the project to take ten years and possibly describe its research modality to evidence the work's educational nature. Brochures, publication lists, and rate sheets can also be attached to convey a picture of the organization's activities.

Section 501(c)(3) and (4) organizations and wholly charitable trusts must (optional for other categories of Form 990 filers) also report the cost of program activities, including the amount of grants and allocations paid to others individuals and organizations. Submission of total expenses by program service category is not required. In other words, the organization must take the expenses reported in column B of Part II and further identify them by particular projects, reporting the total for its four major programs. Functional accounting records maintained by program are clearly a must for completing this part.

27.8 PART IV, BALANCE SHEET AND RECONCILIATION

An exempt organization's beginning and ending assets, liabilities, and fund balances or net assets are reported in Part IV, using the same method it uses for maintaining its normal accounting books and records. Beginning in 1995, this part of Form 990 reflects changes to the Net Asset section to accommodate the financial reporting changes. For organizations not following SFAS No. 117, Lines 70 through 73 combine the former titles and add traditional fund balance titles—endowment and plant fund—as shown on the form in Appendix 27–2. Fair market value of the assets may be reported if the organization's normal accounting method adjusts its carrying value to the current value. The amounts are most often reported at original cost, or "book value." If detailed schedules are requested, they need only be furnished for the year-end numbers. The instructions for this part are quite good and need not be repeated here.

Loans. Certain lines in this part alert the IRS to problem issues, and in those cases detailed schedules are requested. For most loans receivable by or payable by the organization, ten detailed items of information are required: borrower's name and title, original amount, balance due, date of note, maturity date, repayment terms, interest rate, security provided by borrower, purpose of the loan, and description and fair market value of consideration furnished by the lender. Loans to and from officers, directors, trustees, and key employees are presented as a separate total on line 50. The issues discussed in Chapter 20§§4 and 5 may need attention if the organization has such loans. A modest $5000 loan for college education to the vice-president may not cause additional scrutiny, but a $100,000 loan to refinance his credit cards might.

Coordinated schedules. Schedules for depreciable assets should be prepared to coordinate with the information attached for Parts I and II. Likewise, receivable and payable information can be tied to interest expense.

Incomplete information. In its instructions, the IRS cautions the preparer that penalties are imposed for failure to complete this part. The IRS thoughtfully reminds the organization that the reports are open to public inspection, and recommends that an effort be made to correctly complete the report. Labor unions filing Form LM-2 or LM-3 with the U.S. Department of Labor and certain employee benefit plans may substitute those forms for this part.[47]

Part IV-A and IV-B, *Reconciliation of Revenues and Expenses per Audited Financial Statements with Expenses per Return,* were added for 1995 to clarify items for which there are reporting differences (some not necessarily due to FASBs) for tax and financial purpose similar to Schedule M on a Form 1120. These parts are completed by an organization receiving an audited financial statement. They are optional for a group return.

A common reconciling item is revenue from donated services or the use of facilities and the corresponding expense for professional services, rent, or similar item. This part reminds organizations that such revenues are not deductible contributions for tax purposes.[48] Unrealized gains or losses on investments recognized for financial reporting purposes are not shown as revenue in Part I but instead as a change in fund balance on line 20. Charitable pledges reported as revenue under the accounting rules explained in §27.3 are reported as tax revenues. The instructions say SFAS No. 116 may be used for tax purposes, but is not required. Note that Schedule A of Form 990 must be prepared on the cash basis. Similarly, a public charity that records promises to pay out grants can reflect such grants on page 2 as a current-year expense. A private foundation instead reports grants paid only on a cash basis.

27.9 PART V, LIST OF OFFICERS, DIRECTORS, AND TRUSTEES

Part V calls for the names, addresses, titles, and times devoted to the positions for all members of the exempt organization's governing body and key employees, or "those persons having responsibilities or powers similar to those of officers, directors, or trustees,"[49] regardless of whether they are compensated. All such persons are to be listed, even if there are 50 board members. If an attachment is prepared, consider entering totals across the bottom of the form or noting "none" in each column where applicable.

Total compensation paid to persons serving on the governing board, for all services rendered, is to be reported, whether they are employees or independent contractors. For persons serving in more than one position—for example, both as a director and officer or staff member—the compensation for each respective position should be separately presented. Three distinct types of pay are reported. This part contains five columns of information to be listed about each official, regardless

---

[47] IRS Instructions to 1998 Form 990, General Item F, at page 4.
[48] IRC §170(e).
[49] IRS Instructions to 1998 Form 990, Part V, at page 22.

of whether they are compensated. The title of the part was revised in 1992 to add "Key Employees."

Column A. Name and Address. The name and address of each person who served at any time during the year as an officer, director, trustee, or key employee is entered. The address at which they want to be contacted by the IRS if necessary is shown; the organization's address can be used. Key employees include the chief management and administrative officials of an organization (such as an executive director or chancellor) but does not include the heads of separate departments or smaller units within the organization. A chief financial officer and the officer in charge of administration or program operations are both key employees if they have the authority to control the organization's activities, its finances, or both. It is extremely important to coordinate the inclusion of persons on this part with the Intermediate Sanction rules discussed in Chapter 20§9.

Column B. Title and Average Hours per Week Devoted to Position. Each person's title and the average hours per week devoted to the position is reported. Often such officials serve as volunteers and may not keep a record of time they spend in carrying out the position. If the persons are uncompensated, it is sufficient to give an estimate such as "4–6 hours," "as needed," or "part-time." For compensated persons (particularly highly paid ones) records substantiating actual time spent are critical.

Column C. Compensation. Salary, fees, bonuses, and severance benefits paid, including current year payments of deferred compensation reported in column D in a year past, are reportable here. Note that this number is not necessarily equal to the amount reported on one's W-2 or Form 1099. Certain taxable benefits and allowances are reported in column E. Cash and noncash payments are counted. For purposes of reporting compensation paid by related organizations to determine if someone receives a combined amount of more than $100,000, stock bonuses or options granted by a taxable subsidiary would be also includible, even if not currently taxable.

Column D. Contributions to Employee Benefit Plans and Deferred Compensation. All forms of deferred compensation—whether funded or unfunded, whether pursuant to a qualified or unqualified plan, whether accrued or earned for the current year—are reportable in this column. Qualified pension plans include defined contribution, defined benefit, and money purchase plans under §401(a), employee plans under §403(b), and IRA/SEP plans under §408. In a duplicative manner, the current year amount set aside is reported in this column as it accrues, whereas the actual payment made in a later year is reported in column C. Medical, dental, disability, and life insurance premiums paid by the organization are included. Tuition, child care, sick leave, and family leave would be counted. All amounts payable under a cafeteria plan, for example, would be included. Estimated cost is to be used if exact amounts per person are not available.

Column E. Expense Account and Other Allowances. Both taxable and nontaxable fringe benefits are reportable. According to the IRS, examples include amounts for which the recipient did not account to the organization or allowances that were more than the person spent serving the organization. A flat automobile, travel, book, or similar allowance would be included (also reportable on Form W-2). The instructions say that payments made under indemnification arrangements and the value of the personal use of housing, automobiles, or other assets owned or leased by the organization (or provided for the organization's use free of charge) should be reported here. The IRS devoted an entire chapter to this subject in its exempt organization specialists' annual training manual for 1996.[50] The chapter reminds the specialists that Internal Revenue Code §§132, 162, and 274 apply to define compensation and fringe benefits. The training materials recommend following the regulations to distinguish between reportable fringes and nonreportable de minimus fringe benefits to tally up total compensation.[51] Reportable benefits include season tickets to the theater or ball games, commuting use of the organization's car, club memberships, below-market loans, group term insurance on spouses or children, weekend use of an apartment or hunting lodge, and spousal travel absent a bona fide business purpose.

The following question appears at the end of this part:

> Did any officer, director, trustee, or key employee receive aggregate compensation of more than $100,000 from your organization and all related organizations, of which more than $10,000 was provided by the related organizations? ☐ Yes ☐ No.

This question allows the IRS to gather statistics and choose candidates for examination due to excessive compensation. Compensation for this purpose includes all of the items reportable in Part V combined for all related entities. When compensation above the $100,000/$10,000 floor is paid, a supporting schedule adding together the total compensation to any one individual must be attached.

Essentially, Part V intends to reveal compensation paid to personnel of an affiliated group on a consolidated basis. There is some question whether the related organization compensation must be revealed for an officer who receives no compensation from the reporting organization. The question literally asks the organization to combine the compensation of its officers with any compensation they receive from others. Certainly that is the intention. Another aspect of this issue is the potential for reallocation of compensation among the members of the controlled group.[52]

A related organization for this purpose is any entity, tax-exempt or not, that is either controlled or owned by or controls or owns the exempt organization. Control and ownership begin at a 50% level, with the Form 990 instructions very specifically providing:

- "Owns" means possessing 50% or more of the voting membership rights, voting stock, profits interest, or beneficial interest.

- "Control" exists where (1) 50% or more of the EO's officers, directors, trustees, or key employees are also officers, directors, trustees, or key

---

[50] *Exempt Organizations Continuing Professional Education Technical Instruction Program Textbook,* 1995 (for 1996) edition, Chapter I, "Reporting Compensation on Form 990," by Ward L. Thomas and James Bloom.

[51] Reg. §1.132-6(e).

[52] IRC §482, discussed by the IRS in the 1996 training manual (see previous note 48) at page 208.

employees of the second organization being tested for control; (2) The EO appoints 50% or more of the officers, directors, trustees, or key employees of the second organization; or (3) 50% or more of the EO's officers, directors, trustees, or key employees are appointed by the second organization.

- Supporting groups operated to benefit another member of the commonly controlled group are treated as controlled or owned, regardless of whether a 50% control level exists. *Supporting* for this purpose includes §509(a)(3) organizations as well as other organizations that "operate in connection with the EO where one of the purposes of the supporting organization is to benefit or further the purposes of your organization." The instructions suggest that a hospital auxiliary that raises funds for the hospital or coordinates volunteer programs would be treated as a supporting organization.

Shares issued to unrelated but closely associated individuals or organizations may be scrutinized. The structure may be challenged if its purpose was to keep the ownership under 50% for purposes of this reporting requirement. The same issue may be raised for §512(b)(13) purposes (more than 50% subsidiary whose rent, royalty, or interest payments are not subject to unrelated business income tax as discussed in Chapter 21). Clearly a broad net is to be cast.

27.10 PARTS VI AND IX, OTHER INFORMATION

Part VI requests information with which the IRS can evaluate an organization's ongoing qualification for tax exemption. The questions survey a wide range of issues. Some of the questions are germane to a particular class of 501(c) organization. Part IX is completed in response to a positive answer to Question 88 in Part VI. Certain answers can cause serious problems for the organization, as outlined in the following discussion.

Line 76 alerts the IRS to review organizational changes by asking if the organization "engaged in any activities not previously reported to the IRS." The question is sometimes hard to answer when the organization's activity has evolved or expanded, but has not necessarily changed in its focus or overall purpose. When there is any doubt, it is prudent to answer "yes" and attach an explanation. The issue raised by this question is whether the organization wants written IRS approval for its evolving or new activity. Simply answering this question "yes" and attaching a detailed description of a change does not result in an IRS response, in most cases. The exempt organization must decide whether to instead report its changes to the Ohio District Director with a request for determination of its impact on exempt status.[53]

Line 77 serves a function similar to line 76 by asking if "changes were made in the organizing or governing documents, but not reported to the IRS?" Conformed copies[54] should be attached if the answer is "Yes." Again, it is not custom-

---

[53] This decision is discussed in Chapter 28§2.
[54] See Chapter 18§2(a) instructions for line 11.

ary to get an IRS response to any information submitted. Consult Chapter 2, 6, 7, 8, 9, and 11 to ascertain whether a change violates the standards for the type of organization involved. Again Chapter 28 should be studied to decide if the Cincinnati, Ohio office should be informed directly.

Line 78 tells the IRS that the organization has unrelated business income in excess of $1,000 and that Form 990T is due to be filed. This answer should be coordinated with Part VII where reportable UBI is input in column (b). Woe to the organization that checks this question "yes" and fails to do so!

Line 79 reveals whether a liquidation, termination, or substantial contraction has occurred. Chapter 26 considers mergers, bankruptcy, and terminations and describes the consequences and constraints placed on such an organization. The instructions provide specific information to be attached if the answer is "Yes," and direct the preparer to read the regulations for special rules and exceptions.[55]

Line 80 asks "Is the organization related . . . to any other exempt or nonexempt organization?" If so, the entity is to be named. Such relationships are permitted and do not necessarily expose the organization to loss of its exemption. Chapter 22 discusses the consequence of such relationships and the constraints within which they are permitted. *Line 88* and Part IX of Form 990 also request information about taxable subsidiaries and Part VII of Schedule A asks about transactions with noncharitable exempt organizations.

Line 81 asks for the amount of political expenditures. "None" *must* be the answer for (c)(2) and (c)(3) organizations. Political activity for this purpose is that aimed at influencing the election of persons who make local, state, or national laws (not to be confused with lobbying, which is influencing the elected persons once they are in office). An excise tax is imposed on any (c)(3) involved in elections[56] and its exemption may be revoked. Such activity is not absolutely prohibited for many types of exempt organizations. *Line 81a* asks if Form 1120-POL was filed. See Chapter 23 for permissible amounts of political activity and tax on political expenditures.

Line 82 allows an organization to voluntarily report any donated services or facilities it receives during the year and to indicate their value.[57] Such donations are not included on page 1 or Schedule A because they are not deductible to the donor and are difficult to value. Because returns are open to public inspection, it is desirable for the organization to reveal such support here. If in-kind donations are reported for financial purposes, the number is also shown in Part IV-A and B.

Line 83a asks whether the organization has complied with the public inspection rules discussed in Chapter 27§2. Failure to comply leads to imposition of penalties.

Line 83b asks, "Did the organization comply with the disclosure requirements relating to quid pro quo contributions discussed in Chapter 24.

Line 84a. "Did the organization solicit any contributions or gifts that were not tax deductible?" *Line 84b* asks if so, were required disclosures made? This question applies to non-(c)(3) organizations with over $100,000 annual gross receipts

---

[55] Reg. §1.6043-3.
[56] IRC §4955.
[57] Discussed in §27§3(b).

that must expressly disclose on solicitations that payments are not deductible as donations under IRC §170. Organizations eligible to receive deductible gifts answer this question "N/A."

Line 85 asks eight questions pertaining to the requirement that 501(c)(4), (5), and (6) organizations disclose the portion of their member dues attributable to nondeductible lobbying. These questions seek to ascertain whether civic associations, unions, and business leagues that conduct lobbying meet the notification and proxy tax issues explained in Chapter 6§4.

Line 86 requests the statistics needed to calculate a social club's ongoing qualification, based upon the proportionate amount of nonmember receipts and investment income, as explained in Chapter 9§4.

Line 87 similarly tests compliance for benevolent life insurance associations, including mutual ditch or irrigation companies, mutual or cooperative telephone companies, and like organizations that must receive 85% or more of their income from members.

Line 88 is related to Line 80 discussed previously.

Line 89 asks requests pertaining to Intermediate Sanctions explained in Chapter 20§10.

Line 90a asks for a list of the states in which Form 990 is filed.

Line 90b asks for the number of employees during the March 12 pay period reported on Form 941 or 943, not 942.

Line 91 asks for the name and number of the person who is in care of the books. This person will receive the call if the IRS wishes to examine the organization's records.

Part IX, Information Regarding Taxable Subsidiaries. This author understands that this part was added at the behest of Congress to gather statistical information. See Chapter 22§4 for standards regarding separateness of such subsidiaries.

27.11   PART VII, ANALYSIS OF INCOME-PRODUCING ACTIVITY

Part VII was added to Form 990 in 1989 and contains a host of pitfalls and traps for the unwary. At the behest of Congress, the IRS designed this part as an audit trail to find unrelated business income (UBI). Selection of the appropriate inclusion (column a) or exclusion (column b) code to identify income is difficult in some cases and can have adverse consequences. Some choices are not absolute, and discretion can be important. For example, a column (c) exclusion code 40 highlights activities conducted for nonexempt purposes and operated at a loss—possibly indicating use of exempt organization funds for private purposes that results in inurement.[58] Such losses are also not available to offset against profit-motivated UBI.[59]

A thorough review of the unrelated business income provisions discussed in Chapter 21 may be very useful before completing this part.[60] An understanding of

---

[58] Discussed in Chapter 20.

[59] The *Portland Golf Club* decision discussed in Chapter 9§5(a) can be studied regarding limitations on a social club's nonmember activities treated as not entered into to produce a profit.

[60] See also IRS Publication 598, *Tax on Unrelated Business Income of Exempt Organizations.*

the terms *regularly carried on, member convenience, related and unrelated,* and *fragmented* is absolutely necessary for correct completion of this page. The form forces the organization to report items of income appearing on page 1, lines 2 through 11 (except for contributions) in one of three categories by columns.

(a) What the Columns Include

Columns (a) and (b), Unrelated business income. Income from unrelated business activities is reported in column (b). Any amounts included here must be reported on Form 990-T and are subject to income tax if a profit is generated from the activity. Column (a) codes are used in Form 990-T (Appendix 27–7) to identify the type of business conducted—mining, construction, manufacturing, services, and so on. The UBI codes (Exhibit 27–1) which are very similar to those used in Forms 1120 and 1065 for corporate and partnership income tax returns were redesigned for 1998.

Columns (c) and (d), Revenues excluded or modified from tax. Income from investments, fund-raising events, and business activities statutorily excluded from tax are included in these columns. The reason for exclusion of the income from tax is claimed by inserting one of 40 code numbers (explained below by line numbers and shown in Exhibit 27–2) in column (c). If more than one exclusion code applies, the lowest applicable code number is used according to the instructions. Certain codes, such as bingo (9), membership lists (13), and royalties (15), which are the subjects of current IRS versus taxpayer battles described in Chapter 21, may be troublesome, as the IRS uses this page to choose the exempt organizations it will examine, such as social clubs during 1997–98.

Column (e), Related or exempt function income. Income generated through charges for services rendered or items sold in connection with the organization's underlying exempt (program) activities are entered in column (e). Student tuition and fees, hospital charges, admissions, publication sales, handicraft or other by-product sales, seminar registrations, and all other revenues received in return for providing exempt functions[61] are included. This column is a safe harbor because it contains income not potentially subject to the UBI tax: that income generated by "substantially related" activities (those with a causal relationship, contributing importantly to the organization's programs). An explanation of the related aspect of each number in this column must be entered in Part VIII, as described in §27.11(c).

Some exempt function income is also described by specific exclusion codes. Rentals from low-income housing fits into code 16 and therefore could also properly be placed in columns (c) and (d). It is preferable to place such an item in column (e) because the taint of UBI character is removed. Interest income earned under a student loan program or by a credit union and royalties from scientific research patents are other examples of potential dual classifications.

(b) Line-by-Line Description

First, note that for certain lines, gross income before any deductions is reported, and for others (lines 97, 98, 100, and 101) net income is reported.

---

[61] IRC §512(a)(3)(B); see §27.5(c).

CODES FOR UNRELATED BUSINESS ACTIVITY

Codes for Unrelated Business Activity

*(If engaged in more than one unrelated business activity, select up to two codes for the principal activities.
List first the largest in terms of unrelated income, then the next largest.)*

AGRICULTURE, FORESTRY, HUNTING, AND FISHING
Code
110000 Agricultural, forestry, hunting, and fishing
111000 Crop production

MINING
Code
211110 Oil and gas extraction
212000 Mining (except oil and gas)

UTILITIES
Code
221000 Utilities

CONSTRUCTION
Code
230000 Construction
233000 Building, developing, and general contracting

MANUFACTURING
Code
311000 Food manufacturing
312100 Beverage manufacturing
312200 Tobacco manufacturing
313000 Textile mills
315000 Apparel manufacturing
316000 Leather and allied product manufacturing
321000 Wood product manufacturing, except furniture
322000 Paper manufacturing
323100 Printing and related support activities
323117 Book printing
323119 Other commercial printing
324110 Petroleum refineries
325000 Chemical manufacturing
325200 Resin, synthetic rubber, artificial and synthetic fiber and filament manufacturing
327000 Nonmetallic mineral product manufacturing
331000 Primary metal manufacturing
332000 Fabricated metal product manufacturing
333000 Machinery manufacturing
334000 Computer and electronic product manufacturing
335000 Electrical equipment, appliance, and component manufacturing
336000 Transportation equipment manufacturing
337000 Furniture and related product manufacturing
339000 Miscellaneous manufacturing
339110 Medical equipment and supplies manufacturing

WHOLESALE TRADE
Code
421000 Wholesale trade, durable goods
422000 Wholesale trade, nondurable goods

RETAIL TRADE
Code
441100 Automobile dealers
442000 Furniture and home furnishings stores
443120 Computer and software stores
444100 Building materials and supplies dealers
445100 Grocery stores
445110 Supermarkets and other grocery stores
445200 Specialty food stores
445291 Baked goods stores
446110 Pharmacies and drug stores
446130 Optical goods stores
447100 Gasoline stations
448000 Clothing and clothing accessories stores
451110 Sporting goods stores
451211 Book stores
451212 News dealers and newsstands
452000 General merchandise stores
453000 Miscellaneous store retailers
453100 Florists
453220 Gift, novelty, and souvenir stores
453310 Used merchandise stores
454110 Electronic shopping and mail-order houses

TRANSPORTATION AND WAREHOUSING
Code
481000 Air transportation
482110 Rail transportation
483000 Water transportation
484000 Truck transportation

485000 Transit and ground passenger transportation
485510 Charter bus industry
487000 Scenic and sightseeing transportation
493000 Warehousing and storage

INFORMATION
Code
511110 Newspaper publishers
511120 Periodical publishers
511130 Book publishers
511190 Other publishers
512000 Motion picture and sound recording industries
513100 Radio and television broadcasting
513300 Telecommunications
514000 Information services and data processing services

FINANCE AND INSURANCE
Code
522110 Commercial banking
522120 Savings institutions
522130 Credit unions
522190 Other depository credit intermediation
522210 Credit card issuing
522290 Other non-depository credit intermediation
523100 Securities, commodity contracts, and other intermediation and brokerage
524113 Direct life insurance carriers
524114 Direct health and medical insurance carriers
524121 Property and casualty insurance carriers
524126 Direct property and casualty insurance carriers
524130 Reinsurance carriers
524292 Third party administration for insurance and pension funds
524298 All other insurance related activities
525100 Insurance and employee benefit funds
525920 Trusts, estates, and agency accounts
525990 Other financial vehicles

REAL ESTATE AND RENTAL AND LEASING
Code
531110 Lessors of residential buildings and dwellings
531120 Lessors of nonresidential buildings, except miniwarehouses
531190 Lessors of other real estate property
531210 Offices of real estate agents and brokers
531310 Real estate property managers
531390 Other activities related to real estate
532000 Rental and leasing services
532291 Home health equipment rental
532420 Office machinery and equipment rental and leasing
533110 Lessors of nonfinancial intangible assets (except copyrighted works)

PROFESSIONAL, SCIENTIFIC, AND TECHNICAL SERVICES
Code
541100 Legal services
541200 Accounting, tax preparation, bookkeeping, and payroll services
541300 Architectural, engineering, and related services
541380 Testing laboratories
541500 Computer systems design and related services
541511 Custom computer programming services
541610 Management consulting services
541700 Scientific research and development services
541800 Advertising and related services
541860 Direct mail advertising
541900 Other professional, scientific, and technical services

MANAGEMENT OF COMPANIES AND ENTERPRISES
Code
551111 Offices of bank holding companies
551112 Offices of other holding companies

ADMINISTRATIVE AND SUPPORT AND WASTE MANAGEMENT AND REMEDIATION SERVICES
Code
561000 Administrative and support services
561300 Employment services
561439 Other business service centers (including copy shops)

561450 Credit bureaus
561499 All other business support services
561500 Travel arrangement and reservation services
561520 Tour operators
561700 Services to buildings and dwellings
562000 Waste management and remediation services

EDUCATIONAL SERVICES
Code
611110 Elementary and secondary schools
611310 Colleges, universities, and professional schools
611510 Technical and trade schools
611600 Other schools and instruction

HEALTHCARE AND SOCIAL ASSISTANCE
Code
621000 Ambulatory health care services
621110 Offices of physicians
621210 Offices of dentists
621300 Offices of other health practitioners
621400 Outpatient care centers
621410 Family planning centers
621500 Medical and diagnostic laboratories
621610 Home health care services
621910 Ambulance services
621990 All other ambulatory health care services
621991 Blood and organ banks
622000 Hospitals
623000 Nursing and residential care facilities
623990 Other residential care facilities
624000 Social assistance
624100 Individual and family services
624200 Community food and housing, and emergency and other relief services
624310 Vocational rehabilitation services
624410 Child day care services

ARTS, ENTERTAINMENT, AND RECREATION
Code
711110 Theater companies and dinner theaters
711120 Dance companies
711130 Musical groups and artists
711190 Other performing arts companies
711210 Spectator sports (including sports clubs and racetracks)
711300 Promoters of performing arts, sports, and similar events
712100 Museums, historical sites, and similar institutions
713110 Amusement and theme parks
713200 Gambling industries
713900 Other amusement and recreation industries (including golf courses, skiing facilities, marinas, fitness centers, and bowling centers)

ACCOMMODATION AND FOOD SERVICES
Code
721000 Accomodation
721110 Hotels (except casino hotels) and motels
721210 RV (recreational vehicle) parks and recreational camps
721310 Rooming and boarding houses
722100 Full-service restaurants
722210 Limited-service eating places
722320 Caterers
722410 Drinking places (alcoholic beverages)

OTHER SERVICES
Code
811000 Repair and maintenance
812300 Drycleaning and laundry services
812900 Other personal services
812930 Parking lots and garages

OTHER
Code
900000 Unrelated debt-financed activities other than rental of real estate
900001 Investment activities by section 501(c)(7), (9), or (17) organizations
900002 Rental of personal property
900003 Passive income activities with controlled organizations
900004 Exploited exempt activities

Exhibit 27–2

EXCLUSION CODES

Exclusion Codes

General Exceptions

01— Income from an activity that is not regularly carried on (section 512(a)(1))

02— Income from an activity in which labor is a material income-producing factor and substantially all (at least 85%) of the work is performed with unpaid labor (section 513(a)(1))

03— Section 501(c)(3) organization—Income from an activity carried on primarily for the convenience of the organization's members, students, patients, visitors, officers, or employees (hospital parking lot or museum cafeteria, for example) (section 513(a)(2))

04— Section 501(c)(4) local association of employees organized before 5/27/69— Income from the sale of work-related clothes or equipment and items normally sold through vending machines; food dispensing facilities; or snack bars for the convenience of association members at their usual places of employment (section 513(a)(2))

05— Income from the sale of merchandise, substantially all of which (at least 85%) was donated to the organization (section 513(a)(3))

Specific Exceptions

06— Section 501(c)(3), (4), or (5) organization conducting an agricultural or educational fair or exposition—Qualified public entertainment activity income (section 513(d)(2))

07— Section 501(c)(3), (4), (5), or (6) organization—Qualified convention and trade show activity income (section 513(d)(3))

08— Income from hospital services described in section 513(e)

09— Income from noncommercial bingo games that do not violate state or local law (section 513(f))

10— Income from games of chance conducted by an organization in North Dakota (section 311 of the Deficit Reduction Act of 1984, as amended)

11— Section 501(c)(12) organization—Qualified pole rental income (section 513(g))

12— Income from the distribution of low-cost articles in connection with the solicitation of charitable contributions (section 513(h))

13— Income from the exchange or rental of membership or donor list with an organization eligible to receive charitable contributions by a section 501(c)(3) organization; by a war veterans' organization; or an auxiliary unit or society of, or trust or foundation for, a war veterans' post or organization (section 513(h))

Modifications and Exclusions

14— Dividends, interest, payments with respect to securities loans, annuities, income from notional principal contracts, loan commitment fees, and other substantially similar income from ordinary and routine investments excluded by section 512(b)(1)

15— Royalty income excluded by section 512(b)(2)

16— Real property rental income that does not depend on the income or profits derived by the person leasing the property and is excluded by section 512 (b)(3)

17— Rent from personal property leased with real property and incidental (10% or less) in relation to the combined income from the real and personal property (section 512(b)(3))

18— Gain (or loss, to the extent allowed) from the sale of investments and other non-inventory property and from certain property acquired from financial institutions that are in conservatorship or receivership (sections 512(b)(5) and (16)(A))

19— Income or loss from the lapse or termination of options to buy or sell securities, or real property, and from the forfeiture of good-faith deposits for the purchase, sale, or lease of investment real property (section 512(b)(5))

20— Income from research for the United States; its agencies or instrumentalities; or any state or political subdivision (section 512(b)(7))

21— Income from research conducted by a college, university, or hospital (section 512(b)(8))

22— Income from research conducted by an organization whose primary activity is conducting fundamental research, the results of which are freely available to the general public (section 512(b)(9))

23— Income from services provided under license issued by a Federal regulatory agency and conducted by a religious order or school operated by a religious order, but only if the trade or business has been carried on by the organization since before May 27, 1959 (section 512 (b)(15))

Foreign Organizations

24— Foreign organizations only—Income from a trade or business NOT conducted in the United States and NOT derived from United States sources (patrons) (section 512(a)(2))

Social Clubs and VEBAs

25— Section 501(c)(7), (9), or (17) organization— Non-exempt function income set aside for a charitable, etc., purpose specified in section 170(c)(4) (section 512(a)(3)(B)(i))

26— Section 501(c)(7), (9), or (17) organization— Proceeds from the sale of exempt function property that was or will be timely reinvested in similar property (section 512(a)(3)(D))

27— Section 501(c)(9), or (17) organization— Non-exempt function income set aside for the payment of life, sick, accident, or other benefits (section 512(a)(3)(B)(ii))

Veterans' Organizations

28— Section 501(c)(19) organization—Payments for life, sick, accident, or health insurance for members or their dependents that are set aside for the payment of such insurance benefits or for a charitable, etc., purpose specified in section 170(c)(4) (section 512(a)(4))

29— Section 501(c)(19) organization—Income from an insurance set-aside (see code 28 above) that is set aside for payment of insurance benefits or for a charitable, etc., purpose specified in section 170(c)(4) (Regulations section 1.512(a)–4(b)(2))

Debt-financed Income

30— Income exempt from debt-financed (section 514) provisions because at least 85% of the use of the property is for the organization's exempt purposes (Note: This code is only for income from the 15% or less non-exempt purpose use.) (section 514(b)(1)(A))

31— Gross income from mortgaged property used in research activities described in section 512(b)(7), (8), or (9) (section 514(b)(1)(C))

32— Gross income from mortgaged property used in any activity described in section 513(a)(1), (2), or (3) (section 514(b)(1)(D))

33— Income from mortgaged property (neighborhood land) acquired for exempt purpose use within 10 years (section 514(b)(3))

34— Income from mortgaged property acquired by bequest or devise (applies to income received within 10 years from the date of acquisition) (section 514(c)(2)(B))

35— Income from mortgaged property acquired by gift where the mortgage was placed on the property more than 5 years previously and the property was held by the donor for more than 5 years (applies to income received within 10 years from the date of gift) (section 514(c)(2)(B))

36— Income from property received in return for the obligation to pay an annuity described in section 514(c)(5)

37— Income from mortgaged property that provides housing to low and moderate income persons to the extent the mortgage is insured by the Federal Housing Administration (section 514(c)(6)) (Note: In many cases, this would be exempt function income reportable in column (E). It would not be so in the case of a section 501(c)(5) or (6) organization, for example, that acquired the housing as an investment or as a charitable activity.)

38— Income from mortgaged real property owned by: a school described in section 170(b)(1)(A)(ii); a section 509(a)(3) affiliated support organization of such a school; a section 501(c)(25) organization, or by a partnership in which any of the above organizations owns an interest if the requirements of section 514(c)(9)(B)(vi) are met (section 514(c)(9))

Special Rules

39— Section 501(c)(5) organization—Farm income used to finance the operation and maintenance of a retirement home, hospital, or similar facility operated by the organization for its members on property adjacent to the farm land (section 1951(b)(8)(B) of Public Law 94-455)

40— Annual dues not exceeding $106 (subject to inflation) paid to a section 501(c)(5) agricultural or horticultural organization (section 512(d))

Trade or Business

41— Gross income from an unrelated activity that is regularly carried on but, in light of continuous losses sustained over a number of tax periods, cannot be regarded as being conducted with the motive to make a profit (not a trade or business)

Line 93: Program service revenue. Revenues produced from activities forming the basis for exemption, described under column (e), are considered program service revenues. As a general rule, all revenues on this line would be reportable in column (e). One important exception is fees for social club services charged to nonmembers, which must be reported in column (b) and labeled with UBI code 713900.

A short description of the type of income—student tuition, admission fees, and so on—is entered under line 93 (a–f). Program service revenue in the form of interest, dividend, rent, or royalty is entered on this line. Sales of goods or "inventory items," such as student books, blood bank sales, or museum gift shop items are not entered here but on line 102, except for hospitals and colleges. According to the instructions to page 1, they may include inventory sales items as program services revenue when it is consistent with their overall reporting system under GAAP.

Governmental grants for services rendered, not entered as contributions on line 1(c) of page 1, are entered on line 93(g). Contractual services, such as research, student testing, medical and food services, child welfare program fees, and similar services performed on a fee basis for governmental agencies are to be included here.

Line 94: Membership dues and assessments. Dues and other charges for services rendered to members are included on this line. When a member pays dues primarily to support the organization's activities, rather than to derive benefits of more than nominal monetary benefit, that dues payment represents a contribution. To the extent that a (c)(3) organization's membership dues are treated as a contribution because they have no monetary value, they are not included here. See Chapter 24§3 for a description of member items to be included, such as commercial quality publications, discounts on admission or store purchases, free admission, educational classes, referral services, and other items of value given to members in return for their dues.

A business league, labor union, social club, veterans group, or similar organization would report its members' dues, not including any portion allocable to inventory items sold or program services, such as decals or group insurance. Varying levels of membership with different amounts of dues, such as associate or junior members, raise a question. As long as the privileges given to a different class of member do not provide special benefit to any individuals, all types of dues can be aggregated.[62]

Dues would be most commonly placed in column (e). To the extent that member services (such as group insurance or job placement services) are considered UBI, they would be included in column (b) and labeled with a UBI code (524292–524298 for insurance and 561300 for placement services).

Line 95: Interest on savings and temporary cash investment. Payments from savings and loan, bank, and credit union cash deposits are entered on this line. Typically, this income is entered in column (d) and identified with code 14. Interest income on student, low-income housing, and other program-related loans are reported on line 93. Interest on a loan to an officer or employee would be reported as other revenue, line 103, in column (d), unless the loan is in the nature of com-

[62] Priv. Ltr. Rul. 8515061.

pensation (e.g., a temporary loan to buy a new home), in which case it could be reported in column (e).

Line 96: Dividends and interest from securities. Dividends earned on common or preferred stock, money market accounts, mutual fund shares, U.S. or local government and corporate bonds, and any other securities are usually reported on line 96 in column (d) and are also labeled with code 14. Dividends received from an 80 percent-owned for-profit subsidiary would also be reported in column (d). However, interest, rent, or other payments deductible to the subsidiary go in column (b). Capital gains distributed by a mutual fund are reported on line 100.

Securities purchased with borrowed funds, either through a margin account or other debt (called "acquisition indebtedness"), produce UBI. Income from such indebted securities is reported in column (b); in the case of partial indebtedness, only the portion calculated in the ratio of the cost to the debt would be reported in column (b) (UBI code 900000), with the balance reported in column (d).

Line 97: Net rental income (loss) from real estate. The net income, calculated after deduction of expenses such as depreciation, interest on debt, and other direct costs of maintaining real property, is reported on line 97 (code 16). This line does not come directly from page 1. On page 5, real estate and personal property rentals are separated. Also, this is the first line on page 5 where the net income, instead of gross, is entered in column (b), (d), or (e).

Real estate rentals can be classified under one of ten exclusion codes, and careful study of IRC §§512–514 may be necessary to ensure correct property classification under particular facts and circumstances. The majority of real property rentals are received on nonindebted property held for investment, the income from which is reported in column (d) and identified with code 16. Lease rentals dependent upon the tenants' profits are classed as UBI and must be reported in column (b). Rents on program-related real estate properties are placed in column (e) on line 93.

Codes 30–38 apply specifically to debt-financed income reportable in column (d) but excludable from UBI classification due to a statutory exception. The portion of income attributable to acquisition indebtedness which is not excluded (see Chapter 21§12) is reported in column (b), line 97a (513110 series code).

Rents paid by a 50% or more owned subsidiary are reported in column (b) as taxable UBI. If services are rendered to benefit the individual occupant, such as in a hotel, boarding house, parking lot, or storage facility, the rental is also classed as UBI (531110 series code). Services customarily provided for all tenants, such as utilities, security, cleaning of public entrances, elevators, and other common areas do not constitute services rendered to individual tenants.

Line 98: Net rental income (loss) from personal property. Rentals from personal property earned for purely investment purposes create UBI (whether indebted or not) and are reported in column (b) and identified with the appropriate business code, such as 532420. Such rentals could be program-related, in which case they are reported on line 93 in column (e) with no code.

If more than 50% of a combined real and personal property lease revenue is attributable to personal property, the rental is reported on line 98, column (b), and is subject to UBI. A manufacturing or printing plant, a scientific research facility, and an exhibition hall with booths are examples of the types of rentals that might fall into this category. A Form 990-T code again applies and this income, net of directly allocable expenses, is entered in column (b).

Line 99: Other investment income. Royalty income from mineral or intellectual property interests are entered on this line. In most cases such income is entered in column (d) and identified with modification code 15. Royalties from educational publications or research patents might be classed as program service revenue on line 93 and entered in column (e) instead. (See line 103 for certain royalties.)

Changes in unrealized gain or loss on an investment portfolio is not considered as current income on page 1 or page 5, but is entered as a surplus adjustment on line 20 of page 1.

Line 100: Gain (loss) from sales of assets other than inventory. Capital gains and losses reported on line 8 of page 1 from the disposition of all organization assets, other than inventory, are reported on this line (code 18). Gains and losses from the sale of investment portfolio assets, real estate, office equipment, program-related assets, partnership interest, and all sorts of property are included.

Most gains or losses are reportable in column (d), except for debt-financed property that must be shown in column (b). Exempt organizations with sophisticated UBI activity may realize gain from sale of assets used in that business which would also be reportable in column (b). Gain (loss) from the sale of program-related assets is reported in column (e).

Gain or loss on purchase, sale, or lapse of security options can be reported on this line (code 19). It has been suggested that revenue attributable to lapsed options, as distinguished from options sold or "covered" before maturity, should be reportable on line 99. However, the IRS instructions are silent and for convenience all option activity can be combined.

Line 101: Net income from special fund-raising events. Fund-raising event net income, excluding any portion allocated to donations (not reported in this part), is technically UBI. The typical charitable event is excepted from UBI under the irregular (code 01) or volunteer (code 02) exception, and the net profit is reported in column (d). When the primary purpose of the event is educational or otherwise exempt, such as a cultural festival, it is conceivable that the profits could be reported as related income in column (e). Any other fund-raising profits must be reported as UBI in column (b) (711110). (See Chapter 24§2 for more information about fund-raising event revenue calculations.)

Line 102: Gross profit (loss) from sales of inventory. Gross revenues from the sale of inventory, less returns and allowances and cost of goods sold (line 10c on page 1), is entered here. Inventory includes objects purchased or made for resale, rather than held as an investment. In contrast to the instruction for rents and interest produced from program-related investments, exempt function inventory sales are to be reported on this line, rather than on line 93.

Line 103: Other revenue. Revenues not suitable for inclusion on lines 93–102 are entered here. Two particular types of revenue that fit on this line are the subject of constant battles between the IRS and exempt organizations. Advertising revenues not classified as program-related can be entered in either column (b) or (d). Ads produce unrelated income (column (b), code 541800) unless the irregular or the volunteer exception applies. Likewise, royalties from use of the organization's name, logo, or mailing list could be entered in either column. If the organization disagrees with the IRS's current position that such income is unrelated, such revenue would be entered in column (d) with modification code 15. See code 13 for the narrow exception available to (c)(3)s and certain veterans organizations for exchanges or rentals of lists between similar types of organizations.

Some have speculated that use of code 15 is an invitation to be examined, because the IRS will scrutinize organizations claiming modification of royalties, despite the fact that some royalties are clearly passive income.

Recoveries of prior year expenditures, interest on loans not made for investment or program purposes (e.g., to employees or managers), and any other items of revenue not properly reported elsewhere would also be entered on line 103.

For further information on specific lines on this page, consult Chapter 27§5 and the instructions for the page 1 lines that provide the best IRS guidance.

(c) Rationale for Column (e) Amounts

Part VIII, *Relationship of Activities to the Accomplishment of Exempt Purposes*, asks the organization to explain how each activity for which income is reported in column (e) fosters the accomplishment of its exempt purposes (other than by providing funds for such purposes). Dues payments providing funds to support the organization's exempt activities are included here. Not much room is provided and it is hard to know how much information to submit. There are two possible answers to this question, depending on the nature of the income. For clearly and unquestionably related types of revenue, such as student tuition, hospital room fees, symphony performance admission tickets, and member dues, the answer can simply be such a description. For revenues received in activities that might arguably produce UBI, such as charges for computer services, sale of standard forms, advertising, or logo sales, a more convincing description is recommended.

The IRS sample contained in the instructions suggests sentences like: "Fee from county for finding foster homes for two children—this furthers our exempt purpose of ensuring quality care for foster children," and "Members are social services workers who receive information and advice on problem cases from our staff as part of our counseling, adoption, and foster care programs." The explanation here need not repeat the same information, but can refer back to Part III, Statement of Program Service Accomplishments, where very similar information is furnished.

(d) The Codes

Each numerical entry on page 6 is individually explained either with a code or literal description. The type of revenue in Column (b) is identified by column (a) codes (Exhibit 27–1) that mimic those used for the unrelated business income tax return, Form 990-T. These codes describe the type of business and are easy to assign because they are so literal—dance studio, or physical fitness facility, for example. Each major category has a miscellaneous number. There is little harm from choosing the wrong code, because the organization is already admitting that the income is UBI.

Column (d) is described by *exclusion* codes (Exhibit 27–2), and the correct choice of these is very important. These codes explain that, although the organization is admitting it has unrelated business income, it claims that the UBI is not taxable for one of forty different reasons. A review of Chapter 21§9 and 21§10 is extremely useful in making the choices.

27.12   SCHEDULE A: FOR §501(C)(3) ORGANIZATIONS ONLY

With Schedule A, IRC §501(c)(3) organizations and nonexempt IRC §4947(a)(1) wholly charitable trusts furnish information to let the IRS review their ongoing qualification for tax-exempt status and for some, public charity status. See Appendix 27–3.

(a) Parts I and II, Compensation

Both of these parts look for private benefit to highly paid personnel and consultants. Technically private benefit (to those that control the organization) in the past was thought not as damaging to the organization's exempt status as private inurement (to those that do control). However, as explained in Chapter 20, the IRS considers excess compensation to persons *not* controlling an exempt to be almost as bad as such payments made to insiders. See §27.9 for the meaning of the columns in these parts. The compensation level above which compensation must be reported by name was raised in 1994 to $50,000. Payments to employees are reported in Part I. Payments to independent contractors of all sorts, including corporations, who performed personal services of a professional nature for the organization are reported in Part II. Only the fee portion of contractor payments, not expense reimbursements are reported.

(b) Part III, Statements about Activities

Part III canvasses for a host of sins. The sections of this book that apply to each question are.

- *Question 1,* Lobbying. See Chapter 23.

- *Question 2,* Self-dealing. See Chapter 20. Transactions with the persons who control a public charity are not strictly prohibited, but are subject to scrutiny to prove that the insiders do not unfairly benefit at the expense of the exempt. Is too high a price paid for property sold to the executive director? Does the organization need to maintain a New York apartment for its treasurer to monitor the investments? If such a transaction occurred, the organization must explain in this part how its exempt purposes were served.

- *Questions 3 and 4,* Individual grants. See the questions asked in Schedule H of Form 1023 in Appendix 18–1 to get a flavor of the appropriate and expected answers to these questions. A new question was added for 1998 that asks if the EO has a §403(b) plan for its employees.

(c) Part IV, Reason for Non-Private Foundation Status

The "reason for non-private foundation status" rests on the organization's ability to qualify as a public charity and to fit into one of the ten boxes (presented as items 5 through 14) on page 2. For organizations checking boxes 10, 11, or 12, public status is based upon sources of revenue and lines 15 through 27 are completed. Each of the box categories is discussed in Chapter 11. This part repeats the information originally furnished with Form 1023, and the materials at Chapter 18§2(c) can be reviewed for suggestions.

This part was revised in 1995 to add a calculation of the organization's ongoing qualification as a public charity under §509(a)(1) or §509(a)(2). Among the questions raised by this part are the following:

Q: When and how can an exempt organization change its status from a §509(a)(1) to a §509(a)(2) organization, or vice versa?

A: An organization might change annually, depending on the category into which it fits. The consequence is minimal, except (c)(2) organizations are not qualified recipients for a private foundation (PF) terminating distribution and its grants to an (a)(1) is subject to the 2% limit. Only loss of public status is harmful.

Q: For what period after selling its major assets and ceasing operation can a hospital or school maintain its public status? When would it convert to a private foundation?

A: The *facts and circumstances* of each situation determine the organization's status. Technically it would cease to qualify as a school or hospital once it stopped conducting such activities. Due to its revenue sources, however, it is likely it can qualify as a §509(a)(2) or 170(b)(1)(A)(vi) for at least one if not two years after the sale.[63] If the exempt organization permanently invests funds and begins to make grants to other organizations, it will become a PF in the second succeeding year after it fails one of the public support tests.

Q: If the organization fails the test mechanically, are there any exceptions or alternatives to becoming classified as a private foundation?

A: An exempt organization receiving as little as 10% of its support from public sources can be permitted to qualify as a public charity under a facts and circumstances test. Large, nonrecurring, grants may be excluded from the calculation if they qualify as *unusual*. Chapter 11§2 outlines the requirements for these alternatives.

Timing can be extremely important for an organization that inadvertently loses its public status. The organization can make an application to terminate PF status under a 60-month termination. However, as explained in Chapter 12§4, such a conversion must be filed prior to the period for which it is effective. An inattentive organization may not realize its need to file until after the end of the year in which the failure occurs.

Serious record-keeping problems may confront the ill-prepared charitable organization that adopts FSAS No. 116 when completing Schedule A. Revenues are reported solely on a cash basis on Schedule A, rather than the accrual method. Pledge revenues are not counted. Organizations that qualify as public charities under IRC §509(a)(1) or (2) on the basis of their revenue sources tally up four years of revenue on Schedule A. A system for reconciling the cash-to-accrual contributions is needed. Considerable organizational time, as well as the time of outside

---

[63] Regs. §1.170A-9(e)(4) and §1.509(a)-3(c).

accountants, can be saved if year-end reports are prepared in view of this reporting requirement. Lines 15 through 22 on Part IV A—contributions, exempt function revenues, investment income, net income from unrelated businesses, and all other revenues—are also reported on a cash basis.

Coordination of the reporting functions can be particularly important for an organization with major contributors. Schedule A, line 26a, asks §509(a)(1) organizations for the total amount received for the past four years from individual donors in excess of 2% of line 24. For §509(a)(2) organizations, similar details for its disqualified persons[64] (major donors, board members, and their families) are completed on line 27. To complete this report, each donor's total annual cash gifts for four years must be available. An organization's donor databases may need retooling to track pledges on both a cash and accrual system. For accrual purposes, the present value increments of unpaid pledges is reported. These numbers bear no relation to the required Schedule A details. An organization does not necessarily know in any one year which donors will, over the succeeding four-year period, fall into this special reporting category. Alas, the cash-to-accrual details certainly must be maintained on those donors potentially capable of becoming major donors—and to be safe, on all donors.

(d) Part V, Private School Questionnaire

Part V requests information on the nondiscrimination policies of private schools, as discussed in Chapter 5§1. Action taken to publicize such policies to the community served by the school must be reported at item 31. Form 5578 (Appendix 27–4) can be used to furnish the information, but is not specifically required. The Form is designed for use by church and government schools that do not file 990s. The questions in this part reflect the school discrimination policy adopted by the IRS in 1975.[65] It is imperative that all private schools correctly answer them to ensure continued qualification for exemption. Questions 29 through 32 need a "Yes" answer. All parts of question 33 must be answered "No."

(e) Part VI-A, Lobbying Expenditures by Electing Public Charities and Part VI-B, Lobbying Activity by Nonelecting Public Charities

Part VI is completed to allow the IRS to evaluate the levels of an organization's lobbying efforts. Those charities that elect the mathematical lobbying limitations of IRC §501(h) complete part VI-A, which reflects the specific numerical test that is applied. Successful completion of this part depends on good accounting and an ability to identify direct expenses and to allocate indirect ones. The terms are defined in Chapter 23. Appendix 23–1 is Form 5768, which is to be used for making or revoking the election during the reporting period.

Capital expenses are not included in the calculation of lobbying expense limitations. Only straight-line depreciation on assets directly used in connection with lobbying efforts are included as lobbying expenses.

Part VI-B asks nine questions of organizations that do not elect to conduct limited lobbying. Such organizations face a subjective and qualitative measure to ascertain if the lobbying comprises a *substantial part* of their activities, as discussed

---

[64] IRC §4946.
[65] Rev. Proc. 75-50, 1975-2 C.B. 587.

in Chapter 23§4(a). There are over 2½ pages of instructions to this part of Schedule A, and they should be read in detail if the answer to any of the items (a) through (h) is "Yes."

(f) Part VII, Information Regarding Transfers, Transactions, and Relationships with Other Organizations

Part VII was added in 1988 in response to a congressional mandate to the IRS to search for connections between public charities and non-501(c)(3) organizations. Particularly in regard to organizations that lobby or enter the political arena, the IRS is scouting for relationships that allow benefits to the noncharitable organization.

This part looks for use of exempt organization assets to benefit non-(c)(3) organizations and asks the organization to report any financial transactions, such as sales, transfers, or rentals of assets to or from another organization. The reportable transactions are those with affiliated or related organizations. Again, the instructions are very specific and should be consulted if transactions are to be reported. To answer, consider that the following factors must be present to have a related organization:

- A historic and continuing relationship between two organizations evidenced by sharing of facilities, staff, joint effort, or other work in concert towards accomplishing a common goal.

- Common control whereby one or more of the officers, directors, or trustees (managers) of one organization is elected or appointed by those of the other. Similarly, control is found when 25 percent or more of the managers are interlocking.

The few transactions that need *not* be reported include

- Any transaction totaling $500 or less annually

- Specific transactions totaling less than one percent of the organization's annual gross receipts involving subscriptions, conferences, seminars, or other functionally related services or goods

This part indicates yet another type of special records required to be kept by an exempt organization. To answer this part correctly, an organization having the described relationship will want to establish subcodes or new departments in its chart of accounts to tabulate the answers. See Chapter 22§2 for more discussion of such relationships.

27.13 SPECIAL CONSIDERATIONS FOR FORM 990-PF

In addition to reporting financial activity for the year, the 12-page Form 990-PF enables the IRS to evaluate a private foundation's compliance with the IRC §4940 and §4945 sanctions and limitations on activities. Form 990-PF is reproduced as Appendix 27–5. The Form 990-PF instructions are 28 pages long and exemplify the complexity of reporting and compliance requirements for a private foundation.[66] The technical aspects of the sanctions applied to PFs, presented in Chapters 12 through 17, should be studied along with the following suggestions for completion of the form. It should be particularly useful to study Chapter 13. The applicable sections of this book will be referred to throughout this discussion.

Each private foundation, including a §4947(a)(1) trust, must file a Form 990-PF, regardless of gross revenues received during the year. Even a PF with a non-interest-bearing checking account making no disbursements is theoretically required to file Form 990-PF, make it available to the general public, and submit the form to the state attorney general (if its assets are greater than $5,000). A PF converting its status to public under IRC §507[67] also must file Form 990-PF rather than Form 990.

Form 990-PF has evolved over 20 years as the law of private foundations has developed, retaining original concepts and adding new ones. Certain interdependent calculations do not follow in logical order. The most efficient order in which to prepare the form is the following:

1. Parts IV, I, II, and III

2. Skip to Parts VII-A and B, VIII, IX-A and B, XV, XVI-A and B, XVII, and XVIII

3. Part X

4. Part XII

5. Part V

6. Part VI

7. Part XI

8. Part XIII or XIV

Proper allocation of expenses among administrative, investment, and program costs is a significant aspect of the form, so the accounting practices discussed at the beginning of this chapter are recommended. A PF has only two types of expenses—investment-related and disbursements for charitable purposes or exempt function expenses.[68] Similar to the issue of maximizing UBI deductions,[69] investment expenses reduce the PF excise tax on investment income. Ordinary and necessary expenses of producing investment income are deductible to arrive at net investment income. Basically, the rules are the same as the individual and business expense provisions of IRC §162 and §212 pertaining to deductible expenses. The PF must ascertain what portion of a director's salary or bank trustee, legal, or accounting fees are allocable to investment management, oversight, or consulta-

---

[66] The instructions for the 1990 form contained 22 pages—proof that this form is not getting simpler.
[67] See Chapter 12§4.
[68] Defined in §27.6.
[69] Discussed in §27.14.

tions. A reasonable portion, usually one-fourth to one-half of such fees, is customarily allotted to investment income. Upon examination, the IRS will request substantiation of this allocation.

From 1985 through 1990, Congress placed a limit on a PF's administrative expenses. General and administrative (G&A) expense over the limit (.65 percent of assets) essentially fell through the cracks—it did not reduce tax nor count toward the distribution requirements. Based on a study, the IRS found the limits ineffective. They were designed to curb abusive situations often found in larger organizations, such as excessive compensation, but the formula missed that mark. It was the smaller PFs who had high G&A, but had correspondingly high qualifying distributions. Finally, the IRS admitted that the calculations were complicated and burdensome to PFs, and did not recommend their continuance.

(a) Part I, Analysis of Revenue and Expenses

Each of the columns in Part I serves a different purpose in the IRS regulatory scheme for private foundations. Deciding what goes where and why is not a logical process. Different accounting methods are used for reporting information in different columns, and some items are included in more than one column, while others are not.

Column (a), Revenue and expenses per books. This column agrees with financial reports prepared for the board or for public dissemination by the organization. The cash or accrual method of accounting is permitted, again in keeping with the system regularly used to prepare financial statements for other purposes. In-kind contributions of services or use of property, even though properly booked for financial statement purposes, are excluded. Capital gains are calculated using book basis rather than tax basis, which is reported in column (b), line 7 or 8.

Column (b), Net investment income. This column reports the income less associated deductions[70] used to arrive at income subject to the excise tax. Only interest, dividends, rents, and royalties and capital gains from the properties producing such income are reported.[71] This column does not include

- UBI separately reported on Form 990-T
- Program service revenue
- Gain from sale of exempt function assets
- Profits from fund-raising events

Column (c), Adjusted net income. This column became obsolete for most PFs in 1976, although it is still important for two types of PFs:

- Private operating foundations (POFs) must spend 85% of their adjusted net income[72] on charitable projects they conduct directly. This column essentially includes investment income plus short-term capital gains and unrelated business income, less long-term capital gains.

[70] See Chapter 13§3.
[71] See Chapter 13§1.
[72] Reg. §53.4942-2(d); see Chapter 15§5.

- Private foundations receiving program service income also use the column to isolate the income. It is not subject to excise tax. Expenses associated with a program are also reported in column (c). Only the excess expenses over the revenues are reported in column (d).

Column (d), Disbursements for charitable purposes. The cash method must be used for this column. Amounts reported in this column are significant because they count toward calculation of the required charitable expenditures, called the minimum distribution.[73] As a rule, any expenses claimed as allocable to investment income would not also be reportable in this column. Column (d) includes direct charitable expenditures, grants, and administrative and fund-raising costs not allocable to investment income.

Line 1. The total amount of gifts, grants, and other voluntary donations are reported on this line.[74] Details are reported for gifts of $5,000 or more. Distributions from split-interest trusts are included here for column (a) purposes.

Line 2. Split-interest trust distributions for amounts placed in trust after October 26, 1969, are taxed.[75] Amounts earned on trust assets owned prior to that date, when the PF tax was introduced in Congress, are not subject to the excise tax.

Lines 3 and 4. Interest from tax-exempt government obligations is excluded from column (b) and associated expenses are excluded.

Line 5. Gross rent is reported from investment and program-related property. Associated expenses are reported in lines 13–23.

Line 6. The PF's capital gains or losses per the books are entered on this line and entered only in column (a).

Line 7. Note that this line carries only to column (b). Gains (short- and long-term) from the sale of property that ordinarily produces interest, dividends, royalties, or rents are taxed even if the property never produced any income. The gain on a growth stock producing no dividends is also taxed. Program-related investments are not taxed because they are not held for investment. Special exceptions apply for certain gains listed in Chapter 13§2(c).

It is very important to note that property received by the foundation as a donation retains the donor's basis.[76] Since the wealth of PF creators often comes from business interests that are highly appreciated, the PF ends up paying tax on its contributor's gains, albeit at a much lower rate. There had been disagreement for years about the taxability of property sold immediately after its receipt and which never produced income, but the debate is now settled.[77] Capital losses are deductible only to the extent of gains, and there is no carryover. PFs need careful year-end tax planning[78] for this purpose.

Line 8. The short-term capital gains are separately reported for column (c) purposes only, with the amount carrying from Part IV, line 3.

---

[73] See Chapter 15§4.
[74] Definitions and issues involved with contributions are discussed in §27.5(b).
[75] See Chapter 13§1(f).
[76] Reg. §53.4940-1(f)(2)(i)(B), which refers to IRC §1015.
[77] See Chapter 13§2(b).
[78] See Chapter 13§4.

Line 9. Income modifications also pertain only to column (c), and include repayments of amounts previously treated as qualifying distributions[79] that must be added back to the distributable amount in the current year.

Line 10. This line is rarely used. A foundation conducting a self-initiated project might generate sales, such as an educational store selling books or similar items of inventory. A program-related business operation, such as a handicapped worker factory, might have such sales. The instructions suggest reporting fundraising events[80] on this line. This income is not subject to the excise tax, but might be subject to the UBIT.

Line 11. All other types of income, including royalties and interest not reported on line 3 or 4, income from a partnership, and any other investment income not reported on lines 2 through 7, are reported here.

Line 13. Officer, trustee, and director salaries must not result in excessive compensation or self-dealing[81] may occur. The concerns facing public charities about insider compensation and the reporting questions can be reviewed to ensure proper reporting here.[82]

Lines 14–17, 20–23. See the suggestions at §27.6(e)–(g). Also, note that a POF reports its direct expenditures in column (d) on these lines by expense type, not on line 25.

Line 18. Taxes of all sorts are reported in column (a), including excise taxes on investment income, property taxes on real estate, and any unrelated business income tax. Only taxes paid on investment property are reported in column (b). POFs include both excise taxes and investment property taxes in column (c). Only taxes paid on exempt function property is reported in column (d). For nonoperating PFs, the excise tax is taken into account in Part XI, line 2a.

Line 19. Depreciation is reported in column (a) using the PF's book method. Column (b) depreciation must be calculated using the straight-line method and only cost depletion is allowed for mineral properties, not percentage depletion. The basis of property for this purpose is the same as that for calculating gain without a December 31, 1969, step-up to value.[83]

Column (c) depreciation for POFs would usually be the same as column (d). Note that column (d) has no depreciation because asset acquisitions (Section 15.4(b)) are treated as qualifying distributions. Thus, asset cost is essentially written off as a charitable distribution in the year the asset is purchased.

Line 21. Only 50% of the cost of meals is deductible in column (b). This limitation parallels the individual income tax rules for deductible meals.

Line 25. Grants paid to other charitable organizations are reported on this line.[84] Nonqualifying grants are not included, such as those paid to a controlled organization and certain pass-through grants. Such grants would be reported in Part III, line 5. The following omissions are also made:

---

[79] See Chapter 15§3.
[80] See §27.5(j).
[81] See Chapter 14§4.
[82] See §27§6(d) and §27.9.
[83] IRC §4940(c)(3)(B).
[84] See Chapter 15§4.

- Returned grant funds are not entered here but in Part X.
- No set-asides are entered; see Part XIII.

Line 26. The total of disbursements for charitable purposes in column (d) is transferred to Part XII, line 1 to measure compliance with the minimum distributions requirement test.[85]

(b) Part II, Balance Sheets

Both the book value of the foundation assets and liabilities and the ending fair market value are presented in Part II. The total in column (c), line 16, must agree with item I on page 1, top left side. Column (c) need not be completed for a PF with under $5,000. A considerable amount of detail is requested. The instructions should be read carefully for the following lines on the balance sheet.

- Line 6. Insider receivables
- Line 10. Investments—securities
- Line 11. Investments—land, buildings, and equipment
- Line 13. Investments—other
- Line 14. Land, buildings, and equipment
- Line 15. Other assets
- Line 19. Support and revenue designated for future periods
- Line 20. Insider payables
- Line 21. Mortgages and other notes payable

(c) Part III, Analysis of Changes in Net Assets or Fund Balances

This schedule reconciles the fund balances. Examples of matters that might be reflected here include

- A prior-period accounting adjustment not corrected on an amended return.
- Adjustment to unrealized gain or loss on investment assets recorded for book purposes but not reported in column (a) on page 1.
- Nonqualifying grants not reported on page 1.

See Chapter 28 for issues involved in amended returns and reporting back to the IRS. Since a PF pays an excise tax on its investment income, reporting of any corrections or restatements of those amounts must be carefully considered.

(d) Part IV, Capital Gains and Losses for Tax on Investment Income

This schedule reports only investment property. Note that the totals from this schedule carry only to columns (b) and (c) of Part I. Transactions involving exempt function assets or program-related investments (Chapter 15.1(c)) are not included.

---

[85] See Chapter 15.

Basis for property received by the foundation as a gift is reported in column (g) and equals the donor's basis. This schedule accommodates the so-called carry-over basis rules for calculating gains and losses for excise tax purposes. Property received through a bequest is valued as of the date of death or the alternate valuation date for the decedent. Purchased property is reported at its actual cost.[86] Short-term gains are significant only for POFs and carry to column (c), Part I. Note again a net capital loss for the year is not deductible or carried over to the next year.

(e) Part V, Qualification for Reduced Tax on Net Investment Income

A private foundation can cut its tax in half (from 2% to 1% of net investment income) by essentially giving the tax to charity.[87] If the PF's current-year qualifying distributions (Part XII) exceed its past five-year average payout plus a 1% tax for the current year, the tax is reduced to 1%. Achieving this reduction is complicated because not all of the factors are known until the last day of the taxable year, such as line 4 (the average month end value of investment assets). Except for the most generous foundations, reducing the excise tax requires very careful planning. A private foundation cannot qualify for this tax reduction in its first year. See Chapter 13§4 for more discussion and examples of long-range planning to achieve this tax savings.

(f) Part VI, Excise Tax on Investment Income

Except for exempt private operating foundations, PFs pay a tax of two percent, or possibly one percent, on their net investment income reported in Part I, column (b), line 27b. Foreign PFs that receive more than 15% of their investment income from U.S. sources pay a 4% tax on such income. The capital gain inherent in property distributed to a charitable grant recipient, rather than being sold for cash to pay the grant, is not taxed. See Chapter 13§4 for discussion and examples of these tax saving possibilities.

If the annual tax is under $500, it can be paid with a check accompanying the return as it is filed. If the tax is over $500, it is paid in advance through the estimated tax system, using depository receipts or electronic deposit. If the foundation deposited more than $50,000 of payroll or more than that amount in other taxes (including the excise tax) in the prior year, Form 990-W can be used to compute the estimated tax. Private Foundations with over $1 million of taxable income in one of the preceding tax years must make quarterly payments based on actual income earned during the second, third, and fourth quarters, similar to the large corporation rules. Form 990-W contains worksheets and detailed instruments to be used for this purpose.

Penalties are due for failure to pay a sufficient amount by the quarterly due date—the 15th day of the 5th, 6th, 9th, and 12th month of each year.[88] The due date for the first quarterly payment of estimated tax for a private foundation was changed, effective for fiscal years beginning after August 5, 1997, to correspond with

---

[86] The income tax rules contained in IRC §§1011, 1012, 1014, 1015, and 1016 apply in completing this part.

[87] IRC §4940(e).

[88] IRC §6655(g)(3) as amended by Taxpayer's Relief Act of 1997.

the filing deadline for Form 990-PF, or the 15th day of the 5th month after the end of its fiscal year (May 15 for a calendar year foundation). See *Private Foundations,* Chapter 13§6, "Timely Payment of Excise Tax," for more details. A copy of the foundation's Form 1023 must be made available under the standards outlined. Form 2220 is attached to Form 990-PF to calculate the penalty. Penalties are also imposed for failure to deposit taxes with a federal tax deposit coupon (Form 8109) at a qualified bank or to make the payment electronically.

(g) Part VII-A & B, Statements Regarding Activities

A Questions *Line 1.* Answering this question "Yes" is tantamount to admitting that the exempt status should be revoked. Private foundations are, just like all (c)(3) organizations, prohibited from participation in an election.[89]
    Lines 2–5. See answers to lines 76–79 at §27.10.
    Line 6. The private foundation must answer this question "Yes" and would not have been recognized as exempt if it had not.
    Line 8a. Even if a private foundation is not registered to do business in a particular state, filing may be required if it has donations from certain states, such as New York.
    Line 9. See Chapter 15§5. Part XIV must be completed by private operating foundations.
    Line 10. See Chapter 12§2(c) for definition of substantial contributor.
    Line 12. This line asks for the name and number of the person who is in care of the books. This person will receive the call if the IRS wishes to examine the organization's records.

B Questions These questions probe for violations of the excise tax sanctions. All "No" or N/A answers reduce reporting requirements. Any "Yes" answers require details. Certain "Yes" answers reveal the need to file Form 4720 (Appendix 27–6) to report transactions subject to excise tax. Consult the following chapters for guidance:

- Line 10: Chapter 14, Self-Dealing.

- Line 11: Chapter 15, Minimum Distribution Requirements.

- Line 12: Chapter 16, Excess Business Holdings.

- Line 13: Chapter 16, Jeopardizing Investments.

- Line 14: Chapter 17, Taxable Expenditures.

(h) Part VIII, Information about Officers, Directors, Trustees, Foundation Managers, Highly Paid Employees, and Contractors

To assist the IRS in detecting self-dealing and private inurement, details of compensation are to be reported. This part must be completed even if officers and di-

---

[89] See Chapters 17 and 23.

rectors receive no compensation or benefits. All persons in each category, even if they number fifty or more, must be listed. Make an entry in each column, even if the answer is "None." If an attachment is required, submit totals for each column again at the bottom of this part. See §27.9 for the meaning of the column titles.

(i) Parts IX-A and B, Summary of Direct Charitable Activities and Program-Related Investments

The foundation's four largest direct charitable projects[90] are to be reported, including "relevant statistical information such as the number of organizations and other beneficiaries serviced, conferences convened, research papers produced, etc." This part is a welcome addition to permit PFs, particularly POFs, conducting projects to describe their activities. This part parallels the Form 990 exempt function activity report and the same suggestions apply (§27.7).

Program-related investments made during the year are reported in Part IX-B. For a foundation with ongoing investments, this report can be coordinated with the balance sheet reporting and expenditure responsibility reporting requirements.

(j) Part X, Minimum Investment Return

Refer to Chapter 15 for definitions and parameters before completing this part. Line 6 represents the PF's required amount of annual charitable giving. The number is entered in Part XI, line 1. The amount on Part X, line 5 is entered in Part V, line 4.

(k) Part XI, Distributable Amount

Private operating foundations do not complete this part; they answer "N/A—private operating foundation."[91]

(l) Part XII, Qualifying Distributions

Again, see Chapter 15 for definition of the terms; §15.4(c) discusses set-asides that are reported on line 3. The number on line 4 carries to Part V, line 8; Part XIII, line 4; and Part XIV, line 2c.

(m) Part XIII, Undistributed Income

This part surveys five years of grant-making history to determine if the PF has expended sufficient funds on charitable giving to meet the IRC §4942 tests. If this schedule reflects a balance remaining on line 2(b), 6(d), or 6(e), Form 4720 (Appendix 27–6) should be filed to calculate the penalty on under-distributions. The order in which distributions are applied is important. See Chapter 15§6 for examples of payment application.

---

[90] See Chapter 15§4(b).
[91] See Chapter 15§5.

Qualifying distributions entered on line 4 should be the same as on line 4 of Part XII, but the trick is knowing how to apply the total among the four columns and when a distribution is charged to corpus. As the form's design indicates, current-year distributions are first applied to column (c), the remaining undistributed income from the immediately preceding year. This can create a cash flow problem when a PF (or the IRS) finds that deficient distributions from the past must be corrected. The current-year required payments must be paid before the correction can be made. Next, corrections of prior-year deficiencies are applied to line 4(b) (not required).

A PF might elect to apply current-year grants to corpus on line 4c, column (a) under certain circumstances. For example, the corpus election is appropriate for a PF redistributing a donation for which the contributor desires the maximum deduction.[92] Some suggest that this adjustment be made to Part XI, line 6. The point is that the PF cannot count a gift attributable to a pass-through contribution as part of its qualifying distributions. Other instances when a corpus election is appropriate involve grants paid to a controlled public charity and pass-through grants to another PF. The instructions should be read carefully before making this choice.

To make the corpus election, a PF manager signs a statement declaring that the PF is making an election and designating whether it is out of a specific year's prior income or corpus. It is useful to know that the source of line 5 distributions is always from line 3f.

(n) Part XIV, Private Operating Foundations

Private operating foundations submit information to calculate their ongoing qualification based on a four-year average of their qualifying distributions, income, and assets.

(o) Part XV, Supplementary Information

This part is completed for foundations with assets of $5000 or more. It lists the names of substantial contributors.[93] Grant application details, including the name and address, application form requirements, deadlines, and grant restrictions and limitations are also reported. Grant seekers use the information submitted in this part to select the PFs to whom they will make applications for funding. The Foundation Center and other organizations publish books and electronic information containing this information. Public libraries in many cities cooperate in making Forms 990-PF available for public inspection. Most often, inspectors look at this and the following part to find out what kind of grants a PF makes.

Foundations that make grants only to preselected charities and do not accept unsolicited requests for funds can check the blank on line 2. Because the paper load for some PFs is immense, there is a temptation in some cases to check the box although it does not necessarily apply. There are ongoing philosophical discussions about the pros and cons of the box: The question is whether a PF with unrestricted funds should close the door to grant applicants by checking the blank.

---

[92] IRC §170(b)(1)(E).
[93] Defined in Chapter 12§2(c).

(p) Grants and Contributions Paid During the Year or Approved for Future Payment

This part lists grants paid to individuals and to organizations (list separately) during the year and approved for future payment. The total under 3a should agree with the amount reported on line 25, column (d). The line 3b total of future grant commitments is provided for public inspection purposes only, and does not carry to any other part of the form. Grant recipients' relationships to the foundation must be entered to alert the IRS to possible disqualifying grants to controlled organizations.[94]

(q) Parts XVI-A and B, Analysis of Income-Producing Activities and Relation of Activities to the Accomplishment of Exempt Purposes

Since 1989 when these parts were added, private foundations must characterize their income according to its relatedness to their exempt purposes, to allow the IRS to find unrelated business income not identified in Part I. The columns, lines, and codes are thoroughly described at §27.11. The typical PF will only submit information in column (d). Part XVI-B explains how the income-producing activity reported in column (e) furthers the organization's exempt purposes.

(r) Part XVII, Information Regarding Transfers, Transactions, and Relationships with Noncharitable Exempt Organizations

This part was designed for Form 990, and does not apply to most private foundations. See §27.12(f) for the meaning and import of the requested information.

(s) Part XVIII, Public Inspection

The Omnibus Consolidated and Emergency Supplemental Appropriations Act approved on October 21, 1998, makes private foundations subject to the same disclosure rules as those described for public charities discussed in §27.2 Former IRC §6104(d) will no longer apply. PFs will not be required to publish the availability of its Form 990-PF in a newspaper. Instead they will have to make copies of the form for the most recent three years continually available to anyone that asks for a copy. Additionally a copy of Form 1023 and any correspondence issued by the IRS in response to the application must be provided.[95]

Through 1998, Form 990-PF had to be made available to the general public for inspection at the foundation's principal office for 180 days after a notice of its availability is published in a newspaper of general circulation in the area where the PF operates. The penalty for failure to make proper notice is $20 a day until the notice is filed, with a $10,000 maximum for each return.[96] The penalty is imposed on the person under a duty to act. This former PF inspection system was much less onerous than the system imposed on public charities since 1987.

---

[94] See Chapter 15§4.
[95] IRC §6104(a), pending publication of regulations expected by May 1999.
[96] IRC §6652(c).

27.14 FORM 990-T: EXEMPT ORGANIZATION BUSINESS INCOME TAX RETURN

Proper preparation of this form is mostly a matter of remembering that for this purpose an exempt organization is a normal taxpayer subject to tax code provisions applicable to for-profit taxpayers in addition to the UBI rules. The 990-T must be coordinated with Part VII of Form 990 where the organization reports the amount and type of its unrelated income. Hopefully, the following suggestions will help minimize the tax burden. Exhibit 27.3 provides a table of income source references that ties the lines of the form to Chapter 21.

All domestic and foreign exempt organizations, including churches, state colleges and universities, trusts, IRA accounts, and others not required to file Forms 990, must file Form 990-T, Exempt Organization Business Income Tax Return,[97] to report gross income from UBI over $1000 that is not excluded for one of the reasons outlined below.[98] The rules pertaining to UBI are discussed in Chapter 21; references to that chapter are noted in brackets throughout this discussion of preparation of the form for reporting UBI. An *unrelated business* means:

> Any trade or business the conduct of which is not substantially related (aside from the need of such organization for income or funds or the use it makes of the profits derived) to the exercise or performance by such organization of its charitable, educational, or other purpose or function constituting the basis for its exemption.[99]

Not included in the term unrelated business is any trade or business that:

- Is 85% operated by a volunteer workforce [§21.9(a)]

- Sells donated merchandise [§21.9(b)]

- Conducts public fairs and conventions [§21.9(e)]

- Sponsors certain bingo games [§21.9(d)]

- Is operated for the convenience of members, students, patients, and others participating in the activities of IRC §501(c)(3) organizations [§21.9(c)]

- Produces passive income in the form of interest, dividends, capital gains, rentals, royalties, and certain research income [§21.10]

- Distributes low-cost articles and certain mailing lists [§21.9(g) and (h)]

Trade or business is any activity carried on for the production of income from selling goods or performing services. An activity does not lose its identity as a trade or business merely because it is carried on within a larger group of similar

---

[97] See Appendix 27–7.
[98] Reg. §1.6012-2(e). Gross income for this purpose means gross receipts less cost of goods sold as provided in Reg. §1.61-3. Instrumentalities of the United States exempt under IRC §501(c)(1) are also exempt from this tax.
[99] IRC §513(a).

Exhibit 27–3

TABLE OF INCOME SOURCES REFERENCES		
Type of Income	Form 990-T Line Number	Book Section Reference
Advertising	11	21.8(d) & (e); 21.15(a)
Affinity cards	1 or 10	21.8(c) & 21.10(d)
Bingo games	1	21.9(d)
Capital gains	4	21.10(b)
Bookkeeping services or credit counseling for small businesses	1 or 10	21.8(b)
Computer time charges	1 or 10	21.8(b)
Dividends from wholly owned subsidiaries	8	21.10(e)
Exploited exempt functions	10	21.4(c); 21.11; 21.13(a)
Gift shop sales	1 or 10	21.4(c), 21.13
Insurance	1 or 10	21.8(f)
Mailing list sales	1 or 10	21.9(h) & 21.10(d)
Member services	10	21.8(b)
Merchandise sales	1 or 10	21.7, 21.9(b) & (c); 21.13
Partnership distributions	5	21.10(g)
Rent from real and personal property (unindebted)	6	21.10(c)
Rental debt-financed property	7	21.12
Social club charges for meals, golf, or other club activities	1	Chapter 9
Social club investment income	9	Chapter 9
Sponsorships	1 or 11	21.8(e)
Study tours	1	21.14

activities that may or may not be related to the exempt purposes of the organization [§21.4].[100] Taxable UBI is defined as

> Gross income derived by any organization from any unrelated trade or business (as defined in IRC §513) regularly carried on by it, less the deductions allowed by this chapter which are directly connected with the carrying on of such trade or business.[101]

The bottom line question is whether the income-producing activity contributes importantly to, aids in accomplishing, or has a nexus to the organization's mission. Exhibit 27–4 provides a comprehensive checklist on this form.

---

[100] Reg. §1.513-1(b). The term is defined in reference to IRC §162.
[101] IRC §512(a)(1).

Exhibit 27–4

CHECKLIST FOR PREPARATION OF FORM 990-T

Name of organization _____ prepared by _____

☐ 1. Complete Unrelated Business Income portion of Annual Compliance Checklist (Checklist 19-1 for (c)(3) and 19-2 for other 501(c)s) and review Chapter 21 to determine if the organization conducts a trade or business with the following characteristics: _____

- Unrelated, not relevant, or not necessary to accomplish the organization's exempt purposes, _____

- Regularly carried on or occurring for a period of time a normal business would conduct a similar business activity, and _____

- Producing more than $1000 of business, rather than dividends, interest, capital gains, rents or royalties (passive income). _____

☐ 2. Consider whether an exception applies (§21.9): _____

- Goods or services being sold are donated to the organization. _____

- Most of the work (more than 85%) is performed by volunteers. _____

- Public entertainment event or qualified convention or trade show. _____

- Facility or store operated for member or participant convenience. _____

- Sponsors certain bingo games. _____

☐ 3. Review §27.14 for suggestions on preparing Form 990-T. _____

☐ 4. Review page 5 of Form 990 for types of income to be reported. _____

☐ 5. Review any Forms 990-T filed in prior years. _____

☐ 6. Look for carryovers due to one of the following situations: _____

- Charitable contribution deduction, _____

- Section 179 depreciation, _____

- Net operating loss, _____

- Excess capital loss, _____

- Passive activity loss or credit, _____

- At-risk limits due to lack of invested funds, _____

- Minimum tax credit, _____

Exhibit 27-4 *(continued)*

- Foreign tax credit, or   _____

- General business credit.   _____

☐ 7. Consider application of special income tax provisions for: _____

- Method of accounting adopted? Should it be changed?   _____

- Inventory systems used to account for goods sold.   _____

- Accelerated depreciation methods available (only straight line for debt-financed property).   _____

- Profit motive must be present to claim deductions.   _____

- Ordinary and necessary criteria applied to expenses.   _____

- Income from partnerships retains its character.   _____

- Dividend deductions not available.   _____

☐ 8. Categorize expenses as one of three types before deciding whether to claim expenses in Part I or II (first read §27.14(c)).   _____

- Directly related expenses—no limitation.   _____

- Dually used facility costs.   _____

- Exploited (or exempt functions incidentally producing income) activity expenses.   _____

☐ 9. Compare consequences of reporting periodical income separately or combined.   _____

☐ 10. Review accounting systems with these questions in mind: _____

- Does documentation of personnel time, space usage, or other bases for expense allocations seem reasonable and complete?   _____

- Can related income produced alongside unrelated income be identified?   _____

- Could unrelated income become related?   _____

- If accounting system is not adequate, devise new systems.   _____

☐ 11. Consider benefit of filing consolidated return with affiliates.   _____

☐ 12. Verify amount and payment dates for estimated tax.   _____

☐ 13. Prepare Form 2220, if necessary.   _____

☐ 14. Calculate estimated tax requirements for coming year.   _____

☐ 15. Prepare Form 1139 to carry back current year loss.   _____

(a) Filing Dates, Tax Rates, and Accounting Methods

Due Date. Most Forms 990-T are due to be filed on the same day as the other Forms 990—the 15th day of the fifth month following the close of the organization's fiscal year. (It used to be the third month). Trusts, employee trusts, and IRAs file by the 15th day of the fourth month. Corporations may obtain an automatic six-month extension of this time to file by submitting Form 7004, Application for Automatic Extension of Time to File Corporate Income Tax Return. Others use Form 2758, Application for Extension of Time to File Certain Excise, Income, Information, and Other Returns, to obtain a two- to three-month extension.

Payment of Tax. The tax liability is paid in advance through the quarterly estimated tax system if the annual tax is in excess of $500. Estimated tax deposits are due the 15th day of the 4th, 6th, 9th, and 12th month of the tax year. Note the first payment is due before the return deadline though the amount due is almost always based upon the prior year tax liability. Payments are either made using Form 8109, Federal Tax Deposit Coupons, or through electronic transfer.[102] Exempt organization taxpayers with taxable income of $1 million or more must use the *actual* method and pay tax for its second through fourth quarter based on actual income earned for the year, rather than basing the payment on the prior year. The rates of tax for 1998 are shown in Exhibit 27–5.

Although the impact may be reduced by the charitable deduction (using §170 individual limitations), the significantly higher tax rate imposed on trusts reflects a need for good planning by a tax-exempt trust. For this reason such a trust would create a for-profit subsidiary from which to conduct unrelated business activity. Affiliated exempt organizations that are commonly controlled must combine their incomes. The 15% bracket applies only to the first $50,000 of their combined income; the 25% applies to the next $25,000, and so on. The exempt organizations can apportion the tax brackets among themselves as they please, or they can share the lower brackets equally.[103] An apportionment plan must be signed by all members and attached to their Forms 990-T.

Credits and Alternative Minimum Tax. Since an exempt organization earning UBI is taxed just like for-profit corporations and trusts, the general business and foreign tax credits and alternative minimum taxes (AMT) may apply.[104] The AMT was repealed effective for 1998 for corporations with average gross receipts of $5,000,000 for the past three years. A discussion of these tax rules is beyond the scope of this book; a prudent organization seeks the help of competent consultants in this regard.

Proxy Tax. Expenses of attempts to influence legislation—lobbying—are not deductible. A civic association, labor union, or business league has a choice of either informing its members of the portion of their dues so expended or paying a tax of 35% of its lobbying expenses.[105]

---

[102] The depositing method is determined by reference to the organization's payroll tax payment method as discussed in Chapter 25§3(e).

[103] Reg. §1.1561-3(b).

[104] IRC §§27, 28, 29, 38–44, 51, 55–59, and 59A.

[105] IRC §6033(e)(2); see Chapter 6§4.

Exhibit 27–5

1998 TAX RATE SCHEDULE FOR CORPORATIONS

(Section 11 of the Internal Revenue Code)

If the taxable income is:		The income tax equals:
Over—	but not over—	
$0	$50,000	15% of the amount
50,000	75,000	$7,500 plus 25% of amount over $50,000
75,000	100,000	$13,750 plus 34% of amount over $75,000
100,000	335,000	$22,250 plus 39% of amount over $100,000
335,000	10,000,000	$113,900 plus 34% of amount over $335,000
10,000,000	15,000,000	$3,400,000 plus 34% of amount over $10,000,000
15,000,000	18,333,333	$5,150,000 plus 35% of amount over $15,000,000
$18,333,333	—	35% of the amount

1998 Tax Rate Schedule for Trusts
(Section 1(e) of the Internal Revenue Code)

If the taxable income is:	The income tax is:
Not over $1,700	15% of the amount
Over $1,700 but under $4,000	$255 plus 28% of amount over $1,700
Over $4,000 but under $6,100	$899 plus 31% of amount over $4,000
Over $6,100 but under $8,350	$1,550 plus 36% of amount over $6,100
Over $8,350	$2,360 plus 39.6% of amount over $8,350.

Interest and Penalties. Several different charges are imposed when a return is filed late. The failure to file penalty of 5% of the tax due per month the return is late, up to 25% maximum,[106] unless the organization can show reasonable cause for the delay. The IRS has been lenient to first time filers who voluntarily submit Forms 990-T and pay the tax, though rumor has it that the Ogden Service Center may not continue this policy. For the penalty to be abated, the failure to file cannot be due to willful neglect; ordinary business care and prudence must be used to ascertain the requirement.[107] An explanation seeking abatement should be attached to the return requesting relief and explaining why the return was filed late, particularly if the organization regularly engages independent accountants who failed to advise it of its obligation to do so.

Next, a penalty may be assessed for failure to pay of 0.5% (½%) of the unpaid tax (i.e., an annual rate of 6% up to a maximum of 25% of the amount due. Additionally, a penalty may be due for failure to pay the tax in advance through the estimated tax system described above. Form 2220 is used to calculate this penalty, which is assessed on a daily basis at the prevailing federal rate.

---

[106] IRC §6651. When the return is delinquent over 60 days, the minimum tax for failure to file is the smaller of the actual tax or $100.

[107] Reg. §301.6651-1(c) explains the acceptable excuses.

(b) Normal Income Tax Rules Apply

Accounting Methods and Periods. Taxable income is calculated using the method of accounting regularly used in keeping the exempt organization's books and records.[108] Organizations with more than $5 million of annual gross receipts must use the accrual method.[109] Also, an organization selling merchandise or goods that are accounted for piece by piece must maintain inventory records and also use the accrual method.[110] Any change in method results in *§481 adjustments.* Form 3115 is filed to seek permission for the change and to spread the effect of the change over five years.[111]

"Ordinary and Necessary" Criteria. Deductions claimed against the unrelated income must be "ordinary and necessary" to conducting the activity and must meet the other standards of IRC §162 for business deductions. "Ordinary" means common and accepted for the type of business operated; "necessary" means helpful and appropriate, not indispensable. Ordinary does not necessarily mean required, but can mean appropriate or customary. Thus, an organization can deduct expenses commonly claimed by commercial businesses operating similar businesses. Special issues concerning deductible expenses for UBI purposes are discussed in §27.14(c).

Profit Motive. To be deductible, an expenditure must also be paid for the production of income, or in a business operated for the purpose of making a profit.[112] IRC §183 specifically prohibits the deduction of hobby losses, or those activities losing money for more than two years out of every five. In the social club arena, the IRS and the clubs battled for several years over the deductibility of nonmember activity losses against investment income. Ultimately, the clubs lost. The exploitation rule disallows deduction of related activity expenses against UBI, partly because exempt activities are not conducted with a profit motive.

Depreciation. Equipment, buildings, vehicles, furniture, and other properties that are used in the business are deductible over their useful lives through the depreciation system. As a simple example, one-third of the cost of a computer that is expected to become obsolete within three years is deductible for three years. Unfortunately, Congress uses these calculation rates and methods as political and economic tools and the revenue code prescribes rates and methods that are not simple. IRC §§167, 168, and 179 apply and must be studied to properly calculate allowable deductions for depreciation.

Inventory. If the organization keeps an inventory of items for sale, such as books, drugs, or merchandise of any sort, it must use the inventory methods to

---

[108] IRC §446(a).

[109] IRC §448(c).

[110] IRC §§263A and 471.

[111] Rules pertaining to seeking approval for a change in method are presented in Chapter 28§2(c).

[112] IRC §162; Reg. §1.512(a)-1(b); *Iowa State University of Science & Technology v. U.S., infra* n.51; *Commissioner v. Groetzinger,* 480 U.S. 23 (1987); Reg. §1.513-1(4)(d)(iii); *Portland Golf Club v. Commissioner,* 110 S. Ct. 2780 (1990); also see Chapter 9§5(e).

deduct the cost of such goods. The concept is one of matching the cost of the item sold with its sales proceeds. If the organization buys ten widgets for sale and as of the end of a year only five have been sold, the cost of the five is deductible and the remaining five are capitalized as an asset to be deducted when in fact they are sold. Again, the system is far more complicated than this simple example, and an accountant should be consulted to ensure use of proper reporting and tabulation methods. IRC §§263A and 471–474 apply.

Capital and Nondeductibles.   A host of nondeductible items contained in §§261 to 280H might apply to disallow deductions either by total disallowance or required capitalization of permanent assets. Again, all the rules applicable to for-profit businesses apply, such as the luxury automobile limits, travel and entertainment substantiation requirements, and 50 percent disallowance for meals.

Dividend Deduction.   The dividends-received deductions provided by §§243–245 for taxable nonexempt corporations are not allowed. Normal corporations are allowed to exclude 70% of the investment dividends; exempt organizations are not. Note that this rule presents a problem only for dividends received from investments that are debt financed. Most dividends received by exempts are excluded from the UBI under the *Modifications* for passive income.[113] For certain thinly capitalized subsidiaries, IRC §163(j) can remove the passive income exception.

Charitable Deduction.   Up to 10% of an exempt corporation's and 20–50% of a trust's unrelated taxable income before the deduction UBI is deductible for contributions paid to another charitable organization.[114] Note that the deduction is not allowed for an organization's internal project expenditures or gifts to a controlled subsidiary. Contributions in excess of allowable amounts are eligible for a five-year carryover. Social clubs, voluntary employee business associations, unemployment benefit trusts, and group legal service plans can take a 100% deduction for direct charitable gifts and qualified set-asides for charitable purposes.[115]

Net Operating Losses.   A net operating loss can be applied to offset income on which income tax was paid for the two tax years preceding the loss by filing a carryback claim. Any remaining losses can be carried forward to offset net income for 20 years following the loss year.[116] Thus it can be important for an exempt to file Form 990-T to establish a loss potentially available to offset future income.

(c) 990-T's Unique Design

Form 990-T has evolved over the years to accommodate the unique fashion in which deductions against certain types of income are claimed. The sequence of lines is somewhat different from other tax forms with special schedules for rentals, debt-financed UBI, payments from controlled subsidiaries, exploited exempt

[113] IRC §512(b).
[114] IRC §512(b)(10 and 11).
[115] IRC §§170(b)(2), 512(a)(3)(B)(i), and 642(c).
[116] IRC §172(b).

activities, and advertising. The form is designed to enforce the general concept that no portion of the organization's underlying mission-related expenses are deductible.

Part I. Part I was revised for 1992 by adding a column to present the direct expenses alongside gross income for which supporting schedules are completed. Previously, only the net income was carried to this part. This redesign reflects the IRS intention to evaluate deductible expenses. However, for line 1 income, the direct expenses other than cost of goods sold are deducted in Part II and may cause some confusion, particularly in relation to lines called *Excess Exempt and Excess Readership Expenses*. Exhibit 27–5 can be used as a guide for placement of different type of income on the lines of Part I and to find the sections of this book that discuss each type of income. The suggestions for this part will therefore be presented according to the various types of UBI, rather than line by line. Modest organizations whose gross unrelated income does not exceed $10,000 need not play the line game; the total UBI is entered on line 13. For Form 990 and 900-PF filers, line 13 should equal the total on line 15, column (b).

Part II, Deductions Not Taken Elsewhere. On Form 990-T, expenses are deducted either in Part I or Part II, not due to the nature of particular types of expenses, but strictly according to the form's design and the type of income. As the title implies, allocable expenses not deducted in Part I are claimed here. The IRS instructions for this part contain guidance for preparation. Helpful schedules designed to apply the different limitations for certain types of deductions flow into both Part I and II and serve the following functions:

- Schedule A reports cost of goods sold for those organizations required to maintain inventories. There is no Schedule B, D, or H.

- Schedule C calculates the portion of taxable personal property rentals. [§21.10(c)]

- Schedule E calculates the taxable portion of revenues attributable to debt-financed income. [§21.12]

- Schedule F calculates the taxable portion of revenues from controlled subsidiaries. [§21.10(e)]

- Schedule G calculates the taxable income of social clubs, voluntary employee benefit associations, and supplemental employee benefit trusts setting aside part of their income for charitable purposes. [§9.5(g)]

- Schedule I applies a deduction limitation for unrelated income exploited from an exempt activity, such as green fees paid by nonstudents to play on a school's golf course or commissions for nonmember insurance. [§21.4(c)]

- Schedule J applies the deduction limitations and income allocations necessary to arrive at taxable advertising revenues. [§21.14(a)]

- Schedule K reports officer, director, and trustee compensation attributable to unrelated business income. [§27.9]

(d) Categories of Deductions

The complexity of Form 990-T goes beyond the task of understanding the income tax system. Exempt organizations, in their efforts to raise funds, have devised creative methods to make money utilizing their tangible and intangible assets and their staffs. In the words of the regulations, such money-making schemes "exploit" the exempt functions. People and things are mingled and used for both exempt and income-producing purposes. Whatever method is used to arrive at the deductible expenses, including overhead or general and administrative costs, the method must not permit the amalgamation of for-profit and nonprofit activities.[117] If followed consistently from year to year, an organization can use the method it uses for financial statement purposes as a reasonable basis for claiming UBI deductions. Regarding joint costs the accounting profession says, "The cost allocation methodology used should be rational and systematic, it should result in an allocation of joint costs that is reasonable, and it should be applied consistently given similar facts and circumstances.[118] The UBI sections of the code "do not specifically address how expenses are to be allocated when exempt organizations are computing their UBI."[119] The regulations provide three specific types of deductible expenses.[120]

- Type 1. Expense solely attributable to business activities
- Type 2. Dual-use property or project expenses
- Type 3. Exploited activity expense

Type 1.   Expenses attributable solely to unrelated business activities are fully deductible.[121] Such expenses are those reasonably allocable under good accounting theory consistently applied using a method that evidences its connection with the production of unrelated gross income.[122] Two classic business expense deduction concepts are applied:

- A "proximate and primary relationship" between the expense and the activity is the standard for deduction.[123] Proximate means near, close, or immediate, such as the full-time personnel devoted solely to the business.
- A *but for* test can be applied by asking the question, "Would the expense be incurred if the unrelated activity was not carried on?"

---

[117] *Iowa State University of Science and Technology v. U.S.,* 500 F.2d 508 (Ct.Cl. 1974).
[118] Statement of Position 98-2, *Accounting for Costs of Activities of Not-for-Profit Organizations and State and Local Governmental Entities That Include Fund Raising,* issued March 11, 1998 as an amendment to the AICP Audit and Accounting Guide.
[119] 1991 *Exempt Organizations Continuing Professional Education Technical Instruction Program,* at page 20.
[120] Reg. 1. 512(a)-1.
[121] IRC §512(a)(1); Reg. §1.512(a)-1(b).
[122] *Iowa State University of Science and Technology v. U.S.,* 500 F.2d 508 (Ct.Cl. 1974).
[123] Reg. §1.512(a)-1(a).

Type 2. A portion of *dual-use,* or shared, employees, facilities, equipment, and other overhead expenses is also deductible. Shared costs are allocated between related and unrelated activities on *a reasonable basis.* The only example given in the IRS regulations allocates 10% of an organization president's salary to the business activity to which he devotes 10% of his time.[124] This type presents a classic chicken and egg or tail wagging the dog situation. Is the UBI activity an afterthought, or was a facility built to be dually used? When the exempt activity would be carried on regardless of the UBI funds and essentially came first, the dual-use type of expense allocation is not applicable.

It is sometimes difficult to decide whether the type 2 or 3 category should apply. It is important to note in making this choice that the exploitation method often yields a higher level of expense deduction. Conceivably, 100% of an exploited activity's expenses are allocable to the unrelated income, but subject to an income limitation. As shown in §27.14(e), the denominator of the formulas used to make the allocations may also influence the choice of category.

Type 3. The third type is an allocated portion of the expense of a program related, or exempt function, activity that produces income from an unrelated aspect such as the sale of advertising, and is said to exploit the exempt activity. Under specific conditions that depend on the character of the exploited activity, the deduction of exempt function cost is allowed but may be limited by the income generated. The general rule is expressed negatively and disallows such deductions because they are not considered to have a proximate and primary relationship to the revenue. Nonetheless, to the extent of the revenue, a portion of a type 3 expense is deductible. The deductible portion of a type 3 expense is calculated through a series of steps in Schedules I and J that do not allow a loss from an exploited activity to be deducted. To compute UBI, no expense attributable to the conduct of the exempt activity is deductible, *except* in specified circumstances and with limitation.[125] To be deductible, three conditions must be satisfied:

- *Condition 1:* The unrelated trade or business activity is of a kind carried on for profit by taxable organizations and the exempt activity exploited by the business is a type of activity normally conducted by taxable organizations in pursuance of such business.

- *Condition 2:* Expenses, depreciation, and similar items attributable to the exempt activity exceed the income (if any) derived from or attributable to the exempt activity.

- *Condition 3:* The allocation of such items to the unrelated trade or business activity does not result in a loss from such unrelated trade or business activity.[126] Schedules I and J of Form 990-T illustrate Condition 3 (Appendix 27–7).

---

[124] Reg. §1.512(a)-1(c).
[125] Reg. §1.512(a)-1(d)(1).
[126] Reg. §1.512(a)-1(d)(2).

Fund-raising activity in pursuit of voluntary contributions is a good example of a revenue activity that is not normally considered businesslike.[127] Generally, the cost of maintaining an organization's contributor or member lists is not deductible against the proceeds of sales of the list. The IRS says the regulation "is somewhat helpful in trying to decide whether the sale of a mailing list is a dual related/ unrelated use or an exploitation of an exempt function."[128] The IRS admits there "seems to be a significant question of whether exempt function expenses that exceed exempt function income may be deducted." A list developed and maintained for a symphony society's ticket sales instead might be dual-use property.

Publications are less troublesome. The regulations anticipate that periodicals are businesslike and the exploited activity costs can be deducted. A framework for allocating exempt function, or readership, costs against the advertising revenues is provided in the regulations,[129] and shown in Schedule J of Form 990-T.

Advertising has long been treated as businesslike revenue. The proposed sponsorship regulations [§21.8(e)] expand that category.[130] Examples concern an organization conducting an annual bowl game and an art museum. The exploitation method for allocating expenses, rather than the dual-use method, is followed, yielding high deductions. These examples were the first time the IRS has applied the exploitation rule beyond advertising.

Sales of merchandise or products, scientific research, health care service, and many other categories of revenue production are conducted by both exempts and for-profit businesses. Some activities, such as education and cultural performances (dance and theater), are conducted primarily by exempts but also by businesses, and technically qualify under Condition 1.

Type 3 (exploitation) deductions can be financially valuable. Essentially, program service costs, also known as *exempt function costs,* of an inherently businesslike exempt activity can be deducted for UBI purposes, despite the general rule that they cannot be. When the allocation is permitted, the organization essentially earns tax-free income to cover its exempt function costs.

Treating an expense as type 3 can result in a higher deduction than a type 2 that only allows a calculated portion of the exempt function costs. Type 2 (dual-use) expenses may be advantageous in some circumstances, however, because the Type 3 allocable expense must first be reduced by exempt function revenues. Also,

---

[127] Reg. §1.513-1(c)(iii) says, "Income derived from the conduct of an annual dance or similar fund-raising event for charity would not be income from trade or business regularly carried on." In *U.S. v. American Bar Endowment,* 477 U.S. 105 (1986), an insurance sales program, the profit from which reportedly was dependent upon member generosity, was determined to be a taxable business, not a fund-raising effort. The "donated" portion of the member premium was not voluntary and the program was conducted with the intention of producing a profit. Note that because of this decision, the ABA's total cost in relation to the insurance program would be deductible.

[128] 1992 *Exempt Organizations Continuing Professional Education Technical Instruction Program* (published annually and ordered from the IRS Reading Room in Washington, DC or the IRS website), at 74, in discussion of the example found in Reg. §1.512(a)-1(e).

[129] Reg. §1.512(a)-1(f).

[130] Prop. Reg. §301.512(a)-1(e), Examples 2, 3, and 4.

a loss deductible against other UBI cannot result from Type 3 expenses,[131] whereas a dual-use facility loss may be deducted against other types of UBI.

(e) Cost Allocations

The UBI code sections "do not specifically address how a dual-use or exploited expense is to be allocated when exempt organizations are computing UBI."[132] The IRS Manual instructs examining agents that any reasonable method resulting in identifying relationship of the expenses to revenue produced is acceptable.[133] Different allocation methods are available, but once a method is chosen it must be consistently followed from year to year and for all purposes.[134] The choice of method depends on the organization's complexity and the nature of its activities. The AICPA (American Institute of Certified Public Accountants) and the NACUBO (National Association of College and University Business Officers) in response to the time spent and controversies resulting from IRS examinations suggest the adoption of standards of cost allocations for UBI purposes.

The IRS has prescribed the fashion in which a (c)(4), (5), or (6) organization allocates its expenses to compute the cost of its lobbying activity.[135] Two simplified methods—a *direct gross-up* of labor costs (take total salaries and add 175 percent for indirect costs) and a *ratio* method (take total costs and allocate them based on number of hours personnel spend on various functions)—are suggested in addition to the complex rules of IRC §263A. Those rules should be carefully studied as a harbinger of future IRS rules. The AICPA Tax Exempt Organization and the National Association of College and University Business Officers have suggested this sort of guidance be issued.

Whatever method an exempt organization chooses to follow to allocate costs, the method should clearly reflect the economic realities of the organization and the UBI it receives and should be evidenced by suitable documentation. Actual time records must be maintained to reflect the effort devoted to related versus unrelated activities by all personnel and professional advisors. Absent time records, an allocation based on *relative gross income* produced might be used. Direct and indirect expenses must be distinguished.

Direct expenses are those that increase proportionately with the usage of a facility or the volume of activity and are also called *variable*. For example, the number of persons attending an event influence the number of ushers or security guards and represent a direct cost, or, in other words, a cost attributable to that specific use that would not have been incurred *but for* the particular event. *Indirect costs* are incurred without regard to usage or frequency of participation, and are also called *fixed expenses*. An organization's building acquisition costs or annual audit fee, for example, do not necessarily vary with usage. Management and general expenses are normally of this character.

---

[131] Reg. §1.512(a)-1(d)(1); *West Virginia Medical Association v. Commissioner,* 882 F.2d 123 (4th Cir. 1989).
[132] 1991 *Exempt Organizations Continuing Professional Education Technical Instruction Program,* at page 20.
[133] *Exempt Organizations Examination Guidelines Handbook,* Internal Revenue Manual, §720(7).
[134] *Portland Golf Club, supra* n.112.
[135] Reg. §1.162-28.

A *gross income method* of cost allocation is sometimes used to calculate cost of goods sold when costs bear a relationship to the revenue produced from exempt and nonexempt factors. The regulations say, "Such allocations based on receipts from exempt activities may not be reasonable since such receipts are not normally reflective of cost."[136]

A proration based on the number of participants might be suitable in some circumstances. This type of formula is used in calculating allocations for social clubs and publications charging different prices to members and nonmembers. The hours a facility is used might be applied. The proper denominator of the fraction used to calculate costs allocable to UBI is also significant in reducing or increasing allowable deductions. Arguably, no fixed costs of an exempt institution should be allocated to UBI, but to date the courts have allowed allocation among both the exempt and nonexempt functions that benefit from building use. In a football stadium case, the court allowed for example:[137]

$$\frac{\text{number of hours or days used for unrelated purposes}}{\text{total number of hours or days in } use}$$

The IRS argues that fixed costs were allocated (produces a much smaller number) by:

$$\frac{\text{number of hours or days used for unrelated purposes}}{\text{total number of hours of days in } year}$$

The United Cancer Council's (UCC) allocation system for identifying the public education, fund-raising, and generic content of its direct mail materials was reviewed by the tax court. The UCC failed the commensurate test [Chapter 2§2] because less than 10% of its publication, measured by the linear and square inches of material, contained educational information. It was ultimately found to also provide private inurement to fund-raising managers.[138]

The IRS has said it prefers a system that allocates costs to all activities similar to a GAAP functional expense statement. One commentator suggests reference to the foreign tax credit allocation rules for guidance in allocating dual-use facility costs.[139] Take, for example, a hospital pharmacy. A portion of the revenue is generated from sales to patients and is considered as related income. The nonpatient sales are instead classified as unrelated income. The objective is to assign the expenses of the pharmacy operation to the appropriate category of revenue. The easy way is apportion the expenses using the relative percentages of related and unrelated revenue. Revenues, however, can be dissected and leveled for market and other differences. If the patient sales, for example, are made at a 20% percent discount under the amount charged over the counter, patient sales would be grossed back up, or the nonpatient revenue discounted, before calculating the

---

[136] Reg. §1.512(a)-1(f)(6).

[137] *Rensselaer Polytechnic Institute v. Commissioner*, 732 F.2d 1058 (2d Cir. 1984), *aff'g* 79 T.C. 967 (1982).

[138] *United Cancer Council, Inc. v. Commissioner*, 109 T.C. 326 (December 12, 1997).

[139] Special report of Laura Kalish entitled "Allocation of Expenses—A Foreign Solution," *The Exempt Organization Tax Review*, February 1995, p. 283.

ratio. This example follows the fragmentation rules that require unrelated sales be segregated from related sales in an activity that embodies both (§21.4(c) and §21.13). Readers should be alert to developments on this topic.

(f) In-Kind Donations

Three different types of in-kind donations are quantified and reported as revenue and corresponding expense by tax-exempt nonprofits—donated services, facility use, and material goods. FSAS No. 116 contains specific standards for valuing and reporting such gifts.[140] Donations of the first two types are not reported for Form 990 purposes,[141] presumably to remind taxpayers that the donations of services and facilities are not deductible. Tangible goods are reported and may be deductible.[142]

Donated services and use of facilities (as well as tangible goods), in the author's opinion, are reportable as deductions for UBI purposes. This tax planning opportunity can be significant. Booking the in-kind donations does not produce taxable gross income if they are voluntary gifts not subject to income tax.[143] The corresponding expense, to the extent that it is directly associated with or partly allocable to an unrelated business activity, can result in a saving of UBIT.

---

[140] See §27.3(b).

[141] There is no published precedent for this position. An IRS EO specialist's informal opinion was that there could be no deduction because no cash changed hands. There are several precedents in the tax code for imputed income. Under IRC §482, income can be allocated between related companies, essentially on paper. Interest income is imputed to certain below-market rate loans under IRC §7872. Although the analogy is not perfect (because it is not an exchange transaction in which the EO earns its side of the donated services), the value of goods or services received in a barter transaction are reportable income as outlined in IRS Publication 525, *Taxable and Nontaxable Income*.

[142] IRC §170(e).

[143] IRC §102.

Appendix 27–1

FORM 990EZ

Form **990-EZ**	**Short Form**	OMB No. 1545-1150
	Return of Organization Exempt From Income Tax	**1998**

Under section 501(c) of the Internal Revenue Code (except black lung benefit trust or private foundation) or section 4947(a)(1) nonexempt charitable trust

For organizations with gross receipts less than $100,000 and total assets less than $250,000 at the end of the year.

Department of the Treasury
Internal Revenue Service

The organization may have to use a copy of this return to satisfy state reporting requirements.

This Form is Open to Public Inspection

A For the 1998 calendar year, OR tax year beginning _____, 1998, and ending _____

B Check if:
- Change of address
- Initial return
- Final return
- Amended return (required also for state reporting)

C Name of organization
Mock-Up Form 990-EZ referenced to Chapter 27

Number and street (or P.O. box, if mail is not delivered to address) | Room/suite

City, town, or country | State | ZIP code

D Employer identification number

E Telephone number

F Check if ☐ exemption application is pending

H Enter four-digit group exemption number (GEN)

G Accounting method: ☐ Cash ☐ Accrual ☐ Other (specify)

I Type of organization — ☐ Exempt under Section 501(c) ( ) (insert no.) ☐ section 4947(a)(1) nonexempt charitable trust

Note: Section 501(c)(3) organizations and section 4947(a)(1) nonexempt charitable trusts MUST attach a completed Schedule A (Form 990).

J Check if the ☐ organization's gross receipts are normally not more than $25,000. The organization need not file a return with the IRS; but if the organization received a Form 990 Package in the mail, the organization should file a return without financial data. Some states require a complete return.

K Enter the organization's 1998 gross receipts (add back lines 5b, 6b, and 7b, to line 9) . . . . $ _____ 27

If $100,000 or more, the organization must file Form 990 instead of Form 990-EZ.

Part I — Revenue, Expenses, and Changes in Net Assets or Fund Balances (See instructions on page 30.)

R e v e n u e	1 Contributions, gifts, grants, and similar amounts received (attach schedule of contributors)	**1** 27.5(b)
	2 Program service revenue including government fees and contracts	**2** 27.5(c)
	3 Membership dues and assessments	**3** 27.5(d)
	4 Investment income	**4** 27.5(e-h)
	5a Gross amount from sale of assets other than inventory . . . . . **5a** 27.5(i)	
	b Less: cost or other basis and sales expenses **5b**	
	c Gain or (loss) from sale of assets other than inventory (line 5a less line 5b) (attach schedule)	**5c**
	6 Special events and activities (attach schedule):	
	a Gross revenue (not including _____ of contributions reported on line 1) . . . . . . **6a** 27.5(j)	
	b Less: direct expenses other than fundraising expenses . . . **6b**	
	c Net income or (loss) from special events and activities (line 6a less line 6b)	**6c**
	7a Gross sales of inventory, less returns and allowances . . . . . **7a** 27.5(k)	
	b Less: cost of goods sold **7b** 27.14	
	c Gross profit or (loss) from sales of inventory (line 7a less line 7b)	**7c**
	8 Other revenue (describe _____)	**8** 27.5(l)
	9 Total revenue (add lines 1, 2, 3, 4, 5c, 6c, 7c, and 8)	**9**
E x p e n s e s	10 Grants and similar amounts paid (attach schedule)	**10** 27.6(a)
	11 Benefits paid to or for members	**11** 27.6(c)
	12 Salaries, other compensation, and employee benefits	**12** 27.6(d-e)
	13 Professional fees and other payments to independent contractors	**13** 27.6(g)
	14 Occupancy, rent, utilities, and maintenance	**14**
	15 Printing, publications, postage, and shipping	**15**
	16 Other expenses (describe _____) . . .	**16**
	17 Total expenses (add lines 10 through 16)	**17**
Net As-sets	18 Excess or (deficit) for the year (line 9 less line 17)	**18** 0
	19 Net assets or fund balances at beginning of year (from line 27, column (A)) (must agree with end-of-year figure reported on prior year's return)	**19**
	20 Other changes in net assets or fund balances (attach explanation)	**20** 27.5(o)
	21 Net assets or fund balances at end of year (combine lines 18 through 20)	**21**

Part II — Balance Sheets

If Total assets on line 25, column (B) are $250,000 or more, file Form 990 instead of Form 990-EZ.

		(A) Beginning of year		(B) End of year
22	Cash, savings, and investments		**22**	27.8.
23	Land and buildings		**23**	
24	Other assets (describe _____)	0	**24**	0
25	Total assets	0	**25**	0
26	Total liabilities (describe _____)		**26**	
27	Net assets or fund balances (line 27 of column (B) must agree with line 21)	0	**27**	0

For Paperwork Reduction Act Notice, see page 1 of the separate instructions.　　(HTA)　　Form 990-EZ (1998)

Appendix 27–1

FORM 990EZ (*continued*)

Form 990-EZ (1998)   Mock-Up Form 990-EZ referenced to Chapter 27   00-0000000   Page 2

Part III   Statement of Program Service Accomplishments   (See Specific Instructions on page 34.)   **Expenses**

What is the organization's primary exempt purpose?
Describe what was achieved in carrying out the organization's exempt purposes. In a clear and concise manner, describe the services provided, the number of persons benefited, or other relevant information for each program title.

(Required for 501(c)(3) and (4) organizations and 4947(a)(1) trusts; optional for others.)

28 _____

     See Chapter 27.7

_____ (Grants $) | **28a**

29 _____

_____ (Grants $) | **29a**

30 _____

_____ (Grants $) | **30a**

31 Other program services (attach schedule) . . . . (Grants $) | **31a**

32 Total program service expenses (add lines 28a through 31a) . . . . | **32**   0

Part IV   List of Officers, Directors, Trustees, and Key Employees   (List each one even if not compensated.)

(A) Name and address	(B) Title and average hours per week devoted to position	(C) Compensation (If not paid, enter -0-.)	(D) Contributions to employee benefit plans & deferred compensation	(E) Expense account and other allowances
See Chapter 27.9				

Part V   Other Information   (See Specific Instructions on page 35.)   **Yes or No**

33 Did the organization engage in any activity not previously reported to the Internal Revenue Service? If "Yes," attach a detailed description of each activity . . . .   see 27.10

34 Were any changes made to the organizing or governing documents but not reported to the IRS? If "Yes," attach a conformed copy of the changes . . .   27.10.

35 If the organization had income from business activities, such as those reported on lines 2, 6, and 7 (among others), but NOT reported on Form 990-T, attach a statement explaining your reason for not reporting the income on Form 990-T.

   a Did the organization have unrelated business gross income of $1,000 or more or 6033(e) notice, reporting, and proxy tax requirements? . . . .   27.14 & Ch. 21

   b If "Yes," has it filed a tax return on Form 990-T for this year? 27.14

36 Was there a liquidation, dissolution, termination, or substantial contraction during the year? (If "Yes," attach a statement) . . . .   see Ch. 26

37a Enter amount of political expenditures, direct or indirect, as described in the instructions . | **37a**

   b Did the organization file Form 1120-POL for this year? . . . .   see Ch. 23

38a Did the organization borrow from, or make any loans to, any officer, director, trustee, or key employee OR were any such loans made in a prior year and still unpaid at the start of the period covered by this return? . . . . .   see Ch. 20

   b If "Yes," attach the schedule specified in the line 38 instructions and enter the amount involved . . . | **38b**

39 501(c)(7) organizations. - Enter: **a** Initiation fees and capital contributions included on line 9 | **39a**   see Chapter 9

   b Gross receipts, included on line 9, for public use of club facilities . . . . | **39b**

40a 501(c)(3) organizations. - Enter: Amount of tax imposed on the organization during the year under:
section 4911   see Ch. 23 .5   ;section 4912   see Ch. 23.5   ;section 4955   see Ch. 23 .3

   b 501(c)(3) and (4) organizations. - Did the organization engage in any section 4958 excess benefit transaction during the year? If "Yes," attach an explanation . . . . . .   see Ch. 20.9

   c Enter: Amount of tax imposed on the organization managers or disqualified persons during the year under sections 4912, 4955, and 4958 . . . . . . _____

   d Enter: Amount of tax in 40c, above, reimbursed by the organization . . . . _____

41 List the states with which a copy of this return is filed. _____

42 The books are in care of _____ Telephone no. (000) 000-0000

     Located at _____ ZIP + 4

43 Section 4947(a)(1) nonexempt charitable trusts filing Form 990-EZ in lieu of Form 1041- Check here and enter the amount of tax-exempt interest received or accrued during the tax year . . . . | **43**

Please Sign Here — Under penalties of perjury, I declare that I have examined this return, including accompanying schedules and statements, and to the best of my knowledge and belief, it is true, correct, and complete. Declaration of preparer (other than officer) is based on all information of which preparer has any knowledge. (See General Instruction U, page 12.)

Signature of officer	Date	Type or print name and title.	Title

Paid Preparer Use Only	Preparer's signature	Date	Check if self-employed	Preparer's SSN
	Firm's name (or yours) and address		EIN	
			Phone	
		State	ZIP + 4	

Appendix 27–2

FORM 990

Form **990**	**Return of Organization Exempt From Income Tax**	OMB No.1545-0047
Department of the Treasury	Under section 501(c) of the Internal Revenue Code (except black lung benefit trust or private foundation) or section 4947(a)(1) nonexempt charitable trust	**1998**
Internal Revenue Service	Note: The organization may have to use a copy of this return to satisfy state reporting requirements.	This Form is Open to Public Inspection

A For the 1998 calendar year, OR tax year period beginning **July 1st**, 1998, and ending **June 30th**, 19 **99**

B Check if:	**C** Name of organization	**D** Employer identification number
Change of address	**Campaign to Clean Up America**	44-4444444
Initial return	Number and street (or P. O. box if mail is not delivered to street address) Room/suite	**E** Telephone number
Final return	**1111 Any Street**	**(444) 444-4444**
Amended return	City or town State or Country ZIP code	**F** Check ☐ if exemption
(required also for State reporting)	**Hometown** **Texas** 77777	application is pending

G Type of organization ☒ Exempt under section 501(c)(**3**)(insert no.) ☐ section 4947(a)(1) nonexempt charitable trust

Note: Section 501(c)(3) exempt organizations and 4947(a)(1) nonexempt charitable trusts MUST attach a completed Sch. A (Form 990).

H(a) Is this a group return filed for affiliates? **No**

I If either box in H is checked "Yes," enter four-digit group exemption number (GEN)

(b) If "Yes," enter the number of affiliates for which this return is filed:

(c) Is this a separate return filed by an organization covered by a group ruling? **No**

J Accounting method: ☐ Cash ☒ Accrual ☐ Other (specify)

K Check here ☐ if the organization's gross receipts are normally not more than $25,000. The organization need not file a return with the IRS; but if it received a Form 990 Package in the mail, it should file a return without financial data. Some states require a complete return.

Note: Form 990-EZ may be used by organizations with gross receipts less than $100,000 and total assets less than $250,000 at end of year.

Part I   Revenue, Expenses, and Changes in Net Assets or Fund Balances (See Specific Instructions on page 13.)

R e v e n u e	1 Contributions, gifts, grants, and similar amounts received:			
	a Direct public support	1a	974,700	
	b Indirect public support	1b		
	c Government contributions (grants)	1c		
	d Total (add lines 1a through 1c) (attach schedule of contributors) (cash $ _____ noncash $ _____)	1d		974,700
	2 Program service revenue including government fees and contracts (from Part VII, line 93)	2		37,700
	3 Membership dues and assessments	3		
	4 Interest on savings and temporary cash investments	4		5,000
	5 Dividends and interest from securities	5		4,000
	6a Gross rents	6a	2,000	
	b Less: rental expenses	6b		
	c Net rental income or (loss) (subtract line 6b from line 6a)	6c		2,000
	7 Other investment income (describe	7		
	8a Gross amount from sale of assets other than inventory (A) Securities (B) Other	8a		
	b Less: cost or other basis and sales expenses	8b		
	c Gain or (loss) (attach schedule) 0 0	8c		
	d Net gain or (loss) (combine line 8c, columns (A) and (B))	8d		0
	9 Special events and activities (attach schedule)			
	a Gross revenue (not including _____ of contributions reported on line 1a)	9a		
	b Less: direct expenses other than fundraising expenses	9b		
	c Net income or (loss) from special events (subtract line 9b from line 9a)	9c		0
	10a Gross sales of inventory, less returns and allowances	10a	40,000	
	b Less: cost of goods sold	10b	10,000	
	c Gross profit or (loss) from sales of inventory (attach schedule) (subtract line 10b from line 10a)	10c		30,000
	11 Other revenue (from Part VII, line 103)	11		
	12 Total revenue (add lines 1d, 2, 3, 4, 5, 6c, 7, 8d, 9c, 10c, and 11)	12		1,053,400
Expenses	13 Program services (from line 44, column (B))	13		496,700
	14 Management and general (from line 44, column (C))	14		130,800
	15 Fundraising (from line 44, column (D))	15		83,500
	16 Payments to affiliates (attach schedule)	16		
	17 Total expenses (add lines 16 and 44, column (A))	17		711,000
Net Assets	18 Excess or (deficit) for the year (subtract line 17 from line 12)	18		342,400
	19 Net assets or fund balances at beginning of year (from line 73, column (A))	19		43,800
	20 Other changes in net assets or fund balances (attach explanation) . Increase in value of securities	20		5,200
	21 Net assets or fund balances at end of year (combine lines 18, 19, and 20)	21		391,400

For Paperwork Reduction Act Notice, see page 1 of the separate instruc   (HTA)   Form 990 (1998)

Appendix 27–2

FORM 990 (continued)

Form 990 (1998)   Campaign to Clean Up America   44-4444444   Page 2

Part II   **Statement of Functional Expenses**

All organizations must complete column (A). Columns (B), (C), and (D) are required for section 501(c)(3) and (4) organizations and section 4947(a)(1) nonexempt charitable trusts but optional for others. (See Specific Instructions on page 17.)

Do not include amounts reported on line 6b, 8b, 9b, 10b, or 16 of Part I.		(A) Total	(B) Program services	(C) Management and general	(D) Fundraising
22 Grants and allocations (attach schedule) (cash $_____ noncash $_____)	22	0			
23 Specific assistance to individuals (attach schedule) . .	23	0			
24 Benefits paid to or for members (attach schedule) . .	24	0			
25 Compensation of officers, directors, etc.	25	50,000	30,000	15,000	5,000
26 Other salaries and wages	26	270,000	205,000	50,000	15,000
27 Pension plan contributions	27	0			
28 Other employee benefits	28	25,000	18,000	5,000	2,000
29 Payroll taxes	29	25,000	17,000	5,000	3,000
30 Professional fundraising fees	30	20,000			20,000
31 Accounting fees	31	10,000		10,000	
32 Legal fees	32	10,000		10,000	
33 Supplies	33	15,000	12,000	2,000	1,000
34 Telephone	34	18,000	12,000	4,000	2,000
35 Postage and shipping	35	0			
36 Occupancy	36	60,000	43,000	14,000	3,000
37 Equipment rental and maintenance	37	10,000	10,000		
38 Printing and publications	38	62,000	52,000	2,000	8,000
39 Travel	39	25,000	16,000	3,000	6,000
40 Conferences, conventions, and meetings	40	7,000	6,000	1,000	
41 Interest	41	0			
42 Depreciation, depletion, etc. (attach schedule)	42	26,000	24,700	800	500
43 Other expenses (itemize): a _____	43a	0			
b Advertising	43b	50,000	29,000	3,000	18,000
c Dues/library	43c	5,000	2,000	3,000	
d Outside consultants	43d	18,000	16,000	2,000	
e Miscellaneous	43e	5,000	4,000	1,000	
f	43f	0			
44 Total functional expenses (add lines 22 through 43) Organizations completing columns (B) - (D), carry these totals to lines 13 - 15	44	711,000	496,700	130,800	83,500

Reporting of Joint Costs.   Did you report in column (B) (Program services) any joint costs from a combined educational campaign and fundraising solicitation? . . . . [X] Yes   [ ] No

If "Yes," enter (i) the aggregate amount of these joint costs $31,500 ; (ii) the amount allocated to Program services   20,500

(iii) the amount allocated to Management and general _____ ; (iv) the amount allocated to Fundraising   11,000

Part III   **Statement of Program Service Accomplishments**   (See Specific Instructions on page 20.)

What is the organization's primary exempt purpose?   Charitable - to promote civic betterment

All organizations must describe their exempt purpose achievements in a clear and concise manner. State the number of clients served, publications issued, etc. Discuss achievements that are not measurable. (Section 501(c)(3) and (4) organizations and 4947(a)(1) nonexempt charitable trusts must also enter the amount of grants and allocations to others.)

Program Service Expenses (Required for 501(c)(3) and (4) orgs., and 4947(a)(1) trusts; but optional for others.)

	Program Service Expenses
a VOLUNTEER TEAMS: To prevent litter and organize pick-up teams, the campaign holds community meetings to recruit volunteers. Teams are provided equipment, including rakes, shovels, gloves, trash bags and safety signs with which to clean up their communities. Over 300 pesons volunteered this year. (Grants and allocations $)	261,900
b PUBLIC EDUCATION: Literature describing Campaign purposes to rid America of litter and clean up our cities, towns and countrysides is prepared and distributed. Mailings, newspaper and magazine advertisements and pamphlet packages are used. (Grants and allocations $)	146,600
c PROGRAMS AND SEMINARS: The Campaign sponsors educational meetings to bring together government officials, businesses and citizens to discuss new methods of trash collections, recycling and litter reduction. Over 2000 persons participated in programs this year. (Grants and allocations $)	78,200
d LEGISLATIVE ACTIVITY: The Campaign promotes the passage of legislation to reduce litter, including a recent bottle ordinance to require use of returnable bottles. (Grants and allocations $)	10,000
e Other program services (attach schedule) . . . . (Grants and allocations $)	
f Total of Program Service Expenses (should equal line 44, column (B), Program services)	496,700

Appendix 27–2

FORM 990 (*continued*)

| Form 990 (1998) | Campaign to Clean Up America | 44-4444444 | Page 3 |

Part IV Balance Sheets (See Specific Instructions on page 20.)

Note: Where required, attached schedules and amounts within the description column should be for end-of-year amounts only.			(A) Beginning of year		(B) End of year
Assets					
45	Cash - non-interest-bearing			**45**	
46	Savings and temporary cash investments		12,000	**46**	29,000
47a	Accounts receivable	**47a** 2,000			
b	Less: allowance for doubtful accounts	**47b**		**47c**	2,000
48a	Pledges receivable	**48a**			
b	Less: allowance for doubtful accounts	**48b**		**48c**	0
49	Grants receivable			**49**	12,000
50	Receivables from officers, directors, trustees, and key employees (attach schedule)			**50**	
51a	Other notes and loans receivable (attach schedule)	**51a**			
b	Less: allowance for doubtful accounts	**51b**		**51c**	0
52	Inventories for sale or use			**52**	
53	Prepaid expenses and deferred charges			**53**	
54	Investments - securities (attach schedule)		19,000	**54**	255,400
55a	Investments - land, buildings, and equipment: basis	**55a**			
b	Less: accumulated depreciation (attach schedule)	**55b**		**55c**	0
56	Investments - other (attach schedule)		0	**56**	0
57a	Land, buildings, and equipment: basis	**57a** 152,000			
b	Less: accumulated depreciation (attach schedule)	**57b** 27,000	18,000	**57c**	125,000
58	Other assets (describe _____)		0	**58**	0
59	Total assets (add lines 45 through 58) (must equal line 74)		49,000	**59**	423,400
Liabilities					
60	Accounts payable and accrued expenses		5,200	**60**	14,000
61	Grants payable			**61**	
62	Deferred revenue			**62**	18,000
63	Loans from officers, directors, trustees, and key employees (attach schedule)			**63**	
64a	Tax-exempt bond liabilities (attach schedule)			**64a**	
b	Mortgages and other notes payable (attach schedule)			**64b**	
65	Other liabilities (describe _____)		0	**65**	0
66	Total liabilities (add lines 60 through 65)		5,200	**66**	32,000
Net Assets or Fund Balances					
Organizations that follow SFAS 117, check here [X] and complete lines 67 through 69 and lines 73 and 74.					
67	Unrestricted		25,800	**67**	261,200
68	Temporarily restricted			**68**	
69	Permanently restricted		18,000	**69**	130,200
Organizations that do not follow SFAS 117, check here [ ] and complete lines 70 through 74.					
70	Capital stock, trust principal, or current funds			**70**	
71	Paid-in or capital surplus, or land, bldg., and equipment fund			**71**	
72	Retained earnings, accumulated income, endowment, or other funds			**72**	
73	Total net assets or fund balances (add lines 67 through 69 OR lines 70 through 72; column (A) must equal line 19 and column (B) must equal line 21)		43,800	**73**	391,400
74	Total liabilities and net assets/fund balances (add lines 66 and 73)		49,000	**74**	423,400

Form 990 is available for public inspection and, for some people, serves as the primary or sole source of information about a particular organization. How the public perceives an organization in such cases may be determined by the information presented on its return. Therefore, please make sure the return is complete and accurate and fully describes, in Part III, the organization's programs and accomplishments.

Appendix 27–2

FORM 990 (*continued*)

Form 990 (1998)	Campaign to Clean Up America	44-4444444	Page 4

Part IV-A Reconciliation of Revenue per Audited Financial Statements with Revenue per Return

a	Total revenue, gains, and other support per audited financial statements	**a**	1,058,600
b	Amounts included on line a but not on line 12, Form 990:		
(1)	Net unrealized gains on investments	5,200	
(2)	Donated services and use of facilities		
(3)	Recoveries of prior year grants		
(4)	Other (specify):		
	Add amounts on lines (1) thru (4)	**b**	5,200
c	Line a minus line b	**c**	1,053,400
d	Amounts included on line 12, Form 990 but not on line a:		
(1)	Investment expenses not included on line 6b, Form 990		
(2)	Other (specify):		
	Add amounts on lines (1) and (2)	**d**	0
e	Total revenue per line 12, Form 990 (line c plus line d)	**e**	1,053,400

Part IV-B Reconciliation of Expenses per Audited Financial Statements with Expenses per Return

a	Total expense and losses per audited financial statements	**a**	711,000
b	Amounts included on line a but not on line 17, Form 990:		
(1)	Donated services and use of facilities		
(2)	Prior year adjustments reported on line 20, Form 990		
(3)	Losses reported on line 20, Form 990		
(4)	Other (specify):		
	Add amounts on lines (1) thru (4)	**b**	0
c	Line a minus line b	**c**	711,000
d	Amounts included on line 17, Form 990 but not on line a:		
(1)	Investment expenses not included on line 6b, Form 990		
(2)	Other (specify):		
	Add amounts on lines (1) and (2)	**d**	0
e	Total expenses per line 17, Form 990 (line c plus line d)	**e**	711,000

Part V List of Officers, Directors, Trustees, and Key Employees (List each one even if not compensated; see Specific Instructions on page 22.)

(A) Name and address	(B) Title and average hours per week devoted to position	(C) Compensation (if not paid, enter -0-)	(D) Contributions to employee benefit plans & deferred compensation	(E) Expense account and other allowances
John J. Environmentalist	President Part-time	None	None	None
Jane D. Environmentalist	Secretary/Treas. Part-time	None	None	None
James F. Friend	Vice-President Part-time	None	None	None
Samantha Engineer	Board Member Part-time	None	None	None
Andrew Organized	Executive Director +40 hrs week	50,000	5,000	None
All persons listed may be contacted at: 1111 Any Street, Hometown Texas 77777				

75 Did any officer, director, trustee, or key employee receive aggregate compensation of more than $100,000 from your organization and all related organizations, of which more than $10,000 was provided by the related organizations? . . . . ☐ Yes ☒ No
If "Yes," attach schedule - see Specific Instructions on page 22.

FORM 990 (*continued*)

Form 990 (1998)	Campaign to Clean Up America	44-4444444	Page 5

Part VI   Other Information (See Specific Instructions on pages 21.)

			Yes or No
76 Did the organization engage in any activity not previously reported to the Internal Revenue Service?		**76**	No
If "Yes," attach a detailed description of each activity.			
77 Were any changes made in the organizing or governing documents, but not reported to the IRS?		**77**	No
If "Yes," attach a conformed copy of the changes.			
78a Did the organization have unrelated business gross income of $1,000 or more during the year covered			
by this return?		**78a**	Yes
b If "Yes," has it filed a tax return on Form 990-T for this year?		**78b**	Yes
79 Was there a liquidation, dissolution, termination, or substantial contraction during the year? If "Yes,"			
attach a statement		**79**	No
80a Is the organization related (other than by association with a statewide or nationwide organization)			
through common membership, governing bodies, trustees, officers, etc., to any other exempt or			
nonexempt organization?		**80a**	No
b If "Yes," enter the name of the organization			
.... and check whether it is ☐ exempt OR ☐ nonexempt.			
81a Enter the amount of political expenditures, direct or indirect, as described			
in the instructions for line 81	**81a** None		
b Did the organization file Form 1120-POL for this year?		**81b**	N/A
82a Did the organization receive donated services or the use of materials, equipment, or facilities at			
no charge or at substantially less than fair rental value?		**82a**	Yes
b If "Yes," you may indicate the value of these items here. Do not include this amount as revenue			
in Part I or as an expense in Part II. (See instructions for reporting in Part III.)	**82b** Not valued		
83a Did the organization comply with the public inspection requirements for returns and exemption applications?		**83a**	Yes
b Did the organization comply with the disclosure requirements relating to quid pro quo contributions?		**83b**	Yes
84a Did the organization solicit any contributions or gifts that were not tax deductible?		**84a**	No
b If "Yes," did the organization include with every solicitation an express statement that such			
contributions or gifts were not tax deductible?		**84b**	N/A
85 Section 501(c)(4), (5), or (6) organizations. - (a) Were substantially all dues nondeductible by members?		**85a**	N/A
b Did the organization make only in-house lobbying expenditures of $2,000 or less?		**85b**	N/A
If "Yes" to either 85a or 85b, do not complete 85c through 85h below unless the organization			
received a waiver for proxy tax owed for the prior year.			
c Dues, assessments, and similar amounts from members	**85c** N/A		
d Section 162(e) lobbying and political expenditures	**85d** N/A		
e Aggregate nondeductible amount of section 6033(e)(1)(A) dues notices	**85e** N/A		
f Taxable amount of lobbying and political expenditures (line 85d less 85e)	**85f** N/A		
g Does the organization elect to pay the section 6033(e) tax on the amount in 85f?		**85g**	N/A
h If section 6033(e)(1)(A) dues notices were sent, does the organization agree to add the amount			
in 85f to its reasonable estimate of dues allocable to nondeductible lobbying and political			
expenditures for the following tax year?		**85h**	N/A
86 Section 501(c)(7) organizations. - Enter: (a) Initiation fees and capital contributions			
included on line 12	**86a** N/A		
b Gross receipts, included on line 12, for public use of club facilities	**86b** N/A		
87 Section 501(c)(12) organizations. - Enter: a Gross income from members or shareholders	**87a** N/A		
b Gross income from other sources. (Do not net amounts due or paid to other			
sources against amounts due or received from them.)	**87b** N/A		
88 At any time during the year, did the organization own a 50% or greater interest in a taxable			
corporation or partnership? If "Yes," complete Part IX		**88**	No
89a 501(c)(3) organizations - Enter: Amount of tax paid during the year under:			
section 4911 None ; section 4912 None ; section 4955 None			
b 501(c)(3) and 501(c)(4) organizations. - Did the organization engage in any section 4958 excess benefit			
transaction during the year? If "Yes," attach a statement explaining each transaction		**89**	No
c Enter: Amount of tax imposed on the organization managers or disqualified persons during the			
year under section 4912, 4955 and 4958.		None	
d Enter: Amount of tax in 89c, above, reimbursed by the organization		None	
90a List the states with which a copy of this return is filed California and New York			
b Number of employees employed in the pay period that includes March 12, 1998 (See instructions.)		**90b**	10
91 The books are in care of Joan Controller	Telephone no.	(444) 444-4444	
Located at 1111 Any Street, Hometown, Texas	ZIP + 4	77777-1111	
92 Section 4947(a)(1) nonexempt charitable trusts filing Form 990 in lieu of Form 1041-- Check here		☐	
enter the amount of tax-exempt interest received or accrued during the tax year	**92**		

FORM 990 (*continued*)

Form 990 (1998)   Campaign to Clean Up America   44-4444444   Page 6

Part VII   Analysis of Income-Producing Activities   (See Specific Instructions on pages 27.)

Enter gross amounts unless otherwise indicated.	Unrelated business income		Excluded by section 512, 513, or 514		(E) Related or exempt function income
	(A) Business code	(B) Amount	(C) Exclusion code	(D) Amount	
93 Program service revenue:					
a Seminars					23,900
b Publication sales					13,800
c					
d					
e					
f Medicare/Medicaid payments.					
g Fees and contracts from government agencies . . .					
94 Membership dues and assessments					
95 Interest on savings and temporary cash investments . .			14	5,000	
96 Dividends and interest from securities			14	4,000	
97 Net rental income (loss) from real estate:					
a debt-financed property					
b not debt-financed property					
98 Net rental income or (loss) from personal property	900002	2,000			
99 Other investment income					
100 Gain or (loss) from sales of assets other than inventory					
101 Net income or (loss) from special events					
102 Gross profit or (loss) from sales of inventory					30,000
103 Other revenue					
b					
c					
d					
e					
104 Subtotal (add cols. (B), (D), and (E)) . . .		2,000		9,000	67,700
105 TOTAL (add line 104, columns (B), (D), and (E))					78,700

Note: (Line 105 plus line 1d, Part I, should equal the amount on line 12, Part I.)

Part VIII   Relationship of Activities to the Accomplishment of Exempt Purposes   (See Specific Instructions on page 28.)

Line No.	Explain how each activity for which income is reported in column (E) of Part VII contributed importantly to the accomplishment of the organization's exempt purposes (other than by providing funds for such purposes).
93a	Community meetings were held in Texas, California, and New York. An average of of 80 people attended one-day meetings where educational information was presented.
93b	Pamphlets on recycling, litter campaign organizational procedures, and volunteer recruitment skills are sold for $5.00 each.
102	The Campaign sells garbage bags bearing its logo and slogan "CLEAN UP AMERICA". Bags are sold in 50 count boxes for $5.00 each.

Part IX   Information Regarding Taxable Subsidiaries   (Complete this Part if the "Yes" box on line 88 is checked.)

Name, address, and employer identification number of corporation or partnership	Percentage of ownership interest	Nature of business activities	Total income	End-of-year assets
Not Applicable				

Please Sign Here	Under penalties of perjury, I declare that I have examined this return, including accompanying schedules and statements, and to the best of my knowledge and belief, it is true, correct, and complete. Declaration of preparer (other than officer) is based on all information of which preparer has any knowledge. (See General Instruction U, on page 12.)		
	Jane D. Environmentalist		
	Signature of officer Date	Type or print name	Title
Paid Preparer's Use Only	Preparer's signature *Accountant*	Date 5-10-xx Check if self- X employed	Preparer's SSN 400-00-0000
	Firm's name (or yours) and address A Qualified CPA Firm 1001 Main Street Hometown Texas	EIN 45-5555555	Phone (444) 422-2222
		ZIP + 4	44444-4222

Appendix 27–3

SCHEDULE A

SCHEDULE A **(Form 990)**	**Organization Exempt Under Section 501(c)(3)** (Except Private Foundation), and Section 501(e), 501(f), 501(k), 501(n), or Section 4947(a)(1) Nonexempt Charitable Trust	OMB No. 1545-0047
Department of the Treasury Internal Revenue Service	Supplementary Information See separate instructions Must be completed by the above organizations and attached to their Form 990 or 990-EZ.	**1998**

Name of the organization	Employer identification number
Campaign to Clean Up America	44-4444444

Part I Compensation of the Five Highest Paid Employees Other Than Officers, Directors, and Trustees
(See instructions on page 1. List each one. If there are none, enter "None.")

(a) Name and address of each employee paid more than $50,000	(b) Title and average hours per week devoted to position	(c) Compensation	(d) Contributions to employee benefit plans & deferred compensation	(e) Expense account and other allowances
None				

Total number of other employees paid over $50,000 . . . . None

Part II Compensation of the Five Highest Paid Independent Contractors for Professional Services
(See instructions on page 1. List each one (whether individuals or firms.) If there are none, enter "None.")

(a) Name and address of each independent contractor paid more than $50,000	(b) Type of service	(c) Compensation
None		

Total number of others receiving over $50,000 for professional services . . None

For Paperwork Reduction Act Notice, see page 1 of the Instructions to Form 990 and Form 990-EZ.   (HTA)   Schedule A (Form 990) 1998

Appendix 27–3

SCHEDULE A (*continued*)

Part III   Statements About Activities | | **Yes** | **No**

		Yes	No
1 During the year, has the organization attempted to influence national, state, or local legislation, including any attempt to influence public opinion on a legislative matter or referendum?	1	X	
If "Yes," enter the total expenses paid or incurred in connection with the lobbying activities. 2,000			
Organizations that made an election under section 501(h) by filing Form 5768 must complete Part VI-A. Other organizations checking "Yes," must complete Part VI-B AND attach a statement giving a detailed description of the lobbying activities.			
2 During the year, has the organization, either directly or indirectly, engaged in any of the following acts with any of its trustees, directors, officers, creators, key employees, or members of their families, or with any taxable organization with which any such person is affiliated as an officer, director, trustee, majority owner, or principal beneficiary:			
a Sale, exchange, or leasing of property?	2a		X
b Lending of money or other extension of credit?	2b		X
c Furnishing of goods, services, or facilities?	2c		X
d Payment of compensation (or payment or reimbursement of expenses if more than $1,000)? . . . . See Part V Form 990	2d	X	
e Transfer of any part of its income or assets?	2e		X
If the answer to any question is "Yes, " attach a detailed statement explaining the transactions.			
3 Does the organization make grants for scholarships, fellowships, student loans, etc.?	3		X
4a Do you have a section 403(b) annuity plan for your employees?	4a		X
b Attach a statement to explain how the organization determines that individuals or organizations receiving grants or loans from it in furtherance of its charitable programs qualify to receive payments. (See instructions on page 2.)			

Part IV   Reason for Non-Private Foundation Status   (See instructions on pages 2 through 4.)

The organization is not a private foundation because it is (please check only ONE applicable box):

5 ☐ A church, convention of churches, or association of churches. Section 170(b)(1)(A)(i).

6 ☐ A school. Section 170(b)(1)(A)(ii). (Also complete Part V, page 4.)

7 ☐ A hospital or a cooperative hospital service organization. Section 170(b)(1)(A)(iii).

8 ☐ A Federal, state, or local government or governmental unit. Section 170(b)(1)(A)(v).

9 ☐ A medical research organization operated in conjunction with a hospital. Section 170(b)(1)(A)(iii). Enter the hospital's name, city, and state ....

10 ☐ An organization operated for the benefit of a college or university owned or operated by a governmental unit. Section 170(b)(1)(A)(iv). (Also complete the Support Schedule in Part IV-A.)

11a ☒ An organization that normally receives a substantial part of its support from a governmental unit or from the general public. Section 170(b)(1)(A)(vi). (Also complete the Support Schedule in Part IV-A.)

11b ☐ A community trust. Section 170(b)(1)(A)(vi). (Also complete the Support Schedule below.)

12 ☐ An organization that normally receives: (1) more than 33 1/3% of its support from contributions, membership fees, and gross receipts from activities related to its charitable, etc., functions- subject to certain exceptions, and (2) no more than 33 1/3% of its support from gross investment income and unrelated business taxable income (less section 511 tax) from businesses acquired by the organization after June 30, 1975. See section 509(a)(2). (Also complete the Support Schedule in Part IV-A.)

13 ☐ An organization that is not controlled by any disqualified persons (other than foundation managers) and supports organizations described in: (1) lines 5 through 12 above; or (2) section 501(c)(4), (5), or (6), if they meet the test of section 509(a)(2). (See section 509(a)(3).)

Provide the following information about the supported organizations. (See instructions on page 4.)

(a) Name(s) of supported organization(s)	(b) Line number from above

14 ☐ An organization organized and operated to test for public safety. Section 509(a)(4). (See instructions on page 4.)

Appendix 27–3

SCHEDULE A (*continued*)

Schedule A (Form 990) 1998	Campaign to Clean Up America		44-4444444		Page 3

Part IV-A Support Schedule (Complete only if you checked a box on line 10, 11, or 12 above.) Use cash method of accounting.

NOTE: You may use the worksheet in the instructions for converting from the accrual to the cash method of accounting.

Calendar year (or fiscal year beginning in)	(a) 1997	(b) 1996	(c) 1995	(d) 1994	(e) Total
15 Gifts, grants, and contributions received. (Do not include unusual grants. See line 28.)	260,000	Organization not in existence			260,000
16 Membership fees received					0
17 Gross receipts from admissions, merchandise sold or services performed, or furnishing of facilities in any activity that is not a business unrelated to the organization's charitable, etc., purpose					0
18 Gross income from interest, dividends, amounts received from payments on securities loans (section 512(a)(5)), rents, royalties, and unrelated business taxable income (less section 511 taxes) from businesses acquired by the organization after June 30, 1975	10,000				10,000
19 Net income from unrelated business activities not included in line 18					0
20 Tax revenues levied for the organization's benefit and either paid to it or expended on its behalf					0
21 The value of services or facilities furnished to the organization by a governmental unit without charge. Do not include the value of services or facilities generally furnished to the public without charge					0
22 Other income. Attach a schedule. Do not include gain or (loss) from sale of capital assets					0
23 Total of lines 15 through 22	270,000	0	0	0	270,000
24 Line 23 minus line 17	270,000	0	0	0	270,000
25 Enter 1% of line 23	2,700	0	0	0	

26 Organizations described in lines 10 or 11: **a** Enter 2% of amount in column (e), line 24	**26a**	5,400
b Attach a list (which is not open to public inspection) showing the name of and amount contributed by each person (other than a governmental unit or publicly supported organization) whose total gifts for 1994 through 1997 exceeded the amount shown in line 26a. Enter the sum of all these excess amounts	**26b**	194,600
c Total support for section 509(a)(1) test: Enter line 24, column (e)	**26c**	270,000
d Add: Amounts from column (e) for lines: 18 10,000 19 0 22 0 26b 194,600	**26d**	204,600
e Public support (line 26c minus line 26d total)	**26e**	65,400
f Public support percentage (line 26e (numerator) divided by line 26c (denominator))	**26f**	24.22%

27 Organizations described on line 12:   **a** For amounts included on lines 15, 16, and 17, that were received from a "disqualified person," attach a list to show the name of, and total amounts received in each year from, each "disqualified person." Enter the sum of such amounts for each year:

     (1997) ....   (1996) ....   (1995) ....   (1994) ....

b For any amount included in line 17 that was received from a nondisqualified person, attach a list to show the name of, and amount received for each year, that was more than the larger of (1) the amount on line 25 for the year or (2) $5,000. (Include in the list organizations described in lines 5 through 11, as well as individuals.) After computing the difference between the amount received and the larger amount described in (1) or (2), enter the sum of all these differences (the excess amounts) for each year:

     (1997) ....   (1996) ....   (1995) ....   (1994) ....

c Add: Amounts from column (e) for lines: 15 0 16 0 17 0 20 0 21 0	**27c**	0
d Add: Line 27a total 0 and line 27b total 0	**27d**	0
e Public support (line 27c minus line 27d total)	**27e**	0
f Total support for section 509(a)(2) test: Enter amount on line 23, column (e) **27f** 0		
g Public support percentage (line 27e (numerator) divided by line 27f (denominator))	**27g**	0.00%
h Investment income percentage (line 18, column (e) (numerator) divided by line 27f (denominator))	**27h**	0.00%

28 Unusual Grants: For an organization described in line 10, 11, or 12, that received any unusual grants during 1994 through 1997, attach a list (which is not open to public inspection) for each year showing the name of the contributor, the date and amount of the grant, and a brief description of the nature of the grant. Do not include these grants in line 15. (See instructions on page 4.)

Appendix 27–3

SCHEDULE A (*continued*)

Part V   **Private School Questionnaire**   (See instructions on page 4.)

(To be completed ONLY by schools that checked the box on line 6 in Part IV)   Not Applicable

		Yes	No
29	Does the organization have a racially nondiscriminatory policy toward students by statement in its charter, bylaws, other governing instrument, or in a resolution of its governing body? **29**		
30	Does the organization include a statement of its racially nondiscriminatory policy toward students in all its brochures, catalogues, and other written communications with the public dealing with student admissions, programs, and scholarships? **30**		
31	Has the organization publicized its racially nondiscriminatory policy through newspaper or broadcast media during the period of solicitation for students, or during the registration period if it has no solicitation program, in a way that makes the policy known to all parts of the general community it serves? **31**		
	If "Yes," please describe; if "No," please explain. (If you need more space, attach a separate statement.)		
32	Does the organization maintain the following:		
a	Records indicating the racial composition of the student body, faculty, and administrative staff? **32a**		
b	Records documenting that scholarships and other financial assistance are awarded on a racially nondiscriminatory basis? **32b**		
c	Copies of all catalogues, brochures, announcements, and other written communications to the public dealing with student admissions, programs, and scholarships? **32c**		
d	Copies of all material used by the organization or on its behalf to solicit contributions? **32d**		
	If you answered "No" to any of the above, please explain. (If you need more space, attach a separate statement.)		
33	Does the organization discriminate by race in any way with respect to:		
a	Students' rights or privileges? **33a**		
b	Admissions policies? **33b**		
c	Employment of faculty or administrative staff? **33c**		
d	Scholarships or other financial assistance? **33d**		
e	Educational policies? **33e**		
f	Use of facilities? **33f**		
g	Athletic programs? **33g**		
h	Other extracurricular activities? **33h**		
	If you answered "Yes" to any of the above, please explain. (If you need more space, attach a statement.)		
34a	Does the organization receive any financial aid or assistance from a governmental agency? **34a**		
b	Has the organization's right to such aid ever been revoked or suspended? **34b**		
	If you answered "Yes" to either 34a or b, please explain using an attached statement.		
35	Does the organization certify that it has complied with the applicable requirements of sections 4.01 through 4.05 of Rev. Proc. 75-50, 1975-2 C.B. 587, covering racial nondiscrimination? If "No," attach an explanation **35**		

Appendix 27–3

SCHEDULE A (*continued*)

Schedule A (Form 990) 1998   Campaign to Clean Up America   44-4444444   Page 5

Part VI-A   Lobbying Expenditures by Electing Public Charities   (See instructions on page 6.)

(To be completed ONLY by an eligible organization that filed Form 5768)

Check here   **a** ☐   If the organization belongs to an affiliated group.

Check here   **b** ☐   If you checked "a" and "limited control" provisions apply.

Limits on Lobbying Expenditures (The term "expenditures" means amounts paid or incurred)		**(a)** Affiliated group totals	**(b)** To be completed for ALL organizations
36 Total lobbying expenditures to influence public opinion (grassroots lobbying)	36		
37 Total lobbying expenditures to influence a legislative body (direct lobbying)	37		2,000
38 Total lobbying expenditures (add lines 36 and 37)	38	0	2,000
39 Other exempt purpose expenditures	39		709,000
40 Total exempt purpose expenditures (add lines 38 and 39)	40	0	711,000
41 Lobbying nontaxable amount. Enter the amount from the following table -			
If the amount on line 40 is - **The lobbying nontaxable amount is -**			
Not over $500,000 . . . . 20% of the amount on line 40			
Over $500,000 but not over $1,000,000 . . . . . $100,000 plus 15% of the excess over $500,000			
Over $1,000,000 but not over $1,500,000 . . . . $175,000 plus 10% of the excess over $1,000,000	41	0	131,650
Over $1,500,000 but not over $17,000,000 . . . . $225,000 plus 5% of the excess over $1,500,000			
Over $17,000,000 . . . . $1,000,000			
42 Grassroots nontaxable amount (enter 25% of line 41)	42	0	32,913
43 Subtract line 42 from line 36. Enter -0- if line 42 is more than line 36	43	0	0
44 Subtract line 41 from line 38. Enter -0- if line 41 is more than line 38	44	0	0

Caution: If there is an amount on either line 43 or line 44, file Form 4720.

4 - Year Averaging Period Under Section 501(h)

(Some organizations that made a section 501(h) election do not have to complete all of the five columns below.
See the instructions for lines 45 through 50 on page 7.)

Calendar year (or fiscal year beginning in)	**Lobbying Expenditures During 4-Year Averaging Period**				
	(a) 1998	**(b)** 1997	**(c)** 1996	**(d)** 1995	**(e)** Total
45 Lobbying nontaxable amount	131,650	42,000	not in existence	not in existence	173,650
46 Lobbying ceiling amount (150% of line 45(e))					260,475
47 Total lobbying expenditures	2,000	0			2,000
48 Grassroots nontaxable amount	32,913	10,500			43,413
49 Grassroots ceiling amount (150% of line 48(e))					65,120
50 Grassroots lobbying expenditures	0	0	n/a	n/a	0

Part VI-B   Lobbying Activity by Nonelecting Public Charities

(For reporting by organizations that did not complete Part VI-A) (See instructions on page 8.)   Not Applicable

During the year, did the organization attempt to influence national, state or local legislation, including any attempt to influence public opinion on a legislative matter or referendum, through the use of:	Yes	No	Amount
a Volunteers			
b Paid staff or management (include compensation in expenses reported on lines c through h.			
c Media advertisements			
d Mailings to members, legislators, or the public			
e Publications, or published or broadcast statements			
f Grants to other organizations for lobbying purposes			
g Direct contact with legislators, their staffs, government officials, or a legislative body			
h Rallies, demonstrations, seminars, conventions, speeches, lectures, or any other means			
i Total lobbying expenditures (add lines c through h)			

If "Yes" to any of the above, also attach a statement giving a detailed description of the lobbying activities.

Appendix 27–3

SCHEDULE A (*continued*)

Schedule A (Form 990) 1998   Campaign to Clean Up America   44-4444444   Page 6

Part VII   Information Regarding Transfers To and Transactions and Relationships With Noncharitable Exempt Organizations

51 Did the reporting organization directly or indirectly engage in any of the following with any other organization described in section 501(c) of the Code (other than section 501(c)(3) organizations) or in section 527, relating to political organizations?

				Yes	No
a Transfers from the reporting organization to a noncharitable exempt organization of:					
(i) Cash			**51a(i)**		X
(ii) Other assets			**a(ii)**		X
b Other transactions:					
(i) Sales of assets to a noncharitable exempt organization			**b(i)**		X
(ii) Purchases of assets from a noncharitable exempt organization			**b(ii)**		X
(iii) Rental of facilities or equipment			**b(iii)**		X
(iv) Reimbursement arrangements			**b(iv)**		X
(v) Loans or loan guarantees			**b(v)**		X
(vi) Performance of services or membership or fundraising solicitations			**b(vi)**		X
c Sharing of facilities, equipment, mailing lists, other assets, or paid employees			**c**		X

d If the answer to any of the above is "Yes," complete the following schedule. Column (b) should always show the fair market value of the goods, other assets, or services given by the reporting organization. If the organization received less than fair market value in any transaction or sharing arrangement, show in column (d) the value of the goods, other assets, or services received.

(a) Line no.	(b) Amount involved	(c) Name of noncharitable exempt organization	(d) Description of transfers, transactions, and sharing arrangements
		Not Applicable	

52a Is the organization directly or indirectly affiliated with, or related to, one or more tax-exempt organizations described in section 501(c) of the Code (other than section 501(c)(3)) or in section 527? . . . . ☐ Yes ☒ No

b If "Yes," complete the following schedule.

(a) Name of organization	(b) Type of organization	(c) Description of relationship
	Not Applicable	

Appendix 27–3

SCHEDULE A (*continued*)

Campaign to Clean Up America   **EIN #: 44-4444444**
1998 Form 990

Part I, Line 1 - Contributions, gifts, grants and similar amounts received
  and Schedule A, Part IV-A, line 26b

	Total - 1988	Excess in '97
John & Jane Environmentalist 333 First Street Hometown, Texas 77777	$ 200,000	0
Friendly Corporation 101 Business Tower Hometown, Texas 77777	200,000	0
Environmentalist Fund 111 Any Street Hometown, Texas 77777	160,000	194,600
Waste Disposal Company 290 Allied Tower Chicago, IL 60555	50,000	0
All others, under $5,000 each	364,700	0
Total contributions and grants	$ 974,700	
Excess contributions for public support purposes		$ 194,600

Part I, Line 10 Sales of Inventory

Sale of recycling bags	40,000
Less: Cost of goods sold	-10,000
Gross profit from sales of inventory	$30,000

Attachment to Part I, Lines 1 and 10b
Attachment to Schedule A, Part IV-A

Appendix 27–3

SCHEDULE A (*continued*)

Campaign to Clean Up America   **EIN #: 44-4444444**
1998 Form 990

Part II, Line 42 and Part IV, Line 57b - Depreciation

	Cost	Reserve 6/30/98	Current Provision	Reserve 6/30/99
Office furnishings	12,000	400	800	1,200
Computers	18,000	600	1,300	1,900
Vans	30,000		6,000	6,000
Lawn equipment & tools	92,000		17,900	17,900
	$ 152,000	$ 1,000	$ 26,000	$ 27,000

Part IV, Line 54 - Investments - securities

Short-term government securities	$ 160,000
Readily marketable equity securities	95,400
Total investments	$ 255,400

Schedule A, Part VI-A

The Campaign's executive director, Andrew Organized, contacted state legislators several times during the year to request their support for proposed legislation. Organized maintained a diary of time spent and phone costs incurred. The allocable portion of his salary for the year based upon time expended was $1,700; long distance charges totalled $300.

Attachment to Part II Line 42, Part IV Lines 54 and 57b and Schedule A, Part VI-B

Appendix 27–4

FORM 5578

Form **5578** (Rev. June 1998) Department of the Treasury Internal Revenue Service	**Annual Certification of Racial Nondiscrimination for a Private School Exempt From Federal Income Tax** (For use by organizations that do not file Form 990 or Form 990-EZ)	OMB No. 1545-0213 **For IRS use ONLY**

For the period beginning _____ , and ending _____

1a Name of organization that operates, supervises, and/or controls school(s).	**1b** Employer identification number

Address (no. and street or P. O. box no., if mail is not delivered to street address)	Room/suite	

City, town or post office, state, and ZIP + 4 (If foreign address, list city or town, state or province, and country. Include postal code.)

2a Name of central organization holding group exemption letter covering the school(s). (If same as 1a above, write "Same" and complete 2c.) If the organization in 1a above holds an individual exemption letter, write "Not Applicable."	**2b** Employer identification number

Address (no. and street or P. O. box no., if mail is not delivered to street address)	Room/suite	**2c** Group exemption number (see instructions under Definitions)
City, town or post office, state, and ZIP + 4		

3a Name of school. (If more than one school, write "See Attached," and attach list of the names, complete addresses, including postal codes, and employer identification numbers of the schools). If same as 1a above, write "Same."	**3b** Employer identification number, if any

Address (number and street or P. O. box number, if mail is not delivered to street address)	Room/suite

City, town or post office, state, and ZIP + 4 (If foreign address, list city or town, state or province, and country. Include postal code.)

Under penalties of perjury, I hereby certify that I am authorized to take official action on behalf of the above school(s) and that to the best of my knowledge and belief the school(s) has (have) satisfied the applicable requirements of sections 4.01 through 4.05 of Revenue Procedure 75-50, 1975-2 C.B. 587, for the period covered by this certification.

_____ (Signature)	_____ (Title or print name and title.)	_____ (Date)

For Paperwork Reduction Act Notice, see instructions. (HTA) Form 5578 (Rev. 6-98)

Appendix 27–5

FORM 990-PF

Form **990-PF**	**Return of Private Foundation** or Section 4947(a)(1) Nonexempt Charitable Trust	OMB No. 1545-0052
Department of the Treasury Internal Revenue Service	**Treated as a Private Foundation** Note: The organization may be able to use a copy of this return to satisfy state reporting requirements.	**1998**

For the calendar year 1998, or tax year beginning _____ , and ending _____

Use the IRS label. Otherwise, please print or type.	Name of organization **Environmentalist Fund**				**A**	Employer identification number 77-7777777
	Number and street (or P.O. box number if mail is not delivered to street address) **1111 Any Street**		Room/suite		**B**	Telephone number (see page 9 of the instr.) **(444) 444-4466**
	City or town **Hometown**	State **Texas**	Zip + 4 **77777-7777**		**C**	If exemption application is pending, check here . . . ☐

H Check organization: ☒ Section 501(c)(3) exempt private foundation
☐ Section 4947(a)(1) nonexempt charitable trust ☐ Other taxable private foundation

I Fair market value of all assets at end of year (from Part II, column (c), line 16)
2,281,200

J Accounting method: ☒ Cash ☐ Accrual
☐ Other (specify) _____
(Part I, col. (d) must be on cash basis.)

D 1. Foreign organizations, check here . . . . . . ☐
2. Organizations meeting the 85% test, check . . . ☐
E If private foundation status was terminated under section 507(b)(1)(A), check here . . . . . ☐
F If the foundation is in a 60-month termination under section 507(b)(1)(B), check here . . . . . ☐
G If address changed, check here . . . . ☐

Part I	Analysis of Revenue and Expenses (The total of amounts in columns (b), (c), and (d) may not necessarily equal the amounts in column (a).)	(a) Revenue and expenses per books	(b) Net investment income	(c) Adjusted net income	(d) Disbursements for charitable purposes (cash basis only)
R e v e n u e	1 Contributions, gifts, grants, etc., received	300,000			
	2 Contributions from split-interest trusts . . .				
	3 Interest on savings and temporary cash investments . .	4,000	4,000		
	4 Dividends and interest from securities . .	160,000	160,000		
	5a Gross rents				
	b (Net rental income/loss _____) .				
	6 Net gain or (loss) from sale of assets not on line 10 .	30,000			
	7 Capital gain net income (Part IV, line 2) . . .		50,000		
	8 Net short-term capital gain			0	
	9 Income modifications				
	10a Gross sales less returns				
	b Less: C.O.G.S.				
	c Gross profit or (loss) (attach schedule) .				
	11 Other income (attach schedule)				
	12 Total. Add lines 1 through 11	494,000	214,000	0	
E x p e n s e s	13 Compensation of officers, directors, trustees, etc. . .				
	14 Other employee salaries and wages . . .				
	15 Pension plans, employee benefits . . .				
	16a Legal fees (attach schedule) . . .	5,000	2,500		2,500
	b Accounting fees (attach schedule) .	5,000	2,500		2,500
	c Other professional fees	6,000	6,000		
	17 Interest				
	18 Taxes (attach schedule)	4,000			
	19 Depreciation and depletion . . .				
	20 Occupancy				
	21 Travel, conferences, and meetings .	2,000	500		1,500
	22 Printing and publications	2,800	600		2,200
	23 Other expenses (attach schedule) . .				
	24 Total operating and administrative expenses. Add lines 13 through 23	24,800	12,100	0	8,700
	25 Contributions, gifts, grants paid . .	310,000			310,000
	26 Total expenses and disbursements. Add lines 24 and 25	334,800	12,100	0	318,700
	27 Subtract line 26 from line 12:				
	a Excess of revenue over expenses and disbursements	159,200			
	b Net investment income (if negative, enter -0-)		201,900		
	c Adjusted net income (if negative, enter -0-)			0	

For Paperwork Reduction Act Notice, see the instructions. (HTA) Form 990-PF (1998)

Appendix 27–5

FORM 990-PF (*continued*)

Form 990-PF (1998)	Environmentalist Fund		77-7777777	Page 2

Part II	**Balance Sheets** Attached schedules and amounts in the description column should be for end-of-year amounts only.	Beginning of year (a) Book Value	End of year (b) Book Value	End of year (c) Fair Market Value
	1 Cash - non-interest bearing			
	2 Savings and temporary cash investments	82,000	111,200	111,200
	3 Accounts receivable			
	Less: allowance for doubtful accounts			
	4 Pledges receivable			
	Less: allowance for doubtful accounts			
	5 Grants receivable			
	6 Receivables due from officers, directors, trustees, and other disqualified persons (attach schedule) (see page 14 of the instructions)			
A	**7** Other notes and loans receivable			
s	Less: allowance for doubtful accounts			
s	**8** Inventories for sale or use			
e	**9** Prepaid expenses and deferred charges			
t	**10a** Investments - U.S. and state government obligations .			
s	**b** Investments - corporate stock (attach schedule) . . .	535,555	665,555	2,170,000
	c Investments - corporate bonds (attach schedule) . . .			
	11 Investments - land, buildings, and equipment: basis			
	Less: accumulated depreciation			
	12 Investments - mortgage loans			
	13 Investments - other (attach schedule)			
	14 Land, buildings, and equipment: basis			
	Less: accumulated depreciation			
	15 Other assets (describe)			
	16 Total assets (to be completed by all filers - see page 15 of the instructions)	617,555	776,755	2,281,200
Lia-bili-ties	**17** Accounts payable and accrued expenses			
	18 Grants payable			
	19 Deferred revenue			
	20 Loans from officers, directors, trustees, and other disqualified persons			
	21 Mortgages and other notes payable (attach schedule) .			
	22 Other liabilities (describe)			
	23 Total liabilities (add lines 17 through 22)	0	0	
N e t A s s e t s	**Organizations that follow SFAS 117, check here and complete lines 24 through 26 and lines 30 and 31.**			
	24 Unrestricted			
	25 Temporarily restricted			
	26 Permanently restricted			
	Organizations that do not follow SFAS 117, [X] **check here and complete lines 27 through 31.**			
	27 Capital stock, trust principal, or current funds	617,555	776,755	
	28 Paid-in or capital surplus, or land, bldg., and equipment fund			
	29 Retained earnings, accumulated income, endowment, or other funds			
	30 Total net assets or fund balances (see page 16 of the instructions) . .	617,555	776,755	
	31 Total liabilities and net assets/fund balances (see page 16 of the instructions)	617,555	776,755	

Part III Analysis of Changes in Net Assets or Fund Balances

1	Total net assets or fund balances at beginning of year - Part II, column (a), line 30 . . . . (must agree with end-of-year figure reported on prior year's return)	**1**	617,555
2	Enter amount from Part I, line 27a	**2**	159,200
3	Other increases not included in line 2 (itemize)	**3**	
4	Add lines 1, 2, and 3	**4**	776,755
5	Decreases not included in line 2 (itemize)	**5**	
6	Total net assets or fund balances at end of year (line 4 minus line 5) - Part II, column (b), line 30	**6**	776,755

Appendix 27–5

FORM 990-PF (*continued*)

Form 990-PF (1998) Environmentalist Fund 77-7777777 Page 3

Part IV Capital Gains and Losses for Tax on Investment Income

(a) List and describe the kind(s) of property sold (e.g., real estate, 2-story brick warehouse; or common stock, 200 shs. MLC Co.)	(b) How acquired P - Purchase D - Donation	(c) Date acquired (mo., day, yr.)	(d) Date sold (mo., day, yr.)
1a 100 shares Clean Air Industries	D	December 1, 19xx	July 1, 19xx
b			
c			
d			
e			

	(e) Gross sales price minus expense of sale	(f) Depreciation allowed (or allowable)	(g) Cost or other basis	(h) Gain or (loss) (e) plus (f) minus (g)
a	50,000		0	50,000
b				0
c				0
d				0
e				0

Complete only for assets showing gain in column (h) and owned by the foundation on 12/31/69

	(i) F.M.V. as of 12/31/69	(j) Adjusted basis as of 12/31/69	(k) Excess of col. (i) over col. (j), if any	(l) Gains (Col. (h) gain minus col. (k), but not less than -0-) or Losses (from col. (h))
a			0	50,000
b			0	0
c			0	0
d			0	0
e			0	0

2	Capital gain net income or (net capital loss).	If gain, also enter in Part I, line 7 If (loss), enter -0- in Part I, line 7	2	50,000
3	Net short-term capital gain or (loss) as defined in sections 1222(5) and (6): If gain, also enter in Part I, line 8, column (c) (see pages 11 and 16 of the instructions). If (loss), enter -0- in Part I, line 8	3	

Part V Qualification Under Section 4940(e) for Reduced Tax on Net Investment Income

(For optional use by domestic private foundations subject to the section 4940(a) tax on net investment income.)

If section 4940(d)(2) applies, leave this part blank.

Was the organization liable for the section 4942 tax on the distributable amount of any year in the base period? . . . .   Yes No [X in No box]

If "Yes," the organization does not qualify under section 4940(e). Do not complete this part.

1 Enter the appropriate amount in each column for each year; see page 16 of the instructions before making any entries.

(a) Base period years Calendar year (or tax year)	(b) Adjusted qualifying distributions	(c) Net value of noncharitable-use assets	(d) Distribution ratio (col. (b) divided by col. (c))
1997	278,200	1,800,000	0.1546
1996	212,800	1,600,000	0.133
1995	221,800	1,400,000	0.1584
1994	109,200	1,200,000	0.091
1993	90,000	1,000,000	0.09

2	Total of line 1, column (d)	2	0.627
3	Average distribution ratio for the 5-year base period - divide the total on line 2 by 5, or by the number of years the foundation has been in existence if less than 5 years	3	0.1254
4	Enter the net value of noncharitable-use assets for 1998 from Part X, line 5	4	2,019,250
5	Multiply line 4 by line 3	5	253,214
6	Enter 1% of net investment income (1% of Part I, line 27b)	6	2,019
7	Add lines 5 and 6	7	255,233
8	Enter qualifying distributions from Part XII, line 4	8	318,700

If line 8 is equal to or greater than line 7, check the box in Part VI, line 1b, and complete that part using a 1% tax rate. See the Part VI instructions on page 16.

Appendix 27–5

FORM 990-PF *(continued)*

Form 990-PF (1998)	Environmentalist Fund	77-7777777		Page 4

Part VI Excise Tax on Investment Income (Section 4940(a), 4940(b), 4940(e), or 4948 - see page 16)

1a Exempt operating foundations described in section 4940(d)(2), check here and ▢ enter "N/A"			
on line 1. Date of ruling letter: .... *(attach copy of ruling letter if necessary)*			
b Domestic organizations that meet the section 4940(e) requirements in Part V, check here	**1**	2,019	
☒ and enter 1% of Part I, line 27b			
c All other domestic organizations enter 2% of line 27b. Exempt foreign organizations enter 4% of line 27b . . .			
2 Tax under section 511(domestic section 4947(a)(1) trusts and taxable foundations only. Others enter -0-)	**2**		
3 Add lines 1 and 2	**3**	2,019	
4 Subtitle A (income) tax (domestic section 4947(a)(1) trusts and taxable foundations only. Others enter -0-)	**4**		
5 Tax on investment income. Subtract line 4 from line 3. If zero or less, enter -0-	**5**	2,019	
6 Credits/Payments:			
a 1998 estimated tax payments and 1997 overpayment credited to 1998	**6a**	2,400	
b Exempt foreign organizations - tax withheld at source	**6b**		
c Tax paid with application for extension of time to file (Form 2758)	**6c**	0	
d Backup withholding erroneously withheld	**6d**		
7 Total credits and payments. Add lines 6a through 6d	**7**	2,400	
8 Enter any PENALTY for underpayment of estimated tax. Check here if Form 2220 ▢ is attached.	**8**	0	
9 TAX DUE. If the total of lines 5 and 8 is more than line 7, enter AMOUNT OWED	**9**	0	
10 OVERPAYMENT. If line 7 is more than the total of lines 5 and 8, enter the AMOUNT OVERPAID	**10**	381	
11 Enter the amount of line 10 to be: Credited to 1999 estimated tax 381 Refunded	**11**	0	

Part VII-A   Statements Regarding Activities

		Yes	No
1a During the tax year, did the organization attempt to influence any national, state, or local legislation or did it participate or intervene in any political campaign?	**1a**		X
b Did it spend more than $100 during the year (either directly or indirectly) for political purposes (see page 17 of the instructions for definition)?	**1b**		X
If the answer is "Yes" to 1a or 1b, attach a detailed description of the activities and copies of any materials published or distributed by the organization in connection with the activities.			
c Did the organization file Form 1120-POL for this year?	**1c**		X
d Enter the amount (if any) of tax on political expenditures (section 4955) imposed during the year:			
(1) On the organization. _____ **(2)** On organization managers. _____			
e Enter the reimbursement (if any) paid by the organization during the year for political expenditure tax imposed on organization managers. _____			
2 Has the organization engaged in any activities that have not previously been reported to the IRS?	**2**		X
If "Yes," attach a detailed description of the activities.			
3 Has the organization made any changes, not previously reported to the IRS, in its governing instrument, articles of incorporation, or bylaws, or other similar instruments? If "Yes," attach a conformed copy of the changes	**3**		X
4a Did the organization have unrelated business gross income of $1,000 or more during the year?	**4a**		X
b If "Yes," has it filed a tax return on Form 990-T for this year?	**4b**		N/A
5 Was there a liquidation, termination, dissolution, or substantial contraction during the year?	**5**		X
If "Yes," attach the statement required by General Instruction T.			
6 Are the requirements of section 508(e) (relating to sections 4941 through 4945) satisfied either:			
* By language in the governing instrument; or			
* By state legislation that effectively amends the governing instrument so that no mandatory directions that conflict with the state law remain in the governing instrument?	**6**	X	
7 Did the organization have at least $5,000 in assets at any time during the year? If "Yes," complete Part II, column (c), and Part XV	**7**	X	
8a Enter the states to which the foundation reports or with which it is registered (see page 18 of the instructions) Texas			
b If the answer is "Yes" to line 7, has the organization furnished a copy of Form 990-PF to the Attorney General (or designate) of each state as required by General Instruction G? If "No," attach explanation	**8b**	X	
9 Is the organization claiming status as a private operating foundation within the meaning of section 4942(j)(3) or 4942(j)(5) for calendar year 1998 or the taxable year beginning in 1997 (see instructions for Part XIV on page 23)? If "Yes," complete Part XIV	**9**		X
10 Did any persons become substantial contributors during the tax year? If "Yes," attach a schedule listing their names and addresses	**10**		X
11a Did anyone request to see either the organization's annual return or its exemption application (or both)?	**11a**		X
b If "Yes," did the organization comply pursuant to the instructions? (See General Instruction Q.)	**11b**		N/A
12 The books are in care of Mary Goodbooks Telephone no. (444) 444-4555			
Located at 1011 Main Street, Hometown Texas ZIP code 77777-7777			
13 Section 4947(a)(1) nonexempt charitable trusts filing Form 990-PF in lieu of Form 1041. - Check here . . . . ▢ and enter the amount of tax-exempt interest received or accrued during the year	**13**		

FORM 990-PF (*continued*)

Form 990-PF (1998)	Environmentalist Fund	77-7777777		Page 5

Part VII-B Statements Regarding Activities for Which Form 4720 May Be Required

		Yes	No
File Form 4720 if any item is checked in the "Yes" column, unless an exception applies.			

1 Self-dealing (section 4941):

  a During the year did the organization (either directly or indirectly):

    (1) Engage in the sale or exchange, or leasing of property with a disqualified person? . . .   `No`

    (2) Borrow money from, lend money to, or otherwise extend credit to (or accept

      it from) a disqualified person? . . . .   `No`

    (3) Furnish goods, services, or facilities to (or accept them from) a disqualified person? . .   `No`

    (4) Pay compensation to, or pay or reimburse the expenses of, a disqualified person? . . .   `No`

    (5) Transfer any income or assets to a disqualified person (or make any of either

      available for the benefit or use of a disqualified person)? . . . .   `No`

    (6) Agree to pay money or property to a government official? (Exception. Check

      "No" if the organization agreed to make a grant to or to employ the official for a

      period after termination of government service, if terminating within 90 days.) . . . . .   `No`

  b If any answer is "Yes" to 1a(1) - (6), did ANY of the acts fail to qualify under

    the exceptions described in Regulations sections 53.4941(d)-3 or in

    a current notice regarding disaster assistance (see page 18 of the instructions)? . . . . **1b**   N/A

    Organizations relying on a current notice regarding disaster assistance check here . . . . ▸ ☐

  c Did the organization engage in a prior year in any of the acts described in 1a, other than excepted

    acts, that were not corrected before the first day of the tax year beginning in 1998? . . . . . **1c**   X

2 Taxes on failure to distribute income (section 4942) (does not apply for years the organization

    was a private operating foundation defined in section 4942(j)(3) or 4942(j)(5)):

  a At the end of tax year 1998, did the organization have any undistributed income

    (lines 6d and 6e, Part XIII) for tax year(s) beginning before 1998? . . . .   `No`

    If "Yes," list the years ▸ .... , ... , ... , ...

  b Are there any years listed in 2a for which the organization is NOT applying the provisions of section

    4942(a)(2) (relating to incorrect valuation of assets) to the year's undistributed income? (If applying

    section 4942(a)(2) to ALL years listed, answer "No" and attach statement - see page 18 of the instructions) . . . . **2b**   N/A

  c If the provisions of section 4942(a)(2) are being applied to ANY of the years listed in 2a, list the

    years here. ▸ .... , ... , ... , ...

3 Taxes on excess business holdings (section 4943):

  a Did the organization hold more than a 2% direct or indirect interest in any business

    enterprise at any time during the year? . . . .   `No`

  b If "Yes," did it have excess business holdings in 1998 as a result of (1) any purchase by the

    organization or disqualified persons after May 26, 1969; (2) the lapse of the 5-year period (or longer

    period approved by the Commissioner under section 4943(c)(7)) to dispose of holdings acquired by

    gift or bequest; or (3) the lapse of the 10-, 15-, or 20- year first phase holding period? (Use Schedule

    C, Form 4720, to determine if the organization had excess business holdings in 1998.) . . . . **3b**   N/A

4 Taxes on investments that jeopardize charitable purposes (section 4944):

  a Did the organization invest during the year any amount in a manner that would jeopardize its

    charitable purposes? . . . . **4a**   X

  b Did the organization make any investment in a prior year (but after December 31, 1969) that

    could jeopardize its charitable purpose that had not been removed from jeopardy before the first

    day of the tax year beginning in 1998? . . . . **4b**   X

5 Taxes on taxable expenditures (section 4945) and political expenditures (section 4955):

  a During the year did the organization pay or incur any amount to:

    (1) Carry on propaganda, or otherwise attempt to influence legislation (section 4945(e))? . .   `No`

    (2) Influence the outcome of any specific public election (see section 4955); or

      to carry on, directly or indirectly, any voter registration drive? . . . .   `No`

    (3) Provide a grant to an individual for travel, study, or other similar purposes? . . . . . .   `No`

    (4) Provide a grant to an organization other than a charitable, etc., organization

      described in section 509(a)(1), (2), or (3), or section 4940(d)(2)? . . . .   `Yes`

    (5) Provide for any purpose other than religious, charitable, scientific, literary, or

      educational purposes, or for the prevention of cruelty to children or animals? . . . . .   `No`

  b If any answer is "Yes" to 5a(1) - (5), did ANY of the transactions fail to qualify under

    the exceptions described in Regulations section 53.4945 or in a current

    notice regarding disaster assistance (see page 19 of the instructions)? . . . . **5b**   X

    Organizations relying on a current notice regarding disaster assistance check here . . . . ▸ ☐

  c If the answer is "Yes" to question 5a(4), does the organization claim exemption

    from the tax because it maintained expenditure responsibility for the grant? . . . .   `Yes`

    If "Yes," attach the statement required by Regulations section 53.4945-5(d).   Form 4720 filed

Appendix 27–5

FORM 990-PF (*continued*)

Part VIII Information About Officers, Directors, Trustees, Foundation Managers, Highly Paid Employees, and Contractors

1 List all officers, directors, trustees, foundation managers and their compensation (see instructions):

(a) Name and address	(b) Title, and average hours per week devoted to position	(c) Compensation (If not paid, enter -0-)	(d) Contributions to employee benefit plans	(e) Expense account, other allowances
Jane Environmentalist	President Part-time	None	None	None
John J. Environmentalist	Vice-President Part-time	None	None	None
John J. Environmentalist Jr.	Secretary/Treasurer Part-time	None	None	None
All the officers can be contacted at: 1111 Any Street, Hometown, Texas 77777				

2 Compensation of five highest-paid employees (other than those included on line 1 - see page 19 of the instructions). If none, enter "NONE."

(a) Name and address of each employee paid more than $50,000	(b) Title and average hours per week devoted to position	(c) Compensation	(d) Contributions to employee benefit plans	(e) Expense account, other allowances
The Foundation has no employees.				

Total number of other employees paid over $50,000 . . . .   None

3 Five highest-paid independent contractors for professional services - (see page 19 of the instructions). If none, enter "NONE."

(a) Name and address of each person paid more than $50,000	(b) Type of service	(c) Compensation
The Foundation pays no one $50,000 or more.		

Total number of others receiving over $50,000 for professional services . . . .   None

Part IX-A Summary of Direct Charitable Activities

List the foundation's four largest direct charitable activities during the tax year. Include relevant statistical information such as the number of organizations and other beneficiaries served, conferences convened, research papers produced, etc.	Expenses
1 Not Applicable	
2	
3	
4	

Appendix 27–5

FORM 990-PF (continued)

Form 990-PF (1998)   Environmentalist Fund   77-7777777   Page 7

Part IX-B Summary of Program-Related Investments   (see page 20 of the instructions)

Describe any program-related investments made by the foundation during the tax year.	Amount
1 Not Applicable	
2	
3	

Part X Minimum Investment Return   (All domestic foundations must complete this part. Foreign foundations, see page 20 of the instructions.)

1	Fair market value of assets not used (or held for use) directly in carrying out charitable, etc., purposes:	
a	Average monthly fair market value of securities **1a**	1,995,000
b	Average of monthly cash balances **1b**	55,000
c	Fair market value of all other assets (see page 21 of the instructions) **1c**	
d	Total (add lines 1a, b, and c) **1d**	2,050,000
e	Reduction claimed for blockage or other factors reported on lines 1a and 1c (attach detailed explanation) **1e**	
2	Acquisition indebtedness applicable to line 1 assets **2**	
3	Subtract line 2 from line 1d **3**	2,050,000
4	Cash deemed held for charitable activities. Enter 1 1/2% of line 3 (for greater amount, see page 21 of the instructions) **4**	30,750
5	Net value of noncharitable-use assets. Subtract line 4 from line 3. Enter here and on Part V, line 4 **5**	2,019,250
6	Minimum investment return. Enter 5% of line 5 **6**	100,963

Part XI Distributable Amount   (see page 21 of the instructions) (Section 4942(j)(3) and (j)(5) private operating foundations and certain foreign organizations check here ☐ and do not complete this part.)

1	Minimum investment return from Part X, line 6 **1**	100,963
2a	Tax on investment income for 1998 from Part VI, line 5 **2a** 2,019	
b	Income tax for 1998. (This does not include the tax from Part VI.) **2b**	
c	Add lines 2a and 2b **2c**	2,019
3	Distributable amount before adjustments. Subtract line 2c from line 1 **3**	98,944
4a	Recoveries of amounts treated as qualifying distributions **4a**	
b	Income distributions from section 4947(a)(2) trusts **4b**	
c	Add lines 4a and 4b **4c**	0
5	Add lines 3 and 4c **5**	98,944
6	Deduction from distributable amount (see page 22 of the instructions) **6**	
7	Distributable amount as adjusted. Subtract line 6 from line 5. Enter here and on Part XIII, line 1 **7**	98,944

Part XII Qualifying Distributions   (see page 22 of the instructions)

1	Amounts paid (including administrative expenses) to accomplish charitable, etc., purposes:	
a	Expenses, contributions, gifts, etc. - total from Part I, column (d), line 26 **1a**	318,700
b	Program-related investments - total of lines 1-3 of Part IX-B **1b**	0
2	Amounts paid to acquire assets used (or held for use) directly in carrying out charitable, etc., purposes **2**	
3	Amounts set aside for specific charitable projects that satisfy the:	
a	Suitability test (prior IRS approval required) **3a**	
b	Cash distribution test (attach the required schedule) **3b**	
4	Qualifying distributions. Add lines 1a through 3b. Enter here and on Part V, line 8, and Part XIII, line 4 **4**	318,700
5	Organizations that qualify under section 4940(e) for the reduced rate of tax on net investment income. Enter 1% of Part I, line 27b (see page 22 of the instructions) **5**	2,019
6	Adjusted qualifying distributions. Subtract line 5 from line 4 **6**	316,681

NOTE: The amount on line 6 will be used in Part V, column (b), in subsequent years when calculating whether the foundation qualifies for the section 4940(e) reduction of tax in those years.

Appendix 27–5

FORM 990-PF (*continued*)

| Form 990-PF (1998) | Environmentalist Fund | | 77-7777777 | Page 8 |

Part XIII Undistributed Income (see page 22 of the instructions)

		(a) Corpus	(b) Years prior to 1997	(c) 1997	(d) 1998
1	Distributable amount for 1998 from Part XI, line 7				98,944
2	Undistributed income as of the end of 1997:				
a	Enter amount for 1997 only				
b	Total for prior years: 19__, 19__, 19__				
3	Excess distributions carryover, if any, to 1998:				
a	From 1993 10,000				
b	From 1994 9,200				
c	From 1995 102,000				
d	From 1996 146,000				
e	From 1997 163,000				
f	Total of lines 3a through e	430,200			
4	Qualifying distributions for 1998 from Part XII, line 4: $ 318,700				
a	Applied to 1997, but not more than line 2a				
b	Applied to undistributed income of prior years (Election required - see instructions)				
c	Treated as distributions out of corpus (Election required - see instructions)	219,756			
d	Applied to 1998 distributable amount				98,944
e	Remaining amount distributed out of corpus				
5	Excess distributions carryover applied to 1998 (If an amount appears in column (d), the same amount must be shown in column (a).)	0			0
6	**Enter the net total of each column as indicated below:**				
a	Corpus. Add 3f, 4c, and 4e. Subtract line 5	649,956			
b	Prior years' undistributed income. Subtract line 4b from line 2b		0		
c	Enter the amount of prior years' undistributed income for which a notice of deficiency has been issued, or on which the section 4942(a) tax has been previously assessed				
d	Subtract line 6c from line 6b. Taxable amount - see instructions		0		
e	Undistributed income for 1997. Subtract line 4a from line 2a. Taxable amount			0	
f	Undistributed income for 1998. Subtract lines 4d and 5 from line 1. This amount must be distributed in 1999				0
7	Amounts treated as distributions out of corpus to satisfy requirements imposed by section 170(b)(1)(E) or 4942(g)(3)	10,000			
8	Excess distributions carryover from 1993 not applied on line 5 or line 7 (see page 23 of the instructions)	639,956			
9	Excess distributions carryover to 1999 Subtract lines 7 and 8 from line 6a	0			
10	Analysis of line 9:				
a	Excess from 1994 ... 9,200				
b	Excess from 1995. .. 102,000				
c	Excess from 1996 ... 146,000				
d	Excess from 1997 ... 163,000				
e	Excess from 1998 ... 219,756				

Appendix 27–5

FORM 990-PF (*continued*)

Form 990-PF (1998)   Environmentalist Fund   77-7777777   Page 9

Part XIV Private Operating Foundations   (see page 23 of the instructions and Part VII-A, question 9)

1a If the foundation has received a ruling or determination letter that it is a private operating
foundation, and the ruling is effective for 1998, enter the date of the ruling . . . . | Not Applicable

b Check box to indicate whether the organization is a private operating foundation described in section ☐ 4942(j)(3) or ☐ 4942(j)(5)

2a Enter the lesser of the adjusted net	Tax Year	Prior 3 years			
	(a) 1998	(b) 1997	(c) 1996	(d) 1995	(e) Total
income from Part I or the minimum investment return from Part X for each year listed	0				0
b 85% of line 2a	0	0	0	0	0
c Qualifying distributions from Part XII, line 4 for each year listed	0				0
d Amounts included in line 2c not used directly for active conduct of exempt activities					0
e Qualifying distributions made directly for active conduct of exempt activities Subtract line 2d from line 2c	0	0	0	0	0
3 Complete 3a, b, or c for the alternative test relied upon:					
a "Assets" alternative test - enter:					
(1) Value of all assets					0
(2) Value of assets qualifying under section 4942(j)(3)(B)(i)					0
b "Endowment" alternative test - Enter 2/3 of minimum investment return shown in Part X, line 6 for each year listed	0				0
c "Support" alternative test - enter:					
(1) Total support other than gross investment income (interest, dividends, rents, payments on securities loans (section 512(a)(5)), or royalties)					0
(2) Support from general public and 5 or more exempt organizations as provided in section 4942(j)(3)(B)(iii)					0
(3) Largest amount of support from an exempt organization					0
(4) Gross investment income . . .					0

Part XV Supplementary Information (Complete this part only if the organization had $5,000 or more in assets at any time during the year - see page 24 of the instructions.)

1 Information Regarding Foundation Managers:

a List any managers of the foundation who have contributed more than 2% of the total contributions received by the foundation before the close of any tax year (but only if they have contributed more than $5,000). (See section 507(d)(2).)

Jane D. and John J. Environmentalist

b List any managers of the foundation who own 10% or more of the stock of a corporation (or an equally large portion of the ownership of a partnership or other entity) of which the foundation has a 10% or greater interest.

None

2 Information Regarding Contribution, Grant, Gift, Loan, Scholarship, etc., Programs:

Check here if the ☐ organization only makes contributions to preselected charitable organizations and does not accept unsolicited requests for funds. If the organization makes gifts, grants, etc., (see page 24 of the instructions) to individuals or organizations under other conditions, complete items 2a, b, c, and d.

a The name, address, and telephone number of the person to whom applications should be addressed:
Mary Goodbooks, 1011 Main Street, Hometown, Texas 77777-7777

b The form in which applications should be submitted and information and materials they should include:
Grant requests should have up to 6 pages, including mission & budget; also send most recent audit (if any) and Form 990.

c Any submission deadlines:
March 1 and September 1

d Any restrictions or limitations on awards, such as by geographical areas, charitable fields, kinds of institutions, or other factors:
The Foundation supports innovative programs that enhance protection of the environment.

Appendix 27–5

FORM 990-PF (*continued*)

Form 990-PF (1998)	Environmentalist Fund			77-7777777	Page 10

Part XV Supplementary Information (continued)

3   Grants and Contributions Paid During the Year or Approved for Future Payment

Recipient Name and address (home or business)	If recipient is an individual, show any relationship to any foundation manager or substantial contributor	Foundation status of recipient	Purpose of grant or contribution	Amount
a Paid during the year				
Campaign to Clean Up America 1111 Any Street, Hometown Tx 77777		509(a)(1)	General support	160,000
Smart Growth Institute 404 Fourth Street, Houston Tx 70777		509(a)(2)	Support research and dissemination of educational materials regarding livable communities.	100,000
Hometown Public Schools 303 Academic Row Hometown Tx 77333		170(b)(1)(A)(v)	To develop teacher curriculum and support field trips focused on environmental issues.	50,000
Total **3a**				310,000
b Approved for future payment				
Total **3b**				0

Appendix 27–5

FORM 990-PF (*continued*)

Form 990-PF (1998)	Environmentalist Fund		77-7777777		Page 11

Part XVI-A Analysis of Income-Producing Activities

Enter gross amounts unless otherwise indicated.	Unrelated business income		Excluded by sec. 512, 513, or 514		(e) Related or exempt function income
	(a) Business code	(b) Amount	(c) Exclusion code	(d) Amount	
1 Program service revenue:					
a					
b					
c					
d					
e					
f					
g Fees and contracts from government agencies .					
2 Membership dues and assessments					
3 Interest on savings and temporary cash investments			14	4,000	
4 Dividends and interest from securities			14	160,000	
5 Net rental income or (loss) from real estate:					
a Debt-financed property					
b Not debt-financed property					
6 Net rental income or (loss) from personal property					
7 Other investment income					
8 Gain or (loss) from sales of assets other than inventory			18	30,000	
9 Net income or (loss) from special events					
10 Gross profit or (loss) from sales of inventory . .					
11 Other revenue: (a)					
b					
c					
d					
e					
12 Subtotal. Add cols. (b), (d), and (e) .		0		194,000	0
13 Total. Add line 12, columns (b), (d), and (e) 13				194,000	

(See worksheet in line 13 instructions on page 25 to verify calculations.)

Part XVI-B Relationship of Activities to the Accomplishment of Exempt Purposes

Line No.	Explain below how each activity for which income is reported in column (e) of Part XVI-A contributed importantly to the accomplishment of the organization's exempt purposes (other than by providing funds for such purposes). (See instructions.)
	Not Applicable

Appendix 27–5

FORM 990-PF (*continued*)

Form 990-PF (1998)	Environmentalist Fund	77-7777777	Page 12

Part XVII **Information Regarding Transfers To and Transactions and Relationships With Noncharitable Exempt Organizations**

1   Did the organization directly or indirectly engage in any of the following with any other organization described in section 501(c) of the Code (other than section 501(c)(3) organizations) or in section 527, relating to political organizations?

			Yes	No
a	Transfers from the reporting organization to a noncharitable exempt organization of:			
	(1) Cash	1a(1)		X
	(2) Other assets	a(2)		X
b	Other Transactions:			
	(1) Sales of assets to a noncharitable exempt organization	b(1)		X
	(2) Purchases of assets from a noncharitable exempt organization	b(2)		X
	(3) Rental of facilities or equipment	b(3)		X
	(4) Reimbursement arrangements	b(4)		X
	(5) Loans or loan guarantees	b(5)		X
	(6) Performance of services or membership or fundraising solicitations	b(6)		X
c	Sharing of facilities, equipment, mailing lists, other assets, or paid employees	c		X

d   If the answer to any of the above is "Yes," complete the following schedule. Column (b) should always show the fair market value of the goods, other assets, or services given by the reporting organization. If the organization received less than fair market value in any transaction or sharing arrangement, show in column (d) the value of the goods, other assets, or services received.

(a) Line no.	(b) Amount involved	(c) Name of noncharitable exempt organization	(d) Description of transfers, transactions, and sharing arrangements

		Yes	No
2a	Is the organization directly or indirectly affiliated with, or related to, one or more tax-exempt organizations described in section 501(c) of the Code (other than section 501(c)(3)) or in section 527?		X

b   If "Yes," complete the following schedule.

(a) Name of organization	(b) Type of organization	(c) Description of relationship
Not Applicable		

Part XVIII **Public Inspection**   NOTICE NOT REQUIRED after publication of IRC section 6104(d) regulations.

1   Enter the date the notice of availability of the annual return appeared in a newspaper   5/5/xx

2   Enter the name of the newspaper   Daily Newspaper

3   Check here to ☒ indicate that you have attached a copy of the newspaper notice required by the instructions on page 26. (If the notice is not attached, the return will be considered incomplete.)

Under penalties of perjury, I declare that I have examined this return, including accompanying schedules and statements, and to the best of my knowledge and belief, it is true, correct, and complete. Declaration of preparer (other than taxpayer or fiduciary) is based on all information of which preparer has any knowledge.

Please Sign Here

Signature of officer or trustee	Date 5/1/xx	Title President

Paid Preparer's Use Only

Preparer's signature *Accountant*	Date 5/1/xx	Check if self-employed X	Preparer's SSN 400-00-0000
Firm's name (or yours) and address	A Qualified CPA Firm	EIN	45-5555555
	1001 Main Street	Phone	(444) 422-2222
	Hometown TX	ZIP code	77777-4222

Appendix 27–5

FORM 990-PF (*continued*)

Environmentalist Fund   EIN 77-7777777
Attachment to Form 990-PF

Part I, line 1   Contributions Received

Jane D. & John J. Environmentalist	Gift of 1000 shares	$ 300,000
333 First Street	of Clean Air Industries	
Hometown, Texas 77777	NYSE average price	
	on gift date 4/1/xx	

Part I, line 16a   Legal fees

General corporate matters during the year $ 5,000

Part I, Line 16b   Accounting fees

Preparation of Form 990-PF and tax planning consultations
   throughout the year $ 5,000

Part I, line 16c   Other professional fees

Investment management services $ 6,000

Part II, line 10b   Investments - corporate stocks

	Book value	Market value
ABC Securities	$ 100,000	$ 200,000
DEF Incorporated	130,000	200,000
GHI Company	140,000	200,000
JKL Inc.	160,000	200,000
MNO Enterprises	135,555	370,000
Clean Air Industries	nil	1,000,000
Total investment in corporate stocks	$ 665,555	$ 2,170,000

APPENDIX 27–6

Appendix 27–6

FORM 4720

Form **4720**	**Return of Certain Excise Taxes on Charities and Other Persons Under Chapters 41 and 42 of the Internal Revenue Code** (Sections 4911, 4912, 4941, 4942, 4943, 4944, 4945, 4955, and 4958) See separate instructions.	OMB No. 1545-0052 **1998**

Department of the Treasury
Internal Revenue Service

For calendar year 1998 or other tax year beginning .... , and ending ....

Name of foundation or public charity	Employer identification number
Environmentalist Fund	77-7777777

Number, street, and room or suite no. (or P. O. box if mail is not delivered to street address)
1111 Any Street

Check box for type of annual return:
☐ Form 990   ☐ Form 990-EZ

City or town, state, and ZIP code
Hometown , Texas 77777-7777

☒ Form 990-PF   ☐ Form 5227

		Yes or No
A	Is the organization a foreign private foundation within the meaning of section 4948(b)?	No
B	Has corrective action been taken on any taxable event that resulted in Chapter 42 taxes being reported on this form?	Yes

If "Yes," attach a detailed documentation and description of the corrective action taken and, if applicable, enter the fair market value of any property recovered as a result of the correction $ n/a _____ . For any uncorrected acts, or transactions, attach an explanation (see page 3 of the instructions).

Part I   Taxes on Private Foundation or Public Charity (Sections 4911(a), 4912(a), 4942(a), 4943(a), 4944(a)(1), 4945(a)(1), and 4955(a)(1))

1	Tax on undistributed income - Schedule B, line 4	1	0
2	Tax on excess business holdings - Schedule C, line 7	2	0
3	Tax on investments that jeopardize charitable purpose - Schedule D, Part I, column (e)	3	0
4	Tax on taxable expenditures - Schedule E, Part I, column (g)	4	None
5	Tax on political expenditures - Schedule F, Part I, column (e)	5	0
6	Tax on excess lobbying expenditures - Schedule G, line 4	6	0
7	Tax on disqualifying lobbying expenditures - Schedule H, Part I, column (e)	7	0
8	Total (add lines 1-7)	8	0

Part II-A   Taxes on Self-Dealers, Disqualified Persons, Foundation Managers, and Organization Managers
(Sections 4912(b), 4941(a), 4944(a)(2), 4945(a)(2), 4955(a)(2), and 4958(a))

	(a) Name and address of person subject to tax	(b) Taxpayer identification number
a		
b		
c		
d		

	(c) Tax on self-dealing - Schedule A, Part II, col. (d), and Part III, col. (d)	(d) Tax on investments that jeopardize charitable purpose-Schedule D, Part II, col. (d)	(e) Tax on taxable expenditures - Schedule E, Part II, col. (d)	(f) Tax on political expenditures-Sch. F, Part II, col. (d)
a				
b				
c				
d				
Total	0	0	0	0

	(g) Tax on disqualifying lobbying expenditures - Sch. H, Part II, col. (d)	(h) Tax on excess benefit transactions - Schedule I, Part II, col. (d), and Part III, col (d)	(i) Total - Add cols. (c) through (h)
a			0
b			0
c			0
d			0
Total	0	0	0

Part II-B   Summary of Taxes   (See Tax Payments on page 2 of the instructions)

1	Enter the taxes listed in Part II-A, column (i), that apply to self-dealers, disqualified persons, foundation managers, and organization managers who sign this form. If all sign, enter the total amount from Part II-A, column (i)	1	See abatement Request
2	Total tax. Add Part I, line 8, and Part II-B, line 1. (Make check(s) or money order(s) payable to the United States Treasury.)	2	None

For Paperwork Reduction Act Notice, see the instructions.   (HTA)   Form 4720 (1998)

Appendix 27–6

FORM 4720 (*continued*)

SCHEDULE A - Initial Taxes on Self-Dealing (Section 4941)

Part I   Acts of Self-Dealing and Tax Computation

(a) Act number	(b) Date of act	(c) Description of act
1		
2		
3		
4		
5		

(d) Question number from Form 990-PF, Part VII-B, or Form 5227, Part VI-B, applicable to the act	(e) Amount involved in act	(f) Initial tax on self-dealing (5% of col. (e))	(g) Tax on foundation managers (if applicable) (lesser of $10,000 or 2 1/2 % of col. (e))

Part II   Summary of Tax Liability of Self-Dealers and Proration of Payments

(a) Names of self-dealers liable for tax	(b) Act no. from Part I, col. (a)	(c) Tax from Part I, col. (f), or prorated amount	(d) Self-dealer's total tax liability (add amounts in col. (c)) (see page 4 of the instructions)

Part III   Summary of Tax Liability of Foundation Managers and Proration of Payments

(a) Names of foundation managers liable for tax	(b) Act no. from Part I, col. (a)	(c) Tax from Part I, col. (g), or prorated amount	(d) Manager's total tax liability (add amounts in col. (c)) (see page 4 of the instructions)

SCHEDULE B - Initial Tax on Undistributed Income (Section 4942)

1	Undistributed income for years before 1997 (from Form 990-PF for 1998, Part XIII, line 6d)	1	
2	Undistributed income for 1997 (from Form 990-PF for 1998, Part XIII, line 6e)	2	
3	Total undistributed income at end of current tax year beginning in 1998 and subject to tax under section 4942 (add lines 1 and 2)	3	
4	Tax - Enter 15% of line 3 here and on page 1, Part I, line 1	4	

Appendix 27–6

FORM 4720 (*continued*)

SCHEDULE C - Initial Tax on Excess Business Holdings (Section 4943)

Business Holdings and Computation of Tax

If you have taxable excess holdings in more than one business enterprise, attach a separate schedule for each enterprise. Refer to the instructions on page 4 for each line item before making any entries.

Name and address of business enterprise

Employer identification number . . . .

Form of enterprise (corporation, partnership, trust, joint venture, sole proprietorship, etc.) . . . . .

		(a) Voting stock (profits interest or beneficial interest)	(b) Value	(c) Nonvoting stock (capital interest)
1	Foundation holdings in business enterprise 1			
2	Permitted holdings in business enterprise 2			
3	Value of excess holdings in business enterprise 3			
4	Value of excess holdings disposed of within 90 days; or, other value of excess holdings not subject to section 4943 tax (attach explanation) 4			
5	Taxable excess holdings in business enterprise - line 3 minus line 4 5			
6	Tax - Enter 5% of line 5 6			
7	Total tax - Add amounts on line 6, columns (a), (b), and (c); enter total here and on page 1, Part I, line 2 7			

SCHEDULE D - Initial Taxes on Investments That Jeopardize Charitable Purpose (Section 4944)

Part I   Investments and Tax Computation

(a) Investment number	(b) Date of investment	(c) Description of investment	(d) Amount of investment	(e) Initial tax on foundation (5% of col. (d))	(f) Initial tax on foundation managers (if applicable)- (lesser of $5,000 or 5% of col. (d))
1					
2					
3					
4					
5					
Total - column (e). Enter here and on page 1, Part I, line 3					
Total - column (f). Enter total (or prorated amount) here and in Part II, column (c), below					

Part II   Summary of Tax Liability of Foundation Managers and Proration of Payments

(a) Names of foundation managers liable for tax	(b) Investment no. from Part I, col. (a)	(c) Tax from Part I, col. (f), or prorated amount	(d) Manager's total tax liability (add amounts in col. (c)) (see page 6 of the instructions)

Appendix 27–6

FORM 4720 (*continued*)

Form 4720 (1998)　　　Environmentalist Fund　　　77-7777777　　　Page 4

SCHEDULE E - Initial Taxes on Taxable Expenditures (Section 4945)

Part I　Expenditures and Computation of Tax　　　0

(a) Item number	(b) Amount	(c) Date paid or incurred	(d) Name and address of recipient	(e) Description of expenditure and purposes for which made
1	10,000	June 1, 19xx	Citizens Environmental Committee	Pruchase of educational materials & web site
2				
3				
4				
5	See attached explanation of potential taxable expenditure and request for abatement.			

(f) Question number from Form 990-PF, Part VII-B, or Form 5227, Part VI-B, applicable to the expenditure	(g) Initial tax imposed on foundation (10% of col. (b))	(h) Initial tax imposed on foundation managers (if applicable)-(lesser of $5,000 or 2 1 =2 % of col. (b))	
5(c)	See request for abatement		0
	0		0
	0		0
	0		0

Total - column (g). Enter here and on page 1, Part I, line 4 . . . . . .　　　0

Total - column (h). Enter total (or prorated amount) here and in Part II, column (c), below . . . .　　　0

Part II　Summary of Tax Liability of Foundation Managers and Proration of Payments

(a) Names of foundation managers liable for tax	(b) Item no. from Part I, col. (a)	(c) Tax from Part I, col. (h), or prorated amount	(d) Manager's total tax liability (add amounts in col. (c)) (see page 6 of the instructions)
			0
			0
			0

SCHEDULE F - Initial Taxes on Political Expenditures (Section 4955)

Part I　Expenditures and Computation of Tax

(a) Item number	(b) Amount	(c) Date paid or incurred	(d) Description of political expenditure	(e) Initial tax imposed on organization or foundation (10% of col. (b))	(f) Initial tax imposed on managers (if applicable) (lesser of $5,000 or 2 1/2% of col. (b))
1				0	0
2				0	0
3				0	0
4				0	0
5				0	0

Total - column (e). Enter here and on page 1, Part I, line 5 . . . .　　　0

Total - column (f). Enter total (or prorated amount) here and in Part II, column (c), below . . . . . .　　　0

Part II　Summary of Tax Liability of Organization Managers or Foundation Managers and Proration of Payments

(a) Names of organization managers or foundation managers liable for tax	(b) Item no. from Part I, col. (a)	(c) Tax from Part I, col. (f), or prorated amount	(d) Manager's total tax liability (add amounts in col. (c)) (see page 7 of the instructions)
			0
			0
			0

FORM 4720 (continued)

SCHEDULE G - Tax on Excess Lobbying Expenditures (Section 4911)

1	Excess of grassroots expenditures over grassroots nontaxable amount (from Schedule A (Form 990), Part VI-A, column (b), line 43). (See page 7 of the instructions before making entry.)	1
2	Excess of lobbying expenditures over lobbying nontaxable amount (from Schedule A (Form 990), Part VI-A, column (b), line 44). (See page 7 of the instructions before making entry.)	2
3	Taxable lobbying expenditures - enter the larger of line 1 or line 2	3
4	Tax - Enter 25% of line 3 here and on page 1, Part I, line 6	4

SCHEDULE H - Taxes on Disqualifying Lobbying Expenditures (Section 4912)

Part I   Expenditures and Computation of Tax

(a) Item number	(b) Amount	(c) Date paid or incurred	(d) Description of lobbying expenditures	(e) Tax imposed on organization (5% of col. (b))	(f) Tax imposed on organization managers (if applicable) - (5% of col. (b))
1					
2					
3					
4					
5					

Total - column (e). Enter here and on page 1, Part I, line 7 . . . .

Total - column (f). Enter total (or prorated amount) here and in Part II, column (c), below . . . . . .

Part II   Summary of Tax Liability of Organization Managers and Proration of Payments

(a) Names of organization managers liable for tax	(b) Item no. from Part I, col. (a)	(c) Tax from Part I, col. (f), or prorated amount	(d) Manager's total tax liability (add amounts in col. (c)) (see page 7 of the instructions)

SCHEDULE I - Initial Taxes on Excess Benefit Transactions (Section 4958)

Part I   Excess Benefit Transactions and Tax Computation

(a) Transaction number	(b) Date of transaction	(c) Description of transaction
1		
2		
3		
4		
5		

(d) Amount of excess benefit	(e) Initial tax on disqualified persons (25% of col. (d))	(f) Tax on organization managers (if applicable) (lesser of $10,000 or 10% of col (d))

Appendix 27–6

FORM 4720 (*continued*)

Form 4720 (1998)   Environmentalist Fund   77-7777777   Page 6

SCHEDULE I - Initial Taxes on Excess Benefit Transactions (Section 4958) Continued

Part II   Summary of Tax Liability of Disqualified Persons and Proration of Payments

(a) Names of disqualified persons liable for tax	(b) Trans. no. from Part I, col. (a)	(c) Tax from Part I, col. (e), or prorated amount	(d) Disqualified person's total tax liability (add amounts in col. (c)) (see page 8 of the instructions)

Part III   Summary of Tax Liability of 501(c)(3) and (4) Organization Managers and Proration of Payments

(a) Names of 501(c)(3) and (4) organization managers liable for tax	(b) Trans. no. from Part I, col. (a)	(c) Tax from Part I, col. (f), or prorated amount	(d) Manager's total tax liability (add amounts in col. (c)) (see page 8 of the instructions)

Under penalties of perjury, I declare that I have examined this return, including accompanying schedules and statements, and to the best of my knowledge and belief it is true, correct, and complete. Declaration or preparer (other than taxpayer) is based on all information of which preparer has any knowledge.

Signature of officer or trustee	Title	Date

Signature (and organization name if applicable) of self-dealer, disqualified person, foundation manager, or organization manager   Date

Signature (and organization name if applicable) of self-dealer, disqualified person, foundation manager, or organization manager   Date

Signature (and organization name if applicable) of self-dealer, disqualified person, foundation manager, or organization manager   Date

Signature of individual or firm preparing the return	Address of preparer	Date

Appendix 27–6

FORM 4720 (*continued*)

ENVIRONMENTALIST FUND   **# EIN 77-7777777**

Attachment to Form 4720
In reference to Form 990-PF, Part VII-A, Question 5c on page 5

Expenditure Responsibility Statement
For the year 19XX

Pursuant to IRC Regulation §53.4945-5(d)(2), the ENVIRONMENTALIST FUND
provides the following information:

(i) Grantee:	Citizens Environment Committee 1444 Smith Terrace Hometown, TX 77733
(ii) Amount of Grant	December 28, 19xx $ 10,000
(iii) Purpose of grants:	The Citizens Environments Committee (CEC) is an unincorporated nonprofit association operated by Hometown citizens unrelated to the fund's disqualified persons. This grant was for the purchase of educational materials and creation of a web-site. CEC had not sought recognition of its tax-exempt status in 19xx when the Fund made this grant in support of CEC's eduational programs so that an expenditure responsibility agreement was executed.
(iv) & (vi)Reports	The CEC submitted a full and complete report of its expenditures pursuant to the grant on May 1, 19xx.
(v) Diversions:	To the knowledge of the grantor, no funds have been diverted to any activity other than the activity for which the grant was originally made.
(vii) Verification:	The grantor has no reason to doubt the accuracy or reliability of the report from the grantee; therefore, no independent verification of the report was made.

Appendix 27–6

FORM 4720 (*continued*)

ENVIRONMENTALIST FUND   **# EIN 77-7777777**
ATTACHMENT TO FORM 4720
for the year 19xx

STATEMENT regarding CORRECTION OF TAXABLE EXPENDITURE

In submitting its 19xx Form 990-PF, the ENVIRONMENTALIST FUND (Fund) inadvertently failed to submit information regarding an expenditure responsibility grant. This failure is hereby corrected by attaching a complete report of the seven required items. The Fund, during 19xx, made a grant to Citizens Environment Committee(CEC). The CEC is an unincorporated nonprofit association operated by Hometown citizens unrelated to the Fund's disqualified persons. The grant was made before CEC had sought recognition of its tax-exempt status so that the Fund and CEC entered into an expenditure responsibility agreement in a timely fashion.

CEC submitted its follow-up report before the proscribed deadline and the Fund's records indicate a copy of the report was forwarded to Mary Goodbooks to furnish to the accountants for preparation of the Form 990-PF. For unknown reasons, the report was not so furnished and the accountants did not recognize the need for its attachment. Fund had not previously made expenditure responsibility grants and had consulted with its lawyers regarding appropriate documentation for the grant. Although the Fund took reasonable steps to assure its attachment, the accountants did not receive the lawyer's memoranda containing the return attachment regarding the grant.

Pursuant to Internal Revenue Code §4962, the Fund respectfully requests that the first tier §4945 penalty for failure to report, or initial tax of $1,000, be abated because the failure was due to reasonable causes and without willful neglect. The mistake was discovered by the Fund's bookkeeper. In reviewing the tax files to prepare this year's return, she found the expenditure responsibility report had not been forwarded to the accountants. The inclusion of the proper report in this return effectively corrects the failure to report. Therefore the Fund submits it is entitled to an abatement of the tax because it meets the requirements of §4962 and the instructions to Form 4720.

I swear that this information is true and correct and that the Fund's failure to make this report was inadvertent, accidental, and without intention or knowledge on my part or on the part of any of the Fund's other officers.

_____
Jane D. Environmentalist, President

Appendix 27–7

FORM 990-T

Form **990-T**	**Exempt Organization Business Income Tax Return** **(and proxy tax under section 6033(e))**	OMB No 1545-0687

Department of the Treasury
Internal Revenue Service

For calendar year 1998 or other tax year beginning   July 1st   ending   June 30th
See separate instructions.

1998

A ☐ Check box if address changed

B Exempt under section
☒ 501 c(3)
☐ 408(e)   ☐ 220(e)
☐ 408A   ☐ 530(a)
☐ 529(a)

Name of organization
Campaign to Clean Up America

Number, street, and room or suite no. (If a P. O. box, see page 6.)
1111 Any Street

City or town	State	ZIP code
Hometown	Texas	77777

D Employer identification number
(Employees' trust, see instructions for Block D.)
44-4444444

E New unrelated business activity codes
(see instructions for Block E)
900002

C Book value of all assets at end of year **423,400**

F Group exemption number (see instructions for Block F on page 6)

G Check organization type
☒ 501(c) corporation ☐ 501(c) trust ☐ 401(a) trust ☐ 408(a) trust ☐ Other trust

H Describe the organization's primary unrelated business activity.   Rental of personal property

I During the tax year, was the corporation a subsidiary in an affiliated group or a parent-subsidiary controlled group?   ☐ Yes   ☒ No
If "Yes," enter the name and identifying number of the parent corporation.

J The books are in care of: Joan Controller   Telephone number   (444)444-4444

Part I   Unrelated Trade or Business Income

			(A) Income	(B) Expenses	(C) Net
1a	Gross receipts or sales				
b	Less returns and allowances c Balance	1c	0		
2	Cost of goods sold (Schedule A, line 7)	2	0		
3	Gross profit (subtract line 2 from line 1c)	3	0		0
4a	Capital gain net income (attach Schedule D)	4a	0		0
b	Net gain (loss) (Form 4797, Part II, line 18) (attach Form 4797)	4b	0		0
c	Capital loss deduction for trusts	4c	0		0
5	Income (loss) from partnerships and S corporations (attach statement)	5			0
6	Rent income (Schedule C)	6	2,000	1,200	800
7	Unrelated debt-financed income (Schedule E)	7	0	0	0
8	Interest, annuities, royalties, and rents from controlled organizations (see page 7 of instructions)	8	0	0	0
9	Investment income of a section 501(c)(7), (9), or (17) organization (Schedule G)	9	0	0	0
10	Exploited exempt activity income (Schedule I)	10	0	0	0
11	Advertising income (Schedule J)	11	0	0	0
12	Other income (see page 8 of the instructions - attach schedule)	12	0		0
13	TOTAL (combine lines 3 through 12)	13	2,000	1,200	800

Part II   Deductions Not Taken Elsewhere

(See page 8 of the instructions for limitations on deductions.)
(Except for contributions, deductions must be directly connected with the unrelated business income.)

14	Compensation of officers, directors, and trustees (Schedule K)	14	0
15	Salaries and wages	15	
16	Repairs and maintenance	16	
17	Bad debts	17	
18	Interest (attach schedule)	18	
19	Taxes and licenses	19	
20	Charitable contributions (see page 10 of the instructions for limitation rules)	20	
21	Depreciation (attach Form 4562) 21 0		
22	Less depreciation claimed on Schedule A and elsewhere on return 22a	22b	0
23	Depletion	23	
24	Contributions to deferred compensation plans	24	
25	Employee benefit programs	25	
26	Excess exempt expenses (Schedule I)	26	0
27	Excess readership costs (Schedule J)	27	0
28	Other deductions (attach schedule)	28	
29	Total Deductions (add lines 14 through 28)	29	0
30	Unrelated business taxable income before net operating loss deduction (subtract line 29 from line 13)	30	800
31	Net operating loss deduction	31	
32	Unrelated business taxable income before specific deduction (subtract line 31 from line 30)	32	800
33	Specific deduction	33	1,000
34	Unrelated business taxable income (subtract line 33 from line 32). If line 33 is greater than line 32, enter the smaller of zero or line 32	34	0

For Paperwork Reduction Act Notice, see instructions.   (HTA)   Form 990-T (1998)

FORM 990-T (*continued*)

Form 990-T (1998)	Campaign to Clean Up America	44-4444444	Page 2

Part III — Tax Computation

35 Organizations Taxable as Corporations (see instructions for tax computation on page 11).

Controlled group members (sections 1561 and 1563) - check here ☐ See instructions and:

a Enter your share of the $50,000, $25,000, and $9,925,000 taxable income brackets (in that order):

(1) _____ (2) _____ (3) _____

b Enter organization's share of: (1) additional 5% tax (not more than $11,750)		0
(2) additional 3% tax (not more than $100,000)		0
c Income tax on the amount on line 34	35c	0

36 Trusts Taxable at Trust Rates (see instructions for tax computation on page 12) Income tax on

the amount on line 34 from:	☐ Tax rate schedule	☐ or Schedule D (Form 1041)	36	0
37 Proxy tax (see page 13 of the instructions)	37	
38 Total (add line 37 to line 35c or 36, whichever applies)	38	0

Part IV — Tax and Payments

39a Foreign tax credit (corporations attach Form 1118; trusts attach Form 1116)	39a	0	
b Other credits. (See page 13 of the instructions)	39b		
c General business credit - Check if from:			
☐ Form 3800 or ☐ Form (specify)	39c	0	
d Credit for prior year minimum tax (attach Form 8801 or 8827)	39d	0	
e Total credits (add lines 39a through 39d)		39e	0
40 Subtract line 39e from line 38		40	0
41 Recapture taxes. Check if from: ☐ Form 4255 ☐ Form 8611		41	0
42 Alternative minimum tax		42	
43 Total tax (add lines 40, 41, and 42)		43	0
44 Payments: (a) 1997 overpayment credited to 1998	44a		
b 1998 estimated tax payments	44b		
c Tax deposited with Form 7004 or Form 2758	44c	0	
d Foreign organizations - Tax paid or withheld at source (see instructions)	44d		
e Backup withholding (see instructions)	44f		
f Other credits and payments (see instructions)	44e	0	
45 Total payments (add lines 44a through 44f)		45	0
46 Estimated tax penalty (see page 4 of the instructions). Check ☐ if Form 2220 is attached		46	0
47 Tax due - If line 45 is less than the total of lines 43 and 46, enter amount owed		47	0
48 Overpayment - If line 45 is larger than the total of lines 43 and 46, enter amount overpaid		48	0
49 Enter the amount of line 48 you want: Credited to 1999 estimated tax _____ Refunded		49	0

Part V — Statements Regarding Certain Activities and Other Information (See instructions on page 14.)

	Yes or No
1 At any time during the 1998 calendar year, did the organization have an interest in or a signature or other authority over a financial account in a foreign country (such as a bank account, securities account, or other financial account)? If "Yes," the organization may have to file Form TD F 90-22.1. If "Yes," enter the name of the foreign country here	No
2 During the tax year, did the organization receive a distribution from, or was it the grantor of, or transferor to, a foreign trust? . . . . If "Yes," see page 14 of the instructions for other forms the organization may have to file.	No
3 Enter the amount of tax-exempt interest received or accrued during the tax year . . . . . . $	

SCHEDULE A - COST OF GOODS SOLD (See instructions on page 15.) — Not Applicable

Method of inventory valuation (specify) _____

1 Inventory at beginning of year	1		6 Inventory at end of year	6		
2 Purchases	2		7 Cost of goods sold. Subtract line 6 from line 5. (Enter here and on line 2, Part I.)			
3 Cost of labor	3					
4a Additional section 263A costs (attach schedule)	4a			7		0
b Other costs (attach schedule)	4b		8 Do the rules of section 263A (with respect to property produced or acquired for resale) apply to the organization?		**Yes or No**	
5 TOTAL - Add lines 1 through 4b . . .	5	0			Yes or No	

Under penalties of perjury, I declare that I have examined this return, including accompanying schedules and statements, and to the best of my knowledge and belief, it is true, correct, and complete. Declaration of preparer (other than taxpayer) is based on all information of which preparer has any knowledge.

Please Sign Here

Signature of officer or fiduciary: *June D. Environmentalist*	Date: 11/1/XX	Title: *Sec. Treas*

Paid Preparer's Use Only

Preparer's signature: *accountant*	Date: 11/1/XX	Check if self-employed ☒	Preparer's SSN 400-00-0000
Firm's name (or yours, if self-employed) and address	A Qualified CPA Firm	EIN	45-5555555
	1001 Main Street	Phone	(444) 422-2222
	Hometown Texas	ZIP code	44444-4222

FORM 990-T (continued)

Form 990-T (1998)	Campaign to Clean Up America	44-4444444	Page 3

SCHEDULE C - RENT INCOME   **(FROM REAL PROPERTY AND PERSONAL PROPERTY LEASED WITH REAL PROPERTY)** (See instructions on page 15.)

1 Description of property

(1)	0
(2)	Maintenance equipment rented to other organizations
(3)	
(4)	

	2 Rent received or accrued		3 Deductions directly connected with the income in columns 2(a) and 2(b) (attach schedule)	
	(a) From personal property (if the percentage of rent for personal property is more than 10% but not more than 50%)	(b) From real and personal property (if the percentage of rent for personal property exceeds 50% or if the rent is based on profit or income)		
(1)		2,000	Repairs	1,200
(2)				
(3)				
(4)				
Total	0	Total 2,000	Total deductions. Enter here and on line 6, column (B), Part I, page 1	1,200

Total Income (Add totals of columns 2(a) and 2(b). Enter here and on line 6, column (A), Part I, page 1.) 2,000

SCHEDULE E - UNRELATED DEBT-FINANCED INCOME (See instructions on page 16.)

1 Description of debt-financed property	2 Gross income from or allocable to debt-financed property	3 Deductions directly connected with or allocable to debt-financed property	
		(a) Straight line depreciation (attach schedule)	(b) Other deductions
(1)			
(2)			
(3)			
(4)			

4 Amount of average acquisition debt on or allocable to debt-financed property (attach schedule)	5 Average adjusted basis of or allocable to debt-financed property (attach schedule)	6 Column 4 divided by column 5	7 Gross income reportable (col. 2 x col. 6)	8 Allocable deductions (column 6 x total of columns 3(a) and 3(b))
(1)		0%	0	0
(2)		0%	0	0
(3)		0%	0	0
(4)		0%	0	0
			Enter here and on line 7, col. (A), Part I, page 1.	Enter here and on line 7, col. (B), Part I, page 1.
Totals			0	0

Total dividends - received deductions included in column 8 . . . .

SCHEDULE F - INTEREST, ANNUITIES, ROYALTIES, AND RENTS FROM CONTROLLED ORGANIZATIONS (See instructions on page 17.)

1 Name and address of controlled organization(s)	2 Gross income from controlled organization(s)	3 Deductions of controlling organization directly connected with column 2 income (attach schedule)	4 Exempt controlled organizations		
			(a) Unrelated business taxable income	(b) Taxable Income computed as though not exempt under sec. 501(a), or the amount in col. (a), whichever is larger	(c) Column (a) divided by column (b)
(1)					0%
(2)					0%
(3)					0%
(4)					0%

	5 Nonexempt controlled organizations		6 Gross income reportable (column 2 x column 4(c) or column 5(c))	7 Allowable deductions (column 3 x column 4(c) or column 5(c))
(a) Excess taxable income	(b) Taxable income, or amount in column (a), whichever is larger	(c) Column (a) divided by Column (b)		
(1)		0%	0	0
(2)		0%	0	0
(3)		0%	0	0
(4)		0%	0	0
			Enter here and include on line 8, column (A), Part I, page 1.	Enter here and include on line 8, column (B), Part I, page 1.
Totals			0	0

Appendix 27–7

FORM 990-T (continued)

Form 990-T (1998)   Campaign to Clean Up America   44-4444444   Page 4

SCHEDULE G - INVESTMENT INCOME OF A SECTION 501(c)(7), (9), OR (17) ORGANIZATION
(See instructions on page 17.)

1 Description of income	2 Amount of income	3 Deductions directly connected	4 Set-asides (attach schedule)	5 Total deductions and set-asides (col. 3 plus col. 4)
(1)				0
(2)				0
(3)				0
(4)				0
	Enter here and on line 9, col. (A), Part I, p. 1.			Enter here and on line 9, column (B), Part I, page 1.
Totals	0			0

SCHEDULE I - EXPLOITED EXEMPT ACTIVITY INCOME, OTHER THAN ADVERTISING INCOME
(See instructions on page 17.)

1 Description of exploited activity	2 Gross unrelated business income from trade or business	3 Expenses directly connected with production of unrelated business income	4 Net income (loss) from unrelated trade or business (column 2 minus column 3). If a gain, compute columns 5 through 7.	5 Gross income from activity that is not unrelated business income	6 Expenses attributable to column 5	7 Excess exempt expenses (column 6 minus column 5, but not more than column 4).
(1)			0			0
(2)			0			0
(3)			0			0
(4)			0			0
	Enter here and on line 10, col. (A), Part I, p. 1.	Enter here and on line 10, col. (B), Part I, p. 1.				Enter here and on line 26, Part II, page 1.
Column totals	0	0				0

SCHEDULE J - ADVERTISING INCOME   (See instructions on page 18.)

Part I   Income From Periodicals Reported on a Consolidated Basis

1 Name of periodical	2 Gross advertising income	3 Direct advertising costs	4 Advertising gain or (loss) (column 2 minus column 3). If a gain, compute columns 5 through 7.	5 Circulation income	6 Readership costs	7 Excess readership costs (column 6 minus column 5, but not more than column 4).
(1)						
(2)						
(3)						
(4)						
Column totals (carry to Part II, line (5))	0	0	0	0	0	0

Part II   Income From Periodicals Reported on a Separate Basis
(For each periodical listed in Part II, fill in columns 2 through 7 on a line-by-line basis.)

	2	3	4	5	6	7
(1)						
(2)						
(3)						
(4)						
(5) Totals from Part I	0	0				0
	Enter here and on line 11, col. (A), Part I, p. 1.	Enter here and on line 11, col. (B), Part I, p. 1.				Enter here and on line 27, Part II, page 1.
Column totals, Part II	0	0				0

SCHEDULE K - COMPENSATION OF OFFICERS, DIRECTORS, AND TRUSTEES   (See instructions on page 18.)

1 Name	2 Title	3 Percent of time devoted to business	4 Compensation attributable to unrelated business
Total - Enter here and on line 14, Part II, page 1			0

CHAPTER TWENTY-EIGHT

Communicating with the Internal Revenue Service

The Internal Revenue Service (IRS) is an important player throughout the life of an exempt organization (EO). The qualification for receipt of tax-deductible donations and member dues, the privilege of receiving tax-free contributions, member dues, investment income, and exempt function income, and other special advantages granted by federal, state, and local governments are of significant economic value to exempt organizations. Tax-exempt status typically begins with recognition of qualification by the IRS, making it important to understand how that division of the IRS functions.

28.1 REORGANIZATION OF IRS EXEMPT ORGANIZATION DIVISION

As a result of the Internal Revenue Service Restructuring and Reform Act of 1998, the IRS division previously known as Employee Plans/Exempt Organizations was divided into three parts: exempt organizations, employee plans, and government taxpayers. This division is expected to enhance direct accountability within each program, technical excellence, and interactive customer service efforts. While not finalized as this third edition is being written, the consultants engaged by the IRS to aid in the restructuring suggested simplification of the IRS hierarchy and elimination of regions and districts and their directors and assistant commissioner positions.[1] Readers should be alert to current developments.

Until 1996, nine key district offices were responsible for tax issues for exempt organizations in their assigned area under the guidance of a national office in Washington, D.C. The exempt organizations division of the IRS actually began its reorganization in October 1996. The EO functions were centralized and divided as follows:

- Forms 1023, Application for Recognition of Exemption, are filed with the Ohio Key District Office (see Chapter 18).

- Annual information returns (Forms 990, 990-PF, 990EZ, 990-T, and 5227) are all filed with the Utah Service Center (see Chapter 27).

- Field audit responsibility is assigned to the key district offices for the four regions illustrated in Exhibit 28–1.

- Technical guidance, training, and overall supervision of the exempt organization matters are directed from a national office in Washington, D.C.

The 1997 filing season was a little rocky as the Utah Service Center familiarized itself with the exigencies of the Forms 990 and special rules pertaining to exempt organizations. The time frame for approval of Forms 1023 and 1024 also slowed down. In connection with centralization of the determination process, a plan to recruit EO technicians experienced with Form 1023 to move to Ohio was unsuccessful. As a result the Ohio office was understaffed. After initial screening for completeness in Ohio,[2] many applications were forwarded to other key district offices for review—a procedure adding at least a month to the processing in the author's experience. This situation is changing; 20 trainees were hired for the Ohio office in mid-1998 and a computer upgrade began.

Concurrent with, and one of the causes of, the reorganization were significant cuts in IRS funding during the 1990s while the number of exempt organizations doubled. Positions of departing personnel were unfilled due to a hiring freeze placing burdens on those remaining. Personnel in the IRS Exempt Organization group are nonetheless well trained, cooperative, and knowledgeable. While not resulting from a directive, the attitude is normally supportive. They seem to assume most exempt organizations operate in good faith as they are supposed to—to benefit the public or their members. Their customary approach is to be helpful and to explain; the publications and handbooks are well written and available on the Internet; and they offer good telephone assistance, as a rule. As a part of the IRS restructuring, it is expected 990s will be electronically filed by the year 2007. Meanwhile, the EO Division is cooperating with the Urban Institute of Washington, D.C. to make the forms actually filed available on CD-ROM.

---

[1] Report of consultants, Booz-Allen & Hamilton, reported in *Exempt Organization Tax Review*, Vol. 21, No. 2, August 1998, pp. 179–184.
[2] See Chapter 18§1.

Exhibit 28–1

INTERNAL REVENUE SERVICE REGIONS

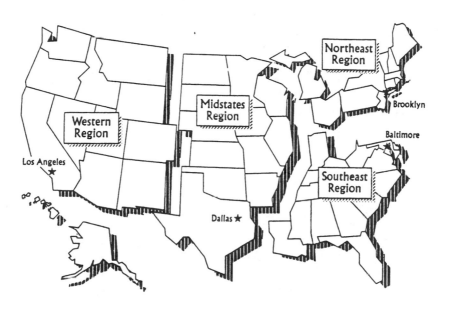

Continuing Professional Education

Exempt Organizations

Technical Instruction Program for FY 1997

This is the 20th Edition of the **EO CPE** textbook prepared by the IRS Exempt Organizations Division. This copy has been reprinted by Tax Analysts for subscribers to *The Exempt Organization Tax Review.*

28.2 HOW TO REPORT CHANGES TO THE IRS

As an exempt organization grows and evolves over the years, it faces the question of how to report changes to the IRS. Annually on Forms 990, the organization is asked the following questions regarding changes:

- Did the organization engage in any activity not previously reported to the IRS? If 'Yes,' attach a statement.

- Were any changes made in the organizing or governing documents but not reported to the IRS?

The procedure for reporting changes is to simply furnish the information and leave it up to the IRS to decide whether the change is acceptable. Commonly no communication—acceptance or rejection—is issued in response to "yes" answers and accompanying attachments to Forms 990.

An exempt organization may also report changes in its organizational documents and/or activities to the Ohio Key District Office with a letter requesting that they determine whether the changes have any impact upon the organization's exempt status.[3] This method of informing the IRS brings a response—the documents and plans are actually read and written approval is issued or questions asked. This submission is not treated as a formal ruling request; no user fee is charged unless a new Form 1023 is required. The dilemma faced by an EO making changes is therefore where to report them, with the decision primarily influenced by the managers' desire for written approval of the organizational change(s). The fact that Form 990 attachments are not necessarily scrutinized may also sway the decision.

Exhibit 28–2 lists actions that constitute a "substantial change in purpose, support or operation" that must be reported to the IRS. Each X indicates the manner and place in which particular changes can be reported. The following subsections discuss various types of changes that might occur, their consequence, and how to report them to the IRS.

(a) When to Request a Ruling

In terms of IRS procedures, it is important to distinguish between gaining approval in advance of a change, rather than risk a sanction for a fait accompli. Once a change has occurred in the form of organization or a major new activity is undertaken, the organization should choose the best method to inform the IRS, based on the succeeding discussion. Such action is taken when the relevant tax laws are clear and established precedents exist, and there is little or no doubt that the change is acceptable.

However, there may be proposed changes for which the organization wishes advance approval because there is a lack of published rulings or other authoritative opinions on the subject. The procedure for obtaining sanction for prospective changes is to request a ruling from the Exempt Organizations Division in the IRS National Office. When significant funds are involved or if disapproval of the change would mean that the organization could lose its exemption, filing of a ruling request may be warranted.

A decision to request a ruling must be made in view of the cost and time involved in the process. The IRS issues a series of revenue procedures each spring to update procedures for seeking guidance in the form of private letter rulings, determination letters, and technical advice. A schedule of fees charged and ad-

---

[3] Internal Revenue Service, P. O. Box 192, Covington, Kentucky 41012-0192 is the mailing address; Internal Revenue Service, 201 West Rivercenter Blvd., Attn: Extracting, Stop 312, Covington, KY 41011 is the delivery address; IRS Announcement 97-87, 1997-36, I.R.B. 1.

Exhibit 28–2

ACTIONS THAT CAUSE SUBSTANTIAL CHANGE IN STATUS

REPORT	KEY DISTRICT DIRECTOR			IRS SERVICE CENTER
	New Form 1023	Letter		Attachment to Form 990 or 990-PF
Conversion from:				
Trust to corporation	X			
PF to public support		X		
PF to private				
operating foundation		X	or	X
School to educational				
organization		X		
Change from 509(a)(1) or (2)		X	or	X
Amendment to:				
Corporate charter		X	or	X
Trust instrument		X	or	X
Bylaws				X
Creation of an endowment				X
Symphony starting				
record publishing business		X	or	X
Shift in major source of				
donations from individuals				
to United Way funding				X

dresses for submitting requests is provided. The most recent pronouncements set the user fee for a letter ruling at $2,100 ($600 for organizations whose gross receipts are under $150,000).[4]

The Ohio Key District Office is first and foremost assigned the responsibility for determining initial qualification for exemption.[5] As a part of that job, the office can also make determinations that fall short of formal ruling requests. In addition to responding to submission of changes in operations and organizing documents as discussed previously, the Ohio office can also act on the following matters:[6]

- Classification of private foundation status

- Recognition of unusual grants[7]

---

[4] Rev. Procs. 99-1, 99-2, 99-3, 99-4, 99-5, 99-8, 1999-1 IRB 7-255.
[5] Process described in Chapter 18.
[6] Rev. Proc. 99-4, 1999-1 IRB 115.
[7] Discussed in Chapter 11§2.

- Advance approval of a PF's grant-making procedures[8]
- Classification as exempt operating foundation[9]
- Advance approval of voter registration activities[10]

(b) Fiscal or Accounting Year

A common change that might occur during the life of an exempt organization is a change in its tax accounting year. Although some commercial, tax-paying businesses must secure advance IRS approval under Internal Revenue Code (IRC) §446(e) to change their tax year,[11] a streamlined system is available for EOs. The EO simply files a "timely filed short period" Form 990 (or 990EZ, 990-PF, or 990T).[12] If a short-period return is filed by the 15th day of the fifth month following the end of the new year end, approval for the change is not required and it is not necessary to submit Form 1128 to Washington.

Say, for example, a calendar year EO wishes to change its tax year to a fiscal year spanning July 1 to June 30. By November 15, a six-month return is filed to report the financial transactions for the short period year (the six months ending June 30 of the year of change). If the organization has not changed its year within the past ten years (counting backward to include the prior short period return as a full year), the change is automatic. The words *Change of Accounting Period* are simply written across the top of the front page. A private foundation that changes its tax year must prorate certain calculations.[13]

Form 1128, Application to Adopt, Change, or Retain a Tax Year, must be filed in two situations: (1) the organization has changed its year end within the past 10 years or (2) the return for the short period is not timely filed. When the organization has previously changed its year, the automatic procedure is still followed if the return is filed within 5 ½ months of the new year end. In that case, Form 1128 is attached to the short period return.

When the filing is late, the organization must first file Form 1128 with the IRS Service Center in Ogden, Utah, to request permission to change its year. If the request is filed within 90 days of the new filing deadline (February 15 in the foregoing example), the organization can request the IRS consider it timely filed. If possible, the organization should explain that it acted reasonably and in good faith.[14] A filing fee of $130 (as of January 1, 1999)[15] is due to be paid. The appropriate Form 990 is not filed using the new tax year until IRS approval is received.

Affiliated organizations holding a group exemption must follow Rev. Proc. 79-3 to effect a change.[16]

---

[8] See Chapter 17§3(e).
[9] See Chapter 13§7.
[10] See Chapter 17§2.
[11] IRS Publication 538, *Accounting Periods and Methods,* can be consulted for more information.
[12] Rev. Proc. 85-58, 1985-2 C.B. 740
[13] See Chapter 15§§1 and 2(b).
[14] Under Reg. §301.9100-1.
[15] Rev. Proc. 99-8, 1998-1 IRB 229; this procedure lists user fees for exempt organization filings and is updated annually.
[16] Rev. Proc. 79-3, 1979-1 C.B. 483.

(c) Accounting Method Change

Generally accepted accounting principles (GAAP) recommend that the accrual method of accounting be used for financial statement reporting; thus, a certified public accountant (CPA) cannot issue a "clean" or "unqualified" opinion on financial statements prepared on a cash receipts and disbursements basis. Because it is simpler, many organizations in their early years use the cash method, which is perfectly acceptable for filing Form 990 and (possibly) for reporting to boards and contributors. Maturing organizations commonly face the need to change to the accrual method, in order to secure an audited statement or to satisfy the requirements of its grantors.

Before 1996, many nonprofits followed what was essentially a hybrid method of accounting. Although they used the accrual method for disbursements, the cash method was used to report donation revenues because pledges of donative support are not enforceable in most cases. Such organizations, therefore, choose not to record pledges as assets with a corresponding showing of income. The Financial Accounting Standards Board in SFAS No. 116, effective beginning in 1995, began to require that such donations be reflected as revenues. A large number of nonprofits were impacted by this (and other) change of reporting. For 1996 and 1997 Form 990s, the IRS excused those organizations that adopted SFAS No. 116 from filing Form 3115.[17]

As a rule, Form 3115 is filed to obtain IRS approval for a change in accounting method. Since an EO is not commonly paying tax, it is deemed to have IRS approval for such a change if it follows the "simplified change procedures." To essentially receive automatic approval, Form 3115 must be timely filed as outlined in the following list:[18]

- Form 3115 is filed within 270 days after the start of the year in which the change is effective. No response or approval for the change is returned to the EO. Form 3115 is filed by mail (effective January 1, 1999) with:

  Internal Revenue Service
  Assistant Commissioner of Employee Plans and Exempt Organizations
  Attention E:EO, Box 120, Ben Franklin Station,
  Washington, DC 20044

- The designated private delivery service address is:

  111 Constitution Avenue NW
  Washington, DC 20224

- No user fee is due.

- A copy of Form 3115 is included with the return filed for the year of accounting method change.

Late applications can be filed, but will only be considered upon a showing of "good cause"[19] and if it can be shown to the satisfaction of the commissioner that

---

[17] Notice 96-13, 1996-1 C.B. 378.
[18] Rev. Proc. 85-37, 1985-2 C.B. 438, modified by 98-60, 1998-51 IRB 16.
[19] The guidelines for showing good cause are found in IRC §6110.

granting the extension will not jeopardize the government's interests. Since EOs typically do not pay tax, the possibilities for such approval are good. A user fee of $130 must accompany late forms.

A change of accounting method necessitates reporting deferred or accelerated income or expenses that would have been reportable in the past if the new method had been used. Items "necessary to prevent amounts from being duplicated or omitted be taken into account" over a period of years and to mitigate the burden to a taxpaying entity are calculated.[20] In most cases, the change has no tax consequence for an EO filing its Form 990 or 990-PF; as a practical matter, the income or expense adjustments for an EO can be made instead in one year. There is no published guidance on this point, but IRS representatives agree with this suggestion, absent tax distortion. An EO whose unrelated business income is affected by an accounting method change should, however, reflect the adjustments. Careful study is appropriate for any organization making such a change that impacts tax liability.[21]

Since there is often no tax consequence of making such a change, an organization may be tempted to forego formal approval for a change in its accounting method. Because the procedure is simple and no fee is due, it is advisable to seek approval. The period of limitation for examining Form 990 might remain open, if the change is significant. Particularly if unrelated business income tax (UBIT) is involved, the time for payment of any tax involved in the change might be accelerated, if approval has not been secured.

(d) Amended Return

If a mistake is discovered after Form 990 has been filed, the question arises whether an amended return should be filed or whether the change can simply be reflected in the next year's fund balance section as a prior-period adjustment. This decision can be difficult to make. There is usually no tax involved, so in accountants' language, the change is not *material*. The extra efforts involved in preparing an amended return may not be necessary.

Amendment is appropriate when correction would cause a change in public charity status or when unrelated business income[22] would increase or decrease, causing an impact on the tax liability. As a rule, for an insignificant correction with no effect on retention of exempt status or tax liability, complete disclosure on the following year's return, along with inclusion of the omitted amounts, is acceptable. Importantly for certain public charities, the correction to revenue should not only be reported in Part I of Form 990 but also in Part IV of Schedule A.

(e) Change in §509 Classification

IRC §509(a)(1) to (a)(2) or Vice Versa. Exempt organizations classified as publicly supported organizations under IRC §509(a)(1) or (a)(2) can often qualify for both categories. Sometimes changes in an organization's sources of support and exempt function revenues cause it to change its qualification from one subsection

---

[20] IRC §481.
[21] Reg. §1.481-5.
[22] Discussed in Chapter 21.

to another. The distinctions between qualification for one category or another are described in detail in Chapter 11§4. For purposes of this discussion, the issue is what the organization must do if it experiences such a change. In order to be classified as a publicly supported organization and not as a private foundation, passage of either test suffices. In one narrow circumstance, it is preferable to be classified as a §509(a)(1) organization: Only (a)(1)s qualify to receive terminating distributions from private foundations.[23]

Qualification is based upon percentage levels of public support calculated using a four-year moving average of financial support received annually. The calculation is made annually when the organization completes Schedule A of Form 990.[24] Checking the (a)(1) blank rather than the (a)(2) blank has not, in the past, prompted a response or notice from the service center that processes Forms 990. The organization must decide whether, in addition to informing the Utah service center, to report the change to the Ohio office to request recognition or written approval. The question is whether the determination letter[25] should be updated. Sometimes it is a matter of the organization's officers and directors being tolerant of uncertainty. In some situations support might change from year to year. The factors to consider in making the choice include the following:

- The IRS does not customarily issue amended or new determination letters when Form 990, Schedule A, indicates that a change has occurred.

- Private foundations need not exercise expenditure responsibility[26] in making a grant to either category, so a new determination letter is not critical.

- IRS Publication 78 makes no distinction in its labeling of public charities, so the information is not entered into that IRS record.

- As of November 1998, the key district office does not charge a user fee for submission of the information with request for a new letter.

Ceasing to Qualify as a §509(a)(3) Organization. Failure to maintain qualification under IRC §509(a)(3) as a supporting organization[27] could occur for either of two reasons:

- The organizational documents are altered in a manner that removes the requisite relationship with one or more public charities and the organization becomes a private foundation supporting grantees of its choice.

- A sufficient level of public support is obtained to allow the organization to convert to a §509(a)(1) or (2) organization.

In the first case, conversion to a private foundation (PF) requires no IRS approval though most would favor overt sanction for the change. Preferably, the conversion

[23] IRC §507(b)(1)(A).
[24] Illustrated in Appendix 27-3, Schedule A, page 3.
[25] Reproduced as Exhibit 18-3.
[26] See Chapter 17§5.
[27] See Chapter 11§6.

is timed to occur at the end of the fiscal year. If not, a short period final Form 990 would be filed at the end of the (a)(3). A short period Form 990-PF would then be filed beginning with the date of the change. Required minimum distributions,[28] excise tax on investment income,[29] and other PF sanctions would apply as if the organization were newly created upon the date of conversion. Full disclosure of the changes would be furnished to the IRS in filing both returns.

In the second situation, the organization would continue to file Form 990 and the change would again be fully disclosed with the return for the year the change occurred. The dilemma discussed regarding a change from (c)(1) to (c)(2) or vice versa also applies in the case. No new determination letter is issued in response to the 990 filing. The exempt organization should analyze its need to furnish evidence of its new status to potential supporters. This situation is rather unusual, and prudence would dictate reporting to the Ohio office to ensure approval of the new category of public status.

Ceasing to Qualify as a Public Charity. An organization classified as a public charity may become reclassified as a private foundation for one of two reasons:

- Its sources of support might fall below requisite amount of public support needed to qualify under IRC §509(a)(1) and (2).

- It ceases to conduct the activity qualifying it as a public charity.

As to an EO the public status of which is based upon revenues, the calculation is made at the end of each year and impacts the next succeeding year. Say, for example, the 1998 Form 990 shows an EO's public support fell to 25% of its total support (based on revenues received 1994–1997). Unless the facts and circumstances test applies,[30] beginning in the year 1999, the EO would be reclassified as a private foundation. Similar to a 509(a)(3) organization converting to private, all of the special rules applicable to private foundations would become applicable on the first day of 1999.

A church, school, or hospital qualifies as a public charity because of the activity it conducts without regard to its sources of revenue. When such an exempt organization ceases to so operate, it potentially becomes a private foundation on the date the change occurs. As the health care industry reformed itself during the 1990s, the assets of tax-exempt hospitals were purchased by for-profit hospitals. Typically the proceeds of the asset sale were then invested to produce income to conduct a charitable grant-making program. For up to two years following the sale, it is conceivable for the hospital to reclassify itself as a public charity based on its sources of support during the time it operated the hospital. Subsequently, it would become a private foundation unless it reformed its organizational structure to qualify as a supporting organization.

[28] See Chapter 15.
[29] See Chapter 13.
[30] See Chapter 11§2.

28.3 WEATHERING AN IRS EXAMINATION

After securing tax exemption from the IRS Key District office and filing Forms 990 annually with the Internal Revenue Service Center, a call may be received from the IRS Exempt Organization Office in the organization's area. Ongoing qualification as an exempt organization may be questioned by the specialist who wants to look at the organization's financial books and records. The knock on the organization's door comes in the form of a phone call from the IRS agent assigned to the case to the person identified as the contact person on Form 990. The agent will request to arrange an appointment to examine a particular year's return. Many EOs will refer such a call to their professional advisors, usually the accountant who prepared the Forms 990. The author is grateful to Jason Kall, Exempt Organizations Chief, Houston office of the IRS Midwest Region, for his contribution to this subsection. He generously reviewed the second edition manuscript and aided in updating IRS examination procedures.

The manner in which the IRS chooses EOs to examine varies from year to year and is always a matter of speculation. In some years, the IRS looks at business leagues, some years at unrelated business activity, and in other years it may examine hospitals, related clinics, and doctors. In 1990 and 1991, the IRS conducted a program to examine over-claimed deductions for fund-raising events, with companion examinations of the income tax returns of EO supporters of such events. During the 1990s, the IRS initiated a Coordinated Examination Program (CEP) to bring together a pool of experts to work on complicated cases involving significant charitable institutions. As a part of a large case initiative, conglomerate EOs with subsidiaries and for-profit and nonprofit related entities, particularly colleges and hospitals, were targeted. Lawyers, accountants, IRS income tax agents, and other specialists join the IRS EO specialists in conducting such examinations. As of September 1998, the CEP programs continue and should be expected to be a significant part of the IRS EO work plan for years to come.

An IRS examination tool called RICS (Return Inventory Classification System) is now being used to evaluate examination candidates. All the information transcribed off of Forms 990 (reputedly about 20 percent of the information) goes into a quereable database. According to Evelyn Petschek, Assistant Commissioner for Employee Plans and Exempt Organizations, RICS enables the IRS to segment the universe of exempts to regulate and determine compliance problems based on statistical samples. During the 1997/98 fiscal year, for example, they contacted social clubs identified by the system as reporting investment income on Form 990 that failed to file the correspondingly required Form 990-T.[31] The IRS 1998/99 work plan included a sampling of political action committees (PACs) chosen by the IRS national office from the Federal Election Commission's Web page containing reports on such organizations. The IRS easily identified PACs with investment assets and resulting income that should have been filing Form 1120-POL. A sampling of organizations with low-income housing projects, travel tours, and tax-exempt bonds were similarly chosen for examination.

---

[31] Remarks at a meeting of the American Bar Association Exempt Organization Committee, May 9, 1997.

(a) How the IRS Examines Returns

The examination procedures are outlined in the IRS *Exempt Organizations Guidelines Handbook*.[32] Before making contact with the exempt organization to be examined, IRS agents are directed to perform the following procedures:

- *Pre-examination.* Review the returns to identify any large, unusual, or questionable items that should be examined for determining the correct tax liability and exempt status. The balance sheet and revenue sources are to be scrutinized for unidentified unrelated business activity. The return is checked for completeness and to identify information to be secured during the examination.

- *Administrative file.* The exempt organization's administrative file (if available) is checked for possible caveats in an exemption letter, and to familiarize the agent with the reasons for which the EO was originally exempt. Prior examinations, technical advice, and correspondence with the EO are reviewed. If a prior examination recommended some changes in operations, the agent is to be alert during the current examination to ensure that corrective action was taken.

- *Examination guidelines.* Agents are responsible for developing issues raised in the examination. They are to study the relevant portions of the *Exempt Organizations Handbook* concerning the particular type of organization they are examining, and are to gather facts to apply the statutes.

- *Preliminary work.* The examination is to be conducted at the organization's place of business with an authorized representative. Before the books and records are reviewed, the agent conducts an initial interview with the principal officer or authorized representative. The agent looks into programs and activities, sources of income, purchases of assets, receipts and payments of loans, noncash transactions, internal controls, and any large or unusual items.

- *On-site tours.* The agent most likely will request a tour of the facilities. During this time, other employees who may be able to provide a more detailed description of operations can be interviewed.

- *Routine examination.* After the appointment is made, the examiner will send a letter specifically listing the items to be reviewed. A sample letter for a routine examination follows as Exhibit 28–3. The basic list is standardized, but is sometimes supplemented with additional items. Publication 1 is furnished and notification required by IRC §7602(c) are expected in the future.

  The records will be sampled by the auditor. All of the board of director meeting minutes are usually read, but not all of the canceled checks are scanned. The breadth of the materials reviewed depends on some extent upon the quality of the accounting workpapers and ledgers, and on the nature of the organization's operations. When accounting records and

[32] IRM 7(10)69.

Exhibit 28–3

SAMPLE LETTER FOR A ROUTINE EXAMINATION

Internal Revenue Service   Department of the Treasury
District Director
Date: Form:
                                Tax Year Ended:
                                Date of Appointment:
                                Time:
                                Place of Appointment:
                                My Telephone Number:

I am writing to confirm our appointment, as shown above, for the examination of the form indicated.

To help make the examination as brief as possible, please have the following records available for the year to be covered by this examination:

- Governing instruments (articles of incorporation, by-laws, etc.)
- Minutes of meetings
- All books and records of your assets, liabilities, receipts and disbursements
- Check register, cancelled checks, and bank statements
- Auditor's report
- Copies of prior and subsequent year returns
- Copies of any other Federal tax returns filed
- Pamphlets, brochures, and other literature printed
- Correspondence files
- Other:

We realize some organizations may be concerned about an examination of their returns. We hope we can relieve any concerns you may have by briefly explaining why we examine exempt organization returns and what your appeal rights are if you do not agree with the results.

We examine returns to verify the correctness of income or gross receipts, deductions, and credits and to determine that the organization is operating in the manner stated and for the purpose set forth in its application for recognition of exemption. An examination of a return does not suggest a suspicion of any wrongdoing. In many cases, the return is closed without change.

At the completion of the examination, an explanation will be made of any proposed recommendation and how it affects your exempt status or tax liability, such as excise taxes or unrelated business income tax. You should understand fully

Letter 1126(DO) (Rev. 9-84)

Exhibit 28–3 *(continued)*

any recommended change, so please do not hesitate to ask questions about anything not clear to you.

If changes are recommended involving your tax liability and you agree with them, you will be asked to sign an agreement form. By signing, you will indicate your agreement to the amount shown on the form as a refund due you or additional tax you owe, and this will simplify closing your case.

You do not have to agree with the recommendations made. You may ask for a conference at a higher level, as explained in the copy of appeal procedures which you will receive.

It will not be necessary for someone to be present throughout the examination, unless that is your wish. I would, however, appreciate your having an officer or your representative available at the beginning of the examination to give me a brief orientation of the operations of the organization and again at the end for a discussion of the results of the examination.

If the examination is conducted with your representative, a power of attorney or tax information authorization must be filed before your representative can receive or inspect confidential information. Form 2848, Power of Attorney and Declaration of Representative, or Form 2848-D, Tax Information Authorization and Declaration of Representative, as appropriate (or any other properly written power of attorney or authorization), may be used for this purpose. Copies of these forms may be obtained from any Internal Revenue Service office.

If you have any questions or need to reschedule our appointment, please contact me at the telephone number shown in the heading of this letter.

Thank you for your cooperation.

Sincerely yours,

Internal Revenue Agent

Letter 1126(DO) (Rev. 9-84)

original source documents can easily be traced to the numbers reported on the Form 990 being examined, the amount of detailed work will be limited and the examination scope may be limited.

- *Rollover Audits.* Sometimes the motivation for the audit is another IRS audit, such as a review of a substantial contributor's or a related organization's return. For example, the IRS examined Pittsburgh doctors in connection with its CEP examination program for hospitals. In such a case, the organization must ask to be informed about all of the facts and circumstances, and should do everything possible to cooperate with the other taxpayers involved.

(b) Who Handles the Examination?

The first question to ask in connection with the examination is its location. If a professional firm or advisor is involved, the examination might take place in his or her office, depending on the sophistication of the organization's accounting staff and the volume of records to be examined. The IRS has the authority to choose the site, although they are cooperative in that regard. Whatever the examination site, the IRS agent will want to visit the physical location in which the organization's programs are conducted.

For an exam conducted in the organization's facilities, a private office should be provided as the examiner's workspace, rather than a nook near the coffee bar or copy machine. Affording some privacy will prevent organization staff from involving themselves in the examination and minimize any distractions that would waste the examiner's time. Particularly when a paid professional is assisting in the examination, it is useful to limit the scope of the work and make the review as efficient as possible, to save professional fees.

(c) How to Prepare for the Audit

Good judgment is called for in culling through an organization's records to prepare for the auditor's appointment. For example, the auditor will ask to see correspondence files. In the case of a United Way agency in a major city, this cannot possibly mean every single correspondence file. Perhaps the correspondence of the chief financial officer or the executive director would be furnished, with an offer to furnish more correspondence if desired.

Too often, some of the requested records are not in appropriate condition to be examined. The most troublesome records are often the board minutes. It is important to carefully prepare minutes of the board of directors' meetings. Optimally, such minutes reflect the exempt nature of the organization's overall concerns. If, for example, a commercial-type operation is undertaken because it helps to accomplish exempt purposes, the minutes should reflect that relationship. Why did the organization enter into a joint venture with a theatrical show producer? Was it because the business put up all the working capital so that the organization experienced no financial risk for producing an avant garde opera production? Proving the relatedness of the venture for purposes of avoiding the unrelated business income tax may be easier with carefully documented minutes.

For private foundations, public charities, and civic associations, it is extremely important that the minutes of director and committee meetings document the basis on which salaries, fees, and benefits of personnel are approved. What the IRS calls *contemporaneous documentation of process* is required to evidence an exempt organization is paying reasonable compensation and not excess benefits subject to sanctions or self-dealing penalties.[33]

Pamphlets, brochures, and other literature are also an open-ended category. In some cases, the volume of such literature is staggering, so choosing those examples that portray the organization in the best light is acceptable. According to Jason Kall, agents look for a variety of matters in reviewing these items:

- *Nature of exempt activities.* The agent reviews the organization's publications with an eye to the exempt purpose of programs conducted. The EO representatives should review the criteria outlined in Chapters 2–10 alongside the EO's Form 1023 and 1024 for descriptions of activities originally approved by the IRS.

- *Unrelated business income.* The exempt organization's pamphlets and publications will be perused for advertisements and for donor acknowledgments that constitute advertising.[34] Contracts and agreements relating to joint ventures,[35] licensing of intellectual property, affinity cards, and exclusive marketing agreements,[36] rentals of property and other arrangements with exempt and nonexempt entities will be evaluated in this regard. Descriptions of fund-raising activities would be also studied to discern their character as related or unrelated.

- *Disclosures.* For schools, the agent looks for disclosure of their nondiscrimination policy.[37] For 501(c)(4),(5), and (6) organizations, disclosure of nondeductibility as a charitable entity and for lobbying expenditures would be sought.[38] Fund-raising invitations, member brochures, and other solicitations for donations are reviewed for quid pro quo disclosures.[39]

Obviously, the examiner cannot and will not look at every shred of paper produced by the organization in a three-year period. Someone knowledgeable about the issues involved in ongoing qualification for exempt status should review the materials and choose those most suitable to be furnished to the auditor. Or, such a person should develop guidelines for persons gathering the information, to ensure that the best possible case is presented to the IRS.

---

[33] See Chapter 14§4 for private foundations and Chapter 20§9 for public charities and civic leagues.
[34] See Chapter 21§8(e).
[35] See Chapter 22.
[36] See Chapter 21§10(d) and (f).
[37] See Chapter 5§1.
[38] See Chapter 6§4.
[39] See Chapter 24.

(d) Achieving Positive Results

There are three rules for achieving positive results in an IRS examination:

- *The less said the better.* Answer only the specific question asked. Do not provide more information than is requested. One person in the organization should be identified as the lead contact through whom all answers are to be funneled. If an outside professional is conducting the examination, he or she would be the contact. The examiner should be given specific answers to specific questions. He or she should not be allowed to go through the organization's file cabinets.

- *Do not answer a question if you are unsure of its import.* Problem issues should be identified ahead of time, and the materials to be furnished to the IRS should be organized for presentation in the most favorable light. New materials, reports, or summaries of information found lacking can be prepared to better reflect the organization's purposes and accomplishments. If you are unsure of the answer to any question, say that you are not sure and that you will find out. Make a list for further consideration, consult a professional, or simply get better prepared to present the best picture for the organization. Agents commonly prepare an information request for answers to such questions and for data not readily furnished during the first visit.

- *Expect the best from the examiner.* The IRS agents who examine exempt organizations are knowledgeable, experienced, cooperative (usually), and sympathetic with the spirit of the nonprofit community. They perceive their purpose as different from that of income tax examiners. Their examination can often be a positive experience for an organization. It can validate the exempt organization's qualification, and can sometimes help the organization staff to understand why in fact the organization is exempt. Another very useful aspect is the reminder it serves of the need to document and preserve a clear record of accomplishments, both from a financial and philosophical standpoint.

(e) The Desired Result: A "No Change"

The desired end product of an examination is a "no change" letter stating that the organization will continue to qualify for exempt status. If the examiner finds no reason to challenge the status of the organization, he or she will normally convey this conclusion to the organization's representative in the field. The examiner then returns to the office to "write up the case." The report is reviewed by the examiner's superiors and, some months later, the organization should receive a letter similar to Exhibit 28–4.

In the event that the IRS examiner finds the organization is not operating in an entirely exempt fashion, several consequences might follow. Changes with no consequences to the basic exempt status could be suggested. A change from §509(a)(2) to 509(a)(1) could result from an analysis of the sources of revenue, but

Exhibit 28–4

SAMPLE "NO CHANGE" LETTER

Internal Revenue Service   Department of the Treasury
District Director   MIDSTATES KEY DISTRICT
                                  OFFICE(EP/EO)
Date: September 22, 1998

                                  Form Number: 990
                          Exemption under section 501(c)(3)
                                  of the Internal Revenue Code
                          Person to Contact:
                                  Thomas McDonough
                          Contact Telephone Number:
00000   (281)721-7969
                          Period Ended:
                                  December 31, 1992

Our recent examination of the above information return
disclosed that your organization continues to qualify for
exemption from Federal income tax. Accordingly, the return is
accepted as filed.

However, the following item(s) were noted:

Our review of your return, Form 990, and related records
indicated that you did not file Forms 1099. Under section
6041 of the Internal Revenue Code, you are required to issue
Forms 1099 to recipients of prizes, awards, or fees of $600
or more during a calendar year. Even though we have now
obtained these returns, your organization may be responsible
for filing similar forms in future years.

During the examination, it was determined that you did not
file when due Forms 940, Employer's Annual Federal
Unemployment Tax Return, or 941, Employer's Quarterly Federal
Tax Return, for wages paid to employees. Under section 6011
of the Internal Revenue Code, you are required to file Forms
940 and 941 when wages are paid for services rendered.

Our examination of your organization indicates that you
did not file Form 990 (or 990-PF) by the due date. Section
6652(d) of the Internal Revenue Code provides for a penalty
of $10 for each day the return is late (not to exceed
$5,000), unless there is reasonable cause for late filing.

You established that you had reasonable cause for filing
this return late; therefore, the $10 a day penalty will not
be charged. However, there may be a penalty if your return is
not filed when due for future years.

Our examination of your organization indicates that you
did not file Form 990 (or 990-PF) by the due date. Section

1100 Commerce, Dallas, TX 75242   Letter 1656-DO(1-93)

Exhibit 28–4 (continued)

6652(d) of the Internal Revenue Code provides for a penalty of $10 for each day the return is late (not to exceed $5,000), unless there is reasonable cause for the late filing.

You were previously billed for this penalty by the service center and there will be no additional penalties. Please be sure to file your return when due to avoid a penalty in the future.

Our examination of your organization indicates that you did not file Form 990 (or 990-PF) by the due date. Section 6652(d) of the Internal Revenue Code provides a penalty of $10 for each day the return is late (not to exceed $5,000), unless there is a reasonable cause for the late filing.

You did not establish a reasonable cause for filing late. Therefore, you will receive a bill from the service center for the late filing penalty.

Although no adjustment was made at this time, for future years expenses must be properly allocated between exempt and investment activities.

During the examination of your Form 990, we noted that you combined income from different sources instead of reporting the separate amounts as required. When filing future returns, please show each source of income and amount on the appropriate line of your return.

Your current records do not appear to comply with Revenue Procedure 80-53, 1980-2 C.B. 848, which requires you to include fringe benefits in gross income reported on Forms W-2 even if these benefits are not subject to income tax withholding. To avoid a penalty in the future, full compliance is required.

During the examination of your Form 990, we noted that some amounts shown on the balance sheet did not reflect those recorded on your books of account. For future years, you should provide accurate figures on your return to avoid a possible penalty under section 6652(d)(1) of the Internal Revenue Code.

During the review of your Form 990, we determined that your organization did not identify its special fundraising activities. When future returns are filed, you should complete Part 1, Line 9 of Form 990 and prepare the required schedule for fundraising activities, including the amount of receipts and expenses. Omitting material information on your Form 990 may subject you to a penalty under section 6652(d)(1) of the Internal Revenue Code.

We will appreciate your compliance with the above requirements.

Sincerely Yours
Glenn E Henderson
Director

1100 Commerce, Dallas, TX 75242   Letter 1656-DO(1-93)

this change often has no adverse consequence. More seriously, the agent could discover failure of the support test for public charity status and could reclassify the exempt organization as a private foundation. Even so, the basic exempt status as a §501(c)(3) organization is not revoked.

If the agent finds unreported or underreported unrelated business income[40] (UBI), the consequences depend upon the amount of the UBI in relation to the organization's total revenues. If the UBI is not considered excessive, the organization's exempt status is not challenged. However, excessive UBI may trigger an exemption challenge. If Form 990-T has not previously been filed, its preparation will be requested and any delinquent income taxes, penalties, and interest will be assessed. Deductions claimed for UBI are also reviewed.

The agent often comments on documentation policies. Are invoices available to evidence all disbursements? What about expense reimbursements reports, particularly for travel and entertainment? Payments for personal services paid to individuals are closely scrutinized to evaluate employee versus independent contractor classifications.[41]

Private schools must prove that they do not operate in a racially discriminatory manner and present proof of publishing notice of the nondiscrimination policy in a widely circulated publication in the community.[42] Additionally, the agent will seek statistical information about the student and teacher population and scholarship grants that might evidence lack of racial balance. Failure to publish the proper notice by a school that does not in fact discriminate will probably be forgiven. However, such a failure in a school whose students are all one race may cause the agent to recommend revocation of status.

The most serious challenge, of course, is a revocation of exemption. The reasons for revocation could include violations of any of the restraints and sanctions discussed in this book. The organization has the right to appeal the examiner's report. Specific procedures must be followed, and some policy decisions will affect the outcome. For example, appeals can be filed either with the regional or the national office in Washington, D.C. Resisting a proposed revocation of exempt status demands the assistance of a trained professional and is beyond the scope of this book.

28.4 WHEN AN ORGANIZATION LOSES ITS TAX-EXEMPT STATUS

The national office of the IRS issued General Counsel Memorandum 39813 in April, 1990, which extensively describes the consequences and tax filing requirements when a public charity's exempt status is retroactively revoked. Such revocation occurs after the IRS has found that an organization has operated to benefit a limited group of insiders, received excessive unrelated business income, engaged in excess lobbying or political activity, or has otherwise failed to serve its charitable or public constituents. The memorandum was reportedly issued to explain the IRS's response to the tax court's opinion in *The Synanon Church v. Commissioner*.[43]

---

[40] See Chapters 21 and 27§14.
[41] See Chapter 25.
[42] See Chapter 5.
[43] *The Synanon Church v. Commissioner* 57 T.C.M. 602 (1989).

(a) Classification of the Organization

For federal income tax purposes, an organization losing its exempt status is treated as a corporation effective on the date of revocation; a charitable trust will be taxed as trusts. Some relief is provided for innocent failures. Contributions received by a former exempt organization reclassified as a taxable corporation are to be treated as nontaxable gifts under IRC §102, during the years the organization considered itself exempt (or, arguably, under IRC §118 or 362(c) as capital received from nonshareholders).

Consequences to Individual Contributors

Contributions received under false pretenses are taxable. If an organization misrepresented itself in its solicitations by stating that it was tax exempt and was devoting the gifts to exempt purposes when the facts indicate otherwise, the gifts can be deemed taxable income. The tax basis for calculating gain or loss or donated goods and property is carried over from the donors.

Regarding *deductions* that can be claimed against the retroactively taxed income, the memorandum fortunately provides for the deduction of expenses related to the production of business or investment income. To the extent that income is excluded as gifts or contributions to capital, the allocable expenses would not be deductible. Expenditures not otherwise allowable under the normal income tax rules, such as political expenditures or expenses of an activity not entered into for profit motives (such as a hobby), are also not deductible.

Excise taxes could be due and payable by the organization and its officers and directors, if the revocation is due to excess lobbying expenses or political campaign activities[44] or excess benefits paid to disqualified persons.[45]

One major concern when an organization loses its exempt status may be who is liable for the tax on the unfairly sheltered income. Should the individual contributors lose their tax deductions? Should the organization pay the tax due on the funds? The memorandum makes it clear that the official who diverts funds to his or her own use (resulting in individual financial gain) realizes personal ordinary income to the extent of the economic benefit so derived. Innocent and unknowledgeable contributors do not lose their deductions until notice of revocation is published in the IRS Revenue Bulletin.

[44] See Chapter 23.
[45] See Chapter 20.

Table of Cases

TABLE OF CASES

TABLE OF CASES

Table of IRS Revenue Rulings and Revenue Procedures

Revenue Rulings	Sections	Revenue Rulings	Sections	Revenue Rulings	Sections
54-394, 1954-2 C.B. 131	§6.2	65-195, 1965-2 C.B. 164	§6.2	68-118, 1968-1 C.B. 261	§6.2
55-70, 1955-1 C.B. 506	§24.3(b)	65-244, 1965-2 C.B. 167	§20.7(b)	68-165, 1968-1 C.B. 253	§5.1(e)
55-230, 1955-1 C.B. 71	§7.2(a)	65-270, 1965-2 C.B. 160	§5.1(e)	68-168, 1968-1 C.B. 269	§§9.1(b),
55-311, 1955-1 C.B. 72	§6.2	65-271, 1965-2 C.B. 161	§5.1(f)		9.2(b)
55-406, 1955-1 C.B. 73	§4.1	65-298, 1965-2 C.B. 163	§§4.5, 5.1(e),	68-182, 1968-1 C.B. 263	§8.3(b)
55-587, 1955-2 C.B. 261	§5.1(e)		5.3(a)	68-222, 1968-1 C.B. 243	§10.3(a)
56-84, 1956-1 C.B. 201	§8.4(b)	65-299, 1965-2 C.B. 165	§6.2	68-224, 1968-1 C.B. 222	§6.2
56-138, 1956-1 C.B. 202	§4.1	65-432, 1965-2 C.B. 104	§24.3	68-263, 1968-1 C.B. 256	§23.7
56-185, 1956-1 C.D. 202	§4.6	66-79, 1966-1 C.B. 48	§8.11	68-265, 1968-1 C.B. 265	§8.4(b)
56-245, 1956-1 C.B. 204	§7.2(a)	66-102, 1966-1 C.B. 133	§10.3(b)	68-306, 1968-1 C.B. 257	§3.1(b)
56-305, 1956-2 C.B. 307	§9.1(b)	66-103, 1966-1 C.B. 134	§4.5	68-307, 1968-1 C.B. 258	§5.1(i)
56-403, 1956-2 C.B. 307	§§2.2(a), 4.5	66-105, 1966-1 C.B. 145	§7.2(c)	68-371, 1968-2 C.B. 204	§§10.3,
57-574, 1957-2 C.B. 161	§3.4	66-147, 1966-1 C.B. 137	§§5.1(i), 5.3,		10.3(c)
58-224, 1958-1 C.B. 242	§8.4(b)		5.3(a)	68-372, 1968-2 C.B. 205	§5.1(g)
58-293, 1958-1 C.B. 146	§8.11	66-150, 1966-1 C.B. 147	§§9.1(b),	68-373, 1968-2 C.B. 206	§5.4
58-294, 1958-1 C.B. 244	§8.3(b)		10.3(a)	68-432, 1968-2 C.B. 104	§24.3(b)
58-455, 1958-2 C.B. 261	§10.3(a)	66-178, 1966-1 C.B. 138	§5.1(g)	68-438, 1968-2 C.B. 609	§4.2
58-501, 1958-2 C.B. 262	§§9.2, 9.2(a)	66-179, 1966-1 C.B. 139	§§6.2, 8.3(c),	68-504, 1968-2 C.B. 211	§5.1(e)
58-588, 1958-2 C.B. 265	§9.3(b)		9.1(b),	68-534, 1968-2 C.B. 217	§7.1(b)
58-589, 1958-2 C.B. 266	§§9.1(a),	66-223, 1966-2 C.B. 224	§8.4(a)	68-535, 1968-2 C.B. 219	§9.2(b)
	9.2(a)	66-295, 1966-2 C.B. 207	§10.3(a)	68-563, 1968-2 C.B. 212	§3.1(c)
59-6, 1959-1 C.B. 121	§7.1(b)	66-338, 1966 2 C.B. 226	§20.7(b)	68-609, 1968-2 C.B. 227	§20.6
59-129, 1959-1 C.B. 58	§3.2(b)	66-354, 1966-2 C.B. 207	§7.1(c)	68-639, 1968-2 C.B. 220	§9.2
59-234, 1959-2 C.B. 149	§§8.4(b),	66-358, 1966-2 C.B. 216	§24.3	68-655, 1968-2 C.B. 613	§4.2
	20.7(b)	66-359, 1966-2 C.B. 219	§5.6	69-68, 1969-1 C.B. 153	§9.1(b)
60-106, 1960-1 C.B. 153	§20.7(b)	67-4, 1967-1 C.B. 121	§§4.5, 5.1(i)	69-106, 1969-1 C.B. 153	§8.4(a)
60-144, 1960-1 C.B. 636	§27.1(c)	67-6, 1967-1 C.B. 135	§6.3, 23.4(a)	69-174, 1969-1 C.B. 149	§4.1
60-384, 1960-2 C.B. 172	§10.2	67-7, 1967-1 C.B. 137	§§7.1(b),	69-175, 1969-1 C.B. 149	§20.7(b)
61-87, 1961-1 C.B. 191	§4.5		7.1(c)	69-247, 1969-1 C.B. 303	§27.1(c)
61-170, 1961-2 C.B. 112	§8.4(b)	67-8, 1967-1 C.B. 142	§§2.2(a),	69-253, 1969-1 C.B. 151	§2.1(d)
61-177, 1961-2 C.B. 117	§§8.4(a), 8 9,		9.1(b)	69 256, 1969-1 C.B. 151	§2.2(a)
	23.1, 23.6	67-71, 1967-1 C.B. 125	§23.2(c)	69-257, 1969-1 C.B. 151	§4.5
62-10, 1962-1 C.B. 305	§27.1(c)	67-77, 1967-1 C.B. 138	§8.3(b)	69-266, 1969-1 C.B. 151	§20.6
62-17, 1962-1 C.B. 87	§7.1(b)	67-138, 1967-1 C.B. 129	§4.2	69-279, 1969-1 C.B. 152	§§2.1(d),
62-23, 1962-1 C.B. 200	§5.1(a)	67-139, 1967-1 C.B. 129	§9.1(b)		2.2(a)
62-113, 1962-2 C.B. 109	§2.2(a)	67-148, 1967-1 C.B. 132	§5.1(e)	69-381, 1969-2 C.B. 113	§10.3(a)
62-167, 1962-2 C.B. 142	§6.2	67-150, 1967-1 C.B. 133	§4.1	69-383, 1969-2 C.B. 113	§§4.6(a),
62-191, 1962-2 C.B. 146	§7.1(b)	67-151, 1967-1 C.B. 134	§5.6		20.2(c)
62-73, 1963-1 C.B. 35	§24.1(d)	67-176, 1967-1 C.B. 140	§8.4(b)	69-384, 1969-2 C.B. 112	§6.2
63-156, 1963-2 C.B. 79	§25.2.(a)	67-217, 1967-2 C.B. 181	§4.5	69-386, 1969-2 C.B. 123	§7.1(c)
63-190, 1963-2 C.B. 212	§§9.1(b),	67-246, 1967-2 C.B. 104	§§24.1(a),	69-441, 1969-2 C.B. 115	§4.1
	9.2(b)		24.2(c)	69-464, 1969-2 C.B. 132	§21.12(a)
63-220, 1963-2 C.B. 208	§4.5	67-248, 1967-2 C.B. 204	§9.3(b)	69-526, 1969-2 C.B. 115	§5.3(a)
63-235, 1963-2 C.B. 210	§4.5	67-250, 1967-2 C.B. 182	§4.2	69-527, 1969 2 C.B. 125	§9.1(b)
64-118, 1964-1 (Part 1)	§9.1(b)	67-251, 1967-2 C.B. 196	§§7.2(c), 8.7	69-528, 1969-2 C.B. 127	§10.3(a)
C.B. 182		67-252, 1967-2 C.B. 195	§7.2(c)	69-545, 1969-2 C.B. 117	§§4.6, 4.6(d)
64-174, 1964-1 (Part 1)	§5.1(f)	67-284, 1967-2 C.B. 55, 58	§21.9(f)	69-635, 1969-2 C.B. 126	§§9.1(a),
C.B. 183		67-292, 1967-2 C.B. 184	§§4.2, 5.1(g)		9.1(b)
64-175, 1964-1 (Part 1)	§5.1(f)	67-293, 1967-2 C.B. 185	§23.4(a)	70-31, 1970-1 C.B. 130	§8.6
C.B. 185		67-294, 1967-2 C.B. 193	§6.2	70-32, 1970-1 C.B. 140	§9.1(b)
64-182, 1964-1 C.B. 186	§§2.2(d),	67-295, 1967-2 C.B. 197	§8.4(b)	70-47, 1970-1 C.B. 49	§24.3(b)
	2.2(e)	67-325, 1967-2 C.B. 113	§4.6(f)	70-48, 1970-1 C.B. 133	§9.2
64-187, 1964-1 (Part 1)	§6.2	67-392, 1967-2 C.B. 191	§§5.1(e),	70-79, 1970-1 C.B. 127	§23.4(a)
C.B. 354			5.1(f)	70-81, 1970-1 C.B. 131	§8.8
64-195, 1964-2 C.B. 138	§23.4(a)	68-14, 1968-1 C.B. 243	§6.2	70-95, 1970-1 C.B. 137	§8.4(b)
65-1, 1965-1 C.B. 226	§5.3(a)	68-15, 1968-1 C.B. 244	§4.2	70-129, 1970-1 C.B. 128	§5.3(a)
65-14, 1965-1 C.B. 236	§8.4(b)	68-68, 1968-1 C.B. 51	§25.2(a)	70-186, 1970-1 C.B. 128	§4.2
65-61, 1965-1 C.B. 234	§5.4	68-70, 1968-1 C.B. 248	§4.2	70-187, 1970-1 C.B. 131	§8.4(a)
65-64, 1965-1 C.B. 241	§9.2(a)	68-72, 1968-1 C.B. 250	§3.1(c)	70-285, 1970-2 C.B. 115	§4.1

TABLE OF IRS REVENUE RULINGS AND REVENUE PROCEDURES

Revenue Rulings	Sections	Revenue Rulings	Sections	Revenue Rulings	Sections
70-372, 1970-2 C.B. 118	§7.2(c)	74-125, 1974-1 C.B. 327	§17.3(b)	76-81, 1976-1 C.B. 156	§6.2
70-533, 1970-2 C.B. 112	§§4.1, 5.1(a)	74-148, 1974-1 C.B. 138	§9.1(b)	76-147, 1976-1 C.B. 151	§§4.2, 6.3
70-534, 1970-2 C.B. 113	§§5.1(e),	74-167, 1974-1 C.B. 134	§7.1(e)	76-167, 1976-1 C.B. 329	§5.1(a)
	21.13(c)	74-168, 1974-1 C.B. 139	§9.3(c)	76-204, 1976-1 C.B. 152	§4.2
70-583, 1970-2 C.B. 114	§4.1	74-183, 1974-1 C.B. 328	§13.5	76-207, 1976-1 C.B. 1578	§8.8
70-585, 1970-2 C.B. 115	§4.2(a)	74-194, 1974-1 C.B. 129	§5.6	76-208, 1976-1 C.B. 161	§11.6(c)
70-591, 1970-2 C.B. 118	§8.4(b)	74-195, 1974-1 C.B. 135	§7.2(c)	76-232, 1976-2 C.B. 62	§24.1(a)
70-641, 1970-2 C.B. 119	§§8.3, 8.9	74-224, 1974-1 C.B. 61	§3.2(c)	76-248, 1976-1 C.B. 353	§§13.3(a),
71-17, 1971-1 C.B. 683	§9.3(c)	74-246, 1974-1 C.B. 130	§4.3		15.5(e)
71-29, 1971-1 C.B. 150	§4.3	74-287, 1974-1 C.B. 327	§12.2(c)	76-296, 1976-2 C.B. 141	§5.3(a)
71-97, 1971-1 C.B. 150	§4.5	74-361, 1974-2 C.B. 159	§4.3	76-298, 1976-1 C.B. 161	§11.6(c)
71-99, 1971-1 C.B. 151	§4.3	74-403, 1974-2 C.B. 381	§13.2(a)	76-335, 1976-2 C.B. 141	§10.3(a)
71-155, 1971-1 C.B. 152	§8.4(b)	74-404, 1974-2 C.B. 382	§13.2(b)	76-384, 1976-2 C.B. 57	§5.1(a)
71-395, 1971-2 C.B. 228	§§5.1(g),	74-425, 1974-2 C.B. 373	§9.1(b)	76-399, 1976-2 C.B. 147	§7.2(b)
	18.2(b),	74-489, 1974-2 C.B. 169	§9.3(c)	76-401, 1976-2 C.B. 175	§8.2
	20.7(b)	74-498, 1974-2 C.B. 387	§15.1(c)	76-410, 1976-2 C.B. 155	§8.4(b)
71-421, 1971-2 C.B. 229	§9.1(b)	74-518, 1974-2 C.B. 166	§7.2(c)	76-419, 1976-2 C.B. 146	§§4.2, 4.2(b)
71-504, 1971-2 C.B. 231,	§§8.2, 8.11	74-553, 1974-2 C.B. 168	§§8.4(a),	76-420, 1976-2 C.B. 153	§7.1(c)
232			8.11	76-424, 1976-2 C.B. 367	§13.2(a)
71-505, 1971-2 C.B. 232	§8.11	74-560, 1974-2 C.B. 389	§15.4(b)	76-440, 1976-2 C.B. 58	§11.2(h)
71-506, 1971-2 C.B. 233	§8.11	74-572, 1974-2 C.B. 82	§11.2(c)	76-441, 1967-2 C.B. 147	§20.4
71-544, 1971-2 C.B. 227	§10.3(a)	74-574, 1974-2 C.B. 160	§23.2(b)	76-443, 1976-2 C.B. 149	§§5.1(f),
71-545, 1971-2 C.B. 235	§5.1(g)	74-575, 1974-2 C.B. 161	§3.1(b)		22.5(a)
71-580	§21.7(a)	74-579, 1974-2 C.B. 383	§13.3(b)	76-456, 1976-2 C.B. 151	§23.2(b)
72-102, 1972-1 C.B. 149	§6.3	74-587, 1974-2 C.B. 162	§4.2(b)	76-459, 1976-2 C.B. 369	§14.7(b)
72-124, 1972-1 C.B. 145	§4.6(h)	74-595, 1974-2 C.B. 164	§5.1(e)	76-460, 1976-2 C.B. 371	§17.3(a)
72-147, 1972-1 C.B. 147	§20.7(b)	74-596, 1974-2 C.B. 167	§7.1(b)	76-461, 1976-2 C.B. 371	§17.3(a)
72-228, 1972-1 C.B. 148	§4.2	74-600, 1974-2 C.B. 385	§§2.1(f),	77-4, 1977-1 C.B. 141	§5.1(i)
72-391, 1972-2 C.B. 249	§7.2(c)		14.2(c)	77-7, 1977-1 C.B. 354	§15.4(c)
72-430, 1972-2 C.B. 105	§5.1(a)			77-7, 1977-1 C.B. 540	§15.4(a)
72-462, 1972-2 C.B. 76	§25.2(a)	75-25, 1975-1 C.B. 359	§14.1(c)	77-44, 1977-1 C.B. 118	§17.3(b)
72-512, 1972-2 C.B. 246	§23.2(b)	75-38, 1975-1 C.B. 161	§12.2(a)	77-46, 1977-1 C.B. 147	§7.1(c)
72-513, 1972-2 C.B. 246	§§23.2(b),	75-42, 1975-1 C.B. 359	§14.5(e)	77-47, 1977-1 C.B. 156	§21.12(a)
	23.4(a)	75-47, 1975-1 C.B. 152-154	§4.2(c)	77-111, 1977-1 C.B. 144	§§4.2, 4.2(a)
		75-74, 1975-1 C.B. 152	§4.0	77-112, 1977-1 C.B. 149	§8.2
72-606, 1972-2 C.B. 78	§3.2(c)	75-75, 1975-1 C.B. 152-154	§4.2(c)	77-114, 1977-1 C.B. 153	§18.1(b)
73-104, 1973-1 C.B. 263	§21.13	75-76, 1975-1 C.B. 152-154	§4.2(c)	77-153, 1977-1 C.B. 147	§7.2(c)
73-105, 1973-1 C.B. 265	§21.13	75-85, 1975-1 C.B. 150	§4.2	77-154, 1977-1 C.B. 148	§§7.1(b),
73-126, 1973-1 C.B. 220	§20.2	75-159, 1975-1 C.B. 48	§6.2		7.1(e)
73-128, 1973-1 C.B. 222	§§4.1. 4.5,	75-196, 1975-1 C.B. 155	§5.1(g)	77-160, 1977-1 C.B. 351	§§14.5(c),
	5.1(e),	75-198, 1975-1 C.B. 157	§§4.1,		14.5(d)
	21.7(a)		22.5(c)	77-164, 1977-1 C.B. 20	§10.2
73-129, 1973-1 C.B. 221	§4.5	75-200, 1975-1 C.B. 163	§21.6(a)	77-165, 1977-1 C.B. 21	§10.2
73-285, 1973-2 C.B. 174	§4.2	75-201, 1975-1 C.B. 164	§21.6(a)	77-206, 1977-1 C.B. 149	§8.7
73-320, 1973-2 C.B. 385	§§13.2,	75-207, 1975-1 C.B. 361	§15.1(c)	77-213, 1977-1 C.B. 357	§17.5(d)
	15.5(e)	75-283, 1975-2 C.B. 201	§4.1	77-246, 1977-2 C.B. 190	§4.1
73-363, 1973-2 C.B. 383	§14.2(c)	75-285, 1975-2 C.B. 203	§4.2	77-259, 1977-2 C.B. 387	§§14.2,
73-407, 1973-2 C.B. 383	§§14.5(e),	75-286, 1975-2 C.B. 210	§6.2		14.4(d)
	24.3	75-288, 1975-2 C.B. 212	§7.1(b)	77-272, 1977-2 C.B. 191	§5.1(e)
73-411, 1973-2 C.B. 180	§8.3(b)	75-336, 1975-2 C.B. 110	§13.1(c)	77-288, 1977-2 C.B. 388	§14.4(d)
73-424, 1973-2 C.B. 190	§21.5(a)	75-384, 1975-2 C.B. 204	§§4.2, 6.2	77-331, 1977-2 C.B. 388	§§14.5,
73-434, 1973-2 C.B. 71	§5.1(a)	75-387, 1975-2 C.B. 216	§11.5(c)		14.5(e)
73-440, 1973-2 C.B. 177	§23.4(a)	75-392, 1975-2 C.B. 447	§15.1(c)	77-366, 1977-2 C.B. 192	§§3.1(b),
73-452, 1973-2 C.B. 183	§8.4(b)	75-393, 1975-2 C.B. 451	§17.3(a)		21.13(c)
73-520, 1973-2 C.B. 180	§§7.2(a),	75-410, 1975-2 C.B. 446	§13.3(a)	77-379, 1977-2 C.B. 387	§§14.2(b),
	9.1(b)	75-435, 1975-2 C.B. 215	§11.2(f)		14.3
73-546, 1973-2 C.B. 384	§14.4(d)	75-442, 1975-2 C.B. 448	§15.5(e)	77-380, 1977-2 C.B. 419	§17.3(a)
73-563, 1973-2 C.B. 24	§10.2	75-470, 1975-2 C.B. 207	§5.1(g)	77-429, 1977-2 C.B. 189	§10.3(b)
73-564, 1973-2 C.B. 28	§17.3(f)	75-471, 1975-2 C.B. 207	§5.1(f)	77-430, 1977-2 C.B. 1914	§3.1(b)
73-567, 1973-2 C.B. 178	§§8.4(a),	75-473, 1975-2 C.B. 213	§7.1(b)	78-41, 1978-1 C.B. 148	§2.2(h)
	8.11	75-492, 1975-2 C.B. 80	§5.1(a)	78-51, 1978-1 C.B. 165	§8.4(b)
73-595, 1973-2 C.B. 384	§14.4(d)	75-494, 1975-2 C.B. 214	§9.1(b)	78-68, 1978-1 C.B. 149	§4.3
73-613, 1973-2 C.B. 385	§§14.5(a),	75-495, 1975-2 C.B. 449	§15.4(b)	78-69, 1978-1 C.B. 156	§6.2
	14.5(b)	75-511, 1975-2 C.B. 450	§15.4(c)	78-77, 1978-1 C.B. 378	§14.2(a)
74-16, 1974-1 C.B. 126	§5.1(e)	76-4, 1976-1 C.B. 145	§5.1(f)	78-82, 1978-1 C.B. 70	§5.1(a)
74-17, 1974-1 C.B. 130	§6.2	76-10, 1976-1 C.B. 355	§14.7(b)	78-90, 1978-1 C.B. 380	§16.2(b)
74-30, 1974-1 C.B. 137	§9.1(b)	76-18, 1976-1 C.B. 355	§14.2(a)	78-102, 1978-1 C.B. 379	§15.4(b)
74-99, 1974-1 C.B. 131	§6.3	76-21, 1976-1 C.B. 147	§4.1	78-111, 1978-1 C.B. 41	§23.4(a)
74-116, 1974-1 C.B. 127	§5.1(e)	76-22, 1976-1 C.B. 148	§4.1	78-112 1978-1 C.B. 42	§23.4(a)
74-117, 1974-1 C.B. 128	§23.2(c)	76-31, 1976-1 C.B. 157	§7.1(b)	78-113 1978-1 C.B. 43	§23.4(a)
74-118, 1974-1 C.B. 134	§7.2(b)	76-47, 1976-2 C.B. 670	§17.3(d)		

TABLE OF IRS REVENUE RULINGS AND REVENUE PROCEDURES

Revenue Rulings	Sections	Revenue Rulings	Sections	Revenue Procedures	Sections
78-114 1978-1 C.B. 44	§23.4(a)	81-94, 1981-1 C.B. 330	§3.1(e)	77-32, 1977-2 C.B. 541	§17.3(d)
78-225, 1978-1 C.B. 159	§§8.3(b), 8.8	81-95, 1981-1 C.B. 332	§§6.1, 23.1	79-3, 1979-1 C.B. 483	§28.2(b)
78-248, 1978-1 C.B. 154	§23.2(a)	81-108, 1981-1 C.B. 327	§10.3(a)	79-63, 1979-3 C.B. 578	§18.1(b)
78-288, 1978-2 C.B. 179	§§7.1(c), 7.1(e)	81-125, 1981-1 C.B. 515	§17.4	80-27, 1980-1 C.B. 677	§18.1(f)
		81-127, 1981-1 C.B. 357	§8.4(a)	80-31, 1980-1 C.B. 646	§18.1(b)
78-301, 1978-2 C.B. 103	§25.2(a)	81-138, 1981-1 C.B. 358	§8.8	80-39, 1980-2 C.B. 772	§17.3(d)
78-305, 1978-2 C.B. 172	§5.1(e)	81-175, 1981-1 C.B. 337	§8.4(b)	81-6, 1981-1 C.B. 620	§17.4(a)
78-315, 1975-2 C.B. 271	§15.5(b)	81-178, 1981-2 C.B. 135	§21.8(c)	81-7, 1981-1 C.B. 621	§11.2(h)
78-385, 1978-2 C.B. 174	§3.1(c)	81-217, 1981-2 C.B. 217	§17.3(f)	81-65, 1981-2 C.B. 690	§17.3(d)
78-395, 1978-2 C.B. 270	§14.3	81-276, 1981-2 C.B. 128	§§4.3, 4.6(g)	82-2, 1982-1 C.B. 367	§2.1(b)
78-426, 1978-2 C.B. 175	§5.4	81-284, 1981-2 C.B. 130	§4.2(b)	82-39, 1982-17 I.R.B. 18	§18.6(a)
78-428, 1978-2 C.B. 177	§§4.1, 5.4	81-295, 1981-2 C.B. 15	§21.9(f)	84-47, 1984-1 C.B. 545	§2.1(a)
79-12, 1979-1 C.B. 208	§23.3(a)	81-811, 1981-1 C.B. 509	§16.1(b)	85-37, 1985-2 C.B. 438	§28.2(c)
79-13, 1979-1 C.B. 208	§23.3(a)	82-136, 1982-2 C.B. 300	§14.5(e)	85-51, 1985-2 C.B. 717	§17.3(d)
79-18, 1979-1 C.B. 152	§4.6(h)	82-137, 1982-2 C.B. 303	§15.1(d)	85-58, 1985-2 C.B. 740	§28.2(b)
79-71, 1979-1 C.B. 249	§5.1(e)	82-138, 1982-2 C.B. 106	§8.6	89-23, 1989-1 C.B. 844	§§17.4(a), 18.6(a)
79-319, 1979-2 C.B. 388	§15.4(a)	82-223, 1982-2 C.B. 301	§§14.5(a), 17.6	90-12, 1990-1 C.B. 471	§§21.9(g), 27.5(b), 27.5(d)
79-321, 1979-1 C.B. 129	§23.2(b)				
79-359, 1979-2 C.B. 226	§§3.1(c), 21.7(a)	83-74, 1983-1 C.B. 112	§§6.3(a), 6.3(c)		
79-375, 1979-2 C.B. 389	§15.4(a)	83-104, 1983-2 C.B. 46	§21.1(a)	90 12 (Fcb. 1990)	§24.3(a)
79-630, 1979-2 C.B. 236	§4.6(f)	83-153, 1983-2 C.B. 48	§11.5(c)	90-27, 1990-1 C.B. 514	§§18.1(b), 18.4(c)
80-18, 1980-1 C.B. 103	§13.1(a)	83-157, 1983-2 C.B. 94	§4.6		
80-63, 1980-1 C.B. 116	§6.3	83-164, 1983-2 C.B. 95	§8.3(a)	91-20, 1991-10 I.R.B. 26	§3.3
80-69, 1980-1 C.B. 55	§24.1(b)	83-170, 1983-2 C.B. 97	§9.1(b)	92-58, 1992-2, I.R.B. 10	§§21.9(g), 24.3(a)
80-97, 1980-1 C.B. 257	§17.6	85-1, 1985-1 C.B. 177	§4.3		
80-110, I.R.B. 1980-16, 110	§25.2(b)	85-2, 1985-1 C.B. 178	§4.3	92-59, 1992-29 I.R.B. 11	§4.2(c)
80-114	§21.7(a)	85-175, 1985-2 C.B. 276	§17.3(c)	92-85, 1992-42 I.R.B.	§18.1(b)
80-118, 1980-1 C.B. 254	§13.1(b)	86-23, 1986-1 C.B. 564	§3.2(c)	92-94, 1992-46 I.R.B. 34	§17.4(c)
80-132, 1980-1 C.B. 255	§14.3	86-43, 1986-2 C.B. 729	§5.1	93-23, 1993-1 C.B. 538	§17.3(e)
80-133, 1980-1 C.B. 258	§16.2(a)	86-49, 1986-1 C.B. 243	§4.2	94-78, 1994-52 I.R.B. 38	§17.3(d)
80-205, 1980-1 C.B. 184	§6.2	86-63, 1986-1 C.B. 88	§24.1(a)	95-21, 1995-15 I.R.B. 1	§§7.1(e), 8.6
80-206, 1980-2 C.B. 185	§6.2	86-95, 1986-2 C.B. 73	§23.2(a)	95-35, 1995-32 I.R.B. 1	§6.4(f)
80-215, 1980-2 C.B. 174	§§5.1(e), 5.5	86-98, 1986-2 C.B. 74	§6.2	95-48, 1995-47 I.R.B. 13	§§10.2, 27.1(c)
80-278, 1980-2 C.B. 175	§4.2	87-41, 1987-1 C.B. 296	§25.1		
80-279, 1980-2 C.B. 176	§4.2	87-119, 1987-2 C.B. 151	§23.3(a)	96-10, 1996-1 C.B. 577	§3.2(c)
80-282, 1980-2 C.B. 154	§23.2(a)	88-56, 1988-2 C.B. 126	§6.3(a)	96-32, 1996-20 I.R.B. 1	§4.2(a)
80-286, 1980-2 C.B. 179	§§4.5, 5.1(e)	90-100, 1990-2 C.B. 156	§18.4(e)	96-40, 1996-32 I.R.B. 8	§27.1(e)
80-287, 1980-2 C.B. 185	§§8.4(a), 8.11	94-16, 1994-1 C.B. 19	§21.9(f)	97-12, 1997-4 I.R.B. 1	§8.6
		95-8, 1995-14, I.R.B. 1	§21.10(a)	97-37, 1997-33 I.R.B. 18	§28.2(c)
80-295	§21.7(b)	97-21, 1997-18 I.R.B. 115	§4.6(a)	97-57, 1997-52 I.R.B. 20	§§21.9(g), 24.3(a)
80-296	§21.7(b)	98-15, 1998-12 I.R.B. 6	§4.6(b)		
80-301, 1980-2 C.B. 180	§2.2(a)			98-1, 1998-1 I.R.B. 225	§18.1(g)
80-302, 1980-2 C.B. 182	§2.2(a)			98-4, 1998-1 I.R.B. 113	§§17.3(e), 18.1(d), 28.2(a)
80-310, 1980-2 C.B. 319	§14.5(c)	**Revenue Procedures**	**Sections**		
81-29, 1981-1 C.B. 329	§4.5				
81-40, 1981-1 C.B. 508	§§14.2(b), 14.10(a)	71-17, 1971-1 C.B. 683	§§9.4(a), 9.4(b)	98-8, 1998-1 I.R.B. 7-225	§§28.2(a), 28.2(b)
81-60, 1981-1 C.B. 335	§8.7	72-5, 1972-1 C.B. 709	§3.4	98-16, 1998-5 I.R.B.	§25.1(c)
81-61, 1981-1 C.B. 355	§4.6(h)	75-50, 1975-2 C.B. 587	§§5.1(b), 27.12(d)	98-19, 1998-7 I.R.B. 30	§6.4(f)
81-69, 1981-1 C.B. 351	§9.5(c)				

Index

INDEX